# Jamaica

## Christopher P Baker

LONELY PLANET PUBLICATIONS
Melbourne • Oakland • London • Paris

# JAMAICA

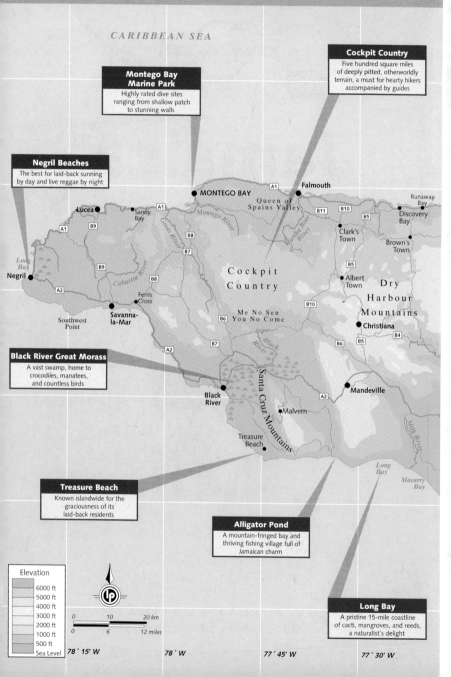

CARIBBEAN SEA

**Montego Bay Marine Park**
Highly rated dive sites ranging from shallow patch to stunning walls

**Cockpit Country**
Five hundred square miles of deeply pitted, otherworldly terrain, a must for hearty hikers accompanied by guides

**Negril Beaches**
The best for laid-back sunning by day and live reggae by night

**Black River Great Morass**
A vast swamp, home to crocodiles, manatees, and countless birds

**Treasure Beach**
Known islandwide for the graciousness of its laid-back residents

**Alligator Pond**
A mountain-fringed bay and thriving fishing village full of Jamaican charm

**Long Bay**
A pristine 15-mile coastline of cacti, mangroves, and reeds, a naturalist's delight

MONTEGO BAY · Falmouth · Runaway Bay
Queen of Spains Valley
Discovery Bay
Lucea · Sandy Bay · A1
Clark's Town · Brown's Town
Montego River
Great River
Martha Brae River
Negril
Cabarita River
Ferris Cross
Savanna-la-Mar
Southwest Point
Cockpit Country
Me No Sen You No Come
Albert Town
Dry Harbour Mountains
Christiana
Black River
Black River
Santa Cruz Mountains
Mandeville
Malvern
Treasure Beach
Long Bay
Macarry Bay
Milk River

A1 A2 B9 B8 B7 B6 B4 B5 B10 B11

## Elevation
- 6000 ft
- 5000 ft
- 4000 ft
- 3000 ft
- 2000 ft
- 1000 ft
- 500 ft
- Sea Level

0    10    20 km
0    6    12 miles

78° 15' W    78° W    77° 45' W    77° 30' W

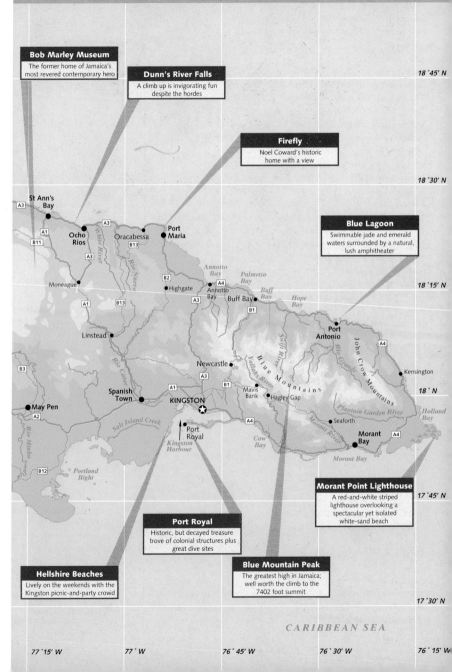

JAMAICA

**Bob Marley Museum**
The former home of Jamaica's most revered contemporary hero

**Dunn's River Falls**
A climb up is invigorating fun despite the hordes

**Firefly**
Noel Coward's historic home with a view

**Blue Lagoon**
Swimmable jade and emerald waters surrounded by a natural, lush amphitheater

**Morant Point Lighthouse**
A red-and-white striped lighthouse overlooking a spectacular yet isolated white-sand beach

**Port Royal**
Historic, but decayed treasure trove of colonial structures plus great dive sites

**Blue Mountain Peak**
The greatest high in Jamaica; well worth the climb to the 7402 foot summit

**Hellshire Beaches**
Lively on the weekends with the Kingston picnic-and-party crowd

18°45' N
18°30' N
18°15' N
18° N
17°45' N
17°30' N

St Ann's Bay
A3
A1
B11
Ocho Rios
White River
Oracabessa
A3
B13
Port Maria
A3
Moneague
Rio Nuevo
B2
Highgate
Annotto Bay
A4
Annotto Bay
A3
Palmetto Bay
Buff Bay
Hope Bay
A1
B13
Buff Bay
B1
Port Antonio
A4
John Crow Mountains
Linstead
Rio Cobre
Newcastle
Swift River
Blue Mountains
Yallahs River
Rio Grande
Kensington
A3
B1
Mavis Bank
Hagley Gap
Plantain Garden River
18° N
Spanish Town
A1
KINGSTON
May Pen
A2
Salt Island Creek
Port Royal
Kingston Harbour
A4
Cow Bay
Seaforth
Morant River
Morant Bay
A4
Holland Bay
Rio Minho
B12
Portland Bight
Morant Bay

CARIBBEAN SEA

77°15' W
77° W
76°45' W
76°30' W
76°15' W

Jamaica
**2nd edition** – January 2000
**First published** – August 1996

**Published by**
**Lonely Planet Publications Pty Ltd**  A.C.N. 005 607 983
192 Burwood Rd, Hawthorn, Victoria 3122, Australia

**Lonely Planet Offices**
**Australia** PO Box 617, Hawthorn, Victoria 3122
**USA** 150 Linden St, Oakland, CA 94607
**UK** 10a Spring Place, London NW5 3BH
**France** 1 rue du Dahomey, 75011 Paris

**Photographs**
Lee Abel, Christopher P Baker, Jon Davison, Lee Foster, Robert Fried,
Jamaica Tourist Board (Jamaica), Lonny Kalfus/International Stock,
Holger Leue, Michael Ochs Archive (Venice, CA), Roger Steffens

Some of the images in this guide are available for licensing from
Lonely Planet Images.
email: lpi@lonelyplanet.com.au

**Front cover photograph**
Schoolchildren in Spanish Town (Robert Fried)

ISBN 0 86442 780 8

text & maps © Lonely Planet 2000
photos © photographers as indicated 2000

Printed by SNP Pte Ltd, Singapore

# Contents

## 2    Contents

## NEGRIL & WEST COAST

## SOUTHWEST COAST

## CENTRAL HIGHLANDS

## 4 Contents

# MAP INDEX

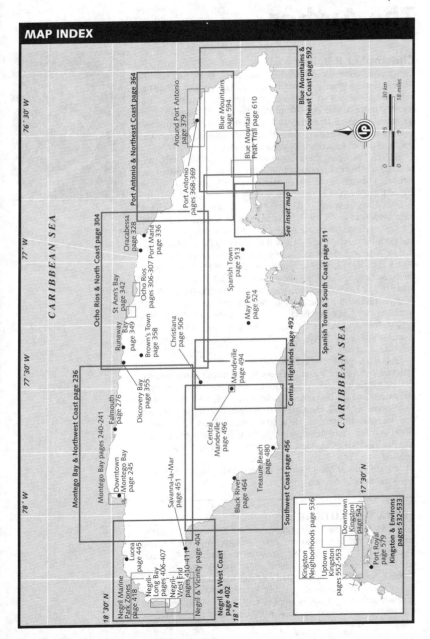

18°30'N

18°N

17°30'N

78°W

77°30'W

77°W

76°30'W

0   15   30 km
0   9   18 miles

# The Author

## Christopher P Baker

Christopher grew up in Yorkshire, England. He earned his BA (Honours) in geography at the University of London and gained his first serious suntan in Morocco on a research expedition. He returned to the Sahara in 1976 and also participated in an exchange program at Krakow University in Poland. He later earned masters' degrees in Latin American Studies (Liverpool University) and education (Institute of Education, University of London).

In 1978 Chris spent six months bumming around the Caribbean, Mexico, and North America before settling in California, where he received a Scripps-Howard Foundation Scholarship in Journalism to attend the University of California, Berkeley.

Since 1983 Chris has made his living as a professional travel and natural sciences writer for publications such as *Newsweek*, *Islands*, *Elle*, BBC's *World Magazine*, *National Wildlife*, *Los Angeles Times*, and *Caribbean Travel & Life*. He authored Lonely Planet's *Bahamas, Turks & Caicos* guidebook, has written guidebooks on Cuba, Costa Rica, and California, and has contributed chapters to *The Beginner's Guide to Getting Published*, Time-Life's *World Travel: A Guide to International Ecojourneys*, *Voyages: The World's 100 Most Exciting Ports of Call*, and *I Should Have Stayed Home*, an anthology of works by travel writers. His latest book is *Mi Moto Fidel: Motorcycling Through Castro's Cuba*, a literary travelogue about a four-month journey by BMW Paris/Dakar motorcycle through his favorite Caribbean isle.

Chris is a member of the Society of American Travel Writers and National Writers Union and has been honored with many awards, including (four times) the prestigious Lowell Thomas Travel Journalism Award and the Benjamin Franklin Award 1995 for 'Best Travel Guidebook.' In 1998, the Caribbean Tourism Organization named him 'Journalist of the Year.' He appears frequently on national television and radio talk shows, regularly lectures aboard cruise ships, and has escorted group tours to New Zealand, Hong Kong, Korea, England, and Cuba.

To learn more about the author and his work, visit his website at www.travelguidebooks.com.

## FROM THE AUTHOR

I'd like to express my sincere thanks to the many friends, acquaintances, and industry personnel who facilitated my research and helped make this book possible. Above all, thanks to Fay Pickersgill and the staff of the Jamaica Tourist Board and, likewise, to Alison DeRosa, Scott Croft and the staff of Peter Martin Associates, and Karyn Millet of Victoria King Public Relations. Also deserving of special thanks are Michael Campbell and Dulcie Moody of Island Car Rentals; John Issa, Suzanne McManus, and all the staff of

SuperClubs; Gordon 'Butch' Stewart and all the staff of Sandals; and Chris Blackwell, Elaine Hokin, and all the staff of Island Outpost.

Several friends lent invaluable help, notably Johnny Abbott (and Arlene Campbell) who selflessly shepherded me around Kingston and turned me on to key contacts; and dearly loved Andrea Hutchinson of Network Public Relations, Ginny Craven of Progressive Public Relations, and Laura Davidson of Laura Davidson Public Relations, who each opened their hearts and homes to me in addition to providing consistently professional assistance.

I also wish to thank Shireen Aga and Barbara Walker of Hotel Mocking Bird Hill; Cheryl Andrews and Jane Watkins of Cheryl Andrews Marketing; Roderic Crawford of Plantation Inn; Josef Forstmayr of Round Hill; Roberta Garzaroli of Jensen Boga Public Relations; Elena Girvan of Le Meridien Pegasus; Pamela Grant and Ralph Pearce of Bloomfield Great House; Blaze and Tammy Hart of Good Hope; Sally and Jason Henzell of Jake's Place; Perry Henzell; Micky Haughton James of Miss Jamaica pageant; Pauline Houghton of Morgan's Harbour; Richard Kahn and Hilarie Dobbs of Kahn Associates; Barbara Lulich of Sunset Beach Resort & Spa; Marcella Martinez of Martinez Public Relations; Malcolm and Ilean McInnes of Blue Mountain Taverna; Yulit Patrick-Gordon of Terra-Nova Hotel; Shantini Ramakrishnan of Spring O'Brien Public Relations; Paul Salmon of Rock House; Jane Watkins of Wyndham Rose Hall Beach Resort; Monica Zidjermans of Hotel Villa Bella; and any and all others, to whom I offer my apologies for my oversight.

Thanks, too, to many other acquaintances and travelers who shared insights and experiences along the way.

Special hugs go out to my wonderful friend Sheri Powers, and to Melonie Bradshaw, Shona Chin, Natasha Johnson, and Claudia Sansome, each of whom brightened my time in Jamaica in their own special ways.

## Dedication
This book is dedicated with love to Sheri.

# This Book

The 1st edition of *Jamaica* was written by Christopher P Baker in 1996.

## FROM THE PUBLISHER

This book was edited and proofread by Robert Reid and Rachel Bernstein in LP's proud Oaktown office, with guidance from Tom Downs. David Zingarelli and Kevin Anglin helped proof and keep the text real. Kate Hoffman and Brigitte Barta chipped in, too. Guphy drew and corrected the lovely maps, with guidance from Tracey Croom and Amy Dennis and extra help from Colin Bishop, Ivy Feibelman, Mary Hagemann, Patrick Huerta, Monica S Lepe, Kimberly Moses, and John 'S-P-E' Spelman. Designers Wendy Yanagihara and Ruth Askevold made the book beautiful, under the guidance of Margaret Livingston. Meanwhile, Wendy further earned her nickname 'Five-star Wendy Y' by designing the grand reggae section. Beca Lafore put the color wraps together, defined the essence of prelayout (notably for the reggae section), and blasted Lady Saw CDs. Illustrations were researched and created by the great artistic forces of Hayden Foell, Shelley Firth, Wendy Yanagihara, Hugh D'Andrade, Jim Swanson, and Lara Sox Harrison. Rini Keagy made many great covers, including the final pick. Josh Schefers got the slides. Ken DellaPenta indexed the book. John Spriggs offered insight into the worlds of reggae and Rastafarianism.

A big thanks and a cold Red Stripe goes to reggae archivist Roger Steffens (Rasrojah@aol.com) who dug through his vast collection of photos, records, and memorabilia to help make this guidebook's Reggae'n'Riddims section so special. Roger photographed the album covers and 45rpm singles that appear in the book, and compiled the Essential Reggae CDs list. Thanks also goes to photographer Lee Abel for her contribution to the reggae section.

Thumbs up to author Chris Baker for the lively text and making a long project fun.

**THANKS**
Many thanks to the travelers who used the last edition and wrote to us with helpful hints, advice and interesting anecdotes. Your names appear in the back of this book.

# Foreword

## ABOUT LONELY PLANET GUIDEBOOKS

The story begins with a classic travel adventure: Tony and Maureen Wheeler's 1972 journey across Europe and Asia to Australia. Useful information about the overland trail did not exist at that time, so Tony and Maureen published the first Lonely Planet guidebook to meet a growing need.

From a kitchen table, then from a tiny office in Melbourne (Australia), Lonely Planet has become the largest independent travel publisher in the world, an international company with offices in Melbourne, Oakland (USA), London (UK) and Paris (France).

Today Lonely Planet guidebooks cover the globe. There is an ever-growing list of books, and there's information in a variety of forms and media. Some things haven't changed. The main aim is still to help make it possible for adventurous travelers to get out there – to explore and better understand the world.

At Lonely Planet we believe travelers can make a positive contribution to the countries they visit – if they respect their host communities and spend their money wisely. Since 1986 a percentage of the income from each book has been donated to aid projects and human-rights campaigns.

**Updates** Lonely Planet thoroughly updates each guidebook as often as possible. This usually means there are around two years between editions, although for more unusual or more stable destinations the gap can be longer. Check the imprint page (following the color map at the beginning of the book) for publication dates.

Between editions, up-to-date information is available in two free newsletters – the paper *Planet Talk* and email *Comet* (to subscribe, contact any Lonely Planet office) – and on our website at www.lonelyplanet.com. The *Upgrades* section of the website covers a number of important and volatile destinations and is regularly updated by Lonely Planet authors. *Scoop* covers news and current affairs relevant to travelers. And, lastly, the *Thorn Tree* bulletin board and *Postcards* section of the site carry unverified, but fascinating, reports from travelers.

**Correspondence** The process of creating new editions begins with the letters, postcards and emails received from travelers. This correspondence often includes suggestions, criticisms and comments about the current editions. Interesting excerpts are immediately passed on via newsletters and the website, and everything goes to our authors to be verified when they're researching on the road. We're keen to get more feedback from organizations or individuals who represent communities visited by travelers.

Lonely Planet gathers information for everyone who's curious about the planet – and especially for those who explore it firsthand. Through guidebooks, phrasebooks, activity guides, maps, literature, newsletters, image library, TV series and website, we act as an information exchange for a worldwide community of travelers.

**Research** Authors aim to gather sufficient practical information to enable travelers to make informed choices and to make the mechanics of a journey run smoothly. They also research historical and cultural background to help enrich the travel experience and allow travelers to understand and respond appropriately to cultural and environmental issues.

Authors don't stay in every hotel because that would mean spending a couple of months in each medium-size city and, no, they don't eat at every restaurant because that would mean stretching belts beyond capacity. They do visit hotels and restaurants to check standards and prices, but feedback based on readers' direct experiences can be very helpful.

Many of our authors work undercover; others aren't so secretive. None of them accept freebies in exchange for positive write-ups. And none of our guidebooks contain any advertising.

**Production** Authors submit their raw manuscripts and maps to offices in Australia, the USA, the UK or France. Editors and cartographers – all experienced travelers themselves – then begin the process of assembling the pieces. When the book finally hits the shops, some things are already out of date, we start getting feedback from readers and the process begins again....

---

## WARNING & REQUEST

Things change – prices go up, schedules change, good places go bad and bad places go bankrupt – nothing stays the same. So, if you find things better or worse, recently opened or long since closed, please tell us and help make the next edition even more accurate and useful. We genuinely value all the feedback we receive. Julie Young coordinates a well-traveled team that reads and acknowledges every letter, postcard and email and ensures that every morsel of information finds its way to the appropriate authors, editors and cartographers for verification.

Everyone who writes to us will find their name in the next edition of the appropriate guidebook. They will also receive the latest issue of *Planet Talk*, our quarterly printed newsletter, or *Comet*, our monthly email newsletter. Subscriptions to both newsletters are free. The very best contributions will be rewarded with a free guidebook.

Excerpts from your correspondence may appear in new editions of Lonely Planet guidebooks, the Lonely Planet website, *Planet Talk* or *Comet*, so please let us know if you *don't* want your letter published or your name acknowledged.

Send all correspondence to the Lonely Planet office closest to you:

**Australia:** PO Box 617, Hawthorn, Victoria 3122
**USA:** 150 Linden St, Oakland, CA 94607
**UK:** 10A Spring Place, London NW5 3BH
**France:** 1 rue du Dahomey, 75011 Paris

Or email us at: talk2us@lonelyplanet.com.au

**For news, views and updates, see our website: www.lonelyplanet.com**

## HOW TO USE A LONELY PLANET GUIDEBOOK

The best way to use a Lonely Planet guidebook is any way you choose. At Lonely Planet, we believe the most memorable travel experiences are often those that are unexpected, and the finest discoveries are those you make yourself. Guidebooks are not intended to be used as if they provided a detailed set of infallible instructions!

**Contents** All Lonely Planet guidebooks follow the same format. The Facts about the Country chapters or sections give background information ranging from history to weather. Facts for the Visitor gives practical information on issues like visas and health. Getting There & Away gives a brief starting point for researching travel to and from the destination. Getting Around gives an overview of the transport options available when you arrive.

The peculiar demands of each destination determine how subsequent chapters are broken up, but some things remain constant. We always start with background, then proceed to sights, places to stay, places to eat, entertainment, getting there and away, and getting around information – in that order.

**Heading Hierarchy** Lonely Planet headings are used in a strict hierarchical structure that can be visualized as a set of Russian dolls. Each heading (and its following text) is encompassed by any preceding heading that is higher on the hierarchical ladder.

**Entry Points** We do not assume guidebooks will be read from beginning to end, but that people will dip into them. The traditional entry points are the list of contents and the index. In addition, however, some books have a complete list of maps and an index map illustrating map coverage.

There may also be a color map that shows highlights. These highlights are dealt with in greater detail later in the book, along with planning questions. Each chapter covering a geographical region usually begins with a locator map and another list of highlights. Once you find something of interest in a list of highlights, turn to the index.

**Maps** Maps play a crucial role in Lonely Planet guidebooks and include a huge amount of information. A legend is printed on the back page. We seek to have complete consistency between maps and text, and to have every important place in the text captured on a map. Map key numbers usually start in the top left corner.

Although inclusion in a guidebook usually implies a recommendation, we cannot list every good place. Exclusion does not necessarily imply criticism. In fact, there are a number of reasons why we might exclude a place – sometimes it is simply inappropriate to encourage an influx of travelers.

# Introduction

Jamaica enjoyed a reputation for exoticism long before Harry Belafonte lauded it as the 'Island in the Sun.' Swashbuckling movie hero Errol Flynn and his Hollywood pals cavorted here in the 1930s and 1940s, and England's equivalents – Noel Coward, Lawrence Olivier, and Sean Connery – had a penchant for this vibrant and colorful Caribbean island. Their interest attracted others, but even before the turn of the 19th century, visitors flocked to its shimmering beaches, ethereal mountains, and tropical climate.

Why choose Jamaica when there are more than 30 other Caribbean islands? Well, Jamaica still has a diversity and an allure that few other islands can claim.

Each of the island's four major resort areas and several minor ones has its own mood and character. Compare, for example, sleepy Port Antonio with its air of tropical lassitude, to Negril, every beach bum's idea of paradise, with its 7-mile, crescent-shaped, white-sand beach, carnal red sunsets, and reputation for bacchanalian living.

Many islands have lovelier beaches (and more of them), but Jamaica has its fair share of stunners fringed by coral reefs. It also has the widest range of accommodations in the Caribbean, with something for every taste and budget. You can camp atop a coral cliff, choose a private villa with your own private beach, laugh your vacation away at a party-hearty, all-inclusive resort, or pursue a genteel lifestyle at a secluded retreat.

Water sports are well developed. So, too, are horseback riding, sport fishing, golf, and lazy river runs by bamboo raft. There are ample opportunities for birding, hiking, and many other offbeat adventures. You'll find colonial-era estates and work-a-day plantations to explore, along with centuries-old botanical gardens, forts, and other historical sites. And the bustling markets are a whirligig of color and motion.

Stray from the north-coast resorts, and you'll discover radically different environments and terrain – perfect for exploring when you burn out on the beach.

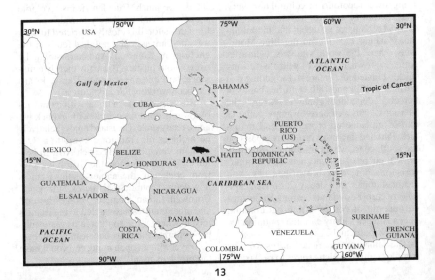

Unfortunately, the 'real' Jamaica often battles to be seen amid the glare of the stereotypical image of big-spending commercial marketers: a sanitized playground of cocktails and water sports and pampered indulgence where everything is on the house and problems don't exist. The trend has fueled (and been fueled by) the runaway success of all-inclusive resorts that aim to package a total Caribbean experience without guests needing to leave the property. As a result, and pummeled with images of drugs and violence, fewer and fewer travelers have been exploring the island serendipitously. Many small hoteliers are hurting for business, particularly those away from Montego Bay, Negril, and Ocho Rios.

Take to the backroads and hills and, taking humility with you, you might discover how gracious and hospitable Jamaicans can be. Buy some jerk chicken or 'pepper swimp' from roadside vendors, share time at sea with a local fishermen, learn about herbal remedies from a 'market mammie' or a guide in 'de bush.' These are a few of the experiences that will give you a greater appreciation of the island and its flavorful, hard-pressed people. Fortunately, there are hints that the pendulum is beginning to swing toward ecotourism, cultural discovery, and 'alternative' types of travel.

Most of Jamaica is rugged and mountainous, reaching 7200 feet in the Blue Mountains, where the world's most sought-after coffee is grown. Pockets of wild, mysterious, thickly jungled terrain are so forbidding that during the 17th and 18th centuries bands of fiercely independent runaway slaves – the Maroons – survived here. Swampy wetlands harbor endangered crocodiles and manatees. Parched cactus-covered savannas line the south coast, where traditional fisherfolk draw their pirogues and nets up on otherwise lonesome dark-brown beaches. And visitors familiar with sleepy Caribbean capitals are surprised to find bustling Kingston a cornucopia of cosmopolitan culture that belies Jamaica's justly earned reputation for laid-back, parochial ease.

The Jamaican experience arises from its complex culture, which aspires to be African in defiance of both the island's location and colonial heritage. Jamaica's evocative and somber history is rooted in the island's sugar-plantation economy: the slave era weighs heavy still in the national psyche.

To many people, Jamaica means reggae and Rastafarianism, both full of expressions of hope, love, anger, and social discontent. Behind the Jamaica Tourist Board's clichés lies a country beset with widespread poverty and angst. Jamaica is a densely populated island struggling to escape dependency and debt. Colorful music and religion are opiates during hot nights, when Jamaicans move with a sensual ease, and everyone – dreadlocked local and clean-cut visitor alike – finds their nirvana in various combinations of reggae, reefers, and rum.

If you don't like reggae music (you can't escape it!), can't cope with poverty or power outages, and hate being hustled, then Jamaica is definitely not for you. To savor Jamaica properly, to appreciate what it is that makes people passionate about the place, it pays to be idiosyncratic. To rest content here you have to 'get' Jamaica, to take the punches in stride. If you can handle that, if you like travel with a raw edge, you'll love it here.

Much has been written about crime and safety. Too much. True, Jamaica is a volatile society, but violence rarely intrudes on the foreign visitor. It is mostly restricted to drug wars and impassioned political feuds in the ghettoes of Kingston. And harassment by overzealous hustlers is usually merely a nuisance, and one the Jamaica Tourist Board has been working hard to address.

Most visitors return home with memories of a warm, gracious people with a quick wit and a ready smile. The island enjoys relatively harmonious race relations: its motto is 'Out of many, one people.' The rich African heritage runs deep. So, too, the British legacy – from cricket to the names of the island's now defunct counties: Middlesex, Surrey, and Cornwall. Indian, Chinese, Middle Eastern, and other cultures have added to the island's mix, nowhere more so than in its zesty cuisine – another fabulous Jamaican highlight.

Travel with an open mind, and you'll have 'no problem, mon!'

# Facts about Jamaica

## HISTORY

Jamaica has a colorful and painful history, marred by an undercurrent of violence and tyranny since European settlement in the early 1500s. The Spanish who arrived in 1510 quickly decimated the peaceful indigenous population and established a plantation-based economy, which the English would later perfect. Three hundred years of slavery – of blood, sweat, and tears under feudal colonial tutelage – left a legacy of antagonism, cultural malaise, and destitution, spurring a push for national dignity. These conditions have shaped many events since emancipation, and profoundly molded the national psyche and character.

## The Arawaks

Around 700 AD, an Amerindian group, the Arawaks, arrived and settled the island now known as Jamaica. The Arawaks had originated in the Guianas of South America perhaps 2000 years earlier. After developing seafaring skills, they gradually moved north through the Caribbean island chain over several centuries.

The Arawaks were a short, slightly built race averaging a height of about 5 feet. They had bronze skin, broad faces, and shiny black hair. They prized pointed skulls (to attain this exalted shape, babies' heads were pressed between slats of wood) and wore their hair in a topknot.

The Arawaks lived in conical thatched shelters located near river mouths. Their egalitarian villages were comprised of several family clans and headed by a *cacique*, whose hereditary yet largely nominal title was passed down by primogeniture. Arawak society was communal, and materialism an alien concept. (They gladly gave what gold they had to the greedy Spaniards who arrived in Christopher Columbus' wake; the Arawaks had only a limited amount of gold for ornamentation, obtained mostly in trade with the people of other islands.)

Columbus described the gentle Arawaks as 'honest and content with what they have…a peaceful and generous people.' They thrived on an abundance of fish and shellfish, fruit, and cassava. The women gathered food, while the men hunted, fished, and tilled the fields. The Arawaks were skilled agriculturalists who rotated their crops to prevent soil erosion. Jamaica's fertile soils yielded yams, maize, beans, spices, and cassava, which they leached of poison and baked into cakes and even fermented into beer.

The Arawaks had neither the wheel nor a written language, and they used neither beasts of burden nor metals (except for crude gold ornamentation). They evolved skills as potters, carvers, weavers, and boat builders. (Columbus was impressed with the scale of their massive canoes hewn from silk cotton trees – some were up to 100 feet long and capable of holding up to 50 people.) The Arawaks were particularly adept at spinning and weaving cotton into clothing (which they traded with neighboring islands) and hammocks – an Amerindian invention. The Spanish even had the Arawaks weave sailcloth for their ships. The Amerindians also wove ropes, carpets, and watertight roofs from the stringy bark of the calabash tree.

A ball game called *batos* formed an important focus of social life. The game, roughly resembling volleyball, was played in stone plazas called *bateyes* using a ball made of rubber, which itself was a novelty to the Spaniards. The Arawaks bet on the games. The Spaniards also noted other habits: the Indians would get fired up by maize alcohol, smoke dried leaves, and snort a powdered drug through a meter-long tube called a *tabaco*.

Religion played a central role in Arawak life. They worshipped various gods who were thought to control rain, sun, wind, and hurricanes, and were represented by *zemes*, idols of humans or animals. One god was supreme: Yocahú, the sun god (also the 'giver of cassava'). The Arawaks believed in a glorious afterlife and would sometimes strangle their dying chieftains to speed them to heaven, an idyllic place known as *coyaba*. The deceased were buried in caves, where their bones were often placed in large jars.

More than 230 Arawak sites have been unearthed in Jamaica, most notably at White Marl, 3 miles east of Spanish Town (now the site of the Arawak Museum). The little that remains of their culture is limited to pottery shards and petroglyphs of frogs, lizards, turtles, humans, and abstract designs (most notably on the ceiling of Mountain River Cave near Guanaboa Vale in St Catherine parish). Another important legacy are some Arawak words such as canoe, cannibal, hammock, hurricane, and tobacco.

## The Coming of Columbus

On his second of four voyages to the New World, Columbus 'discovered' Jamaica on May 5, 1494. Perhaps as many as 100,000 Arawaks already inhabited the island they called Xaymaca ('Land of Wood and Water'). Columbus landed in today's St Ann's Bay, which he named Santa Gloria 'on account of the extreme beauty of its country.'

At the time of Columbus' landing, the easternmost islands of the Caribbean had been swept by warlike Caribs, from whom the region gets its name. Like the Arawaks before them, the Caribs had originated in northern South America and swept north through the Caribbean, slaughtering and enslaving Arawaks wherever they found them. The Caribs never reached Jamaica where, it is claimed, the Arawaks had never experienced war and had no weapons.

The newcomers from the Old World, however, encountered a hostile reception. After anchoring for the night offshore in Bahía Santa Gloria (today's St Ann's Bay), Columbus sailed down the coast to a horseshoe-shaped cove (today's Discovery Bay), where he had his crossbow men fire on another hostile group of Arawaks, killing several. He also set a fierce dog – the first the Arawaks had ever seen – on the Indians, thus

Columbus' crew hated it when he did this.

establishing the vicious tone of future colonial occupation. Columbus took possession of the island for Spain and christened it Santo Jago. The Arawaks soon reappeared with peace offerings and feasted the strange newcomers throughout their brief stay.

On May 9, Columbus sailed on to El Golfo de Buen Tiempo (the Gulf of Good Weather; today's Montego Bay) and then on to Cuba. He returned later that year and explored the west and south coasts before again departing.

Columbus came back nine years later on his fourth and final voyage, still seeking a passage to Asia. Columbus – named the 'Viceroy of the Indies' – was by now out of favor at court. Quantities of gold, ivory, or other wealth had not been found during his explorations, and the Spanish Crown and other underwriters of his expensive expeditions wished to see a return on their investment. Unfortunately, Columbus' worm-eaten ships were falling apart. He abandoned one, the *Gallega*, off Panama. Another sank off Hispaniola (which makes up today's Dominican Republic and Haiti). Later, as he headed back to Hispaniola, storms forced him to seek shelter in Jamaica, and he barely made it to Bahía Santa Gloria. The two remaining vessels were so worm-riddled that Columbus and his 120 crewmen (including his son Ferdinand and brother Bartholomew) were forced to abandon ship and watch both vessels sink.

The luckless explorers spent almost a year marooned. The Arawaks wisely gave them a wide berth. Melancholy set in for the stranded crew, and they suffered desperately from disease and malnutrition. Finally, two officers paddled a canoe 150 miles to Hispaniola, where they were imprisoned by the jealous governor, who then sent a vessel to Jamaica to see if Columbus were dead. The skipper passed by Bahía Santa Gloria, where he left a message for Columbus that no vessel could be spared to rescue him. Eventually the officers were released from jail and chartered a ship to rescue the now broken explorer and his men. On June 29, 1504, Columbus sailed away, never again to return to Jamaica or the New World.

## Spanish Settlement

For a while, Jamaica was Columbus' personal property. When he died in 1506, the title passed to his son Diego, whose descendants to this day carry the honorary title of Marquis of Jamaica. Diego appointed one of his father's lieutenants, Don Juan de Esquivel, governor. In 1510, Esquivel began to colonize the island. He established a capital called Nueva Sevilla (New Seville) near present-day St Ann's Bay, where Columbus' vessels are believed to have sunk in 1503. Unfortunately, Nueva Sevilla was built near a swamp and proved to be an unhealthy and unproductive site. In 1534, the Spanish uprooted and created a new settlement (little remains of it today) on the south coast, to serve as their capital, Villa de la Vega (today's Spanish Town). The new capital grew quickly.

The settlers raised cattle and pigs on large ranches on the savanna of the south coast. They shipped lard derived from the fat of wild pigs, which roamed in large numbers in the interior hills. They also introduced two things that would profoundly shape the island's future: sugar and slaves imported from Africa.

### The First Slaves

The Spaniards had exacted tribute from the Arawak, whom they enslaved and killed off through hard labor and ill-treatment. Many Arawaks chose to kill their children and commit suicide by drinking poisonous cassava juice, rather than succumb to Spanish rule. European diseases decimated the Amerindians, too, for they had no resistance to the common cold, influenza, and more deadly ailments. Within a few decades the Indian population had been virtually wiped out. The Spaniards began importing slaves to Jamaica, the first arriving in 1517. The Spaniards converted their slaves and attempted to convince themselves that the bleak life of a Christian slave was superior to that of a free heathen.

Rivalry between the governor, *cabildo* (an independent council of elected members), and the Church weakened the colony, which received little support from the Spanish

Crown. The Spaniards never developed Jamaica. It languished as a post for provisioning ships en route between Spain and Central America. The weak colony was constantly harassed by French, English, and Dutch pirates, who had begun to operate in Caribbean waters even before the first Spanish settlement in Jamaica was lain.

## The English Invasion

In 1654, Oliver Cromwell, Lord Protector of England, devised his ill-fated 'Grand Western Design' to destroy the Spanish trade monopoly and accrue English holdings in the Caribbean. He amassed a fleet, jointly led by Admiral William Penn (father of the founder of the US state of Pennsylvania) and General Robert Venables, to conquer the Spanish-held Caribbean islands. The expedition was ill-equipped, badly organized, and was severely repulsed in April 1655 by Spanish forces on Hispaniola. The two leaders were as ill-chosen as the men they commanded. Historian Germán Arciniegas recorded that 'Penn smiled every time Venables made a blunder, and Venables made a blunder every time he gave an order or mapped a campaign.'

Intent on a prize to appease Cromwell after their disastrous debacle, Penn and Venables sailed to thinly populated, weakly defended Jamaica. On May 10, 1655, this expeditionary force of 38 ships landed 8000 troops at Caguaya, near the Spanish capital of Villa de la Vega (later known as St Jago de la Vega). The Spaniards stripped the town of possessions and simply retreated north over the mountains, from where they set sail to Cuba. Thus they abandoned the island to the English, who promptly destroyed the Spanish capital.

Before leaving, the Spanish also freed their slaves and encouraged them to harass the English. These *cimarrones* ('wild' runaways) took to the hills, where they mastered guerrilla warfare and fiercely defended their freedom, until finally granted autonomy a century later. A small band of Spanish loyalists under General Cristobal Ysassi also fought a guerrilla war against the English. In 1658 Spanish forces arrived from Cuba to assist Ysassi. The decisive battle at Rio Bueno on the north coast was won by the English under Colonel Edward D'Oyley. Ysassi escaped, and after two futile years of guerrilla warfare he, too, fled to Cuba.

## English Settlement

Cromwell sought to consolidate his new holding by enticing settlers with promises of land grants and supplies. In December 1656, some 1600 English arrived from Antigua to settle the area around Port Morant near the eastern tip of Jamaica. The region proved too swampy: within one year, three-quarters of the settlers had succumbed to disease.

Other settlers fared better and a viable economy began to evolve as trade was established with neighboring islands and the home country. The island was under military rule, and many soldiers wished to settle down as colonists. This desire, and the tensions between supporters of Cromwell and those who favored restoration of the monarchy, helped spawn a mutiny of troops in August 1660, which was quickly suppressed by D'Oyley.

In 1661, the monarchy in England was restored, and D'Oyley was appointed governor of Jamaica, accountable to King Charles II. He was directed to release the military forces from duty and to promote economic prosperity on the island. By 1662, 4000 colonists had arrived, forming an electorate whose governing council soon found itself at odds with the governor. The English government encouraged investment and further settlement, which hastened as profits began to accrue from cocoa, coffee, and sugarcane production.

In 1687, Sir Hans Sloane, a prominent London physician, published a scholarly description of Jamaica that did much to popularize the island. A new wave of settlers began arriving, including felons exiled to Jamaica as punishment, and impoverished Scots and Welsh who arrived as indentured laborers.

## Rise of the Buccaneers

During the 17th century, Britain was constantly at war with France or Spain. Because the Royal Navy couldn't effectively patrol the Caribbean, the Crown sponsored individual captains – privateers – to do the job. It authorized privateers to capture enemy vessels and plunder enemy cities. Jamaica, lying so close to Cuba and Hispaniola, was an ideal base.

Many of the privateers – buccaneers (from *boucan*, a French word for smoked meat, which the privateers often sold) – had evolved as a motley band of seafaring miscreants, political refugees, and escaped criminals who had gravitated to the tiny French-held isle of Tortuga, northwest of Hispaniola. Here they coalesced and established a thriving trade with passing ships. They lived a relatively sedentary life, raising hogs and cattle, and hunting wild boar in the hills of Hispaniola.

The Spanish authorities resented their presence. When the Spanish made a savage attempt to suppress them, the buccaneers were forced from Tortuga to Tortola. Hounded, they formed the Confederacy of the Brethren of the Coast, committed to a life of piracy against the Spaniards. Gradually they replaced their motley vessels with captured Spanish ships and grew into a powerful and ruthless force, feared throughout the Antilles.

Initially, the newly appointed governor of Jamaica, Sir Thomas Modyford, joined with the Spanish in attempts to suppress the buccaneers. But the outbreak of the Second Dutch War against Holland and Spain in March 1664 caused England to rethink its policy. Jamaica was vulnerable to attacks. Hence, Modyford contrived for the Brethren to defend the island. Port Royal and Kingston Harbour became their base, and their numbers swelled astronomically.

Port Royal prospered, and within a decade was Jamaica's largest city. It became an immensely wealthy den of iniquity, reportedly with more brothels and alehouses than any other city on earth.

At sea the buccaneers adopted strict rules of honor, as well as insurance policies for those wounded in battle – the loss of an eye or a finger earned 100 pieces of eight or one slave, the loss of a right arm earned 600

## Pesky Pirates

Even after being forced out of Port Royal following the 1692 earthquake, pirates added to the colony's problems, plundering ships of all nations and coming ashore to raid the sugar plantations that were sprouting all over Jamaica. Several pirates rose to infamy for their cruelty, daring, and, occasionally, their flamboyant ways.

Every English schoolchild has heard of 'Blackbeard,' whose real name was Edward Teach. This brutal giant of a man terrorized his victims by wearing flaming fuses in his matted beard and hair. And 'Calico Jack' Rackham, although equally ruthless, became known for his fondness for calico underwear (see 'Calico Jack' in the Negril & West Coast chapter). Like many pirates, Rackham was captured and executed, his body hung on an iron frame on a small cay off Port Royal (the cay is still called Rackham's Cay).

For the next hundred years, pirates plagued the Caribbean.

Blackbeard

pieces of eight or eight slaves, and so on. They were also ruthless against the Spanish. The privateers' extremes of violence and debauchery are hinted at by John Esquemeling, in his eye-witness description of the sacking of Porto Bello:

Having shut up all the Soldiers and Officers, as prisoners, into one room, they instantly set fire unto the powder...and blew up the whole Castle...with all the Spaniards that were within. This being done, they...fell to eating and drinking after their usual manner, that is to say, committing in both these things all manner of debauchery and excess. These two vices were immediately followed by many insolent actions of Rape and Adultery committed upon many very honest women, as well married as virgins; who being threatened with Sword, were constrained to submit their bodies to the violence of these lewd and wicked men.

A ruthless young Welshman, Henry Morgan, quickly established his supremacy over the mercenary mob and guided the buccaneers and Port Royal to their pinnacle. (Morgan, it appears, had been shipped from Wales to Barbados as an indentured servant and made his way to Tortuga to join the Brethren.)

Morgan and his cutthroats pillaged many Spanish towns throughout the Americas before crowning an illustrious career by sacking Spain's premier New World city: Panama. Spain and England had just signed a peace treaty, however, and Morgan's actions earned the ignominy of King Charles. After being recalled to England to stand trial, the daring buccaneer and his mentor were cleared of disgrace (Modyford was imprisoned for a brief term as a salve to Spain) and reunited in Jamaica, Morgan as governor and Modyford as chief justice. Morgan, now knighted, became a rich landowner with property throughout Jamaica. He was responsible for suppressing privateering as an officially sanctioned activity. Even so, he caroused in Port Royal, where he succumbed to dropsy (edema) and was entombed at Port Royal in 1688.

With England at peace with Spain, buccaneers were now regarded merely as pirates. Mother Nature lent a hand in their suppression when a massive earthquake struck Port Royal on June 7, 1692, toppling much of the city (and Morgan's grave) into the sea. More than 2000 people – one-third of Port Royal's population – perished. Many of the survivors pitched camp across the bay at the site of today's Kingston. Although Port Royal was rebuilt, the pirates were evicted and forced back to sea.

## French Invasions

The island was seen as a worthy prize by France, with whom England remained in near-constant war. In 1694 a French invasion fleet under Admiral Jean du Casse, the buccaneer governor of St-Domingue (Haiti), raided several points along the Jamaican coast, laying waste to many plantations. In August 1702, du Casse's fleet met English fleets under Admiral John Benbow, sailing from Port Royal, and fought a six-day battle to a stalemate off Colombia. Benbow obstinately refused to retire, despite desertion by four of his captains.

## The First Maroon War

By the end of the 17th century, Jamaica, which the English had consolidated as a slave colony, was also under siege from within. The first major slave rebellion occurred in 1690 in Clarendon parish, where many slaves (mainly of fiercely independent Cormorante tribes of the African Gold Coast) escaped and fled into the mountains. They joined the descendants of slaves who had been freed by the Spanish in 1655 and had eventually coalesced into two powerful bands in the Blue Mountains and in the Cockpit Country of southern Trelawny (then part of St James parish).

In 1663, the English had offered full freedom and land grants to all the African slaves brought over by the Spanish who would surrender, but the Maroons (from the Spanish word *cimarrón*, or 'wild one') refused. For the next 76 years the communities of Maroons plagued the English. They raided the plantations from their remote redoubts and attracted runaway slaves. Their daring grew with their numbers.

For decades the English militia skirmished with bands of Maroons in what came to be known as the First Maroon War. In 1729 the English launched an offensive to eradicate the Maroons, but the thickly jungled mountains were ill-suited to English-style open warfare. The Maroons had perfected ambush-style guerrilla warfare, and operated in bands that communicated with secret calls and by *abeng* horn.

After a decade of costly campaigning, the English (aided by dogs and *mestizo* trackers brought in from Central America) gained the upper hand. As the English soldiers squeezed the hardy Maroons into smaller and smaller territories, the Maroons decided to come to terms. On March 1, 1739, Colonel Guthrie and Cudjoe, the Cormorante leader of the Maroons of Cockpit Country, signed a peace treaty granting the Maroons autonomy and 1500 acres of land. In return, the Maroons agreed to chase down runaway slaves as bounty hunters and to assist the English in quelling rebellions. The Maroons of the Blue Mountains, under a leader named Quao, signed a similar treaty one year later. Though the Maroons were temporarily spent as a force, they had sealed their status as the symbol of Jamaica's fierce independence (see 'Windward Maroons' in the Port Antonio & Northeast Coast chapter).

## King Sugar

Many officers in Cromwell's army had received land grants. They and subsequent English settlers used slaves to clear the land for raising indigo, tobacco, and cocoa. But one crop was best suited to the soil and climate: sugar. During the course of the 18th century, Jamaica became the largest sugar producer in the world.

Throughout the period, Jamaica was jointly ruled by a governor appointed by the monarch and an elected assembly of planters, who were usually at loggerheads with the governor and whose main interest lay in fostering the sugar and slave economy. The island was divided into 13 parishes (their boundaries remain today). The Crown's interests at the parish level were looked after by an appointed custos.

Many Jamaican planters were absentee landlords who lived most of the year in England, where they displayed an ostentatious lifestyle and formed a powerful political lobby. Aided by protective tariffs in England, they fostered and maintained an importance that was out of proportion to the size of the West Indian 'sugar colonies.' The planters built sturdy and handsome mansions – 'great houses' – often in the latest Georgian fashion, high above their canefields. These plantations usually consisted of boiling houses, distilleries, other factory buildings made of stone, aqueducts to supply water, and rows of squalid barracks and huts for the slaves. Towns grew up around the major ports, which were centers for trade with North America and Europe. Jamaican sugar, rum, and molasses were exchanged for lumber, pickled fish, salted meats, flour, and other supplies.

The planters lived a life of indolence, with retinues of black servants to cater to their every whim. Many over-indulged in drink and sexual relations with slave mistresses, frequently siring mulatto children. Those who held various estates often kept a favored mistress at each. The economic and political life of the times was an exclusively male arena. The planters' wives lived their own lives of indulgence, divorced from the day-to-day functioning of the estates that drew their husbands' attentions. These women spent much of their time playing cards, arranging balls, and otherwise socializing, while the daily care of their children was given to wet nurses and female slaves. (Not a few planters' wives are known to have taken slave lovers, too, but such liaisons were usually arranged with the utmost secrecy and great pains were taken to avoid an unwanted pregnancy.)

## The Heyday of Slavery

Slavery came to dominate Jamaican life. By 1700 there were perhaps 7000 English in Jamaica and 40,000 slaves. One century later, the number of whites had tripled, and they ruled over 300,000 slaves.

The transition to plantation labor obviously wasn't easy for slaves newly arrived from Africa. The average slave had to be 'broken in' for two or three years. More than

## The Slave Trade

English merchants dominated the sordid trade that supplied the West Indies with slaves from West Africa. They operated an immensely profitable triangular route. The ships normally set sail from Bristol or Liverpool for Africa carrying trinkets to barter for blacks captured or sold into slavery in their homelands. Most were from the Ashanti, Cormorante, Mandingo, and Yoruba tribes.

Many African tribes kept slaves, and at first traders bought captured warriors and other prisoners of local chieftains. As demand soared, however, huge raids swept through West Africa, and captives were chained together and driven like cattle to the coast. There they were held in stockades before being loaded onto ships for the grueling 'middle passage' across the Atlantic.

The voyage lasted anywhere from six to 12 weeks. The captives were kept chained below, where they lay amid their excrement and vomit, shoulder to shoulder. Not an inch of space was wasted. Inevitably, they weakened and sickened, and many died of disease in the festering holds. Others committed suicide. The captives who were still alive were fattened up as the boat reached port.

The slaves were oiled to make them appear healthy before being auctioned. Their prices varied between £25 and £75 for unskilled slaves; slaves who had been trained as carpenters and blacksmiths fetched a premium – often £300 or more. The most wretched had a worth of no more than a shilling.

Kingston served as the main distribution point for delivery to other islands. Of the tens of thousands of slaves shipped to Jamaica every year, the vast majority were re-exported.

The slave ships then returned to England carrying sugar, molasses, and rum.

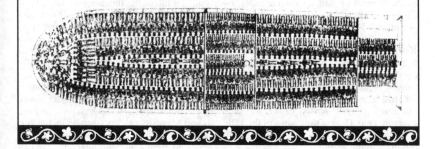

500,000 slaves were imported during the 18th century, yet six slaves died for every one born. Tens of thousands were worked to death. Other slaves died of exposure, disease, or malnutrition. Both men and women slaves were put to work in the fields. Although the majority of slaves were field laborers, others were put to work building factories, houses, and roads. Others were domestic servants, cooks, footmen, butlers, and grooms.

During their few free hours, slaves cultivated their own tiny plots. Sunday was a rest day, and slaves gathered to sell yams and other produce at the bustling markets. If fortunate, a slave might save enough money to buy his freedom, which a master could also grant as he wished (free blacks were issued a pass and had to wear a blue cross on their shoulders). The offspring of white men and slave women were known as 'free coloreds' and were accorded special rights.

The planters ran their estates as vicious fiefdoms under the authority of an overseer (the 'busha'), who enjoyed relatively free reign. White planters lived in constant fear of slave revolt. To forestall ferment, slaves were denied permission to congregate, and families were separated to break down clan systems. Some planters were relatively kind and nurtured their slaves, but most resorted to violence to terrorize the slave population into obedience. The extreme treatment was eventually regulated by slave codes, but plantation society remained tied to the rule of the whip.

## Rebellions & Revolutions

Naturally, the slaves despised their 'massas' (masters) and struggled against the tyranny imposed on them at every opportunity. Insurrections were put down with the utmost severity.

Tacky's Rebellion, the first major uprising, erupted on Easter Monday in 1760 in Port Maria in St Mary parish. Tacky was a tribal leader of the Cormorante tribe from the African Gold Coast. Before dawn, he and a small band of followers murdered a fort storekeeper and stole a supply of muskets and arms. They then moved inland, murdering white settlers and urging slaves to revolt. The rebellion rippled through the western parishes as slaves joined the uprising. When word reached Spanish Town, the governor dispatched troops and called upon the Maroons to aid in suppressing the revolt. Tacky was killed, and many of his followers committed suicide rather than face capture. But the flames of rebellion flickered for months before finally being extinguished. White society enacted a swift and violent retribution (see 'Easter Rebellion' in the Ocho Rios & North Coast chapter).

The spirit of independence fomenting abroad also affected Jamaica, such as during the American War of Independence, which began in 1775. Colonialists' sympathies in Jamaica lay with the 13 American colonies. When the colonies declared independence, the Jamaican House of Assembly petitioned King George on their behalf. Britain reacted by blockading North America's eastern seaboard, cutting it off from trade with Jamaica, which relied on food imports from North America. As many as 15,000 slaves may have died of starvation from the food shortages, which prompted the introduction of breadfruit from the South Seas as a staple for slaves.

Meanwhile, France and Spain took advantage of Britain's preoccupation with its North American colonies to recapture Caribbean islands that Britain had acquired during the preceding half-century of rivalry. By the end of the War of Independence in 1781, Britain had lost all its possessions in the West Indies except Antigua, Barbados, and Jamaica. France and Spain, now in alliance, attempted to invade Jamaica in April 1782. Admiral George Rodney set sail from Port Royal with a naval fleet and soundly defeated the enemy fleet in the Battle of the Saints, in a three-day running engagement off Dominica. Rodney was rewarded with a barony and a £2000 annual pension. His feat is commemorated by a grand marble monument and statue in Spanish Town square.

## The Tide Turns

In Europe, the French Revolution of 1789 spread a spirit of subversion worldwide, not least in the French colony of St-Domingue (Haiti), where slaves, under the black general Toussaint l'Ouverture, ejected the French colonialists and established their independence, becoming the first free black state. In 1793, England attempted to turn back the tide by invading Haiti and managed to hold on to it for four years before again being repulsed.

The example of Haiti fostered a sense of black pride and spurred new uprisings throughout the Caribbean. In Jamaica, Maroon sentiments were running high. A Second Maroon War broke out in 1795 after two Trelawny Maroons were sentenced to flogging for stealing pigs. The slaves who inflicted the punishment had been runaways that the Maroons had captured and returned to the British authorities. The proud Maroons were incensed at the insult, and simmering tensions boiled over. When threats against the residents of Montego Bay were issued in Trelawny Town, the new governor, the Earl of Balcarres, declared martial law and sent troops to destroy the Maroons' provision grounds. The troops were caught in a fatal ambush, and a full-scale war broke out that lasted five months.

Eventually, colonial authorities brought in trained bloodhounds to hunt down the Maroons. The Maroons quickly surrendered on a pledge that they could retain their land. In a betrayal of good faith, Balcarres banished the Maroons to Nova Scotia, from which they were eventually sent to Sierra Leone, becoming the first New World Africans ever repatriated to Africa (about 60 later returned to Jamaica as free men). An English barracks was erected in Trelawny Town, forever ending the Maroon threat.

## The Demise of Slavery

The beginning of the 19th century saw growing anti-slavery sentiment, influenced in part by the liberal shock waves of the French Revolution. A humanitarian spirit and a sense that slavery conflicted with Christian ideals was evolving in England, supported by abolitionist parliamentarians such as William Wilberforce.

Throughout the 1700s, the Church of England, the sole denomination in Jamaica,

## Capt Bligh & Breadfruit

During the epoch of slavery, few colonial islands were self-sufficient in food. Their productive lands were tilled for sugar and the plantations relied heavily upon imported foodstuffs from North America and, to a lesser degree, Europe, to feed their vast slave populations. Jamaica was no exception. It suffered dramatically when supplies were severed during the American War of Independence (1775-81). Tens of thousands of slaves died of starvation.

As a result, planters lobbied the British government to supply breadfruit to be grown cheaply en masse on the island. The government agreed, and in 1787 voted monies for a vessel – the HMS *Bounty* – commanded by Capt William Bligh to bring breadfruit trees from Polynesia, where the starchy, vegetable-like fruit helped sustain the local populations. The fruit, about the size of a small melon with a mealy pulp that can be baked, boiled, or dried and ground, had been recently 'discovered' by Capt James Cook, who recorded: 'If a man plants ten of them…he will completely fulfill his duty to his own and future generations.'

The *Bounty* set sail on December 23, 1878, and arrived in the South Seas after an arduous seven-month voyage. The ship remained for many months in these paradisiacal isles, where the sailors earned the favors of beautiful island girls in exchange for nails and other trinkets. Eventually, with the vessel laden with breadfruit trees, Bligh set sail. But part of the crew, led by Master's Mate Fletcher Christian, felt unhappy about leaving the islands, so mutinied and seized the vessel near the Tonga Islands on April 28, 1789. Capt Bligh and 18 officers were set adrift in a rowboat. (The famous novel, *Mutiny on the Bounty*, by Charles Nordhoff and James Norman Hall, incorrectly depicts Bligh as a tyrannical captain who cared little for the welfare of his crew.)

By a remarkable feat of navigation – and considerable good luck – the 19 men reached Malaysia and were able to return to England. A British frigate was sent in pursuit of the mutineers (they weren't apprehended until 1808, when a settlement they had founded on remote Pitcairn Island was discovered). Meanwhile, Capt Bligh was exonerated of blame and in 1791 set sail again for the South Seas with a new vessel – HMS *Providence*. In February 1793, Bligh finally landed at Navy Island with breadfruits that were sent to Bath Botanical Garden in St Thomas parish for propagation and eventual distribution throughout the island.

supported slavery. By the early 19th century, the arrival of Nonconformist missionaries and the emergence of the evangelical clergy within the established Church fostered a rising movement for abolition. They faced violent reaction from the 'plantocracy.' The Colonial Church Union (an unholy alliance between the planters and church establishment) hoped to delay emancipation by silencing the missionaries and destroying their places of worship. Several missionaries were killed by hired thugs.

British Parliament banned the slave trade in 1807. Although the planter-dominated Jamaican House of Assembly vigorously opposed efforts to end slavery, sentiment in England was shifting against the intransigent planters.

## The Christmas Rebellion

The last and largest of the slave revolts in Jamaica erupted in 1831. The Christmas Rebellion was inspired by 'Daddy' Sam Sharpe, an educated slave and lay preacher who used his prayer meetings to incite passive resistance.

Though Sharpe had hoped for a peaceful uprising, the rebellion turned violent. As many as 20,000 slaves joined the revolt, which spread throughout the island, leaving in its wake enormous destruction. Plantations were razed to the ground and planters murdered. Once again, martial law was declared and troops were employed with vicious force to suppress the uprising. The governor persuaded the slaves to surrender on a promise of full pardon using the ruse that Parliament had voted to abolish slavery. Once the slaves had lain down their arms, more than 400 were hanged; hundreds more were whipped.

The accounts of retribution fostered a wave of revulsion in England and helped the abolitionist cause. Parliament finally abolished slavery throughout the empire on August 1, 1834. (See 'Preaching Resistance' in the Montego Bay & Northwest Coast chapter.)

## The Era of Emancipation

To ease the transition from a slave economy to one based on wage labor, Parliament conditioned the slaves' freedom: slaves had to serve a six-year unpaid 'apprenticeship' for their previous masters. It was untenable. Slaves simply left the estates. The apprenticeship system was soon abandoned, and the slaves were set free unconditionally in 1838.

Economic chaos followed. Although Parliament allotted £20 million to compensate the former slave owners, the planters now had to pay their laborers. They offered starvation wages, and most slaves chose instead to fend for themselves. They lived a harsh life as subsistence farmers – the forebears of today's still impoverished agrarian class. Aided by missionaries, many slave communities formed 'free villages.'

The plantocracy attempted to sustain the crippled estates by importing indentured laborers from China and India (indentured laborers also built the island's first railroad, which opened in 1845). Other laborers came from Germany, Ireland, and Scotland. Many thousands of free Africans were also attracted. Few of these immigrants, however, chose to work the plantations. Instead, they too, tilled their own plots of land.

Jamaican sugar production had peaked in 1814 at 34 million pounds. The planters in Jamaica, however, were facing a number of setbacks: growing competition from Brazil, Cuba, and other islands; cheaper beet sugar grown in Europe; Britain's Free Trade policy, which dissolved the protection Jamaican sugar had previously enjoyed; and the Sugar Equalization Act of 1846, which removed all protective measures on sugar imports to Britain. Many Jamaican estates ceased cultivation and were overrun by natural vegetation or broken up into smaller holdings.

The old order had been toppled, undermining the white plantocracy's economic power, but not its vested political power. Blacks, though free, had no political voice. By law, only titled property owners could vote. Blacks were routinely denied land claims by courts still lorded over by white magistrates schooled in the plantation mentality. The magistrates continued to mete out harsh 'justice' to a free but marginalized peasantry relegated to the least fertile lands.

The majority of the population endured miserable economic conditions and squalor. Rural settlements were entirely lacking in sanitation, and epidemics of cholera and smallpox washed across the island in 1850 and 1852, affecting 32,000 people among the destitute black underclass.

Jamaica's mulattos, however, had been enfranchised in 1830 and granted full rights equal to English citizens in 1832. Many mulattos received a good education and rose into the middle classes. Most looked up to the white society of their fathers (no white women dared bear a mulatto child). Others, understandably, sided with the oppressed, whose cause was taken up vociferously in the 1860s by a mulatto lawyer and liberal assemblyman, George William Gordon.

## Morant Bay Rebellion

Jamaica's economy, already weakened by emancipation, degenerated further during the American Civil War (1861-65), when naval blockades cut off vital supplies that sustained the island. Desperation over economic conditions, high food prices, and injustice finally boiled over in 1865. A demonstration in Morant Bay, led by a black Baptist deacon named Paul Bogle, descended on the town courthouse. The militia fired into the crowd, killing dozens of people, and a violent rebellion ensued. Several planters were murdered.

Governor Edward Eyre and his followers used the Morant Bay Rebellion as a pretext to get rid of mulatto assemblyman Gordon. He was arrested, shipped to Morant Bay, swiftly tried by a kangaroo court, and promptly hanged alongside Paul Bogle. More than 430 other rebels were executed, countless scores were flogged, and thousands of homes razed in retribution (see 'Morant Bay Rebellion' in the Blue Mountains & Southeast Coast chapter).

The brutal repression provoked an outcry in Britain. Eyre was recalled to England and dismissed from the colonial service, but not before being forced to persuade the Jamaican Assembly to vote its own dissolution. The island's internal affairs reverted to Parliament's control as a Crown colony, with ultimate power in the hands of a series of liberal governors, marking the beginning of a more enlightened era.

The British government began to invest in the island's infrastructure: an educational system and civil service were founded; lowland marshes were converted to productive land, and a Lands Department was established to assist local farmers in buying government land. Telegraph communications were established in 1869. Money was allocated for an extensive new road system. And the nation's capital was even moved from Spanish Town to Kingston in 1872. Jamaica's economy began to recover, thanks to, not least, the lowly banana.

## Banana Boom & Bust

In 1866 a Yankee skipper, George Busch, arrived in Jamaica and loaded several hundred stems of bananas, which he transported to Boston and sold at a handsome profit. He quickly returned to Port Antonio, where he encouraged production and soon had himself a thriving export business. Captain Lorenzo Dow Baker followed suit in the west, with his base at Montego Bay. Within a decade the banana trade was booming, so much so that Port Antonio was a busier port than Liverpool. Everyone rushed to grow 'green gold.' Throughout Jamaica, the coming of banana boats was announced by the blowing of a conch shell – a signal for country farmers to cut the fruit and rush down to the harbor by river or donkey.

Baker's small enterprise evolved into the Boston Fruit Company, and eventually, through merger, into the United Fruit Company, the giant that would control the economies of Central America's 'banana republics.' Production peaked in 1927, when 21 million stems were exported. By then the big US corporations had succeeded in squeezing out small-scale Jamaican farmers from the lowlands and dictating the terms of a monopoly trade.

To help pay the passage south to Jamaica, banana traders promoted the island's virtues – notably its warm climate – and took on passengers. Thus, the banana-export trade gave rise to the tourism industry.

'Mr Tally Mon, tally me bananas...'

## Labor Unrest

Despite general progress, conditions for the working poor in Jamaica had remained appalling. A series of natural disasters added salt to the wound. A great earthquake toppled much of Kingston on January 14, 1907, killing more than 800 people. Hurricanes devastated the island in 1915, 1916, and 1917, adding to the hardships suffered during WWI through demise of trade.

In the 1930s, ripples from the Great Depression were felt around the world. Sugar sales plummeted, and banana exports followed suit. The vast majority of Jamaicans were unemployed and destitute; fewer than 20% earned any income at all. Strikes and riots erupted throughout the Caribbean, spilling over in Jamaica in 1938 when a demonstration at the West Indies Sugar Company factory at Frome, in Westmoreland, got out of hand. A battle between police and thousands of unemployed seeking work left several people dead. Strikes and looting erupted throughout Jamaica. (See the Frome section in the Negril & West Coast chapter.)

## Birth of Modern Politics

Jamaican nationalism was growing. Native son Marcus Garvey's call for black self-reliance was a stirring resistance to paternalistic colonial government. In 1938 amid the clamor, a charismatic labor leader, Sir Alexander Bustamante (son of an Irish woman and a mulatto man), formed the Bustamante Industrial Trade Union (BITU), the first trade union in the Caribbean (see 'National Hero Busta' in the Negril & West Coast chapter). That same year, Bustamante's dissimilar cousin, Norman Manley, formed the People's National Party, or PNP, the first political party in the colony (Bustamante would form his own party – the Jamaica Labor Party, or JLP – in 1943). Unlike his headstrong, intuitive, oratorical cousin, Manley was an analytical introvert and advocate. Though rivals, they complemented each other perfectly. Separately they campaigned for economic and political reforms. Say writers Philip Sherlock and Barbara Preston, 'Bustamante swept the Jamaican working class into the mainstream of Jamaican political life and Norman Manley secured the constitutional changes that put political power in their hands.' Prompted by the exigencies of WWII, when the Caribbean islands supplied food and raw materials to Britain, the British government enacted a policy to stimulate economic and social development in the Caribbean. Adult suffrage for all Jamaicans and a new constitution, which provided for an elected government, were introduced in 1944 (Bustamante's JLP won Jamaica's first election). In 1947 virtual autonomy was granted, though Jamaica remained a British colony under the jurisdiction of Parliament and the Crown – a prelude to full independence.

## Independence

Manley had said as early as 1945 that he didn't believe any island in the region could be an independent, modern state. In 1955, when the PNP took power, Manley began to steer Jamaica toward independence within a Caribbean federation. Finally, the British government established the West Indies Federation in January 1958 to unite the former Caribbean colonies as a single political entity.

Bustamante, however, declared the JLP opposed to membership and pressured for secession from the federation. In 1961, Prime Minister Manley allowed voters to decide by referendum. Bustamante was vindicated, Jamaica seceded, and a new constitution was drawn up. When Jamaica withdrew from the federation, the self-interest of its remaining members led to its collapse.

On August 6, 1962, Jamaica gained its independence in a ceremony witnessed by US Vice President Lyndon Johnson and Princess Margaret. At midnight, the union jack came down in the National Stadium in Kingston, replaced by Jamaica's new flag with three new colors: black (for the people), green (for the land), and gold (for the sun).

## Turbulent Years

Immediate post-independence politics were dominated by Bustamante and Manley, whose parties grew more ideologically apart. The JLP – back in power – tilted toward the USA and free-market policies while the PNP leaned left. Buoyed by the rapid growth of the bauxite industry, Jamaica experienced a decade of relative prosperity and growth, which continued under the administration of Bustamante's successors: Donald Sangster (who died shortly after taking office) and Hugh Shearer (who was a blood relative of both Bustamante and Manley).

Nonetheless, the buoyant mood of the early 1960s swiftly passed as the hopes of Jamaica's poor majority went unanswered. A growing radicalism was brewing. Jamai-

MICHAEL OCHS ARCHIVE

Selassie in Kingston, 1966

cans were acutely aware of the emergence of independent black nations in Africa, as well as the rise of black consciousness and the struggles in the USA. In 1964, the body of Marcus Garvey was shipped from England to Jamaica and interred in National Heroes Park in Kingston. The following year, Jamaicans gave a resounding welcome to Martin Luther King, Jr. Also in 1965, Kingston erupted in riots when Black Power advocate Walter Rodney, a Guyanese lecturer at the University of the West Indies in Kingston, was denied re-entry to Jamaica. And Haile Selassie's April 1966 visit to Jamaica was an event of long-term significance that fueled a growing interest in Rastafarianism among the Jamaican poor, helping produce a more positive self-image and focusing a radical outlet for the expression of discontent.

Following Manley's death in 1969, the PNP espoused increasingly radical social policies under the leadership of his son, Michael. In 1972, the PNP came to power under the theme 'Time for a Change.' During the 1972 election, Manley took on the persona of the biblical 'Joshua,' complete with the 'rod of correction,' the walking stick given him by Selassie in Ethiopia in 1970.

Manley had earned the moniker in 1964 when, as a trade union leader, he led a group of striking workers outside the Jamaica Broadcasting Company office and declared, 'These are the walls of Jericho.' The image fitted well with the PNP campaign, which addressed promises of justice and equality for the ghetto dwellers and tapped into the desire for radical social change then being voiced in 'rebel' lyrics by Bob Marley and other reggae singers. Though the moment seemed radical, the PNP carefully avoided offering 'power to the people' and preferred the less radical 'power for the people.'

Manley attempted to make Jamaica a 'democratic socialist' nation. He initiated greater state control over the economy, resulting in a greater share of revenues for the island. Manley introduced a statutory minimum wage and legislation favoring workers' rights. A literacy campaign, socialist health care, and other liberal economic and social reforms proved popular with the masses.

Unfortunately, the move toward socialism caused a capital flight at a time when Jamaica was reeling from the shock of the world's oil crisis and worldwide depression. Inflation roared above 50%, foreign investors pulled out, unemployment skyrocketed, Jamaican society became increasingly polarized, and an anti-white climate prevailed.

Outbreaks of violence erupted and finally boiled over into full-fledged warfare during the campaigns preceding the 1976 election. Heavily armed gangs of JLP and PNP supporters began killing each other in the partisan slums of Kingston. Still, the PNP won the election by a wide margin, which Manley took as a mandate supporting his socialist agenda.

Foreign companies continued to pull out. Tens of thousands of skilled Jamaican workers and professionals also fled the island. The economy went into precipitous decline. Scores of businesses went bankrupt. Severe scarcities of even the most basic consumer items became common. The IMF and World Bank refused to provide further loans to support the government deficit or to finance Manley's social programs. In 1977 the banks demanded a draconian austerity program.

The US government was also concerned over the socialist path Manley was taking. He particularly antagonized the US by developing close ties with Cuba: Manley declared that he would go 'all the way to the mountaintop with Fidel.' A six-day state visit by Castro in 1977 and the arrival of Cuban doctors, educators, and technical experts were seized upon by conservatives determined to thwart the communist association. Cuban planes began arriving in larger numbers. Manley even began recruiting a 'home guard' outside the regular police and army, and a Financial Intelligence Unit was set up, both trained by Cuban advisers. When a Suppression of Crime Act was enacted, giving special powers to the security forces, Jamaica's middle class feared the worst. Polls showed the Cuban presence was viewed favorably by a majority of citizens, however, because of the contributions to development that Cuba was apparently willing to make.

The USA couldn't stomach a second 'Cuba' in the Caribbean. The CIA developed plans to topple the Jamaican government, and deployed officers to train the JLP in the use of violent and destabilizing tactics (Philip Agee's *CIA Diaries: Inside the Company* provides a good exposé).

Kingston was replete with weaponry. Crack cocaine had also come to Kingston, and political posses had turned into gangsters engaged in deadly battles for control of the trade. The ghettoes had become enclaves of lawlessness ruled by 'rude boys.' The situation was exacerbated by a tide of rural migrants flooding to the capital. Mounting resentment with Michael Manley's PNP government found its outlet. Political violence flared. Gun battles raged in Kingston. The government responded by sending in special army squads. They razed the Back-A-Wall ghetto to the ground and dispersed its inhabitants. Armed police and soldiers patrolled the streets, and army helicopters whirred overhead. Street searches became routine. A small right-wing clique of the Jamaica Defense Force even attempted an unsuccessful coup d'etat. The violence of the 1980 election brought Jamaica to the verge of civil war.

With the economy in free fall and society in dangerous disarray, Manley stepped back from the brink of disaster and began to reverse his policies. The reversal alienated much of the PNP rank and file. But many middle-class Jamaicans still speak with animosity of the Manley years.

## About Face

In 1980, the voters decided it was time for a change, but not before witnessing the most violent year since the 1865 Morant Bay Rebellion. Tourism withered.

Under Boston-born, Harvard-educated Edward Seaga, the PLP inherited a country on the verge of bankruptcy and mired in domestic unrest. Seaga had promised 'deliverance.' He set himself to the task of reversing Manley's policies. His efforts to restructure the economy included an austerity program and a painful devaluation of the dollar that created further hardships. Seaga also severed diplomatic relations with Cuba and nurtured strong ties with the Reagan administration, which enacted the Caribbean Basin Initiative offering Jamaica (and other Caribbean islands) financial support in exchange for political loyalty. Jamaican troops even participated in the US military invasion of Grenada in the autumn of 1983. Soon, a faint recovery began.

Nonetheless, Seaga's popularity waned due to the social costs of his retrenchment policies, which included severe cuts in education and health spending. (He also has the dubious credit of introducing 'garrison' politics and thuggery to Jamaican politics, tactics that seem to reflect Seaga's own, at times, brutish personality.) When Jamaica joined the US invasion of Grenada, Seaga called a sudden election to take advantage of a surprise boost in popularity and the absence of Manley, who was touring abroad. The PNP boycotted the snap election and thus the JLP 'won' all 60 seats.

For the next six years (1983-89), Jamaica had a corrupt one-party parliament. It was also a one-man show: Seaga held the position of Prime Minister, as well as the head of the ministries of finance, planning, information, culture, and defense. The cult of personality, government corruption, and growing poverty and unemployment in the midst of an economic revival turned the electorate against him. (Jamaica was still a polarized society, but one in which the middle and upper classes alone had benefited from the economic recovery; the vast majority of Jamaicans were poorer.)

In September 1988, Hurricane Gilbert tore across the island – the first such storm to do so since 1951. The hurricane devastated crops islandwide, damaged over US$300 million of property, and left one-quarter of Jamaica's population homeless.

## Mark Manley II

Meanwhile, Manley had undergone a political reformation, from anti-American firebrand to middle-of-the-road populist promoter of free enterprise and tourism. Manley dubbed himself a 'mainstream realist.' In 1989, voters gave him a second term (the election period was relatively violence-free), during which he took a leaf from Seaga's book, further deregulating the economy, reducing the

scope of state involvement, pursuing liberal-conservative economic policies, and initiating an anti-drug program. (The US government linked a commitment to millions of dollars in aid to a pledge that Jamaica would initiate a drug eradication program.)

Manley retired from politics in 1992 due to ill health, handing the reins to his deputy, Percival James Patterson – Jamaica's first black prime minister. PJ, as he is colloquially called, continued Manley's blend of left-liberal, free-market policies. In the March 1993 election, the PNP won by a landslide (it took 52 out of 60 seats) against an ailing JLP.

Ensuing years have been marked by modest yet steady economic growth. Tourism, with a few hiccups, has continued to blossom. The period has also seen a dramatic increase in the number of returnees to the island: many educated Jamaicans who had fled the island during the early Manley years had made good abroad and returned to invest in their homeland's future. By 1997, however, Jamaica was again in the midst of a financial crisis, exemplified by crippling interest rates. The economic woes were exacerbated by the international financial crisis of 1997-98, fueling a growing dismay over the economic climate and a palpable political tension. In mid-1998, the IMF issued a rebuke to the Jamaican government, warning that its policies were badly off-course for stability and long-term prosperity.

PJ Patterson is not regarded as a particularly creative or accomplished prime minister and has only tenuous support among the middle classes. Nonetheless, in December 1997 voters delivered the PNP an unprecedented third term – and landslide victory – with 56% of the national vote. The victory reflected the intense disarray and in-feuding within the JLP; it is said that the PNP did not *win* the election, but the JLP *lost* it. The following year, the JLP – against Seaga's recommendation – chose not to contest the national municipal elections of September 1998 and got trounced.

In spring 1999, Jamaica erupted in nationwide riots after the government announced a 30% increase in the tax on gasoline. Three days of looting, arson, and riots left nine people dead, including a Jamaican Defense Force soldier brutally murdered (14 policemen were also shot and injured, and several police stations were bombed with Molotov cocktails). Kingston and Montego Bay, where sugarcane fields were set ablaze, were particularly badly hit. Cruise ships canceled their calls, and leading airlines were forced to halt service to Jamaica, which lost several million dollars in potential revenue. The government rescinded the tax.

## GEOGRAPHY

At 4411 sq miles, about equal to the US state of Connecticut, or one-twentieth the size of Great Britain, Jamaica is the third largest island in the Caribbean and the largest of the English-speaking islands. It is one of the Greater Antilles, which make up the westernmost and largest of the Caribbean islands. (The Lesser Antilles, made up of dozens of smaller islands, lies farther east and curl south like a shepherd's crook.)

Jamaica lies 90 miles south of Cuba, 100 miles west of Haiti, and 600 miles south of Miami. It is within the tropics, 18° north of the equator between latitudes 17° 43' and 18° 32' north and longitudes 76° 11' and 78° 23' west.

The island is roughly egg-shaped, with a sagging underbelly, and measures 146 miles east to west; widths vary between 22 and 51 miles. Despite its relatively small size, Jamaica boasts an impressive diversity of terrain and vegetation. Columbus described it as 'the fairest isle that eyes beheld; mountainous…all full of valleys and fields and plains.' It *is* beautiful, with views worthy of a Winslow Homer painting.

### The Coast

Jamaica is rimmed by a narrow coastal plain pitted with bays everywhere except in the south, where broad flatlands cover extensive areas. Mountains (and resorts) edge against white-sand beaches on the north, west, and northeast coasts. North coast vegetation is lush, more so to the east along the island's windward coast.

The south coast offers sharply contrasting terrain, including several areas of parched savanna where cacti are common, plus two large swampy areas: the vast Great Morass, a wetland fed by the Black River; and Long Bay, a remote strip of marshland. In places, mountains muscle right up to the coast, dividing broad plains dominated by market gardens and sugarcane fields. Beaches are, with few exceptions, composed of gray-brown sand.

Isolated, uninhabited coral cays speckle the sea off the south coast, including the Pedro Cays – important nesting sites for colonies of seabirds.

### The Uplands

Inland Jamaica is mostly mountainous. Almost half the island is at elevations of over 1000 feet. The mountains run through the island's center, rising gradually from the west and culminating in the tortuous Blue Mountains in the east, which are capped by Blue Mountain Peak at 7402 feet. Mountainous spurs and plateaus extend from the central chain to the south coast.

The limestone interior is dramatically sculpted of deep vales and steep ridges. Much of the central uplands is dominated by basket-of-egg topography, highlighted by the Cockpit Country, a virtually impenetrable tract full of irregular karstic, limestone hummocks, vast sinkholes, underground caves, and flat valley bottoms. The drama of this 500-sq-mile region in northwest Jamaica is not obvious from ground level, but from a plane its eerie grandeur is startling. Similar topography blankets much of Jamaica's interior spine.

The limestone plateau rises to the island's backbone, which has a distinctly alpine feel at higher elevations, notably around Mandeville and Christiana. Here the terrain, deep-valed and wooded in deciduous and coniferous trees, is reminiscent of parts of central Europe.

## GEOLOGY

Jamaica and the other islands of the Greater Antilles were first formed by a great volcanic welling about 140 million years ago. Gradually, weathering wore the new land down. The island subsided beneath the sea about 100 million years ago before reemerging some 80 million years later during renewed tectonic activity, creating anew the Blue Mountains, and the 24,720-foot-deep Cayman Trench west of Jamaica. Today, the island is still rising, in places as much as one foot every 1000 years.

Jamaica is in an earthquake zone. Frequent quakes shake the island, often with devastating effect: Port Royal was destroyed in 1692, and Kingston was devastated in 1907. Many thermal springs usher from fissures along the south coast.

The island is cut by about 120 rivers, many of which are bone dry for much of the year but become raging torrents after heavy rains, washing silt onto the lowland plains and causing great flooding. Only 12 are major – if still modest – rivers.

Two-thirds of the island's surface is composed of limestone (the compressed skeletons of coral, clams, and other sealife). In places, limestone is several miles thick and covered by thick red-clay soils rich in bauxite (the principal source of aluminum). Most was lain down during the geological period when Jamaica was under the sea and conical clams up to 6 feet across built great colonies on the seabed.

Limestone is soft and porous, and rainfall tends to soak into the rock rather than form rivers. As water soaks in, it dissolves the calcium carbonate, creating a tortuously pitted surface and great networks of dramatically sculpted underground caverns. (Water is aided in this action by reacting with limestone and carbon dioxide in the air to form a weak solution of carbonic acid, which speeds the erosion process; vegetation grows in the cracks and further breaks down the rock.) Where the caverns have become too large, the roofs collapse to form vast sinkholes or depressions.

The limestone performs a service, too, by filtering rainfall, which purifies Jamaica's water supply.

## CLIMATE

One of Jamaica's greatest allures is its idyllic tropical maritime climate. (English playwright and entertainer, Noel Coward, called

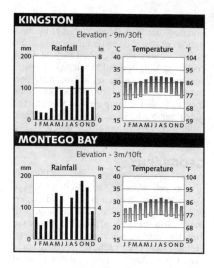

his adopted home 'Dr Jamaica.') Seasons are virtually nonexistent, but weather patterns can change quickly, especially during hurricane season.

There are two weather hotlines visitors can call in Jamaica: ☎ 924-0760 for north coast weather information, or ☎ 924-8055 for south coast.

## Temperatures

Coastal temperatures average a near-constant 80° to 86°F year-round. Temperatures fall steadily with increasing altitude but even in the Blue Mountains average 65°F or more. Monthly temperatures vary less than 6°F, with February and March usually the coolest months. Down by the shore, days are cooled by warm trade winds – known as 'doctor breeze.' A less noticeable nocturnal offshore breeze is known locally as 'the undertaker.' Cool 'northers' can also blow December to March, when cold fronts that bring freezing conditions to Florida can affect Jamaica (on extreme occasions, temperatures may drop near 50°F).

## Rainfall

Annual rainfall averages 78 inches, but there are considerable variations nationwide, with

Montego Bay artisan horsing around

ROBERT FRIED

Yup, it's another hot one

LEE ABEL

At home near Woodstock, Westmoreland

HOLGER LEUE

What to buy in Jamaica – a parrot wood carving from Lou Lou in Cambridge, a roadside cup of soup, or something more potent for the 'drive'

the eastern (or windward) coast receiving considerably more rain than elsewhere on the island. Parts of the John Crow and Blue Mountains receive an average of 300 inches a year (Bowden Pen, in the Upper Rio Grande Valley, holds the record with 496 inches in 1959–60).

A 'rainy season' begins in May or June and extends through November or December, with the heaviest rains in September and October. Rain can fall at any time of year, however, and normally comes in short, heavy showers, often followed by sun.

By contrast, the south coast sees little rain and in places is semi-barren. The Treasure Beach area is particularly dry and can even experience drought in some years, as in 1994, when a drought afflicted the entire island.

Humidity is relatively high year-round, ranging from 63% to 73% in Kingston, and 71% to 77% in Montego Bay.

### Hurricane Season

Although Jamaica lies in the Caribbean 'hurricane belt,' relatively few touch Jamaica. The last great storm to hit the island was Hurricane Gilbert, which roared ashore in 1988, causing immense damage and killing 45 people. The two giant storms of 1998 – Hurricanes George and Mitch – were both near misses.

Officially the hurricane season lasts from June 1 to November 30; August and September are peak months. (All the hurricanes that have struck Jamaica this century have done so before mid-September.) A traditional rhyme is 'June too soon, July stand by, August prepare you must, September remember, October all over.'

## ECOLOGY & ENVIRONMENT

Ecotourism has come late to the Caribbean. Only a decade ago, visitors had to look hard for protected areas. Today, national parks and wildlife reserves are continuing to rise on the neap of an eco-sensitive wave between Miami and Maracaibo, Venezuela. Jamaica has been especially slow in discovering that its wilderness is something to safeguard, but – at last – is waking up.

Coastal mangrove and wetland preserves, montane cloud forests, and other wild places are strewn across Jamaica, yet most travelers stick to beach resorts instead. Those who do get close to nature are as yet poorly served by wildlife reserves: ecological treasures such as Long Bay's stunning swamplands – the last refuge of endangered manatees – remain untapped.

Ecologically, Jamaica is in dire straits. Many of Jamaica's endemic (unique to the island) wildlife species are endangered or gone forever. According to the World Conservation Union, in 1998 Jamaica ranked ninth in the world for number of endangered amphibians. Jamaica also made the top ten

### The Big Blows

Caribbean hurricanes originate off the coast of Africa, forming as winds rush toward a low-pressure area and begin to swirl around it due to the rotational force of the earth's spin. They move counterclockwise across the Atlantic, fed by warm winds and moisture, building up force in their 2000-mile-run toward the Caribbean.

On the islands, the first stage of a hurricane's approach is called a 'tropical disturbance.' The next stage is a 'tropical depression.' When winds exceed 40mph, the system is upgraded to a 'tropical storm' and is usually accompanied by heavy rains. The storm becomes a hurricane if winds exceed 74mph and intensifies around an eye (a center of calm).

Hurricanes can range from 50 miles in diameter to devastating giants more than 1000 miles across. Their energy is prodigious – far more than the mightiest thermonuclear explosions.

For more on hurricanes, see Dangers & Annoyances in the Facts for the Visitor chapter.

for countries with the most endangered plant species. Fishermen using dynamite threaten fish stocks and coral reefs, particularly in western Jamaica. Crocodiles and marine turtles, though protected, are routinely killed by locals, and turtle nests are raided for eggs. Other endangered species are also captured or killed for sale to tourists.

Many other species, including those that inhabit coral reefs, are endangered by such threats as pesticides, siltation, toxic by-products of the bauxite industry, and urban development. For example, the government Urban Development Council is blithely pushing the massive planned city of Portmore into the Hellshire Hills – a forbidding, parched habitat of jagged limestone covered with the last remnant of 'dry limestone forest,' which serves as home to the last of the endangered Jamaican iguanas. Sadly, most existing legislation has been largely ineffectual: authorities are underfunded, laws lack teeth, and fines are absurdly low. Still, there have been a few signs of hope.

The Wildlife Protection Act (1974) gave protection to crocodiles, manatees, the yellow snake, and several other endangered species. The Beach Protection Act was enacted in 1978 to forestall removal of sand by hotel developers creating artificial beaches. But only in 1992 was the Natural Resources Conservation Authority (NRCA) entrusted with responsibility for 'effectively managing the physical environment of Jamaica so as to ensure conservation.' The NRCA also has the duty of promoting ecological consciousness among Jamaicans and of managing the national parks and protected areas under the Protected Areas Resource Conservation Project (PARC), a joint venture between the Jamaican government and the US Agency for International Development (USAID). NRCA's efficacy has been weak, but has scored a few noteworthy victories, such as stopping the Coffee Expansion Project in the Rio Grande Valley. Its theme is 'A Fi Wi It...Tek Care' (It is for all of us...Preserve it).

The past few years have seen a stirring of eco-awareness. Educated Jamaicans are beginning to adopt a more cautious attitude toward unrestrained hotel construction.

Modern-minded entrepreneurs are beginning to open up nature spots for those wanting to escape the resort routine. And numerous nongovernmental organizations born in recent years have become the spearhead of conservation efforts, such as the Jamaica Association of Dive Operators (JADO) and the Negril Coral Reef Preservation Society.

In 1996 Jamaica held its first Green Expo, a forum featuring a 50-foot-long nature trail with wildlife exhibits. A certification program to enhance environmental tourism – 'Greening Negril 2000' – was also launched in 1998, established by the World Travel & Tourism Council as a pilot project for the Caribbean. For information on future Green Expos, contact the Jamaica Conservation & Development Trust (☎ 960-2848, fax 960-2850, jamcondt@uwimona.edu.jm), at 95 Dumbarton Ave, Kingston 10.

The NRCA (☎ 923-5155, fax 923-5070), at 53 Molyne Rd, Kingston 10, has a toll-free hotline – ☎ 0888-991-5005 – on which you can report environmental abuse.

Other information resources include:

Friends of the Sea
(☎ 974-9832, fax 974-6494) 6 James Ave, Ocho Rios

Jamaica Environment Trust
(☎ 960-3693, fax 929-1074) 58 Half Way Tree Rd, Kingston 10

National History Society of Jamaica
(☎ 927-1202) Dept of Zoology, UWI, Mona Campus, Kingston 7

National Environmental Societies Trust
(☎ 960-3316, 922-0667, fax 922-0665) 46 Duke St, Kingston 8

Negril Coral Reef Preservation Society
(☎ 957-3735, fax 957-4473) PO Box 27, Negril

Portland Environment Protection Association
(☎ 993-9632, fax 993-3407) 6 Allen St, Port Antonio

South Coast Conservation Foundation
(☎ 978-4047, 978-4050, fax 927-3754) 91a Old Hope Rd, Kingston 6

Southern Trelawny Environmental Agency
(☎ 919-6992) Albert Town PO, Trelawny

St Elizabeth Environmental Association
(☎ 965-2074, fax 965-2076) 2 High St, Black River

Trelawny Environment Protection Agency (☎/fax 954-4087) c/o Trelawny Chamber of Commerce, Shop 6, Albert George Shopping Centre, Falmouth

Wildlife & Environmental Conservation Action Now (☎ 927-1085) Hope Zoo, Royal Botanical Gardens, Kingston 7

## Ecological Treasures

The Caribbean has beaches, but it also has bush. Within the region, no other island's interior gives its beaches as much competition as Jamaica's.

Visitors to the island can forsake sandals for hiking boots to follow mountain trails, shower in remote waterfalls, and shoot birds through the lens of a camera.

To date, however, the only area that has been developed as a steadfast ecotour destination is Black River's Great Morass, a swampland – with easily seen crocodiles – penetrated by boat from the town of Black River.

Creative entrepreneurship, however, is finally putting the Rio Grande Valley on the map as *the* destination for hiking. The lower folds of the Blue and John Crow Mountains have forests of towering antediluvian tree ferns, rhododendron dells, and cloud-swathed thickets dripping with mosses;

## Tips for Environmentally Conscious Travelers

**Don't litter.** Take only photographs, leave only footprints. If you see litter, pick it up. Support recycling programs.

**Respect the property of others.** Never take 'souvenirs' such as shells, plants, or artifacts from historical sites or natural areas. Treat shells, sea urchins, coral, and other marine life as sacred.

**Don't buy products made from endangered species.** By buying products made of tortoise shell, coral, or bird feathers, you are contributing to the decimation of wildlife. (See 'Shopping with a Conscience' in the Facts for the Visitor chapter.)

**Keep to the footpaths.** When hiking, always follow designated trails. Natural habitats are often quickly eroded, and animals and plants are disturbed by walkers who stray from the beaten path.

**Don't touch or stand on coral.** Coral is extremely sensitive and is easily killed by snorkelers and divers who make contact. Likewise, boaters should never anchor on coral – use mooring buoys. It's the law!

**Sponsor environmental consciousness in others.** Try to patronize hotels, tour companies, and merchants that act in an environmentally sound manner. Consider their impact on waste generation, noise levels, energy consumption, and the local culture.

**Support community tourism.** Many local communities derive little benefit from Jamaica's huge tourism revenues. Educate yourself on community tourism and ways you can participate (see 'Community Tourism' in the Central Highlands chapter). Use local guides wherever possible.

**Respect the community.** Learn about the customs of the region and support local efforts to preserve the environment and traditional culture.

**Tell others.** Politely intervene when you observe other travelers behaving in an environmentally or socially detrimental manner. Educate them about the potential negative effects of their behavior.

orchids are easily seen along trails through Hollywell National Park, as well as on the climb up Blue Mountain Peak (7402 feet). And Negril's Great Morass (still virtually untapped, yet literally a stone's throw from the beaches) has finally gained badly needed protection and is being developed as a prime eco-attraction, with timid crocodiles, fabulous birdlife, and diverse ecosystems.

Other prize areas include the totally uncharted Cockpit Country and the Font Hill Reserve, which teem with crocodiles and waterfowl. Long Bay's as-yet-untapped swamps harbor crocodiles, exotic birdlife, and other unique and much-imperiled wildlife that could be seen with comparative ease – if only some bright entrepreneur would cotton on. At the east end of Long Bay, and receiving few visitors, is Canoe Valley (Alligator Pond), another wetland that harbors endangered manatees.

Much of the north coast, of course, is fringed by coral reefs more beautiful than a casket of gems. (See the Outdoor Activities chapter for diving and hiking options.)

## Felling the Forests

Virtually the entire island was smothered with forest and marshland when Columbus landed, but the island has been ravaged during the intervening 500 years. Forests were felled and wetlands drained for sugar and, later, for bananas. Jamaica's hardwoods were logged, too, to supply English (and Jamaican) furniture designers and craftspeople. Tourist resorts and teeming populations engaged in survival are edging up against much that remains.

Saving Jamaica's forests is not simply an aesthetic consideration: the nation's water supply depends on halting deforestation and protecting watersheds.

Jamaica has protected a greater percentage – 22% – of its 2667 sq miles of forest cover than any other Greater Antillean island; most of this is mangroves and upper montane forest. The sad news is that the island has been losing its forest cover at a rate of more than 5% per year, according to a 1994 study, making Jamaica's rate of deforestation among the highest of any country in the world – more than twice that of Costa Rica and more than four times that of Mozambique, the highest in Africa. The Plant Conservation Centre says well-forested areas in Jamaica have fallen from 32% in the 1920s to 18% in the 1950s and a mere 5% today. Jamaica also loses an estimated 20,930 tons per sq mile per annum: wherever the slopes have been denuded (stripped), rains quickly tear away the topsoil, a situation exacerbated in the Blue Mountains by the Coffee Industry Board, which planted coffee without due regard for conservation techniques. In the Yallahs Valley, the denudation of land is so bad that torrential floods frequently tear down the valley, stripping soils and inundating croplands. In 1961, the Yallahs Valley Land Authority began replanting pines, mahoe, and eucalyptus to stabilize the slopes, but it has been an arduous battle against continued slash-and-burn smallholders and lack of funds.

Explaining to a destitute farmer that he can't cut trees to grow crops is difficult at best. Enforcement of regulations is virtually nonexistent, and the government has no official tree-planting program to replace what is lost (the Forest Dept's tree nursery at Twickenham Park produces only a fraction of its seedling-producing capability). Such efforts have relied on nonprofit organizations such as the Jamaica Agricultural Society, which initiated a massive tree-planting campaign in 1995, but the program has yet to bear fruit.

## Community Involvement

'Meet the People' has been the recent cry of Caribbean governments wishing to stimulate tourism that complements and supports local communities and thereby helps preserve the cultural heritage. For example, Jamaica's Community Tourism efforts urge visitors to take meals, outings, work-visits, and accommodations with local villagers.

Rural communities are also being encouraged to partake in preserving their natural heritage and, by doing so, to benefit from the ecotourism boom. Nature-guide training, and environmental and cultural awareness programs, are growing, as in the Blue Mountains, where PARC is attempting to

## Meet the People

Two decades ago, the JTB developed the Meet the People program, so that visitors to the island could interact with Jamaicans in their home environment and gain an appreciation for island life. Normally this involves being invited to an afternoon tea, dinner, or cocktail party; joining a family at a church service; sightseeing; or even a few hours of sharing the host's work environment.

About 600 volunteer families participate. JTB officials interview the families and inspect their premises to ensure that they meet the program's standards. The JTB tries to match ages, professions, and hobbies of host and visitor. Since the JTB wishes to put Jamaica in the most positive light, you can expect to see middle-class or even upper-class life (the governor's wife regularly participates in the program).

There's no charge, but a small gift (or picking up at least a portion of any tab) is considered a common courtesy.

encourage community involvement in the evolution of the Blue Mountains: with John Crow National Park as a potential eco-escape. Most notable, however, is the success of tour operator Valley Hikes in training guides and fostering eco-consciousness in the Rio Grande Valley in Portland parish.

Similar efforts are being made nationwide. The Jamaica Tourist Board (JTB) is actively involved in programs that sponsor community awareness of the importance of tourism (27% of the nation's populace derives an income from tourism).

## FLORA & FAUNA
### Flora
Jamaica has a perennial summer, a source for year-round flamboyants to bloom. Jamaica boasts more than 3000 species of flowering plants (including 237 species of orchids), of which at least 827 are endemics found nowhere else. The British Isles, many

times larger, can manage only one-twentieth that number. Jamaica is also renowned for having some 60 bromeliad species; dozens of epiphyte species (air plants) such as Old Man's Beard, which grows along power lines; and 550 species of ferns. A quarter of the orchids are endemic, including the diminutive 'Lady Nugent's purse.' Most are epiphytic, living attached to other plants and tree limbs.

Gingers are common and come in various forms, including the ubiquitous and showy torch ginger, with clusters of thick, deep crimson petals. Anthuriums are another dazzling flower, with heart- shaped leaves of pink, white, or blood-red overhung by a pendulous stamen. Heliconias are also abundant, as much in their numbers as in their variety – it's a 40-member family. Bananas are members of the heliconids, all with thick, waxy, vividly colored, pendulous flowers. Likewise, the spectacular bird of paradise, whose scintillating blue stamen and deep orange petals rise like a cockatoo's crest from a mauve, rod-like stem.

Impatiens color roadsides at cooler heights. Periwinkle grows everywhere and is commonly used in bush medicines. Hibiscus is a tropical favorite whose gorgeous flowers brighten many hotel and household gardens. It comes in pink, yellow, white, and vermilion varieties and is distinguished by its long, pollen-tipped stamen jutting up through the center (although there are dozens of exotic variants). The poinsettia is also common and is favored during Christmas season, when it turns blood-red. Many other native plants are used in herbal medicines, teas, and spices, among them cerasee, a climbing vine of the cucumber family; and pimento, Jamaica's only indigenous spice and a member of the myrtle family (periwinkle also belongs to this family).

A native pineapple from Jamaica was the progenitor of Hawaii's pineapples (the fruit even appears on the Jamaican coat of arms).

A great many species are exotics introduced from abroad. Two of the most obvious are the ubiquitous bougainvillea, whose tissue-paper-like 'petals' are actually leaves that blaze purple, pink, and orange; and the equally widespread poinciana, introduced from London's Kew Gardens in 1858. Ackee, the staple of Jamaican breakfasts, was brought from West Africa in 1778. The first mango tree arrived in 1782 after Admiral George Rodney captured a French ship taking the plants from Mauritius to the French West Indies. Capt William Bligh arrived in Jamaica in 1779 bearing 700 breadfruit trees aboard the *Providence* (his first vessel, the *Bounty*, had ended with the famous mutiny). But cocoa and cashew are natives of Central America and the West Indies, as is cassava, a root crop that was once a staple for indigenous peoples. Bombay mango, despite its name, flourishes only on Jamaica, having evolved from its earlier progeny.

Another true-blooded native is bladderwort, a carnivorous plant that lures insects into its bladder where they trigger a trap door and are gradually digested. Likewise, the endemic duppy flytrap – a climbing vine that bears an 8-inch-wide, heart-shaped purple flower (the largest in Jamaica) – has a hollow flower that exudes a noxious smell that attracts flies. The flies enter through a tiny hole and are trapped inside by hairs pointing inward. The duppy plant doesn't consume the fly, however. In its struggle to escape, the fly becomes smothered with pollen – a crafty reproductive device. Eventually the hairs collapse, allowing the fly to escape.

Many visitors are surprised to find cacti flourishing in the parched south, especially in the Hellshire Hills and around Treasure Beach. The opuntia cactus, or prickly pear, is popular with many poor Jamaicans, who roast and eat it (it tastes like roast pork).

Jamaica has several unique cactus species, including the queen of the night cactus, which blooms spectacularly, and god okra, an endemic climbing cactus that bears a scarlet edible fruit called 'vinepear.' Other endemics are the melon cactus, which has a melon-like base topped by a magenta flower; dildos, commonly used as hedges in the Treasure Beach region; the *Rhipsalis baccifera* cactus, locally called spaghetti cactus; and the Turk's Head cactus, resembling a *fez*.

**Tree Species** The national flower is the dark blue bloom of the lignum vitae tree, found mostly in the dry southern plains and coastal foothills. Its timber is the heaviest of all known woods and much in demand by carvers, but the bark, gum, fruit, leaves, and blossoms also serve other useful purposes, including medicines for gout and syphilis. The hefty wood was once popular with shipbuilders (though it is so dense that it sinks in water) and by British policemen, whose sturdy truncheons were made of the painfully solid wood. Its beautiful blossom attracts large numbers of butterflies.

The national tree is blue mahoe, an endemic form of hibiscus with a ruler-straight trunk reaching 70 feet. It derives its name from the blue-green streaks in its beautiful wood, which is favored by carvers and craftspeople. Mahoe also blossoms splendidly, with blooms blazing from yellow to red. Another dramatically flowering tree is the vermilion 'flame of the forest' (also called the 'African tulip tree').

Jamaica has long been known for the quality of its hardwoods. The native mahogany, which grows predominantly in limestone areas, is considered the highest grade mahogany in the world. It and ebony (known for its dark heavy wood, perfect for carving) have been logged and decimated during the past two centuries. Both are now extremely rare. Ebony can be recognized by its burst of bright vermilion flowers after rains.

Other native trees include the massive silk cotton, the huge buttress flanks of which are unmistakable. It's said to be a favored habitat of *duppies* (ghosts). Another dramatic tree is the strangler fig, or ficus, which begins life as an ephiphyte on the branches of other trees. It sends down woody roots that attach themselves to the ground and expand – as if from some Hollywood horror movie – to totally engulf the host tree. Eventually they smother the host, which may die and rot away, leaving a thriving free-standing ficus, whose hollow trunk sometimes serves as a habitat for bats or rodents.

The native calabash tree can be recognized by its large gourd, which is dried and carved into crafts such as storage dishes or 'shake-shakes' (maracas) filled with stones. Logwood, introduced to the island in 1715, grows wild in dry areas. Its wood produces a dark blue dye. Logwood was grown commercially in great quantities during the 19th century, when the value of logwood exports briefly exceeded that of sugar. Another intriguing tree is boarwood, named for a folk belief that wild boars, when injured, will gash the bark with their tusks and rub their wounds on the sap. It is found in the Blue Mountains.

Palms are everywhere, except at the highest reaches of the Blue Mountains. There are many species, including the stately royal palm (a Cuban import), which grows to over 100 feet and even has a reserve named for it in the Great Morass near Negril. Other species are endemic, such as the thatch palms, the leaves of which produce fiber rope used in wicker.

Much of Jamaica's west coast is fringed by mangroves – the only tree able to survive with its roots in saltwater. All four New World species are found here. The hardy plant puts down a circumference of slender stilt roots, forming a great tangle that helps build up the shoreline and prevent erosion by trapping sediment. It also provides a rich compost for algae and other microorganisms, which draw crustaceans and spawning fish in vast numbers. Many creatures are specially adapted to survive in the mangroves; 80% of popular seafood species (such as snapper and shrimp) spend a portion of their juvenile life in the mangroves. Mangroves have suffered immense devastation at the hands of humans, but are now protected as a vital resource.

## Fauna

**Mammals** Jamaica has very few mammal species. Small numbers of wild hogs still roam remote pockets of the John Crow Mountains, Cockpit Country, Portland Ridge, and a few other isolated wilderness areas. There are also feral goats, which have reverted to their long-horn form, and, though rarely seen, are strikingly different from their ubiquitous, domesticated cousins. There are 23 species of bats (called 'rat-bats') but not the vampire bat. These furry mammals usually hide by day inside caves or beneath tree limbs, then emerge at night to feed on fruit or insects.

Otherwise the only native land mammal is the endangered Jamaican hutia, or coney, a large brown rodent akin to a guinea pig. Once a favorite food source of Arawaks, it has since been hunted to near extinction by man and mongoose. Habitat loss now restricts the highly social, nocturnal beast to the Blue Mountains, Hellshire Hills, and a few other remote areas of eastern Jamaica. It lives underground and is rarely seen.

The hutia: social but underground

The most obvious mammals are all imports, such as cattle and the common goat. Jamaica has its own hardy cattle hybrids, such as red poll. The mongoose is the animal you are most likely to see, usually scurrying across the road. This weasel-like mammal was introduced from India in the late 19th century to control rats, but it reproduced quickly and turned its attention on domestic fowl and native animal species. It's now considered a destructive pest. By destroying the harmless yellow snake, birds, lizards, and other species, the mongoose has disturbed the ecological balance. Even the rat, the scourge of sugar plantations, was introduced from abroad (albeit accidentally), as a stowaway aboard the first ships.

**Amphibians & Reptiles** Jamaica harbors plenty of slithery and slimy things. The largest and most enthralling to see are crocodiles (incorrectly called 'alligators' in Jamaica).

They're found in wetlands and mangrove swamps along the south coast, most notably Font Hill Reserve, Black River's Great Morass, and Long Bay, but also in and around Negril's Great Morass and adjacent rivers. Ruthless hunting in recent centuries has reduced their numbers considerably. Although protected, they are still taken illegally due to prejudice (see 'What a Croc!' in the Southwest Coast chapter).

Lizards are everywhere in their bright green, dusky brown, or speckled, rainbow-colored suits. Jamaica has 24 species of lizards, mostly small but some attaining up to 20 inches or more, and even 5 feet for the iguana. The Jamaican iguana hangs on to survival in the remote backwaters of the Hellshire Hills (see 'Jamaican Iguana' in the Kingston & Environs chapter). Some lizards – the anolids – can change color as camouflage. The male anole lizard, when courting, has his own silent rendering of the wolf-whistle: he blows out his throat-fan, brilliantly liveried in saucy vermilion.

My favorites are the geckos, charming but noisy little creatures that can often be seen hanging on your ceiling by their suction-cup feet. Locals call the gecko the 'croaker' and attribute a dark side to the harmless critter, from which Jamaicans superstitiously recoil. (Jamaican folk say: 'when croakin' lizard sing, sign de rain soon come'.) Likewise, the harmless, smooth-scaled galliwasp is superstitiously considered to have a fatal bite. Some Jamaicans still believe that if bitten, you must reach water before the lizard to avoid death (a West African belief).

Jamaica has five species of snakes, none poisonous. All are endangered thanks mostly to the ravages of the mongoose, which has entirely disposed of a sixth species – the black snake. Count yourself lucky to see the nocturnal yellow snake (a constrictor called 'nanka' locally), which can grow to 8 feet in length. Most other species rarely exceed a foot long.

The island also harbors 17 species of frogs (including four tree-frog species and two species of whistling frogs) and one toad. The giant toad, called the 'bull frog,' was introduced from Barbados in 1844 by a planter who hoped that the species would eat rats that were destroying his cane. The plump toad, which weighs up to 2.5lb, is an equal-opportunity consumer: anything bite-size and animate is food. Uniquely, all Jamaica's 14 species of endemic frogs don't undergo a tadpole stage; instead, tiny frogs emerge in adult form directly from eggs.

**Insects** There are mosquitoes and bees and wasps, but most bugs are harmless. For example, a brown scarab beetle, called the 'newsbug,' flies seemingly without control and when it flies into people, locals consider it a harbinger of important news. One species of wasp is particularly noteworthy: *Aullopus bellus*, a meat-eater that makes itself a larder of interconnected mud chambers, like jail cells, to store its stock of food – spiders and other insects, which the wasp keeps alive after chewing off their legs or wings. Diamond-shaped 'stinky bugs' are exactly that, advertising their exotic nature with a lime green color and offensive smell.

Many insect species are quite beautiful, particularly the 120 butterfly species and countless moth species, of which 21 are endemic. My favorite is a large dark brown moth, which has a predilection for flitting in through open windows and is often mistaken by frightened tourists for a vampire bat (locals call it a 'rat-bat'). It's quite harmless. The most spectacular butterfly is the giant swallowtail, *Papillio homerus*. The 6-inch wingspan of this native qualifies it as one of the world's largest butterflies. It flies only at higher altitudes, and lives in the John Crow Mountains and the eastern extent of the Blue Mountains (and in the Cockpit Country in smaller numbers). Though the species is endangered, many hustlers around the Blue Mountains try to sell swallowtails to tourists. Don't buy! If you purchase, you are encouraging a destructive mentality and participating in an anti-environmental, illegal act.

In late summer, you'll also witness yellow butterflies migrating westward by the tens of thousands like a storm of sweet peas. No one seems to know where they gather, but at times the sky is as thick as a blizzard.

You're sure to come across fireflies (called *blinkies* and *peeny-wallies*) flashing luminously in the dark. The phosphorescent green flashing is used as a signal to guide potential mates. About 50 species are found in Jamaica, each of which has its own individual gender-specific signal so that males and females can tell each other apart and prevent mating with other species. Upperclass women used to wear live fireflies as necklaces. Peeny-wallies were also placed en masse in jars to act as lanterns.

Spiders, there are aplenty (though less than one might expect in the tropics). There are some fearsomely large arachnids such as the gargantuan black, red, and orange silk spider, reaching the size of a grown man's hand. It spins an appropriately expansive web – spanning a meter and tethered by 'cables' twice as long – capable of entrapping small birds.

**Birds** Jamaica is popular with birdwatchers. The island has more than 255 bird species, of which 25 species and 21 subspecies are endemic (found nowhere else on earth), and 113 species breed on the island. Several endemic species have become extinct in recent years, including the Jamaican black-capped petrel and parakeet. Others, such as the Jamaican blackbird and ring-tailed pigeon, are endangered. Almost every species of Jamaican bird is now protected by law.

Stilt-legged, snowy-white cattle egrets are a common sight. They usually accompany cattle – often riding piggyback, their long bills jabbing at flies. John crows are also found all over Jamaica. The ungainly bird is actually a vulture, known in the US as the turkey buzzard. It is feared in Jamaica, perhaps because of its undertaker plumage, bald red head, and hunched shoulders. It's a subject of several folk songs and proverbs, including one of a poor man pretending to be well-to-do: 'John Crow say 'im a dandy man but 'im only have so-so feather.' Local lore states that you can predict the approach of rain when John Crows take to the air. Infrequently, albino John Crows are born. Jamaicans call them 'John Crow Headman' and have a saying that warns 'every John

Crow t'ink his pickney white,' meaning everyone thinks their child (or other creation) is the best in the world.

In the mountains you may hear the mournful note of the solitary Jamaican eleania or Blue Mountain vireo. Lower down are the Jamaican euphonia; rare yellow-billed and black-billed parrots; grassquits; the beautiful little black-cloaked, yellow-breasted banana quit (also called the 'beany bird' or 'sugarbird'); and the mockingbird, which imitates the calls of other birds and sings by night (earning the moniker 'nightingale'). It is particularly vocal before sunrise, when its poetic songs may be rebutted by some unpoetic terms in the Jamaican dialect.

That sneaky thief on your breakfast table fearlessly sampling your butter is the kling-kling, or shiny black Greater Antillean grackle (also called the 'tinglings'), with eyes like Spanish beads and a kleptomaniac's habits in hotel dining rooms. They are gregarious beasts and noisy too. Another bird with questionable ethics is a shiny black member of the oriole family known as the cowbird. The female practices 'brood parasitism' – she seeks out a suitable nest of another species and adds her own egg to those of the builder, who incubates the entire clutch. The cowbird's egg usually hatches first and dominates the nest so that the host's nestlings starve. Introduced only in recent years, the cowbird is already having a deleterious effect on other bird species.

*Patoo* (a West African word) is the Jamaican name for the owl. Many islanders superstitiously regard owls as a harbinger of death. Jamaica has two species: the screech owl and the endemic brown owl. There are also four endemic species of flycatchers, a woodpecker, and many rare species of doves, including the crested quail dove, or 'mountain witch,' which wears a multihued cloak of black, purple, cinnamon, and bronze. The ground dove is considered to be a ghost and is generally safe from children's slingshots because it's believed harming a 'duppy bird' brings disaster. Many resident species have developed behavior patterns unique to the island. The Jamaican tody (locally called 'robin redbreast'), a wren-size, lime-green bird with white chest and scarlet throat, nests underground at the end of a 2-foot-long tunnel.

Jamaica, which lies on a migration route, is visited in both spring and autumn by dozens of bird species en route between summer and winter habitats. Birdwatchers can also spot West Indian whistling ducks, herons, gallinules, and countless other waterfowl in the swamps. The long-necked whistling duck, uniquely, cannot quack. Instead it has a high-pitched, eerie whistling call. Jamaica has one of the Caribbean's largest populations of this rare bird: there are fewer than 8000 in the world.

Large, graceful pelicans can be seen diving for fish, while frigate birds soar high above. They have a wingspan of over 6 feet; long, hooked beaks add to their sinister appearance. Offshore cays vibrate with the honking and caterwauling of seabirds such as boobies and noddy terns.

Enchanting hummingbirds are immediately identifiable by their vivid plumage and the buzz of their rapid wings. They can fly sideways, backward, and even upside-down, their wings a filmy fast-beat blur.

Jamaica has four of the 16 Caribbean species of hummingbirds (all hummingbirds are found only in the New World). The crown jewel of West Indian hummingbirds is undoubtedly the streamertail, the national bird, which is indigenous to Jamaica. This beauty boasts shimmering emerald feathers, a velvety black crown with purple crest, and long, slender, curved tail feathers. It is known locally as the 'doctorbird,' apparently for its long bill that resembles a 19th-century surgical lancet. The red-billed streamertail inhabits the west, while the black-billed lives in the east. It adorns Jamaican two-dollar bills and the logo of Air Jamaica.

The Jamaican mango hummingbird is particularly abundant around Kingston and Montego Bay. Another dazzler is the vervain hummingbird, dark-green and so small and quick in flight that it is almost invisible (it is the world's second smallest bird – the smallest lives in Cuba).

Folklore says that hummingbirds have magical curative powers, and Jamaican sorcerers still turn the birds' tiny bodies into charms to protect their possessions from thieves. The mango hummer is known also as 'black magic' because a dried powder from its body is used as a love potion.

See the Outdoor Activities chapter for a list of birdwatching sites.

**Marine Life** Jamaica's immense undersea world is enthralling: its marine life is as varied as its habitats. Leaf-like orange gorgonians (named for the trio of snake-haired Greek goddesses) spread their fingers upward toward the light. There are contorted sheets of purple staghorn and lacy outcrops of tubipora resembling delicately woven Spanish *mantillas*, sinuous boulder-like brain corals, and soft-flowering corals that sway to the rhythms of the ocean currents.

Over 700 species of fish zip in and out of the exquisite reefs and swarm through the coral canyons: wrasses, parrotfish, snappers, bonito, kingfish, jewelfish, and scores of others. The smaller fry are ever-preyed upon by barracudas, giant groupers, and tarpon. Sharks, of course, are frequently seen among the coral ledges, though most of these are harmless nurse sharks. Farther out, the cobalt deeps are run by sailfish, marlin, and manta rays.

**Coral Ecology** Corals are tiny animals with a great gaping mouth at one end surrounded by tentacles to gather food. The polyps live protected by an external skeleton, the production of which is dependent upon algae that live inside the polyp's tissue. The creatures live in vast colonies that reproduce both asexually by budding (many species are dimorphic – both male and female), and sexually through a synchronous release of spermatozoa (when this happens the surrounding waters become milky). Together they build up huge frameworks – the reefs.

A reef is usually composed of scores of different species and shapes, each occupying its own niche. All corals can flourish only close to the ocean surface, where they are nourished by sunlight in clear, unpolluted waters above 70°F.

When it dies, the coral's skeleton turns to limestone, which another coral polyp may use as a foundation to cement its own skeleton. The entire reef system is gnawed away by parrotfish and other predators that browse on the coral. A reef can repair itself, but much of Jamaica's reef system has been severely damaged (and continues to be) by the discharge of waste and agricultural runoff and destructive habits of some fishers.

Coral reefs are the most complex and sensitive of all ecosystems and take thousands of years to form. The rainbow-hued reefs are divided into life zones gauged by depth, temperature, and light; each zone harbors distinct fish, coral, and other species. Jamaica's reefs are prodigal places, especially along the north coast, where the reef is almost continuous and much of it is within a few hundred yards of shore.

Off the south coast, reef systems are broken and far from shore.

**Marine Turtles** Three species of marine turtles – the green, hawksbill, and loggerhead – migrate hundreds of miles to nest and lay eggs at Jamaica's beaches (as they have done for at least 150 million years). Only the relatively small hawksbill does so regularly.

Arawaks considered turtles a delicacy. The Arawaks' subsistence needs had as little impression on the vast aquatic herds as the Plains Indians of North America had on the buffalo. Columbus' 'discovery' of the West Indies, however, opened up the waters to rapacious hunting of turtles, which are now endangered.

Unfortunately, Jamaican fishers still catch turtles for meat, and the hawksbill's lustrous shell is much sought after for jewelry. You may see turtle shells hanging in bars or even for sale. Remember: it is strictly illegal to sell or purchase turtle products of any kind. To do so only encourages their decimation.

**Marine Mammals** The Caribbean monk seal, once common in Jamaican waters, was last seen in 1952 on the Pedro Cays. Unfortunately, the endangered West Indian manatee is heading for a similar fate. The shy and gentle creatures were once common around the island and formed a staple of the Arawaks' diet. Only about 100 still survive in Jamaican waters, exclusively in the swamps of Long Bay on the south coast. (You can see them with relative ease at Alligator Pond, also known as Canoe Valley.) Occasional manatee sightings are reported at Negril's Great Morass, where environmentalists are hoping to reintroduce the species.

Manatees are warm-blooded marine mammals with a huge bloated body (like plump wine sacks), a blunt snout, and a paddle-like tail. They have a voracious appetite and can consume 100lb of water hyacinths and other floating vegetation daily. They can reach up to 12 feet in length and weigh over 1000lb (see 'Mermaid or Manatee?' in the Southwest Coast chapter).

The ever-smiling dolphins are frequently seen swimming alongside boats, particularly off the south coast.

## National Parks

Jamaica's embryonic park system comprises three national parks: the Blue Mountains-John Crow National Park, the Montego Bay Marine Park, and the Negril Marine Park.

The 300-sq-mile Blue Mountains-John Crow National Park (Jamaica's largest) includes the forest reserves of the Blue and John Crow mountain ranges and spans four parishes. Forty percent of the higher plant species are endemic to the area, and the forests harbor many endangered species, including the Jamaican hutia, giant swallow-tail butterflies, and yellow-billed parrots. Despite its many attractions, the park remains virtually unnoticed by nature lovers.

Both marine parks, meanwhile, are situated around resort areas and were developed to preserve and manage coral reefs, mangroves, and offshore marine resources. The 15-sq-mile Montego Bay Marine Park stretches from the Donald Sangster International Airport to the Great River. Fishing is banned in its perimeter, and water sports are restricted to designated areas. The latest national park lying within the separate yet contiguous Negril Environmental Protection Area, the Negril Marine Park is also zoned for varying uses.

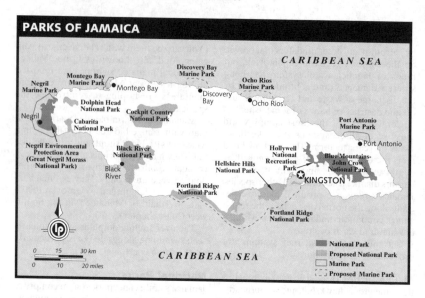

## PARKS OF JAMAICA

There are also a fistful of other wilderness areas granted varying (relatively minimal) degrees of protection. Several additional national parks are being conceptualized and have been touted for years. Notable among the proposed territorial parks is the Cockpit Country National Park. (The local Maroon population, however, opposes creating the park on the premise that it would challenge their regional autonomy.) It is anticipated that Negril's Great Morass, currently an official game sanctuary (hunting is prohibited) and part of the Negril Environmental Preservation Area, will be named a wildlife refuge or national park within the near future. (See the National Parks map for proposed sites.)

Several vital pristine regions are threatened with commercial development due to lax enforcement of regulations.

For information about hiking in Jamaica's national parks, see Hiking in the Outdoor Activities chapter.

### Botanical Gardens

Jamaica has more botanical gardens than any other Caribbean island, and with good reason. Most were established during the colonial era to propagate exotic fruit crops introduced from England's far-flung empire.

Leading gardens include Castleton in the mountains above Kingston; Hope Botanical Gardens, in Kingston; Cinchona, in the Blue Mountains; and Coyaba and Shaw Park, both in Ocho Rios. The Natural History Division of the Institute of Jamaica (☎ 922-6020), at 12 East St in Kingston, has a herbarium of over 125,000 plant specimens.

## GOVERNMENT & POLITICS

Jamaica inherits its political institutions from Britain. It is a stable parliamentary democracy within the Commonwealth – in many regards a miniature England, attested to by the black parliamentary speaker wearing his white wig, with a gold scepter at his side.

Although Jamaica is independent, its titular head of state is Queen Elizabeth II of England. She is represented by a Jamaican-born governor general (often referred to as 'GG' by islanders) appointed on the advice of the prime minister and a six-member Privy Council. Sir Howard Felix Cooke has been governor since 1991. The governor's duties are largely ceremonial and include appointing the prime minister, who is always the leader of the majority party after each national election.

Executive power resides with a cabinet appointed and led by the prime minister, and responsible to Jamaica's Parliament. Parliament consists of a bicameral legislature – a 60-member elected House of Representatives, and a nominated 21-seat Senate, of which 13 members are appointed by the prime minister and eight by the leader of the opposition. The Senate's main function is to review legislation sent forward by the elected House. The House may override a Senate veto, but a two-thirds vote in both houses is required to change Jamaica's constitution.

A full parliamentary term is five years. The governor, however, may call a national election at any time the prime minister requests (that usually means when timing seems propitious for the ruling party). Jamaica has a 'first past the post' electoral system; there is no proportional representation. All Jamaicans aged 18 and over can vote.

## International Relations

Jamaicans have a great affinity with the United Kingdom, which is still regarded fondly by many as the 'mother country' due to the historical relationship, and antagonistically by others (such as Rastafarians) for the same reasons. Part of the Commonwealth, Jamaica has understandably close and amicable political relations with the UK.

Relations with the USA, however, have tended to shift with the times. Currently, the USA is Jamaica's most important trading partner, even after the US withdrew much of its economic commitment to Caribbean nations following the collapse of the Soviet bloc.

Under the current government, Jamaica retains strong ties with Cuba, with whom it trades. Fidel Castro visited Jamaica in 1997 and was warmly received; the Jamaican population, which in general resents the USA's heavy-handedness, holds Castro in high esteem as someone who has shown genuine concern for the impoverished.

## Political Parties

Post-independence Jamaican politics has been largely a struggle between two parties: the presently in power People's National Party (PNP) and the Jamaica Labour Party (JLP). There are also a handful of minor parties, including the National Democratic Movement and the communist Worker's Party of Jamaica.

**People's National Party** The PNP is a social-democratic party closely affiliated to the National Worker's Union. It was formed in 1938 under the leadership of barrister (attorney) Norman Washington Manley, who headed the party for 31 years before being succeeded by his son Michael, a prominent journalist and trade unionist, considered a hero by the poorer classes, but despised by many among the middle classes for the devastating economic impact that his socialist policies had on the nation.

The PNP's leader is PJ Patterson, the current prime minister and a soft-spoken man whose political philosophy blends free-market economics with a large dose of government largesse. Although less controversial than Manley, 'PJ' is regarded with equal disdain by the same people, who worry that inept government policies are drawing Jamaica back to the brink of ruin.

**Jamaica Labour Party** Despite its name, the JLP is a conservative party with ties to the Bustamante Industrial Trade Union. Founded in 1943 by labor leader Sir Alexander Bustamante, it is currently led by ex-prime minister Edward Seaga, a dynamic yet bullying, often slack-mouthed self-promoter who preaches limited government involvement in the economy. Violent flare-ups in and around Seaga's West Kingston constituency continue to remind voters that the party leader was instrumental in the creation of explosive, one-party enclaves (called 'garrisons').

Despite his economic successes, in recent years Seaga has alienated many of his followers, turned away voters, and faced opposition from fellow MPs (members of Parliament) and party members. Infighting riddles the party. In the December 1997 elections, voters delivered Seaga a sound beating. Seaga seems psychologically unable to relinquish power, has fought off several party coups, and retains his hold on the JLP, which in 1998 was in considerable disarray.

### National Democratic Movement
In October 1995, Bruce Golding, former JLP chair and Seaga's heir-apparent, resigned and formed a new party: the National Democratic Movement. Golding launched his new party with a promise to enact radical constitutional changes to ensure greater accountability and continuity in government policies. Third parties have never won significant support in Jamaica. The party fared so badly in the December 1997 elections that even Golding lost his seat.

### Local Government
Jamaica is divided into three counties (Cornwall, Middlesex, and Surrey) and subdivided into 12 parishes – Clarendon, Hanover, Manchester, Portland, St Ann, St Catherine, St Elizabeth, St James, St Mary, St Thomas, Trelawny, and Westmoreland. The political

subdivision also includes two contiguous corporate areas – Kingston and St Andrew.

Local government is administered by two bodies: elected members of parish councils and elected members of city or municipal councils presided over by an elected mayor. The parishes were initially created by British colonialists and headed by a Custos Rotulorum (Keeper of the Rolls), the monarch's representative. The honorary title is now largely ceremonial and granted to the senior justice of the peace.

In September 1998 the PNP won three-quarters of parish council seats in local government elections, with the promise of enacting local government reforms to give more power back to local governments and parish councils (election turnout was a paltry 31%). Seaga called for his JLP members to boycott the elections, though most defied him. Still, the JLP lost Portland, the only parish council it controlled.

### Corruption & 'Garrison' Politics
The one thing the PNP and JLP have in common is a flair for corruption and pandering – what Jamaicans call 'politricks.'

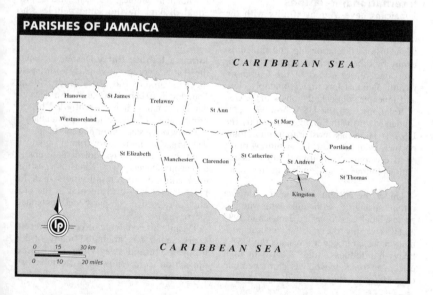

**PARISHES OF JAMAICA**

CARIBBEAN SEA

Hanover · St James · Trelawny · St Ann · St Mary · Westmoreland · St Elizabeth · Manchester · Clarendon · St Catherine · St Andrew · Portland · St Thomas · Kingston

0  15  30 km
0  10  20 miles

CARIBBEAN SEA

**Largesse & Intimidation** Election time in Jamaica is often an explosive affair. Kingston often becomes victim of what travel writer Lynn Ferrin calls Jamaica's 'drop-dead politics,' though things have calmed down since the late 1970s and early 1980s, when scores of Jamaicans lost their lives in partisan killings in 'garrison constituencies,' a term coined to describe zones where political parties maintain their dominance through thuggery and pork-barrel favoritism. Ex-prime minister Edward Seaga is credited with creating the phenomenon.

During the heady 1970s, individual politicians developed strangleholds over some low-income areas in Kingston by pandering to 'dons' (gang leaders) who would deliver blocks of votes in exchange for government contracts and other largesse such as jobs and housing. Political discipline was enforced by bullying and the barrels of Armalite and M16 rifles. Even reggae superstar Bob Marley was a target of a machine-gun attack on his home on the eve of the December 1976 election. Kingston became a city at war with itself. Tivoli Gardens, for example, is a JLP stronghold, while neighboring Arnett Gardens is a PNP garrison. Residents of inner-city communities such as Rema, Concrete Jungle, and Mexico, don't dare pass into neighboring areas for fear of violence. (None of these areas is in the tourist beat.)

Politicians could once claim that they controlled the gangs by rewarding them on a partisan basis. Budgetary constraints in recent years, however, have reduced what they can dole out, and power passed to the dons, who are often arch-criminals. Efforts were made in 1998 to thaw the ice between rival areas, but political killings still mar Kingston and, at their worst, make international headlines. In September 1998, for example, the arrest of a leading don – Donald 'Zeeks' Phipps – on murder and other charges led to six deaths and millions of US dollars of damage when his community members in West Kingston rioted (successfully) to demand his release.

Voter intimidation is common. Former US president Jimmy Carter fielded a team of 60 observers during Jamaica's December 1997 elections and witnessed ballot boxes being stolen and transferred to the opposition party's strongholds, while some polling stations closed early with 100% of the votes declared to one party and 'no correlation between the votes cast and the final results.'

**Corruption** Graft is a way of life in Jamaican politics, and cronyism is entrenched in the system. Many of the funds of the government's so-called social and economic support program, for example, become a gravy train for contractors with political connections. The pork-barrel problem is compounded by the fact that leading officials of government agencies are usually political appointees eager to cash in for themselves before the next change of government. Jamaica is also big on government (a quarter of the workforce is directly employed by the government), with an entrenched and politically vocal bureaucracy. Examples abound of large-scale, get-rich-quick schemes and shameless conniving worthy of Anancy, the Jamaican folktale spider-hero.

One of the biggest areas for graft is in road construction. Each administration announces massive road reclamation programs, but corrupt contractors usurp the money. According to a 1995 article in the *Jamaica Herald*, 'more than half of the J$3 billion (US$78.9) allocated to road construction will go directly into the pockets of a cabal of road contractors.' In 1988, scheming politicians even usurped international relief funds after Hurricane Gilbert 'mashed up' Jamaica.

As of yet, little progress seems to have been made to eradicate the entrenched problem.

## The Judiciary

Jamaica's judicial system is based on English common law and practice.

Local justices of the peace and resident magistrates' courts administer justice at the parish level. Each parish has one magistrate's court (St Andrew has three and Kingston four). In addition, there is a special family court, revenue court, traffic court, and a gun court that handles crimes involving firearms.

There is also a court of appeals; cases can then be appealed to the Supreme Court. The final appeal body is the Judicial Committee of the Privy Council in the United Kingdom. However, PJ Patterson has lent his support to a growing expression of desire to create a Caribbean Court of Appeal.

There are five prisons, and conditions are notoriously bad, particularly in St Catherine Prison in Spanish Town. In 1994 the United Nations' Committee on Human Rights condemned Jamaica for prison conditions and the ill-treatment of prisoners.

## Military

Ostensibly, Jamaica has no army, navy, or air force. The Jamaica Defense Force, comprising 2500 members, however, is a well-armed and highly efficient military unit with its own Coast Guard and Air Wing. It's modeled after the West Indian Regiment of the British Army. It works closely with the US DEA in drug interdiction.

## Police

The police force comes under the responsibility of the Ministry of National Security. Reminiscent of English bobbies, the average policeman or policewoman on the street is exemplary: civil, courteous, mature, and dedicated to upholding the law.

Yet respect for the police among much of the lumpen classes is tenuous. Branches of the police have a reputation for criminal misconduct and, at the highest levels, political manipulation. The charges against the force resulted in reform in 1993 and the first-ever appointment of a civilian police commissioner and a commission intended to place the police service beyond the reach of politicians.

In the past few years, the force has received an injection of capital for new vehicles, and boasts a well-armed, militaristic component that does duty in a vigorous battle against drug lords and syndicated crime figures. Most police carry guns, and it is not unusual to see heavily armed patrols (usually during drug searches) bearing fearsome weaponry.

The JTB has also created the Resort Patrol Services – uniformed patrols at the major resorts whose purpose is to guard the

### Hang 'em High!

In January 1995 the government announced that it was reintroducing hanging after a six-year hiatus. At the time, 272 people were on death row in Spanish Town's notoriously ghastly prison. The first prisoners brought to the gallows were Earl Pratt and Ivan Morgan, convicted of murder in 1979. Although the Jamaican Court of Appeals ruled that capital punishment was legal, lawyers for the convicted murderers managed to earn an 11th-hour reprieve from the UK Privy Council, which commuted the death sentence. The judgment was highly unpopular among Jamaicans (who overwhelmingly favor harsh punishment for anyone convicted of murder or violent crime), resulting in calls for an end to the role of the English House of Lords as final arbiters in Jamaica's legal system.

welfare of tourists. They wear maroon berets and navy blue fatigues.

## ECONOMY

Jamaica's economy is highly developed compared to those of most Caribbean islands. It has a vitalic financial sector with many international banks, a large skilled workforce, and a relatively broad-based economy. The economy, however, is dependent on imported consumer goods and raw materials, which have exceeded earnings from tourism and bauxite (which account for three-quarters of Jamaica's foreign exchange earnings), plus sugar and bananas, all of which are susceptible to erratic worldwide demand. The island has had to confront an acute balance-of-payments crisis and is beleaguered by a massive foreign debt (which stands at US$4.2 billion). Jamaica has also suffered from high inflation and persistent unemployment.

The USA is Jamaica's major trading partner, accounting for more than one-third of the island's exports and more than one-half of its imports.

## Government Policy

There was a marked decline in prosperity during the 1970s and 1980s, which witnessed a flight of capital, and gross domestic product (GDP) fell considerably. Since then a highly successful privatization plan sharply reduced the government's role in the business sector. Beginning in 1992, the government sold off almost 300 of its in-the-red agencies, most notably the national airline, Air Jamaica. Also, incentives were offered to foreign businesses, which began to return to the island, bringing over US$1 billion in investment and creating a burgeoning export-oriented industrial base.

As a result, Jamaica's external debt was reduced considerably and the nation was able to meet the IMF's requirements, which brought Jamaica renewed funding.

It wasn't painless, however. In 1992, government efforts to reduce the budget deficit and inflation in compliance with IMF conditions caused social and industrial unrest.

As Brazilian economist Roberto Campos said, statistics are like bikinis: 'They show what's important but hide what's essential.'

Devaluation hampered economic growth, which stalled in 1993. Another rapid slide in the value of the Jamaican dollar began in mid-1993. By the end of 1995, the Jamaican dollar had lost almost half of its value, and stood at J$38 to the US dollar. Nonetheless, the Patterson administration had accumulated US$435 million in international reserves at the close of 1995 – the first foreign reserves since 1977.

The early Patterson administration had accomplished a dramatic economic turnaround through economic liberalization and tight macroeconomic policies. The Jamaican dollar has remained stable and inflation was only 9% in 1997 (the first single-figure drop in more than a decade).

However, tight economic policy slowed the economy, which has gone into recession (in 1998 interest rates averaged about 40%, and businesses were failing at an unprecedented rate). The Asian financial crisis had ripple effects that washed ashore in Jamaica, exacerbating domestic problems. International investment stalled and, again, began to flee. Reverting to old-style ameliorations, the Patterson administration has increased government jobs by 11% at a time when other nations are slashing the size of government. With the economy in decline, the 1998–99 budget faced a deficit of US$30 billion. In September 1998, the PNP-controlled Parliament voted to increase Jamaica's debt ceiling from J$100 billion (US$2.86 billion) to J$170 billion (US$4.86 billion) – in the same week that it was pleading with the United Nations for debt relief.

In November 1998, the IMF cautioned the Jamaican government about its economic policies, which they said threatened long-term economic stability.

## Hamstrung by Poverty

Despite its relatively developed economy, Jamaica is one of the poorest islands in the Caribbean. Although its GDP was at US$8.4 billion in 1996 (CIA estimate), its per capita GDP of US$3260 reflects the nation's continuing battle with poverty. The UN ranked Jamaica 79th in the world for per-capita income in 1996 (US$3260 per person; by comparison, the Bahamas had a GDP of US$15,900). One-third of Jamaican families officially live below the poverty line. A significant number of these work a small patch of land, coaxing scallions, yams, some carrots, thyme, a little coffee, and perhaps some *ganja* from subsistence-size plots of poor quality. And unskilled workers are abysmally paid (the average minimum wage is US$18 for a 40-hour week). As much as one-third of the working population is unemployed, with another one-third freelancing in what is called the 'informal sector' – prostitution, higgling (bargaining), and hustling.

Although Jamaica has a highly educated middle class, the majority of workers lack any vocational training. Even for trained tradespeople, there is limited work in the boondocks: when a large-scale project arrives, outside contractors usually bring in their own crews. Many adults remain in the boonies, earning pennies but not starving, and unable to significantly better their lives. The ambitious are lured by the city, where the lucky few find work. A life of disappointment, however, lies ahead for a huge percentage of young men and women with no jobs but plenty of dreams.

The slide in the value of the Jamaican dollar has had a devastating impact on the purchasing power of poor families in an economy reliant on imported goods. The population has grown faster than the economy that sustains them. Although middle-class incomes have risen, real incomes have gradually declined since 1980 for the low-paid and irregularly or casually employed. Many families can no longer afford even the basic necessities. Jamaica has no general unemployment benefits (about 125,000 of the abject poor do receive food coupons, however).

## Major Industries

**Tourism** The country's most important source of foreign currency is tourism, which accounts for 45% of Jamaica's foreign income. It also directly employs over 72,000 Jamaicans, plus 217,000 indirectly (a quarter of all jobs).

Jamaica receives more visitors than all but three other Caribbean nations: the Bahamas, Puerto Rico, and – despite the continued embargo – Cuba, whose recent tourism boom has ousted Jamaica into fourth place.

During the early 1980s, tourism withered due to political violence on the island. The decline spurred an aggressive 'Come Back to Jamaica' advertising campaign. Arrivals topped one million for the first time in 1987.

In 1997 almost 1.2 million visitors arrived, a 2.6% increase over 1996. And 1998 saw a 4.4% increase over 1997. More than half of these visitors are cruise-passengers calling in at Ocho Rios and Montego Bay. Jamaica's long-touted and much-delayed development of Port Royal as a third cruise destination will undoubtedly boost these figures even more. Over 30% of visitors come on charter packages. About 65% of visitors come from the USA; 12% come from the UK.

Tourism has changed in recent years, most markedly with a shift toward all-inclusive resorts, and many EP hotels – EP for European Plan, or rooms only – today face parlous times. In 1998 the JTB initiated an aggressive marketing campaign to promote small EP hotels. Jamaicans who rely on passing trade bemoan the impact of all-inclusives, although a JTB study in 1998 showed that all-inclusive guests tend to spend more on tours and incidentals *outside* the resorts than those staying at other types of properties.

The Ministry of Tourism established a Tourism Action Plan (TAP) in 1988 to manage tourism growth, including polishing and restoring Jamaica's attractions, alleviating hustling, and making Jamaica more user-friendly.

Improvements are ongoing: Montego Bay's Gloucester Ave underwent a US$2 million overhaul, as a part of a tourism program that gave a face-lift to Ocho Rios and has targeted Negril, Port Antonio, and the south coast, too. Air Jamaica's positioning of Montego Bay as a rival Caribbean hub to Miami also promises to give Jamaica a long-term boost.

In addition, the JTB initiated a National Tourism Awareness Week in September 1996 with a series of activities to heighten community awareness and appreciation of tourism.

In 1999, the ministries of tourism and education were to introduce tourism studies into the school curriculum for all grades in an effort to generate support at a grassroots level. Tourism Action Clubs will allow children to work on tourism projects. And 'Hello Tourism' programs will link specific schools to specific hotels, all part of concerted efforts by the JTB.

In 1999, the JTB developed a new master plan, which focused on ecotourism, highlighting each region's distinct appeal, and a 'cultural tourism' promotion with none other than Grace Jones as the spokesperson.

The JTB has also long touted the restoration of historic towns such as Falmouth, Port Royal, and Spanish Town as Jamaican Williamsburgs, though no progress has been made to date. And the JTB and Kingston's hoteliers, who have traditionally relied on business traffic, are hoping that the restoration of Port Royal – which finally seemed set to begin in 1999 – and its rebirth as a cruise-ship stop-over will create spillover effects that can revitalize tourism in Kingston.

**Bauxite** For the three decades following WWII, bauxite – 'red gold' – was the bedrock of the Jamaican economy. Jamaica has estimated reserves of 2.5 billion tons – 7% of world reserves and enough to last another century at current production rates.

The industry was born during WWII, when mining grew rapidly to supply the aircraft industry. The rapid post-war expansion of the world's civil aviation industry maintained the momentum. By 1957 Jamaica was the world's number one source of bauxite. During the 1970s it accounted in certain years for over 45% of Jamaica's net earnings and almost 30% of the GDP, and it supplied nearly two-thirds of US requirements for aluminum.

The industry was controlled by a handful of US and Canadian companies. Since the bauxite companies were selling to their parent companies, which processed the ore abroad, they vastly undervalued the bauxite and thereby reduced their royalty and tax payments to the Jamaican government. The crafty device, called transfer pricing, robbed Jamaica of a reasonable share of its natural wealth. In 1974, the Manley administration resolved this by indexing the price of bauxite to the price of aluminum ingots (the government also gained a 51% controlling influence).

A collapse of the worldwide market in the late 1970s to mid-1980s had a devastating impact on the Jamaican economy, but the industry began to recover in the mid-1980s. Earnings, however, have not kept pace due to the reduction in the world price of bauxite.

Today, Jamaica is the world's third largest producer of bauxite and processed alumina. (Only Australia and Brazil produce more.) The industry accounts for one-quarter of the government's income, yet only employs 1% of the workforce.

**Agriculture** Agriculture is by far the most important source of employment (22.5% of the labor force), despite its relatively low contribution to the GDP (less than 10%). Agriculture's share of export earnings has fallen from about 50% in 1970 to just 8.1% in 1996. Some 20% of the land area is given to arable farming and permanent crops; another 24% is in pasture.

However, most necessary foodstuffs for domestic consumption are imported or produced in small quantities by subsistence farmers on marginal, usually mountainous, land.

Two systems have evolved side by side, reflecting ownership patterns that are a legacy of the slave epoch. The fertile plains are the domain of large holdings producing sugar and other crops for export. The rocky hillsides and mountains are the domain of the black peasant smallhold farmer, as they have been since plantation days when hillside plots were allotted to slaves to grow bananas, 'breadkind,' and other subsistence produce.

The small plots of peasant farmers are still the backbone of Jamaica's economy: the vast majority of Jamaica's 160,000 farmers cultivate less than 5 acres (the average holding is 1½ acres). Owning one's 'own likkle piece of rockstone' is still the ideal in a nation where 55% of the land – almost exclusively the most fertile flatlands – is owned by 5% of the population. The archetypal image of the Jamaican countryside is the sun-blackened farmer in rubber boots, dirt-stained pants, with a machete in hand. A few coffee trees might provide some shade beside a simple house built in the bush, where plantain and its relative, the banana, are grown, alongside citrus, avocado, and maybe an ackee tree. Often a few pigs are kept, tethered on a leash, while goats and chickens scamper free until the day that they are killed for the pot. Men till the land, but it is the women who command the produce trade in this matriarchal society. The produce are brought to market along hillside tracks and dirt roads (formerly by donkey and today by truck), to be set upon the ground on a blanket or sold at wooden stalls heavy with ginger, scallion, oranges, yams, 'glossy-green pears' (avocados), papayas, and a rainbow of other vegetables and whatever fruits are in season.

Most of the nontraditional export crops are supplied by small-scale farmers, though individual productivity is relatively insignificant. (The exception is St Elizabeth parish – Jamaica's 'breadbasket' – and the uplands of Clarendon and Manchester parishes, where relatively prosperous small farmholders till the flatlands and slopes with market-garden produce.) Small-scale farmers are hampered by poverty. They cannot afford the debilitating loans or the high cost of fertilizers, fuel, mechanized equipment, and other agricultural inputs.

The Jamaica Agricultural Society acts as a farmer's union and extension agency nationwide.

In the late 1800s, Jamaica was the world's largest banana producer, but the industry has gradually declined during this century and today faces severe hardships as a result

## Hallowed Grounds

Since coffee grows best on well-watered, well-drained slopes in cooler yet tropical climates, it is no surprise that it thrives in Jamaica's Blue Mountains. The region's distinctly flavored coffee is acclaimed by many connoisseurs as the best in the world.

To be designated 'Blue Mountain,' it must be grown – and roasted – in a prescribed area within the parishes of St Thomas, St Andrew, and Portland between 2000 and 5000 feet above sea level. Coffee grown elsewhere is called 'High Mountain' or 'Jamaica Prime.' About 12,000 acres of Jamaica's 30,000 acres under coffee cultivation lie within the designated zone.

Blue Mountain coffee is lighter and sweeter than other coffees and yet more robust, with a unique woody flavor. (Typically, the cherry stays on the bush two to four months longer than lower-elevation beans, and the lengthy ripening process imbues a richer flavor.) It also has less caffeine. There is enormous variation in quality, however, even within the Blue Mountains. Not all Blue Mountain coffee lives up to its reputation or its astronomical price, much of which is due to marketing hype.

Coffee plants, which are native to Ethiopia, were first cultivated in the French West Indies in 1717; virtually the entire Caribbean coffee stock is derived from a single plant introduced to Hispaniola that year. In 1728, governor Sir Nicholas Lawes introduced coffee to Jamaica at Temple Hall Estate, and other planters followed suit, prompted by the growing demand in Europe, where coffee shops were the rage. Production was boosted by the arrival of French planters fleeing the revolution in St-Domingue (Haiti) in 1801, and it peaked in the boom years – 1800 to 1840 – when production rose to 17,000 tons a year. For a time Jamaica was the world's largest exporter.

Emancipation in 1838 doomed the plantations. Many slaves left the estates and planted their own coffee. As steeper slopes were planted, coffee quality began to decline. The upsurge of free trade and the end of England's preferential tariffs for Jamaican coffee further damaged the industry at a time when high-quality coffee from Brazil, a relative newcomer, was beginning to sap Jamaica's market share. A series of hurricanes this century did further inestimable damage. By the close of WWII, Jamaica's coffee industry was on its last legs.

There has been a resurgence in the popularity of Blue Mountain coffee in recent years under Japanese stimulus and aided by the Jamaican Coffee Industry Board (CIB), set up in 1950 to, ostensibly, ensure quality. Blue Mountain coffee is a treasured commodity in Japan, where the beans sell for US$60 or more per pound. To stimulate production, Japanese companies offered growers development loans at 4% and 5% interest. They also bought plantations, such as Craighton Estate. In doing so they have cornered the market. More than 90% of Blue Mountain coffee is sold to Japan at a preferential rate of about US$9 a pound (of which farmers get only US$5 a pound). The Japanese sell it to the domestic market at more than a 600% premium. A pound produces 100 cups of coffee, each of which sells for US$15 in Japan.

of the cessation of privileged access to European markets. Exports averaged 78,000 tons annually during the 1970s but dropped to 28,000 tons the following decade. The industry has since seen a recovery: Jamaica exported 78,577 tons of bananas in 1994, earning US$40 million. Production is dominated by multinational corporations such as Dole and Del Monte – companies that rely on inundating the environment with herbicides and other industrial poisons, and on paying low wages to desperate workers.

Sugarcane is another important crop – almost one-third of Jamaica's agricultural

## Hallowed Grounds

It's a classic colonial situation. The Japanese loaned money to Jamaica's coffee industry and want to be repaid in coffee only. Claiming recent struggles of the economy at home, Japanese sellers have been able to browbeat coffee board prices down.

Although the CIB purports to maintain strict standards and regulates the use of the name 'Blue Mountain coffee,' the policy is a farce. The board oversees four processing plants in the region and acts as the sole exporter of 'Blue Mountain coffee.' The factories are supplied by scores of small-scale farmers who are required by law to sell to them at whatever price the coffee board chooses to pay (about half what the Japanese buy it for) – regardless of the world market value. Blue Mountain coffee growers cannot legally sell their coffee anywhere else. Only beans processed at the four plants may be sold as 'Blue Mountain coffee.' (Alas, though 51% government-owned, JABLUM, the coffee processing company whose factories hold the 'Blue Mountain' monopoly, is also incestuously made up of the same people who sit on the board, several of whom – surprise! – happen to be government ministers. JABLUM went bankrupt in 1997 and was bailed out by the government before going into receivership.)

The four factories blend the high-quality beans with lesser-quality Lowland and Mountain beans. Many independent producers complain that their superior beans are thus degraded and even poor beans end up being sold as 'Blue Mountain coffee.' Hence, many small holders refuse to sell to the central processors and cure and roast their own beans (often over a smoky wood fire), which they sell privately (and illegally) at bargain prices. Only in 1997, after a protracted battle, was a license granted to an independent roaster – the Old Tavern Estate, run by the Twyman family – to roast, package, and sell its own coffee as 'Blue Mountain' coffee (see the Section section in the Blue Mountains & Southeast Coast chapter).

For more information, contact Coffee Industries Ltd, (☎ 929-2227, fax 926-7266), 9 Barbados Ave, Kingston 5.

Life's a coffee break

land (203 sq miles) is planted in sugar. The sugar economy remains the largest employer in Jamaica, but the foreign companies that dominate the industry pay subsistence wages. Formerly the engine of the Jamaican economy, the industry has declined steadily since 1965, when production peaked at 501,000 tons. Production began to increase again in the early 1990s and reached 240,000 tons in 1994 (export earnings were US$98 million). In 1993 and 1994 the Jamaican government sold off four of its five state-owned sugar factories, and it is anticipated that modernization should lead to an increase in production.

The sugar and banana industries are susceptible to devastation by both rain and wind, and the vicissitudes of market prices. (Coffee – an important crop in the Blue Mountains and highland areas throughout the island – is also susceptible to fluctuating world market prices. Jamaica produces about 6 million lb annually.)

Jamaica is growing more and more food for export and less and less for domestic consumption. Unfortunately, preferential trade benefits for sugar and bananas are being lost as the European Union (EU) phases out preferred trade agreements. Increasing attention is being given to allspice (pimento), citrus, coffee, ginger, cocoa, rum, ornamental flowers, and cattle, which together amounted for about US$30 million in exports in 1995. Citrus projects, in particular, have expanded rapidly in the past 20 years.

Alcan, the bauxite giant, is also a major player in agriculture. It established an agricultural division in 1946 (two years after it acquired its first land holding in Jamaica) and in 1998 spent US$4.1 million assisting 2600 tenant farmers. It owns the largest herd of beef cattle in Jamaica (its dairy operations have reverted to the Jamaican government).

And then there's ganja! Between 1972 and 1986, ganja was 'king' in Jamaica and a major contributor to the country's economic development, especially among rural communities. The days are gone when ganja farmers and traffickers built sprawling mansions, thanks to a committed anti-narcotics drive by the Patterson government. Many farmers who once relied on the crop now struggle to make a living (it is estimated that 85% of ganja cultivation has been destroyed), and there is deep resentment among a large segment of the population. Despite the eradication program, ganja is sold over the counter alongside bottles of beer at rum shops in virtually every village. (For more on ganja, see 'Holy Smoke!' later in this chapter.)

**Fishing** Although Jamaica has a fishing industry, it is mostly comprised of small-scale, village-level entrepreneurs in small, flimsy craft who find it difficult to compete with the large mechanized fleets of competing nations that fish the nearby waters. Hence, Jamaica imports about 50% of fish sold on the island at a cost of about US$23 million a year. The waters of the Caribbean have been overfished, adding to local woes.

Jamaica is developing a commercial aquaculture, with fish farms raising tilapia and tarpon. Many are concentrated in the Clarendon flatlands, to which Kingstonians drive out to scoop up the weekend dinner.

**Manufacturing** Manufacturing, which has grown at an average of 2.5% per year since 1990, contributed 36% of the GDP in 1996 and employs about 19% of the active workforce.

Jamaica's low per capita GDP and the island's relatively small population provide a limited consumer base for domestic industry. Nonetheless, investment incentives have resulted in the growth of sizable processed-goods and textile industries. Jamaica's garment exports increased 159% from 1992 to 1994, when they earned US$474 million (Jamaica is one of the biggest suppliers of underwear to the US market). However, since 1994 the garment industry has been affected negatively by Mexico's NAFTA agreement with the USA. (Making matters worse, in 1998 the USA also withdrew its promise to extend NAFTA parity to Caribbean nations.)

**Service Industries** Kingston is one of the Caribbean's leading financial centers. Jamaica has 19 banks and dozens of buildings societies (the equivalent of the USA's savings and loans institutions), plus an important stock market.

Together with government, computing, and other services, the broader service industry employed 41% of the working population and comprised 55.7% by value of Jamaica's GDP in 1996.

## POPULATION & PEOPLE

Jamaica's population is currently estimated at 2.615 million (2.37 million in the 1991 census), of which about 800,000 live in Kingston. At least another two million Jamaicans live abroad. Emigration has served as an escape valve to help balance the high birthrate of 21.56 per 1000. This rate has also been reduced by vigorous programs implemented by the National Family Planning Board in association with the USAID and UN Population Fund. Sadly, in 1997 international aid was withdrawn, leaving the National Family Planning Board to fend for itself. Jamaica's population grew 1.7% annually in the 1980s (it had declined to 0.78% in 1996), but without emigration the growth rate would have been 2.3%. One-third of the population is under 14 years of age. Life expectancy was over 75 years in 1997, when the infant mortality rate was 15 deaths per 1000 live births (compared to eight in Cuba and 11 in both the USA and UK). About half of the island's population lives in urban environments.

## A Diverse People

The nation's motto – 'Out of Many, One People' – reflects the nation's diverse heritage. Tens of thousands of West Africans, plus large numbers of Irish, Germans, and Welsh arrived throughout the colonial period, along with Hispanic and Portuguese Jews. Following emancipation in 1838, Chinese and Indians arrived as indentured laborers from Hong Kong and Panama. The majority remained when their contracted service was over and intermarried with Africans.

Still, Jamaica is overwhelmingly black. Some 76.3% of the population is classified as being of pure African descent. Another 15% are of Afro-European descent, with the remainder white minorities (3.2%), East Indian and Middle Eastern (3%), and Afro-Chinese and Chinese (1.2%).

Jamaica proclaims itself a melting pot of racial harmony. Indeed, the island seems refreshingly free of overt racial tensions. Still, insecurities of identity *have* been carried down from the plantation era. Class divisions in Jamaica are still related to color, and there is much lingering resentment – and prejudice – against whites, particularly among the poorer segment of society. Many white expatriates say that they live with a side glance over their shoulder.

## Minorities

**Whites** Whites are divided into 'white Jamaicans' and 'Jamaican whites.' Many of the former (immigrants from Europe, mostly England) seem to cling to a grandiose illusion of the 'good old days' when Britannia ruled the waves and Jamaica. Most Jamaican whites (island-born) are really 'off-whites.' They contain a trace of black blood but prefer to be considered white; many are very sensitive about this. Their greatest misfortune would be to sire a 'throwback' child of dark complexion or to break out in brown pigmented patches (known as 'mulatto blasts') as these Jamaican whites approach middle age.

The island also has a significant number of poor Jamaican whites: the descendants of Welsh, Scottish, Irish, and German indentured laborers who arrived following emancipation and never made good. Many are the offspring of about 1100 Germans who arrived between 1834 and 1838. A large colony settled in Seaford, in Westmoreland, where for many generations they have refused to intermarry with blacks. This unique extant enclave of Germans is now much-diminished and affected by inbreeding.

You'll also come across many brown-skinned, green-eyed, blond-haired mulattos (so-called 'red' people, a pejorative term) around Treasure Beach in St Elizabeth – the descendants of Scottish seamen, it is said, who were stranded here in the 19th century.

**Indians** East Indians constitute one of the largest ethnic minorities in Jamaica. About 36,400 Indians (mostly Hindus from northern India) migrated to Jamaica as contract laborers in return for cash or land – between

1838 and 1917. They were concentrated in the old sugar parishes of Westmoreland, Clarendon, and St Thomas. They lived a life of semislavery: conditions were so appalling – with much malnutrition and tuberculosis – that the Indian government forbade further migration in 1917. After serving their tenure of indentureship, many Indians moved to Kingston where they rented land, eventually hired laborers, and generally prospered as merchants. The arrival of new migrants ensured that cultural practices such as the *pujas* (prayers) and religious celebrations were kept alive, although many families changed their names to escape the stigma of the caste system. Later this century, another group of independent immigrants arrived and formed a mercantile community known as the 'Bombay Merchants.'

Though small in numbers, the Indians' legacy is profound. Their contributions include the curries that are now an island staple and ganja, which they introduced to the island along with the word itself.

**Chinese** The descendants of the Chinese who arrived as indentured laborers during the post-emancipation era are predominant in the restaurant trade, real estate, and the business community, notably in Kingston. Several family dynasties are among the wealthiest of Jamaicans. Jamaica's Chinese population is now only about 5000; the vast majority – as many as 35,000 by some estimates – left during the turmoil of the 1970s (most headed for the USA).

**Jews** Jews have a long heritage in Jamaica. Sephardic Jews first arrived in significant numbers from Spain and Portugal during the 16th century, when they were forced to flee the Inquisition. The 'Portugales' or 'Morranos,' as they were called, were also persecuted in Spanish Jamaica, where they

## The Black Color Scale

Jamaicans will tell you that they measure people not by the color of their skin but by the depth of their integrity. Not quite! Color in Jamaica is the ultimate status symbol in a society that exhibits great admiration for status symbols. This is a legacy of the plantation era, when whites sired mulatto ('brown') children with slave mistresses By law they were 'free-colored' and eventually held the same legal rights as their fathers.

The plantocracy developed a scale of 'whiteness' that described the mulattos' relative status. Though originally used by the colonial planters, the lexicon passed into general parlance that expressed the percent of black blood: 'sambo' (three-quarters), mulatto (half), 'quadroon' (one-quarter), 'octaroon' (one-eighth), and 'musteefino' (one-sixteenth). Jamaicans still have a name for every nuance of shade. A partial list includes white, 'off-white,' 'high yellow,' 'coolie-royal,' 'chinee-royal,' 'red,' 'brown,' 'high brown,' and black. 'She black, black, black, so 'til' means she's *very* dark indeed.

Today, there is still a general scale by which the lighter one's shade of skin, the more skilled and prosperous one is assumed to be. Jamaican politics and businesses have always been dominated by whites and light-skinned 'browns.' The first 'black' prime minister was elected only in 1992. The very poorest Jamaicans are usually very dark. Even many of the most successful black Jamaicans are not comfortable with their blackness. Many darker Jamaicans still attempt to 'lift' their color by marrying a lighter-skinned person, and it's not uncommon for newspapers and magazines to attempt to slander or flatter public figures by darkening or lightening their photographs. It's a standing joke in Jamaica, which prides itself on the beauty of its women, that the safest bet at the Miss Jamaica contest is the contestant with the lightest skin.

assumed new identities and had to practice their religion in secret. Hence, many Jews assisted the English during the 1655 invasion. As a reward, the English not only permitted the Jews to remain and practice Judaism freely, but even granted them British citizenship and voting rights. Jews quickly established an early influence in political affairs. In 1849, when eight of the 47 members of the House of Assembly were Jewish, the Assembly became the first legislative body in the world to adjourn for Yom Kippur. In the late 19th century a new wave of Jews – called 'Syrians' – migrated to Jamaica from the Middle East, bringing entrepreneurial skills that helped establish their prominence in the financial and political spheres.

There are probably fewer than 1500 Jews in Jamaica today, though their influence has remained strong.

**Middle Easterners** The term 'Syrians' is used in Jamaica as a generic term for all those of Levantine extraction (the JLP party leader and ex-prime minister Edward Seaga is Lebanese). Most are descendants of Lebanese who arrived around the turn of the century and established themselves in the garment industry and as general merchants.

## EDUCATION

During the late 19th century, the British established in Jamaica the foundations of what developed into an admirable education system, based on the British model of schooling. In the 1970s, the Michael Manley administration gave priority to enhancing educational standards, and Jamaica still boasts some of the finest schools in the Americas, many of them private institutions. But critics say the Jamaican public education system has since gone to the dogs.

The main problem is money. Per-student spending has steadily fallen during the past few decades. Today it averages only about US$100 (compared to US$600 in Barbados and US$550 in Trinidad), and the portion of the government budget spent on education has dwindled from 18% in 1980 to 11% in 1999. Low salaries fail to attract quality teachers. Few schools have computers or advanced teaching aids now commonplace in schools in more developed countries. Many rural schools lack even basic sanitation. In many schools, the student-teacher ratio is very high – often with one teacher for all grades. Lack of transportation compounds the problem. Many children in rural areas must travel many miles to reach school, and it is common to see groups of schoolchildren walking barefoot, rain or shine. To solve this, the government has attempted to get private industry involved through its Adopt-a-School Program, launched in 1989.

Although primary education is free and compulsory to the age of 15, about 60% of Jamaican schoolchildren (mostly in rural areas) drop out early. Of those who do stay in school, more than half are functionally illiterate (officially, adult literacy is estimated at 85%, though this includes a great percentage who can do little more than sign their name). Intriguingly, literacy among females is noticeably higher (89.1%) than for males (80.9%). There's a shortage of secondary schools, so primary-school graduates must take competitive exams for placement, as must secondary-school graduates hoping to attend a university or vocational college.

Jamaican schoolchildren perform at miserably low levels in math and English in the Caribbean Examinations: in the 1994 examinations, only 23% of Jamaican students attained the Grade II level of proficiency required by private-sector companies and tertiary institutions.

Nonetheless, there are some splendid schools, and many students receive a fine education. Case in point: Jamaica produced the winner of the 1998 US National Spelling Bee championship (another Jamaican student came in eighth). In general, the best schools are acknowledged to be parochial schools.

## ARTS

Jamaica has evolved a powerful artistic and cultural expression deep-rooted in African traditions. Jamaica is a center of Caribbean art. Kingston, in particular, has a vitalic cultural energy. The island's rich artistic heritage reaches back to pre-Columbian days, when the Arawaks etched petroglyphs on the ceilings and walls of caverns. Today there's a strong intellectual tradition and a large middle class to support the arts. Music, dance, and drama have flourished tremendously since independence in 1962, while quintessentially Jamaican styles have evolved across the spectrum of arts.

Anyone limiting themselves to resort entertainment could leave the island assuming that fire-eaters, limbo dancers, calypso bands, painted fish, and carved gourds are Jamaica's artistic staples, but a much richer artistic tapestry awaits discovery.

In addition, Jamaica's crafts industry supports tens of thousands of artisans, who offer a cornucopia of leatherwork, ceramics, shell art, beadwork, and basket-weaving. Although much of it is tawdry kitsch, mass-produced with little skill or pride, some is surprisingly sophisticated – even museum quality. One company, Things Jamaican Ltd, has worked successfully for more than 30 years to expand Jamaica's crafts industry by accepting only the highest quality works.

## Dance & Theater

Jamaica has a rich heritage of dance and theater, which are intertwined and receive substantial government support. Amateur theater and dance companies are scattered throughout Jamaica, and Kingston-based companies often tour the parishes. Kingston's scene is vibrant enough to sustain half a dozen or more concurrent productions. Many of the larger, upscale hotels also feature their own productions.

Jamaica shuns classical Shakespearian theater, preferring farces and homilies that draw on local traditions, including dance forms from the slave era. Theater productions, often performed in *patois* (Jamaica's local dialect), are difficult for visitors to understand. They're often bawdy and farcical, and tend to portray the trials of the poor.

Dance embraces classical, contemporary, and African forms. Among Jamaica's many internationally acclaimed groups are the Little Theater Movement, the National Dance Theater Company, the Jamaica Folk Singers, the National Chorale, and the University Players. Much of the cultural movement has been at the grassroots level, as epitomized by Sistren (Sisters), a women's cultural group started by working-class women in 1977, which aims at 'advancing the awareness of its audiences on questions affecting Caribbean women.' Through theater, it tells graphic and frank stories – in dialect – of what life is like for many Jamaican women. It deals with sexuality, the legacies of slavery, and other topics honoring the spiritual strength of Jamaican women.

Another dynamic company is L'Acadco, founded by its artistic director, L'Antoinette Stines, and unique in being Jamaica's only full-time, fully salaried dance company. Its works meld Jamaican folklore into modern dance styles such as reggae and dancehall.

**National Dance Theater Company** The NDTC, Jamaica's most acclaimed dance troupe, is based in Kingston's Little Theater. Its dancers, musicians, and singers have earned praise around the world under the direction of Professor Rex Nettleford, who founded the company in 1962 as an offshoot of Jamaica's independence celebrations. It explores African themes and forms, often in vividly imaginative costumes, through performances based on Jamaican history and daily life. The NDTC's season usually runs mid-July to mid-August, with a weeklong miniseries in November and December and a medley of religious works at dawn on Easter Sunday.

**National Pantomime** Begun in 1941, the National Pantomime is the oldest annual production in Jamaica and is traditionally held in Kingston's Ward Theater. The production – a monument of folk theater and irreverent family entertainment – is staged by the Little Theater Movement, the oldest theatrical company in the Caribbean. The performers are all volunteers.

The pantomime has its roots in the British tradition, in which performances are based on childhood fairytales and stories such as 'Cinderella' and 'Jack and the Beanstalk.' But over the years, folkloric characters, such as Anancy and Tacooma (both originated in

West Africa), began to appear on stage, as did adapted versions of Jamaican folktales.

Contrary to its name, the performance has nothing to do with mime. Pantomime is a musical comedy – a blend of lively song, dance, and words that lampoon Jamaican foibles, historic events, and well-known figures in Jamaican life. The audience gets drawn in, volubly so. The lyrics are in patois, so most visitors have difficulty understanding.

A pantomime of a different sort is a 'Bruckins Party,' a village celebration (most commonly found in Portland parish) held on Emancipation Day (August 1) as a parody of British royalty. Bruckins is a dance in which villages divide into two courts (red and blue), each with a king and queen with attending courtiers dressed in satin and fake jewels (the men also carry cardboard swords). Everyone bobs and weaves with a *kutchie* (curtsey) as they sing 'de Queen a comin',' making laughter from the pain of enslavement.

## Music

From hotel beach parties to the raw 'sound-system' discos of the working-class suburbs, Jamaica reverberates to the soul-riveting sounds of calypso, soca, and, above all, reggae. Music is everywhere. And loud! Buses are practically mobile discos. Streetside stores blast rap-reggae to wake the dead. Story-tall speakers in village squares make the telegraph poles shake. (The notion of peace and quiet is not something the average Jamaican can relate to. Once, while savoring the silence of a quiet oceanfront setting, I told a Jamaican friend how much I enjoyed the serenity. 'Yeah, mon,' he replied, 'you get de Jet Skis to yourself.')

Reggae may have put Jamaica on the musical map (see the Reggae'n'Riddims special section), but the nation's musical heritage runs much deeper. And Kingston has become the 'Nashville of the Third World,' with recording studios pumping out dozens of new titles each month.

Jamaica's music scene isn't static. Soca – fast-paced dance music fusing soul and calypso which hails from Trinidad – gained prominence in Jamaica only recently at Carnival.

It is now the music of choice at resort discos and upscale discos in 'uptown' Kingston (dancehall, meanwhile, is 'downtown' music).

Jamaica isn't famous for its jazz, but it has its fans as well as influential world-class performers, notably Ernest Ranglin, who has played a pivotal role in Jamaican music. His jazzy riffs have made classics out of songs for Millie Small ('My Boy Lollipop') and the Wailers ('It Hurts to Be Alone'). Ranglin rose to fame on the London club scene as an exponent of the six-string guitar. (Ranglin invented the up-on-the-down-stroke of Jamaican guitar.) Bob Marley sought Ranglin's tutorial services in the 1970s when the latter was Jimmy Cliff's musical director. He expresses his African roots, melding Afro-Cuban music, reggae, soukous, and jazz – relaxed and grooving. More recently, Ranglin has worked with David Sanborn and has released such critically acclaimed albums as *Below the Bassline*. The old maestro still packs a punch: in 1998, Blackwell's new record company, Palm Pictures, released Ranglin's 17th album, *In Search of the Lost Riddim*.

Jamaica also has a strong heritage in military bands. The Jamaica Military Band, perhaps the country's best, dates back to the first England's West India Regiment in 1795, recruited mainly from Jamaicans. The regiment saw action in the Napoleonic wars and many colonial wars, plus WWI, but was disbanded for economy in 1926, when its band played its last performance (at Buckingham Palace) and turned in its instruments after the performance. Sentiment prevailed and the band was reformed as the Jamaica Military Band, which still uses its unique Zouave (light infantry of North African origin) uniform.

## Pottery

Jamaican ceramists have been making a name for themselves of late, led by Cecil Ball, an octogenarian potter who uses Egyptian motifs. Look, too, for the ceramics of Jag Mehta (also a well-known hotelier), with a monumental quality that belies their small size. Munchi is an outstanding fourth-generation Afro-Caribbean potter, who chooses as her creative ground the shady earth beneath the same mango tree that her mother, Ma Lou, used for inspiration. Wassi Art, in Ocho Rios, has a stable of young artists being trained to self-expression of the highest caliber. And a Montegonian, David Pinto, is another ceramist of note, working from his base at Good Hope, Falmouth, where he teaches wood-fired workshops arranged through Anderson Ranch Arts Center (☎ 970-923-3181, fax 923-3871 in the USA), PO Box 5598, Snowmass Village, CO 81615.

## Literature

While the island has not produced any writers of world-renown, Jamaica does have its literati. Most are well known in the Caribbean but not much farther afield, including John Hearne (*Sure Salvation*), Roger Mais (*Brother Man*), and Orlando Patterson.

Many writers and playwrights are haunted by the ghosts of Jamaica's past, mostly its slave history and the ambiguities of Jamaica's relationship to Mother England. Novels tend to focus on survival in a grim colonial landscape and escape to Africa, which often proves even more grim.

Also see the Books section in the Facts for the Visitor chapter.

**Novels** The classic *White Witch of Rose Hall* by Herbert de Lisser has as its setting the plantation era and tells the tale – now an established part of Jamaican lore – of Annie Palmer, the wicked mistress of Rose Hall who supposedly murdered three husbands and several slave lovers.

*Children of Sisyphus,* by Orlando Patterson, was one of the first novels ever to treat Rastafarianism fairly. It is set in Kingston's ghettoes and tells of a young prostitute's efforts to elevate herself from life on the edge.

Perry Henzell's *Power Game* is a tale of power politics throughout Jamaican society, told by the director of the brilliant cult movie, *The Harder They Come.* The poignant novel of that name, written by Michael Thewell, tells the story of a country boy who comes to Kingston, turns into a 'rude boy,' and becomes fatally enmeshed in the savage drug culture. Likewise, *Yardie,* by Victor Headley, tells of a drug-running 'mule' (childless woman) who makes it to the top of the UK drug trade.

Anthony Winkler's *Lunatic* is a sad but amusing tale of the relationship between Inge, a sex-craved German tourist, and a Jamaican madman who communes with the trees and bushes.

In recent years, a number of Jamaican women have gained notice: Christine Craig (*Mint Tea*), Patricia Powell (*Me Dying Trial*), Michelle Cliff (*Abeng, Land of Look Behind*), and Vanessa Spence (*Roads Are Down*), for example. Coping is still the main theme, as it was in the 'migrant literature' of the 1950s, but the setting is mostly contemporary, and the oppressors are the men within the characters' lives.

**Short Stories** Lorna Goodison's *Baby Mother and the King of Swords* (Longman) is a collection of short stories on Jamaica, in generally somber tone. Another anthology that deals with Jamaica's disturbing societal keynotes is *22 Jamaican Short Stories* (Kingston Publishers), with pieces by several leading local authors.

**Poetry** Jamaican literature has been widened and deepened primarily by a group of women poets. *From Our Yard*, edited by Pamela Mordecai, is a splendid collection of works by Jamaican poets that exemplifies the preoccupying theme of the island: a sober valuing on the real lives of ordinary people 'requiring us,' says Mordecai, 'to look to the condition of our part of this yard, this world.'

**Folk Tales** *Jamaican Folk Tales & Oral Histories* by Laura Tanna (Institute of Jamaica Publications) includes tales of Anancy, the popular spider-hero of Jamaican folklore, as does Louise Bennett's *Anancy and Miss Lou* (Sangster) and *Anancy Stories and Dialect Verse* (Pioneer Press).

*Duppy Talk: West Indian Tales of Mystery & Magic,* by Gerald Hausman, appeals to the Jamaican's innate love of a good duppy story.

## Sculpture

Many noted artists left their legacy in stone during the colonial era, such as John Bacon's monument to Admiral George Rodney in Spanish Town, and John Flaxman, England's 18th-century sculpting virtuoso, who carved a monument to planter Simon Clarke that still stands in Lucea's Hanover church.

The foremost sculptor this century is undoubtedly Edna Manley, the multitalented wife of ex-prime minister Norman Manley (see 'The First Lady of the Jamaica School,' later in this chapter). Her works in wood, metal, and stone are displayed in a magnificent collection in the National Gallery in Kingston. Rastafarian Everald Brown, another noted painter, creates sculptures in stone kindled by 'divine inspiration,' especially from the stones that 'speak' to him near his home in Murray Mountain, St Ann (also see Painting, below).

In addition to fine artists, thousands of self-taught woodcarvers hew intuitive carvings in lignum vitae, blue mahoe, and other hardwoods. The crafts stalls that line north coast roads are menageries of palette fishes, toads, sphinx-like cats, and magnificent roosters, often painted with bright pointillist dots. The most popular subjects are giant Rasta heads and oversized fish and giraffes.

## Film

Jamaica has not been known for its film industry, although things are stirring. Only one homemade movie has garnered international renown. Native-born singer Jimmy Cliff rocketed to fame in *The Harder They Come* (1973), in which he starred as a 'rude boy' (armed thug) in Kingston's ghettoes. The brilliant movie – which has become a cult-icon – was produced by Kingstonian Perry Henzel, who later moved to documentaries but was at press time working on a sequel: *The Harder They Come II*.

The most emotionally engaging – and successful – movie in years is *Dancehall Queen*, a powerful tale of redemption (a bit of Cinderella without a Prince Charming) for a struggling, middle-aged street vendor who finds a novel way of escaping the harrowing, violence-prone mean streets of Kingston

Jimmy Cliff in *The Harder They Come*

through the erotic intoxication of dancehall. The movie is one of a crop of powerful Jamaican productions coming from Chris Blackwell's Palm Pictures studio, which at press time was working on *Third World Cop*, a tale of corrupt police.

In addition, Jamaica has had star billing in dozens of films (pronounced 'flims' in Jamaica) and its status as a favored location for Hollywood and music video shoots has fostered a minor industry, pumping in as much as US$10 million a year into the economy.

A movie of Bob Marley's life was in production at press time.

## Painting

Kingston's National Gallery is the starting point for any understanding of Jamaican art. It houses the nation's largest collection of historical and contemporary art. The

## The First Lady of the 'Jamaica School'

Edna Manley, a leader of the so-called Jamaica School, was instrumental in the radical change in Jamaican art. Manley – the island's leading sculptor – was born in England to a Jamaican mother. As the wife of Norman Manley, Jamaica's first prime minister, she was very much an establishment figure but no less Jamaican for it.

During the formative years between 1922 and 1940, Manley and artist Koren der Harootian nurtured the fine-art movement by freeing themselves from English aesthetics.

Manley organized art classes at the Institute of Jamaica (which evolved into the Jamaican School of Art and later into the Edna Manley School of the Visual Arts). This resulted in the opening of commercial galleries, which, in turn, encouraged self-taught artists. Manley's successor, Karl Craig, expanded the school in the 1970s. It became the embryo for the National Gallery of Jamaica, which today houses a splendid collection of Manley's works in the Roy West Building on Kingston's waterfront. Manley herself remained at the forefront of sculpture and art until her death in 1987 at the age of 86.

larger towns and cities also support commercial art galleries.

Jamaican art has its origins in the 18th and 19th centuries, when itinerant artists such as Philip Wickstead, Joseph Bartholomew Kid, and George Robertson roamed the plantations, recording life in an idyllic, romanticized light – always from a Eurocentric point of view that totally ignored the African heritage. Satirist William Hogarth was one of few artists to portray the hypocrisy and savagery of plantation life.

Until the 1920s, leading artists were establishment figures who looked to Europe for inspiration. That turbulent decade, however, was a heady time of growing nationalism and black pride, and a new national consciousness and artistic movement arose.

Artists of the so-called Jamaica School began to develop their own expressions on canvas, most strongly shaped by themes of poverty, bondage, striving, and other realities of Jamaican life.

A pivotal event occurred in 1939 in Kingston, when about 40 well-known artists stormed the annual meeting of the Institute of Jamaica, an organization established to encourage the arts, science, and culture. The artists demanded an artistic unshackling from European aesthetic prescriptions. One of the artists, a lawyer named Robert Braithwaite, pointed to the portraits of the English governors on the wall and exclaimed, 'Gentlemen! We have come to tell you to tear down these pictures and let the Jamaican paintings take their place.'

The Jamaican School evolved two main groups: the island-themed primitives (labeled 'intuitives') and a more international group of painters schooled abroad. The term 'intuitives' was coined by David Boxer, former director of the National Gallery, and is used for 'pure and sincere' self-taught artists such as Bishop Mallica 'Kapo' Reynolds and John Dunkley, whose explorations of Biblical and folkloric icons have been inordinately influential. Many self-taught intuitive artists have risen from the ghettoes.

Dunkley (born in 1881) was a Kingston barber who painted his entire shop – furniture, walls, and all – in tangled vines, flowers, and abstract symbols. Dunkley later turned to canvas. His untempered interpretations of Jamaican life inspired many subsequent intuitive, homegrown artists. Like many artistic geniuses, Dunkley did not grow rich on his art. Today, years after his death, collectors pay big money for his works.

'Kapo' Reynolds is the most renowned of the intuitive artists. Kapo was a leading Revivalist cult leader (see the Religion section, later in this chapter) who painted mystical landscapes and visions. Though he was imprisoned in the 1930s for practicing *obeah* (black magic) and later suffered a seizure, which left him paralyzed below the waist, his career spanned 50 years. One of his works was presented to Ethiopian emperor Haile Selassie in 1966; another – *New Spring* – was a wedding gift to Prince Charles and Princess Diana. He died at 78 in 1989.

Contemporary Jamaican artists such as Gloria Escoffrey, Michael Escoffrey, Carl Abrahams, Ken Abendana Spencer, Barrington Watson, Osmond Watson, and Christopher Gonzalez have earned world-renown for their museum pieces, although a common complaint has been that their predominant style was influenced by Postimpressionism and other European forms. Gonzalez and many other avant-garde artists studied abroad in the 1960s and 1970s and returned inspired by new ideas that they wedded to their nationalist spirits. Gonzalez's life-size memorial bust of National Hero George William Gordon and 8-foot bronze statue of Bob Marley can be viewed at the National

Gallery. And the works of Osmond Watson, suggests art critic Annie Paul, might be seen as a personification of Jamaica in the 1990s, 'an entire nation cynically clothing itself in pretty packaging, prostituting itself for the sake of a few tourist dollars.'

No collective visual style defines Jamaican painters, but many emphasize historical roots in their works. More recently, reggae and Rastafarianism have had profound effects on Jamaican visual arts. Rastafarians are common subjects, as are market higglers, animals, and religious symbols merged with the myths of Africa. The intuitive works of Everald Brown (a priest in the Ethiopian Coptic Church) and Albert Artwell especially concentrate on Rastafarian symbolism, portraying, for example, exalted black deities living an idyll in heaven. Brown is one of the more unusual artists and has an unmistakable niche. He also creates unique musical instruments, such as his Talking Drum and Star Guitar. Petrona Morrison also pervades an Afro-spiritual side and is known for large metal sculptures that assume shapes representing totems and symbols of mystical worship from ancient Africa. The works of Anna Henriques have been described as projecting a 'gilded religiosity' and hidden meaning.

Jamaica has a comparatively large crop of female artists, many of them expatriates (the director of the Jamaican Artists and Craftsman's Guild is Pat Ramsay). Judy Macmillan is renowned for a Rembrandt-like use of light in her portraits. Samere Tansley's portrayals of women are much admired. The works of Roberta Stoddart, an Australian, are pervasive with satirical humor. Elizabeth Roberts is known for her tropical murals (many grace the lobbies of upscale hotels).

Englishman Graham Davis is perhaps the best-known and most influential of foreign-born male artists now resident in Jamaica.

John Dunkley's influence is perhaps greater than all other artists combined, for the 'common man' across the island has adopted the style. These anonymous artists lavish their métier on murals, which are everywhere. Bars, shops, restaurants, and rum shops islandwide copy Dunkley's

Jungian style (usually with vines crawling along a black wall) or display whimsical alfresco trompe l'oeil cartoons dramatizing Jamaican life. Colloquially, the pop-style wall murals are known as 'yard art,' after the 'yards' of Kingston ghettoes, where powerful politically inspired murals are painted in big, bold colors that can be absorbed at a glance. Many are threatening, no-nonsense parochial messages. Others are more cheery, adding color and humor to otherwise depressing environments.

More developed muralist skills are exemplified by the giant mural on the Assembly Hall at the University of the West Indies (UWI) campus in Kingston.

See the Books section in the Facts for the Visitor chapter for suggestions on reading more about Jamaican art.

## SOCIETY & CONDUCT
### Traditional Culture

Few traces remain of the original Jamaican people, the Arawaks, though many Arawak words have been passed down into common parlance, including the island's Arawak name: Xaymaca.

Jamaica's strongest legacy has descended from the African slaves. Many African traditions from West Africa (where most slaves came from) survive in various guises. 'Jamaica talk' is laced with African words. Storytellers have maintained an oral literature of folk tales, such as Anancy stories. And superstitions (often derived from a belief in obeah) have remained particularly undiluted, for which reason, when asked about their health, a Jamaican usually replies 'not too bad,' expressing an unwillingness to tempt fate and the intervention of duppies with overly positive statements.

The African Caribbean Institute of Jamaica (ACIJ) was established in 1972 to study the island's African heritage.

**Anancy** This devious spider is Jamaica's unlikely leading folk hero. Anancy is the subject of many tales, still frequently told to children at bedtime. The folktales originated with the Ashanti tribe of Ghana but have become localized through the centuries.

Many of Jamaica's traditional folksongs derive from Anancy stories. Tales usually end with the cryptic 'Jack Mandora me no choose none,' a saying of obscure origin that refers to Mandora, the keeper of heaven's gate, and symbolizes that the teller is disassociating himself or herself from Anancy's machiavellianism.

Like Brer Rabbit, Bredda (brother) Anancy survives against the odds in a harsh world by his quick wit, sharp intelligence, cunning, and ingenuity. Anancy, his wife Crooky, and his son Tacooma frequently appear in the annual Christmas pantomime.

Several books trace the evolution and meaning of Anancy stories, including *Jamaican Folk Tales & Oral Histories* by Laura Tanna.

**Folk Healing** Traditional folk healing is still very much alive. Healers, called 'balmists,' can be either male or female. They rely on native herbs mixed into concoctions – bush medicines – the recipes for which span many generations. Colored flags (usually red) and other talismans hang outside their 'balmyards' to chase away evil spirits. Some are associated with obeah cults and are involved in witchcraft, both good and bad to foil duppies, or evil ghosts (grave dirt mixed with secretive oils is often prescribed), or perhaps dispensing 'Oil of Come Back' to win back an errant lover.

Bush medicine is widely practiced, notably among Maroon descendants, and the average Jamaican has a reasonably profound knowledge of herbal remedies.

**Day Work** Jamaicans also still participate in 'day work,' in which villagers perform a common task such as building a house or planting a field. The custom, which originated from the Dahomey region of West Africa, was an early source of many Jamaican folk songs created to lighten the work. These songs utilize the African-derived call-and-response pattern, with verses sung by a *bomma* (leader), and a *bobbin* (chorus). The tradition is translated on Labour Day into community effort when everyone pitches in to paint road markings or pick up litter.

Finger food for the streamertail hummingbird at Rocklands Feeding Station

Climbing up the famous Dunn's River Falls, outside Ocho Rios

Black River celebrity: Charley the crocodile stops to shake a fan's hand

Papaya trees

Cassava fruit

Jackfruit seller

Blooming poinciana tree

**Names & Name-Calling** Some Jamaicans still give a child a 'born day name,' a West African tradition of naming by the day of the week. For example, the name Cudjoe (the name of the 18th-century Maroon leader) meant 'Monday.' However, such names are still in use as uncomplimentary descriptive terms. For example, someone born on Friday is often called a *cuffee* (stupid); a *quashie* (bumpkin) is someone born on Sunday.

**Nine Nights** Many Jamaican elders still observe nine nights, a 'wake' held on the ninth night after someone's death to ensure that the spirit of the deceased departs to heaven. If such a ceremony is not performed, their

## Dealing with Duppies

Many Jamaicans believe in duppies, the ghosts or spirits of the dead that appear only at night. The term is derived from the Twi tribal word *dupon* (from Africa) for the roots of a tree. The superstition is based on an African belief that humans have two souls. One goes to heaven for judgment; the other lingers on earth, where it lives in trees and sends shivers down the spines of superstitious Jamaicans.

Duppies are a force of either good or evil, and can be captured and used to either help, as in *myal*, or harm, as in obeah. Talismans are used to manipulate them. For example, many Jamaicans still place a crossed knife and fork and a Bible near young babies at night to keep away an evil, blood-sucking, witch-like duppy called Ol' Hige, who casts aside her skin at night before setting out on her wicked forays. If you want to be rid of her for good you have to find her skin and douse it with salt and pepper. Like vampires, evil duppies are also terrified when folks 'cut ten' (make the sign of the cross).

You may even come across rural Jamaicans carrying a handful of matches or stones that they drop on the road if they think they're being followed by a duppy. Duppies are incurably curious and will stop to see what has been dropped; since they can't count beyond three, local folklore says that they'll count the first three objects and then have to

start at the beginning again. Many rural Jamaicans remain terrified of another nocturnal duppy – the Whistling Cowboy, whose breath can kill. He rides a three-legged horse, so be careful if you hear 'itty-itty-hop-itty-itty-hop.' Another legendary duppy is the River Mumma, a beautiful maiden who appears near deep riverine pools, where she can be seen sitting on a rock combing her ravishing hair, and enticing males with her looks. Once enchanted, the lovelorn victims are lured to the river and drowned.

spirit will hang around to haunt the living. The wake is usually accompanied by hymns and superstitious rituals, such as turning over the mattress of the deceased or sweeping out the house.

## Modern Culture

Jamaica has a complex and challenging culture, with layer upon layer of complexity shaped by an agonized past. Most visitors have very limited contact with Jamaicans, and the social reality remains hidden. It is easy to go home without the faintest feel for differences between the classes, or for the roots of Jamaican culture. Your interaction with Jamaicans will be richer if you try to understand the social conditions and dilemmas that have shaped the unique Jamaican character. An appreciation for the ironic helps, as do empathy and compassion.

Jamaica has a profound class system despite a unifying sense of national pride. At its heart is an unwritten color code that may not be very noticeable to foreign visitors (see 'Black Color Scale,' earlier in this chapter). Certain profoundly Jamaican stereotypes are keenly noticed, particularly among the poorer classes, but Jamaica is *not* a homogeneous society, and the educated middle classes are very touchy about the idea that 'one size fits all.' From strutting 'rude boys' and Rastafarians clutching their 'cutchie' ganja pipes to besuited city sophisticates driving BMWs and Mitsubishi jeeps; and from cheery market 'mammies' to dancehall queens in 'batty rider' shorts and high-heeled secretaries in designer fashions – Jamaica is a complex potpourri.

**The Jamaican Character** Jamaicans are an intriguing contrast. Much of the population comprises the most gracious people you'll ever meet: hard-working, happy-go-lucky, helpful, courteous, genteel, and full of humility. The majority of Jamaicans are poor, and they are lovely people. If you show them kindness, they will give it back in return. Jamaican children are almost without exception well behaved and extremely polite: most have an English-style civility that they share with a majority of senior citizens.

However, a significant minority (notable among the poorer, uneducated classes) is composed of the most sullen, cantankerous, and confrontational people you could ever wish not to meet. Foreign visitors are often shocked at the surliness they so often encounter.

The Jamaicans' renowned belligerent independence can trace its roots all the way back to the Maroons. Charged memories of slavery and racism have continued to bring out the spirit of anarchy latent in an ex-slave society divided into rich and poor. Whereas North Americans are also imported people, most were transplanted of free volition, whereas the ancestors of the vast majority of Jamaicans were forcibly uprooted. While all were African, they came from vastly diverse regions and tribes – the Mandingos, Ashanti, Yorubas, Dahomey, Ibo, and scores of others – spanning an area as large as Western Europe. Once landed, they were separated and kept apart from their compatriots to lessen the danger of fomented rebellion. Their spirit is shaped by the quest for survival in a harsh world, by a past of suffering and neglect, and by a deep affinity with their African roots. Bob Marley's plaintive words of 'no woman, no cry' and 'by de rivers of Babylon' echo through the valleys and across the mountain tops, touching the aching heart of Jamaica.

Jamaicans struggling hard against poverty are disdainful of talk about a 'tropical paradise.' There is fire in the Jamaican soul. The Jamaicans have a firm identity and understand who they are. Their concern is with the future and their security. Understandably, a seething mistrust runs through society like an undercurrent.

Jamaican culture also owes much to the role model of their Machiavellian folk hero – Anancy. Guileful, cheating, double-dealing, and subtle theft are how a large segment of the underprivileged get by. If someone can get away with it, he earns respect among some peers. Hence, Jamaicans are superb readers of people – they have to be. Jamaicans have, above all, learned to be assertive to survive. It takes a long time to earn their trust. They give a piece one day, another the next. Often, poorer Jamaicans are very slow to warm to strangers and trying to get a smile can be like pulling teeth.

Jamaicans love to debate, or 'reason.' You'll not meet many Jamaicans without strong opinions, and they tend to express themselves forcefully, inflecting and spitting out words like cannon shots and turning differences of opinion into voluble arguments. The clash of opinions sometimes boils over into violence. Private differences don't stay that way for long – part of the national psyche is an instinct to get involved in others' 'bisniss.' There is little reserve. When Jamaicans are not pleased, they tell you in no uncertain terms.

Thus, to foreigners, the Jamaican character can seem schizophrenic and perplexingly volatile. Many Jamaicans are particularly quick to take imagined offense. Their in-your-face response is often quite aggressive and psychologically disturbing for visitors. Hustlers use this to devastating effect on tourists: 'What matter? You got sometin' against me? You racist?' The best defense is to defuse the situation by joking back. Jamaicans appreciate a quick wit. Alas, the tendency to sudden violence is prone to erupt during mob scenes, such as street dances, as in December 1995 when a US businessman was beaten to death after he had accidentally knocked over a street-vendor's pot of soup.

Many, too, among the poorer Jamaicans think for the instant and immediate future – often with little projection and association between act and longer-term consequence. They live to squeeze whatever benefit they can from the moment.

Jamaicans make light of their own foibles, which are a source of humor in theater and pantomimes. But Jamaicans love their island (the success of the Reggae Boyz, Jamaica's national soccer team, in reaching the 1998 World Cup, for example, united Jamaica in a massive outpouring of national pride). In general, Jamaicans are defensive of themselves with foreigners. Countless Jamaicans have accomplished great things. But the society as a whole is deeply insecure, and self-esteem is low among the uneducated classes.

Young males, in particular, are severely challenged and often mask or counter this by putting on a hard-nosed face or by displaying bravado, such as behind the wheel of a car. They rarely shake hands, but prefer to 'thump off de fist' – literally to knock fists – as a greeting, parting, or to show respect for a comment that's appreciated. Sensitivity is rarely displayed for fear of being regarded as 'sissy.' Heroic models are drawn from a musical world that belts out a message exhorting misogyny, violence, and profit from rip-offs or laziness. Unemployment exacerbates the problem, and for every hardworking youth there now seems to be another wanting to be paid for doing nothing.

**Wit & Humor** Jamaicans' sarcastic and sardonic wit is legendary. The deprecating humor has evolved as an escape valve that hides their true feelings. The saying that 'everyt'ing irie' is 'black' humor, because life *is* a problem. Somehow, they know, they'll find a way.

Often Jamaican wit is laced with sexual undertones. Jamaicans like to make fun of others, often in the most subtle yet no-punches-pulled way, but they accept being the source of similar humor in good grace. Individual faults and physical abnormalities inspire many a knee-slapping jibe.

The lusty humor will sometimes be directed at you. Take it in good humor. Their deprecating and self-deprecating jabs are never meant to sting. You'll be an instant hit if you give as good as you get, but the key is subtlety, not malice.

**Sex & Family Life** Many Jamaicans are sexually active at an early age (5% of mothers have their first child before they are 15 years old, and a lower-class woman is considered a 'mule' – sterile – if she hasn't had a child by her twenties). Noncommittal sexual relationships are the norm, especially among the poorer classes. As in many aspects of Jamaican life, this is a carryover from slave days, when slaves were encouraged to have children but were denied permanent relationships, and 'husband' and 'wife' were commonly separated.

## Pumping It Up

Many Jamaican men are preoccupied with their libido, or 'nature,' and have concocted all kinds of juices ('sex potents') for enriching the semen and bolstering their sexual stamina. With names like 'Front-End Lifter,' 'Tear-Up Mattress,' and 'Brek-Down Bed,' they leave little to the imagination. Most look like bottled diarrhea and are usually made of Irish moss (a type of sea algae that's boiled and strained) mixed with other herbal ingredients. 'Pep-up' is made of Dragon stout, Red Label wine, and pureéd green corn. 'Roots wine' is another steadfast health tonic made from varying combinations of roots (and often ganja), boiled with honey or molasses.

Most Jamaicans – male and female – have their own favorite recipes, and markets are full of bottles of odd concoctions to improve health or sexual function (interestingly, many 'juice men' – specialists in selling preparations – won't sell to woman, as 'Dis a man's t'ing!').

It is still common for a poor couple to marry only late in life, if at all. Most live together on a short-term basis. Typically, a Jamaican woman will have a limited number of men in her life to whom she is loyal – one at a time. She may return to each briefly, with long hiatuses between involvements with a particular man. (A woman who has too many boyfriends, however, is termed a *sketel*, or flirty; the male equivalent is a *mantel*.) It is not unusual for women to have children by several men and for men to sire families with several women. An astonishing 80% of children are born out of wedlock. Middle-class Jamaicans, in general, display more spousal loyalty.

Jamaicans are comfortable with – and direct about – sex, displaying few of the hang-ups prevalent in North America and Northern Europe. At weddings or other respectable social occasions, for example, even the most prim and proper Christian females, regardless of age, will gleefully 'wine' (to make overt sexual motions with a member of the opposite gender) on a dance floor, sure to raise roars of approval.

Though true-blue Christians are conservative, Jamaicans as a whole are at ease with their bodies. After all, this is a tropical climate where not-a-little skin is exposed, women bathe naked in mountain streams, and it is not unusual to see naked men poling bamboo rafts upriver. In a society where men are extremely concerned with projecting their libido and women are used to uncommitted relationships, Jamaicans have plenty of casual, quickie sex.

If a Jamaican wants to sleep with you, he or she will let you know. On the Lonely Planet travel video, the *Jamaica Experience*, host Ian Wright is asked by the woman giving him an aloe massage: 'So shorty, you wanna go in de bushes?' You'll need to be just as direct with your response to get a 'No!' across. Don't beat about the bush in the hope of not hurting someone's feelings. It doesn't work. If love beneath the palms sounds enticing, expect to be asked for a 'likkle sometin' to help feed the kids (this is true of men and women). Jamaicans like to cut to the chase. Romance takes a backseat to raw physical passion. Says one of my middle-class Jamaican female friends: 'Jamaican men? Dem is chest-beaters, mon. Dem attitude is 'beat it down an' mash it up!'

**Women in Jamaica** Jamaica is a macho society and in general, life for women is extremely challenging. It is also a matriarchal society in the African (and slave plantation) tradition. The sexes lead independent lives, at least among the lower classes. In the slave system, men were commonly sold and separated from their lovers and children. Even women slaves were commonly sold, never to see their children again. When that happened, the grandmother, aunt, or another family member would care for the child – termed a 'keeper family.' The tradition continues. It is common for a woman to leave her children in the care of a relative for months or even years at a time while she takes up with another man, or for reasons of employment or hardship. Men traditionally factor little in a child's upbringing, though the Family Court exists primarily to enforce palimony payments (the Jamaican government also pays child support stipends to mothers). Violent confrontations are common, including marital rape, which is not recognized as a crime under Jamaican law.

The ideal to a Jamaican woman is autonomy. They are strong and independent. Many couples in relationships maintain their own separate property. Numerous Jamaican women complain that this brings men's insecurities to the surface, and that men give them only begrudging respect. A large percentage of Jamaican men expect women to play a subservient role; they feel threatened by Jamaican women, especially educated women, whom they consider too independent. Hence, a common sight in late afternoon is to see adolescent girls and women struggling along with buckets of water while young men laze around on the roadside. Women do the cooking, the housework, the child-rearing, and, frequently, the breadwinning (in 40% of households, a woman is the sole provider).

This independent spirit translates into a self-assured striving. Jamaican women attain far higher grades in school and have higher literacy rates, and middle-class women have attained levels of respect and performance commensurate with their counterparts in North America and Europe. Women comprise about 46% of Jamaica's labor force, although the majority are in extremely low paying jobs (the average weekly wage is less than US$30). Some 13% of the women in the labor force have reached senior management and professional level, compared to only 8% of male workers, and more than three-quarters of UWI students are women.

The hit movie *Dancehall Queen* deals with self-worth and the role of women in Jamaican culture – the spirit of a strong, independent woman fighting to succeed against adversity. (The story, which tells of a woman's quest to better her life, could be the story of the lead actress, Audrey Reid, who was raised in a ghetto, forced to drop out of high school due to pregnancy, and through determination worked her way to the peak of Jamaica's acting profession.)

Jamaican women look to several role models, particularly Merlene Ottley, the Olympic gold-medal sprinter born in a poor rural village and today a virtual national hero.

**Work & Living Conditions** The two generations since independence have seen a remarkable change, most notably the growth of a significant middle class, but also in a growing disparity in incomes. There has been a steady move away from an agrarian society to an increasingly industrialized and urbanized one marked by massive migration into urban centers, notably Kingston, where a large middle class lives a lifestyle familiar to its counterpart in Europe and North America, while a vast and burgeoning underclass lives in slums.

There is marked regional diversity. Jamaica boasts several regions – the uplands of Manchester parish and the lowlands of St Elizabeth parish, for example – where living conditions tend to be far better than the national average. And everywhere, large sectors of the community live a middle-class life. The majority of Jamaicans, however, live in the hills, out of sight of tourists: many get by quite adequately, living in aged wooden homes in Caribbean style or concrete cinder block (preferred for contemporary dwellings since Hurricane Gilbert); others eke out a marginal existence in ramshackle villages and rural shacks, sometimes in pockets of extreme poverty. There are areas of malnutrition but little starvation – the island is too fecund for that. Jamaicans have only to reach out and pluck bananas or coconuts, and fish is available on the end of a line. On market days, country higglers get up before dawn, load up their yams, carrots, and *chocho* (a native squash), trek from the hills to the main roads, and catch rides to the main market towns – all to earn a few pennies.

It is hard for many Jamaicans to gather even the most meager resources. They languish under economic hardships. The aspirations of most poorer Jamaicans remain compromised, and despite notable exceptions, individuals are generally reluctant to take risks. Some sociologists have suggested that one of the reasons behind this can be traced back to slavery, when blacks were robbed of their sense of initiative and browbeaten into resignation to circumstance. Many low-income Jamaicans have been unable to find a way out of poverty, so they hustle. They hang out on the streets waiting for an opportunity to present itself. (It is difficult to say how much lassitude and indolence is due to ganja, but a vast percentage of the poorer population spend much of their waking life stoned.)

A general malaise prevalent among a large segment of the male underclass seems fired by a belief that a subtle apartheid force is purposely holding them back (many poor Jamaicans do not trust a 'whitey,' and expatriate residents frequently comment on what you may conclude by observation: the presence of whites is tolerated, but they are secretly despised). The police also face a serious PR problem and are not respected by a huge percent of the poorer populace, notably in Kingston, where politically savvy drug barons and area dons are regarded highly by the local populace, which benefits from their largesse and is in debt as surely as if it has received a loan from a bank. Sociologists suggest that a welling crisis in Jamaican society reflects a deep frustration fueled by the trend of 'globalization' in the information age, which has created an expectation of the 'good life' and suggests the possibility of instant gratification. For the majority of the population – poor and relatively illiterate – it is a good life denied.

In contrast, Jamaica has a significant middle and upper class, who conspicuously live in the hills above Kingston and Montego Bay. Everyone knows the scoop about everyone else: Jamaica is amazingly 'small' and has a vibrant grapevine among the intellectual class and social elite. However, many among these classes live with a surprising lack of contact with the harsh reality in which the majority of Jamaicans live, and seem to muster little empathy. Not infrequently you'll hear defensive denials that poverty even exists in Jamaica. They are, as a whole, well educated with vivacious and well-honed intellects, entrepreneurial, and contemporary looking, with a preference for shopping trips to Miami or New York, and a newfound love of Havana, Cuba, as their in-vogue vacation destination. There are differences even here between upperechelon families from Montego Bay and those from Kingston. The former have always felt superior because – for white Jamaicans – their wealth, traditionally, was derived from a plantation heritage, whereas Kingstonian wealth is more recent, derived from trade and banking and, most recently, insurance. The cultural and political elite is drawn from a relatively small number of families. White families are still predominantly in charge of business and political affairs.

This is a legacy of colonial days, when whites ran the administration and businesses. Historians argue that in the postemancipation period, the British exploited color gradations in hiring and the associated social privilege, because a 'divide and rule' policy had become an imperative for running the British Empire. Jamaica became a color-coded socity. Available school places, for example, were reserved for whites and 'high browns,' or 'outside *piknis*' (mulatto children, usually the illegitimate offspring of a white man and a black woman). As late as the 1950s, black women were rarely employed in offices, which led to demonstrations for change. The police force was white, as were the Anglican and Catholic Church clergy.

On the eve of independence, whites were still at the top. The middle-class businesspeople, traders, and professionals were mostly minorities or of mixed ethnic background. The vast pool of labor, subsistence farmers, and the unemployed were black. Thus status, self-esteem, and stigmas became associated with work. Menial and manual labor is still abhorred by many non-blacks as a symbol of inferior status.

**Crime** Jamaica has witnessed a dramatic increase in violent crimes in the past three decades. The Pan American Health Organization reported that in 1990 there were 55 murders per million people worldwide; Jamaica's murder rate is four times higher, second only to the USA.

Much of the violence is related to political rivalry or to the drug trade, particularly in Kingston. There are even parts of Kingston where the police dare not venture. Police officers are frequently brutally murdered. In turn, many police officers are guilty of summary justice and violent excesses; 145 of the 700 reported murders in Jamaica in 1990 were victims who died in police custody. Since then the murder rate has risen. The problem has been exacerbated in recent years by the repatriation of Jamaicans convicted of violent crimes abroad: about 1500 criminals are returned from the USA each year, to be released to the streets as they have not committed a crime in Jamaica and cannot be incarcerated. Many of these thugs represent the most vicious elements of Jamaican society.

Also see Crime in the Dangers & Annoyances section of the Facts for the Visitor chapter.

## Dos & Don'ts

*Do be direct.* Jamaicans prefer it. If you beat around the bush, they may not only not get your point, but also take advantage of you. Be firm to earn respect but also be diplomatic, as some Jamaicans may turn violent.

*Do relax.* Tropical time happens at a slower pace. 'Soon come' is a favorite expression often translated at face value by foreigners but really meaning 'it'll happen when it happens.'

*Do be empathetic.* Try to understand the hardships that the majority of Jamaicans face. Don't try to take advantage of an individual's plight.

*Don't call Jamaicans 'natives.'* Jamaicans may be natives of the island, but the term is laden with racial connotations that can be taken as slurs. 'Islanders' or simply 'Jamaicans' is more appropriate.

*Do be formal with strangers.* Jamaicans are more formal than many foreigners,

particularly North Americans used to quickly reaching a first-name basis. To show respect, address Jamaicans you meet with 'Mr' or 'Miss,' or even 'Sir' or 'Lady.' Using a first name can be taken as treating someone as inferior.

*Do ask before snapping a photo.* Many Jamaicans enjoy being photographed, sometimes for a small fee, but others prefer not to pose for tourists and can respond angrily. Always respect the privacy of others.

## Treatment of Animals

Jamaicans are not sentimental, and particularly not toward animals (most of which will end up in the pot or sizzling on a jerk rack). Again, a vast disparity is evident between the more cultured middle classes, many of whom keep pets, and the less-incomed classes who, in general, have a utilitarian view of animals and pets. Dogs are usually kept to guard property and are trained to be vicious. Countless other dogs roam free and bear the brunt of callous treatment, such as stonings. Do not be surprised to see male Jamaican drivers deliberately aim to hit dogs. The waysides are littered by dead animals (you'll smell their decomposing bodies from afar), which remain until the stench is such that someone will eventually throw a tire over the carcass and set it afire.

## RELIGION

You don't have to peer inside the *Guinness Book of Records* to discover that Jamaica professes to have the greatest number of churches per sq mile in the world. There seems to be a church every few hundred yards, with virtually every imaginable denomination in the world represented. More than 80% of Jamaicans identify as Christians. Atheists are few and far between.

Jamaicans are deeply religious, and in much more than a church-going sense. The Church serves as an important social center in Jamaican communities. In this poverty-ridden society the gospel is a source of hope, with its talk of equality and redemption in the afterlife. Most everyone believes in a life after death and in a spirit world – a legacy of African animism. Jamaicans are inordinately superstitious and firm believers in ghosts and evil spirits. (Many islanders, for example, still recoil from harmless lizards as if they were ferocious dragons, especially the diminutive yet much-feared croaking lizard.)

Religious tolerance has evolved only as a modern Jamaican tradition. The English colonial plantocracy (including the Church) didn't believe slaves had souls, thus was indifferent to slaves' spiritual welfare. Everfearful of slave uprisings, the plantocracy attempted to vanquish the slaves' African heritage by banning religious gatherings and aggressively thwarting missionary efforts at religious conversion. Nonetheless, missionary zeal gathered pace in the half-century preceding emancipation in 1834, as Baptist and Methodist preachers arrived to spread abolitionism alongside their own word of God. A period of Christianization known as the Great Revival followed emancipation.

Foreign visitors are welcome at Christian religious services, but are expected to act in accordance with local wishes. Most importantly, dress both modestly and respectfully to God, which means, at a minimum, no tank-tops and shorts. Dig out your best togs. In general, the revivalist religions are not so welcoming, and visitors wishing to attend a cult meeting should attempt to make arrangements in advance.

## Christianity

On any day of the week, but notably on weekends, it's common to see adults and children walking along country roads, holding Bibles, and dressed in their finest outfits – the girls in white, the men and boys in somber suits, and the women in heels, hats, and bright satins. On Sundays every church in the country seems to overflow with the righteous, and the old fire-and-brimstone school of sermonizing is still the preferred mode. Bible-waving congregations sway to and fro, roll their heads, and wail and shriek 'Hallelujah!' and 'Amen, sweet Jesus!' while guitars, drums, and tambourines help work the crowds into a frenzy.

The most popular denomination, the Anglican Church of Jamaica (formerly the Church of England), accounts for 43% of the population and has dominated religious life since 1655; the English ruling class ensured that each parish had an Anglican church. Church of God (18.4% of the population), Baptists (10%), Presbyterians (5.2%), and Methodists (3%) claim significant adherents, as they have since slavery. Every town of any significance also has a Roman Catholic Church. About 5% of the population today is Catholic, mostly Chinese, East Indians, and Middle Easterners. There are also Pentecostals, Quakers, Christian Scientists, Seventh Day Adventists (6.9%), and other fundamentalists, who have made serious inroads in recent years at the behest of aggressive proselytizing.

## Revivalist Cults

Jamaica has several quasi-Christian, quasi-animist sects. Their spiritual beliefs and practices resemble the voodoo religions of Haiti. They are generically named Revivalist cults after the post-emancipation Great Revival, during which many blacks converted to Christianity. Revivalism is popular among the poorest classes, but is looked down on by most educated Jamaicans.

The cults are derived from animist beliefs of West Africa. (Animism has nothing to do with animal spirits; the name is derived from the Latin word *anima*, for soul.) These beliefs are based on the tenet that the spiritual and temporal worlds are a unified whole. A core belief is that spirits live independently of the human or animal body and can inhabit inanimate objects. These earthly spirits, which can communicate themselves to humans, are usually morally neutral; how humans call them determines whether they will be a force for good or evil.

Many Jamaicans, regardless of religious faith, commonly consult practitioners who claim to be able to invoke the assistance of spirits and duppies. Some practitioners operate as 'balmists,' using black magic (called obeah, an Ashanti word from West Africa) for medicinal purposes or in more subversive or evil ways, such as enacting revenge, influencing impending court cases, or ensuring a successful romance on behalf of a supplicant. Firm believers will sometimes heal, fall sick, or even die due to their faith in the power of obeah. Since it is occasionally used for murder and other evil, obeah has been banned since slave days. Although usually associated with evil practice, obeah can also be used for good, when it is called myal.

**Pocomania** The most important Revivalist cult is Pocomania, a uniquely Jamaican cult mixing European and African religious heritages. The cult is organized into hierarchical bands, which hold meetings at consecrated 'mission grounds' (or 'seals') and are overseen by a 'leader' or 'shepherd' (or 'mother' if female), who often doubles as an herbalist healer.

The ritual meetings are lively, colorful, and frenzied affairs involving prayers, dances, and rhythmic drumming. Adherents often go into a trance, frequently aided by rum and ganja. Then, a worshipper sometimes becomes 'possessed' by a spirit who becomes his or her guardian. Dancers who have fallen into a trance utter incomprehensible bleats and screams, sometimes causing themselves serious injury.

**Kumina** This is the most African of the Jamaican religious cults. It was introduced by free Africans who arrived as laborers following emancipation and settled predominantly in St Thomas, where the cult remains strongest.

Based on the worship of hundreds of ancestor spirit-deities, Kumina focuses on appeasing wandering spirits of dead people who did not receive proper rites and are a menace to society. Kumina ceremonies are performed for all sorts of social occasions. Goats are frequently sacrificed. Drums are particularly powerful during Kumina ceremonies, which use a ritual Bantu language from the Congo, where the cult originated. As with Pocomania, dancers often become possessed by spirits.

## Rastafarianism

Jamaica is often summed up as 'reggae, rum, and Rastas.' The Rastafarians, with their uncut, uncombed hair grown into long sun-bleached tangles known as 'dreadlocks' or 'dreads,' are synonymous with the island in the sun. There are perhaps as many as 100,000 Rastafarians in Jamaica. They adhere to an unorganized religion – a faith, not a church – that has no official doctrine or dogmatic hierarchy and is composed of a core of social and spiritual tenets that are open to interpretation. Not all Rastafarians wear dreads, for example, and others do not smoke ganja. All adherents, however, accept that Africa is the black race's spiritual home to which they are destined to return.

Most of the world became aware of Rastafarianism in the mid-1970s through the superstardom of reggae musicians Bob Marley & the Wailers (see the Reggae'n'Riddims special section). Reggae draws much of its enduring strength from its connections to praise for a perceived deity. Rastafarianism and its use of reggae have been pivotal in the process of freeing the captive minds of a people recovering from centuries of enslavement, 'removing de shackles from de minds of de people,' says top Irie FM broadcaster Queen Elise Kelly. The Rastafarians' profound influence has far outweighed their small numbers. The movement has evolved greatly since the early days, when it was held in public contempt and adherents endured police harassment.

**Garveyism** Rastafarianism evolved as an expression of poor black Jamaicans seeking fulfillment during the 1930s, a period of growing nationalism and economic and political upheaval. It was boosted by the 'back to Africa' zeal of Jamaican Marcus Garvey's Universal Negro Improvement Association, founded in 1914 (see 'One God, One Aim, One Destiny' in the Ocho Rios & North Coast chapter). Rastafarians regard Garvey as a prophet. The black nationalist had predicted that a black man – a 'Redeemer' – would be crowned king in Africa. Haile Selassie's crowning as emperor of Abyssinia (now Ethiopia) on November 2, 1930, fulfilled Garvey's prophecy and established a fascination with Ethiopia that lies at the core of Rastafarianism.

Many Garvey supporters saw their Redeemer in Selassie, and they quoted Biblical references in support of Selassie's claim to be the king of all Africans, and the 225th descendant from King David. He traced his family tree back to King Solomon and the Queen of Sheba, and took the title 'King of Kings, Lord of Lords, Conquering Lion of the Tribe of Judah.' These Garveyites believed Selassie was God incarnate. They adopted Selassie's precoronation name, Ras Tafari: Ras (prince) and Tafari (to be feared).

One charismatic leader, Leonard Percival Howell, consolidated his Rastafarian faith and began a proselytizing tour. Howell preached allegiance to Haile Selassie, not the British Crown. In 1933, he was arrested and sentenced to two years hard labor for sedition. Freed from jail, Howell attracted a following and in 1940 established the first Rastafarian community – the Pinnacle – at Sligoville, northwest of Kingston. His followers adopted the 'dreadlocked' hair style of several East African tribes – an allegory of the mane of the Lion of Judah.

Howell developed the tenets of Rastafarianism, many of which were derived from the *Voice of Ethiopia*, a newspaper of the Ethiopian Orthodox Church, which proclaimed Haile Selassie as the 'Elect of God.' The church was boosted by a Jamaican branch of the Ethiopian World Federation founded in New York in 1937 by Haile Selassie's cousin, Dr Malaku Bayen, to organize support for Ethiopia following its invasion by fascist Italy.

Numerous charlatans have been involved with the faith, such as Claudius Henry, an early sympathizer and head of the African Reform Church, who allied himself with Rastafarianism in its early days. In 1959 he began selling tickets for passage to Africa. Scores of Jamaicans bought tickets and sold their property and belongings and arrived at Kingston dock on October 5, expecting to sail. Alas, they'd been duped. A police raid on Henry's church uncovered a mass of armaments,

**The Lion of Judah**

leading to rumors that Rastafarians were planning to overthrow the government. It was a public relations disaster and inspired much of the fear that marked the widespread response to the faith in its early days.

Howell's self-sufficient commune at Pinnacle endured numerous police raids, and many members were arrested on ganja charges. In 1954, the Pinnacle community was broken up by police. Many of the members settled the squatter camps of West Kingston, such as the Dungle and Back-A-Wall (so-called because it was behind a wall), and the still-extant commune at Bull Bay, east of Kingston (Orlando Patterson's novel *Children of Sisyphus* tells of this epoch). By the end of the decade there were perhaps 15,000 Rastafarians in Back-A-Wall. As their militancy increased, leftist political activists and criminals penetrated their ranks and, in 1958, a pitch battle broke out on Coronation St between Rastafarians and the police.

That same year, followers of Rastafarian Reverend Claudius Henry fled to the hills following his arrest and began plans to initiate a Cuban-style guerrilla campaign. The deaths of two British soldiers in skirmishes that ensued did much to demonize Rastafarianism, although a subsequent report characterized the movement, correctly, as pacifist. In 1961, a fact-finding mission that included Rastafarian representatives was sent to Africa to investigate the possibility of repatriation.

At least 15 different sects had emerged by the 1960s, when Rastafarianism evolved a firm philosophy and solid foundation in the face of continued police harassment that included regular beatings. Communes were frequently bulldozed.

Poor Jamaicans had long sought solace in the Bible, which lent itself to reinterpretation by Kingston's sufferers ('Weep not, behold the Lion that is of the tribe of Judah,' says the Book of Revelation). Disillusionment helped turn ghetto youth toward the social and spiritual salvation implicit in Rastafarianism. They could connect with the philosophy's empathy for the underdog and its militant attacks on injustice, and

many grasped at a faith that offered a positive alternative to the despair of the ghetto. By the 1970s Rastafarianism's influence was far-reaching among Jamaica's underclass, and even members of the middle classes were adopting Rastafarianism. Savvy to a political opportunity, Michael Manley, campaigning to be prime minister, saw advantage in wooing the island's growing sympathy. Manley lent legitimacy to the movement by adopting its lexicon and electioneering with a sacred 'rod of correction' (given to him by Selassie in 1970). Rastafarianism really came of age with Bob Marley's ascendancy to international fame and acceptance. Suddenly, Rastafarianism was hip.

**Rastafarian Tenets** A document began to circulate in the 1950s outlining the 'Twenty-One Points,' which defined the Rastafarian philosophy and creed. One tenet was that the African race was one of God's chosen races, one of the Twelve Tribes of Israel descended from the Hebrews and displaced. Jamaica is Babylon (after the place where the Israelites were enslaved), and their lot is in exile in a land that cannot be reformed. A second tenet states that God, whom they call *Jah*, will one day lead them from Babylon to Zion (the 'Promised Land,' or Ethiopia). A third addresses Selassie's status as the Redeemer chosen to lead Africans back to Africa.

Rastafarians have also adapted traditional Christian tenets to fit their philosophical mold or 'reasoning,' the term used to cover their distinctive discourse. They believe that the original Bible told the history of the African peoples, but was stolen and rewritten by whites to suppress and dominate blacks. This interpretation underpins the Rastafarians' mistrust of white society and elements of Christian philosophy, especially of redemption after death (their discourse is full of bitterness about injustices based on race and social class). Rastafarians believe that heaven is on earth in the present. (They also casually dismiss Selassie's appalling human rights record and harsh, despotic rule.) Though Selassie died in 1975, a commonly held belief is that he still lives among them unidentified in a new guise.

Rastafarian leaders continue to petition England's Queen Elizabeth to repatriate them to Africa. Meanwhile they wait for redemption. Reggae – a music born of their nonviolent protest against oppression – and ganja (the holy herb) kill the time. Soon come!

**Ganja & Good Living** Rastafarians believe that ganja provides a line of communication with God. Again, they look to the Bible, specifically Psalm 146:8, which says,

Who covereth the heaven with clouds, and prepareth rain for the earth. Who maketh grass to grow on the mountains, and herbs for the service of men.

Herb could, of course, be sage, rosemary, or thyme but, hey, they don't do the trick! Most but not all adherents smoke ganja copiously from cigar-size *spliffs* (reefers) and the holy *chalice*, a bamboo pipe made of a goat's horn. Through it they claim to gain wisdom and inner divinity through the ability to 'reason' more clearly. The search for truth – 'reasoning' – is integral to the faith and is meant to see through the corrupting influences of 'Babylon' and its pernicious

## Holy Smoke!

Ganja (marijuana) is an omnipresent fact of a Jamaican vacation. The weed, which grows throughout the island, has been cultivated for its narcotic effect since 1845, when indentured

Indian laborers brought the first seeds from Asia (the English called it 'Indian hemp'). Its use spread rapidly among the plantation workers. Since it induced indolence and reduced productivity, it was outlawed at an early stage. Nonetheless, islanders have used it ever since. Today, an estimated 60% of Jamaicans smoke it on a regular basis.

Ganja use crosses all social strata; it is no less common for friends of the highest income levels to offer guests an after-dinner 'tote' than it is for the urban poor, who often smoke spliffs the size of bazookas. Many Jamaicans don't see ganja as a drug but as a medicinal and religious herb. To Rastafarians it is a source of wisdom.

For Jamaica's impoverished farmers, growing 'poor man's friend' is one of the few sure ways of earning money. The remote interior provides ideal conditions; the

HOLGER LEUE

denigration of black people and, in particular, of Rastas.

In recent years, Rastafarianism has concerned itself less with redemption than with resolution of the problems of the poor and dispossessed on the island. It advocates a peaceful fight against oppression, against 'Babylon,' defined as the 'establishment' and powerfully exemplified by Bob Marley in his song 'Babylon System':

Babylon system is the vampire
Sucking the blood of the sufferers
Building church and university
Deceiving the people continually

Me say them graduating thieves
And murderers, look out now
Sucking the blood of the sufferers.

Despite its militant consciousness, Rastafarianism is not a political movement (its adherents refuse to vote or work within the existing political system), although many of its members, most notably exemplified in the 1970s by singer Peter Tosh, become militantly radical in their denunciations of 'Babylon.' True Rastas preach love and nonviolence and live by strict Biblical codes that advocate a way of life in harmony with Old Testament traditions. They are

## Holy Smoke!

five-lobed plant thrives in Jamaica's rich red soil. And the main export market – the USA – is nearby.

First the seedlings are meticulously raised under protective cover and then transplanted into fields (*guano*, or bat dung, used as a fertilizer supposedly produces the most prolific plants). There they mature in five or six months, reaching heights as great as 10 feet. Ganja is planted between other crops by small-scale farmers, and in larger plots by more serious entrepreneurs. Once harvested, the plants are pressed to extract hash oil, and the leaves are then dried. Distributors collect the dried and baled ganja, which they transport to lonesome boat docks and remote airstrips for rapid shipment to the USA. Legitimate businesses sometimes act as covers (many respected businesspeople in Jamaica reportedly got their start in drug trafficking).

The US embassy estimates that during the early 1980s, the annual wholesale value of Jamaica's ganja crop exceeded US$1.5 billion – possibly Jamaica's major source of foreign exchange! – and there are reasons to believe that the ganja trade had tacit approval at the government level. Nonetheless, since 1986 the Jamaican government has cracked down on drug trading at the behest of the US Drug Enforcement Agency (DEA). Efforts to eradicate the crop include spraying nurseries with weed killers. The DEA claims that Jamaica's ganja production has fallen by 80%, and that exports have fallen by two-thirds. But poverty-ridden small farmers have borne the economic crunch, and the demise of ganja has fostered the use and trading of other drugs, especially crack and cocaine.

Illicit drug sales on the streets are commonplace, and most street hustlers and roadside stalls will have a small spliff or bag of ganja on hand. If they like you, some Jamaicans may even give you a 'small sometin' of ganja – often enough to get the entire hotel high. The strongest varieties are Burr, Cotton, and Lamb's Breath, which are marketed in the USA as *sinsi* (short for *sinsemilla*, Spanish for seedless), the highest grade (pardon the pun).

If you're tempted to sample the local crop while on the island, remember that the possession, use, or sale of any drug is strictly illegal, and foreigners are not exempt from the heavy punishments.

vegetarians who follow strict dietary laws. Strict adherents are teetotalers, too. They also shun tobacco and the staples of western consumption. Those who copy Rastafarian style but bring ill-repute are referred to as 'wolves.'

**Rastafarian Sects** Adherents are grouped into regional sects, which cleave to the strict codes to greater or lesser degrees. The Bobo Ashantis, who live above Bull Bay, follow a strictly ascetic and reclusive life, shunning interactions with Babylon, hoping intently for the day of repatriation, and relegating women to a subservient role. (For more on Bull Bay, see the Kingston & Environs chapter.) A sect known as the Twelve Tribes of Israel (Bob Marley was a member) is composed primarily of more accomplished, well-to-do Jamaicans who have managed a greater accommodation with Babylon and honor women if not quite as equals, then almost. It has branches around the world. The Ethiopian Zion Coptic Church is a fringe sect that has become heavily involved in the drug trade (the sect's leaders were recently jailed). It's shunned by traditional Rastafarians, who deem the Coptics as 'wolves.'

Rasta 'yards' or communes are distinguished by the presence of flags and a figure of a lion representing Haile Selassie. Here they hold their *nyabinghis*, organized gatherings also known as 'groundations.'

Divisions between the sects have intensified in recent years. Attempts to unify the varying sects have met with little success. The most recent effort involves the Rastafarian Centralization Organization, which sponsors conferences in hopes of evolving common ground.

**A Unique Lexicon** One of the 21 tenets of Rastafarianism is the belief that God exists in each person, and that the two are the same. Thus the creed unifies divinity and individuality through the use of personal pronouns that reflect the 'I and I.' ('One blood. Everybody same, mon!') 'I' becomes the *id* or true measure of inner divinity, which places everyone on the same plane.

Thus 'I and I' can mean 'we,' 'him and her,' 'you and they.' (The personal pronoun 'me' is seen as a sign of subservience, of acceptance of the self as an 'object.')

Rastafarians have evolved a whole lexicon of their own, which has profoundly influenced 'Jamaica talk' (see the Language chapter) and is laced with cryptic intent and meaning. This revisionist 'English' is inspired by Rastafarian reasoning that sees the English language as a tool in the service of Babylon designed to 'downpress' the black man. In short, they believe the language is biased. Every word is analyzed and in this frame, even the most insignificant word can seem tainted. A well-meant greeting – 'Hello!' – may elicit an angry response: 'Dis not 'ell and I not low!' Conversely, where a word favors their faith, naive interpretations lend a meaning out of all proportion. Thus, Selassie-I can be interpreted as Selassie-eye, showing proof of the Ethiopian emperor's omniscience.

An excellent resource for understanding Rastafarian lingo is *Dread Talk* by Velma Pollard.

## LANGUAGE

Officially, English is the spoken language. In reality, Jamaica is a bilingual country, and English is far more widely understood than spoken. The unofficial lingo, the main spoken language of poor Jamaicans, is patois (PA-twah) – a musical dialect with a uniquely Jamaican staccato rhythm and cadence, laced with salty idioms and wonderfully and wittily compressed proverbs designed, often, to outwit whomever a Jamaican is speaking to, particularly during verbal battles.

Patois evolved from Creole English and a twisted alchemy of the mother tongue peppered with African, Portuguese, and Spanish terms and, in this century, Rastafarian slang. Linguists agree that it is more than simplified, pidgin English, and it has its own identifiable syntax.

The widest differences are in the grammar of the common folk. Patois is deepest in rural areas, where many people do not know much standard English. Although it is mostly the lingua franca of the poor, all sectors of Jamaica understand patois, and even polite, educated Jamaicans (who tend to speak with a lilting Queen's or Oxford English accent) lapse into patois at unguarded moments. Most Jamaicans vary the degree of their patois according to whom they're speaking with.

Jamaicans are generally more emphatic with language than most English-speaking people. They tend to shout a lot, often stressing key words with an apparent rudeness or volatility that takes soft-spoken foreigners by surprise.

See the Language chapter for vocabulary and phrases.

Reggae'n'Riddims

# REGGAE'N'RIDDIMS

Whether you've been inspired by Bob Marley's lyrics or scandalized by Lady Saw's, skanked the night away at a ganja-smoke-filled rum shop, or wined groin-to-groin at a steamy dancehall, you can't help but feel the punchy pulse of Jamaican music, hitting you in the gut like a shot of over-proof rum. It is everywhere. Intense and asser-tive. The pulsing undercurrent of Jamaican life.

Jamaican music is associated above all with reggae, and reggae is synonymous with one man: Robert Nesta Marley. Marley laid the foundation, beginning with the Wailers (the island's 'Beatles'). But reggae is actually only one of several distinctly Jamaican sounds, which have evolved through six clear stages, each defined by a specific beat: ska (about 1960-66), rock-steady (1966-68), early and 'rebel' reggae (1969-74), 'roots' reggae (1975-79), dancehall (1979-85), and, more recently, ragga.

Pivotal in the evolution and ever-shifting currents has been the 'sound system,' a simple arrangement of high-powered amplifiers and gargantuan speakers blaring bass-dominated tunes at open-air venues that remain the most notable social fixture on the contemporary music scene. (See 'Sound Systems & the Rise of DJs.')

The scene is impressively fecund: Jamaica has spawned more than 100,000 records, and Kingston has dozens of recording studios. About 500 45s pour out of Kingston pressing plants monthly (the 7-inch 45rpm vinyl remains the dominant format in Jamaica). The production scene has always been highly competitive and fluid; a producer builds a small studio, scouts

LEE ABEL

**Previous page:** Bob Marley takes it easy backstage in 1979 (photograph by Roger Steffens).

**Left:** Keepin' it real at Reggae Sunsplash

Note: All record label photographs by Roger Steffens

out a skilled arranger to manage the auditions and recording sessions, hires established musicians to form a studio session band to lay down rhythm tracks, then selects the right song and vocalist to record over the rhythm. Competing producers have traditionally used the same rhythm bands (or at least the same musicians under nominally different logos) and rhythm tracks, rehashed over and over with new interpretations to give old rhythms a fresh feel. Then it's off to press.

The sheer creativity and productivity has produced a profound effect around the world. International stars such as Eric Clapton, the Rolling Stones, and Paul Simon incorporated reggae tunes into albums in the 1970s. In the early 1980s UK reggae bands such as Steel Pulse often shared concert billing with the Clash and other punk bands, exemplifying

## Essential Reggae CDs

For newcomers to the music, here's a list of some of reggae's most definitive recordings.

*Best of Studio One, Volume 1* – Various Artists (Heartbeat)
*Black Woman* – Judy Mowatt (Shanachie)
*Blackheart Man* – Bunny Wailer (Island)
*Cry Tough* – Alton Ellis (Heartbeat)
*Equal Rights* – Peter Tosh (Columbia)
*Foundation Ska* – Skatalites (Heartbeat)
*King Tubby Meets the Rockers Uptown* – Augustus Pablo (Shanachie)
*Legend* – Bob Marley & the Wailers (Polygram)
*Marcus Garvey/Garvey's Ghost* – Burning Spear (Island)
*Natty Dread* – Bob Marley & the Wailers (Island)
*Reggae Greats* – Lee 'Scratch' Perry (Mango)
*Right Time Come* – the Mighty Diamonds (Shanachie)
*Rivers of Babylon: The Best of the Melodians 1967-73* – Melodians (Trojan Records)
*Ska Boo-Da-Ba* – Skatalites (Westside)
*Super Boss* – U-Roy (Culture Press)
*The Harder They Come* – soundtrack featuring Jimmy Cliff and various artists (Mango)
*Tougher Than Tough: The Story of Jamaican Music* – 4-CD compilation (Island)
*Two Sevens Clash* – Culture (Shanachie)
*Where There Is Life* – Luciano (Island)

— **Roger Steffens**

their commonality in uncompromising lyrical assaults on the 'system.' And the contemporary rap, rave, and hip-hop cultures owe much to Jamaica's sound-system-based dancehall culture.

The varying musical forms have reflected the changing mood of the Jamaican people. From early mento to dancehall, Jamaican music is the cultural synthesis and expression of a people struggling against adversity and in quest of freedom. The musical roots are sunk deep in a national psyche steeped in an African heritage and fired by the pain and humiliation of colonialism, enslavement, and latter-day poverty.

# African Roots

Jamaican music draws on its rich heritage of folk music introduced by African slaves, influenced through contact with white culture.

Although slaveowners attempted to suffocate African culture, traditional music survived and evolved its own forms. Particularly important were the *burru* ('talking drums'), which were used to pass information, and folk songs derived from the cane fields, which were most often based (as in Central and West African tradition) on 'call-and-response' singing where a *bomma* (lead singer) chanted verses and the *bobbin* (chorus) responded. These musical forms were given a boost during the Great Revival of the 1860s, when Jamaica revivalist religions, such as Pocomania and Kumina, had a passionate resurrection.

The songs have been kept alive this century by day workers (see Day Work in the Society & Culture section in the Facts about Jamaica chapter), and by professional groups such as the Jamaica Folk Singers and National Dance Theatre Company singers.

Over generations, European elements such as the French quadrille introduced by planters were absorbed and fused into the African music and dance accompanied in time by fife and flute, then fiddles and horns, creating a uniquely Caribbean style that slave communities made their own (often in subtle parody of the mores of the slave-owning class). In the 18th-century, fife-and-drum bands melded military march tempo to the quadrille and other dance forms and found their most colorful expressions in Jonkanoo celebrations held at Christmas (see 'Jonkanoo' in the Facts for the Visitor chapter). Almost from the beginning, the violin joined the hourglass-shaped African drum to give island music its distinctive form.

The drum, however, has always lain at the heart of African music, as exemplified by the burru drummer who performed in the cane fields to keep slaves at labor or performed at fertility rites and, after emancipation, roamed the Jamaican countryside much like a European troubadour. The burru man usually delivered licentious ditties played over a three-drum set called the *akete*.

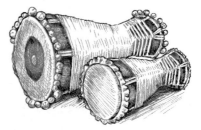

Few recordings of this musical genre were ever made. You can still witness country dances being performed in remote villages, with melodies played on banjo and violin accompanied by small accordions, kettledrums, gourds, and calabashes. And Jamaicans still play tambour drums, bamboo flutes, and other African instruments in revivalist religions. The use of akete and *funde* drums, cymbals, and rattles of revivalist religions entered into reggae music, notably in the 1960s with the Maytals.

# Mento

The earliest original Jamaican musical form was mento, a simple folk calypso that emerged at the turn of the 20th century as an accompaniment to a dance derived from the French quadrille and English-inspired maypole dances. (The terms 'mento' and 'calypso' were used interchangeably in Jamaica during the period. Calypso is often associated with Jamaica, partly because of Harry Belafonte's fame, but it really belongs to Trinidad, where it derived based on the steel drum.)

Mento was rooted in a hard country life and was a hybrid between folk and the commercial sounds that were to follow. The music fused burru-based calypso with Cuban influences – guitar, banjo, shakers, and rumba box (adapted from the African thumb piano, with metal straps for strings) – introduced by Jamaican migrant workers. Mento was slow and rhythmic, perfectly suited to the undulating groin-to-groin 'dubbing' of the African-derived dance styles. Most songs were underwritten by a wry, often raunchy, humor that dealt with the material discomforts of everyday life.

Mento developed a faster pace during the 1940s and 1950s and became as popular throughout Jamaica as reggae is today. It even became a staple of entertainment for tourists at the north coast hotels.

By the late 1950s, the music was fading under a wave of popular North American music, particularly early boogie-woogie and R&B brought back to Jamaica by seasonal workers or carried on radio signals from New Orleans and Miami. Nonetheless, mento's influence has lingered and many Jamaican musicians in ensuing years have given a nod to its themes, as with Phyllis Dillon's rock-steady hit 'Don't Touch My Tomato' in the mid-1960s and the recordings of DJs Lieutenant Stitchie and Admiral Bailey in the 1990s.

JAMAICA TOURIST BOARD

**Left:** Beat-busting in the parking lot

Today, mento is mostly played for tourists by traditional groups in the lobbies of upscale hotels. It is also kept alive during Heritage Week's 'Mento Yard,' hosted in a different parish each October. Most recordings were made for a local market in the era of the 78rpm, and finding mento discs today is difficult.

## The Transition to Ska

As North America shifted to rock'n'roll in the 1950s, producers such as Coxsone Dodd, Duke Reid, and Prince Buster faced a shortfall of suitable music (Jamaicans hankered for New Orleans' hard-edged, 'blacker' style of jump blues) and in 1957 began to bring Jamaican performers into local studios to record the shuffling sounds their listeners wanted to hear.

The promoters created their own labels and also sponsored radio shows to get airplay. Plenty of other budding entrepreneurs set up their own labels, including Chinese-Jamaicans Justin and Duke Yap; Chris Blackwell, a Harrow-educated white Jamaican who got his start with his R&B label in 1958 (he would later rise to fame with his London-based Island Records in the early 1960s); and future prime minister, Edward Seaga, who founded West Indies Records the same year.

Though still driven by shuffle boogies, the Jamaican R&B musicians lent the rhythm guitar on the offbeat more prominence (echoing the rhythm of the banjo in mento) and charged the third beat with an emphatic bass-drum kick that created a 'more Jamaican' sound and more befitted the bass-heavy sound systems for which the recordings were intended. Gradually, the emphasis switched to the after-beat that would become the hallmark of Jamaican syncopation, conjuring ska out of American-influenced R&B by late 1961.

# Ska

Ska was the first distinctive style of Jamaican music, synonymous with the aspirations and concerns of a proud yet impoverished people at a time when independence from England was imminent. Ska's buoyant rhythms captured perfectly the sense of pride and optimism, reflected in celebratory songs such as Jimmy Cliff's 'Miss Jamaica,' Derrick Morgan's 'Forward March,' and Lord Creator's 'Independent Jamaica.' Appropriately, ska was the first music to be internationally recognized as exclusively Jamaican.

Ska's enigmatic beat was born in economically depressed areas of Kingston and adopted by the poor and dispossessed who were then falling under the spell of Rastafarianism. The sentiments of the apocalyptic cult echoed the lyrics of the revivalist gospel tradition, which lent yet another source of inspiration, and many singers of the day infused Old Testament themes into their work. Owen Gray's 'Sinner's Weep' and Laurel Aitken's 'Zion' and 'Judgement Day' exemplify the conscious thematic concerns that would burst more fully onto the music scene a decade later.

Ska incorporated elements from all the indigenous musical traditions. Though short-lived, it was uniquely inventive. While boogie-based R&B was a catalyst for the evolution of ska, the form was also molded from African music, mento banjo strumming, hand-clapping of the Revival church, and the cadence of the Rasta funde drum, inspired by the music of Count Ossie. Ska's fast, upbeat tempo blended mento's folk derivatives with elements from jazz, merengue, the Kumina religion, and fervid nyahbinghi rhythms expressed in such Rastafarian-inspired tracks as 'Lion of Judah.' (Nyahbinghi sounds involved relentless drumming and chanting, usually employing a three-drum set – the akete – of different sizes.)

ROGER STEFFENS

**Right:** Derrick Morgan

It was, however, mostly instrumental: horn-driven, with a danceable double-time beat (12-bar blues shuffle accented on the second and fourth beats and a syncopated afterbeat provided by the guitar and piano, lending the form its onomatopoeic name from the *skat, skat, skat* sound of the guitar). Drummer Lloyd Knibb is credited with giving ska its distinctive beat.

The music's own unique bobbing dance style (also called ska, or skanking) became an overnight sensation, with shuffling feet seemingly moving like crankshafts and arms pumping like pistons.

LEE ABEL

Prince Buster was the most prolific ska producer and personified the 'one-man record company' that remains a staple of the Jamaican record production scene. He produced soulful singer Derrick Morgan and had ska's biggest hit in the early years with Eric Morris' 'Humpty Dumpty,' an insinuating nursery rhyme lyric that set off a brief trend. Another key figure was Leslie Kong, a Chinese-Jamaican producer whose Beverly label was named for his restaurant on Orange St in Kingston. Morgan also had a string of hits for Kong, who also signed on three young singers who would rise to later prominence: Jimmy Cliff, Desmond Dekker, and Bob Marley.

Coxsone Dodd found his own golden boy in Delroy Wilson, a teenager who put out several spiritual-cum-dancehall numbers, including the Rasta hit 'Lion of Judah,' and several songs attacking Prince Buster. Dodd also scored big with Toots & the Maytals and the Skatalites, a 13-member band (including Lloyd Knibb on drums and Ernie Ranglin on bass guitar), most of whom had received their formal training at an orphanage – Kingston's Alpha Boys School – that emphasized music education.

**Left:** Skatalites Tommy McCook and Roland Alphonso in 1990

## Count Ossie

A prominent Rastafarian activist during the 1950s and 1960s was Count Ossie (Oswald Williams), a master drummer who spread positive cultural values at nyahbinghi sites such as his Renock Lodge in the Wareika Hills, where hopeful musicians such as the young Don Drummond and teenage Bob Marley often hung out. Count Ossie and his band, the Mystical Revelation of Rastafari, infused their African-centered music with the sustained two-beat rim of the funde drum that still provides the hypnotic effect of the reggae beat.

Count Ossie was featured in the Independence Day celebrations on August 5, 1962, and produced the first-ever recording by the Jamaica Broadcast Corporation.

## The Alpha Boys School

Many of Jamaica's top-notch musicians are graduates of Kingston's Alpha Boys School, on South Camp Rd. The school was founded in 1880 as a Catholic school for delinquent boys and run by nuns as a no-nonsense institution. It quickly developed a great reputation for the quality of its musical tuition and the discipline it instilled in the wayward youth sent there.

Its influence on Jamaica's musical development cannot be overstated. Many of the players in the early dance bands of the 1940s and 1950s, who were forerunners of ska, studied here, including several key figures who would become members of the Skatalites, notably trombonist Don Drummond. The school has continued to pour out talent, most notably Yellowman, the 1980s ragga sensation (though the nuns are probably feverishly crossing themselves at the words that pour out of his mouth!).

Although they were together formally for only two years, the Skatalites (who were at one time managed by current Prime Minister, PJ Patterson) produced hundreds of 45s, and their influence on the island music scene was inestimable. The band's leading influence was trombonist Don Drummond, whose compositions defined ska in the same manner that Bob Marley's music would later dominate reggae. Many of the Skatalites converted to Rastafarianism, influencing dozens of other musicians. Drummond was a committed Rasta whose career tragically ended when he murdered his lover and was committed to a mental asylum in 1969. (When the Skatalites disbanded in 1966, half the members formed the Supersonics and went to work for Duke Reid's Treasure Isle label, while the rest formed the Soul Brothers and became the house band for rival Coxsone Dodd's Studio One.)

The Skatalites were also the backing group for the Wailing Rude Boys (later the Wailers), a youthful band led by Bob Marley that had signed with Dodd in late 1963. The group took its name for the lawless youths – 'rude boys' – of Kingston's ghettoes. They recorded 'It Hurts to be Alone' and 'I'm Still Waiting,' which were well received on local sound systems. Dodd then had the band record

'Simmer Down' with Don Drummond pushing things along on a fast ska rhythm. The song, one of the first records to express Rastafarian viewpoints, was a hit, topping the Jamaican charts for two months. More 'rudie' songs followed, including 'Rude Boy,' although the group branched out to doo-wop, spirituals, and even a take on Burt Bacharach's theme from the film *What's New Pussycat?* In the early days many performers looked north: for example, Jimmy Cliff (who enjoyed great success with 'King of Kings') copied Otis Redding, while Marley and the Wailers had modeled themselves on Curtis Mayfield and the Impressions. (Mayfield has been dubbed the 'godfather of reggae' for his abiding influence.)

Despite chart-busting hits, ska was the music of shantytown dwellers and was dismissed by local media. Abroad, however, radio stations spread ska to North America and Europe, and performers such as Toots & the Maytals ('Six and Seven Books of Moses') and Byron Lee & the Dragonaires became household names. In England, ska found a strong following among Jamaican immigrants and gained prominence with Millie Small's 1964 hit 'My Boy Lollypop,' produced by renowned guitarist Ernie Ranglin. That year, Small also led a ska delegation to the World's Fair in New York City that included Jimmy Cliff and Byron Lee & the Dragonaires. (Marley and the Wailers were branded as 'rude boys' and had to stay home, while the Skatalites and the Maytals were deemed 'too religious,' a euphemism for Rastafarians, then still considered too controversial by authorities.)

# Rock-Steady

Ska had a therapeutic effect on a nation still in its infancy. But as socio-economic pressures swiftly mounted, discontent set in, and musicians began to address a younger, more militant ghetto audience, charging their music with angrier lyrics that reflected the changing times.

Many sounds of the times glamorized the 'rudies,' including Peter Tosh's 'I'm the Toughest,' Bunnie Livingstone's 'Let Him Go,' the Clarendonians' 'Rudie Gone A Jail,' and a series of hits by Derrick Morgan and Desmond Dekker, including '007 (Shanty Town).' Others unequivocally condemned the rudies, such as Prince Buster's 'Judge Dread' and, more notably, Alton Ellis, who condemned Bob Marley and the Wailers for having previously glorified the rudies. However, the Wailers also were in tune with the rising influence of Rastafarianism and recorded several more positive numbers: the Wailers were one of several ska groups that sang moralistic messages aimed at the 'rudies,' but it was their slow-paced

LEE ABEL

**Left:** Jimmy Cliff really wanting it

**Right:** Rastafarians await Haile Selassie's arrival at the Kingston airport in 1966.

MICHAEL OCHS ARCHIVE

1966 hit, 'Jailhouse,' that crystallized the new style that became known as 'rude-boy music.' Tosh's 'Rasta Shook Them Up,' which celebrated Haile Selassie's visit in 1966, combined the pumping piano riffs of rude-boy music with a traditional Rasta chant. This, and the group's subsequent recordings, presaged the move toward 'reality,' or social-consciousness songs of the forthcoming decade. These songs would find their greatest expression through the voice of Bob Marley, Black Uhuru, and Burning Spear, and become known as 'rebel' or 'roots' music (the term 'roots reggae' is often used by Jamaicans to imply *any* music that concerns itself with the life or 'reality' of the oppressed).

Lyrics began to take greater prominence, and the music slowed and the basslines became broken up to keep pace allegorically with the broken dreams of the people. A pumping piano typified the genre. Gradually the drums and bass came to prominence, slowing ska down still further to half speed so that it became a more syncopated, melodic, and slick music that harked back to mento. The dance style was more languid, with minimal movements that gave the new 'ska' its own name: rock-steady. Almost overnight, it became the in-vogue sound of the all-important dancehall.

## The Rock-Steady Comet

Musicologists look to Delroy Wilson's 'I'm in a Dancing Mood' as a seminal song that defined the juncture, while drummer Winston Grennan's unique approach to rhythm also helped inaugurate the slow groove of Jamaican rock-steady. As the creator of the 'one-drop' beat (with a hard blow on the third beat that cuts the beat in half), Grennan was a profound influence on the island's popular music.

Other leading exponents were Leroy Sibbles and his band, the Heptones, who gave the sound a heavy bass, and Jimmy Cliff ('You Can Get It If You Really Want'), whose uniquely positive and catchy style rings with a clarity and power of true talent still in evidence today.

Among producers, long-established Duke Reid commanded the scene. Rock-steady reached its sudden maturity in 1967 with an outpouring of cool, romantic sounds from Reid's Treasure Isle studio above his liquor store on Bond St. Alton Ellis, Phyllis Dillon, and such harmony trios as the Paragons,

## Sound Systems & the Rise of DJs

The uniquely Jamaican sound system has been the driving force behind the evolution of Jamaican popular music. Sound systems – essentially mobile discos – became the main source of entertainment for the vast majority of Jamaicans and continue to be so.

Sound systems evolved in the mid-1940s and were concentrated in central Kingston in an area known as 'Beat Street.' The systems were set up at outdoor fenced-in plots (called 'lawns' or dancehalls), usually next to bars or liquor stores, whose owners were the main promoters. The promoter set up food and drink for sale inside the gate and made his money off the sales. Sound systems are still run this way, with smoke rising from jerk stands and steam rising from bubbling vats of mannish water mingling with thick clouds of ganja.

**Part of Duke Reid's sound system in the 1960s**

In the early days, most sound systems were very basic: a record player or jukebox with one or two speakers. During the 1950s, the systems became more sophisticated with wardrobe-sized speakers (known as 'House of Joy') able to blast the tunes several blocks. Gradually they evolved into megawatt giants capable of playing belly-wobbling bass frequencies at 30,000W.

The selectors (DJs), who introduced and played the music, gradually gained immense stature by 'chatting' over tunes at dances and 'toasting' the crowd. Count Machuki is considered the first of the jive-talking DJs. He began by making up spoken introductions to records, copying the slang of US radio DJs interspersed by clicking and other sounds. This caught on and became known as 'peps.' Typical of his jives is his first, inspired by *Jive* magazine:

If you dig my jive
You're cool and very much alive
Everybody all round town
Machuki's the reason why I shake it down
When it comes to jive
You can't whip him with no stick

By the mid-1950s, three promoters – Clement Seymour 'Coxsone' Dodd, Arthur 'Duke' Reid, and Vincent 'King' Edwards – dominated the scene with their Downbeat, Trojan, and Giant sound systems. By 1960, a fourth giant – Prince Buster – had asserted himself onto

## Sound Systems & the Rise of DJs

the scene with his Voice of the People sound system. Their rivalry is legendary and generated fierce, and often violent, loyalty among their fans. The promoters traveled the American south to seek out R&B singles to introduce to Jamaica as their own material. Rival sound systems would often set up on opposite sides of the street and attempt to poach each others' fans through exclusive music pumped out over a more powerful bass. The greatest battles of all occurred at pre-arranged 'sound clashes' when DJs and sound systems vied to see who could 'flop' the opponent and earn the sound-system crown. DJs still square off in fierce battles in deafening arenas where freshly pressed 'dub plates' become lethal weapons for DJs seeking the ultimate 'burial tune.'

Duke Reid was a daunting figure: a former policeman who often appeared in a sequined leather outfit and carried two pistols wherever he went, setting a tone for egotistical DJs down the line. His aggressive style attracted 'enforcers,' violent men who often attacked opponents' dances and even destroyed their sound systems. Reid had the baddest boys, but Coxsone had the better music, aided by Count Machuki as DJ. By 1959, Edwards had become king of sound systems thanks to a supreme collection of rare US sounds.

Today's undisputed top dog on the sound-system scene is Stone Love, with a stable of A1 selectors and DJs and an islandwide reach. Increasingly, urban dancehall is giving way to an out-of-town scene in response to a crackdown by authorities implementing noise-abatement laws. Several key dancehall sites in Kingston and other cities have been closed, and those in Negril now operate under time restrictions that have all but spelled their doom.

Sweet dreams are made of discs: a DJ takes a break
at Reggae Sunsplash

**Left:** Leroy Sibbles (center) and the Heptones

LEE ABEL

the Silvertones, and the Melodians had a string of pioneering, soulful hits. Coxsone Dodd's Brentford Rd studio tended toward instrumentals, although Dodd also produced the teenage heartthrob Delroy Wilson; the harmony group, the Heptones; and Marcia Griffiths, who, as part of the Bob & Marcia duo, would shoot to fame in 1969 with 'Young, Gifted, and Black.'

Among the important new producers to arrive on the scene were Joe Gibbs, Bunny 'Striker' Lee, and Sonia Pottinger, the most successful of Jamaica's female producers. Pottinger's backing group was Lynn Taitt & the Jets, led by Taitt's brilliant guitarwork.

Rock-steady was short-lived, basically spanning 1966 to 1968, but helped shift Jamaica's music away from the dominant big sound-system bosses.

# Reggae

Reggae – one of the world's few living folk musics – is the heartbeat of Jamaica, and as strongly identified with the island as R&B is with Detroit or jazz with New Orleans. It's a major factor in the Jamaican economy, at no time better demonstrated than during Reggae Sunsplash (held in Ocho Rios) and Reggae Sumfest (held in Montego Bay), when tens of thousands of visitors arrive to dance and sway in delirious union. (Also see the Special Events section in the Facts for the Visitor chapter.)

To Jamaicans, reggae has two distinct meanings: first, a generic term for *all* popular Jamaican music and, more particularly, a specific beat and style popular from about 1969 to 1983.

Reggae evolved from romantic-themed rock-steady, but (being sired in the ghettoes of Kingston) it was fired in a crucible of tensions and social protest simmering violently in the late 1960s and early 1970s. Jamaicans will tell you that reggae means 'comin' from de people,' a phrase coined (as was the name *reggae* itself) by Frederick 'Toots' Hibbert of Toots & the Maytals in the single 'Do The Reggay' in 1968, although others claim the term 'reggae' was coined by singer-producer Clancy Eccles and is derived from 'streggae,' a slang term for a prostitute. Devout Rastafarians, meanwhile, claim that 'reggae' comes from *rex*, the Latin word for King. Jamaicans also say that reggae is about 'truth and rights.' The music expresses a yearning for respect, self-identity, and affirmation amid poverty: the word itself means 'down to earth,' or a 'ragged' way of life. Its lyrics are distinct in their political, social, and religious messages full of metaphor, expressions of anger, and praise of Jah.

Reggae is really a culture, specifically Jamaican, expressive of aspirations and spiritual triumph in the face of adversity. Though it has spiraled in unforeseen directions, it is as resilient as the Jamaican people.

## Early Reggae

Early reggae had a faster rhythm than rock-steady, with a more insistent electric bass guitar at the fore. Although it swiftly evolved in diverse directions, the commonality was a hard-edged roughness and lyrics that addressed the topic of black self-determination. It was experimental and ranged widely, incorporating the jerky instrumentals of session bands and the sweet harmonies of established vocal groups, while inventing new types of rhythms and, for the first time, the appearance of 'toasting' on record (no one had previously thought to record the phenomenon of rapping DJs). Many musicologists consider Larry & Alvin's 'Nanny Goat' to be the first true reggae record.

**Below:** 'Hey, did anyone see my Red Stripe?'

LEE ABEL

As ever, the established producers, notably Coxsone Dodd, led the way using veteran performers who proved capable of adapting to the evolving rough-edged sound, as well as new talent that was setting the trend. Duke Reid struggled to make the crossover to reggae until 1970, when he spawned the 'toasting' craze with DJ U-Roy. Producers such as Lee 'Scratch' Perry, Bunny Lee, Leslie Kong, Sonia Pottinger, and Joe Gibbs filled the vacuum, the latter gaining his greatest success with

Dennis Brown, who hit it big in 1972 with 'Money in My Pocket.' Most rock-steady musicians made the crossover with relative ease, including Toots & the Maytals (who had missed the rock-steady era due to a two-year jail term for ganja possession), the Melodians, the Heptones, and Delroy Wilson.

Many new producers also entered the scene – what Bob Marley termed 'small axes' to whittle away at the big trees – and forged their own unique styles, including Harry Johnson, Alvin Ranglin, and Keith Hudson, whose hauntingly enigmatic *Flesh of My Skin, Blood of My Blood* (1973), is considered reggae's first concept album.

LEE ABEL

These were radical times and during the 1972 election Jamaica seemed on the cusp of a revolutionary moment. Although Jamaican singers wisely forswore publicizing their political affiliations, Clancy Eccles openly backed Manley's PNP by putting out a series of songs from artists such as Max Romeo, Junior Byles, and Delroy Wilson, whose 'Better Must Come' title became a PNP slogan. Within a few years, when disillusionment and resentment set in, these same singers had changed their tune, and Manley was being attacked on vinyl.

**Left:** 'Toots,' leader of the Maytals and the man who – some say – gave reggae its name

## 'Rebel Music'

Rastafarians came to dominate the scene by the mid-1970s with their 'rebel music,' filled with lyrics reflecting the mood of discontent and black self-determination as the central theme. Rebel singers such as Max Romeo, the anguished Junior Byles, the Abyssinians, and Winston 'Niney' Holness expressed their Rastafarian beliefs forcefully, imbuing their recordings with traditional Rasta chants (often alongside variants of nyah-binghi drumming), with the Upsetters as the regular backing band. Instrumental to their success was the influence of radical producer Lee 'Scratch' Perry, who tinged their music with a slow, edgy mood of 'dread,' a foreboding style suggestive of impending violence. Byles' intensity, militancy, and spiritual faith combined on albums such as *Beat Down Babylon*, but severe mental problems curtailed his career (he attempted suicide after learning of the death of Haile Selassie). Niney's masterful 1970 *Blood and Fire* most forcefully represents the early rebel genre, and its success showed that the vengeful message resonated among the island populace.

Perhaps the most profound rebel entrée was the eye-popping debut, in 1969, of Burning Spear (Winston Rodney) whose 'Door Peeper' begins with a Rasta declamation, the likes of which had not been heard before:

I and I, the son of the Most High
Jah Rastafari
Whose heart shall correspond
And beat in harmony
Sounds from the Burning Spear

Rodney had renamed himself Burning Spear after Jomo Kenyatta, the leader of the Kenyan independence movement. Burning Spear invoked a unique, sobering, reflective chant that would forever cast the performer as one of

**Right:** Rebel rebel Burning Spear

LEE ABEL

a kind. Burning Spear found great commercial success and attained international status in the mid-1970s on the coat-tails of Bob Marley, but he remained uncompromisingly rebel in style. His epochal *Marcus Garvey* album in 1975 would establish him unequivocally as the quintessential rebel singer. He performed 'solo,' backed by two harmony singers. His enduring performances two decades later remain capable of hypnotizing his audience. More importantly, Burning Spear remains true to his original message.

In 1970, the Wailers, whose Wail'n Soul'm label had failed, also joined Perry, who coached Marley toward a new voice and led to an outpouring of relatively unknown recordings that musicologists acclaim as representing the Wailer's finest embodiments of the slow, raw, spiritual style, showing the band members at their peak. Exemplary was the *African Herbsman* album released on Trojan records.

All three of the Wailers had become Rastafarians and now sported dreadlocks. As disillusion with Manley's PNP government deepened, Rastafarianism gained ground among the general populace. By the mid-1970s the genre of music concerned with the life of the ghetto sufferer, colonialism, repatriation, Haile Selassie as living deity, the Babylon system, and the 'reality' of the downpressed had become dominant. Nyahbinghi drumming and Rasta chants were common rhythm elements, played in an updated, in-vogue version of the rock-steady rhythm, known as 'rockers.' ('Steppers' was a more aggressive take honed for a military, high-stepping dance style that would become dominant in the late 1970s, taking over from 'skank' moves that had become in-vogue in the dancehalls to a slow rhythm called the 'John Crow.')

The genre had also earned a new moniker – 'roots reggae' – and was poised for international acclaim.

## Bob Marley & 'Roots Reggae'

In 1972, the Wailers visited London and came under the wing of genius promoter Chris Blackwell, whose Island Records was the UK's top independent label. Blackwell was keen to promote reggae and that year had released Jimmy Cliff's soundtrack to the movie *The Harder They Come*, a cult classic that helped thrust reggae onto the world stage. Blackwell saw that with a little tinkering, the Wailers could be promoted to a worldwide audience. Island produced the Wailers' *Catch a Fire* (1972) as the first reggae album aimed at the album-buying rock audience, followed by a UK tour in the manner of a rock band. Blackwell's gamble paid off. Within a year, they headlined with Marvin Gaye in Kingston, and toured the USA with Sly & the Family Stone. *Catch A Fire* and a second album, *Burnin'* (1973), rocketed up the charts and put reggae – and the Wailers – on the map.

The group's two Island albums (on which Marley dominated) set the stage for Marley's solo career, which was boosted in 1974 when Eric Clapton had a hit with a remake of 'I Shot the Sheriff,' a Marley song on the *Burnin'* album. Most influential of the songs was 'Get Up, Stand Up,' co-written by Marley and fellow Wailer Peter Tosh, which has become an anthem for protest groups worldwide.

The group's success led, perhaps inevitably, to the disintegration of the group. There was just too much energy and individual ability to be contained in one outfit. Tosh – the outspoken rebel – and Bunny Wailer – the soulful, dedicated Rasta – were jealous that Blackwell was focused on promoting Marley, who seemed more marketable than his musical partners (Marley considered Blackwell his 'interpreter' not his producer). And Tosh's egotistical ways and simmering rage clashed with Marley's gentler character. By 1974 the group had separated, ending an 11-year musical partnership, but allowing the three to develop their own ways and unleashing a tremendous outpouring from each.

Meanwhile, Marley took the band's name and performed with a new group as Bob Marley & the Wailers, and a trio of female back-up singers, the I-Threes, comprising his wife Rita, Judy Mowatt, and Marcia Griffiths, who each continue to perform as soloists two decades later. The women

**Right:** Rita Marley, still smiling after all these years

LEE ABEL

## Bob Marley – Reggae Royalty

ROGER STEFFENS

Robert Nesta Marley was born on February 6, 1945, in the tiny village of Nine Mile in St Ann parish. His 17-year-old mother, Cedella, was a Jamaican, and it was she who raised him after his 51-year-old father, Norval Marley – a white, English-born, former army captain then acting as an overseer of Crown lands in the Dry Harbour Mountains – deserted the family while Bob was still a youngster.

Marley's early years, surrounded by a tight-knit extended family, had a profound effect on his evolution, and he became intensely aware of his African roots. In his teens, Marley moved to Trench Town, a poverty-ridden ghetto in Kingston that would be his home for most of his life. Kingston's ghettoes reverberated with the experimental sounds of young kids with musical aspirations, and the teenage *bhuttu* (country bumpkin) from Nine Mile followed suit.

Marley had begun singing in informal sessions on Third St, in Trench Town, where he was mentored by a musician called Joe Higgs. Here, in 1960, he met Bunny 'Wailer' Livingston, Peter Tosh, and Junior Braithwaite. In 1961 they formed the Teenagers with two backing singers, Beverley Kelso and Cherry Smith. In February 1962, Marley was introduced to singing star Derrick Morgan, who invited Marley to Beverly's, the restaurant owned by record producer Leslie Kong. At this stage, Marley was a weak singer. Nonetheless he was allowed to cut three solo records – 'Judge Not,' 'One Cup of Coffee,' and 'Terror' – which were released under the name Bob Martell. They flopped.

Lyricists had by now begun marrying the music to social protest and Marley and his cohorts had renamed themselves the Wailing Rude Boys, later shortening it to the Wailers. In mid-1963, the group auditioned for Coxsone Dodd, and recorded ska hits such as 'Rude Boy,' '400 Years,' 'Bus Dem Shut,' and 'Craven A Go Choke Puppy.' They had their first modest hit with 'Simmer Down,' which urged the rude boys to cool their heels during a period of rising tensions in Kingston.

In February 1966, Marley left for Wilmington, Delaware, where he lived with his mother and found work in a car factory. Later that year, Marley married Rita Anderson. In 1967 Marley returned to his home parish where he tried farming. During the heyday of ska, Marley had established himself as an early leading influence, with his creative style and unique stage presence. Texan rock-steady singer Johnny Nash, who had seen Marley perform on Jamaican TV, set out to find the reclusive singer. Nash signed Marley to his JAD label and, unsuccessfully aiming at the US market, began producing Marley's groundbreaking melodies that the world now knows as reggae. In ensuing years, Marley's Rastafarian philosophies injected his music with greater soul and more poignant lyrics – roots reggae – that helped spark a worldwide 'Third World consciousness.'

## Bob Marley – Reggae Royalty

In the 1970s reggae soared to the top of the world charts. Marley followed the Wailers' success with solo blockbuster albums, including *Exodus*, his greatest seller, which spent 56 weeks in the Top 10 UK album charts.

Marley was now a member of the liberal Rastafarian Twelve Tribes of Israel sect, which gave him the name 'Joseph.' He was instantly recognizable with his thick dreads, but not afraid to be photographed haloed in clouds of ganja. And his womanizing was well known: although he and Rita remained man-and-wife until his death 15 years later, he is known to have fathered at least 11 children by other women, including Junior Gong, his son by former Miss Jamaica and Miss World, Cindy Brakespeare.

Marley's stature was such that he was courted by politicians at times when Jamaica was seething with violence and animosities. In 1976, the bile of the election campaign spilled over into a mayhem of murder, and Prime Minister Michael Manley declared a state of national emergency and staged a Smile Jamaica concert intended to calm the situation. Marley was headlined, but on the eve of the concert he and Rita were nearly killed when gunmen burst into his home in Kingston and opened fire. Two days later, a bandaged Marley went on stage and induced political archrivals Edward Seaga and Michael Manley to link arms (unenthusiastically) with him in a plea to stop the sectarian violence.

After recuperating at Strawberry Hill, Chris Blackwell's home in the Blue Mountains, Marley left Jamaica and spent two years recording and performing in Europe and North America, where reggae lovers greeted him as a demigod. By 1978, when he returned to Jamaica, multimillionaire Marley had attained superstardom.

Despite his revered stature, Marley never forgot nor forsook his roots. He remained intensely spiritual and pervaded an almost tangible aura and energy that emanated naturally from deep within, not from his demigod status. A consistent voice against racism, oppression, and injustice, Marley became the musical conscience of the world. Throughout the Third World, he was received as a messiah, with his crowning moment on April 17, 1980, when Marley led a triumphant concert to celebrate Independence Day at the transformation of colonial Rhodesia into Zimbabwe.

While touring the USA in 1980, Marley was diagnosed as having brain cancer. On the eve of his death, he was awarded the Order of Merit, Jamaica's highest honor. The Honorable Robert Nesta Marley, OM, died at the age of 36 on May 11, 1981, at Miami's Cedars of Lebanon Hospital. Dressed in a blue denim suit and a tam of red, green, and gold, his body lay in state at Kingston's National Arena, a Bible in one hand, a guitar in the other. He was laid to rest in a crypt within a whitewashed chapel next to the one-room cottage where he lived as a boy. The cortege stretched for 50 miles!

Marley died without making a will. His fortune – estimated at about US$50 million – has been the source of ongoing legal battles between family members.

Two decades after his death, Bob Marley continues to be reggae's biggest seller (his *Legend* album is nearing 10 million sales). Jamaicans never tire of his songs. They relate to the lyrics, which act as emotional outlets. Where others hear the rhythm, they hear the message in the words.

Marley's wife, Rita, and four of their children (performing as the Melody Makers) have continued to hold aloft the family flame; see 'Ziggy Marley' later in this chapter.

For more information in Jamaica, contact the Bob Marley Foundation (☎ 978-2991).

added a more 'acceptable' sound to rock audiences and lent a softer visual note when touring – all part of Blackwell's vision for crossover market success. Marley shared the vision and showed willingness to adopt elements that would widen his worldwide acceptance.

Ten albums followed the initial success, beginning with *Natty Dread* in 1975, Marley's first solo album featuring more rebel lyrics and named for the dreadlocks that he displayed on the album cover. The proven formula included more live concerts in the UK, followed by a live album. The next year Marley entered the US album charts with *Rastaman Vibration*, which the mainstream US media proclaimed as 'Jamaican rock and roll.' Marley was catapulted to superstardom.

Following an assassination attempt in December 1976, Marley left Jamaica and spent two years touring, bolstering his international stature; more than 100,000 fans attended a 1980 show in Milan. His death to cancer in 1981 was a tremendous loss to the musical world, but by then Marley had stamped reggae upon the world.

## The Other Players

Marley's songs initially received relatively little airplay in Jamaica, where the music – redolent with menacing social protest – was anti-establishment. (Reggae was actually banned from the airwaves; true reggae still rarely

### Peter Tosh

Jamaica's most iconoclastic reggae singer was born in Belmont on October 19, 1944, and christened Hubert McIntosh. While still a young boy he was sent to Kingston to be raised by an aunt in the poverty-ridden 'yards' that left him embittered for life. Here he met fellow teen wanna-be musicians Bob Marley and Bunny Livingstone and together they formed the Wailing Rude Boys (also see 'Bob Marley – Reggae Royalty').

The trio was formative in the evolution of reggae and was bathed in limelight in 1972 when they signed with Chris Blackwell's Island Records and shot to fame with *Catch a Fire* and *Burnin'*. Tosh, perhaps the most accomplished musician in the group, was always the militant, more strident voice beginning with his early version of 'Go Tell It on the Mountain.' (Tosh was perhaps the first Jamaican to tour Africa on a musical journey aimed at tearing down the apartheid regime, synonymous with Marley's later participation in the struggles for freedom in Zimbabwe.) Tosh sought to express his seething anger through music and penned solo songs that he put out on his own label, Intel Diplo HIM (Intelligent Diplomat for His Imperial Majesty). Resentful of Blackwell, whom he called 'Whiteworst,' and embittered by Jamaica's 'Babylon shitstem,' Tosh parted company with the Wailers and poured out his bile on vinyl, using his razor-sharp wit to slash at politicians and other hypocrites. Most of his songs were imbued with outrage at past and present injustices against blacks.

His raging outbursts against the social and political elite and his forthright and lifelong advocacy of the legalization of marijuana (including a habit of smoking huge spliffs onstage) led him inevitably into a confrontation with police. Arrested in 1975 on a drug charge, he barely survived a severe beating and after his release taunted the police and finds its way onto the play lists of commercial pop, rock, or easy-listening stations.) Marley shot to international fame by touring and national acclaim followed. Radio's indifference to roots reggae forced other artists to follow Marley's example by performing in Europe where the musical form gained early acceptance. But Bob Marley & the Wailers were an exception: self-contained bands were a rarity in Jamaica. Dancehall sound systems ruled; most producers utilized pre-recorded rhythm tracks (often used time and time again) and not 'bands.'

The only other self-contained Jamaican reggae band to reach stardom was Third World (Burning Spear was essentially a solo performer), a rarity for being from the middle class. Black Uhuru, who debuted in 1978 with *Black Sounds of Freedom*, also signed to Island Records – as did Third World – and proved perhaps the most dynamic reggae act of the late 1970s and early 1980s (especially after they were joined by a slinky US-born female singer, Puma Jones). However, they proved too uncompromisingly militant in their roots music to fill the vacuum left by Marley's departure.

Practically every singer of the epoch addressed socially conscious topics on vinyl and most, it seemed, felt it de rigueur to appear on their album covers sporting 'natty dreads' (called 'fashion dreads' when used by non-Rastas). Dozens of 'Garveyite' singers made their mark, including veterans such as Cornell Campbell and Joe Higgs and newcomers such as Jacob

## Peter Tosh

other authorities with *Legalize It!* and *Whatcha Gonna Do*, which were promptly banned from the airwaves.

Tosh recorded several songs with Mick Jagger and Keith Richards and gained worldwide acclaim on the EMI label. Most notable, perhaps, is *Equal Rights*. Tosh's backing group, Word, featured two performers who would remain among the most influential musicians in Jamaican music: Sly Dunbar and Robbie Shakespeare.

Fame and wealth seemed to fuel his paranoia, however (he believed, for example, that the government was out to kill him). As it was, Tosh was murdered along with two friends on September 11, 1987, when gunmen burst into his home. Many Jamaicans still idolize Tosh, who put out a documentary – *Stepping Razor Red X* – in which he explained his own mantra while staring into a camera in a shadowed room.

ROGER STEFFENS

Miller, whose exciting stage presence boosted him to a brief popularity (he starred in *Rockers*, a campy movie about reggae).

The Rastafarian community, notably the Twelve Tribes of Israel sect (which had its own record label, Janikmikmusik), produced a host of performers – many of them quite artless – whose 'consciousness' ran deep in their veins, among them Pablo Moses (renowned for his herb-smoker's anthem, 'I Man A Grasshopper'), Bim Sherman, and Pablove Black. Fred Locks represents the most quintessentially non-commercial of the successful artists, epitomized on his 'Black Star Liner,' an enduring, anthemic roots classic. Perhaps the most influential, though, was Little Roy, whose most notable recording, 'Tribal War,' was later re-recorded by various artists and in various guises.

LEE ABEL

Yabby You, an intensely spiritual Rastafarian who launched his Prophet label in 1974 and has since gained cult status among followers of roots music, was among the most noteworthy – and enigmatic – producer-performers (such numbers as 'Chant Jah Valley,' 'Warn the Nation,' and 'Jah Vengeance' are considered classics of Rastafarian-inspired music). Yabby You also produced the successful roots singer Michael Prophet, as well as 'toasting' tunes by Big Youth, Dillinger, and other up-and-coming DJs, including the profound 'Judgement' by Jah Stitch.

Augustus Pablo, a scrawny Rastafarian and accomplished keyboard player and sessions musician, also contributed mightily to roots music, creating the so-called 'Far East' sound reliant on minor chords. In 1979, his Rockers International label debuted the youthful Junior Reid, who would become a leading vocalist through the 1980s. Fellow producer Lee 'Scratch' Perry also managed to formulate his own unique sound at Black Ark Studios and had notable hits with the accomplished singer Max Romeo, whose 'rootsy' tirades (often gospel-inspired) were overshadowed by the fame of his lewd 'Wet Dream,' a harbinger of things to come.

**Above:** Experimentation is key for Augustus Pablo

'Niney' Holness also contributed greatly to roots music using leading singers such as Gregory Isaacs, Junior Byles, Delroy Wilson, and Dennis Brown, whose message-oriented songs culminated with his 1975 'Tribulation' and the 1977 album, *Wolf & Leopard*. Isaacs lent a sense of the wounded sufferer to his roots laments, typified by 'Village of the Under Privileged' and 'Black Kill A Black.' Niney also produced cultural classics with such DJs as Big Youth and Dillinger, whose most notable hits include '6 Dead 19 Gone to Jail' (a diatribe against Kingston's violence) and

'Flat Foot Hustling,' which masterfully wove elements of mento into the weft of a ghetto narrative.

The era was dominated by male performers, although the I-Threes – Rita Marley, Judy Mowatt, and, above all, Marcia Griffiths – had solo hits.

Harmony groups (usually trios), a steadfast product of rock-steady, also made the transition to roots music, converting to trendy cultural lyrics and updating established rhythms with varying combinations of 'dread' vocal tones and US-inspired soul. This was the era of the Stylistics, Delfonics, and Chi-Lites, sporting suave Chicago and Philadelphia sounds. Most Jamaican groups, however, infused African-inspired melodies and rhythms to achieve a more genuinely 'dread' Jamaican sound.

## Non-Roots Reggae

Although the Rastafarian influence dominated the reggae scene in the latter 1970s, 'cultural' music was a limited market and many artists re-corded more mainstream sounds focusing on the vocal harmonies of the 1960s. Mid-1970s masters were Gregory Isaacs, Freddie McGregor, and Dennis Brown, who crafted romantic lovers' laments while producing evocative roots classics embracing social commentary in their lyrics. The trio became the most popular reggae artists of the late 1970s (although all three would have their greatest successes in the 1980s and 1990s) and popularized this beautifully melodic, romanticized reggae – called 'lovers rock.'

While Isaacs is revered for his 'consciousness' music, he was also the consummate Jamaican 'crooner' whose smooth tones and inimitable style were as well-suited to lovers rock as to empathetic expressions of the sufferer's lot. Isaacs relied on a suave projection as the lonely, suffering romantic who gets hurt by love, a theme of masculine vulnerability that

**Right:** Crooner
Gregory Isaacs

LEE ABEL

## Dub & the Rhythm Track

'Dub,' a term used internationally to mean a remix, in Jamaica means a 'raw riddim,' a rhythm without the voice track.

Dub was born in Jamaica in 1967 among DJs seeking sound-system exclusivity. The first dubs were instrumentals with the vocal tracks removed and intended strictly for sound-system play. The genre was spawned when Duke Reid's studio inadvertently left the vocal track off a B-side dub of a Paragon's tune, 'On the Beach,' being cut for Rudolph 'Ruddy' Redwood's sound system – Supreme Ruler of Sound – which ruled the Spanish Town roost. Ruddy played the remixed track, and the crowd loved it.

Ruddy then cut stripped-down 'versions' of several established Duke Reid vinyls and soon other producers followed suit. By 1968, the instrumental rhythm tracks from the A side began appearing as B-sides on singles, with new instrumentation overlaid. 'Versions' were ideal for dancehalls, as the DJs could take the spotlight and invent their own lyrics to chant over the pre-existing rhythms of rock-steady classics.

By 1972, one man reigned supreme: King Tubby (Osbourne Ruddock), a skilled sound engineer and aural perfectionist whose high-tech Home Town Hi-Fi sound system was the best in Kingston. Tubby's DJ was U-Roy. U-Roy's spontaneous and brilliant 'toasting' used Count Machuki-inspired jive lyrics peppered with whoops and screams. In 1970, Duke Reid wisely recorded him. U-Roy's B-side singles shot up the charts. Soon most established producers were producing dub flip sides. In 1971, they hit on a new formula:

dropping parts of the rhythm in and out of the mix and adding in special effects that, inspired by Tubby's ground-breaking creativity, would eventually include snatches of vocals, organ stabs, and massive thunderclaps, and a sense that the rhythm track – steeped in delay and reverb effects – was ceaselessly mutating. These 'version' tracks became so popular, and Tubby so renowned, that singles often sold on the basis of a record label bearing a B-side credit such as 'King Tubby Version.'

## Dub & the Rhythm Track

ROGER STEFFENS

'Scientist' mixes it up.

Other producers evolved their own mixing styles. Soon entire albums of dub versions appeared featuring Tubby's work, as well as other notable dub technicians such as Bunny Lee, Sylvan Morris, Yabby You, and Augustus Pablo, whose collaboration with Tubby on the *King Tubby Meets Rockers Uptown* album is considered the pinnacle of the genre. Re-released in the UK, the album introduced the sound-system craze to a wider world.

By 1975, Joseph 'Joe Joe' Hookim at Channel One had moved to the forefront of dub based on fresh, horns-dominated rhythm tracks from the Revolutionaries, with Sly Dunbar effecting a radical new drumming style. Errol Thompson contributed extremism to the genre by adding barking dogs, blaring car horns, and other vulgar sound effects. Even wilder trends and a medley of styles evolved in ensuing years as mixing technology advanced, and a tidal wave of dub albums flooded the market, driven by demand from the dancehalls.

The late 1970s saw new mixing talent, notably the brilliant Prince Jammy, the masterful Hopetown 'Scientist' Brown, and Mikey Dread (Michael Campbell), who transferred his rootsy style honed through his radio show onto vinyl. By 1980, however, the craze had become almost formulaic and the emergence of dancehall DJs with an ability to improvise lyrics live over beloved rhythm tracks spelt the gradual demise of the traditional dub album, bringing the genre full-circle.

LEE ABEL

**Left:** The late 'Crown Prince of Reggae,' Dennis Brown

he established with 'My Only Lover,' a self-produced, easy-skanking hit that set the tone for most of his future recordings that would earn him the title 'the Cool Ruler.'

Dennis Brown's rich, soulful voice and the strength of his repertoire (notably his work with 'Niney' Holness, beginning with the love song, 'Westbound Train,' in 1973) of both roots music and lovers rock earned him the title, 'Crown Prince of Reggae.' Brown sold more reggae albums than any other singer during the period. He maintained his own label, DEM, yet recorded for several producers and even recorded on Gregory Isaacs' African Museum label. (Brown died in 1999 of respiratory failure, aged 41.)

And Freddie McGregor, who was a member of the Twelve Tribes of Israel and put out such roots classics as 'I Man A Rasta' and 'Rastaman Camp,' managed the crossover to songs of the heart with consummate ease. He perhaps came closer than any other Jamaican performer of the era in approaching US-style soul-pop, as best represented by his suave 1976 version of George Benson's 'Love Ballad.'

Homegrown reggae lost much of its direction with the death of Marley in 1981, and roots music deteriorated. In any event, Marley's music had veered sharply away from the majority of music then being recorded and played in Kingston, where pure rhythms were most important. By the early 1980s, local audiences were tiring of the conscious lyrics that were an integral part of roots reggae, often made for an international audience. By the close of the decade, Jamaican music was taking a new direction more in tune with the changing focus of ghetto youth. After a decade of hardships, Jamaicans craved a dance beat; the DJs answered their call, inventing their own lyrics to 'dub' over vintage rhythm tracks, evolving during the early 1980s into dancehall.

# Dancehall

The term 'dancehall,' although used to mean a sound-system venue, is also used specifically to refer to the energetic musical genre dominant from 1979 to 1985. Singers and jive-talking DJs pumped-up with braggadocio performed live over instrumental rhythm tracks reliant on a succession of horn riffs and juggernaut basslines from the rock-steady heyday. Dancehall is a kind of Caribbean 'rap' music that focuses on earthly themes dear to the heart of young male Jamaicans, principally 'gal business,' gunplay, and ganja. This is hardcore music, named for the loosely defined, outdoor venues at which outlandishly named 'toasters' (rapper DJs) set up mobile discos, usually comprising two decks, an amplifier and mixer, and enormous speakers loud enough to bring a Boeing 747 home.

## Dancehall Antecedents

The form harks back to the 1950s when DJs traveled about the island with their sound systems and chatted over the music they played (see 'Sound Systems & the Rise of DJs,' earlier).

During the 1960s, the DJ was still largely confined to the dancehalls and worked to promote the sound systems that employed them, and to encourage the dancers by compliments or 'toasts.' One of the best was King Stitt, who used his gargoyle looks to promote himself as 'the Ugly One.' Stitt had several hits on record. Most DJs still derived their inspiration from the style of US radio DJs, with lyrics in an MC style interjected over songs and instrumentals. All that was to change in 1969 with the arrival of 'dubbing,' which shot to prominence in 1970 when Duke Reid recorded U-Roy, termed the 'Originator' for the immense influence of his new style and his popularization of recording a DJ on vinyl. (See 'Dub & the Rhythm Track.')

Instead of merely interjecting a few hip, catchy phrases, U-Roy rode instrumental tracks down the line, saturating the tune with excitable jive-lyrics in a baritone voice that held crowds in sway. As a DJ for King Tubby's Home Town Hi-Fi sound system, U-Roy soon propelled DJ records to the top of the Jamaican charts (at one point he had the top three records on the charts with 'Wake the Town,' 'Rule the Nation,' and 'Wear You to the

Ball'). Reid also found success, with Dennis Alcapone, who half-sung his lyrics in rhyming style spiced with whoops and the sounds of crowing cockerels.

A stampede of DJs jumped onto the bandwagon, including the dreadlocked Big Youth, and a Spanish Town spinmeister called I-Roy, possessed of a worldly erudition that set him apart as one of the most influential of the roots DJs that would follow. In 1975, I-Roy and another accomplished DJ, Prince Jazzbo, got into a serious feuding match using 45s in a latter-day take on past 'sound wars.'

During the 1970s, the dancehalls continued to inspire parallel sounds pioneered by producers such as Joe Gibbs, Joseph 'Joe

**Right:** U-Roy, the 'Originator'

LEE ABEL

Joe' Hookim, and Bunny Lee, who showed the way with his 'flying cymbals' rhythm developed by drummer Carlton 'Santa' Davis in reply to an in-vogue style of Philadelphia soul, engendering the 'flyers' dance style. Hookim's Channel One Studio, meanwhile, focused on 'rockers' rhythms using a house band, the Revolutionaries, centered from 1975 on the drum-and-bass partnership of the 'Riddim Twins' – Sly Dunbar and Robbie Shakespeare. The new rhythm they created – a militant version of rocksteady rhythms – soon set the tone of the dancehalls and was widely copied. The long-lasting Wailing Souls (led by Winston Matthews), the Mighty Diamonds, Black Uhuru, and John Holt were among the performers who sang rebel and roots lyrics over Revolutionaries' dancehall rhythms.

Channel One dominated the Kingston music scene during the mid-1970s, when Sly & Robbie reigned supreme. In 1975, the 'Mighty Two' – Joe Gibbs and dub pioneer Errol Thompson – pumped out hit after hit ranging from romantic blues-dance records (epitomized by singer Dennis Brown) to DJ 'dread' epitomized by Prince Far I's hard-hitting critique of Manley's get-tough policy toward violent crime, 'Under Heavy Manners.'

The roots movement was so pervasive that leading 'toasters,' such as Dillinger (who had a UK hit with 'Cocaine Running Around My Brain'), Big Youth, and I-Roy championed the cause of the ghetto dwellers, going as far as lacing their commentaries with chanted psalms. Although most toasters recorded for numerous producers with money and rhythms to lure them into their studios, Big Youth was so successful that he set up his own label and managed a crossover to the mainstream rock audience with his *Dread Locks Dread* album. Competing DJ U-Roy also gained international exposure, eventually setting up the Stur-Gav Hi-Fi sound system that became a de facto proving ground for many future top-notch DJs.

## The Dancehall Heyday

By the close of the 1970s, a new wave of sound systems and a fresh crop of DJs had emerged from among the Jamaican youth who had tired of radical lyrics on a political and social theme, and were seeking a new focus on issues closer to their heart: dance, drugs, and sex. Producers had begun adopting computerized effects such as echo and reverb machines,

**Above:** The two sides of DJ I-Roy

## Sly & Robbie

The famous rhythm duo, Lowell 'Sly' Dunbar and Robbie Shakespeare (the 'Riddim Twins'), helped sculpt the reggae sound from the beginning and are the most sought-after producers and rhythm-makers in Jamaica. Read the credits on any top reggae artist's CD album today and you're likely to find Sly & Robbie somewhere. If they haven't produced a single, they've mixed it or played drums and bass, respectively.

The duo have been around for more than three decades and have always forged an independent path, bridging existing styles with their own unique sounds. They were driving forces behind the Revolutionaries, the resident band at the cutting edge Channel One Studio in Kingston during the 1970s, when the duo honed the sound of big acts such as Wailing Souls and Black Uhuru. During the roots heyday, they evolved a trademark 'metallic' sound that presaged the digital revolution that they helped bring to Jamaica.

Sly & Robbie have been sought out by many leading international performers, including such unlikely stars as Bob Dylan and Grace Jones. Interestingly, one of the duo's earlier albums of classic 'riddims' (as their heavily imitated drum-and-bass combinations are called) was inspired by a poster of Grace Jones that hung in a recording studio.

More recently they incorporated East Indian sounds into their compositions and released *Friends,* a CD featuring performers such as Simply Red, Maxi Priest, and Ali Campbell.

LEE ABEL

producing 'dub' music that helped usher in a new era. The popularity of dancehall 'version' tracks (also see 'Dub & the Rhythm Track') had permitted DJs to move to center stage. Indisputably, the 1980s was the decade of the DJs, who replaced the 'cultural' chants of the mid-1970s with more carnal and materialistic dancehall chatter interspersed with animalistic sounds such as 'oinks' and 'ribbits,' showing how creative new lyrics could be seamlessly grafted onto proven rhythms.

**Left:** Reggae Sunsplash dancer in the slack age

**Below:** Yellowman, Jamaica's best-selling DJ

Sexually explicit lyrics had been a popular staple of dancehall for many years, but during the 1980s songs gradually became mired in lewd lyrics, called 'slack.' General Echo and Clint Eastwood set the tone in the early years with their respective albums, *The Slackest LP* and *Sex Education*, followed by the incalculably influential Lone Ranger, who had a smash hit with 'Barnabus Collins,' which reached the top of both the Jamaican and UK reggae charts and was inspired by a vampire character from the US TV program *Dark Shadows*. (Other artists countered slackness with socially conscious lyrics known as 'dub poetry.')

None of the rough-and-tough rapping DJs, however, could compete with a previous unknown called Yellowman (Winston Foster), who rose against all odds to become the undisputed king of slack – and the first dancehall artist to attain international status.

An albino black (the lowest of the low on Jamaica's class totem) and orphaned as a child, 'King Yellow' went to the famous Alpha Boys School in Kingston. His rap is focused on his questionable sex appeal, claiming women were crazy for him, leading Jamaicans to respect his humor, wit, and courage.

He and Fat Head became the first rapper DJs to appear on a live dancehall recording with *Live at Aces*. The talented Yellowman became the best-selling DJ of all time and was also the first Jamaican DJ signed by a major US label (CBS). Although he has lost his prominence, he remains a staple of the island's music scene.

U-Roy, already well-established, rode the dancehall craze, mainly via his own Stur-Gav Hi-Fi sound system, which also promoted other DJs, notably Charlie Chaplin who, rare among rapping DJs, stayed true to a roots dancehall theme. Brigadier Jerry, a member of the Twelve

LEE ABEL

**Right:** Bunny Wailer

ROGER STEFFENS

Tribes of Israel, also refused to veer from 'reality' lyrics, demonstrated with his 1982 hit, 'Pain.' Other DJs (such as Peter Metro and Ranking Toyan) flunked on vinyl; for their best performances they relied on spontaneous interactions with live audiences.

The dancehall genre was so dominant that the eruption of DJ records soon outnumbered 45s by singers, and the only singers who could compete with DJs were those such as Junior Reid and Barrington Levy who had risen through the DJ sound-system ranks. It was the adolescent Levy, with his powerful voice backed by the Roots Radics, who had established the musical sound of early dancehall lyrics, veering away from Garveyite militantism toward a more hedonistic theme. He had a series of strong singles in 1979 that appeared as a debut album, *Bounty Hunter,* and pointed the way for a new genre of dancehall vocalists. Levy pumped out scores of hits, including his 1984 'Under Mi Sensi,' adopted as a ganja smoker's anthem, and 'Living Dangerous' in 1996.

Gregory Isaacs and Bunny Wailer swiftly followed suit with gently rocking dancehall hits in 1981 that combined the new, sweeter mood with a certain gruffness typical of the dancehall genre. Similarly, Freddie McGregor had a hit with 'Bobby Babylon,' and Dennis Brown's hard-hitting 'They Fight I,' produced by Prince Jammy, proved a winner. Most dancehall vocalists delivered in a roughhouse style, perhaps best exemplified by adolescent singing star Little John and songster Sammy Dread.

Just as the Revolutionaries had dominated the 1970s scene, the new ranking session band was the Roots Radics, formed in 1978, who forged vintage rhythms into a fresh, melodic yet stark style adapted to the mood of the times. The band relied upon established rhythms remixed into infinite variations, as did the DJs, who rapped over versions of classic rock-steady rhythms. The phenomenon lent new vitality to the 1970s craze for dub 'versions' and during the mid-1980s few hits sported an original rhythm track.

## Dancehall Divas

Jamaican women have had to work doubly hard to break into the island's musical scene. They have traditionally been relegated to the role of back-up singers or just to moan on 'slack' numbers.

Dancehall has provided a vital venue, however, for a few talented female DJs, such as Lady Saw and Lady G. Lady Saw is the island's top female DJ chatter, with massive stage presence. She earned her name from dancehall fans in the early 1980s when she began as a rapper working a sound system called the Romantics. She is renowned for her aggressive sexual overtures and slack lyrics offered from a woman's perspective, as in 'Condom,' advising safe sex. But she can run with the most obscene of male DJs, as in 'Stab Out the Meat,' and her proclamations of her own sexual prowess, often aimed as put-downs of boastful men.

Lady G has also made a name for herself at the top of the charts as a cultural DJ with incisive ghetto reality lyrics, notably with 'Nuff Respect' which aimed barbs at misogynist male DJs and became an anthem for Jamaican women, notably within the dancehall sorority.

Super-talented Chevelle Franklyn got her first taste of music (as did many other female singers) in a church choir. She shot to fame locally in 1991 with 'Here I Am,' which won seven music industry awards, followed by recordings with Shabba Ranks ('Mr Loverman'), Cyndi Lauper, Maxi Priest, and other top performers. She is featured on the soundtrack for the movie *Dancehall Queen*.

But other than the inimitable Marcia Griffiths, whose long pedigree (dating from the 1960s) assured her success with several ragga hits, no female ragga singer has yet made a mark on the crossover market, and most talented dancehall divas – such as Nadine Sutherland, Twiggy, and Foxy Brown – still await debut albums. Relatively few vinyls by women singers have appeared.

Lady Saw

Marcia Griffiths

LEE ABEL

**Right:** Half Pint

Although the digital era has spawned flexibility and freedom to experiment with a host of new styles, the motif of basslines and chord sequences first laid down during the heyday of rock-steady and reggae remains the foundation for contemporary Jamaican music, with the best chord and bassline combinations reappearing ad nauseum in fresh remakes that can inspire a yawning sense of deja vu. Dub continues to influence hip-hop and other dance styles, and the tradition of a dub version remains a B-side convention today.

## The Producers

The dancehall craze spawned scores of new sound-system operators and producers, who remixed these favorites in true Jamaican manner, without heed for any copyright concerns. Studios such as Channel One and Studio One (which had supplied a huge percentage of the original rock-steady hits) cut countless versions of their own well-loved rhythms, which were released with new names.

LEE ABEL

Chief among the producers was Henry 'Junjo' Lawes, who had spearheaded the direction of the new dancehall style with the early recordings of Barrington Levy and, later, a string of vocalists that included Michael Prophet, a honey-voiced singer named Cocoa Tea, and veteran singers Alton Ellis, Johnny Osbourne, and John Holt, but Junjo had his greatest success with Yellowman. Junjo bowed out in 1985 when he emigrated to the USA.

Junjo's crown was seized by Prince Jammy (later renamed King Jammy) who apprenticed with King Tubby before setting up his own studio and label. Jammy had successes with a young dancehall singer named Half Pint; Junior Reid, a roots-oriented singer whose rough-edged style took a leaf from the fast-talking DJs; and Johnny Osbourne, whose 1983 hit, 'Water Pumping,' spawned its own eponymous dance style. Jammy also produced songs by Lincoln 'Sugar' Minott, a gifted all-rounder who took the dancehalls by storm with his honey-hued voice and who exposed many young, up-and-coming performers through his own Youth Promotion sound system, with Jah Stitch as DJ.

Many of Jammy's successful numbers featured backing rhythms by the High Times Band, whose sound overlaid a brash modern dancehall beat of classic rock-steady rhythms culled from decades before. Their hegemony was challenged by the irrepressibly experimental and in-demand duo of Sly & Robbie, whose own Taxi label put out scores of hits by songsters as diverse as Gregory Isaacs, Sugar Minott, Barrington Levy, Freddie McGregor, and an exciting debut singer, the Rastafarian Ini Kamoze.

Jamaican music is never static, and dancehall has proven no exception. Sly & Robbie's experimentation with electronic 'robotic' rhythms in the mid-1980s was a signal of the radical new direction that dancehall was about to take as sound engineers switched from analog to digital recording formats.

**Left:** Shabba Ranks, Jamaica's biggest icon since Bob Marley

LEE ABEL

# Ragga

Ragga (considered part of the 'dancehall' genre) is the ever-evolving, techno-driven, in-vogue music of the current dancehall generation – an often angry, in-your-face musical form echoing the restlessness of Jamaican youth. The music – 'reggae' played with digital instrumentation – reflected a technological rather than aesthetic leap and derived its diverse form from a variety of inspirations spanning spiritual hymnals and romantic crooning to coarse DJ music.

For all its digital engineering, this technological music also draws on the rhythms of African cults and has been 'rootsier' than the dancehall music of the 1980s. Nonetheless, to the lay-listener ragga remains associated most strongly with egotistical DJs spouting crass lyrics over a usually monotonous yet always fast-paced, compulsive, computerized, two-chord beat.

Dancehall ragga has had a phenomenal impact on the world music scene. You can trace the bloodline of ragga as it reaches out to influence rap, dub, drum-and-bass, hip-hop, and any of today's riddim-heavy club sounds. While a few ragga artists have reached high levels of popularity outside Jamaica (notably Shabba Ranks, with his hits, 'Mr Loverman,' 'Twice My Age,' and 'Wicked in Bed'), far greater numbers of North American performers have incorporated the ragga style into their own music, fusing and helping form the USA's rap/hip-hop culture of the urban ghettoes.

## Digital Revolution

Ragga was spawned in the mid-1980s by the revolution in digital music technology which permitted pioneers such as Sly & Robbie, the Roots Radics, and another studio band, Paul Blake & the Blood Fire Posse, to generate recycled drum-and-bass rhythms, significantly lowering production costs. Though 'versioning' of established tracks continued, the revolution fostered experimentation with original sound tracks that resulted in an astonishingly fecund blossoming of producers and labels that continues to this day.

The revolution also assured the demise of traditional session bands; computerization permitted just one or two musicians to make a 'band.' The duo of Wycliffe 'Steely' Johnson and Cleveland 'Clevie' Browne proved the masters of the newly popular 'combination' style and Steely & Clevie became the sought-after maestros of digital rhythm tracks during the ragga era.

It remained for the top producer, King Jammy, to take the lead with Wayne Smith's 'Under Me Sleng Teng,' which auditioned at a historic sound clash between Jammy and rival sound system Black Scorpio on February 23, 1985. The digitized disc spun Jamaica around and was an instant smash. Almost immediately it was 'versioned,' while other producers, seeing the writing on the wall, rushed to dump their traditional rhythms in favor of a new synthetic beat. The mood was captured later that year in Junior Delgado's 'Ragamuffin Year.' The word – an identification with ghetto youth – was shorted to 'ragga' and adopted as the generic term for the new dancehall music.

The ever-astute King Jammy herded the best talent of his day (including a harmonic duo, Brian & Tony Gold) into his studio and became the 'don' of early ragga. Jammy produced most of the well-known leading vocalists, such as Delroy Wilson, Alton Ellis, Dennis Brown, and Gregory Isaacs. New talent such as King Kong, Nitty Gritty, and Tenor Saw wed their expressive, wailing voices to ragga rhythms, while Thriller U and Sanchez melded their powerful tenors.

Jammy's chief engineer, Bobby Digital, set out alone with his Digital B label, immediately providing a friend and relatively unknown, gravel-voice DJ called Shabba Ranks his first break with 'Peanie Peanie' (built atop the rhythm of Junior Byles' classic 'Fade Away') and other numbers that helped launch Shabba to ragga stardom. Bobby Digital's reputation helped launch other stellar DJs, including Ninjaman, Beenie Man, Bounty Killer, and a sharp storyteller named Lieutenant Stitchie.

As ragga evolved, it was producers such as Bobby Digital, Dave 'Rude Boy' Kelly, Sly & Robbie, and the more sophisticated Donovan Germain and Augustus 'Gussie' Clarke who set the tone. In 1988 Clarke's state-of-the-art Music Works studio produced an evolutionary hit with Gregory Isaacs' 'Rumours,' blending a 'dread' feel drawn from the roots reggae heyday onto a modern hi-tech rhythm that also gave female ragga singer JC Lodge a club hit in the USA with 'Telephone Love' and would re-emerge in 1997 with lovers lyrics as a UK reggae chart topper for Freddie McGregor.

While Clarke eschewed DJs, rival producer Winston Riley hit it big with DJs Red Dragon and Super Cat, who spun Marcia Griffith's rock-steady rhythm of 'Feel Like Jumping' into gold with 'Boops,' setting off a dancehall fervor for songs about sugar-daddies. And Germain's Penthouse studio promoted such up-and-coming DJs as Buju Banton, Lieutenant Stitchie, Buccaneer, Spragga Benz, former butcher Cutty Ranks, 'rude boy' rapper Cobra, and Tony Rebel, who focused on 'cultural' themes and came to prominence with such 45s as 'Mandela Story.' Oddly mismatched, Cobra and Rebel shared their first Penthouse album, *Die Hard*.

LEE ABEL

**Left:** JC Lodge calls out

Steely & Clevie, meanwhile, had established *their* own studio. Though working up magical rhythms for rival producers, they saved their most inspirational treatments – drawn from elements of musical tradition, including Pocomania – for the singers and DJ rappers who sought them out on their home turf. Their virtuosity produced wide-ranging hits, from Foxy Brown's remake of Tracy Chapman's 'Fast Car' and Freddie McGregor's interpretation of Little Roy's 'Prophecy' to brash DJ Cutty Ranks' 'Retreat' and Ninjaman's 'Murder Dem.'

## Bad Boys

Kingston's sound systems have never feared for a shortage of limelight-seeking DJs from the rougher-than-rough ghettos, and ragga has brought its fair share to the fore in the international market where consumers who would never conceive of attending a ragga dancehall have bought albums by luminaries such as Shabba Ranks, Jamaica's first international icon since Bob Marley two decades prior.

Shabba first recorded with King Jammy but rose to fame in 1988 with producer Bobby Digital at this Digital B studio. Shabba started as a slack DJ of the first order: his favorite topics were his own sexual prowess, typified by 'Hard and Stiff.' Shabba's endorsement of Buju Banton's homophobic 'Boom Bye Bye' in 1992 sealed his image as a bad boy DJ, although he matured in ensuing years, veering from slackness, exposing a greater creativity and even humor, and making a huge crossover leap to success under producer Gussie Clarke's Music Works studio and, later, the US major label, Epic, which in a rare rethink on normal policy, permitted Shabba to express himself freely. Fortunately, hip-hop had prepared the US market for rapping 'singers,' and Shabba hit the big time with 'Mr Loverman,' which boosted him into international fame.

Although Digital B has continued to release 45s from Shabba that play to the rough-and-tumble world of the ghetto dancehall, Shabba's move to Epic permitted Ninjaman and Buju Banton to fill his shoes. Ninjaman established for himself a unique style that propelled him to the front in 1990. Rather than harnessing the rhythm track in the normal manner, he pitted himself against it in a stuttering, conversational style, as if he were 'reasoning' aloud. He expounded on every topic, but his favored topic has been a veneration of gun violence including his own outlaw past (he has twice been arrested for firearms felonies and has been a long-term crack addict), the subject of his 1990 song album, 'My Weapon.' The outspoken, gold-toothed DJ – whose many self-given titles include 'Original Gun Tooth' and '48 Gun Bad Bwoy Talker' – has swum with the current, attempting to clean up his image with claims at a spiritual faith (reflected in 'Fulfilment') and, in 1997, jumping on the consciousness bandwagon by claiming to be a born-again Christian called Brother Desmond.

Buju Banton also made girls and guns his dancehall staples. He started in his teens, recording with veteran producers such as Winston Riley and Bunny Lee. In summer 1991, the then 18-year-old had his first hit with 'Love Mi Browning.' Darker skinned women took offense at this overt celebration of light-skinned women, to which Buju replied with 'Love Black Woman.' He found even bigger success with producer Dave Kelly and the

LEE ABEL

singles 'Big It Up' and 'Batty Rider.' His star briefly faded in 1992 after his anti-gay 'Boom Bye Bye' exploded in his face, but he rebounded in 1993. Now a Rastafarian and powerfully 'conscious' rapper, Buju remains a leading force in the new ragga.

**Above:** A ragga record comes together at Kingston's Music Works studio.

Buju's shoes were filled by Beenie Man, a witty and sagacious DJ who began his career at the age of eight when he beat out all contenders in a DJ and singing contest. By 1993 he was rated one of Jamaica's top DJs.

That year a memorable clash with Bounty Killer at the Sting music festival made him Kingston's top DJ and a household name. But the well-publicized, ongoing feud with Bounty Killer has deflated Beenie Man's bubble. Bounty Killer has made commentary on ghetto life his main forté. After a series of hits under King Jammy, he set up his own Priceless label in 1995 and has reached crossover fame with hip-hop fans.

To be fair, several of the 'bad boy' rappers occasionally offered lyrics decrying the gun culture or, more ambivalently, warning of its dire consequences. And DJs such as Yami Bolo and Admiral Tibet were always true to 'conscious' lyrics and would find their forté in vogue with the 'roots' renaissance that lay ahead.

## Balladeers

DJ music enjoyed a dominant reign through the 1980s and early 1990s, and live singers were in danger of becoming obsolete. Although popular DJs still outnumber current popular singers by a wide margin, ragga re-established vocalists – including lovelorn crooners – at the fore. Where the 'bad boy' DJs took the low-ground in lyrics and gave ragga a bad name, many of the soulful singers given a boost by ragga's development took the high ground and lent their syrupy voices to romantic ballads, acquiring staunch female followings along the way.

Beres Hammond established himself as perhaps the finest soulful singer of lovers ragga, drawing inspiration from his Rastafarian faith.

## Watch Yo' Slack Mouth

At the dawn of ragga a decade ago, cultural sentiments had virtually disappeared from the dancehall scene and boastful DJ gangsta rappers weighed down by gold chains had come to dominate ragga. Many DJs had become over-reliant on gimmickry and the easy option of unbridled pornographic lyrics (known as slack) spewed out, rapid-fire over a thumping, two-chord beat. Year by year, lyrics leaned ever more sharply toward no-holds-barred sexual explicitness, most often centered on female anatomy, such as Shabba Ranks' 'Love Punaany Bad.'

The crass lyrics evolved by 1992 into a Buju Banton-led round of 'matey songs,' which relied on cussing and glorification of drug lords and gun culture. Violence-charged dancehall-rap, often homophobic and misogynist, was epitomized by Banton's 'Boom Bye Bye,' which was denounced for advocating murdering gays and caused the police commissioner to issue a decree banning radio and TV stations from playing songs that encourage gun violence.

Ability in front of the microphone has brought many Jamaican youngsters out of the shantytowns and 'yards.' Many of the DJs, however, are tainted by gangsterism – as witnessed by the scores of performers who have died in shoot-outs – and have idolized the gun as a symbol of power, and women as mere sexual objects to be abused. These sewer-mouthed exponents of titillation are charged with fostering moral decay among Jamaican youth. Apologists argue that the pernicious lyrics merely reflect the harsh facts of the ghetto, born during a period when drug-dealing posses and political gangsters were in a virtual civil war with each other and with army E-squads (colloquially called E-Radication) determined to squash them by fair means or foul.

Several female performers give as good as they get, notably Lady Saw, who also addressed the arching question – 'what is slackness?' – head-on in her eponymous song, which says slackness is 'when government brek dem promise…when politicians issue out guns, so de two party a shoot one another down.'

# The Contemporary Scene

Music critics claim that the pilgrimage of Jamaican music has covered less ground internationally than many believe it deserves. Certainly, sagging sales of 'pure' reggae music worldwide suggests that the vitality has gone. To uninitiated ears, reggae might seem dormant, with an avid inclination to recycle rhythms and a lack of creativity in lyrical content.

The accusations, however, are unfair. The past few years have seen an explosion of experimentation, not least in a rejection of 'rude boy' lyrics in favor of a return to issues of 'cultural' concern.

## Roots Resurgence

The foundation that Marley had built has proved so solid that pockets of good 'pure' reggae music endured and today there is a new dynamism. Roots music is again the lick. In the early 1990s Jamaica began to witness a resurgence in the Rastafarian influence and with it a rebirth in the conscious focus that was the lifeblood of early reggae. Spearheading the renaissance was a group called Christian Souljahs, a trio comprising DJ-dubber Tony Rebel, a dub-poet Yasus Afri, and the soulful singer Garnett Silk, hailed at the time as their 'heir apparent' to Marley.

Silk's 'doctrine-steeped music' produced hits such as 'It's Growing,' 'Mama Africa,' and 'I Saw Zion in a Vision.' His Rasta-tinged tunes with songwriter Anthony 'Fire' Rochester caught the national conscience and wrested the musical initiative from boastful dancehall 'dons' such as Beenie Man. Although Silk tragically died when a cooking gas cylinder exploded during a shoot-out in December 1994, the Rastafarian influence survived, inspiring a recent return to the days when Jamaican music was ruled by live horns, drums, and bass. Anthony B, for example, now goes for an authentic sound similar to old time Marley classics, and Luciano and Buju Banton have moved back to live instrumentation.

Banton sets a standard of excellence with his ability to bridge the gap between the reggae of the 1970s and early 1980s and the brash new 1990s sounds of dancehall. He has also crossed a deep river socially and spiritually. Following the brutal murders of two friends and prominent musicians, Dirtsman and Pan Head, Banton wrote 'Murderer' decrying the senseless violence that claims the lives of so many Jamaican youths. The song marked the watershed of Banton's conscientious rebirth as a Rastafarian. *Billboard* magazine credits his song 'Murderer' as turning the 'lyrical tide' of dancehall away from gangsterism and sexual themes. To prove Banton (and reggae) had come full circle, his song 'Untold Stories' won Jamaica's award for 'Song of the Year' in 1995 and is often compared to Bob Marley's 'Redemption Song.'

Shabba Ranks has also adopted 'cultural' ragga that even incorporates nyahbinghi drumming ('Kettle Drum') and a remake of Bob Marley's 'Heathen.' Similarly, Capleton – the slackest of all DJs in the early 1990s – discovered Rastafarianism and has incorporated nyahbinghi drumming in his cultural lyrics for the dancehall. Sizzla is another DJ chanter who transitioned from dancehall to 'culture' and whose 'Praise Ye Jah' is already a classic.

## Ziggy Marley

David 'Ziggy' Marley was born in Kingston in 1968 as the second child of Bob and Rita Marley. Ziggy looks and sounds like his famous father. He grew up immersed in music and with his siblings – Cedella, Sharon, and Stephen – formed the Melody Makers in 1979. That year the progeny recorded 'Children Playing in the Streets' (composed by their father) followed in 1980 by 'Sugar Pie' and 'Trodding,' and in 1981, following Bob Marley's death, by 'What A Plot.'

*Play the Game Right*, the group's debut album, appeared in 1985 and featured a medley of top-notch session players.

Ziggy Marley & the Melody Makers are the most commercially successful of all Jamaican musical acts, with a crossover audience that even Ziggy's dad would be proud of. Though the imprint has no doubt helped, Ziggy is a gifted musician in his own right. Although the vast majority of Jamaican musicians have been fired in the crucible of West Kingston dancehalls, Ziggy was removed from the milieu and has etched his own sound – albeit heavily influenced by his father – aimed at the international market, with little regard for ragga or other evolutions in the dancehall market. He has most recently experimented with acoustic reggae.

LEE ABEL

LEE ABEL

The Xterminator label, owned by Phillip 'Fatis' Burrell, is at the forefront of 'roots ragga,' utilizing innovative drum-dominated rhythms conceived by master drummer Sly Dunbar as well as revitalized favorites from the past. Burrell has lent his shoulder to muscling roots music forward and has been instrumental in the leap to fame of the deeply religious, multi-talented Luciano, who is edging toward superstardom with culturally conscious reggae evoking a universal message of spiritual hope, as in his album *Where There Is Life*, featuring his chart-topping hit, 'It's Me Again Jah.'

**Left:** Michael Rose, formerly of Black Uhuru

Tony Rebel is considered the 'father' of the cultural revolution that began in earnest in 1995 and is still sweeping the dancehalls, inspiring a revisit to the protest chamber where reggae began. (Rebel is also one of many contemporary dancehall artists who now sport dreads.) Rebel is one of the most far-reaching of contemporary Jamaican musicians. His work spans a double feature on the Grammy-nominated *Stir It Up* album to success on the soundtrack of the movie *Cool Runnings* and the hit single 'Weekend Love' with artist Queen Latifa. Look for Tony Rebel's CD-set *La La Bella* delivering 14 cuts from veteran and up-and-coming roots artists.

This resurgence of roots music is exemplified, too, by Everton Blender, syrupy of voice and who broke big with his 1995 'Lift Up Your Head'; former Black Uhuru member Michael Rose; and Ini Kamoze's dancehall hits, 'Jah Never Fail I Yet' and 'No Watch No Face.' Junior Reid is another former Black Uhuru songster who has performed some of his best work in the digital era (notably 'All Fruits Ripen' and 'One Blood').

## An Explosion of Sounds

The roots renaissance has also spun-off new success for the 'old bloods,' prompting a growing demand for ska and rock-steady music from the 1960s. (Today, Jamaica's social calendar is etched with 'oldies' sound-system shows, traditionally held on Sunday, with live performers such as Alton Ellis and John Holt earning overdue paychecks.) But the renaissance is also fueling a search among studio producers for suitable *new* platform rhythms. The constant experimentation with new drum beats sets the tone for evolving trends, resulting in ragga rhythms that in age-old Jamaican style are being 'versioned' as classics, as with Dave Kelly's influential 1995 hit, 'Pepper Seed,' and Malvo & Redrose's 'Quarter to Twelve.'

Recent experiments have also yielded intriguing hybrids. In 1996, the Taxi Gang's 'Western Farm' utilized country and western (even Lady Saw has blended country into dancehall ragga). Buccaneer's outrageous 'Sketel Concerto' brought opera into ragga. Reggae artist Gibby discovered heavy metal. The venerable Wailing Soul invoked a psychedelic tinge. And Sly & Robbie have created 'latinreggae,' reflecting how Jamaica's new-found fondness for Cuba is having an effect on the music scene; salsa is stirring new commotions in the music industry.

Jazz has also begun to influence reggae in a big way, beginning in 1995 when jazz-propelled recordings were released by leading artists such as Spragga Benz, Papa San, and Beenie Man, who has finally begun to explore new styles (his 1997 album, *Many Moods of Moses,* includes an endearing country-and-western melody with 'Ain't Gonna Figure It Yet,' recorded in Nashville). That year, too, Island Records established a new label: Island Jamaica Jazz Records. (In 1998, Island Records was dissolved and replaced by the new Palm Pictures label.)

And ska has had an enduring albeit malleable renaissance that in the late 1980s brought back Jamaican ska greats to a younger generation of enthusiastic fans and, more recently, has been melded with jazz into a style called 'skazz' (popular throughout Europe), a free-form hip-hop/ska/jazz combo, and even Christian ska bands, ska/punk called 'ska-core,' and a fusion of ska with Latin sounds called 'salska.'

Alas, money talks and the Jamaican music scene remains fettered by unprofessional influences. Much of ragga is rebel music, operating on the fringe of big companies – it relies on independent label support – and virtually outside the law. Jamaica's ghetto-derived music industry has always been edged with violence, and continues to suffer from often explosively violent elements going into the 21st century. The scene is very corrupt, and promoters offer large pay-offs to get airplay: dancehall dominates the airwaves, leaving little room for broader music with a more creative edge.

**Right:** Natty dread or radio head?

LEE ABEL

REGGAE'N'RIDDIMS

## The International Scene

Many of the hottest reggae artists of the past two decades have been non-Jamaicans. Reggae even has a huge following in Scandinavia and Japan, where homegrown performers have burst onto the scene (even the Norwegian band Irie Darlings – led by Gambian, Papa Abdou – hit the spotlight in 1994 with their *Xaymaca* album).

### The UK Beat

Britain already had a well-versed market of emigré Jamaicans dating from the 1950s (many Kingston-cut ska recordings of the era were aimed at this relatively affluent market), producing successful singers such as Laurel Aitken and Jackie Edwards.

During the heyday of reggae, UK-born musicians charted a course distinct from their island-born brothers'. Compared to many artists from the dancehall-inspired Kingston scene, they were relatively affluent and less inclined toward Rastafarianism. Musically, though, they have tended to take their cue from Bob Marley. Successful 'roots' groups included Aswad, Matumbi, the Cimarons, Black Slate, and UB40. The most notable is Birmingham's Steel Pulse, which had tremendous crossover appeal with a white audience (including in the USA), and in the 1990s became more commercial.

The 1970s also saw reggae basslines merged with soft-soul styles to produce the uniquely British lovers rock. The trio Brown Sugar, Carroll Thompson, and Janet Kay were notably successful, followed by Deborahe Glasgow and Kofi in the 1980s, and Janet-Lee Davis and Sylvia Tella in the 1990s.

During the 1980s dancehall craze, England produced its own DJ 'dons,' many of whom rose up with London-based Sir Coxsone's and the Saxon Sound International sound systems, and Birmingham's Wassifa sound system, which all kept abreast of the Kingston scene.

Attempts to mix reggae with fast rolling drums produced jungle and its successor, drum-and-bass. Contemporary exponents include Starkey Banton, Top Cat, the rough-edged General Levy, boy-wonder Glamma Kid, and Birmingham's Apache Indian. Britain also produced Maxi Priest, the biggest name in reggae since Marley.

As in Jamaica, 'roots' music has had a revival in the digital 1990s, spearheaded by Adrian Sherwood's On-U-Sound label and Rastafarian Jah Shaka's sound system, and more recently Danny Red. 'Dub-poet' Linton Kwesi Johnson was also at the forefront during the later 1990s.

### Down in Africa

African reggae is vibrant and spans a breadth of influences almost as large as the continent. The genre dates back to the 1960s, when Millie Small initiated a wave of tours by Jamaican musicians, who were often received as demigods (Jimmy Cliff sold out the Lagos football stadium). Most important was Bob Marley's appearance at the Zimbabwe independence concert in 1980.

## The International Scene

Typically, African performers have fused reggae with local styles and tribal traditions. Marley has remained the abiding influence, although incongruous with the times. Hence, African musicians remain relatively unknown in Jamaica, where the audience responds best to up-to-the-moment dancehall dictates. Two African superstars to reach international acclaim are Senegalese reggae-maestro Alpha Blondy and South African Lucky Dubé, both of whom rose to prominence during the 1980s with their Marley-inspired music. Thomas Mapfumo, from Zimbabwe, and Nigerian Majek Fashek also sell well abroad.

### Reggae in the States

Jamaican immigrants brought reggae to the USA and formed an important market for Kingston-born music. Although the US was a fertile market for sounds that shaped Jamaica's own musical course, it produced very few reggae performers of note. Johnny Nash was the sole star during the 1960s and 1970s, based in, of all places, Texas. The first reggae recording studio set up in New York appeared only in the mid-1970s: Lloyd Barnes' Bullwackie's.

The established sound-system scene of Brooklyn and the Bronx produced few US reggae stars until the mid-1980s. Then, Shinehead hit it big with a remake of Michael Jackson's 'Billie Jean' and secured his stature with his debut album, *Rough & Rugged*, melding dancehall beats with hip-hop and R&B.

A decade later Jamaican-born Shaggy hit it big, beginning with his 1993 debut album, *Pure Pleasure*, featuring 'Oh Carolina,' a remake of a 1958 Folks Brothers classic. His 1995 album, *Boombastic*, went platinum and won the 1996 Grammy for 'Best Reggae Album.'

Jamaican dancehall has been mammothly influential in rap music, which is said to have been introduced to the USA by Jamaican-born DJs, such as DJ Cool. Most recently, the Fugee's impassioned reggae covers and Spearhead's rhythmical, rootical sensibilities have captured the attention of the record-buying masses.

Shinehead

REGGAE'N'RIDDIMS

## Resources

**Online Resources** The best online resource is Jammin Reggae Archives site at www.niceup.com, with links to reggae record companies and plenty of sound samples. It also includes information on concerts, lyrics, books, clubs, and radio shows.

**Publications** The definitive book on the topic is Rough Guide's *Rough Guide to Reggae* by Steve Barrow and Peter Dalton.

*Reggae Routes* (Ian Randle), published in 1997 by Wayne Chen and Kevin O'Brien Chang, is required reading. This copious, lavishly illustrated volume is an insider's guide to reggae and popular Jamaican music in general, demystifying the music and correcting many misconceptions.

Two other books to look for include *The Virgin Encyclopedia of Reggae* (Colin Larkin), a superb A-Z encyclopedia; and *Reggae Island: Jamaican Music in the Digital Age* by Brian Jahn and Tom Weber (Kingston Publishers).

For books on Bob Marley, see the Music section of Books in the Facts for the Visitor chapter.

**Below:** Reggae Sunsplash hangover

LEE ABEL

# Facts for the Visitor

## HIGHLIGHTS

The Jamaica Tourist Board (JTB) has divided the island into seven 'resort' areas: Kingston, Mandeville, Montego Bay, Negril, Ocho Rios, Port Antonio, and Runaway Bay. (Mandeville and Manchester parish are marketed by the JTB together with Treasure Beach and St Elizabeth parish as the 'South Coast,' a misleading term.)

## Beach Resorts

Visitors to Jamaica always ask, 'Which is the best beach?' The answer is elusive, partly because many of the finest beaches are privately owned and access is limited. Others are fronted by hotels that jealously guard them.

The most important resort areas (in order of size) are Montego Bay, Ocho Rios, Negril, and Runaway Bay, and all are associated with the island's best beaches. Virtually the entire crop of hotels is found in these locales. The coast immediately east of Port Antonio also has an enclave of resort hotels, and others are dotted along the north coast.

Still, some of my favorite beaches are in nonresort areas, including Negril's Long Bay, Port Antonio's San San Beach, and Long Bay on the east coast. All boast scintillating white sand melding into turquoise shallows, though each is as distinct as a thumbprint.

**Montego Bay** The second largest city in Jamaica, MoBay, as Montego Bay is popularly called, has more hotel rooms than any other part of the island. It's the principal gateway to Jamaica and the main tourist center, with several modest public beaches and a good choice of hotels and all-inclusive resorts, concentrated in a touristy strip north of the historic city core (the downtown is of modest interest). Despite recent enhancements, I consider the town itself overrated – an idealized marketers image of a tropical vacation for Middle America and budget-minded Europeans.

A fistful of interesting historic sites lie close at hand, as do plantations, bamboo raft trips, and Cockpit Country for hardy hikers.

A short distance east of MoBay is Falmouth, boasting the largest collection and some of the finest examples of Georgian architecture in Jamaica.

**Ocho Rios** Situated along the north coast, 'Ochi' is the main destination for cruise ships. The town itself is unappealing despite its two beaches, but there are plenty of historic sites, botanical gardens, and other attractions within a few minutes' drive. Accommodations range from budget guest houses to some of Jamaica's finest all-inclusive and old-style resorts. Like MoBay, it has received a recent facelift.

**Negril** Jamaica's liveliest resort, Negril also boasts the longest (and one of the most stunning) beaches on the island. It's far enough from everywhere else to have its own unique, fun-in-the-sun appeal. Live reggae shows, spectacular sunsets, and a let-your-hair-down attitude make this a favorite of budget and college-age travelers. Some of the finest all-inclusive resorts are also here, including Hedonism II (the wildest resort in Jamaica) and Swept Away (the island's pre-eminent fitness resort). Negril is also renowned for scuba diving and water sports, and is an evolving center for ecotourism based on the Great Morass, a wetland harboring crocodiles and fabulous birdlife. Accommodations run the gamut.

**Runaway Bay** This small, secluded resort town, midway between MoBay and Ocho Rios, is famous for its coral reefs and polo facilities. Here you'll find nice beaches and many hotels and all-inclusives, including family resorts. The one-street town itself has no appeal whatsoever, however, and tourist infrastructure outside the resorts is minimal (nightlife, for example, is a bomb), but the

1999 opening of Hedonism III is sure to give the resort the major boost that it needs.

**Port Antonio** Secluded at the lush northeastern tip of Jamaica, this formerly bustling banana port has long been popular with Hollywood stars and other luminaries, but has remained small and relatively undeveloped. Offbeat Port Antonio is a center for bamboo raft trips and hiking in the Rio Grande Valley. It has an intriguing historic core of an architectural style unique on the island, but its highlights are its fully staffed, upscale villas and deluxe resorts tucked into coves east of town.

**South Coast** Most of the beaches along the south coast are long gray-sand beaches, less pretty than their northern neighbors, but appealing for their isolation and a lifestyle that still revolves around fishing. The best selection is around Treasure Beach, an invogue spot for travelers seeking an off-beat experience. Nearby, Whitehouse has one of the few white-sand beaches along the south coast and, in 2000, will burst onto the resort scene with the south coast's first true resort: Beaches (part of the Sandals chain). Near at hand lie the Great Morass (a swamp area good for crocodile-spotting safaris), the YS waterfalls, Appleton rum estate, Lover's Leap, an ostrich farm, and interesting forays into Cockpit Country. Other beaches can be found at Morant Bay, Alligator Pond, and Bluefields.

## Other Escapes

**Kingston** The nation's bustling capital is more of a business locale than a tourism center. However, it *is* the center of island culture and is surprisingly sophisticated. Most of Jamaica's museums and art galleries are here, as well as some important historic buildings. Kingston receives few tourists and gives visitors a strong sense of Jamaican reality.

Nearby, you'll find the attractive Hellshire beaches, popular with Kingstonians on weekends, and Lime Cay, a short boat ride from Port Royal, a funky town replete with historic buildings and a fascinating history as the former pirate capital of the Caribbean.

## Scenic Drives

For anyone who loves driving, Jamaica is a delight (forsaking the appalling driving habits of locals). Here is my top-five choice of the best routes:

**Mandeville to Maggotty** – This superlative drive follows the B6 and leads through valleys that transport the visitor viscerally through the Lake District of England, with grassy meadows edged by fieldstone walls and shaded by oaks tucked in the folds of a tight valley that spills westward into a second valley lush with sugarcane.

**Alexandria to Claremont** – This backroads route in St Ann takes you through the Dry Harbour Mountains, and past dramatic limestone 'cockpits' that lend an otherwordly contrast to the north coast.

**Kingston to Buff Bay** – Jamaica's mountain drive par excellence is the B1, which demands the driver's undivided attention, yet reveals phenomenal vistas of Kingston and (if the weather behaves) the northeast coast, with lush foliage emboldened by color at the crest of the Blue Mountains.

**Treasure Beach to Milk River** – I call this a triptych drive, combining the patchwork quilt of southern St Elizabeth's market gardens; a dramatic descent from Bull Savannah to Alligator Pond, and a long, winding, lonesome drive along Manchester's Long Bay at the base of cliffs edging up against a swampy morass shaded by stately Royal palms. En route, stop for lunch at Little Ochi, in Alligator Pond.

**Rio Nuevo to Port Maria** – Choosing the best coastal drive is difficult, but this brief section of the A3 east of Ocho Rios is my vote, offering the most dramatic vistas with waves crashing up against scalloped headlands best seen on a foray inland to Firefly.

Spanish Town, close by, also has a fabulous wealth of historic buildings in various states of decrepitude.

**Blue Mountains** Kingston is set in the lee of the Blue Mountains, which offer unique physical settings and an idyllic escape from the package-tour syndrome. Birders, hikers, and most other kinds of independent travelers will find something of interest. The Blue Mountains-John Crow National Park has well-developed hiking trails.

**Mandeville** This historic agricultural and residential town lies in the cool upland interior, appealing to visitors who shun the beach resorts in favor of birding, scenic mountain drives, hiking, and interactions with local families. (Mandeville is the center for community-based tourism.)

## The Best

Air Jamaica Jazz & Blues Festival – Jamaica has other classy jazz festivals, but this (held in November in Oracabessa) takes the prize, with a line-up of artists that reads like a Who's Who from the world of jazz, blues, and R&B.

Alligator Pond – Hidden away from the world in its own mountain-fringed bay, this atmospheric fishing village is uniquely Jamaican. Sure, the beach is an unappealing brown, but it's marvelously lonesome, intriguing for its local fishing community and one of the finest funkiest eateries in Jamaica, plus a wildlife-rich marshland lies to the east.

Black River Boat Trip – A leisurely cruise into the Great Morass with a naturalist guide brings you face to face with crocodiles, waterfowl, and other critters.

Cuba Excursion – A 90-minute flight north of Jamaica, Cuba is drawing Jamaica's middle class in droves – and more and more travelers, too. Several tour companies offer easy excursions of varying lengths. (See '¡Cuba Sí!' in the Montego Bay & the Northwest Coast chapter for more information.)

Dunn's River Falls – Cruise passengers swarm like lemmings to this tumbling cascade outside Ocho Rios, but climbing its slippery limestone tiers is exhilarating fun, hordes or not.

Firefly – Jamaica has many fine historic attractions, but the former home of Noel Coward, near Port Maria, is my favorite.

Gloria's Rendezvous – On Saturday nights, the inhabitants of Port Royal (a funky, time-warp fishing village southeast of Kingston) flock to get down and dirty on the dance floor. The rum flows. The place is hopping. And age is distinctly no object. The pirate legacy lives on!

Helitour over Cockpit Country – Jamaica's most dramatic landscape is difficult to access, so seeing it from above is the way to go. Helicopters leave from MoBay or Ocho Rios.

Hellshire Beaches – The place to schmooze with Jamaicans on sunny weekends, when Kingstonians flock to swim and flirt.

Hiking to Blue Mountain Peak – When a break from the beach is required, a walk on the wild side will introduce you to another Jamaica. Highlights include cloud-shrouded forests and a view from the 7450-foot summit that makes all others seem like fainthearted efforts. For those flush with money, a night or two at Strawberry Hill seems like heaven.

Negril – Jamaica's best beach, best sunsets, best nightlife. What more could you want?

Reggae Festivals – Both the Reggae Sunsplash (held in Ocho Rios) and Reggae Sumfest (in Montego Bay) feature world-class entertainment and color-blind revelry, elevating these shindigs to an almost religious experience.

Treasure Beach – Oozing with laid-back, off-the-beaten-track ambience, this loosely knit south coast community is a haven of calm. A great place to leave pretentions at home and go fishing with locals.

YS Falls – The 'Dunn's River' of the South Coast, this series of dramatic cascades attracts fewer visitors but offers a smashing setting and the opportunity for swimming.

## The Worst

This is where I lose friends and make enemies. Many much-lauded hotels, resorts, and attractions are dismal letdowns. Here are a few:

Accompong – It's hyped, but there's little that's unique or different about this tiny hamlet that touts itself as the capital of Maroon culture. It's a harpy to get to and after your troubles, disappointment might be the only reward – unless you come on January 6, when the village comes alive with festivities.

Folly – One of Port Antonio's much-praised attractions is nothing more than a derelict, mildewed wreck. It's a favorite for fashion shoots and music videos. But if you're not a model or professional photographer, skip it.

Montego Bay – Sure, the shopping is good, the golfing is excellent, splendid attractions lie close at hand, and several of the resorts outside town are top-notch. But as Jamaica's *premier* resort, I can't understand the appeal. The main drag is only marginally attractive. The public beaches are mediocre. And entertainment is lackluster. Where you stay makes the difference.

Ocho Rios when the cruise ships are in – There's plenty to see and do within minutes of Ocho Rios and great options for accommodations, but the town itself is quite dull, and the main drag is packed when the cruise ships are in and passengers flood Main St in search of cheap souvenirs.

Runaway Bay – While the resorts are exceptional, the town of Runaway Bay is dreary, inspiring an 'Oh my God, what have we done!' response from anyone seeking a vitalic town.

# PLANNING
## When to Go

Jamaica is a year-round destination, though there are seasonal differences to consider. Weatherwise, temperature isn't an impor-

tant factor in determining when to go (winter is usually warm by day and mild to cool by night; summer months are hot), but rainfall is – especially if you plan on spending time in the east coast and Blue Mountains. The so-called rainy season extends from May to November, with two peaks: in May and June, and in October and November. Although the rainy season is a little more humid than others, rain usually falls for short periods (normally in the late afternoon), and it's quite possible to enjoy sunshine for most of your visit. In Portland parish, however, it can rain for days on end.

Tourism's 'high season' runs from mid-December to mid-April, when hotel prices are highest. This is the busiest (and driest) season, when 'snowbirds' from Canada and the USA flock south. Some hotels are booked solid during Christmas and Easter, when many charge 'peak season' rates.

You can save wads of money (40% or more at some hotels) and will find fewer foreign visitors if you visit 'off-season,' the remainder of the year. This is when Jamaicans take their vacations, more Europeans arrive, and there are relatively few North Americans.

## What Kind of Trip

Options range from bumming around on the cheap to pre-paid packages at a ritzy beach resort where butlers and valets wear white gloves.

There's nothing wrong with visiting Jamaica simply to laze on a beach, sip rum cocktails, and get a tan. Most visitors opt for this type of vacation. The island's home-grown 'all-inclusive' resorts provide particularly good options for escapism and are favored by North Americans. The downside is that your contact with the *real* Jamaica is at a minimum. The experience is a 'canned' idealized version of paradise: reggae bands, rum swizzles, and never a care in the world.

A more enriching experience comes from immersing yourself in Jamaica. Meeting Rastafarians, playing dominoes in a rum shop, exploring off the beaten track, visiting a Kingston dancehall – such experiences will allow you to know and appreciate the colorful Jamaican character.

---

### Spring Break Fever

Beach parties, free concerts, and fun in the sun lure thousands of North American college students every spring. The JTB launched its 'Spring Break' program in 1989, with a host of activities specifically designed for the spring-break crowd and sponsored by Appleton Rum and Red Stripe beer.

For information, contact Apple Vacations/Sunbird Vacations (☎ 800-727-3400 east coast; 800-365-2775 west coast), Reggaejam & Calypso Tours (☎ 813-985-7944, 800-873-4423), or Student Travel Services (STS; ☎ 410-859-4200, 800-648-4849). Companies such as Sunsplash Tours and Island Flight Vacations/Sunburst Holidays (see Charter Flights in Getting There & Away) also cater to the party-hearty crowd with weeklong packages to Negril and Montego Bay, starting at about US$450 per person, including roundtrip airfare, airport transfers, accommodations, parties, and concerts. Trips are generally offered throughout March and April.

Jamaica is not well set up for special-interest vacationers in, say, the way Costa Rica is, although golfing and horseback riding are well-developed. Other than crocodile and bird-viewing safaris on the Black River, ecotourism is nascent. Birders, hikers, cavers (spelunkers), artists, and others with special interests will find relatively few tour companies catering to their needs, though this is changing. (Also see the Tours section in the Getting There & Away chapter.)

## Maps

The JTB publishes a 'Discover Jamaica' road map (1:350,000) in association with Esso. No topographical details are shown, and some of the sites of tourist interest are incorrectly marked. The same is true of a similar road map published in association with Texaco, which has the advantage of showing topographical detail and greater road details. Both include separate street maps (1:34,000) of Kingston and major towns. Shell also publishes a road map to Jamaica. You can pick these maps up at the respective gas stations or at any JTB office.

The best maps are Hildebrandt's Jamaica map (1:300,000), and ITMB Publishing's maps (1:250,000) – both show topographic detail. You can find them in many travel bookstores.

The most accurate maps are the Jamaica Ordnance Survey maps published by the Survey Dept (☎ 922-6630), 231-1/2 Charles St, PO Box 493, Kingston 10. (The US$5, 1:50,000-scale topographical maps are most useful.) Unfortunately, only a few of the 20 sheets are currently in print. You'll need to pay at the cashier's office on the 3rd floor; it's open 9 am to 1 pm and 2 to 3 pm Monday to Thursday.

The Survey Dept also sells larger-scale topographical and planimetric city and regional maps, and provides photographic map services. A single-sheet topographical map (1:250,000) costs a whopping US$150, but you can also order this reduced to 1:500,000 scale for US$50, plus US$2 per 100 sq inches.

You can order individual Ordnance Survey sheets (plus the Hildebrand and ITMB maps) from:

Australia
 Travel Bookshop (☎ 02-241-3554)
 20 Bridge St, Sydney, NSW 2000
Canada
 ITMB Publishing (☎ 604-687-5925)
 736A Granville St, Vancouver BC V6Z 1G3
France
 Espace IGN (☎ 01-43-98-85-00)
 107 rue la Boétie, 75008 Paris
New Zealand
 Specialty Maps (☎ 9-307-2217)
 58 Albert St, Auckland
UK
 Sanfords (☎ 020-7836-1321, fax 7836-0189)
 12-14 Long Acre, London WC2E 9LP
USA
 Omni Resources (☎ 800-742-2677, fax 910-227-3748, www.omnimap.com)
 PO Box 2096, Burlington, NC 7216

 South Trek (☎ 512-440-7125, fax 512-443-0973)
 1301 Oxford Ave, Austin, TX 78704

 Treaty Oak (☎ 512-326-4141, fax 443-0973, maps@treatyoak.com)
 PO Box 50295, Austin, TX 78763

For information about maritime maps and charts, see the Sea section in the Getting There & Away chapter.

## What to Bring

Travel light! Jamaica is a hot, tropical country and you shouldn't need much clothing. My motto is: if you can't take your main bag as a carry-on onto an aircraft, you've packed too much for a one-week visit. This depends on where you stay, however. The fancier the resort, the more you may need fancy clothes.

Airlines are strict about baggage allowance and carry-ons. The dimensions of checked luggage should not measure more than 62 linear inches (length plus width plus height), with a 70lb weight limit. The maximum size for a carry-on bag is usually 45 linear inches. A duffel bag with zippered pockets is handiest, though small suitcases are also good. Garment bags are ideal if you plan on staying at one resort. It's best to avoid backpacks with external metal straps. Make sure your luggage is padlocked before parting with it, and don't leave anything of value in external pockets. Theft from baggage at the

Montego Bay airport is very high. A small daypack is also handy.

**Clothing** Loose-fitting, lightweight cotton clothing is best because it allows air flow in the hot humid climate. Tight clothing tends to make you sweat more and can get uncomfortable, as will synthetics like nylon. T-shirts and tank-tops are the perfect wear for outdoors and are best worn untucked, allowing air to circulate. You are going to sweat!

White is the best color for reflecting the sun's rays, but gets dirty quickly. A long-sleeved shirt and long pants are useful in case you get a sunburn. You'll also need long pants for the more upscale discos and restaurants.

Don't forget one or two pairs of shorts, which can be your normal daywear, and swimwear, which should be restricted to the beach. Dress more modestly in towns. This is particularly true of conservative Kingston, where women may attract unwanted attention commensurate with the amount of flesh they expose. Topless bathing (even a birthday suit) is allowed at some resort hotels and on the beach in Negril, but elsewhere is frowned upon and may even result in hostility from shocked locals.

A light sweater might prove handy at night – you'll certainly need one in the upland areas.

Some hotels require casual evening wear at dinner. Several of the ritzier hotels even require jackets (and ties in winter) for men, and elegant dresses for women while dining. Such hotels *do not* allow shorts or jeans in the dining room. Elsewhere, however, fancy togs are taken more as a statement of the wearer's insecurities or snootiness. They also mark you as wealthy, leaving you more open to potential robbery or higher prices when bargaining for souvenirs.

Speaking of money, it's a good idea to carry your cash in a money-belt beneath your clothing.

You'll get by with a pair of sneakers, sandals, or flip-flops (thongs), and a pair of lightweight casual shoes for evening wear. In the interest of conservation *and* for personal safety, you should refrain from walking on coral, but elasticated canvas and rubber 'reef-walking' shoes are ideal for wading.

If you plan on hiking, prepare for variable weather conditions. Rain can fall at any time of year, especially in mountainous areas. Pack a windproof jacket, a sweater, and, ideally, a lightweight rainjacket. At lower altitudes, lightweight cotton clothing will suffice. (Also see the Hiking section in the Outdoor Activities chapter.)

**Toiletries & Supplies** You should bring all toiletries with you. But you don't need to overdo it. For example, you may find an excess of make-up is uncomfortable in the humid tropical heat. At a minimum, your basic kit should include toothpaste, toothbrush, dental floss, deodorant, shampoo, skin creams, make-up, tampons, contraceptives, and a basic health kit (see the Health section later in this chapter).

Few hotels in Jamaica provide complementary toiletries. Don't forget a washcloth: many hotels don't have them. Unless you're staying at an upscale hotel, consider bringing a beach towel. Better yet, buy one in Jamaica. You can also buy any toiletry you may need in Jamaica, although at a higher price than North America or Europe.

Don't forget a spare pair of glasses or contact lenses, and any medicines you may require. Pharmacies should be able to fill any prescriptions you require. Many drugs that are available by prescription-only in the USA can be bought over the counter in Jamaica.

A flashlight is useful in the event of an electrical black-out (very common), or to find your way along unlit streets or paths at night. I also consider a Swiss Army knife essential.

Other essentials include resealable plastic bags (handy for toiletries), a small laundry bag (for dirty underwear and wet clothes), a fold-up umbrella (which will also prove a handy parasol), plus a hat for shade (or buy a straw hat in Jamaica).

It's better to bring items such as laundry detergent, notepads, pencils, and batteries with you; they're available in major towns, but don't rely on finding them when you want to buy them.

**Camping Supplies** Jamaica does not cater to campers. A few places rent tents, but you should bring everything you need, most importantly a bug-proof tent that can withstand a good downpour. Only a few campsites have cooking facilities though most are near inexpensive restaurants, so there should be no need to bring cooking gear unless you plan on camping in the boondocks.

Essential supplies are a flashlight, mosquito repellent, Swiss Army knife (with corkscrew), water bottle, thin rope to use as a washing line, and a lightweight sleeping bag. Also consider a lantern or candles and bring waterproof matches. (See Camping in the Accommodations section, later in this chapter.)

## RESPONSIBLE TOURISM

While tourism brings desperately needed foreign income, it has many potentially negative side effects. How you behave abroad is critical. For example, visitors are often tempted to buy souvenirs made from endangered wildlife – such as swallowtail butterflies, stuffed baby crocodiles, and black coral

---

### Getting Married in Jamaica

Jamaica is a popular destination for honeymooners, many of whom tie the knot on the island. It's often promoted as an ideal place to get married, and its requirements to do so are easily met. There is no blood test requirement, for example, and unlike many other Caribbean destinations which require residency of up to one week, Jamaican law allows couples to marry after only 24 hours on the island.

In addition to proof of citizenship (such as a certified copy of a birth certificate that includes the father's name), you'll need certified copies of the appropriate divorce or death certificates, if one or both of you is divorced or widowed, and written parental consent if either partner is under 21 years of age. These documents must be notarized.

Most major hotels and tour operators will make arrangements, although they usually ask couples to send notarized copies of required documents at least one month in advance. Major resorts usually have special package prices that include the wedding ceremony, government tax, and wedding expenses (SuperClubs' Grand Lido and Sans Souci Grand Lido will even pick up the entire tab if you choose to get married while staying at either resort). They can also arrange a wedding at short notice with a justice of the peace. If you prefer a religious ceremony, advance planning with a member of the clergy is required.

Alternately, you can apply in person at the Registrar Office, at 37 Market St, Montego Bay, or the Ministry of National Security & Justice (☎ 922-0080), at 12 Ocean Blvd, Kingston, which is open 8:30 am to 5 pm Monday to Thursday, 8:30 am to 4 pm Friday. The paperwork costs US$150.

jewelry – without realizing the devastating impact this has on local ecology. (See Ecology & Environment in the Facts about Jamaica chapter.)

Drug use also raises certain moral dilemmas. Buying ganja or cocaine not only is illegal but also helps foster drug trafficking and its concomitant handmaiden, crime.

Prostitution is tolerated and exists quite openly in tourist resorts, where it is often difficult to distinguish between romantic liaisons and sex-for-cash transactions. The women and men are independent and, as opposed to places in Asia, for example, where many prostitutes are forced into the trade, the women plying their bodies in Jamaica do so of their own free will. However, some females choosing to engage in sex with tourists are underage (16 is the legal age of sexual consent in Jamaica). Sexual activity with a minor carries heavy penalties, as well as being morally reprehensible. (Also see Prostitution in the Dangers & Annoyances section, later in this chapter.)

The Center for Responsible Tourism (CRTourism@aol.com), 1765-D LeRoy Ave, Berkeley, CA 94709, publishes guidelines for tourists and works to mitigate the negative impacts of tourism in promoting prostitution. Among the publications available is *What You Should Know About Sex Tourism Before You Go Abroad.*

## TOURIST OFFICES

The Jamaica Tourist Board (JTB) has six offices in Jamaica plus offices in key cities around the world. These serve as information centers, and their staff members are usually very helpful in answering questions. You can request maps and literature, including hotel brochures, but they do not serve as reservation agencies. In Jamaica, the JTB has a Tourism Information Helpline (☎ 929-9200, 881-991-4400) and a hotline for emergency assistance (☎ 888-991-9999). The website (www.jamaicatravel.com) features a 'J-Mail Dispatch,' which automatically updates you via email about new events and happenings in Jamaica. The JTB email address is jamaicatrv@aol.com.

### Local Tourist Offices

The JTB headquarters (☎ 929-9200, fax 929-9375), at 2 St Lucia Ave, PO Box 360, Kingston 5, is surprisingly poorly stocked with literature, perhaps because Kingston isn't a major tourist destination. In addition, you'll find JTB offices in Montego Bay, Negril, Ocho Rios, Port Antonio, and Black River (see regional chapters).

Roadside information booths have also recently been established in major resorts along the north coast and Negril.

### Tourist Offices Abroad

There are a number of JTB offices worldwide, including the following:

Canada
  (☎ 416-482-7850, fax 482-1730)
  1 Eglinton Ave E No 616, Toronto,
  ON MAP 3A1

France
  (☎ 01-45-61-90-58, fax 01-42-25-66-40)
  c/o Target International, 32 rue de Ponthieu
  75008 Paris

Germany
  (☎ 6184-99-0044, fax 6184-99-0046)
  c/o Postfash 90 04 37, 60444 Frankfurt/Main 1

Italy
  (☎ 6-686-9112, fax 6-687-3644)
  c/o Sergat Italia SRL,
  Via Monte Dei Cenci 20 7/A 01186, Rome

Japan
  (☎ 3-3591-3841, fax 3-3591-3845)
  Chigusa Building, 1-5-9 Nishi-Shinbashi
  Minato-ku, Tokyo 108

UK
  (☎ 020-7224-0505, fax 020-7224-0551)
  1-2 Prince Consort Rd, London SW7 2BZ

USA
  Atlanta (☎ 770-452-7799, fax 452-0220)
  Boston (☎ 617-335-6931, fax 335-6291)
  Chicago (☎ 312-527-1296, fax 527-1472)
  500 N Michigan Ave No 1030
  Chicago, IL 60611
  Coral Gables, FL (☎ 305-666-0557, fax 666-7239) Doral Executive Office Park, 3785 NW 82nd Ave suite 403, Miami, FL 33166
  Dallas (☎ 214-553-5118, fax 553-5183)
  Los Angeles (☎ 213-384-1123, fax 384-1780)
  3440 Wilshire Blvd No 1207
  Los Angeles, CA 90010

New York (☎ 212-856-9727, 800-233-4582,
fax 212-856-9730) 801 Second Ave
New York, NY 10017
Philadelphia (☎ 800-233-4582)

## VISAS & DOCUMENTS
### Passports
US and Canadian citizens do not need passports for visits up to six months. However,
they *do* need two pieces of identification,
including proof of citizenship or permanent
residency, such as a passport, birth certificate, voter's registration card, or driver's
license with photo ID.

All other visitors *must* arrive with a passport. British citizens need passports that will
still be valid six months from their date of
arrival. (Check its expiration date before
departing for Jamaica.)

It's a good idea to carry your passport –
or, better yet, a photocopy – with you, out of
the reach of thieves. Otherwise, leave it in a
safety-deposit box in your hotel, along with
your other valuables.

If you don't have a passport, allow at least
six weeks for getting one.

### Visas
No visas are required for entry to Jamaica
for citizens of European countries (including Turkey), the USA, Canada, Mexico, Australia, New Zealand, Japan, and Israel.

### Travel Permits
No travel permits are required. However,
you'll need to fill out an immigration card
upon arrival. You will need to show it when
you depart. Cruise passengers are cleared
en masse by the cruise company.

### Onward Tickets
Immigration formalities require that you
show a return or ongoing airline ticket when
arriving in Jamaica.

### Travel Insurance
However you're traveling, it's worth taking
out travel insurance. You may not want to
insure that grotty old army surplus back-
pack, but everyone should be covered for
the worst possible case: an accident, for

example, that requires hospital treatment
and a flight home. Travel insurance may
seem rather expensive, but certainly is
cheaper than paying for a medical emergency overseas.

A travel insurance policy that covers
theft, loss of baggage, and medical treatment
is a good idea. You might also consider trip
cancellation insurance if you have booked a
pre-paid package with cancellation penalty
clauses. Any travel agent can recommend an
appropriate package.

When purchasing medical insurance,
consider a policy that pays for medical
services immediately and directly. Otherwise you may have to pay on the spot, then
claim for reimbursement once you return
home. Check if the policy covers ambulances or an emergency flight. If you have
to stretch out, you will need two seats and
somebody has to pay for them. Also check
if there are exclusions for any 'hazardous
activities' you may be contemplating, such
as renting motorcycles or scuba diving.

In the USA, the following companies are
leading travel insurance suppliers:

American Express (☎ 800-234-0375)
    PO Box 919010, San Diego, CA 92190
Travelers (☎ 203-277-0111, 800-243-3174)
    1 Tower Square, Hartford, CT 06183
TravelGuard International (☎ 715-345-0505)
    1145 Clark St, Stevens Point, WI 54481

In the UK, contact Campus Travel (☎ 020-7730-
8111), Endsleigh Insurance (☎ 020-7436-4451),
or STA Travel (☎ 020-7361-6262). The Association of British Insurers (☎ 020-7600-3333), 51
Gresham St, London, EC2V 7HQ, can recommend other travel insurance brokers.

In Australia, call AFTA (☎ 02-9956-4800),
Cover More (☎ 02-9968-1333, 800-251881),
or UTAG (☎ 02-9819-6855).

### Driver's License & Permits
To drive in Jamaica, you must have a valid
International Driver's License (IDL) or a
current license for your home country or
state, valid for up to six months. You can
obtain an IDL by applying with your current
license to any Automobile Association office.

In the USA, it costs US$18 (US$16 for AAA members) and can be issued on the spot at AAA offices.

A North American driver's license is valid for up to three months per visit from the date of entry; a UK license is valid for up to one year; and a Japanese license is for one month.

## Hostel Card

Jamaica has no youth hostel system. Unless you plan on combining your visit to Jamaica with other destinations that have youth hostels, leave your IYHF card at home.

The same is true for student, youth, and seniors' cards. Other than Air Jamaica Express' discount flights for students and

## Embassies & Consulates

### Jamaican Embassies & High Commissions

Unless otherwise noted, details are for embassies.

**Canada**
High Commission:
(☎ 613-233-9311)
Standard Life Bldg,
275 Slater St suite 402
Ottawa, Ontario
K1P 5H9
Consulate General:
(☎ 416-598-3008)
214 King St W suite 402
Toronto, ON M5H 1KA

**UK**
High Commission:
(☎ 020-7823-9911,
fax 7408-2545)
1-2 Prince Consort Rd
London SW7 2BZ

**USA**
(☎ 202-452-0660,
fax 452-0081)
1520 New Hampshire Ave
NW, Washington, DC

Consulate Generals:
(☎ 212-935-9000,
fax 935-7507)
767 Third Ave
New York, NY 10017
(☎ 305-374-8431,
fax 577-4970)
842 Ingraham Bldg
25 SE Second Ave
Miami, FL 33131

### Embassies & Consulates in Jamaica

At press time, more than 40 countries had official representation in Jamaica. Except for a couple of Montego Bay consulates, all are located in Kingston. If your country isn't represented in this list, check 'Embassies & High Commissions' in the yellow pages of the Greater Kingston telephone directory.

**Australia**
High Commission:
(☎ 926-3550, 926-3551)
64 Knutsford Blvd, Kingston 5

**Austria**
Consulate:
(☎ 929-5259)
2 Ardenne Rd, Kingston

**Barbados**
Consulate:
(☎ 977-2854)
561-1/2 Duke St, Kingston

**Brazil**
(☎ 929-8607)
64 Knutsford Blvd, Kingston

**Canada**
High Commission:
(☎ 926-1500)
Royal Bank Limited Bldg,
30 Knutsford Blvd,
Kingston 5
Consulate:
(☎ 952-6198) 29 Gloucester
Ave, Montego Bay

**China**
(☎ 927-3871) 8 Seaview
Ave, Kingston 10

**Chile**
(☎ 968-0260)
1 Holborn Rd, Kingston 10

**Cuba**
(☎ 978-0931)
9 Trafalgar Rd, Kingston 10

**Denmark**
Consulate General:
(☎ 923-5051) 449 Spanish
Town Rd, Kingston

**France**
(☎ 927-7430) 13 Hillcrest
Ave, Kingston 6

**Germany**
(☎ 926-6728) 10 Waterloo
Rd, Kingston 10

**Haiti**
Consulate General:
(☎ 927-7595)
2 Munroe Rd, Kingston

seniors (see Domestic Airlines in the Air section of the Getting Around chapter), nobody in Jamaica honors discount cards.

## Photocopies

Before leaving home, make two photocopies of your most valuable documents, including your passport, driver's license, airline ticket, hotel vouchers, and health insurance. Keep one copy at home. Carry the second copy with you, but separate from the originals.

## CUSTOMS
### Entering Jamaica

You are allowed to import the following items duty-free: 25 cigars, 200 cigarettes,

---

### Embassies & Consulates

**Honduras**
(☎ 969-5082)
7 Lady Kay Drive, Kingston

**Israel**
Consulate:
(☎ 926-8768) 60 Knutsford
Blvd, Kingston 5

**Italy**
(☎ 978-1273)
10 Rovan Drive, Kingston 6

**India**
(☎ 927-3114)
4 Retreat Ave, Kingston 6

**Japan**
(☎ 929-7534)
32 Trafalgar Rd, Kingston 10

**Mexico**
(☎ 926-6891)
36 Trafalgar Rd, Kingston 10

**Netherlands**
(☎ 926-2026) 53 Knutsford
Blvd, Kingston 5

**Norway**
Consulate:
(☎ 923-9811)
6 Newport Blvd, Kingston

**Russia**
(☎ 924-1048) 22 Norbrook
Drive, Kingston 8

**Spain**
(☎ 929-6710) 25 Dominica
Drive, Kingston 5

**Sweden**
Consulate:
(☎ 922-3347)
105 Harbour St, Kingston 5

**Switzerland**
Consulate:
(☎ 922-3347)
105 Harbour St, Kingston 5

**Trinidad & Tobago**
High Commission:
(☎ 926-5730) 60 Knutsford
Blvd, Kingston 5

**Venezuela**
(☎ 926-5510)
36 Trafalgar Rd, Kingston 10

**UK**
High Commission:
(☎ 926-9050)
26 Trafalgar Rd, Kingston 10
Consulate:
(☎ 953-2231) Montego Bay

**USA**
(☎ 929-4850, 926-5679, fax
926-6743)
Jamaica Mutual Life Centre,
2 Oxford St, Kingston 2
Consulate:
(☎ 952-0160, 952-5050)
St James Plaza, 2nd floor,
Gloucester Ave, Montego Bay

---

### Your Own Embassy

As a tourist, it's important to realize what your own embassy – the embassy of the country of which you are a citizen – can and can't do.

Generally speaking, it won't be much help in emergencies if the trouble you're in is remotely your own fault. Remember that you are bound by the laws of the country you are in. Your embassy will not be sympathetic if you end up in jail after committing a crime locally, even if such actions are legal in your own country.

In genuine emergencies you might get some assistance, but only if other channels have been exhausted. For example, if you need to get home urgently, a free ticket home is exceedingly unlikely – the embassy would expect you to have insurance. If you have all your money and documents stolen, it might assist in getting a new passport, but a loan for onward travel is out of the question.

Embassies no longer keep letters for travelers or have a small reading room with home newspapers.

one pint of liquor (except rum), one pound of tobacco, and one quart of wine. The following items are restricted: firearms, drugs (except prescription medicines), flowers and plants, honey, fruits, coffee, and meats and vegetables (unless canned).

You are allowed to bring in a reasonable amount of personal belongings free of charge. However, you may need to show proof that laptop computers and other expensive items (especially electronics) are for personal use, otherwise you may be charged General Consumption Tax (GCT) of 6.25% to 15% plus duty. You should declare these upon arrival.

Only animals born and bred in the UK may be brought in freely; all others must be quarantined for six months upon arrival.

## Leaving Jamaica

US citizens can purchase up to US$600 duty-free per person, provided they have not used the allowance within the last 30 days. In addition, you may import 200 cigarettes, 100 cigars (except Cuban cigars, which are *not* permitted to be taken into the USA), plus 1L of liquor or wine. Art, handicrafts, antiques, and certain other items are exempt from duties under the Generalized System of Preferences (GSP). For more information, contact the US Customs Service (☎ 202-566-5268), 1301 Constitution Ave NW, Washington, DC 20229, which publishes *GSP and the Traveler,* explaining what may and may not be imported.

Canadian citizens are allowed an annual allowance of C$500, plus 200 cigarettes, 50 cigars, 2lb of loose tobacco, and 40oz of liquor. In addition, you can mail unsolicited gifts valued up to C$40 per day. The booklet *I Declare* provides more information: contact the Revenue Canada Customs Dept (☎ 613-993-0534), Communications Branch, Mackenzie Ave, Ottawa ON, K1A 0L5.

British citizens may import goods worth up to £200 in addition to 200 cigarettes, 50 cigars or 250g of loose tobacco, and 2L of wine plus 1L of spirits (depending on alcohol proof). For further information, contact Her Majesty's Customs & Excise Office (☎ 020-

7202-4227), New King's Reach House, 22 Upper Ground, London SE1 9PJ.

Australian citizens are permitted to bring back A$400 of gifts and souvenirs, plus 250 cigarettes or 250g of tobacco, and 1125ml of alcohol. For specifics, contact the Australian Customs Service (☎ 02-9213-2000, fax 9213-4000), Box 8, Sydney, NSW 2001.

New Zealand citizens may bring back NZ$700 worth of souvenirs, plus 200 cigarettes or 50 cigars, and 4.5L of beer or wine and 1125ml of spirits. For specifics, contact the New Zealand Customs (☎ 09-359-6655), Custom House, 50 Anzac Ave, Box 29, Auckland.

If you need the services of a licensed customs broker, contact the Customs Brokers Association of Jamaica (☎ 962-0744), in Kingston.

If you need assistance with immigration formalities, contact the Jamaican Immigration Office (JIO; ☎ 952-5381), Overton Plaza, Union St, in Montego Bay. Its hours are 8 am to 1 pm and 2 to 4 pm, Monday to Thursday. The JIO also has an office at Montego Bay's Donald Sangster International Airport (☎ 952-5645).

## MONEY
### Currency

The unit of currency is the Jamaican dollar, the *jay*, which uses the same symbol as the US dollar ($). Jamaican currency is issued in bank notes of J$10, J$20, J$50, J$100, and J$200. Coins are issued for 10 cents, 25 cents, J$1, and J$5. You may still find old 20-cent and 50-cent coins in circulation, but one-cent and five-cent coins have been phased out. The symbol for cents (¢) is also the same as in the US.

The smaller denomination coins are virtually valueless, and many cashiers simply round up to the nearest dollar when giving change.

Rarely you hear old names used, such as *quattie*, the name for the 1½ penny coin introduced in 1834, *fippance* (three-pence coin), and *mac* (shilling). They most often appear in folksongs and tales.

Prices for hotels and valuable items are often quoted in US dollars, which are widely accepted. It's always wise to check whether a quoted price is in Jamaican or US dollars, particularly when using taxis. (Duty-free goods must be purchased with foreign currency). European currencies are usually frowned upon. You can bring in as much money as you wish and take out Jamaican dollars.

## Exchange Rates

The Jamaican dollar has been stable for about two years, with a few wild swings here and there. The official rate of exchange fluctuates daily and as of August 1999 was about J$40 to US$1, and J$64 to £1. Long-term, the Jamaica dollar has been in gradual and steady decline against the US dollar.

## Exchanging Money

Although not essential, it's a wise idea to purchase some local currency (or US dollars, which are universally accepted in Jamaica) before departing home.

To change Jamaican dollars back into US dollars or other foreign currency, you will need to show exchange receipts for the Jamaican dollars you purchased.

**Cash** Nine major commercial banks maintain branches throughout the island, so you will rarely be far from a bank. Those in major towns maintain a foreign exchange booth, and foreign currency may be exchanged for Jamaican dollars during regular business hours. Bank hours are generally 9 am to 2 pm Monday to Thursday, and 9 am to 4 pm Friday. Some banks close at 2 pm and reopen from 3 to 5 pm on Friday. A few local banks also open 9 am to noon on Saturday.

You'll usually get the best exchange rate at banks. You can also change money at most hotels, or at licensed exchange bureaus in the airports and at a few other select locations in major resort towns. Many hotels offer the same rates as banks. Others offer rates between 2% to 5% lower.

Often you'll be given big denomination bills (J$500 and up). Smaller bills, however, are preferable, especially if you intend to explore the boondocks, where change for such large bills may be in short supply.

**Traveler's Checks** Traveler's checks are widely accepted in Jamaica, although some hotels, restaurants, and exchange bureaus charge a hefty fee for cashing them. You can purchase them prior to departing for Jamaica at virtually any bank, lending institution, or currency exchange service.

Three of the most popular and widely accepted traveler's checks are American Express, Barclays Bank, and Thomas Cook. To report lost American Express traveler's checks, call ☎ 800-221-7282. For lost Thomas Cook checks, call ☎ 800-223-7373.

**ATMs** Automated teller machines (ATMs) are a good way to obtain incidental cash using a credit or debit card. Most city branches throughout Jamaica now have 24-hour ATMs in secure booths.

Don't rely on your ATM card, however. As yet, few Jamaican banks are linked to international networks such as Cirrus or Plus. Some Scotiabank branches have this facility, but I've found my ATM cards don't work at all locations. National Commercial Bank has a hotline (☎ 888-991-2419) for customers using its Midas 24-hour ATM service. Check with your local bank before departing for Jamaica to find out how you may be able to utilize your ATM card.

**Credit & Debit Cards** Major credit cards are widely accepted throughout the island. Visa and MasterCard are the most commonly accepted, followed by American Express, Diners Club, and Discover.

You can use your credit card to get cash advances at most commercial banks for a small interest or transaction fee. You can opt to receive US or Jamaican dollars. When using your card for purchases, don't let the store add a processing fee (which is forbidden by the card companies). And note that credit-card purchases are subject to a government sales tax that might not otherwise apply.

American Express is represented by Stuart's Travel Service. Stuart's offices include Kingston (☎ 929-2345), 9 Cecelio Ave; Montego Bay (☎ 952-4350), 32 Market St; Negril (☎ 957-4887), Coral Seas Plaza; and

Ocho Rios (☎ 974-2288). See regional chapters for more local offices.

To report lost or stolen credit cards, call:

| | |
|---|---|
| American Express | ☎ 800-528-4800 |
| AmEx Gold | ☎ 800-528-2121 |
| MasterCard | ☎ 800-826-2181 |
| Visa | ☎ 800-336-8472 |
| Visa Gold | ☎ 800-847-2911 |

**International Transfers** If you need emergency cash, you can arrange a telegraphic or mail transfer from your account in your home country, or from a friend or family member. You also can arrange a transfer in advance through your local bank, and while you're in Jamaica at most major banks via MoneyGram.

Western Union has offices in Kingston (☎ 926-2454) and in towns islandwide (call ☎ 888-991-2056 for the nearest location).

**Black Market** Many young Jamaican men are eager to change Jamaican dollars in street transactions, particularly in Ocho Rios when the cruise ships disembark passengers. It's strictly illegal, however, and hardly worth it: the black market rate is rarely 5% better than the official exchange rate, and street trading is full of risks.

If you trade on the street, be very cautious: *never* hand over your money until you have counted every Jamaican bill handed to you. The following trick is often used on foreigners: as you each hand over your money, the black marketeer shouts 'Police!' and runs; the foreigner usually beats a hasty retreat, but upon counting the money finds a few Jamaican dollar bills enfold bill-sized pieces of newspaper.

You're not helping the struggling Jamaica economy, however, by trading on the black market. By doing so you'll undermine the government's attempts to stabilize the Jamaican dollar's official value.

**Money-Changers** Foreign exchange is a big business in Jamaica, and virtually every town and village has at least one or more licensed money-changers, known as 'cambios.' They deal in most major currencies, offer rates slightly lower than those of banks, and usually charge a processing fee that is between 2% and 5% of the transaction. All kinds of outlets operate as 'cambios,' including supermarkets and general stores. Look for the 'cambio' sign.

## Security

Carry as little cash as needed when away from your hotel. Keep the rest in a hotel safe. You can rely on credit cards and traveler's checks for most of your purchases. However, you'll need cash for most transactions in rural areas and at gas stations.

Don't carry your cash where it can be seen. Keep your wallet in your front pocket. Even better, stash your money in a money belt or pouch, worn inside your clothing. Set a small sum (say US$100 or so) aside for emergencies in case you get ripped off.

A significant number of counterfeit bills – mostly high denomination bills (particularly US$50 and US$100 bills) – are in circulation, and banks and shopkeepers are fairly savvy at identifying them. Many places won't accept the new US$100 bills, which were supposed to be counterfeit-proof, but are treated with disdain in Jamaica.

## Costs

Jamaica is relatively expensive, about on par with North America or the UK. How much you spend, however, depends on your sense of style. Even hard-core budget travelers will need at least US$20 a day if you stick to street stalls and local produce. Roadside stalls and budget restaurants sell patties for US$0.50 and jerk pork and other local meals for as little as US$2. A hand of bananas or half a dozen mangoes will cost about US$0.50. More touristy restaurants, however, can be expensive, as many of the ingredients they use are imported: expect to pay at least US$8, and as much as US$50 per head for the finest restaurants. Grocery shopping can be expensive for the same reason; stick to local produce if possible.

Transport costs vary. Car rentals are expensive by North American standards, beginning at about US$45 a day for the smallest vehicle. Bus travel is inordinately cheap (a 50-mile journey is as little as US$1). Licensed taxi service is expensive (typically US$7 for even short rides in downtown Montego Bay, Negril, and Ocho Rios), but unlicensed taxis will carry you for whatever fare you can bargain.

Accommodations will be your biggest expense. Most budget accommodations charge US$20 or more, even for spartan conditions. Mid-range hotels range from about US$30 to US$60, while some resorts charge US$300 or more.

**Discounts** If you want to save money, consider visiting in 'summer,' or low season (mid-April to mid-December), when hotel prices plummet and airfares are often reduced. Another good way to stretch your dollars is to rent a villa or cottage with several other people.

*Jamaica's Practical Pocket Guide* by Jacqueline Marie Tschetter (US$19.95) is a discount voucher book covering tours, sights, and attractions throughout the island.

The Traveler Club offers discounts on items from fast food to insurance, and new members receive a free US$10 phone card. For information, contact ITS Tours (☎ 926-6540), 18 Ripon Rd, Kingston 5, or any CIBC Ltd bank.

See Reservations in the Accommodations section, later in this chapter, for organizations offering discounts on hotel rooms.

### Tipping & Bargaining
Tipping hasn't reached the crazed levels of the USA. However, a 10% tip is normal in hotels and restaurants, and bellhops at most hotels expect a tip for bringing baggage to your room (US$0.50 per bag is plenty). Many all-inclusive resorts have a strictly enforced no-tipping policy; their staff can lose their jobs for accepting tips.

Some restaurants automatically add a 10% to 15% service charge to your bill, in which case there's no need to leave an additional tip. Check your bill carefully, as often the charge is unscrupulously hidden.

Most prices in shops are fixed. However, bargaining – *higgling* – is a staple of street and market life in Jamaica. Sometimes the bargaining gets a bit brisk, even testy.

Remember that Jamaica is a poor country, and many of the Jamaicans you encounter may be counting upon your tip for their livelihood. Be generous as seems fitting.

### Taxes & Refunds
The government charges a General Consumption Tax (GCT) of 15% on most hotels, plus restaurant bills, and most purchases in stores. The GCT charge varies according to type of hotel, from 6.25% to 15%. Most hotels also add a 10% service charge.

## POST & COMMUNICATIONS
### Postal Rates
Every town and most villages have a post office; there are over 300 nationwide. The smaller ones (called postal agencies) issue stamps and receive and send letters and parcels, but otherwise have few facilities. Larger post offices are full-service, with telegram facilities, a philatelic bureau, and savings' bank bureau. Some have fax facilities.

Post offices are open 8 am to 5 pm Monday to Friday. Postal agencies are usually open Monday, Wednesday, and Friday mornings only, although times vary.

Postcards cost J$25 to anywhere in the world. Airmail letters to the USA and Canada cost J$25 per ounce for letters; to the UK and Europe it costs J$30 per ounce; and to Africa, Asia, or Australia, J$40.

### Sending Mail
Public postboxes are few and far between. You will need to go to a post office to mail your postcards and letters. Alternately, you can leave them with the front desk clerk at most hotels.

The stamps may be pretty and cheap, but the service is *sloooow*! Always use airmail unless you have a valid reason not to. Airmail to North America usually takes about 10 days to two weeks, and a few days longer to Europe. Surface mail can take forever (at least two months). Even a letter from Montego Bay to Kingston can take a week.

Ensure that any parcels are adequately secured. Postal theft is common, so don't tempt fate by mailing loosely taped packages. Never mail cash or valuables. If you want to mail valuable documents, use an express mail service that ensures security.

When sending mail to Jamaica always include the addressee's name, address or post office box, town, and parish, plus 'Jamaica, West Indies.'

**Express Mail Services** Express mail services are listed in the yellow pages and include AirPak Express (☎ 923-0371 in Kingston), UPS (☎ 968-8288 in Kingston), Federal Express (☎ 952-0411 in Montego Bay; ☎ 960-9192 in Kingston), or DHL (☎ 922-7333, 929-2554 in Kingston). All four have offices nationwide.

UPS offers a money-back guarantee of 24-hour delivery to North America and parts of Europe, plus free customs clearance. Their offices are open 7 am to 7 pm daily.

## Receiving Mail

You can have mail addressed to you marked 'Poste Restante' care of a major central post office. Thus, you should have a letter or package addressed with (your name), Poste Restante, General Post Office, Montego Bay No 1, St James, Jamaica, West Indies. Letters can likewise be addressed to Kingston.

## Telephone

Jamaica has a fully automated, digital telephone system. The service is not consistent, however, and crackles and other strange noises are frequent, and disruptions are not unknown. Telecommunications of Jamaica (TOJ; ☎ 926-9700), 47 Half Way Tree Rd, Kingston 5, a privately owned member company of the UK's Cable & Wireless group, has offices islandwide. Offices are usually open 8 am to 4 pm Monday to Friday, and until noon on Saturday. TOJ's Kingston headquarters has a toll-free customer information number (☎ 888-926-9700), and other TOJ offices islandwide also have toll-free numbers, including the following:

Black River
    (☎ 888-965-9700) 3 North St
Falmouth
    (☎ 888-954-9700) 23 Market St

Mandeville
    (☎ 888-962-9700) Shop 16, Leaders Plaza
Montego Bay
    (☎ 888-952-9700) 20 Church St
Negril
    (☎ 888-957-9700) Shop 27, Negril Plaza
Ocho Rios
    (☎ 888-974-9700) Mutual Life Bldg, Graham St
Port Antonio
    (☎ 888-993-9700) Shop 4C, Portmore Mall

You can make direct calls at TOJ offices or at privately run 'call-direct centers,' where an operator places a call on your behalf and you're directed to the appropriate phone booth. You will be charged 'time and charge,' in which the operator will advise you of the cost upon completion of your call. Many hotels work this way also.

Jamaica's country code is ☎ 876.

**Public Telephones** You'll find public telephones at TOJ offices – usually bearing the Cable & Wireless logo – in most major towns. Even remote villages are served by public telephones, which often serve the entire community.

To use a public phone, pick up the receiver and wait for the clicking tone before dialing. You deposit your coins *after* a connection, after which you can begin talking.

Most public phones now use TOJ phone cards – CardPhone – which have virtually replaced coin-operated public call boxes. The cards can be handy if you're making several calls, but it can be a hassle if you want to make one quick call and you have to go scout out where to buy a phone card.

The plastic cards are available from Cable & Wireless offices, retail stores, hotels, banks, and other outlets displaying the 'phone cards on sale' sign. There's always an outlet close by the phone, even in the boondocks. The card is paid for in advance in denominations of J$20 to J$500. When calls are made, the telephone shows the balance remaining on a digital screen, and deducts the charges from the value of your card. Some phones are cantankerous and don't always accept the cards, at least not at first try.

To make a call using the CardPhone, simply lift the receiver and insert the card (picture-side up) into the special slot. Then dial ☎ 113; when you hear the tone, press the # button, then dial your number. Then wait for the other party to start talking before pressing the 'Press to Talk' button.

**Domestic Calls** All domestic calls cost J$0.15 per minute for calls within parishes, and J$0.38 (off-peak) or J$0.76 cents (peak) for inter-parish calls.

Jamaican numbers all have seven digits, which you dial for calls within the same parish. For calls to other parishes, dial ☎ 1 then the seven-digit number.

There are many toll-free numbers in Jamaica, which can be dialed from any phone. Toll-free numbers begin with ☎ 800 or 888.

**International Calls** The easiest way to call home is usually from your hotel. Almost all the larger or more upscale hotels have direct-dial calling; elsewhere you may need to go through the hotel operator, or even call from the front desk. Note, however, that hotels add a 15% government tax for overseas calls. They also impose their own service charge, often at sticker-shock rates. Some hotels even block access to 'home-direct' service so that they can jack up your bill. The more expensive the hotel, the higher the service charge.

Outside major hotels, direct dial is a bit of a circus and usually requires that you call ☎ 113, wait for a tone, then press the # button, wait for a tone, and finally dial your desired number.

You can save money by using a 'home-direct' service such as AT&T USADirect, MCI CallUSA, or Sprint Express. Dial an access number from any telephone to reach a US operator who links your call. You can bill your home phone, phone card, or call collect. AT&T USADirect phone booths are located at several key locales in Jamaica, and most upscale hotels have signed up with AT&T to offer direct service from room phones. Many Jamaican operators still tell you that you can't use your calling card to call internationally. If this happens, try another operator. Scams are frequent; *never* give your calling-card number to anyone other than the operator.

To place collect or calling-card calls, simply dial the appropriate code below:

| country/service | code |
| --- | --- |
| USA | |
| AT&T USADirect | ☎ 872 or 800-872-2881 |
| MCI CallUSA | ☎ 873 or 800-674-7000 |
| Sprint Express | ☎ 875 or 800-877-8000 |
| Canada | |
| Canada Direct | ☎ 876 or 800-222-0016 |
| UK | |
| BT Direct | ☎ 874 or 800-364-5263 |

Note that MCI no longer permits calling card calls from Jamaica due to a large volume of fraud cases.

Alternately, you can also buy World-Talk Calling Cards in Jamaica, available in various denominations and good for use on any telephone, including public call boxes and cellular phones. To use, dial the access number (☎ 958-2273), wait for a tone, then enter the card account number, wait for a tone, then dial the number you are calling. Intra-island calls cost J$0.75 per minute (J$6.50 using cellular phones). International calls cost J$30 to J$180 per minute, depending on destination.

You can make international collect calls (reverse charges) using World-Talk Calling Cards. However, you can no longer receive collect calls from overseas. And the process for connecting to 'home-direct' service is different.

| country | service | code |
| --- | --- | --- |
| USA | AT&T USADirect | ☎ #1 |
| | MCI CallUSA | ☎ #2 |
| | Sprint Express | ☎ #3 |
| Canada | Canada Direct | ☎ #4 |
| UK | BT Direct | ☎ #5 |

For countries that cannot be dialed direct, call the international operator toll-free (☎ 113, 888-922-2170).

**Calling Jamaica from Abroad** If you wish to call Jamaica from abroad, dial your country's international dialing code, then

☎ 876 (Jamaica's country code), and finally the seven-digit local number.

**Cellular Phones** You can bring your own cellular phone into Jamaica, but you'll be charged a customs fee upon entry (this is refunded when you leave). You can also rent cellular phones from the TOJ (☎ 888-865-2355), which has four Cellular Customer Care centers:

Kingston
  (☎ 969-9855) 116-1/2 Constant Spring Rd
Mandeville
  (☎ 962-9855) 24 Hargreaves Ave

Montego Bay
  (☎ 979-9855) 36 Fort St
Ocho Rios
  (☎ 974-9855) Mutual Life Bldg

Cellular coverage is available only in specific areas. The airtime charge is J$3.60 per minute.

Cable & Wireless Caribbean Cellular also provides a cellular network throughout the Caribbean for yachts and cruise ships. By dialing ☎ *0 then 'SND' in Jamaica, you can register your cellular phone for instant service, or you can pre-register (☎ 800-262-8366 in the USA, ☎ 800-567-8366 in Canada,

## Internet Resources

The explosion in recent years of communications in cyberspace has fostered dozens of travel sites on the Internet. They are no substitute for a good guidebook, but many provide excellent information for planning your trip. They also give you a chance to exchange information and otherwise gossip via email with other travelers in-the-know.

Addresses (URLs) for hotels, tour companies, and the like are listed throughout the book. Meanwhile, here are good starting points for general information about Jamaica or travel:

**Lonely Planet**
*www.lonelyplanet.com*
Especially good for practical tips on preparing for your trip
**GNN Travel Center Global Network Navigator**
*http://nearnet.gnn.com/gnn/meta/travel/index.htm*
One of the largest and most far-reaching resources
**American Society of Travel Agents**
*www.ASTAnet.com*
Helps you find out which companies specialize in particular types of trips
**Adventure Travel Society**
*www.adventuretravel.com/ats/*
Lists reputable adventure-travel companies by activity and destination
**Specialty Travel Index**
*www.spectrav.com*
Also lists adventure-travel companies

**Great Outdoor Recreation Page**
*www.grop.com*
If you plan on hiking, mountain biking, or the like, try this site with extensive listings on maps, gear, and outfitters
**TravelMag**
*www.travelmag.co.uk/travelmag/*
For independent, down-to-earth travelers
**TapOnlIne**
*www.taponline.com*
More information on independent travel
**Shoestring Travel**
*http://turnpike.net/metro/eadler/index.html*
A forum for budget travelers
**Council Travel**
*www.ciee.org/cts/ctshome.htm*
Lists international airfares from US cities
**Air Charter Guide**
*www.guides.com/acg*
Find student airfares in the directory on worldwide charter aviation

☎ 1-758-453-9922 elsewhere). You can arrange billing direct to your credit card. For information, call ☎ 800-262-8366 from the USA; ☎ 800-567-8366 from Canada. In Jamaica, call ☎ 968-4000. The company offers discount rates for use over a six-week period or longer, and rents cellular phones and fax machines.

## Fax
Many towns have private fax services, which are listed in regional chapters. You can send faxes from hotels, major post offices, and TOJ centers, which send telegrams, too.

## Email & Internet Access
Only a few of the more modern, upscale hotels provide in-room, dial-up access for laptop computers. However, most upscale

---

## Internet Resources

### Specific to Jamaica
There are dozens of Jamaica-specific sites. Your starting point should be the JTB's website.

**Jamaica Tourist Board**
*www.jamaicatravel.com*
Covers most of the bases for travelers and has numerous links
**National Library of Jamaica**
*www.nlj.org.jm*
The largest online directory of Jamaican websites
**International Development Institute**
*www.idicalif.com*
Links to more than four dozen Jamaica-specific sites, from travel to music
**Virtual Voyages**
*www.virtualvoyages.com/jamaica/jam_guide.htm*
Has links to more than four dozen sites, from travel to music
**Jamweb**
*www.jamweb.com*
Also provides links, though far less comprehensive than the above site
**Jamaica Information Service**
*www.jamweb.com*
This government organization provides news and information

**Jamaica Observer**
*www.jamaicaobserver.com*
Jamaica's leading newspaper's site with current day's paper online, plus archives
**Jamaica Travel Net**
*www.jamaica-tours.com*
A list of attractions, hotel reviews, flight information, and booking services
**Jamaica Today**
*www.jamweb.com*
This site of Jamaica Online Information Service has pages serving news, environment, music, society and culture, economy and business, politics, sports, arts, and vacations, all with breaking news plus links to related sites
**Jamaica! Yellow Pages**
*www.jamaica-yp.com*
Has a listing of all businesses in Jamaica
**CPSCaribNet**
*www.cpscaribnet.com*
Has facts and things to see and do for more than two dozen Caribbean islands, including Jamaica. Includes listings of accommodations, special interest activities, real estate, and investing

hotels are connected to the Internet and offer guests email and Internet access through business centers via the hotel's own computer system.

The TOJ offers Internet access via its Voyageur Internet Service. You can sign up online (www.toj.com) or at any TOJ business office.

Most cities have at least one commercial entity where you can access the Internet. See regional chapters for details, or look in the phone directory.

## BOOKS

Information on bookshops throughout Jamaica can be found in the regional chapters.

Most books are published in different editions by different publishers in different countries. As a result, a book might be a hardcover rarity in one country while it's readily available in paperback in another. Fortunately, bookstores and libraries can search by title or author, so your local bookstore or library is the best place to find out about the availability of the following recommendations.

Macmillan Caribbean, a division of Macmillan Press, publishes a wide range of books about the Caribbean. For a catalog, contact its office (☎ 0256-29242, fax 0256-20109), Houndmills, Basingstoke, Hampshire RG21 2XS, England.

### Guidebooks

There are about one dozen English-language travel guidebooks to Jamaica, plus many other Caribbean guidebooks with chapters on Jamaica.

Lonely Planet's *Eastern Caribbean* by Glenda Bendure and Ned Friary is invaluable if you're planning to do some island hopping.

*Passport's Illustrated Travel Guide to Jamaica from Thomas Cook* by Christopher P Baker is a handy pocket-size sightseeing guide. The author offers signed copies of this illustrated guide at a discount, available at www.travelguidebooks.com.

*Insight Guides' Jamaica* is another richly illustrated guide. It also has a detailed introduction to the country, which was written by

a team of native writers. Unfortunately, it is weak on nitty-gritty details.

*Tour Jamaica* by Margaret Morris (Gleaner Company) is an excellent guide for anyone exploring by car. The book, recently re-released in small format, has 19 recommended tours.

*Adventure Guide to Jamaica* by Steve Cohen (Hunter Publishing) is an indispensable guide for anyone interested in off-the-beaten-track exploration and activities.

*Diving & Snorkeling Guide to Jamaica* by Hannie & Theo Smitt (Lonely Planet) is the most comprehensive guide for underwater enthusiasts, with lavishly illustrated regional sections and maps complementing an introductory overview.

Kay Showker's *Outdoor Traveler's Guide to the Caribbean* (Stewart Tabori & Chang, New York) is an excellent guide for ecotourists, with detailed information on specific locales in Jamaica for birders, hikers, and nature lovers.

The US Dept of State publishes *Tips for Travelers to the Caribbean* (Publication No 9906, BCA), available from the Superintendent of Documents, US Government Printing Office (☎ 202-783-3238), Washington, DC 20402.

### Travel

Very few travel books have been written about Jamaica, at least during this century.

An early travelogue that provides a colorful insight into the life and times of colonial Jamaica is Lady Maria Nugent's *Journal of Residence in Jamaica, 1801-5*, which tells an often patronizing tale from a preferential perspective. In a similar vein is *Journal of a West Indian Proprietor* by Matthew Lewis, written in 1834.

Patrick Leigh Fermor's *Traveller's Tree* (Penguin UK) is a classic tale and includes a chapter describing his visit to Jamaica in the 1940s.

*Jamaica the Blessed Island* by Lord Sydney H Olivier (Faber & Faber) recalls the noted actor's viewpoints and experiences at a favored vacation spot. Likewise, swashbuckling Hollywood hero Errol Flynn, who lived in Jamaica for many years, recalls some of his colorful experiences there in his auto-biography *My Wicked Wicked Ways*.

Anthony Winckler's *Going Home to Teach* (Penguin UK) tells of the novelist's time in Jamaica as a teacher during an epoch of anti-white sentiment in the tension-filled late 1970s.

*Ian Fleming Introduces Jamaica*, published in 1965 and edited by Morris Cargill, is a collection of essays in which various authors describe aspects of Jamaican life.

## History & Politics

*Views of Jamaica* (Institute of Jamaica, Kingston) features rare illustrations of plantations and townscapes by 19th-century artist Joseph Bartholomew Kidd.

In a similar vein is *A Picturesque Tour of the Island of Jamaica*, originally published in 1825 (recently reprinted by Mill Press), and featuring beautiful illustrations of an idealized Jamaica by James Hackle.

Edward Long's three-volume *The History of Jamaica*, written in 1774, remains a definitive study of the early colonial era. *The Annals of Jamaica* is a similar, two-volume work by George Bridges, published in 1828. *A Short History of the West Indies* by Anthony Maingot, J H Parry, and Philip Sherlock (Macmillan) is a concise work that puts the Jamaican context in a regional perspective, from colonial to contemporary times.

Mavis Campbell's *The Maroons of Jamaica* (Africa World Press) is a serious study of the origins of the Maroons and their evolution as a culture through to the end of the last century. Two other recommended books that tell the fascinating tale of the Maroons are *The History of the Maroons* by RC Dallas, a two-volume set published in 1803, and Carey Robinson's *The Fighting Maroons of Jamaica* (Collins).

*Buccaneers of America*, first published in 1684, is an entertaining eyewitness account of the sordid acts of the infamous buccaneers told by John Esquemeling, who partook in the misdeeds. Surprisingly little has been written on the pirate era. However, the period is covered well in *Port Royal* by Clinton V Black (Institute of Jamaica Publications). Black also authored *Tales of Old*

*Jamaica* (Longman Caribbean), which tells the tale of 10 of Jamaica's most notorious scoundrels, including Annie Palmer, the 'White Witch of Rose Hall.'

Tony Sewall's *Garvey's Children: The Legacy of Marcus Garvey* (Macmillan Caribbean) provides a look at the rise of black nationalism inspired by National Hero Marcus Garvey, as does *Garvey: His Work and Impact*, edited by Ruper Lewis and Patrick Bryan (Africa World Press).

*Alexander Bustamante and Modern Jamaica* by George Eaton (Kingston Publishers) follows the rise of nationalism to its logical conclusion: independence and the birth of a nation under the fostership of National Hero Alexander Bustamante.

The biography of Jamaica's most controversial prime minister is traced in Darrell E Levi's *Michael Manley: The Making of a Leader*, although it is scant on the charismatic leader's failures and could be considered unduly favorable. Manley's own *Politics of Change – A Jamaican Testament* was written as a philosophical treatise as his PNP government began the social experiment that shook the island nation to its roots.

## General

**Flora & Fauna** There's no shortage of books on the natural history of Jamaica and the Caribbean islands. *Flowering Plants of Jamaica* by C Dennis Adams (University of the West Indies) has detailed descriptions of individual species, accompanied by illustrations. *Caribbean Flora*, by the same author (Nelson), is in a similar vein, as are *Wild Flowers of Jamaica* by Alex D Hawkes, and *Flowers of the Caribbean* and *Trees of the Caribbean*, both by GW Lennox. All three are published by Macmillan Caribbean.

Lepidopterists should refer to *An Annotated List of Butterflies of Jamaica* by A Avinoff and N Shoumatoff.

Birders are well informed by the authoritative *Birds of Jamaica: A Photographic Field Guide* by Audrey Downer and Robert Sutton (Cambridge University Press).

James Bond's classic *Birds of the West Indies* is another reference for serious bird-watchers. It was recently republished as

*Peterson's Field Guide to Birds of the West Indies* (Houghton Mifflin) in a lavishly illustrated version.

Other books on birds include *The Birds of Jamaica* by DB Stewart (Institute of Jamaica Publications), *Familiar Jamaica Birds* by Anna Black (Jamaica Information Services), and *Gosse's Jamaica 1844-45* by Philip Henry Gosse, first published in 1851.

If you're into snorkeling or diving, a standard reference should be Eugene Kaplan's *Peterson Field Guide to Coral Reefs: Caribbean and Florida* (Houghton Mifflin). In the same series is *Fishes of the Caribbean Reefs, the Bahamas and Bermuda* by Ian Took.

**Culture & Society** *Jamaica In Focus: A Guide to the People, Politics & Culture* by Marcel Bayer provides an accurate and concise account of Jamaican society and contexts. *Roots of Jamaican Culture* by Mervyn Alleyne is a scholarly but readable treatise on Afro-Jamaican culture dealing with themes from language to religion.

Barrett's *Rastafarians* (Beacon Press) offers a comprehensive review of the movement, with origins, evolution, and philosophies explored. The sympathetic *Dread: The Rastafarians of Jamaica* by Joseph Owens (Sangster, Kingston) and *Rastafari: For the Healing of the Nation* by Dennis Forsythe (Ziaka Publications) are also noteworthy books on Jamaica's most talked-about creed.

*Revival Cults in Jamaica,* by former prime minister Edward Seaga, is the classic on the theme of Pocomania, Kumina, and other cults. Meanwhile, ex-prime minister Michael Manley's *A History of West Indian Cricket* is considered *the* text on the contribution of Caribbean cricketers to this most popular of island sports.

*Color, Class and Politics in Jamaica,* by Aggrey Brown, relates issues of race to Jamaica's political development.

The dark side of the Jamaican drug trade is chillingly explored in Laurie Gunst's *Born Fi' Dead.*

For an understanding of the hardships of motherhood in Jamaica, read Andrea Taylor's *Baby Mother*, the autobiographical report of a single parent's ordeals. *Baby Father* by Patrick Augustus tells the Jamaican male's point of view.

**Cuisine** Galloping gourmands should refer first and foremost to *Classic Jamaican Cooking* by Caroline Sullivan. A century after it was first released, it remains the gastronomic equivalent of Mrs Beeton.

Two of the best are *Real Taste of Jamaica* by Enid Donaldson, and *Traveling Jamaica with Knife, Fork & Spoon: A Righteous Guide to Jamaican Cooking* by Robb Walsh and Jay McCarthy. The latter is a collection of anecdotes and recipes from the backcountry and the kitchens of snooty resorts.

*Jerk: Barbecue from Jamaica* by Helen Willinsky is a must for preparing a sizzlingly successful barbecue, while *Cooking with Caribbean Rum* by Laurel-Ann Morley (Macmillan) and *Cooking with Red Stripe* by the brewing company, Desnoes & Geddes, provide intriguing recipes using beer and rum.

Vegetarians should seek out *The Rasta Cookbook* by Laura Osbourne, a gourmand's guide to I-tal cooking.

**Art & Architecture** *Jamaica Art* by Kim Robinson and Petrine Archer Straw (Kingston Publishers) is a well-illustrated treatise on the evolution of the island's art scene. Likewise, *Modern Jamaican Art* by David Boxer and Veerle Poupeye is a 206-page coffee-table book providing an overview of the works of 82 Jamaican painters and sculptors.

Several books have been written on Caribbean and Jamaican architecture. *Jamaican Houses: A Vanishing Legacy* by Geoffrey de Sota Pinto (de Sota Pinto Publishers) has brief descriptions and black-and-white prints of Jamaica's most important historic houses.

*Caribbean Style* by Suzanne Slesin and Stafford Cliff and its pocket-size companion, *Essence of Caribbean Style*, explain the evolution and elements of the Caribbean vernacular in architecture. The lively text is supported by stunning photography.

**Language** *Jamaica Talk, 300 Years of the English Language in Jamaica* by Frederic Gomes Cassidy (Macmillan) will provide you with an understanding of English as spoken in Jamaica, as will *Understanding Jamaican Patois* by Emilie Adams (Kingston Publishers).

Cassidy and RB LePage's *Dictionary of Jamaican English* (Cambridge University Press) is the definitive lexicon on *patois*, while Chester Francis Jackson's *Dancehall Dictionary* (Kingston Publishers) is a glossary of cuss words, buzz words, and phrases that pervade the dancehall culture.

*Jamaican Proverbs* by Martha Beckwith (Negro University Press) will help you translate the esoteric sayings that Jamaicans are sure to throw your way.

**Literature** Terry McMillan tells a semi-autobiographical tale of holiday romance in *How Stella Got Her Groove Back*, the tale of a mature black woman and her unexpected relationship with a much younger man. Russell Banks has produced two noteworthy novels with Jamaica as their setting: *Book of Jamaica* and *Rule of the Bone*.

For a list of books by Jamaican authors, see Literature in the Arts section of the Facts about Jamaica chapter.

**Music** *Rough Guide to Reggae* by Steve Barrow and Peter Dalton is the definitive guide to reggae music. *Reggae Island* by Brian Jahn and Tom Weber, and *Reggae – Deep Roots Music* by Howard Johnson and Jim Pines, focus on the contemporary and historical scenes, respectively.

*Dancehall,* by Anton Marks, lays it bare, from the sordid under-the-table deals of musical politics to the steamy backstage scene.

Cedella Booker's *Bob Marley* (Penguin UK) is an anecdotal account of the reggae superstar's life as told by his mother. Then read the definitive and engaging *Catch a Fire: The Life of Bob Marley* by Timothy White, which analyzes the forces that shaped Marley's political and spiritual evolution. A more sensational albeit poorly written text is *Marley & Me: The Real Bob Marley Story* by Mike Henry and Marley's ex-manager, Don Taylor, who tell an oft-controversial, behind-the-scenes tale. Perhaps the best biography, though one full of salacious gossip, is *Bob Marley* by Stephen Davis. One of the most recent texts is *Bob Marley: Reggae King of the World* by Dermot Hussey and Malika Lee Whitney.

**Coffee-Table** Ray Chen's *Jamaica: The Land and the People* is the most lavish book of photographs on Jamaica, focusing on landscapes. Also look for the now out-of-print *Beautiful Jamaica* by Evon Blake; and *Jamaica: Babylon on a Thin Wire*, a black-and-white coffee-table book with text by Adrian Boot and Michael Thomas, who explored Kingston during the 1970s with camera in hand.

*Reggae Bloodlines: In Search of the Music and Culture of Jamaica*, by Stephen Davis and Simon Peter, focuses on the island culture, notably the Rastafarians. The same authors also produced *Reggae International*.

**Other** The *A-Z of Jamaican Heritage* by Olive Senior (Gleaner Company) is an encyclopedia on Jamaica. It's been out of print for some years.

The *Statistical Yearbook of Jamaica* provides facts and figures on every aspect of the economy and demographics. It's available from the Statistical Institute (☎ 967-2680), 84 Hanover St, Kingston.

Likewise, look for *Who's Who & What's What in Jamaican Art & Entertainment* by Louis Marriott.

A series of short pocket-guides designed to help visitors understand Jamaican life is published by Jamrite Publications, Kingston, including the *How to be Jamaican Handbook* by Kim Robinson, Harclyde Walcott, and Trevor Fearon. *Ganja in Jamaica* by Vera Rubin and Lambros Comitas (Moulton & Co) will edify you on the mysteries of 'de holy 'erb.'

## FILMS

Dozens of movies are set in Jamaica, many of which give a taste of the island, and its people, culture, and music.

Jamaica has had strong links to James Bond movies ever since novelist Ian Fleming concocted the suave, macho spy 007 at his home near Oracabessa. The Bond movies *Dr No* and *Live and Let Die* were both shot on location on Jamaica's north coast.

Portions of *20,000 Leagues Under the Sea* were filmed in Jamaica, as were scenes from *Papillon* with Steve McQueen and Dustin Hoffman, employing many of Seaford's residents of German heritage as extras. *Lord of the Flies, Flipper, Prelude to a Kiss*, and *Search for Tomorrow* were also filmed in Jamaica. Reggae star Jimmy Cliff starred alongside comedian Robin Williams in the movie *Club Paradise*, filmed around Port Antonio. In recent years Port Antonio has become something of an international star in its own right. *Clara's Heart* (starring Whoopie Goldberg), *Hammerhead* (starring Denzel Washington), *Cool Runnings* about Jamaica's improbable bobsled team, *Cocktail* (starring Tom Cruise), *Mighty Quinn, Blue Lagoon* (starring Brooke Shields), *Treasure Island* (starring Burt Lancaster), and *Wide Sargasso Sea* (a sultry tale of post-emancipation Jamaica), were filmed wholly or in part around Port Antonio, which is also a favorite location spot for music videos.

Most recently, *How Stella Got Her Groove Back*, starring Whoopi Goldberg and Angela Bassett, was filmed throughout Jamaica, showing the island as a paradise. Following the movie's success, scores of middle-aged North American women have followed Angela Bassett's example, descending on Jamaica to find their youth in the arms of much younger men.

Also see Film in the Arts section of the Facts about Jamaica chapter.

## NEWSPAPERS & MAGAZINES
### Foreign Publications

Leading international newspapers such as the *International Herald Tribune*, the *Times* (of London), *Figaro*, and *USA Today*, plus leading magazines such as *Newsweek, Time*, and the *Economist* are stocked by many hotel gift stores, pharmacies, and stationery stores throughout Jamaica. You'll also be able to find many international consumer magazines. However, they're pricey – usually two to three times the cost at home.

Before you go, take a look at some magazines about Jamaica and the Caribbean. *Caribbean Travel & Life* is a beautiful, full-color, bi-monthly magazine; *Caribbean World,* published quarterly in the UK, profiles the lifestyles of the rich and famous. Its less-snobbish US equivalent is *Unfold: The Soul of the Caribbean*. And *Caribbean Week* is a high-quality, bi-weekly news magazine that covers the region. *Caribbean Today*, published in Trinidad, is similar.

### Jamaican Publications

The *Gleaner* is a high-standard, conservative daily that has been around since 1834. Coverage is mostly national, but international events also get reasonable coverage, often from a perspective that differs from the general US viewpoint.

The *Gleaner's* rival is the *Jamaica Observer*, a middle-of-the-road daily tabloid.

The Gleaner Company also publishes a trashy afternoon tabloid – the *Star* – in a similar vein as the major English tabloids and the slightly more erudite *New York Daily News* and *National Enquirer*. The *X-News* is another gutter tabloid – a 'social newspaper' – in similar salacious vein, heavy on sports, entertainment, and flesh, as is the *Sunday Punch*. The dregs of the sewer is *ExS* – consider the anagram.

There are several regional newspapers, including the *North Coast Times*, which serves St Ann and St Mary parishes. The *Western Mirror* serves Montego Bay and is published on Wednesday and Saturday.

The *Jamaica Tourist Guide* is a 16-page newspaper geared to international visitors. It's published monthly by the Gleaner Company. It features news reports, articles, and personality profiles, plus regional listings of things to do and see. You can obtain free copies in many hotel lobbies. *Jamaica International* is a multi-language quarterly tourist newspaper also printed by the Gleaner Company.

Published bi-weekly, the *Vacationer* is a newsletter-style publication for travelers, similar to the *Jamaica Tourist Guide*. Complementary copies are available at hotel desks and JTB offices. And the *Tourism Talk* newsletter, published by the JTB, provides an update on the latest happenings on the tourism scene.

Domestic magazines are few. One of the finest is *SkyWritings*, the bi-monthly in-flight magazine of Air Jamaica.

A new publication, *Caribbean Gourmet,* hit the newsstands in 1999, aimed at gourmands.

## RADIO & TV
Though television was privatized in 1997, most Jamaicans still prefer radio over TV, and you can learn a lot about the island by listening to Jamaica's radio stations.

### Radio
In 1997 there were some 16 radio stations. Music stations tend toward reggae and rap. Call-in talk shows are very popular, and there is considerable political debate on the air. As the island is so small and parochial, radio serves as a kind of community service grapevine. Deaths, for example, are announced with somber details (and muted morguelike music behind) followed by a long roll call of relatives and friends requested to attend the funeral.

Radio Jamaica Rediffusion (RJR) bought the national radio station run by Jamaica Broadcasting Corporation (JBC) in 1997. The station (91.1 FM) is now a 24-hour public broadcast station, with content provided by the Ministry of Education, the Jamaica Information Service, and others. It mixes talk shows, political analysis, and cricket coverage with reggae and popular music. RJR also broadcasts FAME FM (91.5/98.1 FM), a popular music station.

Reggae lovers should tune-in to Irie FM (105.5/107.7 FM), which plays nonstop reggae (it usually starts out with moody ska and gradually winds into more hardcore reggae and dancehall) and is the most popular station. It has a fairly rebellious political content. Love FM (101.1 FM) plays a lot of North American and romantic reggae. KLAS (89.5 FM), Power 106 (106.5 FM), and Radio Waves (102.9 FM) are alternatives.

Talkshows to take note of include Beverly Manley's 'Breakfast Club' (KLAS, weekdays 6 to 9 am), Ronnie Thwaites' 'Independent Talk' (Power FM, weekdays 5:30 to 9 am), and Wilmott Perkins' 'Straight Talk' (KLAS, weekdays 10:30 am to 2:30 pm).

Reception is variable throughout the island and is affected by terrain.

## Television
The government-owned JBC was privatized and sold in 1997 to RJR, the island's oldest broadcast outlet, which promptly renamed the TV station Super Supreme Television. CVM is a second private TV company.

The Public Broadcasting Corporation established to produce quality TV materials (its productions were of relatively low standard) continues to function. News coverage is in-depth and follows the BBC style, with broad international coverage. The island even has its own soap: *Royal Palm Estates*.

Few Jamaicans in the countryside have a TV, although most urban Jamaicans have access to TV and are familiar with US programming (private cable companies have operated in Jamaica since 1996). Most hotels offer satellite or cable TV, and CNN and ESPN are staples. However, many hotels have poor or only limited reception and receive only local stations, which broadcast only at certain hours. If you must have a TV, you should ensure that it receives cable programming.

## PHOTOGRAPHY & VIDEO
Jamaica is about as photogenic as a destination gets, and there are no restrictions on taking photographs, even at airports. (Police officers and other officials are generally happy to be photographed, too.) The landscapes and seascapes are fabulous, as are the sunsets. Be sure to ask permission before taking somebody's picture; see Photographing People, below.

### Film & Equipment
Bring the equipment you'll need from home. If you do have to buy something, you'll find camera stores in most major towns, especially in Montego Bay and Ocho Rios, where

duty-free stores sell cameras and lenses at prices that offer only marginal savings. Most shops sell a range of basic filters, including UV and polarizing filters – essentials for getting the most out of Jamaica's tropical conditions – but don't count on it.

Film is extremely expensive – about double what you'd pay in the USA or Canada – so ensure you bring enough to last. Most photo supply stores and drugstores sell a limited range of film. Print film is widely available, but slide (transparency) film is extremely rare, and usually limited to Ektachrome or Agfachrome. Fuji film is virtually impossible to find in Jamaica.

Many places leave film sitting in the sun; avoid this like the plague, as heat and humidity rapidly deteriorate film. Don't forget to check the expiration date, too. Once you've finished a roll of film, try to keep it cool and have it developed as soon as possible. One or two weeks is OK, but if you'll be traveling around for several weeks, consider having your film developed on the island, or mailing it home for development (you can purchase pre-paid mailers for this purpose). You'll find processing studios in most towns islandwide.

Every photographer has the same enemy in Jamaica – humidity. Carry silica gel packages in your camera bag to soak up moisture.

## Technical Tips

Jamaica's bright sunlight can fool even the most sophisticated light metering systems, resulting in disappointing, washed-out photographs due to overexposure. Your meter may not be set up to register the dazzling ambient light surrounding the subject it's reading from. Sand and water are particularly reflective (you can use a polarizing filter to cut the glare).

A separate hand-held meter can provide more accurate readings. It's also often a good idea to 'stop down' one F-stop to reduce the light and thereby get richer color saturation. Most effective of all is to take photographs in early morning and late afternoon, to avoid the harsh shadows and the sun's glare.

The type of film you use will also make a huge difference. Fujichrome gives the best color saturation of any film, matched by Kodak's newest series of professional films. It's not cheap, but it pays big dividends. Kodachrome 25 and 64 give excellent color rendition; the former – as with any ASA/ISO 25 film – is great for bright conditions, but is too 'fast' to handle dark conditions or great contrasts of light and shade. Slide film requires fairly exact exposure (it is less tolerant of error than other film types). To compensate you should bracket – take a frame one F-stop underexposed and one overexposed in addition to the metered exposure.

When photographing people, you'll need to compensate for the contrast between dark faces and bright backgrounds; otherwise they may turn out as featureless black shadows. The darker a person's skin is, the more light you will need to reflect onto their faces. Many modern cameras have a fill-in flash for this purpose. Alternately, you could invest in a small hand-held reflector. If you're taking really close-up shots, you can even ask your subject to hold the reflector (out of the camera frame, of course).

## Video Systems

Video cameras and tapes are widely available in photo supply stores in main resort towns and in Kingston. Prices are significantly higher than in North America or Europe. Most video supplies sold in Jamaica are to North American standards. UK citizens should check carefully to ensure that any tapes are PAL compatible.

## Photographing People

The majority of Jamaicans delight in having their photographs taken, and will be happy to pose for you. However, many Jamaicans of all ages object to having their picture taken. Older people may object if they're not dressed in their Sunday best. Some have religious proscriptions. Others may even fear that you're a police informer or similar. If they don't want to be photographed, they may let you know this in no uncertain terms, and can get quite volatile if you persist. Depending on the circumstances, you should honor their wishes with good grace. There's no reason not to take a photo over their objections if, for example, the person happens to be part of a broader subject of interest, in which case you have every right to take photos. They'll move!

Still, it is a common courtesy to ask permission. Expect to be asked to pay a small 'donation' to take photographs. Whether you agree to this or not is a matter of your own conscience, but honor that person's wishes in this regard: if you don't want to pay, don't take the shot.

In markets it is considered good manners to purchase a small item from whomever you wish to photograph. Don't forget to send a photograph to anyone you've promised to do so.

### Airport Security

Your baggage will be inspected when you depart Montego Bay and Kingston airports. It's a good idea to have your film hand-inspected, since X-ray machines can fog films. Most modern X-ray machines will not produce any noticeable fogging if your film passes through only once or twice, but why take the risk? If your baggage will be passed through several X-ray machines during the course of your travels, you should definitely have it hand-checked. Otherwise, invest in a lead-lined film pouch, which you can buy at most camera stores.

Don't forget to have your camera hand-inspected if it has film inside.

### TIME

Jamaica is five hours behind Greenwich Mean Time. In autumn and winter, the time in Jamaica is five hours behind London, and the same time as in New York (Eastern Standard Time). Jamaica does not adjust for daylight saving time. Hence, from April to October Jamaica is six hours behind London and one hour behind New York.

### ELECTRICITY

Most hotels operate on 110 volts and 60 cycles, the same as in the USA and Canada. A few establishments operate on 220 volts and 50 cycles, as in the UK.

Sockets throughout Jamaica are usually two or three-pin – the US standard. Occa-sionally, particularly in older establishments, you may find three-square-pin sockets. The more upscale hotels can usually provide a transformer and adapter.

### WEIGHTS & MEASURES

Jamaica has been gradually converting from the Imperial system to the metric. Distances are still shown on some maps in miles and inches, although official documents now speak of kilometers and centimeters, and road signs now give speed limits and distances in kilometers. Because of this period of transition, information in this book tries to follow local usage – sometimes in metric, sometimes in Imperial. There is a conversion chart at the back of the book.

The antiquated English 'chain' – based on the cricket pitch – is still the most commonly used measure of distance in Jamaican parlance. It equals 22 yards, but few Jamaicans have the foggiest notion of that. 'Jus' a couple o' chains' can mean anywhere from exactly that to a couple miles or more.

Liquids are generally still measured in pints, quarts, and (Imperial) gallons; and weights in grams, ounces, and pounds. However, metric measures are increasingly used. Most imported food items are in metric.

### LAUNDRY

Self-service, coin-operated laundries are as rare as the Mauritian dodo. Drop-off laundries are more widely available in major resort towns. Elsewhere local women may offer to clean your clothes.

Most hotels – though not all – can arrange next-day or two-day laundry. Usually they will send your clothes out to be washed. For the better hotels, this will be to a professional laundrette. For more modest establishments, expect your laundry to be washed in a river and beaten over rocks (don't expect your clothes to be ironed).

Many establishments that advertise 'dry cleaning' don't use a chemical treatment. Often this means that your garment will be hand-washed in cold water. Be sure to check.

## TOILETS

There are very few public toilets. Those that do exist are places to avoid.

Many Jamaican men think nothing of urinating in public, even on the main streets of towns. Don't follow suit.

## HEALTH

Jamaica poses few health risks. The water is chlorinated and potable (though it's still wise to drink purified water), and food hygiene standards are generally high. The greatest threats are usually dehydration and an excess of sun and booze.

Travel health depends on your predeparture preparations, your day-to-day health care while traveling, and how you handle any medical problem or emergency that develops. Few travelers experience more than upset stomachs.

In Jamaica, if a medicine is available you can generally get it over the counter, and the price will be much cheaper than in Europe or North America. However, be careful to ensure that the expiration date has not passed and that correct storage conditions have been followed. It may be a good idea to leave unwanted medicines, syringes, and the like, with a local clinic, rather than carry them home.

If you require a particular medication, take an adequate supply, as it may not be available locally. Take the prescription with you to show that you legally use the medication, and consider taking part of the packaging showing the generic rather than the brand name (which may not be locally available), as it will make getting replacements easier.

While the following discussions of diseases may provoke anxiety, they are provided for your enlightenment and are not necessarily a reflection of the prevalence of particular diseases or threats.

### Travel Health Guides

There are a number of worthwhile books on travel health:

*Staying Healthy in Asia, Africa & Latin America,* Moon Publications – Probably the best all-around guide to carry, as it's compact but very detailed and well organized.

*Travelers' Health,* Dr Richard Dawood, Oxford University Press – Comprehensive, easy to read, authoritative and also highly recommended, although it's rather large to lug around.

*Travel with Children,* Maureen Wheeler, Lonely Planet Publications – Includes basic advice on travel health for younger children.

### Predeparture Preparations

**Health Insurance** An insurance policy to cover theft, loss, and medical problems is a wise idea. For more details about health insurance, see Travel Insurance in the Visas & Documents section, earlier in this chapter.

**Immunizations** No vaccinations are required to enter Jamaica unless you have visited the following locations within the previous six weeks: Asia, Africa, Central and South America, Dominican Republic, Haiti, and Trinidad & Tobago. Check with the JTB or your travel agent before departure to see what current regulations may be. Yellow fever is not a threat in Jamaica, but immunization may be required of travelers arriving from infected areas, chiefly in Africa and South America. Protection lasts 10 years.

All vaccinations should be recorded on an International Health Certificate, which is available from your physician or government health department. Tetanus and diptheria, typhoid, and infectious hepatitis are vaccinations you may want to look into. Your doctor may still recommend booster shots against measles or polio, diseases still prevalent in many developing countries. The period of protection offered by vaccinations differs widely and some are contraindicated if you are pregnant.

Plan ahead for getting your vaccinations: some require an initial shot followed by a booster, while others cannot be given together. It is recommended you seek medical advice at least six weeks prior to travel.

### Basic Rules

Taking care in what you eat and drink is the most important health rule; stomach upsets are the most likely travel health problem

## Medical Kit Checklist

A small, straightforward medical kit is a wise thing to carry. A possible list of kit supplies includes:

- ❏ **Aspirin** or **Panadol** – for pain or fever.
- ❏ **Antihistamine** (such as Benadryl) – useful as a decongestant for colds, allergies, to ease the itch from insect bites or stings or to help prevent motion sickness.
- ❏ **Antibiotics** – carry the prescription with you.
- ❏ **Kaolin preparation (Pepto-Bismol), Imodium,** or **Lomotil** – for stomach upsets.
- ❏ **Rehydration mixture** – for treatment of severe diarrhea. This is particularly important if traveling with children, but recommended for everyone.
- ❏ **Antiseptic** (such as Betadine) – for cuts and grazes.
- ❏ **Calamine lotion** – to ease irritation from bites or stings.
- ❏ **Bandages** and **Band-Aids**
- ❏ **Scissors, tweezers** and a **thermometer** (note that mercury thermometers are prohibited by airlines).
- ❏ **Throat lozenges** and **cold and flu tablets** – pseudoephedrine hydrochloride (Sudafed) may be useful if flying with a cold, to avoid ear damage.
- ❏ **Insect repellent, sunscreen, lip balm** and **water purification tablets.**
- ❏ **Multivitamins** – consider for long trips, when dietary vitamin intake may be inadequate.

The best medical kits on the market are made by Adventure Medical Kits (☎ 510-261-7414, 800-324-3517, fax 510-261-7419, amkusa@aol.com, www.adventure medicalkits.com), 5555 San Leandro, Oakland, CA 94624 USA.

(between 30% and 50% of travelers in a two-week stay experience this) but the majority of these upsets will be relatively minor. Don't become paranoid; trying the local food is part of the experience of travel.

**Water** Jamaica has its own natural purification system in its limestone base through which rainwater percolates. Water is generally safe to drink from faucets throughout the island. However, sanitation conditions in some outlying and backcountry areas are poor, and in the more extreme areas of the eastern parishes you should avoid drinking the water. The same is true for ice, particularly ice sold at street stands as *bellywash, snocones* or *skyjuice*, shaved-ice cones sweetened with fruit juice. If you are not certain that the water is safe, assume it isn't.

Reputable brands of bottled water or soft drinks are generally fine. Only use water from containers with an unbroken seal – not caps or corks. Take care with fruit juice, particularly if water may have been added. Milk should be treated with suspicion, as it is often unpasteurized. Boiled milk is fine if it is kept hygienically, and yogurt is always good. Tea or coffee should also be OK, since the water should have been boiled.

**Water Purification** This is rarely needed in Jamaica. However, if you're camping or using hovel-like budget accommodations and are unsure of your water supply, then purify it. The simplest way is to boil it vigorously for five minutes.

If you cannot boil water it should be treated chemically. Chlorine tablets (Puritabs, Steritabs, or other brand names) will kill many but not all pathogens, including giardia and amoebic cysts. Iodine is very effective in purifying water and is available in tablet form (such as Potable Aqua), but follow the directions carefully and remember that too much iodine can be harmful. Tincture of iodine (2%) can also be used. Four drops of tincture of iodine per liter or quart of clear water is the recommended dosage; the treated water should be left to stand for 20 to 30 minutes before drinking.

**Food** Jamaican restaurants pose relatively few hygiene problems. Salads and fruit should be washed with purified water or peeled where possible. Ice cream is usually OK, but beware of street vendors selling ice cream that has melted and been refrozen. Thoroughly cooked food is safest, but not if it has been left to cool or if it has been reheated. Shellfish such as oysters and clams should be avoided as well as undercooked meat, particularly in the form of mince. Steaming does not make shellfish safe for eating.

**Nutrition** Make sure your diet is well balanced. Eggs, tofu, beans, lentils, and nuts are all safe ways to get protein. Fruit you can peel (bananas or oranges, for example) is always safe and a good source of vitamins. Try to eat plenty of grains (rice) and bread. Remember overcooked food loses much of its nutritional value. If your diet isn't well balanced or if your food intake is insufficient, it's a good idea to take vitamin and iron supplements.

**Everyday Health** In Jamaica's backwaters, clean your teeth with purified water rather than tap water. Wash your hands before eating. Avoid overexposure to extremes: keep out of the sun at its peak, and dress warmly if hiking to Blue Mountain peak. Avoid potential diseases by dressing sensibly. You can get worm infections from walking barefoot. Seek local advice. In situations where there is no information, discretion is the better part of valor.

Normal body temperature is 98.6°F; more than 4°F higher indicates a high fever. The normal adult pulse rate is 60 to 100 per minute (children 80 to 100, babies 100 to 140). As a general rule, the pulse increases about 20 beats per minute for each 2°F rise in fever.

Respiration (breathing) rate is also an indicator of illness. Count the number of breaths per minute: between 12 and 20 is normal for adults and older children (up to 30 for younger children, 40 for babies). People with a high fever or serious respiratory illness breathe more quickly than normal. More than 40 shallow breaths a minute may indicate pneumonia.

## Medical Treatment

An embassy or consulate can usually recommend a good place to go. So can five-star hotels, although they often recommend doctors with five-star prices. (This is when that medical insurance really comes in useful!) Jamaica's medical standards are fairly high, but for the most serious ailments, the best advice is to go home.

## Climatic & Geographical Considerations

**Sunburn** In the tropics you can get sunburned surprisingly quickly, even on cloudy days. Many people ruin their holiday by getting badly burned soon after they arrive in Jamaica. Don't underestimate the power of the tropical sun, no matter how dark your skin color. Use a sunscreen with a protective factor of 15 or more. Take extra care to cover areas that don't normally see sun – such as your feet. Be *very* careful if going topless or nude. Build up your exposure to the sun gradually. A hat provides added protection, and you should also use zinc cream or some other barrier cream for your nose and lips. If you do end up with a burn, calamine lotion and aloe vera will provide soothing relief.

**Prickly Heat** Prickly heat is an itchy rash caused by excessive perspiration trapped under the skin. It usually strikes people who have just arrived in a hot climate and whose pores have not yet opened sufficiently to cope with increased sweating. Keeping cool and bathing often, using a mild talcum powder, or resorting to air-con may help alleviate symptoms.

**Dehydration & Heat Exhaustion** You'll sweat profusely in Jamaica. Make sure you drink enough – don't rely on feeling thirsty to indicate when you should drink. Not needing to urinate or very dark yellow urine is a danger sign. Always carry a water bottle with you on hiking trips. You'll lose quite a bit of salt through sweating. Salt deficiency is characterized by fatigue, lethargy, headaches, giddiness, and muscle cramps, and in this case salt tablets may help. Vomiting or

---

### Healing Powers of 'Sinkle Bible'

Jamaicans call aloe vera the 'healing plant' (and also 'sinkle bible,' from its botanical name, *Sempervivum*) and swear by aloe's curative powers. Jamaicans use it to cure sunburn, heat rash, burns, insect bites, eczema, psoriasis, and other ailments. The plant grows profusely on the island and is easily recognized by its thick, hard-cased, spiny-edged leaves, which are sliced in half to reveal a mauve jelly that is simply wiped on the skin (it stains clothes, so don't spill any). Mixed with water, it is also used as an eye wash to soothe conjunctivitis. I don't recommend another local treatment – mixed with garlic and drunk to cleanse the blood. You'll find plenty of Jamaicans selling aloe on beaches at major resorts. I do recommend a massage using a peeled aloe leaf for US$5 or so – it feels great.

---

diarrhea can also deplete your liquid and salt levels. Anhydrotic heat exhaustion, caused by an inability to sweat, is quite rare. Unlike other forms of heat exhaustion, it is likely to strike people who have been in Jamaica's hot climate for some time, rather than newcomers.

Avoid booze by day, as your body uses water to process alcohol. Drink water, soft drinks, or – best of all – coconut water straight from the husk.

**Heat Stroke** This serious, sometimes fatal, condition can occur if the body's heat-regulating mechanism breaks down and the body temperature rises to dangerous levels. Long, continuous periods of exposure to high temperatures can leave you vulnerable to heat stroke. You should avoid drinking binges or strenuous activity when you first arrive in Jamaica.

The symptoms are feeling unwell, not sweating very much (or at all), and a high body temperature. Where sweating has ceased the skin becomes flushed and red. Severe, throbbing headaches and lack of coordination will also occur, and the sufferer may be confused or aggressive. Eventually the victim will become delirious or convulse. Hospitalization is essential, but meanwhile get victims out of the sun, remove their clothing, cover them with a wet sheet or towel, and fan them continually.

**Fungal Infections** Hot weather fungal infections are most likely to occur on the scalp, between the toes or fingers (athlete's foot), in the groin (jock itch or crotch rot), and on the body (ringworm). You get ringworm (which is a fungal infection, not a worm) from infected animals or by walking on damp areas, such as shower floors.

To prevent fungal infections, wear loose, comfortable clothes, avoid artificial fibers, wash frequently, and dry carefully. If you do get an infection, wash the infected area daily with a disinfectant or medicated soap and water, then rinse and dry well. Apply an antifungal powder such as the widely available Tinaderm. Try to expose the infected area to air or sunlight as much as possible, and wash all towels and underwear in hot water (as well as changing them often).

**Motion Sickness** Eating lightly before and during a trip will reduce the chances of motion sickness. Find a place that minimizes disturbance – near the wing on aircraft, close to midship on boats, near the center on buses. Fresh air usually helps. Commercial anti-motion-sickness preparations, which can cause drowsiness, have to be taken before the trip commences; when you're feeling sick it's too late. Ginger is a natural preventative and is available in capsule form.

**Jet Lag** Travelers arriving in Jamaica from North America will feel relatively minor effects, if any. Those coming from Europe and farther afield will be more susceptible.

The effects will usually be gone within three days of arrival, but there are ways to minimize the impact of jet lag:

- Rest for a couple of days prior to departure; try to avoid late nights and last-minute dashes.

- Try to select flight schedules that minimize sleep deprivation; arriving late in the day means you can go to sleep soon after you arrive. For very long flights, try to organize a stopover.
- Eye drops and nasal sprays can help alleviate the ill effects of 'dry,' recirculated cabin air.
- Avoid excessive eating and alcohol during the flight. Instead, drink plenty of non-carbonated, non-alcoholic drinks such as fruit juice or water.
- Make yourself comfortable by wearing loose-fitting clothes and perhaps bringing an eye mask and ear plugs to help you sleep.

## Diseases of Poor Sanitation

**Diarrhea** A change of water, food, or climate can all cause the runs. Despite precautions, you may still have a bout of mild travelers' diarrhea; a few rushed trips to the toilet with no other symptoms is not indicative of a serious problem. Dehydration is the main danger with any diarrhea, particularly for children. Fluid replacement remains the mainstay of management. Weak black tea with a little sugar, soda water, or soft drinks allowed to go flat and diluted 50% with water are all good. For severe diarrhea, a rehydrating solution is necessary to replace minerals and salts. Commercially available oral rehydration salts are very useful. Stick to a bland diet as you recover.

Lomotil or Imodium can be used to bring relief from the symptoms, although they do not actually cure the problem. Only use these drugs if absolutely necessary – if you *must* travel. For children, Imodium is preferable, but under all circumstances fluid replacement is the main message. Do not use these drugs if diarrhea is accompanied with a high fever or severe dehydration.

**Giardiasis** The parasite causing this intestinal disorder is present in contaminated water. The symptoms are stomach cramps, nausea, a bloated stomach, watery, foul-smelling diarrhea, and frequent gas. Giardiasis can appear several weeks after you have been exposed to the parasite. The symptoms may disappear for a few days and then return; this can go on for several weeks.

Tinidazole, known as Fasigyn, or metronidazole (Flagyl) are the recommended drugs for treatment. Either can be used in a single-treatment dose. Antibiotics are of no use for giardiasis.

**Dysentery** This is caused by contaminated food or water and is characterized by severe diarrhea, often with blood or mucus in the stool. There are two kinds of dysentery: bacillary, characterized by a high fever and rapidly onset headache, vomiting, and stomach pains; and amoebic, which is often more gradual in the onset of symptoms, with cramping abdominal pain and vomiting less likely, and fever may not be present. A stool test is necessary to diagnose which kind of dysentery you have, so you should seek medical help urgently.

Flagyl or Fasigyn can be used as presumptive treatment in an emergency.

**Cholera** Jamaica has not had a cholera outbreak in many years, although it is present on Haiti and in nearby Central American countries.

**Viral Gastroenteritis** This is caused not by bacteria but, as the name suggests, by a virus. It is characterized by stomach cramps, diarrhea, and sometimes by vomiting or a slight fever. All you can do is rest and drink lots of fluids.

**Hepatitis** Hepatitis A is a very common problem amongst travelers to areas with poor sanitation. With good water and adequate sewage disposal in most industrialized countries since the 1940s, very few young adults now have any natural immunity and must be protected with the new vaccine Havrix or the short-lasting antibody gamma globulin.

The disease is spread by contaminated food or water. The symptoms are fever, chills, headache, fatigue, feelings of weakness, and aches and pains, followed by loss of appetite, nausea, vomiting, abdominal pain, dark urine, light-colored feces, jaundiced skin, and the whites of the eyes may turn yellow. You should seek medical advice, but in general there is not much you can do apart from rest, drink lots of fluids, eat lightly and avoid fatty foods. People who have had hepatitis must forego alcohol for six months after the illness, as hepatitis attacks the liver and it needs that amount of time to recover.

Hepatitis B, which used to be called serum hepatitis, is spread through contact with infected blood, blood products, or bodily fluids, for example through sexual contact, unsterilized needles, and blood transfusions. Other risk situations include having a shave or tattoo in a local shop, or having your ears pierced. The symptoms of type B are much the same as type A except that they are more severe.

Although there is no treatment for hepatitis B, an effective prophylactic vaccine is readily available in most countries. Persons who should receive a hepatitis B vaccination include anyone who anticipates contact with blood or other bodily secretions, either as a health care worker or through sexual contact with the local population.

Hepatitis Non-A and Non-B is a blanket term formerly used for several different strains of hepatitis, which have now been separately identified.

Tests are available for these strands, but are very expensive. Travelers shouldn't be too paranoid about the apparent proliferation of hepatitis strains; they are fairly rare (so far), and following the same precautions as for A and B should be all that's necessary to avoid them.

**Typhoid** Contaminated water and food are responsible. Vaccination against typhoid is not totally effective and it is one of the most dangerous infections, so medical help must be sought. The last major outbreak of typhoid struck the southwest corner of Jamaica in 1992 and was attributed to contaminated dairy products.

In its early stages typhoid resembles many other illnesses: sufferers may feel like they have a bad cold or flu on the way, as early symptoms are a headache, a sore throat, and a fever that rises a little each day until it is around 104°F or more. The victim's pulse is often slow relative to the degree of fever present – unlike a normal fever when the pulse increases – and gets slower as the fever rises. There may also be vomiting, diarrhea, or constipation.

In the second week, the high fever and slow pulse continue and a few pink spots may appear on the body; trembling, delirium, weakness, weight loss, and dehydration are other symptoms. If there are no further complications, the fever and other symptoms will slowly fade during the third week. But you must get medical help before this because pneumonia (acute infection of the lungs) or peritonitis (perforated bowel) are common complications, and because typhoid is very infectious.

The fever should be treated by keeping the victim cool, and dehydration should also be watched for.

**Worms** These parasites are common in rural, tropical areas. A stool test when you return home is not a bad idea. They can be present on unwashed vegetables or in undercooked meat, and you can pick them up through your skin by walking barefoot. Infestations may not show up for some time, and although they are generally not serious, if left untreated they can cause severe health problems.

## Diseases Spread by People & Animals

**Tetanus** This potentially fatal disease is present in Jamaica as in other undeveloped tropical areas. It is difficult to treat, but is preventable with immunization. Tetanus occurs when a wound becomes infected by a germ that lives in the feces of animals or people; clean all cuts, punctures, or animal bites. Tetanus is also known as lockjaw, and the first symptom may be discomfort in swallowing, or stiffening of the jaw and neck; this is followed by painful convulsions of the jaw and whole body.

**Sexually Transmitted Diseases** There's a high prevalence of venereal diseases in Jamaica. While sexual abstinence is the only certain preventative, using condoms is also effective. Gonorrhea and syphilis are the most common of these diseases; sores, blisters, or rashes around the genitals, and discharges or pain when urinating are common symptoms. Symptoms for women may be less marked or not observed. Syphilis symptoms eventually disappear, but the disease continues and can cause severe problems – even death – in later years. The treatment of gonorrhea and syphilis is by antibiotics.

There is no cure for herpes.

Condoms are widely available in pharmacies and general stores throughout Jamaica. Nonetheless, they may not be available when you need them. Take condoms with you.

**HIV & AIDS** The Human Immunodeficiency Virus (HIV) may develop into Acquired Immune Deficiency Syndrome (AIDS). HIV is a relatively small yet not insignificant problem in Jamaica. (As of September 1997, 1265 people had died of AIDS in Jamaica. It is particularly prevalent in Montego Bay and St James parish, with nearly 229 HIV cases per 100,000 people, compared to 144 in Kingston, and 24 in Manchester.) Any exposure to blood or bodily fluids puts the individual at risk. In Jamaica, transmission is predominantly through heterosexual sexual activity. Apart from abstinence, the most effective preventative is always to practice safe sex using condoms. It is impossible to detect the HIV-positive status of an otherwise healthy-looking person without a blood test.

HIV can also be spread through infected blood transfusions; Jamaica cannot afford to screen blood for transfusions. The virus can also be spread by dirty needles – vaccinations, acupuncture, tattooing, and ear or body piercing can potentially be as dangerous as intravenous drug use if the equipment is not clean. If you do need an injection, ask to see the syringe unwrapped in front of you, or better still, take a needle and syringe pack with you when you go overseas – it is a cheap insurance package against infection.

Jamaica has a toll-free information line on AIDS, HIV, and STDs (☎ 0888-991-4444, 967-3764, 967-3830). Singer Buju Banton's Operation Willy helps children with AIDS through Jamaica AIDS Support (☎ 968-8867), 11a Osbourne Rd, Kingston 10.

## Insect-Borne Diseases

**Malaria** Fortunately malaria isn't present in Jamaica. It's spread by mosquito bites, but among Caribbean islands is relegated to Hispaniola (Haiti and the Dominican Republic) and parts of Cuba.

**Dengue Fever** Although extremely rare, dengue fever is present in Jamaica, notably in Portland parish and around Kingston, where serious outbreaks occurred in 1998. There is no prophylactic available for this mosquito-spread disease. A sudden onset of fever, headaches, and severe joint and muscle pains (hence its colloquial name, 'broken bone disease') are the first signs. Later a rash starts on the trunk of the body and spreads to the limbs and face. After another few days, the fever will subside and recovery will begin. Serious complications are not common.

The mosquitoes that transmit dengue fever most commonly bite from dusk to dawn, when travelers are advised to wear light-colored clothing, long pants and long-sleeved shirts, and use mosquito repellents containing the compound Deet (diethyl-metatoluamide) on exposed areas, avoid highly scented perfumes or after-shave, and use a mosquito net and coil.

**Chagas' Disease** In rural areas this parasitic disease is transmitted by a bug that hides in crevices, palm fronds, and often the thatched roofs of huts. It comes out to feed at night. A hard, violet-colored swelling appears at the site of the bite in about a week. Usually the body overcomes the disease unaided, but sometimes it continues and can eventually lead to death years later. Chagas' disease can be treated in its early stages, but it is best to avoid thatched-roof huts, sleep under a mosquito net, and use insecticides and insect repellents.

**Typhus** Typhus is spread by ticks, mites, or lice. It begins as a bad cold, followed by a fever, chills, headache, muscle pains, and a body rash. Often a large painful sore appears at the site of the bite, and nearby lymph nodes can become swollen and painful.

Check your skin carefully for ticks after walking in a danger area, such as a tropical forest. A strong insect repellent can help.

## Cuts & Scratches

Skin punctures can easily become infected in hot climates and may be difficult to heal. Treat any cut with an antiseptic such as Betadine. Where possible, avoid bandages and Band-Aids, which can keep wounds wet. Coral cuts are notoriously slow to heal, as the coral injects a weak venom into the wound. Clean any cut thoroughly with sodium per-oxide if available.

## Bites & Stings

Bee and wasp stings are usually more painful than dangerous. Calamine lotion will give relief, and ice packs will reduce the pain and swelling. There are some spiders with dangerous bites, but antivenins are usually available.

Various fish and other sea creatures can sting or bite dangerously or are dangerous to eat. Fortunately, Jamaica has no venomous snakes.

**No-See-'Ums** These well-named irritants are almost microscopically small fleas that hang out on beaches and appear around dusk (especially after rain) with a voracious appetite. Their bite is out of all proportion to their size. You'll rarely, if ever, see the darn things, despite the fact that they seem to attack en masse, seemingly when you're not looking. They prefer the taste of ankles. Cover your ankles if possible. Most insect repellents don't faze them. A better bet is a liberal application of Avon's Skin So Soft, a cosmetic that even the US Army swears by.

**Jellyfish** Local advice is the best way to avoid contact with these sea creatures with their stinging tentacles. Dousing in vinegar will deactivate any stingers that have not 'fired.' In addition to calamine lotion, anti-histamines and analgesics may reduce the reaction and relieve the pain.

**Bedbugs & Lice** Often, microscopic bed-bugs live in dirty mattresses and bedding. Spots of blood on bedclothes or on the wall around the bed can be read as a suggestion to find another hotel.

All lice, which are larger and easy to see, cause itching and discomfort. They make themselves at home in your hair (head lice), your clothing (body lice), or in your pubic hair (crabs). You catch lice through direct contact with infected people or by sharing combs, clothing, and the like. Powder or shampoo treatment will kill the lice; infected clothing should be washed in very hot water.

**Scabies** Scabies is an infestation of micro-scopic mites and is acquired through sexual contact, bed linen, towels, or clothing. Scabies is ubiquitous in Jamaica, notably among people living in rustic conditions.

The first signs – severe itching caused by infestation of eggs and feces under the skin – usually appear three to four weeks after infestation (as soon as 24 hours for second infestations) and is worse at night. Infesta-tion appears as tiny welts and pimples, often in a dotted line, most commonly around the groin and lower abdomen, between the fingers, on the elbows, and under the armpits. Other bacterial skin infections may occur.

Treatment is by pesticidal lotions (prescription-only in the USA) sold over-the-counter at local pharmacies in Jamaica. The entire body must be covered. Often two treat-ments within 48 hours are required. Personal hygiene is critical to exterminating the mites. At the same time as using the treatment, you must wash *all* your clothing and bedding in hot water (don't forget your luggage and any other item where mites might be present).

## Women's Health

Poor diet, lowered resistance due to the use of antibiotics, and even contraceptive pills can lead to vaginal infections. Wearing skirts or loose-fitting trousers and cotton under-wear will help to prevent infections while traveling in hot climates.

Yeast infections, characterized by a rash, itch, and discharge, can be treated with a vinegar or even lemon-juice douche, or with yogurt. Nystatin suppositories are the usual medical prescription.

Trichomoniasis is a more serious infection; symptoms are a discharge and a burning sensation when urinating. Sexual partners must also be treated, and if a vinegar-water douche is not effective, medical attention should be sought. Metronidazole (Flagyl) is the prescribed drug.

If you are pregnant, note that most miscarriages occur during the first three months of pregnancy, so this is the most risky time to travel.

Periods often become irregular, or even cease, while on the road. There are health posts and family planning clinics in urban centers throughout Jamaica, where you can seek advice and have a urine test to determine whether you are pregnant or not.

## Health Facilities

Jamaica's health service is administered jointly by parish councils and the Ministry of Health and Environmental Control. Together they operate 23 general hospitals and seven specialist hospitals, plus about 350 regional clinics. There are also several private hospitals. Hospitals are located in most major towns and cities, but note that the nearest hospital to Ocho Rios is in St Ann (about 7 miles west) and the nearest hospitals to Negril are 20 miles away, in Lucea and Savanna-la-Mar. Most maintain 24-hour emergency wards.

You'll find private and government health clinics in towns throughout the island. In addition, most large hotels have resident nurses, plus doctors on call. If it's within your budget, private medical clinics and hospitals are to be preferred, as the public health system has suffered significant budgetary cutbacks in recent years, and service is notoriously slow and less efficient.

You can help contribute to Jamaica's welfare by donating to the Rebecca Pike Foundation for Sick Children (☎ 962-3265, fax 962-1461), c/o Diana McIntyre-Pike, Astra Country Inn, 62 Ward Ave, PO Box 60, Mandeville, which works to improve facilities at the Hargreaves Memorial Hospital in Mandeville; and Food for the Poor (☎ 984-5005), c/o Christian Ferdinand Mahfood, PO Box 557, White Marl Arawak Museum, Spanish Town, which is Jamaica's largest charity.

See regional chapters for hospital listings.

## Ambulances

The emergency number for public ambulances is ☎ 110.

The St John's ambulance brigade also provides a free ambulance service in Kingston (☎ 926-7656) and Ocho Rios (☎ 974-5126). Deluxe Ambulance Service has a 24-hour emergency service in Kingston (☎ 923-7415), as does AmbuCare (☎ 978-2327).

Wings Jamaica also provides a local and overseas 24-hour air ambulance service (☎ 923-6573, 923-5416), as does Karvinair Air Ambulance (☎ 978-4913).

## Medical Assistance Organizations

Many companies offer a range of medical assistance for travelers. Most maintain 24-hour emergency hotline centers that connect travelers to professional medical staff worldwide. Many also provide emergency evacuation, medical attention, and payment of on-site medical treatment. Some companies provide services for a set annual membership fee; others offer varying coverage levels for you to choose from.

The Council on International Education Exchange (CIEE) offers low-cost, short-term insurance policies called 'Trip Safe' to holders of the International Student Identification Card (ISIC), International Youth Card (IYC), and International Teachers Identification Card (ITIC).

North American medical assistance organizations include:

Air Ambulance Professionals
    (☎ 954-491-0555, 800-752-4195)
    Ft Lauderdale Executive Airport,
    1575 W Commercial Blvd, Annex 2
    Ft Lauderdale, FL 33309
    You can receive 24-hour worldwide medical transportation, with all flights staffed by 'aeromedically certified medical attendants.'

International Association for Medical Assistance for Travelers (IAMAT)
(☎ 716-754-4883)
417 Center St, Lewiston, NY 14092
IAMAT is an information service to assist travelers needing medical attention.

International SOS Assistance
(☎ 215-244-1500, 800-523-8662, fax 244-0165, individual@intsos.com, www.intsos.com)
PO Box 11568, Philadelphia, PA 19116
This service provides 24-hour emergency services for insured members, with various plans at reasonable rates.

## WOMEN TRAVELERS
### Attitudes toward Women

'Political correctness' hasn't yet filtered down from the educated Jamaican middle class to the male masses. Many Jamaican men display behavior and attitudes that might shock visiting women, often expressing disdain for the notion of female equality or women's rights. Rape is common in Jamaica, although it rarely involves female tourists. You can expect to receive heaps of attention and no-holds-barred compliments on your bodily assets.

If you're single, it will be assumed that you're on the island seeking a 'likkle love beneat' de palms.' Any remonstration to the contrary will likely be met with wearying attempts to get you to change your mind. Black women can expect to hear a 'roots' trip.

If you go along with the flirting, don't expect a Jamaican man to understand if you've no intent of going all the way. Your innocent acceptance will be taken as a sign of acquiescence. The Jamaican male has a fragile ego and is likely to react strongly to feeling like a fool. If this behavior is offensive, don't beat about the bush for fear of hurting the man's feelings. He'll most likely take your rejection in good humor, with a bawdy jibe at your lack of good taste.

Many foreign women welcome these advances, as evidenced by the proliferation of 'rent-a-Rastas' – semi-professional good-time guys, or gigolos – on the arms of North American and European women. Very frequently, the man is excited more by your economic clout than your looks – a foreign catch brings status and the possibility for wheedling some cash. You'll be the money-bags in any romantic encounter, however brief. Don't expect your Jamaican 'boyfriend' to stand up for you in tricky circumstances, including with other males.

In the resort areas, be prepared for constant approaches.

You are far less likely to engage with Jamaican women, except higglers and others working in the tourist trade, partly because most women's lives are taken up with domestic duties and breadwinning. Perhaps for this reason, many younger Jamaican women also seem to hold a stereotypical image of foreign females and resent what they see as poaching. A clear exception is in Kingston, where thousands of educated professional women live a cosmopolitan lifestyle and are less tethered by the hardships of raising children in dire economic circumstances. Such women range more freely throughout society and more fully engage with foreigners as equals.

Also see Women in Jamaica in the Society & Culture section in the Facts about Jamaica chapter.

### Safety Precautions

Women traveling alone can reduce unwanted attention by dressing modestly when away from the beach. You should avoid walking alone at night and otherwise traveling alone in remote areas. If you take a fishing or diving trip with a local fisherman, do not go unaccompanied.

Women travelers should *not* attempt to hitchhike. And, if driving, be extremely cautious about whom you choose to pick up roadside.

### Organizations & Resources

Women's organizations in Jamaica include:

Association of Women's Organizations in Jamaica
(☎ 968-8260) 2 Waterloo Rd, Kingston 10

Jamaica Federation of Women
(☎ 926-7726) 74 Arnold Rd, Kingston 5

The Woman's Club
(☎ 927-7076) 101 Hope Rd, Kingston 6

Woman's Crisis Center
(☎ 929-2997) 18 Ripon Rd, Kingston 5

Women's Center of Jamaica Foundation
(☎ 929-7608) 42 Trafalgar Rd, Kingston 10

Women's Resource & Outreach Center
(☎ 929-6945) 47 Beechwood Ave, Kingston 5

Good resources abroad include the International Federation of Women's Travel Organizations (☎ 602-956-7175), 4545 N 36th St No 126, Phoenix, AZ 85018. The *Handbook for Women Travelers* by Maggie and Gemma Ross and the *Traveling Woman* by Dena Kaye are also replete with handy tips and practicalities. Two other compulsory compendiums are *Travelers' Tales: Gutsy Women, Travel Tips & Wisdom from the Road* and *Travelers' Tales: A Woman's World*, both by Mary Beth Bond.

## GAY & LESBIAN TRAVELERS

Jamaica is an adamantly homophobic nation. Homosexual intercourse between men is illegal, and anti-gay hysteria is a staple of musical lyrics, such as Buju Banton's *Boom Bye Bye* ('bum him up like an ol' tyre wheel') and those of Shabba Ranks, whose advocacy of 'gay bashing' reflects – and no doubt sponsors – the bigoted mind-set. Homosexuality is a subject that evokes extreme reactions among Jamaicans, and it is difficult to hold a serious discussion on the topic.

Likewise, the attitude of the majority of Jamaicans toward HIV and AIDS – which is considered a 'gay disease' – is insufferably narrow, and sympathy for those struck by the disease is pitifully lacking.

Most Jamaican gays are still in the closet. You rarely see overtly gay Jamaicans – intolerance is too great. Nonetheless, many hoteliers are gay or gay-tolerant, and you should not be put off from visiting the island. Just don't expect to be able to display your homosexuality openly without an adverse reaction.

### Organizations & Resources

I'm not aware of any gay and lesbian support groups in Jamaica, but the following organizations can provide information and assistance in planning a trip and will point you toward specialist travel agents and tour operators:

International Gay & Lesbian Association
(☎ 212-620-7310, fax 924-2657,
ltcscnyc@aol.com, www.gaycenter.org)
1 Little West 12th St, New York, NY 10014

International Gay & Lesbian Travel Association
(☎ 954-776-2626, 800-448-8550, fax 776-3303,
iglta@iglta.org, www.iglta.org)
4431 N Federal Hwy No 304
Ft Lauderdale, FL 33308

Travel Alternatives Group
(☎ 415-552-5140, 800-464-2987, fax 552-5104)
2300 Market St No 142
San Francisco, CA 94114

Ferrari Publications produces several travel guides for gays and lesbians, including the *Spartacus International Gay Guide* (☎ 602-863-2408, 800-962-2912, fax 602-439-3952, ferrari@q-net.com), PO Box 37887, Phoenix, AZ 85069. Another valuable resource is *Odysseus: The International Gay Travel Planner* (☎ 516-944-5330, 800-257-5344, fax 516-944-7540, odyusa@odyusa.com), PO Box 1548, Port Washington, New York, NY 11050.

## DISABLED TRAVELERS

Disabled travelers will need to plan their vacation carefully, as few allowances have been made in Jamaica. Things have begun to improve in recent years, however, partly as a result of lobbying by Derrick Palmer, director of Disabled Persons International (☎ 931-6155), 9 Tunbridge Terrace, Kingston 9. Another useful resource is the Combined Disabilities Association (☎ 929-1177, fax 920-9389), PO Box 220, Liguanea, Kingston 6, which acts as an umbrella organization.

Two other organizations include the Jamaica Association for Mentally Handicapped Children (☎ 955-4849) and the Jamaica Association for the Deaf (☎ 926-7709).

Most hotels built in recent years have taken account of disabled travelers, but overall only a small percentage of hotels in Jamaica have facilities. The JTB or Derrick Palmer can provide a list of hotels with wheelchair ramps. Check with the individual hotel before making your reservation.

New construction codes mandate ramps and parking spots for disabled people at shopping plazas and other select sites.

## Organizations & Resources

Contact the following for more information:

Society for the Advancement of Travel for the
Handicapped
(☎ 212-447-7284, fax 725-8253)
347 Fifth Ave No 610, New York, NY 10016
Annual membership costs US$45.
They publish a quarterly magazine *Open World*
(subscriptions cost US$13).

American Foundation for the Blind
(☎ 212-502-7600, 800-232-5463,
afbinfo@afb.org, www.afb.org)
11 Penn Plaza No 300, New York, NY 10001

Flying Wheels Travel
(☎ 507-451-5005, 800-535-6790, fax 507-451-1685)
PO Box 382, Owatanna, MN 55060
A full-service travel agency for the physically
challenged.

## SENIOR TRAVELERS

One-third of travelers worldwide are over
50, and travel companies court seniors with
discounts, usually passed on to members of
seniors' organizations. Most US airlines
offer senior discount programs for travelers
62 or over. Some car-rental companies also
extend discounts – ask and you may receive.

Air Jamaica Express offers a seniors' fare
of US$35 between Montego Bay and
Kingston, and similar discounts on other
routes. Otherwise, Jamaica is virtually
devoid of seniors' discounts.

## Organizations & Resources

The American Association of Retired
Persons (AARP) offers discounts on hotels,
car rentals, and the like through its Purchase
Privilege Program (☎ 800-424-3410), 601 E
St NW, Washington, DC 20049. It also
arranges travel for members through AARP
Travel Experience. Annual membership
costs US$8. The Golden Age Travelers Club
(☎ 415-296-0151, 800-258-8880, fax 415-776-
0753, youleisure@msn.com), Pier 27, Embar-
cadero, San Francisco, CA 94111, offers
similar services and has special programs
aboard cruise ships.

You'll find another handy source of tips
on seniors' discounts in the monthly
newsletter of the National Council of Senior
Citizens (☎ 301-578-8800, 800-373-6407, fax

301-578-8999), 8403 Colesville Rd No 1200,
Silver Spring, MD 20910-3314.

## TRAVEL WITH CHILDREN

Jamaica courts the family traveler aggressively, and the larger hotels compete by providing facilities for children. Most hotels
provide a babysitter or nanny by advance
request. Several all-inclusive resorts, such as
Poinciana (Negril), FDR Resort (Runaway
Bay), SuperClubs Boscobel Beach (Boscobel, near Ocho Rios), and Sandals Beaches
(Negril and Whitehouse) cater specifically
to families and have an impressive range of
activities and amenities for children. Most
hotels also offer free accommodations or
greatly reduced rates for children staying in
their parents' room (a child is usually
defined as being 12 years or younger, but
some count those 16 or younger).

It's a good idea to pre-arrange necessities
such as cribs, babysitters, cots, and baby food
at hotels other than family resorts.

Villas and apartments are good options
for families. Most come fully staffed, allowing you to leave the children with the housekeeper if you feel comfortable doing so
(check that this is in accordance with rental
terms).

Rascals in Paradise (☎ 415-978-9800, 800-
872-7225 in the USA) offers all-inclusive,
family-vacation group trips (limited to six
families). Premier Cruises (☎ 407-783-5061,
800-327-7113, 800-990-7770) specializes in
family cruises that include Jamaica on its
itineraries.

*Travel with Children*, by Lonely Planet
co-founder Maureen Wheeler, gives you the
low-down on preparing for family travel.
Other handy resources are the *Family Travel
Guide Catalog* and *Family Travel Times
Newsletter*.

## USEFUL ORGANIZATIONS

The Jamaica Information Service (☎ 926-
3740, 888-991-2327, fax 926-6715), 58a Half
Way Tree Rd, Kingston 10, dispenses information geared to domestic issues such as
housing law, government regulations, and
health issues. The head office (☎ 926-3740,
888-991-2327, fax 926-6715) is at 58a Half

Way Tree Rd, Kingston 10, and there are also local offices in most major cities.

The Institute of Jamaica (☎ 922-0620), 12 East St, Kingston, has reading rooms. It publishes the *Jamaica Journal* and is responsible for maintaining museums in the Kingston area.

A branch of the Institute of Jamaica, the Jamaica National Heritage Trust (☎ 922-1287, fax 967-1703), Headquarters House, 79 Duke St, PO Box 8934, Kingston, is responsible for preserving, restoring, and maintaining more than 300 declared monuments nationwide. It maintains the Jamaica Archives (☎ 984-2581) and Archives Record Dept (☎ 984-3041) in Spanish Town.

Brits who sorely miss their favorite newspaper will find the latest dailies in the information library of the British Council (☎ 929-6915, fax 929-7090), First Mutual Life Bldg, 64 Knutsford Blvd, Kingston.

## DANGERS & ANNOYANCES

For all its tropical beauty and charm, Jamaica has plenty of petty annoyances – mostly harassment – that can be psychologically intimidating and scary. It helps to have a sense of humor.

To help make Jamaica more user-friendly, JTB has started training government staff (such as immigration officers, airport porters, and others who liaise with tourists), with a new industry-wide training program – 'Team Jamaica' – which will emphasize customer service.

The JTB also publishes a pocket-size pamphlet, 'Helpful Hints for Your Vacation,' containing concise tips for safer travel. The JTB has a hotline (☎ 888-991-9999) for emergency assistance.

The US State Dept publishes travel advisories (☎ 202-647-5225, fax 647-3000) that advise US citizens of trouble spots. Contact Citizens Emergency Center, Room 4811, Dept of State, Washington, DC 20520-4818. US embassies and consulates abroad can also be consulted.

Likewise, the British Foreign & Commonwealth Office (☎ 020-7238-4503, fax 020-7238-4545), Travel Advice Unit, Consular Division, Foreign & Commonwealth Office, 1 Palace St, London SW1E 5HE, issues travel advice warnings.

**Cockroaches** This being the tropics, cockroaches are everywhere. Many are veritable giants! Even the fanciest hotels have them. You may not be used to them, and many visitors find the ugly bugs repugnant. However, they're not really a health problem, except in restaurants, where they can contaminate food.

**Crime** The island as a whole is generally safe, and the vast majority of travelers return home without having suffered any mishaps whatsoever. Most Jamaicans are extremely law-abiding citizens. Their sense of honor and pride runs deep, and their tolerance of thieves and criminals is extremely low. Jamaicans have even been known to stone or beat to death thieves caught in the act.

Nonetheless, the island's pervasive poverty fosters crime, and the volatile nature of the Jamaican psyche adds its own catalyst. Jamaica, and in particular Kingston, has the worst reputation in the Caribbean for violent crime. But violent crime intrudes very little on the visitor. The majority of crime is related to drug wars fought in ghettoes far from tourist centers.

Among Jamaica's underclass, however, resentment against whites can run deep. Many seem permanently 'pissed off' and – as one reader reported – 'at war' with foreigners, whom they are often intent to rip off. (In 1998 in St Ann, a spate of incidents erupted – many readers have written of instances there involving attacks with machetes!)

But, on the whole, crime against visitors has dropped significantly since the initiation of 'Operation Shining Armour' in June 1994 – a collaborative effort by the Ministry of Tourism and Ministry of National Security to combat crime. Police operations were beefed up in tourist resorts. Villas and apartments were required to be fitted with security systems wired to a central police command. And major hotels also have security guards to protect the grounds (unfortunately, some 'guards' dress like ragamuffins and many have the disconcerting habit of skulking around in the undergrowth – often with knives in hand – while shadowing guests arriving back at the hotel late at night). If you're renting an out-of-the-way private villa or cottage, check in advance with the rental agency to establish whether security is provided.

Most crime against travelers is petty, opportunistic crime. Take sensible precautions with your valuables. Carry your wallet in your front pocket, or better, in a money belt or similar pouch beneath your clothing. Steer clear of ghettoes, where you can easily get into serious trouble. Try to avoid walking at night, but if you do, stick close to main thoroughfares. The US State Dept and British Foreign & Commonwealth Office travel advisories also warn against taking public transport and visiting downtown Kingston unless absolutely necessary. However, downtown Kingston is usually quite safe by day (it's certainly *not* an area to be wandering around alone at night).

Muggings do occur, and several visitors have been robbed in their cars or hotel rooms. You should take adequate precautions. Keep hotel doors and windows securely locked at night. Don't open your door to anyone who cannot prove his or her identity. If you camp, take care in choosing your site. It is very unsafe to camp in the wild, especially alone or in small groups. Be cautious if invited to see the 'real Jamaica' by a stranger. And be constantly wary of young Jamaican males with whom you may strike up a seeming friendship; many readers have written to tell of being assaulted and robbed by locals whom they've come to trust. Use your discretion.

**Critters to Beware** Sea urchins cluster in great numbers on the seabed and on coral walls. Their porcupine-like spines are designed for defense. If you step on one, the 'quills' will pierce your skin and break off. They're agonizingly painful.

Jamaica's benign-looking reef system harbors other nasty critters, not least the bristleworm, whose brittle bristles act like those of a prickly pear cactus: one touch and you're impaled by tiny needles that detach as

keepsakes. A white-tipped, yellowish brown coral-look-alike fire coral actually isn't a coral, but is so named for the severe burning sensation it causes when brushed up against. Two-thirds of coral species are poisonous – another reason to remember, *hands off!*

Moray eels like nothing so much as an undisturbed life in their nooks and crannies amid the reef. They're curious creatures, though, and pop their heads out to keep an eye on things. Mindless divers often reach out to pet them. *Don't!* Their bite can do devastating damage.

The deadly scorpionfish is also present. It sits on the seabed and resembles the rocks and corals around it, thus is difficult to spot. Its raised spines inflict venom that can be fatal to humans. Likewise, stingrays often lie buried in sand; if you tread on one, its tail may slash you with a venomous spike. When wading in sandy shallows, it's a good idea to *slide* your feet along the sea bed to avoid stepping on the otherwise harmless rays.

Poisonous jellyfish also pulse in Jamaica's waters in late summer.

Swimming is usually no problem in the presence of sharks – mostly, harmless nurse sharks. Fortunately, these dangerous-looking beasts (which can grow up to 12 feet long) are well fed and wary. Still, they'll attack in self-defense if provoked or cornered. Give them plenty of room.

Jamaica's crocodiles are fish-eaters, not human-killers. But use caution if swimming in river estuaries, as a crocodile that feels threatened is sure to prove me wrong.

See the Health section, earlier in this chapter, on how to help relieve stings and scratches.

**Driving Hazards** Driving in Jamaica – or even being near highways and streets – can be dangerous. Pedestrians should take heed of many drivers who would as soon hit you as appear 'sissy' and slow down. If you drive, always be on the lookout for people alongside the roads or animals that might dash in front of you.

For tips on driving conditions, see the Car & Motorcycle section in the Getting Around chapter.

**Drug Trade** Ganja (marijuana) is everywhere in Jamaica, and you're almost certain to be approached by hustlers selling drugs on the streets. Cocaine has become widely available, too.

Be warned that possession and use of drugs in Jamaica is strictly illegal and penalties are severe. In recent years, Jamaica has become serious about combating the trade (in 1998 it was acclaimed by the US Drug Enforcement Agency (DEA) as one of only two countries in the developing world with a serious and effective anti-drug policy). Roadblocks and random searches of cars are common, undertaken by squads of well-armed police in combat gear (I can vouch from personal experience that such searches are taken seriously; be prepared for every nook and cranny to be gone over with a fine-toothe comb). Few Jamaicans carry drugs in their cars, knowing they can find ganja for a pittance when they 'reach.' Foreigners are more blithe at their own risk. Almost every day of the year, visitors carrying drugs are arrested for street trading or possession by undercover agents, including at Kingston and Montego Bay airports. The arrests are announced on radio news shows. If you *do* buy drugs in Jamaica, don't be stupid enough to try to take any out of the country. If you get caught in possession at the airport, you will *not* be getting on your plane home, however small the amount.

A first offense is usually good for a stiff fine (and the costs of an attorney), though if you're caught with a significant amount of dope, you can expect to do some time in the pokey.

Also be aware that smoking a Jamaican *spliff* or *chillum* will pack an almighty punch compared to those skinny little joints you're used to back home. Many Jamaicans – you can recognize them by their yellowed eyes – are used to smoking cigar-sized joints with their first breath of air every morning without noticeable side effects. You can't. It's not unknown, too, to find cocaine is actually Ajax, or ganja sprayed with paraquat or laced with crack cocaine – or that it is really dried croton.

If you plan on hiking or exploring the off-the-beaten path, it's wise to do so with a local guide. Many areas in the hinterland are

centers for ganja production. The DEA works closely with the Jamaican government to suppress the trade, and strangers (especially white travelers) are often suspected of being undercover DEA agents. If you accidentally stumble across a large ganja plantation, you could put your life in jeopardy.

Travelers should be aware that US Customs are more likely to single out individuals arriving from Jamaica because of a high level of drug smuggling, and that certain racial groups receive closer surveillance based on statistical profiles.

**Fearsome Flora** The manchineel tree, which grows along the Jamaican shoreline, produces small applelike green fruits. Don't eat them – they're highly poisonous. Take care not to sit beneath the tree either, as the raindrops running off the leaves onto your skin can cause blisters.

**Garbage** The Jamaican countryside is terribly polluted by garbage, and many town centers are even worse – places of true squalor that conjure up images of Haiti at its worst. Very few among the Jamaican masses seems bothered about fouling their own yards. Relatively few Jamaicans display the cleanliness of, say, Cuba, and all manner of debris litters yards and public spaces. There is no more appalling site than a Jamaican produce market, where offal, spoiled produce, and other trash lies rotting underfoot in huge piles that attract flies, cockroaches, and rodents.

**Harassment** One of Jamaica's biggest ongoing problems is the vast army of hustlers (mostly male) who harass visitors, notably in and around major tourist centers. A hustler is someone who makes a living by seizing opportunities, and the biggest opportunity in Jamaica is *you*!

Hustlers walk the streets looking for potential buyers of crafts, jewelry, or drugs, or to wash cars, give aloe vera massages, or offer any of a thousand varieties of services. A sibilant 'sssssst!' to catch your attention is the first indication that hustlers have their eyes on you. If you as much as glance in their direction, they'll attempt to reel you in like a flounder.

Aggressive persistence is key to their success and shaking them off can be a wearying process. Hustlers often persist in the hope that you'll pay them just to be rid of them. A sale for many Jamaicans is a matter of economic survival; the ideal victory is to achieve a 'rip-off.'

Don't underestimate the hustlers' understanding of the human mind. Jamaican hustlers are experts in consumer psychology. They have an instant answer for any excuse you might throw. And in no other context are they as adept at using the Jamaicans' renowned aptitude for artful wordplay, or 'lyrics,' designed to part you from your dough. A guilt trip is a favorite trick. 'Hey mon, remember me?' is another clever line to link themselves to you. If you say 'No' expect to hear: 'Yeah, I work at your hotel.' If so, ask 'which hotel?' Many hustlers show a total disrespect for visitors who reject their services by saying: 'Hey mon, why you disrespect me?'

The problem is so severe that one Jamaican hotelier told me that many older people who've been coming to Jamaica for years no longer visit because they are still being hassled by the same hustlers who hassled them the last time. 'Jamaicans have ruined their own show,' he told me.

To its credit, the JTB pulled its head from the sand in 1997 and began to aggressively tackle the problem. Tourist police were introduced to patrol key resort areas; fines for harassing tourists were increased 100 times to J$2700 (about US$80) for first offenders; new laws forced street merchants to relocate to established market sites; and night courts were established so that police officers could appear in court without missing their patrols.

Still, it's a never-ending battle, and the problem persists, exacerbated by the fact that 40% of visitors to Jamaica are cruise passengers whose short visits account for the aggressive sales pitch. The situation grew so bad that in 1998 several cruise ships canceled visits to Jamaica, and the threat of a boycott by members of the Florida Caribbean Cruise Association in August 1998 prompted the government to announce plans to establish 'safe zones' in resort areas. Police sweeps literally lifted hustlers off the main streets of Montego Bay and Ocho Rios. Today things are much better in the main resort areas. By 1998, the two main problem areas – Montego Bay's Gloucester Ave and Ocho Rios's Main St – were relatively hassle-free.

If you're hassled, play to the Jamaicans' innate sense of humor. A wisecrack can often break the icy confrontation and earn you respect. Alternately, a good defensive gambit is to play like a savvy local: 'Cho mon, doan't harass de touris'!' Most hustlers are aware of the JTB's efforts to eradicate the problem.

If you want to insure a hassle-free time, check into an all-inclusive resort. And away from touristed areas and in off-the-tourist-beat Kingston, you'll rarely be hassled.

The curious local who approaches you in the boondocks is not likely to try to sell you anything. In Kingston, hustlers tend to gravitate to captive audiences, such as at traffic lights, where a couple of young men will feverishly wash your car at a red light, even if you adamantly say 'No!' Keep your window closed.

Anywhere you go, you'll be seen as a moneybags. At some stage you're sure to be befriended by wily Jamaicans professing to aid you or proffering friendship, but really intent on getting some of your money. You stop, say, to admire a beauty spot or swim in a refreshing pool and almost magically a self-appointed attendant will emerge with suggestions for an even better spot to enjoy or looking to become your buddy. The service is never free. In resort areas *any* unsolicited approach by a stranger is suspect. The goal is most frequently to make you feel indebted as a prelude to importuning. Sometimes – you'll have to use your own conscience – it's worth it to pay and achieve a strategic retreat. At other times, you should stand up for principles. Ironically, the firmer you are, the more respect you'll probably earn. Anything other than saying 'no' will lead by default into a commitment. Fortunately, there *is* always the possibility that a genuine friendship might emerge; at the very least you'll learn the ropes.

If you hire a guide, don't expect him to do more than keep you from getting lost or keep other hustlers at bay. Establish parameters up front, such as what he'll provide and for how much.

To prepare yourself and learn the full scope of the tricks of the trade, refer to *The How to be Jamaican Handbook* by Trevor Fearnon, Kim Robinson, and Harclyde Walcott (Jamrite Publications), which provides humorous lessons in dealing with harassment. It's widely available islandwide.

**Hurricanes** Public warnings will be issued if a hurricane is due to come ashore (though it is difficult to predict a storm's path).

If a hurricane warning is announced, seek shelter in the sturdiest structure you can find, and stay sober. A hurricane is no time to be partying. You'll need your wits about you both during and after the storm.

The Office of Disaster Preparedness (☎ 972-9941), at 12 Camp Rd, Kingston 5, issues guidelines for what to do if a hurricane strikes.

For current weather information, call WeatherTrak (☎ 900-370-8725).

For more on hurricanes, see 'Big Blows' in the Facts about Jamaica chapter.

**Prostitution** Sex work is rife among the young female underclass (and the 'rent-a-Rasta' trade – foreign females seeking Jamaican gigolos – was given a significant boost in 1998 by the hit movie *How Stella Got Her Groove Back*). Negril, in particular, attracts large numbers of Jamaicans eager to attach themselves to foreigners. Some clearly hope for the ultimate reward – marriage. Single foreigners (male and female) are likely to be approached at some stage in not-too-subtle terms. Go-go dancers usually double as prostitutes and most clubs have private rooms to facilitate this. Resist any temptations, as AIDS and other STDs are noted risks, and many street-walkers are also crack addicts. Many dancers also live in relatively unsanitary, sometimes scabies-ridden conditions (even a lap dance is sufficient to pass along scabies).

**Soon Come!** In Jamaica things happen when they happen, and if you can't handle slow (and occasionally surly) service, you're in the wrong place. A phrase you'll hear often is 'Soon come!,' which really means: 'Hey, relax…what's the rush?' 'Soon come!' could be one minute or a darn long time.

Sometimes this is mixed with a shockingly lackadaisical attitude toward you, the client. Jamaican-born photographer Cookie Kincaid told me a story that exemplifies Jamaicans' lackadaisical approach to life:

A tourist had arrived at Kingston airport and went to a car rental company to pick up a car he'd reserved through his travel agency. There was no record of his reservation, and no cars were available. The receptionist was no help: 'Me know not'n' about it, mon!' she said, brushing him off disdainfully. Eventually he persuades her to call her head office. She sits with the phone to her ear for an eternity. He watches, exasperated, as she files her nails with the phone all the while tucked in the crease of her neck. Eventually he asks her if anyone has answered yet. 'No, mon,' she replies, 'de phone line is busy!'

**Undertows** Those gorgeous coral reefs beg to be explored, and the turquoise waters are seductive sirens. But be aware that many places have dangerous undertows. This is particularly true along the east and south coasts, where you should never

Soon come!

swim alone off isolated beaches. Long Bay is especially dangerous for its whipping undertows. Seek local advice about conditions before swimming.

## DISCRIMINATION

Jamaica is overwhelmingly a black society and one that prides itself on an apparent ease of relationships between the black majority, the white minority, and shades in-between: the island's motto is 'Out of Many, One People.' Overt displays of racial discrimination are not tolerated, and foreign visitors who attempt to treat black Jamaicans as subservient will usually meet a forthright remonstration.

Nonetheless, all is not as it seems and there are undercurrents of racial unease in Jamaican society (see Population & People in the Facts about Jamaica chapter). A small yet not insignificant percentage of Jamaicans, for example, display open or barely hidden hostility toward whites.

Everywhere, white visitors will find themselves a tiny minority. This can be unnerving if their's is the only white face for miles around and Jamaican children and even adult men begin calling out 'whitey!' or 'Jake!' (I've been unable to ascertain where this came from). Such epithets are common in more remote areas, but the individuals usually mean no offense. It's usually a matter-of-fact statement of surprise, not a term of abuse.

Tourists should be cautious about using Jamaican terminology, as the interpretation can vary according to context and may carry a pejorative connotation, much as the word 'nigger' in the USA has different connotations when used by whites (always derogatory) and blacks (sometimes considered humorous). Interestingly, black visitors to Jamaica are easily and rapidly identified as tourists and are treated just like white tourists.

## LEGAL MATTERS

Jamaica's drug and drunk-driving laws are strictly enforced. Don't expect leniency because you're a foreigner. Jamaican jails are Dickensian hell-holes, and a stay here can ruin your vacation…and your life! Still, if you run afoul of the law and are arrested, insist on your rights to call your embassy in Kingston to request their assistance. They should be able to help with finding a lawyer, advising relatives, and providing counsel.

If you need legal assistance, the Jamaica Bar Association (☎ 967-1528) can recommend an attorney.

## BUSINESS HOURS

Most business offices are open 8:30 am to 4:30 pm Monday through Friday. Very few offices are open on Saturday.

Most stores open at either 8 or 9 am and close at 5 pm, except Saturday, when they are open until noon. Generally shops are closed on Sunday, except pharmacies, which are open every day.

## PUBLIC HOLIDAYS & SPECIAL EVENTS
### Public Holidays

Public holidays are the following:

January
  New Year's Day (January 1)
February
  Bob Marley Day (February 6)
  Ash Wednesday
March-April
  Good Friday
  Easter Monday
August
  Emancipation Day (August 1)
  Independence Day (August 6)
September
  Labor Day
October
  National Heroes' Day (October 19)
December
  Christmas (December 25)
  Boxing Day (December 26)

### Special Events

Jamaica hosts a full calendar of musical, artistic, cultural, and sporting events. The JTB publishes an annual 'Calendar of Events,' available from their offices worldwide.

The two biggest events are Ocho Rios' Reggae Sunsplash, held in February, and Montego Bay's Reggae Sumfest in August.

(See the regional chapters for more on these concerts.) Several international tour operators have special packages built around the two musical events. In the USA, Sunburst Holidays (☎ 800-426-4570) specializes in tour packages to both events.

**Carnival** In recent years Jamaica has enthusiastically adopted the Carnival of the eastern Caribbean. Although it began only in 1991, Kingston's carnival is now a tourist attraction in its own right. Mostly, however, it is a big blow-out for the Jamaican masses, when costumed revelers take to the streets in droves. There's reggae and calypso, of course, but soca is king.

Designers seek to make their bands the most outstanding, the most glittering, the most daring. Some designers choose controversial topics, while others go for fun and fantasy. It wouldn't be Carnival without the outrageous. Hence some designers (and many of the crowd) strip down their creations to near nudity. Be prepared to throw inhibitions to the wind. Jamaica's Carnival crowd is not shy. The fun turns salacious and not a little promiscuity is obvious (a noteworthy custom befitting Carnival's pagan roots is for otherwise platonic friends to consummate any pent-up sexual fantasies they may have felt for each other, for which reason, one suspects, Kingstonians look forward feverishly to Carnival as the highlight of the year).

The event – held in mid-April – has a different theme each day, ending with the 'Last Hurrah.' The 1998 carnival was an eight-day affair.

**Other Events** Most of the events below follow a predictable schedule. Many annual events occur at the cusp of months and the specific month may vary year to year. Two of the biggest are the Ocho Rios Jazz Festival, and the recently initiated Air Jamaica Jazz & Blues Festival, both attracting the biggest names in jazz.

The JTB can provide phone numbers and dates for specific events (see Tourist Offices, earlier in this chapter), of which the following are the most important:

## January

Accompong Maroon Festival, Accompong, St Elizabeth (January 6)

White River Reggae Bash, Ocho Rios

High Mountain 10K Road Race, Williamsfield, Manchester

Negril Sprint Triathlon, Negril

Red Stripe Cup Cricket Competition, Kingston

Jamaica School of Dance Concert Season, Kingston

## February

Carib Cement International Marathon, Kingston

Pineapple Cup Yacht Race, Miami to Montego Bay

Bob Marley Birthday Bash – Reggae Sunsplash, Ocho Rios

Shell/Sandals Limited Overs Cricket Competition, Kingston

UWI Carnival, University of West Indies campus, Kingston

## March

JAMI (Jamaica Music Industry) Awards, Kingston

Jamaica Orchid Society Spring Show, UWI, Kingston

Miss Universe Jamaica Beauty Pageant, Kingston

Negril Music Festival

Bowden Marina Invitational Fishing Tournament, near Morant Bay

## April

Montego Bay Yacht Club Easter Regatta

Harmony Hall Easter Crafts Fair, Ocho Rios

Devon House Easter Craft Fair, Kingston

Jake's Triathlon, Treasure Beach

Kite Festival, Drax Hall, near Ocho Rios

Motor Sports Championship Series, Dover Raceway, Runaway Bay (April through December)

Cable & Wireless Test Cricket, Kingston

Jamaica Beachfest, Negril

## May

Manchester Horticultural Society Show, Mandeville

Portland Annual Flower Show, Crystal Springs

## June

All-Jamaica Tennis Championships, Kingston
(late May through mid-July)

Ocho Rios Jazz Festival

## July

National Dance Theater Company's Season of
Dance, Little Theater, Kingston

## August

Denbigh Agricultural Show, May Pen

Reggae Sumfest, Montego Bay

Independence Day Parade, Kingston (August 6)

Hi-Pro Family Polo Tournament & International
Horse Show, Mammee Bay

Portland Jamboree, Port Antonio

## September

Miss Jamaica World Beauty Pageant, Kingston

Panasonic Golf Championship, Ocho Rios

Fossil Open Polo Tournament, Chukka Cove,
St Ann

Montego Bay Marlin Tournament

Ocho Rios International Marlin Tournament

## October

Jamaica Open Pro Am Golf Tournament,
Montego Bay

Great Jamaican Canoe Race and Hook'n'Line
Fishing Tournament, Treasure Beach

SuperClubs World Cup Qualifier, Runaway Bay

Shell/Sandals Cricket Competition, Kingston and
Montego Bay

Oktoberfest, Jamaica German Society, Kingston

All That Heritage & Jazz Festival, Montego Bay

Port Antonio International Marlin Tournament

Caribbean Heritagefest, Portmore, near Kingston

African Dance and Drum Retreat, Negril

James Bond Oracabessa Marlin Tournament

National Heroes Weekend, Frenchman's Cove,
near Port Antonio

## November

Air Jamaica Jazz & Blues Festival, James Bond
Beach, Oracabessa

International Karting Road Race, Kingston

Harmony Hall Anniversary Crafts Fair, Ocho
Rios (mid-November)

Holland Bamboo Run, Bamboo Avenue,
St Elizabeth

## December

Jam-Am Yacht Race, Montego Bay

Esso International Rally, Dover Raceway,
Runaway Bay

Best of Harmony Hall, Ocho Rios

Devon House Christmas Fair, Kingston

Johnnie Walker World Golf Championship, Tryall
Estate

LTM National Pantomime
December 26 (through April), Kingston

## WORK

Visitors are admitted to Jamaica on the condition that they 'not engage in any form of employment on the island or solicit or accept any order for goods or services, for or on behalf of any persons, firm or company not carrying on business with the island.' (So says the immigration stamp placed in your passport.) Professionals can obtain work permits if sponsored by a Jamaican company, but casual work is very difficult to obtain.

## ACCOMMODATIONS

For accommodations meeting every budget and style, few Caribbean islands can match Jamaica for diversity.

Where you stay can make or break your vacation, so it pays to research thoroughly. Price is only one guide – many hotels of similar price vary dramatically in ambience and value. Far too many hotels in Jamaica are overpriced or soulless. But there are also some splendid bargains at all price levels, from cozy budget guest houses for US$20 nightly to ritzy, US$500-a-night, all-inclusive resorts, where maids float hibiscus petals in the toilet bowl before turning down the linens.

Twice a year the JTB publishes a guide and rate sheet to leading hotels and guest houses nationwide. You can obtain it from JTB offices worldwide or the JTB information booths at the airports in Montego Bay or Kingston. The 140 or so establishments

## Jonkanoo

Jonkanoo is a traditional Christmas celebration in which revelers parade through the streets dressed in masquerade. It was once the major celebration on the slave calendar.

The festivity, which originated among West African secret societies, evolved on the plantations among slaves who were forbidden to observe their sacred traditions. The all-male cast

of masqueraders hid their identity: some dressed as demons, others wore papier-mâché horse heads, and many were on stilts. The elaborate carnival was accompanied by musicians with drums, fifes, flutes, and rattles.

At first, Jonkanoos were suppressed by the colonial government, which feared they might lead to slave uprisings. Later, planters encouraged Jonkanoos as safe outlets for pent-up energies, which gradually adopted European traits (though many whites contemptuously referred to Jonkanoos as 'Pickaninny Christmas'). Creole elements found their way into the ceremony, and Morris dancing, polka, and reels were introduced. During its early 19th-century heyday, the Jonkanoo featured processions of 'set girls,' groups of young women dressed identically and elaborately in a specific color (also according to color of skin). Following emancipation, the Church and state suppressed the Jonkanoo as a vulgar pagan rite. It was discouraged throughout this century, too, until recent years. It is now being revived as an important part of Jamaican culture and is reappearing in towns and villages at Christmas.

Christiana, in Manchester parish, hosts perhaps the liveliest Jonkanoo on the island: the 'Grand Market Night,' held on Christmas Eve.

Costumed spectators are expected to offer donations, food, and drink to the performers.

---

listed have been inspected and are 'JTB approved,' as are at least 300 guest houses nationwide. Many accommodations that are not JTB licensed are perfectly OK.

In 1998 the JTB began to redefine its approved properties according to 'character,' not price, as part of a campaign to promote small hotels. Four categories were to be created: the Boutique Collection, representing first-class hotels with special character; the Countryside Collection of off-the-beaten-path properties; the Seascape Collection, located on riverbanks or shorefront; and the Town Collection, in urban centers.

GoGo Worldwide Vacations, the Caribbean's largest US wholesaler, has an 'Intimate Hotels of the Caribbean' program featuring about 30 of Jamaica's smaller properties, as well as 'Inns of Jamaica.' Caribbean Vacation Network (☎ 305-673-8822, 800-423-4095, fax 305-673-5666) has a similar 40-page catalog showing dozens of properties.

Unfortunately, many small hotels, lacking funds, have had a hard time maintaining standards (or they cater to a domestic market that is undemanding). In 1998 the JTB hoped to secure government funding to help small hoteliers make the necessary improvements to remain competitive. In 1999 the JTB introduced 'Insider's Jamaica,' offering packages at small hotels (five-night minimum stay starting at US$459, including roundtrip airport-hotel transfers, accommodations, a 'Jamaica House Party,' plus discounts on admission to participating attractions and restaurants, and a free upgrade at select car-rental companies.

## Rates & Seasons

Hotel prices throughout this book are given in US dollars. Unless otherwise stated, prices are for double rooms in low season and refer to European Plan (EP), or room only.

Low season (summer) is usually mid-April to mid-December; high season (winter) is the remainder of the year, when hotel prices increase by 40% or more. Some hotels have even higher rates for 'peak' season: usually at Christmas and Easter. Some hotels have year-round rates. Others also discount room rates based on the number of nights you stay. Ask what discounts may be available, and feel free to suggest your own.

There are several advantages to traveling in low season, not the least of which is the price discounts. The more popular hotels are often booked solid in high season; at other times of the year, you not only can find rooms, but are also often given the run of the house.

Many hotels have a local rate for Jamaicans and a higher rate – in US dollars – for foreigners. Most hotels accept payment by credit card or traveler's check.

Accommodations rates range from US$10 to US$20 budget guest houses and US$30 to US$60 mid-range hotels to ritzy top-end resorts for US$300 a night, or more. All-inclusive packages can be a great bargain if

you choose wisely. Such packages are usually based on three-day minimum stays.

Note that some hotels will quote rates as Continental Plan (CP; room and breakfast), Modified American Plan (MAP; room plus breakfast and dinner), or American Plan (AP; room plus three meals daily). Don't forget to check if the quoted rate includes tax and service charge; if not, the compulsory 6.25% to 15% GCT (and possibly a 10% to 15% service charge) may be added to your bill.

It is advisable to book several months in advance. This is especially true if you're reserving by mail, which can take several weeks. It's best to phone, fax, or use a travel agent or hotel representative when making reservations from your home country.

Many hotels also charge for the privilege of bringing guests to your room, even if it's a friend whom you've invited for a beer on the porch.

## Reservations

You can make reservations directly with hotels, but it's just as easy to use an agency such as TravelJam Reservation & Information Service (☎ 800-554-7352), 1449 Lexington Ave No 3A, New York, NY 10128, which represents almost two dozen upscale properties islandwide.

In North America, the JTB operates a JRS Tours (☎ 800-526-2422 in the USA, ☎ 800-432-7559 in Canada), Doral Executive Office Park, 3785 NW 82nd Ave suite 403, Miami, FL 33166.

Several Jamaican hotels that do not anticipate filling their rooms sell blocks of rooms in advance to wholesalers at bulk discounts, which the latter pass along as huge savings. Try the Room Exchange (☎ 800-846-7000 in the USA, fax 212-760-1013, www.hotelrooms .com), which has more than 75 properties in Jamaica to choose from at up to 50% discount – including US$79 summer rates for the top-end Negril Cabins Resort.

The Jamaica Hotel & Tourism Association (☎ 926-3635, fax 929-1054), 2 Ardenne Rd, Kingston 10, represents hoteliers and other lodgings owners and tourism service providers.

Independent-minded travelers might consider booking through the Ring of Confidence, a group of select, family-style hotels (and a few other tour-related companies) that work together to help visitors plan the next stage of their trip by 'handing' guests on to another property within the ring. You reserve your first night's accommodations in advance, then pay a 10% deposit for bookings – handled by your current host – which is deducted from the bill of each subsequent property. Contact Malcolm McInnes (☎ 977-8223, fax 977-8440, be@in-site.com), the Square, Mavis Bank, St Andrew, or check out the website (www.in-site.com/ring) for links to all participating properties.

## Camping

With few exceptions, Jamaica is not developed for campers. Negril is the only resort area with a choice of camping facilities, although a few isolated campsites are also scattered elsewhere. Many budget properties will let you pitch a tent on their lawns for a small fee. Some even rent tents. Most have shower, toilet, and laundry facilities. Costs begin at about US$5 per night, but US$10 per tent is the average. (Also see Camping Supplies in the Planning section, earlier in this chapter.)

It is unsafe to camp in the wild in Jamaica: the threat of robbery or rape is too great. This includes beaches. If you insist on camping away from organized sites, ensure that you're within sight and sound of other visitors or hotels. The JTB or JATCHA (see Hiking in the Outdoor Activities chapter) can provide information on safe sites.

## Hostels

Jamaica has no youth hostel association, and there are no hostels on the island. The closest contender is Maya Lodge, in Jack's Hill on the outskirts of Kingston. The YMCA in Kingston was being rebuilt at press time.

## Guest Houses

Guest houses are the lodgings of choice for Jamaicans when traveling. Usually they're small, fairly simple, no-frills, family-run properties with a live-in owner who provides breakfast and sometimes dinner. What they lack in facilities they make up for in character – or at least, they should.

Unfortunately, the term 'guest house' is much abused in Jamaica. Some so-called guest houses are no more than a couple of dingy rooms with shared bathrooms (most guest houses have shared bath). Others are self-contained apartments. Still others are indistinguishable from hotels or faceless motels. Standards and prices vary enormously. A few offer their own versions of all-inclusive packages.

If what you need is a roof over your head, guest houses are an inexpensive option for value-wise lodgings, and they're good places to mix with locals. Don't expect to be right on the beach, though.

The JTB publishes an annual 18-page *Inns of Jamaica* catalog, which also includes JTB's fly-drive packages offering vouchers for 48 participating inns. (See the Fly & Drive Packages in the Car & Motorcycle section of the Getting Around chapter.) Several newspapers list guest houses in their classified sections.

## B&Bs

A B&B ('bed and breakfast') usually is a lodging where the owner plays live-in host and provides breakfast in the quoted room rate. In Jamaica the term is often misused, and true B&Bs are few and far between.

## Hotels

Jamaican hotels run the gamut, but terms such as 'deluxe' or 'first-class' have been so abused that it is unwise to rely on a hotel's brochure. Reporting on whether a hotel has air-con, TV, and a swimming pool tells you nothing about its ambience. Hence, I've tried to provide in-depth descriptions of hotels to help you make a more informed decision.

Some of the first, and certainly the most elegant, hotels in the Caribbean were established in Jamaica. It still has a large selection of unbeatably stylish hotels, many still attracting a Who's Who of Hollywood and royalty.

Several exude an old world charm, with butlers and white-gloved waiters who call you 'm'lady,' though they're not all so stuffy. Some – Jamaica Inn (outside Ocho Rios) comes to mind – are sublime. The Elegant Resorts of Jamaica represents a handful of these exclusive properties, including Half Moon Golf, Tennis & Beach Club, Round Hill Hotel & Villas, and Trident Villas & Hotel. Membership has been in flux.

Jamaica is also at the forefront of establishing a more modern, quintessentially Caribbean style of boutique hotel epitomized by the Island Outpost properties (☎ 305-672-5254, 800-688-7678, fax 305-604-5182; ☎ 0800-614-790 in the UK, questions@ islandoutpost.com, www.islandoutpost.com), 1330 Ocean Drive, Miami Beach, FL 33139. Avant-garde, refined, and irresistibly charming, these gems – it is an insult to call them hotels – evoke the finest in unpretentious and gracious living. Stay once at Strawberry Hill, Goldeneye, or the Caves and you'll understand.

A consortium of more than three dozen smaller intimate hotels recently formed the Inns of Jamaica group for marketing pur-poses. Most are upscale. The biggest of these has 50 rooms. Contact JTB offices for a brochure.

**All-Inclusive Resorts** All-inclusive resorts are cash-free, self-contained hotels or village resorts: you pay a set price and (theoretically) pay nothing more once you set foot inside the resort. Even unlimited booze is usually included.

All-inclusives offer a pampered vacation, but tend to shelter guests from mingling with locals and discovering the colorful, gritty, real Jamaica. To be fair, most resorts offer a wide range of shopping and tours. And if you want to get out and explore on your own, you're free to do so, of course.

All-inclusive resorts were invented in Jamaica and perfected to suit the needs of couples, families, and singles. Two companies dominate the scene: Sandals and Super-Clubs. The renowned rivalry between them has fostered the highest standards based on supreme service. Together they set the benchmark that others attempt to reach, with varying degrees of success.

A guest house can be anything from a grandiose plantation house to a modest room.

Outside these two chains (and the reliable Couples chain, with three properties), caution is needed when choosing an appropriate resort, as all may not be as it seems. Many properties have jumped onto the 'all-inclusive' bandwagon for marketing purposes. Check carefully for hidden charges for water sports, laundry, and other activities or services *not* included in the price. Rates begin at about US$100 per day for the less expensive resorts.

All-Inclusive Travel (☎ 800-405-4787, www.all-inclusivetravel.com) specializes in discounted packages to all-inclusives, beginning at US$799 for one week including roundtrip airfare from Atlanta, GA.

A recent development has been the emergence of all-inclusives targeting specialist markets, such as fitness buffs.

**Sandals** Sandals started out as a couples-only chain. It operates six couples resorts: three in Montego Bay, two in Ocho Rios, and one in Negril. No singles or families are allowed (nor gay or lesbian couples, for that matter). In 1995 the company introduced its 'Beaches' resorts for couples, singles, and families (gay men and lesbians are accepted). Negril has a Beaches, and another is slated to open in 2000 outside Whitehouse. Guests at any Sandals have free access to the golf course at the Ocho Rios Sandals. The Sandals resorts in Negril and Dunn's River have splendid, full-service spas (also free to use for guests at any Sandals).

Sandals markets its resorts as 'ultra-inclusives.' Guests staying at one resort get full access privileges to all the others. And guests who book suites get special 'concierge' treatment.

The company's various resorts boast the highest occupancy rates of any hotels in the Caribbean.

For more information on Sandals (www.sandals.com), contact:

Canada
   (☎ 416-223-0028, 800-545-8283, fax 416-223-3306)
France
   Tropic Travel
   (☎ 01-42-36-42-52, fax 01-42-36-48-35)

UK
   (☎ 020-7581-9895, 0800-742742, fax 020-7823-8758)
USA
   Unique Vacations
   (☎ 305-284-1300, 800-726-3257, fax 305-284-1336)

**SuperClubs** SuperClubs' seven 'super-inclusive' resorts cater to specific market segments. Its three 'Grand Lido' properties are luxury resorts with full-menu, 24-hour room service and a gamut of amenities aimed at couples and singles. Its Hedonism II, in Negril, has long been legendary for a free-spirited – OK, libertine – lifestyle and was to be joined in 1999 by a sister property – Hedonism III – in Runaway Bay. SuperClubs also operates Boscobel Beach (for families) and three budget-oriented properties under the 'Breezes' title for middle-income couples and singles.

It markets its properties as 'super-inclusive' and is constantly innovating to define the term. Even full-service weddings are on the house (brides actually earn credits for free flights). SuperClubs offers a money-back guarantee against bad weather – even a hurricane. And the Grand Lido properties are renowned for their award-winning cuisine.

For more information on SuperClubs (☎ 974-5424, www.superclubs.com), contact:

Canada
   ☎ 800-553-4320
UK
   ☎ 01749-677200
USA
   ☎ 954-925-0925, 800-467-8737, fax 954-925-0334

## Homestays

You can also make your own arrangements to stay with individuals or families that do not rent rooms as a normal practice. You should use your discretion. There are many scalawags eager to part visitors from their money, or worse; if you don't feel secure, don't accept an offer. The JTB's 'Meet the People' program, while not specifically designed to provide accommodations with Jamaican families, is a good starting point. (See 'Meet the People' in the Facts about

Jamaica chapter.) Diane McIntyre-Pike can also arrange family stays through her community tourism program based at the Astra Country Inn in Mandeville (☎ 962-3265).

## Rentals

Jamaica boasts hundreds of private houses for rent, from modest cottages to lavish beachfront estates. In fact, more than 40% of the island's accommodations are 'self-catering,' a higher ratio than any other Caribbean island. Most are located in the north coast tourist resorts and, to a lesser degree, the coastal strip between Savanna-la-Mar and Treasure Beach. Many villas near Montego Bay, Ocho Rios, and Runaway Bay are in self-contained villa communities. They're a great way for self-sufficient travelers to establish their independence and are very cost-effective if you're traveling with family or a group of friends. Many self-catering rentals include a cook and maid. Deluxe villas sometimes have an army of staff. Others come with a kitchenette, and you do your own cooking and laundry.

You can rent cottages and villas directly from owners or through villa-rental companies. Good sources are the classified ad sections of *Caribbean Travel & Life* and *Islands* magazines. The JTB's *Travel Agents Reference Guide* lists 28 villa representatives in North America. The best starting point is the Jamaican Association of Villas & Apartments (JAVA; ☎ 974-2508, fax 974-2967), PO Box 298, Ocho Rios, which represents about 80% of the 400 or so properties available islandwide, and is responsible for marketing rental units. Other offices include:

UK
    TC Resorts
    (☎ 020-7486-3560, fax 7486-4108)
    21 Blandford St, London W1H 3AD
    You can make bookings through JAVA.

USA
    (☎ 305-673-6688, 800-845-5276, fax 305-673-5666)
    1680 Meridian suite 504, Miami Beach, FL 33139

Other villa-rental companies include:

At Home Abroad
    (☎ 212-421-9165, 212-752-1591, athomeabroad@aol.com, http://members.aol.com/athomabrod/index.html)

Elegant Resorts Villas
    (☎ 876-953-9562, 800-337-3499 in North America, fax 876-953-9563) PO Box 80, Montego Bay

Villas by Linda Smith
    (☎ 301-229-4300, fax 301-320-6963, linda@jamaicavillas.com, www.jamaicavillas.com)

Villawise
    (☎ 974-5877, fax 974-5362)

VHR Worldwide
    (☎ 201-767-9393, 800-633-3284, fax 201-767-5510, vhrww@juno.com, www.vhrww.com)

Several of Jamaica's most elegant resorts offer villa rentals in privately owned homes with access to all resort facilities. These include Half Moon, Round Hill, and the Tryall Club, all near Montego Bay, and Trident Villas and Goblin Villas near Port Antonio.

Usually, upscale villas have a private pool, TV with VCR, stereo, and often a tennis court. They're almost always fully staffed with a maid, cook, and gardener. Some even include a butler and laundress.

Your villa-rental agency should supply you with complete details on staff arrangements, including guidelines for tipping. It's customary to give the staff one night off per week. You should also tip each staff member separately according to the service they've provided. However, an unwritten ranking states that the cook gets the largest tip and the laundress the least. Most villa-rental agencies recommend that the combined gratuity should total about 7% to 15% of the villa rental cost.

Rental rates vary, starting as low as US$100 per week for budget units with minimal facilities. More upscale villas usually begin at about US$750 weekly for a two-bedroom cottage and can run US$5000 or more for a four-bedroom estate sleeping eight or more people. Rates fall as much as 30% in summer. A large deposit (usually 25% or more) is required to confirm your reservation; full payment is normally required one month before your rental begins.

Villas in the hills offer the advantage of cool breezes and spectacular views. They're usually cheaper. You'll pay a premium for being down by the beach. Expect to pay more, too, if your villa is pre-provisioned with food. It's usual to buy your own food (costs generally run about US$100 per person per week). Your cook may stock the food for your first dinner and breakfast, and should be reimbursed. He or she normally accompanies you on your shopping spree – a great way to learn about local food items and Jamaican dishes. If you let the cook do your shopping, be sure to give *explicit* written instructions, and ask for a strict accounting.

## FOOD

Jamaica's homegrown cuisine is a fusion of many ethnic traditions and influences, and the product of generations of women who as children apprenticed alongside their mothers and grannies who cooked using *yabbas* (clay pots) and iron pots, black from soot, on a raised stove fired by wood. The Arawaks were the first island residents to grill meats and fish. They also brought callaloo, cassava, corn, sweet potatoes, and several tropical fruits to the island. The Spanish adopted native spices, later enhanced by spices brought by slaves from their African homelands. East Indian immigrants brought hot and flavorful curries, often served with locally made mango chutney. *Roti*, a bread of Indian origin, is also popular served with a dollop of curried goat or chicken in the middle and eaten folded. Middle Eastern dishes and Chinese influences have also become part of the national menu. And basic roasts and stews followed the flag during three centuries of British rule, as did Yorkshire pudding, meat pies, and hot cross buns.

The Jamaicans have melded all these influences into dishes with playful names, including Solomon Grundy.

A fair amount of Jamaican cuisine is an adventure in tongue-lashing. A key ingredient is pimento (or 'allspice'), which is indigenous to Jamaica and grows most profusely in hilly limestone areas.

A key island condiment is savory, piquant Pickapeppa sauce, the recipe for which is a closely guarded secret. The basic ingredients, however, include tomatoes, onions, raisins,

CHRISTOPHER P BAKER

Roadside snacks (and Red Stripe) for sale

tamarind, mangoes, red hot peppers, cane vinegar, thyme, and other spices.

Two cultural events – the weeklong Terra Nova Heritage Food Festival, in Kingston each October; and the two-day Jamaica Spice, in Ocho Rios each July – celebrate Jamaican cuisines.

## Out to Eat

Dining in Jamaica ranges from wildly expensive restaurants to humble roadside stands and bamboo shacks where you can eat simple Jamaican fare for as little as US$1. Hole-in-the-wall restaurants often serve fabulous local fare; don't be put off by their often basic appearance (unless they're overtly unhygienic). Most serve at least one vegetarian meal (often called I-tal, a Rastafarian inspiration for 'pure' or health food).

Restaurants geared to the tourist trade are generally overpriced (often outrageously so), partly because much of the food they serve is imported. Most hotels incorporate Jamaican dishes in their menus, although these are often tame versions of the spicy island cuisine.

Food bought at grocery stores is usually expensive. Many of the canned and packaged goods are imported and cost up to three times what you might pay at home. Bottled water is also expensive. You'll find plenty of dirt-cheap fresh fruits, vegetables, and spices on sale at markets and roadside stalls islandwide. (Many produce markets are filthy, with piles of rotting garbage plagued by flies; in October 1998, Mandeville market was closed by health inspectors. Wash all produce thoroughly!)

Likewise, you can buy fish (and lobster, in season) from local fishermen. If you have some favorite food items, consider taking them with you, just make sure they're preserved, or otherwise not 'live' agricultural products.

Many of the more popular upscale all-inclusive resorts sell evening passes that allow you to eat and drink in their restaurants, bars, and nightclubs for a single fee.

Plenty of restaurants serve continental cuisine, and virtually every town of any size has fast-food joints such as McDonald's,

Burger King, and Kentucky Fried Chicken. Their local equivalents are Mother's, King Burger, and Juici-Beef Patties.

Dress is casual at even the most exclusive restaurants, where you will be expected to dress 'elegantly casual,' meaning no jeans. A few of the more traditional upscale resorts may require jackets for men at dinner.

## Snacks

The staple and most popular snack is a patty – a thin, tender yet crisp crust filled with highly spiced, well-seasoned beef or vegetables. 'Stamp and go' are saltfish cakes eaten as appetizers.

Avoid turtle eggs in red wine (a specialty snack of Clarendon parish). Endangered turtles and their eggs are protected by law.

### Nouvelle Jamaican Cuisine

Recent years have witnessed the beginnings of an evolution in nouvelle Jamaican cuisines. A new generation of local chefs is reinterpreting traditional dishes and creating new ones that provide the finest dining experiences on the island (the recherché influences have not yet filtered down to the masses). You owe it to yourself to search out a handful of trendsetting restaurants. Here's my top ten (see regional chapters for details):

Blue Mountain Taverna, Mavis Bank (Blue Mountains)

Bloomfield Great House, Mandeville

Café Aubergine, Moneague, near Ocho Rios

Culloden Café, near Whitehouse

Hotel Mocking Bird Hill, Port Antonio

Hotel Villa Bella, Christiana

Good Hope Estate, near Falmouth

Norma's at the Wharf, Reading, Montego Bay

Red Bones Blues Café, Kingston

Strawberry Hill, Irish Town (Blue Mountains)

The same is true of booby eggs, taken (illegally) from the rookeries on Goat Island.

## Main Dishes

Jamaicans typically forsake corn flakes for more savory fare at breakfast: ackee and saltfish is typical. The average Jamaican eats a light lunch. Other dishes could be pepper pot stew, fried fish, or 'jerk' pork, or another national dish using island ingredients simmered in coconut milk and spices.

Many meals are accompanied by starchy vegetables – 'breadkinds' – such as plantains and yam that replace bread; or with bread substitutes such as pancake-shaped cassava bread or *bammy*, and *johnny cakes* (the name derives from 'journey cakes,' or fried dumplings, an original Jamaican fast-food).

The island staple is rice and 'peas' (red beans), most often served with pork, the staple meat. Goat is also an island staple. It is usually served curried, chopped into small bits with meat on the bone, but it is also the main ingredient of *mannish water* (or 'goat head soup') made from goat offal. You may turn your nose up, but it is considered an aphrodisiac. The essence of soup is that is has to have substance and be heavily flavored. Thus Jamaican soups are thick, more like stews, and loaded with vegetables and 'breadkind.' *Dip and fall back* is a salty stew served with bananas and dumplings.

Jamaica's most popular dish (now finding its way onto the world market) is *jerk*, a term that describes the process of cooking meats smothered in tongue-searing marinade. Chicken, pork, or fish are first washed with vinegar or lime juice, then marinated in a hot sauce of island-grown spices (including volatile Scotch bonnet pepper), and barbecued slowly in an outdoor pit – usually an oil drum cut in half, cleaned out, and hinged so that one half forms a lid – over a fire of pimento wood, which gives the meat its distinctive flavor. The pits are covered with a sheet of galvanized tin, which reflects the heat. Jerk is best served hot off the coals wrapped in paper. You normally order by the pound (US$2 should fill you up).

Jerk supposedly derives from the John Crow Mountains, where the runaway slaves known as Maroons first 'jerked' wild pigs, then cooked the meat over a *barbacoa*, from which comes the word 'barbecue.' It is commonly associated with Boston Bay, in Portland parish. Jerk stalls are interspersed along most major roads throughout the country, often advertised with hand-painted signs. You'll find them in the center of towns, too.

In general, avoid steaks unless the meat is imported. Jamaican steaks are tough, and meant for stewing. Beef most commonly finds its way into patties.

Naturally, there's a strong emphasis on seafood. Snapper and parrot fish are two of the more popular species. Kingfish, grouper, and marlin are also common. Many fish

### Ackee & Saltfish

A typical Jamaican 'plantation breakfast' is ackee and saltfish, the national dish. Ackee is a tree-grown fruit (native to Africa), the golden flesh of which bears an uncanny resemblance to scrambled eggs when cooked. Served with johnny cakes (delicious fried dumplings), and callaloo (a leafy vegetable), and flaked escovietched fish, it makes a fantastic breakfast.

If you attempt to cook it yourself, be aware that the fruit is highly toxic when unripe (known as 'Jamaica poisoning'), and can be eaten only after the pods have fully opened to reveal the canary yellow arils within.

LEE ABEL

dishes are heavily spiced or salted. A favorite is *escoveitched* fish, which is pickled in vinegar, then fried and simmered with peppers and onions. Bammy is a popular accompaniment, as is *festival*.

Pickled herring bears the improbable name of *solomon grundy*. *Rundown* is

mackerel that's cooked in coconut milk, and usually eaten at breakfast.

The term 'lobster' is also used for the local clawless freshwater crayfish, usually served grilled with butter and garlic, or curried, for as little as US$5 at stalls. Likewise, freshly caught and highly spiced

## Fruits

Jamaica is a tropical Eden ripe with native fruits such as the peachlike naseberry, banana, pineapple, coconut, the star apple, soursop, ugli, and the ortanique (a citrus crossbred from oranges and tangerines). Tiny roadside shacks also proffer fresh papayas, mangoes, and young or unripe bananas.

The starchy, rather bland-tasting plantain, closely related to the banana, cannot be eaten in its raw state, but must be cooked. It is treated somewhat like a potato and is usually fried or baked and served as an accompaniment to a main dish. In its unripe form it is used to make delicious chips. More mature plantains can develop a delicate sweetness.

Jamaica's fruits include:

**Guava** – The guava is a small ovoid or rounded fruit with an intense, musky sweet aroma. It has a yellow-green skin and pinkish, granular flesh studded with regular rows of tiny seeds. It is most commonly used in nectars and punches, syrups, jams, chutney, and even ice cream.

**Guinep** – This small green fruit (pronounced GI-neps) grows in clusters, like grapes, and can be bought July through November. Each 'grape' bears pink flesh that you plop into your mouth whole. It's kind of rubbery, and juicy, and tastes like a cross between a fig and a strawberry. Watch for the big pit in the middle.

**Mango** – Mangoes are a lush fruit that come in an assortment of colors, from yellow to black. Massage the glove-leather skin to soften the pulp, which can be sucked or spooned like custard. Select your mango by its perfume. Some are hairy; some are small, such as Sweetie mango, the size of an egg and sweet to boot; others are fat, such as Governor mango. Alas, some taste diabolical. Don't cross the street for Turpentine mango. Over the years select breeding has produced true aristocrats: the Julie, Bombay, and East Indian mangoes.

**Papaya** – The papaya's cloaks of many colors (from yellow to rose) hide a melon-smooth flesh that likewise runs from citron to vermilion. The central cavity is a trove of edible black seeds. Tenderness and sweet scent are key to buying papayas. They are commonly served with breakfast plates and in fruit salads, and in jams, ice cream, and baked in desserts.

**Soursop** – This is an ungainly, irregularly shaped fruit with cottony pulp that is invitingly fragrant yet acidic. Its taste hints at guava and pineapple. It's most commonly used for pudding, ice cream, syrup, and canned drinks.

**Star apple** – Star apples are leathery, dark-purple, tennis-ball-sized, gelatinous fruits of banded colors (white, pink, lavender, purple). Its glistening seeds form a star in the center. The fruit is mildly sweet and understated. Immature fruits are gummy and unappetizing: feel for some give when buying.

**Sugar apple** – Sugar apple is a strange name for a fruit that resembles a giant pine cone, with bractlike sections that separate when the fruit is ripe. The gray, juicy flesh is sweet and custardlike and shot with watermelon-like seeds.

**Ugli** – This fruit is well-named. It is ugly on the vine – like a deformed grapefruit with warty, mottled green or orange skin. But the golden pulp is delicious: acid-sweet and gushingly juicy.

'shrimp' (called *pepper* '*swimp*,' though actually *janga* or crayfish) is a favorite in the Black River area, particularly in the village of Middle Quarters.

## Vegetables

Yams (they come in several kinds) are the island staple, along with carrots and scallions. Pumpkin is another staple side dish served boiled and mashed with butter. You may also come across breadfruit in various guises. This starchy vegetable – any starchy vegetable is referred to as 'breadkind' – grows wild throughout the island but was first landed in Jamaica only in 1793 (see 'Capt Bligh and Breadfruit' in the Facts about Jamaica chapter). The round 'fruits' weigh up to 4lb. Young or immature fruit is eaten as a staple – either added to soups or served as an accompaniment to the main dish. The mature (but not yet ripe) vegetable is roasted or deep-fried.

Callaloo is a spinachlike vegetable and is usually served shredded and steamed or lightly boiled as a side vegetable. It also finds its way into spicy pepper pot stew, which dates back to the Arawak period and has been altered over the centuries to become a soup. Local lore says pepper pot can be generations old, as the pot is reheated each day with fresh ingredients added.

*Cho-cho* (also known as *christophine*) is a pulpy squashlike gourd that hangs on a luxuriant vine in the same way as the cucumber. Cho-cho is served as an accompaniment to meats, in soups, and for making hot pickles.

## Desserts

Jamaicans have evolved their own desserts, too, such as *matrimony*, a salad of pulped orange and star apple (and sometimes other fruits) with cream; and *duckunoo* (or 'blue drawers'), a pudding made of cornmeal, green bananas, and coconut, and enlivened with sugar and spices.

## DRINKS

Jamaica has a variety of refreshing drinks – both alcoholic and nonalcoholic. Tap water is generally safe, as Jamaica's limestone base serves as a natural purification system. But sanitation conditions in some backcountry areas (particularly in eastern parishes) can be poor; stick with bottled water if you're in doubt. (Also see Water in the Health section, earlier in this chapter.)

## Nonalcoholic Drinks

**Coffee** Jamaican Blue Mountain coffee is considered among the most exotic coffees in the world. It's also the most expensive, fetching up to US$35 a pound in retail shops in the USA and Europe, and double that in Japan. You can buy it in Jamaica for US$2 a pound.

The coffee is relatively mild, light-bodied, and lacks an acrid aftertaste. It has a musty, almost woody flavor, and its own unmistakable aroma. It's delicious.

Most upscale hotels and restaurants serve it as a matter of course. Unfortunately, the majority of lesser hotels serve either lesser coffees from other parts of the country or – sacrilege! – powdered instant coffee. Be careful if you ask for white coffee, which Jamaicans interpret to mean 50% hot milk and 50% coffee. For more about Blue Mountain coffee, see 'Hallowed Grounds' in the Facts about Jamaica chapter (also see Old Tavern Estate in the Section section of the Blue Mountains & Southeast Coast chapter).

**Tea** Coffee is not Jamaica's drink of choice. Locals prefer herbal teas such as 'fevergrass,' said to bring down a fever, or soursop leaves for calming the nerves. 'Tea' is a generic Jamaican term for any usually hot, nonalcoholic drink, commonly referring to popular herbal 'teas' used by locals as medicines and aphrodisiacs. But the term is also used for other ingredients. 'Fish tea' is made from boiled fish broth, usually seasoned and with vegetables added. Jamaicans will make teas of anything: Irish moss is often mixed with rum, milk, and spices; and ginger, mint, ganja, and even fish are brewed into teas. Be careful if innocently tempted by 'mushroom tea,' the fungus in question is hallucinogenic, and unless you're in search of an LSD-like buzz, steer clear.

'Chocolate tea ball' is a tea-free beverage made from a chocolate paste rolled into a hard ball with a touch of nutmeg and cinnamon (they're now rare, but you'll find them around Port Antonio, where they're still made by the Fairy Hill's Long Road Co-operative).

**Cold Drinks** A Jamaican favorite for cooling off is skyjuice. This shaved-ice cone is flavored with sugary fruit syrup and lime juice, and is sold at streetside stalls, usually in a small plastic bag with a straw. Sanitation is sometimes questionable. The same is true of snocones and bellywash, the local name for limeade.

Your best bet for quenching a thirst is to drink coconut water straight from the nut. You'll find them for sale for about US$0.50 from streetside vendors, who will lop off the top and provide a straw. Coconut water is one of the healthiest of drinks (full of iron), and it's a diuretic that flushes out the bloodstream. (It is not the same as coconut milk, which is squeezed from the dry nut.)

Another refreshing and nutritious drink to combat the heat is a fruit punch of blended ripe fruits. Countryfolk also drink *wash* (brown-sugar water, often with lime or orange juice) for an energy boost. Another popular drink with locals is ginger beer, which isn't a beer at all, but a zesty soda – delicious, slightly spicy, and a perfect tonic for hot days. And watch for *sorrel*, traditionally a bright red Christmas drink made from flower petals.

Ting is Jamaica's own soft drink, a bottled grapefruit soda. Pepsi and Coca-Cola are also available almost everywhere.

Be mindful of milk, which is often unpasteurized (boiled milk is fine).

## Alcoholic Drinks

Red Stripe is the beer of Jamaica. In fact, it's synonymous with the island. (Jamaicans seem inordinately proud of their national brew.) Crisp and sweet, it's perfectly light and refreshing. It's also the only known antidote to hot spicy jerk meats. If you hear locals calling for 'policemen,' don't panic: the beer is named for the 'natty trim' – a conspicuous red seam – on the trouser leg of the uniform of the Jamaican police force. It's not a *great* beer by anyone's standard, but it's perfect for the tropics.

Heineken is also brewed in Jamaica. Malty Dragon Stout is also popular, and is a favorite of Jamaican women, as is bottled Guinness, brewed under license locally.

Rum ranges from dark rums to a mind-bogglingly powerful white (clear) rum, the libation of choice for poorer Jamaicans.

Jamaica produces many liqueurs, mostly of rum, but also of coffee beans and fruits. Sangster's rum-based 'Old Jamaica' liqueurs are among the more famous and use natural extracts of Caribbean fruits and spices. (Also see the World's End section in the Blue Mountains & Southeast Coast chapter.)

The original coffee liqueur is Tía Maria, which was developed in 1946 by Morris Cargill and a government pathologist, Ken Evans, using Blue Mountain coffee. The liqueur is named after Cargill's aunt *(tía* is Spanish for aunt). It makes an excellent additive in cakes, soufflés, and pastry creams. The caffeine 'neutralizes' the depressant effect of the alcohol.

## ENTERTAINMENT

Jamaica has plenty to keep you amused, from ear-shattering 'stageshows' for the masses to ballet for the social elite. Most of the high culture, including theater, and the best discos and upscale bars are to be found in Kingston. Elsewhere the key word is reggae (see the Reggae'n'Riddims special section), although jazz is growing in popularity. The various elements of Jamaican society each has its own genre, including rum shops and ubiquitous go-go clubs, the staples of island life for the male masses.

Few outlets cater specifically to women. Elderly Jamaicans, in general, have few social outlets. There are few clubs and few formal organizations. Certainly none in the boondocks.

Any Ticket (☎ 937-1279), 3 Lancelin Ave, Kingston 10, is a ticket office for entertainment and sporting events.

**Rum Shops** Rum shops are the staple of island entertainment and can be found on virtually any street and in every village. They are funky bars and clubs catering to poorer Jamaicans; the drink of choice is Dragon stout, Red Stripe, or white rum (often laced with milk). Locals will swear to you that the overproof rum doesn't give you a hangover, but expect to wake up with a sore head and misty memories. Rum shops are patronized almost exclusively by men, and de rigueur decor includes Christmas lights and girlie pinups.

**Go-Go Clubs** Go-go clubs are another staple of Jamaican nightlife, often as an adjunct to the village rum shop. Almost every village has at least one; sometimes several cluster together. Usually it's simply a bar, often quite rustic, with a mirrored stage where young women dance in lingerie, string bikinis, or topless (even naked) dance and perform – often quite raunchy – contortions. None is upscale in the style of US 'gentleman's clubs.' Most have private rooms for one-on-one 'private dances' (the dancers are paid an average of J$600 a night – about US$18 – plus whatever they can gain for private lap-dances or for other services rendered). Although the

## The Story of Rum

Jamaican sugar has been turned into alcohol since Spanish times, when *meleza* (cane molasses) was fermented to make a liquor called *aguardiente*. The British introduced distillation to produce a cane liquor called *saccharum*, from which the term 'rum' is derived.

Making rum involves three stages: fermentation, distillation, and aging. The traditional distillation process used copper pots and produced a heavily flavored rum containing 85% alcohol and 15% water. The distilled liquor was then poured into 40-gallon, charred-oak barrels and matured from three to 20 years. Rum derived its distinct flavor and color from the charred barrel as it aged. A small percentage was lost every year to evaporation: the 'angel's share.'

Very little rum is produced in this manner today. The modern, continuous-still method produces a more lightly flavored rum of higher alcohol content. Most modern rum is aged in stainless steel vats for no more than three years, and since all rums are clear after distillation, the color and flavor are 'manufactured' with caramel and other additives.

'White overproof' is the rum of the poor Jamaican, and it's an integral part of island culture. Overproof rum from homemade stills is virtually pure alcohol (legally overproof rum is 151 proof, but bootleg liquor can be a brain-melting, throat-searing 170 proof).

It is used as a remedy for all sorts of maladies, from toothaches to colds (it was originally called 'Kill Devil'). It's also used to clean newborn babies and to baptize them. Of course, it drowns sorrows and is imbibed liberally at wakes to chase away duppies. Jamaican gravediggers still sprinkle rum on the ground before digging to consecrate it. White rum is also supposedly good for a man's libido (a popular version is the 'Front End Loader').

clientele is mostly young and male, it is not unusual to see Jamaican couples in the crowd. They're generally non-threatening places, but see Prostitution in the Dangers & Annoyances section, earlier in this chapter, for warnings.

**Stageshows** Concerts – 'stageshows' – are as integral a feature of Jamaica as ackee and saltfish. Usually held at open-air venues, they draw big crowds, catered to with itinerant vendors selling beer and rum. The distinct smell of ganja drifts through the air, amidst the deafening noise from banks of speakers the size of double-decker buses. The larger, better organized concerts are a marvelous slice of Jamaican life. The billing often includes several top-name reggae or dancehall performers, such as Third World, Buju Banton, Gregory Isaacs, and Lady Saw.

Jamaicans really get into their concerts and often throw fireworks to show appreciation.

'Sound-system parties' or 'jump-ups' are smaller, impromptu concerts ubiquitous on weekends throughout the island, often at improvised 'lawns' and often in remote locations where the music can be cranked up until the earth trembles (literally!) and noise restrictions are not likely to be enforced. Music is supplied by DJs – 'selectors' – who often 'dub' or improvise lyrics over prerecorded sound tracks. Often, rival DJs vie against each other at 'clashes.' DJ-based shows are nowhere near as appealing as those where live bands play. Sound-system parties are popular with a young, often unruly male crowd and violence is always a possibility. Security guards usually frisk for weapons, but often someone will sneak in a gun to let off as a bravado demonstration of appreciation. City-based clashes are best avoided.

**Discos & Nightclubs** Kingston has more than a dozen discos ranging from earthy dancehall discos frequented mostly by the urban poor to upscale discos playing mostly US and European chart-toppers plus soca for tourists and the local middle classes. The leading resort towns each have a choice of two or three discos. Many hotels also have their own discos open to everybody.

The better discos usually have theme nights. Thursday is traditionally 'ladies nite,' offering either free entry or free drinks to women. Sunday is traditionally oldies night, with a selection of R&B, old-time reggae, and ska.

The best of the bunch are heaps of fun and usually quite safe. Cover charge rarely exceeds US$5 and is often free mid-week.

Many clubs get jam-packed and are sweaty, horribly smoky affairs with the music cranked up full-bore, beer bottles (often broken) littering the floor, and the omnipresent gigolos and salacious females ever-ready to hit up on foreign tourists.

**Theater** Although small-scale theater can be found in all the major towns, Kingston is where the real action is. Jamaica's most beloved theater company is the National Dance Theater Company, which performs at the Little Theater. Almost every performance is sold out.

The company tours the island, along with smaller repertoire companies catering to a local audience, often in patois and most commonly performing 'roots plays' rather than Shakespeare. Roots plays make much of Jamaican traditions and folklore and involve plenty of audience participation. And tongue-in-cheek, salacious content is common. Also see Arts in the Facts about Jamaica chapter.

**Cinemas** Jamaicans are not big moviegoers (given the paucity of cinemas, Jamaicans tend to rent videos). Nonetheless, most large cities have at least one cinema showing top-run Hollywood movies, usually only a month or two after their release in the USA. Most movie houses are now smoke-free, but anticipate a lot of booing and screams and other audience interruptions. Entrance generally costs US$2 or US$5.

**Gambling** There are no casinos in Jamaica. Although hoteliers have lobbied for gambling, in February 1995 the government voted not to allow the introduction of gambling in the country. However, several larger hotels have video slot-machines (one-arm bandits), which are legal. By far the largest is the recently opened Coral Cliffs Gaming Room in Montego Bay (it's a casino by any other name), with 100 gaming machines and all the flashing-bulbs and neon glitz of Vegas.

Betting on horse racing is permitted at Caymanas Park (see Spectator Sports, below) and at betting shops nationwide. Charles Off Betting (☎ 922-3124) and Western Track Ltd (☎ 952-8721) are two of the leading chain branches.

## SPECTATOR SPORTS

Jamaica is relatively devoid of spectator sports. Cricket is by far the most important sport on the island, and games between leading regional and international teams are played frequently at Sabina Park, Kingston. Horse racing often draws large, enthusiastic crowds. Polo is played at St Ann Polo Club and at Chukka Cove Farm, both in St Ann parish.

The Dover Raceway, south of Runaway Bay, hosts the Motor Sports Championship Series of car and motorcycle racing, held from April to December. See Motor Racing in the Runaway Bay section of the Ocho Rios & North Coast chapter for more details on the race.

### Cricket

Cricket, played virtually year-round, is as much a part of Jamaica's cultural landscape as is reggae. You'll come across small fields in even the most remote backwaters, where boys with makeshift bats practice the bowls and swings that may one day take them from rural obscurity to fortune and fame.

Cricket is a legacy of British rule. The late 19th-century colonialists sponsored cricket as a game of true gentlemen. It was a handy tool for spreading English culture and an admiration for the 'mother country.' In his book *Beyond a Boundary*, CLR James postulated that the level of maturity of cricket was used by the British in the first half of this century as a measure of whether a colony was prepared for self-rule. There is no doubt that cricket has helped cement a sense of

regional identity and unity throughout the English-speaking Caribbean islands.

Jamaica has no national team. Instead, the best players from the cricketing nations of the Caribbean form the West Indies team, which has dominated world cricket for two decades. Cricket fever boils over when the West Indies plays England. Regional competitions feature teams from individual islands.

Jamaicans turn what is in England a game without spirit into the most exhilarating cricket in the world. Leading tournaments ignite holy passions. They're also a social occasion. Entire families arrive with coolers of beer and hampers stuffed with Jamaican food. Plenty of rum is consumed, and the calls of the crowd make for great theater.

The rising Jamaican star is Jimmy Adams, who follows in the footsteps of such heroes as George Headley. In the 1930s, Headley dazzled the world with his unique skills (he is considered Jamaica's Babe Ruth) and is still the only man to score two centuries (a century is 100 runs) in one test match at Lord's, the London cricket ground that is the sport's world headquarters and the most hallowed ground of cricket.

See the Public Holidays & Special Events section, earlier in this chapter, for a listing of cricket matches played on the island.

**George Headley**

## Understanding Cricket

It's easy to get the gist of the game of cricket. Here are the basics:

Two teams of 11 players compete. As in baseball, one team fields its entire team while the other team has individuals come up to bat against a bowler (pitcher). The batsman attempts to protect a wicket – three wooden stumps (posts), on top of which sit two precariously balanced bails (crosspieces) – with a three-foot-long, five-inch-wide bat, flat on one side and ridged on the other. The bowler attempts to knock the bails from the wicket (home plate), which stands at the end of a 22-yard-long grass pitch – wicket-to-wicket – in the center of a circular field (this is the origin of the 22-yard 'chain,' a traditional measure still beloved of Jamaicans). The batsman attempts to hit the ball, which may be delivered relatively slowly or at 100mph. The ball usually bounces in front of the batsman on delivery, the bowler having usually put a tricky spin on the ball. The batsman can send the ball in any direction, including behind, and may choose to run to the end of the pitch to score a run. Four runs are automatically earned if the ball passes the boundary of the cricket field; six if it does so without touching the ground (the equivalent of a home run in baseball).

If a fielder catches the ball before it hits the ground, the batsman is out (the batsman may also be called out at the umpire's discretion if the ball hits his leg instead of the wicket). A second batsman stands at the far end of the pitch. The two batsmen must run past each other to opposite ends to score a run, and can do so as many times as prudence allows while the ball is being fielded (the equivalent of 'stealing bases'; as in baseball, if the ball is fielded to the wicket before the batsman reaches it, then he is out). After every six balls (pitches), or 'over,' a second bowler bowls from the opposite wicket.

Each team usually plays two innings. A single innings (in cricket, there is no singular 'inning' as in baseball) is complete when all the team members are 'out' (there are various other ways in which they can be called 'out' by one of two umpires). The team can choose to retire before all its members have batted, in which case the average number of runs per batsman can prove strategically useful in calculating a winner (the best batsmen usually bat first). To hit a 'century' (100 runs) in an innings is considered great – the equivalent of a 'grand slam' in baseball. To be 'bowled for a duck' (0 runs) is a disgrace.

One-day matches are common. However, test matches (games between international teams) are played over the course of three to five days, not least because the batsmen are so skilled that it can take a long time to get them out.

## Soccer

Soccer is Jamaica's second sport and was given a huge boost by the success of the Reggae Boyz – Jamaica's national soccer team – in qualifying for the 1998 World Cup finals in Paris. The team lost badly in the finals (though finished better than the US team), but in the process they had become national heroes. On any day in any village, a soccer ball is sure to be kicked around, and weekend games between village teams draw large crowds of spectators (all male). International matches are played at the National Stadium in Kingston (☎ 929-4970).

## Athletics

Jamaica is a leader on the international athletics scene, regularly producing track and field athletes of world record caliber dating back to sprinter Arthur Wint, Jamaica's first Olympic gold medal winner (in 1948) through the more recent successes of Merlene Ottey (gold medal winner in 1996). Most major meets are hosted at Kingston's National Stadium, though important international championship meets are infrequent.

## SHOPPING

Jamaica has a wide range of arts, crafts, and duty-free items, plus food items and drinks such as Blue Mountain coffee, rum liqueurs, Pickapeppa sauce, and marinades such as Busha Brown's gourmet pickles, relishes, and other gourmet products. I am not aware of any Jamaican foods, drinks, or spices that cannot be exported, though you should check with your home country's customs to see what restrictions they might impose on imports. (See the Customs section earlier in this chapter for more information.)

### Crazy about Horses

Jamaicans have always been passionate about horse racing, which takes place twice-weekly at Caymanas Park, at Portmore, outside Kingston. In 1687 the governor of Jamaica even dissolved the House of Assembly following a riot when the Speaker denied a member permission to attend a horserace.

Horse racing takes place at Caymanas Park (☎ 939-0848), in Portmore, 10 miles west of Kingston, each Wednesday and Saturday and on public holidays. Track Tours Ltd (☎ 952-4657), PO Box 19, Montego Bay, offers tours from Montego Bay on race days, and JUTA Ltd (☎ 974-2292, fax 974-5406), in Coconut Grove Plaza, offers tours from Ocho Rios.

JAMAICA TOURIST BOARD

Every resort area has a choice of duty-free stores, crafts shops, and roadside stalls selling a full range of goods. Kingston has a world-class range of shopping centers.

## Cigars

The past few years have seen an explosion in the popularity of Cuba as a tourist destination for Jamaicans – and of smoking Cuban cigars as a hip pastime. Most gift stores in upscale hotels sell premium Cuban cigars. (Technically it's illegal for US citizens to purchase Cuban cigars unless they hold a Treasury Dept license to travel to Cuba, in which case purchase of any Cuban item is restricted to the island. Thus it remains illegal to buy Cuban cigars in Jamaica.)

Fine handmade Jamaican cigars give Havana cigars a run for their money though. Cinfuentes y Cia Ltd (a subsidiary of General Cigar Co of Connecticut) has been operating in Jamaica for over 40 years. The company specializes in premium Macanudo cigars. You can even buy direct from the factory (☎ 924-7052) in Kingston. You can also buy Cinfuentes or Royal Jamaica cigars at gift shops, duty-free outlets, Kingston and Montego Bay's international airports, or the Jamaica Tobacco Retail Store (☎ 925-1547), 31 Upper Waterloo Rd, Kingston 10.

## Duty-Free Goods

Resort towns feature a plethora of duty-free and in-bond shops, and most upscale hotels sell duty-free items – from name-brand colognes and Gucci watches to Mont Blanc pens and Colombian emeralds (at up to 30% below US or European retail prices). The same is true of island-made products such as rums, liqueurs, and cigars, which you can buy for 50% or greater savings. Prices vary between stores and resorts, however, so it pays to comparison shop.

By law you must pay for duty-free goods in foreign currency. You can use credit cards or traveler's checks. In certain cases you may find that you cannot walk out with your purchase; instead, the goods will be delivered to your hotel or cruise ship.

## Arts & Crafts

Tens of thousands of Jamaicans make a living as artists selling to the tourist trade. Much of the artwork is kitsch, paintings of and intuitive hardwood carvings of Bob Marley, glistening with oil, and fishes and animals, often painted in rainbow hues and touched with pointillist dots for anywhere from US$5 to US$50.

There's plenty of first-rate art, too (see Arts in the Facts about Jamaica chapter). Jamaican art is sought after by collectors worldwide. The best works are bought by local galleries for resale at fixed prices. Kingston has an excellent selection of galleries to choose from. (Jamaica's middle classes are enthusiastic about art.)

You should look far and wide before making a purchase. You should carefully examine wood carvings. Avoid green wood, as the carving will split when the wood dries out. Minute holes betray woodworm.

Colorful bead jewelry is a good buy, including bracelets in Rasta colors: red, yellow, and green. Baskets and other straw goods are also great bargains. Styles of baskets are as varied as their uses. The traditional *bankra* is an all-purpose rectangular basket of woven palm thatch – an integral part of the rural Jamaican scene. The word bankra, which is derived from the Ghanaian *bonkara*, is now synonymous with basket. Of course, you may need a good straw hat to guard against the sun. Look for 'jippi-jappa' hats (pronounced hippy-happa) from St Catherine parish, beautifully woven from fine strips of palm-leaf in the style of Panama hats and named for the town of Jipijapa in Ecuador. Jamaicans once called them 'trash hats' or 'wha-fi-do hats' (what to do?) because they were all they could afford.

The greater the distance from a craft market or resort town, the lower the prices in general.

Never pay the asking price. Higgle! It's expected; if you pay the first price quoted, you'll pay over the odds. Expect to settle on a price at least 20% below the initial asking price. The eventual price is dependent on your patience and bargaining skills. Keep your cool and good humor, which will go a long way toward getting a fair price.

Remember, however, that the life of most higglers is hard and you should be willing to pay a fair price. Leave your ego behind when bargaining – it is not a battle. Don't get involved in a serious bargaining if you don't intend to buy – to do so displays crass insensitivity.

Genuine higglers can be trusted, but the more aggressive and crafty hustlers who accost you with crafty schemes – called 'runnings' – cannot in general be trusted. Expect to find an agreed upon price jacked up a few minutes later.

Most roadside stalls accept cash only. Few will be able to ship your item home for you.

See regional chapters for specific locales.

## Furniture

Jamaica has a rich stock of skilled carpenters and furniture makers, a legacy of colonial days when skilled craftsworkers from Europe came to supervise construction and outfitting of plantation homes and passed on their skills to the locals. Jamaican carpenters are among the world's best at making antique reproduction furniture, and there are several top-notch furniture-making factories that manufacture in mahogany, wicker, and exotic woods, such as blue mahoe, aloe, lignum vitae, and guango. Furniture produced for the export market is top of the line, with an emphasis on Chippendale and Queen Anne styles. Medallion Galleries (☎ 923-9017), 1 Nanse Pen Rd, Kingston 11, is one of the leading producers.

High-quality, handmade wicker has also been winning a market for itself in North America. Creative Wicker Ltd (☎ 929-3019), Shop 1, 6 St Lucia Ave, Kingston, is geared for export and can fulfill orders within a few weeks.

The Jamaica Furniture Guild (☎ 929-1292), 13 Dominica Drive, Kingston 5, represents the leading exporters. Call for a recommendation and reference if you plan on shipping furniture home.

## Shopping with a Conscience

Many souvenirs sold in Jamaica are made from protected species of plants and animals that have been acquired illegally. By collecting or purchasing these items, you undermine the wildlife conservation efforts of the Jamaican government and wildlife organizations.

Most sea turtle products, including 'tortoise shell' jewelry and combs, are made from the highly endangered hawksbill sea turtle. Other turtle species are killed for eggs, food products, taxidermy, leather, and oil for creams. And eggs are poached for baking and for downing raw in rum-shops as aphrodisiacs. All are prohibited in trade. And all products made of endangered American crocodile are prohibited, as are black and white coral products, and swallowtail butterflies, commonly offered for sale in and around the Blue Mountains. Many species of plants – especially orchids – are endemics, also protected by law. Under US and international laws, violation of a foreign wildlife law is automatically a violation of domestic law.

Everywhere you drive along the north coast, you'll see Queen conch shells for sale. The species is of great ecological importance to Caribbean seagrass ecosystems, but is heavily overcollected in some areas. Historically, the meat has been a staple food item. Today the shells are popular ornaments and the conch population is now declining. Sure, they look pretty, but don't buy!

For more information, contact the World Wildlife Fund (☎ 800-225-5993, www.wwf.org), 1250 24th St NW, Washington, DC 20037 USA.

# Outdoor Activities

Jamaica has a number of sports and activities for those for whom bumming around on the beach spells boredom. Some facilities are world-class, such as the golf courses. Others, such as hiking and bicycling, are relatively undeveloped as organized activities.

## HIKING

You can spend weeks exploring the countryside. Jamaica's embryonic organized trail system, which is relegated mainly to the Blue Mountains-John Crow National Park, is popular for hiking. Elsewhere, there are rough bridle tracks used by locals spanning remote areas nationwide. Thousands of miles of these narrow trails bustle with foot traffic. Following them to the interior is a tremendous way to meet Jamaicans who have been little touched by outside influences.

The rugged and dramatic Cockpit Country and Hellshire Hills are little explored, yet tailor-made for experienced backcountry hikers. You'll also find plenty of bridle trails close to the major north coast resorts. The most developed area, however, is the Rio Grande Valley in Portland parish, where local tour guides offer a series of one to three-day hikes that lead to easily accessible waterfalls and caves, and to more remote destinations such as Nanny Town, the Blue Mountains, and John Crow Mountains.

Most trails are hilly, rugged, and often overgrown by bush. You'll find even a short hike demanding: oppressive heat and humidity can turn what seems like an easy stroll into a grueling trudge. Allow considerably more time than you would in temperate climates to cover a similar distance, especially since distances can appear deceptively short on a map. And take locals' assurances that your destination is 'jus' around de corner' or 'a likkle distance' with a grain of salt.

Travel light. Always carry plenty of water, as you're sure to sweat profusely and dehydration can set in quickly. Don't attempt to hike farther than your state of health will allow. Bear in mind that many isolated roads and paths become overgrown quickly (consider buying a machete for off-the-beaten-path hiking). And remember that weather conditions can change quickly, especially in mountainous areas where sudden torrential downpours can turn hiking trails into mud. Carry a windbreaker and a sweater or jacket in hilly areas. Long pants, rather than shorts, are best for hiking through bush, as they protect against thorns. Generally, sneakers or tennis shoes are fine for hiking. Even better are the new breed of lightweight canvas hiking boots. You'll want something sturdier than sneakers to handle the sharp limestone of the Cockpit Country and Hellshire Hills. And be sure to take plenty of insect repellent, plus a small first-aid kit.

You will rarely be far from habitation, but don't succumb to a false sense of security. It's easy to injure yourself in Jamaica's back-country, and phones and first aid will seldom be close at hand. Always follow established trails: Jamaica's mountainous terrain is too treacherous to go wandering off the track, as thick vegetation hides sinkholes and crevasses. Seek advice from locals about trail conditions before setting out.

Consider hiring an experienced local guide, if only because the danger of stumbling upon a commercial patch of ganja is ever-present; in these days of determined efforts by authorities to destroy ganja cultivation, your discovery carries with it the potential of serious consequences. You can hire guides at many local rum shops.

The Jamaica Alternative Tourism, Camping & Hiking Association (JATCHA) remains the best source of information on hiking, although Peter Bentley, the founder, now lives in Australia. (Bentley was the father of commercial hiking in Jamaica and is missed for many reasons, not the least of which is his colorful, devil-may-care persona – he used to hike naked except for a bush hat and tattered sneakers!) JATCHA (☎ 702-0314, 702-0112, 800-532-2271), PO Box 216, Kingston 7, is based at Maya Lodge, at Jack's Hill in the hills north of Kingston. It is now run by Valerie Phipps and her assistant, Michael 'Sweet Pea' Barrett. Bentley's former company, Sense Adventures, is now known as Destinations, and is really the alter ego of JATCHA. It provides a reservation service for guides, sells maps, has a good reference library on hiking and Jamaica's natural history, offers guided hikes, and will plan an itinerary according to your desires (see the Blue Mountains & Southeast Coast chapter for details).

The Touring Society of Jamaica (☎ 975-7158, fax 975-3620, lyndalee@islandoutpost .com, www.touringjamaica.com), c/o Island Outpost, PO Box 118, Ocho Rios, also offers guided hikes into the Blue Mountains, with visits to coffee plantations, botanical gardens, and other offbeat sites, including an option for a helicopter ride from Ocho Rios. The company caters to more moneyed folk. Travelers of impecunious means should try Nature N U Tours (☎ 977-5607), 3 University Drive, Elleston Flats, Kingston 7, which offers weekend trips for US$28.50 to US$43 per person, using the cabins at Portland Gap.

See regional chapters for information on Sun Ventures (☎ 960-6685) for tours of Kingston and the Blue Mountains, and Rasta Mountain Eco-Adventures (☎ 956-9092), for hill hikes in Negril.

Stuart's Travel, which acts as an adventure travel specialist and has offices islandwide, can be reached at the following offices:

| | |
|---|---|
| Brown's Town | ☎ 975-2566 |
| Linstead | ☎ 985-2781 |
| Kingston | ☎ 929-2345, 929-4222 |
| May Pen | ☎ 986-4542 |
| Montego Bay | ☎ 952-3448, 952-4350 |
| Ocho Rios | ☎ 974-2288 |
| Spanish Town | ☎ 984-3285 |

Many individuals nationwide freelance as hiking guides. See regional chapters for contact information and prices.

Steve Cohen's *Adventure Guide to Jamaica* provides details on hiking routes in the Blue Mountains and elsewhere.

## Hiking in the National Parks

The potentials are immense. Many hardy hikers have trod the Blue Mountain pathways, and most choose the path to the summit of Blue Mountain Peak (see the Blue Mountains & Southeast Coast chapter). The Blue Mountains, however, embrace hundreds of miles of bridle trails used by locals. The Protected Areas Resource Conservation Project has been developing this fascinating complex of pathways into a trail system (including a Blue Mountain Ridge Trail, akin to the Appalachian Trail of the eastern USA), with hiking trails categorized as 'guided,' 'nonguided,' and 'wilderness trails.' Routes vary from an easy morning stroll to minor expeditions.

There are a few trails suited only to experienced trekkers; a couple require advance planning, such as the path to Nanny Town, the remote Maroon redoubt on the wild, totally uninhabited, mid-level northern slope of Blue Mountain Peak. The path is cleared occasionally, but then quickly retaken by undergrowth. See both the Port Antonio & Northeast Coast and the Blue Mountains & Southeast Coast chapters for details on hikes in the Rio Grande Valley (which separates the Blue Mountains and the Jim Crow Mountains) and into the Blue Mountains.

The Cockpit Country offers vast potential that remains as yet untapped; National Park status is pending. And the Negril Conservation Area is evolving as a center for hikes.

*A Hiker's Guide to the Blue Mountains,* by Bill Wilcox, is an indispensable guide for serious hikers.

## SCUBA DIVING

Jamaica's shores are as beautiful below the water as they are above, especially along the north coast where the treasures range from shallow reefs, caverns, and trenches to walls and drop-offs just a few hundred yards offshore. Jacques Cousteau described the Montego Bay area as having 'some of the most dramatic sponge life in the Caribbean.' Negril, on the west coast, is another favorite spot with a diverse reef system. There are ship wrecks (plus aircraft and even cars), especially around the rarely dived Hellshire cays (near Kingston) and Port Royal, which boasts a sunken pirate city (currently off limits).

All the favorite stars are on show: moray eels, grunts, barracudas, stingrays, turtles, nurse sharks, and an impressive array of hard and soft coral formations. Most dive locations are within a 20-minute boat ride from shore. Most of the reefs off the southern coast, where the island shelf extends up to 20 miles, are much farther out to sea.

Jamaica's waters offer exceptional visibility and water temperatures above 80°F year-round. Wet suits are not required for warmth, though a body wet suit (without arms and legs) is recommended and a full wet suit comes in handy to prevent scrapes on coral.

The Jamaica Dive Extravaganza (☎ 800-815-5019) was hosted along the north coast in spring 1998 and featured seminars, photo competitions, and a wide variety of dives. The two-week event is set to become annual; look for special promotional packages.

An excellent resource for exploring Jamaica underwater is the *Diving & Snorkeling Guide to Jamaica* by Hannie and Theo Smitt (Lonely Planet).

## Organizations

The following dive organizations are good to know:

Divers Alert Network (DAN)
 (☎ 919-684-2948, 919-684-8111 24-hour emergency line) PO Box 3823, Durham NC 27710. Offers divers' health insurance, covering evacuations and treatment in emergencies

National Association of Underwater Instructors (NAUI)
 (☎ 813-628-6284, fax 813-628-8253) 9942 Currie Davis Drive, suite H, Tampa, FL 33619-2667

Professional Association of Diving Instructors (PADI)
 (☎ 714-540-7234, 800-729-7234, fax 714-540-2609) 1251 E Dyer St No 100, Santa Ana, CA 92705

## Operators

By law, all dives in Jamaican waters are guided dives. There are dozens of licensed dive operators offering rental equipment and group dives led by qualified dive masters. Many hotels also offer dive facilities, including virtually all the major all-inclusive

resorts. Since 1986, when Jamaica enacted water-sport licensing laws, dive operators have been required to adhere to strict safety standards. All are regulated by the Jamaica Tourist Board and require a license to operate. Most belong to the Jamaica Association of Dive Operators (JADO; ☎ 974-6900).

'Resort courses' for beginners (also called 'Discover Scuba' or 'Intro to Scuba') are offered at most major resorts. They usually last a few hours. You can also take a PADI or NAUI certification course (plus more advanced courses) that last several days. You can't rent tanks or scuba equipment for unsupervised diving.

*Never* go diving with one of the freelance guides who solicit business on beaches.

The cost averages about US$35 per dive, or US$60 a day for a two-tank dive. Introductory half-day resort courses normally cost about US$50, and a full PADI certification course will cost US$350 to US$375. Certified divers should be sure to bring their dive cards.

The *Traveling Diver's Chapbook* (Elephant Socks Publishing, PO Box 1658, Sausalito, CA 94966) is a compendium of opinions on and recommendations for dive resorts and operators written by customers. It's a handy reference for comparing resorts and making your choice based on ostensibly unbiased critiques.

Many dive packages are available from specialist dive-tour operators in North America or Europe. Package tours can offer considerable savings. Reputable companies include the following:

Caribbean Adventures
 (☎ 800-934-3483, fax 954-434-4282) 10400 Griffin Rd No 109, Cooper City, FL 33328

Tropical Adventures Travel
 (☎ 206-441-3483, 800-348-9778, fax 206-441-5431, dive@divetropical.com)

Most of the upscale all-inclusive resorts have their own scuba operations, including Beaches, Breezes, Couples, Grand Lido, Hedonism II, and Sandals. Other well-known operators can be found in the regional chapters.

## Safety

Although all dives are guided, you are responsible for your own safety. Always check your equipment thoroughly, and ensure you know how to use it. If you haven't dived for some time, it's wise to take a refresher course either before or during your vacation. And rigidly adhere to maximum depth and time limits. Dives are restricted in Jamaica to 100 feet.

See the Health section in the Facts for the Visitor chapter for information on hazardous marine life.

The only decompression chamber on the island is at the University of West Indies Marine Laboratory in Discovery Bay (☎ 973-3274, 24 hours; ☎ 973-2241, 9 am to 5 pm).

## Recommended Sites

See the regional chapters for more suggested diving sites, prices, and diving course information.

### Montego Bay & Northwest Coast

Jamaica's first marine sanctuary was at Montego Bay. Most dive sites are close to shore – one is as close as 200 yards in – and range from teeming patch reefs to awe-inspiring walls that begin in as little as 35 feet of water.

There are three main areas near Montego Bay: offshore from Reading, north of Donald Sangster International Airport, and offshore at Rose Hall.

Reading has a few primary diving spots. Spanish Anchor is known for its anchors, caverns, and tunnels, and coral heads where eagle rays hang out. Nearby, Garden of Eels is named for a species of conger eel that inhabits the seabed, but there's superb wall diving, too. Novice divers might try Chatham Reef, offshore from Sandals Montego Bay and carpeted with gorgonians. Another great shallow dive is Rose Hall Reef, known for its tall columns of pillar coral and walls, divided by sand flats, that begin in as little as 10 feet of water. There are many overhangs, and you're likely to come across a harmless nurse shark or two dozing under a ledge.

For advanced divers, the Point, north of the airport, is considered 'the ultimate wall dive,' due to the dense corals and fish that are fed by crystal-clear waters scoured by currents. The wall here starts at 70 feet and drops to at least 300 feet. The Airport Reef, off the southwestern edge of the airport, is considered by many to be the best site on the island, with masses of coral canyons, caves, and tunnels.

Farther east, the wall at Falmouth runs within half a mile of shore and is riddled with tunnels and caverns. A favorite is Chub Castle, which starts fairly shallow with a top decorated by soft corals and basket sponges; its wall is strung with rope sponges and black coral.

**Negril** Miles of coral reefs, now protected within the Negril Marine Park, make Negril a popular dive site. The best diving is a 10-minute boat ride from shore. Visibility reaches up to 100 feet. There are no real wall dives, but the coral reefs more than make up for that in diversity (clusters of dwarf tube sponges are a noteworthy feature not common elsewhere in Jamaica), with shallow reefs perfect for novice divers and mid-depth reefs right off the 7-mile-long main beach at Long Bay.

There are even plane wrecks off Long Bay. At the north end of the bay, near Booby Cay at a site called the Arches, is a small plane – called 'Shallow Plane' – whose hull harbors soldierfish, sentinels of a ghostly aluminum carcass. Nurse sharks and moray eels also call this home. Another plane, this one a small Cessna called 'Deep Plane,' lies nearby off Booby Cay Reef. You can even enter the cockpit for a dandy photo.

The reefs along the West End cliff-face are literally at your doorstep. The West End offers caves and tunnels, and its overhangs are popular for night dives because of their proximity to shore. Hawksbill turtles are common here.

**Ocho Rios & North Coast** Some of the best diving in Jamaica lies off the north central coast, where wrecks (some of which date back centuries, while others are quite recent) add intrigue, and classic wall dives remain superb.

Ocho Rios offers a great opportunity to spot nurse sharks, which are commonly seen snoozing on the sandy bottom at Jacks Hall Reef, near the egress of Dunn's River. Nearby, rising from the depths, is Top of the Mountain, boasting dozens of coral species, some quite rare in Jamaica, including grooved-blade sea whip. A few miles east of town is Devil's Reef, a pinnacle that drops more than 200 feet and is popular with commercial dive groups. Devil's Reef is a ridge, about 700 yards offshore, beginning at about 60 feet and dropping to the inky black brine.

Snorkelers and novice divers are delivered a gem at Caverns, a shallow reef about a quarter-mile long. Nurse sharks are often around and the wreck of the 140-foot minesweeper, *Kathryn*, remains intact, permitting divers to swim inside. Eerie! Various fishes and other sealife have already claimed their space among the crowded condominium. The reef is named for the nearby caves where harmless sharks and elkhorn coral are highlights.

To the west, Runaway Bay shares the same wall as Falmouth and offers similar conditions plus sunken planes and even two Mercedes cars! Here, too, is the *Reggae Queen*, a 100-foot tugboat with a wooden hull that has been the seed for an artificial reef. A fabulous wall dive – Pocket's Reef (named for Colin Hamilton, alias Mr Pocket or 'Mr P,' the dive master who discovered it) – begins nearby and boasts seven species of black coral among many other coral types. Ricky's Reef is another popular deep wall. It drops to a sandy shelf at 140 feet that is home to stingrays, and there are lobsters and king crabs in the coral crevices. Want to feed the fish? Head to Silver Spray, another favorite of local scuba outfitters where the fish, including snappers, are used to hand outs.

Potty Reef, also at Runaway Bay, will have you flush with excitement. JamAqua Watersports sank this toilet for a lark. Divers can't resist having their photo taken sitting on, er, King Neptune's throne.

**Port Antonio & East Coast** The east coast isn't as well developed for scuba diving, and the shallow reefs were badly damaged by

Hurricane Gilbert in 1988 (by now most have recovered nicely). Nonetheless, there are some excellent sites and several marine species that are rare elsewhere off Jamaica. The best sites are east of Port Antonio, notably at Alligator Long (not to be confused with two other sites called Alligator Head and Alligator Deep), boasting marvelous arrays of coral plus sand flats with stingrays; and Dragon Bay, a shallow reef being repopulated by staghorn coral.

Farther east, on the windward coast, the seas are rough and visibility is reduced.

**Kingston & Port Royal** This is Jamaica's unexplored coast. Since the area is off the mainstream tourist map, much of the area has yet to be dived, and new dive sites are still being discovered. The area's position and prevailing winds normally mean that diving is a morning affair only, when seas are calm and visibility good. Lying in the lee of the island, however, these waters do not suffer the adverse effects of midwinter 'northers' that sometimes force dives to be canceled on the north coast.

Several prime sites are well established. Some of the best reef development in Jamaica is in this area, with small cays separated by clear blue water no deeper than 50 feet, surrounded by an outer reef with a drop-off point at 80 feet.

The Southeast Cay Wall is a drift dive (in an easterly direction) that follows a wall beginning at 50 feet and descending to 90 feet before a gradual ascent back to 30 feet. It is marked by deep crevices overhung with plate coral (a dive light is recommended for peering inside the recesses). Nurse sharks are common.

For a true blue-water dive, head out to Windward Edge, about 7 miles south of Kingston Harbour. The distance from shore guarantees fabulous visibility during calm days, and the condition of the reef, which begins at 70 feet, is pristine, with plentiful staghorn coral, vase sponges, and even the possibility of encounters with dolphins.

The reefs off Hellshire, southwest of Kingston Harbour, have been much bashed about by storms but are recovering, with elkhorn and staghorn both well represented. Barracuda and nurse sharks are common. The wreck of the Cayman Trader, a burnt-out vessel that sank here during a storm when being towed from Kingston Harbour in 1977, lies scattered about the reef and flats, having been broken up by ensuing storms. The seas here are subject to storm surges, and divers are advised not to enter the enclosed wreck sections, which are inhabited by many species of fish.

If the thought of searching for pirate treasure appeals to you, you should dive at Port Royal, site of the former pirate capital of the Caribbean (much of the original city sank below the ocean, where it remains, in the 1692 earthquake). However, dives of the Sunken City are currently by permit only (see Port Royal in the Kingston & Environs chapter for further information).

## Sharks & Dolphins

It's common to see sharks in the waters and reefs around Jamaica. Mostly these are harmless nurse sharks. There is no more exhilarating experience for a diver than staring eye-to-eye at a shark. Don't worry! The critters are wary of humans and usually give divers a wide berth. Currently, no commercial dive operators feed the sharks, as they do in the Bahamas.

Dolphins are seen increasingly in Kingston Harbour and in the waters off southeast Jamaica, though they're not frequently spotted in other Jamaican waters. The animals (they're air-breathing mammals, not fish) are far more approachable if you have a snorkel than if you have noisy scuba gear. Remember, though, that they're also unpredictable wild creatures, despite their cute smiles. If you see one, heed the following advice:

- Remain passive if a dolphin approaches.
- Do not swim or chase after dolphins. They may perceive you as a threat and bite you.
- Never touch a dolphin, for the same reason.
- Do not lie or swim on your back, as this can make dolphins unpredictable.
- If a dolphin becomes aggressive or unpredictable, exit the water.

## GOLF

Jamaica is known for its golf courses. The island has more courses than any other Caribbean island, and has been attracting golfers since the mid-1800s when the first course was laid in the cool highlands at Mandeville.

Jamaica has 10 championship courses, some of which are regular stops for the PGA and LPGA tours. Green fees range from US$5 to US$150 in summer, and US$8 to US$180 in winter. Most courses rent out clubs (which cost US$5 to US$20 depending on the course), and have carts and caddies for hire. Most courses require that you hire a caddy – a wise investment, as they know the layout intimately. Don't be surprised to see caddies carrying golf bags on their heads! Tee times are usually easy to find out.

At least two additional championship courses are scheduled to open within the next few years, including at Whitehouse, on the southwest coast. For more information, contact the Jamaica Golf Association (☎ 925-2325). For the stats on Jamaica's courses, costs, and further details, see regional chapters.

Jamaica hosts several leading international golf tournaments, including the Johnnie Walker World Championship held each mid-December at Tryall Golf Club. (The championship is the richest in golf, with a first prize of US$550,000 and a total purse in excess of US$3 million.) Spectator admission is free, and a free shuttle runs from the Montego Bay Parish Library and selected hotels.

See the Special Events section in the Facts for the Visitor chapter for information on other tournaments.

Golfing Around in Jamaica, Ltd (☎ 926-7206, fax 929-5078), 54 Brentford Rd, Kingston 5, offers four, five, and eight-day golf packages.

## HORSEBACK RIDING

This is a great way to explore Jamaica. Stables are located in most resort areas, and hotels usually can arrange rides. Many lead through working plantations; others venture farther afield along bridle trails that lead into the rugged mountains. Riding times vary from one to six hours. Prices range from

## Bird Watching Sites

Good sites include Marshall's Pen (outside Mandeville), Font Hill Reserve and Great Morass (near Black River), the Great Morass and Royal Palm Reserve (Negril), Rockland Bird Feeding Station (near Montego Bay), and Salt Pond and Great Salt Pond (near Treasure Beach). There's an aviary in Hope Botanical Gardens in Kingston, and Enchanted Gardens (a resort in Ocho Rios) has a large walk-in aviary. The largest collection of caged birds – unfortunately the cages are unconscionably tiny – is at Serenity (near Spanish Town), with species from around the world. Heck, there's even Cashoo Ostrich Park (near Lacovia, in St Elizabeth), which, in

addition to its approximately three dozen ostriches, has a menagerie of avifauna.

The Gosse Bird Club – named for Philip Henry Gosse, the 'Father of Jamaican Ornithology' – is a valuable information source (see Bird Watching). It publishes a semi-annual *Broadsheet* about endemic birds of Jamaica and resident and migratory birds (US$8 annually for foreigners). It also offers field trips and educational programs.

A list of organizations that offer birding tours is in the Getting There & Away chapter. Recommended books and field guides to Jamaican birds are listed in the Facts for the Visitor chapter.

US$20 to US$40 for two-hour rides, and lessons can be arranged. See regional chapters for additional details.

### BIRD WATCHING

Jamaica is a birder's haven (see Flora & Fauna in the Facts about Jamaica chapter). The Blue Mountains, the Cockpit Country, the Black River Great Morass, and Negril Great Morass are the best spots.

All you need in the field is a good pair of binoculars and a guide to the birds of the island (see Books in Facts for the Visitor).

The Gosse Bird Club (☎ 922-2253), c/o Audrey Downer, PO Box 1002, Kingston 8, offers field trips and educational programs and is the best overall birding resource in Jamaica.

### SNORKELING

If you can swim you can snorkel, which means donning a swim mask (for better viewing), flippers (for easier propulsion in water), and a breathing tube that lets you

keep your face in the water full-time. It is amazing how different the undersea world looks through a snorkel mask.

There are dozens of sites suitable for snorkeling that are accessible from public beaches. Shallow dive sites are also perfect for snorkeling. Most scuba dive operators offer snorkeling trips, as do cruise outfitters.

Snorkeling equipment can be rented at most scuba dive operators and at beach hotels and resorts, typically for US$5 one hour or US$10 to US$15 a day. See regional chapters for recommended snorkeling sites and rental locations.

### SAILING

Most beachside resorts provide small sailboats called Sunfish, either as part of the hotel package rate or for a small hourly rental fee. These tiny craft are easy to handle and perfect for short forays from shore. Hotel staff will give basic instruction and away you go. They typically rent for US$15 to US$20 per hour.

Larger sailboats, yachts, and cruisers can be rented by the day or week from marinas and small beachside companies almost anywhere along the north coast, as well as at Morgan's Harbour and the Royal Jamaican Yacht Club, both at Port Royal near Kingston. (See Chartering, below.)

## Sightseeing & Theme Cruises

Jamaica's shoreline, indented with coves and backed by forested mountains, translates into a perfect sightseeing cruise ground. Short sailing cruises – usually three hours – are offered at all the major resorts in various permutations, from snorkeling cruises and 'wet'n'wild' party cruises, to sunset trips and romantic dining experiences. Half-day cruises cost about US$25 to US$35. Special theme cruises cost from US$35 to US$50.

See regional chapters for details about cruises.

## Chartering

All the major resorts have marinas where you can charter yachts or motorboats, either with a crew or 'bareboat.' (See the Charter Yachts section in the Getting There & Away chapter for explanations and caveats. Also see regional chapters for further details on rental opportunities.)

You can arrange a yacht charter on the island from:

Heave-Ho Charters
(☎ 974-5367, fax 974-5461)
11a Pineapple Place, Ocho Rios
Montego Bay Yacht Club
(☎ 979-8038) Montego Freeport, Montego Bay
Morgan's Harbour Yacht Club
(☎ 924-8464, fax 924-8146)
Marina Morgan's Harbour, Port Royal
Royal Jamaican Yacht Club
(☎ 924-8685) Palisadoes Park, Kingston 1

## SPORT FISHING

Jamaica's waters are a pelagic playpen for schools of blue and white marlin, dolphin fish, wahoo, tuna, and dozens of other species. Deepwater game fish run year-round through marlin alley, the deep Cayman Trench that begins just 2 miles from shore

and plummets to fathomless depths. Sport fishing is popular and rewarding.

Blue marlin is the most prized catch and can be hooked at fishing grounds all around the island. Though present all year, the largest fish are usually caught in late summer and autumn, notably off Port Antonio and the north coast. June and August are the prize months for sailfish and marlin.

## Tournaments

Almost a dozen fishing tournaments are held annually, highlighted by the prestigious Port Antonio International Marlin Tournament that caps a monthlong calendar each October. The fishing calendar includes the following:

### March

Bowden Invitational Tournament
(☎ 977-1078, fax 977-2061)
Bowden, near Port Morant

### September

Ocho Rios International Marlin Tournament
(☎ 922-7160)
Montego Bay Marlin Tournament
(☎ 979-8038, fax 979-8490)

### October

Falmouth Tournament
(☎ 954-3229, fax 954-4529)
Discovery Bay Marlin Tournament
(☎ 925-0893, fax 925-9673)
James Bond Oracabessa Marlin Tournament
(☎ 968-6792, fax 968-6779)
Great Jamaican Canoe Race and Hook'n'Line Fishing Tournament
(☎ 965-0552) Treasure Beach
Port Antonio International Marlin Tournament
(☎ 923-7683, 923-8724, fax 901-4179)

## Operators

Several operators set out from Montego Bay, Ocho Rios, and Port Antonio (most provide hotel transfers) and most other resort destinations. Morgan's Harbour and the Royal Jamaica Yacht Club at Port Royal, near Kingston, have fine marinas with sport fishing boats for hire.

In general, sport fishing in Jamaica is slightly cheaper than elsewhere in the Caribbean. Rates range from US$350 to US$400 for half a day to US$600 or more for a full day, with bait and tackle provided. You usually provide your own food and drinks. Most charter boats require a 50% deposit (if you cancel, do so at least 24 hours before departure to avoid losing your deposit). Some boats keep half the catch, so discuss terms with the skipper prior to setting out. Never book your trip or negotiate arrangements with bystanders on the dock or beach. (See regional chapters for details on chartering vessels.)

Freshwater fishing is popular among locals, but Jamaica remains untapped as a freshwater and fishing destination for foreigners. A growing number of inland resorts, however, raise tilapia, tarpon, and snook.

Few foreigners fish the south coast, where Jamaica's major fishing banks are located. This is the preserve of local fishermen who use 'canoes' (long, narrow longboats with outboards) and hand-lines – a spartan experience promoted in the annual Hook'n'Line Fishing Tournament (see above). You can hire one of the rustic fiberglass or wooden 'canoes' at Alligator Pond, Treasure Beach, or Whitehouse.

## RAFTING

Raft trips are a staple of the Jamaican tourist menu, offering a calming trip aboard slender rafts made of sturdy bamboo poles lashed together (there is no white-water rafting). The 36-foot-long rafts are 3 feet wide. You sit on a raised seat with padded cushions while an experienced 'captain' poles you through the washboard shallows and small cataracts.

Most trips take between 90 minutes and three hours. It's a marvelous experience, and grants you a sample of outback Jamaica. Often, you'll pass villagers bathing or doing their laundry in the river. Usually you're welcomed with a cocktail before departing. Most trips feature a stop for a refreshing drink of coconut juice or rum punch at waystops where a mento band might perform and you may be hustled to buy souvenirs. Transfers are provided.

A hat to guard against the sun is a wise idea. And don't forget your sunscreen and an umbrella in case of rain.

Trips are offered on the following four rivers (single companies hold a monopoly at each): Great River, Martha Brae, Rio Grande, and the White River. A trip costs about US$35 to US$45 for up to four people. (See regional chapters for details.)

## SPELUNKING

Jamaica is honeycombed with limestone caves and caverns, particularly in the western parishes. Some 400 of an estimated 900 caves on the island have been at least partly explored and mapped by the Geological Survey Dept and Jamaica Caving Club.

A few caves are steadfast tourist attractions, with guided tours and occasional refreshment stands. These include Green Grotto near Runaway Bay, Roaring River near Savanna-la-Mar, and Nonsuch Caves near Port Antonio. Lesser-known caves include Ghourie Caves, Coffee River Cave, Ipswich Caves, Windsor Caves, and Oxford Caves. All are located on the fringe of Cockpit Country; guides are available, but there are few other facilities. Many of the caves were used by Arawaks at one time for burial and ceremonial purposes, and petroglyphs

LEE FOSTER

**Watch your head! Stalactites (and sometimes bats) hang from the roofs of Jamaica's caves.**

add to the artistic appeal of the caverns, most of them boasting fine stalagmites and stalactites, underground streams, and even waterfalls. The most important of the ancient ceremonial caves is Mountain River Cave, in the Guanabacoa Valley north of Spanish Town. Many of the caves are also roosts for bats.

Use extreme caution if exploring non-commercial caves. Many rivers and streams disappear underground and flow through the cave systems. During heavy rains the water level can rise rapidly, trapping and drowning unwary spelunkers.

Take powerful flashlights and spare bulbs and batteries.

An indispensable guidebook is *Underground Jamaica* by Professor Alan Fincham. For further information, contact the Jamaica Caving Club (☎ 927-2728, 927-6661), c/o Dept of Geology, University of the West Indies, Mona, Kingston. The club was once very active, but apparently is somewhat quiescent these days.

The only company that specializes in spelunking is Sun Ventures (☎ 960-6685, fax 929-7512), 30 Balmoral Ave, Kingston 10, which offers caving trips to Cockpit Country from US$50 for four people.

## KAYAKING

Despite its immense potential, Jamaica has barely been tapped as a venue for canoeing and kayaking. There are more than 120 rivers, many with white-water sections that provide challenging runs for kayakers. The Great River, west of Montego Bay, is one of the few that has been scouted.

Since the departure of Peter Bentley, whose nude canoe trips were legendary, no tour operator has picked up the baton. But Destinations (formerly Sense Adventures) at Maya Lodge (☎ 702-0314, 702-0112, 800-532-2271), at Jack's Hill north of Kingston, may still rent inflatable 'Sea Eagles' for canoeing.

## CYCLING

Relatively few people explore Jamaica by bicycle, although large numbers of Jamaicans use bicycles to get around. The island is perfect for mountain biking if you can stand the heat and humidity. Mountain bikes can be rented at most major resorts. For serious touring, bring your own mountain or multi-purpose bike (you'll need sturdy wheels to handle the potholed roads). See the Getting Around chapter for more details about getting your bike from home to Jamaica.

There are very few bicycle repair shops. If you intend to roam off the beaten track, carry an adequate repair kit plus plenty of spare parts, such as inner tubes. Travel as light as possible. Be sure to have plenty of water with you (a Camelback is ideal; these plastic water containers strap to your back and allow you to sip through a tube as you cycle). And wear a helmet! Conditions are hazardous. Roads are covered with loose gravel and are narrow and twisting, with many potholes and blind spots where a car could easily surprise you.

### Organized Tours & Bicycle Rental

Cycling trips that range from a half day to three days are offered by touring companies in Ocho Rios, St Ann's Bay, Apple Valley, and Mammee Bay.

Bicycles can be rented at some resort properties and motorcycle rental concessions at major resorts. (See regional chapters for bike supply, rental, and repair shops.)

### SURFING

Jamaica is *not* a surfer's paradise. If you're seeking the ultimate wave, look elsewhere. There are a few spots on the east coast, however, where surfers can find decent waves coming in from the Atlantic. Boston Beach, 9 miles east of Port Antonio, is recognized as the best spot. Other worthwhile places nearby include Long Bay and tiny Christmas Beach, about 4 miles farther south.

### RUNNING

More and more runners, mostly middle-class Jamaicans, are taking to the streets (primarily in Kingston, where a choice spot is the breeze-swept Palisadoes; see the Kingston & Environs chapter). You'll need lots of stamina to handle the tropical conditions.

Jamaica is also making a name for itself with its marathons and triathlons. (See the regional chapters for dates and details for some of the major road races.)

## TENNIS

Most upscale hotels have tennis courts, many of which are lit for nighttime play. Several are splendidly endowed with Laycold courts, while others have let their courts go to seed. You can rent rackets for about US$5 per hour. (See regional chapters for details.)

You should take to the courts in the cool of early morning or evening.

## OTHER ACTIVITIES

Most large beach hotels provide an array of water sports, often free of charge for guests. Independent concessions also provide water sports on the beach, from jet-skiing and waterskiing to windsurfing and banana boat

rides. Windsurfing is usually rather tame, depending on wind conditions, although things liven up for serious adherents when northers kick in. The best conditions for windsurfing are along the eastern – windward – shore.

Typical rates are as follows: glass-bottom boat rides (US$15 to US$25 for 30 minutes to one hour); waterskiing (US$35 to US$40 for 20 minutes); windsurfing (US$15 to US$25 per hour).

The Touring Society of Jamaica offers private, full-day 4WD trips from US$250 for up to four people. Safari Tours Jamaica (☎/fax 972-2639, Safari@toj.com, www.jamaica-irie .com/safari), Arawak PO, Mammee Bay, offers separate daylong 'jeep safaris' of Orange Valley and the Blue Mountains using zebra-striped Land Rovers. It even has a two-day mule ride and trekking tour in the Blue Mountains.

# Getting There & Away

Jamaica is easy to get to. Dozens of airlines and charter companies offer direct service to the island. It's a regular port of call on cruise ship itineraries, and yachters find Jamaica an easy hop from neighboring islands and the eastern seaboard of North America.

## AIR

From both North America and Europe, Jamaica enjoys one of the best air feeds in the Caribbean. Its proximity to Florida means regular, relatively inexpensive flights from Miami, Fort Lauderdale, and Orlando, as well as other US gateways.

### Airports & Airlines

Jamaica has two international airports: the Donald Sangster International Airport near Montego Bay, and Norman Manley International Airport at Kingston.

There are four additional airports for which the government has responsibility: Tinson Pen in Kingston, Boscobel near Ocho Rios, Negril Aerodrome, and Ken Jones Aerodrome at Port Antonio. Plans to expand a private airport at Mandeville to handle international flights have yet to come to fruition. Numerous other small airstrips are scattered around the island, although many have been blockaded with concrete slabs to foil drug-runners.

### Montego Bay

The vast majority of visitors to Jamaica arrive at Donald Sangster International Airport, about 2 miles north of Montego Bay. The airport is Air Jamaica's hub for its services through MoBay to islands throughout the Caribbean. Construction on a new terminal, begun in 1996, was ongoing at press time. When completed there will be 12 gates. Air-conditioned hallways are gradually replacing the open-air walkways that were a sweaty introduction for passengers. The domestic terminal has a snack bar and restrooms.

There's a Jamaica Tourist Board (JTB) information booth before the immigration checkpoint in the arrivals hall. The staff can recommend hotels and even make reservations. A 24-hour money-exchange bureau is immediately beyond immigration, before the stairs down to the baggage claim and customs. The airport has a branch of the National Commercial Bank (☎ 952-2354). There's a local transport information desk immediately in front of the exit from customs. Desks representing specific tour companies and hotels are on the left and rental cars on the right. An airport information desk, on the right next to the exit, also provides information on transportation and makes announcements. Porters are available.

Customs is usually a breeze for foreign visitors, although there can be a lengthy wait if many Jamaican nationals are on the flight; customs officials tend to go through their baggage with a fine-tooth comb. Beware if you travel with heavy carry-on baggage: you may have a long walk to the arrivals hall, depending on where your aircraft berths.

Theft from baggage is a problem at the airport. Ensure your luggage is locked and don't leave valuables in unlocked pockets.

For flight arrival and departure information, call the airport (☎ 952-5530) or call the airline directly.

A separate, smaller terminal serves domestic flights. Though adjacent, the domestic and international terminals are not linked by walkway. They're a 10-minute walk apart. The charter airlines (Timair, Jamaica Airlink, and Air Negril) provide connecting shuttles.

### Kingston

Norman Manley International Airport is on the Palisadoes, a long sand spit about 11 miles southeast from downtown.

You'll find a JTB information desk facing you immediately after you enter the arrivals hall. There's a money-exchange bureau before (and to the left of) customs. Immigration and customs formalities are straightforward and usually without long lines. There's a taxi information booth on the left as you exit customs, beyond which an alley (also on the left) leads to a bank and Island Car Rentals. Straight ahead is the JUTA taxi office and, beyond, a police station, an ATM, Cable & Wireless telephone office, and the airport's only eatery – the Otaheitis Café.

Fortunately, the airport is hassle-free. There are porters and plenty of public telephones. For flight arrival and departure information, call the airport (☎ 924-8452, 924-8024) or call the airline directly.

The departures lounge features a range of duty-free stores and cafés, plus a well-stocked magazine store in the check-in area.

**Airlines** The following major airlines have offices in Jamaica:

Air Canada
  (☎ 924-8211) 7 Trafalgar Rd, Kingston
  (☎ 952-5160) Montego Bay
Air Jamaica
  (☎ 922-4661) 51 Knutsford Blvd, Kingston 5
  (☎ 952-4300) Montego Bay
  (☎ 957-4210) Negril
  (☎ 974-2566) Ocho Rios
Air Jamaica Express
  (☎ 923-8680, 922-4661) Kingston
  (☎ 952-4300) Montego Bay
  (☎ 957-5251) Negril
  (☎ 974-2566) Ocho Rios
  (☎ 993-3692) Port Antonio
ALM Antillean
  (☎ 926-1762) 23 Dominica Drive, Kingston 5
  (☎ 952-5530) Montego Bay
American Airlines
  (☎ 920-8887) 26 Trafalgar Rd, Kingston 10
  (☎ 952-5950) Montego Bay
British Airways
  (☎ 929-9020) 25 Dominica Drive, Kingston 5
  (☎ 925-3771) Montego Bay
BWIA International Airways
  (☎ 929-3770) 19 Dominica Drive, Kingston 5
Cayman Airways
  (☎ 926-1762) 23 Dominica Drive, Kingston 5
COPA Airlines
  (☎ 926-1762) 23 Dominica Drive, Kingston 5
  (☎ 952-5530) Montego Bay
Cubana
  (☎ 978-3410) 22 Trafalgar Rd, Kingston 10
Northwest Airlines
  (☎ 952-4033, 800-225-2525) Montego Bay

TWA
  (☎ 952-7262) Montego Bay
US Airways
  (☎ 940-0172, 800-622-1015) Montego Bay

## Buying Tickets

The plane ticket will probably be the single most expensive item in your budget, and buying it can be an intimidating business. There is likely to be a multitude of airlines and travel agents hoping to separate you from your money, and it is always worth putting aside a few hours to research the current state of the market. Start early: some of the cheapest tickets have to be bought months in advance, and some popular flights sell out early. Talk to other recent travelers – they may be able to stop you from making some of the same old mistakes. Look for special offers in newspapers and magazines, consult reference books, and phone several travel agents for bargains. Find out the fare, the route, the duration of the journey, and any restrictions on the ticket (see restrictions in the 'Air Travel Glossary,' later in this chapter), then decide which is best for you.

You may discover that those impossibly cheap flights are 'fully booked, but we do have another one that costs a bit more...' Or they may claim to have 'the last two seats available' for the period of your travels, which they 'can hold for a maximum of only two hours.' Don't panic – keep phoning around.

An alternative is to search online for the best deals. Dozens of websites now promote discount airfares worldwide. Most permit you to make reservations online. However, you are likely to be quoted rates offered to wholesalers and consolidators, for which special conditions and restrictions apply (see Discount Tickets, later in this chapter).

Most airlines charge different fares according to the season (highest fares are normally in the high season, from mid-December through mid-April, with even higher fares for peak times such as Christmas and around the New Year). You can save 20% or more by traveling off-season; sometimes weekday flights offer savings, too.

If you are traveling from the UK or the USA, you will likely find that the cheapest flights are advertised by obscure 'bucket shops' (called 'consolidators' in the USA). Most such firms are honest and solvent, but there are a few rogues who will take your money and disappear, to reopen elsewhere a month or two later under a new name. If you feel suspicious about a firm, don't give them all the money at once – leave a deposit of 20% or so and pay the balance when you get the ticket. If they insist on cash in advance, go somewhere else. And once you have the ticket, phone the airline to confirm that you are actually booked on the flight. Bucket shops act as clearinghouses for 'unsold' seats, selling tickets for seats that an airline anticipates being unable to fill. Such tickets are discounted at up to 35% – a handy savings! Before committing to a purchase, call the airline to see if it can match the consolidator's price with a promotional fare.

You may decide to pay more than the rock-bottom fare by opting for the safety of a better known travel agent. Firms such as Student Travel Services (STS; ☎ 800-648-4849), which has offices worldwide, Council Travel (☎ 800-226-8624) in the USA or Travel CUTS (☎ 416-979-2406) in Canada are not going to disappear overnight, leaving you clutching a receipt for a nonexistent ticket, and they do offer good prices to most destinations. These three companies specialize in fares for students, but no discount student fares are available to Jamaica from North America.

Once you have your ticket, write down its number, together with the flight number and other details, and keep that information separate from your ticket. If the ticket is lost or stolen, this will help you get a replacement.

It's sensible to buy travel insurance as early as possible (see Visas & Documents in the Facts for the Visitor chapter). If you buy it the week before you fly, you may discover, for example, that you're not covered for delays to your flight caused by industrial action.

If you plan on visiting additional Caribbean destinations, consider buying an airpass that permits any number of stopovers. Air Jamaica, BWIA International Airways, and Liat all offer such passes, which can be purchased in North America, the UK, Asia,

or Australia in conjunction with international tickets to Jamaica or other Caribbean islands (see the Caribbean & South America, later in this chapter).

## Travelers with Special Needs

If you have special needs of any sort – you've broken a leg, you're vegetarian, traveling in a wheelchair, taking the baby, terrified of flying – you should let the airline know as soon as possible so that they can make arrangements accordingly. You should remind them when you reconfirm your booking (at least 72 hours before departure) and again when you check in at the airport. It may also be worth it to ask airlines, prior to booking, how they might handle your particular needs.

Airports and airlines can be surprisingly helpful, but they do need advance warning. Most international airports will provide escorts from check-in through boarding, and there should be ramps, lifts, accessible toilets, and reachable phones. Aircraft toilets, on the other hand, are likely to present a problem; travelers should discuss this with the airline at an early stage and, if necessary, with their doctor. (See the Disabled Travelers section in the Facts for the Visitor chapter for more information.)

Guide dogs for the blind will often have to travel in a specially pressurized baggage compartment with other animals, away from their owner, though smaller guide dogs are sometimes admitted to the cabin. Only animals born and raised in Britain are currently allowed into Jamaica.

Deaf travelers can ask that airport and in-flight announcements be written down for them.

Children under two travel for 10% of the standard fare (or free, on some airlines), as long as they don't occupy a seat. They don't get a baggage allowance either. 'Skycots' should be provided by the airline if requested in advance; these will take a child weighing up to about 10kg. Children between two and 12 can usually occupy a seat for half to two-thirds of the full fare, and do get a baggage allowance. Strollers and wheelchairs can often be taken as hand luggage.

## Departure Tax

As of June 1999, Jamaica's departure tax was J$1000 (approximately US$30), payable at the airport when you check in for your flight. You can pay in foreign currency or in Jamaican dollars (cash only). The tax is subject to change.

## The USA

The most popular routings are via Miami and New York, but Jamaica is also served by direct flights from a dozen or so other cities.

The big boy is Air Jamaica, which uses Montego Bay as a hub for the Caribbean and has code-sharing with Delta Airlines. The following US carriers also fly to Jamaica, so you can use their 'frequent flyer' and other discount promotions: American Airlines, TWA, US Airways, and Northwest Airlines. American Airlines has the most frequent service to Montego Bay, with continuing service to Kingston. It also services many other Caribbean islands, with Puerto Rico as a main connecting hub. The major carriers usually offer spring and autumn discounts up to 35%. Also look for joint promotions with major package wholesalers offering discounts up to 35% on land and air portions seasonally.

Fares quoted around press time for roundtrip travel to Montego Bay originating on a weekend averaged US$445 low season, US$505 high season from New York, and US$267 low season, US$347 high season from Miami. There are many variables that go into determining a fare, however, so these fares should be used only as a ballpark figure.

The following toll free airline information and reservation numbers are valid anywhere in the USA, Canada, Mexico, and the Caribbean:

| | |
|---|---|
| Air Jamaica | ☎ 800-523-5585 |
| American Airlines | ☎ 800-433-7300 |
| Delta Airlines | ☎ 800-221-1212 |
| Northwest/KLM | ☎ 800-225-2525 |
| TWA | ☎ 800-892-4141 |
| US Airways | ☎ 800-622-1015 |

Privately owned Air Jamaica flies more people to the island than any other airline (about 45% of all arrivals), and from more USA gateways (10) than any other, using Airbus jets. It offers more than 150 flights weekly, plus connecting flights through Montego Bay at no extra charge to destinations throughout the Caribbean. All flights are smoke-free. Free champagne breakfasts are offered in every class, plus free champagne, beer, and wine with lunch or dinner. Some flights even have a fashion show!

Air Jamaica offers direct service to Jamaica from Atlanta, Baltimore/Washington, Chicago, Fort Lauderdale, Miami, Orlando, New York (Newark and JFK airports), Philadelphia, Los Angeles, and San Francisco. (Nonstop flights from the West Coast take approximately as long as flying to Hawaii – about five to six hours.)

Air Jamaica also offers joint fares with Carnival Airlines from Los Angeles via Miami, with daily flights.

It also promotes a 'Seventh Heaven Fly Free Program': If you buy six roundtrip tickets in any two-year period, you get the seventh free (if three tickets were first class, then the free ticket is first class also). Alternately, you'll receive a 50% discount on a fifth ticket if you purchase four roundtrip tickets within two years. Look for Air Jamaica's special fall savings, when prices drop 30% or so.

Some airlines offer special rates at select hotels in conjunction with the purchase of an airline ticket. In exchange for staying at least three nights, Sandals, a leading resort chain, awards 1000 miles to guests who are members of American Airlines' AAdvantage frequent flyer program.

The *New York Times*, the *LA Times*, and most other major city newspapers all produce weekly travel sections in which you'll find any number of ads quoting airfares. The monthly *Travel Unlimited* newsletter, PO Box 1058, Allston, MA 02134, publishes details of some of the cheapest airfares and courier possibilities for destinations all over the world, departing from the USA.

**Charter Flights** Large-body jets can be chartered for exclusive use by large tour operators. These flights generally offer the lowest fares for confirmed reservations (sometimes more than one-third lower than regular airline prices) and can be booked through most travel agencies. You can sometimes also book one-way tickets with charter airlines for less than half the roundtrip fare. Often the charter price is for a package that includes the flight and accommodations. They are usually direct flights, without the hub-stop common on standard

## Air Travel Glossary

**Apex** Apex, or 'advance purchase excursion,' is a discounted ticket that must be paid for in advance. There are penalties if you wish to change it.

**Baggage Allowance** This will be written on your ticket: usually one 44lb (20kg) item to go in the hold, plus one item of carry-on luggage.

**Bucket Shop** An unbonded travel agency specializing in discounted airline tickets.

**Bumped** Just because you have a confirmed seat doesn't mean you're going to get on the plane (see Overbooking).

**Cancellation Penalties** If you have to cancel or change an Apex ticket, there are often heavy penalties involved; insurance can sometimes be taken out against these penalties. Some airlines impose penalties on regular tickets as well, particularly against 'no show' passengers.

**Check-In** Airlines ask you to check in a certain time ahead of the flight departure (usually 1½ hours on international flights). If you fail to check in on time and the flight is overbooked, the airline can cancel your booking and give your seat to somebody else.

**Confirmation** Having a ticket written out with the flight and date you want doesn't mean you have a seat. The agent has to check with the airline that your status is confirmed. Meanwhile you are 'on request.'

**Discounted Tickets** There are two types of discounted fares – officially discounted (see Promotional Fares) and unofficially discounted. The lowest prices often impose drawbacks like flying with unpopular airlines, inconvenient schedules, or unpleasant routes and connections. A discounted ticket can save you things other than money – you may be able to pay Apex prices without the associated Apex advance booking and other requirements. Discounted tickets exist only where there is fierce competition.

**Full Fares** Airlines traditionally offer 1st-class (coded F), business class (coded J), and economy class (coded Y) tickets. These days there are so many promotional and discounted fares available from the regular economy class that few passengers pay full economy fare.

**Lost Tickets** If you lose your airline ticket, an airline will usually treat it like a traveler's check and, after inquiries, issue another one to you. Legally, however, an airline is entitled to treat it like cash – if you lose it, it's gone forever. Take good care of your tickets.

**No Shows** No shows are passengers who fail to show up for their flight, sometimes due to unexpected delays or disasters, sometimes due to simply forgetting, sometimes because they airlines. Few charters are listed in airline computer reservations systems, as they're operated by wholesale tour operators with whom you or your travel agent will have to deal directly.

There are drawbacks to this mode of travel. Although you can buy the ticket without an advance-purchase requirement, you do have to fix your departure and return dates well ahead of time; a substantial fee

---

## Air Travel Glossary

made more than one booking and didn't bother to cancel the one they didn't want. Full-fare passengers who fail to turn up are sometimes entitled to travel on a later flight. The rest are penalized (see Cancellation Penalties).

**On Request** This is an unconfirmed booking for a flight.

**Onward Tickets** An entry requirement for many countries is that you have an onward or return ticket, in other words, a ticket out of the country. If you're not sure what you intend to do next, the easiest solution is to buy the cheapest onward ticket to a neighboring country or a ticket from a reliable airline that can later be refunded if you do not use it.

**Open Jaws** A return ticket that allows you to fly to one place but return from another. If available, this can save you backtracking to your arrival point.

**Overbooking** Airlines hate to fly with empty seats and since every flight has some passengers who fail to show up (see No Shows), airlines often book more passengers than they have seats. Usually the excess passengers balance those who fail to show up, but occasionally somebody gets 'bumped.' If this happens, guess who it is most likely to be? The passengers who check in late.

**Promotional Fares** Officially discounted fares, like Apex fares, that are available from travel agents or directly from the airline.

**Reconfirmation** At least 72 hours prior to departure time, you must contact the airline and 'reconfirm' that you intend to be on the flight. If you don't do this, the airline can delete your name from the passenger list and you could lose your seat. You don't have to reconfirm the first flight on your itinerary or if your stopover is less than 72 hours. It doesn't hurt to reconfirm more than once.

**Restrictions** Discounted tickets often have various restrictions on them – advance purchase is the most common (see Apex). Others are restrictions on the minimum and maximum period you must be away, such as a minimum of 14 days or a maximum of one year (see Cancellation Penalties).

**Transferred Tickets** Airline tickets cannot be transferred from one person to another. Travelers sometimes try to sell the return half of their ticket, but officials can ask you to prove that you are the person named on the ticket.

may apply for any changes or cancellations (you should consider cancellation insurance in the event of illness, etc). Seating may be more cramped, as planes are usually full; service isn't always up to par with scheduled airlines; and flights often depart at inconvenient hours. And though US charter operators are bonded with the US government, if the tour operator or airline defaults, you may have problems getting your money back. Also, charter flights are often less organized than the standard carriers, and processing at airline counters often is more confusing and time-consuming.

Before buying, compare charter prices with an airline's 'sale' fare and a discount ticket from a consolidator. Typically, three, five, or seven-night packages are offered in conjunction with flights.

Dozens of charter operators fly to Jamaica from the USA. Apple Vacations has weeklong charters from New York starting at US$719 per person low season. It will not quote prices over the phone; instead you must book through a travel agent. GoGo Worldwide Vacations is the biggest Caribbean wholesaler, with many options for Jamaica spanning all budgets. Sun Splash Tours specializes in spring break and student travel, and has packages starting at US$399 with charter flights from cities throughout North America. STS also offers seven-night charter packages from US$399 (based on quadruple occupancy), with nonstop flights from 26 cities across the USA, plus 'Spring Break Jamaica' packages, also from US$399.

The Sandals hotel chain operates 'Champagne Express' charters to other Caribbean destinations using Miami Air from JFK, Baltimore, and Philadelphia. It may add Jamaica.

Check the Sunday travel section of major city newspapers. Your travel agent should be able to provide a listing of charter companies and flights. A good resource is the *Worldwide Guide to Cheap Airfares: How to Travel the World Without Breaking the Bank* by Michael McColl (☎ 800-782-6657, www .travelinsider.com), Insider Publications, 2124 Kittredge St, Berkeley, CA 94704. It provides details of charter tour operators. Its evolving website is good for sleuthing bargain airfares and travel fares.

Some key charter operators to Jamaica include:

American Trans Air
    ☎ 800-293-6194

Apple Vacations/Sunbird Vacations
    ☎ 800-727-3400 for east coast gateways,
    ☎ 800-365-2775 for west coast

Council Travel (CIEE)
    ☎ 212-822-2600, 800-226-8624, fax 212-822-2699,
    info@ciee.org, www.ciee.org

GoGo Worldwide Vacations
    ☎ 800-333-3454

Funjet
    ☎ 800-558-3060

Island Flight Vacations/Sunburst Holidays
    ☎ 800-426-4570, 800-223-1277, fax 310-410-0830

Student Travel Services (STS)
    ☎ 410-859-4200, 800-648-4849, fax 410-859-2442

Sun Splash Tours
    ☎ 212-366-4922, 800-426-7710, fax 212-366-5642

**Courier Flights** If you're willing to fly on short notice and travel light, courier flights are one of the cheapest ways to go – about half the standard fare or less. As a courier, you 'deliver' an item, such as a parcel or document, on behalf of a company. Usually the courier company takes care of handling the item; you merely act as its agent by occupying a seat. In exchange, you usually give up your baggage allowance, which the courier company uses for the item to be delivered.

The leading booking agency for courier companies is NOW Voyager (☎ 212-431-1616), 74 Varick St, No 307, New York, NY 10013. You must pay a one-time US$50 registration fee. There are few other courier options to the Caribbean.

Two good resources are *Courier Air Travel Handbook: Learn How to Travel Worldwide for Next to Nothing*, by Mark Field, and Michael McColl's *Worldwide Guide to Cheap Airfares* (see above).

**Discount Tickets** Several discount ticket agencies sell reduced-rate tickets to the Caribbean. One of the leading brokers specializing in the area is Pan Express Travel (☎ 212-719-9292, 800-518-7726), 55 W 39th St, New York, NY 10018.

You'll find numerous other discount travel sites on the World Wide Web by searching for 'discount+airfares.' A good starting point is the author's website (www.travelguidebooks .com) with links to several discount ticket agents. Also try Airfares For Less (☎ 954-565-8667, www.airfares-for-less.com) and Discount Airfares (www.discount-airfares.com).

The Worldwide Discount Travel Club (☎ 305-534-2082), 1674 Meridian Ave, Miami Beach, FL 33139, arranges discounted vacations for members – it costs US$40 for your first year, US$30 for each subsequent year – but does not issue airline tickets.

Also try Airtech (☎ 212-219-7000, 800-575-8324) or TFI Tours International (☎ 212-736-1140).

**Standby & Last Minute** If you can fly on very short notice (usually within seven days of travel), then consider buying a ticket from a 'last-minute' ticket broker. These companies buy surplus seats from charter airlines (and sometimes standard carriers) at hugely discounted prices. The airline would rather fill the seat than fly empty – you reap the reward. Discounts can be as great as 40% for a confirmed seat.

Last Minute Travel Club (☎ 617-267-9800, 800-527-8646), 1249 Boylston St, Boston, MA 02215, specializes in air/hotel packages to the Caribbean.

Other last-minute ticket agencies require that you become a member of their club; annual fees are about US$40, for which you receive regular updates.

Also check out Moment's Notice (☎ 212-486-0500, www.moments-notice.com), 7301 New Utrecht Ave, Brooklyn, NY 11204.

## Canada

Air Canada (☎ 800-776-3000, 800-869-9000) serves Montego Bay four times weekly from Montreal, and Montego Bay and Kingston from Toronto daily in peak season. Air Jamaica (☎ 416-229-6024, 800-523-5585), 4141 Yonge St, Willowdale ON, M2P 2A6, flies nonstop from Toronto and Montreal.

Canadian Universities Travel Service (Travel CUTS; ☎ 416-979-2406), 187 College St, Toronto, Ontario M5T 1P7, sells discount airfares to the general public as well as to students. It has 25 offices throughout Canada.

Major city newspapers such as the *Toronto Globe & Mail* and the *Vancouver Sun* carry travel agents' ads.

**Charter Flights** Air Transat (☎ 514-987-1616, fax 987-9750) offers weekly charter flights from Toronto, with plans to introduce them from Montreal. Canada 3000 (☎ 416-674-2661) also flies from Toronto. Tickets on both are issued only via travel agencies.

Regent Holidays (☎ 905-673-3343), 6205 Airport Rd, Building A, No 200, Mississauga, ON L4V 1E1, offers charter flights and air/hotel packages using Air Transat. Conquest Tours (☎ 416-665-9255, 800-268-1925, fax 416-665-6811), 85 Brisbane Rd, Downsview, ON M3J 2K3, has charter flights plus hotel packages from Ottawa and Toronto. Signature Vacations (☎ 416-967-1510, fax 967-4951), 160 Bloor St, suite 400, Toronto, ON M4W 1B9, has charters on Tuesday and Sunday from Toronto.

## Australia & New Zealand

There is no direct service to Jamaica; travelers from Australia or New Zealand must fly via the USA. The best routes are via San Francisco or Los Angeles, where you can connect to direct flights to Jamaica with Air Jamaica, or via Dallas or Miami with American Airlines or another major US carrier. Direct service between Australia, New Zealand, and California is provided by the following airlines:

Air New Zealand
   ☎ 02-9223-4666 in Sydney
   ☎ 09-366-2400 in Auckland

Delta Airlines
   ☎ 02-9262-1777 in Sydney
   ☎ 09-379-3370 in Auckland

Qantas
   ☎ 02-9957-0111 in Sydney
   ☎ 09-357-8900 in Auckland

United Airlines
   ☎ 02-9237-8888 in Sydney
   ☎ 09-307-9500 in Auckland

You can also fly via Santiago, Chile, or Buenos Aires, Argentina.

Fares from Australia to Los Angeles begin at about A$1600 for special fares, and about A$2300 for regular APEX fares. From New Zealand, fares begin at about NZ$2495.

Consider a round-the-world (RTW) ticket, which offers the option of several additional stopovers at marginal cost. You can also save money by buying a Liat or BWIA International Airways (☎ 02-9223-7004) air-pass if you plan on exploring other islands of the Caribbean (see the Caribbean & South America, later in this chapter). Air Jamaica also offers additional Caribbean stopovers.

In Australia, STA Travel (☎ 800-637-444) and Flight Centre International (☎ 13-1600) are major dealers in cheap airfares. Other good sources for discount tickets include Anywhere Travel (☎ 02-9663-0411) and Thomas Cook (☎ 13-1771, 800-064824).

In New Zealand try the following for discount fares:

| | |
|---|---|
| Brisbane Discount Travel | ☎ 09-366-0061, |
| | ☎ 800-808040 |
| Destinations Unlimited | ☎ 09-373-4033 |
| Flight Centre | ☎ 09-309-6171 |
| STA Travel | ☎ 09-309-0458 |
| Thomas Cook | ☎ 09-379-3920 |

One of the few tour agencies that specialize in the Caribbean is Caribbean Destinations (☎ 800-816717), Level 4, 115 Pitt St, Sydney, which offers packaged and customized programs in Jamaica. Also try Contours (☎ 03-9329-5211), 466 Victoria St, N Melbourne, or Cubatours (☎ 03-9428-0385), 235 Swan St, Richmond, Victoria 3121, which specialize in air/land packages to Cuba.

Check the travel agents' ads in the yellow pages and phone around.

## The UK

Jamaica is well served by flights from the UK. Air Jamaica offers direct service to Montego Bay and Kingston from Heathrow, with four flights weekly at press time (scheduled to increase to five weekly). British Airways also offers direct service to Montego Bay and Kingston from Gatwick three times

weekly (Wednesday, Saturday, and Sunday), and was planning six flights weekly, using Boeing 777s. It's advisable to check seasonal variations.

You can buy a BWIA International Airways air-pass to combine your visit to Jamaica with explorations of other Caribbean islands; see the Caribbean & South America, later in this chapter. Air Jamaica also offers additional Caribbean stopovers at no extra cost.

| | |
|---|---|
| Air Jamaica | ☎ 020-8570-9171, |
| | ☎ 020-8570-7990 |
| British Airways | ☎ 020-8897-4000 |
| BWIA International Airways | ☎ 020-8577-1100 |

Quoted return fares for 1998 ranged from £405 to £495 in low season, £675 to £865 in high season.

It may be cheaper to fly through the United States, changing aircraft in Miami (return fares between London and Miami can be as low as £200 in low season). Several airlines feed Miami and Fort Lauderdale from the UK, including American Airlines (☎ 800-433-7300), Delta Airlines (☎ 800-221-1212), and Virgin Atlantic (☎ 800-862-8621). American Airlines has connecting service to Jamaica, while British Airways has onward service from Nassau, Bahamas.

Two of the leading air-only travel specialists are Caribbean Gold (☎ 020-8741-8491) and Caribbean Travel (☎ 020-8969-6230), 367 Portobello Rd, London W10.

For discount tickets, try the following travel agencies:

Trailfinders
   (☎ 020-7937-5400)
   194 Kensington High St, London W8 7RG

STA Travel
   (☎ 020-7361-6262)
   86 Old Brompton Rd, London SW7

Council Travel
   (☎ 020-7437-7767) 29a Poland St, London W1V

London Flight Centre
   (☎ 020-7244-6411)
   131 Earls Court Rd, London SW5

Travel Bug
   (☎ 020-7835-2000)
   125A Gloucester Rd, London SW

Look in the magazine *Time Out,* the Sunday papers, and *Exchange & Mart* for ads. Most newspaper stands stock these. Also look for the free magazines widely available in London – start by looking outside the main railway stations.

Most British travel agents are registered with ABTA (Association of British Travel Agents). If you have paid for your flight through an ABTA-registered agent who then goes out of business, ABTA guarantees a refund or an alternative. Unregistered bucket shops are riskier, but sometimes cheaper, too.

**Charter Flights** Jamaica is a major charter destination from the UK, and many charter operators have contracted with airlines since Airtours first tested the market in 1988. All charter flights are into Montego Bay. They are usually considerably cheaper than scheduled fares, although departure and arrival times are often inconveniently scheduled in the middle of the night. You should be able to find fares as low as £250 in low season, and £550 in high season.

Thomson Holidays (☎ 020-7387-9321, 0990-502555, fax 020-7387-8451), Greater London House, Hampstead Rd, London NW1 7SD, has weekly charters year-round with Britannia Airways from Manchester and Gatwick. Airtours (Sunday) and Unijet (Monday) also offer weekly charters from Manchester and Gatwick. Airtours has two-week packages as low as £349. Unijet has weeklong packages from £399.

All-Jamaica specializes in travel between the UK and Jamaica. The company uses Air UK Leisure from Manchester to Montego Bay on Sunday, and London Gatwick to Montego Bay on Monday, connecting with flights to Cuba.

In Northern Ireland, Chieftain Tours (☎ 028-9023-3547, fax 9024-7490), 155 Northumberland St, Belfast, Northern Ireland BT13 2JF, offers charter flights from Belfast and Dublin, year-round.

Leading charter operators include:

| | |
|---|---|
| Airtours | ☎ 01706-260000 |
| All-Jamaica | ☎ 0161-796-9222, fax 0161-796-9444 |
| British Airways Holidays | ☎ 01293-617000 |
| Caribbean Connection | ☎ 01244-341131 |
| Caribtours | ☎ 020-7581-3517, fax 020-7225-2491 |
| Cosmos | ☎ 0161-480-5799 |
| Harlequin Worldwide | ☎ 01708-852780, fax 01708-854952 |
| Jetlife Holidays | ☎ 01322-614801 |
| Kuoni | ☎ 01306-742222 |
| Simply Caribbean | ☎ 01423-526887 |
| Thomas Cook | ☎ 01733-332255 |
| Thomson Holidays | ☎ 020-7387-9321 |
| Tropical Places | ☎ 01342-825123 |
| Unijet Travel | ☎ 01444-459191 |
| Virgin Holidays | ☎ 01293-617181 |

## Europe

There are few direct flights to Jamaica from continental Europe. The following are your best bet:

### Denmark

Cruise & Travel
  (☎ 45-33-119-500, fax 119-501)
  Bredgade 35C, Copenhagen, 1260 K.
  Specializes in travel to the Caribbean

### Ireland

Aeroflot
  (☎ 020-7491-1764 in London,
  ☎ 06-47-2299 in Eire)
  70 Piccadilly, London W1V 9HH.
  Weekly service from Shannon Airport in Eire

Budget Travel
  (☎ 01-661-1403)
  134 Lower Baggot St, Dublin 2

Thomas Cook Holidays
  (☎ 01-677-1721)
  118 Grafton St, Dublin 2

### France

Alternative Travel
  (☎ 01-42-89-42-46, fax 42-89-80-73)
  8 Ave de Messine, Paris 75008 Austral
  (☎ 02-99-85-94-94, fax 99-30-66-77)
  29 Rue Du Puits Mauger, Rennes 35000

### Italy

Ventaclub
  (☎ 39-2-467-541, fax 4675-4999)
  Via Dei Gracchi 35, Milano 20146.
  Operates its own charters

Viaggidea
(☎ 39-2-895-291, fax 895-00406)
Via Lampedusa 13, Milano 20141.
Operates a weekly charter flight from Milan
to Montego Bay year-round

Hotelplan Italia
(☎ 39-2-721-3655, fax 877-558)
Corso Italia 1, Milano 20128

**Switzerland**

Carib Tours
(☎ 1-463-8863, fax 463-9261)
Malzstrasse 21, Zurich 8036.
Offers charters with Balair to Montego Bay

In Germany, LTU Airways (☎ 0211-9-41-8888, fax 9-41-8881) flies from Düsseldorf and Munich to Montego Bay on Monday. LTU offers a sky-shuttle service between Düsseldorf and the Frankfurt airport. Contact LTU at the following branch offices:

Düsseldorf
(☎ 021-9-41-0952) Parsevalstrasse 7a, D-40468

Munich
(☎ 89-57-09-29-30) Eisenhelmerstrasse 61,
D-80687
(☎ 89-97-59-19-16) Modul A, Munich Airport

## Asia & Africa

There are no direct flights; travelers fly via London or the USA.

From Asia, Hong Kong is the discount plane ticket capital. Ask other travelers for advice before buying a ticket. STA Travel has branches in Hong Kong, Tokyo, Singapore, Bangkok, and Kuala Lumpur.

In Japan, try one of the following companies:

Alize Corporation
(☎ 03-3407-4272, fax 3407-8400)
Aoyama Kyodo Bldg, No 803, 3-6-18 Kita
Aoyama Minato-ku, Tokyo 107

All Nippon Airways World Tours
(☎ 03-3581-7231, fax 3580-0361)
Kasumigaseki Bldg, 3-2-5 Kasumigaseki
Chiyoda-ku, Tokyo 100

Island International
(☎ 03-3401-4096, fax 3401-1629)
4-11-14-204 Jingumae, Shibuya-ku, Tokyo 15

L & A Tours
(☎ 03-5474-7723, fax 3746-2478)
No 608, 3-1-19 Nishi Azabu, Minato-ku,
Tokyo 106

## The Caribbean & South America

Air Jamaica (☎ 800-523-5585) uses Montego Bay as a hub for connecting its US flights with service to and from Antigua, the Bahamas, Barbados, Cuba (Havana and Santiago de Cuba), Grand Cayman, St Lucia, and Turks and Caicos, with more than 150 connecting flights a week. Passengers are permitted a stopover in Jamaica, or may continue to a second or third Caribbean destination at no extra cost.

Flights from the USA arrive at Air Jamaica's Montego Bay hub between 10 and 10:30 am, with connecting flights to Caribbean islands departing between 11 and 11:30 am. Flights arrive in Montego Bay from Caribbean islands between 3 and 3:30 pm and depart for the USA between 4:30 and 5 pm.

Jamaica is also linked by BWIA International Airways (☎ 929-3770, 800-327-7401 in Kingston; ☎ 305-371-2942, 800-538-2942 in North America) to Antigua, Barbados, Haiti, and Trinidad. It also serves Puerto Rico, as does ALM Antillean Airlines, which has flights to Aruba, Bonaire, Colombia, Panama, and St Martin. Cayman Airlines connects Jamaica with the Cayman Islands. COPA (☎ 952-5530 in Jamaica, ☎ 227-5000 in Panama), has service to and from Panama five times weekly. And Cubana has flights from Montego Bay and Kingston to Santiago, Varadero, and Havana in Cuba (see Organized Tours, later in this chapter).

Liat (☎ 268-462-0700, fax 462-2682) offers a 'Caribbean Explorer Pass' (US$249), which permits stops at any three of the 26 islands that it services, with purchase of a ticket from North America or other international gateway to either Antigua, Barbados, Miami, Puerto Rico, St Thomas, St Croix, St Martin, St Lucia, or Trinidad. It costs US$80 per extra island. Unlimited stopovers are permitted for US$449. Trinidadian-based BWIA has a similar 30-day pass with unlimited stops at its Caribbean destinations (from US$399). You have to specify the routing (but not the dates) in advance, with a US$20 fee for each change.

**Charter Flights** Air Jamaica's domestic airline, Air Jamaica Express (☎ 923-8680,

922-4661 in Kingston; ☎ 305-670-3222, 800-523-5585, fax 305-670-2992 in the USA) offers charter service to Cuba, Grand Cayman, Haiti, and other Caribbean isles. Air Jamaica's service permits easy passage from Miami to Havana, Cuba, although the Cuban leg cannot be booked or purchased in the United States (see '¡Cuba Si!' in the Montego Bay & Northwest Coast chapter).

In the Dominican Republic, General Air Services (☎ 809-686-3130, fax 686-3353), Juan Sanchez Ramirez No 40, Santo Domingo, represents Martinair Holland, Alitalia, and other airlines for Jamaica.

Tropical Airlines (☎ 920-3770 in Kingston, ☎ 979-3565 in Montego Bay) flies 19-seater Beechcraft on 'scheduled' charter service ('scheduled' charters depart at set predetermined times) from Jamaica to Varadero and Santiago de Cuba, plus charter service to Cancún, Mexico and several other Caribbean destinations.

## SEA
### Departure Tax
Cruise passengers are charged a US$15 departure tax (cruise companies normally take care of this).

### The USA
**Cruise Ship** If all you want is a one-day taste of Jamaica, then consider arriving by cruise ship. A cruise is a good way to get a feel for several Caribbean destinations, and can even help you select a site for a future land-based vacation. Jamaica is one of the most popular calls on Caribbean cruising itineraries, recording 711,699 cruise visitors in 1997. Visits are usually one-day stopovers on longer Caribbean itineraries. The cruise companies provide buses for passengers, and taxis are available (US$7 to downtown). Ocho Rios (532,408 passengers in 1997) and Montego Bay (178,637 passengers) are Jamaica's two major cruise ship ports.

Cruise ships are floating resorts, with all meals, activities, and entertainment included in one price. Most feature a swimming pool, spa, health club, beauty shop, duty-free stores, theater, card room, library, bars and lounges, dining rooms, and medical facilities. Larger,

ritzier ships will usually have a casino, orchestras, and lavish Las Vegas-style revues.

Cruise experiences vary vastly according to the cruise company and ship you choose. While some cruise lines are relaxed, others are regimented, with neatly choreographed dining and entertainment. Princess Cruises, for example, requires formal wear for dinner (remember scenes from the *Love Boat*?), but Carnival's ships are all kitschy, Las Vegas-style glitz, and appeal to a younger, more budget-conscious party crowd.

The Cruise Line International Association (CLIA; ☎ 212-921-0066, fax 921-0549), 500 Fifth Ave No 1407, New York, NY 10110, can provide information on cruising and individual cruise lines, originating in the USA or abroad. The following included Jamaica in their 1999 itineraries:

| | |
|---|---|
| Carnival Cruise Lines | ☎ 800-327-9501 |
| Celebrity Cruises | ☎ 800-437-3111 |
| Commodore Cruise Lines | ☎ 800-237-5361 |
| Costa Cruise Lines | ☎ 800-462-6782 |
| Crystal Cruises | ☎ 800-446-6620 |
| Cunard Line | ☎ 800-528-6273 |
| Holland America Line | ☎ 800-426-0327 |
| Mediterranean Shipping | ☎ 800-666-9333 |
| Norwegian Cruise Line | ☎ 800-327-7030 |
| Premier Cruises | ☎ 800-990-7770 |
| Princess Cruises | ☎ 800-421-0522 |
| Royal Caribbean Cruise Line | ☎ 800-327-6700 |
| Star Clippers | ☎ 800-442-0551 |
| World Explorer | ☎ 800-854-3835 |

Prices vary according to how deluxe a ship is, length of cruise, and which cabin you choose. Most ships have a range of accommodations. The cheapest cabins are usually in the center of the vessel – midships – and often lack windows, but are less prone to rolling and pitching. You'll pay more for an ocean view and more still for an upper-deck cabin. The Vacation Store (☎ 800-825-3633) offers discounted cabins.

Seven-day cruises begin at US$1500. Remember, you get what you pay for, including all meals and entertainment. You'll save money by booking early. Don't forget to budget for tips. Cruise lines promote tipping to an extreme.

Most cruises that call in Jamaica depart from Florida, less frequently from New York. A few depart Los Angeles and travel via the Panama Canal.

Most days are spent partaking of optional short excursions, or you can sightsee on your own. World Explorer Cruises offers the widest range of shore excursions, and features Ocho Rios and Montego Bay on its eight and 14-day midwinter educational cruises aboard the SS *Universe Explorer*.

In 1997, the Jamaican government approved a US$35 million project to rebuild the cruise berths in Kingston, formerly a vital cruise hub. More likely, the investment will go into the US$60 million reconstruction of Port Royal – slated to begin in 1999 – which will be converted into Jamaica's third port of call and is intended to be a cruise destination rivaling the best in the Caribbean. Don't hold your breath! (See 'Restoring Port Royal' in the Kingston & Environs chapter.)

**Freighter** Gone are the good ol' days when passengers could buy passage aboard the banana freighters that plied between Jamaica, North America, and Europe. But freighters still call in on Jamaica, and several take paying passengers. Most have plush cabins – often as few as two per vessel – and passengers are well looked after by stewards. Book early!

The *Maritime Reederei* offers service from New Orleans and Houston, and stops at Kingston on its 56-day voyages down the eastern seaboard of the Americas (US$5040 per person).

The Columbus Lines' vessels frequently stop in Kingston on Pacific cruises that depart monthly from Savannah, GA (US$5280 single, US$4620 per person double occupancy, March through September; US$7260 and US$6270, October through February).

*Ford's Freighter Travel Guide* (☎ 818-701-7414), 19448 Longelius St, Northridge, CA 91324, lists freight ships that take passengers. You can also find listings in *TravelTips* (☎ 800-872-8584), PO Box 580188, Flushing, NY 11358.

Freighter World Cruises (☎ 626-449-3106, 800-531-7774, fax 626-449-9573, www.freighterworld.com), 180 S Lake Ave, No 335, Pasadena, CA 91101, is a travel agency specializing in freighter cruises.

**Private Yacht** Many yachters make the trip to Jamaica from North America. If you plan to travel in summer, keep fully abreast of weather reports; mid to late summer is hurricane season.

Marinas are located in all major resorts and other select points around Jamaica's coast. Upon arrival in Jamaica, however, you *must* clear customs and immigration at either Montego Bay (Montego Bay Yacht Club), Kingston (Royal Jamaican Yacht Club, Port Royal), Ocho Rios (St Ann's Bay), or West Harbour in Port Antonio. In addition, you'll need to clear customs at *each* port of call in Jamaica. It's a hassle, but Jamaica's troubles with drug trafficking are so extensive that you should be willing to cooperate with this policy. Anticipate the possibility of being boarded and searched by the Coast Guard.

You'll need the regular documentation for foreign travel (see Visas & Documents in the Facts for the Visitor chapter). An invaluable resource is *Cruising Guide to the Leeward Islands*, published by Cruising Guides Publications (☎ 813-733-5322, 800-330-9542, fax 813-734-8179), PO Box 1017, Dunedin, FL 34697-1017. Two other publishers of cruising guides to the Caribbean are White Sound Press (☎ 904-423-7880, fax 217-423-0522), 1615 W Harrison Ave, Decatur, IL 62526, and Tropic Isle Publishers (☎ 305-893-4277), PO Box 610938, N Miami, FL 33261.

**Charter Yacht** Both experienced sailors and novices can charter sailboats, yachts, and cruisers by the week in Florida and elsewhere for sailing to the Caribbean, although Jamaica is not a major destination. Most marinas offer boats with a skipper and crew, as well as 'bareboat' vessels on which you're your own skipper. Obviously you'll need to be a certified sailor to charter bareboat, and you'll have to demonstrate proficiency before being allowed to sail away. Boats are normally fully stocked with linens and other supplies. You provide your own food, however. (You can hire a cook for about US$100 daily.) A security deposit will be required.

Bareboat charters begin at US$1200 per week, depending on size. Crewed charters normally cost about double that. Skippers can be hired for about US$200 a day.

Two leading companies are Florida Yacht Charters (☎ 305-532-8600, 800-537-0050, boat@floridayacht.com), 1290 5th St, Miami Beach, FL 33199, and the Moorings (☎ 813-535-1446, 800-535-7289, fax 813-530-9747), 19345 US Hwy 19 N, Clearwater, FL 33764.

You can also use the services of a broker, who will secure an appropriate yacht based on your specific requirements. They work on commission and therefore won't charge you a fee.

The following are reputable brokerages:

Ed Hamilton & Co
(☎ 207-549-7855, 800-621-7855, fax 207-549-7822)
PO Box 430, N Whitehead, ME 04353

Lynn Jachney Charters
(☎ 800-223-2050, fax 617-639-0216)
PO Box 302, Marblehead, MA 01945

Nicholson Yacht Charters
(☎ 617-225-0555, 800-662-6066, fax 617-661-0554, nikyacht@tiac.net, www.yachtvacations.com)
29 Sherman St, Cambridge, MA 02138

Boat charter companies within Jamaica are listed under Chartering in the Sailing section of the Outdoor Activities chapter.

**Maps & Charts** You'll need accurate maps and charts for any voyage through the Caribbean's reef-infested waters. British Admiralty charts, US Defense Mapping Agency charts, and Imray yachting charts are all reliable. You can order them in advance from Bluewater Books & Charts (☎ 954-763-6533, 800-942-2583), 1481 SE 17th St, Causeway, Fort Lauderdale, FL 33316.

US government charts of the region can be ordered through most marine stores, as can detailed National Oceanic & Atmospheric Administration (NOAA) charts. Contact NOAA (☎ 301-436-8301, 800-638-8972, fax 301-436-6829, distribution@noaa.gov, www.nws.noaa.gov), NOAA Distribution Division, National Ocean Services, Riverdale, MD 20737-1199; or Better Boating Association, PO Box 407, Needham, MA 02192.

**Crewing** A popular way of getting to Jamaica is to crew aboard a yacht that's destined for the West Indies or Europe. Inquire in ports or yacht marinas about any irregular passenger services, via yacht or cargo boat, between Jamaica and other Caribbean islands. Check the notice boards at marinas; often you'll find a note advertising for crew, or you can leave one of your own. Yachting magazines are also good resources.

Yacht charter companies may be able to assist you.

## The UK & Continental Europe

**Cruise Ship** Several companies that operate summertime cruises in European waters must reposition their vessels to the Caribbean in winter, and vice versa. Passengers can participate in weeklong repositioning cruises.

**Freighter** *Cap Blanco* sails from Hamburg to South America, calling at Kingston (price is DM8970 for 69 days). Contact Hamburg-Sud Reiseagentur (☎ 0403-705-155, fax 7-052-420), Ost-West Strasse 59-61, 20457 Hamburg.

Harrison Line offers passenger service from England to the West Indies aboard the MV *Author*, a 27,631-ton vessel that carries eight passengers in two suites, one twin, and two single cabins, each with bath and shower. There's a small swimming pool, plus a lounge with TV and VCR. The vessel sails on 42-day roundtrip voyages from Felixstowe, with calls throughout the Caribbean and South America, including Kingston, before it returns to England. The cost for the full voyage is US$4275 to US$4725. Normally you must book the full roundtrip, although you may be able to book one-way passage in summer.

The Geest Line (☎ 023-8033-3388, fax 8071-4059), PO Box 154, Southampton, Hampshire SO1 OXP, accepts passengers aboard its banana freight ships that ply between Southampton and the West Indies. Book at least a year in advance through Strand Cruise & Travel Centre (☎ 020-7836-6363, fax 7497-0078), Charing Cross Shopping Concourse, the Strand, London WC2N 4HZ.

**Private Yacht** You'll need impressive sailing experience to make – or be hired for – an Atlantic crossing.

For information on crewing or charters in the UK, contact Alan Toone of Compass Yacht Services (☎ 020-8467-2450), Holly Cottage, Heathley End, Chislehurst, Kent BR7 6AB.

## ORGANIZED TOURS
There are dozens of organized tours to Jamaica. The vast majority are sun-and-sand package tours offered by charter tour operators and featuring roundtrip airfare, airport transfers, hotel accommodations, breakfasts, and certain other meals, all for a guaranteed price. Sightseeing tours, entertainment, and other extras may also be included.

### Package Tours
Dozens of tour companies offer package tours to Jamaica, usually using charter airlines (see Charter Flights, earlier in this chapter). The biggest companies operate on a regular basis, often every week. Most offer a selection of hotels to choose from, with prices varying accordingly.

Most per-person rates are quoted based on double occupancy. An additional charge ('single supplement') applies to anyone wishing to room alone.

**The USA** GoGo Worldwide Vacations and Air Jamaica Vacations are the two biggest package operators, but there are dozens more. The following tour operators are among those most active in the Jamaican market:

Adventure Tours USA
   (☎ 214-210-6132, 800-999-9046, fax 214-210-6191)
   10726 Plano Rd, Dallas, TX 75238

Air Jamaica Vacations
   (☎ 305-670-1177, 800-523-5585, fax 305-663-8291)
   9200 S Dadeland Blvd, No 800,
   Miami, FL 33156

American Airlines FlyAAway Vacations
   (☎ 800-433-7300, fax 817-967-4328)
   Mail Drop 1000, Box 619619,
   DFW Airport, TX 75261

Apple Vacations
   (☎ 800-727-3400 for east coast gateways, ☎ 800-365-2775 for west coast)
   101 NW Point Blvd,
   Elk Grove Village, IL 60007

Caribbean Collection
   (☎ 813-969-2140, 800-969-8222, fax 813-264-5912)
   13902 N Dale Mabry Hwy, No 230,
   Tampa, FL 33618

Caribbean Concepts
   (☎ 800-423-4433, fax 516-496-9880)
   575 Underhill Blvd, No 140, Syosset, NY 11791

Caribbean Travel Plus
   (☎ 215-474-5211, fax 877-8016)
   5243 W Berk St, Philadelphia, PA 19131

Caribbean Vacation Network
   (☎ 305-673-8822, 800-423-4095, fax 305-673-5666)
   1680 Meridian Ave, No 504,
   Miami Beach, FL 33139

Changes in L'Attitudes
   (☎ 813-573-3536, 800-330-8272, fax 813-573-2497)
   11681-49th St N, No 11, Clearwater, FL 33762

Delta Vacations
   (☎ 954-359-8388, 800-872-7786, fax 954-359-8386)
   1100 Lee Wagener Blvd, No 338,
   Fort Lauderdale, FL 33315

Friendly Holidays
   (☎ 800-221-9748, fax 516-358-1350)
   1983 Marcus Ave C-130,
   Lake Success, NY 11042

Funjet Vacations
   (☎ 414-351-3553, 800-558-3050, fax 414-351-1453)
   Box 1460, Milwaukee, WI 53201

GoGo Worldwide Vacations
   (☎ 800-333-3454, fax 800-821-3731, 201-944-3821)
   69 Spring St, Ramsey NJ 07446

Island Flight Vacations
   (☎ 310-410-0558, fax 410-0830)
   6033 W Century Blvd, No 807,
   Los Angeles, CA 90045

Island Resort Tours
   (☎ 212-476-9451, 800-251-1755, fax 212-476-9452)
   300 E 40th St, New York, NY 10016

Jamaica Travel Specialists
   (☎ 510-489-9552, 800-544-5979, fax 510-489-2318)
   2827 Mann Ave, Union City, CA 94587

Sunburst Holidays
   (☎ 212-567-2050, 800-426-4570, fax 212-942-9501)
   4779 Broadway, New York, NY 10034

Sun Splash Tours
   (☎ 212-366-4922, 800-426-7710, fax 212-366-5642)
   236 W 27th St, No 700, New York, NY 10001

Travel Impressions
(☎ 516-845-8000, 800-284-0044, fax 516-845-8095)
465 Smith St, Farmingdale, NY 11735

TravelJam
(☎ 301-429-9730, 800-554-7352, fax 301-429-9736)
9470 Annapolis Rd, suite 406,
Lanham, MD 20720

TWA Getaway Vacations
(☎ 609-985-4100, 800-438-2929, fax 800-264-8673)
10 E Stow Rd, Marlton, NJ 08053

US Airways Vacations
(☎ 407-857-8533, 800-544-7733, fax 407-857-9764)
7200 Lake Ellenor Drive, No 241,
Orlando, FL 32809

Wild Side Destinations
(☎ 503-760-4395, fax 760-0655,
JOTT399102@aol.com)
11306 SE Clinton, Portland, OR 97266

Vacation Express
(☎ 404-321-7742, 800-486-9777, fax 404-248-1237)
2957 Clairmont Rd, No 120, Atlanta, GA 30329

**Canada** Canadian package tour operators
include:

Air Transat Holidays
(☎ 514-987-1616, fax 987-9750)
300 Leo Pariseau, No 400,
Montreal, QC H2W 2P6

Albatours
(☎ 416-746-2890, fax 746-0397)

Conquest Tours
(☎ 416-665-9255, fax 665-6811)
85 Brisbane Rd, Downsview, ON M3J 2K3

Regent Holidays
(☎ 905-673-3343)
6205 Airport Rd, Building A, No 200,
Mississauga, ON L4V 1E1

Signature Vacations
(☎ 416-967-1510, fax 967-4951)
111 Avenue Rd, No 500, Toronto, ON M5R 3J8

Sunquest Vacations
(☎ 416-485-1700, fax 485-9479)
130 Merton St, Toronto, ON M4S 1A4

World of Vacations
(☎ 416-620-8050, fax 620-8700)

**Australia & New Zealand** Contours
Travel (☎ 3-9329-5211, fax 9329-6314), 466
Victoria St, N Melbourne, Victoria 3051, is
Australia's largest tour operator/wholesaler
to the Caribbean islands.
   Innovative Travel (☎ 3-365-3910, fax 365-
5755), PO Box 21, 247 Edgeware, Christ-

church, New Zealand, has a nascent Caribbean specialty.

**The UK** The following companies specialize in Jamaica and the Caribbean:

Caribbean Centre
(☎ 020-8940-3399, fax 8940-7424)
3 the Green, Richmond, Surrey TW9 1PL

Caribbean Expressions
(☎ 020-7794-1480, fax 7431-4221)
104 Belsize Lane, London NW3 5BB

Club Caribee: The Travel Shop
(☎ 020-8682-1115, fax 8682-2308)
2 Selkirk Rd, London SW17 0ES

First Choice Holidays House
(☎ 1293-588-437, fax 588-309)
London Rd, Crawley, W Sussex RH10 2GX

Sunworld
(☎ 020-8290-1111, fax 8218-3369)
29-31 Elmfield Rd, Bromley, Kent BR1 1LT

Thomas Cook Holidays
(☎ 0173-3417-000, fax 3417-784)
12 Coningsby Rd, Peterborough,
Cambs PE3 8XP

Unijet Sandrocks
(☎ 1444-255-600, fax 459-298)
Rocky Lane, Haywards Heath,
W Sussex RH164RH

**Continental Europe** Tour companies that
offer tours from Europe to Jamaica include:

**France**

LVO Collections du Monde
(☎ 01-42-93-61-16, fax 42-93-79-92)
43 Rue La Conadmine, Paris 75017

Le Grand Golf
(☎ 47-26-19-171, fax 26-19-172)
18 Rue Servient, Lyon 69003

**Germany**

Dertour GMBH
(☎ 69-9588-3231, fax 9588-3250)
Emil-von-Behring Strasse 6, Frankfurt 60424

**Hungary**

Mercator Travel
(☎ 53-311-500, fax 311-859)
Gubody U 17, Cegled 2700

**Netherlands**

Far Holidays International
(☎ 70-511-6092, fax 514-0796)
Van Carlingenlaan 16, Wassenaar 2241 SC

Indigo Tours
(☎ 70-360-1602, fax 362-1622)
Noordeinde 136A,
Den Haag 2514 GP

**Switzerland**
Carib Tours
(☎1-463-8863, fax 463-9261)
Malzstrasse 21, Zürich 8036

**Ukraine**
Yana Travel & Tours
(☎ 44-246-6213, fax 246-6061)
42 Saksagunskogo St, Kiev 252033

**Israel**  Sky Hakikar Tours (☎ 3-511-1999, fax 517-0932) 4 Bugrashov St, Tel Aviv, handles trips to Jamaica.

**Japan**  Island International (☎ 03-3401-4096, fax 3401-1629), 4-11-14-204 Jingumae, Shibuya-ku, Tokyo 150, specializes in travel to Jamaica.

## Specialty Tours
Very few companies offer specialty tours to Jamaica. The Association of Jamaican Attractions (☎ 940-0704, fax 979-7437, attractions@jamaica-irie.com) can provide you with a list of all the island's major attractions.

An excellent resource is *Specialty Travel Index* (☎ 415-459-9000, 800-442-4922), 305 San Anselmo Ave, suite 313, San Anselmo, CA 94960. Tours are cross-referenced in both a geographical and subject index. The *Island Vacation Guide* (☎ 203-655-8091, 800-962-2080, fax 203-655-6689), PO Box 2367, Darien, CT 06820, also lists tours to Jamaica.

**Birding & Ecological Tours**  Several companies offer special interest programs focusing on birding, nature, and hiking, including the following:

Calypso Island Tours
(☎ 510-366-5116)
3901 Grand Ave, No 304, Oakland, CA 94610.
Offers an eight-day 'Eco-Adventure,' featuring hiking, birding, and trips to rarely visited sites
Caligo Ventures
(☎ 800-426-7781)
156 Bedford Rd, Armonk NY 10504.
Offers a weeklong nature tour that includes

visits to the Cockpit Country, the Great Morass, and the Blue Mountains

Experience the Adventure Tours
(☎ 305-267-6644, fax 261-6648)
1350 SW 57th Ave, No 315, Miami, FL 33144.
Offers ecotours to Jamaica

Field Guides
(☎ 512-327-4953, 800-728-4953, fax 512-327-9231, fgileader@aol.com, www.fieldguides.com)
PO Box 160723, Austin, TX 78716.
Offers birding tours to Jamaica

Victor Emanuel Nature Tours
(☎ 800-328-8363)
Offers birding tours to Jamaica

The Touring Society of Jamaica (☎ 975-7158, fax 975-3620, lyndalee@islandoutpost.com, www.touringjamaica.com), c/o Island Outpost, PO Box 118, Ocho Rios, has a seven-day 'Bird Watcher's Jamaica Tour' for groups of 10 or more. During the tour you'll visit Cockpit Country and the Blue Mountains with noted birding authorities Robert Sutton and Audrey Downer (co-authors of *Birds of Jamaica*) as guides; the tour costs US$3345. You can also contact Robert Sutton (☎ 904-5454) in Mandeville for personalized birding tours.

In England, Discovery Initiatives (☎ 020-7299-9881, fax 7229-9883), 68 Princess Square, London W2 4NY, offers birding and ecotours.

The Gosse Bird Club (☎ 922-2253), c/o Audrey Downer, PO Box 1002, Kingston 8, offers educational programs and birding field trips.

**Cultural Tours**  Ecotours for Cures (☎ 203-598-0400, 800-829-0918, fax 203-598-0164, Naturalalt@juno.com), PO Box 525, Oyster Bay, NY 11771, offers 10-day ecotours to Jamaica during which guests spend time with the Maroons, learning hands-on natural healing remedies (US$1875 includes round-trip airfare from New York). It also offers 'Roots & Culture' tours, which arrange travel with Rastafarian teachers and healers.

Also consider SERVAS (☎ 212-267-0252), 11 John St, suite 706, New York, NY 10038, an organization that acts as a clearinghouse for travelers concerned with international welfare.

**Music Tours** Several companies offer package tours to the various music festivals. For example, Sunburst Holidays offers a 'Mind, Body & Soul' package to the Air Jamaica Jazz & Blues Festival in early November, with three-night packages as low as US$280 from Miami, and US$390 from New York.

Also see Special Events in the Facts for the Visitor chapter for companies offering tours to Reggae Sumfest and Reggae Sunsplash festivals.

**Clothing-Optional Tours** Several resorts welcome nudists, notably the all-inclusive resorts of the Sandals, SuperClubs, and Couples chains, most of which have nude beaches (see regional chapters for details). SuperClubs' deluxe Grand Lido Braco has a special nude wing, with bar, grill, pool, and other facilities. SuperClubs' Hedonism II is often booked by Lifestyle Tours & Travel (☎ 714-821-9939, fax 821-1465), 2641 W La Palma, suite A, Anaheim, CA 92801, which offers tour programs for adults with a 'sex-positive' attitude. Sandals' properties are not gay-friendly; SuperClubs is more liberal-minded.

At least three other US companies cater to travelers seeking an all-over tan:

Bare Necessities
   (☎ 512-499-0405, 800-743-0405)
   1502-A West Ave, Austin, TX 78701

Go Classy
   (☎ 888-825-2779, goclassy@sprynet.com)
   2676 West Lake Rd, Palm Harbor, FL 34684

Travel Au Naturel
   (☎ 800-728-0185)
   35246 US 19 N, suite 112, Palm Harbor, FL 34684

# Getting Around

## AIR
### Domestic Airports
Montego Bay's Donald Sangster International Airport has a domestic terminal adjacent to the international terminal; note, though, that these two terminals are not connected by a walkway. (See the Montego Bay & Northwest Coast and Getting There & Away chapters for details.)

In Kingston, most domestic flights use Tinson Pen, Kingston's intra-island commuter airport, handily situated 2 miles west of the downtown oceanfront at the west end of Marcus Garvey Drive, but a 40-minute ride from Norman Manley International Airport. (See the Kingston & Environs chapter for details.)

There is no departure tax for domestic flights.

### Domestic Airlines
Air Jamaica Express (☎ 923-8680, 800-523-5585, 305-670-3222 in the USA) has daily service between Montego Bay, Kingston's Tinson Pen, Negril, Ocho Rios, and Port Antonio, using 30 to 40-seat Shorts turboprops, 19-seat Dorniers, and nine-passenger Britten Norman Islanders. Plans were afoot to add service to Mandeville. See regional chapters for specific information.

Typical one-way fares (for purchase outside Jamaica) are:

| | |
|---|---|
| Kingston-Montego Bay | US$49 |
| Kingston-Negril | US$52 |
| Kingston-Port Antonio | US$37 |
| Montego Bay-Negril | US$37 |
| Montego Bay-Port Antonio | US$49 |
| Negril-Port Antonio | US$52 |

Air Jamaica Express offers a student fare (a student ID is required) of US$25 one-way for students up to 25 years of age (up to 30 years for UWI and UTECH students), plus senior citizens' fares of US$35 one-way. Air Jamaica Express also has a 'Cloud 9 Special'

air-pass – buy a book of nine tickets and get the 10th free.

Jamaica AirLink (☎ 923-0486, 877-359-5465 toll free, fax 923-0264, 954-564-7667 in the USA) connects MoBay with Kingston, Negril, Ocho Rios, and Port Antonio with nonscheduled charter service, as does Aero Express (☎ 927-4921).

Air Negril (☎ 940-7747, fax 940-6491 in Montego Bay; ☎ 957-5325, fax 957-5291 in Negril; airnegril@cwjamaica.com), also offers nonscheduled charter service from MoBay, Kingston, Ocho Rios, and Negril.

SuperClubs operates Air SuperClubs, a shuttle service for the resort's own guests, promising to get them to their final destination within an hour of landing at Montego Bay (US$60 per person each way to Negril, and US$84 each way to Ocho Rios, including hotel transfers). Flights operate sunrise to sunset and can be booked up to 24 hours in advance (return flights require 48 hours confirmation, and no-shows are charged a 50% cancellation fee). Service is provided by Air Negril, which has nine new planes emblazoned with the SuperClubs logo. For bookings, contact SuperClubs (☎ 800-467-8737), or send a fax marked 'Attention: Air Desk' to 954-925-0334.

### Charter Flights
A handful of companies offer charter services aboard Cessnas and other small aircraft, including the following:

Airspeed Express
☎ 937-7072, fax 923-0264 in Kingston

Airways International
☎ 923-6614 in Kingston, ☎ 952-5299 in Montego Bay, ☎ 957-4051 in Negril

Aero Express
☎ 937-4921 in Kingston, ☎ 952-5807 in Montego Bay, ☎ 957-9108 in Negril

Timair
☎ 952-2516

Wings Jamaica
☎/fax 923-6573, 923-5416 in Kingston

These companies offer customized sightseeing tours plus one-way charter flights to airports islandwide. Airways International also offers charter services that include Miami, Nassau, Turks and Caicos, Haiti, and Puerto Rico.

## Helicopter

Helitours (☎ 974-2265, 974-1108, fax 974-2183), based in Ocho Rios, offers sightseeing tours by Bell 206B Jetranger III helicopters. A 15-minute 'Fun Hop' around Ocho Rios costs US$50 per person. Longer journeys take in the coast east of town, including Firefly and Tacky Falls beyond Port Maria (US$95). The hour-long 'Jamaican Showcase' costs US$190 per person and will take you across the island, over Kingston and Port Royal, and across the Blue Mountains. A daylong 'Island Delight' costs US$2500 for up to four people, and includes breakfast in Port Antonio, a city tour in Kingston, a gourmet lunch, and beach time in Negril.

The company maintains helipads in Montego Bay, Negril, and Port Antonio. Each chopper seats four passengers and holds up to 250lb of cargo.

You can charter a helicopter for transport to any airport or for personalized tours. From Montego Bay, transfers are about US$400 to Negril, US$550 to Ocho Rios, US$750 to Kingston, and US$1200 to Port Antonio. Charter rates begin at US$500 per hour.

## BUS

Traveling by bus could be the best – or worst! – adventure of your trip to Jamaica. The island has an extensive bus network – there are public buses and private minibuses ('coasters') – that links virtually every village in the country, and which many Jamaicans use frequently. Traveling by bus is a great way to meet locals and get a feel for Jamaican lifestyles. It's also remarkably inexpensive. Buses are seldom used by foreign travelers, as the ride can be a demanding experience. Buses normally run on reduced schedules on Sunday.

## Public Buses

Jamaica's public bus 'system' is in many regards the epitome of chaos, worsening every year since, after independence, the efficient British system was replaced by the government-run Jamaica Omnibus Service.

Every town has a bus waiting area, usually near the main market, often in intimidating, crowded areas. There's no order or plan to most, however, and you'll usually be on your own to figure out where your desired bus leaves from. Each bus should have its destination marked above the front window. Bus stops are located at most road intersections along the routes, but you can usually flag down a bus anywhere except in major cities, where they're inclined to stop only at designated stops.

Buses rarely run on set schedules. They depart when they're full, often literally overflowing, with people hanging from the open doors. The problem is particularly bad in Kingston. While there's still room to squeeze a few more souls on board, the impending departure is typically announced with a continuous bleating of the horn. Once the bus sets off, the driver usually manages to scare passengers to death with a hair-raising display of reckless driving. Time is money!

You pay a conductor (or 'sideman'). You should ascertain the fare from an independent traveler, as conductors often quote an

There's always room for one more

HOLGER LEUE

inflated price to foreign passengers (it also helps to have the correct change ready). Alas, rates for tourists are often based on how much the driver thinks he can squeeze out of you. And you'll be charged an extra seat if you put your baggage on the seat next to you. Most Jamaicans are scrupulously honest and may pitch in on your behalf if you're having a hard time agreeing on a fare. Guard your luggage carefully against theft and to avoid having it seized by an overeager tout, who will maneuver you aboard his bus in a fait accompli.

Many buses are antiquated Hungarian contraptions that have hard seating and pump out clouds of black smoke. Passengers are usually laden down with sacks of produce or even a live piglet or poultry. When you want to get off, simply shout, 'One stop!' The conductor will usually echo your request with, 'Let off!'

In recent years, the Transport Authority has become aggressive in attempting to make Jamaica's bus system user-friendly. A new bus terminal in Montego Bay has considerably eased the burdens of departing and alighting there. Ground was broken for a new terminal in Negril in late 1998, and new terminals are planned for other key cities, including Kingston, where 150 gleaming new Mercedes-Benz buses and a creative new cashless bus system are being phased in (see the Kingston & Environs chapter).

Expect to pay less than US$1 for bus travel within town, and approximately US$1 per 50 miles for longer journeys

## 'Coasters'

Private minibuses are the workhorses of Jamaica's public transport system, and far outnumber buses. These 'coasters' operate like the larger buses, and all the caveats for buses apply.

Hundreds of private minibus operators are licensed by the Transport Authority, and all major towns and virtually every village in the country is served. Licensed minibuses display red license plates with the initials PPV (public passenger vehicle) or have Jamaican Union of Travelers Association (JUTA)

insignia (JUTA buses are exclusively for tourists).

The badly worn wrecks that used to serve as minibuses have mostly been retired and replaced in recent years with sleek new Japanese models. All are driven by men, most of whom spice up the ride with daredevil driving.

Expect your coaster to be jam-packed and for the radio to be blaring reggae so loud you can't hear yourself think. Take water and try to get a window seat as the buses can get stiflingly hot. Although most passengers are heading to the final destination, the bus may stop along the route to drop off and pick up people.

Coasters usually cost two to three times more, about US$3 or so for a 50-mile journey.

## Hotel Transfers

Many hotels include airport transfers in their room rates. Leading tour operators and car-rental companies also offer minibus transfers. The following are typical one-way fares from Montego Bay Airport to various destinations:

| Downtown | US$8 |
| Negril | US$20 |
| Mandeville | US$23 |
| Ocho Rios | US$25 |
| Port Antonio | US$30 |
| Kingston | US$30 |

JUTA is the largest transfer provider, with services islandwide (☎ 927-4534 in Kingston, ☎ 952-0813 in Montego Bay, fax 952-5355).

Major car-rental companies also offer private transfers. (See Rental Companies, later in this chapter, for more information.)

## TRAIN

Those railway tracks marked on maps don't mean very much. Gone are the days when, for a few pennies, you could travel aboard the now defunct Jamaica Railway Corporation's daily service between Kingston and Montego Bay. The unprofitable railway system was shut down in 1992. There have been rumors for years that private investors might resurrect train service, but nothing has yet emerged.

## CAR

Exploring on your own is one of the greatest joys of Jamaica, and renting a vehicle is a great way to do it. There are some fabulously scenic journeys, and with your own wheels you can get as off-the-beaten-track as you wish, discovering the magic of Jamaican culture beyond the pale of the touristy areas.

Jamaica has about 9500 miles of roads, about 2400 miles of which are paved. Virtually any part of the island is accessible by car. A paved coastal highway circles the entire island (except in St Elizabeth, Manchester, and Clarendon parishes, where it runs about 20 miles inland, parallel to the shore between Black River and Spanish Town). Three main (and numerous minor) roads cross the central mountain chains, north to south, linking all the main towns. A web of minor roads, country lanes, and dirt tracks provides access to more remote areas. Most roads are narrow with frequent bends, and often are overgrown with foliage on the edges.

There are no freeways (motorways). A new two-lane highway linking Montego Bay and Negril was nearing completion at press time. And there's another two-lane highway linking Kingston with Spanish Town. With few other exceptions, most roads are single lane each direction.

Road conditions range from excellent to awful. The main roads are usually in good condition, although you're likely to find deep potholes everywhere, especially toward the end of rainy season. Keep your speed down! Many of the secondary roads, or B-roads, are in appalling condition and best tackled with a 4WD vehicle. Minor, unpaved roads are usually rutted by rains and lack of repairs. Don't underestimate how badly washed out backcountry roads can be. In places you might wish for a Humvee!

The following list indicates distances and approximate driving times between a few major destinations:

| route | distance | duration |
|---|---|---|
| Montego Bay-Negril | 52 miles | 2 hours |
| Montego Bay-Ocho Rios | 67 miles | 2½ hours |
| Ocho Rios-Port Antonio | 66 miles | 2½ hours |
| Ocho Rios-Kingston | 55 miles | 2 hours |
| Port Antonio-Kingston | 61 miles | 2½ hours |

Also see Scenic Drives in the Highlights section of the Facts for the Visitor chapter.

### Road Rules

Always drive on the *left*. Remember: 'Keep left and you'll always be right.' Here's another local saying worth memorizing: 'De left side is de right side; de right side is suicide!' The speed limit is 30mph in towns and 50mph on highways. Observe it. Jamaican traffic police frequently use radar as part of a crackdown on speeding and drunk driving. You'll usually have fair warning, since Jamaican drivers flash their headlights at oncoming traffic to indicate a police patrol ahead.

Jamaica has no compulsory seatbelt law (few old cars have seatbelts anyway) nor is it compulsory to wear helmets when riding motorcycles. However, read the section on Driving Conditions, below, for many reasons why you *should* wear a seatbelt or a helmet.

### Driving Conditions

Take a deep breath! Jamaican drivers rank high among the world's rudest and least cautious drivers. Expect to be honked at frequently and to hear the foulest cuss words yelled at other drivers for any real or imagined slight. A huge percentage drive dangerously, particularly when you consider local road conditions. Cars play hopscotch with one another, overtaking with daredevil folly, often passing long lines of cars even on blind curves! 'No mon can pass me when me drive 'ard down de road,' boasts taxi driver Clifford Edwards, whose 15-year-old Lada looks like it should have been junked years ago.

Thus, Jamaica has the third highest auto fatality rate in the world – behind Ethiopia and India – with a staggering 343 fatalities per 100,000 cars (compared to 26 per 100,000 in the US, and 22 per 100,000 in the

UK). And accident and fatality rates are rising, with a 19% increase in 1997 over 1996. The fearsome statistics are compounded because few Jamaicans use seatbelts, which are considered 'sissy.'

Use extreme caution and drive defensively, especially at night when you should be prepared to meet oncoming cars that are either without lights or blinding you with their high-beams! (A huge percentage of Jamaicans use high-beams as statements of power – wonderful fodder for sociological study but a nightmare for other drivers.) Don't drive after drinking: Jamaican police give random Breathalyzer tests.

Use your horn liberally, especially when approaching blind corners and in heavily congested urban areas, where you may need to weave your way through crowds. Traffic jams are particularly frequent in Montego Bay, Spanish Town, May Pen, Ocho Rios, and Kingston, especially on market days.

## Directions

Signage on main roads is very good (in recent years, the government's Tourism Action Plan has initiated a program to place road signs on all major routes). But a good road map is still essential; directional signs are few and far between as soon as you leave the main roads. Maps are usually available at car-rental companies. Only a fraction of B-roads are shown on maps, however, and many newer roads are not shown. And what may appear on a map to be a 30-minute journey may take several hours due to windy roads. (See Maps in the Facts for the Visitor chapter.)

Locals will be more than happy to help with directions, but take their instructions with a grain of salt. Few Jamaicans own cars, so many tend to underestimate distance and are overly optimistic about road conditions. You may be blithely told that your destination is 'straight ahead,' for example, only to discover that the road peters out into a walking track. Believe any Jamaican, however, who tells you a road is bad.

Many Jamaicans still measure distance in 'chains,' the old British measure of 22 yards, though few seem to know its length. All too often 'a few chains' can turn out to be a mile

or more. You may also need to phrase your question carefully. Avoid asking, 'Is this the way to so-and-so?' A better question is, 'Where does this road go?' Often, too, whomever you're asking directions of will answer only your specific question. Thus, if you ask, 'Is this the way to so-and-so?' and it isn't, they may tell you 'No, mon!' without then pointing you in the right direction unless you specifically ask them to.

Likewise, Jamaicans tend to say 'left' for both left *and* right when giving directions. Ask to have directions repeated with a hand signal ('Turn left a mile up de road,' will often be accompanied by a hand signal to turn *right*). And anyone telling you to continue 'straight' – which usually means 'ahead' – is sure to have forgotten to point out the Y-fork just around the bend. Ask if there are any forks in the road…and then ask which direction you should take.

## Driver's License

Although the minimum age to obtain a driver's license in Jamaica is 17, renters must be 21 (some companies will rent only to those 25 or older). For additional details, see the Driver's License & Permits section under Visas & Documents in the Facts for the Visitor chapter.

## Gasoline

Esso, Shell, Texaco, and PetCom maintain gasoline stations across the island. In rural areas, stations usually close on Sunday. Almost everywhere, gas stations may close after 7 pm or so. Fortunately, gasoline is very inexpensive by international standards: about US$1.80 per gallon (J$140 per liter) in early 1999. However, in mid-1999 the government introduced new levies on gasoline that virtually doubled the price of gasoline, resulting in islandwide riots. The tax was rescinded, but expect prices to rise.

Cash only, please! Credit cards are not accepted.

Both leaded and unleaded fuels are sold.

## Security

It's always best to park in hotel (or other secure) car parks. Wherever you park, whether on the street or in a secure parking lot, be sure to always remove your belongings. At the very least, keep them locked in the trunk. Even 'secure' hotel parking lots are rarely fully secure.

Women should consider not driving alone in remote areas. (See Women Travelers in the Facts for the Visitor chapter.)

The majority of Jamaicans – man, woman, and child – get around by standing at the side of the road and flagging down passing cars. As a visitor with a car, you're a privileged person. Any empty seats in your car will go a long way toward easing the burden of Jamaicans forced to rely on buses and passing cars. However, your rental policy may specifically forbid giving rides to strangers; check the fine print.

You can feel secure giving rides to children and women, who will wave you down with a lackadaisical sweep of the outstretched hand. Use common sense and caution when offering rides to men.

## Mechanical Problems

There is no national roadside service organization to phone when you have car trouble. Most car-rental agencies have a 24-hour service number in case of breakdowns and other emergencies. That's a good enough reason to choose an agency that is a member of JUDA (the Jamaica U-Drive Association), which sets minimum standards for members. If you do break down, use a local mechanic only for minor work, otherwise the car-rental company may balk at reimbursing you for work they haven't authorized. If you can't find a phone or repair service, seek police assistance. Use common sense in dealing with offers of unsolicited help. *Never* give your keys to strangers.

## Accidents

Hopefully you won't have one, but if you 'mash up' there are a few rules to obey. Don't move the vehicles, and don't let anyone else do so, including the other driver. Have someone call the police, and remain at the scene until a police officer arrives. Make sure to get the name and address of anyone else involved in the accident, as well as their

license number and details about their vehicle. Take photos of the scene if possible, and get the names and addresses of any witnesses. Above all, don't be drawn into an argument. Jamaican emotions are volatile, so you should do your best to keep tempers calm. Call your rental company as soon as possible.

You'll be lucky to find any witnesses who'll admit to having seen the accident. Jamaicans are loath to get involved where the police are concerned. Unfortunately, there's a tendency, too, to point a finger at tourists. If you're the victim of an accident caused by someone else, be prepared to defend your position vigorously.

If you hit and kill an animal such as a goat, morally you should stop and offer to compensate the owner. I'm told that US$100 is the going rate for a goat. Killing a chicken is a lesser 'crime.' However, be aware that volatile tempers can erupt in unrestrained anger even where the cause is purely accidental (in 1995, a US businessman was beaten to death by a mob after he accidentally knocked over a vendor's pot). Try to judge your circumstances. Balance your sense of obligation against any fears for your safety. If the situation turns nasty, get out of there fast.

## Rental

All the major international car-rental companies operate in Jamaica, along with dozens of smaller local firms. Car-rental agencies are listed in the local yellow pages, and the Jamaica Tourist Board (JTB) publishes a list of JUDA members. You'll find plenty of rental companies at the two international airports, in major cities, and even in smaller towns.

Rental rates may give North Americans sticker shock (Europeans will find prices on par with home). In general, companies away from airports tend to be less expensive. High-season rates begin at about US$48 per day and can run as high as US$125, depending on the vehicle. You may be able to find slightly cheaper rates in low season. Some companies include unlimited mileage, while others set a limit and charge a fee for excess miles driven. You may be able to negotiate to receive unlimited mileage if this is not automatically included. Most firms require a deposit of at least US$500, but will accept a credit card imprint. Keep copies of all your paperwork.

You can reserve a car upon arrival, but in high season you may find that most vehicles are taken and that the vehicle of your choice is not available. Consider making your reservation in advance. It's wise to reconfirm before your arrival, at which time your car will be delivered to the airport (or your hotel).

Rental companies can arrange a driver, for an extra fee.

Before signing, go over the vehicle with a fine-tooth comb to identify any dents and scratches. Make a note of each one before you drive away. You're likely to be charged for the slightest mark that wasn't noted before. Don't forget to check the cigarette lighter and interior switches, which are often missing.

**Type of Vehicle** Most companies utilize modern Japanese sedans. A small sedan is perfectly adequate for paved roads. A big car can be a liability on Jamaica's narrow, winding roads. Most companies also rent 4WD vehicles, which are recommended if you intend to do *any* driving away from main roads and certainly for any backcountry exploring, where the roads can be terribly potholed and extra ground clearance may be required. A Suzuki Samurai is an economical and versatile vehicle, perfect for Jamaican conditions (for two people). A Suzuki Samurai Jeep costs about US$60 a day.

Your options are standard (stick) or automatic transmission, and with or without aircon. Stick shift is preferable because frequent and sudden gear changes are required when potholes and kamikaze chickens appear out of nowhere; automatic transmissions do not give you the control you'll need. Remember, though, that you'll be changing gears with your *left* hand. If this is new to you, don't worry; you'll soon get the hang of it.

**Insurance** Check in advance to see whether your current insurance or credit card covers you for driving while abroad. All rental companies will recommend damage-waiver insurance, which limits your liability in the event of an accident or damage. It should cost about US$12 to US$15 per day and is a valuable investment. American Express cardholders can waive this damage-waiver option; most Jamaican car-rental companies recognize AmEx's policy.

**Rental Companies** Jamaica's largest and most reputable car-rental company is Island Car Rentals. Nine categories of vehicles cost from US$48 to US$99 daily in low season, US$65 to US$130 high season. You'll find information at www.islandcarrentals.com or through the following offices:

Kingston
  Main office (☎ 926-8861, 926-5991, fax 929-6787) 17 Antigua Ave, Kingston 10
  Norman Manley International Airport (☎ 924-8075, fax 924-8389)

Montego Bay
  Sangster International Airport (☎/fax 952-5771)

Ocho Rios
  (☎/fax 974-2334)

You can also make arrangements from abroad at the following numbers:

Canada                    ☎ 800-526-2422
USA                       ☎ 800-892-4581

Most car-rental companies are reliable, although the smaller the company, the greater the risks involved.

The major international companies are also represented by these offices in Jamaica:

Bargain
  (☎ 888-991-2111, ☎ 800-348-5398)
  (☎ 926-8237, 926-8021) Norman Manley International Airport, Kingston
  (☎ 952-0762) Montego Bay
  (☎ 974-5298) Ocho Rios
Hertz
  (☎ 800-654-3131)
  (☎ 924-8028) Norman Manley International Airport, Kingston
  (☎ 979-0438) Sangster International Airport, Montego Bay

It's best to make reservations before your arrival in Jamaica. The following major car-rental companies have offices in Jamaica:

**North America**

| | |
|---|---|
| Budget | ☎ 800-527-0700 |
| Dollar | ☎ 800-421-6868 |
| Hertz | ☎ 800-654-3001 |
| Island Car Rentals | ☎ 800-892-4581 |

**The UK & Ireland**

| | |
|---|---|
| Budget | ☎ 0800-181181 |
| Hertz | ☎ 0990-996699 |

**Australia & New Zealand**

| | |
|---|---|
| Budget | ☎ 13-2727 in Australia<br>☎ 9-375-2222 in New Zealand |
| Hertz | ☎ 13-3039 in Australia<br>☎ 9-309-0989 in New Zealand |

**Fly & Drive Packages** If you want to explore Jamaica fully, consider a prepurchased package combining car-rental and hotel vouchers. You simply arrive at the airport, pick up your car, and set off to roam the island armed with vouchers good at 48 participating hotels. The program, called 'Fly-Drive Jamaica,' is sponsored by Inns of Jamaica and offered by Caribbean Vacation Network (☎ 305-673-8822, 800-892-4581 in Jamaica, ☎ 800-423-4095 in the USA, ☎ 800-526-2422 in Canada, fax 305-673-5666), 1370 Washington No 301, Miami Beach, FL 33139. The company will reserve your first night's accommodations in advance (you choose the place), plus additional nights for a fee. Alternately, you can book your next stop as you check out of each one, or be spontaneous and show up unannounced.

If you choose to stay at the most upscale places, the package can promise discounts of up to 20% off hotels and car rentals booked separately. Low-season rates for a one-week package start at US$952 single, US$476 double occupancy, US$353 triple occupancy. The standard high-season package costs US$581 per person double occupancy (US$1162 single, US$448 triple), including a two-door, subcompact car with standard transmission and unlimited mileage. Add an extra US$12 daily for a four-door car, US$15 for an automatic, and US$32 for an automatic with air-con.

## MOTORCYCLE

There's a special thrill to exploring on two wheels, with the sun and wind on your skin. Dozens of companies rent motorcycles and scooters, available at any resort town. They're far more lax than car-rental companies; you may not even have to show your driver's license (if you've seen the Lonely Planet video, the *Jamaica Experience*, the scene of negotiating for a motorcycle won't inspire you with great confidence). If you're not an experienced motorcycle driver, you could rent a scooter, which is far easier to handle. Motor scooters cost about US$25 per day. Motorcycles cost more, according to size. Expect to pay about US$45 a day for a 750cc machine.

*Ride cautiously!* Road conditions are extremely hazardous, particularly for novice riders. Especially away from major resorts, you'll encounter potholes, loose gravel, narrow roads, reckless drivers, free-roaming cattle and goats, and other hazards. Check if the rental agency has helmets. If they do, *wear one!*

## BICYCLE

Cycling is a cheap, convenient, healthy, environmentally sound, and above all, fun way of traveling. Many Jamaicans use bicycles and most resorts have at least one bike rental shop. Bicycle supply shops can be found in most large towns.

If you do take your own bicycle to Jamaica or plan to rent one while you're there, augment your repair kit with every imaginable spare before you leave home. You won't necessarily be able to buy that crucial gizmo when your bicycle breaks down in the backcountry as the sun sets.

Bicycles can travel by air. You can pack a bike in pieces in a bike bag or box, but it's much easier simply to wheel your bike to the airline's check-in desk, where it should be treated as a piece of baggage. You may have to remove the pedals and turn the handlebars sideways so that it takes up less space in the aircraft's hold; check all this with the airline well in advance, preferably before you pay for your ticket.

Note the caveats about road conditions and driving habits given in Driving Conditions, earlier in this chapter. Most roads are extremely narrow and Jamaican drivers are not very considerate about bicyclists.

Purchasing a bicycle in Jamaica is not practical. Outside Kingston, bicycle stores are few and far between, with a limited selection. Bicycles are also far more expensive than their equivalents in North America or Europe, and it is usually cheaper to transport your bicycle from home at no extra cost.

For practicalities, plus information on bike rentals, see Cycling in the Outdoor Activities chapter.

## HITCHHIKING

Most Jamaicans do not own vehicles and the bus service is unreliable, so the majority of Jamaicans who live outside major towns hitch rides. Jamaican drivers are therefore used to giving rides to strangers as a matter of course.

That said, hitching is never entirely safe in any country in the world, and we don't recommend it. Travelers who decide to hitch should understand that they are taking a small but potentially serious risk. Women are especially at risk. Travel in pairs and let someone know where you are planning to go.

## BOAT

If you want to prearrange a yacht rental, there are several respected companies that offer both crewed and bareboat charters. (See Charter Yacht in the Getting There & Away chapter and Chartering in the Outdoor Activities chapter for details on cruising in Jamaican waters.)

A ferry service links Kingston to Port Royal. See the Kingston & Environs chapter for details.

## TAXI

Taxis are widely available throughout the island. Hiring a taxi is a handy, albeit expensive, way of traveling between resorts and for getting around larger towns such as Kingston or Montego Bay. Taxis range from beat-up Russian-made Ladas to sleek new Toyota Corollas. Note that there are usually both tourist rates and local rates for fares, which differ vastly.

### Licensed Taxi

Licensed taxis – called 'contract carriages' in Jamaica – have red PPV license plates (a blue plate indicates that the owner has applied for a license; those without such plates are unlicensed). They're not cheap by the standards of other developing countries, but are affordable if you share the cost with up to three other passengers.

There's no shortage of licensed cabs, which you'll find at all the major resorts and towns. JUTA (☎ 927-4534) operates islandwide, using a vast government-approved fleet of taxis and minivans. JUTA services the cruise lines and hotels and is geared almost exclusively to the tourist business. Its vehicles are recent-model, white Toyota Corolla station wagons (estate cars). Dozens of other taxi cab companies are listed in the yellow pages and in the regional chapters of this book.

The government has established fixed rates according to distance. Licensed cabs should have these posted inside. Ostensibly you can obtain a copy from any JTB office (but few have them). If not, ask to see some documented evidence that the fare you're being charged is correct. Taxis are also supposed to have meters, but few drivers use them.

Fares on the touristic north coast are expensive. In Kingston and nontouristy areas, fares are more reasonable.

The following were typical fares in late 1998, based on up to four people per taxi:

| | |
|---|---|
| Sangster International Airport to Montego Bay | US$7 |
| Around Montego Bay | US$7 to US$15 |
| Montego Bay to Ocho Rios or Negril | US$70 |
| Negril Aerodrome to Negril | US$7 |
| Norman Manley airport to Kingston | US$15 to US$21 |
| Kingston to Ocho Rios | US$100 to US$120 |
| Kingston to Port Antonio | US$100 to US$120 |

**'Robots'** If you're penny-pinching, consider hailing a 'robot' – a shared taxi that picks up and drops off as many people as it can squeeze in along the route. Usually these are beat-up old cars. They are much cheaper than other taxis (fares are slightly higher than bus rates, with whom they compete). Few tourists use them, which means you're likely to be charged the local rate rather than an inflated tourist rate. If your driver attempts to throw other passengers out, you can assume that he thinks that you – the wealthy tourist – want to charter the taxi, in which case the fare will shoot up exorbitantly.

Many robots are licensed (look for the red PPV plate); others operate as unlicensed taxis.

## Unlicensed Taxi

You won't find meters in unlicensed taxis, which are operated illegally by freelancers who rent out their own vehicles, usually old heaps.

Many freelance taxi drivers try to charge the same amount as licensed cabs, but you can normally get the price down substantially. Bargain hard! Your hotel desk clerk or concierge should be able to give you a good idea of a fair fare. Be sure to agree on a fare *before* getting in (this is a good rule even for licensed cabs). If you don't, you're most likely going to get ripped off. Be sure to determine if the driver means Jamaican or US dollars, and whether 'three bills' means three *hundred* Jamaican dollars.

Guard your belongings carefully: freelance taxis have a reputation for theft. And don't let yourself be talked into visiting specific shops, where the driver can expect to receive a commission on anything you purchase.

## ORGANIZED TOURS
### General Interest

There are plenty of organized sightseeing tours to choose from. Scores of reputable Jamaican companies offer guided excursions and tours to leading attractions islandwide (see 'Sightseeing Tours' in the yellow pages). Popular tours include rafting trips on the Martha Brae and Rio Grande Rivers, and visits to Croydon Plantation and other working plantations. The JTB can provide you with information, and virtually every hotel lobby displays brochures. Tour excursions typically cost from US$20 half-day to US$70 full-day, but prices can vary widely according to the destination and itineraries.

A good resource is the Association of Jamaican Attractions (☎ 940-0704, fax 979-7437, attractions@jamaica-irie.com), which lists all the major attractions islandwide.

One of the most popular tours is the Appleton Estate Rum Tour (☎ 997-6077, 952-5013, fax 923-6981, 952-0981), a motorcoach tour over the rugged mountains and into the Siloah Valley to visit the famous rum factory. The Appleton tour costs US$62 from Montego Bay and US$65 from Ocho Rios, and includes rum tasting and a small bottle of rum.

One of the biggest tour operators is Caribic Vacations, with offices in Montego Bay, Negril, and Ocho Rios (see below).

At the deluxe end, Island Car Rentals (see Rental Companies, earlier in this chapter) offers a series of personally chauffeured tours, such as historic and cultural tours of Kingston (US$43 to US$51 per person), Port Royal (US$50), the Blue Mountains (US$64), Port Antonio (US$134), Black River (US$121), and Ocho Rios (US$100).

The following are among the leading tour companies (the addresses listed are the companies' headquarters):

Blue Danube Tours
    (☎ 952-0886, fax 952-5018)
    55 Gloucester Ave, Montego Bay

Caribic Vacations
    (☎ 953-9878, 979-9387, fax 953-9897, 979-3421)
    1310 Providence Drive, Ironshore Estate,
    Montego Bay

Galaxy Tours
    (☎ 968-8122, fax 925-6975)
    75 Red Hills Rd, Kingston 20

Gemini Tours
    (☎ 968-2473 in Kingston, ☎ 952-8202 in
    Montego Bay)
    2 Eastwood Ave, Kingston 10

Glamour Tours
    (☎ 979-8207, fax 953-2619)
    Montego Bay Shopping Centre, Montego
    Freeport

Greenlight Tours
(☎ 952-2636, fax 952-0564)
Bogue Industrial Estate, Montego Bay

Infinity Tours
(☎ 960-9290, fax 960-9301,
infinity@infochan.com)
12-14 Oxford Terrace, Kingston 5

Intimate Jamaica
(☎ 960-3598, fax 960-3599,
intimjam@infochan.com)
12 Worthington Terrace, Kingston 5

JUTA Tours
(☎ 927-4534, fax 929-0648)
49 Lady Musgrave Rd, Kingston 10

Pleasure Vacation Tours
(☎ 924-4140, fax 924-1756)
1531-1/2 Constant Spring Rd, Kingston 8

Pro Tours
(☎ 978-6113, fax 978-6139)
7 Lady Musgrave Rd, Kingston 5

Tourwise
(☎ 974-2323, fax 974-5362)
103 Main St, Ocho Rios
(☎ 979-1027)
Sangster International Airport

## Special Interest Tours

Many companies offer special interest tours. For activities such as bicycling, hiking, and bird watching, see the Outdoor Activities and Getting There & Away chapters.

One of the best – and costliest – companies is the Touring Society of Jamaica (☎ 975-7158, fax 975-3620, lyndalee@islandoutpost.com, www.touringjamaica.com), c/o Island Outpost, PO Box 118, Ocho Rios, which has a series of tours for birders, botanists, hikers, and anyone seeking a deeper appreciation of island culture. It specializes in groups and customized tours. Want to check out the Kingston dancehall scene? Trips range from US$75 per person for half-day trips, and start at US$250 for groups of four.

Destinations (☎ 702-0314, 702-0112, 800-532-2271), PO Box 216, Kingston 7, specializes in hiking and is the progeny of Sense Adventures, the original Jamaican alternative tour operator. Sense Adventures is still a handy information resource, but these days limits its offerings to hiking in the Blue Mountains.

The Touring Society of Jamaica has a five-day 'Jamaica's Historic Gardens' tour into the Blue Mountains with stays at Strawberry Hill, plus customized itineraries based on stays at Island Outpost properties islandwide.

**Safaris** By far the most popular outings in Jamaica are river safaris up the Black River in search of crocodiles and birdlife. Three major outfitters operate floating excursions aboard pontoon boats from the town of Black River into the heart of the Great Morass, and close-up crocodile sightings are virtually assured. Most of the major tour companies listed above offer excursions from resort towns that use the services of one of these outfitters, often in combination with a visit to YS Falls, a beautiful spot nearby. (See the Southwest Coast chapter for details; also see regional chapters for Black River excursions offered from specific resorts.)

Safari Tours Jamaica (☎/fax 972-2639, safari@toj.com, www.jamaica-irie.com/safari), Arawak PO, Mammee Bay, offers separate daylong 'jeep safaris' of Orange Valley and the Blue Mountains using zebra-striped Land Rovers. It even has a two-day mule ride and trekking tour in the Blue Mountains.

The Touring Society of Jamaica offers private 4WD trips from US$250 for a full day for up to four people.

# Montego Bay & Northwest Coast

Montego Bay is the second largest city on the island and by far Jamaica's most important tourist resort. More than 30% of the country's hotel rooms are here, including those in several of Jamaica's most exclusive hotels, nestled up against their own gilded shores.

The resort town of Montego Bay is as far from the 'real' Jamaica as you can get, though behind the narrow coastal plain is hill country where you can immerse yourself in mountain-village life. The region boasts a greater concentration of well-preserved colonial houses than any other, many of which are working plantations that welcome guests on guided tours. And several championship golf courses, a number of horse stables, and the island's best shopping add to the region's appeal.

You'll discover Falmouth, a town of intriguing historical interest and the gateway for rafting on the Martha Brae River; Good Hope, known for horseback riding and fine dining and site of Jamaica's only 'country house hotel'; and the fascinating Cockpit Country, one of the island's most scenic regions and one that is still virtually inaccessible.

## Montego Bay

Montego Bay (population 82,000), capital of St James parish, is dependent on tourism. It's also a thriving port city, based on the container-shipping trade farther west at Montego Freeport. The town, colloquially called 'MoBay' by locals (native-born Montegonians are called 'bawn-a-bays'), spreads tentacles of light industry west as far as Reading, 4 miles away. An equal distance to the east, Ironshore, formerly a sugar estate, is now a burgeoning resort (see Ironshore, later in this chapter).

MoBay's primary attractions are its golf courses, historic great houses, and the beautiful private beach resorts outside of town. Also worth a visit are the waters, coral reefs, and mangroves offshore, protected within the Montego Bay Marine Park. Many admirable Georgian stone buildings and timber houses still stand downtown. The duty-free shopping is excellent. Every kind of water sport is represented. And there are several good restaurants to choose from. Those seeking a budget holiday with a lively nightlife and shops and craft markets packed with bargains will be right at home, as will those seeking to spend a week idly sunning at an all-inclusive upscale resort. However, if you're seeking authentic, offbeat Jamaica, move on. Many guidebooks

## Highlights

- Reggae Sumfest, Jamaica's world-class midsummer reggae festival
- Barnett Estate and Belvedere Estate for firsthand glimpses of working plantations
- Magnificently restored Rose Hall, embellished by an eerie legend
- Rocklands Bird Feeding Station, where you feed birds by hand
- Sunset sailing trips, for the party crowd
- Bamboo rafting expedition on the Great River and Martha Brae River
- Horseback ride and a meal or overnight at Good Hope Estate
- A hike in Cockpit Country – not for the faint-hearted

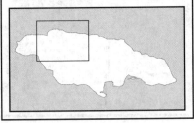

# MONTEGO BAY & NORTHWEST COAST

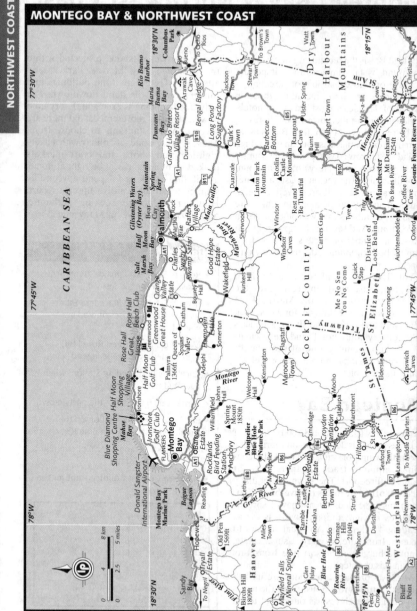

tout MoBay's natural beauty, and reggae artists have sung the city's praises to the world, though frankly, the city lacks much soul.

South of Gloucester Ave's tourist strip, you'll find downtown to be a crowded, chaotic mishmash of one-way streets full of honking cars, storefronts pumping out dancehall music, and a press of pedestrians. By some historic quirk, two of the city's three 'public' beaches – Doctor's Cave and Cornwall – are in the hands of private owners who hold a monopoly lease. The wire fences and tall concrete walls they erected effectively divorced the beaches from the resort. Fortunately the grotesque wall that precluded a glimpse of Doctor's Cave Beach was being replaced at this writing by another fence that – at last – offered MoBay's best beach to view, promising to change the entire mood of the strip. Walter Fletcher Beach, run by the Urban Development Council, began to get a much-needed facelift in 1998. To boot, the full length of Gloucester Ave has been paved (as part of a US$2 million overhaul). Proud of its new liverie, Gloucester Ave has officially been christened the 'Hip Strip.'

Most resort hotels around Montego Bay have their own private beaches – and they are some of the best beaches around.

## HISTORY

Columbus anchored in Montego Bay in 1494 and called it El Golfo de Buen Tiempo (Gulf of Good Weather). Only in 1655 did a settlement first appear on Spanish maps: Manterias, after the Spanish word *manteca*, or lard, from the days when the Spanish shipped 'pig's butter' derived from herds of wild hogs that flourished in the nearby hills. English maps later showed the area as 'Lard Bay.' Following the British takeover in 1655, the parish of St James was established and named for the Duke of York, later known as King James II. The tiny port, however, languished for over a century under constant threat both from pirates and the fearsome Maroons, who maintained their autonomy in the wild Cockpit Country southeast of MoBay.

As sugar was planted in the 18th century, Montego Bay took on new importance, encouraged by a peace settlement with the Maroons. Sugar was planted on every valley floor and St James became the most important sugar-producing parish on the island. More than 150 ships a year arrived in Montego Bay, bringing slaves and supplies. Wealthy planters and merchants erected lavish townhouses and the parish church. And a cultural life developed: by 1773, the city had the island's only newspaper outside Kingston, the *Cornwall Chronicle*. Unfortunately, many of the original buildings perished in fires and hurricanes that also destroyed many valuable records in the western part of the island, obscuring this early history.

## Emancipation & the Launch of Tourism

Montego Bay and its hinterland were the setting for the slave rebellion of Christmas 1831, when estates throughout St James were put to the torch. Militia and regular troops stationed in Montego Bay quickly quelled the revolt, and the courthouse (now in ruins) became a center for savage retribution. (See 'Preaching Resistance.')

Following emancipation in 1834, the sugar trade slipped into decline. The city once again languished until revived by the development of the banana trade, pioneered by the local firm of JE Kerr & Co, and by the early tourist trade that developed in the late 1880s when Dr Alexander G McCatty founded a sanitarium at what is today Doctor's Cave Beach. Rich Americans and British flocked on the banana boats to 'take the waters.' Many later bought homes here, adding luster to the name Montego Bay.

When a famous British chiropractor, Sir Herbert Baker, published an article touting the curative powers of Doctor's Cave, the beach became an overnight hit. The Casa Blanca Hotel became a favorite of the elite during the mid-January to mid-March season (it closed its doors for the rest of the year). The diesel train that carried tourists who had arrived by sea in Kingston became known as the 'Casa Blanca Special.' Alas, the famous cave was destroyed along with the original Casa Blanca Hotel (since rebuilt) during a 1932 hurricane.

## The Jet-Set Age

During WWII, the US Air Force built an airstrip east of town, which, in the post-war years, served to open up Montego Bay to tourism on a larger scale. Round Hill and Tryall Resorts were built west of town and became emblematic of a new breed of exclusive resorts that cemented Jamaica's reputation for chic. In the 1960s, the government lent its financial muscle to sponsoring the tourism trade, and hotels have been going up ever since.

In the late 1960s the west side of the bay was dredged and Montego Freeport was constructed on 35 acres of fill (today the freeport is a center of light industry). Later,

a separate cruise-ship terminal appeared, launching a new breed of visitor.

Tourism's success has had its negative side. MoBay earned a justified reputation as a hustler's city: until a year or two ago, it was impossible to walk even a few yards without being approached and hassled. To its credit, the Jamaican Tourist Board (JTB) has made enormous inroads to reduce the numbers of touts and prostitutes who once hung out casually along Gloucester Ave. The makeover is remarkable.

## ORIENTATION

There are two Montego Bays. The tourist quarter, north of the town center, arcs along Gloucester Ave, a narrow shoreline boulevard lined with hotels, restaurants, and public beaches. Gloucester Ave becomes Kent Ave, which stretches along what used to be called Chatham Sea Wall and ends at tiny Dead-End Beach, with the airport just beyond. The airport is accessed from Sunset Blvd, which stretches east from the junction of Gloucester and Kent Aves and continues east, beyond the airport (at the roundabout junction with the Queen's Drive), as the A1 to Ironshore and the resorts on the north coast.

A steep hill – Miranda Hill – rises behind the tourist strip. The Queen's Drive traverses the hill: it begins at the airport roundabout (traffic circle) and ends at another roundabout at the southern end of Gloucester Ave.

The town center lies immediately south of the roundabout, with the downtown accessed by Fort St, a bustling thoroughfare that leads from the roundabout to Sam Sharpe Square, MoBay's vibrant heart. En route, you'll pass the clamorous William Street Market – commonly called the Gully – spilling down Union St from the junction of Orange St (Orange St parallels Fort St and leads uphill past a motley array of rum shops and stores into the hovels of the Canterbury squatters' settlement).

The compact historic center is laid out as a rough grid of narrow one-way streets. St James, the bustling main street, runs south from Sam Sharpe Square and ends at Barnett St, which is the main thoroughfare into town when approaching from the west.

---

## Hour of Emancipation

'On the evening of July 31st the chapel at Falmouth…was opened for worship…It was crowded. An hour before midnight some verses of a dirge composed for the occasion were sung by the congregation, who then continued in devotional exercises till within a few minutes of 12 o'clock. After a short silence Knibb began to speak: his hearers were wrought to a pitch of extraordinary excitement. He pointed to the face of the clock, and said, "The hour is at hand, the monster is dying." Having heard its first note, he cried out, "The monster is dead: the Negro is free." During these few moments the congregation had been as still as death, and breathless with expectation: but when the last word had been spoken they simultaneously burst into exaltation. "Never," says Knibb, writing to a friend, "never did I hear such a sound. The winds of freedom appeared to have been let loose. The very building shook at the strange yet sacred joy."'

– Anonymous, 1834

(Barnett St is famous for its old jail, attached to the police station – officers appeal for donations to help maintain the jail, which keep the jailees in notoriously appalling conditions.) South of Barnett St is the predominantly industrial area of Catherine Hall, the sugarcane fields of Bogue, and Bogue Lagoon.

East of Barnett St is Montego Bay's least salubrious quarter, where factories meld into squalid housing and residents live in the smelly lee of the slaughterhouse. Barnett St becomes the A1 heading west to Reading and Negril.

Barnett St is prone to traffic jams. The alternate route into and out of town is Howard Cooke Drive, a downtown bypass that begins at the Gloucester Ave roundabout and runs south along the bayfront, parallel to St James St, to Alice Eldemire Drive, linking the A1 with Montego Freeport, the industrial and port area backing onto the marshlands of

## Preaching Resistance

The weeklong Christmas Rebellion that began on Kensington Estate on December 27, 1831, and engulfed much of the Montego Bay region was the most serious slave revolt to rock colonial Jamaica. Its impact and the public outcry over the terrible retribution that followed were catalysts for British Parliament passing the Abolition Bill in 1834.

The instigator of the revolt was Samuel Sharpe (1801-32), the slave of a Montego Bay solicitor. Sharpe acted as a deacon of Montego Bay's Burchell Baptist Church and became a 'daddy,' or leader, of native Baptists. Religious meetings were the only legal gatherings for slaves, and Sharpe used his forum to encourage passive rebellion. He also formed a secret society dedicated to securing emancipation. After reading about debates over slavery in the British Parliament, he became convinced (incorrectly) that emancipation had already been granted.

In 1831 Sharpe counseled fellow slaves to refuse to work during the Christmas holidays unless estate owners agreed to address their grievances.

Word of the secret, passive rebellion spread throughout St James and neighboring parishes. Inevitably, word leaked out and war ships and extra troops were sent to Montego Bay.

The rebellion turned into a violent conflict when the Kensington Estate was set on fire. Soon, plantations and great houses throughout northwest Jamaica were ablaze, and Sharpe's noble plan was usurped by wholesale violence. Fourteen colonialists were murdered. The superior military might of the colonial authorities, however, soon suppressed the revolt. Swift and cruel retribution followed.

It is thought that the militia killed more than 1000 slaves during and after the conflict. Day after day for six weeks following the revolt's suppression, magistrates of the Montego Bay Courthouse handed down death sentences to scores of slaves, who were hanged two at a time on the Parade, among them 'Daddy' Sam Sharpe. He was later named a national hero.

NORTHWEST COAST

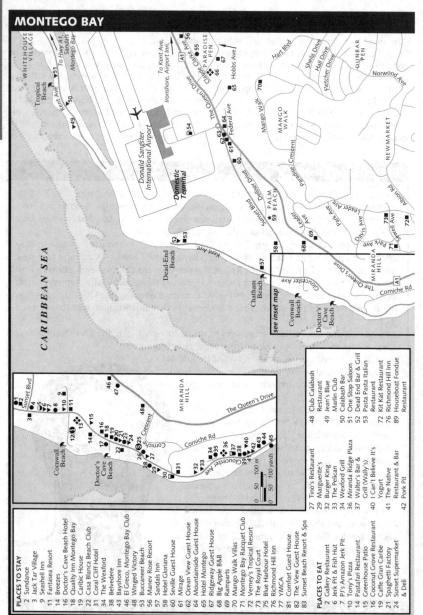

# MONTEGO BAY

**PLACES TO STAY**
2 Sundance
3 Jack Tar Village
5 Seashell Inn
9 Fantasea Resort
11 Breezes
14 Doctor's Cave Beach Hotel
16 Quality Inn Montego Bay
18 Caribic House
19 Casa Blanca Beach Club
22 Coral Cliff Hotel
31 The Wexford
34 Belvedere
38 Bayshore Inn
43 El Greco, Montego Bay Club
46 Winged Victory
48 Buccaneer Beach
53 Manev Rose Resort
56 Sandals Inn
57 Hotel Gloriana
58 Seville Guest House
60 Mirage
61 Ocean View Guest House
62 Mountainside Guest House
64 Hotel Montego
65 Ridgeway Guest House
67 Big Apple B&B
68 Ramparts
69 Mango Walk Villas
71 Montego Bay Racquet Club
72 Verney's Tropical Resort
73 The Royal Court
75 Blue Harbour Hotel
76 Richmond Hill Inn
77 YMCA
81 Comfort Guest House
82 The View Guest House
83 Sunset Beach Resort & Spa

**PLACES TO EAT**
2 Gallery Restaurant
6 Jerk Pit & Fish Hut
7 PJ's Amazon Jerk Pit
10 Tony's Pizza
14 Pastafari Restaurant
15 Greenhouse Patio
16 Coconut Grove Restaurant
19 Caffe Gran Caribe
21 Spaghetti Factory
24 Sunset Supermarket & Deli
27 Tino's Restaurant
29 Marguerite's
32 Burger King
33 The Pelican
34 Wexford Grill
36 Miranda Ridge Plaza
37 Walter's Bar & Grill (Wally's)
40 I Can't Believe It's Yogurt
41 The Native Restaurant & Bar
42 Pork Pit
48 Club Calabash Restaurant
49 Jean's Blue Marlin Club
50 Calabash Bar
51 One Stop Saloon
52 Dead End Bar & Grill
53 Pasta Pasta Italian
72 Kit Kat Restaurant
76 Richmond Hill Inn
89 Houseboat Fondue Restaurant

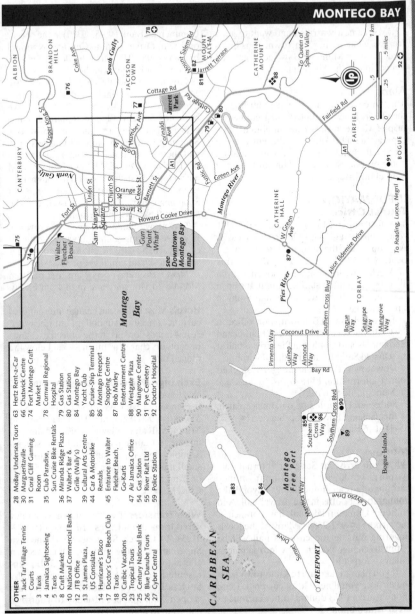

**OTHER**

| | | | |
|---|---|---|---|
| 1 | Jack Tar Village Tennis Courts | 28 | MoBay Undersea Tours |
| 3 | Taxis | 30 | Marguerittaville |
| 4 | Jamaica Sightseeing | 31 | Coral Cliff Gaming Room |
| 5 | Taxis | 35 | Club Paradise, Sun Cruise Bike Rentals |
| 8 | Craft Market | 36 | Miranda Ridge Plaza |
| 10 | National Commercial Bank | 37 | Walter's Bar & Grille (Wally's) |
| 12 | JTB Office | 39 | Cultural Arts Centre |
| 13 | St James Plaza, US Consulate | 44 | Car & Motorbike Rentals |
| 14 | Hurricane's Disco | 45 | Entrance to Walter Fletcher Beach, Go-Karts |
| 17 | Doctor's Cave Beach Club | 47 | Air Jamaica Office |
| 18 | Taxis | 54 | Gas Station |
| 20 | Caribic Vacations | 55 | River Raft Ltd |
| 23 | Tropical Tours | 59 | Police Station |
| 25 | Century National Bank | | |
| 26 | Blue Danube Tours | | |
| 27 | Cyber Central | | |

| | | | |
|---|---|---|---|
| 63 | Hertz Rent-a-Car | | |
| 66 | Chatwick Centre | | |
| 74 | Fort Montego Craft Market | | |
| 78 | Cornwall Regional Hospital | | |
| 79 | Gas Station | | |
| 80 | Gas Station | | |
| 84 | Montego Bay Yacht Club | | |
| 85 | Cruise-Ship Terminal | | |
| 86 | Montego Freeport Shopping Centre | | |
| 87 | Bob Marley Entertainment Centre | | |
| 88 | Westgate Plaza | | |
| 90 | Mangrove Center | | |
| 91 | Pye Cemetery | | |
| 92 | Doctor's Hospital | | |

Bogue Lagoon. The Pye Cemetery is at the junction of the A1 and Alice Eldemire Drive.

If you're newly arrived and want to get a feel for what's where in town, consider a guided tour of Montego Bay (see Organized Tours, later in this chapter).

## Maps

The 'Discover Jamaica' map published by the JTB includes a detailed and accurate city map of Montego Bay. You can obtain a free copy at the JTB office at the entrance to Cornwall Beach, at the JTB information booth on Fort St, or at the one at the Craft Market downtown.

## INFORMATION
## Tourist Offices

Your first stop in MoBay should be the JTB, which runs a regional office off Gloucester Ave, opposite the entrance to Cornwall Beach (☎ 952-4425, fax 952-3587), PO Box 67. Much of their literature is hidden away in file cabinets, but the staff is helpful. It's open 8:30 am to 4:30 pm weekdays and 9 am to 5 pm Saturday.

There's also a JTB information office in the Craft Market on the corner of Market and Harbour Sts, and another in the arrivals hall at the Donald Sangster International Airport.

Downtown, there's a meagerly stocked tourist information bureau inside the Cage on Sam Sharpe Square.

For general information on Jamaica, call in at the Jamaica Information Service (☎ 952-0544) at 16 East St.

## Money

When you arrive at Sangster International Airport, you'll find a 24-hour money exchange bureau immediately beyond the immigration booths in the arrival hall. And National Commercial Bank has a branch at the airport (☎ 952-2354). Many of the locals lingering outside the customs hall will be happy to change your money into Jamaican dollars – forget it!

If you plan to take the bus into town from the airport, you'll need local currency. Taxis, though, accept US dollars (other currencies are frowned upon).

**Banks** There are plenty of banks in town, including two on Gloucester Ave: National Commercial Bank (☎ 952-6320) at the corner of Ewin Drive, and a Century National branch (☎ 952-9485) at 166 Gloucester Ave, just north of Burger King.

Downtown, Scotiabank (☎ 952-4440), Mutual Security Bank, and the National Commercial Bank (☎ 952-3640) have branches on Sam Sharpe Square. Jamaica Citizens Bank has a branch in the MoBay Shopping Centre on Howard Cooke Drive, and there's a National Commercial Bank in the Bay West Centre. All have 24-hour ATM machines. A branch of National Commercial Bank (☎ 979-8060) at Montego Freeport Shopping Centre also serves passengers who arrive at the cruise-ship terminal.

Downtown banks can get very crowded. If you're seeking a cash advance against a credit card, be sure to ask for the customer service desk and you'll get prompt service.

Most banks are open 9 am to 2 or 3 pm Monday to Thursday and until 4 pm Friday.

**Hotels** Most hotels can change international currency for Jamaican dollars, but rates vary. A few hotels convert at the official exchange rate; others charge as much as 5% below the official rate.

**Exchange Bureaus** Numerous officially sanctioned money exchange bureaus advertise on Gloucester Ave. The biggest is King Midas (☎ 940-0000, fax 940-1111), next to Miranda Ridge Plaza, which claims to handle 'all currencies.' You'll see several 'cambio' signs on St James St, and there's a small money exchange bureau in the Cage, on Sam Sharpe Square and another in the Craft Market.

**Wire Transfers** If you need to have money wired from abroad, Western Union (☎ 979-9125), 19 Church St, is above Hometown Supermarket, at the corner of Orange St. An alternative is Moneygram (☎ 952-3448), represented (as is American Express) by Stuart's Travel at 40 Market St; Moneygram is open 9 am to 2 pm Monday to Thursday, and 9 am to noon and 2 to 5 pm Friday.

## Post & Communications

The main post office (☎ 952-7016) is on the west side of Fort St. It's open 9 am to 4:30 pm Monday to Saturday. The lines can be long. If you want to mail only postcards or letters, do it through your hotel's front desk. (See Sending Mail in the Facts for the Visitor chapter for information about express mail services and sending packages from Jamaica. Also see the yellow pages for air-courier services.)

Most hotels offer telephone service. Cyber Central (☎ 953-4318), on Gloucester Ave, charges US$1 per minute for calls to the USA and US$2 per minute to the UK. It charges US$1 per five minutes of email access. The Teleworld Services Telephone Centre (☎ 940-7415) in Miranda Ridge Plaza, charges US$2.20 per minute for calls across North America (less for Florida) and to the UK. It's open 8 am to 10 pm Monday to Saturday. The same company also has an office downtown at Shop No 158, upstairs in the City Centre Building; it also offers 'mini postal' and courier services. There's also a small telephone center in the Cage, on Sam Sharpe Square, charging J$20 (about US$0.60) for a three-minute long-distance call.

Cable & Wireless has racks of public phones outside its offices on either side of Church St.

The Jamaica International Telecommunications office (☎ 888-952-9700), 20 Church St, just east of the fort on Fort St, is open 9 am to 7 pm Monday to Friday. This is where most locals make their calls. Lines are long; when too many people are inside, the mirrored doors are often locked on a whim (since you can't see inside, you might incorrectly assume that the office is closed).

Also see the Telephone section in Facts for the Visitor.

## Internet Resources

A good starting point is www.montego-bay-jamaica.com, which lists a calendar of events, provides information on accommodations, activities, sightseeing, and a plethora of other information. A commercial site, www.mobay.com/town4.htm, offers descriptions of various attractions in town ranging from activities to restaurants.

## Travel Agencies

Montego Bay has plenty of travel agencies. Two of the more reputable ones are International Travel Services (☎ 952-2485) at 14B Market St and Stuart's Travel (☎ 952-4350) at 32 Market St. Concierges at upscale hotels can make most of the same reservations as a travel agency.

## Bookstores & Libraries

Most gift stores and pharmacies sell a limited selection of leading international magazines, newspapers, and books. For a wider variety, including novels, try Sangster's Bookshop (☎ 952-0319) at 2 St James St, which is the largest bookstore in town. Also try Ray of Light Bookshop (☎ 979-9154) at 11 King St, or Henderson's Book Store (☎ 952-2551) at 27 St James St. Most 'bookshops' in Jamaica are stationers first and foremost.

The parish library (☎ 952-4185), opposite the City Centre Shopping Centre on the south side of Fort St, has quiet reading rooms and an impressive collection of books in English on Jamaica.

## Laundry

Most hotels arrange laundry and dry cleaning. The only coin-operated laundry in town is Wonder Wash (☎ 940-1143) in Westgate Plaza on the A1, south of downtown. There's a drop-off laundry at the Fabricare Centre (☎ 952-6897) at 4 Corner Lane, which offers one-hour dry cleaning plus laundry service, as does Ucon Laundry & Dry-Cleaners (☎ 952-6105) at 3 Love Lane.

## Medical Services

Montego Bay has two public hospitals. The main hospital is Cornwall Regional Hospital (☎ 952-5100), above town just off Mt Salem Rd. It has a 24-hour emergency department. Eldemire Hospital (☎ 952-2620) is at 3 Orange St. Expect lengthy delays for all but emergencies.

Doctor's Hospital (☎ 952-1616) is a private hospital atop a hillock in Fairfield, southeast town; it accepts most international insurance coverage.

There are dozens of doctors to choose from. Try Cornwall Medical Centre (☎ 979-6107) at 19 Orange St. Doctors on Call (☎ 979-0283), a physicians group, will send a doctor to your hotel. The staff at Blue Cross of Jamaica (☎ 952-4448, fax 979-7868) at 3 King St may be able to offer referrals.

Is that filling coming loose? Try the Montego Bay Dental Clinic (☎ 952-1080) at 19 Gloucester Ave, or Dr Marlene Foote (☎ 952-3016) at 14c Market St.

Pharmacies are a dime a dozen downtown. Try the well-stocked Bay Court Pharmacy in the Bay West Centre.

## Emergency

The town has four police stations. The main station is at 14 Barnett St (☎ 952-2333, 952-1557). Downtown stations are at 49 Union St (☎ 940-3500) and 29 Church St (☎ 952-4396). The Tourism Liaison Unit is in the Summit Police Station (☎ 952-1540) on Sunset Blvd.

In the case of an emergency call:

| | |
|---|---|
| Air-Sea Rescue | ☎ 119 |
| Ambulance | ☎ 110 |
| Fire | ☎ 110, 952-2311 |
| Police | ☎ 119 |
| Rape Crisis Centre | ☎ 929-2997 |

## Dangers & Annoyances

Montego Bay has earned a reputation for tourist harassment: often pushy importuning by male hustlers trying to sell you something or attach themselves to you as a guide as you walk down the street. In 1996, the JTB initiated a campaign to allow less harassment on Gloucester Ave. Hustlers have moved on, as have petty vendors. And the tourist police have a strong presence and are ever-watchful for harassment. Still, away from Gloucester Ave, harassment is a pervasive annoyance and serious crime is, as everywhere, always a possibility.

Many hustlers will accept 'no thanks' for an answer. A few will attempt to make foreigners feel guilty: 'You a racist?' You'll hear

a gamut of crafty lines to get you to open your wallet. Often a hustler will approach you with his hand extended in a greeting. The natural temptation is to shake it, but once you do you're on the hook. 'Remember me?' is one of the favorite lines used on naive tourists, even though you know you've never set eyes on the person before. 'Yeah, mon, I work at your hotel,' to which your best response (if you choose not to ignore the person completely) is, 'Oh yes, which hotel would that be?' Both male and female visitors can expect to be approached in none-too-subtle terms by locals offering their services as gigolos and 'good-time girls.'

Uniformed members of the Montego Bay Resort Patrol police the strip in male-female pairs (they wear dark blue military-style uniforms, with black berets). Downtown is not patrolled, but by day there is really no danger to foreign visitors. However, avoid the Flankers area, across the highway from the Sangster International Airport. Many of the city's drug dealers are based here and its residents are notably antagonistic toward outsiders.

At night don't walk downtown or on any backstreets, especially alone. The streets are ill-lit and you risk being mugged.

Your greatest danger is from traffic. Montego Bay's roads are narrow and often you'll be forced to step into them. Cars are often driven at breakneck pace. Don't expect the driver to give way, use extra caution when crossing streets, and watch for deep gutters and potholes.

The JTB gives out a little pamphlet on 'Helpful Hints for Your Vacation,' which discusses practical pointers to help you avoid trouble.

## WALKING TOUR

Montego Bay's downtown is replete with edifices of historical interest, and compact enough to warrant a walking tour. Allow two hours for roaming.

### Fort Montego

Begin your tour at Fort Montego. Virtually nothing remains of the main fort, which once stood atop the hill above Gloucester

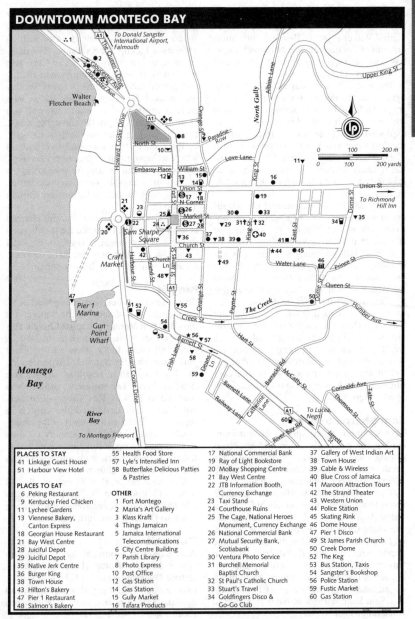

# DOWNTOWN MONTEGO BAY

To Donald Sangster International Airport, Falmouth

Walter Fletcher Beach

North St

Embassy Place

Sam Sharpe Square

Craft Market

Pier 1 Marina

Gun Point Wharf

*Montego Bay*

*River Bay*

To Montego Freeport

To Lucea, Negril

To Richmond Hill Inn

Union St

The Creek

| PLACES TO STAY | | OTHER | |
|---|---|---|---|
| 41 Linkage Guest House | 55 Health Food Store | 1 Fort Montego | 17 National Commercial Bank |
| 51 Harbour View Hotel | 57 Lyle's Intensified Inn | 2 Maria's Art Gallery | 19 Ray of Light Bookstore |
| | 58 Butterflake Delicious Patties | 3 Klass Kraft | 20 MoBay Shopping Centre |
| PLACES TO EAT | & Pastries | 4 Things Jamaican | 21 Bay West Centre |
| 6 Peking Restaurant | | 5 Jamaica International | 22 JTB Information Booth, |
| 9 Kentucky Fried Chicken | | Telecommunications | Currency Exchange |
| 11 Lychee Gardens | | 6 City Centre Building | 23 Taxi Stand |
| 13 Viennese Bakery, | | 7 Parish Library | 24 Courthouse Ruins |
| Canton Express | | 8 Photo Express | 25 The Cage, National Heroes |
| 18 Georgian House Restaurant | | 10 Post Office | Monument, Currency Exchange |
| 21 Bay West Centre | | 12 Gas Station | 26 National Commercial Bank |
| 28 Juicial Depot | | 14 Gas Station | 27 Mutual Security Bank, |
| 29 Juicial Depot | | 15 Gully Market | Scotiabank |
| 35 Native Jerk Centre | | 16 Tafara Products | 30 Ventura Photo Service |
| 36 Burger King | | | 31 Burchell Memorial |
| 38 Town House | | | Baptist Church |
| 43 Hilton's Bakery | | | 32 St Paul's Catholic Church |
| 47 Pier 1 Restaurant | | | 33 Stuart's Travel |
| 48 Salmon's Bakery | | | 34 Goldfingers Disco & |
| | | | Go-Go Club |

| | |
|---|---|
| 37 Gallery of West Indian Art | |
| 38 Town House | |
| 39 Cable & Wireless | |
| 40 Blue Cross of Jamaica | |
| 41 Maroon Attraction Tours | |
| 42 The Strand Theater | |
| 43 Western Union | |
| 44 Police Station | |
| 45 Skating Rink | |
| 46 Dome House | |
| 47 Pier 1 Disco | |
| 49 St James Parish Church | |
| 50 Creek Dome | |
| 52 The Keg | |
| 53 Bus Station, Taxis | |
| 54 Sangster's Bookshop | |
| 56 Police Station | |
| 59 Fustic Market | |
| 60 Gas Station | |

Ave. The sole remnant, a small battery with three brass cannons on rails, is on Fort St behind Walter Fletcher Beach at the southern end of Gloucester Ave. Not much effort has gone into sprucing up even this morsel for the tourist trade.

The erstwhile fort that guarded the bay figured in the history books only for two tragic mishaps. In 1760, during celebrations for the capture of Havana, a cannon exploded, killing the gunner. The only time the fort's cannons were fired on a ship (in 1795) proved equally lamentable. The ship – the friendly schooner *Mercury* – had been mistaken for an enemy vessel. Fortunately no damage was done.

Immediately south of the fort is a roundabout that marks the beginning of downtown. Follow Fort St as it curls around near the **Gully market**, a veritable Caribbean souk with stalls brimming with glossy, sweet-smelling fruits and vegetables. After browsing, walk one block east along Union St to the **Georgian House**, at the corner of Orange St. This venerable brick and stone house with its bow-shaped frontage is today the Georgian House Restaurant. There are actually two buildings here: the original owner, a wealthy merchant, apparently housed his wife in one and his mistress in the other.

Retrace your steps to Fort St and continue one block south to arrive in the heart of Montego Bay.

## Sam Sharpe Square

This bustling, cobbled square – an important center for political rallies and speeches during election times – is centered on a small bronze fountain dedicated to Captain J Kerr, a pioneer in the banana trade.

The square, formerly called the Parade, is named for national hero the Right Excellent Samuel Sharpe (1801-32), leader of the weeklong Christmas Rebellion that erupted on December 28, 1831, engulfing much of the region (see 'Preaching Resistance,' earlier in this chapter). At the square's northwest corner is the National Heroes Monument, an impressive bronze statue of Paul Bogle and Sam Sharpe, Bible in hand, speaking to three admiring listeners.

Also on the northwest corner is the most notable monument, **the Cage**, a tiny cutstone and brick building. It was built in 1806 as a lockup for vagrants, disorderly seamen, and runaway slaves. The Cage also was where slaves were imprisoned if they overstayed their welcome in town: Sunday was market day for plantation slaves, who were permitted to come into town to sell their produce. At 2 pm the constable would ring the bell in the tiny belfry to warn country slaves that they had one hour in which to leave town or face imprisonment. The Cage is still in use. At this writing it served as a cambio (currency exchange booth) with motley information bureau attached.

At the southwest corner is the charred ruin of the colonial **courthouse** that burned down a few years ago. There is no local calling for the old courthouse to be restored, for it is a reminder of a history of pain.

## King St

From the square, head east along Market St. Two blocks east of Sam Sharpe Square, you pass **Burchell Memorial Baptist Church**. This red brick structure, which dates to 1835, is not at all pretty but it plays an important part in local history. Samuel Sharpe, who led the Christmas slave revolt of 1831, was a deacon here. The original church was founded in 1824 by Rev Thomas Burchell. An angry mob destroyed the church in reprisal for Burchell's support of the emancipation cause, but the missionary escaped to sea. Sam Sharpe's remains are buried in the vault. The concrete hulk across King St is **St Paul's Catholic Church**.

Continue up Market St one block and turn south onto East St. This brings you to Church St. Turn left and follow it uphill one block to Dome St, and turn right.

## Dome St

About 100 yards south, at the junction with Water Lane, is **Dome House**, a recently restored plantation home of classical stature in cut stone, with large sash windows and an opulent interior. It's now a dance and theater space (☎ 952-2571).

The street names hereabouts – Creek St, Water Lane, S Montego Gully – hint at the importance of water in the city's history. A stone's throw south of Dome House, at the corner of Dome and Creek Sts, is **Creek Dome**, built in 1837 above the underground spring that supplied the drinking water for Montego Bay. Until 1894, when piped water was introduced, slaves would line up at the Dome with *yabbas* (traditional wicker baskets) on their heads. Despite its name, the structure is actually a sextagon with a crenelated castle turret in which the 'Keeper of the Creek' lived in yesteryear, collecting a toll from users of the city's only freshwater supply.

Retrace your steps along Dome St or Water Lane and walk down Church St.

## Church St

Many of the most interesting buildings in town are clustered along Church St, the most picturesque street in MoBay. At the corner of Water Lane is a two-story plantation-style octagonal structure that today houses a **police station**. Its wide veranda is supported by square, fluted columns. Fifty yards west, at the corner of King St, is a splendidly maintained, white-fronted, cut-stone Georgian building that houses the First Life Insurance Co. Its lofty doorway is lit by brass lamps. Equally impressive is the three-story, pink-stuccoed Georgian building with a soaring hardwood door at 25 Church St, also on the corner of King St – this is the headquarters of Telecommunications of Jamaica.

The highlight, however, is **St James Parish Church**. Once regarded as the finest church on the island, it remains impressive. It is *not* named for James II, King of England, as the parish is; the English adopted the name of the original Spanish church on the site, which was dedicated to Santiago (St James), the patron saint of Spain – a handy coincidence. The current church was built between 1775 and 1782 in the shape of a Greek cross but was so damaged by the earthquake of March 1, 1957, that it had to be rebuilt. By the look of the toppled and desecrated tombs, the graveyard was also badly knocked about.

With luck the tall church doors will be open (if not, call ☎ 952-2775 to arrange a visit) and you can view the beautiful interior, which contains a stunning stained-glass window behind the altar. Note the intriguing marble monuments, including fine works by John Bacon, the foremost English sculptor of the late 18th century. One is a memorial to Rosa Palmer, whose virtuous life was upended in literature to create the legend of the White Witch of Rose Hall. Look carefully at her neck and you'll detect faint purple marks. Locals consider this proof of the fable that the 'witch' was strangled.

Facing the church is the **Town House** at 16 Church St with a handsome red brick frontage buried under a cascade of bougainvillea and laburnum. It dates from 1765, when it was the home of a wealthy merchant. It has since served as a church manse and then as a townhouse for the mistress of the Earl of Hereford, Governor of Jamaica circa 1850. In this century, it has been used as a hotel, warehouse, Masonic lodge, lawyer's office, and synagogue. An intriguing curiosity is the bullet hole in the mahogany staircase – the result of a feud between a man and his wife's lover during the period when the house was a hotel. Today the Town House is home to a splendid restaurant (see Places to Eat, later in this chapter).

An equally absorbing historic building next to the Town House, on the corner of Orange St, houses the Gallery of West Indian Art. Continue west two blocks to Strand St and you will see the 1930s-era, art-deco **Strand Theater**.

## BARNETT ESTATE

The sea of sugarcane south of Montego Bay is part of Barnett Estate (☎ 952-2382, fax 952-6342), PO Box 876, a plantation owned and operated since 1755 by the Kerr-Jarretts, one of Jamaica's preeminent families, whose holdings once included most of the Montego Bay area. Today the family (now in its 11th generation) holds the land in trust for the government and manages it accordingly.

Tours begin at a visitor's center. This was formerly the plantation manager's house, which doubles as a museum charting the development of the area since the day that Colonel Nicholas Jarrett arrived with Cromwell's invasion army in 1655. The family has been at the vanguard of Jamaican history ever since. The **Bellfield Great House**, built in 1735, has been exquisitely restored and is now a showcase of elite 18th-century colonial living. Well-informed guides in period costume lead you from room to room, each furnished in period detail. Mannequins representing members of the Kerr family add a little 'life' to the settings.

You'll then hop aboard a jitney for a ride through the 3000-acre estate to see how bananas, coconuts, mangos, and other exotic crops are grown commercially. Before leaving, take time to sample jerk chicken or pork at the thatched Sugar Mill Bar & Jerk Centre. A botanical garden, aviary, and gourmet restaurant are in the works. There's also a children's playground with pony rides.

Horseback rides (90 minutes) are also offered from Barnett Point Stables, 10 am to 2 pm daily (US$40 to US$60).

Entrance with guided tour costs US$15. Barnett Estate is open 9 am to 4 pm, Monday to Friday.

The estate is located along Barnett St, about 800 yards east of Doctor's Hospital. It's poorly signed: take the right turn at the Y-fork marked for Day-O Plantation, then turn right at Granville Police Station.

## BOGUE LAGOON

Much of the bay south of Montego Bay is lined with mangroves that are a vital breeding ground for fishes and birds. For centuries, fishermen harvested the mangrove to make fishpots and charcoal, while the bark was used to make dye. Later, developers cleared the swamps for waterfront properties. Only three islands remain of the chain of islands that once formed the vast mangrove system. They are now protected within the Montego Bay Marine Park (☎ 952-5619, mbmp@n5com.jm, www.montego-bay-jamaica.com/mbmp), Pier 1, Howard Cook Blvd. By filtering sediment and runoff before they can enter the sea, the mangroves are key to protecting the coral reefs and to maintaining the delicate balance of the marine ecosystem.

### Montego Bay Marine Park

Destruction of mangroves, sewage and industrial-waste runoff, overfishing, and depletion of coral and shells by collectors have all contributed to a decline in the health of the Montego Bay reef ecosystem in recent decades. In 1992, the Montego Bay Marine Park was established as the first national park in Jamaica with an aim to conserve and manage the coral reefs, seabed grasses, and shoreline mangroves (see the Coral Ecology section in Facts about Jamaica).

The park extends from the eastern end of Sangster International Airport westward (almost 6 miles) to the Great River and covers an area of some 15 sq miles of bay to a depth of 100 feet. It encompasses the mangroves of Bogue Lagoon, a vital breeding ground for fishes and birds.

Several government agencies shared responsibility for the park until September 1996, when authority was handed to the Montego Bay Marine Park Trust (MBMPT; ☎ 952-5619, mbmp@n5com.jm, www.montego-bay-jamaica.com/mbmp), Pier 1, Howard Cook Blvd. MBMPT is a local non-governmental organization whose members have a vested interest in park protection.

MBMPT has initiated 24-hour ranger patrols to reduce destructive and illegal practices and enforce regulations.

Fishing is banned within its perimeter, allowing fish populations to recover; water sports are also limited to designated areas. Boats are required to use mooring buoys and can no longer anchor at will atop the coral. And collecting shells or coral or otherwise interfering with or molesting wildlife is prohibited.

You can hire canoes or kayaks and set out with a guide to spot herons, egrets, pelicans, and waterfowl, while below, in the tannin-stained waters, juvenile barracudas, tarpon, snapper, crabs, and lobsters swim and crawl.

The Mangrove Centre, opposite the entrance to Montego Freeport Cruise Ship terminal, provides educational displays on the vital ecosystem; it's open 8 am to 6 pm daily.

## BEACHES
### Cornwall Beach

This 100-yard-wide swath of white sand is enclosed within a wire-fence compound behind St James Shopping Plaza. The beach (☎ 952-3463) is popular with a younger tourist set, including topless bathers and gigolos eager to serve them. At its core is the Bird Watcher's Bar, built around a massive almond tree. On the left are changing rooms, plus a snack bar, an ice cream shop, a hair-braiding and manicure shop, and a crafts stall. The snack bar serves sandwiches, steamed fish fillet, and fish-and-chips for less than US$5. There's a volleyball court in the sand, and a dance stage for nighttime concerts. Water sports include jet-skiing (US$40 per hour), parasailing (US$40 per hour), and a glass-bottom boat ride (US$12). Hustling here is minimal, but you may still be importuned to buy jewelry, trinkets, or drugs. If tempted by the latter, discretion is advised; the beach is small and very public. Entrance costs US$2 (children US$1). Lifeguards are on duty from 9 am to 5 pm.

### Doctor's Cave Beach

MoBay's main beach is immediately south of Cornwall Beach and is owned by the Doctor's Cave Bathing Club (☎ 952-1140, fax 952-2566), which administers it as a private bathing club. It gets crowded on weekends when locals flock. The deep, wide, white-sand beach has seen ongoing improvements in recent years: a beach grill has been added, and the grotesque wall that hid the beach from view was being replaced at press time by an attractive see-through fence. There's a bar, snack bar, gift shop, and water sports, plus changing rooms (which are rather grubby), and a new food court was being built at press time. It's open 8:30 am to 6 pm. Entrance costs US$2 (children US$1). You can rent shade umbrellas and inflatable 'lilos' for US$5, and chairs for US$4.

Breezes (see Places to Stay), an all-inclusive resort that opens onto the beach, sells a day pass for US$45, including all meals, drinks, and access to the beach and the resort's water sports.

### Walter Fletcher Beach

This long sliver of white sand is mostly the domain of locals. This is true partly because of its distance from the hotels, but also because it *seems* inaccessible and unwelcoming due to the high wire fences enclosing an unkempt seaside park that was unimaginatively laid out by the Urban Development Council. The park, however, received a radical facelift in 1998, lending it greater appeal. The beach (☎ 979-9447) is floodlit at night.

Swimming is not advisable after heavy rain, for the overflow of sewer pipes in the gully washes out to sea nearby – that's not brine you're smelling! Reef Keepers (☎ 979-0102) is a dive operator at the beach.

You'll find netball (US$3.50 per team) and tennis courts (US$1.75 per couple), and a small go-cart track was being laid out at this writing. Lockers are available for US$3, beach mats for US$1.75, and chairs for US$3. It's open 9 am to 10 pm, and entrance is US$1.50 for adults, US$0.80 for children. There's free parking.

### Other Beaches

**Dump-Up Beach** lies immediately south of Walter Fletcher Beach and is hardly the most salubrious place. Expect to be hustled. Locals dump their garbage here and goats and pigs rummage the refuse piles scattered on the grass behind the narrow beach. Worse, rainwash gullies dump their human effluvia, while the Catherine Hall sewage plant adds its overflow.

Also free are pocket-size **Chatham Beach** and **Dead-End Beach** (also called Sunset Beach), both on Kent Ave. Chatham Beach is opposite Sandals Inn; Dead-End is at the end of the road. At night they're popular with locals who cool off after dark.

A beautiful beach – **Tropical Beach** – lies on the north side of the airport. Sandals Montego Bay resort takes up the best section, but other portions are accessible. A relatively impoverished fishing village, White-house, is here and there are basic food shacks and rum shops.

## WATER SPORTS

New Wave Water Sports (☎ 991-2021) offers water sports on Cornwall Beach. Take your pick of activities, from jet-skiing and parasail-ing (US$40) to a glass-bottom boat ride (US$12) out to the reef, where the snorkeling is good amid the turquoise and azure shal-lows. MoBay Windsurfing (☎ 952-5505) runs a similar concession at Doctor's Cave Beach.

The resort hotels bordering the beach, including Breezes, offer their own water-sports concessions, as do the resorts east of town. Resort Divers (☎ 974-5338) is a dive operator at Jack Tar Village.

## SPORT FISHING

The waters off Jamaica's north coast are especially good for game fishing. Beyond the north-shore reefs, the ocean floor plummets steeply for thousands of feet. The abyss is part of the Cayman Trench, the deepest ocean canyon in the Caribbean. You can see it from shore, a great river of deep indigo against the lighter blues. Deep-water game fish use it as a migratory freeway. Kingfish, yellowfin tuna, wahoo, and barracuda run through the channel year-round, as do blue marlin, the grand prize of sport fishing. Sep-tember to April is best for marlin (June and August are peak months), but 'Marlin Alley,' as the trench is known, offers weighty catches in all months. The Montego Bay Marlin Tournament (☎ 979-8038, fax 979-8490) is held in late September.

Half and full-day charters can be booked through hotels or at Pier 1 Marina. Expect to pay about US$300 for a half-day charter. Be sure to clarify in advance what the fee includes. A day's notice and a 50% deposit are usually required.

Rhapsody Cruises (☎ 979-0104) charges US$250 half-day, US$400 full-day for up to four people (US$350 half-day, US$550 full-day for five or six people) aboard the *Rose Bud* and *Jamaica Rose*.

Also see the Ironshore section, later in this chapter.

## SAILING & CRUISING

A large selection of yachts and small cruise boats operate party cruises. Most companies charge US$35 for three-hour party cruises, and US$25 to US$35 for sunset and dinner cruises. Prices vary. Most vessels sail from Pier 1.

One of the better known vessels is the *Jamaica Queen IV* (☎ 953-3992), a double-deck, 61-foot-long, glass-bottom catamaran specially designed as a party boat. You can dance to the pulsating beat of soca and reggae on a day cruise, sunset cruise, or dinner cruise with open bar. It even has a Saturday night disco cruise.

Try North Coast Cruises' *Calico* (☎ 952-5860), a 55-foot ketch faintly resembling an old pirate ship. Party cruises sail from Pier 1 at 10 am and 3 pm daily, except Monday. A sunset cruise is also offered at 5 pm Wednes-day to Saturday. Rhapsody Cruises (☎ 979-0104, fax 979-0101), 42 Fort St, offers three-hour 'fun' cruises (US$50) and two-hour sunset cruises (US$25) aboard the *Montrose*. Likewise, *Tropical Dreamer* (☎ 979-0102) hosts a 'wet'n'wild cruise party' at 10 am and 3 pm daily except Sunday, which includes snorkeling (US$40). Rhapsody Cruises (☎ 979-0104) offers sunset cruises (US$25), including a 'Sunset with Dinner' cruise (US$50).

Also contact No Problem Cruises (☎ 995-3912) or try Jamaica Queen Cruises (☎ 953-3992).

You can charter yachts for private group sailing trips from any of the above compa-nies, or from the Montego Bay Yacht Club (☎ 979-8038, fax 979-8262).

Also see Ironshore, later in this chapter.

## SCUBA DIVING

The site of Jamaica's first marine sanctuary, MoBay offers highly rated dive sites, most of which lie close to shore and vary from shallow patch reefs to awe-inspiring walls. Visibility is usually 60 to 100 feet; water tem-perature never falls below 68°F.

The large sponges at deeper sites such as **Basket Reef** are spectacular. Another choice site is **Black Coral Alley**, a canyon lined with black coral trees. **Widowmakers Cave** is famous for being swarmed by wrasses, barracuda, and parrot fish. If nurse sharks, hammerheads, and rays appeal, head out to the Point. There's even a DC-3 wreck at **Airport Reef**. Beginners explore the shallow reef close to shore off Doctor's Cave Beach.

Also see the Outdoor Activities chapter.

## Organized Diving

Operators are in constant flux. Most offer dive courses from beginner to dive master and will certify you through the PADI Open Water Dive Course, which costs US$350 to US$375. Most companies charge US$35 for a single dive and US$55 to US$65 for two dives. Many large resorts have their own operations.

A Dutch couple, Hannie and Theo Smit, operate Poseidon Divers (☎ 952-3624, 800-880-5224, fax 952-3079), PO Box 152, Reading, St James, at Marguerite's Restaurant on Gloucester Ave. Besides offering dive courses, they also rent scuba equipment for US$15 per item between 8:30 am and 3 pm daily (closed Sunday). Resort Divers Pro-Shop (☎ 952-4285, fax 952-4288), Shop No 8 in the MoBay Shopping Centre, Reef Keeper Divers (☎ 979-0104, fax 979-0101), Fun Divers (☎ 953-2650) at Wyndham Rose Hall, and Rhapsody Cruises (☎ 979-0104) offer a range of snorkeling and diving excursions, as well as certification courses; they also rent equipment.

All the above companies offer one-hour snorkeling trips, usually for US$15. Also see the Ironshore and Reading sections, later in this chapter.

**Dives for Nondivers** Don't swim? Consider the 'Undersea Semi-Submarine Tour' aboard a semi-submersible that operates from Margueritaville. Contact MoBay Undersea Tours (☎ 997-2893, fax 940-2493). Tours depart at 9 and 11 am and 1:30 pm daily (US$30 adults, US$15 children). The vessel doesn't dive – you look at the marine life through bubble-dome windows beneath the boat. You can also snorkel and hand-feed fish.

## GOLF

If MoBay lives up to any boast, it's the excellent golfing. There are three championship golf courses east of town at Ironshore (see Ironshore, later in this chapter). A fourth course, the site of the Johnnie Walker World Championship, lies within easy reach at Tryall, a 30-minute journey west.

## TENNIS

Most major resort hotels have tennis courts for guests. The Jack Tar Village tennis courts, at the junction of Sunset Blvd and Kent Ave, cost US$4 per hour for nonguests. The Montego Bay Racquet Club (☎ 952-0200, fax 921-5335) charges US$10 per hour for use of its Laykold tennis courts, and US$10 extra at night.

## HORSEBACK RIDING

Three entities offer horseback riding from Ironshore and Rose Hall. See the Ironshore section, later in this chapter.

## RAFTING

Mountain Valley Rafting runs river trips down the Great River, beginning in Lethe. Likewise, there's rafting on the Martha Brae. (See the Great River and Martha Brae sections, later in this chapter.)

## ORGANIZED TOURS
### Guided City Tours

If you've just arrived and want to get a feel for the town, consider a guided tour of Montego Bay. Several local companies offer half-day tours. JUTA (Jamaica Union of Travelers Association) Tour Company (☎ 952-0813, fax 952-5355), in the Chatwick Centre on Claude Clarke Ave, PO Box 1155; and JCAL Tours Ltd (☎ 952-7574, fax 952-7575), at 80B Queens Drive, PO Box 265, have 'Montego Bay Highlight' tours, as does Tropical Tours (☎ 953-9100) on Gloucester Ave.

### Farther Afield

More than a dozen companies slate options for touring locally and afield. Caribic Vacations (☎ 953-9878, 979-9387, fax 953-9897, 979-3421), 69 Gloucester Ave, offers a wide range of tours, including excursions to Ocho Rios, Croydon Plantation, and Negril, plus a two-day all-Jamaica tour every Monday. The company also operates the 'Appleton Estate

## ¡Cuba Sí!

You won't be long in Jamaica before noticing posters advertising excursions to Cuba, which lies just 90 miles to the north of Jamaica. The two islands are as different as chalk and cheese, one reason that Jamaica's middle-classes flock to Cuba for weekend visits. For US citizens, the temptation to visit an island that Washington has dubbed off-limits holds a compelling allure (more than 85,000 US citizens visited Cuba in 1997 – mostly through gateways such as Jamaica).

Despite Cuba's hardships and faults, visiting is a profound experience that far exceeds most travelers' expectations. It stirs one's passions and deeply touches the heart and soul.

The US government's Trading with the Enemy Act, while not actually banning US citizens from traveling to Cuba, prohibits them from spending money there or otherwise engaging in financial transactions with Cuba. To spend even one cent, a US citizen must have a Treasury Dept license, which is granted only to journalists, academic researchers, and Cuban-Americans with family in Cuba. Yet, *if you purchase an all-inclusive package in Jamaica and don't actually spend any money in Cuba, your visit is entirely legal!*

All you need is your passport and a tourist visa issued on the spot by any of the Jamaican companies that specialize in excursions to this intriguing island of socialism and sensuality. The Cuban government has an open-door policy and welcomes US tourists. Cuban immigration officials don't stamp passports.

Getting there is easy. Air Jamaica flies from Montego Bay and Kingston to Havana on Monday, Friday, and Saturday, with connecting service from the USA (you must purchase your Cuban portion separately in Jamaica).

Several Jamaica tour companies offer weekend and longer excursions from Montego Bay and Kingston using Cubana Airlines and Air Jamaica Express charters. Most trips include airfare, transfers, city tours, some meals and entertainment, and accommodations for overnight trips. You can pay for your tour with a US credit card. (US credit cards cannot be used in Cuba.)

Keep an eye out for Lonely Planet's Cuba guidebook. The best online source for reading material is www.cubabooks.com.

Rum Tour' in association with Jamaica Estate Tours (every Tuesday and Wednesday, US$62 to US$65). It also arranges car rentals, transfers, and specialty excursions and tours.

Its main rival is Tourwise, which offers tours nationwide and has five offices in town, including at Sangster International Airport (☎ 979-1027) and on Gloucester Ave (☎ 940-5634).

Jamaica Sightseeing (☎ 952-4370, fax 979-3821) at 1 Kent Ave, opposite the Sundance, also runs a series of day tours, as well as two-day tours (US$244) and three-day tours (US$320) into the Central Highlands and Blue Mountains. Vernon Chin, the owner, is very knowledgeable and helpful. His company specializes in personalized tours and special interest groups (especially nature-oriented). Write Jamaica Sightseeing at PO Box 467.

Maroon Attraction Tours (☎ 952-4546, fax 952-6203), 32 Church St, offers a 'cultural, educational, and historic tour' into Maroon Country. It claims to be 'the only legal tour' to Accompong (see the Southwest Coast chapter).

Other local tour and travel arrangers include Blue Danube Tours (☎ 952-0886, fax 952-5018), 55 Gloucester Ave, and Glamour Tours (☎ 979-8207, fax 979-8168) in the MoBay Shopping Centre on Howard Cooke Drive; Jamaica Co-Op Auto & Limousine Tours (☎ 940-4555) on Claude Clarke Avenue; Pro-Tours Ltd (☎ 978-6113, fax 978-5473) in Kingston; and Greenlight Tours (☎ 952-2636, fax 952-0564), Bogue Industrial Estate, Montego Bay.

Ian Robinson offers personalized tours through his company, Intrepid Explorers (☎ 997-5798), PO Box 188, Reading, St James, using his somewhat beaten-up Land Rover, which holds up to six people (US$200 per day). He'll customize tours for any variety of interests with several days' notice.

Also see Ironshore, later in this chapter.

## SPECIAL EVENTS
### Reggae Sumfest
This internationally acclaimed reggae festival was first held in 1993, at the same time that Reggae Sunsplash fatefully moved from MoBay to Kingston. (It's now in Ocho Rios.) The five-day festival, held each August, begins on the first Tuesday after Independence Day (August 6) with a beach party on Walter Fletcher Beach, followed by four theme nights, including a 'street jam' on Gloucester Ave. Locals look forward to dancehall night, when dancing is almost X-rated.

The 1998 festival included more than 50 world-class reggae artists – including Ziggy Marley, Beenie Man, Lady Saw, and Bunny Wailer – and expanded into R&B and other musical grooves.

Several venues are used for Sumfest. The main venue is the Bob Marley Entertainment Centre (also known as the Catherine Hall Entertainment Centre) on Howard Cooke Drive. At this writing, tickets cost from US$15 to US$30 per night. The street jam is free. Tickets go on sale in Jamaica about two weeks before the concert. Full-week bracelets that allow you to attend all events cost US$100 to US$150. Contact Summerfest Productions (☎ 952-8592, 800-979-1720, www.sumfest.com).

Many tour operators run special Sumfest packages. In the USA, contact Jamaica Travel Specialist (☎ 510-489-9552, 800-544-5979), 2827 Mann Ave, Union City, CA 94587, or Calypso Tours (☎ 510-366-5116, 800-852-6242), 3901 Grand Ave No 304, Oakland, CA 94610. Both companies have special week-long packages, as does Island Flight Vacations (☎ 310-410-0558, 800-426-4570, fax 310-410-0830), 6033 W Century Blvd No 807, Los Angeles, CA 90045, which in past years has been the official tour operator for Sumfest.

In England, Music Travel Centre (☎ 020-7138-37518) offers organized Sumfest tours.

### All That Heritage & Jazz Festival
The All That Heritage & Jazz Festival (☎ 979-2567, fax 979-2584) is part of National Heritage Week. It's held in mid-October during Heroes Weekend at the Half Moon Conference Centre (US$23 in advance, US$28 at the gate; see Ironshore, later in this chapter); and at the Great River Theme Park (US$15) at Nature Village Farm (see Lethe, later in this chapter). The festival features a

Heritage Village, Food Village, and Country Fair, with stalls displaying the culture, cuisine, and arts and crafts of Jamaica. Gates open at 11 am. It's preceded by cultural arts workshops, and followed by a 'Family Fun Fair' (US$3, children US$1.60).

## Miami to Montego Bay Yacht Race

Sailors flock to Jamaica for this 800-mile race, colloquially called the Pineapple Cup Yacht Race, which takes place in mid-February. It has been an annual event since its conception in 1961. The challenging race is a mandatory event in the World Ocean Racing Championships. Entries are varied by size. The event is also an excuse for four days of partying. For information, call the Montego Bay Yacht Club (☎ 929-7029).

The Montego Bay Yacht Club hosts an Easter Regatta, or Jamaica Sailing Week, each March or April. It also sponsors the Jam-Am Yacht Race (☎ 979-8262) in December, another three days of races and regattas.

## Other Happenings

The annual five-day Montego Bay International Marlin Tournament is held in September. Contact the Montego Bay Yacht Club (☎ 979-8038).

An International Horse Show & Polo Match is held each February at Rocky Point Stables (☎ 953-2286) at Half Moon.

The MoBay No Problem 10K foot race, first held in January 1996, was intended to be an annual event, but I haven't heard of it being repeated. Contact the JTB for more information.

## PLACES TO STAY

Montego Bay boasts the largest number of guest rooms of any resort area in Jamaica: over 5000. The great majority of hotels are clustered along Gloucester Ave, with more deluxe resorts nestled on their own beaches east of town at Ironshore and Mahoe Bay. Many older hotels are above town on Queen's Ave, where they catch the breezes.

Although many hotels are listed as guest houses, the definition is nebulous; the majority are no different than hotels (and are cat-

egorized as such, below, according to price), and the only self-proclaimed B&B in town does *not* include breakfast!

You can choose from a large selection of private villas, and there is also a wide choice of all-inclusive resorts. You need to research carefully if booking an all-inclusive hotel, however; standards vary markedly, and some resorts do not include water sports and certain services in their rates. Many of the town's older hotels are dowdy and seem to be having difficulty competing with the newer all-inclusive hotels.

Where only summer season rates (mid-April to mid-December) are quoted, add 20% to 40% for high season. A 10% service charge and 6.25% to 15% General Consumption Tax are automatically added to the bill at most hotels. Reservations are advised for more upscale properties. If you arrive without reservations, the JTB information booth in the arrivals hall at Sangster International Airport can provide a list of approved hotels and guest houses. They'll call and make reservations for you.

## Places to Stay – Budget

**Downtown** Downtown, the cheapest place I know is *Guest House* (☎ 952-4546, 39 Church St). The 14 rooms in the old wooden house are simple but clean and have fans, louvered windows, and hot water in the shared bathrooms. Rates begin at US$15/20 single/double. Discounts are offered for stays of a week or longer. Meals are served, and the owners offer Maroon heritage tours to Accompong and Cockpit Country.

The *YMCA* (☎ 952-5368, 28 Humber Ave) maintains a hostel on the south side of town, well away from the tourist beat. Its 15 basic rooms have shared bathrooms (cold water) in the hallway and cost US$15 to US$25. Fans can be rented. There's a TV lounge and table tennis.

**Farther Afield** Alternately, try *Mountainside Guest House* (☎ 952-4685) on the Queen's Drive, at the corner of Federal Ave. Rooms cost around US$15 and are simple but adequate, and *camping* is allowed for US$5 per person.

The cheapest hotel near the airport is *Ocean View Guest House* (☎ 952-2662, 26 Sunset Blvd). It's a bargain at US\$23/30 single/double, although rooms are no-frills. It has a TV lounge. Free airport transfers are available on request. You could even walk to the airport 400 yards away if your bags are light.

On the southeast edge of town, in the slopes of Mt Salem, are two other guest house options recommended by readers: *Comfort Guesthouse* (☎ 952-1238, 55 Jarrett Terrace), whose Christian owners offer home-cooked meals; and, across the road, the *View Guesthouse* (☎ 952-3175), also with home-cooked meals, basic yet adequate rooms, plus views and a swimming pool and Friday night party.

## Places to Stay – Mid-Range

**Downtown** The only option downtown is the *Harbour View Hotel* (☎ 952-1100, fax 952-2873, 1 Harbour St). It's a modern and modest option charging US\$60 double, but you can do better for the price, and the location offers no advantage.

**Gloucester Ave** The *Seashell Inn* (☎ 979-2983, fax 979-9836) is perfectly located off Gloucester Ave, opposite Cornwall Beach. Some of its spacious, albeit sparsely furnished, air-conditioned rooms are ready for a renovation and cost US\$35/40 single/double; you pay US\$5 extra for a superior room, but at this writing owner Vernon Chin was preparing to upgrade the entire property to a three-star hotel with suites. Huge showers are a plus. Request rooms in a newer block. It has a dining terrace beneath a huge fig tree next to a pool.

The *Hotel Gloriana* (☎ 979-0669, fax 979-0698) is a five-minute walk from Gloucester Ave, in the midst of a roadside shopping complex on Sunset Blvd. It has 40 quaint, large, carpeted rooms with verandas, air-con, cable TV, and telephones, though bathrooms are small. It operates a tiny downstairs restaurant, plus a breezy rooftop restaurant. Rates are US\$35 to US\$50 single or double.

The *Bayshore Inn* (☎ 952-1046), on Gloucester Ave facing Walter Fletcher

Beach, is a pleasant modern place with 15 rooms with fans and air-con for US\$40 single or double (US\$225 per week). Some have TV (with poor reception).

A favorite of budget-minded Europeans is the compact, no-frills *Caribic House* (☎ 979-6073, fax 979-3421, 69 Gloucester Ave), above the Caribic Vacations' office directly opposite Doctor's Cave Beach. It has 17 basically furnished, overpriced rooms with fans, TVs, and large bathrooms from US\$40 to US\$54 single, US\$44 to US\$62 double, year-round. Some rooms smell sour.

Nearby is the *Belvedere* (☎ 952-0593, fax 979-0498, 33 Gloucester Ave) near Walter Fletcher Beach, with 19 rooms with air-con, telephones, and hot and cold water (from US\$50 single or double low season, US\$65 high season). Larger top-floor rooms with balconies cost US\$10 more. Some of the rooms have heaps of light and views over the bay. Others are cellarlike, and bathrooms are small, the furniture is basic, and one reader thought the air-con sounded like a B-52. You can cool off in a little dipping pool with poolside bar.

My favorite in this price range is the *Sundance* (☎ 952-4370, fax 952-6591, PO Box 467, sundance@cwjamaica.com) on the corner of Gloucester Ave and Sunset Blvd. The 72 air-conditioned rooms are in several two-story units surrounding a pool and sundeck with bar. Rooms vary, but all are nicely furnished, with faux-marble floors and pine-and-rattan furniture. Most have small verandas. Facilities include a game room, modestly elegant Gallery Restaurant (food quality is average), the pool bar, and an elevated 'treehouse bar' with a lounge and large-screen TV. The hotel – which charges US\$60/70 single/double in low season, and US\$70/80 in high season – is popular with German tour groups and young Europeans. It has live entertainment, including limbo and folkloric shows.

A nearby alternative is the *Coral Cliff Hotel* (☎ 952-4130, fax 952-6532, PO Box 253), a venerable hotel built in 1906 and feeling its age. The 30-room colonial-style hotel is a charming, modestly furnished warren. Some rooms remain desperately in need of renovation. Still, you might like its funky charm. There's an oval swimming pool at the back, and the atmospheric Veranda Restaurant is enjoyable for its broad, breezy terrace. Rates for standard rooms are US$65 to US$95 in low season, US$75 to US$115 in high season. The flamboyant casino-style Coral Cliff Gaming Room is here.

The **Buccaneer Beach** (☎ 952-6489, fax 952-7658), on Kent Ave, is a small, modest property with a homey feel. Rooms – US$75 single or double – have tile floors, phones, TVs, and safety boxes, plus large balconies. There's a plunge pool in each of the front and back courtyards, plus a piano bar with large-screen TV. Its reclusive location at the end of Kent Ave is a five-minute walk from Gloucester Ave.

**Miranda Hill** A popular option is **Blue Harbour Hotel** (☎ 952-5445, fax 952-8930, PO Box 212), on Sewell Ave midway up Miranda Hill. Free shuttles to the beach are available, but it's a stiff climb back up from town. Its air-conditioned rooms are spacious, well lit, and airy. All have TVs; some have king-size beds. Room rates begin at US$29/40 single/double in low season, US$48/58 in high season, and range to US$75/80 low season, US$90/98 high season. A pool and bar are set in a courtyard. Breakfasts are served, but not lunch or dinner. It also has family units for up to 10 people.

By far the most atmospheric place is the 10-room **Ramparts** (☎ 979-5258, fax 979-5259), on Ramparts Close, boasting lots of dark timber and natural stone. Its intimate little bar and the TV lounge that serves as a dining room are exquisitely Old World English. The small pool is a satisfying place to catch some rays. Rates begin at US$50 single or double. **Big Apple B&B** (☎ 952-7240, 18 Queen's Drive), nearby, has 12 carpeted, air-conditioned rooms, all with two double beds and views. Furnishings are modest and bathrooms are small. Rates are US$40 for a double with fans (US$45 with TV, US$50 with TV and air-con) but do *not* include breakfast.

Kathleen and Ernest Sterling are your delightful hosts at the euphemistically named **Verney's Tropical Resort** (☎ 952-2875, fax 979-2944, 3 Leader Ave), offering a secluded spot in the hills with views inland over the sugarcane fields. The 25 rooms are very modest and homey, albeit clean; double rooms cost US$45 low season, US$55 high season. Some have air-con, though check first to see that the one in your room is working. TVs can be rented. The open-air bar is pleasant and there's a large pool, but the Kit-Kat Restaurant is rather dull. Verney's is popular with Jamaican families.

If you prefer a breezy hilltop setting, Miranda Hill has plenty of options. At the north end is **Mirage** (☎ 979-0359, fax 952-6980, 6 Queen's Drive), a cozy hotel complex with 22 spacious, carpeted rooms with rattan furniture for US$60 single or double. The rooms overlook a small amoeba-shaped pool. Upper-floor rooms have skylights but get warm.

**Farther Afield** The **Palm Bay Restaurant and Guest House** (☎ 952-1795, fax 940-0411) at Bogue Crossing, 2 miles south of town, has nine rooms with louvered windows, fans (air-con was to be added at press time), telephone, high ceilings, and spacious bathrooms, but fuddy-duddy decor. There's a modest restaurant serving sandwiches and Jamaican dishes (US$3.50 to US$15). Rooms cost US$35 single or double, or US$42 with satellite TV.

The **Ridgeway Guest House** (☎ 952-2709, 940-0637, fax 940-0636), directly opposite the airport, is popular with Europeans. The 10 rooms are large and attractive (some have air-con) and feature private bath with hot water. Rates run from US$30/45 single/double, or US$60 double with air-con, including continental breakfast. You can rent TVs. Free shuttles to the beach and airport are provided. A worthy alternative is the nearby **Airport Inn** (☎ 952-0260) which has 10 clean and adequate little rooms for US$45, and US$50 with kitchenette.

Hotels on the Queen's Drive, near the airport, offer modest accommodations at reasonable prices, good for overnighting in transit, but the beaches are far away. **Seville Resort Guest House, Villas & Apartments** (☎ 979-0098, 800-486-2738, fax 952-5509) offers four rooms that are clean and air-conditioned with utility decor for US$45 single, US$51 double, including tax. There's a TV lounge. No meals are served. It also has apartments near the Blue Harbour Hotel for three months or longer at US$550 per month.

The grand looking **Hotel Montego** (☎ 940-6009, fax 979-0351) is less appealing close up, though its position is convenient to the airport, over which it sits. Its 33 air-conditioned rooms and suites have TV and telephone plus king-size beds, but the decor is frumpy. There's a breeze-swept veranda pool, plus a bar and restaurant. Rates are US$57 single or double, and US$88 for suites.

## Places to Stay – Top End

**Gloucester Ave** The 88-suite **Quality Inn Montego Bay** (☎ 952-4420, 800-228-5151 in North America, fax 952-8088, PO Box 86, www.hotelchoice.com), formerly the Gloucestershire Hotel, is directly across the street from Doctor's Cave Beach. Most rooms feature a balcony. All have air-con and direct-dial phones, room safes, and satellite TV. It offers a pool deck with Jacuzzi beneath the cliffs out back, and there's a restaurant and tour desk. Rates range from US$80 to US$90 single or double in summer, and US$95 to US$115 in winter.

The family-run **Doctor's Cave Beach Hotel** (☎ 952-4355, fax 952-5204, PO Box 94, info@dcbh.com) offers a good location on Gloucester Ave. Its labyrinthine corridors lead to 78 rooms and 12 suites. Some rooms are dowdy and in need of repair. The lush gardens at the back are tight up against the cliff face, where there's a whirlpool under a gazebo. Other facilities include a small gym, the Coconut Grove Restaurant, and a piano bar that opens onto a small swimming pool. A standard room costs US$80/105 single/double in low season, US$110/130 in high season; a superior room costs US$90/115 and US$120/140 respectively. Suites cost US$140 double in low season, US$160 in

high season. Breakfast and dinner cost an additional US$35 daily.

Another hotel in the same price bracket is the **Wexford** (☎ 952-2854, fax 952-3637, PO Box 108) on Gloucester Ave. Though recently remodeled, it remains run-of-the-mill. The 61 carpeted rooms are modestly furnished and have balconies, telephones, and TVs for US$104 to US$110. One wing has one-bedroom apartments with kitchenettes for US$120. There's a pool, the Zee Bar, and the Wexford Grill.

Several all-inclusive properties stand out on Gloucester Ave, each with its own distinct mood. The first is the low-rise **Casa Blanca Beach Club** (☎ 952-0720, fax 952-1424, PO Box 469), above the coral shore south of Doctor's Cave Beach. This former hotel of choice for the rich and famous has re-emerged as one of MoBay's finest hotels after a long decline. It has its own pocket of sand where free water sports (sailing, surfing, and snorkeling) are offered. The 80 air-conditioned oceanfront rooms and suites with queen-size bed, private bath, and balcony cost US$120/190 single/double, all-inclusive in low season. Facilities include two pools, a game room, TV lounge, and seaside dining terrace.

An appealing mid-range resort in the heart of Montego Bay is **Breezes** (☎ 940-1150, 800-467-8737 in North America, ☎ 01749-677200 in the UK, fax 940-1160), a contemporary four-story structure that towers over Doctor's Cave Beach, to which guests have free access (the hotel also has its own private water-sports section). It promises the luxury of a 'cruise ship on land,' with 124 graciously appointed but cramped rooms and suites on an L-shaped pool that at night forms the foreground for a high-tech stage. The standard rooms are small and have queen-size beds; other rooms have king-size beds. All have satellite TVs, VCRs, and CD players, hair dryers, and in-room safes. The lively entertainment features theme nights epitomized by a toga party on Thursday nights. Facilities include two restaurants, beach grill, four bars, rooftop Jacuzzi, game room with pool tables, water sports, a beauty salon and massage, 24-hour fitness center, and an upscale nightclub. Breezes is managed by SuperClubs: *everything* is included in the cost. Low-season rates (per person, double occupancy) begin between US$319 and US$549 for a two-night package, depending on the type of room; high-season rates range from US$409 to US$639.

My favorite in the breed is ***Jack Tar Village*** *(☎ 952-4340, fax 940-5646, PO Box 144; ☎ 800-858-2258, fax 305-444-4848 in North America; www.allegroresorts.com)*, a welcoming, low-rise beachfront hotel with 128 rooms (recently renovated with lively tropical decor) and its own private extension of Cornwall Beach, onto which a breezy, elegant restaurant faces. All rooms have ocean views and wide French doors opening onto a private balcony. The hotel offers a full range of activities and water sports, plus complimentary massage daily. It also hosts a crafts fair each week with vendors setting up stalls along the beach. Rates for a standard room begin at US$185/270 single/double in low season, US$245/360 in high season.

A stone's throw north on Kent Ave is ***Sandals Inn*** *(☎ 952-4140, fax 952-6913, PO Box 412, www.sandals.com)*, a 52-room couples-only resort. It's run to exacting standards, and offers a range of entertainment, water sports, and top-notch cuisine. Guests get privileges at the other Sandals' resorts, including golf at the Sandals Golf Course near Ocho Rios. The beach, across the road, is tiny – much smaller than the hotel brochure suggests – and open to everyone. Three-night packages begin at US$505 per person in low season. (See Sandals, under Hotels in the Facts for the Visitor chapter, for international contact information.)

Another all-inclusive on Gloucester Ave – the 119-room ***Fantasea Resort*** *(☎ 952-4150, fax 952-3637, PO Box 161)* – was closed for renovations at press time. And the much-troubled ***Vista Ambassador*** has closed to await yet another facelift and renaissance.

**Miranda Hill** The ***Montego Bay Racquet Club*** *(☎ 952-0200, fax 921-5335, PO Box 245)*, above town at the corner of Sewell and Park Aves, has traditionally operated as a

hotel. At press time, however, it was being leased by the government for its employees. It may convert to condos with kitchenettes. Nearby is the ***Winged Victory*** *(☎ 952-3891, fax 952-5986, 5 Queen's Drive)*, another elderly property with a lush hillside setting, lots of tilework and wrought-iron in the public areas, and a pool with views. Carpeted rooms are modestly furnished. It was devoid of guests (and life) when I last called in. No smoking is allowed in bedrooms. Rates begin at US$60 single or double. All-inclusive packages are available. The Club Calabash Restaurant is here.

***Mango Walk Villas*** *(☎ 952-1473, fax 979-3093)* has attractive modern units that include six studios costing US$60 high season, 14 one-bedroom units for US$80, and two two-bedroom units for US$140. All are air-conditioned and furnished in rich fabrics, and have kitchen, living room, and patio. It's centered on a deep pool and bar, and is in a reclusive hilltop district that's 10 minutes by car to the town and beaches.

Also for self-caterers is ***Montego Bay Club Resort*** *(☎ 952-4310, 212-840-6636, 800-223-9815 in the USA)*, a 14-story high-rise apartment complex rising from the Queen's Drive. Apartments are clean and spacious and clinically white, with kitchenettes and balconies with good views. There's a swimming pool and restaurant atop the cliff. Rates begin at US$66/78 single/double low season, US$96/114 high season. Montego Bay Club shares its clifftop setting with El Greco Resort (see below).

A hilltop option is the ***Royal Court Hotel & Natural Health Resort*** *(☎ 952-4531, 800-509-1133 in the USA, fax 952-4532)* at Sewell and Leader Aves. This old 25-room hotel caters to the health and fitness market. Hence, the old alcohol bar is now a juice and herbal tea bar, the restaurant serves fish and vegetarian dishes exclusively, and the in-house Wellness Centre offers everything from colon therapy to weight-loss programs. The suites are attractive and homey. Even the standard rooms, which are carpeted, have king-size beds. Rates start at US$60/70 single/double in summer, US$70/90 in winter. Royal Court also offers three to seven-night packages (from US$430 per person). Free airport transfers and shopping trips are offered. Views face inland.

*El Greco Resort* (☎ 940-6116, 888-354-7326 in the USA, ☎ 800-597-7326 in Canada, fax 940-6115, PO Box 1624, www.montego-bay-jamaica.com/jhta/elgreco), on the Queen's Drive, is a new complex with 96 one and two-bedroom air-conditioned suites with kitchenettes, satellite TV, tile floors, rattan furniture, and floral prints. French doors open to balconies. There's a swimming pool, restaurant, and tennis courts. An elevator provides direct access to Gloucester Ave. Rates begin at US$90 (one-bedroom) and US$120 (two-bedroom) year-round.

The *Richmond Hill Inn* (☎ 952-3859), on Union St, is a venerable hotel built of limestone and molasses and is chock-full of antiques. It's noted for its restaurant, which has attracted many among the great and famous, but the rooms are a letdown, especially for the US$110 price tag. A six-person penthouse costs US$440.

**Farther Afield** *Sandals Montego Bay* (☎ 952-5510, fax 952-0816, PO Box 100, www.sandals.com) takes up 19 acres of splendid beachfront on the airport's north side and is a superb all-inclusive couples resort where you and the one you love – as long as you're heterosexual – can put aside the noise of children, seek out the honeymoon sparkle, and snorkel, sail, or soak up the sun to your heart's content. The scintillating white-sand beach seems endless. Be prepared for lots of social activity. Couples are here to have fun! The food is superb, and the live entertainment is top-notch. Every kind of water sport is available, including scuba (resort course only, not certification). Sandals has 244 rooms in nine categories. Three-night packages begin at US$625 per person. (For international contact information, see Sandals, under Hotels in the Facts for the Visitor chapter.)

There's much to recommend about the 420-room *Sunset Beach Resort & Spa* (☎ 979-8800), a twin high-rise complex in a reclusive setting west of town at the end of the Montego Freeport Peninsula. The former

Seawind was scheduled to reopen in spring 1999, after a thorough remake as an upscale all-inclusive resort with a state-of-the-art spa and the 'largest lobby in Jamaica.' Choose from five categories of rooms with ocean or bay view. All are air-conditioned, with one king-size or two double four-poster mahogany beds, hair dryer, telephone, cable TV, in-room safes, and private balconies. There are 32 suites, including 12 with Jacuzzis. The sumptuous lobby opens directly to a massive pool bar. It also has a boardwalk with four restaurants (one Italian, another Japanese with *teppanyaki*), Harry's Café, five bars, a disco, nightly entertainment, as well as four tennis courts, three swimming pools, state-of-the-art gym and spa, a game room featuring Sega computer games, water sports, a high-tech business center, plus three beaches with a nudist's section and water sports. A Kiddies Club caters to families. Summer rates will range from US$250 to US$320 double.

## PLACES TO EAT

MoBay has dozens of restaurants of every stripe, including a selection of sidewalk cafés along Gloucester Ave. Many tourist-oriented restaurants offer free hotel transfers, but far too many eateries geared to the tourist trade serve bland cuisine at high prices. Be prepared to pay top dollar – say, US$20 minimum per person – for meals that satisfy your palate. Many of the best restaurants are associated with the upscale resort hotels, and most are open to nonguests (also see the Ironshore and Montego Bay to Tryall Estate sections, later in this chapter). But there are also plenty of inexpensive, down-to-earth downtown restaurants catering mostly to the local trade.

### Jamaican

The open-air *Jerk Pit & Fish Hut* (☎ 952-6072) at the north end of Gloucester Ave, serves jerk pork and chicken from US$2.50. It offers an 'all you can eat' barbecue on Wednesday nights. It's next to *PJ's Amazon Jerk Pit*, with live reggae music at night. A more authentic experience is the internationally known *Pork Pit* (☎ 952-1046), on Gloucester Ave, where you're served

Got jerk?

through a hole in the wall and can eat at open-air picnic tables beneath a shade tree. Finger-lickin' jerk chicken and pork costs from US$3 with yams, *festival,* and sweet potatoes extra. Downtown, try the *Native Jerk Centre* (☎ 940-5522) in an old house at the south end of Market St. It has a pool table and video games.

*Tino's* (☎ 952-0886), outdoors on Gloucester Ave, has a Jamaican menu and a Rastafarian I-tal Special dish for US$5.

*Walter's Bar & Grill* (☎ 952-9391, 39 Gloucester Ave) serves Jamaican specials as well as American favorites such as buffalo wings.

The food at *Greenhouse Patio* (☎ 952-7838), next to Doctor's Cave Beach Hotel, is bland, but it's open at 7 am for breakfast. It can be ice-cold inside, but there's a small road-front patio. The western menu has Jamaican hints, such as callaloo omelette (US$3). Here, too, in the Caribic House hotel, is *Caffe Gran Caribe,* serving lunch specials for US$5 including drink.

Downtown, you can fill up for under US$3 at *Lyle's Intensified Inn* (☎ 952-4980, 36 Barnett St). It sells pastries, patties, fried fish, and bammy. Note the mural outside

showing police officers harassing a Rasta. 'No loafers, prostitutes & Pimps Read & Run or Else?' says the sign. Another bargain spot for curried goat, pumpkin soup, and so on, is *Smokey Joe's,* off St James Ave.

For spicy meat and vegetable patties, try *Butterflake Pastries*, *Delicious Patties & Pastries*, opposite Lyle's on Barnett St, and the *Viennese Bakery* on the corner of Fort and William Sts.

*Pier 1* is a great place to savor Jamaican Sunday brunch (about US$15) on a breezy wooden deck overlooking the pier. The *Pelican* (☎ 952-3171) is a steadfast good-value favorite of upscale locals for over three decades. Its menu of Jamaican dishes includes stew peas with rice, and stuffed conch with rice and peas (US$7), but it also serves sirloin steaks and seafood. Take a sweater. It offers free shuttles. In the nearby Wexford hotel is the *Wexford Grill*, specializing in seafood and steak and ribs (including sweet-and-sour ribs and honey garlic ribs) for US$17 to US$22. It's open 7 am to 11 pm.

Farther afield in Reading, *Norma's at the Wharf* is even better – it's one of the best dining experiences in the Caribbean (see the Reading section, later in this chapter).

*Day-O Plantation Restaurant* (☎ 952-1825), a mile along the Fairfield Road just past Doctor's Hospital, east of town, enjoys a breezy hilltop setting, and serves entrees such as pork scallopini and plantation chicken (US$12 to US$28), as well as salads (US$3 to US$5). It has a marble dance floor, plus a small pool and sundeck. It offers free hotel transfers.

Guests at Sandals Montego Bay wishing to discover the *real* Jamaica will find several offbeat local eateries – *One Stop Saloon*, *Calabash Bar*, and *Jean's Blue Marlin Club* – a short walk west.

## Fast Food

There are plenty of fast-food outlets, including the typical US chains. For burgers try *Raine's Burger Bar* in St James Plaza, or *Hemingway's Pub* at Miranda Ridge Plaza between Walter Fletcher and Doctor's Cave Beaches. Hemingway's also serves buffalo wings, fish-

and-chips, and shepherd's pie. There's a food court in the MoBay Shopping Centre.

*Tony's Pizza (☎ 952-6365)* has traded in its famous mobile-home-turned-kitchen outside the National Commercial Bank on Gloucester Ave for a shopfront at the same location. It stays open until 2 am (3 am on Friday and Saturday).

Downtown, *McDonald's* has an outlet in the Bay West Centre. The *Dead End Bar & Grill*, at the north end of Kent Ave, offers patties and snacks.

## I-tal & Vegetarian

There's a *health food store (☎ 952-4952)* on the corner of St James and Creek Sts, and a vitamin store in the MoBay Shopping Centre on Howard Cooke Blvd. *Juiciful Depot,* in a cul-de-sac off Market St, serves natural juices.

There are numerous cheap food shacks on the A1 east of town, although the area – Flankers – is full of unsavory characters. The *I'N'I Food Shack* is recommended for good I-tal food and natural juices. Downtown, *Ray's Vegetarian Top Tasting Restaurant*, on Railway Lane, has been recommended for I-tal food that runs from tofu sandwiches and stew peas to callaloo loaf and veggie burgers.

## Continental

The *Coconut Grove Restaurant (☎ 952-4355),* at Doctor's Cave Beach Hotel, mixes 'European, Italian traditional, and Jamaican nouvelle.' The elegant poolside setting offers piano music, but the food is expensive and of moderate quality. Typical dishes are curry of the day with coconut and fried plantain (US$10), and shrimp creole in a spiced tomato and sweet sauce (US$17).

*Marguerite's (☎ 952-4777),* adjoining Margueritaville on Gloucester Ave, is a great place to watch the sunset over cocktails, followed by dinner on the elegant cliff-top patio with views west across the bay. The pricey menu edges toward nouvelle Jamaican, but execution is lacking. It's open 6 to 10 pm.

Downtown are two splendid options with a unique historic ambience. The first is the *Georgian House* at the corner of Orange and Union Sts. This elegant restaurant features

silverware, crystal, lace curtains, and gilt chandeliers. You can also dine alfresco at wrought-iron tables in a courtyard shaded by palms. Entrees such as shrimp creole, lobster Newburg, and tenderloin of pork begin at about US$20. The courtyard boasts the *Georgian House Food Court,* serving less expensive take-out local fare, such as curried chicken (US$4) and 'Rasta pasta' (US$5).

In a similar vein, the *Town House (☎ 952-2660, fax 952-3432, 16 Church St)* offers a choice of dining in the brick-walled cellar or more elegantly upstairs in the Blue Room of this 18th-century structure. Choose from red snapper papillot (US$23) or stuffed lobster (US$30) and the like. Maybe you'll sit at the same table where such notables as Paul McCartney, Charlton Heston, Barbra Streisand, Marlon Brando, and other illustrious figures have dined.

The modestly elegant *Native Restaurant & Bar (☎ 979-2769),* newly located on Gloucester Ave, features live music. The menu ranges from salads to 'goat in a boat' (curried goat in a pineapple half; US$9) and a 'seafood royale' (US$31).

Another longtime favorite is the *Richmond Hill Inn (☎ 952-3859),* off of Union St, where you can dine in an 18th-century great house attended by white-gloved waitstaff. It specializes in continental seafood and offers grand views over town.

For something out of the ordinary, try the *Houseboat Fondue Restaurant (☎ 952-7216),* anchored in Bogue Bay at Montego Bay Freeport. It bills itself as a place 'for dippers, dunkers, and people who like to eat what they cook and cook what they eat.' A three-course meal (US$20) includes a choice of cheese, filet mignon, chicken, and 'chocolate festival' fondue. It's open for dinner only from 6 to 10 pm and offers free shuttle service.

## Chinese

The most popular Chinese restaurant is the *Guangzhou Restaurant (☎ 952-6200, 39 Gloucester Ave)* in the Miranda Ridge Plaza. It's open noon to 10 pm weekdays and 5 to 10 pm on weekends. It serves a huge variety of Chinese dishes (US$5 to US$15) but also has Thai and Mongolian dishes. Discounts are offered between noon and 4 pm. Downtown, the elegant **Lychee Gardens** (☎ 952-9428, 18 East St) is recommended for Szechuan cuisine. It's open noon to 10 pm daily. More basic and cheaper options are the **Peking Restaurant** at Shop No 132 in the City Centre Building; and **Canton Express**, upstairs, opposite the Shell gas station on Fort St.

### Indian
The **Delicious Roti Restaurant** (☎ 940-6646), upstairs in the City Centre Building, serves basic Indian fare.

### Italian
A steadfast favorite for gourmet Italian is **Julia's** (☎ 952-1772) on Bogue Hill, south of town. It offers a tremendous view. Free hotel shuttles are provided.

Guests at Breezes, on Gloucester Ave, are offered the **Pastafari Restaurant**, mediocre Italian fare in a faux-Italianate air-conditioned environment lacking windows.

Although the waiters can be pushy, I like the atmospheric **Spaghetti Factory** (☎ 940-7514) opposite Doctor's Cave Beach, with filling pastas and an attractive bar with TV. Entrees cost US$6 to US$60. Also consider the **Pasta Pasta Italian Restaurant** at the north end of Kent Ave.

### Cafés, Ice Cream & Yogurt
**I Can't Believe It's Yogurt**, on Gloucester Ave, serves nonfat frozen yogurt priced from J$40 (a little over US$1) for a tiny cup – expensive but delicious. And, 200m away, **Jen's Coffee Shop and Ice Cream** serves Devon House I-Scream plus various coffees, as does the **Celebration Coffee Bar** in Miranda Ridge Plaza. **Country Creams** is downtown on Union St, and a **Devon House I-Scream** outlet is in the Bay West Centre.

### Groceries
You can buy fresh produce downtown at the **Gully** (the colorful market is on Orange St between Union and William Sts) and at the bustling **Fustic Market** (also called Charles Gordon Market), off Barnett St. Street vendors sell patties and other fast-food fare, including roasted peanuts, from push carts;

listen for the peanut sellers' mobile roasters whistling away like steaming kettles.

There are plenty of grocery stores and supermarkets downtown, particularly at the MoBay Shopping Centre at Howard Cooke Drive and Market St, and the Westgate Plaza south of town on Barnett St (the A1). Several mini-marts on Gloucester Ave sell groceries at touristy prices. The best is the **Sunset Supermarket & Deli**, opposite the Casa Blanca Beach Club.

There are plenty of bakeries downtown, including the **Viennese Bakery** on Fort St, **Hilton's Bakery** on Church St, and **Salmon's Bakery**, on St James St.

## ENTERTAINMENT
Montego Bay's nightlife is surprisingly unsophisticated compared to Kingston's and less developed than Negril's. Most upscale hotels have live bands and limbo and carnival-style floor shows for dinner and post-dinner entertainment, and if you're staying at an all-inclusive resort, you may never be tempted to prowl outside the compound at night.

Avoid walking alone downtown at night; if you're unsure of an area, take a taxi.

### Bars
The king of the night scene is **Margueritaville** (☎ 952-4777), on Gloucester Ave. This brazen, hip-hopping place has four open-air bars, 15 big-screen TVs, and dance floors on decks overhanging the water. It even has a 110-foot waterslide and an outdoor hot tub. Music is piped in, and there's a CD jukebox. Theme nights are common: Monday is Red Stripe beer fest; Tuesday is 'Marguerita Madness'; a wet T-shirt and bikini contest is hosted on Wednesday; and Sunday is karaoke night. Entry costs US$3 after 9 pm.

Margueritaville's success has knocked the wind out of the sails of **Walter's** (also known as **Wally's**), also on Gloucester Ave, once the most popular hangout in town. The TV at the bar is always tuned to sports. For a sedate option, try the **piano bar** at Doctor's Cave Beach Hotel, or **Hemingway's Pub** (☎ 952-8606) in the Miranda Ridge Plaza on Gloucester Ave, which also offers live entertainment.

*The Brewery*, also in the Miranda Ridge Plaza, is a popular spot with the beer-loving crowd. It has sports on the TV.

## Beach Parties & Stage Shows

Montego Bay is famous for *boonoonoonoos*, or 'beach parties,' which are only-in-Jamaica affairs with live reggae bands. At boonoonoonoos, the DJs crank it up until you can feel the vibrations loosen your fillings. The crowds crush shoulder-to-sweaty-shoulder; the air is thick with ganja smoke; and the whole street is full of revelers *wining* ('dirty dancing') en masse. The location changes; check with JTB (☎ 952-4425) for the latest venues. In 1999, the JTB was considering resurrecting its weekly street carnival on Gloucester Ave, from 7 pm until midnight Monday evening. Check with JTB.

Cornwall Beach hosts a 'Jammin' on the Beach' party on Mondays (US$4.50). A *Boonoonoonoos Beach Party* (☎ 952-5719) is also held every Friday night at Walter Fletcher Beach. The US$29 entrance includes buffet and open bar.

Reggae Sumfest in August is the big daddy of stage-shows (see Special Events, earlier in this chapter). The main venue, the *Bob Marley Entertainment Centre* (also called the Catherine Hall Entertainment Centre) on Howard Cooke Drive, also occasionally hosts 'sound systems'; look for posters advertising forthcoming performances.

## Discos

The most urbane place in town is *Hurricane's Disco* (☎ 940-1150), atop Breezes on Gloucester Ave. It's small but high-tech and gives you an option beyond reggae music (it's open 10 pm to 4 am; entry costs a steep US$14, but guests at other hotels can purchase a pass for US$25 that includes all drinks). The new *disco* in the Sunset Beach Resort & Spa at Montego Freeport promises to be another hot spot.

The yin to Hurricane's yang is the funky *Club Paradise*, a reggae club with mirrored dance stage above the Miranda Ridge Plaza (entry US$2.50), favored by MoBay's less sophisticated crowd. *The Keg*, an earthy club opposite the fire station at the base of St

James St, has soca on Wednesday and Friday nights. And the *Bottle Inn (11 Union St)* is another unsophisticated spot for a taste of 'real' Jamaican clubbing. It has dancehall on Wednesday.

*Goldfingers* (☎ 952-1684, 51 Market St) is an earthy dancehall club downtown. Go-go dancers are one of its fortés; see the caveats in the section on Go-Go Clubs in Facts for the Visitor. You're likely to be hustled in the neighborhood. Entry costs US$2.

On Fridays, everyone heads to *Pier 1 Disco* (☎ 952-2452) off Howard Cooke Drive, where you can dance to reggae and R&B beneath the stars. It gets packed with tourists and locals (US$5 entrance); live bands also play. Rent-a-dreads really make their plays on foreign women. The dancing goes on well into the wee hours. It's open nightly and plays a mix of oldies, world-beat, and reggae midweek.

Also see the Ironshore section, later in this chapter.

## Cinemas

The only modern cinema is at Ironshore (see Ironshore, later in this chapter). You might also try the *Roxy* on Barnett St and the *Strand* (☎ 952-5391, 8 Strand St), though both are dingy and are not in the best areas for nighttime walking.

## Gaming

There's a hint of Las Vegas to the *Coral Cliff Gaming Room* (☎ 952-4130) on Gloucester. The place has over 100 video slot machines, plus a big-screen TV and bar, to draw the cigarette-and-Budweiser crowd. It's open 9:30 am to 1:30 am.

## Other Options

*PJ's Amazon Jerk Pit* (☎ 952-6072), at the north end of Gloucester Ave, has live reggae loud enough to wake the dead. It's the most popular outdoor spot, but attracts gigolos and drug hustlers. PJ's was planning on introducing a skating rink in 1999. Downtown there's a small upstairs *skating rink (39 Church St)*.

If you love jazz, you can make an evening of it with *Twilight Time at Rose Hall*

(☎ 953-2323), starting at 6:30 pm on Fridays. Dinner and drinks are also available. The bar at **Doctor's Cave Beach Hotel** is a mellow place to hear a jazz trio on Thursday and Sunday evenings. The **Belvedere** (☎ 952-0593, 33 Gloucester Ave), across from Walter Fletcher Beach, also has live jazz at 6:30 pm on the last Sunday of the month. The **Orange River Ranch** (see the Montego Bay to Maroon Town section, later in this chapter) was planning to introduce monthly live jazz, reggae, and traditional music.

Montego Bay's Little Theater Company performs at the **Fairfield Theater** (☎ 952-0182). Watch for advertisements for this as well as for dance and theater performances at **Dome House** (☎ 952-2571) on Dome St. Both the **Strand** (see Cinemas above) and **Chatwick Centre** (☎ 952-2147, 10 Queen's Drive) host 'roots plays.'

The tiny **Club Paradise,** on Gloucester Ave, has pool tables and a small gaming room, as does the **Native Jerk Centre,** downtown.

Also see Ironshore, later in this chapter.

## SHOPPING

You can shop till you drop, with no shortage of duty-free stores. And the competition among crafts vendors is so great it's amazing that they all make a living. At least half a dozen major shopping plazas are in town and at Ironshore (see the Ironshore section, later in this chapter).

Bargaining is the norm on the street at crafts markets but *not* in duty-free stores.

### Arts & Crafts

MoBay's streets are spilling over with stalls selling wooden carvings, straw items, jewelry, ganja pipes, T-shirts, and other touristy items.

For the largest selection, head to the downtown Craft Market that extends for three blocks along Harbour St between Barnett and Market Sts (open 7 am to 7 pm daily), or the Fort Montego Craft Market, behind the fort on Gloucester Ave.

There's also a crafts market hidden behind the National Commercial Bank on Gloucester Ave, where a small streetside shopping center sells everything from duty-free goods to souvenirs. And for cruise-ship passengers who have left things to the last minute, there's Harry's Art & Craft Gallery (☎ 979-8024) at Montego Freeport Shopping Centre, which has several other duty-free stores and, handily, a bank. Prices are higher than in town.

The hard-sell hustlers who were once the plague of Gloucester Ave are a thing of the past (all crafts vendors have been forced to set up shop in the sanctioned markets). Some of the all-inclusives, such as Jack Tar Village, allow local vendors to set up a crafts market one day a week. A few vendors have hit on a nifty way to bring their wares to tourists ensconced in all-inclusives: they paddle in and sell their jewelry and carvings from within wading distance of the beaches.

Most upscale hotels have their own arts-and-craft stores. One of the best stores is at Half Moon (see Ironshore, later in this chapter).

The Gallery of West Indian Art (☎ 952-4547) at 1 Orange St, downtown, has quality arts and crafts from around the Caribbean. Maria's Art Gallery (☎ 952-7919) and Things

**Montego Bay vendor**

Jamaican (☎ 952-5605), both on Gloucester Ave southeast of the fort, also sell high-quality works ranging from about US$25 to US$1500. Bay Gallery (☎ 952-7668), in Shop No 16 of the St James Shopping Plaza, exhibits works by well-known local artists.

Also check out the Cultural Arts Centre (☎ 940-3174) on Gloucester Ave; the Budha's Art Gallery (see Reading, later in this chapter); and Tafara Products (☎ 952-3899), 38 Union St, an African/Rastafarian cultural center. The latter sells books, arts and crafts, and natural foods. And the offbeat Natural Apparel Shop at 8 Filandy Plaza, off Barnett St, specializes in clothing and apparel made of hemp.

Klass Kraft (☎ 952-5782), next to Things Jamaican, sells a variety of leather sandals (US$12 to US$35).

### Duty-Free Goods
The City Centre Building – a modern shopping plaza opposite the library on Fort St – has several duty-free shops including Bijoux (☎ 952-2630), Chulani (☎ 952-2158), and Casa de Oro (☎ 952-3502), which also has an outlet at the Holiday Village Shopping Centre, east of town. You'll also find a good selection of duty-free shops in the departure lounge of Sangster International Airport and at the cruise ship terminal at Montego Freeport. Most duty-free stores open at 10 am.

You can buy quality rums at almost any store that sells souvenirs. If penny-pinching, head to Harbour St where you can buy it wholesale at C&J Liquors. Many in-bond stores also sell discounted rums, available in pre-packed 'Jamaica Farewell' boxes with handles.

### Reggae Reminders
If the colorful concert posters around town have caught your eye, nip down a narrow driveway on Union St to Party Magic (☎ 952-6331), at 5 Sewell Ave, where Mansion, Dain, Danny, and Whizzy hand-paint banners for Reggae Sumfest and other key events. You can buy small-scale signs as souvenirs for US$3.

Reggae tapes are widely available, but for the biggest selection check out Tee Pee Records & Tapes at Shop No 17 in the City Centre Building; Top Ranking Record Shop (☎ 952-1216) at Shop No 4 in the Westgate Shopping Centre; or the Caribbean Reggae Shop (☎ 971-6658) at 39 Gloucester Ave, up the hill behind Wally's. El Paso, at 3 South Lane, off Sam Sharpe Square, is another good option. You can have custom compilation tapes made for US$2 to US$5.

### Film
Gift stores along Gloucester Ave sell a limited range of film. In town try Green's Computer & Photographic Services (☎ 940-1395) at 14 Market St, Ventura Photo Service (☎ 954-5864) at 22 Market St, Salmon's Colour Lab (☎ 952-4527) at 32 St James, or Stand Photo Express (☎ 952-3120) at 57 Fort St. Don't expect the counter clerks to be the least bit knowledgeable about photography.

Ventura, which also has a store 3 miles east of town in the Half Moon Shopping Centre, has a 15-minute passport and visa photo service.

Also see Photography in the Facts for the Visitor chapter.

## GETTING THERE & AWAY
### Air
Air Jamaica Express (☎ 922-4661, 952-5401, fax 952-1877; ☎ 305-670-3222, fax 670-2992 in the USA), operates scheduled flights between MoBay and Kingston (eight flights daily; US$49 each way), Negril (twice daily; US$37), and Port Antonio (once daily; US$49). Service was planned for Ocho Rios and Mandeville. Air Jamaica's main office is on the Queen's Drive.

Jamaica Airlink (☎ 923-0486, fax 923-0264; ☎ 954-564-9014, fax 564-7667 in the USA) offers charter air service from MoBay to resorts islandwide using Air-Speed Jamaica's Cessnas. Likewise, Aero Express (☎ 952-5807) offers charter transfers to or from MoBay, as does Timair (☎ 952-2516). Air Negril and Timair also offer charters from Sangster International Airport.

See the Getting There & Away chapter for a description of international service into Sangster International Airport.

## Bus

Montego Bay is served by buses from towns islandwide. They arrive and depart from a new bus station at the south end of St James St, considerably easing the chaotic situation that used to exist. There's an inspector's office (open 7 am to 6 pm) inside the gate, where you can ask the departure point of the bus you're seeking.

Major bus routes include the following:

| route | duration | cost |
|---|---|---|
| Catadupa | 1 hour | US$0.60 |
| Christiana | 1½ hours | US$1.50 |
| Duncans | 1 hour | US$1 |
| Kingston | 4 hours | US$2.50 |

**Minibuses** Minibuses – 'coasters' – serve dozens of towns islandwide, picking up and dropping passengers en route. They also depart from the bus station at the end of St James St. Touts will descend upon you like flies to hustle you to 'their' bus. (See the Getting Around chapter for information about minibuses.)

Minibus routes include the following:

| route | duration | cost |
|---|---|---|
| Duncans | 1 hour | US$3 |
| Falmouth | 30 minutes | US$2 |
| Frome | 1 hour | US$3 |
| Kingston | 3½ hours | US$8 |
| Little London | 2 hours | US$5 |
| Lucea | 1¼ hours | US$3 |
| Negril | 1½ hours | US$4 |
| Ocho Rios | 2 hours | US$6 |

## Taxi

If you're traveling with two or more additional passengers, taxis are a feasible and cost-effective way to travel between towns. The fare for a licensed taxi is about US$70 to Ocho Rios or Negril. Make sure you and the driver reach an agreement on a fare and what it includes *before* setting off.

Private taxi stands are opposite Jack Tar Village and Doctor's Cave Beach on Gloucester Ave, downtown at the junction of Market and Strand Sts, and by the bus station. The Market St stand (☎ 952-6329) operates 6 am to 1 am. You can also call for cabs from Doctor's Cave Taxi (☎ 952-0521), In Your Hands (☎ 952-4863), and JUTA (see below), which caters almost exclusively to tourists.

Unlicensed taxi drivers usually drive battered old cars. Fares are negotiable but should be significantly lower than for licensed taxis. Hammer out an agreeable fare before setting off. If you feel you're being ripped off, get out and hail another cab.

Several companies offer private taxi transfers by minibus. JUTA, the biggest taxi operator, has a fleet of minibuses and full-size motor coaches. The main office is on Claude Clarke Ave (☎ 952-0623, fax 952-5355), PO Box 1155, with another office at 6 Queen's Drive (☎ 979-0778). One-way transfers with Caribic Vacations (☎ 953-9878, 979-9387, fax 953-9897, 979-3421) or Pleasure Tours (☎ 952-5383) cost US$21 to Negril, US$25 to Ocho Rios, US$35 to Port Antonio, and US$25 to Mandeville, based on two or more people.

Many resort hotels offer airport transfers, either free or for about US$15 per person.

## Car & Motorcycle

Several companies are represented at the airport. Other companies have outlets on the Queen's Drive adjacent to the airport, on Sunset Blvd, and downtown at the southern end of Gloucester Ave.

All companies offer discounted rates (usually about 15% to 20% lower) April to December, as well as free pickup and delivery service.

The following companies have offices at Sangster International Airport:

| | |
|---|---|
| Bargain Rent-a-Car | ☎ 952-0762 |
| Budget | ☎ 952-3838 |
| Hertz | ☎ 979-0438 |
| Island Rental Car | ☎ 952-5771 |

Companies with offices in Montego Bay include:

Budget (☎ 953-9765)
   Ironshore Industrial Estate
Caribbean Car Rental (☎ 952-664, fax 974-5760)
   19 Gloucester Ave

Fiesta Car Rentals (☎ 953-9444)
　Ironshore Industrial Estate

Hertz (☎ 979-0439)

Island Car Rentals Estate (☎ 953-9694)
　Ironshore Industrial

Sunbird Car Rentals (☎ 952-0055, fax 940-0328)
　17 Hobbs Ave

At least a dozen outlets along Gloucester Ave rent motorbikes varying in size from 50cc to 750cc. Motorbikes begin at about US$40. If you're not an experienced rider, try getting a scooter; they rent for about US$30 a day. Try the following three companies on Gloucester Ave: Kryss Bike Rental (☎ 940-0476) next to Wally's; Montego Bay Bike Rentals (☎ 952-4984) at 21 Gloucester Ave, where you can also rent bicycles; and Sun Cruise Bike Rentals (☎ 979-0614) next to the Wexford Hotel. Downtown, Hewitt Motorcycle Rentals (☎ 979-0393) has an outlet at 68 Barnett St.

### Boat
Cruise ships berth at Montego Freeport, about 2 miles south of town. Taxis and minibuses will be waiting to whisk you downtown (US$10) and to major sites if you haven't already signed up for a tour offered by the cruise-ship company. (See the Getting There & Away chapter for details on cruise companies serving Montego Bay.)

If arriving under your own steam (or sail), you can berth at Montego Bay Yacht Club (☎ 979-8038, fax 979-8262) at Montego Freeport. It has both 110V and 220V electrical hookups, plus gasoline and diesel. There's a pool and a very attractive bar and restaurant.

### GETTING AROUND
You can walk between any place along Gloucester Ave and downtown (it's about 1½ miles from Kent Ave to Sam Sharpe Square). It can be hot going, but it's level. You'll need a vehicle for anywhere farther.

**To/From the Airport** You'll find plenty of taxis outside the arrivals lounge at Donald Sangster International Airport. A few freelance taxi touts may descend on you imme-

diately as you exit the arrivals lounge, though the blight of a few years ago has eased. Don't let yourself be hassled, however. An official taxi dispatcher should be on hand to assign you a licensed JUTA taxi. If not, there's a dispatcher booth on the sidewalk to the left as you exit.

A US$7 taxi fare applies between the airport and downtown Montego Bay. It may be the most expensive taxi ride you'll take, mile for mile. Even nonlicensed drivers may quote you this rate. You should be able to share a 'robot' (a collective taxi taking several people) for less than US$1, but the wait can be long; they leave from the gas station just outside the airport. If you have much luggage, you may have to pay extra.

Buses don't serve the airport, but you can catch a bus or minibus into town from the roundabout on the main road 400 yards from the terminal. The fare is about US$0.20.

I'm not aware of any regular transfer service between Sangster International Airport and Norman Manley Airport in Kingston (five hours). Most tour operators offer such transfers by arrangement, as does Island Car Rentals, which charges US$120 for one or two people, and US$150 for three to seven people. A licensed taxi ride will also cost US$120.

### Bus
Alas, there's no effective bus service within MoBay, nor is there a tourist shuttle service. Fortunately, most tourist places on Gloucester Ave are within walking distance, but if you need wheels you're at the mercy of taxi drivers who managed to kill a tourist shuttle bus service – Soon Come Shuttle – that was introduced briefly in 1996.

### Taxi
Plenty of licensed taxis cruise up and down Gloucester Ave for a rip-off of US$7 for virtually any distance along the strip (although the same fare also takes you downtown – a better bargain). Licensed taxis (mostly white Toyota Corolla estate-wagons) have red license plates and meters. Government-determined rates should be posted inside the cab and at major taxi points.

Published fares from outside Jack Tar Village include the following:

| | |
|---|---|
| Airport | US$7 |
| Ironshore | US$10 |
| Montego Freeport | US$10 |
| Rose Hall | US$15 |
| Tryall | US$30 |

Dozens of taxi drivers hang out on Gloucester Ave. Recommended drivers include Patrick Clarke (☎ 819-5832) and Richard Hutchinson (☎ 952-7032).

'Robots' (collective taxis that pick up and drop off along set routes) cruise the town and set off from the bus station near the junction of St James and Barnett Sts. A good place to catch one on Gloucester Ave is by the straw market near Walter Fletcher Beach. You should be able to travel anywhere in town for less than US$1.

### Horse-Drawn Carriage

All Nations Carriage Tours (☎ 979-2514) charges US$25 per hour for city tours by canopied horse-drawn cab, beginning at the fort at the south end of Gloucester Ave.

### Bicycle

Biking around town is simple, but beware the crazy drivers. You'll want a mountain bike for forays away from town. Beware that most bikes rented locally are flimsy and old. Local bicycle rental specialists include Tropic Ride Car & Bike Rental (☎ 952-7096) and Montego Bay Rentals (☎ 952-4984). Rapid & Sheffield (☎ 979 8158), 30 Pimento Way, is a bike supply and repair shop.

# The Coast: Montego Bay to Trelawny

East of Montego Bay, the A1 hugs the coast all the way east to Falmouth, 23 miles away. It's not a particularly scenic drive, although there are small beaches tucked away behind the shoreline mangroves. The narrow coastal plains were once covered in sugarcane, but in recent years the sugar estates have given way to private homes, villas, and resorts. Two fabulous great houses – Rose Hall and Greenwood – still stand foursquare on the hills, and each is worth a visit. Greenwood Great House (17 miles east of MoBay) spans the boundary of St James and Trelawny parishes.

A more adventurous option is to head inland from Montego Bay by following the Montego River east to the pancake-flat Queen of Spains Valley, where a sea of rippling green sugarcane sweeps off into the distance, hemmed in by a serrated bowl of the wild, unexplored Cockpit Country.

## IRONSHORE

This upscale residential suburb about 5 miles east of Montego Bay is a center for deluxe resorts and villas, several of which are at scintillating Mahoe Bay while others command their own diamond-dust patches. It is based around the 1000-acre Ironshore Resort Estate and golf course and the nearby Half Moon golf course.

Don't bother following the sign on the A1 that points inland to **Blue Hole Plantation** (the turnoff is beside the Coral Gardens Police Station, half a mile east of Coyaba Beach Resort). This fieldstone-and-timber house, 1200 feet above sea level, served until recently as a nature lodge, but is no longer open to visitors.

### Information

There's a Transport Centre & Visitor Information Centre (☎ 953-9007) in the Blue Diamond Shopping Centre. A Scotiabank is in the new Half Moon Shopping Centre. The Northwestern Medical Service & Microlab (☎ 953-9299) is in the Blue Diamond Shopping Centre. For the police, call ☎ 119 or 953-2229.

### Activities

**Sport Fishing & Sailing** Seaworld (☎ 953-2180, fax 953-2550), PO Box 610, offers deep-sea fishing from the Cariblue Beach Resort at Ironshore.

Princess Cruises (☎ 953-2180, fax 953-2550), at the Cariblue Beach Resort, offers a variety of cruises as far afield as Negril, and includes a 'snorkeling safari.' A similar option is the *Mary Ann*, a 57-foot ketch that also offers day and evening party cruises from Sandals Royal Caribbean (☎ 952-5505).

**Scuba Diving & Snorkeling** Jamaica Scuba Divers is based at the Half Moon Golf, Tennis & Beach Club (☎ 953-2211, fax 953-2731), and Seaworld (see above) is nearby at the Cariblue Beach Resort.

**Golf** Most noteworthy is the Half Moon Golf, Tennis & Beach Club (☎ 953-2560, 953-3105), conceived by world-renowned course-designer Robert Trent Jones. About 3 miles east of Ironshire, the course is 18 holes, 7115 yards, par 72. The first nine holes are laid out along the shore; the back nine ripple sensationally uphill through Running Gut, a narrow limestone gorge (green fees cost US$95 year-round, plus US$30 for cart rental and US$14 for a caddy). The former sugar factory is now a club house.

Ironshore Golf & Country Club (☎ 953-2800) is a links-type course (6633 yards and par 72) known for its blind-shot holes. Green fees are US$52 in summer, US$58 in winter, plus US$29 for cart rental and US$13 for a caddy. Reservations are essential.

**Horseback Riding** The Double A Ranch (☎ 936-6106), opposite the Holiday Inn Sunspree, offers trail rides. A more comprehensive facility is Rocky Point Stables (☎ 953-2286, fax 953-9489), PO Box 35, Falmouth. Rocky Point is a full-blown equestrian center just west of the Half Moon Shopping Village. Daily rides include a 90-minute ride into the mountains at 9 and 10 am and 3 pm (US$40), and a 2¹/₂-hour ride combining mountain and ocean – yes, you ride the horse into the Caribbean – for US$50. Rocky Point also offers riding and polo lessons. You must wear long pants and shoes or sneakers.

Also try L&M Riding Stable (☎ 953-2002), which has rides along the Coral Gardens Woodland Trail and up into the hills above Ironshore and Rose Hall.

## Organized Tours

Utas Tour (☎ 979-0684, fax 979-3465), PO Box 429, in the Transport Centre in Blue Diamond Shopping Centre, has a series of full-day excursions to Dunn's River Falls (US$24), Kingston (US$60), and various attractions islandwide, plus a three-day 'Jamaica Land We Love' tour of the whole island (US$391).

Other tour companies include Blue Danube Tours, in the Cariblue Beach Resort (☎ 953-2550), and Jamaica Tours Ltd (☎ 953-3727) at Shop 4, Half Moon Shopping Village.

## Places to Stay

**Resorts** *Manev Rose Resort (☎ 979-9584, fax 940-3188, 17 Claude Clarke Rd)*, in the hills east of town, is a modern complex with 20 rooms with fans, TV, refrigerator, and hot water for US$40 to US$57. There's a swimming pool, plus bar and restaurant upstairs.

*Cariblue Beach Resort (☎ 953-2022, fax 953-2550, PO Box 610)*, 400m east of Coyaba Beach Resort (see below), offers 22 spacious though meagerly furnished air-conditioned rooms. Most have a balcony. It has a restaurant, pool, dive shop, a wide range of water sports, plus excursions aboard its 47-foot *Princess* motor-yacht. Rates are US$50 to US$55 single, US$61 to US$66 double in summer; US$61 to US$66 single, US$83 to US$93 double in winter.

At the east end of Claude Clarke Rd, is *Relax Resort (☎ 979-0656, 800-742-4276 in North America, fax 952-7218, 26 Hobbs Ave)*, a breeze-swept, 41-room property that is an adequate place to rest for a night. All rooms are ocean-view, with floral prints, tile floors, spacious bathrooms, tiny TVs, and telephones (they also smell permanently of fresh plaster). It has a sumptuous three-bedroom villa. Rates in summer range from US$60 single or double for a superior room, and from US$85 to US$190 for one to three-bedroom suites. Winter rates are US$78, and US$110 to US$215, respectively.

*Sandals Royal Jamaican (☎ 953-2231, fax 953-2788, PO Box 167, Montego Bay)*, at Mahoe Bay, is a sedate couples-only property that attracts a slightly older age group than other Sandals resorts. Its beach is relatively small, but water sports, land sports, entertainment, and cuisine are up to par. Highlights include Kokomo Island, with the Indonesian-style Bali-Hai Restaurant (one of four restaurants on the property) and its own swimming pool and Jacuzzi. It offers 190 rooms in seven categories. Three-night packages begin at US$675 per person, low season, and US$730 high season. Weeklong packages begin at US$1370 and US$1485, respectively. (See Hotels in the Facts for the Visitor chapter for international contact information for Sandals Resorts.)

Also at Mahoe Bay is **Coyaba Beach Resort & Club** (☎ 953-9150, 800-330-8272, fax 953-2244, Little River PO, coyaba@n5.com.jm, www.coyabajamaica.com), a compact family-run resort with 50 luxurious rooms furnished 'plantation style' with hand-carved beds, floral drapes, and rich mahogany reproduction antiques. All rooms have French doors opening onto oversized verandas, and feature an in-room safe, telephone, and satellite TV. It sits on a narrow beach in the cusp of a lagoon with a reef just 100 yards offshore. Water sports are offered. It's a quiet property blending contemporary elegance with a New York clubby feel. One of three restaurants, the elegant Vineyard Restaurant – offers splendid (yet pricey) nouvelle Jamaican cuisine. Summer rates are US$120/150 single/double for garden-view, US$150/180 ocean-view, US$180/210 deluxe. Winter rates are US$210/240, US$260/290, and US$310/330, respectively. An all-inclusive plan is offered for US$130 extra. Junior suites were to be added.

Among my top-five Jamaica resorts is **Half Moon Golf, Tennis & Beach Club** (☎ 953-2211, 800-626-0592, 800-424-5500 in the USA, fax 953-2731, PO Box 80, www.halfmoon.com.jm), one of the most beautiful and exclusive colonial-style resorts in Jamaica. This world-renowned resort is named for its private crescent beach that stretches more than a mile, behind which are 400 acres of beautifully landscaped gardens containing 42 rooms and 179 suites in stunning Georgian plantation-era decor. Per person rates (double occupancy) range from US$110 to US$300 in summer, and US$165 to US$550 in winter, including tax. Special

packages are offered. Adjacent to the hotel are 20 super-deluxe, five, six, and seven-bedroom villas with private pools. Each comes with its own cook, maid, gardener, and even its own rental car – for US$1500 a night. Facilities include four squash courts, 13 tennis courts, an equestrian center, a championship golf course, and the Half Moon Shopping Village, comprising a bank, coffee shop, English pub, six specialty restaurants, and 30 upscale shops. It was even named 'Green Hotel of the Year' by the Caribbean Hotel Association for its eco-sensitivity, which includes upkeep of a 20-acre bird reserve.

Coyaba and Half Moon are members of Elegant Resorts of Jamaica, which has an all-inclusive Platinum Plan that allows you to mix and match accommodations at these and any of its other properties: Round Hill Hotel & Villas, Blue Lagoon Villas, Prospect Villas, and Russell Villas (see below). For information call ☎ 800-237-3237 in the USA, ☎ 020-7730-7144 in the UK.

The nearby **Holiday Inn Sunspree** (☎ 953-2485, 800-465-4329 in North America, fax 953-9480, PO Box 480, Rose Hall), is the second largest property on the island, with 516 air-conditioned rooms and 26 family suites in ungainly seven-story buildings around a vast, handsomely conceived sundeck and free-form pool. The place underwent a total renovation in 1997 and is now an all-inclusive family resort with special facilities for children, including supervised activities, a kiddies' disco, game parlor, and kids-only restaurants. Mom and dad are also catered to with a fitness spa, tennis and volleyball courts, disco, and four bars. The rooms are tastefully decorated. Rates (all-inclusive) in summer start at US$155/240 single/double for a garden-view room and rise to US$185/270 for an oceanfront room; in winter, rates are US$215/300 to US$245/330, respectively. Children 12 and under stay free. You can reach a dive operator at ☎ 953-2486.

**Jamaica Rose Resort** (☎ 953-3993, 205-836-2929, 800-358-3938 in the USA, fax 205-836-2931, 427 Ferguson Ave), in the hills of Ironshore Estate, offers 10 deluxe air-conditioned rooms with TVs and private bath.

There's a sundeck and private pool, plus two terrace bars. Guests can use the Ironshore Golf & Country Club. Rates are US$149 per person double (three-night minimum; breakfasts and dinner are US$15 extra).

At this writing the Ritz-Carlton Hotel Corp planned to build a 400-plus room luxury resort at Rose Hall with a new 18-hole golf course, to open in 2000.

**Villas & Apartments** The Ironshore hills are replete with snazzy villas and apartments for rent. One of the most exquisite is *Tranquility Villa*, a large three-bedroom house with its own private beach and stunning decor. It rents for US$4500 per week December to April, and from US$1950 to US$2800 during low season. For information on this and other villas, contact Exclusive Villa Resorts (☎ 951-6232, fax 951-6236, PO Box 1372, Montego Freezone).

*Russell Villas of Rose Hall* (☎ 953-3707, 800-238-5289, fax 953-2732, rrussell@infochan .com), is a conglomeration of 10 deluxe, fully staffed two to six-bedroom luxury hillside villas, each in its own landscaped grounds and costing US$400 to US$700 nightly in summer. Each comes with transportation services and full membership privileges at Half Moon Golf, Tennis & Beach Club, which they overlook. In a similar mode, *Elegant Resort Villas* (☎ 953-9562, fax 953-9563, PO Box 80, Montego Bay), includes temporary membership at the Half Moon club – US$4500 to US$7500 weekly low season, US$7500 to US$8050 high season – for its luxury four and five-bedroom villas overlooking the golf course.

*Sunshine Villas* (☎ 953-2253, fax 953-9228, PO Box 400, Montego Bay), has tastefully appointed upscale villas, most with private swimming pool, whirlpool spa, or a private section of beach. Many have stereos, TVs, and VCRs and come fully staffed.

The *Atrium at Ironshore* (☎ 953-2605, fax 953-3683, PO Box 604, Montego Bay), also offers a selection of upscale apartments of various sizes and amenities.

Villas by Linda Smith (☎ 301-229-4300, fax 320-6963, 8029 Riverside Drive, Cabin John, MD 20818, linda@jamaicavillas.com) represents the *Oscar Hammerstein Estate* plus 22 other exquisite villas near Montego Bay. More modest three-bedroom villas are available through *Ironshore Resort Villas* (☎ 953-2501, PO Box 108) and *Seville Resort Villas & Apartments*, (☎ 952-2814, fax 952-5509, 19 Sunset Ave). The latter also has a guest house for US$30/35 single/double.

## Places to Eat

For nouvelle Jamaican cuisine with an international flavor, head to the *Vineyard Restaurant* at Coyaba Beach Resort (☎ 953-9150). The menu is creative and the fare among the best on the island. Budget a minimum US$20 per person for dinner.

If you're craving Japanese cuisine, check out *Sakura* (☎ 953-9686) in the Half Moon Village. It specializes in teppanyaki cooked at hibachi-grill tables. Meals start at US$20 per person. The Half Moon Shopping Village also features an English steak house in the same price range.

Everyone raves about the *Sugar Mill Restaurant* (☎ 953-2314) at the prestigious Half Moon Golf Club. It serves Caribbean and international cuisine in an elegant setting. Free shuttles are offered from Sandals and Comfort Inn & Suites (for pickup reservations, call ☎ 953-2228).

Roadside stalls sell fried fish, jerk, and other staples of work-a-day Jamaican fare. There's also a *McDonald's* and a *Baskin Robbins* beside the A1, catercorner to the Blue Diamond Shopping Centre.

## Entertainment

The modishly upscale *Planet Xaymaka Disco* (☎ 953-3840), in the Half Moon Shopping Village, attracts MoBay's elite. A more modest option is the *Diamond Roof Disco* in Blue Diamond Shopping Centre.

The *Blue Diamond Cinema* (☎ 953-9020) at the Blue Diamond Shopping Centre shows first-run movies. The *Atlanta Night Club*, also here, has video games and darts, plus blackjack, poker, and pool.

The *Flamingo Nightclub* (☎ 953-2257), in an old stone building at Sugar Mill Rd in Ironshore, has erotic go-go dancing nightly except Monday (US$3 entry including one beer). It occasionally hosts live bands.

Want to learn more about Bob Marley? Check-out the **Bob Marley Experience & Theater** (www.bobmarleyexperience.com) which has daily showings of a documentary on Marley's life, on the hour every hour, in a 68-seat theater at the Half Moon Shopping Village. Admission is free.

## Shopping

Images Art Gallery in the Half Moon Club (☎ 953-9043) displays watercolors, antique collectibles, and selected crafts from Jamaica's foremost artists. Most of the other resorts also have gift stores, and the A1 is lined with makeshift stalls where artists sell wood carvings and sea-shells.

For CDs, tapes, or vinyl reggae recordings, check out Reggae Rhythms in the Blue Diamond Shopping Centre.

## ROSE HALL TO GREENWOOD

East of Ironshore, the A1 hugs the coast, dipping and rising past scrubland and meadows and residential estates of modern, middle-class housing, with finer villas ascending the forested scarp slope that faces the ocean. The Bob Marley School for the Arts, at Greenwood, is the island's premier training ground for up-and-coming musicians. There are few beaches, but history makes its mark. Colonial-era great houses dot the hillsides, including Cinnamon Hill Great House, now the private home of country and western singer Johnny Cash, who is admired locally as a major contributor to local charities.

## Rose Hall Great House

This stunning mansion (☎ 953-3513), PO Box 186, Montego Bay, with its commanding hilltop position 2 miles east of Ironshore, is the most famous house in Jamaica. It's also one of the most magnificent, enticing over 100,000 callers a year. The imposing house was built in the 1770s by John Palmer, a wealthy plantation owner. Palmer and his wife Rose (after whom the house was named) hosted some of the most elaborate social gatherings on the island. Slaves destroyed the house in the Christmas Rebellion of 1831, and it was left in ruins for over a century. In 1966 John Rollins, a former lieutenant governor of the US state of Delaware, bought the property and lavished over US$2.5 million on it to restore it to haughty grandeur.

The three-story building has wings enclosing a courtyard, and a double staircase backed by an arcade leading up to a front door beneath a Palladian portico. Inside, the house is a bastion of 18th-century style, with a magnificent mahogany staircase and doors, and silk wall fabric that is an exact reproduction of the original designed for Marie Antoinette during the reign of Louis XVI. Unfortunately, the fabric is now badly torn and worn by the hands of unthinking visitors. *Don't touch!* Many of the antiques are the works of leading English master woodworkers of the day, including Hepplewhite, Sheraton, and Chippendale.

Part of the attraction is the legend of Annie Palmer, a multiple murderer said to haunt the house (see 'White Witch of Rose Hall'). Her bedroom upstairs is decorated in crimson silk brocades. The cellars now house an old-English-style pub and a well-stocked gift shop. There's also a snack bar on the grounds.

The White Witch story is gruesome enough, but violence of another sort mars the history of Rose Hall. In 1963 a deadly exchange known as the 'Coral Gardens Massacre' occurred here while the property was being restored. A group of Rastafarians had settled and were farming the land. Tensions over property use erupted when the Rastafarians fought against the police who had come to evict them. A petrol station was set ablaze, troops were called in, and in the ensuing battle, eight Rastafarians were killed.

Tours of the house commence every 15 minutes, 9 am to 6 pm daily. Entrance costs US$15 (US$10 for children under 12).

## Greenwood Great House

Greenwood (☎ 953-1077), PO Box 169, Montego Bay, sits high on a hill 5 miles east of Rose Hall. It's a more intimate property.

## The White Witch of Rose Hall

John Rose Palmer, grandnephew of John Palmer who built Rose Hall, married Anne May Patterson in 1820. Although the young woman was half English and half Irish, legend has it that she was raised in Haiti where she learned voodoo. Legend also says that Anne May was a murderous vixen. The lascivious lady allegedly practiced witchcraft, poisoned John Palmer, stabbed a second husband, and strangled her third. Her fourth husband escaped, leaving her to dispose of several slave lovers before she was strangled in her bed.

This tale – Jamaica's most famous legend – is actually based on a series of much distorted half-truths. The inspiration for the story, originally told in writing in 1868 by John Costello, editor of the *Falmouth Post*, was Rose Palmer, the initial lady of Rose Hall. She *did* have four husbands, the last being John Palmer, to whom she was happily wed for 23 years (she died before her husband at age 72). Anne Palmer, wife to John Rose Palmer, died peacefully in 1846 after a long, loving marriage.

In 1929, novelist HG DeLisser developed the fable into a marvelous suspenseful romance, the *White Witch of Rose Hall*.

Many Jamaicans believe the legend, and various attempts have been made to contact Anne's ghost. The most famous was a séance held on Friday, October 13, 1978, when a psychic named Bambos claimed to have made contact. Apparently, Anne's ghost led him by the hand to a nearby tree where, in full public view, he found a voodoo doll.

The two-story stone-and-timber structure was built about 1760 by Sir Richard Barrett, whose family had arrived in Jamaica in the 1660s and amassed a fortune from their sugar plantations. (Barrett was a cousin of the famous English poet, Elizabeth Barrett Browning, whose poetry was supported by the sweat of more than 2000 slaves, a fact over which Browning herself expressed great shame.) Greenwood was intended primarily for entertaining guests, hence the large ballroom. Barrett was custos (the English monarch's representative) of St James and a member of the Jamaican Assembly. In an unusual move for his times, however, he educated his slaves, as the guides in period costume will tell you (they neglect to tell you that Barrett died in compromising circumstances in a 'rooming house' – brothel – in Falmouth).

Unique among local plantation houses, Greenwood survived unscathed during the slave rebellion of Christmas 1831. The house today boasts what it claims is 'the finest antique museum in the Caribbean.' The original library is still intact, as are oil paintings, Dresden china, a rare collection of musical instruments, a court jester's chair, and such somber antiques as a man-trap used for catching runaway slaves. The master bedroom is still used by the current owners. Have your camera ready for the spectacular views of the coast from the veranda.

Sir Richard once won the prize for the best constructed mile of the new tarred road between Montego Bay and Falmouth. If he could see the state of the road up to the house today, he would turn over in his grave.

Entrance costs US$12. The house is open 9 am to 6 pm daily. Buses traveling between Montego Bay and Falmouth will drop you off along the A1.

### Rose Hall Beach Club

This private beach, 2 miles east of the Wyndham Rose Hall resort, is open to the public (US$8) 9 am to 6 pm daily and offers water sports, volleyball, banana boat rides, jet-skiing, parasailing, and snorkeling. There's a restaurant and bar.

### Golf

Wyndham Rose Hall Golf & Country Club (☎ 953-2650), home to the Jamaica Open and the International Junior Golf Championship, is known for its tricky windage and superb coastal vistas. The sharp doglegs and windy conditions put a premium on club selection. Vital statistics: 18 holes, 6598 yards, par 72. Green fees are US$50 year-round, plus US$27 for cart rental and US$15 for a caddy.

### Other Activities

If your love life is lackluster, call on Raphael Brown, the Jamaican Bush Doctor, who has a roadside healing center on the A1 east of Greenwood, at the diminutive roadside community of Lilliput. His aphrodisiac juice should do the trick, though the ingredients – seamoss, sarsaparilla, Irish moss, bloodwist vine, ginseng, and 'chenny root' blended and fermented with honey – will probably make you wilt (US$5 per mini bottle, US$18 for half a pint). Raphael also has herbal teas for various illnesses (US$1 per cup). He'll read your palm, dispensing scant clairvoyant advice for a 'mere' US$21 (30 minutes), and he'll even don white robes and perform a soul-sealing voodoo wedding ceremony.

White Witch Stables (☎ 953-2746) is located at Wyndham Rose Hall Golf & Country Club.

Jamaica Tours Ltd (☎ 953-3700), at 1207 Providence Drive, Rose Hall, has an outlet in the Wyndham Rose Hall Beach & Golf Resort (☎ 953-2597).

## Places to Stay

The *Bob Marley School for the Arts* (☎ 954-5252, fax 953-3683), just east of Greenwood, offers rooms boasting Rasta-inspired 'roots' decor, wicker furniture, ceiling fans, and doors opening to patios with coastal vistas for US$30 to US$40.

The *Wyndham Rose Hall Golf & Beach Resort* (☎ 953-2650, 800-996-3426 in the USA, 020-8367-5175 in the UK, fax 953-2617, PO Box 999, Montego Bay, www.wyndham .com), on the shore just west of Rose Hall Great House, is an elegant 488-room resort on 400 acres fronted by a beautiful 1000-foot-long beach. This twin-tower, seven-story hotel offers elegant furnishings in spacious rooms with king-size beds, and top-notch amenities – including a choice of restaurants, video game room, the Cricketer's Pub, and the Jonkanoo nightclub. Families are catered to with the Kids Klub. The resort boasts its own 18-hole golf course and six tennis courts. The entire property was to be upgraded at this writing, when a major water complex – Sugar Mill Falls – was due to open as a kind of mini-Disneyland.

If you prefer a place in the hills, consider *Dunn's Villa Resort Hotel* (☎ 953-7459, 718-882-3917 in the USA, fax 953-7456, 718-882-4879, Rose Hall, Little River PO, Montego Bay) in the village of Cornwall, 2 miles inland from the Wyndham. This well-kept, homey hotel has 11 air-conditioned rooms with satellite TV and wide balconies for US$65 double, including breakfast. The spacious public areas are minimally but attractively furnished. There's a pool and Jacuzzi on a raised sundeck. It's run by Howard and Gloria Dunn, gracious hosts who offer a local tour by horse and buggy (they also rent mountain bikes for US$8). The Dunns offer lunch, dinner, and weekend brunch poolside.

The *All Seasons Beach Resort* (☎ 953-1448, fax 953-1449, allseasons@cwjamaica .com), alongside the A1 and east of the

Wyndham, has 12 two and three-bedroom air-conditioned townhouses with kitchens and handsome 'mini-suites.' There's a small pool, plus a restaurant and bar where meals are cooked to order. It has sea kayaks. The tiny beach, however, is horrid and being reclaimed by mangroves. Rates are US$70 double year-round, or US$30 nightly for monthlong stays.

A short distance east of Wyndham Rose Hall is *Comfort Inn & Suites* (☎ *953-3250, 800-228-5150, fax 953-3062*), a luxury all-suite resort centered on a plantation-style great house at the heart of a 14-acre estate on a private beach. It offers 150 air-conditioned studios and one, two, and three-bedroom units with kitchenette, satellite TV, telephone, and balcony or patio. There's a pool with poolside cafés where entertainment is hosted. Facilities include volleyball, tennis, and water sports. The property, formerly called Sea Castles, is a good place for families, offering a Kiddies Club and nanny service. Low-season rates range from US$90/102 single/double for studios to US$342 for a three-bedroom penthouse that sleeps six.

*Royal Reef Hotel & Restaurant* (☎ *952-1704*), on the A1 at Greenwood, is a modern, ochre-colored, Mediterranean-style hotel. Its decor includes classical wrought-iron furnishings as well as exquisite tropical murals. An elevated amoeba-shaped pool is inset in the terra-cotta terrace that has an outside grill overlooking a tiny, unappealing beach overgrown by mangroves.

### Places to Eat
The resorts cater to their guests with a selection of restaurants. There are few food-stops around Rose Hall. *White Witch's Hideaway Pub & Grill* serves typical Jamaican meals by the shore (US$2 to US$5).

At the *Far Out Fish Hut*, just east of Greenwood, you can get steamed fish and bammy and other seafoods that draw the locals.

'Bredda' (brother) Brown also serves vegetarian dishes at his rustic *restaurant* and bar at Lilliput.

### Entertainment
MoBay's middle classes mingle with guests at the *Jonkanoo Lounge* at the Wyndham Rose Hall Golf & Beach Resort (☎ *953-2650*), which also has a video game room.

# The Coast: Falmouth to Rio Bueno

Much of Jamaica's history was written along this section of coast, notably around Falmouth, an active market town that has been largely ignored by tourist development. Its attractions are largely historical. East of Falmouth, the A1 runs parallel to the shore about 2 miles inland. It again hits the coast at Rio Bueno, a charming historic little town 13 miles east, at the border with St Ann parish. Few roads lead down to the shore, which remains relatively undeveloped. Good beaches are relatively few and far between. Inland, however, the scenery is terrific. See the Cockpit Country (North) section, later in this chapter.

## FALMOUTH
Few other towns in Jamaica have retained their original architecture to quite the same degree as Falmouth (population 4000), which has a faded Georgian splendor. The city, on the west shore of Glistening Waters (see Glistening Waters, later in this chapter), 23 miles east of Montego Bay, has been the capital of Trelawny parish since 1790. It's still an active market town. On Wednesdays, the downtown bustles with clothiers and craft retailers, and on weekends farmers come in from miles around to sell their produce, recalling the days when Falmouth was Jamaica's major port for the export of rum, molasses, and sugar. Many of the buildings dating back to that era are now decrepit. Although slate roofs have long since been replaced with zinc and tin, upper stories of timber atop cut-stone bases remain, as does the arcade along Market St, with its upper story supported by fat Doric columns.

There have been several plans to restore the town as a tourist attraction, but very little effort has been undertaken. One exception occurred during the early 1970s, when several of the buildings along Market St received a tuck-and-fold for the filming of *Papillon*, starring Steve McQueen and Dustin Hoffman. And several individuals have done fine restoration work, such as Tony Hart, who is working to restore the Baptist Manse; Geoffrey Pinto of the Jamaica Georgian Society; and Heinz Simonitsch (managing director of the Half Moon Club), who has restored a twee Regency house near the courthouse. A

North American, Jim Parrent, has been instrumental in raising local consciousness to restore the town through the Jamaican Heritage Trail (☎ 954-3033, 999-4674), but his efforts to establish an open-air Slave Museum have not gained local support, as many people hereabouts would prefer to forget about their painful past.

Farther away, a lonesome 2-mile-long beach begins east of town at the tip of the spit in Glistening Waters (see below) and stretches eastward past the Trelawny Beach Hotel. For more intrepid explorers, there's

**FALMOUTH**

*Half Moon Bay*

To Montego Bay

Charlotte St
Rodney St
Old Harbour St
Trelawny St
Cornwall St
Duke St
George St
Seaboard St
Pitt St
Newton St
Princess St
Queen St
King St
Market St
Thorpe St
Lower Harbour St

To St Ann's Bay, Ocho Rios

To Martha Brae, Good Hope Estate

Winns Morass

0    100    200 m
0    100    200 yards

**PLACES TO STAY & EAT**
10  Salmon's Pastries
20  Falmouth Resort
23  Wally's
25  Spicy Nice Bakery

**OTHER**
1   Hospital
2   Police Station
3   Library
4   Fort Balcarres
5   Methodist Manse
6   Scotiabank
7   Barrett House
8   Doctor's Clinic
9   Joy's Craft & Gift Shop
11  Baptist Manse
12  Post Office
13  Cable & Wireless / TOJ

14  Police Station
15  Vincy's Pharmacy
16  National Commercial Bank
17  Gas Station
18  Courthouse
19  St Peter's Anglican Church
21  Knibb Memorial Church
22  Cinema
24  Scotiabank
26  Water Square
27  Albert George Shopping
    & Historical Centre
28  Buses and Taxis
29  Tharp House
30  Orion Pharmacy
31  Phoenix Foundry
32  Gas Station
33  Big J's Supermarket

bamboo rafting on the Martha Brae, horseback riding at Good Hope, and hiking in the Cockpit Country close at hand (see Cockpit Country, later in this chapter).

The Falmouth Tournament (☎ 954-3229, fax 954-4529) is held in early October, attracting fisherfolk chasing prize marlin.

## History

The land on which Falmouth was founded once belonged to Edward Barrett, who owned a number of estates locally. In 1770 a new parish was formed from the eastern portion of St James. The first capital was Martha Brae, a small port inland from the mouth of the Martha Brae River, a mile south of present-day Falmouth. Gradually, the rivermouth silted up, making Martha Brae unsuitable for cargo traffic. In 1790, Falmouth was laid out as the new parish capital. The town was named for the English birthplace of Sir William Trelawny, then the island's governor, after whom the parish was named. The streets were planned as a grid and patriotically named after members of the royal family and English heroes.

Lots were sold and eagerly bought up by wealthy planters, who erected their townhouses in a simple but charming style using Georgian elements adapted to Jamaican conditions.

Advantageously positioned, Falmouth quickly grew into the busiest port on the north coast. Most of the outbound trade consisted of hogsheads (large barrels) containing wet sugar, and puncheons (casks) of rum, while slaves were off-loaded for sale in Falmouth's slave market. Despite this market, Falmouth was described as a 'pleasant, fashionable seaport' in 1830, when it had a population of almost 3000 – the same as today. Back then, the town was a relatively urbane place, and the city weekly newspaper, the *Falmouth Post*, even had subscribers in England.

It was not unusual for two dozen ships to be in port at a time, alongside scores of smaller vessels that ferried goods to towns along the coast. While the ships waited for the winds by which to depart, the sailors carE= carE=carE=caroused, creating such uproar that they were banned from the town after dark.

The town's fortunes degenerated when the sugar industry went into decline during the 19th century, and were dealt a further blow with the advent of steamships, which the harbor was incapable of handling. By 1890 the port was dead.

## Orientation

The town's center is Water Square, a wide plaza at the east end of town with a roundabout. The A1 from Montego Bay runs along Duke St into Water Square, from which it zigzags east before continuing to Ocho Rios. Market St, one block west of Water Square, runs south to Martha Brae and Good Hope.

## Information

**Money** You can cash traveler's checks at Scotiabank (☎ 954-3357) at 20 Market St at the corner of Duke St, the Scotiabank at Market and Seaboard Sts, and at the National Commercial Bank (☎ 954-3232) on Water Square. Western Union is represented by Big J's Supermarket (☎ 954-3278) on Lower Harbour St.

**Post & Communications** The post office is at the corner of Cornwall and Market Sts. The Cable & Wireless/TOJ office (☎ 954-5910) at 23 Market St is open 8 am to 4 pm Monday to Friday.

**Medical Services & Emergency** Emergency services are available in the Falmouth Hospital (☎ 954-3250) on Rodney St. Dr Diane Glasgow runs a clinic (☎ 954-4580) at 1 Trelawny St, open 8:30 am to 2:30 pm Monday to Friday. Pharmacies include Vincy's on Water Square and the Orion Pharmacy (☎ 954-3392) at 35 Market St.

The main police station (☎ 954-3222) is on Rodney St. There's also a police station downtown on Market St between Duke and Cornwall Sts.

## Historic Downtown

Any walking tour of Falmouth should begin at the spacious **Water Square**, at the east end of town, named for an old circular stone reservoir (dating to 1798) that stored water raised from the Martha Brae River. Slaves would arrive in early morning to draw water, which they carried to their owners' townhouses. In 1955, a formal garden and fountain were erected atop the site, which today forms a traffic roundabout. The fountain is topped by an old waterwheel.

Albert George Market, a grand old market facing Water Square, was built in 1894 and named for two of Queen Victoria's grandsons. Renamed the **Albert George Shopping & Historical Centre**, it still functions as a market with crafts stores, but also contains an historic museum with a motley colonial-era collection.

From here follow the main road east one block to peruse the strange, conical structure at the corner of Thorpe and Lower Harbour Sts. It was once the **Phoenix Foundry**, built in 1810. Among other things, it supplied iron bedsteads for the British army. Behind the foundry, guarded by locked metal gates, is the **Central Wharf** where slaves were brought ashore, replaced in the holds by sugar, rum, and other victuals born of their back-breaking labor. The crumbling warehouses are on their last legs, as are the fading remains of plasterboard erected as sets for the 1993 movie *Wide Sargasso Sea*. Some 50 yards west, on Thorpe St, is **Tharp House**, sagging from age yet still one of the best examples of elegant period townhouses. Today housing the tax office, it was formerly the residence of John Tharp, at one time the largest slaveholder in Jamaica.

Retrace your steps to Water Square and turn east for one block to Seaboard St. Here stands the most imposing building in Falmouth – the grandiose Georgian **courthouse** – in Palladian style, fronted by a double curling staircase and Doric columns, with cannons to the side. The current building, dating from 1926, is a replica of the original 1815 structure that was destroyed by fire. The town council presides here.

History buffs might follow Seaboard St west one block, then turn right onto Market St, which soon brings you to **Fort Balcarres** – now a school – on Charlotte St. The fort was

originally near the courthouse in the town center. But apparently, the firing of ceremonial salutes set neighboring roofs ablaze, prompting the fort's move. The remains are hidden by a high stone wall, and there's little to see.

By following the wall around you get to Rodney St, which runs west along the shore past the historic **police station**. It was constructed in 1814 as the Cornwall District Prison: a 'house of correction' for defiant slaves, with a separate cell for debtors. The prison once contained a 'treadmill,' a huge wooden cylinder with steps on the outside, installed to replace flogging (a punishment that the governor, Lord Sligo, thought too inhumane). Shackled above the mill, slaves had to keep treading the steps as the cylinder turned. If they faltered, the revolving steps battered their bodies and legs. The ancient lockups are still in use.

At the bottom of Market St is the **Methodist manse**, a stone-and-wood building with wrought-iron balconies and Adam friezes above the doorways. A diversion along Trelawny St leads one block west to **Barrett House**, handsome in the extreme, as may be expected of the former home of wealthy planter Edward Barrett. Almost derelict in 1996, it has since been renovated.

Nearby is the **Knibb Memorial High School**, at the corner of Market and Trelawny Sts. Built in 1798, it was originally a Masonic hall. One of the most stately edifices is the **Baptist Manse**, at Market and Cornwall Sts, recently restored to its earlier grandeur. It was formerly the residence of nonconformist Baptist preacher, William Knibb, an active abolitionist. Knibb came to Jamaica from England in 1825 and was branded a troublemaker by privileged whites. His first chapel was burned by the militia following the Christmas Rebellion of 1831; Knibb was arrested, but later released. He was instrumental in lobbying for passage of the Abolition Bill that ended slavery. The porticoed **post office** is adjacent.

On Duke St, turn right one block then left on King St, where you come to **Knibb Memorial Church**, at the corner of King and

George Sts. Here, on July 31, 1838, slaves gathered outside the rebuilt chapel for an all-night vigil, awaiting midnight – the most pregnant moment in Jamaican history – and the dawn of full freedom, when slave shackles, a whip, and an iron collar were symbolically buried in a coffin. The scene is depicted in sculpture relief on a marble panel above the baptismal trough inside the chapel. Knibb and other Baptist ministers are buried here.

The oldest extant building in town – **St Peter's Anglican Church** – built in 1785 and enlarged in 1842, lies four blocks west on Duke St. Take time to browse the graveyard, which has tombs spookily sun-bleached like bones and dating back over 200 years.

## Orange Valley Estate

The ruins of this sugar estate are 5 miles southwest of Falmouth. The boiling house and slave hospital are in particularly good shape, though slowly being reclaimed by tropical foliage. To get there, turn inland off the A1 at Dundee toward Adelphi; turn east after 2 miles. The road is horribly deteriorated.

## Charles Swaby's Swamp Safari

The place was closed for renovation at press time, but should be reopened before 2000.

This crocodile breeding farm, nature reserve, and family park (☎ 954-3065), formerly Jamaica Safari Village, is at the eastern end of Salt Marsh Bay, a mile west of Falmouth. Crocs bask in the sun, eyeing you leerily from behind wire fences. Other animals include mongooses and snakes, and there's a bird sanctuary, plus a petting zoo for the kids. The scene in the movie *Live and Let Die,* in which James Bond ran across the backs of crocodiles, was filmed here; a five-minute clip of the film is shown on arrival.

You can take a short boat tour of the mangrove swamp behind the village. With luck you might even get to see Mr Swaby himself wrestling crocodiles, which through the years he has learned to manhandle and hog-tie with ease.

Post-renovation entrance cost and times were to be announced.

## Places to Stay

*Greenside Villa* (☎ 954-3127, PO Box 119, Falmouth), 2 miles west of Falmouth, has studio apartments. They rent for US$25 single or double with refrigerator only; US$28 with kitchenettes fitted with small gas stoves (US$5 extra person). The rooms are simple but spacious and clean and have private bath and ceiling fans. Meals are cooked on request. You can rent bicycles and cars here.

Nearby *Roi's Villas & Travel Halt* (☎ 954-3852, fax 954-3324) rents furnished studios and small cabins for about US$30.

In town, the only place is *Falmouth Resort* (☎ 954-3391, 22 Newton St), with 12 modest rooms with private bath and hot water for US$34 double, and a popular restaurant.

My heartiest recommendation is *Good Hope Estate*, 8 miles south of town on Route 6. See the Cockpit Country (North) section, later in this chapter.

## Places to Eat

Falmouth is devoid of good eateries. Check out your options near Glistening Waters (see below) or, for the best food for miles, at *Good Hope Estate*. See Cockpit Country (North), later in this chapter.

You can buy fresh baked breads, pastries, and spicy meat and vegetable patties at *Spicy Nice Bakery* or *Salmon's Pastries* in Falmouth. For ice cream, head to *Wally's* on Market St, between Duke and George Sts.

## Entertainment

The *Country Club Restaurant* has a disco nightly. East of town, it's opposite the Trelawny Beach Hotel (see Glistening Waters, below), which also has a disco. A tiny *cinema* (☎ 954-4191, 33 Market St) shows current-run movies for US$2. Otherwise you're relegated in town to the rum shops such as *One Love People Club* (4 Lower Harbour St).

## Shopping

The venerable Albert George Shopping & Historical Centre contains several crafts shops. Joy's Craft & Gift Shop at 48 Duke St, opposite the church, is also worth a browse.

For ceramics, head to Good Hope Estate, where acclaimed artist David Pinto runs the Good Hope Pottery & Gallery in an old plantation building next to the stables. Also see Glistening Waters, below.

## Getting There & Away

Falmouth is served by regular buses and minibuses plying between Montego Bay (about 30 minutes) and Ocho Rios (90 minutes) and you should rarely need to wait more than 30 minutes between 6 am and 7 pm, with a reduced schedule on Sunday. Buses arrive and depart from Water Square and cost about US$0.50 to Montego Bay and US$1 to Ocho Rios.

From Kingston, buses and minibuses depart for Falmouth from the Parade. Expect to pay about US$6.

Minibuses also run between Falmouth and Brown's Town, Duncans, Mandeville, and other destinations.

## MARTHA BRAE

Two miles due south of Falmouth, this small village astride the Martha Brae River served as the first capital of Trelawny parish. Then the rivermouth at Rock silted up and Falmouth was planned and built as the new capital in 1790.

The Martha Brae River rises at Windsor Caves in the Cockpit Country and flows 32 miles to Glistening Waters, east of Falmouth. Tropical fish are bred commercially and ornamental water plants are raised in the marshland behind the rivermouth.

The river is named for an Arawak priestess who, according to legend, knew the location of a secret gold mine in a cave by the river. She is said to have lured Spanish gold-seekers to the cave, which she sealed by diverting the course of the river, drowning the conquistadores and securing her secret.

From Martha Brae, a well-maintained road winds scenically through the river gorge to Sherwood. Another rougher road leads west to Good Hope Estate and the Queen of Spains Valley (see the Port Antonio & Northeast Coast chapter).

Buses run to Martha Brae from Falmouth, just east of Water Square.

## Rafting

The rafting trip down a 3-mile stretch of the Martha Brae is one of the most exhilarating in Jamaica. The journey takes 90 minutes on long bamboo rafts poled by a skilled guide. The upper reaches tumble at a good pace before slowing farther downriver where you stop at 'Tarzan's Corner' for a swing and swim in a calm pool. At the end, you'll be driven back to your car.

Trips begin from Rafters Village, situated on a great loop of the river about a mile south of Martha Brae. There's a picnic area, bar, restaurant, a swimming pool, bathrooms, changing rooms, and a secure parking lot, plus a large gift store where you can buy miniature rafts and T-shirts.

A raft trip costs US$40 per raft (one or two people). Contact River Raft Ltd (☎ 952-0889, fax 979-7437, rafting@montego-bay-jamaica .com), 66 Claude Clarke Ave, Montego Bay. Your raft guide will expect a tip.

Canoeing is possible farther upriver. Good Hope is said to be a good put-in site, although no one is currently offering commercial trips.

## GLISTENING WATERS

By day it's rather ugly, but at night Glistening Waters (also called Luminous Lagoon and, in guidebooks, Oyster Bay, though no one locally seems to know that name) boasts a singular charm – it glows an eery green when disturbed. The glow is due to the presence of microorganisms that produce photochemical reactions like fireflies. The concentrations are so thick that fish swimming by look like green lanterns. The bioluminescence will last up to three days when a sample is kept in a jar.

The bay, which is one of the largest lagoons of its type in the world, is surrounded by mangroves, many of which were destroyed in the 1970s as part of an aborted plan to develop the bay for tourism, almost killing off the microorganisms, which have only recently recovered.

The lagoon begins about a mile east of Falmouth and extends almost 2 miles past the hamlet of Rock.

Boat trips are offered from the wharves at Falmouth Yacht Club (US$7 per person).

## Bear Cay & World Beach

Bear Cay is a spit of land that hooks around the north side of the bay. World Beach, the lonesome white-sand beach on the north side is good for snorkeling and sunbathing, and although popular with locals on weekends, attracts virtually no foreign tourists. You can access it at Time 'n Place (see Places to Stay, below), or you can rent a boat at Glistening Waters and Fisherman's Inn; picnic meals are available.

## Sport Fishing & Boating

The Caribbean Amusement Co (☎ 954-2123) at Fisherman's Inn (see Places to Stay, below) has a dive boat, and you can charter sport fishing boats to set out in search of marlin and other game fish. The rivermouth in Glistening Waters is one of the few places in Jamaica that still offers good fishing for tarpon, known as the 'silver bullet' for its feisty defense on a line. No license is required.

The ramshackle wharf at Rock doubles as the Falmouth Yacht Club and has gasoline and water for boats. You can hire a boat here to take you to World Beach.

## Places to Stay

*Bodmint Villas & Resort (☎ 954-3551)*, about 2 miles east of Falmouth, is a rather jaded property with air-conditioned rooms in landscaped gardens overlooking Glistening Waters. The carpeted rooms are clean and simply furnished, with walls of pine and whitewash for US$35 double year-round. A cook is provided if you rent the full four rooms (US$50 double). There's also a two-bedroom wooden cottage with kitchen.

*Paradise Guest House (☎ 997-5372)*, a mile farther, has eight rooms for US$40 double. It's half a mile from the shore. There's a pool in the courtyard.

Anyone seeking offbeat seclusion should head to *Time 'n Place (☎/fax 954-4371, PO Box 93, Falmouth, timenplace@cwjamaica .com)*, a funky beach bar at the east end of Bear Cay, with deserted World Beach at your doorstep. Its delightful and knowledgeable owners, Sylvia and Tony, have three quaint all-hardwood cottages for rent right on the beach, with louvered windows plus hot water,

radios, and eclectic furniture. They charge US$65 for up to three people, or US$75 for one with air-con. The rustic restaurant and bar is a great place to hang out. Ask Tony to take you to the 'bottomless' Blue Hole.

*Fisherman's Inn (☎ 954-4078, fax 954-3257; ☎ 800-767-3009, fax 310-671-8954 in the USA)* is a quaint hotel at Rock Wharf, 2 miles east of Falmouth. The 12 gleaming air-conditioned rooms are spacious and pleasingly furnished, with big bathrooms and private patios. There's a pool and two restaurants (one inside, one out). It's not really worth the US$75/100 single/double rate, however, and the location has no great appeal.

The venerable *Trelawny Beach Hotel (☎ 954-2450, 800-336-1435 in North America, fax 954-2149, PO Box 54, Falmouth)*, 4 miles east of town, is a twin-tower high-rise hotel dating back to the 1960s, with 350 nicely decorated rooms and a full complement of amenities. It caters to families and is popular with tour groups and a middle-of-the-road crowd. It has its own white-sand beach and a full range of water sports and activities, including a dive operator. Rates begin at US$115/170 single/double for standard in low season, US$210/310 in high season. It also has cottages ranging from US$170/270 low season to US$310/440 high season.

At press time, FDR resorts was building a new resort next to Time 'n Place.

## Places to Eat

*Time 'n Place* (see above) resembles a set from *Popeye*, the movie starring Robin Williams, and has been featured in movies and fashion shoots. The bamboo beachside hut has tables on the sand. Driftwood sculptures decorate a ramshackle wharf. There are swings and hammocks at the bar. Take your pick of burgers with fries (US$5), vegetarian pizza (US$4), and an array of Jamaican dishes. Leave room for some key lime pie (US$3). Look for the road sign: 'If you got the time, we got the place.'

Craving Chinese? Check out the *Ponderosa Restaurant (☎ 954-4153)*, 200 yards west of the Trelawny Beach Hotel. The Trelawny Beach Hotel itself offers continental and Jamaican fare in the *Jamaican Room* (☎ 954-2450), with a prix fixe menu for US$25. The restaurant is closed on Tuesday and Thursday. Shorts are not allowed, but there's a second, more casual open-air restaurant – *Palm Terrace* – that also has entertainment nightly. Entrees range from US$12 to US$25.

*Jamaica Hut* and *Country Club Restaurant*, both opposite the Trelawny Beach Hotel, are modestly expensive seafood restaurants.

Another option for stylish dining is the *Fisherman's Inn* (☎ 954-3427), which has elegant indoor seating. You can also eat outside on the terrace overlooking Glistening Waters. The menu ranges from salads and seafood to creole specialties such as brown stew; it's also heavy on steaks and lobster. Entrees range upwards of US$10. It's open from 7 am to 10 pm.

## Shopping

A comprehensive selection of arts and crafts is available at Bamboo Village, 200 yards west of the Trelawny Beach Hotel, next to the Ponderosa Restaurant.

Caribatik (☎ 994-3314), the showroom of the late Muriel Chandler, has its name prominently displayed on the outside wall beside the A1 just east of town at Rock Wharf. You can tour the workshop and watch the rainbow-hued batiks being made with hot wax and dye by artists-in-training. It's open 9 am to 4 pm Tuesday to Saturday.

Farther east, at Hague, a mile inland from the A1, is the factory and outlet of Reggae to Wear (☎ 954-3552), selling hand-painted batik resort wear. It's open 7 am to 5 pm Monday to Thursday, and 7 am to 2:30 pm Friday. It's well signed.

## DUNCANS

This small town is centered on an old stone clock tower in the middle of a three-way junction, on a hillside 7 miles east of Falmouth – a good halfway stop en route from MoBay to Ocho Rios.

**Kettering Baptist Church**, built in 1893, commemorates William Knibb, a Baptist missionary and a leading abolitionist who founded an emancipation village for freed slaves here in 1840.

Three miles east of Duncans you'll pass a cleft in the roadside cliff face that opens into **Arawak Cave**, which has fruit bats, intriguing stalagmites and stalactites, plus petroglyphs stenciled onto the glassy walls centuries ago by the Arawaks. Peter, a friendly man who runs the drinks stall across the road, has the key to the gate. He charges US$2 for a short tour.

The road that leads south from the clock tower will take you to Clark's Town, gateway to a splendid adventure drive into the Cockpit Country. See the Cockpit Country (North) section, later in this chapter.

## Places to Stay

The no-frills *Sober Robin Inn* (☎ 954-2202), on the west side of Duncans, is a place of last resort. The 11 rooms downstairs cost US$25. Six upstairs rooms have TVs with local reception only, plus hot water for US$34. There's a small pool and a tiny bar, and breakfast is served in a gloomy restaurant.

*Silver Sands Villa Resort* (☎ 954-2001, 888-745-7245, fax 954-2630, PO Box 1, www .silversands-jamaica.com), a mile west of Duncans, has 85 upscale villas and cottages spread out over 224 acres, plus basic motel rooms for US$35. The enclosed estate backs a private 1000-foot-long white-sand beach. Each unique villa is privately owned and individually decorated. Each has a cook, housekeeper, and gardener. Most have TVs and their own pools. The villas are rated standard, superior, and deluxe. Summer rates range from US$100 to US$120 for a one-bedroom cottage to US$450 for a five-bedroom villa; winter rates range from US$130 to US$150 for a one-bedroom cottage to US$510 for a five-bedroom villa. Weekly rates offer savings and include airport transfers. Features include a gym, four-poster beds, a tiny pool with its own rock garden and waterfall, and two double whirlpool bathtubs.

Seeking self-catering? Try the three-bedroom *Beach Haven* (☎ 954-2423, PO Box 65), which rents for US$800 a week.

## Places to Eat

There are several roadside stalls in town, including the rustic *Nicky Beef Patties*, next to the plaza on the west side of the clock tower. It's good for snacks. The *Hillside Bakery*, also on the plaza, is recommended for its 'cocobreads' (rolls spread with butter before baking). If you're in the mood for seafood, try the *Fishpot*, just west of town. The *Aeroplane Jerk Pit*, opposite Arawak Cave, serves finger-lickin', mouth-searin' jerk pork or chicken for about US\$2.

## Getting There & Away

All the buses plying the route from Montego Bay to Runaway Bay and Ocho Rios stop on the west side of the clock tower. It's one hour and US\$0.80 one way. A minibus will cost about US\$2.50.

## RIO BUENO

If you saw the 1964 movie *A High Wind in Jamaica*, then this tumbledown fishing village, which appeared as a set, may seem familiar. Rio Bueno is an escape from the faster-paced resorts, a somnolent place where fishermen still tend their nets and lobster pots in front of ramshackle Georgian cut-stone buildings.

The town, 32 miles east of Montego Bay, is set on the west side of a deep, narrow bay that may be the site where Columbus first set foot in Jamaica on May 4, 1494, after anchoring his caravels, *Nina*, *San Juan*, and *Cardera*.

The bay became an active port for coastal traffic during the colonial era but has seen a gradual decline this century. The A1 loops around the bay, at one point crossing over **Bengal Bridge**, which marks the border of Trelawny and St Ann parishes. The stretch of coastal road from here to Discovery Bay (3 miles) is known as the Queen's Hwy, as it was officially opened by Queen Elizabeth II in November 1953.

A very narrow and deteriorated road leads inland to Jackson Town.

For an indulgence, call in at Grand Lido Braco (see Places to Stay, below), which issues all-inclusive day passes good from 10 am to 6 pm (US\$75), and evening passes

good 6 pm to 2 am (US\$90) granting full access to all facilities at no extra cost. Be sure to stop off at the Gallery Joe James (see Shopping).

## Historic Sites

The 18th-century ruins of **Fort Dundas** lie behind the school. Old churches of interest include an **Anglican church** dating to 1833 and a **Baptist church** erected in 1901 to replace another destroyed in the anti-missionary riots of the abolitionist era.

## Dornoch Riverhead

Two miles south of Rio Bueno, a river springs from the ground at Dornoch Riverhead, where a steep track leads downhill to a thickly wooded cliff. Beneath, the Dornoch River wells up silently into a deep pool – a blue hole – before rushing off to the sea. It's an enchanting and mysterious place surrounded by trees that hang heavy with epiphytes and lianas.

According to legend, a mermaid lived here. On moonlit nights she would sit on a rock combing her hair with the pool as a mirror. One night, a young girl from Stewart Town supposedly disturbed the mermaid, who dove into the pool, leaving her comb. The girl began combing her hair, which began to grow longer and longer and heavier and heavier until its weight pulled the girl into the pool. She drowned. Many locals believe the legend and are wary of the pool. Nonetheless, the famous Baptist missionary, William Knibb, used the pool to baptize converts.

To get to the riverhead, turn south at Bengal Bridge and drive a mile south. Turn right for Dornoch (1 mile).

## Places to Stay

Things have improved since the 1870s when a visitor to Rio Bueno's only hotel – the Wellington Inn – reported:

Up in the crazy room where I slept I lay upon an antique bed in the company of lizards, and gazed through holes in the roof upon the twinkling stars.

The *Hotel Rio Bueno* (☎ 954-0046, fax 952-5911) has been converted from an old

Georgian wharfside warehouse and has a pleasant decor and unique ambience. The hotel is a museum of Joe James' artwork. All rooms have wide French doors opening onto balconies that overlook the bay. I recommend the huge, atmospheric suite with hardwood floors, open-plan walls and lots of light. Rates are a rather hefty US$100 single or double, and US$200 for a suite. A pool may soon be added.

On the eastern flank of the bay, *Bay Vista Village* (☎ 995-3071, 800-526-2422, fax 997-7023) was closed for renovation at press time. It has 38 modern, carpeted one-bedroom and studio suites in landscaped grounds facing the bay and the hotel's own pretty, pocket-size beach. Some rooms have air-con and kitchenettes; some are noisy due to traffic. Facilities include a pool, tennis court, and game room, plus horseback riding and scuba diving.

*Grand Lido Braco Village Resort* (☎ 973-4882, 800-467-8737 in North America, 01749-677200 in the UK, fax 954-0000) is one of the most impressive all-inclusive beachfront resorts in Jamaica. Imagine a time-warp village with a cobbled square and Georgian buildings of cut stone, red brick, and timber in Jamaican vernacular style with shady, columned verandas and gingerbread trim. Introduce artisans, pushcart vendors, and country higglers dressed in period costume. Create a spectacular, jigsaw-piece-shaped Olympic-size pool, lawns crowded with bougainvillea, and a 2000-foot-long beach. Add low-rise accommodations with 180 rooms and 52 suites in a medley of four handsome plantation styles. The result is this 14-acre all-inclusive resort 2 miles west of Rio Bueno. Low-season rates range from US$770 for a garden view for three nights to US$1950 for an oceanview suite for seven nights, all-inclusive.

There are also several private homes for rent along the bay.

### Places to Eat

The *Lobster Bowl Restaurant* in the Hotel Rio Bueno serves seafood dishes from US$15 in a huge yet elegant hall opening onto a veranda. It's open from 7 am to midnight daily and from 9:30 am on Sunday, when it serves their Old Time Jamaican breakfast. The property also includes *Joe's Bar* in a gloomy stone-and-timber building that has tons of character. At *International Reggae Beach Club* opposite the post office, you can enjoy seafood (about US$5), jerk dishes, and burgers (US$2). The place hops at night.

*Rio Brac Rest Stop* is an upscale roadside restaurant about 400 yards east of Grand Lido Braco. It opens at 7 am and has a gift store and grocery, plus clean bathrooms. *Yow Rest Stop*, a short distance east, offers seafood and jerk by the shore. *Travel Halt*, a government-run crafts market, a half mile east of Rio Bueno, has jerk stalls.

You get more than your money's worth at *Grand Lido Braco* (see above), where a day pass (10 am to 6 pm; US$75) or night pass (6 pm to 2 am; US$90) buys all-you-can-eat plus access to all facilities and entertainment. The cuisine is fantastic at any of five atmospheric restaurants.

### Entertainment

*Hotel Rio Bueno* (☎ 954-0046, fax 952-5911) hosts a 'Day of Jazz' 11:30 am to 3 pm and 6 to 9 pm the first Sunday of each month.

### Shopping

Gallery Joe James, in old wharves beside the Hotel Rio Bueno, displays James' famous naive paintings and carvings. There are some occasional masterpieces, but most pieces are uninspired and overpriced. Small works begin at US$10, and larger, better works sell for US$500 or more.

# Montego Bay to Tryall Estate

West from Montego Bay the A1 follows the coast, offering little in the way of nice beaches or other attractions. Five miles west of town, the road crosses the mouth of the Great River, which forms the boundary between St James and Hanover parishes. After crossing the Great River, the A1 winds uphill to a headland with a sweeping vista back toward Montego Bay, then drops down through a dwarf coconut plantation and passes Round Hill Hotel & Villa (see Places to Stay in the Hopewell section, later in this chapter), one of Jamaica's ritziest resort hotels; and, farther along the A1, Tryall Estate and world championship Tryall Golf Course, beyond which the new highway to Negril begins.

The two villa resorts are centers of gracious living, particularly at Thanksgiving and other holiday seasons, when the homeowners flock and the area is chockablock with socialites, houseguests, and renters who live a high-life most of us can only dream of.

## READING

Reading, 4 miles west of Montego Bay along the A1, is a small crossroads hamlet at the junction of the B8, which leads south to Westmoreland and St Elizabeth parishes. Reading faces onto Bogue Lagoon and has several small resort hotels fronting pocketsize beaches. At the east end of Reading is the Desnoes & Geddes factory where Red Stripe beer is brewed.

In colonial days, Reading was an important shipping port for sugar. During the 1950s, several of the old wharfside buildings metamorphosed into the winter home of Millicent Rogers, an eccentric heir to the Standard Oil Company fortune who arrived in Jamaica with a retinue of Indians from Taos, New Mexico. (Her warehouse is today a top-notch restaurant, Norma's at the Wharf; see Places to Eat, below.) The hills above Reading are still popular with the international elite, who maintain fashionable homes here.

Budha's Art Gallery (☎ 979-2568) is worth a stop; coming from MoBay, it's on the left, in a colonial era house 200 yards west of the junction of the A1 and B8. It boasts fine art from famous artists such as Neville Budha and Ramó Díaz (US$25 to US$6000). Credit cards are accepted.

### Scuba Diving & Fishing

Reading is a good spot for scuba diving: offshore is Reading Reef, at the western extreme of the Montego Bay Marine Park.

Poseidon Divers (☎ 952-3624, 800-880-5224, fax 952-3079), PO Box 152, Reading, St James, has an outlet at Reading Reef Club.

The old wharf at the west end of Reading is the setting for the *Wet'n'Wild* cruise yacht. (See the Outdoor Activities chapter for descriptions of other diving spots in the area.)

### Places to Stay

You'll find oceanfront cottages for rent at *Beach House Apartments*, opposite Budha's Art Gallery. Nearby is *Chalet Caribe Hotel (☎ 952-1365, Box 365)*, which concentrates on scuba diving and offers 30 studios, apartments, and hotel rooms, starting at US$40. Mrs Jarrett runs a *B&B (☎ 952-1327)* on the south side of the road, 2½ miles west of Reading. She has two rooms with single and double beds, plus private bath with hot water. She charges about US$35 including breakfast. Look for the sign.

Two miles west of Reading is *Sahara de la Mer Resort (☎ 952-2366, 213-292-4803 in the USA, fax 979-0847, PO Box 223, Reading)*, a modest two-story hotel built around a coral reef from which the swimming pool – open to the sea – has been cut. The hotel also has its own tiny beach, plus a Jacuzzi. There are 24 spacious rooms with custom furnishings, air-con and ceiling fans, hot water, satellite TV, telephone, and oodles of light. French doors open to a wide terrace; the suite has its own spacious balcony. There's also a beauty shop plus restaurant with wrap-around windows. Summer rates are US$55 for a single or double standard, US$65 to US$85 deluxe, US$125 suite.

*Reading Reef Club (☎ 952-5909; 402-398-3217, 800-315-0379 in the USA; fax 952-7217; PO Box 225, Reading; www.montego-bay-jamaica.com/jhta/reefclub)* is an upscale property tucked cozily on its own small private beach on Bogue Lagoon, opposite the junction of the B8 to Anchovy. Small and intimate, the elegant hotel has 37 oceanfront rooms and two and three-bedroom suites (some with king-size beds). All have verandas and louvered windows, air-con, fans, and telephone. There's a breezy terrace bar plus a pool. There is a five-night minimum Christmas and New Year. Rates are US$75 superior, US$100 to

US$125 ocean-view, US$200 to US$250 suite, in summer; US$100 superior, US$125 to US$150 ocean-view, US$250 to US$300 suite, in winter.

## Places to Eat

The *Safari Restaurant* at the Reading Reef Club is recommended for its seafood, which is delivered fresh each day by local fishermen. Otherwise, for offbeat dining, try the *Oceanside Seafood Restaurant* (☎ 952-2365) opposite Budha's Art Gallery, with a breeze-swept patio and dishes such as stuffed crab (US$10) and curried lobster (US$22).

Exuding ambience is *Norma's at the Wharf* (☎ 979-2745), in the old bayside warehouse of the Montpelier Estate. Norma Shirley has justifiably been acclaimed the 'Julia Child of the Caribbean.' The menu includes such dishes as deviled crab-back (US$8) and Châteaubriand in peppercorn sauce (US$30). It's not cheap, but Norma's food will have you salivating for more. Guests dine on the brick patio and wooden dock with views across the bay or inside the venerable limestone building full of antiques. There's a dark, brackish pool at the entrance where a Rasta squatter requests a fee for a dip, which locals swear by for its rejuvenative powers. It's open May to October only.

## Getting There & Away

Any of the buses or minibuses that ply the A1 between Montego Bay and Negril will let you off. From MoBay, it should cost no more than US$0.10 by bus or US$1 by minibus. A taxi should cost US$12.

## GREAT RIVER

This major river flows down from the hills of Hanover and is popular for scenic bamboo raft trips (see Lethe, later in this chapter). Snook can reportedly still be caught in the lower river course, and tarpon at the rivermouth.

## Entertainment

Each Tuesday, Thursday, and Sunday, *Great River Productions* (☎ 952-3732, fax 971-2435) offers an 'Evening on the Great River.' It costs US$30, including roundtrip

transfers from Montego Bay. You'll travel by fishing boat up the torch-lit river from its mouth, followed by a barbecue dinner with a calypso and limbo show, and dancing to live music. Trips depart Montego Bay at 7 pm.

## HOPEWELL

This small wayside village 5 miles west of Reading has a bustling market, especially on Saturday when the streets are cacophonous with higglers from the hills. Other than to browse the market, there's no need to stop. The rusting skeleton of the *Caribou*, an iron-hulled steamer that ran aground during a storm in the 1890s, still protrudes from the shore a mile west of Hopewell, in front of skinny Steamer Beach, which is popular on weekends with local families.

For an absorbing browse, stop at the Craft Potters, selling wicker, intriguing figurines, and huge pots and vases.

The Dolphin Head Mountains rise to the southwest inland of Hopewell. You can turn inland and follow a rugged road to Chigwell, where a right turn leads to Pondside, set in the midst of glorious mountainscapes in a region abundant with watery cascades. You'd do well to hire a guide if you choose to go swimming, particularly as the area is renowned for ganja production and it is unwise to blithely beat a path through the brush unawares. You can go diving with Jamaqua Water Sports (☎ 956-7050), located at Round Hill (see below), or North Coast Marine Sports (☎ 953-2211), at Half Moon and Round Hill.

## Places to Stay

At *Round Hill Hotel & Villas* (☎ 956-7050, 800-972-2159, fax 956-7505, PO Box 64, Montego Bay, www.roundhilljamaica.com), the roster of guests says it all: Steven Spielberg, Demi Moore, Meryl Streep, Paul McCartney, plus a smattering of Hapsburgs and Borgheses! It's been said that this is where the haughty come to be naughty. The 98-acre resort was created in 1954 as the first cottage-type hotel. Round Hill, about 2 miles west of the Great River and a mile east of Hopewell, bespeaks 'class' and has been lauded one of the best hotels in the world.

You might recognize it from scenes in the movie *How Stella Got Her Groove Back*. Elegant Resorts of Jamaica (☎ 800-237-3237, 020-7730-7144 in the UK) can provide information and reservations.

Pineapple House, the complex's main building, has 36 spacious and exquisitely decorated rooms overlooking the beach, each with massive windows shaded by canopies, plus Georgian antique furniture and mahogany beds, and floral prints (from US$220 to US$270 per room in low season, US$330 to US$420 high season). The 28 privately owned two, three, and four-bedroom villas on the hillside are as individual as thumbprints and cost US$310 to US$480 double in low season, US$520 to US$730 high season. Most are furnished to the owners' own tastes – Ralph Lauren owns one (he recently helped redecorate the resort's public areas) – and many have their own private pools. A meal plan costs US$85 daily.

Facilities include a gym, tennis courts, water sports, and a beauty salon, though everything eventually funnels down to the secluded beach. You can still gather around a piano where Noel Coward and Leonard Bernstein both entertained guests. Calypso is hosted on Monday nights, and there's live jazz three nights a week. The Saturday gala is a formal affair. And the star-studded Sugar Cane Ball is still held here each Christmas to raise money for charity. Otherwise it's serene. It's children-friendly and offers a family program.

### Places to Eat
The *Sports Club Restaurant & Bar* beside the entrance to Round Hill, offers Jamaican fare (US$3 to US$6) served in modestly elegant surrounds.

Hopewell's *bakery*, on the main street, is known for its harddough. Immediately west of Hopewell is the *Jamaica Micrazy Bar & Grill* (☎ 956-5448), a rustic oceanfront eatery where you can sample conch soup, seafood, and jerk pork and chicken with the locals. In a similar vein is *Tavern on the Beach* (☎ 956-5578), a seafood restaurant 50m farther west.

Lunch or dinner in the elegant *Georgian Dining Pavilion & Almond Tree Terrace* at Round Hill will cost at least US$12 for continental and Jamaican dishes. Dining on the shoreline terrace is a romantic indulgence, though entrees begin at US$25 and the menu, alas, uninspired. It's worth the splurge for the setting. Midafternoon tea is a bargain at US$3. Nonguests should call ahead.

### Getting There & Away
There's always a taxi available at Round Hill. Other taxis run constantly between Hopewell and MoBay. A 'robot' (shared taxi) should cost about US$1.

### TRYALL ESTATE
Many travelers whiz by the Tryall Water Wheel, 14 miles west of Montego Bay, without giving it a second glance, but it's well worth checking out. It stands amid the ruins of the old Tryall sugar plantation, 3 miles west of Hopewell. Much of the estate, including the huge wheel that drove the cane-crushing mill, was destroyed in the slave rebellion of Christmas 1831 (see 'Preaching Resistance,' in the Port Antonio & Northwest Coast chapter). Restored to working condition in the late 1950s, the wheel is still turned by water carried by a 2-mile-long aqueduct from the Flint River. (A sideroad just east of the waterwheel follows the river uphill to **Mayfield Falls & Mineral Springs**.)

The great house atop the hill is today the hub of one of Jamaica's most exclusive resort properties: the Tryall Club (see Places to Stay, below). The resort – formerly the Tryall Golf, Tennis & Beach Club – is built atop the remains of a small fort and is still guarded by cannons. The great house and 2200-acre resort complex are closed to nonguests, but you can park by the roadside to see the water wheel.

### Golf
You don't have to stay at the Tryall resort to enjoy a challenging round of golf on the championship, par 71, 6920-yard Tryall Golf Course (☎ 956-5660, 952-5111). The front nine holes parallel the sea; the back nine wind into the rolling hills, with some fabulous views. Green fees for Tryall Club guests are US$40 off season, US$60 in season;

nonguests pay about double. Caddies are available for US$15, as is cart rental (US$27). The splendid clubhouse is down by the sea and features a bar and restaurant. It's open year-round.

The famous course is host to the annual Johnny Walker World Championship, boasting the biggest purse in the world. About 15,000 spectators gather daily in mid-December to watch the world's leading players compete for the coveted title of 'World Champion.' The event is eagerly anticipated by the local community, as it generates hundreds of short-term jobs, and the Scottish whisky company also contributes heavily to local charities and schools.

### Places to Stay & Eat

The *Tryall Club (☎ 956-5660, 800-336-4571 in North America, ☎ 01753-684810 in the UK, PO Box 1206, Montego Bay, tryallclub@ cwjamaica.com, www.connectabltd.co.uk)* is magnificently situated amid 2200 acres of lush hillside greenery. At its heart is the old hilltop great house with a bar and lounge where you can savor a traditional English afternoon tea while enjoying the views.

The house had its roof ripped off by Hurricane Gilbert in 1988. It has since been restored and guest rooms formerly located in the historic house have metamorphosed into one-bedroom Great House Villas, each fully staffed and with kitchen, living room, dining room, and oversized marble bathroom, renting for US$350 to US$650 one-bedroom, US$420 to US$1000 two-bedroom, depending on season. A new wing includes 52 gracious, air-conditioned Junior Suites for US$200 in summer, US$350 in winter, US$450 peak season. More than 55 private villas are scattered throughout the estate and cost US$420 to US$1037 two-bedroom, to US$772 to US$1886 six-bedroom, depending on the season. All are stunning. Choose between up in the hills or down by the water. Each is uniquely decorated by individual owners and staffed with cook, housekeeper, laundress, and gardener. A farmer's market is held on site each Monday for guests to purchase food. There's a large pool set into the hillside beside the gourmet restaurant and bar.

The rustic *Momma Coffies*, just east of Tryall, offers seafood dishes served amid lawns behind a pier with cannons.

### SANDY BAY

This hamlet immediately west of Tryall began as a 'free village' founded by Rev Thomas Burchell for emancipated slaves. His Baptist church, dating to 1848, still stands. Many locals are christened Burchell in the Jamaican custom of honoring people they admire.

West of town, watch for **Blue Hole Estate**, a charming old great house backed by hills, fronted by wide pasture, and with a stump of a windmill at the edge of the former polo field. It was once the home of William DeLisser, former custos of Hanover parish, who owned a sugar estate and factory here. It's not open to the public.

The new high-speed highway to Negril, still in progress at press time, begins at Sandy Bay.

### Places to Stay & Eat

*Lollypop on the Beach (☎ 953-5314)* has two small, basic, but clean air-conditioned rooms with cold water. They're overpriced at US$27 per night and are directly above the stage and dance area, but there's no denying the place has offbeat atmosphere!

Lollypop is very popular with locals for its mouth-searing jerk pork and chicken, and as a well-known dance hall. It gets packed to the beams on Fridays, when its reggae and dancehall night pulls tourists from as far afield as MoBay and Negril. It offers packages from Negril, including Carnival Nite on Tuesdays (US$20), Jamaica Beach Party Nite on Wednesdays (US$45 including unlimited beer, glass-bottom boat cruise, and roundtrip transfers from hotels in Negril), a Friday night seafood fiesta, and 'golden oldies' on Sunday.

# Inland: South of Montego Bay

The hill country south and east of MoBay is replete with attractions, including a variety

View of Cockpit Country at Good Hope Estate

Local architecture, Falmouth

Round Hill, Montego Bay

Oh, the options at the Montego Bay market

Albert Town, a market center at the edge of Cockpit Country

Bamboo rafting down the Martha Brae River

of working plantations, several great houses, evolving eco-resorts, and a village of poor white farmers that is one of Jamaica's strangest anomalies. Most points of interest are reached either via the B8, which winds south from Reading and crosses a broad upland plateau before dropping onto the plains of Westmoreland, or the B6, which leads southeast from Montpelier (6 miles south of Reading).

The southeast quarter of St James parish culminates in the wild Cockpit Country accessed from Montego Bay by the Queen of Spains Valley or via the road to John's Hall and Maroon Town. See Cockpit Country (North), later in this chapter.

## LETHE

This small village is the starting point for raft trips on the Great River. Lethe is in the hills about 4 miles south of Reading; signs show the way. The graceful stone bridge spanning the Great River was built in 1828. The overgrown remains of an old sugar mill remain on the riverbank.

Driving west, you'll arrive at a Y-junction 2 miles east of Lethe. The fork to the left leads to Lethe; that to the right leads to **Nature Village Farm**, a farm-turned-family-resort that offers fishing and other attractions. The site is the venue for the annual 'All That Heritage & Jazz Festival' (☎ 979-7963, 952-6231), held in mid-October. (See Special Events in the Montego Bay section, earlier in this chapter.)

### Rhea's World

Rhea's World (which doubles as the main office for Mountain Valley Rafting), on the west bank of the river on the north side of Lethe, has a water garden and mini-botanical gardens where anthuriums are grown for export (don't stroke the snapper turtles kept in a small pool; their bite can take a finger off). A jitney tour leads into the adjacent banana plantation. Kids can take a donkey ride while adults laze in a hammock with a rum cocktail or coconut water. It's part of Lethe Estate, owned by Francis Tulloch, Minister of Tourism. A restaurant provides hot lunches for US$10.

### Rafting

Mountain Valley Rafting (☎ 956-4920, fax 956-4927), c/o Great River Rafting & Plantation Tour Ltd, PO Box 23, Montego Bay, offers tranquil two-hour river trips from Lethe. You're punted 9 miles downstream to the mouth of the river aboard long, narrow bamboo rafts poled by an expert raftsman. The waters are generally calm and, depending on river conditions, good for swimming beside the raft or in calm pools. The journey includes a stop at Lethe Estate. An optional plantation tour is also offered. Trips cost US$45 for two passengers (children under 12 are half price), including lunch and transfers, or US$36 for the raft trip alone. The company has an office on Gloucester Ave in Montego Bay.

### Kayaking

The section from Lethe to the estuary also provides one of Jamaica's best white-water kayak runs. The journey was pioneered in 1983 by Peter Bentley (of now-defunct Sense Adventures) and John Yost of Sobek Expeditions in California, though locals implored the 11-man team not to canoe downstream.

The first 5 miles lead through spectacular gorges with sheer rock walls festooned with foliage. The waters are usually calm, with a few white-water sections (Class 2 or 3). A sharp bend in the river announces a change of pace. The river tumbles through more than a dozen rapids that increase in difficulty (some are Class 5, listed as 'extremely challenging') and require scouting. The run varies markedly throughout the year. During heavy rains the river can rise as much as 25 feet, reaching the graceful old stone bridge in Lethe. Inflatable rafts are recommended because of the many sharp rocks.

### Places to Stay

An Italian woman (Francesca) and Rastafarian (Neville) offer *camping* for US$10 per tent on their lawn at Copse, a mile southwest of Lethe.

*Busha's Country Resort & Farm* (☎ 952-0712) is a modest and rather run-down retreat on the site of a former sugar plantation and slave village (you can still see rusting sugar kettles and graying gravestones), but marvelously out of the way and surrounded by 200 acres of farmland and forest good for hiking. The place is popular with religious groups on weekends. Facilities include an outside bar under shade and kiddie swings, but the swimming pool was derelict at this writing. Rooms cost US$24 single or double, US$30 for studio with kitchenette. To reach it, take a dirt road that begins a mile west of the junction with the B8 on the road to Lethe.

*Lethe Estate* (☎ *956-4920, fax 956-4927, PO Box 23, Montego Bay)* is a delightful riverside hotel with 14 elegantly furnished air-conditioned rooms in an old two-story building boasting a large open lounge, a bar with piano and TV, and patio dining under an arbor over the river. Rooms have wooden floors, four-poster mahogany beds, and reproduction antiques, plus fans and balconies. Rates are US$190 double in winter, including breakfast.

### Getting There & Away

The turnoff for Lethe is 2 miles south of Reading. Drive carefully up Long Hill, a steep and narrow ascent southward from Reading; the serpentine road is heavily trafficked with buses and trucks.

## ROCKLANDS BIRD FEEDING STATION

Rocklands (☎ 952-2009) is a favorite of birders who have flocked here since 1958 when it was founded by Miss Lisa Salmon, who has tamed and trained over 20 bird species to come and feed from your hand. A variety of birds show up reliably at 3:15 pm: ground doves, orange quits, saffron finches, and hummingbirds, including the 'doctorbird.' Unfortunately the elderly Miss Salmon, with her amazing repertoire of bird lore and a renowned keen humor, is limited by ailing health. Her replacement guide, Fritz, is also an expert on birds.

Fritz, or another attendant, will pour birdseed into your hand or provide you with a sugar-water feeder with which to tempt birds. Seats are arranged theater-style on a stone patio festooned with orchids and other plants and from where there is a miraculous view over Montego Bay. Guests sit in religious awe as a hummingbird streaks in to hover like a miniature helicopter before finally perching on an outstretched finger – hopefully yours. Soon, half a dozen or more birds may be feeding. Over 140 birds have been recorded. When I last called in, *three* doctorbirds came streaming in.

Rocklands is open 2 to 5 pm or longer, depending on the lighting. No calls are accepted after 6 pm, as Miss Salmon is early to bed. You can make a special appointment for an early morning walk with Fritz. Entrance costs US$5.

The turnoff to the east from the B8 is 200 yards south of the signed turnoff for Lethe. The dirt road to Rocklands (400 yards) climbs steeply. You can also take a bus from Montego Bay for Savanna-la-Mar or Black River. There's a bus stop on the B8 near the turnoff for Rocklands.

## ANCHOVY

The only reason to stop at this nondescript village is to view **Mt Carey Baptist Church** on a knoll on the right, about a mile south of town. The church was the headquarters for Rev Thomas Burchell (1799-1846), a leading missionary in the fight for emancipation. An obelisk commemorates the abolitionist, who founded the Baptist movement in western Jamaica.

In town there is a post office, police station, and several restaurants, including the *Anchovy Progressive Pork Shop* serving jerk pork, grilled fish, and so on.

You might call in at Anchovy Furniture Factory, where you can order handcrafted four-poster beds and other large hardwood pieces for delivery, but at least one couple prepaid for furniture and had not received anything two years later. It's on the B8, a mile south of the village.

## MONTPELIER

South of Anchovy, you drop down into a broad valley planted in the citrus trees of Montpelier Estates, formerly an important sugar estate now owned by the Jamaica

Orange Company. The Ministry of Agriculture also maintains an important cattle research station, assisted by the New Zealand government. It was here, in the 1890s, that Zebu cattle (from Africa) and Mysore cattle (from India) were first crossed with native stock to produce a Jamaican breed of draft cattle.

The great house of the old Montpelier sugar plantation burned down a few years back, but St Mary's Anglican Church still stands on a knoll overlooking the remains of the sugar factory.

The B8 splits at a gas station, a stone's throw south of the church. The main road continues south. The road to the southeast (the B6) leads toward Seaford Town.

### Montpelier Blue Hole Nature Park

This 800-acre 'eco-park,' (☎ 909-9002), PO Box 26, Cambridge, St James is 3 miles south of Anchovy in the hills east of the valley. A guided plantation tour is offered, and horseback rides are planned through the groves of interspersed pineapple and citrus. There are botanical gardens and picnic groves, plus an impressive 60-foot-wide circular swimming pool with meandering cascades. A bird and wildlife sanctuary is in the planning stage. Meals are served alfresco at a thatched restaurant and bar. The park is open 8 am to 5 pm and costs US$3 (children US$1).

The park owners permit camping (bring your own tent) and have toilets and cooking facilities.

Look for the signed turnoff 400 yards north of the gas station at Montpelier. You'll see St Mary's Church ahead; keep to the right and follow the potholed road steeply uphill for 2 miles.

About 400 yards beyond the park entrance is the Blue Hole – a jade-colored sinkhole measuring 164 feet deep (but only 12 feet wide). It's been tapped by the Water Commission to supply local communities, so iron fences have spoiled the setting. No swimming!

### CAMBRIDGE

From Montpelier, the B6 follows the Great River Valley 5 miles to this little crossroads

town centered on a railroad station in disuse. Cambridge (population 3000) seems small and insignificant, but it's the second largest town in St James parish and the center of a banana and coffee producing area. It has a bank and gas station. Be sure to call in at Lou Lou's to check out the colorful crafts store run by its equally colorful namesake (see below).

### Places to Stay & Eat

Half a mile south of Cambridge at Mount Faith, just beyond the crest of a hill, is *Lou Lou's*, a gaily painted little crafts shop and restaurant. Don't fail to stop! Lou Lou is a jovial, charismatic figure, with a small, rather basic two-bedroom cottage behind her store. Furnishings are bare, but it's clean and has a small balcony. She says it rents for US$57 per night (overpriced; did I misunderstand her?) or US$114 a week (a bargain), but these rates are probably negotiable.

If you're hungry, try her fried chicken and fish, mutton, and pepperpot soup (US$2 to US$5). You can also buy fresh coconuts to slake your thirst (US$0.60). 'We no rush people here. Leave de visitors to dem mind.' Her grandson, Fitzroy 'Tony' Dove, offers guiding locally.

### MARCHMONT

This crossroads is the gateway to Croydon and Catadupa (east), and Seaford Town (southwest). Just south of Marchmont lies a Rastafarian retreat, unmistakable with its vividly painted walls. Casual camera-touting visitors are discouraged. A grocery store sits at the four-way junction.

### CATADUPA

Twenty years ago, locals had a thriving trade selling crafts and making clothing to order for passengers en route to the Appleton Rum Estate (you were measured for skirts or shirts en route to Appleton and they were finished and ready for pick up on the way back). Today Catadupa is a collection of aging buildings around the railroad station. Locals eke out a living growing coffee and bananas, but the population has dwindled

40% since the Appleton Express stopped calling. Dalkeith Hann, owner of Croydon Plantation, can no longer find workers to pick coffee.

The village is named for some nearby cascades and reflects the Greek name for the Nile cataracts in Egypt.

In Catadupa, the road from Marchmont swings right at the railway station and leads uphill to Mocho and Maroon Town (Mocho is a common place name defined by the *Dictionary of Jamaican English* as 'a place of symbolic remoteness – a rough uncivilized place,' but also used colloquially as an insult, much like the English 'bumpkin'). You'll need a 4WD vehicle to handle the bone-jarring ride. 'Road bad to 'ell, mon,' an old timer told me. What an understatement! You can also get to Catadupa directly by bus from the Parade in Kingston (about US$1.50).

## Croydon Plantation

This working plantation(☎ 979-8267), also named Croydon on the Mountain, has 132 acres of hillside terraces planted in coffee, citrus, and five varieties of pineapples. Honey is produced here, and a hive under glass allows you to see what's buzzing in the bees' world. Croydon, reached via a sideroad from Catadupa (1 mile), has a fabulous setting and spectacular views. The terrain is too hilly for mechanization, as will be explained to you on a 'see, hear, touch, and taste' tour offered from 10:30 am to 3 pm daily (except Sunday). The tour costs US$45, including lunch and transfers.

Advance reservations are advisable. Be sure to call ahead, as the gates may otherwise be padlocked.

Caribic Vacations (☎ 953-9878, 979-9387, fax 953-9897, 979-3421) offers a Croydon Plantation Tour from Montego Bay.

From Montego Bay, the plantation is a 45-minute journey by bus.

## HILTON

This beautiful old plantation home (☎ 952-3343, 952-5642), PO Box 162, Reading, St James, has a splendid hilltop location at St Leonards, 2 miles southwest of Marchmont. The house is overgrown with thumbergia that hangs over the veranda, from which you'll savor tremendous views. Antiques abound.

The house is the venue for the all-day 'Hilton High Day Tour,' which begins with a Jamaican breakfast in the house. You then take a guided walk to Seaford Town (1 mile) and the village of St Leonards. The walk should create an appetite for a roast-suckling-pig luncheon prepared in a brick oven back at Hilton. You're led down to the pigsties, where there are dozens of little piggies. Say 'hi!' to your future lunch. The meal also features a choice of homemade lemonade (fantastic!), shandy (half lemonade, half beer), or rum punch. For the rest of the afternoon, you're free to relax or roam the 100-acre plantation on horseback.

Tours are offered on Tuesday, Wednesday, Friday, and Sunday (US$55 for call-in visitors; US$65, including transfers, from Montego Bay). Horseback rides cost US$10 for 30 minutes using English saddle. The hot-air balloon rides for which Hilton was once famous are no longer offered.

## SEAFORD TOWN

This sprawling village has a singular history. Its scattered tumbledown cottages follow a traditional German design that points to Seaford's unusual origin. The hillside village was settled by German immigrants in 1835 as part of the colonial program of establishing European settlements in Jamaica after emancipation.

Between 1834 and 1838, more than 1200 Germans arrived in Jamaica, of which an initial group of 251 settled Seaford (along with a dozen or so English families). The land – 500 acres on Montpelier Mountain – was donated by Lord Seaford, who owned 10,000 acres locally (the Germans were promised that they would receive title to their land after five years' labor; they toiled for 15 before the land became theirs).

The farmland that the Germans had been promised turned out to be a tangled wilderness. And only a few of the settlers were farmers; most were tradespeople or former soldiers. Fortunately, the immigrants received free rations for the first 18 months, but even before the rations ran out, the Germans had settled into a life of poverty. Tropical diseases and social isolation soon reduced the population to less than 100 within two or three years. Only a fraction of the original settlers stayed. Those that remained established a viable German community whose legacy is felt to this day.

Less than 200 Seaford inhabitants can claim German ancestry; the rest have emigrated over the past few decades. Today, white people are only 20% of Seaford's population. Still, despite 150 years, there are relatively few mulattos in evidence. Socially, Seaford remains segregated in key ways.

The initial community was a mix of Protestants and Catholics, but most were converted to Catholicism by Father Tauer, an energetic Austrian priest who settled here in the 1870s. Seaford's white residents remain practicing Catholics and still practice a few folk customs. German is rarely spoken.

### Seaford Town Historical Mini-Museum

This tiny museum (☎ 995-9399) tells the fascinating tale of Seaford's German origins. There are maps and photographs of the early settlement, plus artifacts spanning 150 years, including such curiosities as cricket bats made from the stems of coconut leaves. Overhead, note the list of original settlers and their trades.

Entrance costs US$1. The town priest, Friar Bobby Gilmore, keeps the key to the museum; he lives in the green-and-white house opposite the museum. However, you should first seek out the caretaker, Spencer Gardner, who lives 100 yards beyond the museum; his house is the last in the row along a dirt road just below the health center. Spencer has plans to publish a history of the Seaford Germans.

### Church of the Sacred Heart

This red, zinc-roofed old stone structure sits atop a rise overlooking Seaford. Its precursor was built by Father Tauer in the late 19th century but was totally demolished in the hurricane of 1912, when even the 1000lb foundation stones were picked up and tossed down the hill. Take time to browse the overgrown graveyard.

The road beyond the church continues uphill to the government-run St Boniface Industrial Training Centre, which provides training in technical trade, and a health clinic.

### Places to Stay & Eat

*Johnson's Circle Tree Bar*, 100 yards west of the turnoff for the church in Seaford Town, has shaded outdoor dining. Mr Johnson rents basic rooms with cold water only. You're sure to find someone else who'll rent a room by asking around.

*Ripple's Grocery, Ice Cream Store & Restaurant* is the only other eatery of note.

### BELVEDERE ESTATE

Belvedere (☎ 956-4710, 957-4170 in Negril, fax 957-4097), PO Box 361, Montego Bay, is a family-owned working plantation of 1000 acres, of which 500 are cultivated with tropical fruits. Red Poll cattle graze the other 500 acres.

The estate offers a fascinating perspective on modern estate life and a touristy but intriguing re-creation of how things were centuries ago. You're welcomed by guides in Jamaican-bandanna prints offering sugarloaf and pineapple and orange samplers, while a farmhand coaxes a donkey in circles to demonstrate the workings of an old sugar press. If you've arrived under your own steam, a guide will come in your car as you drive through the groves of citrus and coconut palms and fields of Scotch bonnet peppers. The guide will also walk you through the botanical gardens and Post-Emancipation Village, featuring huts where a basket-weaver, baker, blacksmith, and coffee and cocoa grinder demonstrate traditional skills.

Trails lead to the Great River. There's a waterfall where you may bathe.

It's open 10 am to 3:30 pm, Monday to Saturday. The entrance with tour costs US$10, or US$25 including a Jamaican lunch in a thatched restaurant where a mento band provides entertainment. A tour by tractor-pulled jitney is in the works, and horseback riding was to be introduced. Pat McGann, the owner, is restoring one of the two old great houses (destroyed in the 1831 slave rebellion) as a guest house.

Belvedere is at Chester Castle, 3 miles southwest of Montpelier (take the B7, which splits from the B8). Excursions to Belvedere are available through tour operators in Montego Bay.

Belvedere is served from MoBay by minibus. You can also take another minibus that travels between MoBay and Darliston; ask the driver to drop you at Chester Castle, and walk the rest of the way.

## STRUIE

Struie, 5 miles south of Chester Castle and 5 miles west of Seaford Town, is known for its roadside tomb of a British solder killed in an ambush during the slave rebellion of Christmas 1831. Legend says that his head was severed and fled the scene. Locals believe the area to be haunted by the soldier's ghost; listen carefully at night and you may be able to hear the clash of swords.

## KNOCKALVA

Following the B8 southwest from Montpelier leads to Knockalva, the center of an agricultural training farm that for over a century has been a leading cattle breeding center. The school is centered on a great house built in 1859 and later modified in Asian-Gothic style by a Scottish freemason, Major Malcolm, with pillars and arches echoing Solomon's Temple. The garden he laid out was his version of Gethsemane.

The hills south of Knockalva are festooned with spectacular groves of bamboo. Five miles south of Knockalva you pass through the village of Whithorn. As you round a bend immediately beyond it, the sugarcane plains of Westmoreland are suddenly laid out below, with the twin white stacks of the Frome sugar plantation in the distance (see the Frome section in the Negril & West Coast chapter).

### Places to Stay & Eat

On a bend just south of Haddo is *Capitol*, a bar and gift store. You can't miss the mural of Bob Marley on the outside wall. Owners Gillian and Marilyn Stewart (he Jamaican, she Canadian) were preparing three simple rooms for rent at this writing.

Restaurants are in short supply. *Leslie's Place* at Haddo is a funky rum shop and restaurant where you can sup a Red Stripe and eat curried goat with locals for about US$3.

## QUEEN OF SPAINS VALLEY

About 2 miles south of Montego Bay, the Montego River twists through a narrow, thickly wooded gorge and eventually deposits you at **Adelphi**, 13 miles east of Montego Bay, at the head of the Queen of Spains Valley. The valley is as flat and green as a billiard table, with sugarcane rippling silver-tipped as far as the eye can see. Adelphi is a modest village of no visual appeal. It was here, however, that a Quaker, Isaac Lascelles Winn, bought an estate known as 'Stretch and Set' (the name was derived from the cruel punishment previously meted out here), named it Adelphi, and hired a free-black Baptist minister, Moses Baker, to administer religious instruction and education to his slaves – the first estate owner ever to do so in Jamaica.

Reggae star Jimmy Cliff, who became an international sensation overnight in the film *The Harder They Come*, has a home near Lima, a mile east of Adelphi.

A number of hiking trails through the Montego River Valley begin at Sign Great House (☎ 979-4394, fax 927-7539), No 5 Sign PO, St James. You'll find streams with large pools for swimming, notably at the Old Bridge – locally called 'the dam' – deep enough for diving.

The valley runs east as far as Good Hope, on the edge of Cockpit Country. See Cockpit Country (North), later in this chapter.

### Hampden Estate

Three miles east of Adelphi, Hampden is a working plantation with a rum distillery, sugar factory, and great house still in the hands of the original family. The property straddles the border of St James and Trelawny parishes. The plantation house is one of the most impressive and beautiful buildings in Jamaica, well worth the drive. It's a highly unusual whitewashed structure with dark timbers and mansard roof. The house dates back to 1799 and is enclosed within dry-stone walls with the factory immediately beside, steaming gently. The factory – built by Krupps, of Germany – processes 160,000 tons of sugar per year, and operates 24 hours a day, seven days a week, between January and July. It closes for renovations in the summer. The distillery operates February through October and produces one million liters of absolute alcohol (double the strength of bottled rum), so you should beware when sampling. It is hotter than Hades within, and 'louder than the hottest disco,' thought writer Gully Wells. Wells described his experience at the distillery:

[Crossing a] bridge that been cunningly constructed from odd bits of leftover metal held together with wire and rusty nails, [I] looked down and saw, a few inches beneath my feet, huge bubbling vats of liquid fire and a rapacious machine that looked like the innards of the kind of garbage truck that munches up old washing machines.

Understandably, children are not allowed upon the rickety gangway.

Today, two brothers, David and Richard Farquharson, hope to squeeze four harvests annually, instead of two, from their land, thus doubling their yield, with the help of a new high-tech Israeli irrigation system.

The factory is open by appointment for guided tours, 9 am to 4 pm Monday to Friday (US$12 adults, US$8 children) in sugar season only and includes a tasting tipple, but be warned that the overproof rum called 'jancro batty' is 170% alcohol – almost strong enough to burn a hole through armorplating. Ask for John Terry, the charming English manager.

If coming from Adelphi, you'll pass through fields of tall sugarcane. Turn left at the road junction with an old steam engine sitting in a triangle. There are no signs. The smell of molasses and 'dunder' (the liquid waste from sugar-making) will guide you through the rippling fields.

## Places to Stay & Eat
A relatively undiscovered gem is *Sign Great House* (☎ 979-4394, fax 927-7539, No 5 Sign PO, St James), 5 miles east of Montego Bay, an old great house that has been brought back from dereliction and recently evolved into an intimate inn. It is set on 40 acres, with a fishing pond, the Montego River, and hiking trails close at hand. It has a swimming pool, bar, and reasonably priced open-air restaurant.

## Getting There & Away
A bus travels through the Queen of Spains Valley via Hampden from Montego Bay (US$0.20).

## MONTEGO BAY TO MAROON TOWN
Few travelers venture into the hills southeast of Montego Bay, accessed by Fairfield Rd, 1½ miles south of town. The potholed road ascends to the western flanks of Cockpit Country. A smattering of attractions may appeal to history buffs.

### Kensington
This hamlet, 13 miles southeast of Montego Bay, is famous as the site where, in 1831, slaves set fire to the ridgetop plantation and initiated the devastating 'Christmas Rebellion' (see 'Preaching Resistance,' earlier in this chapter). A roadside plaque erected by the Jamaica National Heritage Trust commemorates the event.

### Maroon Town
Despite its name, this crossroads village (3 miles southeast of Kensington) was never a center for Maroons. You're now on the edge of the rugged Cockpit Country.

In 1739, after decades of fighting a guerrilla war with the Maroons of St James, Governor Edward Trelawny despatched Colonel John Guthrie to make peace with Cudjoe, the Maroon leader. They signed a treaty that granted the Maroons 1500 acres of land around Petty River, which was renamed Trelawny Town. Cudjoe was named hereditary chief of the Maroons, who were granted virtual autonomy, including the sole right to serve justice on their own people. Peace lasted for half a century. Unfortunately, a second Maroon War commenced in 1795 (see 'The Tide Turns' under History in the Facts about Jamaica chapter).

Over 1500 British soldiers were engaged in the guerrilla war that ensued. Eventually, bloodhounds were imported from Cuba and used to track down the Maroons. Under the ruse of negotiating a peace treaty, the British seized the Maroon leaders and loaded them aboard ships for transport to Halifax, Nova Scotia (many died of the cold, and the survivors were eventually shipped to Sierra Leone, becoming the first Africans ever repatriated from the Americas). Trelawny Town was razed and a barracks built for British soldiers.

In 1992, four locals formed Maroon Pride, a community-based banana-chip-producing enterprise that you can visit. There's little else of interest here, but 2 miles east of town in the tiny hamlet of Flagstaff, on the site of Trelawny Town, a few remains of the military site can today be discerned (the dirt road peters out in the lee of a deep cockpit, about a half mile beyond Flagstaff). Guides will tout themselves to lead you to nearby caves and battle sites; some quote a whopping US$20. Be prepared to bargain.

### Places to Stay & Eat
The **Orange River Ranch** (☎ 979-3294, 995-0780, 914-639-1916 in the USA, Johns Hall PO, Montego Bay, orngervr@infochan.com) is a gracious old plantation house on 998 acres in the hills a mile north of Williamsfield (near Johns Hall, about 6 miles southeast of Montego Bay), with views down the valley awash with bamboo. It focuses on holistic vacations under the direction of metaphysician Alea. The 24 simple, appealingly furnished rooms have half-poster beds, telephones, fans, and small patios. If you arrive for an impromptu meal, it may be cooked to order, which sometimes takes over an hour. A guided walking tour of the banana plantation is available, as is horseback riding (US$28 per hour), and there's a swimming pool and Jacuzzi. The lodge allows camping for US$5 per tent. It also has modest dormitory accommodations for US$10, and the more attractive rooms are US$55 single or double; or US$64/70 single/double, including breakfast, and US$84/106 including dinner. A beach shuttle runs twice daily. A family brunch is hosted each Sunday.

# Cockpit Country (North)

Jamaica's most rugged quarter is a dramatic, sculpted 500-sq-mile limestone plateau taking up the whole of southwest Trelawny, inland of Falmouth. The area, which is pockmarked with deep depressions, is a classic example of karst scenery: an area of eroded limestone features studded with thousands of conical hummocks divided by precipitous ravines. Over millions of years, the limestone accumulated on the seabed before being uplifted about 20 million years ago. It has since been eroded into fantastic formations. Though similar terrain extends east all the way through Trelawny and St Ann parishes to the border with St Mary, nowhere is it as dramatic as in the area known as the Cockpit Country.

The daunting region is overgrown with luxuriant greenery. Most remains unexplored, unexploited, and virtually uninhabited. No roads penetrate the region (although a rough dirt road cuts across the eastern edge between Clark's Town and Albert Town) and only a few tracks make even half-hearted forays into its interior. Even by 4WD you can explore only its outer edges; otherwise it is accessible solely by hiking along overgrown trails. The most dramatic way to see it is from above by plane or helicopter, from which you gain a dramatic sense of the Cockpits' scale and beauty. From the sky, the area looks like a giant upturned egg carton.

Covered in dense vegetation, the reclusive, untamed Cockpit Country proved a perfect hideout for the Maroons, who through their ferocity maintained an uneasy sovereignty from the English colonialists (see 'A Renaissance of Pride' in the Southwest Coast chapter). The southern section is known as 'District of Look Behind,' an allusion to the Maroon practice of ambushing English soldiers. Much of the vegetation around the perimeter has been cleared in recent years by charcoal burners. And a few valley bottoms are cultivated by small-hold farmers who grow bananas, yams, corn, manioc, and ganja in the deep red earth. It's unwise for foreigners to explore here unless accompanied by someone known in the area. You could easily get lost or worse, if you stumble upon a major plot, you're likely to be considered a DEA (Drug Enforcement Agency) agent, and the consequences could be serious (in 1994, a foreign journalist was murdered after such a transgression).

The area – a vital watershed and home to several endangered species – has been earmarked for national park status (it is currently a National Reserve). However, the proposal has received vehement opposition from the leaders of the latter-day Maroons, who claim that its establishment would directly challenge their sovereignty. The Cockpit Country is listed as Crown Land and remains the subject of a long-standing dispute between the Maroons and the government.

Early morning in the Cockpits is magical! Mists float through the eerily silent valley bottoms where you hear only dripping water and birdlife.

The southern portion of Cockpit Country lies in St Elizabeth parish and is accessed from the south by sideroads from the B6. See the Nassau Mountains & Cockpit Country (South) section in the Southwest Coast chapter.

## Flora & Fauna
The Cockpits are virtually unsullied by humans and the area is replete with wildlife – a temptation for birders and nature lovers. Most of the Cockpits are still clad in primary vegetation that in places includes rare cacti and other endemic species known only in that specific locale. Vegetation differs markedly from top to bottom, and from

north to south-facing slopes. Northern slopes typically are more lush, with rain forests draped with epiphytes, ferns, and mosses. The hilltops are relatively sparsely vegetated due to soil erosion. The Cockpits themselves are generally covered in tall scrub, including brambles and scratchbush, the serrated leaves of which can leave you itching for weeks.

Most of Jamaica's 27 endemic bird species are found in the Cockpits, including black and yellow-billed parrots, todies, and the endangered golden swallow. Keep a sharp eye out for the harmless and now rare Jamaican boa. With luck you may also see giant swallowtail butterflies, the largest butterfly in the Western Hemisphere.

## Hiking
A few hunter's tracks lead into and even across the Cockpit Country. You can follow overgrown Maroon trails with a guide to lead the way. Most trails are faint, rocky tracks, often overgrown. Hiking away from these trails can be dangerous going. The rocks are razor-sharp, and sinkholes are everywhere, often covered by decayed vegetation and ready to crumble underfoot. Never travel alone. There is no one to hear your pleas for help should you break a leg or fall into a sinkhole. Don't underestimate how strenuous and hot it can be. Take plenty of water, and drink only sparingly. There is no water to be had locally (except from the bug-filled tanks of bromeliads that are also perfect breeding grounds for mosquitoes) due to the porous nature of limestone.

You'll need a machete and stout walking shoes plus raingear and a powerful flashlight in the event of a delay past sunset. Take warm clothing if you plan on overnighting, as nights can get cold.

The easiest trail across the Cockpits connects Windsor (in the north) with Crown Lands and Troy, about 10 miles as the crow flies. It's a full day's hike with a guide. The southbound trail begins at the fork where you branch right for the Windsor Caves; the trail is the left-hand fork. It is a more difficult hike southbound, leading gradually uphill; an easier option is to begin in Troy and take the downhill route (see Troy in the Southwest Coast chapter).

In Windsor, you can hire either Martell or Franklyn Taylor as guides. (Not many locals know the way across the Cockpits. Ascertain whether your prospective guide really does know the way, as he may merely have convinced himself – and you – that this is the case for the sake of your dollars.)

Albert Town, on the east flank of the Cockpits, is evolving as a base for organized hikes.

## Spelunking

The Cockpits are laced with caves, most of them uncharted. Guides lead trips into the more well-known caverns. Elsewhere, exploring is for experienced and properly outfitted spelunkers only. Many caves harbor underground rivers, which can rise dramatically during rains. There is no rescue organization, and you enter at your own risk. *Jamaica Underground* by Alan Fincham is a rare but essential compendium providing the most thorough information available on the island's charted caves. It's published by the Jamaica Caving Club (☎ 927-6661), c/o Dept of Geology, University of the West Indies, Kingston 7.

## Organized Tours

Few organized tours operate in this fantastic and primitive region, reflecting the undeveloped state of Jamaica's adventure tourism and ecotourism.

Cockpit Country Adventure Tours, in Albert Town, is managed by the Southern Trelawny Environmental Agency (☎ 610-0818) and uses local guides trained by US Peace Corp workers. Tours originate in Albert Town. The 'Burnt Hill Natural History Tour' is a 'light adventure' through the District of Look Behind (US$15 per person, or US$10 per person with groups of more than five people). The 'Rock Spring Cave' tour is a 'medium adventure' that leads you through this cave full of fascinating formations that will get you all wet and muddy (US$40 per person, US$35 with more than five people). The 'Quashie River Sink and Cave' is a 'high adventure' into the rugged Freeman's Hall

district, accessed by steep ladders or a thrilling 150-foot rappel to the Quashie River, including rummaging the 2½-mile-long Quashie Cave with its 'Cathedral Room' and underground waterfall (US$35 per person for more than five people). Two days' notice is required.

Also try Trelawny Adventure Guides (☎ 919-6992, 990-6034) in Albert Town, with a similar range of trips.

Sun Ventures (☎ 960-6685, fax 929-7512), 30 Balmoral Ave, Kingston 10, offers guided hikes into the Cockpits including a 'Serpent Trail' trip that's undertaken, ostensibly, in search of the Jamaican boa.

The Touring Society of Jamaica (☎ 975-7158, fax 975-3620, www.touringjamaica.com), c/o Island Outpost, PO Box 118, Ocho Rios, has a 7-day 'Bird Watcher's Jamaica Tour' for groups of 10 or more, visiting Cockpit Country – focused around Barbecue Bottom – and the Blue Mountains. Noted birding authorities Robert Sutton (co-author of *Birds of Jamaica*) acts as guide; US$3345 includes accommodations at Good Hope, Marshall's Pen, and Strawberry Hill. Company owner, Lynda Lee Burkes, can custom design tours for birders, spelunkers, and hikers. You can also call Robert Sutton in Mandeville (☎ 904-5454). He can organize birding and nature hikes from Mandeville.

Also see Clark's Town and Albert Town, later in this chapter.

## GOOD HOPE ESTATE

This marvelous great house and working plantation is 8 miles south of Falmouth. The property is set on the very northern edge of Cockpit Country, and the views over the Cockpits have no rival. It overlooks the lush Queen of Spains Valley (see, Queen of Spains, earlier in this chapter), with undulating fields of papaya and lime-green sugarcane framed by a rim of mountains.

The estate, which is watered by the Martha Brae River and is called 'Bad Hope' by the locals because of its painful associations with slavery, was settled in 1742 and the house – which is today a hotel and restaurant open only to guests – was built around 1755 atop a hillock. The property was owned by John

Tharp (1744-1804), who became the richest man in Jamaica. At one time he owned 10,000 acres and 3000 slaves in Trelawny and St James parishes (Tharp had seven neighboring estates and reportedly kept a mistress on each). Displeased with all four of his sons, he left his entire estate to his only grandson. Unfortunately, the 21-year-old heir was a simpleton – but a wealthy one! Marriage offers were made and a wedding arranged with a titled lady. The poor fellow apparently found the experience too much and is said to have lost his wits on his wedding night. He lived another 67 years, totally unaware of the constant lawsuits that whittled away at John Tharp's fortune. The property went into decline, mismanaged by a series of agents.

The estate office and slave hospital still stand, as does the sugar works by the riverbank.

### Horseback Riding

Good Hope maintains a fine stable. You can take rides along trails that lead through the plantation and along the banks of the Martha Brae. Guided tours are offered 7:30 am to 4:30 pm (US$30 for 90 minutes; US$25 flat fee for hotel guests).

### Places to Stay & Eat

*Good Hope Country House* (☎/fax 954-3289, 800-688-7678 in the USA, PO Box 50, Falmouth) was recently restored and today operates as a stately 'country house hotel' in the classic English style. You might recognize it from scenes in *How Stella Got Her Groove Back*. I highly recommend staying here, or at least dining, which gives you a chance to admire the architecture: the formal entrance with a double staircase, high-raftered ceilings, Adam frieze, gleaming floor of hardwood the color of pumpkin, and a two-story counting house with a basement once used as a lockup for defiant slaves. Breezes ease through the wide jalousies and keep the house cool as a well. The house is fully furnished with period pieces – time-worn cowhide planter's chairs, antique bookcases, and chintz sofas – that preserve the plantation-era atmosphere.

One of the four generously proportioned bedrooms in the main house has the original plantation owner's lead-and-tile-lined bathtub and a deep copper basin in which water was heated. The former coach house has five rooms (which can be rented as a self-contained villa complete with cook and housekeeper). Lovers should opt for the 'guest house' – a perfect honeymoon suite – set like a jewel box on its own pedestal on the rear lawn. There's a small swimming pool in the stone courtyard, plus tennis courts (in need of restoration at press time). Be sure to get up shortly after dawn to see the valley enshrouded in mist. Service is friendly and relaxed but always professional. Room rates range from US$125 to US$150 in summer; US$150 to US$250 in winter, including breakfast.

The drive from Falmouth is worth it for the meal alone. Lunch and dinner are served by reservation only. Denver 'Wormy' Smith's assured cooking epitomizes the best of nouvelle Jamaican cuisine. Dishes such as jerk roast lamb loin with guava and roasted garlic are worth every cent. Leave room for the sublime cheesecake. Sandwiches and light snacks are also served. Budget US$30 per person for dinner, US$20 for lunch, and US$10 for breakfast.

## WINDSOR

This valley, southeast of Good Hope, is surrounded by towering, lushly foliated cliffs. It was part of John Tharp's vast estate. Tharp built Windsor Great House nearby (half a mile northeast of Windsor Caves), which is today in private hands and has recently been restored. In the 1960s, the Kaiser Bauxite Company bought the estate to resettle farmers displaced by its mining operations. The farmers grow subsistence crops and bananas for sale. From Sherwood at the north end, a narrow 2-mile corridor cuts through the limestone outcrops. The paved road dead-ends at Windsor near the head of the valley, from whence you can hike across the Cockpits to Troy.

### Windsor Caves

Though little visited, these off-the-beaten-track caverns are fascinating. The entrance is a mile-long hike from the road ending with a clamber up a narrow rocky path. About 200 yards beyond the narrow entrance you'll pass into a large gallery full of stalactites (you'll have to step through bat manure, which the locals 'mine' for phosphates). A second passage opens to another huge chamber with a dramatically arched ceiling. In rainy season you can hear the roar of the Martha Brae River flowing deep underground. You can explore safely for more than a mile, beyond which the caves are the terrain of experienced spelunkers only.

I strongly recommend you hire a local guide, as several spelunkers have been lost in the caves. Martell and Franklyn 'Doc' Taylor – two elderly and friendly Rastas – are the best guides. They lead the way with flashlights (thankfully, they've gotten rid of the smoky kerosene-soaked torches that were having a devastating affect on the limestone). You'll find the Taylors at the gaily painted hut at the end of the paved road. They charge US$5 to US$10 per person (depending on group size) to visit Rat Bat Cave and a little more to the Royal Flat Chamber. They offer snacks and cold drinks. Don't rely on your guide's flashlight – bring your own.

Linger at dusk to watch the bats leave the cave, sometimes in dozens, often in a great cloud (the cool air exiting the cave keeps the mosquitoes at bay while you wait). Fireflies wink as you walk back along the trail in the dark.

Until recently, the caves were owned by Lady Rothschild, an etymologist of the famous banking family, who bought them to study the bat population. Now they belong to the Jamaica Tourism Development Council.

### Places to Stay

A Texan, Patrick Childres, has two rooms for rent in a *two-story house* (☎ 409-846-1891 in the USA) at Windsor. He charges US$15 for rooms and US$10 to camp beside the river. The simple place has water from a spring, plus solar panels to power the radio and a battery for lighting. You can cook over a simple stove. Martell and Franklyn act as caretakers and will provide food and even cook lunch and dinner for US$5.

A local fella called Courtney also rents *rooms*, as does 'Sugar Belly,' whose basic I-tal (natural) *rooms* share an outside toilet and bathroom with cold water only for US$35 double including breakfast.

Reportedly, budget travelers can also stay at *Windsor Great House* (☎ 997-3832), which provides meals at extra costs.

### Getting There & Away

There's no bus service to Windsor. But a bus operates between Montego Bay and Brown's Town via Sherwood, from where you can walk or hitch the remaining 3 miles.

If you're driving, the best route is via Martha Brae. From there head south to Sherwood, where Windsor is signed (turn right at Mac's Supermarket, then left 200 yards down the hill). The road dead-ends in Windsor.

Finding the correct route from the Queen of Spains Valley or Good Hope is best done with the aid of a 1:50,000 map. One mile east of Bunkers Hill, you'll reach a staggered crossroads: the turnoff to the left (north) leads to Good Hope. From Bunkers Hill, you can either continue straight ahead to Sherwood, or take the right fork (south), 100 yards farther east of the Good Hope junction; then turn left after half a mile to reach Windsor. The very rough dirt road is partly overgrown with tall grass and often has deep muddy pools; if you miss the turn, you'll end up at an estate called Panteprant.

## CLARK'S TOWN

This small market center sits in the middle of sugarcane fields in a bowl on the northern perimeter of Cockpit Country, 4 miles south of Duncans. The town is centered on St Michael's Anglican Church. Just north of town you'll pass the Long Pond Sugar Factory & Distillery, which manufactures the famous Gold Label Rum. The narrow B11 leads west opposite the factory and winds through sugarcane to Rock, a mile east of Falmouth.

One of the most adventurous drives in Jamaica begins at Barbecue Bottom, 2 miles south of Clark's Town.

## Getting There & Away

Several minibuses operate to Clark's Town from Water Square in Falmouth, from Creek St in Montego Bay, and from north of the roundabout on DaCosta Drive in Ocho Rios.

## STEWART TOWN

This village (population 2000) hangs like a citadel atop a hill 8 miles east of Clark's Town. In the center of a grassy town square stands the Anglican church of St Thomas, built in 1842. An old sawmill stands immediately to the west, with the police station opposite. The Webb Memorial Baptist Church stands on the road that leads west to Discovery Bay.

## BARBECUE BOTTOM

Thickly forested limestone cliffs close in on this flat ravine planted in sugarcane. From here a very rough road snakes south across the eastern edge of Cockpit Country. The scenery is stupendous as you rise onto the flanks of ravines and look out upon the fantastic shapes. In places, the loftily perched track traces the edge of great abysses so deep that if you drop a stone it may take forever to hear it hit bottom.

Beyond Barbecue Bottom there's not a soul for the next 7 miles. It's extremely remote, and you'll feel, correctly, that you're driving along one of the loneliest stretches on the island. A breakdown here is serious business. The rarely used track is overgrown with bush, and vegetation sweeps up against the car on both sides. In places you may have to negotiate deep muddy pools and in parts, where the gravel gives way to big rocks and potholes, you'll wish your car had hooves. A 4WD vehicle is essential.

Eventually you'll emerge at Burnt Hill and a Y-junction. Take the left turn to Spring Garden and Troy for some of the most dramatic scenery in Jamaica. The right turn leads to Albert Town (see below), where you can return to the coast via an easier drive.

If you're arriving via Albert Town and want to drive *north* from Burnt Hill, take the road that begins 50 yards south of the Texaco gas station in Albert Town and leads uphill (southwest) to Spring Garden. After a

mile you'll pass a tiny roundabout at the side of the road. A rough road to the right heads to Barbecue Bottom.

## Ramgoat Cave

This remote cavern lies hidden midway between Barbecue Bottom and Burnt Hill. You'll need a guide to locate it (you can hire a guide in Albert Town). Take a flashlight.

## ULSTER SPRING

South from Rio Bueno, the B5 (linking the north coast with Mandeville) winds uphill via Jackson Town and Vale Royal Mountain, then cuts through a dramatic steep-faced gorge known as the Alps before plunging down through another gorge to Ulster Spring, 20 miles from Rio Bueno. On the edge of Cockpit Country, you'll pass through cockpit bottoms planted in bananas and sugarcane.

About 2 miles south of Ulster Spring, the Quashie River tumbles into an immense sinkhole, where it disappears, reemerging 10 miles to the north (see Dornoch Riverhead, earlier in this chapter).

## ALBERT TOWN

This small market center sits in the hills above and 2 miles southwest of Ulster Spring. The road climbs through cockpits with dramatic views en route. There's a Texaco gas station (it's closed on Sundays, when the nearest gas station is at Christiana). Albert Town is a base for guided hikes into the Cockpit Country, which spreads out immediately to the west (see Organized Tours in the Montego Bay section, earlier in this chapter).

Southeast of Albert Town, the B5 rises into mountains that form the spine of Jamaica. Beyond the hamlet of Wait-a-Bit you enter a whole different realm, with vistas of lush, rolling agricultural land interspersed with pine forest. It's cooler up here, with clouds drifting languorously through the treetops. You'll crest the mountains (and the boundary with Manchester parish) just south of Lorrimers, about 9 miles south of Albert Town. The spot is marked by a radio station.

Christiana is about 2 miles farther south (see the Central Highlands chapter).

Southwest of Albert Town, the B10 rises along the eastern edge of Cockpit Country and, beyond Warsop, drops dizzyingly and dramatically to Troy, a southern gateway to the Cockpits (see the Southwest Coast chapter).

### Information
The Southern Trelawny Environmental Agency (☎ 610-0818) works in liaison with US Peace Corps Volunteers who are helping to train locals to be guides. They can provide information on local conditions, and the Peace Corps volunteers are usually happy to provide other helpful tidbits.

### Places to Stay & Eat
Several locals have opened up their homes as B&Bs catering to the growing influx of hikers. The Southern Trelawny Environmental Agency (☎ 610-0818) or Trelawny Adventure Guides (☎ 919-6992) can offer recommendations.

For one or two dollars you can appease your appetite at *TJ's Snacks & Pastries* at the north end of town, 50 yards north of the post office; or at *Ataurus Restaurant & Bar*, also in the town center (check out the views from the veranda out back). *Sunshine Bakery & Grocery* is nearby. Need a cooling refresher? Call in at *JJ's Ice Cream Parlor*, about 400 yards north of the town center.

### Getting There & Away
Buses and minibuses operate between Albert Town and Falmouth, Mandeville, Kingston, and Spaldings.

There's a gas station in town that's closed on Sundays.

# Ocho Rios & North Coast

Jamaica's north central coast – spanning St Ann and St Mary parishes – is replete with attractions, making its main resort, Ocho Rios, a favorite stop for cruise ships. The region is more lush than Montego Bay and areas farther west, and Dunn's River Falls, plus several botanical gardens, working plantations, and other attractions, are within a few minutes' drive of Ocho Rios. Dozens of resort hotels boast their own private beaches.

Discovery Bay (said to be the site of Columbus' first landing in Jamaica in 1494) and Runaway Bay, both known for their white-sand beaches, are lesser centers of resort development. And smaller hotel enclaves dot the coast west of 'Ochi' (as the locals call it). East of Ocho Rios, cliffs edge up to the shore, making for increasingly dramatic scenery beyond Oracabessa and Galina Point. Here you can escape the crowds and discover gems such as Firefly, Noel Coward's former home, and several plantations open to visitors.

Oracabessa, famous for its association with Bond (…James Bond!), is the site of the most exciting tourism development in Jamaica in years. The long-term project promises to reinvigorate this old banana port and put it squarely on the map as a leading contender in Jamaica's evolving tourism stakes.

Hills rise south of the coast road (which is the A1 west of St Ann's Bay and the A3 to the east) and ascend into the Dry Harbour Mountains. Few travelers venture inland to discover the scenic beauty of the mountains or esoteric attractions, such as Bob Marley's birthplace and mausoleum.

## Ocho Rios

Ocho Rios (population 8200) is Jamaica's third most important region (second if you count cruise ship arrivals). It is located in a deep bowl backed by lushly vegetated hills and fronted by a wide, scalloped, white-sand

### Highlights

- Dunn's River Falls, an invigorating, fun climb, despite the crowds
- Scuba diving or snorkeling amid coral reefs
- Fern Gully, a serpentine, fern-lined gorge that stretches for three miles
- Firefly, Noel Coward's former home
- Golf at the exquisitely landscaped Sandals Ocho Rios Golf & Country Club
- A horseback ride through the ocean at Chukka Cove
- A romantic weekend – or a week – at Goldeneye
- Paying homage at the Bob Marley Museum at Nine Mile
- Green Grotto's musical stalagmites

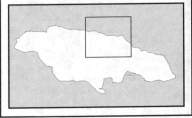

beach – UDC Beach (or Turtle Bay Beach) – and a reef-sheltered harbor. Offshore offers some excellent scuba diving with splendid coral formations slated to be protected within the as-yet-unrealized Ocho Rios Marine Park. Immediately east of town are other nice beaches, most of them hidden in coves that are the private domain of upscale hotels.

Ocho Rios, 67 miles east of Montego Bay, is popular with cruise ships, which gleam white and omnipresent in the turquoise bay with the lush green mountains above.

The town, however, has little charm. Most of the palm trees behind Turtle Beach are

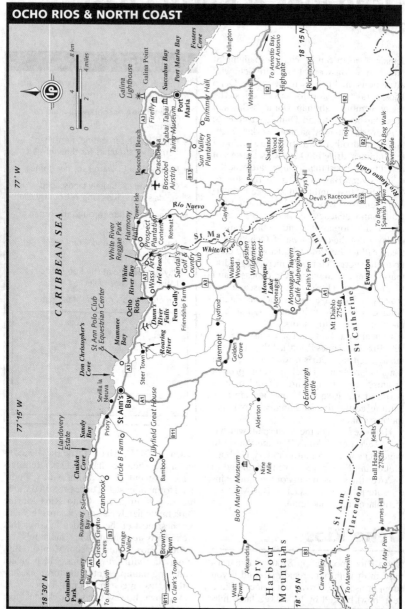

## OCHO RIOS & NORTH COAST

gone, having been replaced by hotels. The otherwise beautiful bay vista is marred by a bauxite-loading area beside the cruise port. In town there are virtually no historic buildings of note. And when the cruise ships call in, the compact streets are thronged with passengers, like bees released from a hive. (Cruise ships rarely arrive on weekends; you would do well to plan your itinerary accordingly.) Almost 600,000 passengers flood the streets annually. Not surprisingly, competition among local hustlers is fierce at these times, though the JTB's recent revitalization project, aimed at reducing harassment of visitors and beautifying the town, has virtually eradicated the hard-core hustling.

Ocho Rios extends its influence west as far as Dunn's River and east to Tower Isle, as well as farther afield through IRIE FM, the home-based national radio station.

## HISTORY

Ocho Rios (Spanish for 'eight rivers') is an English corruption of *chorreras* ('waterfalls'), the name the Spaniards gave to this section of coast. Ironically, neither the Spanish nor the English settled the bay; pirates, however, thought it a perfect base. The pirates were sponsored by plantation owners, partly to keep them focused on foreign and not domestic booty, but also in exchange for a share of the profit.

Although plantations were developed inland and along the coast, Ocho Rios never evolved as a fruit-shipping port of any consequence. Things began to change when Reynolds Jamaica Mines built a deep-water pier west of town in the 1940s. The first shipment of bauxite to leave Jamaica did so in 1952 from the Reynolds Pier. An overhead conveyor belt (which still looms over the road) carried the ore 6.3 miles from the Reynolds open-cast mines at Lydford, in the hills south of town.

Ocho Rios was still just a quiet fishing village in the 1960s when the Jamaican government formed the St Ann Development Council and began a systematic development. The council acquired much of the land surrounding the bay. It dredged the harbor and built a small marina, reclaimed the shore, brought in sand for Turtle Beach, and built a number of shopping complexes and housing schemes. Private developers followed. By the early 1980s, Ochi's character had been established: a meld of American-style fast-food franchises, nondescript shopping malls, an enclave of mediocre hotels in town, and a fistful of more tasteful, upscale English-style hotels a discrete distance east.

Sandals and SuperClubs have since added classy all-inclusives, and the success in the past few years of the Renaissance Jamaica Grande as Jamaica's premier convention hotel has secured Ochi's stature.

## ORIENTATION

Greater Ocho Rios extends for 4 miles between Dunn's River Falls, 2 miles to the west of the town center, and the White River, 2 miles to the east. Almost all the development outside the center is to the east.

The main coast road, the A3, bypasses the town center via a recently opened two-lane east-west highway. Near its western end is a roundabout (traffic circle): DaCosta Drive leads into town from here, while the A3 south leads to Kingston via Fern Gully. The main street downtown is aptly named Main St, which runs in an S-curve along Turtle Bay. Main St and DaCosta Drive meet to the east at a clock tower that marks the busy center of town and casts a shadow on tiny One Love Park, with pretty murals that are an attempt to beautify the otherwise ugly central node. Main St continues east, lined with hotels and shops, and eventually merges with the bypass opposite the IRIE FM radio station.

The town is small enough to walk everywhere.

### Maps

A large fold-out map, *Ocho Rios & Beyond,* is available from street stands. It shows the location of major restaurants, hotels, attractions, and services, and has a handy listing of telephone numbers.

## INFORMATION

The free *Jamaica Tourist Guide*, published weekly by the Gleaner Company and available at most hotels, includes local as well as island-wide updates.

## Tourist Offices

The well-stocked JTB office (☎ 974-2582, fax 974-2559) is upstairs at Shop 7 in Ocean Village Plaza on Main St. Iva Walters, the director, is extremely helpful. The JTB also maintains information booths on Main St, near Turtle Towers, and at the east end of town at Pinegrove Place, opposite Island Car Rentals.

## Money

There are numerous banks, including CIBC (☎ 974-2824), 29 Main St, at the west end of Ocean Village Plaza; Jamaica Citizens Bank (☎ 974-5953) on Newlin St; and Scotiabank (☎ 974-2174) on Main St. All have foreign exchange facilities. The National Commercial Bank (☎ 974-2522) at 40 Main St has a foreign exchange bureau open 2:30 pm to 5 pm Monday to Thursday. You can arrange an urgent remittance of money via Western Union, which is represented at Pier View Plaza (open from 9 am to 5 pm, Monday to Saturday).

If you want to change money illegally on the black market, you'll find a few obliging hustlers on DaCosta Drive, but the going rate is only 5% above the official exchange rate at best and not worth the risk.

## Post & Communications

The post office is on Main St, opposite the Ocean Village Plaza; it's open 8 am to 5 pm, Monday to Saturday. You can send faxes and telegrams from there, as well as from the Cable & Wireless/TOJ office (☎ 974-1574) on Renie St, just off Graham St. There's a Call Direct Centre (☎ 974-7594) at 74 Main St opposite the Island Grill and another (☎ 974-5708, fax 974-3461) tucked off Main St about 50 yards west of the Acropolis Disco. UPS has an office on Renie St (☎ 974-0204); it's open 7 am to 7 pm daily.

## Internet Resources

A good starting point is www.mobay.com/town3.htm, which gives information ranging from the town's history to descriptions of

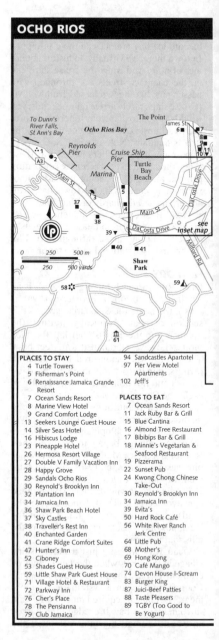

**OCHO RIOS**

*To Dunn's River Falls, St Ann's Bay*

*Ocho Rios Bay*

The Point

James St

Reynolds Pier

Cruise Ship Pier

Turtle Bay Beach

Marina

Main St

DaCosta Drive

see inset map

0  250  500 m
0  250  500 yards

Shaw Park

Millard Rd

**PLACES TO STAY**
4  Turtle Towers
5  Fisherman's Point
6  Renaissance Jamaica Grande Resort
7  Ocean Sands Resort
8  Marine View Hotel
9  Grand Comfort Lodge
13  Seekers Lounge Guest House
15  Silver Seas Hotel
16  Hibiscus Lodge
23  Pineapple Hotel
26  Hermosa Resort Village
27  Double V Family Vacation Inn
28  Happy Grove
29  Sandals Ocho Rios
30  Reynold's Brooklyn Inn
32  Plantation Inn
34  Jamaica Inn
36  Shaw Park Beach Hotel
37  Sky Castles
38  Traveller's Rest Inn
40  Enchanted Garden
41  Crane Ridge Comfort Suites
47  Hunter's Inn
52  Ciboney
53  Shades Guest House
59  Little Shaw Park Guest House
71  Village Hotel & Restaurant
72  Parkway Inn
76  Cher's Place
78  The Pensianna
79  Club Jamaica
94  Sandcastles Apartotel
97  Pier View Motel Apartments
102  Jeff's

**PLACES TO EAT**
7  Ocean Sands Resort
11  Jack Ruby Bar & Grill
15  Blue Cantina
16  Almond Tree Restaurant
17  Bibibips Bar & Grill
18  Minnie's Vegetarian & Seafood Restaurant
19  Pizzerama
22  Sunset Pub
24  Kwong Chong Chinese Take-Out
30  Reynold's Brooklyn Inn
34  Jamaica Inn
39  Evita's
50  Hard Rock Café
56  White River Ranch Jerk Centre
64  Little Pub
68  Mother's
69  Hong Kong
70  Café Mango
74  Devon House I-Scream
83  Burger King
87  Juici-Beef Patties
88  Taste Pleasers
89  TGBY (Too Good to Be Yogurt)

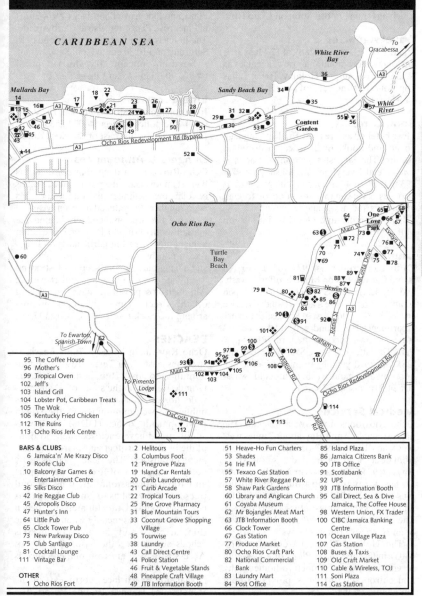

95 The Coffee House
96 Mother's
99 Tropical Oven
102 Jeff's
103 Island Grill
104 Lobster Pot, Caribbean Treats
105 The Wok
106 Kentucky Fried Chicken
112 The Ruins
113 Ocho Rios Jerk Centre

**BARS & CLUBS**
6 Jamaica'n' Me Krazy Disco
9 Roofe Club
10 Balcony Bar Games & Entertainment Centre
36 Silks Disco
42 Irie Reggae Club
45 Acropolis Disco
47 Hunter's Inn
64 Little Pub
65 Clock Tower Pub
73 New Parkway Disco
75 Club Santiago
81 Cocktail Lounge
111 Vintage Bar

**OTHER**
1 Ocho Rios Fort

2 Helitours
3 Columbus Foot
12 Pinegrove Plaza
19 Island Car Rentals
20 Carib Laundromat
21 Carib Arcade
22 Tropical Tours
25 Pine Grove Pharmacy
31 Blue Mountain Tours
33 Coconut Grove Shopping Village
35 Tourwise
38 Laundry
43 Call Direct Centre
44 Police Station
46 Fruit & Vegetable Stands
48 Pineapple Craft Village
49 JTB Information Booth

51 Heave-Ho Fun Charters
53 Shades
54 Irie FM
55 Texaco Gas Station
57 White River Reggae Park
58 Shaw Park Gardens
60 Library and Anglican Church
61 Coyaba Museum
62 Mr Bojangles Meat Mart
63 JTB Information Booth
66 Clock Tower
67 Gas Station
77 Produce Market
80 Ocho Rios Craft Park
82 National Commercial Bank
83 Laundry Mart
84 Post Office

85 Island Plaza
86 Jamaica Citizens Bank
90 JTB Office
91 Scotiabank
92 UPS
93 JTB Information Booth
95 Call Direct, Sea & Dive Jamaica, The Coffee House
98 Western Union, FX Trader
100 CIBC Jamaica Banking Centre
101 Ocean Village Plaza
107 Gas Station
108 Buses & Taxis
109 Old Craft Market
110 Cable & Wireless, TOJ
111 Soni Plaza
114 Gas Station

activities, restaurants, and accommodations, etc. Also try www.fantasyisle.com/ochie.htm, which has travel information on Ocho Rios.

## Travel Agencies

Stuart's Travel (☎ 974-2288), at 12 Main St, is one of the more reputable travel agencies as is the European-run Holiday Travel (alias Top Tours) at the rear of Pinegrove Plaza (☎ 974-1463).

## Bookstores

Most hotel gift stores sell English-language novels and books on Jamaican history and culture. The largest selection of books is available at Everybody's Bookshop (☎ 974-2932) at Shop 44 in Ocean Village Plaza. It also has a reasonable selection of foreign magazines and newspapers.

The town library (☎ 974-2588) is on Milford Rd.

## Laundry

Carib Laundromat (☎ 974-7631), next to Island Car Rentals on Main St, offers a wash-and-dry service (US$5 per load) and is open 10 am to 7 pm. There's also a laundry service (☎ 974-8436), 100m west of Skycastles Luxury Apartments. The Laundry Mart (☎ 974-5519) is east of town opposite the turnoff for Shaw Park. The latter charges US$2.75 per load and US$2.75 for drying. Note that 'dry cleaning' here means hand-washed in cold water (US$4.50 pants, US$3 shirt).

## Medical Services

Ocho Rios does not have a hospital. The nearest is at St Ann's Bay, about 7 miles west of Ocho Rios (☎ 972-0150). Your hotel's front desk can arrange a doctor's visit. Medi-Rays (☎ 974-6251), at Carib Arcade on Main St, has X-ray and ultrasound diagnostics plus the Central Medical Lab (☎ 974-2614) and Dr Michael James' office (☎ 974-5413). There's also a doctor's office in Island Plaza, open 10 am to 5 pm weekdays.

The Holistic Medical Centre (☎ 974-6403), in Ocean Village Plaza, offers 24-hour service, including acupuncture, homeopathy, and chiropractic services, plus a 24-hour ambulance (☎ 999-7425).

Pharmacies include Ocho Rios Pharmacy (☎ 974-2398) in Shop 27 of the Ocean Village Plaza, and Pinegrove Pharmacy (☎ 974-2023) in Pinegrove Plaza, and also at Carib Arcade. The latter is open 9 am to 8 pm, Monday to Saturday, and 10:30 am to 3 pm Sunday.

Need an optician? Try Morris Optical (☎ 974-7032) in Ocean Village Plaza.

## Emergency

In an emergency, call ☎ 119 (police) or ☎ 110 (fire). The police station (☎ 974-2533) is off DaCosta Drive, just east of the clock tower.

## Dangers & Annoyances

Ocho Rios is not a dangerous place and its biggest annoyance – the persistent entreaties of young men selling ganja and cocaine – has been significantly reduced in recent years.

Avoid the area immediately behind the market south of the clock tower. Use caution at night anywhere, but particularly on James Ave, a poorly lit street with two nightspots and a hang-out strip of ill-repute. Just say no to anyone who approaches and move on. Although most prostitutes have been cleared off the streets, some still linger, notably around the clock tower and DaCosta Drive.

## BEACHES

Ocho Rios' main beach is **Turtle Beach.** It stretches east from Turtle Towers condominiums to the Renaissance Jamaica Grande Resort, on the shore of a half-mile-wide, horseshoe-shaped bay. The beach is public and well maintained by the Urban Development Council (UDC). The hotels at either end have enclosed their portions of the beach to protect guests from harassment by hustlers. The beach is backed by hotels, with plenty of licensed water-sport and food concessionaires, plus almond trees and a few palms for shade. It also has changing rooms. Unfortunately, the beach feels cramped – especially when the cruise ships are in – and the noise of Jet Skis echoes across the otherwise calm waters. Access is daily 6 am to 6 pm; entrance is US$1.

**Mallards Beach** faces north, east of the Renaissance Jamaica Grande Resort. The narrow strip of sand is broken into sections dominated by hotels that maintain virtually autonomous control of what are, ostensibly, public beaches.

**Columbus Foot** is the tiny fisherman's beach, squeezed into a nook at the west end of town. You get a real taste of local color here, where colorful pirogues (fishing boats) and nets festoon the beach. You can hang out with the locals who still make a living by fishing and serving up fried fish.

## FERN GULLY

This lush gorge is one of Ocho Rios' prime attractions. A road zigzags uphill through the 3-mile-long canyon of an old watercourse that was planted with hundreds of different fern species about 1880. Trees form a canopy overhead, filtering the aqueous light. Several species of fern have disappeared from the gorge in recent years, killed by traffic fumes that form a thick haze beneath the canopy by late morning. It's best to visit early in the day. Hurricanes have added to the damage, due to the funneling effect of the chasm. Fern Gully is a national park and removing plants is forbidden.

Drive slowly and carefully.

## BOTANICAL GARDENS
### Coyaba River Garden

Coyaba is an Arawak word for 'heaven' or 'paradise.' This paradise has wooden walkways and trails that lead through lush gardens featuring streams, cascades, and pools filled with carp, crayfish, and turtles. Very serene! The **Coyaba Museum** (☎ 974-4568, fax 974-6235), PO Box 18, Ocho Rios, in a Spanish-style villa, traces Jamaica's heritage from early Arawak days to independence. There's also a gift store, and a gallery that holds the works of Jamaica's leading artists. Coyaba is about a mile west of St John's Church (on the A3), just before Shaw Park Gardens. Entrance is US$4.50 and includes a 30-minute guided tour. It's open 8 am to 5 pm, and until midnight on Thursday and Friday.

A Moonshine Festival is held on Thursday nights (5:30 to 10 pm). The US$50 fee buys you a Jamaican buffet, and you enjoy

African drumming and a jonkanoo show, followed by dancing to ska, rock steady, and reggae.

## Shaw Park Botanical Gardens

Ocho Rios' venerable Shaw Park Botanical Garden (☎ 974-2552, fax 974-5042), PO Box 17, is a tropical fantasia of ferns and bromeliads, palms, and exotic shrubs, spread out over the 25 acres that once formed the grounds of the now-defunct Shaw Park Hotel, a converted 18th-century great house. Trails and wooden steps lead past waterfalls that tumble in terraces down the hillside. A viewing platform offers a bird's-eye vantage over Ocho Rios, and a bar and restaurant are on hand. Shaw Park Gardens is open daily, 8 am to 5 pm. Entrance is US$4.

To get there, turn west opposite the public library on the A3, take the right fork at the Shaw Park Dairy, and follow the winding road uphill for a mile.

## OCHO RIOS FORT

The English built this pocket-size fort in the late 17th century. The fortress later did duty as a slaughterhouse before being restored in the 1970s by the Reynolds mining company, which fitted it with four cannons (two from the original fort). It stands next to the Reynolds bauxite installation on the A3 west of town.

## DUNN'S RIVER FALLS & PARK

To visit Jamaica and not climb Dunn's River Falls (☎ 974-5015) is like touring France without seeing the Eiffel Tower. The cascades, 2 miles west of town, are the island's most well-known attraction. Forget about trying to avoid the crowd. Join hands in the daisy chain and clamber up the tiers of limestone that stairstep 600 feet down to the beach in a series of cascades and pools. The water is refreshingly cool and the falls are shaded by tall rainforest.

You must buy a ticket before you can climb, then follow the stairs down to the beach. You have the option of hiring a guide. The powerful current can sweep your feet from the slippery rocks, but your sure-footed guide will hold you by the hand and carry your camera. You climb at your own risk – yes, occasionally people hurt themselves. Hence, there's a first-aid station supervised by St John's Ambulance Brigade. You can always exit to the side at a convenient point if your nerves give out, and there are wooden steps with handrails for the less adventurous. You can also rent rubber sandals for US$5 from booths outside the entrance.

Plan your visit for when the cruise ships aren't in town (weekends are best) otherwise, you may have to line up for some time. It's a 30-minute climb; allow 90 minutes in all. Swimwear is essential. The property is managed by the St Ann Development Council, which maintains changing rooms and lockers (US$5) on the beach. However, it's best to leave any valuables in your hotel safe, as the lockers are reputed to not be secure. At the top there's a huge crafts market – though the hustling can be fierce – and there are jerk stalls, snack bars, and a small restaurant next to the car park. It costs US$6 (children US$3) to climb the falls. The park is open 8:30 am to 4 pm.

The road beyond the car park, which is in terrible condition, climbs steeply for a mile and leads to the top of the falls (turn right just before the green wire-mesh gates; follow a dirt road through brush). Locals use the clearing by the falls for trysting and picnics, fouling it with garbage.

You can walk from Ochi along the 'One Love Trail' (the sidewalk along the A3), but bring water: it's a long, hot walk. There are a few crafts stalls en route, including Michael Clark's Art Studio, which makes for an intriguing stop.

## WASSI ART

This pottery studio (☎ 974-5044, fax 974-8096, wassi.art@cwjamaica.com), PO Box 781, in the Great Pond District, is signed from the Fern Gully road. Visitors see more than 50 employees' individual styles, including some young, supremely gifted, up-and-coming masters such as Homer Brown, a ceramist with a reputation for his erotic works. The pottery was begun in 1990 by Robert and Theresa Lee, who named it for the 'wassi' wasp, or potter wasp, which

makes a mud pot of each of her eggs and stuffs each with a caterpillar for food for her hatchlings. The studio still processes its own clay and is environmentally friendly (it uses lead-free paints and glazes). It's open 9 am to 5 pm Monday to Saturday and, 'unofficially,' on Sunday afternoons. Free tours are offered. There's a store where works sell from US$4 to US$4000. The owners will ship (US$23 per 8lb to the USA; US$30 to the UK). A museum and snack bar are planned.

Wassi Art offers work-experience programs for schoolchildren, plus vacation workshops.

## WHITE RIVER

This slow-moving river marks the boundary between St Ann and St Mary parishes, 2 miles east of town. It's popular for lazy 45-minute journeys by bamboo raft (US$30 per person) operated by Calypso Rafting (☎ 974-2527). En route you'll stop for a refreshing dip in a deep pool. An 'Exotic Night on the White River' is held each Tuesday and Saturday night, when flaming torches are lit along the riverbank; your raft trip ends with dinner and a 'native' cabaret (US$31).

Every Tuesday, Wednesday, and Thursday, Calypso Rafting also features a 'Jungle Bachanaal' (US$40 per person) that includes a buffet on the riverbank beside a lagoon. Drinks cost extra.

To get to Calypso Rafting, turn south at the Texaco station immediately west of the White River bridge. The road curls down to the river past White River Reggae Park. Signs point the way half a mile uphill to Calypso Rafting, to the right up Bonham Spring Rd. It's best to call ahead for reservations. Trips are available between 9 am and 5 pm.

## IRIE BEACH

This isn't a beach, but a series of cascades and deep turquoise pools formed by the White River, high in the hills at Bonham Spring Farm, 2 miles south of the river estuary. It's a serene and secluded place with a fabulous setting. A tourist resort, Irie

Beach, opened in mid-1995 on a beautifully landscaped riverbank garden with a wooden deck beneath shade trees, and a very tiny sand 'beach' with lounge chairs. There's a rope swing over a 25-foot-deep lagoon, and a trail follows the cascades half a mile upriver. A restaurant of natural stone and wood stands above the river.

Unfortunately, the whole area struggled and was 'closed until further notice' at press time. Call ☎ 974-5044 for the latest information.

Bonham Spring is an organic farm owned by a Chinese-Jamaican family who also own the recording studio in the grand house above the entrance to Irie Beach. Reggae stars often hang out on the front porch, but can be cold to foreign visitors.

## PROSPECT PLANTATION

Prospect (☎ 994-1058, fax 994-1468) is a working plantation, 4 miles east of town. It grows pimento and limes commercially and other produce for show. The old great house that sits atop a hill is not open to the public, but from a distance you can make out the fortified loopholes for protection against pirates and rebel slaves. The estate also includes the Prospect Cadet Training Centre, founded to educate the youth of indigent families and prepare them for the police force and Jamaica Defense Force.

The youngsters also act as tour guides. You can tour the plantation by tractor-powered jitney that offers some incredible views of the White River gorge and coast. Cuba, 90 miles away, is visible from Sir Harold's Viewpoint. The tour includes a visit to the nondenominational college chapel, a sturdy stone structure with a timbered roof. You can join such luminaries as Charlie Chaplin, Winston Churchill, and Henry Kissinger by planting a tree for US$50. You'll receive a photo with your name and the date of planting, which is also branded onto the trunk. The tree will be maintained for life. Tours depart at 10:30 am, 2 pm, and 3:30 pm, Monday to Saturday, and 11 am, 1:30 pm, and 3 pm on Sunday. It costs US$12. Three horseback tours are also offered for US$20 to US$50.

## HARMONY HALL

This beautiful great house (☎ 975-4222, fax 974-2651, harmony@toj.com), PO Box 192, on the A3 about 4 miles east of town, dates to 1886 when it was a Methodist manse adjoining a pimento estate. The restored structure is made of cut stone, with a wooden upper story trimmed with gingerbread fretwork, and a green shingled roof topped by a spire. It has been reborn as an arts and crafts showcase. Shows are held in the Front Gallery throughout the year; an exhibition season runs mid-November to Easter. The Back Gallery features arts and crafts from Jamaica's finest artists; the Intuitive Room has 'primitive' works by self-taught artists. There is also a Print Room housing posters and other works on paper; plus the requisite gift store. The downstairs showcases bamboo furniture and Reggae to Wear clothing.

It's open 10 am to 6 pm daily, except Christmas and Good Friday.

The grounds are a venue for events during the Ocho Rios Jazz Festival in June. There's a café (☎ 975-4785), and part of the lower level re-opened in the fall of 1998 as a premier Italian restaurant.

## SCUBA DIVING & SNORKELING

Virtually the entire shoreline, east of Ocho Rios to Galina Point, is fringed by a reef. One of the best sections is **Devil's Reef**, a pinnacle that drops more than 200 feet. Nurse sharks are abundant at **Caverns**, a shallow reef about a mile east of the White River estuary; it has many tunnels plus an ex-minesweeper, the *Kathryn,* that was sunk in 1991 to create a dive site.

You can arrange dives at the water-sport concessions on Turtle Bay Beach (UDC Beach); try Garfield Diving Station (☎ 974-5749), at Shop 1, UDC Beach, offering scuba lessons (US$20) and certification (US$300), plus glass-bottom boat rides (US$15), and snorkeling. Resort Divers (☎ 974-5338, fax 974-0577) at Shop 6, Island Plaza, has dive trips from US$35, plus scuba lessons and PADI certification courses (US$350). It has a full service pro shop and rents gear, as does Sea & Dive Jamaica

(☎/fax 974-5762) at 74 Main St. Fantasea Divers (☎ 974-5344). has a facility at Sans Souci Resort with a Handicapped Scuba Association instructor on staff. Shaw Park Beach Hotel (☎/fax 974-5762) also has a dedicated scuba facility.

All the dive operators offer snorkeling. For information on snorkeling cruises, see Organized Tours, below. Also see the Outdoor Activities chapter.

## SPORT FISHING
Several sport fishing boats are available for half and full-day charters from the marina. Try Free Spirit Charters offered by Resort Divers (☎ 974-5338, 800-317-7310 in the USA) at Shop 6, Island Plaza.

## WATER SPORTS
There are plenty of water-sport concessionaires on Turtle Beach offering jet-skiing, windsurfing, and paddleboating. Water Fever (☎ 974-2587, 819-7093, 974-2391 at night) offers parasailing. It has a facility at Shaw Park Beach Hotel. Most other upscale hotels offer a range of water sports.

## GOLF
The only golf nearby is at Sandal's Ocho Rios Golf & Country Club (☎ 975-0119, fax 975-0180), formerly the Upton Country Club, 700 feet up in the hills, 4 miles southeast of town (turn right at the Texaco gas station beside the White River estuary and follow Bonham Spring Rd uphill past White River Reggae Park). The par 71, 6600-yard, 18-hole course has fairways rippling up and down hills fringed by forest, and there's a driving range and putting green, plus clubhouse, bar, pro shop, and snack bar. It's open 7:30 am to 5 pm. Greens fees are US$70, or US$50 for nine holes (complimentary for guests at Sandals resorts). Caddies are mandatory and cost US$12, and cart rental is US$30. Club rental is US$12. Lessons are offered.

## HORSEBACK RIDING
You can choose from three tours at Prospect Plantation (☎ 994-1058, fax 994-1468), where trails lead through 900 acres. The guided trips vary from one hour to 2½ hours and cost US$20 to US$35. Daniel's Stables at Mammee Bay also offers horse riding.

## ORGANIZED TOURS
### General Tours
JUTA Tour Company (☎ 974-2292), PO Box 160, offers an 'Ocho Rios Highlight Tour' and other day excursions. Tourwise (☎ 974-2323, fax 974-5362) at 103 Main St offers a wide range of day excursions as far away as the Blue Mountains and Negril, as well as locally. Top Tours (☎ 974-1463, fax 974-0005) in Pinegrove Plaza specializes in inbound tours for Italian tourists. Its associate, Holiday Services (☎ 974-2948, fax 974-2817), in the same office, offers sightseeing excursions locally and throughout Jamaica.

Safari Tours (☎/fax 972-2639, safari@toj .com, www.jamaica-irie.com/safari/), Arawak PO, Mammee Bay, specializes in jeep safaris into the local hinterland (Monday and Wednesday), and into the Blue Mountains (Thursday and Friday), using a Land Rover. The German-run company also has bicycling (see below) and horseback riding trips, including a four-hour trip that combines riding at Prospect Plantation and river tubing; trips are scheduled daily except Sunday.

The Touring Society of Jamaica offers special interest tours into Cockpit Country and the Blue Mountains. (See the Outdoor Activities and the Getting Around chapters for more details and contact information.)

Caribic Vacations also offers excursions throughout Jamaica, but it specializes in excursion tours to Cuba (see '¡Cuba Sí!' in the Montego Bay & Northwest Coast chapter). Their local office (☎ 974-9106) is in the Ocean Village Plaza.

You can take a tour of the rum-producing Appleton Estate for US$65. Island Car Rentals offers a series of personally chauffeured tours, including a historic and cultural tour of Ocho Rios (US$100). See Organized Tours in the Getting Around chapter for details on both tours.

## Snorkeling & Sunset Cruises

Resort Divers (☎ 974-5338, fax 974-0577) has snorkeling trips for US$15 and sunset cruises for US$25. Heave-Ho Charters (☎ 974-5367, fax 974-5461), 11A Pineapple Place, also has snorkeling and party cruises aboard the 60-foot catamaran, *Cool Jazz*. Also try the *Windsong* (☎ 974-2446), another catamaran that has snorkeling trips (US$35) plus a 'Soca Sunset Dance Party' (US$25) on weekend evenings. A trimaran called *Freestyle* (☎ 974-2446, redstripecruises@toj .com) sails daily at 9 am and 12:30 pm from the UDC dock on a Dunn's River Cruise (US$45), and at 4:30 pm on a 'Soca Sunset Cruise' (US$25). Likewise, the trimaran *Cool Runnings* offers a party cruise to the falls.

You can act the part of a pirate on the *Jolly Roger*, a brigantine that also hosts parties and sunset cruises; contact Tourwise (☎ 974-2323, fax 974-5362) at 103 Main St. Red Stripe Cruises (☎ 974-2446) offers sightseeing and theme cruises.

## Bicycling

Safari Tours (see General Tours, above) offers a two-hour guided bicycle tour to Dunn's River Falls each Monday at 8 am and noon, beginning with an hour-long downhill ride from Murphy Hill.

Blue Mountain Tours (☎ 974-7075, fax 974-0635), 152 Main St, has an 18-mile downhill bicycling tour in the Blue Mountains for US$80, including transfers, breakfast, and lunch. It's popular and fun, although the company uses uncomfortable, single-gear beach cruisers – a detestable bike with the pedal as a brake.

## Helicopter

Helitours (☎ 974-2265, 974-1108, fax 974-2183) at 120 Main St offers three aerial tours by four-passenger Bell Jetranger helicopters. A 15-minute 'Ocho Rios Fun Hop' costs US$50. Longer journeys take in the coast east of town, including Firefly and Tacky Falls beyond Port Maria (US$95), and as far as the Blue Mountains. You can also charter a chopper. See the Getting Around chapter for details.

## SPECIAL EVENTS
## Reggae Sunsplash

The biggest shindig in Ocho Rios is the four-night annual reggae extravaganza. Featuring performances by such stars as Ziggy Marley, Burning Spear, and Buju Banton, Sunsplash spans reggae, rock, gospel, and 'roots.' Since moving to Ocho Rios in 1995, the event is staged at White River Reggae Park on February 6, coinciding with Bob Marley's birthday.

Sunsplash was initially held in Jarrett Park, an open-air entertainment center in Montego Bay, but it grew so popular – drawing 100,000 or so visitors – that a special forum, the Bob Marley Entertainment Centre (also called the Catherine Hall Entertainment Centre), was built on Howard Cooke Drive.

In 1993, the event (which traditionally spanned five nights in August) moved to another specially built venue, Jamworld, at Portmore outside Kingston. It was a disaster. In 1995 a group of private investors rescued the troubled event and brought it to Ocho Rios.

Formerly – and famously – the music didn't begin until late at night and would continue until dawn. In 1998, a more formal structure was introduced for the now four-night event and concerts have been revised to offer six-hour shows beginning at 8 pm on weekday nights and Saturday, and 7 pm on Sunday. How this will work out is anyone's guess, as the entertainers are renowned for showing up hours late.

The event – like Montego Bay's Reggae Sumfest – has become increasingly geared toward tourists, as is reflected in the move from showcasing exclusively reggae to a greater variety of music. Ticket prices have also increased; today they are prohibitive for many Jamaicans.

A plethora of stalls sell jerk and other Jamaican fare, plus beer, rum, and other essentials.

In the UK, Hammock Leisure Tours (☎ 0171-423-9400, fax 0171-423-9411) has a two-week 'Sunsplash' trip (£629, including roundtrip flights). In Germany, NDR2 radio (☎ 511-394-6661) sponsors a similar package. In the US, Sunburst Holidays (☎ 800-426-4570) offers package tours.

Tickets for the events range from US$15 to US$25 per night. For information, call Reggae Sunsplash International (☎ 960-1904, fax 960-1906, www.reggaesunsplash.com).

## Other Events

Rivaling Sunsplash is the weeklong Ocho Rios Jazz Festival, held mid-June at various venues that include the Renaissance Jamaica Grande Resort, the Little Pub complex, and Harmony Hall and Glenn's Jazz Club, east of town. Many performances are free; afternoon and evening concerts are US$15 and US$20 (US$25 and US$30 for the main concerts on opening and closing days). Island Flight Vacations (☎ 800-426-4570) is the official jazz festival tour operator and offers package tours from North America. For information contact the Jazz Hotline (☎/fax 927-3544).

In late September, sportsfisherfolk flock for the annual Ocho Rios International Marlin Tournament (☎ 922-7160).

The Panasonic Golf Championship is hosted annually in September at Sandals Golf Course (☎ 975-0119, fax 975-0180).

The Jamaica Hotel & Tourism Association hosts an annual fundraiser for charities each May. Contact the JTB (☎ 974-2570) for more information.

## PLACES TO STAY

Ocho Rios flaunts a wide range of accommodations for every taste and budget. Several hotels line Turtle Beach, but they are not particularly appealing. A fistful of Jamaica's most sophisticated hotels extend east for several miles and have their own beaches (also see East of Ocho Rios, later in this chapter).

Self-catering villas are a popular option and can be great bargains if you're with a family or group.

The accommodations below extend westward to Dunn's River Falls and eastward to Tower Isle. For hotels farther away, see the West of Ocho Rios and East of Ocho Rios sections, later in this chapter.

## Places to Stay – Budget

**Camping** You can camp at *Little Shaw Park Guest House* (see Guest Houses, below), near the Shaw Park Gardens in the hills above town. Each site costs US$25 for two, including tents. The owners will cook meals on request.

Also see *Island of Light Centre for Holistic Development* in the East of Ocho Rios section.

**Guest Houses** *Happy Hut B&B* (☎ 994-1223), on the A3, is run by Aston Young, a former producer of 'Sesame Street.' He rents three bedrooms in his homey bungalow above Rivermouth Beach, about 200 yards west of Grand Lido Sans Souci, about 3 miles east of downtown. Each has a private entrance and bathroom and costs US$27; one has a kitchenette for US$30. You can use the spacious TV lounge and a kitchen. There's a bus stop outside.

A cozy option is *Pentus Guest Villa* (☎ 974-2313, 3 Shaw Park Rd) in the hills southwest of town. It has four rooms with shared bath for US$20/30 single/double. *Seekers Lounge Guest House* (☎ 974-5763, 25 James Ave) has 25 rooms with lots of light, but they are basic and a bit run-down. The hotel has a large billiards room. Rates are US$25 with shared bath, US$38 with private bath with hot water, and US$50 with air-con.

A reader recommends the *Pencianna Guest House* (☎ 974-5472, 3 Short Lane) in downtown, which reminded him of an Italian pension. The rooms are small yet immaculately kept, with shiny red tile floors and crisp linens for US$30 to US$35. Some have shared baths. The owners prepare Jamaican meals for US$3 and up.

Nearby is the *Little Shaw Park Guest House* (☎ 974-2177, 21 Shaw Park Rd), a trim place with 10 rooms amid beautifully tended lawns and bougainvillea with a gazebo and hammocks. There's a room in the owner's house, plus seven spacious (though dark) cabins boasting homey – almost fuddy-duddy – decor, lounges, and large walk-in showers, for US$50. Meals are available by request. The owners also offer well-lit studio apartments with nicer furnishings. You can camp here; see Camping, above.

If you prefer to be closer to the town center, consider *Carleen's Villa Apartments*

(☎ 974-5431, 85 Main St) on the waterfront. It offers five rooms at US$50.

Don't be fooled by the advertisements for **Shades Guest House** (☎ 974-4713) at Content Garden. Sure, you can overnight, but most beds are used for 'short-time' with johns by the go-go dancers downstairs; the word is that the place is infested with bedbugs.

**Hotels – City Center** The true budget spot in town is the **Grand Comfort Lodge** (☎ 974-2597), attached to the Roofe Club on James Ave, with nine bare-bones rooms for US$15 with fans, or US$20 with air-con. Those in the center have no windows. Things get real noisy at night when the disco gets thumping. Grand Comfort? I don't think so!

Pool players could be in heaven at **Hunter's Inn** (☎ 974-5627, 86 Main St), which has a huge bar and four pool tables. The eight carpeted rooms have fans and small bathrooms with hot water, but they are rather gloomy and basically furnished for US$30.

**Cher's Place** (☎ 974-1959, 4 Evelyn St) has nine rooms with fans, louvered windows, cable TV, telephone, kitchenettes, and small bathrooms for US$45. They're modestly furnished and have tile underfoot. Air-con was to be added.

**Hotels – Farther Afield** The cheapest rooms are at the **Rum Barrel Motel & Restaurant** (☎ 974-5909), above the 'El Rancho' grocery store, a mile south of town on the road to Fern Gully. The six basic rooms cost about US$12 and have private bathrooms and fans.

**Reynold's Brooklyn Inn** (☎ 974-2480, 188 Main St) has six basic but clean rooms that share two bathrooms with cold water, and cost US$18. Those facing the road are noisy. The restaurant serves Jamaican and Chinese dishes for about US$3.

Another basic option is **Rose Ann Accommodation** (☎ 994-1912), below a hardware store beside the A3, 200 yards west of Grand Lido Sans Souci. It has 14 rooms (some very small) with ceiling fans and private bathrooms with hot water for US$20 to US$34.

At the west end of town, on Main St near the Columbus Foot fisherman's beach, is **Travelers Rest Inn** (☎ 974-7799), a budget hotel with a roadside seafood restaurant and a laundry attached.

**Hummingbird Heaven** – a longtime favorite of budget travelers – has closed.

## Places to Stay – Mid-Range

**City Center** Ocean Sands Resort (☎/fax 974-2605) is an attractive property on James Ave, with an oceanfront setting and its own pocket-size beach, with lots of coral, at your doorstep. A tiny restaurant sits at the end of a wooden wharf – a marvelous spot for enjoying a cool beer, or the splendid 'Jamaican Special' breakfast. The 35 pleasant rooms have French doors that open onto private balconies. It was closed for renovation at press time and may go all-inclusive (rates to be announced). There's a small pool.

The strangely named **Double V Family Vacation Inn** (☎ 974-0173, 109 Main St) is a compact property in lush grounds. Its 13 spacious, air-conditioned rooms have large beds but gaudy red carpets and dowdy furnishings and cost US$30 single/double, small; US$60 large. It features a pool, restaurant, and TV lounge. Self-catering apartments were being added.

**Marine View Hotel** (☎ 974-5753, fax 974-6953, 9 James Ave) has 25 basic rooms for US$35, some with air-con US$45/50 low/high season, or US$50/55 with air-con. All have private bathrooms with hot water. Top floor rooms offer a glimpse (barely) of the sea. There's a small pool and a restaurant.

A downtown option is **Jeff's** (☎ 974-2664, 10 Main St). Air-conditioned rooms with private bathrooms and hot water cost US$40.

Two other options nearby include the **Pineapple Hotel** (☎ 974-2727, fax 974-1706, PO Box 263), behind Pineapple Place, with 23 contemporary rooms with private bathrooms and hot water for US$60; and the **Parkway Inn** (☎ 974-2667), with 21 spacious, air-conditioned, simply furnished rooms for US$65, plus one suite and a family size room for US$75. Rooms at both properties are spacious but bland. The former has a lap pool and children's playground.

*Pier View Motel Apartments* (☎ 974-2607, fax 974-1384, 19 Main St) offers studios for US$50, a range of modestly furnished rooms for US$65 and efficiency apartments for US$70, all with fans, refrigerator, and cable TV; air-conditioned suites go for US$85. It has a small pool. Its neighbor, *Fisherman's Point* (☎ 974-5317, fax 974-2894, PO Box 747; ☎ 516-233-1786, 800-654-1337, fax 516-233-4815 in North America), is a condominium resort with 76 simple, elegant apartments with kitchenettes, satellite TV, and tiny private balconies. A personal cook can be arranged. The complex has a pool, bar, and seafood restaurant. Rates range from US$70 single, US$100 double in summer, to US$100 single, US$120 double in winter.

If you want to cook for yourself, check out the *Hermosa Resort Village* (☎ 974-2660, Lot 8, Hermosa Beach) near Carib Arcade. Its 16 contemporary, one-bedroom, air-conditioned townhouses for US$70 feature kitchens, plus loft bedrooms that sleep up to four. There's a pool and hot tub.

Two self-catering properties are on Turtle Beach. *Sandcastles Apartotel* (☎ 974-5626, 800-562-7273, fax 974-2247, 120 Main St), west of Ocean Village Plaza, has large, pleasantly furnished and well-kept studios and apartments with fully equipped kitchens or kitchenettes surrounding a pool. It has a sterile pub. Rates range from US$84 low season to US$111 high season for a studio; US$95 to US$140 seasonally for a standard; and between US$102 and US$176 low season, and US$154 to US$249 high season for a suite.

One of the best bargains is the *Hibiscus Lodge* (☎ 974-2676, fax 974-1874, PO Box 52). Its breezy clifftop setting on Main St overlooks a coral reef where the snorkeling is superb. It's close to the town center. The rooms, set amid lush grounds, are spacious and modestly furnished. There's a small clifftop pool, an atmospheric bar, plus a fine restaurant – the Almond Tree. Stairs lead down to a boat landing. The hotel offers good value, especially its discounted off-peak rates of US$93 standard, US$105 deluxe, including breakfast and taxes.

**Farther Afield** For a hilltop setting, try *Pimento Lodge* (☎ 974-1899), a handsome, Spanish-style hotel with spacious studios for US$30, and two and three-bedroom units for US$60 to US$90. There's also a dining room and kitchen. The studios have the best views down over the forest towards the distant ocean. A pool provides the same vistas. There's no restaurant, but the staff will cook meals on request. Take the turnoff to the left opposite Mr Bo Jangles Meat Mart and Mae Mae's Drinking Saloon, a mile south of town on the road to Fern Gully; Pimento Lodge is a mile up Breadnut.

*Happy Grove* (☎ 974-4660, 129 Main St) about 2 miles east of downtown, has rooms and studios with modest decor, cable TV, and balconies. Rates are US$40 for studios with fans, US$50 to US$60 for air-conditioned rooms, and US$70 with kitchenettes.

Farther out, *Chrisann's Beach Resort* (☎ 975-4467, 800-526-2422, PO Box 104, Tower Isle PO, St Mary), at Tower Isle near Harmony Hall, has uninspiring condominium apartments around a small pool and overlooking a private beach. Studios rent for US$490 weekly, low season; and one to three-bedroom suites for US$525 to US$1470. Across the road is *Tower Cloisters* (☎ 975-4360), another condo resort. And *Sea Palms* (☎ 975-4400, fax 975-4017, PO Box 70, seapalms@cwjamaica.com), nearby, has handsomely appointed, air-conditioned waterfront apartments with fully equipped kitchens and personal maid and cook service. Weekly rates range from US$735 for a one-bedroom unit to US$2980 for a four-bedroom penthouse in summer; and from US$1000 to US$4000 in winter.

*Bonham Hill Villas* (☎ 974-5454, fax 974-1706, PO Box 263) is on Bonham Springs Rd in the hills below Sandals Golf Course. It has two and three-bedroom units – not villas – with pleasant decor and ocean-view balconies.

## Places to Stay – Top End

You're spoiled for choice, though quality and ambience vary greatly, especially among all-inclusive resorts. Choose wisely.

**City Center** *Silver Seas Hotel* (☎ 974-2755, fax 974-5739) enjoys a breezy location on its own private, pocket-size beach in Mallards Bay. It has a lively atmosphere but was looking jaded at press time. The center of action is a huge semicircular bar facing a pool. Natural stone abounds. The spacious, ocean-view rooms cost US$80 to US$90 low season; US$110 to US$130 high season. It's popular with young German package-tourists.

A little charmer in town is the modern *Village Hotel & Restaurant* (☎ 974-9193, 800-835-9810, fax 974-8894, 54 Main St). Its 34 air-conditioned rooms feature tasteful contemporary decor and vary from standard to deluxe for US$81 to US$126, the latter with hot tubs. Satellite TVs and telephones are standard. Superior rooms and suites have kitchenettes. It also has one and three-bedroom suites for US$140 and US$220. A tiny courtyard restaurant serves Jamaican dishes. Rates drop with longer stays.

There are several options facing onto Turtle Beach. *Club Jamaica* (☎ 974-6632, 800-818-2964, fax 974-6644, PO Box 342), on Main St, is a compact all-inclusive resort with a Club Med theme, centered on a small pool and whirlpool enclosed in a soulless concrete courtyard. It has 95 air-conditioned rooms with satellite TV, telephones, and a vibrant color scheme. Noise echoes down the corridors. Insist on an oceanfront room. The courtyard is used for alfresco dinners (other meals are served in a cafeteria-style dining room). It's small enough that people mingle, but it's devoid of atmosphere and some guests wanted out.

A dive operation is on-site and there are water sports, a bar-hopping tour, karaoke, crab racing, and toga parties. Rates are US$175 to US$270 in summer; US$210 to US$330 in winter.

The gleaming white *Renaissance Jamaica Grande Resort* (☎ 974-2201, fax 974-5378, PO Box 100; ☎ 800-468-3571, fax 216-349-3159 in North America) reclusively lords over the north end of Turtle Beach. It's centered on a grandiose open-air lobby overlooking a massive 'fantasy pool' with swim-up bar, swim-through grotto, and a waterfall fashioned after Dunn's River Falls. There are 720 tastefully decorated rooms and 24 suites in two towers. Facilities include five restaurants, nine bars, the Jamaica'n me Krazy disco, video slots, a fitness center, tennis courts, and Club Mongoose, which keeps children younger than 12 amused. Nonguests may be able to purchase a day pass. It has the largest conference facilities on the island and gets a lot of convention traffic. Theme parties and live entertainment are offered nightly; gregarious folks will love it. All-inclusive plans range from US$220 to US$340 April through late December; US$280 to US$400 double in winter; and US$415 to US$450 single, and are higher at Christmas through New Year's.

**Farther Afield** The epitome of the term gracious is the very beautiful, family-run *Jamaica Inn* (☎ 974-2514, fax 974-2449, PO Box 1; ☎ 804-469-5009, 800-243-9420 in North America, c/o Caribbean World Resorts), exuding yesteryear patrician refinement. The 45-room hotel, under watchful German management, occupies six acres, with manicured lawns falling down to a 700-foot-long beach tucked into a private cove. Rooms are a soothing combination of whites and Wedgewood blues, with mahogany beds and Edwardian furnishings, subdued floral prints, colonial-theme prints, and plentiful French doors and windows, plus elegant, superbly lit bathrooms. All ground-floor rooms have fully furnished veranda suites. The West Wing is especially appealing, with verandas suspended above the sea – perfect when the evening sunlight floods in (East Wing rooms nudge up to the beach). There's a small pool, croquet lawn, games room, and library. The bar boasts a warm clubby atmosphere. Men are required to wear jackets for dinner (plus a tie in winter) and women's dress code is in accordance. No children under 14 are allowed. No programmed activities are on hand, though scuba diving, ocean kayaks, and Sunfish are available, and guests have access to the facilities at Shaw Park Beach Hotel. Rates are from US$170 single, and US$220 to US$245 double, including breakfast and dinner.

At the east end of Main St, 2 miles east of downtown, is *Sandals Ocho Rios Resort & Golf Club* (☎ 974-5691, fax 974-5700, PO

NORTH COAST

*Box 771)*, one of the Sandals chain's two immensely popular, upscale, heterosexual-only couples' resorts hereabouts. The elegant complex has 237 rooms in five categories, all with air-con, king-size beds, satellite TV, telephone, in-room safe, and coffeemaker. Every water sport imaginable is available, as are land activities from bocci ball to basketball. Nightlife means everything from karaoke to toga parties. Rates are all-inclusive, from airport transfers to everything that exists within the gates, including all-you-can-eat meals and drinks, a tour of Dunn's River Falls, and golf at Sandals Golf Course. Guests who book suites get special concierge treatment. The vast facilities embrace four specialty restaurants (including Italian and Southwestern), three pools, a beauty salon, gym, and disco. Low-season rates (three nights) range from US$680/1388 standard to US$840/1708 deluxe. See Facts for the Visitor for Sandals' international contact information.

See West of Ocho Rios, later in this chapter, for information on Sandals Dunn's River Golf Resort & Spa.

***Ciboney*** (☎ 974-1027, fax 974-5838, PO Box 728; ☎ 800-242-6639, fax 305-662-9813 in North America, ciboney@infochan.com), next to Sandals Ocho Rios, is one of only two AAA Four Diamond-award winners in Jamaica (although there are more deserving places), with rooms in the great house, plus 226 one, two, or three-bedroom, red-tile-roofed villa suites, each with a private pool and attendant. Six restaurants each have a distinct mood and cuisine. The resort has its own nightclub, two large pools and a hot tub, plus six tennis courts, two squash courts, and a spa. Water sports include scuba diving through PR Scuba Technologies (☎ 974-1880), and there's entertainment, including video slots. Otherwise, it's a fairly sedate place. All-inclusive summer rates are US$400 double for a standard room, US$420 deluxe, and US$460 to US$540 for suites. Winter rates are US$424 double for a standard room, US$440 deluxe, and US$500 to US$580 for suites.

The other AAA Four Diamond hotel is the ***Grand Lido Sans Souci*** (☎ 994-1353, fax

994-1544, PO Box 103; ☎ 800-467-8737, fax 954-925-0334 in North America, ☎ 01749-677200 in the UK, www.superclubs.com), which sets the tone for contemporary sophistication. Its setting is sublime, with its own golden beach in a secluded, lushly foliated cove backed by lime-green lawns. The resort has a world-class fitness center and emphasizes restorative spa treatments. Every conceivable water sport is featured, as is tennis, and a complete schedule of activities range from scuba lessons to reggae dance classes. A volleyball court and jogging track have been added. All 146 suites are deluxe and feature king-size beds, CD player, cable TV with adult viewing, and direct-dial telephones. Some are set on the cliff face, with dramatic views through the trees. Bathrooms are glorious, with huge showers and tubs (76 have Jacuzzis).

A second beach is for nude bathing and features a grotto with hammocks. Rates (per person, double occupancy) for a three-night package begin at US$820 to US$1390 in low season, depending on room type; high-season rates begin at US$1130 to US$1839. Its 'SuperSummer' packages offer significant savings off published rates.

Another popular option is the reclusive ***Shaw Park Beach Hotel*** (☎ 974-2552, 800-377-1126, fax 974-5042, Cutlass Bay, PO Box 17; ☎ 800-223-6510, fax 402-398-5484 in North America; ☎ 020-7581-4094, fax 7225-2491 in the UK), whose thatch-roofed units are spread along a wide golden-sand beach in a private cove. Choose from 33 standard, 60 superior, and 13 lavish suites, all with air-con and their own private oceanfront balcony or terrace. Features include an oval pool and children's wading pool, two tennis courts, games room, and Silks Disco, plus water sports and floor shows, and a 'crafts fair' on Wednesday.

***Enchanted Garden*** (☎ 974-1400, 800-847-2535 in North America, fax 974-5823, PO Box 284), on Eden Bower Rd in the hills southwest of town, is named for its 20-acre Eden-like setting. The grounds are akin to a lush landscaped park, with 14 waterfalls, huge pools, a fruit orchard, separate fern, spice, cactus, and lily gardens, and a walk-in aviary (the grounds once formed Carinosa Gardens). The 40 suites have mezzanine kitchens and hot tubs on the patio. Facilities include a full health spa with a gym, tai chi and aerobics, a private beach club, plus a restaurant incongruously set on an East Indian pavilion, containing pool tables, slot machines, and three aquariums. Rates are US$280 to US$380 double in low season and US$340 to US$450 double high season. Two and three-bedroom suites cost US$190 to US$200 low season, US$225 to US$235 high season. Day and evening passes for use of the facilities are available for US$45 per person per day, or US$55 evening, including entertainment. Take the winding road that leads south from the roundabout at the western junction of DaCosta Drive and Main St.

Nearby is *Crane Ridge Comfort Suites* (☎ 974-8050, 800-221-2222, fax 974-8070), offering a breezy hilltop location at 17 DaCosta Drive. The modern, all-suite resort features 119 one and two-bedroom suites in six three-story structures. An airy restaurant on stilts looms over a large pool. A shuttle service is offered to the hotel's private beach, and to Shaw Park Gardens and Dunn's River Falls. Per person high-season rates start at US$115 for one-bedroom, US$135 two-bedroom.

If you want your own place with the luxury of being waited on hand and foot, consider *Somewhere Villa* or *Eight Rivers Villa*, both a stone's throw east of Prospect Plantation. The latter is a 5000 sq foot property on 1½ acres fronting the beach. It has four air-conditioned bedrooms, each with its own bathroom. Nearby is the three-bedroom *Wag Water Villa*, opposite the entrance to Prospect Plantation. The three villas share a tennis court. They're represented by VHR Worldwide (☎ 201-767-9393, 800-633-3284, fax 201-767-5510, 235 Kensington Ave, Norwood, NY 07648, vhrww@juno.com, www.vhrww.com).

*Seapalms* (☎ 975-4400, fax 975-4017, PO Box 70) has nicely decorated, fully equipped one, two, three, and four-bedroom units from US$735 to US$2980 per week in summer, US$1000 to US$4000 in winter. *Villa Viento*

*Resort* (☎ 975-4392) is also here, with four air-conditioned villas plus a small pool set in pleasant grounds that slope to the beach. It has an all-inclusive option.

*Elegant Resorts Villas* (☎ 876-953-9562, 800-337-3499 in North America, fax 876-953-9563, PO Box 80, Montego Bay) also has five three to five-bedroom villas at Prospect Plantation, beginning at US$2350 weekly.

*Emerald Seas* (☎ 925-9571, fax 925-2931, c/o 12 Norbrook Rd, Kingston 8) is another elegant two-story, four-bedroom Georgian villa on two acres of lush grounds, adjacent to Grand Lido Sans Souci. Living areas are built around an indoor rock garden. It has its own pool and tennis court, and is staffed by a butler, cook, housemaid, laundress, and gardener. The weekly rate is US$4500/7000 summer/winter.

Many local villas are also represented by Selective Vacation Services (☎ 974-5187, fax 974-2359) at 154 Main St, PO Box 335, Ocho Rios. See Accommodations in Facts for the Visitor for more rental villas and apartments.

## PLACES TO EAT
### Fast Food
For fresh-baked bread, patties, and desserts, head to the *Tropical Oven* bakery, opposite *Kentucky Fried Chicken* on Main St. *Mother's* is a 24-hour fast eatery serving patties and pastries, where you can enjoy a pre-dawn ice cream; it has several outlets.

For cheap patties (US$0.50) try *Juici-Beef Patties* or, behind it, *Taste Pleasers* with tasty callaloo cakes and meat loaf, and *Irie Juice* next to the Little Pub.

There's a *McDonald's* and a *Burger King*, both on Main St, catering to the 'just gimme a bite to eat' crowd.

### Jamaican
The *Island Grill*, on Main St, is a fast-food joint, good for jerk fish. The nearby *Village Café & Jerk Centre* (☎ 974-9193) serves good-value sinus-searing jerk, plus festival, rice and peas, and seafood. And the *Ocho Rios Jerk Centre*, next to the roundabout on DaCosta Drive, is another favorite of locals. It's open 10 am to midnight daily.

The *Jack Ruby Bar & Grill*, on James St, is a whirligig of Caribbean colors, serving the usual Jamaican fare from oxtail soup to ackee and saltfish. It has a pool table and occasional live music in the courtyard out back.

*Jeff's,* a restaurant and lounge toward the west end of Main St, is an American-style diner with Jamaican and American breakfasts (US$2.50 to US$4), burgers (US$2), and sandwiches (US$2 to US$3). Its dinner menu is Jamaican, but the ambience is distinctly middle-American.

Cheap shacks sell all manner of local fare in the produce market on DaCosta Drive, immediately southwest of the clock tower. *Jah Roy's* and *Father Ancient I-tal Food Shop* have been recommended.

For tasty I-tal food, try *Minnie's Vegetarian & Seafood Restaurant* (☎ 974-0236, 795-1655) nearby at the Carib Inn, with a shaded outdoor patio and a menu of seafood, salads, vegetable stew, gunga pea stew, and veggie patties from US$4, plus natural fruit juices and herbal teas made from beets, paw paw, guava, or June plum. For lunch try the veggie run-down with coconut custard and spiced vegetables for US$6, or the curried tofu (US$10.50). Dinner entrées begin at US$14. Minnie (a gracious Rastafarian) used to cook for Bob Marley. Her restaurant is set on three acres, with a stream and a beach – you can swim up for lunch.

## Seafood

In town, the *Lobster Pot*, on Main St, is a homey seafood restaurant with entrées from US$5. And at *Fish World (3 James Ave)*, you can watch your fish being cooked on an open grill. Wash down your steamed, grilled, or fried fish with natural juices. It stays open until 2 am but is closed on Sunday.

Both the *Waggon Wheel* and *Lion's Den Restaurant,* opposite the entrance to Dunn's River Falls, are reasonably priced yet uninspired options for seafood prepared the Jamaican way. For lobster, try *Jungle Lobster House* beside the estuary of the White River. Never mind that it's a rustic shack. The food is superb, cooked before your eyes over an open fire.

## Continental

*Bibibips Bar & Grill* (☎ 974-1287, 93 Main St) is a breezy oceanfront bar and restaurant serving chicken wings (US$6), crab, cajun fries, burgers, and the like. It has a live band on weekends.

A favorite is *Café Mango* on Main St, another colorful place with a large menu that includes spicy hot chicken wings and other finger foods, plus burgers, seafoods, and continental dishes, and good music to boot.

For a meal with a view, head to the *Almond Tree Restaurant* (☎ 974-2676), in the Hibiscus Lodge on Main St, where wooden dining pavilions stairstep down the cliff and candlelit dinners are served alfresco. The huge menu ranges from hamburgers and continental fare to steadfast Jamaican dishes. Entrées aren't cheap (budget a minimum of US$15), but the view makes amends.

The *Little Pub* (☎ 974-2324, 59 Main St) is totally touristy, yet enjoyable, and serves good American breakfasts. An eclectic lunch and dinner menu is strong on steak and seafood at modest prices. It's open 8 am to midnight.

East of town, the *Garden Cafe* (☎ 975-4785), on the terrace at Harmony Hall, is open 10 am to 10 pm and serves jerk fare, sandwiches, burgers, fish and chips, and Jamaican fare. Nearby, *Glenn's Jazz Club* (☎ 975-4360), a swank place at Tower Isle a stone's throw west of Couples, serves breakfast (US$7) as well as lunch and dinner with an international menu that includes fish and chips (US$10).

For upscale dining, you owe it to yourself to dine amid a surfeit of silverware at the *Jamaica Inn* (see Places to Stay). The cuisine is excellent.

## Chinese

*Hong Kong*, on Main St in the heart of downtown, serves inexpensive Chinese, as does *Kwong Chong Chinese Take-Out* (☎ 974-2425), immediately west of Hermosa Resort Village; the *Wok*, at the west end of Main St, serves Chinese staples such as chop suey for US$5.

Caribbean view from Firefly, Noel Coward's home

A peek into downtown Brown's Town

Cruising in Port Antonio

Portland parish inlet, east of Frenchman's Cove

Rio Grande at Berridale

A more expensive touristy favorite is *The Ruins* (☎ *974-2789*) on DaCosta Drive. This former sugar mill is now a Chinese restaurant amid gardens with cascades and pools. The quality is fair, but the setting is splendid. Appetizers begin at US$4, and entrées run US$8 to US$30.

## Italian

For pizza, try *Mr Humphrey Pizza Café* (☎ *974-8318*) in Pinegrove Plaza; *Pizzerama* (☎ *995-5938*) near Carib Arcade on Main St; or *Pineapple Pizza Pub* (☎ *974-6426*), with uninspired pub-style decor but tasty pizzas from US$6 (10 inch), including vegetarian pizza.

The talk of the town is *Toscaninni* (☎ *975-4785*), newly opened at Harmony Hall. The impressive menu ranges from pasta (US$5 to US$12) to shrimp sautéed with garlic and hot pepper flambé with Appleton rum (US$18). It's open 10 am to 3 pm, and 6 pm to 10 pm.

The best views in town are from *Evita's* (☎ *974-2333*), high above Ochi on Eden Bower Rd in a handsome 1860s house. Northern Italian entrees average US$8; half-orders are available.

## Coffee & Ice Cream

*Baskin Robbins* is in Ocean Village Plaza. Better bets are *Devon House I-Scream* and *TGBY (Too Good to Be Yogurt)*, next to each other on DaCosta Drive. *Caribbean Treats* serves ice cream sundaes. The *Coffee House* (☎ *974-2959*) serves espressos, cappuccinos, and fresh-brewed Blue Mountain coffee. For the best coffee, though, head to *JaJava Coffee Bar* (☎ *994-1188*), beside the entrance to Prospect Plantation east of town.

## Groceries

There's a *supermarket* in Ocean Village Plaza and smaller grocery stores scattered along Main St. You can buy fresh fruits and vegetables at the *produce market* on the south side of DaCosta Drive near the clock tower. Plan on some hard bargaining, and ask a local what you should expect to pay before choosing your vendor.

## ENTERTAINMENT
### Discos

The happening scene remains *Acropolis Disco* (☎ *974-2633, 70 Main St*), also known as the 'Crub-Crub,' on the second floor of Mutual Security Mall. It's cramped and dark, and the mostly Jamaican crowd presses shoulder-to-shoulder while rap, world beat, and reggae blare at deafening levels. The dance floor is usually littered with empty beer bottles. Why it's so popular, I'll never know! An outside bar and terrace provide relief. A dress code is strictly enforced. Entrance is US$5 (free on Wednesday). Thursday is 'Ladies Nite,' when women get in free.

An even more down-to-earth option for hardcore reggae fans is the *Roofe Club* (☎ *974-1042, 7 James Ave*); admission is US$3. This rooftop disco is favored by locals and sends earth-shattering music across the roofs of town. This is the place to get down and dirty with the latest dancehall moves. Another earthy spot is the *Irie Reggae Club*, upstairs opposite Carib Arcade.

Attempting to steal the limelight is the *New Parkway* (☎ *974-2667*), a German-run disco that opened in late 1998 at the junction of DaCosta Drive and Main St. Thursday is Ladies Nite, and Sunday is oldies night. Happy hour is from 7 to 9 pm on Friday. There's a dress code.

*Jamaica'n me Krazy* disco in the Renaissance Jamaica Grande Resort is spacious and air-conditioned and done up in squiggly fluorescent, psychedelic decor. Entrance is a steep US$30 but includes all-you-can-drink. A 'Carnival Jump-Up' is held here on Thursday nights. It gets few locals and caters mostly to the hotel guests. *Silks Disco* (☎ *974-2554*), in the Shaw Park Beach Hotel, attracts a more affluent local crowd. The small disco is open from 10 pm until the last guest leaves, nightly except Tuesday. Entrance is US$5. Friday is Ladies Night.

The *Hard Rock Café* (see Bars, below) also has a small disco on Saturday.

Consider buying a night pass to *Sandals Dunn's River* (US$120 per couple), permitting you full access to the disco, plus meals, drinks, and a panoply of other entertainment (valid 6 pm to 2 am; or US$60 per couple

**NORTH COAST**

9 pm to 2 am). A full-day pass costs US$170 (valid 8 am to 3 am; or US$100 8 am to 6 pm). See West of Ocho Rios, later in this chapter.

## Bars

The best-known spot is *Cocktail Lounge* (☎ 974-5371, 47 Main St), formerly Bill's Place, which has changed little and offers tunes off the jukebox and a sports TV above the small bar. It has a mini-disco and serves burgers and Jamaican fare. The *Little Pub* (☎ 974-2324, 59 Main St) is a touristy favorite and also has sports TV and eclectic entertainment to amuse you while you sit at the bar.

The *Hard Rock Café*, at the east end of Main St, is another mellow spot to lounge, surrounded by Tiffany lamps and Hollywood posters, with tunes from an old jukebox. The *Vintage Bar* atop Soni Plaza plays oldies, or soca on Friday.

The *Jack Ruby Bar & Grill*, on James St, has live bands in the courtyard out back. Farther along James St is the rooftop *Balcony Bar Games & Entertainment Centre*, with pool, video games, card games, and live music twice weekly. You'll find several other simple 'entertainment centers' on James St. Use caution at night.

Locals head to the *Corner Hut* (☎ 999-7188), at Steer Town, in the hills above Mammee Bay. It sometimes has live reggae. Thursday is oldies night. The action begins around 10 pm.

## Go-Go Clubs

*Shades* (☎ 974-4713) is a raunchy go-go club at Content Hills, just east of Coconut Grove Shopping Centre. The US$6 entrance includes one drink. The performers tend to plonk themselves in men's laps and may attempt to entice male audience members upstairs for private pleasures, but the place is reputedly unsanitary.

The earthy *Club Santiago* (US$3 entrance) and *Hunter's Inn* also feature go-go dancing. The *Corner Hut* (see above) has go-go dancing on Sunday.

## Live Music

The *Little Pub* offers live entertainment, including an Afro-Carib musical. Tuesday is

karaoke night, and there's a cabaret on Friday. Saturday is Ladies Nite, when women get in free and receive a glass of champagne on the house (men pay US$6 entrance); a dress code applies. It offers free cabs for cruise ship passengers.

Most top-end hotels also have limbo and cabaret shows.

If you're a jazz lover, give *Glenn's Jazz Club* (☎ 975-4360), east of town near Tower Isle, a call for the latest schedule.

*White River Reggae Park* hosts frequent concerts, including the 'White River Reggae Bash,' a one-day event in January. For information, call ☎ 929-4089.

## Other

The *Little Pub* also has a 'casino' with gaming slots.

*Coyaba* (☎ 974-4568, fax 974-6235) hosts occasional 'moonlick' parties during the full moon.

Cigar smokers should head to *Club Aficionado* (☎ 974-6497, fax 974-1222), in Shop 22, Soni's Plaza, where you can savor a fine Cuban stogie and cognac in the company of like-minded souls. Top-notch cigars are for sale.

## SHOPPING

At times you may think Ocho Rios is geared solely toward shoppers pouring off the cruise ships. There's a handful of major shopping centers where stores sell everything from coral and silver jewelry and straw and leather crafts to T-shirts for everyone from grannie to the kids. Don't expect any real bargains, however; free-spending cruise passengers inflate the prices (except for duty-free items). To get the best deals, visit after the cruise passengers have returned to their ships.

Ocho Rios Craft Park, on Main St, and Dunn's River Craft Park, below the parking lot at Dunn's River, each have dozens of craft stalls. Pineapple Place, east of town, and Coconut Grove Shopping Village, opposite the Plantation Inn, also specialize in crafts. Fern Gully is lined with stalls where artists sell paintings and carvings at prices marginally lower than elsewhere.

The two main shopping plazas are Soni Plaza and Ocean Village Plaza, both on Main St. Soni Plaza hosts several top-class duty-free stores, including Taj Mahal (☎ 974-6455), which offers a vast array of watches and jewelry.

There's no shortage of crafts stores and boutiques selling resort wear, although the Beautiful Memories store in Island Plaza has been recommended for good value. Local designer Ruth Clarage has a store (☎ 974-2874) at Shop 46 in Ocean Village Plaza. Also here is Living Wood (☎ 974-2601), with one of the largest and more eclectic ranges of crafts, including wicker furniture. For batiks, try It's a Wrap (☎ 975-0866) in Sandcastles Plaza in front of the Sandcastles Aparthotel, selling sarongs and resortwear.

For the best quality art, check out the Frame Centre Gallery (☎ 974-2374) in Island Plaza, and the gallery at Harmony Hall (☎ 975-4222), 4 miles east of town. The latter sells superb paintings, sculptures, and ceramics, as well as quality kitsch such as painted wooden fish and parrots. It also has a small bookstore (open 10 am to 6 pm) and the downstairs gallery offers fine quality wicker, furniture, etc. Harmony Hall is renowned for its Christmas craft fair; you also can hit the 'Best of Harmony Hall' in January and the 'Harmony Hill Easter Crafts Fair' in April. The 'Harmony Hall Anniversary Crafts Fair,' held mid-November, is an invitational with local artists showcasing their works.

Seeking ceramics? I highly recommend a visit to Wassi Art (see Wassi Art, earlier in this chapter), which has a showroom in the ceramics factory and an outlet on the A3, 200m west of the entrance to Prospect Plantation.

Many stores sell music tapes and CDs. One of the best is Reggae Master, at 71 Main St, drawing (or frightening away) customers with its blaring sound system. Dis N Dat Music (☎ 795-2775) in Island Plaza also has a large stock of reggae albums and will make up compilation tapes. Try Vibes Music Shack in Ocean Village Plaza for more obscure and eclectic sounds.

Exotic Flowers To Go (☎ 974-2201) has a shop in the Renaissance Jamaica Grande Resort. A boxed pack of 30 fresh tropical flowers costs US$25.

## GETTING THERE & AWAY

### Air

Ocho Rios is served by Boscobel airstrip (☎ 975-3101), about 10 miles east of town. No direct international service lands here, but at press time, developer Chris Blackwell had a lease option and was pressuring to get the runway expanded to take international jets and to get the airstrip upgraded as a port of entry.

Air Jamaica Express (☎ 922-4661, 975-3254) serves Boscobel with scheduled flights from Montego Bay, Port Antonio, and Kingston.

Air Negril operates 'scheduled' charters between Montego Bay and Ocho Rios (US$85), and between Negril and Ocho Rios (US$130). Timair (☎ 974-0575, 979-1114) also operates charter service to and from Boscobel.

### Bus

At press time, a new bus station was being planned. Until that comes to fruition, buses and minibuses arrive and depart Ocho Rios from Milford Rd, between Main St and the roundabout on DaCosta Drive. Expect to be hustled by bus touts.

Buses operate sporadically throughout the day between Ocho Rios and both Montego Bay and the main bus terminal in Kingston (about US$2). They're crowded and terribly uncomfortable. Minibuses are almost as cheap (US$3) and certainly more comfortable. It's a two-hour ride from either Montego Bay or Kingston.

Several tour operators provide minibus transfers, including Caribic Vacations (☎ 974-9106, 953-9878 in Montego Bay), which has transfers for US$15 each-way from Montego Bay airport. Tropical Tours (☎ 974-5250, 953-9100 in Montego Bay) has a similar service.

### Taxi

A licensed taxi between Montego Bay and Ocho Rios costs US$70 (one to four people); it's US$150 by limousine. A taxi

NORTH COAST

ride between Ocho Rios and Kingston costs US$80 (US$100 to the airport).

The car park next to Ocean Village Plaza and the vacant lots around the clock tower are unofficial taxi stands. JUTA (☎ 974-2292) is the main taxi agency catering to tourists. You can also call a cab from the Maxi-taxi Association (☎ 974-2971) at Pineapple Place or Ocho Rios Cab Operators (☎ 974-5929) at 1 Newlin Plaza.

Most tour companies charge about US$110 for a chauffeured ride from Montego Bay; try Caribic Vacations (see Bus, above).

Island Car Rentals (☎ 974-2334, 974-2666 in Ocho Rios, ☎ 926-8861 in Kingston, ☎ 952-5771 in Montego Bay), offers transfers to and from Kingston or Montego Bay (US$70 for one or two people; US$90 for up to seven people).

### Hitchhiking

Though never a highly recommended way to get around, the hitching is said to be good between Ochi and both MoBay and Kingston, as many freight trucks use the A1 between the towns. Be cautious of cars whipping by too close for comfort!

### GETTING AROUND
### To/From the Airport

There is no shuttle service from Boscobel to downtown, although local buses pass by and will cost about US$0.30, or US$1 for a mini-bus. A taxi to Ocho Rios will cost about US$14.

### Bus

Ocho Rios has no bus service within town, but you can hop aboard any of the buses that link Ochi and other towns. Within town, most points are within walking distance, but don't be deceived by how spread out the town really is. Main St stretches for 2 miles east of town – a sweaty walk in the heat of midday.

### Car & Motorcycle

Island Car Rentals (☎ 974-2334, 974-2666), Jamaica's largest and most reputable company, at Shop No 2, Carib Arcade on Main St, has competitive rates and offers a variety of vehicles.

Companies with offices in Ocho Rios include the following:

| | |
|---|---|
| Bargain Rent-a-Car | ☎ 974-5298 |
| Caribbean Car Rentals | ☎ 974-2123 |
| Don's Transport Car Rental | ☎ 974-7726 |
| Gemini Car Rental | ☎ 974-1361 |
| Island Car Rentals | ☎ 974-2334, 974-2666 |

Companies that rent scooters or motorcycles include the following:

| | |
|---|---|
| Bikes n Cycles Trading | ☎ 974-8247 |
| Island Scooters | ☎ 974-9510 |
| Jake's | ☎ 974-8838 |
| Motorcycle Rentals/Motor Trails | ☎ 974-5058 |

Bikes 'n Cycles Trading, at 6 James Ave, charges from US$25 for a range of motorcycles up to 750cc Yamaha Viragos.

### Taxi

There's a shortage of licensed taxis (usually Toyota Corolla estate cars), whose prices are regulated. You can negotiate with unregistered taxi drivers, whose cars are often beat-up wrecks, although prices are inflated due to the prevalence of rich cruise passengers. Haggle to get a fair price.

Government established fares from downtown are as follows (one to four people):

| | |
|---|---|
| Dunn's River | US$20 |
| Firefly | US$50 |
| Prospect Plantation | US$20 |
| Shaw Park Gardens | US$20 |
| Sandals Golf Course | US$25 |

Taxi tours are offered, including 'Ocho Rios highlights' (US$60), the 'Garden Parish' (US$100), Blue Mountains (US$180), and Nine Mile (US$100).

### Bicycle

Vacation Wheels (☎ 974-5021), Shop 3 in the Carib Arcade, rents bicycles for about US$10 daily. Cycletronics (☎ 974-1281), 75 Main St, is a bicycle repair shop, as is Rapid & Sheffield (☎ 974-5554), 144 Main St. Also try Abe Rental & Sales (☎ 974-1008) and Jake's Bike Rental (☎ 973-4403).

Blue Mountain Tours (☎ 974-7075, fax 974-0635), at 152 Main St, rents bicycles, but they're not very comfortable. See the Organized Tours section, earlier in this chapter.

# East of Ocho Rios

## TOWER ISLE TO BOSCOBEL BEACH

Don't miss the drive along the A3 east of Ocho Rios; see Scenic Drives in the Facts for the Visitor chapter. East of the White River, habitations begin thinning out. Several beaches lie hidden below the cliffs. Notable among them is Tower Isle, 5 miles east of Ocho Rios, where Jamaica's all-inclusive resort craze began three decades ago with the opening of the first American-style hotel in Jamaica (originally the Tower Isle hotel and now Couples), helping to launch tourism on this part of the island in the 1960s.

Jamaica Beach, between Tower Isle and the Rio Nuevo, is renowned for its dive sites immediately offshore.

An interesting side trip is to follow the Rio Nuevo inland along a glade-shaded valley to **Retreat**, where an imposing church looms over colonial ruins next to a suspension bridge over the river (the turnoff from the A3 is opposite the Unipet gas station). Nearby, the Waterside Hide-Away has swimming, plus live music and food and drink on weekends.

### Rio Nuevo

The Rio Nuevo meets the ocean 5 miles east of Ocho Rios. In 1658, the bluff west of the river's mouth was the site of the most important battle ever fought on the island. Although the colonial Spanish commander had surrendered to the invading British army in 1655, many Spanish soldiers refused to lay down their arms. Under the leadership of a guerrilla and fifth-generation Jamaican, Don Cristobal Arnaldo de Ysassi, the recalcitrant Spaniards continued to harass the British. In May 1658, the King of Spain named Ysassi titular governor and sent reinforcements from Cuba in an attempt to retake the island. They landed at Rio Nuevo, where they built a stockade on the heights west of the river mouth. The English governor, D'Oyley, promptly landed marines, established camp on the opposite bank, and managed to surprise the Spaniards using a classic feint: after sending a small boy under flag of truce to test the depth of the river, D'Oyley's ships made the appearance of launching a full-scale frontal assault while his soldiers sneaked up to the fort from the rear. A plaque records the events:

On this ground on June 17, 1658, was fought the battle of Rio Nuevo to decide whether Jamaica would be Spanish or English. On one side were the Jamaicans of both black and white races, whose ancestors had come to Jamaica from Africa and Spain 150 years before. The Spanish forces lost the battle and the island. The Spanish whites fled to Cuba but the black people took to the mountains and fought a long and bloody guerrilla war against the English. This site is dedicated to them all.

Another memorial stands beneath a gazebo on the site of the old stockade. The site is shaded by pimento trees, beneath which are benches for quiet contemplation. The site is said to be open 9 am to 4 pm daily, but was locked up when I called by. You can hike down to a gray-sand beach where there's a small fishing community.

### Boscobel Beach

Boscobel Beach, 4 miles east of Rio Nuevo, is a hamlet dominated by SuperClub's nearby Boscobel Beach resort. Other tiny coves farther east harbor fishing hamlets nestled in turquoise lagoons protected by coral reefs. The Boscobel airstrip is here.

Boscobel is served by Stewart Town, a small village replete with roadside food shacks and groceries. There's a post office on a road parallel to the A3 running closer to the shore.

### Places to Stay

**Mid-Range** *Skip's Place* (☎ 975-7010), half a mile west of Boscobel Beach, has 16 modest rooms of varying sizes, with cross-ventilation and basic furnishings from US$25 to US$75 double. Skip also rents a three-bedroom flat with kitchen for US$100 double, US$150 up to six people, and offers scuba diving and fishing in a fully equipped boat.

*Island of Light Centre for Holistic Development* (*☎/fax 975-4268, PO Box 6, Retreat, St Mary*) hints at a New Age countercultural sort of place. In fact, it's an exquisite B&B in a tastefully converted colonial cottage in the hills. The five-acre estate was once part of Prospect Plantation and the two guest cottages (one with three bedrooms, the other with one) were formerly the plantation accountant's stables. The place is a tasteful home-away-from-home, with exquisite modern art and antique furnishings. Rooms cost US$40 – a bargain. Vegetarian meals are US$12, and feature produce straight from the garden. There's a plunge pool, plus hammocks under palms in grounds offering sweeping vistas. The American owner, Sally Sherman, hosts workshops in yoga and meditation, massage therapy, and bodywork, as well as art classes for local children. You can also *camp* here for US$15. To get there, turn off the A3 for Retreat, then turn right (east) by the police station in Retreat.

*Cottage by the Beach* (*no telephone*), 400 yards east of Boscobel Beach, is a three-bedroom apartment in its own private cove. Each unit has a kitchenette, TV, and private bath, plus a wide veranda with sofa and hammock for US$40 double.

*La Mer Resort* (*☎ 975-5002, fax 974-2359*) is a modestly upscale hotel on Jamaica Beach, immediately west of the Rio. It was once a dedicated dive resort, but no more, and seems to be struggling to attract business. It has 34 self-contained one, two, and three-bedroom units set in lush landscaped grounds, from US$55 single, US$60 double.

*Jamaica Beach Resort* (*☎ 975-4582*), a short distance east, is a modern roadside option with nine rooms with fans, TVs, and modest decor for US$55 downstairs, US$65 upstairs with kitchenette. It has a pool and sundeck and a breeze-swept bar, but is of only modest appeal. The nearest beach is Reggae Beach, a mile away.

For a self-catering option, consider *Seagrape Villas* (*☎ 975-4406, 800-637-3608 in the USA, c/o West Indies Investments, 640 Pearson St, suite 304, Des Plaines, IL 60016*), perched on the cliff at Jamaica Beach. Each beautiful villa has four bedrooms and four bathrooms, sleeps up to eight people, is centered on a private pool, and comes with its own cook and maid. They rent for US$55 per person nightly in low season, and US$2500 per week, high season.

Another attractive option nearby, similar to Skip's Place, is *Sea Chalets Villa* (*☎ 974-3265*), in landscaped grounds 400 yards east of Boscobel airstrip. Four-bedroom, two-story villas with kitchens share a shell-shaped pool and sundeck (US$60 per room). *Harbour View Manor* (*☎ 926-0029, fax 978-6380*) at Boscobel has also been recommended. The breeze-swept home is set in a garden and boasts antiques and stenciled pastel walls. It also has a self-contained cottage.

**Top End** Lording over Boscobel Beach is the handsome, 207-room, all-inclusive *Boscobel Beach* (*☎ 975-7331, fax 975-7370, PO Box 63, Ocho Rios; ☎ 954-925-0925, 800-467-8737, fax 954-925-0334 in North America; ☎ 01749-677200 in the UK; www.superclubs.com*), Jamaica's most complete family resort, operated by the SuperClubs chain. Resembling a mini-Disneyworld – there's even a family of bears in bear suits – in a lush fantasia of landscaped foliage, the multi-tiered resort cascades to a handsome beach lined by a boardwalk arcade with cafés, stores, and entertainment facilities. It also welcomes singles and couples. The rooms and suites are very elegant and lively, and each boasts king-size bed and terrace. Suites also have a lounge and sofa-bed. Per person rates begin at US$589 to US$1289 for a three-night package low season; high-season rates begin at US$929 to US$1889. Add US$150 per night for single occupancy. Two children under 14 per adult stay and eat free when sharing a room with parents (US$50 each additional child). Educational programs, a petting zoo, computer lab, video games room, a Teens Party HQ disco, nursery, and 24-hour SuperNanny program keep the kids amused. There are adults-only areas, plus five bars, four tennis courts, gym, volleyball, and an Olympic-size family pool.

*Couples (☎ 975-4271, fax 975-4439, PO Box 330, Ocho Rios; ☎ 305-668-0008, 800-268-7537, fax 305-668-0111 in North America; ☎ 020-8900-1913, fax 020-8795-1728 in the UK, www.couples.com),* at Tower Isle, is an upscale all-inclusive resort for couples only. The palm-lined driveway to the porte cochere and the marble lobby hints at the tasteful decor within. Volleyball, squash, horseback riding, tennis, bicycling, catamaran cruises, and a complete array of water sports are on hand, and 'social directors' make sure that the action never stops. A small island is reserved for nude bathing and weddings. The 172 rooms have king-size beds and large balconies. Low season rates (per couple) start at US$1320 for three nights and US$2800 for one week. High season rates start at US$1520 for three nights and US$3220 for one week. The all-inclusive price covers roundtrip airport transfers, three sightseeing tours, and anything that exists inside the gates.

## Places to Eat

In Stewart Town, be sure to stop at *Colette's Café,* a twee little roadside shop where Colette and her mum serve simple Jamaican fare, patties, ice cream, and bottled coconut water (US$3).

*Skip's Place (☎ 975-7010),* enjoys a breezy clifftop setting half a mile west of Boscobel Beach. It serves seafood and Jamaican dishes upwards of US$5, although the surroundings are a bit dour.

*Cliff View (☎ 975-4417),* just west of the Rio Nuevo, is a popular upscale restaurant owned by music promoter Har Richards.

## Shopping

If you're tired of seeing the same old woven straw and carved wood souvenirs, check out Irie Ceramics (☎ 975-4800), also called Lloyd's Ceramics, a local potters' workshop where you can buy wind chimes, casserole dishes, figurines, and vases for a song. It's 400m east of Couples (see Places to Stay, earlier in this chapter).

## ORACABESSA

This small town (population 10,000), which hangs on a hillside 13 miles east of Ocho Rios, takes its name from the Spanish *oro cabeza,* meaning 'golden head,' probably a reference to the way the evening sunlight reflects on the headland. First impressions of Oracabessa are of its Caribbean vernacular architecture along the main street, lined by an open-air market and wooden houses trimmed with old-fashioned fretwork and complete with verandas. There's even the **Old Fort** with cannon (currently overgrown and crying out for landscaping).

In the early 1970s an artificial harbor was built on the shore below Oracabessa. It was ill timed. Banana shipping – formerly the principle trade of Oracabessa – was in decline, and the harbor was never put to use.

Below Oracabessa is the marina, formerly used as a banana-loading port, in the lee of a tombolo on whose western flank pirogues and fishing boats bob at anchor. Until recently you could see lobster cages and nets drawn up on **James Bond Beach,** today the setting for one of the most remarkable urban revival projects ever undertaken on the island. At this writing the entire shorefront was in the midst of a dramatic remake that will put Oracabessa squarely on the tourist map.

The entire waterfront has been bought by the Island Trading Company, which is recreating an entire village on a 19th-century theme down by the shore. The company is owned by Chris Blackwell, the famous music promoter who was born hereabouts and who actively promotes local community development. His plans are ambitious and call for the marina to be relocated and expanded. Two new beaches have been created, a park on the promontory was in the works at press time, and ground had been broken on a major upscale resort that will include a spa on **Santa Maria Island.** The island, in the midst of the harbor channel, will be turned into a 'bird and people sanctuary.' The town center will receive a cantilevered sidewalk, landscaping, civic center, and rehabilitation of the cluster of traditional houses.

NORTH COAST

## ORACABESSA

*Oracabessa Bay*

Low Cay Beach

Snorkeler's Beach

Santa Maria Island

To Port Maria, Port Antonio, Firefly

James Bond Beach

Fisherman's Beach

Wharf Rd

Vernon Ave

Coleraine Rd

Neil St.

Caraoe Pond Rd

Frank Lane

Main Rd

Waterfront Rd

Jack's River

To Ocho Rios

North Coast Hwy

To Jack's River

Jack's River Rd

0   1.5   3 km
0   1   2 miles

| PLACES TO STAY | OTHER |
|---|---|
| 2  Goldeneye Cottages | 1  Lighthouse |
| 3  Goldeneye Villa | 3  Goldeneye |
| 5  Rock Edge, | 4  Jet Ski Base |
| Golden Cloud Villas | 6  Oracabessa Medical Centre |
| 9  Nix-Nax | 7  Gas Station, Supermarket |
| 10  New Feelings Motel | 8  Marina |
| 24  Golden Seas | 10  New Feelings Disco |
| Beach Resort | 11  Feelings Night Club & Disco |
|  | 12  Old Fort |
| PLACES TO EAT | 13  Police Station |
| 15  Jah Willy's Calabash Inn | 14  Public Health Clinic |
| 19  Blue Lagoon Restaurant | 16  Edward's Plaza |
| 20  Big Tree Bar | 17  Library |
| 21  La Shanka Tavern | 18  Supermarket |
| 26  Miss P's | 22  Post Office |
|  | 23  Scotiabank |
|  | 25  Produce Market |
|  | 27  Supermarket |

**NORTH COAST**

The project has involved the setting up of the Oracabessa Foundation to serve as a catalyst for the sustainable development of the town (see 'Community Development'). Locals are being encouraged to set up their own businesses on the waterfront. To learn more, contact Island Communications (☎ 975-3632), Goldeneye, Oracabessa, and order a copy of *Oracabessa: The Town, the People & the Waterfront Development* by Jean and Oliver Cox.

You can hike to caves in the hills east of town. Ask for Percy at Dor's Fish Pot, east of town (see Places to Eat); he'll guide you. There are stalactites and stalagmites and harmless fruit bats. Percy's fee is 'negotiable.'

### Information

A Scotiabank (☎ 975-3203) is in the town center. The private Oracabessa Medical Centre (☎ 975-3304) is opposite the Esso gas station at the east end of town; it's open 7:30 am to 2:30 pm weekdays, and 7 am to 12:30 pm Wednesday and Saturday. One mile farther east, the Natural Health Care Centre offers holistic massage. The Oracabessa Pharmacy (☎ 975-3241) is in Edward's Plaza in the town center; it closes at 12:30 pm on Wednesdays.

There's a Shell gas station 800 yards west of town.

### Goldeneye

Topped by carved pineapples, the gateposts on the A3 immediately east of Oracabessa mark the entrance to Goldeneye, former home of novelist Ian Fleming, inventor of the legendary super-spy, James Bond. Fleming fell in love with Jamaica after a visit and returned to buy this 15-acre beachfront estate (he bought the house for £49 from the Blackwell family), designing most of the house himself in 1946, with huge jalousies to let in the breeze. All 14 of Fleming's James Bond novels were written here, and five were set in Jamaica. 'Would these books have been born if I had not been living in the gorgeous vacuum of a Jamaican holiday? I doubt it,' he wrote in *Ian Fleming Introduces Jamaica*. Noel Coward, who later lived down the road at Port Maria (see Firefly,

## Community Development

Under the umbrella of the Oracabessa Foundation (☎ 975-3393, fax 975-3394), PO Box 38, Oracabessa, St Mary, Oracabessa's community spirit is as energetic as anywhere on the island. The key to the community effort is providing youngsters with alternatives to prostitution and drugs. The International School of Jamaica, PO Box 36, Oracabessa, St Mary, for example, works to promote self-sufficiency through various enterprises like bee-keeping, composting, solid-waste management, and quilt-making from rag scraps.

A group called Lynx works to educate the community about littering and other environmental issues. The group also helps feed the indigent and elderly, mediates in youth disputes, and patrols the community. Another community group, Inner Circle, works to ensure that parents send their children to school and assists with providing school supplies.

The foundation is planning a civic center; has plans to beautify the old fort; and has launched the Oracabessa Sports Trust to supply children with sports equipment (donations are welcome).

later in this chapter), was a frequent visitor, as were Evelyn Waugh, Graham Greene, and others of the beau monde. The house is now part of Goldeneye Villas and can be rented (see Places to Stay, below), but is *not* open to casual visitors.

### Sun Valley Plantation
Sun Valley Plantation (☎ 995-3075), PO Box 20, Oracabessa, is a working plantation at Crescent on the B13, some 3 miles south of Oracabessa and about 5 miles west of Port Maria. Owners Lorna and Nolly Binns will guide you along the Crescent River and on through the groves of coconuts and other tropical fruits and medicinal herbs (US$12 including snack). Tours are offered daily at 9 am, 11 am, and 2 pm. You can see coconut

water – the plantation's main income source – being bottled for sale (the water is considered the purest of drinks and is highly regarded as a diuretic). Hour-long horseback rides are offered (US$20, or US$28 including a plantation tour).

### Sport Fishing
Captain Barry Roper (☎ 975-3312) can take you sport fishing aboard a 42-foot Bertram, the *Renegade*.

### Special Events
The big event of the year is the Annual Air Jamaica Jazz & Blues Festival (☎ 975-36654, fax 975-3399), a three-day event held each November at James Bond Beach and featuring an amazing showcase of international stars. The 1998 program boasted Earl Klugh, Dianne Reeves, Roberta Flack, Chaka Khan, Kool & the Gang, George Duke, George Benson, and Toots & the Maytals, among others. *Imagine!*

The James Bond Oracabessa Marlin Tournament (☎ 968-6792, fax 968-6779) is held in late October.

A great time to visit is Christmas for the town's tree lighting ceremony, when the Oracabessa Youth Ensemble performs and Santa is on hand to give out gifts.

Jason Henzell of Jake's Place (see Treasure Beach in the Southwest Coast chapter) was organizing the 'Golden Man Triathalon,' sponsored by Chris Blackwell and to be initiated in 1999. It will begin and end at James Bond Beach.

Keep your ears and eyes peeled for any future 'James Bond Festival,' first held in 1996 but which has not been continued. For updates, email the Ian Fleming Foundation at news@ianfleming.org, or visit their website (www.ianfleming.org).

### Places to Stay
Dickie (a Jamaican Rasta) and Dominica (from Harlem) offer basic but good-value rooms at *Nix-Nax* (☎ 975-3364) on School St. It's a counterculture kinda place splashed with rainbow motifs, philosophical texts, and colorful, mystical murals (even the pillowcases are rainbow batiks). It's simple, but

has all the essentials, including a communal kitchen. There are two types of rooms: those with shared showers and toilets in the courtyard, and those with private bathrooms, for US$10 to US$15 per person, respectively. One room is a four-bunk dorm. The couple operates the Rainbow Learning Centre here; the kindergarten works for peace and development, rooting young children in 'faith and power and peace.' The kids are present 9 am to 12:30 pm weekdays, when the place may be noisy.

*Lovely Spot Ocean Villas* (☎ 975-3322), also east of town, is a laid-back place with a friendly owner, Len, who offers tours of his farm. His four pink and white villas, for US$24 per person, are modest, spacious, and clean, and sit above a coral shore. Each has a kitchenette, fans, homey furnishings, and hot water. Upstairs rooms have verandas. Little gazebos dot the ramshackle garden.

The *New Feelings Motel & Disco* (☎ 975-3549), on Wharf Rd, also has modest rooms. Other rooms next to the pharmacy beside the A3 are rented by the owners of the *Tropical Hut*, a rustic eatery east of town; they cost US$35.

Here's a gem, and a bargain to boot. Nestled atop a hill four miles south of Oracabessa is the *Tamarind Great House* (☎/fax 995-3252, Crescent Estate, Oracabessa PO, St Mary, tamarind@cariboutpost.com), described as a 'plantation guest house.' Delightful English hosts and owners Gillian and Barry Chambers built this stunner in 1994 in grand colonial style to replace the original plantation house that had burned down. The setting is sublime, with lush valleys and mountains all around. The house boasts gleaming guango wood floors, plus reproduction antiques. There are 10 cavernous rooms, reached by a wide staircase, going for a song: US$45 single, US$65 double. Each opens to a vast veranda with Adirondack chairs for enjoying the views over swaths of bamboo and palms. Squawking parrots flash by. Logs blaze in the fireplace in the TV lounge on chilly nights, and meals are served in an elegant dining room. Tamarind is a working citrus plantation. It has a small swimming pool with sundeck, and a fishpond

stocked with tilapia (a cross between a snapper and freshwater perch) to keep the kitchen supplied (pheasant are also raised). It's a mile south of Sun Valley Plantation (turn right at the first Y-fork, then right at the next fork).

Half a mile west of Oracabessa, the *Golden Seas Beach Resort* (☎ 975-3540, fax 975-3243, PO Box 1, egons@infochan.com) is an attractive hotel of cut stone, with 79 comfortable rooms – done up in mauve floral prints – with patios overlooking a pool where you can sit in hammock chairs at the swim-up bar. It offers water sports, tennis clinics and lessons (US$20 per hour), cabaret shows, and a resident band that plays nightly. Low-season rates are US$83/99 single/double standard, up to US$149/165 for a suite (there are five categories of rooms within this range). High-season rates are US$94/110 single/double standard, up to US$160/175 for a suite.

*Rock Edge* (☎ 975-3232), *Golden Cloud*, and *Golden Acre* are villas at the east end of Oracabessa, east of Goldeneye. They're represented by Villas of Ocho Rios, Practical Solutions LLC (☎ 612-821-9342, 888-625-6007, fax 612-824-2956, 3400 Irving Avenue South, Minneapolis, MN 55408, agent@sunvillas.com, www.sunvillas.com/golden/).

*The* place to be, if you have deep pockets, is *Goldeneye Villa & Cottages* (☎ 975-3354, 800-688-7678 in the USA, fax 975-3679, www.islandoutpost.com). Eight villas, including Ian Fleming's former home, sit in expansive grounds atop one of the quaintest coves and beaches you ever saw. No hoi polloi here! The place attracts the international A-list, including supermodel Naomi Campbell and, appropriately, Pierce Brosnan…Bond himself! Fleming's house, a one-story, three-bedroom affair with Mansard wooden ceiling and massive glassless windows, features spectacular decor heavy on teak and bamboo and Balinese fabrics, plus dramatic ethnic art pieces. You can write your postcards at the original fan-shaped corner desk at which Fleming dreamed up 007 and would unstintingly write 2000 words every day. The main bedroom has a king-size bed beneath a hangar-size canopy. All this costs

US$5000 nightly, all-inclusive of meals and full-time steward service.

Tucked along the cliff face is a 'flexible configuration of eight cottages,' each with its own distinct character. You can rent them individually or collectively (from US$650 to US$2000 nightly). Built of wood and stone and painted in autumnal colors, each is a study in good taste. All have ceiling fans, a kitchen and entertainment/TV room, CD player and a collection of CDs (choose from Mozart, Mapfumo, or Marley), thoughtful extras such as spice colognes and an armory to counter mosquitos, plus pampering yet discreet stewards. Each cottage has its own terrace with dining table, and Adirondack and lounge chairs overhanging the waters, where stewards serve up romantic candlelit meals. Imagine bathing in a deep claw-foot bathtub on a pedestal next to the bed, or showering beneath a massive fig tree in a zen-style garden with torrents of piping hot water pouring down from a showerhead the size of a skillet.

The coup de grâce is an entertainment room with bar and drop-down screen, where 007 movies are shown while you nestle on the biggest sofa you ever saw, with martini (shaken, not stirred) in hand. Water sports are available, as are excursions plus a tennis court lit for night play. A swimming pool was to be added. A larger private beach lies a short swim (or boat ride) across the marina channel, where a 60-room upscale resort was under construction at press time. For a grand entrance, why not touch down on the helipad?

## Places to Eat

The resort development looks like it will shut down business at **Jah Willy's Calabash Inn**, down by James Bond Beach, a cool place to hang for a game of dominoes or volleyball with the locals. Willy serves seafood and jerk for US$2 and less. **Dor's Fish Pot** is a lively yet rustic jerk and seafood eatery atop the breezy cliffs east of town; the equally rustic and charming **Tropical Hut** is 200 yards east. Nearby is **Club Tan Jan Tavern**, serving seafood and I-tal dishes.

---

### Fleming...Ian Fleming

Ian Fleming first came to Jamaica in 1942, while serving for British Naval Intelligence. In 1946 he bought a house on the shore at Oracabessa and named it 'Goldeneye,' where he wintered every year until his death in 1964.

It was here that Fleming conceived his secret agent '007,' alias James Bond, whose creation the author attributes to living in Jamaica.

'I was looking for a name for my hero – nothing like Peregrine Carruthers or Standfast Maltravers – and I found it, on the cover of one of my Jamaican bibles, *Birds of the West Indies* by James Bond, an ornithological classic,' he relates in *Ian Fleming Introduces Jamaica*.

Want to know more? Contact the Ian Fleming Foundation (π/fax 805-683-9525, news@ianfleming.org, www.ianfleming.org), PO Box 6897, Santa Barbara, CA 93160. The foundation, which works to procure, restore, and archive Fleming's legacy, publishes *Goldeneye Magazine*.

---

In the town center, head to **Miss P's**, opposite the supermarket and beside the market. Miss P sells tasty loaves stuffed with callaloo and ackee and saltfish, plus veggie patties and cooked meals. **Big Tree Bar**, nearby on Main Rd, sells zesty pastries and soothing ice cream. And you'll find basic Jamaican fare for US$2 or so at the earthy **Blue Lagoon Restaurant**, opposite Scotiabank.

For a gourmet meal, head to **Tamarind Great House** (see Places to Stay, earlier).

## Entertainment

The only real action around is **Feelings Night Club & Disco** (π 975-3545) on Wharf Rd; it features oldies on weekends. **La Shanka Tavern**, opposite the market on Main St, is a lively rum shop playing ear-bursting music, good for a spirited game of dominoes.

No stay would be complete without sipping a 'Goldfinger' (pineapple and orange juice with two types of rum) or a 'Moonraker' (a strawberry-flavored rum drink) on James Bond Beach.

## Getting There & Away

Buses and minibuses that run between Ocho Rios and Port Antonio, and those that go between Ocho Rios and Kingston via Annotto Bay, pass through Oracabessa. A bus from Ocho Rios will cost about US$0.50; a minibus about US$2.

You can rent a car from Paramount Cars (☎ 994-2357).

## FIREFLY

A visit to Firefly is one of the most interesting excursions in all Jamaica. The English-style cottage, set amid wide lawns high atop a hill 3 miles southeast of Oracabessa and 3 miles west of Port Maria, was the home of Sir Noel Coward, the English playwright, songwriter, actor, and wit. When he died in 1973, Coward left the estate to his friend Graham Payne, who gifted it to the nation. It soon fell into disrepair. In 1990 the property was leased by the Jamaica National Heritage Trust to Island Outpost, owned by Chris Blackwell, who embarked on a meticulous restoration (it was Blackwell's mother who sold the property to Coward, and both she and her son were considered part of the Coward 'family'). In 1993 the house reopened to the public as a museum, looking just as it did on Sunday, February 28, 1965, the day the Queen Mother visited.

You'll be greeted by a guide, who will hand you a fruit punch or rum cocktail and lead you first to Coward's art studio, where he was schooled in oil painting by Winston Churchill. The studio displays Coward's original paintings and photographs of the host and a coterie of famous friends from around the world.

The former garage has been turned into a screening room where a spellbinding film about Coward's life is shown before you tour the house. The upper lounge features a glassless window shaded by a green awning that stretches the full length of the room and offers one of the most stunning coastal vistas in all Jamaica. Contrary to popular opinion, Coward didn't write his famous song 'A Room with a View' here; it was written in Hawaii in 1928. Beyond is the bedroom with his mahogany bed topped by pineapples (symbols of prosperity and peace) and closets still stuffed with his Hawaiian shirts and silk PJs.

Coward lies buried beneath a plain white marble slab on the wide lawns where he

LONNY KALFUS

Firefly, Noel Coward's former home

entertained so many illustrious stars of stage and screen. A stone hut that once served as a lookout for the pirate Henry Morgan has been restored and is now a gift store, bar, and restaurant (Firefly was then part of Morgan's Llanrumney Estate). Today, musical and theatrical performances are hosted regularly, and a Moonlick party (US$25 all-inclusive) with live jazz band is held on weekends closest to the full moon. During the parties, the estate is lit by candles in brown bags to represent the fireflies (locally called peeny-wallies or winkies) after which the house is named.

Entrance is US$10 (or J$100 for Jamaican residents), including a complimentary drink. The museum is open 8:30 am to 5:30 pm daily (☎ 997-7201, fax 974-5830), PO Box 38, Port Maria, St Mary. Firefly is well signed along three different routes that lead inland from the A3, from Oracabessa, Little Bay, and Port Maria.

## GALINA POINT & LITTLE BAY

Three miles east of Oracabessa, the A3 leaves the coast and winds around Galina Point, the northernmost tip of the island. A 40-foot-high concrete lighthouse marks the headland. South of Galina you'll pass Noel Coward's first house, **Blue Harbour** (not open for tours; see Places to Stay & Eat, below) squatting behind a blue-and-white fence on the top of what is called 'the double bend,' where the road and shoreline take a 90 degree turn and open to a view of Little Bay and Cabarita Island. The road drops steeply from Blue Harbour to Cocomo Beach, in Little Bay.

The beach is unappealing, despite being popular in the 1950s and 1960s with Coward and his illustrious friends, but the snorkeling is said to be good above the coral reef 50 yards out (check with locals about swimming conditions).

The **Zabai Tabai Taino Museum**, next to the Hotel Casa Maria on the A3, is an offbeat museum celebrating the Taino culture. Many of the artifacts were dug up on the owner's property, which has a cave with what are purportedly Taino paintings that glow translucent in winter.

## Places to Stay & Eat

Errol Henry offers camping at his *Zabai Tabai Taino Heritage Park.*

*Ocean Villa Guest House* (☎ 994-2390) and *Belretiro Inn* (PO Box 151, Galina District PA, Port Maria) are run by a colorful character, Busta Prendergast. Belretiro has 10 rooms with private baths and cold water for US$30. Nearby, *Malindos Villa by the Sea* (☎ 994-0202), on Galina Point, is run by Canadian Jamaicans and offers marvelous coastal views from atop the raised coral shore. The modern house has homey decor and is cross-ventilated. There's a cozy atrium lounge. The eight mezzanine bedrooms vary in size but all have fans and open to an outside patio; they're US$50 to US$100 single or double.

The attractive *Caribbean Pearl* (☎ 994-2672, fax 994-2043, PO Box 127, Port Maria), which rests on a breezy hilltop at the southern end of Little Bay, is run to excellent standards by the rather dour Hans Jurgens Böcking. This elegant and intimate villa-style hotel is centered on a pool, and its eight rooms and two master suites are furnished with hardwoods and white wicker, and mosquito nets over the beds. Wide windows open to shady verandas where you can relax on wicker hammocks. Ask for Room 2, which has a wicker four-poster bed and Chinese rugs. It costs US$50 per person, including breakfast.

If all else fails, there's the 20-room *Hotel Casa Maria* (☎ 994-2323, PO Box 10, Port Maria; ☎ 509-547-7065, 800-222-6927, fax 509-547-1265 in North America) next to the Caribbean Pearl. The place has lost its panache since Noel Coward and his celebrated guests frequented the bar in the 1950s and 1960s. The rooms are pleasantly though modestly furnished. Cheaper rooms have garden views; superior rooms have private balconies with ocean views. Rates are US$50 single or double standard, US$55 superior. The modestly elegant restaurant advertises 'pizzas and patties.'

Farther along is the modern, motel-style *Tradewinds Resort* (☎ 994-0420, fax 994-0423), cascading down the windswept cliffs to a rocky shore. It has 14 rooms, all with

## Noel Coward's Peeny-Wally

Sir Noel Coward, the multi-talented English actor, playwright, songwriter, and raconteur, first visited Jamaica in 1944 on a two-week holiday. He found so much peace of mind here that he dubbed his dream-island 'Dr Jamaica.' Four years later he rented Ian Fleming's estate, Goldeneye, at Oracabessa, while he hunted for a site to build his own home. He found an incredible view over Little Bay near Galina, 'a magical spot' 10 miles east of Oracabessa.

In 1948 Coward bought the eight-acre estate and set to work building 'Coward's Folly,' a three-story villa with two guest cottages. He then went back to England and returned to Jamaica only when it was complete. Inspired by the view, he named his home Blue Harbour. He had a swimming pool built at the sea's edge and invited his many notable friends, a virtual Who's Who of the rich and famous.

'His was a most extraordinary, charismatic mind,' recalls Chris Blackwell. 'His wit was so sharp that he controlled a room not only by what he was saying, but by the expectation of what he might say next.'

The swarm of visitors, however, eventually drove Coward to find another retreat.

While painting with his friend, Graham Payne, at a place called Lookout (so-named because the pirate Henry Morgan had a stone hut built atop the hill to keep an eye out for Spanish galleons), Coward was struck by the impressive solitude and the vista of bays receding in scalloped relief, backed by distant mountains. The duo lingered until nightfall, when fireflies appeared. Within two weeks Coward had bought the land, and eight years later had a house built, big enough for only himself. He named it Firefly.

Coward's most creative years were behind him when he arrived in Jamaica. At Firefly, however, he could write in peace. His only novel, *Pomp and Circumstance*, his comedy, *South Sea Bubble*, and his musical, *Ace of Clubs*, were all written here. Coward lived a remarkably modest lifestyle in Jamaica; he set up the now-defunct Designs for Living shop in Port Maria, the profits from which were put into the training of local schoolchildren in arts and crafts. Coward himself recorded his love of the island and islanders on canvas, in bright, splashy colors.

Coward had spent 30 'delightful years' in Jamaica when he suffered a heart attack at the age of 73. He is buried on the lawns of Firefly beneath a marble slab that reads simply: 'Sir Noel Coward/Born 16 December 1899/Died 26 March 1973.'

---

splendid views along the St Mary coastline, cool white tiles, modest furnishings, small TVs, phones, and remote air-con. There's a small lap pool and a restaurant. Rooms (including breakfast) cost US$60 upstairs, US$51 downstairs.

A more atmospheric option is ***Reef Point*** (☎ 994-0817, fax 994-0265), a mile west of Port Maria and boasting more magnificent views of the coast and Cabretta Island. This property squats on the cliffside and attempts a budget version of Goldeneye, at Oracabessa: the octagonal wooden cabins feature large walk-in marble showers, remote air-con, fans, cable TV, and radio. Some rooms have a mini-fridge, and a suite has a Jacuzzi. Facilities include a games room and a tennis court, plus a classy restaurant with sponge-washed motifs and Mediterranean hints. The best feature is a small swimming pool on a deck framed by squiggly wrought-iron rails. Sailboat trips are offered. Rates are US$70/75 single/double, small room; US$100 large room; US$110 to US$130 suite.

If you want to sleep in the same room as Marlene Dietrich, Katherine Hepburn, Errol Flynn, or Winston Churchill, rent a villa or room at the rather offbeat and somewhat run-down ***Blue Harbour*** (☎ 994-0289, 505-586-1244 in the USA, PO Box 50, Port

*Maria)*. Coward bought the property in the early 1950s and built the main house, Villa Grande, for himself, and two smaller villas for his guests. Villa Grande has four upstairs bedrooms with wicker and dowdy utility furniture. Meals are served on a wide wraparound veranda with fabulous views over the bay. Villa Rose has four rooms with fairly basic furnishings and decor. Villa Chica is smaller, very private, with more pleasing decor in tropical pastels. Blue Harbour comes fully staffed with cook and housekeeper, though some of the staff appear lackadaisical. Pathways lead downhill through tropical foliage to a shingle beach and a small seawater pool. Rates are US$85 per person, including three meals.

Of an entirely different ilk is *Bolt House* (☎ 975-3620, 800-688-7678 in the USA, 0800-614790 in the UK, c/o Island Outpost, PO Box 118, Ocho Rios, www.islandoutpost .com), a villa set amid 50 cliffside acres across the road from Tradewinds. The villa – once owned by Blanche Blackwell – has a marble-floored living room (with a stupendous view over the coast), three sunlit bedrooms, and a pool overhanging the cliff top. It's part of the Island Outpost empire, and as such boasts exquisite contemporary furnishings – pastel walls and lots of batik – with accents playing on its past as a venue for folks like Charlie Chaplin, Ian Fleming, and Joan Sutherland. Guests have access to facilities at Goldeneye Village, in Oracabessa. It comes fully staffed, and rents for US$4000 weekly (up to six people), including airport transfers and all meals, served in a formal dining room or alfresco on the patio beside the swimming pool.

## PORT MARIA

Port Maria (population 8000) is the capital of St Mary parish. It's merely a place to pass through en route to Port Antonio or Ocho Rios, and has no tourist facilities. As with many other towns along this coast, it prospered in the 19th century as a sugar and banana port. Two centuries prior, the land for miles around was part of Llanrumney Estate, owned by the nefarious Henry Morgan, who rose from fame as a pirate to become lieu-

tenant governor of the island. Nothing much seems to happen here these days, except on weekends when there's a market, turning the main street into mayhem.

When you approach from the west, your first view is spectacular: you round the headland east of Little Bay, and there's Port Maria nestling in its bed of turquoise and aquamarine with mountains rising behind. Have your camera ready.

Port Maria is divided by a bridge over a small river, with a sleepy residential area to the west and a commercial section immediately to the east. Take care at the tiny roundabout immediately east of the bridge; keep left.

### Information

**Money** You can change traveler's checks or get advances against credit cards at Scotiabank (☎ 994-2265) or National Commercial Bank (☎ 994-2219) on Warner St. Western Union has an office in Kong's Store (☎ 994-2218) at 5 Stennet St.

**Post & Communications** The post office (☎ 994-2278) is on the north side of the roundabout.

**Medical Services** The public general hospital (☎ 994-2228) is 1 mile south of town on Stennet St. For less urgent medical attention call Dr Leonard Jones (☎ 992-2622), or Dr Watson, who has a clinic 100m east of the police station. Clare's Pharmacy (☎ 994-2386) and Parkway Pharmacy (☎ 994-2037) are in the town center.

**Emergencies** The police station (☎ 994-2223) is 100 yards north of the roundabout, facing the sea on Main St.

### Things to See

At the extreme west end of town, **St Mary's Parish Church** was built in 1861 of limestone in quintessential English style. Palms loom over the churchyard.

Opposite the church is the roofless ruin of the **old courthouse**, destroyed in 1988 by fire. A plaque on the wall is dedicated to the Right Honorable Alexander Bustamante,

# PORT MARIA

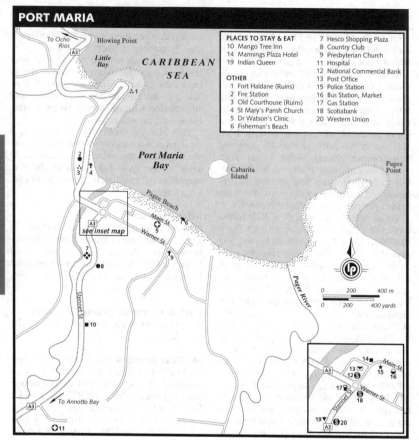

**PLACES TO STAY & EAT**
10  Mango Tree Inn
14  Mannings Plaza Hotel
19  Indian Queen

**OTHER**
1  Fort Haldane (Ruins)
2  Fire Station
3  Old Courthouse (Ruins)
4  St Mary's Parish Church
5  Dr Watson's Clinic
6  Fisherman's Beach
7  Hesco Shopping Plaza
8  Country Club
9  Presbyterian Church
11  Hospital
12  National Commercial Bank
13  Post Office
15  Police Station
16  Bus Station, Market
17  Gas Station
18  Scotiabank
20  Western Union

To Ocho Rios

Blowing Point

Little Bay

CARIBBEAN SEA

Port Maria Bay

Cabarita Island

Pagee Point

Pagee Beach

see inset map

Main St

Warner St

Stennet St

Pagee River

To Annotto Bay

0    200    400 m
0    200    400 yards

Main St
Warner St
Stennet St

---

the labor organizer and former prime minister who once stood trial in the courthouse, which dates back to 1820. A monument in front commemorates 'Tacky of the Easter Rebellion.' The courthouse was being restored with the funding of the Venezuelan government at the time of this writing. It will reopen with an interpretive museum, auditorium, gift shop, and craft center.

Motley remains of **Fort Haldane** can be seen on a bluff beside the A3, half a mile north of town. If you haven't had your fill of churches, check out the stern brick **Presbyterian church** atop a knoll to the east of town. It was built in 1830 to Christianize the slaves of Frontier Estate, where the Easter Rebellion was sparked in 1760.

## Activities

The town beach, Pagee Beach, sweeps eastward for almost a mile from the river's mouth. Fishing pirogues are usually pulled up here. You can hire a guide and boat to go **fishing** or to take you to Cabarita Island.

Pagee Beach is safe for **swimming**. It is also the most westerly spot for **surfing** along the north coast, with long peelers. The rocks are sharp however; local surfers advise surfing in front of the point closest to town. The action is best in the morning before the trade winds kick in.

## Places to Stay & Eat
Pickings are slim and depressing. The very basic *Mango Tree Inn* (☎ 994-2687, *49 Stennet St*) is about 800 yards south of the town center on the road to Port Antonio. The inn doubles as a rum shop and place of coital convenience. It has 13 rooms with bathtubs made of concrete, and with cold water only, for US$8.50. *Mannings Plaza Hotel*, 50 yards north of the roundabout, is another very basic, run-down property which offers rooms with shared bath for US$12.

Try the *Country Club*, a rustic restaurant and bar on Stennet St. It serves ackee and codfish and other Jamaican fare for less than US$3. About the only other decent-looking place in town is *Indian Queen*, on Stennet St, immediately south of the roundabout.

## Entertainment
You can let your own hair down at the *Country Club*, which has open-air dancing to live music. You'll be the only out-of-towner.

## Getting There & Away
You can catch buses to Port Maria from Ocho Rios (40 minutes; US$0.30). A minibus will cost about US$2. Buses also operate from Annotto Bay for about US$0.40, as do minibuses (about US$1.50). Buses travel from Kingston, from both Half Way Tree and the Parade (US$1.50), as do minibuses (US$3.50).

There's a gas station by the roundabout east of the bridge.

## BRIMMER HALL
This 2000-acre working plantation (☎ 994-2309, fax 974-2185) near Bailey's Vale, 6 miles southwest of Port Maria, grows bananas, coconuts, sugarcane, pineapple, and citrus for export. It's centered on a wooden great house with an impressive

---

### The Easter Rebellion

St Mary parish was thinly populated by white people throughout the 18th century, when local sugar estates prospered. Many of the slaves of St Mary were from the Cormorante tribes of Africa's Gold Coast. On Easter Sunday, 1760, those of Frontier Estate, east of Port Maria, revolted. They were inspired by Tacky, an overseer who had been a tribal chief prior to being captured and shipped to Jamaica.

The rebellion was one of the most serious slave revolts to shake Jamaica. The slaves killed their masters at Frontier and at neighboring Trinity Estate before marching on Port Maria, where they murdered the storekeeper of Fort Haldane and seized arms and ammunition. The revolt lasted one month, during which plantations throughout St Mary were destroyed.

Eventually the militia gained the upper hand in the guerrilla war, and, aided by Maroons, captured Tacky. His head was cut off and displayed in Spanish Town. About 60 whites and 300 slaves perished in the Easter Rebellion, and several hundred more slaves were killed in grim retribution.

---

interior of dark hardwoods, furnished with oriental rugs, antique furniture with Chinese inlay, and even an original suit of armor. An educational tour reveals the workings of the plantation. Brimmer Hall is a popular tour stop for groups from cruise ships calling in at Ocho Rios. The one-hour tour costs US$15, including a tour of the plantation by canopied jitney pulled by a tractor. A bar and restaurant serve Jamaican dishes next to a pool surrounded by lush foliage.

It's open 9 am to 5 pm daily. Tours are offered at 11 am and 1:30 and 3:30 pm. It's 2 miles inland and is signed from the gas station half a mile south of Port Maria.

# South of Ocho Rios

Five miles south of Ocho Rios, at the top of Fern Gully, the A3 crests a plateau where you can savor your first stupendous view across the rolling pastures to the hillocks of the Dry Harbour Mountains. For the next 7 miles south to Moneague, the road winds up through sweeping pastoral country with stone walls reminiscent of the Dales of England.

At Moneague, the A3 merges with the A1 from St Ann's Bay. You can continue south, uphill to Mt Diablo, where the road dips dramatically toward Spanish Town and Kingston.

## WALKERS WOOD

This village in the cool hills of St Ann parish is clean and tidy. At first the country village seems sleepy. Yet Walkers Wood has an active community life, financed partly by USAID small-business development grants, and there are several thriving businesses.

**Bromley Great House** sits atop a hill southeast of Walkers Wood. Tucked behind the great house is a small factory where a local cooperative called Cottage Industries makes their world-renowned Walkers Wood sauces and spices. (See 'Spicy Enterprises.')

---

### Spicy Enterprises

For over a decade, worker-owned Cottage Industries (☎ 917-2318) has been making products from local ingredients: bales of fresh scallions from St Elizabeth, nutmeg from St Mary, tomatoes, hot peppers, and assorted dried spices from local fields. Initially it experimented with chocolate fudge and pork sausages, but it was jerk seasoning that took hold, launching the cooperative to success and giving birth to a whole range of products. You can now get everything from canned ackee and callaloo, solomon grundy, jams, and spices, to dried bananas, coconut run-down sauce, and escoveitch marinade.

---

Unfortunately, neither Bromley nor the factory are open to the public.

The playing field in the village center was donated by the Reynolds Mining Company, which had a huge open-cast bauxite mine at **Lydford**, about 2 miles west of Walkers Wood. When the company ceased operation in 1983, it restored its 80,000 acres to pasture. Reynolds actually maintained the largest herd of cattle in the West Indies, and their offspring still graze the lime-green fields.

### Places to Stay & Eat

*Murphy Hill* (☎ 922-0440) is a cozy guest house in the cool hills along Spring Mountain Rd, near Lydford. It has fabulous views and a swimming pool popular with Jamaicans escaping the heat of the lowlands. You can also rent horses. The rooms are clean, boast genuine antiques, and cost US$30 to US$40. There's a small restaurant, but you can also use the kitchen.

The ***Corner Tree Café*** is run by a colorful character, Ralph 'Cowboy' Ellis, who serves inexpensive Jamaican dishes. It's a good place to chat over a Red Stripe beer and maybe even challenge a local to a game of dominoes.

### Shopping

There's a crafts market in the village center, next to Corner Tree Café. Here too is the workshop of the Walkers Wood Woolspinners Cooperative, and the studio and showroom of Art Beat (☎ 917-2154), a small craft shop owned by Nancy Burke, alias Inanci. She sells jewelry, carnival and duppy masks, painted rocks, and other intriguing creations. Another local artist, Laura Facey-Cooper, paints and sculpts in her family home in the nearby hamlet of Bellevue.

If you fancy buying a box of spices and sauces, call ahead to Cottage Industries (☎ 917-2318) at Bromley Great House.

### GOSHEN WILDERNESS RESORT

This lakeside 'wilderness resort,' 4 miles east of Walkers Wood (☎ 974-4613), happily proclaims: 'You catch it, we cook it.' Its prime attraction is 42 large ponds stocked with tilapia just waiting for you to yank them out of the water. Hours are 10 am to 5 pm daily except Monday; admission is US$3.

In the 1860s the property was a sugar and coffee plantation that formed part of a 40,000-acre estate owned by Judge Roper. Goshen was the heart of a prosperous district and had a racetrack, polo field, and showground. It is still owned by a member of the Roper family, Alex Lanigan.

The resort is a good place to take the kids. Attractions include many types of birds, both caged and roaming free, a petting zoo, a pool with freshwater turtles, swings, volleyball, paddleboats, and kayaks (US$1). There are also nature trails and horseback rides around the landscaped grounds and into the surrounding woods. A 30-minute 4WD tour of the plantation and nearby hills costs US$25.

Lanigan has yet to bring to fruition his plans to build cabins and introduce a shuttle from Ocho Rios. He currently offers a fishing package (US$20) that includes a drink, tackle, and a guide – the fee is US$9 for catch and release. The chef will prepare your fish with bammy and festival, but burgers, hot dogs, and jerk dishes are also available at the thatched restaurant and bar.

Getting there from Ocho Rios is easy and the route is well signed. Take the turn-off from the A3 at the White River estuary. Eventually you'll reach a three-way road junction called Goshen. Turn east (left when coming from Ocho Rios) down the deteriorated road. The Wilderness Resort is half a mile beyond the gates for Goshen great house – marked 'Goshen.' They say you can drive there from Moneague, but it is not so easy.

If you don't have a car, you can take a minibus from Ocho Rios. The 30-minute journey should cost about US$1.50.

## MONEAGUE

This small crossroads town, 12 miles south of Ochi, was favored during the 19th century as a hill resort, and before that as a staging post on the three-day journey between Spanish Town and the north coast. It sits at the junction of the A3 and the A1, marked by the Moneague Training Camp of the Jamaica Defense Force. Two Saracen armored cars

are on display at the gate. The Moneague Tavern, erected in 1891 to cater to coach traffic, today boasts one of Jamaica's finest restaurants.

A road leads northeast a mile from the public works (south of the training camp) to **Moneague Lake**, with the local nickname, 'The Swamp.' The lake's level fluctuates according to the subterranean water table (local lore says that it disappears altogether when someone drowns). Turtles and perch flourish in the lake and waterfowl flock in. It's quite beautiful, surrounded by a meniscus of forest-clad hills.

Alcan, the bauxite giant, maintains an orchid sanctuary – **Schwallenburg** – about 5 miles south of Moneague. Two km of trails lead through the 3½ acre facility, where 15,000 plants represent about 60 species.

### Information

Call the police station (☎ 972-3211) in case of an emergency.

### Places to Eat

The *Café Aubergine*, also called Moneague Tavern, (☎/fax 973-0527), half a mile south of town, was voted 'Best North Coast Restaurant of 1998' and is a must visit. It's housed in a 250-year-old tavern granted the island's first-ever liquor license. The place abounds in tasteful art, china, and real silverware. You dine with jazz or New Age music playing softly. The menu, written on parchment and concocted by owners Neville Anderson and Rudolf Schlössel, is Mediterranean-influenced Jamaican nouvelle, such as crayfish provençal (US$8), chicken in coconut curry sauce (US$10), and roast lamb in sauce provençal (US$18). Leave room for the chocolate gateau. It's open 11:30 am to 9 pm, Tuesday to Sunday. It hosts an Octoberfest Party with German fare.

### FAITH'S PEN

South of Moneague, the A1 climbs steadily to Faith's Pen, 17 miles south of Ocho Rios. The roadside is lined with stalls selling citrus fruits and, 400 yards farther south, dozens of jerk stalls at Faith Pen Vendor Centre, where you can try oddities such as cow-cod soup, a concoction made of bull's testes, reputed to be an aphrodisiac. Try the Ragamuffin Juice Centre where you can wash down your jerk with 'roots' wine (don't ask for the ingredients or you may never be able to swallow, but it's also said to be just the tonic for a perky sex life).

Immediately beyond Faith's Pen, a road leads east to the bauxite mine of ALCAN (the Canadian Aluminium Corporation Ltd), which began operations in Jamaica in 1960. The ravaged slopes have been replanted in recent years in Caribbean pine and blue mahoe.

The road continues to rise up the pine-forested slopes of Mt Diablo (2754 feet). At 2250 feet the A1 crests the mountain chain and begins its steep, winding descent to Ewarton and the lush Rosser Valley, beautiful from these heights. The summit marks the boundary between the parishes of St Ann to the north and St Catherine to the south. On your left, just below the summit, is a large lake the color of jade; this is a tailings dam for the ALCAN mine.

# West of Ocho Rios

The coastal plains west of Ochi boast many beaches, mostly hidden from view. The best have been snapped up by upscale resorts. A few historic sites of note line the route, and there's a splendid botanical garden, plus opportunities for horseback riding. The Dry Harbour Mountains rise steeply inland, offering recommended scenic drives.

## MAMMEE BAY

A favorite with Jamaican beachgoers, Mammee Bay – 3½ miles west of Ocho Rios and 2½ miles east of St Ann – receives few tourists. It has several little beaches, some hidden away, including Old Fort Bay. Much of the beachfront is a private residential estate, but access is offered to the public beaches. Sandals Dunn's River resort is here and has its own splendid beach. Locals flock to Fisherman's Beach, immediately east of Sandals. Jet Skis can be rented (US$40 for 30 minutes).

## Laughing Waters

These cascades are not quite a mile west of Dunn's River (and a mile east of Mammee Bay) and are less crowded. Just as at Dunn's River, a river appears from rocks amid a shallow ravine about 2 miles from the sea and spills to a charming little beach. Unfortunately, the falls, which are also known as Roaring River, are not what they once were since they were tapped by a hydroelectricity plant. Parts of the James Bond movie *Dr No* were filmed here (the beach is known as 'James Bond Beach').

To get here, look for the large fenced-in electrical power structure beside the A3. Follow the river to the beach. Public access to the falls is by foot, though you can hire fishing boats from along the coast.

## Horseback Riding

The St Ann Polo Club & Equestrian Centre (☎ 972-2762) at Mammee Bay, offers horseback lessons for US$15 per hour, as well as dressage instruction. Safari Tours (see Organized Tours, earlier in this chapter) offers horseback trips, as does Hooves (☎ 972-0905, fax 972-9204, hooves@cwjamaica.com), 4 Church Crescent, St Ann's Bay, which has 2-hour beach and mountain trips twice daily, with rides through Maima Seville Heritage Park originating at Twickenham Farm, near Beecher Town.

The St Ann Polo Club hosts the Hi-Pro Family Polo Tournament & International Horse Show in August. Contact Leslie-Ann Masterton (☎ 922-8060).

## Organized Tours

Safari Tours offers trips by Land Rover, as well as river tubing and bicycling. See Organized Tours, earlier in this chapter, and the Outdoor Activities chapter for details.

## Places to Stay

*Rose Garden Hotel* (☎/fax 972-2825, 908-583-5463, fax 718-951-6327 in the USA) is a ho-hum place 200 yards from Old Fort Bay, 600m east of Sandals (see below). It has 24 air-conditioned studios with kitchenette, private bathroom with hot water, TV, and balcony. They're modestly furnished and clean, with lots of light, and cost US$60 single/double low season, US$70 high season; US$65/75 with air-con. There's a small pool and sundeck.

There are also several villas at Mammee Bay. Two options are **Drabar Villa** (☎ 972-5762), and the **Villa Orchid**, a five-bedroom villa said to have pleasing decor and a small pool. There are dozens of villas, too, in the Mammee Bay Estate, 200 yards west of Sandals Dunn's River. A luxurious 19th-century villa also commands the headland where the river meets the sea at Laughing Waters. The villa – **Laughing Waters** – is a government-run 'protocol house' for visiting dignitaries, and thus is not usually open to the public. However, you may be able to rent the fully staffed, four-bedroom house through Heave-Ho Charters (☎ 974-5367, fax 974-5461, 11A Pineapple Place, Ocho Rios) for US$6000 a week.

**Silver Palms** features elegant, modern three-bedroom townhouses, plus one and two-bedroom apartments fronting a pool and Jacuzzi for US$70 low season, US$90 high season for studios; apartments run US$100 to US$210 low season, US$130 to US$270 high season. A housekeeper is provided. **Cannon Villas & Silver Palms** (☎ 927-1852, fax 977-6143), adjacent, is at Old Fort Bay on the east side of Mammee Bay. It offers six air-conditioned cottages, each with a living and dining area, satellite TV, fully equipped kitchen, and patio for US$180 low season, US$230 high season. **Condo-Rios Villas** (☎ 972-0731) and **Old Fort Bay Cottage** are nearby.

For an upscale all-inclusive option, I recommend the perennially popular 25-acre, 256-room **Sandals Dunn's River Golf Resort & Spa** (☎ 972-1610, fax 972-1611, PO Box 51, Ocho Rios), fronted by its own sparkling white beach. A dramatic curving staircase and gleaming marble columns in the lobby recreate the opulence of an Italian palazzo, reflected in the ritzy Roman-style full-service spa that opened in 1998. The resort also boasts a huge swimming pool with a cascading waterfall topped by a gazebo, plus a second pool around a huge bar, three Jacuzzis (two big enough for 40 people each),

a pitch-n-putt course, tour desk, four specialty restaurants (including teppanyaki and one serving nouvelle Jamaican cuisine), plus video games room, billiards room, and a theater and disco. The rooms come in seven categories. A resident jazz band plays nightly, and the theater hosts top local entertainers. Low season rates (three nights) range from US$748 to US$1518 standard and US$1133 to US$2300 deluxe. (See Sandals, under Hotels in Facts for the Visitor, for international contact information.)

## ST ANN'S BAY

This small town (population 8500), 7 miles west of Ocho Rios, rises up the hillside above the bay that Columbus christened Santa Gloria for its beauty. Despite a relatively illustrious history, the town has long since been eclipsed by Ocho Rios. Today the provincial market town is centered on an old tumbledown market topped by a wooden clock tower.

West of the turnoff for St Ann's Bay, the A3 becomes the A1, a two-lane bypass called the AGR Byfield highway. It skirts the town, capital of its namesake parish. The main road into town is also the A1, which runs south via Claremont to Spanish Town.

St Ann's has several sites of interest and is worth a brief browse. It is important as the birthplace of Marcus Garvey, founder of the Black Nationalist movement, who is honored each August 7 with a parade through town. There are several interesting old buildings in Caribbean vernacular style, especially along Braco St.

### History

St Ann's Bay figured prominently in the modern history of Jamaica. Christopher Columbus called in here in 1494 during his second voyage to the Americas. Santa Gloria must have seemed far from glorious in 1503, during his fateful fourth and final voyage, when the explorer had to abandon his worm-infested ships in the bay. Columbus and his crew were stranded for more than a year before finally being rescued (see the History section in the Facts about Jamaica chapter).

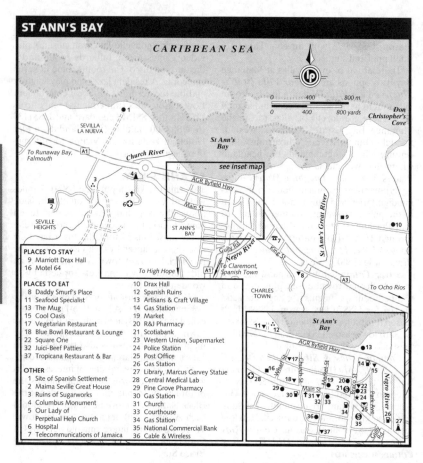

## ST ANN'S BAY

CARIBBEAN SEA

SEVILLA
LA NUEVA

To Runaway Bay,
Falmouth

Church River

St Ann's
Bay

see inset map

AGR Byfield Hwy

Main St

ST ANN'S
BAY

SEVILLE
HEIGHTS

Gully Rd

Negro River

To High Hope

To Claremont,
Spanish Town

Don
Christopher's
Cove

St Ann's Great River

King St

Don

CHARLES
TOWN

To Ocho Rios

St Ann's
Bay

AGR Byfield Hwy

Main St

Negro River

Park Ave

Gully Rd

**PLACES TO STAY**
9   Marriott Drax Hall
16  Motel 64

**PLACES TO EAT**
8   Daddy Smurf's Place
11  Seafood Specialist
13  The Mug
15  Cool Oasis
17  Vegetarian Restaurant
18  Blue Bowl Restaurant & Lounge
22  Square One
32  Juici-Beef Patties
37  Tropicana Restaurant & Bar

**OTHER**
1   Site of Spanish Settlement
2   Maima Seville Great House
3   Ruins of Sugarworks
4   Columbus Monument
5   Our Lady of
    Perpetual Help Church
6   Hospital
7   Telecommunications of Jamaica

10  Drax Hall
12  Spanish Ruins
13  Artisans & Craft Village
14  Gas Station
19  Market
20  R&J Pharmacy
21  Scotiabank
23  Western Union, Supermarket
24  Police Station
25  Post Office
26  Gas Station
27  Library, Marcus Garvey Statue
28  Central Medical Lab
29  Pine Grove Pharmacy
30  Gas Station
31  Church
33  Courthouse
34  Gas Station
35  National Commercial Bank
36  Cable & Wireless

In 1509, the Spaniards built the first Spanish settlement on the island about 800m west of St Ann's, at Sevilla la Nueva. The site was abandoned within four decades and later developed as a sugar estate by a British planter, Richard Hemming. Other planters established sugar estates nearby and a town grew and prospered as a bustling seaport with forts on opposite sides of the bay. Following the slave rebellion of Christmas 1831 (see the Montego Bay and Northwest Coast chapter), the local rector, Reverend George Wilson Bridges, formed the Colonial Church Union in St Ann's Bay. The organization persecuted non-conformist ministers, and its members rampaged through the northern parishes burning Baptist churches and assaulting abolitionist missionaries.

### Information
**Money** National Commercial Bank (☎ 972-2490) and Scotiabank (☎ 972-2531) have branches in the town center with 24-hour ATMs. Western Union is at Triple Super Save Supermarket (☎ 972-1304), on Bravo St.

## The Founding of Sevilla la Nueva

'New Seville' was established in 1509 by orders of Juan de Esquivel, the island's first governor. Esquivel had been with Columbus when returning from Panama on his last voyage in 1503, when Columbus careened his two caravels into this bay and eventually abandoned them side by side (historians agree that this was the same bay where Columbus had first anchored during his discovery voyage in 1494). The ships were so eaten with worms that they immediately filled with water. Unable to repair his vessels, Columbus dispatched his boatswain, Diego Mendez, and a handful of men, who successfully set out in a canoe for Hispaniola. Finally, 369 days after being marooned, Columbus was rescued by Mendez. The *Santiago de Palos* and *Capitana* are thought to be buried under coral and silt to the northwest of the old wharf but have not been found, despite considerable effort.

In November 1509, Don Juan de Esquivel arrived with about 70 colonists. They brought cows, horses, sheep, pigs, and domestic fowl. Christopher Columbus' son Diego was given authority over Jamaica, and it was he who laid out the settlement, which remained the capital until 1534. The settlement spread over 15 acres, with brick-paved streets, a fort, church, sugar mills, and a wharf, where the first African slaves brought to Jamaica were landed.

Sevilla never prospered. It was an ill-chosen site with a marshy shoreline, and malarial fevers were common. Twenty-five years after its founding, the settlers abandoned the city and established a new capital on the site of today's Spanish Town. Sevilla fell into ruin and eventually was entirely reclaimed by vegetation.

**NORTH COAST**

**Post & Communications** The post office (☎ 972-2307) is just east of the police station. You can make international calls and send faxes from the Cable & Wireless office (☎ 972-9701) at 11 King St. It's open 8 am to 4 pm Monday to Friday.

**Library** The parish library (☎ 972-2660) is at 2 Windsor Rd, just west of the town center.

**Medical Services** St Ann's Bay Public General Hospital (☎ 972-2272) has an emergency clinic. It's hidden behind Our Lady of Perpetual Help Catholic church at the west end of town. Several doctors' clinics are concentrated west of the town center on Main St, including the Phoenix Medical Complex, which is open 8:30 am to 4:30 pm Monday to Friday and 8 am to noon Saturday. Pharmacies include Pine Grove Pharmacy (☎ 972-0334) at 55 Main St, and R&J Pharmacy (☎ 972-2242), next to Scotiabank.

**Emergency** The police station (☎ 972-2211) is on the corner of Main and Braco Sts.

### Walking Tour

St Ann's Bay warrants a walking tour, with all the sights of interest along Main St within a span of a mile.

Begin by parking outside the parish library, on King St 100 yards east of Braco St. Its grassy forecourt is dominated by the **Marcus Garvey Statue**, with the national hero portrayed larger than life in pewter-gray bronze (see 'One God, One Aim, One Destiny').

Westward along Main St you'll pass the town's most important edifice – the **Courthouse** – at the corner of Market St. It was erected in elegant cut limestone and red brick in 1866 with a pedimented porch bearing the scales of justice. Visitors are welcome to observe the court when it's in session; take the chance to see a bewigged judge and the venerable British legal system in quasi-Dickensian action. Across the way is the antique **market**, topped by a clock tower and worth a browse.

Nearby, on Hospital Rd just off Main St, is the warehouse of **Seville Pottery** (☎ 972-9517),

## One God, One Aim, One Destiny

Marcus Garvey was born of working-class parents in St Ann's Bay on August 17, 1887. As a young man he traveled extensively throughout Costa Rica, Panama, and England. He returned well educated and a firm believer in self-improvement. Inspired to raise the consciousness and well-being of blacks, he founded the United Negro Improvement Association (UNIA) in 1914 to unite 'all the Negro peoples of the world into one great body to establish a country and a government exclusively their own.' In 1916 he traveled to the US, where he formed a branch of UNIA in New York (at its peak in the 1920s, UNIA had 5 million members) and was influenced by another prominent black nationalist, Booker T Washington.

Marcus Garvey

Garvey, a gifted orator, established a weekly newspaper, the *Negro World*, and built an enormous following under the slogan 'One God! One Aim! One Destiny!'

Garvey set up the Black Star Line, a steamship company the aim of which was to eventually repatriate blacks to Africa. The company, however, failed due to poor management.

The American and British colonial governments considered Garvey a dangerous agitator. They conspired against him and in 1922 arrested him on mail-fraud charges. He served two years in Atlanta Federal Prison before being deported to Jamaica. Back in his homeland, the black nationalist founded the reformist People's Political Party. Universal franchise did not then exist in Jamaica, and he failed to gather enough support at the polls. In 1935 he departed for England, where he died in poverty in 1940.

His remains were repatriated to Jamaica in 1984 and interred with state honors in National Heroes Park. In 1980 the Organization of American States honored him by placing his bust in its Hall of Heroes.

which makes bottles for Sangster's famous liqueurs (see World's End in the Blue Mountains & Southeast Coast chapter). You can purchase superb ceramics, including exquisite blue-glazed bottles.

You'll pass numerous venerable buildings as you continue west to the end of Main St, where stands the impressive **Columbus Monument**, surrounded by bougainvillea in a small roundabout at the far west end of town. Here, a large coral base is topped by a bronze figure of the explorer shown dressed as a Spanish grandee. It was cast by Michele Geurisi in Columbus' native city of Genoa. The pedestal has bronze plaques depicting the caravels that are thought to have sunk in Santa Gloria Bay.

One hundred yards up the hill from the Columbus monument is the exquisite **Our Lady of Perpetual Help Church**, built in contemporary Spanish design by an Irish priest in 1939 of stones recovered from the ruins of

Sevilla la Nueva. It stands amid palms and bougainvillea and is festooned with climbing plants. Inside, great beams support the organ loft.

## Drax Hall

Drax Hall, immediately east of St Ann's, is today the site of one of Jamaica's largest deluxe resort developments. The property, however, has an intriguing history. A Barbadian migrant, Charles Drax, established a sugar estate here in the late 17th century. By his will of 1721, Drax left his property for the founding of a charity school. By devious means, the local Beckford family 'captured' the property and relinquished it only in 1804 following two decades of litigation. In 1802 the school was founded near Kingston, and the disputed property was converted to a coconut and cattle plantation.

On Easter Monday, Drax Hall hosts a colorful kite festival. For information, call ☎ 972-9607.

## Maima Seville Great House & Heritage Park

The modern history of Jamaica began in 1509, less than half a mile west of present-day St Ann's. The park marks the site of the first Spanish capital on the island – Sevilla la Nueva – and one of the first Spanish settlements in the New World. However, the town lasted only 25 years. Not until 1937 was the Spanish settlement discovered. In 1982, Sevilla la Nueva was declared a Site of the Americas by the Organization of American States, which funds ongoing excavations by the Spanish Archaeological Mission and Jamaica National Heritage Trust. The digging has turned up almost as much information on the Arawaks, as this was also the site of an Arawak village.

Scant traces of the original buildings can be seen, though most of the original Spanish settlement remains buried. A grassy track leads down to the ocean from the A1, opposite the entrance to Maima Seville Great House & Heritage Park. Farther east along the A1, fortifications are still visible near the shore behind a restaurant called Seafood Specialist (squatters have turned it into a

fishing hamlet). The eastern extent of the old settlement is marked by the Columbus Monument, in St Ann's Bay. The governor's house stood in the coconut grove that separates the road and the sea. It was decorated with sculptured stone friezes that were removed to Kingston, where they are on display at the National Gallery.

When the English captured Jamaica from the Spanish, the land on which Sevilla la Nueva had been built was granted to Richard Hemming, an officer in Oliver Cromwell's invasion army. Over the next two centuries, Hemming's descendants developed the property as a sugar estate that is today owned by the Jamaica National Trust Commission and is dominated from on high by Seville Great House, built in 1745 by Hemming's grandson. You can explore the 'English Industrial Works' that include the ruins of a sugar mill, copra kiln, waterwheel, and boiling house, plus the Hemmings' tombs.

The original house has been substantially altered, not least by a hurricane in 1944 that lopped off its upper story. The restored building contains an excellent museum depicting the history of the site from Arawak times through slavery and the colonial period (entrance costs US$2). An historical video is shown.

The grounds to the rear boast a thatched 'Afro-Jamaican House' of wattle-and-daub, and a 'Taino house' – both intended as interpretive exhibits – in addition to a 'kitchen garden.'

Horseback rides are offered to the shore (US$60 including lunch). A nature tour allows you to learn about tropical fruits.

## Activities

The offshore diving is said to be splendid. Contact Seascape Dive Village (☎ 972-2573), a local dive operator. Gosh! Maybe *you'll* discover the wrecks of Columbus' sunken vessels.

A local company, Tomorrow's Times Today Bamboo Bicycle Tour (☎ 972-2144), offers a mountain bike tour in the hills above St Ann's Bay (US$50).

High Hope Adventures (☎ 972-2997, fax 972-1607), 16 Top Rd, St Ann's Bay, offers bike trips that are about half a day long. JJ's Tours (☎ 964-2243, fax 964-2765), c/o Hotel Villa Bella, PO Box 473, Christiana, arranges longer mountain bike tours through the central highlands, with nights at the Hotel Villa Bella; one, two, and three-day trips cost US$60, US$70, and US$80.

## Special Events

An emancipation celebration is held on the grounds of Maima Seville every July 29 to August 1.

## Places to Stay

In town, the pickings are slim. *Motel 64* (☎ 972-2308) is very basic. Its 14 small rooms cost US$15 and have minimal furnishings, but they are clean and have fans and private showers.

For a treat, head inland to *High Hope Estate* (☎ 927-2277, fax 972-1607, PO Box 11). This interpretation of an Italianate villa is set on 40 acres of manicured lawns and woodland high in the hills above St Ann's Bay. It has seven rooms, each individually styled. Five look out over the ocean; two face the mountains. All are decorated with priceless antiques: 18th-century Moroccan harem screens, 19th-century Korean silk screens, a Steinway baby grand piano, and marble floors. A squiggly lap pool is inset in a sundeck offering views down along the coast. High Hope was built in 1961 as a private residence for a socialite couple who have welcomed illustrious guests from Charlie Chaplin to Adlai Stevenson. If it's raining, you can settle in the well-stocked library with a good book. Rates range from US$145 to US$225 double, including breakfast. You can also rent the entire place fully staffed. To get there, take Market St south (uphill) three blocks from downtown St Ann's, then turn right, then take the first left and continue uphill a mile.

The long-touted *Marriott Drax Hall* was still not begun at press time, although it is slated to open by 2000. When complete, the project is slated to take up 2400 acres of shorefront overlooking Don Christopher's Cove east of St Ann, and will include the 27-hole Doral Drax Hall Golf Course. A master plan includes single-family villa lots and condominium and townhouse sites, a 100-slip marina and marina village, and a 280-room hotel.

## Places to Eat

There's no shortage of reasonably priced places to eat. Several of the better restaurants are at the west end of Main St, including the *Blue Bowl Restaurant & Lounge*. Nearby, on Braco St, is *Square One,* serving patties, callaloo loaf, and other Jamaican fare.

On the side of the bypass, the rustic *Seafood Specialist* serves excellent steamed or fried fish with yams and rice and peas for US$4. Wash it down with natural juices (US$1). Nearby, *The Mug* (☎ 972-1018) is a respected seafood restaurant in a slightly jaded colonial structure on the shore in the Artisans & Craft Village beside the A1. It serves all manner of seafood, drawing locals from miles around. It has a barbecue on Mondays – 'Mug Night' – when it stays open until 1 am.

*Tropicana Restaurant & Bar* (☎ 972-9139), up the hill on Market St, is attractive, as is the *Cool Oasis*, by the gas station on the A1 east of town. Health food junkies should check out the *Vegetarian Restaurant* at 18 Musgrave St, selling soups, patties, gluten, and beans (US$4), carrot juice and other fruit drinks, etc. 'I'm not boasting, but here are de best tasty food,' says the owner.

In the hills above town, try *High Hope* (see Places to Stay, above), or *Lillyfield Great House* (see Places to Stay in the Priory & Environs section, below), both by reservation only; or *Sleepy Hollow*, a rustic eatery reached by a long winding dirt road, with views down the mountain.

You'll find at least two bakeries on Main St. For jerk, check out *Daddy Smurf's Place* on Windsor Rd at the far east end of town.

## Shopping

The St Ann's Artisans & Craft Village on the north side of the bypass has stalls selling straw items, wooden carvings, jewelry, and the usual array of T-shirts. Among the few stores selling arts and crafts are Gifts Galore

& Book Shop and Mind & Body Boutique, side by side at the west end of Main St.

## Getting There & Away

You can take any of the buses and coasters traveling along the A1 between Montego Bay and Ocho Rios. Ask to be dropped off by the crafts market on the bypass. At least one minibus leaves from the Parade in Kingston.

## PRIORY & ENVIRONS

Priory, about a mile west of St Ann's Bay, has a small beach with water sports and several hotels. You can turn inland and head into the hills for views down the coast. Few travelers take time to explore inland south of St Ann's Bay, much of which is given over to cattle estates and pimento farms.

Most of the land hereabouts was formerly part of Llandovery, a mile west of Priory and one of the largest sugar estates on the island, dating from 1674. Llandovery Factory is still intact (you'll see its brick chimney on the north side of the A1), although it no longer makes rum, as it did for over 300 years. Today it functions as a cattle farm; you can take tours by arrangement (☎ 1-819-7021 cellular). It's 4 miles west of St Ann's; the turnoff is 200 yards east of the turn for Cranbrook (see below).

## Chukka Cove Farm

The name says it all. Polo is the game of choice at Chukka Cove Farm (☎ 972-2506, fax 972-0814, chukka@infchan.com), Laughlands PO, St Ann, a mile west of Priory. This 50-acre equestrian center has a full-size polo field and hosts regular polo tournaments plus occasional jump contests. The Jamaica Polo Association's (☎ 974-2592) tournaments are held here, including the Fossil Open Polo Tournament (☎ 925-0463), a two-day event featuring some of the international polo circuit's top riders.

Chukka offers a three-hour 'Swim Your Horse Trek' along the sand (yes, you go swimming with your horse), ending at Llandovery, where there's a small snack bar. It's offered twice daily at 9 am and 2 pm (US$50). Other rides include going from sea level to

### I Say, Polo Anyone?

Polo was introduced to Jamaica by the British army during the late 19th century and today has a fanatical following among the Jamaican elite. St Ann's Bay is a center for polo (see Chukka Cove above). Although refined English accents abound in the spectator stands, where sandwiches and pots of steaming hot tea are de rigueur, money and the appropriate social pedigree are supposedly *not* a prerequisite to participation. All you need is a horse, which, by Jamaica standards, costs an arm and a leg. The St Ann Polo Club (☎ 972-2762) has polo matches every Saturday at 4 pm at Drax Hall.

almost 2000 feet on Mt Zion (three hours, US$50) A six-hour mountain trek for experienced riders is occasionally offered and includes a visit to Lillyfield Great House (see Places to Stay, later in this section), which is also part of an overnight trip and a three-day trip.

Mountain bike rides were planned from Lillyfield to Chukka Cove.

### Cranbrook

This 130-acre botanical garden is a treat, crafted in the lush valley that carves up into the hills south of Laughlands, immediately west of Priory. It's a little Kew Gardens in the tropics, quite exquisite. The garden, which is built around a colonial-era building thought to have been a veterinary clinic, is the product of a decade-long evolution, but opened only in 1997. The owner, Ivan Linton, is a professional horticulturalist who has developed theme gardens, a hothouse orchid display, pools, and lush lawns fringed by banks of anthuriums and other tropical flowers.

Guided tours are included (and a tip is appreciated). Nature walks (about 90 minutes) lead to the river, reflecting giant tree ferns, spectacular torch ginger, heliconia, Birds of Paradise, begonias, crotons, philodendrons, palms, and other exotic species. Pond fishing is available, as is volleyball, tube riding on the river, and horseback riding. There are gazebos and picnic spots, plus a snack counter.

It's open 7:30 am to sunset, daily (US$5.50, children US$2). For information, contact Lowland Exotic Park (☎ 770-8071, 995-3097), PO Box 8, Laughlands, or the Kingston office (☎ 968-1001, fax 968-1003), PO Box 228, Kingston 10.

### Plantation Tours

If you want to see how a typical Jamaica farm operates, you can take a tour of Circle B Farm (☎ 972-2988), a working plantation that grows avocados, bananas, coconuts, and vegetables (US$10, or US$20 including lunch). It's open 10 am to 5 pm daily. The farm is near Richmond Hill, a mile south of the A1, reached via a turnoff a half mile west of Sevilla la Nueva at Priory, 2 miles west of St Ann's Bay.

Sleepy Hollow Park, at Blowfire Hills, a half mile south of Circle B, also offers guided farm tours. Owners Con and Patsy Pink also host birders, hikers, and picnickers. It's open 10 am to 6 pm. Entrance costs US$2.

The Mammee Ridge Racehorse Breeding Centre (☎ 974-6447), at Bamboo, offers a chance to 'see prize stallions serving at stud.'

### Scuba Diving

The coral reef offshore of St Ann's Bay is said to be one of the most impressive in Jamaica. You can rent equipment from the Island Dive Shop (☎ 972-2519) at Columbus Beach in Priory.

Also see the section on scuba diving in the Outdoor Activities chapter.

### Places to Stay

You can camp on lawns at an offbeat spot called **Starfish** (☎ 972-1028), up the track 400m beyond Jamel Jamaica (see below). There are showers and toilets with cold water for US$5 per person. It has a windswept setting on the shore.

**Jamel Jamaica** (☎ 972-1031, fax 972-0714, 12 Richmond Estate), in Priory, is a compact, recently renovated property with a Mediterranean feel. Bougainvillea spills over white-

washed walls onto a tiled sundeck. Each of the 24 air-conditioned rooms has a TV, telephone, and private balcony overlooking the beach. Water sports are offered. Summer rates are US$55 single, US$67 double. A two-bedroom family suite costs US$80.

Modestly furnished units with kitchens are offered at **Columbus Beach** (☎ 972-2519) for US$60 one-bedroom, US$75 two-bedroom. The facility is affiliated with New York's Hofstra University and is often full of students and faculty utilizing the small library and marine research facility. Sea kayaks are available.

A stone's throw from Jamel is **Priory Beach Cottages** (☎ 972-2323), a complex of five spacious beachfront cottages facing Priory Beach. It's a reclusive place. Each unit costs US$700 per week and has two bedrooms, a full kitchen, and wide jalousie windows. There's a small pool.

Another atmospheric and classy charmer in the hills is **Lillyfield Great House** (☎ 972-6045, 754-0997, fax 754-1021 in Kingston), about 5 miles east of Brown's Town and 2 miles west of Bamboo, a hamlet about 6½ miles uphill from the turnoff on the A1 at Priory. This 18th-century great house, which has a serene hilltop setting, has been graciously restored and boasts elegant antique furnishings. The five rooms, festooned with modern art, are US$100 double, including breakfast. Wooden floors, lofty beamed ceilings, and modern bathrooms add to the appeal. There's a lounge with fireplace (it gets cool at night in winter) a large-screen TV, a bar and elegant dining room, and outside, a recreation room and function room used for dances. A swimming pool was to be added. There are also four cottages. It looks over the valley where cattle nibble in pastures once farmed with pineapples. Pimento is also grown commercially.

At Chukka Cove you'll find five fully staffed, air-conditioned, two-bedroom, two-story villas sleeping four, from US$99 per person. They're arranged around a pool between the coral shore and polo field. There's no beach, just a rocky cove where scenes from Papillon, starring Steve McQueen and Dustin Hoffman, were filmed (it's now called Papillon's Cove). They're privately owned, but the staff at Chukka Cove can forward rental requests.

## RUNAWAY BAY

Despite its diminutive size, Runaway Bay (10 miles west of St Ann's) was the first planned resort development in Jamaica and has a broad array of hotels and tourist facilities, though the place is far from sophisticated and in fact is not particularly appealing. Together with Salem, with which it merges to the east, it's a one-street village stretching along the A1 for 2 miles. Several small beaches are supposedly public, although most are the backyards for a few all-inclusive resorts.

The place's name derives from the legend that the Spaniards fled the island from here in 1655. It is now thought that the escapees were African slaves making their escape to Cuba by canoe.

Hedonism III, a sibling to the renowned Hedonism II in Negril, was due to open in 1999 and is sure to bring a new attention and risqué panache to Runaway Bay.

## Information

**Money** You can arrange wire transfers through Western Union, in Rose Brothers Haberdashery (☎ 973-3456) in Salem.

**Post & Communications** A small post office (☎ 973-2477) is located on the main road in the center of Runaway Bay. You can place international calls or send and receive faxes from the Call Direct Centre (☎ 973-5613, fax 973-5676) in Salem Plaza (it's open 9 am to 10 pm Sunday to Thursday; 9 am to 5 pm Friday; and 7 am to 11 pm Saturday); or from the Worldwide Communication Centre (☎ 973-4830) nearby. The latter permits credit card, calling card, and collect calls.

**NORTH COAST**

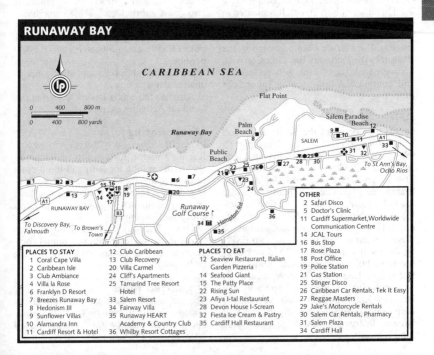

RUNAWAY BAY

CARIBBEAN SEA

Flat Point

Runaway Bay

Palm Beach

Salem Paradise Beach

SALEM

A1

Public Beach

To St Ann's Bay, Ocho Rios

A1
RUNAWAY BAY

To Discovery Bay, Falmouth    To Brown's Town

Runaway Golf Course

Hampton Rd

**PLACES TO STAY**
1   Coral Cape Villa
2   Caribbean Isle
3   Club Ambiance
4   Villa la Rose
6   Franklyn D Resort
7   Breezes Runaway Bay
8   Hedonism III
9   Sunflower Villas
10  Alamandra Inn
11  Cardiff Resort & Hotel
12  Club Caribbean
13  Club Recovery
20  Villa Carmel
24  Cliff's Apartments
25  Tamarind Tree Resort Hotel
33  Salem Resort
34  Fairway Villa
35  Runaway HEART Academy & Country Club
36  Whilby Resort Cottages

**PLACES TO EAT**
12  Seaview Restaurant, Italian Garden Pizzeria
14  Seafood Giant
15  The Patty Place
22  Rising Sun
23  Afiya I-tal Restaurant
28  Devon House I-Scream
32  Fiesta Ice Cream & Pastry
35  Cardiff Hall Restaurant

**OTHER**
2   Safari Disco
5   Doctor's Clinic
11  Cardiff Supermarket, Worldwide Communication Centre
14  JCAL Tours
16  Bus Stop
17  Rose Plaza
18  Post Office
19  Police Station
21  Gas Station
25  Stinger Disco
26  Caribbean Car Rentals, Tek It Easy
27  Reggae Masters
29  Jake's Motorcycle Rentals
30  Salem Car Rentals, Pharmacy
31  Salem Plaza
34  Cardiff Hall

**Laundry** Runaway Self-Service Laundrette (☎ 973-5625) is in the Rose Plaza.

**Medical** There's a doctor's clinic (☎ 973-3409) in the Rose Plaza in Salem. It's open 8 am to 5 pm Monday to Friday, and until noon on Saturday.

**Emergencies** For the police, call ☎ 973-3433.

## Cardiff Hall

This beautiful 18th-century great house, a mile east of Salem, is splendidly preserved. Note the mahogany beam supporting the staircase, cut from one of the enormous trees on the property and shipped to England to be carved with a garland of cattle skulls symbolizing the source of the family's wealth.

The house once overlooked a coconut and cattle estate on property awarded by Oliver Cromwell to Daniel Blagrove, a loyal member of Parliament. It remained in the Blagrove family for over two centuries (the Blagroves are still landowners hereabouts). The estate metamorphosed in the 1960s into the Runaway Bay Golf Course, a luxury beachfront hotel, and residential and commercial lots (now a Superclubs property).

## Golf

SuperClubs operates the SuperClubs Golf Club (☎ 973-7319). It's a low-lying, par 72, 6884-yard course with several elevated tees, well-placed bunkers, and a putting green. The SuperClubs World Cup Qualifier golf tournament comes here in October as a step toward a position in the World Cup of Golf Championship. It's open 6:30 am to 9 pm daily. There's a pro shop and, upstairs, a classy restaurant and sports bar with ESPN on the TV. It's open to all (US$35, or US$23 for nine holes). Caddies are mandatory (US$12, or US$8 for nine holes); carts are optional. SuperClubs also operates the Breezes Runaway Bay Golf School, the island's only golf school, solely for guests at Breezes. Instruction is available for all levels (and is included for guests).

## Scuba Diving & Water Sports

Runaway Bay has some of the best diving on the island. There's a wreck in shallow water in front of Club Ambiance. A reef complex called **Ricky's Reef** is renowned for its sponges; the best diving is said to be below 80 feet. More experienced divers might try the **Canyon**, beginning at about 35 feet and running between two walls; don't be put off by the nurse sharks that gather here. There are two cars and a plane offshore from Club Caribbean – relics of drug busts – that attract fish and are now overgrown with coral.

Jamaqua is a full-service dive facility at Club Caribbean (☎ 973-3507, fax 973-5309). It offers three dives daily, plus PADI certification and other courses. You can rent equipment here. Sundivers PADI scuba facility is located at Club Ambiance (☎ 973-2066).

The German-run Reef Divers (☎ 973-4400, 973-5636), PO Box 137, Runaway Bay, offers dives and certification programs. It also rents snorkel gear (US$5 per hour, US$15 daily), has glass-bottom boat rides (US$10), waterskiing (US$20), banana boat rides (US$8), and sailboat rentals (US$30 per hour).

Breezes also has full scuba diving equipment and instruction.

Also see the Scuba Diving section in the Outdoor Activities chapter.

## Motor Racing

Dover Raceway (☎ 975-2127, c/o Motor Racing Jamaica, Ltd), south of Runaway Bay, is the setting for auto and motorcycle races, including the Motor Sports Championship Series. There are five races, one held every other month, beginning in April and ending in December.

Dover Raceway hosts the Esso International Rally in December, the annual competition of the Jamaica Motoring Club (☎ 929-4451).

## Organized Tours

The major hotels have tour desks and can arrange for you to explore locally or farther afield. JCAL Tours (☎ 973-4106) has a small office outside the Seafood Giant restaurant.

## Places to Stay

**Budget** You can camp for US$10 on the lawns at **Whilby Resort Cottages** (☎ 973-6308, PO Box 111), on a hillside behind Runaway Bay HEART Country Club. It's owned by the colorful Sister Pat Cassier. Facilities include water and toilets, and kitchen privileges are granted. Sister Cassier also rents simple, cozy air-conditioned rooms with kitchenettes and private bath and hot water. The place is modestly furnished, with views down over the coast. Rates begin at US$40.

**Villa la Rose** (☎ 973-3093), at the west end of Runaway Bay, has more modest rooms with beach views for US$35, or US$40 with TV.

**Cliff's Apartments** (☎ 973-2601) offers houses and very simple rooms, several with shared bath, from about US$20. The main house is on the south side of the A1, off Hampton Rd. Another budget option is **Club Recovery** (☎ 973-4361) opposite Club Ambiance. It has five small and basic air-conditioned rooms with private bathrooms and hot water. They're vastly overpriced, however, at US$40 double.

Another self-catering option is **Coral Cape Villa** (☎ 973-2559), 200m west of Caribbean Isle resort. **Sharp's Flats**, set in gardens opposite the post office on the A1, has also been recommended, although rooms are small.

**Mid-Range** The family-run **Salem Resort** (☎ 973-4256, fax 973-5017, PO Box 151) has 24 rooms, each modestly furnished for US$45/50 single/double, or US$50/55 with air-con. It has a bar and restaurant, plus a small pool.

**Alamandra Inn** (☎ 973-4030, fax 973-5195, PO Box 65), in the center of Salem, is modestly charismatic. Its 23 beautiful air-conditioned suites are adorned with bougainvillea. All have TVs. Guests have use of Club Caribbean, nearby. Rates for doubles are US$50/60 low season/high season (or US$120/160 all-inclusive). No children are permitted.

The **Tamarind Tree Resort Hotel** (☎ 973-2678, fax 973-5013, PO Box 235) is a 16-room hotel, 100 yards from the beach. All rooms have air-con and are pleasantly furnished.

The hotel also boasts the Stinger Disco. Rates for a single or double range from US$62 to US$85 for a suite with telephone and color TV. The resort also has three three-bedroom cottages for US$165.

The intimate **Caribbean Isle** (☎ 973-2364, fax 973-4835, PO Box 119) is a modest, contemporary three-story place, with 24 simple yet clean air-conditioned rooms for US$65 single or double. All rooms overlook the pool and beach.

**Sunflower Villas** (☎ 973-2171, fax 973-2381, Box 150) has 80 units that range from one to five bedrooms; some are Spanish-style three-bathroom villas, with private dipping pools. Cooks and housekeepers are available. There are two pools, plus water sports on a rather scruffy beach, and the place looks jaded. Low-season rates for rooms begin at US$65 per person, all-inclusive. Luxury villas range from US$900 to US$2000 weekly. Rates include airport transfers.

For a bargain and a breezy hillside setting, check out **Runaway HEART Academy & Country Club** (☎ 973-2671, fax 973-2693, PO Box 98), a plantation-style manor with 20 spacious, pleasantly furnished, well-lit rooms with TVs, air-con, and coastal vistas from balconies. Some guests report that the service is excellent, as well it should be: next door is the hotel training school. Others say the service is slow, which is also to be expected since trainees are learning the ropes. In essence, you're a guinea pig. It overlooks the SuperClubs Golf Course, to which hotel guests have access. A shuttle runs to Cardiff Hall beach. Amenities include a pool, and an elegant terrace restaurant with faux marble floors and polished hardwood ceilings. A 36-room extension and conference center were planned. Summer rates are US$68 single or double. Winter rates are US$84 including tax and service charge. Meal plans are offered.

The euphemistically named **Cardiff Resort & Hotel** was being built at press time above the Cardiff Supermarket – a far from salubrious setting 10 minutes' walk from a beach.

**Top End** The all-inclusive **Club Ambiance** (☎ 973-2066, fax 973-2067, 800-523-6504 in *the USA, PO Box 20)* is popular with European charter groups. It has only a small beach, so most of your time may be spent around the pool and sundeck. Its air-conditioned oceanfront rooms and junior suites are set back from the beach. All have balconies and telephones, and king-size beds are available on request. It has a restaurant and large open-air oceanfront bar. Four categories of rooms cost from US$90 to US$110 per person in low season, and US$105 to US$150 high season. The Royal Ambience Suite sleeps six people.

Another favorite of European charter groups is **Club Caribbean** (☎ 973-3507, fax 973-3509, PO Box 65, Runaway Bay; ☎ 212-545-8431, 800-223-9815 in North America) in Salem. This all-inclusive has 20 rooms, 130 conical, African-style thatched-roof cottages, and 20 one-bedroom suites spread throughout 15 landscaped acres behind a 1000-foot-wide beach with a nude section. The rooms are spacious, with king-size beds and wooden ceilings. There's plenty of activity and nightlife at the disco and three bars. If you hate crowds, you'll not fit in. Activities include a full range of water sports, a PADI dive center, and party cruises on a 40-foot trimaran for an extra fee. Summer rates start at US$170/190 single/double; winter rates start at US$200/250.

A more upscale option is **Breezes Runaway Bay Golf & Beach Resort** (☎ 973-2436, fax 973-2352, PO Box 58, Runaway Bay; ☎ 800-467-8737 in North America, ☎ 01749-677200 in the UK), a 234-room, 27-acre resort in the SuperClubs chain and flagship of its 'Breezes' brand. It caters to couples and singles, has a massive freeform swimming pool, lush landscaping, and fronts the best beachfront in Runaway Bay. A nude section has its own Jacuzzi (one of three on site). Facilities include scuba diving and a trapeze, plus well-stocked stores, a nightclub and disco, and a wide choice of restaurants (including Japanese), appealing mostly to an unsophisticated crowd. The price is 'super-inclusive' of everything that exists inside the gates, including unlimited golf at the adjacent golf club. It is increasingly promoting itself as a scuba resort. Per

person rates begin at US$629 to US$739 for a three-day package in low season, depending on room type; high-season rates begin at US$809 to US$889. Add US$100 per night for single occupancy.

SuperClubs' 225-room **Hedonism III** (☎ 800-467-8737, www.superclubs.com) due to open in September 1999, is for adults only. This sibling to the renowned Hedonism II in Negril likewise aims toward those 'who fancy a playful and uninhibited vacation.' Translation: leaning toward and beyond the risqué. The 10-acre property will feature the island's first 'swim-up' guest rooms, with verandas featuring steps leading directly into the swimming pool. A panoply of activities will be included.

In a similar vein, but for families, is **Franklyn D Resort** (☎ 973-3067, fax 973-3071, PO Box 201; ☎ 800-337-5437, fax 516-223-4815 in North America; ☎ 020-8795-1718, fax 020-8795-1728 in the UK; www.fdrholidays.com), a Spanish-hacienda-style, all-inclusive property with 67 suites, including two and three-bedroom apartments. Children are provided their own facilities and can participate in a variety of activities. And a 'Girl Friday' is assigned to each suite, to look after the kids and tend to your every need. The resort has a full range of activities and facilities, including three restaurants and five bars. The beach is basic. Rates begin at US$1600 per person per week, including all meals, drinks, and activities. Children under 16 stay free.

**Villa Carmel** (☎ 974-2451, 103 Main St, Ocho Rios), next to Breezes Runaway Bay, is an attractive property with four air-conditioned rooms, each with private bath and pleasing furnishings. It's surrounded by landscaped grounds and has a pool and sundeck overlooking the beach. A staff of five includes a cook and two housekeepers. Access to Breezes Runaway Bay can be arranged.

Another option is **Fairway Villa** (☎ 974-2508, fax 974-2967, c/o JAVA, PO Box 298, Ocho Rios; ☎ 305-673-6688, 800-221-8830, fax 305-673-5666 in the USA), on the Cardiff Hall Estate just west of Salem. It's a five-bedroom villa whose spacious lounge has modern, uninspired furniture. It has its own pool and is fully staffed. Weekly rates range from US$2000 to US$2800 summer and winter.

*Eaton Hall*, a great house built upon the brick foundations of an old English fort that was converted into a hotel in 1948, closed in 1988.

## Places to Eat

You can't miss *Seafood Giant* (☎ 973-4801) – roadside billboards advertise the restaurant for miles around – at the west end of Runaway Bay. Typical dishes are jackfish with spinach roasted in foil (US$4) or fried with bammy, plantain, and rice and peas (US$3); and curried, creole, or braised garlic shrimp (US$12). The filling meals are an excellent value. However, if you pick your own fish you'll be charged 'according to size.'

Another good bargain is the elegant *Cardiff Hall Restaurant* (☎ 973-2671) at Runaway HEART Academy & Country Club. Reservations are essential. The *Seaview Restaurant* and *Italian Garden Pizzeria* are good options at Club Caribbean. Outsiders can buy day or night passes and enjoy the entertainment, too.

More down-to-earth options in Salem include *Hayden's Seafood Restaurant*, *Pizza! Pizza! Pizza!* (☎ 973-4836), the *Northern Jerk & Steak Pit* for succulent jerk, and *Island Queen Patties*, which delivers ackee and saltfish breakfasts, callaloo loafs, burgers, chicken and chips, and an array of savories. The *Rising Sun*, next to the gas station, sells German-inspired Jamaican fare (closed Mondays).

*Afiya* (☎ 973-4266), 100 yards east of the gas station, specializes in health foods and vegetarian cuisine. Typical dishes include tofu with barbecue sauce, vegetarian pastas (US$4), and veggie burgers (US$2). You can also get soups, natural juices, and desserts, plus grains, tofu, soy milk, and herbal teas. It's open 9 am to 7 pm, Monday to Saturday.

There's a *Devon House I-Scream* shop on the A3 in Salem. The *Patty Place*, near the junction from Brown's Town, also serves ice cream and has fresh-baked bread and pastries, as does *Fiesta Ice Cream & Pastry*, opposite the Cardiff Supermarket.

You can stock up on groceries at *Clarke's Grocery* on Main St, and fresh fish is always available, particularly outside Salem Paradise Beach.

## Entertainment

Runaway Bay is not booming with nightlife, although you'll find several rustic rum shops and reggae bars. *Tek It Easy* is the only bar with a hint of sophistication.

There's the usual array of charmless go-go clubs, including *Reggae Masters* (☎ 973-4707). Others include the *19th Hole Club* (☎ 973-5766), in Salem Plaza, which also has pool and live music.

For a more touristy experience, try the shows at *Club Caribbean* or the *Safari Disco* (☎ 973-2066) at Club Ambiance, which has a happy hour from 10:30 pm, and special attractions on weekends. The *Stinger Disco* in the Tamarind Tree Resort Hotel has a happy hour from 6 pm to 8 pm nightly. Monday is rock 'n roll, Wednesday is soca, Friday is dancehall, and Saturday is oldies night.

The *Almond Grove* (☎ 973-4652) hosts occasional amateur dramatics.

You can purchase a night pass to *Breezes* for US$46, granting unlimited food and drinks and access at no extra cost to all bars and entertainment.

## Shopping

You'll find wood carvings, jewelry, and other tourist trinkets for sale on the street.

A selection of swimwear and leisure wear is available at Splash, in the Club Caribbean resort. Mingles (☎ 973-2570), in the Breezes Runaway Bay Resort, sells top designer items, including crafts and clothing. If you're not staying at the hotel, you'll need to call ahead. A daily shopping shuttle picks up guests from larger hotels for trips to Ocho Rios.

## Getting There & Away

All the buses traveling the A1 between Montego Bay and Ocho Rios stop in Runaway Bay, which is about 1½ hours from the former (US$1.20) and 40 minutes from the latter (US$0.50). Buses arrive and depart from the tiny square in front of Patty Place, catercorner to the post office. Poochie's (☎ 973-2509) is a local minibus service.

'Robots' (shared taxis) ply the A1. Try Sir Win's Love Line Taxi Service (☎ 973-4954).

## Getting Around

Jake's Motorcycle Rentals (☎ 973-4403), west of Salem Plaza, rents scooters for about US$30 a day; it's more for larger bikes up to 750cc. Salem Car Rentals (☎ 973-2564, fax 973-5779) and Caribbean Car Rentals (☎ 973-3539) are located on the main road in Salem, and charge US$45 per day for a Toyota Starlet, and US$55 for a Suzuki Samurai.

## DISCOVERY BAY

This wide flask-shaped bay, 5 miles west of Runaway Bay and 5 miles east of Rio Bueno (and the boundary with Trelawny parish), is a popular resort spot for locals drawn to its Puerto Seco Beach. However, the town itself has only marginal appeal. A marine park has been proposed.

It is considered by locals to be the first place where Christopher Columbus landed on Jamaican soil in 1494 (the actual site of the original landing is controversial; see Rio Bueno in the Montego Bay & Northwest Coast chapter).

The Kaiser Bauxite Company's Port Rhoades bauxite-loading facility dominates the town. Large freighters are loaded with bauxite at a pier on the west side of the bay (most of it heads off to Russia). They're fed by conveyor belts from a huge storage dome that holds 125,000 metric tons of bauxite – enough for three ore carriers. The facility, which is covered in rust-colored dust, is a blight on the bay and must surely be a brake on tourism development. You can follow the road signed 'Port Rhoades' steeply uphill half a mile to a lookout point offering fantastic views over the bay (there is a pair of high-power, pay-per-view binoculars).

## Information

There's a gas station in town, as well as a bank and supermarket at Columbus Plaza. The Tretcel Medical Clinic (☎ 973-3568), signed at the turnoff for Kaiser west of town, is open 8 am to 4:30 pm Monday to Friday. It also has a dentist.

You can make calls from Fontana's Direct (☎ 973-2630) in the plaza opposite Puerto Seco Beach. Western Union has an outlet here, and there's a pharmacy.

## Puerto Seco Beach

The eastern side of the bay is rimmed with white-sand beaches. Puerto Seco Beach (☎ 973-2660) is the main one. Open to the public, it has tennis courts and rustic eateries and bars. On weekends and holidays locals flock from miles around, the air is thick with jerk smoke, the reggae music is cranked up, and the beach jams. It's open 8:30 am to 5 pm (entrance costs US$2, children US$1). Enter opposite the gas station.

## Quadrant Wharf

A plaque painted in Rasta colors at the west end of town recalls the history of this old wharf and of Discovery Bay.

## Columbus Park

Kaiser funded the development of this open-air roadside museum atop the bluff on the west side of the bay. The eclectic historic memorabilia include anchors, cannons, nautical bells, sugar-boiling coppers referred to locally as 'taces' and used for heating and concentrating cane juice, and an old waterwheel in working condition that creaks and clanks as it turns. There's also a diminutive locomotive formerly used to haul sugar at Innswood Estate. A mural depicts Columbus' landing.

The site offers superb views over Discovery Bay. You'll find a craft shop, restaurant, and snack bar. The vendors are friendly and their proceeds go to charities. Entrance is free.

## Marine Biology Laboratory

The University of the West Indies (☎ 973-3274 24-hour line, 973-2241) maintains a marine research laboratory on the west side of the bay (immediately west of Columbus Park), where scientists study

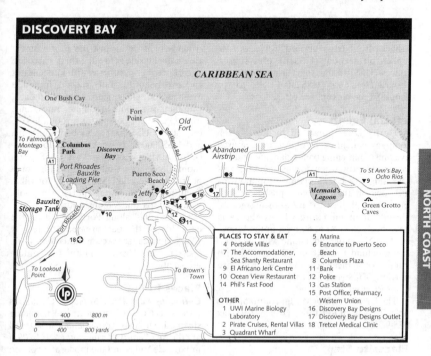

**DISCOVERY BAY**

*CARIBBEAN SEA*

One Bush Cay

Fort Point

Old Fort

To Falmouth, Montego Bay

Columbus Park

Discovery Bay

Abandoned Airstrip

To St Ann's Bay, Ocho Rios

Port Rhoades Bauxite Loading Pier

Puerto Seco Beach

Jetty

Bauxite Storage Tank

Mermaid's Lagoon

Green Grotto Caves

To Lookout Point

To Brown's Town

0    400    800 m
0    400    800 yards

| PLACES TO STAY & EAT | |
| --- | --- |
| 4 Portside Villas | 5 Marina |
| 7 The Accommodationer, | 6 Entrance to Puerto Seco |
| Sea Shanty Restaurant | Beach |
| 9 El Africano Jerk Centre | 8 Columbus Plaza |
| 10 Ocean View Restaurant | 11 Bank |
| 14 Phil's Fast Food | 12 Police |
| | 13 Gas Station |
| OTHER | 15 Post Office, Pharmacy, |
| 1 UWI Marine Biology | Western Union |
| Laboratory | 16 Discovery Bay Designs |
| 2 Pirate Cruises, Rental Villas | 17 Discovery Bay Designs Outlet |
| 3 Quadrant Wharf | 18 Tretcel Medical Clinic |

NORTH COAST

coral reefs. It has Jamaica's only decompression chamber.

## Green Grotto Caves

This system of caves and tunnels extends for about 10 miles and is accessed via a well-marked entrance 2 miles east of Discovery Bay. Steps lead down into the chambers, where statuesque dripstone formations are illuminated by floodlights. The highlight is Green Grotto, a glistening lake 120 feet down. The US$4 entrance fee includes fruit punch and a guided 45-minute tour, with a boat trip across the lake (children under age five get in free; those five to 12 are charged US$2). It's a fabulous experience with the stalactites reflecting on the crystalline waters. Your guide may even tap some of them to produce eerie sounds. Seven miles of caverns are said to be negotiable for spelunkers. Swimming is allowed.

In pre-Columbian days, the caves were used by the Arawaks who left their artwork on the walls. The caves are open 9 am to 5 pm. The *Spicy Nice Kitchen* here provides breakfast and lunch.

## Fishing

Mermaid's Lagoon (also known as Discovery Bay Lake), immediately west of Green Grotto, is 170 feet deep and stocked with tilapia. The commercial fishing enterprise no longer operates but, hey, if you have your own tackle, go for it.

If you want to try your hand at bigger fry, sport fishing boats can be rented from the marina at Puerto Seco Beach.

Also try the following charters for fishing:

| King Fisher | ☎ 974-2726 |
| Mitzy | ☎ 974-2527 |
| Sunfisher | ☎ 994-2294 |
| Triple B | ☎ 975-3273 |

## Cruises

Pirate Cruises (☎ 973-2007), at Portside Villas, offers trips aboard *Liverpool*, a replica pirate boat (US$10), plus sunset cruises (US$10) and sport fishing charters aboard *Don One* (US$250 for up to six people). Free pickups are offered.

## Special Events

A Derby Day sponsored by the Kaiser company is held each August and features live music, marching bands, dancing, and the Pushcart Derby, when dozens of youths representing parish teams compete in a downhill race on their wooden pushcarts that they normally use for transporting goods. Despite their miniature wheels, the carts have been clocked at 60 mph in the homestretch! Now you understand why the road, rising behind Port Rhodes, is marked with lanes like a racetrack and lined with tire barriers. The event is featured in the movie *Cool Runnings*.

The Discovery Bay Marlin Tournament is hosted each mid-October (☎ 925-0893, fax 925-9673).

## Places to Stay

*Spanish Court Apartments* (☎ 972-2235) offers simply furnished units with kitchens. The *Accommodationer* (☎ 973-2559), just east of Puerto Seco Beach, has seven plain rooms with kitchenettes for US$50.

*Portside Villas* (☎ 973-2007, 973-3135, fax 973-2720, PO Box 42) is an attractive little

property with a splendid setting. Thirty of its rooms and apartments are set in pleasant grounds tight up against the shore; others are on the hillside across the road. There are also efficiency apartments with kitchenettes and two beautiful, fully staffed, four and five-bedroom villas sleeping up to 10 each, with their own pools. In summer, rates range from US$65 per person for a room, US$75 for a studio, US$85 for a one-bedroom suite, and US$2000/2500 weekly for a four/five-bedroom villa. Winter rates are US$80 for a room, US$95 for a studio, US$105 for a one-bedroom suite, and US$2500/3250 for villas. Facilities include water sports, two pools, whirlpool spa, and a tennis court.

Other villas, along Portland Rd on the east side of the bay, are represented by JAVA Jamaica (see Accommodations in the Facts for the Visitor chapter for contact information).

## Places to Eat

*Columbus Park Patty Stand,* in Columbus Park, sells a host of Jamaican fare, including steamed fish. Also serving Jamaican seafood are the *Sea Shanty Restaurant* (☎ 973-2007) in Portside Villas and the moderately priced *Ocean View Restaurant* near the cay. Both offer bay views. The Sea Shanty also serves steaks and has a four-course dinner that varies nightly.

For jerk pork or chicken, try *El Africano* (☎ 973-2054) opposite Green Grotto Cave. *Phil's Fast Food* (next to the gas station) has spicy vegetable and meat patties for less than US$1. There's a *supermarket* next door.

## Entertainment

*Coxon's HQ,* near the Discovery Bay Designs Outlet, is the happenin' local night spot, with reggae and go-go drawing local men. The operators of Green Grotto Caves were planning on opening a disco.

## Shopping

Discovery Bay Designs (☎ 973-2565) makes and sells clothing and quality hand-

'My other car is a pushcart.'

crafted wooden housewares. It has a gift shop and factory outlet east of town.

### Getting There & Away
You can catch buses that ply the A1 between Montego Bay and Ocho Rios and stop in Discovery Bay at the junction of the A1 and the B3. A minibus between Kingston and Discovery Bay costs US$7.

### Getting Around
You can walk almost anywhere. Robots ply the coast road. Also see Runaway Bay, earlier in this chapter, for taxi and minibus information.

A company called G&B (☎ 973-3576) reportedly rents bicycles.

# Dry Harbour Mountains

Paved roads lead south from Discovery Bay, Runaway Bay, and St Ann's Bay and ascend into the Dry Harbour Mountains, a rugged, thickly wooded region of Cockpits. In this off-the-beaten track area, the roads twist and turn through fabulous scenic countryside. Genuine attractions are few, with one notable exception: Nine Mile, the birthplace and resting place of reggae superstar Bob Marley.

The roads rise to the island's rugged backbone, then drop away to the south coast parishes of Clarendon and Manchester. The district south of Brown's Town is known as Wilberforce, after the English abolitionist who steered the Abolition Act through Parliament. Many villages in the wooded folds of the Dry Harbour Mountains were founded as 'emancipation villages' by the Reverend John Clark of Brown's Town.

Only two main roads run east-west. The lower, the 'Great Interior Road' (the B11), parallels the coast about 7 miles inland. Built at the turn of the 18th century to facilitate troop movements, it begins at Rock, a mile east of Falmouth, and weaves east across the sugar plains of eastern Trelawny and the tight valleys on the lower slopes of the Dry Harbour Mountains. The drive is gorgeous

all the way through Brown's Town (south of Runaway Bay) to Claremont.

## BROWN'S TOWN
Brown's Town (population 4000) is a large and lively market town 7 miles south of Runaway Bay. Many noble houses on the hillsides hint at its relative prosperity (much of the wealth is still derived from illicit means, though many of the ganja plantations for which the surrounding hills were renowned have been eradicated). The town is at its most bustling during market days (Wednesday, Friday, and Saturday), when the tin-roofed, cast-iron Victorian market overflows with higglers, and the streets throng. Park the car and rummage amid the stalls and sidewalks piled high with gaudy knickknacks, cheap knock-off name-brand clothing, baskets of scallions, dasheen, and yams still red with cloying earth.

Bring your camera, but be warned that not all the market higglers like to have their photo taken.

### Information
**Money** National Commercial Bank (☎ 975-2242), Scotiabank (☎ 975-2237), and Jamaica Citizens Bank (☎ 975-2726) all have branches within a stone's throw of each other on Brown's Town Rd. None have currency exchange booths, but you can cash traveler's checks and arrange advances against credit cards.

**Post & Communications** The post office (☎ 975-2216) is on Brown's Town Rd, opposite the police station. You can make international calls and send faxes from Direct Telecom (☎ 975-2926, fax 975-2925), above KFC at B&H Mini Mall.

**Travel Agencies** The nation's leading travel agency chain, Stuart's Travel Service (☎ 975-2566), has an office in Nam's Plaza on Main St.

**Bookstores** You'll find a small selection of magazines at Grand Pharmacy, and at Brown's Town Books & Stationery in B&H Mini Mall on Main St.

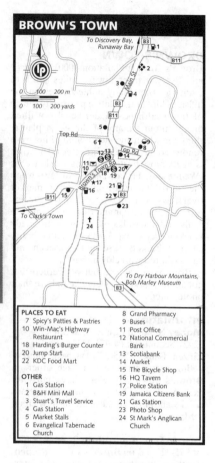

## BROWN'S TOWN

To Discovery Bay,
Runaway Bay

To Clark's Town

To Dry Harbour Mountains,
Bob Marley Museum

0   100   200 m
0   100   200 yards

**PLACES TO EAT**
7   Spicy's Patties & Pastries
10  Win-Mac's Highway
    Restaurant
18  Harding's Burger Counter
20  Jump Start
22  KDC Food Mart

**OTHER**
1   Gas Station
2   B&H Mini Mall
3   Stuart's Travel Service
4   Gas Station
5   Market Stalls
6   Evangelical Tabernacle
    Church

8   Grand Pharmacy
9   Buses
11  Post Office
12  National Commercial
    Bank
13  Scotiabank
14  Market
15  The Bicycle Shop
16  HQ Tavern
17  Police Station
19  Jamaica Citizens Bank
21  Gas Station
23  Photo Shop
24  St Mark's Anglican
    Church

James-Grant, who also has a clinic (☎ 975-2343) on St Christopher's Crescent.

Pharmacies include Brown's Town Pharmacy (☎ 975-2271) in the B&H Mini Mall on Main St and Grand Pharmacy (☎ 975-2613) at 2 Top Rd. The former is open 9 am to 6 pm Friday to Wednesday and until 4 pm on Thursday.

**Emergency** The historic police station (☎ 975-2233) is midway up Brown's Town Rd.

### Things to See
The town is named for its founder, Irish estate owner Hamilton Brown (1776–1843), who represented the parish in the House of Assembly, and owned nine estates locally. Brown financed the building of **St Mark's Anglican Church** in Victorian Gothic style, but allegedly also arranged for the Baptist church to be burned down so that blacks would have nowhere to worship.

Another 19th-century church, the **Evangelical Tabernacle**, is on Top Rd. The founder of the latter, Dr James Johnson (1854–1922), was one of the earliest promoters of tourism to Jamaica.

Other buildings of interest include the fine cut-stone **courthouse** with neoclassical columned portico.

### Places to Stay
**Treasure Trove Guest House** (☎ 975-2371), at Minnard Heights just north of town, features a swimming pool and horseback riding on a farm. Jean Sharpe (☎ 975-2487) apparently also rents out *rooms*. Alternately, try **Meditation Height** (☎ 975-2588), above the Esso gas station on Huntley Ave.

Also see Lillyfield Great House in the Priory & Around section, earlier in this chapter.

### Places to Eat
You can buy patties and pastries at **Spicy's Patties & Pastries**, and fresh produce at stalls along Main St and in the **open-air market** in the center of town. There are several basic budget cateries in town, including **Jump Start**, a rustic 'Boston jerk center'; **Harding's Burger Counter**, 50 yards down the hill from

There's a photo shop on the hill south of the town center, on the B3.

**Cultural Centers** The Jamaica Cultural Development Commission (☎ 975-0578), on Main St, should be able to answer any questions. It's open 9 am to 5:30 pm Monday to Saturday.

**Medical Services** You can get medical attention at the DeCarteret Medical Centre (☎ 975-2265) at the north end of Main St. Or pay a visit to Dr Winsome the market; and the atmospheric, down-to-earth **Win-Mac's Highway Restaurant**, opposite the police station on Brown's Town Rd.

**HQ Tavern** is a funky place to share an ear-shattering game of dominoes over Red Stripe and white rum.

You can buy groceries at the **KDC Food Mart** beside the Epping gas station on the road to Alexandria.

### Getting There & Away
Buses and minibuses arrive and depart from the east end of Top Rd. At least six vehicles operate daily between Brown's Town and Kingston, and more than a dozen ply the Ocho Rios route. At least one bus (US$0.50) and two coasters (about US$1.50) also operate from Discovery Bay.

### Getting Around
Ken 'Keith' Moulton sometimes acts as a guide by special request. He leads hikes and offers chauffeured guiding. Write him c/o Joyce Harris, Minnard Heights, Brown's Town; or PO Box 161, St Ann, or leave a phone message at Headquarters Tavern (☎ 975-2535) on Musgrave St.

If you're cycling, the Bicycle Shop at the bottom of Brown's Town Rd may be able to make repairs or supply parts.

### WATT TOWN
You can count on being the first foreigner in weeks to arrive at Watt Town, 10 miles southwest of Brown's Town in the backwaters of the Dry Harbour Mountains.

The hamlet is known as the birthplace of Revivalism, which began here in the 1880s. It is still a center of the religion, and Revivalists make pilgrimages here to study at the Watt Town Revival Schoolroom. Visitors are welcome. A gatekeeper will determine whether or not you may enter the consecrated grounds. The village is semi-autonomous and ruled over by a body of 'patriarchs.'

### ALEXANDRIA
Alexandria, 9 miles south of Brown's Town, is a small crossroads village that spreads along the B3 for over a mile. It's of little interest except for those heading to the Bob Marley Museum at Nine Mile. (Don't be misled by a roadside sign for Knutsford Great House, 3 miles north of Alexandria. You may think it's open to the public, but it's not.)

### Information
The National Commercial Bank (☎ 975-1229) is open only 9:30 to 11:30 am Tuesday and 9:30 am to 3 pm Friday. There's a small hospital (☎ 975-2372), police station (☎ 975-9011), and gas station.

### Places to Stay & Eat
A reader recommends 'staying with the Rastas' at **Bongo Joe's Place**.

The **Ackee Tree Lawn & Restaurant**, 2 miles north of Alexandria, is a colorful eatery and grocery store that has go-go dancing at night. I recommend a lunch of roast yam, saltfish, and coconut water at the **Roast Yam Centre**, a funky shack 100m south of the Ackee Tree Lawn.

### Getting There
Alexandria is linked by bus (US$1) and minibus (US$3) to the Parade in Kingston. It's a two-hour journey. Minibuses also travel to Alexandria from Ocho Rios.

### NINE MILE
This tiny mountain hamlet is 9 miles east of Alexandria, in the middle of a poor farming district. Despite its totally out-of-the-way location, it is firmly on the tourist map for pilgrimages to Bob Marley's birth site and resting place, which the Bob Marley Foundation has turned into a commercial success.

The community where the 'King of Reggae' was born on February 6, 1945, is set dramatically in the midst of Cockpits. The road continues east from Nine Mile through a rugged landscape with tiny hamlets in the base of the Cockpits, with marvelous views through the canyons. Splendid! The road leads to Claremont (see Claremont & Environs, later in this chapter), where you can turn north on the A1 for St Ann, or south for Spanish Town and Kingston.

## Bob Marley Museum

A visit to the birthplace and crypt of Bob Marley is a must for anyone with the least interest in reggae or the legacy of the 'first Third World superstar.' The site is run by the Bob Marley Foundation, which uses some of the proceeds to advance education, health, and social services in the local community.

Upon arrival you're guided into a secure parking lot, then diverted into the gift shop to pay your US$10 entrance fee before your guide leads you up a steep path lined with international flags. Rastafarian guides lead the 30-minute tours. They speak in reverential tones and often break into renditions of Marley's songs. Between puffs on a spliff of *ganja*, your guide will tell of Marley's childhood and simple lifestyle.

Marley was born in what is now a house below the museum site. He moved into the hut on the hill – called Zion – when he was three months old. The hut, like virtually everything else, is painted green, yellow, and red, representing sunshine (yellow), nature (green), and blood (red). Inside there is merely a bed, and walls covered with adoring graffiti and miscellany left by visitors.

Behind the hut is the 'inspiration stone' (or 'Mt Zion Rock') on which Marley sat and learned to play the guitar. Supposedly Marley even slept on a rock – painted like a tam in Rasta colors – called 'pillow' (made famous in the song, 'Talking Blues') to receive inspiration.

Marley's body lies buried along with his guitar in an 8-foot-tall oblong marble mausoleum inside a tiny church of traditional Ethiopian design that stands next to the hut. You must leave your shoes outside and take your cap off before entering. The sun rising to the east casts its rays on Marley's tomb as it shines through a Star of David-shaped window.

A photo of Haile Selassie takes precedence at the base of the tomb, with a smaller photo of Marley to the side. The crypt also contains a large bronze bust of the musician, a stained glass window of a lion of Judah, some of Marley's musical instruments, and a huge, badly worn leather-bound book full of newspaper clips reporting Marley's funeral.

Before leaving the crypt you may be asked to stand humbly while a prayer is recited.

No video camera or taping equipment is allowed.

The museum shop sells Marley paraphernalia of every description, from T-shirts to music tapes. You can also buy simple crafts from locals who hawk carved gourds and other items opposite the museum entrance. Hustlers who used to offer to guard or wash visitors' cars, or act as guides have for the most part left, and huge wire fences have been erected. Now the place looks like a military compound. Nonetheless, the guides and abundant hangers-on have an annoying habit of hitting you up for extra money. Give them a J$100 (US$3) bill and you're likely to receive a contemptuous stare for being a skinflint! Don't be suckered. Foreign women can expect to be pestered.

## Special Events

A memorial reggae concert is held here each February 6. For information about the concert or the museum, contact Cedella Marley Booker Entertainment (☎ 999-7003), Calderwood, PO Box St Ann, or (☎ 305-665-5379, fax 305-663-1605, cmbe@msn.com), 2809 Bird Ave suite 146, Miami, FL 33133.

## Places to Stay & Eat

You can camp at **Natural Mystic**, 800m east of Nine Mile. It also has basic lodging, serves I-tal food, and offers a 'plantation tour.'

The **Wailer's Villa**, opposite the museum, comes as a surprise: this modern, gleaming white structure looks like a millionaire's home. It has 14 rooms basically furnished in pine, with cool tile floors and attractive bathrooms; upstairs rooms have lofty wooden ceilings plus balconies for US$45 single, US$60 double. A health food store was to be added.

The home of Cedella Booker, Bob Marley's mother, was being rebuilt at press time and may be offered for rental.

The **museum restaurant** serves vegetarian I-tal dishes for US$3 and upwards. **Club Marcus**, opposite the museum, is a lively little bar that serves snacks. And there are also a couple of local rum shops about 100 yards downhill.

## Getting There & Away
A minibus operates between Alexandria and Claremont and should cost no more than US$1 from either.

Several tour companies offer tours from Kingston, Montego Bay, and Ocho Rios. One of the best is Caribic Vacations' guided excursion (☎ 974-9106 in Ocho Rios, ☎ 953-9878 in Montego Bay).

## CAVE VALLEY
This tiny village sits on the border of St Ann and Clarendon parishes, 8 miles south of Alexandria, at the north end of Vera Ma Hollis Savanna, a 7-mile-long valley. During the early years of the British occupation in the late 17th century, the region was a center for the Maroons. The British built a barracks here during the First Maroon War in the 1730s.

A horse trough, erected in the square in 1937 by the Jamaica Society for the Prevention of Cruelty to Animals, hints at Cave Valley's former importance as a horse-trading center. Reportedly, it still hosts a weekend market to which horses and mules are brought from miles around. Tobacco and coffee are also important crops, especially in the valley of the Cave River, which rises in the mountains near Coleyville, 10 miles west of Cave Valley (the Coffee Industry Board has a small factory 3 miles southwest of Cave Valley at Aenon Town; visitors are welcome to look around).

In the dry season you can see the **Cave River Sinks**, two holes into which the river disappears to reemerge 13 miles north near Stewart Town. During heavy rains, however, the valley floods.

The road southeast from Cave Valley begins a precipitous ascent to Corner Shop and the summit of the Central Highlands at about 2800 feet. From here you can descend to Trout Hall in the upper Rio Minho Valley (drive carefully; the road drops 1300 feet in less than 3 miles).

The road through the Cave River Valley eventually reaches Spaldings, Christiana, and Mandeville.

## Getting There & Away
You'll find minibuses to Cave Valley in Ocho Rios north of the roundabout on DaCosta Drive. Other minibuses run from Mandeville and Kingston, from where you can also catch a bus (about US$2). A minibus operates between Albert Town and Cave Valley.

## CLAREMONT & ENVIRONS
The A1 turns inland at St Ann's Bay and runs south 9 miles to Claremont (population 1500), a regional market town that prospered briefly during the 1960s and 1970s on the income generated by the Reynolds Company's bauxite and cattle-ranching activities. The company has since pulled out of Jamaica. The town has an attractive town square centered on a handsome clock tower topped with green shingle.

South of Claremont, the A1 climbs from sea level to 1500 feet in 5 miles and merges with the A3 at Moneague, rising beyond to Mt Diablo (2754 feet) on the border with St Catherine parish before dropping down to Spanish Town and Kingston.

## Golden Grove
Two miles southeast of Claremont at Golden Grove along the A1, a road heads west through pastures and rusting metal structures that are all that remains of the old Lydford Works, a massive bauxite mine and processing plant that was established in 1952 by Reynolds Jamaica Mines, Ltd. The facility was built near the site where a Kingstonian named Sir Alfred D'Costa (the 'Father of Jamaican bauxite') discovered bauxite ore in 1942 (he had soil samples analyzed because he was concerned about the low yield of his crops). The soils from his estate were declared unusually rich in alumina, with a content of 45% to 50%.

At their peak, the conveyors and overhead bucket tramways carried more than three million tons of bauxite annually to the pier at Ocho Rios. Reynolds also engaged in agricultural research and light industry. It owned 80,000 acres locally, most of which was grazed by the largest herd of cattle (16,000 head) in the West Indies. The company sold its land to the Jamaican government in 1980 and finally pulled out of the island altogether in 1984, though the cattle remained.

The genesis of Jamaica's bauxite industry is commemorated by an aluminum plaque beside the road at Phoenix Park, 5 miles south of Claremont. It was cast from the first load of bauxite shipped in 1952.

## Edinburgh Castle

One of Jamaica's more gory and fascinating stories surrounds the ruins of Edinburgh Castle, 8 miles southwest of Claremont, on the northern outskirts of Bensonton. It's a curiosity (and not worth the drive), but the tale is worth telling.

The two-story fortified house with two towers at diagonal corners was built by Lewis Hutchinson, a Scottish mass murderer who settled in Jamaica in the mid-18th century. The 'castle' stood close by what was, at the time, the main coach road between St Ann's Bay and Spanish Town. The deranged Scot invited his victims into the house, where he wined and dined them before

robbing and murdering them. For years, no one presented evidence against him.

Eventually the maniac quarreled with a neighboring planter, whom he almost killed. A soldier was then sent to arrest him. He, too, was shot dead, but the game was up. Hutchinson was hanged from the Spanish Town gallows on March 16, 1773.

Local lore says that Hutchinson disposed of his victims in a 275-foot-deep sinkhole 400 yards south of the castle. No skeletons have been found, but 43 watches that belonged to his victims were discovered.

The ruin sits atop a hillock on the south side of Bensonton (the Bensonton Health Clinic is in the meadow at the base). Bring a machete if you wish to hike to the top.

## Getting There & Away

Claremont is on the main bus route between the north coast and Kingston, and many buses pass through. Ask your driver to drop you in Claremont, which you can also reach by minibus from Kingston (US$5) or Ocho Rios (US$1).

# Port Antonio & Northeast Coast

The northeast coast is Jamaica's undiscovered quarter – one geared toward the traveler rather than the tourist. It's one of the island's least accessible coastal regions and also its wettest. This is the island's windward corner, where surf rolls ashore into perfect beach-lined coves, and waves chew at rocky headlands. White-sand beaches and colonial-era edifices are relatively few, though several beautiful pocket-size beaches line the shore, and Long Bay (farther east) has a spectacular wave-washed, diamond-dust beach. You'll also find several unspoiled fishing villages where budget travelers can rent cottages and ease into a laid-back local lifestyle. The only town of importance is Port Antonio, popular with budget travelers looking for a more offbeat spot. A fistful of world-famous, deluxe resort-hotels 'unfold like a board game of castles and palaces,' says writer Herb Hiller, recalling the days when Errol Flynn and other luminaries lent the area renown and panache.

The mountainous east coast parish of Portland (population 160,000) receives far fewer tourists (and a more selective breed, too) than rival resort areas. That's the appeal. North American visitors are few and far between. Instead, the area relies on European – mostly German – traffic, which tends to be more exploratory and adventurous. (The German connection dates back decades.) The sparsely populated region is also ruggedly beautiful, with the Blue Mountains forming a handsome spine to the south. Exploring is easy, as the A4 hugs the coastline with brief forays inland. The hinterlands of the John Crow Mountains and Blue Mountains are for serious adventurers only, though the Rio Grande Valley offers easy access and is of great appeal.

Portland's natural beauty prompted the foundation of the Portland Environmental Protection Association (PEPA), a volunteer organization that has gained stature and the support of the Nature Conservancy and other international bodies. One of PEPA's

## Highlights

- Boston Bay for the best – and hottest – jerk in Jamaica
- Guided hiking in the Rio Grande Valley
- Enchanting Blue Lagoon for swimming, a fine meal, and live jazz
- Exhilarating Reach Falls for cooling fresh water dips
- A soothing bamboo raft trip on the Rio Grande

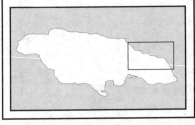

goals is to create a protected 'conservation corridor' from the Blue Mountains to the Port Antonio Marine Park. Local hoteliers and other tourism figures are marketing the region to an eco-conscious niche market. The new environmentalism reflects a broader intent that includes the sponsorship of local craft industries and the training of fishermen as snorkeling guides (the fishermen are being supplied with snorkel gear in the hope that organized snorkeling will come to replace fishing as a source of income, as the waters are desperately overfished).

A new and vigorous effort to market and limelight the Port Antonio area as a distinct destination – 'Port Antonio *Naturally*' – has been born in recent years thanks to the efforts of concerned hoteliers and tour operators who are showing Jamaica the value of eco-conscious development (the Port Antonio Destination Marketing Program

# PORT ANTONIO & NORTHEAST COAST

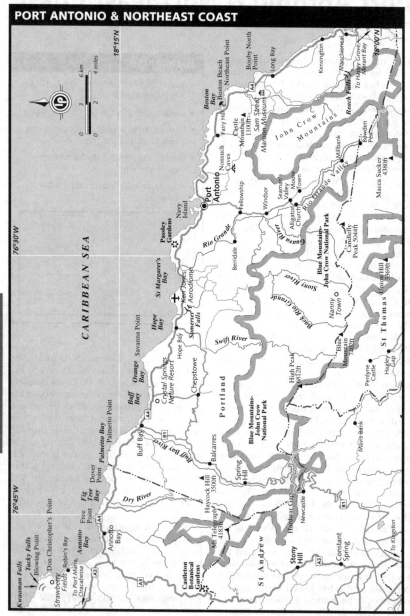

CARIBBEAN SEA

18°45'N

76°30'W

76°45'W

18°00'N

0    3    6 km
0    2    4 miles

Kwaaman Falls
Tacky Falls
Blowing Point
Don Christopher's Point
Strawberry Fields
Robin's Bay
To Port Maria, Oracabessa
Free Point
Fig Tree Bay
Dover Point
Palmetto Point
Palmetto Bay
Savanna Point
Annotto Bay
Buff Bay
Orange Bay
Hope Bay
St Margaret's Bay
Passley Gardens
Navy Island
Port Antonio
Boston Bay
Boston Beach
Northeast Point
Booby North Point
Long Bay
Kensington
Manchioneal
To Happy Grove, Morant Bay
Reach Falls
Bowden Pen
Macca Sucker 4380ft
Millbank
John Crow Mountains
Sam Street Maroon Museum
Castle Mountain 1100ft
Fairy Hill
Nonsuch Caves
Fellowship
Windsor
Seaman's Valley
Moore Town
Alligator Church
Rio Grande Valley
Candlefly Peak 5044ft
Union Hill 3369ft
St Thomas
Nanny Town
Blue Mountain 740ft
High Peak 4612ft
Blue Mountains–John Crow National Park
Stony River
Back Rio Grande
Buck Rio Grande
Cuna River
Berridale
Rio Grande
Swift River
Somerset Falls
Ken Jones Aerodrome
Hope Bay
Crystal Springs Nature Resort
Hope Resort
Chepstowe
Portland
Balcarres
Spring Hill
Buff Bay
Buff Bay River
Dry River
Haycock Hill 3500ft
Mt Telegraph 4183ft
Castleton Botanical Gardens
St Andrew
Stony Hill
Constant Spring
Newcastle
Hardwar Gap
Mavis Bank
Penlyne Castle
Hagley Gap
To Kingston
Annotto Bay

A4    A3    B1    B3

## Fickle & Feverish

It is best not to pre-book (and especially not to pre-pay) excursions, as the weather is fickle. It's easy to book rafting trips, etc, once you arrive.

Take and apply mosquito repellent. In 1998 the area suffered from a bout of dengue fever, which is particularly common in autumn.

involves seven hotels and Rio Grande Attractions). For more information, contact Unique Destinations (☎/fax 934-3398, Marylou@portantoniojamaica.com, www.portantoniojamaica.com), 120 Elmdalè Rd, North Scituate, RI 02857 USA, which offers vacation and hotel packages. And a group of guest house owners recently came together to form the Port Antonio Guest House Association (☎/fax 993-7118, www.in-site.com/portant).

## History

Portland parish was one of the last areas of Jamaica to be populated. In the 18th century the government was eager to settle the area as a buffer against raids by marauding Maroons. The English offered inducements to settlers, including tax-free land grants. Few settlers accepted the colonial government's offer. In 1739 the Maroons were finally subdued, a peace treaty was signed, and it became possible to settle the hinterland.

The rich alluvial soil and damp climate of Portland was suitable for growing bananas, which the Spanish had introduced from the Canary Islands. For two centuries the banana was grown chiefly for domestic consumption. A Yankee skipper, Captain Lorenzo Dow Baker (1840-1908), began the banana trade that would boost the economic prospects of eastern Jamaica when he loaded his vessel with the fruit in 1870 and sold them at a fantastic profit in Boston. The following year he sailed into Port Antonio and traded his cargo for coconuts and 1450 stems of bananas that earned him a profit of

US$2000. Dow Baker and his Boston Fruit Company went on to own 40 banana plantations from Port Antonio to Buff Bay. He also bought up much of Port Antonio and developed Boundbrook Wharf. Bananas were planted throughout the island, but Portland parish remained unrivaled.

Portland's brief heyday was doomed in the 1930s by the onset of Panama disease, which ravaged the crops. More resistant strains of banana have since been planted.

By this time Port Antonio had been discovered by moneyed vacationers seeking an escape from the snows of North America and Europe. Jamaican tourism, in a way, began here. Errol Flynn's arrival and, later, that of numerous blue bloods and Hollywood stars, assured rainy Port Antonio a spot in the sun. See the History section

## PEPA's Park Projects

Declining fish stocks, damage to the ecology of Port Antonio's coral reefs, and threats to Portland parish's natural resources led to the formation of the non-profit Portland Environment Protection Association (PEPA) in 1988.

PEPA is made up of representatives from over 40 civic and citizens' groups that spearhead environmental projects within their communities. PEPA has worked to foster public awareness of their fragile resources, including setting up 14 Environmental Education Clubs in local schools.

The group's most notable achievement has been the establishment of the Port Antonio Marine Park, with boundaries extending over an area of 11 miles, from Ship Rock, west of Port Antonio, to Northeast Point, south of Boston Bay. Within these limits are two reserves – at Turtle Crawle Bay and San San-Blue Lagoon – where fishing is prohibited. USAID has contributed funds for ranger training and buoy installation. You can contact PEPA (☎ 993-9632) at 6 Allan Ave, Port Antonio.

NORTHEAST COAST

## Errol Flynn

Errol Flynn (1909-59), the infamous Hollywood idol, arrived in Portland parish in 1946 when his yacht *Zacca* washed ashore in bad weather. Flynn fell in love with the area and made Port Antonio his playground and home (his acting career was already washed up). In his autobiography, *My Wicked, Wicked Ways*, he described Port Antonio as 'more beautiful than any woman I've ever seen.'

Flynn bought the Titchfield Hotel and Navy Island, where he threw wild, extravagant parties – locals tell exaggerated tales of Flynn's exploits: 'Remember de day 'im drove de Cadillac into de swimming pool?' Flynn's beguiling ways inevitably attracted the attention of other stars of stage and screen, like Clara Bow, Bette Davis, and Ginger Rogers.

With his third wife, Patrice Wymore, Flynn later established a cattle ranch at Boston Estate. He also planned a lavish home at Comfort Castle, and he had grandiose plans to develop Port Antonio into a tourist resort. But heavy drinking and a profligate lifestyle – he spent much of his final years on Navy Island in the arms of the teenage actress Beverley Aadland – added to the toll of his ill-health. He died in 1959 before his plans could be brought to fruition. The wild parties are no more, but his legend lives on.

---

under Port Antonio, later in this chapter, for more details.

## Climate

Portland is famed for its high rainfall, and though most falls at night, the scent of a recent shower always hangs in the air. Seasonal variations are less pronounced in Portland than elsewhere in the country. Here, year-round, moist northeast trade winds meet the John Crow and Blue Mountains, which force the saturated air to rise and cool. The moisture condenses and falls in torrents. Parts of upland Portland have recorded more than 300 inches of rain a year, some of the heaviest rainfall in the world.

Kenneth Pringle, writing in his *Waters of the West*, describes how, while he was hiking in the John Crow Mountains, the rains began to come down:

It started around midnight, quietly, a long sigh like the breaking of a wave, and streamed down in a steady sheet. It did not stop, although it lightened from time to time, for four days.

Fine weather is locally termed 'backra luck.'

## Flora & Fauna

The vegetation is correspondingly lush. The forested mountains with their deep gorges and rushing rivers beckon invitingly, but remain virtually inaccessible to all but hardy hikers. Fortunately, new trails and recreational activities are opening up the Rio Grande Valley and newly formed Blue Mountains-John Crow National Park, which is being linked to the Port Antonio Marine Park by a 'conservation corridor.' The upland regions are a last refuge for the guinea pig-like Jamaican coney, and for the world's largest butterfly, the giant swallowtail.

# Port Antonio

Port Antonio (population 19,000), 68 miles east of Ocho Rios, has been the capital of Portland since 1723 when the parish was founded. Poet Ella Wheeler Wilcox (1855–1919) described the town as the 'most exquisite port on earth.' Back then it was Jamaica's main banana port. Melancholic Port Antonio still has the rakish air and tropical lassitude of a maritime harbor, and there is little of the hustle of Montego Bay or Ocho Rios. Goats snoozing in the shade of verandas sum it all up.

Port Antonio has long resisted efforts to develop it as a tourist resort, despite the limelight provided by socialites who have vacationed here for the past 50 years. In the past decade, it was also the setting of various movies, including *The Mighty Quinn*, *Club Paradise*, *Cocktail*, and a remake of *Lord of the Flies*. The town comes half-alive each October during the International Marlin Tournament, considered Jamaica's most prestigious deep-sea fishing tournie.

The upscale resorts and private villas east of town still help keep Port Antonio resolutely old-fashioned. More broad-based tourism has seemed jinxed. Commercialism hasn't yet found this pocket of paradise, and Port Antonio and the surrounding area are pretty much as they were 30 years ago.

But things are stirring. In 1996, the **Portland Heritage Foundation** was founded by local citizens concerned about preserving Port Antonio's past. Thanks to its pleas, the entire Titchfield Peninsula has been named a National Heritage treasure, with plans to restore many buildings, including Fort George. Modern commercial buildings are arising downtown, providing a newfound sense of vitality, crowned by a splendid commercial complex called Village of St George. A fistful of new hotels have opened nearby

of late. And creative marketing schemes have emerged from local hoteliers eager to see their prospects brighten.

Economically, things are definitely looking up for the town.

## HISTORY
The Spanish named the town in the late 16th century when they christened the bay 'Puerto Anton,' after the governor's son. The Spanish, however, made no serious effort to settle. It wasn't until 1723 that the British laid out a rudimentary town on the peninsula and named it Titchfield after the estate in Hampshire of the Duke of Portland (then Jamaica's governor). The British Navy established a careening station on the island in West Harbour, and in 1729 a fort was built at the tip of Titchfield. However, rampant fevers in the swampy coastlands and constant raids by marauding Maroons deterred all but a few settlers.

Once peace with the Maroons was established in 1739, Titchfield expanded. Much of the land passed into the hands of peasants who grew sustenance crops, including bananas. Enter Lorenzo Dow Baker, fruit shipping magnate, who arrived in 1871 and established the banana trade that created a boomtown overnight and established Port Antonio as the 'banana capital of the world.' In 1879 an observer candidly noted:

But for the fruit trade with America which has sprung up within the last few years, it would now, in all probability, have become as effete and valueless as any part of the whole island.

### Banana Bonanza
In its heyday, 17 steamer lines were operating here and Port Antonio grew so wealthy that, it is said, planters would light their cigars with US$5 bills. (Actually, only the fat-cat traders and planters, who soon controlled much of the land, amassed the wealth; the Jamaican laborers who performed backbreaking work were paid a pittance, as they still are.) Dow Baker, himself from Cape Cod, staffed his company with New Englanders who lent Port Antonio Yankee airs. Lorenzo Dow Baker was not the first shipper of bananas from Jamaica, but he was by far the most successful.

NORTHEAST COAST

NORTHEAST COAST

# PORT ANTONIO

**PLACES TO STAY**
1 Navy Island Marina Resort
5 Little Reef Guest House
6 Ivanhoe's
8 Scotia Guest House
10 DeMontevin Lodge
11 Holiday Home
12 Sunny Side Guest House
14 In & Out Guest House
15 Way Valley Guest House
16 Shadows
24 Bonnie View Plantation Hotel
65 Triff's Inn

**PLACES TO EAT**
1 Bounty Restaurant
18 Food Stalls
19 Centrepoint Club
  & Restaurant
23 Rainbow Country Kitchen
30 Golden Happiness
36 Sabrina's Restaurant & Bar
38 New Debonere
46 Three Star Lion Bakery
47 Daddy Dee's
48 Devon House I-Scream
56 Delicious Delites
58 Cream World

**OTHER**
1 Crusoe Bar
2 Fort George Ruins
3 Folly
4 Titchfield School
7 Bobby's Bar
9 Bamboo Bike,
  Car & Jeep Rental
13 Folly Oval Cricket Ground
16 Shadows
17 Texaco Gas Station
20 Port Antonio Hospital
21 Rolex
22 Mandela Open Ground
25 Village of St George
26 Shell Gas Station
27 Portland Parish Library
28 Craft Market
29 Portland Communication, Ltd
31 Clock Tower
32 Public Telephones, Courthouse
33 Post Office
34 Goebel Plaza, Jamaica
  Information Service
35 Jamaica Arcade
37 Huntress Marina & Charter
  Services
39 Gallery Art Ambokile
40 Valley Hikes
41 Kamal Supermarket
42 Musgrave Market
43 CIBC Jamaica Banking Centre
44 Scotiabank
45 Bus Station, Taxis
49 Roof Club
50 National Commercial Bank,
  Attractions Link
51 Cenotaph
52 Direct Telecom
53 A&E Pharmacy
54 Police Station
55 JTB Office & City Centre Plaza

57 Texaco Gas Station
59 Eastern Rent-a-Car
60 Citizens Bank
61 Ekklesia Supermarket
62 Jamaica National Building
  Society, Currency Exchange
63 Agape Family Medical Clinic
64 Christ Church

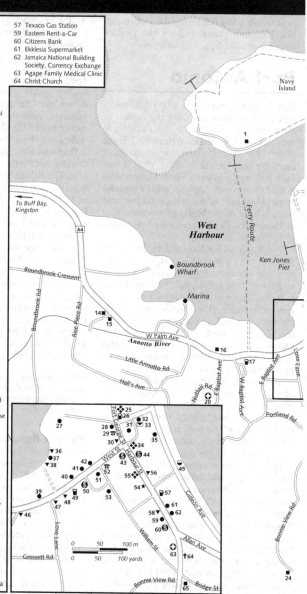

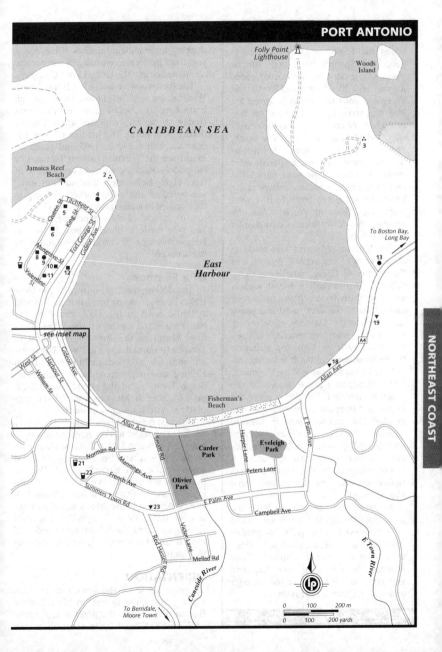

**PORT ANTONIO**

Folly Point
Lighthouse

Woods Island

CARIBBEAN SEA

Jamaica Reef
Beach

Titchfield St

Queen St

King St

Fort George St

Gideon Ave

Musgrave St

Valentine St

East
Harbour

To Boston Bay,
Long Bay

see inset map

West St

Gideon Ave

Harbour St

William St

Allan Ave

Fisherman's
Beach

Allan Ave

A4

Norman Rd

Smatt Rd

Mannings Ave

French Ave

Summers Town Rd

Carder
Park

Olivier
Park

Harper Lane

Peters Lane

E Palm Ave

Eveleigh
Park

E Palm Ave

Campbell Ave

Victor Lane

Red Hassell Rd

Mellad Rd

Caneside River

E Town River

To Berridale,
Moore Town

0          100          200 m
0          100          200 yards

NORTHEAST COAST

## The Windward Maroons

When the English invaded Jamaica in 1655, the Spanish freed their African slaves, who under their own elected leader, Juan de Serra, fled to the wild Rio Grande Valley and Sierra de Batistas (renamed the Blue Mountains by the English). Another group became concentrated in the equally wild Cockpit Country of Trelawny parish. They formed fierce bands known as Maroons, from *cimarron*, a Spanish word meaning 'untamed' or 'wild ones.' The eastern community became known as the Windward Maroons; those further west were called Leeward Maroons (see the Montego Bay & Northwest Coast chapter for more details).

The Windward Maroons were made up of members of the warlike Ashanti and Fante tribes of Ghana, who were highly skilled in guerrilla warfare. English soldiers were no match for the Maroons in their jungle terrain. The thick forest and heavy rainfall aided the Maroons in defending their territory from their remote headquarters at Nanny Town, high atop a spur on the northern slopes of the Blue Mountains.

In 1739, Quao, leader of the Windward Maroons, signed a peace treaty with the British government. The pact ensured the Maroons' freedom. They were also granted 500 acres of land in the Rio Grande Valley. The Windward Maroons split; one group went with Quao to establish Crawford Town near the coast. A second group, under the warrior-priestess Nanny, founded New Nanny Town (now Moore Town).

Modernity has caught up with the Maroons, although they retain vestiges of autonomy even today via a 24-member council headed by an elected 'colonel' who arbitrates minor disputes. They attempt to keep alive their lore and legends, and still bring out their *abengs* and talking drums on occasion.

His initially small trade blossomed into the Boston Fruit Company, which, at its peak, was shipping three million bunches of bananas a year from Jamaica. Eventually, by merger, the company became the United Fruit Company.

The bananas were loaded at Boundbrook Wharf, at the west end of town. Freighters still berth here to supply Europe with bananas (today, all bananas exported from Jamaica depart from here). The loading of fruit has been mechanized since 1963 and you'll no longer see the Tallyman tallying bananas or stevedores 'working all night on a drink of rum.' Harry Belafonte's 'Banana Boat Song' was based on truth: the workers *did* sing as they carried bananas on their heads. The clusters, or 'hands,' of each bunch were tallied, and nine made a 'bunch.' Thus the line in Belafonte's song, 'Six hand, seven hand, eight hand, *bunch*!'

### Of a Feather

In the 1890s, the ever-enterprising Dow Baker began shipping three million bunches of bananas from the cold Atlantic coast of the USA in his empty banana boats. It was he who built the Titchfield Hotel as the first tourist hotel in Jamaica (it burned down in 1969). The international set followed, including Rudyard Kipling, newspaper magnate William Randolph Hearst, and the world's wealthiest man, financier JP Morgan, who called in regularly aboard his yacht *Corsair III*.

Movie star Errol Flynn and a high-society entourage flocked to Port Antonio throughout the 1940s and 1950s. Flynn settled here. In the 1960s, a new, brief heyday occurred when a millionaire named Garfield Weston built a luxurious resort with villas overlooking Frenchman's Cove. He was followed by Prince Alfonso Hohenlohe's equally exclusive Marbella Club at Dragon Bay. The regal resorts attracted the jet-setting crowd, and the coves east of town were colonized by the very rich.

### ORIENTATION

To get a sense of the town's marvelous setting, you have to get up high. Follow Bonnie View Rd to the hotel of that name or, better yet, head up to the well-named

Jamaica Heights. The compact town center is nestled between twin harbors separated by the Titchfield Peninsula. A narrow channel separates the peninsula from Navy Island, half a mile offshore, at the mouth of West Harbour (all the commercial activity centers here). To the east is the almost circular, mile-wide East Harbour.

W Palm Ave runs along West Harbour. Allen Ave runs along East Harbour. The town center lies at the base of the Titchfield Peninsula, where the two main drags meet at a right angle in front of the main plaza and courthouse. Fort George St runs from this junction uphill along the Peninsula. The roads in the town center follow a complicated one-way pattern.

Summers Town Rd (marked incorrectly on the JTB's *Discover Jamaica* map as W Palm Ave) leads south from the town center to the Rio Grand Valley.

## Maps

You can obtain the *Discover Jamaica* road map, which includes a small street map of Port Antonio, from the JTB office (see below). The clock tower in front of the courthouse has a city directory painted on it.

## INFORMATION
## Tourist Offices

The JTB has an office (☎ 993-3051, fax 993-2117) on the second floor of City Centre Plaza at the west end of Harbour St. It's open 8:30 am to 4:30 pm Monday to Friday, and 9 am to 1 pm Saturday. It's poorly stocked with literature, but manager Cynthia Perry is helpful. If you're seeking generic information on Jamaica, try the Jamaica Information Service (☎ 993-2630) across the street in Goebel Plaza.

## Money

You'll find branches of CIBC (☎ 993-2708) at 3 West St, Scotiabank (☎ 993-2523) at 3 Harbour St, National Commercial Bank (☎ 993-9822) at 5 West St, and Citizens Bank (☎ 993-9755) at 28 Harbour St. All have foreign exchange counters; there's also a foreign exchange booth across the street from Citizens Bank (open 9 am to 2 pm

Monday to Thursday, until 3 pm Friday, and until noon Saturday). Western Union has an outlet in Ekklesia Supermarket (☎ 993-2140), next to the Jamaica National Building Society, which has a foreign exchange counter.

## Post & Communications

You can place overseas calls and send faxes from the Portland Communication, Ltd (☎ 993-4192, fax 993-4149) next to the market facing Port Antonio Square, or at Direct Telecom at William and West Sts (both are open 8 am to 10 pm Monday to Saturday, and 10 am to 10 pm Sunday). The Telecommunications of Jamaica office (☎ 993-2775) is on Allan Ave.

The post office (☎ 993-2158) is next to the courthouse.

## Internet Resources

See 'Internet Resources' in the Facts for the Visitor chapter. Also try www.portantonio .com/portmain.htm and www.fantasyisle.com.

## Travel Agencies

There are several travel agencies in town, including Travel Experts (☎ 993-2645).

## Libraries

The Portland Parish Library (☎ 993-2793) is in the town center.

## Laundry

The Town Talk (☎ 993-9847), next to the library on Harbour St, offers a drop-off laundry service.

## Medical Services

The Port Antonio Hospital (☎ 993-2646) is above town on Naylor's Hill, south of West Harbour. Doctors' clinics are located in the City Centre Plaza, which also has a dental office (☎ 993-9611) and an optician; and at 1 Harbour St (☎ 993-3578), 6 Harbour St (☎ 993-3742), 17 Harbour St (☎ 993-2559), and 50 William St (☎ 993-2338). The Agape Family Medical Clinic (☎ 993-7516) on Harbour St is open 9 am to 4:30 pm Monday to Saturday, and has emergency service.

Pharmacies include A&E Pharmacy (☎ 993-9348) on Port Antonio Square; in City Centre Plaza on Harbour St (☎ 996-3624); and on W Palm St (☎ 993-3629).

## Emergency

The police station (☎ 993-2546) is on Harbour St.

## Dangers & Annoyances

Port Antonio is relatively free of the hard-core hustlers and prostitutes associated with other resort areas. Nonetheless, many locals make a living from scamming tourists and you should always remain vigilant (any overt attempt, by a total stranger, to befriend you is possibly a prelude to a scam). Guard your valuables if browsing Musgrave Market, and use caution if walking the ill-lit streets at night. Stick to the main streets.

The Resort Patrol Services (☎ 993-7482) patrol the streets of town to guard the welfare of tourists.

## WALKING TOUR

It takes two hours at the most to see the few sites of note in the town center. You can easily walk, but watch for fast-moving traffic along sinuous West St.

Port Antonio's heart is the **main square** at the junction of West St and Harbour St. It's centered on a clock tower (out of order) and backed by a handsome red-brick Georgian courthouse topped by a cupola. From here walk 50 yards down West St to the junction of William St, where the smaller **Port Antonio Square** has a cenotaph honoring Jamaicans who gave their lives in the two World Wars.

Opposite is the main entrance to the lively and colorful **Musgrave Market**, which has operated since the late 18th century and is supported by thick limestone columns. It is clamorous and yet congenial and colorful. The higglers spill out onto the crowded pavement.

When you can tear yourself away, follow William St south to the end, where it meets with Bonnie View Rd, Bridge St, and Harbour St. The superhuman might turn right onto Bonnie View Rd and hike the dauntingly steep road that leads half a mile to the aptly named Bonnie View Hotel. All others should

turn left onto Harbour St and peek inside **Christ Church**, a red-brick Anglican building with a belfry festooned with epiphytes. It was built in neo-Romanesque style around 1840 atop a hillock overlooking East Harbour, though much of the present structure dates from 1903. The interior architecture is simple; the singular item of note is the brass lectern donated by Captain Lorenzo Dow Baker.

From here, follow Harbour St past the shops and historic **police station** until you emerge back on the main square. You will be drawn to the north side by the imposing facade of the **Village of St George**, a beautiful three-story complex built in 1997 with an exquisitely frescoed exterior in Dutch style and an atrium courtyard surrounded by an array of boutiques, eateries, and even a disco in a pastiche of traditional European architectural styles. Take a refreshing break in the Gallery Café before continuing up Fort George St, along the **Titchfield Peninsula**, enjoying the fragrance of 'June plum' perfuming the air and the redolence of a historic charm found nowhere else on the island. This hilly peninsula (known locally as 'the Hill') supports several dozen Victorian-style gingerbread houses, most notably **DeMontevin Lodge**, an ornate rust-red mansion. The peninsula is now a National Heritage Trust Site, which includes more than 15 buildings hereabouts and will soon experience a grand restoration. Many of the finest homes line King St, which runs down the center of the peninsula (parallel to Queen and Fort George Sts) and conjures up images of the American Deep South, with tall shade trees festooned with mosses known as old-man's-beard.

Fort George and King Sts lead north to the remains of **Fort George** at the tip of the peninsula, dating from 1729. The parade ground and former barracks today house **Titchfield School**. Beyond the school, several George III-era cannons can still be seen mounted in their embrasures in 10-foot-thick walls (they bear the hallmark of Carron Ironworks, Edinburgh, and were cast in 1813). You can roam freely when class is out, but a few nice words to the security guard may earn you permission to enter at any time. The Portland Heritage Foundation is pressing to get the fort restored and turned into a 'Jamaican Williamsburg.'

Return to town via Gideon Avenue, which lines the harbor and offers views.

## NAVY ISLAND

The island itself holds no great appeal, but it is well worth your time to hop on a ferry to Navy Island for the sake of the ride and the marvelous views across the bay. The lushly vegetated, 60-acre island is popular with egrets and other waterbirds, as well as local day-trippers on weekends.

It was originally called Lynch's Island, after Governor Lynch received the island as a gift for services to the Crown. It bore his name until 1728, when the British Navy took over. They used it to careen ships for repair, and eventually built a small battery, plus jetties and warehouses. Nothing remains of their presence. In 1793, Captain William Bligh (of HMS *Bounty* fame) brought the first breadfruits to Jamaica from the South Seas. They were landed here before being sent to Bath Botanical Garden to be propagated and distributed all over Jamaica.

This century, the island has had several owners, including Errol Flynn. A local legend says that he won it in a poker game, but the truth is less glamorous: he bought it. Some say his ghost can be seen at night at the dock enjoying sushi and whisky! Flynn's former home is now a run-down hotel (see Navy Island Marina Resort in Places to Stay, later in the Port Antonio section) with a jaded restaurant. Three beaches are reached by trails, but only one – it's a five-minute walk to the left of the jetty – holds any appeal. No food or drink is allowed on the island.

Water taxis depart from the wharf on W Palm Ave every 15 minutes or so, 8 am to 5 pm, and after 5 pm they are on call (there's a phone on the wall to connect you with Navy Island). It costs US$3 roundtrip. Of course, you can always swim, but beware the strong currents.

## FOLLY

According to legend, a millionaire built this classical mansion for his bride. Alas, he built it out of concrete and the cement began to crumble the moment he carried her over the threshold. She fled in terror at the omen and never returned. The legend is nonsense! The two-story, 200-foot-long, 60-room mansion *was* built entirely of concrete in pseudo-Grecian style by a North American millionaire. But Alfred Mitchell and his family lived there happily between 1905 and 1912 (his wife – one of the Tiffany family of famous New York jewelers – was already a grandmother), and it was in use until 1936, when the roof collapsed. Sea water had been used in the construction, causing the iron reinforcing rods to rust.

Today the shell remains, held aloft by limestone columns. The ugly ruin is smothered with graffiti and stained by tropical mire, and despite being a popular spot for magazine photo-shoots, there is little to recommend about it.

The legend also says Mitchell stocked nearby **Woods Island** with albino monkeys and peacocks. He did turn it into a menagerie, but not all the animals were white.

Folly is on the peninsula east of East Harbour. Follow the dirt road parallel to the coast past Folly Oval cricket ground, and veer right at the first Y-junction. The second junction will lead you to the bright orange Folly Point Lighthouse, built in 1888. Visitors are allowed to roam the grounds.

## BEACHES

Both the dark-sand beach fronting East Harbour, and tiny Jamaica Reef Beach at the northwest tip of Titchfield are unappealing and made more so by garbage. There's also a small but pleasant beach on Navy Island, popular on weekends with locals. Also consider little Mother Beck's Beach at Norwich, one mile west of Port Antonio.

For the best beaches, head east to San San and Frenchman's Cove (see East of Port Antonio, later in this chapter).

## ACTIVITIES

You can charter sport fishing boats from the Port Antonio Marina (☎ 993-3209), with facilities for yachters. Here, Port Antonio Villas & Charters (☎ 993-7333, fax 993-7387,

LEE ABEL

**Port Antonio's West Harbour**

PAVCltd@aol.com) offers a 48-foot sport fishing boat, *B'Tween*, for charter. Expect to pay from US$250 half-day or US$400 full-day, including bait and tackle. The owners of Villa Paola Guest House (☎ 993-7525) also have fishing and cruise boats for rent (US$240 half-day; US$450 full-day). The *Bonita II* (☎ 993-3086) is available for sport fishing charter.

Other boats can be charted at Huntress Marina & Charter Services (☎ 993-3318) on West St.

## ORGANIZED TOURS

JD Tours (☎ 993-4618) has a daily, four-hour tour (US$15) of their 22-acre working fruit and flower plantation. It also offers a Blue Mountains tour (US$35), plus horseback rides into the Shotover Mountains (US$30 per person) and other destinations nearby (US$5 per person per hour). Advance reservation is needed.

Mocking Bird Tours (☎ 993-3370) specializes in putting visitors in touch with the local community, especially women in the arts. The company is based in the Hotel Mocking Bird Hill (see Places to Stay, under East of Port Antonio).

Valley Hikes (☎/fax 993-3881, ☎ 993-7267, uniquedest@aol.com), PO Box 89, Port Antonio; or (☎/fax 401-934-3398), c/o Unique Destinations, 120 Elmdale Rd, North Scituate, RI 02857, offers organized hikes in the Rio Grande Valley (see Rio Grande Valley, later in this chapter). It also offers half-day horseback riding (US$40), birdwatching (US$30), and other trips. Its office is upstairs at 12 West St in Port Antonio, near Kamal's Supermarket.

Attractions Link (☎ 993-2102, fax 993-4828), at Shop 1 above the National Commercial Bank, offers Blue Mountain coffee plantation tours, bicycle tours, and trips to Reach Falls, etc. The company is very trustworthy and is recommended.

Maria Carla Gullotta of the Port Antonio Guest House Association (☎/fax 993-7118) also arranges a variety of tours, including horseback riding, hiking, beach trips, and a visit with Bobo, a Rastaman known for his medicinal powers (US$10 plus transportation). Island Car Rentals offers a series of personally chauffeured tours, such as historical and cultural tours of Port Antonio (US$134).

## SPECIAL EVENTS

The weeklong Portland Jamboree is held mid-August, featuring a float parade, street dancing, food fair, and live music. Contact the JTB for information.

Contestants are lured here each October for the weeklong Port Antonio International Marlin Tournament, one of the Caribbean's most prestigious sport fishing events (☎ 923-7683, fax 901-4179). Local fishermen compete in an annual canoe tournament.

Middle-class Jamaicans flock from far and wide to Frenchman's Cove during National Heroes Weekend in mid-October for a wild party that is one of Jamaica's premier social events of the year (in 1998 tickets cost US$85, all-inclusive of food and booze).

## PLACES TO STAY

There's something for every budget. Consider staying east of town, where a wide choice of accommodations are located near the beaches (see East of Port Antonio, later in this chapter).

### Budget

There are a few basic guest houses in historic homes on the Titchfield Peninsula. The *Scotia Guest House* (☎ 993-2681, 15 Queen St) has 10 bare-bones rooms with fans and shared bath for US$9, or private bath for US$12. Also on Queen St is the comfy *Little Reef Guest House* (☎ 993-9743). It has eight small, basic rooms, some with private bathroom, for US$10 to US$19 for up to four people. Meals are cooked to order, but guests can also use the kitchen. Nearby, *Sunny Side Guest House* (☎ 993-9788, 13 West St) is a two-story house with 14 basic, clean, comfortable rooms, with shared bath with cold water, for US$6 to US$34.

One of the best is *Ivanhoe's* (☎ 993-3043, 9 Queen St), a gracious property with 12 well-lit rooms with fans, louvered windows, and private bathrooms with hot water. It's well-run, spotless, and quiet, and has a breezy patio and homey TV lounge. Rooms cost US$25 to US$50 single or double. Breakfasts cost US$5, and lunch and dinner are cooked to order.

Another option is *Way Valley Guest House* (☎ 993-3267, 11 W Palm Ave), a gloomy and basic option with rooms with private bath with cold water only for US$12 to US$18.

The charming *Holiday Home* (☎ 993-2425, PO Box 11), on King St, has nine rooms. They're basic and small and some have shared bathrooms with cold water, but they're spic-and-span and cost US$50 double. Meals are cooked to order.

Next door to Way Valley is *In & Out* (☎ 993-3468, 17A W Palm Ave), a guest house with six rooms for US$40, each with its own outside entrance; plus a two-bedroom cottage with kitchen for US$100. The latter is cozy, albeit dark, and nicely furnished, and has a family room with TV, plus a small dining room in which breakfast is served.

### Mid-Range

*DeMontevin Lodge* (☎ 993-2604, 21 Fort George St, PO Box 85) is a virtual institution. This venerable Victorian guest house boasts a homey ambience and a blend of modern kitsch and antiques reminiscent of grannie's parlor. A carved stairway leads upstairs to 13 simple bedrooms (three with private bathrooms) that are time-worn, but clean as a whistle. Two rooms have a balcony with views over the bay. Rates are US$39 single or double with shared bath, US$52 with private bath. The place is well maintained by Fay Johnson.

The best place to stay is the *Jamaica Heights Hotel* (☎ 993-2156) on Spring Bank Rd southwest of Boundbrook. Housed in an exquisite hilltop plantation home, Jamaica Heights is set amid lush lawns with a spectacular setting. Columned verandas, whitewashed walls, aged brick and dark hardwoods floors, and sky-blue louvered windows and French doors all around provide a gracious environment. Rooms are tastefully furnished with white wicker and antiques, including four-poster beds. Two gazebo decks (one inset with a pool) have hammocks and lounge chairs. The office (☎ 993-3563) is at 1 Morris Ave.

A more modest option is *Triff's Inn* (☎ 993-2162, fax 993-2062, 1 Bridge St). This well-run hotel has 17 spacious and clean air-conditioned rooms with telephone, and private bath with hot water for US$55 single or double, US$85 three beds, US$110 four beds. Furnishings are minimalist.

*Shadows* (☎ 993-3823, 40 West St) has five air-conditioned rooms with private bathroom and satellite TVs and telephones for about US$30.

An alternative is *Bonnie View Plantation Hotel* (☎ 993-2752, fax 993-2862, PO Box 82; ☎ 309-659-2358, fax 659-2395 in the USA), which occupies an alluring spot astride a ridge 600 feet above town, offering a spectacular view. Bonnie View is surrounded by well-tended gardens and a plantation backed by the soaring Blue Mountains. The back garden contains a pool and, amazingly, a small beach. The spotless, modest rooms are done up in pinks and white. Rates are US$54 to US$84 standard; US$60 to US$88 deluxe. A cottage costs US$60. A complete meal plan is US$30 extra, daily, though the food can sometimes be bland and the service laid-back, even by Jamaican standards. Maurice, the archetypal barman, is full of apocryphal tales.

*Navy Island Marina Resort* (☎ 993-2041, 993-2667, 968-5731 in Kingston, fax 960-1533, PO Box 188, Port Antonio) is a cottage resort on Navy Island that is unkempt and poorly managed (by the government's Urban Development Council). Accommodations are in cabins (that sleep six people) for US$75 single to US$150 triple for studio villas; US$225 triple to US$325 six people for two-bedroom villas. The resort features a tennis court, volleyball court, freshwater pool (crammed with locals on weekends), plus the meager Bounty Restaurant and Crusoe Bar. Kitchenettes allow self-catering.

## Top End

Port Antonio is renowned for its exclusive rental villas, almost all of which are concentrated east of town. *Evra Jam Villa Rentals* (☎ 993-2325, fax 993-2328, 38 West St, Shop 10) represents local owners. Send mail to PO Box 180, Port Antonio.

## PLACES TO EAT

The best dining is outside town (see East of Port Antonio, later in this chapter).

In town, *Daddy Dee's*, on West St, serves Jamaican staples such as ackee and codfish and curried goat for as little as US$2. Similar prices may tempt you to *Kingslee Bar & Restaurant*, also on West St and also serving traditional Jamaican breakfasts for under US$2. *Delicious Delites* (☎ 993-2169, 9 Harbour St) leans toward fried chicken, burgers, hot dogs, and ice cream. Another good bet for budget meals is *Centrepoint Club & Restaurant*, on a breezy hillside location at the east end of East Harbour. It's a dance club at night. The gaily painted *Caribbean Hut*, one of several stalls facing the waterfront on Allen Ave, is also recommended for jerk and other simple fare for a

few dollars. There are other huts nearby, including *Jah Mek Yah*.

There's nothing debonair about the *New Debonere*, though the fried chicken, conch soup, jerk, and other Jamaican staples are good, and served on a waterside patio. You can dine for less than US$5. It has live music (US$3 entrance).

The *Mandala Restaurant*, on West St, serves omelettes, plus steamed fish, fish with coconut, creole chicken, and the like starting at US$2. For patties try *Rainbow Country Kitchen*, which also sells staples such as fried fish.

Craving Chinese? *Golden Happiness*, on the corner of Harbour and West Sts, has reasonable quality dishes – including a vast menu of chop sueys and sweet and sour dishes – for less than US$5, and you can request half-orders. For more cosmopolitan fare, try the bistro-style restaurant at Bonnie View (see Places to Stay, above), which serves an eclectic variety of dishes, from American to Italian.

*Sabrina's* is a popular wooden bar and restaurant at Huntress Marina, next to New Debonere. The owner, Sabrina, who calls herself a 'Germaican,' serves steamed fish and other seafood for US$5 to US$15. The ambience is spoiled by deafening DJ music.

*DeMontevin Lodge* (☎ 993-2604) makes budget meals for guests and also has a Wednesday night feast of ackee and codfish, suckling pig, and other Jamaican delicacies (US$20). You must phone in your order 24 hours ahead.

For pizza, head to the middle floor of the Village of St George building, where a *pizzeria* also offers vanilla milkshakes.

For savories, desserts, and fresh-baked bread, try *Coronation Bakery* and *Three Star Lion Bakery* at 18 and 27 West St.

Don't fail to savor a cappuccino and bowl of delicious ice cream at the German-run *Gallery Café*, upstairs in the Village of St George. This tasteful coffee shop has exquisite art deco glass tables, heaps of light, original artwork, and exquisite desserts and coffees. *Delicious Delites* sells ice cream and yogurts, as does *Devon House I-Scream*

*Shop*, opposite Huntress Marina, and *Cream World*, also on Harbour St.

## ENTERTAINMENT
The *Roof Club* (☎ 993-3817, 11 West St) is Port Antonio's infamous hang-loose, rough-around-the-edges reggae bar and has attracted the likes of Linda Evans and Tom Cruise. You can't hear yourself think, but you're guaranteed a great time. Young men and women move from partner to partner dancing sensually. You're fair game for any stranger who takes a fancy to you. (Be prepared to withstand the incessant sponging of locals – male and female – hitting on tourists to buy them drinks.) The place is small, crowded, and decorated with mirrors, Day-Glo squiggles, and UV lighting. Stoned Rastas slow-jive on the spot, heads bowed, beer in one hand, and spliff in the other. As elsewhere in Jamaica, the reggae scene at the Roof Club has been usurped by dubbing, which is intensely annoying. It's relatively dead mid-week, when entry is free. But on weekends it hops, especially after 11 pm (US$3), and especially on Thursday, which is 'Ladies Nite' (free entry to women). Beers are expensive (US$3), but the panoply of cocktails offer a bargain. It's best to go with a partner, as the place can get rough.

Maria Carla Gullotta of Draper's San Guest House escorts guests to the Roof Club for US$10. She also arranges a 'Drumming Night' with dancing to the traditional jumina (US$13).

The Roof Club has a poor reputation among educated Jamaicans, who prefer the more upscale air-conditioned disco at the *Jamaica Crest* on weekends (see East of Port Antonio, later in this chapter). *Shadows* (☎ 993-3823, 40 W Palm Ave) is another option and has oldies on Sunday. Other happening dance spots include the *Mandela Open Ground* for reggae, and *Rainbow Country Kitchen*, which has a disco on Thursday.

On Titchfield Peninsula, you may be tempted to drink at *Bobby's Bar*, a rustic thatched place at the south end of Queen St. Locals gather to play dominoes and cards.

Bobby Jones and his pals are full of pally charm...until the sponging begins.

If you're looking for go-go dancing, the in place is *Rolex* (☎ 993-9432, 33 Summers Town Rd), with exotic dancers Thursday to Sunday. Entry costs US$1.50 on weekends (free on weekdays). It gets crowded on Fridays. Other options include *Blue Jays*, on Bamboo Crescent in the Boundbrook district (US$1.60 cover).

## SHOPPING
Musgrave Market, on West St, is a cacophonous slice of Jamaican life. The colorful and aromatic produce section faces onto West St. At the back is a craft market that opens onto the town square. Thursday and Saturday are liveliest. Jamaica Arcade also has craft stalls tucked in a courtyard immediately east of the courthouse. Also check out the sculptures and paintings of Renford Stewart at his studio on 5 William St.

Gallery Art Ambokile (☎ 993-3162, 931-5803), 22a West St, offers a wide selection of art, ceramics, and sculptures, plus framed prints, much of it of high quality. And be sure to call in at the Gallery Carriacou in the Hotel Mockingbird Hill (☎ 993-7267, fax 993-7133, www.negril.com/mhmain.htm); see East of Port Antonio, later in this chapter.

Don't leave without checking out the Spencer Gallery, in the Village of St George, featuring works by local artist Ken Abendana Spencer (you can visit his 'studio' in Long Bay; see the Long Bay section).

There's also a duty-free shop in City Centre Plaza that sells liquors and the like.

The Photo Bank, next to the Roof Club, has a good supply of film that the owners keep cool, as it should be.

## GETTING THERE & AWAY
### Air
Port Antonio is served by the Ken Jones Aerodrome (☎ 913-3692, 913-3173), 6 miles west of Port Antonio and 2 miles west of St Margaret's Bay. The small airport has a phone and a waiting room but no other services, although there's a small grocery and the

*Seaview Bar Jerk Centre* within a 10-minute walk.

Air Jamaica Express (☎ 922-4661, 993-2405 at Ken Jones Aerodrome) operates two flights daily from Kingston's Tinson Pen (US$37 each way), and once daily from MoBay (US$49) and Negril (US$52 each way).

### Bus

A bus station extends along the waterfront on Gideon Ave. Buses and 'coasters' leave regularly for Annotto Bay and Port Maria (where you change for Ocho Rios). At least half a dozen buses and even more minibuses operate between Kingston via Buff Bay and via Manchioneal and Morant Bay (US$1.60 to Kingston). Other minibuses operate from the central square on West St. A journey from Ocho Rios or Kingston takes about 2½ hours.

### Taxi

Licensed taxi fares from Kingston to Port Antonio cost US$100 to US$120 (one to four people). JUTA (☎ 952-0623 in Montego Bay, ☎ 993-2684 in Port Antonio) offers transfers from Montego Bay airport (US$50 one way), and from Kingston airport (US$35 one way). Island Car Rentals (☎ 926-8861 in Kingston, ☎ 924-8075 at Norman Manley International Airport) can arrange a car and driver from Kingston (US$80 one way for one or two people, US$110 for up to seven people). Transfers (per vehicle) from Ocho Rios cost US$100, and it's US$180 from Montego Bay.

### Boat

The Port Antonio Marina (☎ 993-3209, fax 993-9745) offers customs clearance if you arrive aboard your own vessel. It charges US$0.25 per foot (US$0.20 for monthlong stays). Power costs US$3 (110V) or US$8 (220V); water costs US$2 daily.

### GETTING AROUND
### To/From the Airport

Most upscale hotels offer free transfers to/from the Ken Jones Aerodrome for their guests. There's no shuttle bus service, although you can flag down any bus or minibus passing along the A4.

### Car & Motorcycle

Eastern Rent-a-Car (☎ 993-3624) has an office at 26 Harbour St, and Don's Car Rental (☎ 993-2241) has an office in the Trident Hotel.

Scooters and motorcycles are available from Bamboo Bike, Car, & Jeep Rental (☎ 993-3053), on Musgrave St, on the Titchfield Peninsula. Expect to pay US$30 to US$50 a day.

### Taxi

'Robots' (shared taxis) run along the A4 on a regular basis as far afield as Boston Beach. Fares should be less than US$1.50. For licensed taxis, call the Port Antonio Cab Drivers' Co-op (☎ 993-2684) or JUTA (☎ 993-2684), which operates with new Toyota Corolla station wagons (estate cars). Taxis (including unlicensed cabs) hang out by hotels. A typical charge is US$7 to or from San San or the Blue Lagoon. Your taxi driver will gladly wait for you at no charge if you're dining or out for a night of entertainment.

### Bicycle

East Coast Rentals (☎ 993-9330) rents bicycles in the Huntress Marina. You can rent a bicycle for two-wheeled exploring from D&L Rentals (☎ 993-3282).

# East of Port Antonio

## PORT ANTONIO TO FAIRY HILL

For decades, international society figures have made the 10-mile strip east of town a home-away-from-home. Hugging Jamaica's northeastern coastline, the A4 winds around a series of deep bays and privately owned tiny coves where chic hotels and homes are hidden from view amid dramatically lush foliage that brushes up against your car.

# AROUND PORT ANTONIO

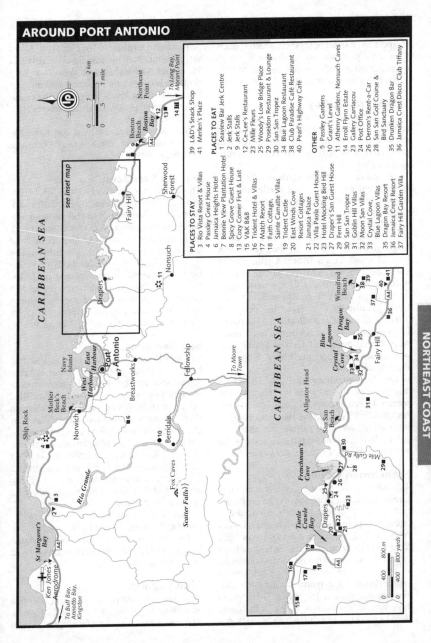

*see inset map*

**PLACES TO STAY**
3 Rio Vista Resort & Villas
4 Passley Great House
6 Jamaica Heights Hotel
7 Bonnie View Plantation Hotel
8 Spicy Grove Guest House
13 Cozy Corner First & Last
15 V&K B&B
16 Trident Hotel & Villas
17 Match Resort
18 Faith Cottage,
   Sainte Camatte Villas
19 Trident Castle
20 East Winds Cove
   Resort Cottages
21 Jamaica Palace
22 Villa Paola Guest House
23 Hotel Mocking Bird Hill
27 Draper's San Guest House
29 Fern Hill
30 San San Tropez
31 Goblin Hill Villas
33 Moon San Villas
33 Crystal Cove,
   Blue Lagoon Villas
35 Dragon Bay Resort
36 Jamaica Crest Resort
37 Fairy Hill Garden Villa

**PLACES TO EAT**
1 Seaview Bar Jerk Centre
2 Jerk Stalls
9 Jerk Stalls
12 Ce-Lee's Restaurant
23 Mille Fleurs
25 Woody's Low Bridge Place
29 Poseidon Restaurant & Lounge
30 San San Tropez
34 Blue Lagoon Restaurant
38 Club Paradise Café Restaurant
40 Pearl's Highway Café
39 L&D's Snack Shop
41 Merlen's Place

**OTHER**
5 Passley Gardens
10 Grant's Level
11 Athenry Gardens, Nonsuch Caves
14 Erroll Flynn Estate
23 Gallery Carriacou
24 Post Office
26 Derron's Rent-a-Car
28 San San Golf Course &
   Bird Sanctuary
35 Drunken Dragon Bar
36 Jamaica Crest Disco, Club Tiffany

NORTHEAST COAST

## Information

Immediately west of Frenchman's Cove, Drapers has a small post office, which is open 8 am to 4 pm Monday to Friday, 8 am to noon Saturday, and a police station (☎ 993-3220) half a mile east of Frenchman's Cove.

## Turtle Crawle Bay

Two miles east of town, the road circles around this deep bay, an important fish nursery that is rimmed by mangroves and protected as a part of the Port Antonio Marine Park.

Squatting atop the western headland is a magnificent gleaming-white castle, an Austrian-style, rococo whimsy with flamboyant stonework (including a pair of enormous crocodiles flanking the front door) built in the 1980s by Baroness Elisabeth Siglindy Stephan von Stephanie Thyssen (now Mrs Nazar Fahmi). This is **Trident Castle**, part of the Trident Villas resort, nicknamed Folly II because it lay unfinished for several years due to financial problems. The architect, Earl Levy, eventually took over the property after a well-publicized tiff with the Baroness. It's now his home. Scenes from *Clara's Heart* were filmed here, and Denzel Washington was seduced by hotel guest Mimi Rogers in the *Mighty Quinn*.

On the east shore of Turtle Crawle is another fantasy in stone – this one the pseudo-Grecian **Jamaica Palace** – built by the Baroness in 1989. Thus the Baroness trumped the Earl; he has only a castle, but she has a palace. It, too, has appeared on screen: as the setting for Playboy's *Playmates in Paradise*.

## Frenchman's Cove

This small cove, just east of the hamlet of Drapers, 5 miles from Port Antonio, boasts one of the prettiest beaches for miles. It became famous in the 1960s when a luxury resort called Frenchman's Cove was built atop the tall headland. The hotel has been closed for some years and seems constantly in the throes of redevelopment. A stream winds lazily to a white-sand beach that shelves steeply into the water. Bring insect repellent, as mosquitoes thrive in the moist dale behind the beach. There's a snack bar

and a secure parking lot where you pay US$3 to use the beach. It's closed Tuesday.

In mid-October, Frenchman's Cove attracts hundreds of middle-class revelers for a wild National Heroes Weekend party that locals consider a nuisance, and not just because of noise levels. People use the ocean as a toilet, and post-party drunk drivers are a lethal menace.

The cove is reached by a dirt road 200 yards south of the San San Golf Course & Bird Sanctuary.

## Gallery Carriacou

This marvelous art gallery (☎ 993-7267, fax 993-7133, www.hotelmockingbirdhill.com), at the Hotel Mocking Bird Hill, boasts a fabulous array of paintings, ceramics, sculptures, and other quality works of fine art by local artists, all lit by large glass windows. The gallery offers regular exhibitions of works by Cuban artists from Santiago de Cuba, twin city to Port Antonio. It also serves as a center for cultural interchange, and hosts workshops and cultural events. It's open 10 am to 5 pm daily, except Wednesday.

## San San Beach

San San Beach, which was used as a setting for the cable movie *Treasure Island*, is a preferred spot for the rich and famous, whose opulent homes are on the peninsula called Alligator Head. A stairway descends through thick greenery to the private beach used by guests of Goblin Hill, Fern Hill, and Jamaica Palace hotels. Passersby, however, may be able to gain day use for US$8. It has a bar and restaurant and snorkeling equipment. The entrance gate is easy to miss; it's 500m east of San San Tropez restaurant. It's open 10 am to 4 pm daily.

San San Beach has terrific waves for **surfing**, if conditions are right.

Offshore is a tiny islet: **Pellow Island**. Watch out for spiny sea urchins if you swim out to the island.

## Blue Lagoon

Yes, this *is* where 14-year-old Brooke Shields swam in the movie *Blue Lagoon*, in which she and a young Christopher Atkins played child castaways. Aptly named, it's embraced by a deep, natural amphitheater with forest-clad sides. It's open to the sea through a narrow funnel, but is fed by freshwater springs that come in at about 140 feet deep. Its color changes through every shade of jade and emerald during the day. The 180-foot-deep lagoon periodically undergoes a significant rise in temperature. It's refreshing to swim here, passing through cold and warm patches. You may be tempted to swim with your mouth open once you learn from locals that the waters are said to have aphrodisiac properties. Another piece of local baloney says that Hollywood hero Errol Flynn once dived to the bottom using only a snorkel.

Millions of tiny fish and even barracuda and squid can also be seen swimming around. Hibiscus *(puia)* drop their pink leaves, which float out on the receding tide. At night, floodlights add to the romantic ambience.

Bamboo raft trips are available from the Blue Lagoon Restaurant – a handsome stone-and-hardwood structure with terraces overhanging the water – which has all access rights to the lagoon, though you can also get there by boat or by swimming along the channel from Dragon Bay. It's a great place to while away time over chess and backgammon boards. You can rent snorkeling equipment and paddle-boats (US$10). A US$3 entrance fee for day use is added to your bill with any purchase. It even has a helicopter pad for bigwigs to arrive and depart in style.

The oceanfront immediately west of the lagoon is lined with fabulous rental villas.

## Dragon Bay

This beautiful little cove is immediately east of Blue Lagoon, 7 miles east of Port Antonio. It's the private property of the Dragon Bay Resort, but the small beach is open to the public for day use (US$1). This is where Tom Cruise set up his beach bar in the movie *Cocktail*. A scuba diving concession is here. The boatman will take you to Frenchman's Cove and San San Beach with a stop for a swim in the Blue Lagoon, which you can also reach by a path along the western shore of the Dragon Bay.

## Fairy Hill & Winnifred Beach

Fairy Hill, 8 miles east of Port Antonio, is a small clifftop hamlet composed of private vacation homes juxtaposed with squalid shacks. A dirt road leads steeply downhill to **Winnifred Beach**. The beach is a secluded golden-sand crescent catering mostly to locals and is a great place to hang with 'real' Jamaicans.

The beach was used as a setting for the Robin Williams movie *Club Paradise*. A coral reef offshore provides snorkeling. Parties are held here on some weekends. There are toilets and changing rooms to the right, where there's a small fishing community. Locals will rent boats or bamboo rafts to take you to another tiny beach hidden around the headland, 'if you want a private moment with your loved one.'

There's a homespun paper-making factory where local artisans turn banana leaves and other natural materials into paper crafts.

The turnoff to the beach is opposite the Jamaica Crest Resort.

## Activities

**Scuba Diving** The shoreline east of Port Antonio boasts 8 miles of interconnected coral reefs and walls at an average of 100 to 300 yards offshore. No site is more than 15 minutes away by boat. All dives are drift dives in waters at a near constant 75°F and minimum 60-foot visibility. Dive sites average 30 to 110 feet, with drop-offs of over 300 feet, and little current or surge. Many of the sites are largely unexplored, and the reef, which was recently protected in the Port Antonio Marine Park, remains relatively undisturbed. **Alligator Head** is known for big sponge formations and black corals on a banking reef that drops to extreme depths. You stand a good chance of seeing hammerhead sharks and large pelagic fish at **Fairy Hill Bank**.

Lady G'Diver (☎ 993-3281), PO Box 81, Port Antonio, a full-service dive shop at Dragon Bay Resort, offers dives from a Boston whaler and flat-bottom boat (US$65 for two same-day dives). You can rent equipment here. San San Beach (see San San Beach, earlier in this section) also has a scuba facility.

NORTHEAST COAST

## San San Golf Course & Bird Sanctuary

This nine-hole course (☎ 993-7645, fax 993-7644) was laid out in the 1960s and reopened in 1998 after lying idle for some years. It has been beautifully restored and work on the back nine holes was almost complete when I called by (it will be a 18 hole, 6000-yard course). The fairways ripple along valleys surrounded by rain forest. The ocean is visible from the top of the course. Fabulous! There's a clubhouse, a small pro shop, and bistro dining. It offers unlimited golf for US$30. A round of nine holes costs US$20 (US$30 for 18 holes). Caddies cost US$7 (US$12), a pull-cart costs US$5 (US$7), and golf club rental is US$10 (US$12).

## Places to Stay

**Budget** At Winnifred Beach you can camp on the beach for no charge, although I wouldn't recommend doing so alone. Pablo, at the far east end of the beach, rents tents for about US$5.

At Fairy Hill, *Merlen's Place* (☎ 993-8079) has rooms for rent for about US$20 in a pleasant little concrete cottage. *L&D's Snack Shop* also has a small room for rent 100 yards above Winnifred Beach.

Several guest houses can be found at Turtle Crawle: try *Sainte Camette Villas* (☎ 993-2140, fax 993-9393) or *V&K B&B* (☎ 993-2945, Lot 89, Daffodil Ave, Anchovy Gardens, Port Antonio).

*Draper's San Guest House* (☎/fax 993-711) is a spic-and-span place that sits atop the headland above Frenchman's Cove and is run by a charming Italian woman, Maria Carla Gullotta, who is president of the Port Antonio Guest House Association. Her rambling little house has five doubles and one single room (two share a bath), all with fans, louvered windows, and hot water and twee decor for US$22 per person, including breakfast. One unit is two-story, with a thick wooden staircase and a kitchen. A minimum two-night stay is required. It's all very family-oriented. Bobo, the chef, will show you how to cook local fare. Maria, who knows the island like the back of her hand, offers tours with 'respected, trustworthy guides.' She also

takes guests under her wing, including to local parties and concerts.

*Villa Paola Guest House* (☎ 993-7525), next to the Jamaica Palace, is a genteel hilltop guest house with four rooms with ceiling fans, private bath with cold water for US$50 single or double including breakfast cooked by Paola, a Jamaican woman (she prepares dinner on request). The owners have fishing and cruise boats for rent, and offer snorkeling (US$55 per hour, including boat).

*East Winds Cove Resort Cottages* (☎ 993-7482), on a hillside facing west across Turtle Crawle Bay toward Trident Castle, was leased by the Resort Patrol Services at press time.

**Mid-Range** *Faith Cottage* (☎ 993-3703, PO Box 50, Port Antonio), inland of Trident Villas at Turtle Crawle, is a gracious, pink-painted hotel with turrets and gables that lend a French provincial feel. It has five rooms, which are spacious and pleasant and have small TVs, fans, modern, modest decor – some even have columned bedrooms. Rooms cost US$51 single, US$86 double. There's a pool in the courtyard. Guests get access to the nearby resorts.

The old great house above *Frenchman's Cove* (☎ 993-7270) was recently renovated and has 12 air-conditioned rooms including two suites for US$50 and 18 cottages for US$100 one-bedroom, US$128 two-bedroom.

At San San, a breezy hilltop option is *Fern Hill* (☎ 993-7374, fax 993-7373, PO Box 100, Port Antonio; ☎ 800-263-4354, fax 416-620-4843 in North America), '15 chains' up Mile Gully Rd. It offers fabulous views down over San San Beach. The 16 spacious, elegant, twin-level units are spread across the luxuriant hillside and each has a balcony beyond French doors. There are also three villas. Suites have mezzanine bedrooms and their own hot tubs. An airy dining terrace atop the hill offers tremendous views. Fern Hill offers a poolside buffet with a dance cabaret when there's a full house. Rates range from US$60 single or double for standard, air-conditioned rooms, to US$110 for a suite or one-bedroom villa. The resort offers an all-inclusive option (from US$145 single, US$230 double for a standard to US$195 single, US$280 double for a suite or villa), and a breakfast plan is offered. It was in the midst of a much-needed renovation at this writing.

The Italian-run **San San Tropez** *(☎/fax 993-7399)* offers gracious, well-lit, cross-ventilated, air-conditioned rooms for US$60 to US$90 double (suites cost US$70 to US$100). The furnishings are modern and graced by bright tropical decor. There's a pool and sundeck in the concrete courtyard.

The modern **Match Resort** *(☎ 993-9629, fax 993-2700, 993-4044, Lot 30, Dolphin Bay, Port Antonio)* is a five-cottage complex with a swimming pool on a limb 200m inland from Trident Villas. All rooms are nicely furnished, with soft pastels, air-con, and TV. Rates are US$62 to US$69.

**Top End** Sitting above Crystal Cove is **Moon San Villas** *(☎ 974-7075, c/o Blue Mountain Tours)*, a tastefully decorated three-level house with a TV/VCR lounge (with a large tape library), a large terrace, and four bedrooms with wide windows, fans, and its own utterly romantic decor. Two rooms have king-size beds. Fluffy towels adorn the bathrooms. The master suite is done up in ocean blues. The bargain rates – US$85 single or double – include a gourmet breakfast and two passes to both San San Beach and Blue Lagoon. French-inspired dinners cost US$13. Three dining areas provide options both for gregarious folks and for guests preferring privacy.

**Goblin Hill Villas** *(☎ 925-8108, 800-472-1148 in North America, fax 925-6248, 11 East Ave, Kingston 10)* is a 700-acre hilltop estate above San San, popular with families. Its 16 two-bedroom and 12 one-bedroom self-catering villas straddle a ridge and are surrounded by lawns and raw jungle. Those closest to the sea get more breezes and have views down to San San Bay. A nature trail encircles the property. The air-conditioned, townhouse-style villas are huge, have massive open windows and wide verandas, and are superbly cross-ventilated. Each comes with its own private maid and butler (optional). The rooms have neither telephones nor TVs, though the resort has a TV lounge and

reading room, a large pool, two recently resurfaced tennis courts, and a marvelously jungly Tree Bar built around a massive fig tree. Tired furniture and bathrooms and kitchens sorely in need of renovation remained a concern at this writing. Rates start at US$90 summer, US$110 winter for a one-bedroom villa; and US$145 summer, US$185 winter for a two bedroom villa.

**Trident Hotel & Villas** *(☎ 993-2602, fax 993-2590, PO Box 119, Port Antonio; ☎ 800-633-3284 in the USA; ☎ 020-7730-7144, fax 020-7938-7493 in the UK)* has been an eternal favorite of internationals determined to unwind, ever since it opened in the late 1960s. It has a charming, worn-in feel, and sits atop a cliff overlooking a tiny cove. Peacocks stroll about the croquet lawn and around the topiary firs. Stepping through the lofty mahogany front door is like entering a European mansion. It offers 26 deluxe rooms and villa suites, plus the luxurious Imperial Suite. Earl Levy runs his property with an aristocratic flair. Jackets for men and 'cocktail attire' for women are required (men must also wear ties during winter season). Hence, the place is a bit standoffish and snooty. Low-season rates are US$160/220 single/double for deluxe rooms, and from US$220/340 for suites. High-season rates are US$365/385 deluxe, and from US$410/620 for suites. Transfers from Kingston are free for weeklong stays only. Helicopter transfers are also offered from Kingston and Montego Bay for a fee.

Lottery winners can even rent the Trident 'Castle,' in private grounds with its own chapel. Indeed castle-like, it is lit by wall-torches and has eight rather gauche bedrooms. You rent the entire place for US$5500 summer, US$7500 winter, all-inclusive. It is shown by appointment.

For relaxing button-down ambience, check into the romantic, 'eco-chic,' 10-room **Hotel Mocking Bird Hill** *(☎ 993-7267, fax 993-7133, PO Box 254, Port Antonio, www.hotelmockingbirdhill.com)*, in the hills above Frenchman's Cove. This gem – the best hotel in Portland – is run with finesse by a delightful couple – Shireen Aga and Barbara Walker – and their manager. The owners describe it as a 'traditional split-level Caribbean villa' (there are also well-lit bungalows) offering nonsmoking options. All rooms are lovingly appointed with well-chosen fabrics and modern art and appliances. Most boast ocean views from private balconies. Facilities include a small pool, a Caribbean-bright TV lounge, a bar (conducive to lounging with Cuban cigars, enjoyed with the hotel's renowned cocktails), plus a variety of health and wellness services, including massage. The Gallery Carriacou is here (see Frenchman's Cove, earlier).

The owners are environmentalists and culturally sensitive contributors to the local economy. And their gaiety and engaging, erudite conversations are an integral part of what makes a stay here so delightful. The couple are also gourmands, and meals are a sublime experience (see Places to Eat, later in this section). The clientele is mostly European; both Shireen and Barbara speak fluent German. Trails lead through the lush hillside gardens. Room rates are US$110 to US$140, May to mid-December, and US$150 to US$195 in high season. To get there, take the private road that leads inland from the church at Drapers.

Aiming for the same upmarket appeal as Trident Castle is the *Jamaica Palace* (☎ 993-2020, 800-472-1149, fax 993-7759, PO Box 277, Port Antonio, jampal@toj.com), a rambling and gracious neoclassical property fronted by white marble columns on the eastern bluff overlooking Turtle Crawle Bay. Everything but the black-and-white-checkered floor is gleaming white and ascetic. The 24 rooms and 55 suites are cavernous and come with king-size bed, crystal chandeliers, period antiques, and Georgian bay windows. In the landscaped grounds behind the hotel is a 114-foot-long pool shaped like Jamaica, so you can swim from Port Antonio to Negril. Its El Gaucho restaurant serves sizzling steaks from the grill. Room rates (including tax and service charge) are US$140 to US$180 single or double in summer, US$160 to US$200 in winter; suites cost US$210 to US$355 in summer, and US$230 to US$400 in winter. It offers a

'Getaway Package' for US$95 year-round, including room, breakfast, dinner, taxes, and service charge.

The resplendent *Crystal Cove* (for reservations: ☎ 925-8108, fax 925-6248, 11 East Ave, Kingston 10) is adjacent to Blue Lagoon Villas and offers a similar degree of luxury. It has three bedrooms and three bathrooms, cross-ventilated through large picture-windows. There are living and dining rooms, a study, two terraces, and an outdoor living room. It comes fully staffed. Rates are US$230 double, US$270 for three to six people in summer; US$270 and US$355 respectively in winter. What a bargain!

Elegant Resorts Villas (☎ 953-9562, 800-337-3499 in North America, fax 953-9563, PO Box 80, Montego Bay) has three villas at San San Beach, including the luxurious six-bedroom *Tiamo*, formerly owned by Princess Nina Aga Khan. Rates begin at US$4350 for *Belmont*, a three-bedroom villa, and US$5350 for Tiamo.

Other options nearby include the five-bedroom *Shoreham Green* (☎ 403-264-2604, 800-640-7866 in the USA). The 3800-sq-foot, Georgian-style villa has its own pool and staff for US$3000 weekly.

Splayed along the shore immediately west of Blue Lagoon, *Blue Lagoon Villas* (☎ 993-8491, fax 993-8492, PO Box 2, Port Antonio, austria@cwjamaica.com; ☎ 800-822-3274 in the USA; ☎ 416-484-4864, fax 485-8256 in Canada; ☎ 020-7730-7144, fax 7938-4793 in the UK; ☎ 03-5376-0144, fax 5376-5939 in Japan) provides a stunning setting, with a fistful of waterfront villas made famous as a popular locale for fashion shoots. Each of these gleaming white beauties is as individual as a thumbprint. All are exquisitely furnished and include TV and CD player. Each one to four-bedroom villa is staffed with a housekeeper-cook and houseman, and all have a sundeck overlooking the water, with sea kayaks provided. A houseboat is on hand to reach Blue Lagoon – within swimming distance – and other points offshore. Low-season rates are US$3600 to US$8000, and US$4500 to US$10,000 in high season, based on three-night minimum stay, including airport transfers, and temporary membership to Dragon Bay Beach Club. Extra nights are pro-rated. A helicopter pad is on hand.

The **Dragon Bay Resort** (☎ 993-8751, PO Box 176, Port Antonio, www.dragonbay.com; ☎ 201-767-9393, 800-633-3284 in the USA; ☎ 020-7413-8877 in the UK) enjoys a beautiful setting on the hill overlooking the flask-shaped cove and tiny beach of that name. The resort hotel, originally the creation of the Prince of Marbella, was closed for some years, but reopened a few years ago and recently underwent a complete facelift – the construction is a bit jury-rigged – and today caters to a mostly German clientele.

The 30 villas have an attractive quasi-Spanish look. Each villa has silent air-con, a kitchenette, and two downstairs bedrooms that can be rented as separate hotel rooms. Ho-hum decor features heavy bamboo furniture, floral fabrics, and pink granite floors. Villa Sevilla is a secluded twin-bedroom, two-story family villa with a private pool and sundeck. Water sports include paddle boats, windsurfing, beach volleyball, and a full-service dive outfit. There is also a pool, two floodlit tennis courts, a beauty shop, a spa with sauna and small exercise room, two restaurants (meals are a let-down), and two additional bars. It has lots of steps and is not handicap accessible. Rates start at US$100 in summer and US$140 in winter. Villas start at US$290 in summer and US$400 in winter. A full meal plan costs US$55 a day.

**Jamaica Crest Resort** (☎ 993-8400, fax 993-8432, PO Box 165, Fairy Hill, Port Antonio; ☎ 305-573-2006, 800-247-8718 in the USA), at Fairy Hill, has 45 air-conditioned, red-tile-roofed rooms stairstepping a hillside (56 rooms were being added). They have from one to four bedrooms, with kitchenette, cable TV, telephone, and balcony (a housekeeper-cook is optional). Room costs are US$90 to US$100 one-bedroom, US$170 two-bedroom low season, US$100 and US$190 respectively, high season. A full meal plan costs US$25 daily. The complex features an elevated sundeck and pool, plus an elegant, aloof restaurant, bar, disco, conference center, two tennis courts, and a gym. The decor is a strange mix of Chinese and Milanese.

**Fairy Hill Garden Villa** (☎ 993-8205) is one of several private homes for rent at Fairy Hill.

For a complete list, contact the Jamaica Association of Villas & Apartments (JAVA; ☎ 974-2508, fax 974-2967, PO Box 298, Ocho Rios; ☎ 305-673-6688, 800-221-8830, fax 305-673-5666 in the USA).

## Places to Eat

**Woody's Low Bridge Place**, beside the A4 in Drapers, is a rustic and colorful roadside eatery that serves tremendous hot dogs and burgers as well as Jamaican dishes for a couple of bucks.

The **Mille Fleurs** restaurant, in Hotel Mocking Bird Hill, offers the best cuisine in the region using produce grown on the property. It serves superb gourmet nouvelle Jamaican specialties by candlelight on the hillside veranda. A set three-course dinner (US$36), including a vegetarian option, ends with a trolley of Sangster's liqueurs. Even the ice creams are homemade – and superb. If you're lucky, you'll be served by Shernette, whose presentations of the menu are a joy to behold. The special Mille Fleur continental breakfast costs US$12.50.

Also be sure to eat at least once at the **Blue Lagoon Restaurant** (☎ 993-8491), which has wide wooden decks overhanging the lagoon. Trees grow through the decks. It serves a creative, entirely jerk menu, including jerk crayfish, marinated jerk lamb chops, and jerk pork tenderloin. Freshwater lobster is available, and there's spicy honey-garlic conch. You eat with your fingers (a finger bowl and cloth napkin are also provided). Try the potentially lethal Blue Lagoon cocktail, served in a half-pint glass, or the XXX-rated 'Sex in the Lagoon.' Lunch costs US$15, including a to-die-for Tía Maria rum cake dessert. A Sunday dinner special is US$20. You can even request a private dinner on a floating deck in the middle of the lagoon. Fabulous! It's open from 11 am to 5 pm Monday to Wednesday, and 11 am to 10 pm Thursday to Sunday.

**Dragon Bay Resort** offers two dining options: a beach restaurant serving salads and grilled seafood, burgers, and jerk dishes;

and a more elegant restaurant serving consistently mediocre continental cuisine. A dinner buffet costs US$22. An alternative on the theme is Fern Hill's *Poseidon Restaurant & Lounge*.

For Italian cuisine, head to *San San Tropez* (☎/fax 993-7399), whose owner has imbued his hilltop restaurant with a gracious Mediterranean feel. The vast menu runs from US$10 to US$25 for entrees, and there's a large wine list.

At Fairy Hill, try *Pearl's Highway Café* (☎ 993-8445), a pleasant little 'bar and fish place' beside the A4. On the beach take your pick from a dozen rustic jerk stalls. Near the far end is *Club Paradise Café Restaurant* run by Dungus; and Owen cooks crayfish soup and steamed fish under an almond tree.

There are two *groceries* beside the A4 at Zion Hill.

### Entertainment

A *beach party* with limbo and cabaret is held on Monday evenings at San San Beach. Upscale hotels also feature limbo and Caribbean folk shows in season.

*Woody's Place*, at Drapers, hosts live reggae in its backyard every last Friday of the month. The *Blue Lagoon Restaurant* hosts live jazz and reggae on Saturday evenings (US$25, including dinner), when the *Jamaica Palace* also hosts a poolside jam at 8 pm (US$22 including buffet dinner). And there's reggae at the basic *Reggae Pub Restaurant* at Zion Hill.

For a quiet drink, nip into the *Drunken Dragon Bar*, at Dragon Bay Resort.

The Jamaica Crest has the *Club Tiffany* disco. Entrance costs US$1.50 to US$3, depending on the day of the week. Thursday is Ladies Nite. Oldies are played on Sunday.

The *Gallery Carriacou*, at Hotel Mocking Bird Hill (☎ 993-7267, fax 993-7133), also hosts cultural events and musical performances.

### Shopping

All the resort hotels have craft and gift stores. The best quality crafts are sold at Patricia Wymore Flynn's Designer's Gallery,

in the Jamaica Palace; and at the Gallery Carriacou at Hotel Mocking Bird Hill in Frenchman's Cove. You should also take time to check out the women's paper-making project in Fairy Hill, and the Long Road Co-Operative, where women make traditional Jamaica 'chocolate tea balls' – a perfect nightcap with a shot of rum and cream.

Near Turtle Crawle Bay you'll pass Renford Stewart's ramshackle studio. He's a well-known artist and can be seen on almost any day sitting by the roadside, brush in hand, daubing at a canvas upon which an intuitive scene is being hatched. His works are gradually being acknowledged and now fetch upwards of US$100.

### Getting There & Away

Minibuses and buses run between Port Antonio and Boston Bay, Golden Grove, and points beyond. It should cost you no more than US$0.50 by bus, double that by minibus.

At Drapers, Derron's Rent-a-Car (☎ 993-7252, fax 993-7253) charges from US$70 daily. It also has an outlet at Trident Villas (☎ 993-4180).

Dragon Bay Resort rents bicycles.

### BOSTON BEACH

There are several good reasons to stop at Boston Beach, half a mile east of Fairy Hill. First is the pretty, pocket-size, golden-sand beach shelving into jewel-like turquoise waters. High surf rolls into the bay and you may join locals who spend much of their time surfing (you can rent boards on the beach). Many think Boston Beach is the best surfing spot in Jamaica. The beach is tucked in a little cove and is easy to drive past without noticing.

In the 1950s the beach was owned by Robin Moore (author of the *Happy Hooker* and the *Green Berets*), who 'donated' it to the government.

The overriding first impression, however, is of rows of chickens and slabs of pork – even heads and hooves – sizzling away roadside on smoky barbecue pits, for you have arrived at the center of jerk.

## Boston Jerk

Jerk pork, Jamaica's informal national dish, first gained notoriety here as a 'hand-me-down' from the Maroons, who hunted wild boars in the hills of Portland and cooked the meat, well-seasoned, over pimento wood fires. Boston jerk, sold wrapped in paper, is searing. Don't underestimate how *hot* Boston Beach pepper sauce can be. You'll need plenty of Red Stripe beer as an antidote.

## Errol Flynn Estate

Much of the land locally was once owned by Errol Flynn. His widow, Patryce Wymore Flynn, still farms red poll cattle on this estate, called the Priestman's River Plantation, where coconuts are also commercially grown. Locals whisper that Mrs Flynn feeds crocodiles to keep intruders away, but you can tour the plantation on horseback for US$30 by reservation (☎ 993-3294). She still lives in the house Flynn built for her before he died in 1959.

## Places to Stay

*Cozy Corner First & Last* (☎ 993-8450) has two simple but nicely appointed rooms with fans and TV for US$28.50 double. Two rooms have hot water. It's half a mile south of Boston Beach, on the roadside about 200 yards from the shore. It has a small bar, but doesn't serve food. Stay a week and the weekend is free.

A reader recommends the *Sweet Harmony Guest House* (☎ 993-8779, fax 993-3178), run by a friendly French couple, Candida and Jean-Michel. The place has three clean rooms with double beds with mosquito nets, wall fans, and shower-bath with cold water only for US$35 single/double, including breakfast and dinner. One room has air-con. The couple also has a two-story villa for five people (US$100). Spanish and French cuisine is served on a rooftop patio. You've gotta love dogs though, which abound underfoot. It's about 400 yards inland from the A4.

Alternately, consider the very basic *Spicy Grove Guest House* (☎ 993-8515) at the west end of Boston Beach.

## Places to Eat

There are plenty of jerk stalls, but the most significant is *Sir G HQ*, which is popular with tour groups as well as locals. You can't miss it. It's roadside and has a huge barbecue pit heaped with meats and fish being smoked (US$3 to US$5 for a jerk meal served with roasted breadfruit and yam). Get there early, as food tends to be sold out by mid-afternoon.

A good place to buy your searing hot sauce is *Spirit Farmer's Production Spice & Garden Number One*. For the hottest sauce, buy from Harris 'Lawless' Grace, whose homemade concoction will burn a hole through your tongue. Expect to pay no more than US$1.

*Ce-Lee's Restaurant* serves seafood dishes, as does *Club Favorita*, a beachside 'party center' that plays ear-splitting music on weekends.

## Getting There & Away

Boston Beach is 9 miles east of Port Antonio. Expect to pay about US$0.50 by bus, or US$1.50 by minibus. In Kingston, buses and minibuses operate from the Parade via Port Antonio and Morant Bay.

## LONG BAY

This is one of the most dramatic settings in all of Jamaica. The aptly named bay is a 1-mile-wide crescent with rose-colored sand, deep turquoise waters, and breezes pushing the waves forcefully ashore. Canoes are drawn up on the beach, with fishing nets drying beside them. You may be able to hire a fisherman to take you out for about US$15 hourly. There's a dangerous undertow. A good place to admire the views is from the headland at the east end of the bay.

Long Bay appeals to budget travelers seeking to ease into a life of leisure in a fishing village that's a total escape from touristy resorts. A few surfers are also drawn, and the sunrises are spectacular. The lifestyle here is laid-back, but the locals are belligerent toward foreign visitors, although several roughneck-type foreigners have settled here and now live a counterculture lifestyle.

Ken Abendana Spencer, a renowned modernist artist, has his studio here. His concrete home is a rambling, multi-storied palace (it reminds me of a 3-D tromp l'oeil by M C Escher) as fanciful as some of his pricey works. It's been under construction for years (it is already being taken over by foliage) which looks like it could continue for years to come. He's a garrulous chap attended by male hangers-on and full of controversial notions. You're welcome to visit if your interest in art is genuine. Take the dirt road inland from the post office near the gas station; follow the track to the right until you reach a high stone wall and castle-like gates.

There were no phones in Long Bay at press time, but lines were being planned to be brought in.

### Dangers & Annoyances

Many inhabitants along the entire east coast take a while to warm to outsiders. Drugs are rife locally, and several readers have confirmed that there is an unusual aggressiveness in the air. You should be very careful when photographing people here. Don't argue the point if you're confronted. Many burglaries have been reported, as have several instances of violent assaults and even rape. Campers should be particularly wary.

### Sam Street Maroon Museum

Local resident Dr Sam Street welcomes visitors to his museum (☎ 993-5560), which is incorrectly marked on the JTB's *Discover Jamaica* road map as being in Moore Town in the Rio Grande Valley. The museum, housed in an old fort at Snow Hill, contains a fascinating collection of African tribal art and artifacts accrued over several decades by Dr Street, who also raises medicinal plants.

Take the road that leads inland from the hamlet of Fair Prospect, just north of Long Bay. You can continue along this road to Reach Falls (see below).

### Activities

The King George Beer Joint at the north end of the village rents bicycles for US$15 a day.

Long Bay is one of the most consistent surf spots on the island. Riptides and currents are common. You should stick to the extreme northern end.

### Places to Stay

**Camping** You can camp for about US$3 at *Fisherman's Park*, a rustic Rasta-owned jerk center on the shore in the village center. In a similar vein is *Cutting Edge Park*, across the street. Both are popular hang-outs for locals. See Dangers & Annoyances, above: you should never camp 'wild' nor leave your gear unattended.

**Guest Houses** If you're on a really tight budget, try *Precious*, which has basic rooms for about US$5. It's next to the post office at the north end of the village.

Many foreigners who now live here rent rooms to travelers. At the north end of Long Bay is *Blue Heaven*, owned by an American, John. It's above a little river estuary with a coral outcrop offshore. The place is basic, but perfect for escape artists who don't mind spartan. John has two bamboo cottages with kitchenette, ceiling fans, and cold water for US$12.50, plus two rooms for US$20, and a cabin with kitchen and sundeck for US$40. You can make reservations through the Roof Club (☎ 993-3817; ask for Antoinette or Curtis) in Port Antonio.

The *Long Bay Chalet* is a two-story beachfront house with two simply furnished rooms with fans, and private bathroom with hot water for US$20 single/double. The well-maintained *Villa Seascape*, nearby, offers two two-story buildings with three modest, nicely furnished rooms each. They have fans, private bathrooms with hot water, and sliding glass doors opening to breezy balconies or patios for US$40 double, or US$80 for two rooms, US$130 for three rooms. Two rooms share a bathroom. Meals are prepared to order.

The *Lovers Hide-Out Cottage* has two bedrooms with fans and cold water for US$25 single/double. A second two-bedroom cottage with kitchen was to be added. Jamaican meals are served in a rustic roadside bar with video games.

Peter Paul Zahl rents his *Rose Cottage B&B* for weeklong stays; it's signed in Long

Bay, but easy to miss. Another couple maintains a **cottage** at Commodore, in the hills above Black Rock. Kris Kristensen rents a four-bedroom **cottage** here (☎ 993-3768, PO Box 166, Port Antonio).

**Rolling Surf** (☎ 993-3232), at the southern end of the bay, has six rooms for US$30, each with two single beds plus ceiling fan and private bathrooms. They're simply furnished and clean. Herman Doswell runs **Herman's Holiday Homes**, with modest rooms for US$20 per person. He also has comfortable two-bedroom cottages for US$320 weekly.

Considerably more upscale is the **Seacliff Resort** (☎ 926-2248), atop the cliffs 2 miles south of Long Bay. It's not a resort at all. A three-bedroom villa is set amid expansive lush lawns with a volleyball court, plus a beautiful stone-fringed swimming pool shaded by palms. The villa is nicely furnished and well-kept (the rate of US$200 is 'negotiable'). Picnics are hosted here.

### Places to Eat
**Fisherman's Park** is a jerk center (see Camping, above). **Bamboo Lawn** is a rustic beachside bar serving seafood dishes for about US$2. It has a disco at night. Another lively spot is the **Sunset Strip Pub**. You can get European-style dishes at the **Hungry Lion**.

If you're catering yourself, the **Ocean View Pub**, opposite the Rolling Surf Guest House, has a grocery. Nearby is **M&M's Pastry Centre**, selling cakes, patties, fudge, and ice cream.

Picnics with live music are occasionally hosted at the **Seacliff Resort** south of Long Bay (US$28 includes all-you-can-eat buffet).

### Getting There & Away
Bus No LS289, which runs between Port Antonio and Golden Grove, will drop you off at Long Bay (US$0.50).

## MANCHIONEAL
This sleepy fishing village is set in a deep, scalloped bay with calm turquoise waters and a wide, shallow beach where colorful pirogues are drawn up. It's a center for lobster fishing. The name is derived from the poisonous manchineel plant (*Hippomane mancinella*) that once grew profusely along the shoreline (see Fearsome Flora in Facts for the Visitor). It's a cool place to hang if you want a rustic, laid-back experience, and the coastal vistas are dramatic hereabouts.

### Places to Stay & Eat
Two miles north of Manchioneal is the **Heartical Roots Corner** (☎ 993-6138) where the tiny Christmas River meets the ocean just south of Kensington. Heartical is run by friendly Stanford Johnson, who has a thatched, family-size room for rent for US$30 in an Arawak-style octagonal cabin with hammocks on a wraparound veranda (additional rooms are being added). Alas, the place is beginning to look neglected since Stanford's delightful wife, Gabrielle, returned home to Austria. You can also camp on the riverbank for US$6 per person. Bring mosquito repellent! The pit latrine was due to be upgraded. Stanford (a 'superone chef') cooks I-tal vegetarian meals. The tiny golden-sand beach is backed by a small lagoon that is safe for swimming. Gabrielle says the surf here is 'killer.' July is said to be the best month. Stanford also rents tents and scooters for US$30.

The **Zion Country Beach Cabins**, south of Manchioneal, are more basic.

There are plenty of jerk stalls and rum shops on the coast road in town. Try **Sultan's Place**, the **Fish Pot** (which is open 24 hours), or **Foxy Legs Inn** (☎ 993-6253), serving steamed fish, fish tea, roast conch, etc. Foxy Legs has a pool table, table football, a working jukebox, and go-go dancing (from 10 pm).

There's a gas station and a Western Union.

## REACH FALLS
Although a traditional favorite of JTB posters, these cascades remained virtually unvisited until a few years ago, when the below-the-falls sex scene in the movie *Cocktail* spawned the waterfall's newfound fame. Now tour buses arrive from as far away as Ocho Rios. Time your visit right and it remains a peaceful spot surrounded by

virgin rain forest. A series of cascades tumble over limestone tiers from one hollowed, jade-colored pool to another. A half-mile hike upriver leads to **Mandingo Cave**, which has a whirlpool and is worth the hike. Note the sign that reads: 'Beware of deep pools and strong currents.'

An erstwhile squatter, Frank Clarke, has parlayed his piece of illicit real estate into a moneymaker. Frank charges around US$1.25 entrance to descend the concrete steps that lead down to the cascades. He also charges about US$3 (negotiable) for a 'tour' that involves wading and scrambling over rocks to a deep pool. There are changing rooms above the parking lot, where Rastafarians will attempt to sell you woolen tams, jewelry, etc.

### Places to Stay & Eat

Frank Clarke (☎ 993-6138) rents two very basic **cabins** with private bath and cold water for US$20 per person. He also has a basic restaurant – **Ranch Bar** – atop the falls serving dishes such as tuna fish stew with potatoes for about US$2. A man called Buckley also rents rooms nearby.

### Getting There & Away

Bus No MB11 operates from the Parade in Kingston (US$1). You can catch any of the buses that run between Kingston and Port Antonio via Morant Bay; get off in Manchioneal, then walk or hitch uphill to Reach. A taxi from Port Antonio costs about US$50 roundtrip.

The well-paved road up to the falls is half a mile south of Manchioneal. It's a spectacular one-mile drive as you follow the valley of the Driver's River into the foothills of the John Crow Mountains.

### HAPPY GROVE

Three miles south of Manchioneal you'll pass Happy Grove High School, which stands atop a wild rocky shore. It's a good place to stop and admire the coastal vistas. The village of **Hector's River** is one mile south, on the border of Portland and St Thomas, where the road drops onto the southeastern flatlands.

# Rio Grande Valley

Fed by torrential rains, the Rio Grande rushes down from 3000 feet in the Blue Mountains and has carved a huge gorge. This exceedingly lush valley forms a deep, V-shaped wedge between the northeastern flank of the Blue Mountains and the John Crow Mountains to the east. Its fertile alluvial soils are well watered, and much of the valley is dominated by banana groves. This area of the valley is renowned for its populations of rare, giant swallowtail butterflies *(Papilio homerus)*, which are particularly abundant in early summer. The valley is now being promoted assiduously and offers plenty of treats. There's a strong sense of Maroon heritage here; 'bush medicine' is still alive.

Red Hassell Rd runs south from Port Antonio and enters the Rio Grande Valley at Fellowship, where the Rio Grande Development Corporation has its headquarters. From Fellowship, the road winds uphill to Windsor (the traditional starting point for arduous hikes to Nanny Town; see Nanny Town, later in this chapter) and Seaman's Valley, where the Maroons massacred an English force in the 18th century. At Seaman's Valley the road forks: to the left is Moore Town, and to the right, it leads up through the upper Rio Grande Valley.

For anyone able to take their eyes off the potholed road, the views up the valley are dramatic.

### Hiking

There are many narrow trails – called 'Parish Council roads' – through the valley. All are off the beaten track and many are known only to farmers. Most link remote hamlets, many of which now exist only in name (ruins can be seen at such places as Brookdale and John's Hall). Most lead past waterfalls, and local guides are keen to tell you about medicinal herbs such as 'fever few' and 'headache-no-more' (cowfoot leaf), which works wonders on hemorrhoids. 'Softbush,' you are advised, makes good toilet paper. One guide in particular, Ivylyn 'Blossom,' knows her herbs like the back of her hand.

One reason to hire a guide is that most trails pass through private property. If you hike alone, be prepared for the unexpected. Some hikes are easy. Popular hikes include one to White Valley, known for its large population of giant swallowtail butterflies; to Dry River Falls, reached on a one-hour hike west from the Rio Grande (it's said that a mermaid lives in the cave behind the falls); and to Scatter Falls and Fox's Caves (see below).

Other hikes are demanding, with muddy, overgrown trails and small rivers that can be chest deep and require fording. Don't attempt to hike off the beaten path without a guide unless you're an extremely experienced hiker. If you do, make sure you have a machete, and take plenty of water! The Corn Puss Gap trail is particularly difficult. So, too, is the wild path that leads from Windsor to the site of Nanny Town.

You can sponsor a tree with Valley Hikes (see Organized Hikes, below), which will plant a hardwood tree seedling on your behalf and guarantee that it will not be cut for at least 20 years.

Huub Gaymans spearheads the Eco-Tourism Action Group, part of the Rio Grande Valley Project that is researching trails, training trail guides, and developing attractions to sponsor development.

**Organized Hikes** Valley Hikes (see Organized Tours, earlier in this chapter) offers a series of organized hikes utilizing 20 local farmers and herbalists trained as guides. The hike to Scatter Falls and Fox Cave costs US$12. Others, lasting no more than four hours, cost US$20 to US$25. Three-day hikes cost US$170, and a strenuous 10-day hike is US$450. Horseback rides (US$40 for four hours) and a cultural show (US$9) are also available. Reservations must be made 24 hours in advance. Valley Hikes publishes a splendid trail guide map and rents hiking boots at its Port Antonio and Fellowship offices. Rubber boots can be rented (US$3) but aren't needed if you have sturdy footwear. Its office is upstairs at 12 West St in Port Antonio, above Kamal's Supermarket.

**Scatter Falls & Fox Caves** A recommended easy hike takes you to Scatter Falls and Fox Caves, among the most accessible attractions in the Rio Grande Valley. They're reached by crossing the Rio Grande on a bamboo raft at Berridale, then hiking 15 minutes through a series of hamlets. (Alternately, you can hike from St Margaret's Bay up to Coopers Hill and Olive Mount, then down to Bourbon and Berridale along the Sarah River.)

Eventually you arrive at the falls, which tumble exquisitely through a curtain of ferns. There are pools for refreshing dips, and a grassy knoll with bench seats for enjoying that well-earned snooze. Streamer-tail hummingbirds flit about.

The owners, the Thaxters, have developed a rest area with toilets and changing rooms, plus a campground, a bamboo-and-thatch bar, and a kitchen serving hot lunch (which must be ordered in advance).

A steep, 15-minute hike from the waterfall leads to the caves, which have interesting formations that your guide will conjure into vivid imaginings: a lion's head, lovers *in flagrante delicto*, and another that resembles a bed and has caused more than one amorous couple to request that the guide depart for a few minutes ('…but please leave the lantern!'). Rufus Thaxter is an excellent cave guide. The passages are narrow, provoking postures like those of a tai chi master, but the roof is high above and pitted with hollows in which tiny bats dangle. One cave, which the Fox River runs through, has a particularly large population of bats.

## Nanny Town

This former stronghold of the Windward Maroons was once a village of more than 140 houses on the brink of a precipitous spur on the northeastern flank of Blue Mountain Peak, about 10 miles southwest of Moore Town as the crow flies. It is named for an Ashanti warrior priestess who led the Maroons during the early 18th century. Today she's a national hero. English soldiers searched for Nanny Town for many years and found it in 1728. They attacked it several times over the ensuing years, but Nanny proved to be a brilliant military tactician. Legend says that she had supernatural gifts, including the ability to catch bullets and return them 'with fatal effect' with her vagina. (See Moore Town, later in this chapter, for more about Nanny.) Eventually, in 1734, a Captain Stoddard led his troops over the Blue Mountains and, armed with swivel guns, finally took Nanny Town.

The village was soon lost to the jungle. Even the Ordnance Survey maps show its location as 'approximate.'

Local superstitions abound. Nanny Town is said to be haunted by a 'whole heap of duppies' who appear as white birds, and a nearby river flows 'red, red like blood,' according to one guide. Another legend says that any European who ventures there will die.

It's a tough 10-mile hike over hill and dale from Windsor, 3 miles south of Moore Town. Valley Hikes (see Organized Hikes, above) has a three-day guided hike that begins in Windsor. Nights are spent in huts. In Moore Town, Shadow (alias 'The Professor') or Lucky can guide you.

### Rafting

Errol Flynn supposedly initiated rafting on the Rio Grande during the 1940s, when he organized raft races among locals, who used to ship bananas downriver to Port Antonio on bamboo rafts. By the 1960s, rafting the Rio Grande had become the rage among the social elite. Moonlight raft trips were considered the ultimate activity among the fashionable…until a formally dressed party (including noted novelist and wild card, Truman Capote) tipped over, and grand ladies in chiffon almost drowned.

Today, paying passengers make the three-hour, 6-mile journey from Grant's Level or Rafter's Village, a mile east of Berridale, to Rafter's Rest, at St Margaret's Bay. The journey is perfectly scenic. You'll get a taste for rural life along the riverbanks, where women and children bathe and wash clothes, shoreside peddlers strum guitars for a tip, and others sell sodas and coconuts, often from other rafts. En route, you'll pass through **Lovers Lane**, a moss-covered narrow stream where you're supposed to kiss and make a wish, and **Betty's**, a lean-to café on a pebbly curve of the river, where you can lunch on Jamaican staples such as ackee and codfish or *janga* (crayfish) soup.

The trips are offered by Rio Grande Attractions Ltd (☎ 993-5778, fax 993-5290), PO Box 128, Port Antonio, which has a monopoly. They're available 9 am to 4 pm, and cost US$45 per raft, double for full-moon rides. It's best to make reservations. You can buy tickets at Rafter's Village at Berridale if you don't have reservations.

If you drive yourself, you can have your car driven back down to Rafter's Rest to await your return (US$5). The drivers are insured, but you should make totally clear to your driver that you expect him to drive slowly and safely.

You can find private rafters touting their services in Port Antonio, but are the risks worth it?

### ATHENRY GARDENS & NONSUCH CAVES

Athenry Gardens, high in the hills southeast of town, is a former coconut plantation and agricultural research center that today, as a lush botanical garden, boasts many exotic and native species. The highlight, however, is the Nonsuch Caves (☎ 993-3740), 14 separate chambers full of stalagmites and stalactites. Steps lead into the caves, which are lit by electricity. The limestone was laid millions of years before Jamaica rose above the sea, as indicated by fossils of fish, coral, and other sea creatures. Now only bats occupy the dank bowels. They hang from the 40-foot-high ceiling in what is called the Gothic-Scale Cathedral. Guides call it the Bat Romance Room, which more accurately portrays what goes on. They'll also point out imaginary stalagmite formations: a pope, a bishop, a man in robes upon a camel, and a naked woman emerging from a shell.

The caves and garden are about 7 miles southeast of Port Antonio via Red Hassell Rd. After 2 miles there's a Y-fork. The right fork leads to Berridale and the Rio Grande; take the left for Nonsuch. The road leads uphill all the way and is appallingly rutted.

Just when you feel like giving up, you'll see a handsome home sitting incongruously atop the hill. A sign to the right of the house points to the caves and Athenry Gardens.

You can also reach Nonsuch Caves via a road that heads uphill via Nonsuch Village and Sherwood Forest from the Fairweather Building at Fairy Hill.

There's a secure parking lot and toll booth. Entrance costs US$5. It's open 9 am to 5 pm.

JD Tours (☎ 993-4618) offers a trip to Nonsuch and Athenry, ending with a swim at Frenchman's Cove (US$15). Other tour companies in Port Antonio also offer tours.

## TAMARIND HILL FARM

This organic farm is run by Vincent and Joanna Slimford, who raise fruits and vegetables, freshwater fish, bees, geese, rabbits, and sheep. They offer guided tours that are especially fun for families, and will make lunch to order. Vincent is particularly knowledgeable about the region and acts as an informal guide.

Take the turn (on the left when heading south) marked 'Tom's Hope Farm,' a mile north of Fellowship, then take the right lane at the Y-fork.

## BERRIDALE

This hamlet is the headquarters for Rafter's Village, 400m east of the village, where dozens of rafts are drawn up along the shore. Further along is Grant's Level, the bamboo-ferry point linking Berridale with the hamlets that line the trail to Scatter Falls and Fox Cave.

At Berridale, there's a small grocery, and a riverside bar and restaurant. Jaming Tour Art & Crafts ('by the one and only Winston') has crafts and hats for sale.

A minibus from Port Antonio to Grant's Level will cost about US$2. Expect to pay about US$15 roundtrip for a taxi.

## MOORE TOWN

This one-street village, 10 miles south of Port Antonio, stretches uphill for several hundred yards along the Wildcane River. It looks like any other Jamaican village, but is important as the former base of the Windward Maroons (see 'The Windward Maroons,' earlier in this chapter). The village was founded in 1739 following the signing of a peace treaty whereby the British colonialists granted the Maroons their independence. Moore Town is still run semi-autonomously by a council of 24 elected members headed by a 'colonel.' The current leader is Colonel Stirling, ably assisted by a revered ex-schoolteacher and Jamaica Labour Party (JLP) senator, Colonel 'Teacher' Harris, who held the post between 1964 and 1995.

You don't have to request prior permission to visit Moore Town as some sources suggest. You might want to give a donation to Colonel Stirling for the Maroon Museum, which still had not materialized at press time.

Trails lead from Moore Town, including one to **Nanny Falls**, about 45 minutes away.

### Information

There's a Workers Savings & Loan Bank and a post office (open 8 am to 4 pm Monday to Friday, and 8 am to noon Saturday).

### Bump Grave

Beyond a recently restored church and graveyard at the southern, uppermost end of town, is Bump Grave (note the intriguing murals on the school wall, opposite the gravesite). A plaque on the oblong stone grave reads:

NANNY of the Maroons/National Hero of Jamaica/Beneath this place known as Bump Grave lies the body of Nanny, indomitable and skilled chieftainess of the Windward Maroons who founded this town.

The grave is topped by a flagpole flying the Maroon and Jamaican flags.

Moore Town's inhabitants are a very Christian people, as the seven churches attest to. On one of my recent visits, one of the colonel's lieutenants, Mr Lucky Osborn, became quite vexed when I asked if Nanny was venerated. 'We worship no idols. We worship GOD!' he boomed. He calmed down later and even offered to be my guide to Nanny Town.

### Faith Healing

Try to visit on Monday, when Mother Roberts, a local faith healer, performs in the

Deliverance Centre. People gather from far and wide for revivalist music, dancing, and lots of hysteria – don't be surprised to see her pull a rusty nail from someone's head! On Wednesday, Mother Roberts holds more serious, private healings in a shack at the back of her house (a substantial ochre-colored affair that reveals how lucrative her trade is). You take a ticket and wait in line. There's a soda stand to ward off any thirst. There could be as many as 40 people waiting to be 'healed.'

### Places to Stay
There are no hotels, but you can try renting a room with a local family.

### Getting There & Away
Moore Town is 2 miles south of Seaman's Castle. The town is unmarked and lies in a hollow to the left of a Y-junction; the road to the right (terribly deteriorated) continues uphill to Cornwall Barracks, where it ends. In Moore Town, the road dead-ends above the school, petering out amid mud in a glade of night jasmine.

A bus operates to Moore Town from Port Antonio in the early morning and again in early afternoon (less than US$1 each way).

In Port Antonio, 'Rev' organizes trips to Moore Town (contact him at Culture Ice, 40 Somestown Rd).

## UPPER RIO GRANDE VALLEY
The road leading west from the T-junction at Seaman's Valley leads via **Alligator Church** (named, according to local legend, for an alligator that was seen entering the church, dressed in black) and Comfort Castle to Bowden Pen, 10 miles or so up the river valley. The paved road ends at Alligator Church and begins to deteriorate, rising gently past heraldic stands of bamboo and, eventually, antediluvian tree ferns and sweet-smelling wild ginger. The dirt road is extremely rough and narrow and you'll need a 4WD.

The Blue Mountains-John Crow National Park ranger station is at **Millbank**, 2 miles before Bowden Pen, near the summit ridge of the John Crow Mountains, which parallels

the valley like a great castle wall. A trail leads to the **White River Fall**, a series of seven cascades. It's a tough trek through the rain forest, often quite wet. The area has received more than 400 inches of rain in some years. Needless to say, the vegetation is as thick as it gets in Jamaica. Be sure to bring waterproof gear!

A short distance above **Bowden Pen**, the track begins rising more precipitously and grows muddy as the vegetation closes in. Don't push too far, for there is nowhere to turn your vehicle back (Ambassabeth Cabins marks the end of the track). Getting stuck here is serious business! You can continue on foot along what was once a road across the Compass Gap.

Sun Venture Tours (☎ 960-6685), 30 Balmoral Ave, Kingston 10, offers guided treks on request from US$50 per person for one or two hikers (US$70 for overnight trips), US$35 per person for more people.

Several locals act as guides, including a gracious fella, Errol Deans (a dead ringer for the boxer Mike Tyson), Errol Francis, and Desmond Gray.

### Places to Stay & Eat
Royce Brimson runs a small, modern guest house called *Rainbow Valley* at Bowden Pen. It is said to boast great views from the porch. Royce cooks I-tal meals. You can camp here, too. Vegetarian meals are served.

You can also rent a room from an elderly woman, Birdie Bifield, opposite the soccer field in Millbank. She'll cook if you bring food.

*Ambassabeth Cabins* (☎ 938-5036) is on the slope above the river near the valleyhead above Bowden Pen. It has two solid and very basic wooden cabins painted in Rasta colors with bamboo seats amid lawns, with views toward Compass Gap, for US$15 per person; meals cost US$6 to US$9 extra. Bring mosquito repellent. Gary Wade, a UWI professor, leads trips here. Contact him at ☎ 929-3236, the Towers, 25 Dominica Drive, Kingston 5.

There's a tiny, well-stocked *grocery store* in Comfort Castle and another at Millbank. There are a few rum shops for supping with locals, notably the *Gingerbread House* in Ginger House, just north of Comfort Castle.

## Getting There & Away
A bus from Port Antonio goes as far as Millbank (US$0.50). You can drive to Bowden Pen only from the north; there's a hiking trail heading south.

# West of Port Antonio

## PASSLEY GARDENS
Passley Botanical Gardens, 2 miles west of Port Antonio, is run by Passley Gardens College, which offers degree courses in agriculture. The 680-acre facility is laid out around a well-preserved great house recently restored and run as a hotel. In addition to well-tended gardens, the grounds include an experimental livestock farm and groves of tropical fruit trees. The college has even initiated mariculture along its 2-mile shoreline. There are even two beaches – one for students, one for staff – and a small palm-tipped island.

Visitors are welcome and admission is free. Students lead tours by appointment only (☎ 993-2631); you travel on a tractor-pulled jitney and visit the slaughterhouse as well as the farm and nearby forest.

### Places to Stay & Eat
The *Passley Great House* (☎ 993-5491, 993-5436) has five air-conditioned bedrooms, each with private bathroom. Recently renovated, they feature terra-cotta floors, lofty ceilings, and adequate furnishings, and cost US$70 double. A living room has cable TV. Maid service is provided, and meals can be prepared for guests, or you can use the kitchen or take meals in the faculty cafeteria.

The rustic *Burru's Restaurant & Pub*, about 1½ miles east of Passley, serves seafood, I-tal stew, and vegetarian dishes.

## HOPE BAY
There's nothing inspirational about Hope Bay, which has an ugly gray beach. A loop drive, however, can be made from here up the Swift River Valley, where plantations grow cacao. You can turn west off the same road and loop inland, taking a scenic drive into the foothills of the Blue Mountains before returning to the coast at St Margaret's Bay, beyond which the A4 crosses the Rio Grande 2 miles west of Passley.

A delightful Rastafarian, Sister P (for Pauline), runs Sundial (☎/fax 913-0690), a colorful store in the center of town: look for the sign reading 'It's Ital. It's Vital.' She sells health products, including the 'Ashanti energy lifter,' and other tonics, plus African jewelry, clothing, and crafts.

On the A4, betwixt Hope Bay and St Margaret's Bay, is the Ken Jones Aerodrome.

## Somerset Falls
These falls (☎ 913-0108), 9 miles west of Port Antonio, are hidden in a deep gorge overhung with thick foliage about 2 miles east of Hope Bay. The Daniels River cascades down through a lush garden of ferns, heliconias, lilies, crotons, and bright purple plumbergia that grow on a former indigo and spice plantation.

The US$3 entrance includes a guided tour to the Hidden Fall that tumbles 33 feet into a jade-colored grotto. You can plunge from a rock into the cool waters. The property has waterfowl. It's open 9 am to 5 pm daily, and has restrooms and a snack bar next to the parking lot (meals are made to order – but it's a long wait). Rafts were to be introduced.

You'll have to negotiate some steep, twisty steps, and when I was last there visitors had to wade through a narrow opening to reach the waterfall.

## Places to Stay
Sister P runs a rustic retreat called *Content Farm* (☎ 913-0690, 953-2387, Content, Hope Bay PO, Portland), at Content, in the mountains above Hope Bay. A stay here offers all-around vistas of the mountains and the coast and provides insight into the real Jamaican lifestyle. Sister P has five bamboo cottages with outhouse toilets, no electricity, and cold water from an outside barrel. You'll bathe in an invigorating mountain stream. Accommodations with all meals (I-tal food and

natural juices) cost about US$30. You can camp, too, for US$5. The 35-acre farm is planted with avocado, coconuts, and citrus. Content Farm is featured on the Lonely Planet video *Jamaica Experience*, though the tiny primary school no longer functions. Sister P and her daughter are delightful people.

To get there, turn south at the police station in Hope Bay, turn right after one mile, and then take the second left. 4WD is recommended.

Mrs Brown runs **Spring Garden Guest House**, a small bed-and-breakfast on the black-sand beach at St Margaret's Bay.

The **Swift River Hotel & Restaurant** (☎ 913-0178) offers uninspired lodging at the mouth of the river. The four rooms have fans and private bathroom, but meager furnishings and cold water only; they cost US$25 to US$50. One has a four-poster bed. The owner, Paula Espuet, also has two self-catering apartments. You can arrange meals with the housekeeper.

**Paradise Inn** (☎ 993-5169, fax 993-5569; ☎ 020-7350-1009, fax 7228-3536 in the UK), at Snow Hill, has modestly furnished, self-catering one-bedroom suites and studios for US$50 to US$90. It's a 20-minute walk to the beach.

A superb option is **Rio Vista Resort & Villas** (☎/fax 993-5444, PO Box 4, St Margaret's Bay PO, Portland), atop a ridge near the turnoff for Rafter's Rest, 4 miles west of Port Antonio. This handsome modern home is built into the remains of an old plantation home – Burlington Estate – and boasts an enviable setting high above a deep bend in the Rio Grande, with the steep, green-carpeted mountains behind. To the fore are 10 acres of tropical fruit trees falling down to the river. There are two rooms in the main house, which has terra-cotta floors and an atrium lounge with circular mezzanine, for US$60 double with breakfast. Antiques and Asian paintings abound. Five genteel villas have lofty ceilings and polished wood floors; three have two bedrooms and kitchen plus TV lounge, and cost from US$100 to US$150. The 'honeymoon' cottage was featured as a 'Room with a View' in *Condé Nast Traveler*. All feature a kitchen,

satellite TV, ceiling fans, and a housekeeper. Meals are made to order, and if you wish you can dine poolside under the gazebo (try the seafood gumbo for US$18, or vegetable platter for US$10). A honeymoon package costs US$1000. Henry, your gracious host, offers airport transfers and represents Island Car Rentals.

**Blue Beyond Villas** (☎ 993-5498, 977-1454, PO Box 7, St Margaret's Bay PO), where four quaint, contemporary, and clean two-bedroom, two-bathroom villas with kitchens cost US$100, or US$110 with air-con, for up to four people. You can rent one room with kitchen for US$50. Rates include a maid, who'll cook for US$15 daily. The property has a rocky shore with pocket-size beach nearby.

## Places to Eat

There are a few funky restaurants and an ice cream stand in Hope Bay, and a fistful of shacks sell jerk chicken and seafood beside the bridge over the Swift River.

For elegant dining, head to **Rafter's Rest** (☎ 993-2778), in a columned Georgian mansion, at the mouth of the Rio Grande, 600 yards downhill from the A4. Rafter's Rest is the traditional end point for the bamboo raft trip from Berridale. You dine on a shady veranda lit at night by wrought-iron lanterns. The menu includes hot dogs (US$2), salads (US$4 to US$10), burgers (US$5), curried chicken (US$9), and steak with garlic butter (US$12), plus espressos and cappuccinos. There's also a well-stocked gift store. It's open 8 am to 7 pm daily.

## Getting There & Away

See Getting Around under Port Antonio, earlier in this chapter, for information on air transportation.

Buses No LS287 and LS997 pass Somerset Falls between Annotto Bay and Port Antonio. Take any of the dozen or so buses that operate between Port Antonio and Kingston.

## ORANGE BAY

West of Hope Bay, the A4 winds inland for several miles past Orange Bay and Spring Gardens Estate.

## Spring Gardens Estate

This former sugar plantation, one of the oldest in the region, is today planted in coconuts. It formerly belonged to Viscount Hailsham, whose grandson renounced the title in 1963. Hailsham's attorney, William Bancroft Espuet, later bought the property and built Jamaica's first railway in 1868 to convey sugarcane from field to factory. The enterprising Espuet also introduced the mongoose to the island. Alas, the four male and five female animals he brought from India to control rats multiplied and their progeny are to blame for the devastation to many native species that's taken place over the past century.

## Crystal Springs

Crystal Springs (☎ 996-1400, 800-523-3782 in the USA), half a mile inland from Spring Gardens, is a bucolic recreational site home to a splendid orchid collection and botanical greenhouses in a 56-acre setting of wide lawns, lush bougainvillea, aracauria palms, fruit trees, and forest linked by pathways. There's superb birding here, too. But at this writing the owners were refurbishing Crystal Springs. Call ahead.

In May, Crystal Springs normally hosts the Portland Annual Flower Show. There's a small folk museum and restaurant, and guided tours are available. Entrance is US$0.50.

### Places to Stay & Eat

*Crystal Springs* (see above) has cabins with electricity and cold water, but call ahead to see if they've reopened. It's a peaceful haven amid lawns and patches of forest. The rustic cottages cost US$40 double, including a Jamaican breakfast. A two-bedroom unit that sleeps four is also available for US$120. You can camp for US$5. Tent rentals, previously offered, are no longer available. Meals are served in an open-sided restaurant.

### Getting There & Away

Buses running between Port Antonio, Annotto Bay, and Kingston pass by the turnoff for Crystal Springs.

## BUFF BAY

This small, neatly laid-out town has been entirely bypassed by tourism. It has several colonial-era buildings of modest interest, centered on the Anglican church. The narrow shingle beach is used by locals as a garbage dump.

There are some modestly attractive beaches west of town, where the road rises away from the coast, with occasional dirt roads leading down to the shore.

Banana plantations extend westward from Buff Bay along the coastal plains spanning the border of St Mary and Portland parishes. The plantations are owned by Jamaica Banana Producers, Ltd, which was founded by the Jamaican government in 1930 to challenge the domination of the United Fruit Company.

The Buff Bay River and Spanish River valleys are also major centers of banana cultivation.

**Fishdone Waterfalls** is a beautiful spot on a private coffee plantation near Buff Bay. The falls are surrounded by rain forest and there are trails for hiking.

The coast between Orange Bay and Annotto Bay is good for surfing.

### Information

The post office is 100 yards east of the church. Buff Bay also has a small hospital (☎ 996-1478), and the police station (☎ 996-1497) is at the east end of town.

### Places to Stay & Eat

The *Sea Palace* (☎ 996-2310), a mile east of town at Blueberry Hill, has *very* basic rooms for US$3. Check to see if the *Seawaves Club* has been opened yet; its construction has been stalled for years.

At the east end of town, opposite Seawaves, is *Kildare Villa Great House* (☎ 996-1214), a restored colonial structure operating a well-stocked gift store selling patties and desserts. The restaurant, with patio dining upstairs, offers Jamaican breakfasts such as ackee and saltfish, and brown stew chicken (US$5), and staples such as fried chicken, and curried goat for lunch and dinner (US$5 to US$12).

For breakfast, head to **Pace Sitter Café** (☎ 996-1240, 22 Victoria Rd). It's run by Earle and Pat Brown, who offer inexpensive meals, including curried goat, rice and peas, and delicious pastries and coffee. At **Rosa's Cantina**, in town, you can savor curried goat, escoveitch fish, and rice and peas for US$2 or so.

### Getting There & Away

Buses operate four times daily from Kingston to Port Antonio via Buff Bay (3½ hours). Buses also operate once daily between Port Antonio and Montego Bay and Ocho Rios, passing through Buff Bay.

A gas station is at the east end of town.

## BUFF BAY RIVER VALLEY

The B1 heads south from the Texaco gas station in the town center and climbs 20 miles through the valley of the Buff Bay River via Balcarres, Spring Hill, and Section to Hardwar Gap, at an elevation of 4500 feet, before dropping down to Kingston. The road narrows, climbs, and grows increasingly sinuous, with more and deeper pot holes (it's in horrendous condition).

These slopes are an important coffee producing area, and you can buy Blue Mountain coffee from roadside stalls for less than US$1 a pound.

Midway between Orange Bay and Buff Bay, a rough road leads inland through banana plantations to the foothills of the Blue Mountains. The area was earmarked for coffee expansion in the late 1980s, funded by the Japanese Ushima Coffee Co. The first plantations appear at Skibo.

A bus from Buff Bay goes as far as Chepstowe (US$0.20).

### Blue Mountain Bicycling

Blue Mountain Tours, based in Ocho Rios, offers a 'Blue Mountain Downhill Bicycle Tour' (see the Outdoor Activities chapter). The thrilling descent begins at the company's handsome restaurant high up in the Blue Mountains at 5060 feet and ends at a waterfall. Take extreme care, as the road is winding, narrow, and full of potholes. US$85 includes roundtrip transfers, breakfast and lunch, refreshments, and a guide.

### Hiking

It's wise to obtain a copy of Sheets 13 and 14 of the Ordnance Survey 1:12,500-series topographical maps of Jamaica, showing the Portland Blue Mountains. You'll need both sheets, as well as Sheet 18 (and possibly 19) if you plan on descending to the south of the Blue Mountain crest. You can buy them for US$5 per sheet at the Survey Dept office (☎ 922-6630), at 23½ Charles St, PO Box 493, Kingston; or in England from the Ordnance Survey, Romsey Rd, Southampton SO9 4DH.

## ANNOTTO BAY

This erstwhile banana port became a main center for banana production in the late 19th century when a Scottish physician, Sir John Pringle (1848-1923), arrived in Jamaica and reaped a fortune in the area by buying up derelict sugar plantations and planting bananas.

Today Annotto Bay is a downtrodden, one-street town that springs to life for Saturday market. It suffered a severe blow in 1985 with the demise of the Gray's Inn sugar factory and the discontinuation of rail service. Hurricane Gilbert added insult to injury in 1988.

The mile-long main street straddles the River Pencar, which effectively divides the town into east and west Annotto Bay. Depressing shanties line the waterfront. At the town's center is an old blue-and-white courthouse that now houses the office of the collector of taxes. There are also some gingerbread colonial-era structures with columned walkways, and the paltry remains of **Fort George**. The most intriguing edifice is the venerable yellow and red-brick **Baptist chapel** built in 'village baroque' style in 1894, with cut-glass windows and curious biblical exhortations engraved at cornice height. Little cannons stand in its gateway.

The town's name derives from the Anatto, a dye plant (Bixa orellana) that once was grown commercially here.

Two miles west of town is the junction of the A4 with the A3.

## Information

The town has a small hospital with a primitive emergency department (☎ 996-2222). The post office is on Main St, 50 yards east of the Baptist chapel; the police station (☎ 996-2244), also on Main St, is a stone's throw east of the chapel.

There's a National Commercial Bank 100m west of the town square; and a Jamaica National Building Society, 50m east of the Baptist Church, has a foreign currency bureau.

## Places to Stay & Eat

Hardy budget travelers might consider the *Octopus Drive Inn*, 200 yards east of the Texaco gas station just east of town. This two-story wooden house facing the Caribbean has very basic, unclean rooms for about US$8.

You can eat for less than US$2 at *Roots Club*, on Main St, a popular local bar which also has go-go dancing at night. *Back to Eden*, across the street, serves I-tal food. Both are good budget eateries, as is the *First & Last Snack Stop* in the old railway station east of town.

You can buy grilled lobster, conch, saltfish, and peppered shrimp from *roadside higglers* who congregate immediately east of town. Wash them down with fruit juices or coconut milk.

## Getting There & Away

A bus from Ocho Rios costs about US$0.50 one way. A mini-bus (US$2) runs between Annotto Bay and Port Maria, as does bus LS287 (US$0.50).

Taxis and buses gather to either side of the tax office in the main square.

A gas station is at the east end of town.

## ROBIN'S BAY

West of Annotto Bay, the A3 forks. One branch turns south through the Wag Water River Valley and winds into the Blue Mountains en route to Kingston. The other continues west to Port Maria and Ocho Rios (see the Ocho Rios & North Coast chapter), passing through Robin's Bay and Don Christopher's Point on the way.

Midway to Port Maria from Annotto Bay, on the A3, you'll pass a turnoff to the north that leads past banana plantations, then hugs a lonesome shoreline with gray-sand beaches fringed by almonds and backed by lagoons. After 2½ miles, you emerge in **Mt Pleasant Heights**, a fishing village atop a wide open plateau with mountains off in the distance. Mt Pleasant Heights is nestled atop **Don Christopher's Point**, named for the Spanish guerrilla leader, Don Cristobal Arnaldo de Ysassi (see Rio Nuevo, in the Ocho Rios & North Coast chapter).

The paved road ends at Strawberry Fields, a small Rastafarian community that welcomes visitors wanting to experience the 'real' Jamaica. You can also reach Strawberry Fields from Port Maria by a hiking trial that leads along one of the few stretches of Jamaican coastline that remains pristine. Locals can lead you to remote Black Sand Beach, and the **Kwaaman and Tacky waterfalls**, where 100-foot falls plummet into deep pools surrounded by forest.

**Whitehall**, about 6 miles west of Don Christopher's Point, is a tiny village once known for its cast-iron pots, though these days most of the pots sold roadside are made of aluminum. It's at the junction with the B2, a rough and lonesome road that leads southwest over the mountains to Bog Walk and Spanish Town.

## Organized Tours

Ecotours for Cures (☎ 203-598-0400, 800-829-0918, fax 203-598-0164, Naturalalt@juno.com), PO Box 525, Oyster Bay, NY 11771, includes a stay at Strawberry Fields plus hikes to Kwamaan Falls during 10-day ecotours that also introduce participants to local knowledge on natural medicines (US$1875 including roundtrip airfare from New York).

## Places to Stay

A few local fishermen and small farmers rent homes. Ask around.

Try *Sonrise Beach Retreat* (☎/fax 999-7169, Sonrise, Robin's Bay PA, St Mary, sonrise@in-site.com, www.in-site.com/son rise), at Robin's Bay, immediately west of Mt

Pleasant Heights, which offers camping, and one and two-bedroom cabins. It specializes in 'peace, beauty, and adventure' and gets lively on weekends when it has a beach party. You can camp beneath the trees; tent sites cost US$15 (or US$10 single). There's a bath and shower complex, plus picnic tables and benches. Tents (US$5) and air mattresses (US$2) can be rented. Or stay in one of six standard cabins with two bunks and a double bed; the two-bedroom deluxe cabins have a kitchenette and loft bedroom. They cost US$50, or US$70 with a bath. Discounts are offered for three nights or more. A charming, two-bedroom 'honeymoon cottage' costs US$120 double and has its own little private beach. Packages are offered. Meals cost US$15 per day. A licensed physical therapist offers massage, and there's a yoga teacher nearby.

Sonrise, run by a charming couple, Kim and Robert Chase, is a serene, unpretentious spot, popular with families from Kingston on weekends (the clientele is mostly Jamaican, and it is popular with church groups). It nestles above a tiny cove with a pretty, pocket-size, golden-sand beach, with clear, shallow waters great for snorkeling. Robert leads eco-adventure tours to hidden waterfalls, and there's horseback riding and other excursions. At night a big campfire is built in a huge stone fireplace on the shore. It's marvelous! Jazz and spiritual music concerts and other special events are hosted. Meals are served in a gazebo restaurant. Day entry costs US$3.

*Bobby's*, next to Sonrise, is a Rasta's basic shack that you can rent for US$15.

About 400 yards west of Sonrise is the quaint, offbeat *River Lodge* (☎/fax 995-3003, *Robin's Bay PO, St. Mary*; ☎/fax 0561-886232, *Mrs Fuchslocher, Fladigenfeld 35, 34128 Kassel in Germany*), an atmospheric mill house on a century-old estate, with white-bleached stone walls, blood-red floors, and five spacious bedrooms lit by skylights for US$25 single, US$40 double. The bathrooms (cold water only) are festooned with climbing ivy. Meals are served in a small thatched restaurant in the courtyard (US$18 for breakfast and dinner). The place is run by Brigitta, who serves I-tal food and offers massage, bush hikes, and boat trips. There's volleyball on the lawn. The place is said to be haunted by the ghost of the Lady of the Manor.

### Places to Eat

Robin's Bay has several reasonably priced eateries, including *A&G Seaview Pastries & Fishstop*, *Miss Pearl's*, selling 'finger-licking jerk chicken,' and the *Front Line*, for ice cream, fish tea, and fried fish. The *Harbour Light Club* and *Sallas Lawn* are rustic entertainment centers that sell steamed fish and jerk for a few dollars. The Harbour Light Club has an old hits party every last Saturday of the month.

*Bobby's* (see Places to Stay, above) has its own health food restaurant serving breakfast (US$5), lunches, and dinner (US$6 to US$12).

*Churchill's* is a rustic I-tal restaurant you'll pass while hiking from Strawberry Fields.

You can also bargain for lobster and other seafood from local fishermen.

### Getting There & Away

Any of the buses between Ocho Rios and Annotto Bay or Port Antonio will let you off at the junction of the A3. It's a 4-mile walk to Robin's Bay. With good timing, you can connect with bus No JR16A, which operates between Kingston and Robin's Bay.

# Negril & West Coast

The stub-nosed west coast is divided through the middle by Jamaica's smallest and flattest parishes: Hanover to the north and Westmoreland to the south. Hanover is virtually undeveloped for tourism, although there's an intriguing museum at Blenheim and the vintage port city of Lucea is a living heritage museum of disheveled colonial facades slated for eventual restoration. In Westmoreland, an appealing countryside resort – Mayfield Falls – is in the heart of the Dolphin Head Mountains. The A1 snakes past lime green cattle pastures and sleepy fishing villages tucked teasingly into coves rimmed by mangroves, with nary a beach of much worth in sight – until you arrive at Negril, sliced through by the parish dividing line.

Negril is Jamaica's hippest, most casual resort, with the island's longest beach (perhaps its most beautiful) and a buzzing nightlife. Offbeat Negril nestles at the westernmost tip of Jamaica, with a grandstand seat for unrivaled sunsets. It also boasts superb coral reefs and excellent scuba diving, plus a large swamp area – the Great Morass – that is a naturalist's paradise with the promise to become an ecotour haven.

Negril's hinterlands are slowly emerging as a destination for cycling, horseback riding, and other 'alternative' experiences. The region's only other town of note – dirty, disheartening Savanna-la-Mar – offers little of sightseeing interest with the exception of a nearby gem: Roaring River.

## Highlights

- Negril, hands down the best spot for laid-back sunning by day and sinning by night
- Scuba diving off Negril
- Peaceful Royal Palm Preserve and the Great Morass, full of wildlife
- Mayfield Falls, for refreshing dips beneath cooling cascades
- Roaring River, for atmosphere and natural beauty

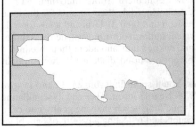

# Negril

Negril (population 3000), 52 miles west of Montego Bay, is Jamaica's fastest-growing resort and the vortex around which Jamaica's fun-in-the-sun vacation life whirls. Tourism is Negril's only industry. The village is so small, however, that hotel workers are drawn from miles around. Despite phenomenal growth in recent years, Negril is still more laid back than anywhere else in Jamaica (it has the only public nude beach in Jamaica), and you are more likely to interact with locals here than in other resort areas.

It's remarkable to think that only two decades ago you could walk a mile on the beach before chancing upon Man Friday footprints. What a pleasure it was to arrive in Negril in the mid-1970s, before the world had discovered this then-remote, sensual Eden. For one buck a night, you could sleep in a Rastafarian's hut beside the jungled shoreline, aided in slumber by thick clouds of ganja and the 'cheep-cheep' of geckos that call from the eaves. Back then Negril was an off-the-beaten-track haven: nirvana to the budget-minded, beach-loving crowd. It was a 'far-out' setting where you could drool over sunsets of hallucinogenic intensity that had nothing to do with the 'magic' mushrooms that still show up in omelettes and teas.

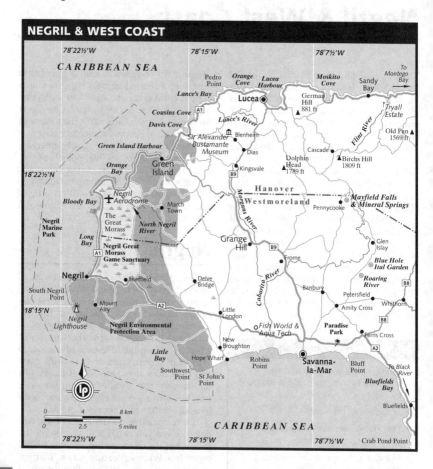

## NEGRIL & WEST COAST

Negril's innocence is long gone. The red-eyed hippies have been joined by neatly groomed youths who whiz about on rented motor scooters, often with a local lass or dreadlocked 'rent-a-Rasta' clinging tightly behind. Topless sunbathers lie semi-submerged on lounge chairs in the gentle surf. And it's impossible to avoid the entreaties of drug-dealing locals: *'Hey, Tom Jones. A likkle smoke for you, mon?'*

Compared to other resort towns, this is the 'real Jamaica,' permissive and unrestrained, drawing Negril devotees from abroad, among them counterculture types colloquially called 'Jahmericans' who put down ephemeral roots, mat their hair in dreadlocks, trade their accents for the local lexicon and their T-shirts and jeans for a de rigeur uniform of string-vest, tie-dyed shorts, and colored tam, and adopt their 'bredren's' barely disguised disdain for more uptight tourists.

You'll soon find yourself falling in love with Negril's insouciance and its scintillating 7-mile-long beach shelving gently into calm waters and reflecting a palette of light blues and greens. Coral reefs lie like a forest of gems just offshore. And you'll want your camera to record the consistently peach-colored sunsets that get more applause than the live reggae concerts for which Negril is equally famous.

## HISTORY

The Spanish called the bay and adjacent headland Punta Negrilla, referring to the black conger eels that used to proliferate in the local rivers. During the colonial era, pirates favored Negril's two bays for safe anchorage. Negril was perfectly situated for preying on Spanish treasure ships passing to and from Havana. And the English pirates, Sir John Hawkins and Sir Francis Drake, used the bay during the 16th century as a base from which to attack Villa de la Vega, the Spanish capital of Jamaica.

Port Royal later displaced Negril as Jamaica's pirate capital, but British naval armadas still used Bloody Bay as an assembly point. In 1702, a fleet under Admiral Benbow sailed from here for its disastrous engagement with a French invasion fleet under Admiral Jean du Casse. Likewise, in 1814 it was the point of departure for another ill-fated expedition – 50 British men-of-war carrying 6600 marines to storm New Orleans during the War of 1812 between England and the USA. A Yankee trader outran the British fleet and warned the defending American general, Andrew Jackson, of the attack. On January 8, 1815, the British were repulsed and lost 2000 lives in the battle.

Bloody Bay was used by 19th-century whalers who butchered their catch here (hence the name). The area languished, however, until the middle of this century.

Only in 1959 was a road cut from Green Island to what is now Negril Square, launching the development of what then was a tiny fishing village. Electricity and telephones came later. The sleepy beachfront village soon became a popular holiday spot for Jamaicans, who utilized the first modest hotels that appeared in the 1960s. About the same time, hippies and backpackers from abroad began to appear. They roomed with local families or slept on the beach, partook in ganja and magic mushrooms, and generally gave Negril its laid-back reputation. In 1977 the first major resort – Negril Beach Village (later renamed Hedonism II) – opened its doors to a relatively affluent crowd in search of an uninhibited Club Med-style vacation. Tales of Hedonism's toga parties and midnight nude volleyball games helped launch

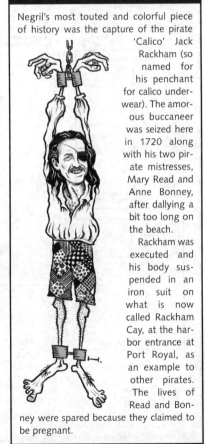

### 'Calico' Jack

Negril's most touted and colorful piece of history was the capture of the pirate 'Calico' Jack Rackham (so named for his penchant for calico underwear). The amorous buccaneer was seized here in 1720 along with his two pirate mistresses, Mary Read and Anne Bonney, after dallying a bit too long on the beach.

Rackham was executed and his body suspended in an iron suit on what is now called Rackham Cay, at the harbor entrance at Port Royal, as an example to other pirates. The lives of Read and Bonney were spared because they claimed to be pregnant.

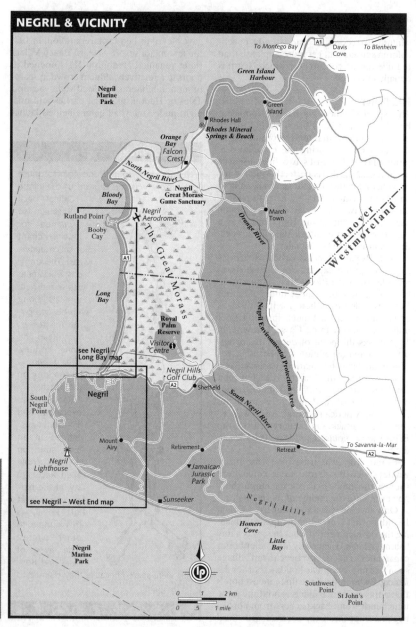

**NEGRIL & VICINITY**

To Montego Bay · A1 · Davis Cove · To Blenheim

*Green Island Harbour*

**Negril Marine Park**

Green Island

Rhodes Hall
*Rhodes Mineral Springs & Beach*

*Orange Bay*
Falcon Crest

*North Negril River*

**Negril Great Morass Game Sanctuary**

*Bloody Bay*

Rutland Point

Negril Aerodrome

Booby Cay

A1

**The Great Morass**

*Long Bay*

March Town

*Orange River*

**Negril Environmental Protection Area**

**Royal Palm Reserve**

Visitor Centre

see Negril – Long Bay map

Negril Hills Golf Club
A2 · Sheffield

*South Negril River*

**Negril**

South Negril Point

Mount Airy

Retirement

Retreat

To Savanna-la-Mar · A2

*Negril Lighthouse*

▼*Jamaican Jurassic Park*

see Negril – West End map

■ Sunseeker

*Negril Hills*

*Homers Cove*

*Little Bay*

**Negril Marine Park**

Southwest Point

St John's Point

Hanover / Westmoreland

0   1   2 km
0   .5   1 mile

NEGRIL & WEST COAST

Negril to fame. By the mid-1980s, Negril was in the throes of a full-scale tourism boom that continues today.

In 1993, mounting concern over the uncontrolled growth and pressure on local resources forced the Jamaican government to establish a two-year moratorium on new construction. The resort has since evolved an active, environmentally conscious spirit under the guidance of expat residents, resulting in the creation of the Negril Marine Park within the Negril Environmental Protection Area (see map), established in late 1997 as part of a broad-based management plan for the region. The park – the newest formalized national park in Jamaica – encompasses the shoreline, mangroves, offshore waters, and coral reefs. The area is being zoned into six environmental zones and eight recreational zones (see the Negril Marine Park Zones map).

Alas, the conservation ethic among the local populace remains weak. Crocodiles – although endangered and protected by law – are routinely killed or captured, usually with the expectation of a reward. And dynamite fishing – also illegal – continues to be widely practiced with devastating results: whole sections of reef are sometimes obliterated. Anyone with information about dynamite fishing should contact the NCRPS Marine Park Headquarters (☎ 957-3735, fax 957-4626).

## ORIENTATION

Negril is basically a one-street town divided in two by the South Negril River, with Long Bay to the north and West End to the south. The apex is Negril Village, which lies immediately south of the river and is centered on a small roundabout from which Norman Manley Blvd leads north, West End Rd leads south, and Sheffield Rd goes east and becomes the A2, then leads to Savanna-la-Mar, 19 miles away.

Long Bay is backed by the Great Morass swamp stretching inland for 2 miles.

### Long Bay

Long Bay and its blindingly white, 7-mile-long beach fringed by sea grapes and palms stretches north from the South Negril River.

Long Bay is paralleled by Norman Manley Blvd, a two-lane highway about 100 yards inland of the beach. There are no sidewalks, so be careful when walking the road; traffic whips past pell-mell. The road is lined with hotels, restaurants, and food shacks for almost its entire length, except for a half-mile section toward its northern end that has been set aside as Long Bay Beach Park (☎ 957-9828). The park has parking, a snack bar, changing rooms (US$1), lockers (US$1), and lounge-chair rentals (US$1). This area is popular for nude bathing.

The beach draws gigolos and hustlers proffering everything from sex to aloe massages and, always, 'sensi.' *'Pssst! Bredda, you want ganja? Negril de place to get high, mon!'* Tourist police now patrol the beach, but by law all Jamaican beaches must permit public access, so the hustlers are free to roam. A few hotels have built walls to keep the hustlers off their property, and most have security guards.

Water-sports concessions line the beach, particularly at the southern end, and the silence is broken by the thrum of flashing Jet Skis. By night this section is laden with the blast of reggae from disco bars and the unmistakable smell of ganja.

Long Bay is anchored to the north by the low rocky headland of Rutland Point. Beyond is a deeply scalloped cove, Bloody Bay, rimmed by a beautiful beach (though not as pretty as that of Long Bay). Negril's upscale all-inclusive resorts are all located here or on the north end of Long Bay.

There's a rather makeshift encampment of low-income housing behind the beach at its southern end. And narrow canoes made from large cotton trees are pulled up on the Bloody Bay beach in the early morning, when local fishermen bring in their catches of parrot fish, red snapper, and angel fish.

### Negril Village

Negril Village consists of two shopping plazas and a handful of banks and other commercial ventures, plus a few score of houses and wood-and-tin shacks that lie dispersed among the forested hills behind in an area known as Red Ground. There is no

# NEGRIL–LONG BAY

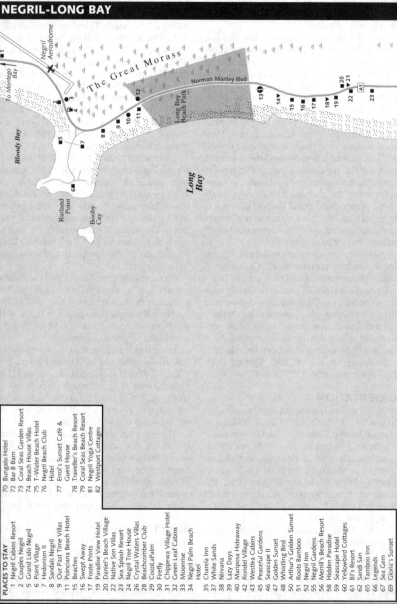

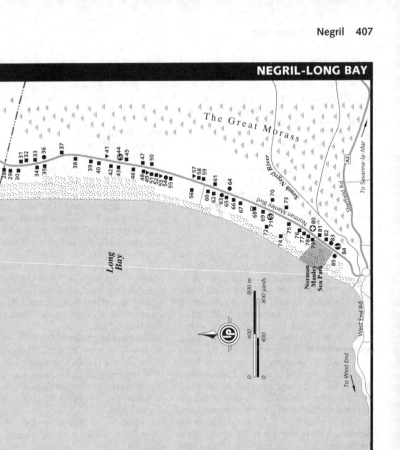

**NEGRIL-LONG BAY**

**PLACES TO EAT**
14 Cosmo's
18 Conch Hill Natural Food Place
21 Ossie's Shack
23 Tan-Yah's
27 Chances'
28 Gambino's Italian Restaurant
40 Ristorante da Gina Italiano
41 Cecile's Café
49 Fun Holiday Beach
53 Red Snapper Deli
54 Mr Slice Pizza
57 Blue Mountain Coffee Shop
65 Tamboo Inn
67 Kuyaba on the Beach
77 Errol's Sunset Café
81 Negril Yoga Centre

**OTHER**
3 Rutland Point
  Craft Center
4 Gas Station
10 Ray's Water Sports
12 Anancy Fun Park
13 JTB Information Booth
18 Blue Lagoon Country Club
25 Margueritaville
36 Christine's Country
43 Salmon's Bike Rentals
44 Century National Bank
49 Vernon's Car Rentals
52 Limits
54 Alfred's Ocean Palace
63 Risky Business
64 Times Square
66 Legends
68 De Buss
71 Timetrend
76 Negril Scuba Centre
78 Club Palm
80 Negril Minor Emergency Clinic
83 Caribic Vacations
84 JTB Tourist Information Booth
85 Negril Watershed Area
  & Coral Reef Conservation
  Project HQ, Negril Marine
  Park Office

town of Negril to speak of. The plazas (Coral Seas Plaza and Negril Plaza) lie immediately south of the roundabout and are fronted by Negril Square, a parking lot where taxis and touts hang out. Two other shopping plazas (King's Plaza and Sunshine Village) and the A Fi Wi Plaza crafts market (also called Negril Vendors Plaza) lie 200 yards west on West End Rd.

The Shell gas station, public health clinic, police station, market stalls, and taxis and buses line Sheffield Rd, which at day's end is thronged with honking traffic and hotel staff jostling for space on the buses.

## West End

A rocky limestone plateau rises south of the South Negril River and extends south for several miles. The area is known as the West End or 'the Rock,' and it plays second fiddle to the beach. The coral cliff top is indented with coves good for swimming in 15 feet of crystal-clear azure waters, providing a dramatic setting for dozens of small hotels and cottages, and restaurants built atop the rockface, which was the setting for scenes from *20,000 Leagues Under the Sea*, *Papillon*, and *Dr No*. You'll find a few pocket-size beaches at the northern end where fishing boats are drawn up, but swimming is not recommended.

Narrow West End Rd snakes south from Sunshine Village along the cliff top (be careful walking – it's narrow, with many blind corners and fast-moving vehicles). About a mile south, the road is renamed Lighthouse Rd, which leads past Negril Lighthouse, 3 miles south of Sunshine Village and beyond which it changes its name again to Ocean Drive. Ocean Drive runs through scrubland for 4 miles to the junction with William Hogg Blvd, which runs inland over the Negril Hills before dropping down to Sheffield Rd. Beyond the lighthouse, accommodations thin out, the cliffs gradually diminish, and southerly winds can whip up the sea.

The mood is more laid-back and less commercial than in Long Bay.

The unbelievably fiery sunsets seem even more stoked from the West End, and gathering at Rick's Café in the evening is a Negril tradition (though the place seems more contrived by the year). Negril's cliffs reach their highest point here (45 feet above the sea), providing opportunities for locals to earn a few dollars with daredevil leaps into the Caribbean.

## INFORMATION
### Tourist Offices

The Jamaica Tourist Board (JTB) office (☎ 957-4597, 957-4243, fax 957-4489) is in Shop 20 on the 2nd floor of Coral Seas Plaza (formerly Adrijan Plaza), on the southwest side of Negril Square. The staff is helpful and can provide information on excursions and hotel availability. The office is open 8:30 am to 4:30 pm Monday to Friday, 9 am to 1 pm Saturday.

The JTB also has visitor information booths at the Negril Crafts Market on Norman Manley Blvd; on West End Rd, south of the turnoff for Summerset Village (200 yards north of Rick's Café); and at Long Bay Beach Park.

The Negril Chamber of Commerce (NCC; ☎ 957-4067, fax 957-4591) publishes an annual *Negril Guide*, a comprehensive compendium that includes a useful map. You can pick it up at hotels or at the NCC office next to the post office (open 9 am to 4 pm Monday to Friday).

*Negril, Negril: Where to Stay, Dine and Party* is published twice yearly (irie@ execulink.com); it's available free at most hotels. Keep your eyes open, too, for *Negril Beat*, another free biannual guide.

### Money

There are several banks, all open 9 am to 2 pm Monday to Thursday, and until 4 pm Friday. The exception is Workers Bank (☎ 957-3001), in Negril Plaza, which is open 9:30 am to 2 pm weekdays and 9 am to noon on Saturday. Scotiabank (☎ 957-4236), fifty yards west of Negril Square, is the most central; the Century National Bank, a quarter way along Norman Manley Blvd, serves Long Bay.

All the banks have money-exchange counters and offer cash advances against Visa or MasterCard. On Norman Manley Blvd, you can also change money at Timetrend

(☎ 995-2538, 997-5655), a money-exchange bureau 20 yards south of De Buss. It's open 9 am to 5 pm weekdays and until 3:30 Saturday. The National Commercial Bank outlets (☎ 957-4117) have 24-hour ATMs, as does Scotiabank.

Most hotels can change money. It's best not to try to save a few pennies by changing money with hustlers near Coral Seas Plaza; rip-offs are frequent.

### Post & Communications

The post office is in King's Plaza on West End Rd. It's open 8 am to 5 pm Monday to Friday. Anticipate long lines.

Airpak Express (☎ 957-5051), at the Negril Aerodrome, handles UPS service, which delivers letters internationally (US$11 to the USA, for example), as well as packages. It also offers photocopy and fax services, as does the Negril Chamber of Commerce (see Tourist Offices, above).

You can make international calls from the main JTB office (the operator will monitor the time and you'll be charged accordingly); or from either the Cable & Wireless office (open 8 am to 4 pm weekdays, and 9 am to 4 pm Saturday) or Negril Calling Service (☎ 957-3212; open 9 am to 11 pm daily), both upstairs in Negril Plaza. Global Communications Network (also called the West End Calling Service; ☎ 957-0724), in the forecourt of the Bougainvillea Hotel on West End Rd, has similar services; it's open 10 am to noon and 2 to 4 pm Monday to Saturday. You can buy phone cards from the Cambio currency exchange (☎ 957-0612), next to Drumville Cove on West End Rd.

### Email & Internet Access

Global Communications Network also offers email service. Beingees Internet (www.negril .com) has a Negril message board and chat room; plus Fantasy Isle (www.fantasyisle .com) on Norman Manley Blvd.

### Internet Resources

A good starting point is www.negriljamaica .com. Also try www.mobay.com/town5.htm. (Some hotels have websites; see Places to Stay.)

### Travel Agencies

Advanced Travel Service (☎ 957-4057), upstairs in Negril Plaza, is the only full-service travel agency. Caribic Vacations (☎ 957-3309, fax 957-3208), on Norman Manley Blvd, can also make travel arrangements.

### Bookstores

Most hotel gift stores sell novels, magazines, and newspapers. Top Spot (☎ 957-4542), in Sunshine Village, is well stocked with international publications, and Ideal Stationery (☎ 957-3325), upstairs in Negril Plaza, has a limited range of newspapers and magazines.

### Library

Negril has a small library (☎ 957-4917) on West End Rd. It's open 10 am to 6 pm Monday, Tuesday, and Wednesday; 1 to 5 pm Thursday; and 10 am to 6 pm Friday.

### Laundry

Most hotels can arrange for laundry and dry-cleaning. Allow up to two days. You can have your dirties washed and ironed at West End Cleaners (☎ 957-0160), 20 yards behind Scotiabank. Laundry costs 50 cents per pound. Pants cost US$4; a shirt costs US$3 for 'dry-cleaning' (which here means hand-washed in cold water). There's also the Village Laundry (☎ 957-0165), behind Coral Seas Plaza. Any number of local women are willing to do your laundry for a lesser price.

### Medical Services

The Negril Minor Emergency Clinic (☎ 957-4888, fax 957-4347), on Norman Manley Blvd, is open 9 am to 5 pm weekdays. It can perform diagnostics, blood tests, and so on (the laboratory is open 9:30 am to 2 pm Tuesday and Friday). Dr Michael Clarke has a clinic (☎ 957-3047), next to Compulseion Disco in Negril Plaza. The clinic is open 8 am to 8 pm Monday to Friday and 9 am to 3 pm every other Saturday. And Dr Henry Blythe (☎ 957-4697) has a clinic at White Swans Plaza. Most clinics accept credit cards.

Your last resort is the Negril Health Centre (☎ 957-4926), 100 yards east of the Shell gas station on Sheffield Rd. It's a government

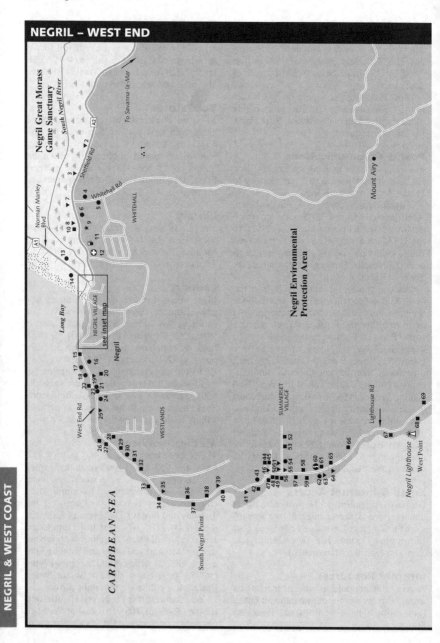

# NEGRIL – WEST END

Negril Great Morass Game Sanctuary

South Negril River

To Savanna-la-Mar

Norman Manley Blvd

Sheffield Rd

Whitehall Rd

WHITEHALL

Mount Airy

Negril Environmental Protection Area

Long Bay

NEGRIL VILLAGE
See inset map

Negril

West End Rd

WESTLANDS

SUMMERSET VILLAGE

Lighthouse Rd

South Negril Point

Negril Lighthouse

West Point

CARIBBEAN SEA

NEGRIL & WEST COAST

# NEGRIL – WEST END

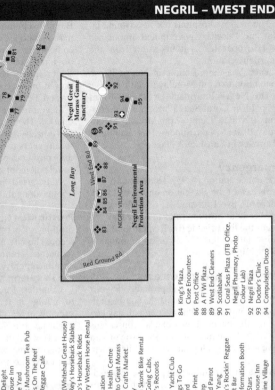

CARIBBEAN SEA

**PLACES TO STAY**
10 Up Front
15 Llanissant
20 Falcon Cottages
22 Negril Yacht Club
26 Heartbeat
27 Milestone Cute Cottages
28 Hotel Villa La Cage
29 Bougainvillea
31 La Mer Resort & Café
32 New Moon Cottages
33 Reefcliff Resort
34 Blue Cave Castle
36 Croton Grove Cottages
37 Hotel Samsara
38 Ocean Edge
40 Xtabi
42 Rockhouse
44 Thrills
45 Primrose Inn
47 Dreamscape Villa
48 Coral Seas Cliff Resort
49 Rock Cliff Resort
52 Addis Kokeb,
   New Star Guest
   House & Cottages
53 Summerset Village
56 Drumville Cove
57 Mariner's Inn & Dive
   Resort
58 Del Rose Villas
59 Tensing Pen
61 Banana Shout
65 Villas Sur Mer
66 Negril B&B
67 The Caves
68 Lighthouse Park
69 Lighthouse Inn
70 Sandy Cliff
73 Tingalaya's B&B
74 Caribbean Dream
75 Sunflower
76 Secret Paradise
77 Jackie's On The Reef
79 Hog Heaven
80 Ibis Too
81 Wendy Lindo's B&B
82 Sunseeker Hotel
83 Sunshine Village
   Apartment Hotel
85 Chris' Donbar Cottages
87 Cotton Tree Place
95 Chuckles

**PLACES TO EAT**
2 Miss Brown's
3 Tedd's One-Stop
7 Sweet Spice Restaurant
8 Country Man
19 Mr Slice Pizza
25 Chicken Lavish
35 Cheap Charlie's Kaffe
37 Hotel Samsara
39 Just Natural
40 Xtabi
41 Pickled Parrot
42 Smoke House, Rockhouse
   Restaurant & Bar
46 Archway Café
50 Hungry Lion
51 Bella Donna
53 Summerset Village
55 Roy & Felix
   Serious Chicken
56 Drumville Cove
63 Rick's Café
64 LTU Pub
66 Doc's Delight
69 Lighthouse Inn
71 Culture Yard
72 Sunset Mushroom Tea Pub
77 Jackie's On The Reef
78 Hard Reggae Café

**OTHER**
1 Ruins (Whitehall Great House)
4 Papa Rey's Horseback Stables
5 Brando's Horseback Rides
6 Country Western Horse Rental
9 Police
11 Gas Station
12 Negril Health Centre
13 Boats to Great Morass
14 Negril Crafts Market
16 Library
17 Indian Skonk Bike Rental
18 Easy-Going Cabs,
   Victor's Records
21 MXIII
22 Negril Yacht Club
23 Sarongs To Go
24 Mi Yard
30 Photo Print
35 Jus Jeep
41 Pickled Parrot
43 Yin & Yang
54 Garcia's Rockin' Reggae
57 Sunset Bar
60 JTB Information Booth
62 Twin Stars
69 Lighthouse Inn
83 Sunshine Village
84 King's Plaza,
   Close Encounters
86 Post Office
88 A Fi Wi Plaza
89 West End Cleaners
90 Scotiabank
91 Coral Seas Plaza (JTB Office,
   Negril Pharmacy, Photo
   Colour Lab)
92 Negril Plaza
93 Doctor's Clinic
94 Compulsion Disco

NEGRIL & WEST COAST

clinic offering free (but slow) treatment 9 am to 8 pm Monday to Friday.

The nearest hospitals are at Savanna-la-Mar and Lucea. A government ambulance (☎ 110) operates 24 hours a day from the Negril fire station.

There's a dental clinic in Negril Plaza, open noon to 6 pm Monday to Saturday.

The Negril Pharmacy (☎ 957-4076), at Shop 14 in Coral Seas Plaza, fills prescriptions. It's open 9 am to 7 pm Monday to Saturday, 10 am to 4 pm Sunday. There's another pharmacy in Sunshine Village.

### Emergency

The police station (☎ 957-4268) is about 200 yards east of the gas station on Sheffield Rd. There are two Tourism Liaison Officers, and a police boat now operates in Long Bay.

For the fire brigade (on Red Ground Rd), call ☎ 110 or 957-4242. For an ambulance, call ☎ 110.

### Dangers & Annoyances

**Sun & Heat** The sun will probably be your biggest headache, or at least the source of it. The temptation is great to spend all day lazing on the beach. Beware! Use sunscreens liberally. If you burn, for US$5 or so you can have a soothing aloe massage on the beach.

**Insects** The Great Morass provides a breeding ground for mosquitoes, but they're not usually a problem by the sea where the breezes blow. Inland, however, you'll be happy to have insect repellent.

**Hustlers & Drugs** The peskiest annoyance is the persistent importuning by touts trying to get you to buy from their stalls, rent a Jet Ski, or a dozen variants on the theme. Most irritating is the constant pitching of drugs, though the presence of tourist police patrol (they're the ones in navy blue fatigues and scarlet berets) has eradicated the most irascible trade. There's a ready market among travelers attracted by Negril's *laissez-faire* reputation. If drug use isn't your thing, the sales pitch can wear on the nerves. Cocaine and crack have appeared in recent years, and ganja is still a steadfast part of the Negril

scene. Tourists and locals alike smoke spliffs openly at concerts and even on the beach. Be more circumspect by day, as undercover narcotics police work the scene and have become more active in recent years. (In a famous incident in 1996, a private plane carrying singer Jimmy Buffet and the band U2 was shot at by the coast guard, which assumed it was on a drug-trafficking mission.)

If you're not interested, give a firm 'no thanks!' The Negril Chamber of Commerce and citizens' groups have taken measures in recent years to cut down on harassment by drug pushers, unlicensed vendors, and 'undesirable elements.' Even the hair braiders are now licensed and relegated to specified booths along the beach.

**Prostitution** Negril is permissive and prostitution is an established part of the local scene. The city attracts a plethora of young Jamaicans – both male and female – seeking an attachment with a dollar-rich foreigner, and short-term holiday liaisons are a staple.

Countless foreign women flock to Negril to indulge in the 'rent-a-Rasta' trade, presumably in search of a sexual adventure that might be considered taboo back home. The typical woman is young and white. Thus scores of Jamaican males – 'rastitutes' – pimp themselves to foreign females, bombarding

### Here's the Dope

Ganja is illegal in Jamaica. Though it's smoked in plain view in Negril, undercover police agents are present, and rarely a day goes by without one or more visitors being arrested.

I've heard reports of tourists suffering harmful or disturbing side effects from ganja or mushrooms, especially from ganja cakes. This is also true of hallucinogenic wild mushrooms, which are legal and grow wild in cow pastures (psilocybin is the active agent). Apparently, drinking alcohol while on mushrooms can induce a 'bad trip.'

women visitors with well-honed lines enticing you to sample some 'Jamaican steel.' It can be wearying if you have no interest.

Female prostitutes are no less forward. Male tourists walking alone are almost sure to be approached, often by a hissing sound: '*pssstt!*' Discos are also favored pick-up spots.

Negril's hoteliers have a far more laissez-faire attitude to these relationships than hoteliers in other resort towns. Most hotels permit you to bring whomever you wish to your room, but they frown on unregistered guests, which usually means you'll have to pay an 'extra guest' charge. Alternately, a discreet tip to the security staff is often what's called for.

(Also see Prostitution in the Dangers & Annoyances section of the Facts for the Visitor chapter.)

**Crime** There is plenty of opportunistic theft. Take particular care of items left on the beach. Burglary is common in budget and mid-range properties. And muggings occur, though infrequently. At night, take a taxi rather than walking long distances on the dimly lit roads (at press time, the Negril Chamber of Commerce was planning to install solar lights along the beach). I've also heard of at least two hotel robberies in which tourists were robbed at gunpoint; never open your hotel door to strangers without ascertaining their identity.

**Crazy Drivers** In Negril, Jamaican males seem to be particularly affected by a need for bravado. Beware! They fly down Norman Manley Blvd and West End Rd with total disdain for other drivers or pedestrians. Neither road has a sidewalk, and West End Rd has many sharp bends. If you take a cab, don't let the driver risk your life as well as his. Order him to slow down.

## NEGRIL LIGHTHOUSE
You won't find much of historical interest in Negril, but the gleaming-white, 66-foot-tall lighthouse (3 miles south of Negril Village on West End Rd) is a worthy place to check out. At 18° 15' north, 78° 23' west, it illuminates the westernmost point of Jamaica.

Negril lighthouse, Jamaica's westernmost point

CHRISTOPHER P BAKER

The lighthouse, erected in 1894 with a prism made in Paris, was powered by kerosene until 1956, when it was replaced by acetylene. It has been solar powered since 1985, and flashes every two seconds. The lighthouse is built atop a tank of pressurized water, which acts as a shock absorber in the event of infrequent earthquakes.

You can visit the lighthouse free of charge. It's open 9 am to sunset daily. Wilson Johnson, the superintendent, will gladly lead the way up the 103 stairs for a bird's-eye view of the coast. Don't touch the brass fittings, however, or Wilson will chew your head off. It is a common courtesy to tip.

A small brass cannon sits on the grounds. Also note the two huge, bulbous silk-cotton trees at the gate.

A precarious wooden ladder leads down to a beautiful cove good for basking.

## BOOBY CAY
This small coral island lies half a mile offshore from Rutland Point. It was used as a South Seas setting in the Walt Disney movie *20,000 Leagues Under the Sea*. The island is named for the colony of blue-footed booby birds that nest here. Unfortunately, the bird population is endangered following years of egg collecting by local fishermen.

**NEGRIL & WEST COAST**

Boat shuttles operate from the all-inclusive resorts at the north end of Long Bay. Watersports concessionaires can arrange boats for about US$20 roundtrip.

## THE GREAT MORASS

Behind the shore of Long Bay, a virtually impenetrable 2-mile-wide swamp of mangroves – the Great Morass – stretches 10 miles from the South Negril River to Orange Bay. The swamp, said to be the remnant of a primeval forest, is the island's second-largest freshwater wetland system and forms a refuge for endangered waterfowl. American crocodiles still cling to life here and are frequently seen at the mouth of the North

---

### The Fragile Coral Reefs

Negril's offshore reefs provide a habitat for over 1000 species of coral, fish, sponges, and other fauna in the near-shore waters. They have been severely damaged by the resort boom and human tinkering with the Great Morass.

Reef restoration is an important part of the NEPA project, and pilot projects were established early on at Banana Shout and Tensing Pen hotels on Lighthouse Rd. Both are sites for artificial coral cultivation. Unfortunately, nothing can be done to bring back the marine turtles that once favored the beach for nesting. A coral reef monitoring program has been established within the boundaries of the Negril Marine Park, officially declared in March 1998.

Scientists recently identified Long Bay as 'one of the most nutrient-stressed tropical marine environments in the world.' The percentage of live coral cover is now so low (6%) that further coral loss could seriously threaten the functioning of the entire ecosystem. The culprit? Poor water quality. Nutrients delivered into the bay by runoff from the watershed are feeding algae that suffocate and starve the corals.

The Negril Coral Reef Preservation Society (NCRPS) has established a code of conduct for snorkelers and scuba divers:

- **Don't touch the puffer fish!** This removes their protective mucous film that prevents infection.
- **Don't turn over rocks.** They form homes for many species.
- **Don't remove or kill long-spined black urchins.** They serve a good cause by controlling algae and are themselves recovering from a devastating virus.
- **Don't catch or purchase lobster between April 1 and June 30.** This is the lobster's peak reproductive time.

Other NCRPS projects include demarcation of a swimmers' lane 300 feet from shore along the beach, and designating areas for Jet Skiing, waterskiing, parasailing, and anchoring large boats. Local children are also being trained as Junior Environmental Rangers and educated to care for the environment they will inherit.

The NCRPS (☎ 957-3735, fax 957-4626, coralreefs@cwjamaica.com), PO Box 27, Negril, Westmoreland, publishes a quarterly newsletter, *Negril Reef Rap*, which you can receive by becoming a member (US$15 per year). The NCRPS headquarters is in the community center, in the car park at the Negril Crafts Market on Norman Manley Blvd.

Divers can help in environmental surveys by joining a Reef Census. Participation for one week costs US$1107, including airfare from Miami and accommodations at the Reefcliff Resort. Contact Phil Carta (☎ 888-437-8456, phil@newadventures.com).

Negril River. No one seems sure if endangered manatees still inhabit the swamp, whose waters are stained a sickly tea color by tannins from the underlying peat that, during the hottest times of year, often bursts into spontaneous combustion.

In 1958, the Norman Manley administration set up the ineffectual Negril Land Authority to drain the 6000-acre morass and develop it as part of the Peat Mining for Energy Project. Excavations in the 1950s washed sediments out to sea, killing large portions of the reef system. The coral has grown back, but the reefs remained at the forefront of an ecological battle between conservationists and the government-owned Petroleum Corporation of Jamaica (PCJ), which wanted to mine the peat. Local opposition to the project gained international support, and the project was shelved in 1987.

Drainage channels cut into the swamp have lowered the water levels, and as a result, water quality has deteriorated. Sewage, pesticides, and other commercial byproducts have seeped into the region's shallow water table, making their way to sea where they have poisoned the coral reefs and depleted fish stocks.

The Great Morass is critical to the Negril environment. It acts like a giant sponge and filters the waters flowing down to the ocean from the hills and mountains east of Negril. It's also a source of much-needed freshwater. During the past two decades, Negril's meteoric, unplanned development has resulted in severe water shortages, alleviated in recent years by construction of a water desalination plant. The creation of the Negril Environmental Protection Area (NEPA) is considered essential to protecting the area's fragile watershed.

Locals have been slow to utilize the Great Morass for tourism, but the creation of the Negril conservation area has provided a focus on natural attractions away from the beach. At press time, the area was on the verge of being declared the Great Negril Morass National Park or Nature Reserve (it was gazetted in August 1997 as the Negril Great Morass Game Sanctuary, where no bird shooting or hunting is permitted).

## Royal Palm Reserve

This 177-hectare reserve (☎ 1-816-9150 cellular), at the southern end of the Great Morass, was created by the PCJ in 1989 to protect the largest population of native 'swamp cabbage palm' (*Roystonea princeps*, or 'morass royal'), which is locally – and mistakenly – called the Royal palm (that title belongs to a species of Cuban palm). Ospreys and sea hawks use the palms for vantage points, and the reserve is a home for the Jamaica parakeet and Jamaica woodpecker. The reserve lay idle for years until 1998 when a Kingstonian entrepreneur – Kenny Benjamin – leased it for development as a wildlife park. Benjamin plans to reintroduce crocodiles and introduce flamingos, tarpon, and possibly manatees, as well as offer fishing.

Wooden boardwalks make a mile loop through a fascinating array of vegetation. Three distinct swamp forest types are present: the Royal Palm forest (covering 81 hectares), buttonwood forest, and bull thatch forest – home to butterflies galore and doctorbirds, herons, egrets, and endangered black parakeets and countless other birds flitting about – almost at arm's reach. Two observation towers provide views over the tangled mangroves, African tulip trees, and stands of blue mahoe that blooms yellow to blood-red.

Illegal logging still takes place in the reserve due to insufficient monitoring (believe it or not, the palms are mulched down to make diapers). The Negril Area Environmental Protection Trust (NEPT) plans to develop it as a center for ecotourism, and is campaigning to make the reserve a national park.

Send a signed letter of support to the Negril Coral Reef Protection Society (NCRPS; see 'Fragile Coral Reefs').

It's open sunrise to sunset year-round (the visitor's center is open 8:30 am to 4 pm). Guided tours – starting at 10 am – cost US$5. The guides (relatively short on knowledge about local ecology) were to receive formal training. There's also a snack bar.

Signs lead to the reserve from the main road. The turnoff is about 400 yards beyond Cool Runnings Entertainment Centre, a

## Negril Environmental Protection Area

This protected wilderness zone, the first of its kind in Jamaica, has come to fruition after years of lobbying by local conservationists.

The conservation area extends from Green Island on the north coast to St John's Point (south of Negril) and inland to the Fish River and Orange Hills. It also includes a marine park extending out to sea. The intention is to protect the entire Negril watershed, including the Great Morass swampland and all land areas that drain into the Caribbean between Green Island and Salmon Point. One of the area's best remaining fish-nursery grounds and the area's most extensive remaining mangrove forest are included, and future hotel construction will be controlled. Once approved, the conservation area will be managed by the NEPT, made up of community activists.

The NCRPS, formed in 1990, spearheaded initial conservation efforts (see 'Fragile Coral Reefs' for contact information) and received a J$22 million (US$620,000) grant from the European Union for hiring and training rangers, community education, mariculture projects, coral reef restoration, water-quality monitoring, placement of zoning and reef-mooring buoys, and the creation of a central sewage system considered vital to the project's success.

The Negril Environmental Protection Area (NEPA) was declared in November 1997, incorporating a Negril Marine Park (established in March 1998 and extending from the mouth of the Davis Cove River in the north to that of the New Savannah River in the south). It embraces uplands, morass, shoreline, offshore lagoon, and reefs, and – of course – the local peoples living within the Negril Watershed (the area drained by the Orange, Fish, Newfound, North Negril, and South Negril rivers). The NEPA plan establishes guidelines for tourism growth. The various agencies involved have established moratoriums on further cutting or draining of mangrove or wetland areas, and are presently setting up 'fish management zones,' providing new sewage systems for outlying communities, and establishing tourism-related activities that will take advantage of the evolving preservation ethic.

For a copy of the *Negril Environmental Protection Plan*, contact NEPT (☎ 957-3736, fax 957-3115), Negril PO, Westmoreland.

mile east of the golf course. After 200 yards, turn left at the Y-fork.

The reserve also has a Kingston office (☎ 978-5760, fax 927-7539), 107 Old Hope Rd, Kingston 6.

### Touring the Great Morass

Caribic Vacations and other local tour operators run trips to the reserve (see Organized Tours, later in this chapter). To explore the Morass outside the Royal Palm Reserve, negotiate with villagers who have boats moored along the South Negril River, or with fishermen at Norman Manley Sea Park, at the north end of Bloody Bay. Alternately, check with Derek at Roots Bamboo (☎ 957-4479), who arranges boat trips. It costs approximately US$35 for two hours.

In 1998, NEPT was planning to introduce bicycle trips into the hills east of Negril, plus boat tours up the North Negril River.

### NUDE BATHING

Topless bathing is common all along the Negril shoreline. A small section of public beach near Cosmo's Restaurant is a favorite of nudists, as is Booby Cay. Hedonism II, Grand Lido, Couples Negril, and Point Village resorts all have nude beaches.

### WATER SPORTS

The waters off Negril are usually mirror-calm – ideal for all kinds of water sports. The beach shelves so gently into the calm waters that you can wade out to the coral reef. Snorkeling is particularly good at the southern end of Long Bay and off the West End, where plentiful coves and deep lagoons with crystalline waters offer excellent coral reefs. Dozens of concession stands along the beach rent masks and fins, as well as Jet Skis and waterskiing equipment. Expect to pay US$5 an hour for snorkeling equipment, and US$10 to US$15 an hour for sailboards and Sunfish.

Jet Skis can be rented along the beach. Try Ray's Water Sports (☎ 957-4349).

## Sea Kayaking

Negril Kayak Tours (☎ 957-4474), at the Mariner's Inn on West End Rd, offers guided sea-kayaking tours to hidden beaches on the south coast.

## Banana Boat Rides

On Long Bay, Irie Watersports (☎ 957-4670) has banana-boat rides – an inflatable raft shaped like a banana and towed by a speedboat. It's great fun, a sort of bucking bronco ride with a cushioned seat instead of a saddle.

## Parasailing

If a bird's-eye view of Negril sounds good, try parasailing (being harnessed to a parachute and towed aloft by a speedboat). Ray's Water Sports (☎ 957-4349), Aqua-Nova Water Sports (☎ 957-4420, 957-4323) at the Negril Beach Club Hotel and Arthur's Ocean Palace; and Pringle's Watersports (☎ 957-4893) offer parasailing on Long Bay.

## SCUBA DIVING

Negril's extensive offshore reef and its coral cliffs with grottoes make it a leading scuba-diving center. Visibility often exceeds 100 feet, and seas are dependably calm, with an unusually high level of marine life. Most dives are in 35 to 75 feet of water. (Also see the Outdoor Activities chapter.)

There are several sites of interest:

Aweemaway, a shallow reef area south of the Throne, has tame stingrays that may allow you to stroke them.

Coral Gardens is a shallow near-shore dive (also good for snorkeling).

Deep Plane is the remains of a Cessna airplane lying at 70 feet in Bloody Bay. Corals and sponges have taken up residence in and around the plane, attracting an abundance of fish, including deadly scorpion fish. Nurse sharks hang out at a nearby overhang. Nearby Shallow Plane is another good dive site.

Sands Club Reef lies in 35 feet of water in the middle of Long Bay. From here, a drift dive to *Shark's Reef* leads through tunnels and overhangs with huge sponges and Gorgonian corals. Placid nurse sharks, moray eels, and spotted eagle rays are commonly seen.

The Throne is a 50-foot-wide cave with massive sponges, plentiful soft corals, nurse sharks, octopi, barracuda, and stingrays.

**Organized Dives** Sundivers Jamaica has a five-star PADI facility at the Poinciana Beach Hotel (☎ 957-4069) and Rock Cliff Resort (☎ 957-4834). PADI certification and introductory 'resort courses' are offered by the following:

Blue Whale Divers
   (☎ 957-4438)
Dolphin Divers
   Negril Gardens (☎ 957-4944)
Mariner's Dive Centre
   (☎ 957-0392, Mariners@infochan.com)
Marine Life Divers
   (☎ 957-4834)
Negril Scuba Centre
   (☎/fax 957-4425, 800-818-2963, neg.scuba
   .centre@cwjamaica.com, www.jamaica-irie.com)
   PO Box 49, at the Negril Beach Club Hotel
Reef Keeper Divers
   (☎ 979-0102)
Resort Divers Swept Away
   (☎ 957-4061)
Scuba World – Orange Bay
   Poinciana Beach Resort (☎ 957-5100)

Expect to pay US$30 to US$50 for introductory one-tank and night dives, and US$300 to US$400 for PADI Open-Water certification.

Some operators also rent underwater video cameras for US$40. The Negril Scuba Centre rents 35mm underwater cameras for US$25. All rent wet suits and equipment. Most all-inclusive resorts have scuba facilities.

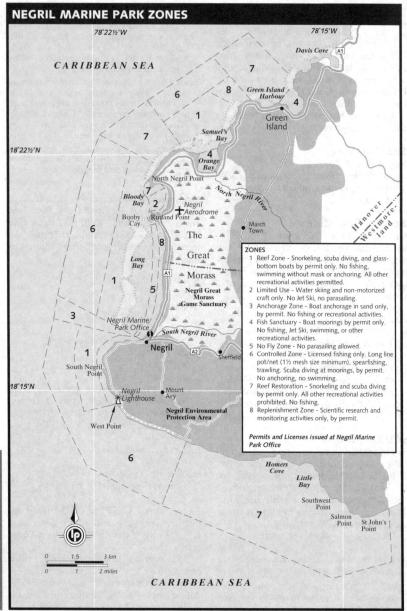

# NEGRIL MARINE PARK ZONES

*CARIBBEAN SEA*

78°22½'W
78°15'W

Davis Cove  A1

7

6
8

1
Green Island Harbour  4

7
Green Island

*Samuel's Bay*

18°22½'N

4
*Orange Bay*

North Negril Point

*North Negril River*

*Bloody Bay*  7
2

Booby Cay  Rutland Point

Negril Aerodrome

March Town

8

The Great Morass

*Long Bay*

6

1

A1

5

**Negril Great Morass Game Sanctuary**

3

Negril Marine Park Office

South Negril River

1

**Negril**  A2

Sheffield

South Negril Point

18°15'N

*Negril Lighthouse*

Mount Airy

**Negril Environmental Protection Area**

West Point

*Hanover*  *Westmore-*  *land*

**ZONES**

1  **Reef Zone** - Snorkeling, scuba diving, and glass-bottom boats by permit only. No fishing, swimming without mask or anchoring. All other recreational activities permitted.
2  **Limited Use** - Water skiing and non-motorized craft only. No Jet Ski, no parasailing.
3  **Anchorage Zone** - Boat anchorage in sand only, by permit. No fishing or recreational activities.
4  **Fish Sanctuary** - Boat moorings by permit only. No fishing, Jet Ski, swimming, or other recreational activities.
5  **No Fly Zone** - No parasailing allowed.
6  **Controlled Zone** - Licensed fishing only. Long line pot/net (1½ mesh size minimum), spearfishing, trawling. Scuba diving at moorings, by permit. No anchoring, no swimming.
7  **Reef Restoration** - Snorkeling and scuba diving by permit only. All other recreational activities prohibited. No fishing.
8  **Replenishment Zone** - Scientific research and monitoring activities only, by permit.

*Permits and Licenses issued at Negril Marine Park Office*

*Homers Cove*

*Little Bay*

Southwest Point

7

Salmon Point

St John's Point

0    1.5    3 km
0    1    2 miles

*CARIBBEAN SEA*

## SPORT FISHING

Stanley's Deep Sea Fishing (☎ 957-0667) offers custom fishing trips with hourly and half-day rates. For a more offbeat experience, head out into the briny with a local fisherman; ask around by the bridge over South Negril River, or with the fishermen near North Negril River. Women should not go on such a fishing trip unaccompanied.

Anancy Fun Park rents paddleboats (US$8 per hour) and tackle for fishing on large ponds adjacent to the Great Morass, where tilapia and perch can be hooked or netted (US$2 per pound).

Another option is to charter a boat for a fishing trip. Good charters include the following:

| | |
|---|---|
| Blue Whale Divers | ☎ 957-4438 |
| Dolphin Divers | ☎ 957-4944 |
| *Sea Raider,* Our Past Time Villas | ☎ 957-4224 |

## BOAT CRUISES

Several companies offer two and three-hour excursions daily aboard yachts and catamarans. Most trips include snorkeling and plenty of booze, but don't mix the two!

You'll find boats lining Long Bay, including *Wild Thing,* a 52-foot cat that offers day and sunset cruises for US$35 including lunch or a light meal from Chances (also called Wild Things Watersports Long Bay; ☎ 957-3977, 957-5392). And *Montrose II* offers a day or sunset 'Wet'n'Wild Cruise Party' for US$30.

Aqua-Nova Water Sports (☎ 957-4323, fax 957-4754, gaynair@hotmail.com) at the Negril Beach Club Hotel has a three-hour island picnic (10:30 am) and a sunset cruise (3:30 pm) daily aboard the *Eclipse,* plus a lunchtime party cruise to Booby Cay. Each cruise costs US$35. The *Checkmate* (☎ 957-4218), a 68-foot yacht, hosts a two-hour sunset cruise at 4 pm daily for US$20, including hotel pickup. *Reggae II* also sets sail at 4 pm daily from Bloody Bay on a sunset cruise.

Glass-bottom boat rides are a great way to see the fish life and coral if you hate getting wet. There are several to choose from, including Best Boat Reef Tours (☎ 957-3357). In the West End, glass-bottom boat rides are offered from the little beach near Heartbeat hotel.

## GOLF

The Negril Hills Golf Club (☎ 957-4638, 957-0221, fax 957-0222) is a 220-acre facility that's landscaped into the base of the Negril Hills at Sheffield, 3 miles east of Negril. The 18-hole, par 72 course borders the Great Morass. This course opened in 1994 and features undulating fairways, water hazards, and swampy surrounds. If you plop your ball in the water, forget it – the crocodiles probably got to it first! There's a clubhouse, a pro shop, and a restaurant. A hilltop villa resort and great house are planned. The green fee is US$58. Carts are mandatory and cost US$35. Caddies cost US$14, club rentals are US$17.

## HORSEBACK RIDING

Babo's Riding Stable, near Sandals, offers lessons and two-hour rides for US$25 into the Negril Hills and the ruins of Whitehall Great House. Babo bills himself as the 'Rasta Cowboy.' Country Western Horse Rental (☎ 957-3250), next to the police station on Sheffield Rd, charges US$30 for rides. Rides are available 8 am to 5 pm daily. Papa Rey's Horseback Stables (☎ 957-4474) and Brando's Horseback Rides, both on Whitehall Rd, also offer guided two-hour rides for US$25. Rhodes Mineral Springs & Beach (☎ 957-4258) has two-hour rides for US$30 at 7 and 10 am, and 1 and 3 pm, including hotel transfers.

## BICYCLING

X-cellent Adventures, a Negril-based company, reportedly offers off-road mountain biking along goat paths and rugged adventure trails using 15-geared, knobby-tired bikes. Not for the faint of heart!

Bike-rental specialists in Negril include the following:

| | |
|---|---|
| Banmark Bike Rental | ☎ 957-0196 |
| Dependable Bike Rental | ☎ 957-4764 |
| DT Bike Rental | ☎ 957-0014 |
| Jah B's Bike Rental | ☎ 957-4235 |
| Rambo Bike Rental | ☎ 957-4711 |
| Salmon's Bike Rental | ☎ 957-4671 |
| Wright's Bike Rental | ☎ 957-4908 |

## ORGANIZED TOURS

Trips to the Royal Palm Reserve are a marvelous option, and bicycle and horseback rides into the Negril Hills are becoming popular. Otherwise, there's not much to see or do locally. The most popular excursions are to Roaring River, Blue Hole, or Mayfield Falls in the west coast region, or farther afield to YS Falls, the Black River Great Morass (not to be confused with Negril's Great Morass), and the Appleton Rum Estate (see the Southwest Coast chapter).

The biggest name in town is Caribic Vacations (☎ 957-3309, fax 957-3208), on Norman Manley Blvd. The agency has local trips into the Negril Hills for US$30, plus jeep tours to the Royal Palm Reserve for US$80, including lunch and a river swim at Paradise Park; and to Mayfield Falls for US$50. It also has a full-day Black River Safari including a visit to YS Falls and the rum factory at Appleton for US$75, plus other trips to farflung spots. It's open 9 am to 6 pm weekdays, and 10 am to 1 pm weekends. Caribic Vacations also specializes in tours to Cuba (see '¡Cuba Si!' in the Montego Bay & Northwest Coast chapter).

Iyoni and Uthman Nicholson run Rasta Mountain Eco-Adventures (☎ 956-9092), at Green Island, offering guided hikes into the bamboo forests and hills east of the Great Morass. You'll learn about Rasta living and swim in mountain streams.

Tropical Tours (☎ 957-4110) offers a range of tours to Dunn's River Falls, Rose Hall, and Belvedere Estate. JUTA Tours (☎ 957-9197), at Negril Crafts Market, offers a range of excursions. Mr Tour Man (☎ 990-9608), near De Buss bar, also runs local trips, plus tours to YS Falls and Black River; it's open 8 am to 10 pm. And Irie Tours (☎ 957-5555) offers a guided scooter excursion for US$70 single (US$110 double) to Mayfield Falls.

## SPECIAL EVENTS

Negril has relatively few special events. The Bob Marley Birthday Bash is hosted each February 6, when top reggae stars perform at MXIII, a concert venue in the West End.

If you want to see the resort at its liveliest, visit in mid-March during the Negril Music Festival (☎ 968-9356), when leading Jamaican and international reggae stars, calypso artists, and other musicians perform for three nights.

The annual Jamaica Beachfest – a four-day excuse to *paaarrty!* – is held each mid-April and features live music, plenty of booze, and wet T-shirt and bikini contests. Anyone is welcome to show. In a similar vein, the Negril Carnival (☎ 957-4220) is held in May and features a float parade, concerts, soca party, competitions, and dancing.

The Negril Spring Triathlon is held each January at the Swept Away resort's sports complex (☎ 957-4040). The event comprises a half-mile swim, 15-mile cycle race, and a 3-mile run. Alfred's Ocean Palace, on Norman Manley Blvd, holds an annual volleyball tournie in January.

The Negril West End Reggae Festival, first held in 1993, has met a demise.

The weeklong African Dance and Drum Retreat is held in mid-October at Negril Tree House (☎ 957-4287) with master drummers from the USA and Jamaica. Contact Rainbow Travel (☎ 957-4287, 957-4386, 516-378-9110 in USA), Negril Tree House, PO Box 29.

## PLACES TO STAY

Negril boasts a dizzying kaleidoscope of hostelries. There's a good selection of budget properties and several places cater to campers.

Many of the hotels and restaurants are operated by foreigners who arrived in the early days and fell under a spell from which they could never escape. The tradition of cottages lingers, though they're no longer cheap. Most of the funky shacks have evolved into guest houses, and the guest houses into hotels, which continue to multiply. A strict building code has kept the resorts from growing taller than the tousled palm trees that rise majestically over the beach. South of the village, hotels continue to spread beyond the lighthouse where the gaps are gradually being filled in.

Negril has few guest houses. Hotels given below are listed within each price range from north to south beginning at Bloody Bay.

In general, beach properties are more expensive than hotels of equivalent standard in the West End. The most exclusive properties congregate at the northern end of Long Bay. Rates quoted are for summer (low season) unless otherwise noted. Winter (high season) rates can be 20% to 60% higher.

Because electricity supply is sometimes interrupted, hotels provide candles in your room. Locate them when you check in, but note that they're not there for romantic nights.

In the USA, Vacation Hotline (☎ 773-880-0030, 800-325-2485) acts as a reservation agent for over 50 properties in Negril.

Prices below do not include hotel tax unless stated.

## Places to Stay – Budget

**Camping** On the Long Bay beach, *Roots Bamboo (☎ 957-4479, c/o Ted Plummer, Negril PO, Westmoreland)* is one of the most popular options, close to all the action, and gets fairly busy. It has a communal shower block. A two-person site is US$16. Tent rental costs US$2. Roots has a small beachside bar and restaurant with pool tables. Also check out *Westport Cottages* (see Hotels, below), where you can camp in the yard for US$6, and use the well-stocked kitchen; and *Seascape II (☎ 957-9225)*, a short distance north. You can camp here for US$10 double, with kitchen facilities, water, outside toilets, and security.

*Peaceful Gardens (☎ 957-9659)* has camping for US$10 per tent with outdoor showers and toilets.

At West End, *New Moon Cottages (☎ 957-4305)* has camping beneath shade trees on rough ground atop the coral cliffs for US$5 per person. There are basic toilets, plus water. *Addis Kokeb* (see below) is planning campsites.

Also atop the cliffs are *One-stop Camping*, with sites for US$10, and *Lighthouse Park (☎ 957-0252, PO Box 3)*, just south of the lighthouse. Lighthouse Park offers tent sites, communal toilets, and cold showers in nicely kept grounds for US$15 for one or two people, US$2.50 additional. No children are allowed.

**Guest Houses** *Errol's Sunset Café & Guest House (☎ 957-3312)*, on Norman Manley Blvd, has 10 cabins with private bath and hot water for US$55 high season (US$10 more with air-con).

There's a true gem in the hills proper: *Wendy Lindo's B&B (☎ 1-999-5793 cellular, fax 957-4591, Westcliff Gardens, Negril PO)*, a quaint guest house that's a great bargain at US$50 double, including breakfast (or US$500 for two weeks). Wendy, an expat from the Isle of Scilly, offers three rooms (two share a bath) in her charming house – a little piece of England built atop a coral outcrop with views slanting down over the forest to the ocean. Her cottage is full of antiques and cozy couches, frilly curtains, and porcelain china. Guests have full use of the house. The clean, airy rooms have private patios, ceiling fan, screened windows, and hot water. Drip-feed hangers attract hummingbirds. The house is on Beaver Ave, about 8 miles south of Negril, off William Hogg Blvd. Airport transfers are offered (US$50 each way). Wendy's husband, John, also offers a taxi service.

**Hotels – Long Bay** *Green Leaf Cabins (☎ 957-4677)*, opposite Chippewa Village Hotel, offers 10 basic two-story cabins with patios (some with private bath), which run from US$20 to US$35. Two villas are available; rates are US$60 to US$70.

The Italian-run *Mariposa Hideaway (☎ 957-3167)* is a twee place with rooms for US$20 per person low season, US$25 high season; plus bungalows with kitchenette, TV, and fans for US$60 low season, US$80 high season. Family-size apartments cost US$120 low season, US$150 high season. It has a restaurant.

A popular no-frills favorite of budget travelers is *Westlea Cabins (☎ 957-4422)*. Its 18 skimpily furnished wooden cabins are clean but overpriced at US$60 high season. Smaller units, sharing outside toilets in scruffy grounds, cost US$45.

*Seascape II (☎ 957-9225)* has nine tiny rooms – basic but clean – for US$20. Another popular option is *Roots Bamboo (☎ 957-4479)*, with 32 soulless but well-kept cabins right on the beach. Some have showers; others share a communal shower block with campers. Rates are US$30 to US$40 double, US$50 with a porch and shower, and US$70 with air-con. There's a small beachside bar and restaurant with pool tables. *BJ's Resort* (☎ 957-4744), south of Seascape II, also has eight small, basic cabins with patios in the same price range.

*Yellowbird Cottages* (no telephone) has four cottages (each with four beds; US$50 low season) plus eight rooms for US$35 and US$45 in low-season; US$45 and US$65 in high season. All are simply furnished, with wicker furniture, ceiling fans, and a refrigerator.

Don't make a decision until you've checked out the eight very rustic yet charming rooms and cottages that make up the *Negril Yoga Centre* (☎ 957-4397, 813-263-7322 in the USA, PO Box 48, aebbra@waterw.com). The rooms surround an open-air, wood-floored thatched yoga center set in a garden. Options range from a two-story, Thai-style wooden cabin to an adobe farmer's cottage for US$25 to US$50 double. The center staff make their own yogurt, cheese, and sprouts and cook on request. Yoga classes are offered thrice-weekly in winter, and on Tuesday and Thursday in summer. A chiropractor is on hand.

*Arthur's Golden Sunset* (☎ 957-4241, 957-9703, fax 957-4761, PO Box 21) is a longtime favorite of the budget crowd. It has expanded from a group of rustic cottages and now offers 'economy' rooms with shared kitchen for US$45 high season; rooms with shared kitchenette but private bath cost US$55; and 'superior' rooms with air-con, kitchenettes, private bathrooms, and hot water cost US$80.

Check out the offbeat *Westport Cottages* (☎ 957-4736), which is popular with the laid-back backpacking crowd (particularly Europeans). A communal feel pervades the place, which owner Joseph Mathews says is approved for 'roach people.' Joseph has very rustic huts with well-kept outside toilet and cold shower. The nine rooms have mosquito nets and fans and cost US$20 double. A communal kitchen is available, and free bicycles and snorkeling equipment are provided. A funky bar is out front.

*Gloria's Sunset* (☎ 957-4741), 100 yards south of De Buss, has small but clean cottages with fans and bathrooms with hot water for US$25 to US$30 (US$5 less a night for four-night stays). Larger rooms have verandas. Barry, the owner, says he wants to preserve the feel of a Jamaican 'yard' rather than a hotel.

*Travellers Beach Resort* (☎ 957-3039, 718-251-9300 in the USA, travellers@cwjamaica .com) has 14 basic cabins amid unkempt grounds, plus 12 rooms in a two-story beachfront block. All have fans and air-con plus private bath with hot water, and enclosed verandas or patios. The rooms have a telephone and cable TV. Downstairs there's a small beachfront restaurant and bar. Summer rates are US$37 for cabins (US$42 with kitchenettes) and US$67 for rooms. Winter rates are US$10 higher.

Two other options are the *Bungalo Hotel* (☎ 957-4400, fax 957-4716), a characterless unit with 40 modestly decorated rooms with kitchenettes for US$40 double low season, US$80 high season.

## Hotels – West End

*Up Front* (☎ 957-3276), on Sheffield Rd east of Negril Square, charges US$30 double for basic units with fans and cold water only. *Chris' Donbar Cottages* (☎ 957-4429), next to King's Plaza, has three basically furnished cottages with ceiling and floor fans for US$25 double low season, US$40 high season. *Hotel Villa La Cage* (☎ 957-4114, fax 957-0217) has 24 rooms in a handsome and clean two-story building. High-season rates are US$42, US$50 with air-con, US$55 with kitchenette (it's about US$10 less in low season). There's an Italian restaurant and a small pool.

A favorite of budget travelers is the oceanfront *Negril Yacht Club* (☎/fax 957-9224, negrilyacht@cwjamaica.com), with 16 rooms with fans, cable TV, refrigerator, and hot water in private bathrooms. Air-con was to be added. Rates for singles or doubles are US$35 low season, US$50 high season. The outside bar and restaurant is popular.

A tremendous option for atmosphere is *Blue Cave Castle* (☎/fax 957-4845, PO Box 66), which looks like a castle from *Ivanhoe*, as Ian White described it in *Jamaica Experience* (a Lonely Planet video). This crenelated concoction squats on the cliff face. It's the creation of a Czech who has spent almost a decade on his pet project. The 14 bedrooms (each with refrigerator) cost around US$45 in summer, around US$65 in winter, and are made of natural stone. A penthouse duplex with kitchen costs US$65 in summer, US$80 in winter. Stairs lead down to Blue Cave, a sparkling grotto with swallows nesting on the overhang.

You'll find several inexpensive cottages for rent along West End Rd. *Milestone Cute Cottages (☎ 957-4442)* has three pleasant two-story cottages in a garden. All have ceiling fans, hot water, and balconies or patios for US$50 to US$65. There's a small bar and restaurant upstairs with a TV. *New Moon Cottages (☎ 957-4305)* has nine simply furnished rooms with ceiling fans in a two-story house; doubles run US$40 in high season. Other nearby options include the *Croton Grove Cottages (☎ 957-4340)*, charging US$50 for little rooms with kitchenettes in a house with garden.

*Thrills (☎ 957-4390, fax 957-4153)*, 200m from the shore, is an attractive property with nicely landscaped grounds. It has a lap pool, volleyball, and carpeted rooms with louvered windows and private balconies for US$50 high season.

The very simple *Primrose Inn* has five rooms with screened louvered windows, fans, and patios with hammocks. Guests share a kitchen. Singles or doubles cost US$30 high season.

The Cinderella of the West End has to be *Addis Kokeb (no telephone, PO Box 78)* also known by a new name, *New Star Guest House & Cottages*, a rustic wooden home steeped in atmosphere. Four rooms in the Colorado-style lodge each have two double beds. Guests share two bathrooms. There's a TV lounge, a small library boasting Persian throw rugs and deep-cushion sofas, an open mezzanine dining room, and kitchen with guest privileges. Rooms are a bargain at US$25 double, or US$100 for the whole house. Three bare-bones cabins by a 3-acre wilderness garden cost US$40, or US$20

nightly for one-month stays. Each has private bath, kitchen, and screened porch with hammocks. Guests have access to a pool and beach shuttle.

*Del Rose Villas (☎ 957-0166)* has 14 rooms with ceiling fans and private bath, though some rooms have only cold water. It has a swimming pool and restaurant. Rates are US$20 low season, US$30 high season; rooms with kitchenette are US$20 more.

South of the lighthouse, *Lighthouse Park (☎ 957-0252, PO Box 3)* offers six rustic but charming and clean bamboo and thatch cabins for US$25 single or double in low season, US$40 high season, and A-frame cottages for US$45 low season, US$60 high season, including some with kitchenettes for US$65 low season, US$80 high season. Breakfast is provided. Steps lead from the sunning platform to the sea.

*Lighthouse Inn (☎ 957-4052)* has two six-person cottages with solar-heated water for US$25 to US$120 low season, US$50 to US$150 high season, depending on number of people. It has a free beach shuttle, plus a restaurant offering candlelit dining.

Nearby options include *Sandy Cliff (☎ 957-4881)*, with 14 cottages for US$40, plus a house for four people for US$80; *Caribbean Dream* (alias Negril Rocks), offering four apartments with lounges, kitchens, and verandas in a two-story building atop the coral shore; and *Sunflower (☎ 957-4874)*, a one-bedroom cottage sitting amid a bamboo grove 100 yards from the shore, with kitchen, fans, and hot water for US$50.

Farther along you'll find *Sunseekers (☎ 1-771-3873 cellular)*, which enjoys a breezy location and is run by a gracious hostess, Beverly Wilcock. Like most other properties at this quiet end of Ocean Drive, it gets few guests. It has 10 spacious, modestly furnished rooms with ceiling fans and large tiled showers with hot water; some rooms have TVs. It has a coral terrace with a pool (empty, unfortunately in late 1998) with a dive platform. Rates range from US$30 to US$40 double, US$50 with kitchenette and king-size bed, and US$60 for a self-contained cottage.

## Places to Stay – Mid-Range

**Hotels – Long Bay** Near the north end is *Our Past Time Villas* (☎ 957-5931, fax 957-5422), with 17 pleasantly furnished rooms – some have air-con – with satellite TV and patios. It has a bar and restaurant. Rates are US$80 to US$90 for rooms or US$150 for a two-bedroom apartment with kitchenette.

*Foote Prints* (☎ 957-4300, fax 957-4301, ☎ 800-742-4276 in the USA, PO Box 100, footeprints@toj.com) has 30 air-conditioned rooms with TV, telephone, and safety box. Some have ceiling fans. Most have balconies. There's a restaurant and bar, plus Jacuzzi, tour desk, water sports, and excursions. Rooms cost US$95 double in summer, and US$145 in winter. Studios with kitchenettes cost US$20 extra, and two-bedroom apartments cost US$185 in summer, US$255 in winter.

A modern property set amid lawns is *Paradise View* (☎ 957-4375, fax 957-4074), with modestly decorated rooms in two-story units, all with TV and telephone. It has a beach bar and oceanside dining. Doubles cost US$88 double in low season, US$120 in high season.

*Daniel's Beach Village* (☎ 957-4394, fax 957-4713) is a gleaming white 45-room structure that seems to have been airlifted from Spain's Costa Brava. You can choose studios or standard or deluxe rooms with kitchenette (from US$60 to US$85). Furniture, alas, is dowdy. It also has apartments with large kitchens and living areas for US$90 to US$130, plus a large pool and the Swamp Thing Bar.

Its neighbor is *Beachcomber Club* (☎ 957-4170, fax 957-4097, PO Box 98), a handsome 45-room hotel with an open-air beachside restaurant, Gambino's Italian restaurant, plus a nightly entertainment schedule, tennis, and water sports. All rooms have air-con, ceiling fans, telephone, and satellite TV. Room rates are US$85 to US$105 in summer, US$130 to US$150 in winter. Apartments cost US$115 to US$210 in summer, US$200 to US$325 in winter.

Nearby, *Firefly* (☎ 957-4358, fax 925-5728, ☎ 800-477-9530 in the USA, PO Box 54, www.jamaicalink.com) rents four handsome,

all-hardwood cottages, plus one-bedroom studios, apartments, and penthouse suites. Each is different but all have kitchenette and veranda and cost US$66 to US$122 double in summer, US$100 to US$160 double in winter. A minimum one-week stay is required in winter. There's a Jacuzzi, and guests get free access to Swept Away resort's facilities.

*Moonrise* (☎ 957-4344, fax 957-4675, PO Box 57) offers six studios and 17 comfortable rooms with private bath. Louvered windows let in light, but the units' utility furniture creates an institutional feel. Rates (single or double) are US$50 winter for a standard room, US$80 for superior, US$110 for deluxe, and US$125 for a studio with kitchenette.

*Negril Palm Beach Hotel* (☎ 957-4218, fax 957-4426, PO Box 41) is a modern beachfront structure, adequate despite shabby furnishings. The living room has a wide-screen TV with VCR and video library, and there's a large bar, restaurant, and Jacuzzi. Summer rates are US$75 to US$100 double, including a cruise and snorkeling trip. Winter rates are US$98 to US$123.

I heartily recommend the *Chippewa Village Hotel* (☎ 957-4676, chippewa@fantasyisle .com), where friendly Californian John Babcock accommodates up to 22 people in three octagonal studio units with screened porches and lofty ceilings. He also has a three-bedroom apartment; plus two two-bedroom apartments with dining room, living room, and kitchen. All are rustic rough-hewn affairs oozing a warm ambience, epitomized by American Southwest decor, throw rugs, and tasteful fabrics. A small swimming pool under a shade canopy is inset in a wooden deck. John was planning to add a fitness center offering aromatherapy in 1999. There's a small restaurant and bar, with American home cooking (for guests only). The property offers superb views of the Great Morass to the rear. John charges US$55 double for cottages, and US$100/120/140 for one/two/ three-bedroom units.

Nearby, *White Sands* (☎ 957-4291, fax 957-4674, PO Box 60, wsnegril@infochan .com) is an attractive property where options range from simple yet elegant one-bedroom apartments to a four-bedroom, four-bath villa. Winter rates based on double occupancy are US$61 for a studio, US$89 deluxe room, US$123 apartment, and US$340 villa that sleeps eight. The units sit in a well-maintained garden with a pool. White Sands is popular with tour groups.

*Lazy Days* (☎ 957-3571) offers five bare-bones all-wood cottages (one beachfront) with fans, stove and refrigerator, and shared showers. There are pool tables. It's overpriced at US$80 double (US$120 beachfront).

*Rondel Village* (☎ 957-4413, fax 957-4915, PO Box 96, wrightc@cwjamaica.com) has nicely appointed studios and beach-front rooms clustered around a small pool and Jacuzzi. You can also choose octagonal-shaped one and two-bedroom villas that sleep up to six and feature air-con, marble floors, French doors, satellite TV, fully equipped kitchenettes, and Jacuzzi. A seafront café and snack bar sells ice cream, cappuccinos, and the like. Summer rates range from US$85 double for a garden studio to US$180 double for a two-bedroom beach-front villa. In winter, rates are US$115 to US$240 respectively.

*Hidden Paradise* (☎ 957-4404, fax 957-9219, PO Box 9) offers four twin-room cottages with air-con, fan, private verandas, and hot water. Two cottages have kitchenettes. It also features eight rooms in a house amid well-tended lawns. Rates (including tax and service charge) are US$78 single, US$102 double high season. A meal plan is offered. Nearby, also in lush gardens, sits the *Seascape Hotel* (☎ 957-4303, fax 957-3489), offering one and two-bedroom studios and apartments. Seascape has a restaurant and bar with Jacuzzi in the backyard. Summer rates are US$40 to US$70 for rooms or US$90 for a self-contained apartment. Winter rates are US$10 extra.

*Sandi San* (☎ 957-4487, fax 957-4234, PO Box 47) is an intimate property; its seven studios, 15 rooms, and one suite all feature air-con with fans, hot water, and attractive decor, including hand-carved beds of native mahoe. It has its own beachside bar and open-air restaurant, plus beach volleyball. Rooms cost US$65 to US$100 double or US$110 for a cottage in summer; and US$115

to US$165 double, or US$170 for a cottage in winter. TVs and refrigerators rent for US$8 apiece.

The *Tamboo Inn* (☎/fax 957-4282) has nine cabins. Rates are US$93 high season for a one-bedroom, and US$175 for a two-bedroom cabin with kitchenette. It also has a smaller unit with kitchenette for US$87.

*Legends* (☎ 957-3834, fax 957-9783, PO Box 23, samsara@cwjamaica.com, www.negrilhotels.com/legends) is a new beach-front resort with 25 gleaming white air-conditioned rooms, modestly furnished, with ceiling fans, two double beds, and balconies. It has a lively and popular restaurant-cum-sports bar. Rates are US$85 summer, US$120 winter, single or double.

I recommend its neighbor, the family-run *Sea Gem* (☎ 957-4318, fax 957-9765), which offers six quaint though rustic wooden cabins with filigree trim, done up in bright Caribbean colors. Patios face onto twee landscaped grounds. There are also three suites upstairs in a handsome stone-and-timber house tastefully decorated with terra-cotta floors. The gracious, eco-conscious owners are gourmands and run the splendid Kuyaba on the Beach restaurant, attached to the property (see Places to Eat). There's also a well-stocked gift store. Rates (including continental breakfast) are US$62 high season for a cottage (US$8 extra for air-con, and another US$8 with kitchen); US$97 to US$106 high season for suites. The owners also have rooms across the street for US$77.

*Beach House Villas* (☎ 957-4731, 800-634-7457 in the USA, BHVillas@aol.com, www.jamaicanegril.com) has nine rooms in three villas. All are unique in configuration and range from a jungleview room for US$110 winter, and one-bedroom suite with sundeck in the treetops for US$150, to one, two and three-bedroom units with kitchens, and an oceanfront beach house with four bedrooms for US$400 summer, US$600 winter. *Bar B Barn* (☎ 957-4755), nearby, is a modest family-run hotel with 22 rooms, all with cable TV and fans for US$80 to US$110 high season.

*T-Water Beach Hotel* (☎ 957-4270, fax 957-4355, PO Box 11) is one of the oldest hotels in Negril and was desperately in need of an upgrade in late 1998. That said, its 70 air-conditioned rooms and beachfront suites are handsomely furnished, with patios or balconies, some with kitchenette. It has a restaurant and beach bar, plus two Jacuzzis, a pool, TV lounge, and water sports. The public areas are jaded in the extreme. Alas, it's overpriced: 'moderate' rooms run US$140 high season; 'deluxe rooms' are US$185, and US$197 for suites, including taxes, breakfast, and lunch.

A better option is its neighbor, the **Negril Beach Club Hotel** (☎ 957-4222, fax 957-4364, PO Box 7). Its smorgasbord of rooms includes 65 modest yet nicely furnished air-conditioned rooms, plus studios and deluxe suites. Facilities include water sports, tennis courts, a pool, coffee shop, boutique, and health club, but the grounds are unkempt. Summer rates are US$68 to US$108 double, in winter US$100 to US$135. One-bedroom suites cost US$138 double in summer, US$175 in winter. Two-bedroom suites are US$50 extra. Rates include tax.

**Coral Seas Beach Resort** (☎ 957-9226, 957-4388, fax 957-4269, ☎ 800-223-6510 in the USA, PO Box 91, coralseas@toj.com) is sequestered beachside amid a garden of bamboo and hibiscus. You can choose from rooms with verandas or fully equipped apartments, or two honeymoon suites. It has a pool with bar. Rates for a double are US$85 summer, US$120 winter. A one-bedroom unit with kitchenette costs US$10 per person extra.

Across the street to the north is its sibling **Coral Seas Garden Resort** (☎ 957-4388, fax 957-4269, ☎ 800-223-6510 in the USA, PO Box 91, coralseas@toj.com), with rooms of a similar standard. Rates are US$62 summer, US$90 winter. Apartments with kitchenette cost US$10 extra.

**Hotels – West End** If you prefer to be in Negril Village, check out **Cotton Tree Place** (☎ 957-4450, fax 957-4773, PO Box 85), 100 yards west of Scotiabank. This modern complex has 35 units with air-con; studios with kitchenettes are US$80 high season. The rooms with fans are better and cost US$60,

although carpeted. All rooms have a TV, sofa, and balcony. Bathrooms are small. A roomy 'Stone House' with lofty wooden ceiling and a loft bedroom sleeps up to five people from US$80 double. There's a restaurant.

On the hillside behind Negril Village is **Chuckles** (☎ 957-4250, fax 957-9150), boasting modern condo-style units in lush landscaped grounds centered on a large pool and sundeck. It has 75 luxury air-conditioned rooms for US$70 to US$105, depending on size and view. More expensive rooms have king-size beds. You can also choose from a pair of two-bedroom villas for US$225. The resort offers a Jacuzzi, tennis courts, bike rental, and a shuttle to the beach. Rates include tax, service charge, and breakfast.

**Sunshine Village Apartment Hotel** (☎ 957-4125, fax 957-4124, PO Box 109; ☎ 800-550-6288 in the USA; ☎ 0800-969459 in the UK; sunshinevillagepathl@toj.com), formerly Singles, has a strange location above Sunshine Village. This modern complex is modestly attractive and of a townhouse design. It has 32 air-conditioned suites with kitchenettes and loft bedrooms, and hosts nightly poolside parties. Rates for doubles are US$80 summer, US$90 winter.

**Falcon Cottages** (☎ 957-4263, fax 957-4921, PO Box 20) has standard rooms or a one-bedroom flat with kitchen for US$44 summer, US$55 winter; deluxe rooms run US$55/US$66. There's a bar, restaurant, and swimming pool.

**Heartbeat** (☎ 957-4329, fax 957-0069, PO Box 95) offers a romantic option atop the cliffs in its thatched, all-hardwood octagonal cabins. You can also choose self-sufficient studio apartments or a three-bedroom cottage, beginning at US$45. Nearby, **Bougainvillea** (no telephone) charges US$40 per night for studios with kitchenette; long-term rentals cost US$400 a double per month.

**La Mer Resort & Café** (☎ 957-4283) has 23 rooms with fans for US$50 low season (US$65 with air-con). Cable TV is extra, on request.

To the south is **Reefcliff Resort** (☎ 957-4478, 800-925-7418 in the USA, PO Box 2), formerly Home Sweet Home, with 13 rooms with private balconies, fans, and private showers. It features a cliff bar and restaurant, a small figure-eight pool, a Jacuzzi, and a boat pick up for fishing or snorkeling trips. It charges US$75 to US$100 high season, and offers a seven-night all-inclusive package for US$995. Suites cost US$160 to US$210.

One of Negril's most popular options is the *Hotel Samsara* (☎ 957-4395, fax 957-4073, PO Box 23, samsara@cwjamaica.com, www.negrilhotels.com). There are 50 air-conditioned oceanfront rooms for US$50 to US$70 summer, US$75 to US$95 winter; or more charming thatched tree houses on stilts for US$75 summer, US$95 winter. Samsara boasts tennis and volleyball courts and PADI scuba-diving center, a pool, a unique water slide into the ocean, plus the Jah Beer Garden/Sports Café with satellite TV. It hosts a sunset happy hour and live concerts on the ugly concrete sundeck spanning the cliff top.

Farther south, *Ocean Edge* (☎ 957-4362, fax 957-0086, PO Box 71) offers 30 rooms – some with air-con – and is also poised on the cliffs, with 20 additional rooms in a block across the road. The hotel has a pool and Jacuzzi, plus glass-bottom boat and water sports. Winter rates are US$60 garden-view, US$75 oceanside, US$80 suite. It suffers from loud music from the bar next door.

A good bargain is *Xtabi* (☎ 957-4336, fax 957-0121, xtabiresort@toj.com, PO Box 19). The name – an Arawak word – means 'meeting place of the gods.' You can choose simple garden cottages or quaint octagonal bungalows perched atop the cliff. The bar is lively and the restaurant is appealing. Steps lead down to sunning platforms by the water's edge. Massage is offered. Economy rooms cost US$45 low season, US$55 high season. Standard rooms are a bit more, and sea-front bungalows cost US$110 low season, US$160 high season.

Another good bargain with a stylish yet off-beat ambience is the recently and dramatically upgraded, Australian-run *Rockhouse* (☎ 957-4373, 708-823-5226 in the USA, PO Box 24, rockhousehotel@toj.com), boasting 13 thatched, hardwood rondavels (two are 'premium villas') of pine and stone, plus 15 studios dramatically clinging to the cliff-side above a small cove. Decor is basic yet adequate, with mosquito-net-draped poster beds, and strong Caribbean colors. Each cabin has a ceiling fan, hot plate, refrigerator, safe, mini-bar, alfresco shower, and sliding glass door opening to private, wrap-around verandas. Catwalks lead over the rocks to an open-sided, multi-level dining pavilion (with one of the best restaurants around; see Places to Eat, later in this chapter) and iron ladders and steps lead down to the ocean. A pool has been added atop the cliffs. Summer rates are US$85 for a studio, US$100 to US$120 for a villa; US$100 studio, US$130 to US$165 villa, in winter.

Farther south, *Coral Seas Cliff Resort* (☎ 957-3147, fax 957-4269, ☎ 800-223-6510 in the USA, PO Box 91, coralseas@toj.com) has elegant villas with nicely furnished rooms with cable TV. I like the hotel's relaxed feel. Rooms in summer cost US$55 to US$95 double, and in winter US$80 to US$110. It has an impressive pool, airy restaurant, and bar in well-tended grounds.

*Drumville Cove* (☎ 957-4369, fax 978-4971, ☎ 800-423-4095 in the USA, ☎ 020-8940-3399 in the UK, PO Box 72) is a dramatically landscaped property. Its 19 rooms – some with air-con – are cramped but clean and romantic; deluxe rooms are larger. Another option is three cozy cabins with four beds (two in a loft) and a kitchenette. You can sunbathe nude atop the rugged limestone crags with a cliff-top bar. Drumville also boasts a saltwater bathing pool and kiddie pool, and a small restaurant. A dive shop was to be added. Singles or doubles in rooms or cabins run US$40 low season, US$60 high season.

Opposite Drumville, a road leads inland about 300 yards to *Summerset Village* (☎ 957-4409, PO Box 80), on 7 acres of landscaped grounds centered on a large pool. Standard rooms cost US$50 summer, US$70 winter. Ten air-conditioned 'superior' rooms costing US$60 summer, US$80 winter are in a condo-style unit; eight others are in a 'chateau.' One-bedroom octagonal cottages are US$5 more. Two-bedroom cottages are US$110 summer, US$130 winter. There's a five-bedroom 'Thatch House' with a suite and kitchen for US$225 summer, US$275 winter; it can also be rented by the room. Summerset offers a shuttle to the beach.

***Rock Cliff Resort*** (☎ *957-4331, fax 957-4108, PO Box 67*) specializes in scuba packages, has a dive center on site, and is popular with European tour groups. Its 33 elegantly furnished, air-conditioned ocean-view rooms and suites cost from US$92 to US$103 double in summer, and from US$132 to US$160 in winter. There's also a two-bedroom suite at double the cost.

Likewise, there is a scuba center at the ***Mariner's Inn & Dive Resort*** (☎ *957-0392, fax 947-0391, PO Box 16, mariners@infochan .com, www.negril.com/mimain.htm*). Its 52 rooms are appealing and represent a bargain at US$44 to US$56 double in summer, US$65 to US$79 in winter, including tax, tips, and an introductory scuba course. It also has apartments for US$68 in summer, US$94 in winter, and features a pool and elevated sundeck, Jacuzzi, bike rental, gift and grocery shop, tour desk, disco, gameroom, and two restaurants.

Among the more acclaimed places is ***Tensing Pen*** (☎ *957-0387, fax 957-0161, PO Box 13, tensingpen@cwjamaica.com*). Owner Richard Murray created the stunning garden – a tropical Fantasia of bromeliads, ferns, orchids, and other flowering plants for which the hotel is renowned. It has 12 thatched cottages on two acres, most 'pillar houses' perched atop the coral cliffs, and all with exquisite bamboo and hardwood beds inside. Guests use a communal rock-walled kitchen. Rooms differ markedly and are priced from US$70 to US$245 in low season, US$105 to US$350 in high season.

***Banana Shout*** (☎/fax *957-0384, PO Box 4, www.negril.com/bananashout*) offers seven cabins: three hidden among tropical foliage and linked by interminably winding paths, and four perched on the cliff face with sundecks built into a cave with a freshwater shower. They're offbeat affairs, with loft bedrooms, ceiling fan, hammocks, and kitchenettes (from US$40 to US$60 double in summer, US$50 to US$100 in winter). A house for four people rents for US$160 in summer, US$200 in winter.

***Villas Sur Mer*** (☎ *957-0342, fax 957-0177*) is a handsome structure atop the cliffs, with tasteful appointments in two one-bedroom and two two-bedroom suites, each with air-con and a kitchen, and a living room and master bedroom that open onto a private balcony. Outside there's a small amoeba-shaped swimming pool and a cantilevered deck inset with whirlpool. Winter rates are US$135 one-bedroom, US$190 two-bedroom, and US$600 six-bedroom.

***Negril B&B*** (☎ *957-4850*), one block from Rick's Café, is surrounded by a beautiful garden. You may choose either a standard or deluxe room with king-size beds plus air-con, two fans, and louvered windows for US$65 and US$75.

South of the lighthouse, hotels thin out. Keep going a couple of miles and you'll reach ***Tingalaya's B&B*** (☎ *957-0126, 416-924-4269, 800-222-0016 in North America*). This is a marvelous creation of an eccentric Canadian, Lynda Perry, and resembles a tiny African village. You can choose from four thatched adobe cottages painted brown and blue. Lynda also rents her beautiful all-hardwood cottage. The property slopes down through a grove of sea grapes to fabulous coral formations with pocket-size sandy areas. There's a beachside cafe and bar serving bush teas and I-tal food. A natural fruit, vegetable, and herb garden supplies the kitchen. Meals are served beneath a high-pitched thatch restaurant. Alas, the grounds were very run-down when I called in by in late 1998, but the rooms are well-maintained by Egbert, a friendly, elderly Rasta. Rates are US$50 to US$60 per room, including breakfast.

Farther along is ***Secret Paradise*** (☎ *957-4882, PO Box 56*), a secluded property that offers one and two-story octagonal units with full kitchens for US$75 double, plus a two-bedroom ranch house for US$85 to US$181, and a five-bedroom house that can be rented by the room for US$48. A cook is available, and there's a small restaurant. A freshwater pool overlooks a small cove.

At the end of Ocean Drive, near the junction with William Hogg Blvd, is ***Hog Heaven*** (☎/fax *957-4991*). It offers 13 clean, well-appointed self-catering units for US$50 low season, US$80 high season, or US$160 for suites, all set in attractive grounds but less salubrious than the prices may suggest. Wide patios have hammocks and chairs. Free snorkeling equipment is available, and you can sunbathe nude. Across the street is the Hard Reggae Café.

## Places to Stay – Top End

**Hotels – Long Bay** For jungly atmosphere, try *Negril Cabins Resort* (☎ 957-4350, 957-4381, 800-382-3444 in North America, PO Box 118), on Bloody Bay. It has 24 standard and 26 air-conditioned superior rooms. The all-hardwood, Thai-style cabins are raised on stilts and set well apart amid lush grounds with abundant waterfalls. Facilities include a fitness center and tennis court plus game room, Jacuzzi, pool with swim-up bar, and Coconut Palm restaurant. A path leads to the beach. It's popular with European tour groups. Summer rates are US$145 to US$220 double, including breakfast, tax, and service charge (children under 16 free). Winter rates are US$165 to US$250 double. A three-night minimum stay is required.

*Couples Negril* (☎ 957-5960, fax 957-5858, PO Box 35; ☎ 305-668-0008, 800-268-7537, fax 305-668-0111 in the USA; ☎ 020-8900-1913, fax 8795-1728 in the UK), at Bloody Bay, boasts the most classy contempo decor of any resort in Jamaica – a statement of ultra-sophistication with a thoroughly in-vogue, retro motif that the company terms 'Negril Chic' and which immediately dated all rivals when the property opened in late 1998. The lobby boasts a huge tapestry by famous Jamaican artist Ireko and opens over a wide pool at the heart of the 18-acre resort. Facilities include four tennis courts, a fitness center, gameroom, spa, beauty salon, and boutiques, plus a full range of water sports. The 216 exquisitely appointed rooms are in nine blocks. Imagine blood-red fabrics, a canary-yellow duvet, iridescent curtains, dark bamboo, cobalt hints, and oh-so-chic furniture. All rooms have TV and CD player. The suites have vast bathrooms with Jacuzzi and 'his and her' sinks. Dining facilities include the Otaheite restaurant serving nou-velle Jamaican. A three-night minimum stay is required. Low-season rates (three nights, per couple) – July to September – range from US$1420 for gardenview to US$1715 for beachfront rooms and US$2110 for beachfront suites. Mid-season rates – April through June and September through Christmas – range from US$1485 to US$2180. High-season rates are US$1635 to US$2395. The 'Couples Double-Take' (seven-night minimum stay) offers an option to stay at both Couples Negril and Couples Ocho Rios, including free air transfer, based on Ocho Rios prices (10% lower than Couples Negril).

Also exuding sophistication is the ritzy *Grand Lido Negril* (☎ 957-5010, fax 957-5517, PO Box 88; ☎ 800-467-8737 in the USA; ☎ 01749-677200 in the UK), a flagship of the SuperClubs chain, and offering a second beach for an all-over tan. The 210 suites and split-level junior suites (some with whirlpool) are spread through 22 acres of gardens featuring nine bars, including three 24-hour bars with Jacuzzis. Grand Lido is the very antithesis of the Caribbean, boasting a chic Mediterranean flair. The spacious rooms feature a lounge and mezzanine bedroom and tasteful furnishings, plus TV and CD player. New luxury suites are especially elegant. Even wedding ceremonies, 24-hour room service, and dry cleaning, laundry, and pedicures are included in the price. Take your pick of several restaurants. A full range of water sports includes cruises in glass-bottom boats. A spa and high-tech gym was added in 1998. Sunset and dinner cruises are offered aboard *M/Y Zien*, a 147-foot motor yacht that was a wedding gift from Aristotle Onassis to Prince Rainer and Grace Kelly. Adult singles are welcome. Per-person rates begin at US$850 to US$1230 for a three-night package in low season; high-season rates are US$1180 to US$1570. Add US$100 per night for single occupancy.

Rutland Point holds the all-inclusive *Point Village* (☎ 957-9170, 957-4351, 877-704-6852 in North America, ☎ 0800-328-9970 in the UK, pt.village@cwjamaica.com, www.pointvillage.com). Studios, and one, two, and three-bedroom suites in Mediterranean-style, two-story limestone villas are scattered throughout the 14 acres. Its wave-pounded shoreline holds pocket-size beaches, including a diminutive nude beach. Furnishings are modest, though kitchens are roomy and well appointed. Water sports, picnic trips to Booby Cay, and guided bicycle rides are all included. Facilities include a pool, tennis courts, barber and beauty shop, boutique, beachside massage 'parlor,' and nanny service. Low-season rates are US$268 double for a studio and US$276 for a one-bedroom unit, rising to US$376 and US$396 respectively in peak season (Christmas and New Year). A minimum weeklong stay is required for peak season.

In 1998, SuperClubs broke ground on a 225-room *Breezes Negril* for middle-income couples and singles on Bloody Bay.

Another SuperClubs property, the aptly named *Hedonism II* (☎ 957-5200, fax 957-4289, PO Box 25; ☎ 800-467-8737 in the USA; ☎ 01749-677200 in the UK) lies nearby. This no-holds-barred adults-only resort (also called the 'Human Zoo') is world-famous for its risqué attitude highlighted by its weekly toga party and lingerie party that are preludes to even more unrestrained antics, proving that 'sex on the beach' is more than the name of a drink. It's always wild – how wild depends on your timing. But it also caters to more conservative folks. Social events revolve around a main dining room-cum-theater. Its 280 air-conditioned rooms and suites have no telephones or TVs, but boast king-size beds (twin beds for singles) and mirrored ceilings and a strange retro decor in beige and sexual-flush. Two beaches (one nude), five bars, a gameroom, tennis and squash courts, volleyball, basketball, and a complete range of water sports are among the attractions. It even has a 'Circus Workshop' and a windsurfing school, plus stores, one of which sells a risqué collection befitting Frederick's of Hollywood. Guests include more single males than females and a surprising proportion of seniors, too. To even the balance, a third female is free if sharing a room. Per-person rates begin at US$559 to US$619 for a three-night package in low season, US$739

to US$829 in high season. Add US$100 per night for single occupancy. The place gets booked solid during national holidays, when Jamaica's party crowd flocks for high-jinx.

Hedonism's neighbor is the ever-popular, recently renovated *Sandals Negril* (☎ 957-4216, fax 957-4338, PO Box 12, www.sandals .com), part of the all-inclusive, couples-only resort chain. The 21-acre deluxe property sprawls over wide lawns trimmed to perfection, with music piping softly from speakers hidden amid the palms. At its node is a huge pool with swim-up bar abuzz with happy guests. In all, there are 227 rooms in six categories, including exquisite honeymoon suites in gracious cottages replete with Edwardian decor, plus new villa-suites with loft bedrooms and marble bathrooms. Sandals also features tennis, squash, racquetball courts, a splendid full-service spa, plus a medley of restaurants playing a calliope on the international and Jamaican theme. There's even a sushi bar. Winter room rates begin at US$980 double for a two-night stay, to US$2870 for a seven-night stay. Rates for the suites range from US$730 double for a two-night stay to US$2190 for a seven night stay. (For worldwide Sandals contact numbers, see the Accommodations section of the Facts for the Visitor chapter.)

Another impressive Sandals' property farther south on Norman Manley Blvd, *Beaches* (☎ 957-9270, fax 957-9269) caters to families, singles, and couples. It is designed loosely to resemble a castle, with thick limestone walls and patinated wrought-iron furniture and lanterns harking back centuries. Facilities wrap around a large free-form pool with a humpback bridge leading to a Jacuzzi. It has 225 air-conditioned rooms, including 39 junior suites, in seven categories in three-story units built in quasi Spanish-hacienda style. All rooms boast king-size bed, in-room safe, and satellite TV, and a colonial feel. There's also a 12,000-sq-foot pool, kiddie pool, five restaurants, including a teppanyaki-style Asian restaurant and a Southwestern-style saloon, plus a huge theater, disco, several bars, a pool room, a 24-hour gym, sauna, and massage and beauty salon, and a panoply of water sports. Facilities for children include a Sega Centre (with state-of-the-art games in six languages), a superbly outfitted Kids Camp, and a 'fun track' with electric bikes and cars. The disco has a teen's night. The Piazza is a separate family area with its own pool. Guests get access to Sandals Negril.

*Poinciana Beach Hotel* (☎ 957-4100, PO Box 44) is a family resort popular with Jamaican couples (one child per adult stays free with parents) that came under the management of the Sandals chain in 1998. Children and teens can make the most of a gameroom, organized activities such as arts and crafts, beach volleyball and Anancy Fun Park, Poinciana's own amusement complex. The resort's 6 acres include three-story accommodation blocks and villas in Georgian-plantation style. The exterior has recently been renovated and has a more upscale, lively feel than in prior years. It has a complicated rate structure, with 12 separate rates periods. All-inclusive rates range from US$310 to US$452 double for a superior room, and from US$396 to US$668 double for a two-bedroom villa. There are also suites and one-bedroom villas. A three-day minimum stay is required.

You could indeed be swept away by *Swept Away* (☎ 957-4061, fax 957-4060, ☎ 800-545-7937, fax 305-666-8520 in North America, info@sweptaway.com, www.sweptaway.com), an all-inclusive, adults-only resort that boasts the island's most replete sports and fitness facility, with endearing accommodations to boot. (It recently reopened as the Swept Away Negril, part of the Issa Resort Collection.) Pathways coil through a 20-acre botanical rush-hour of ferns and heliconias to the 134 suites, housed in 26 two-story villas and boasting terra-cotta tile floors, cream walls, deep-red hardwoods, oversized mirrors, and vast louvered windows. You could host a house-party in the cavernous showers. The gym, aerobics studio, 10 tennis courts (all lighted and open to nonguests), two squash and two racquetball courts all come with professional instruction. When you're done with your workout, you can recuperate in the spa and beauty parlor. The Feathers Restaurant is a gourmand's

delight, and there's a Fruit and Veggie Bar, plus cabaret and other entertainment. Free golf at Negril Hills Golf Club is included. Holistic programs and monthly 'health specials' are offered. The property had been taken over by the Couples chain and was closed for a remake when I called by in late 1998. A three-night minimum stay is required. Rates (per person) range from US$675 (garden suites) to US$855 (beachfront suites) in summer for a three-night stay, and US$750 to US$938 in winter.

*Native Son Villas* (☎ 957-4376, fax 379-1918, ☎ 201-467-1407 in the USA) offers four modern two-story duplex villas sleeping four to nine people. It's a bargain for families or groups at US$115 to US$240 per night (summer), including a housekeeper/cook and a bottle of rum. The elegant *Sea Splash Resort* (☎ 957-4041, 800-254-2786, fax 957-4049, PO Box 123), with 15 spacious suites, each with kitchenette and screened-off bedroom, costs US$120 to US$130 double in summer, US$199 to US$219 in winter, including tax and transfers to and from Montego Bay. Tasteful decor highlights 15 air-conditioned suites, each with large balcony, fully equipped kitchenette, satellite TV, and telephone.

Another of my favorites is the *Negril Tree House* (☎ 957-4287, 957-4386, PO Box 29; ☎ 412-231-4889, 800-634-7451, fax 412-231-5044 in North America, jackson@cwjamaica .com), an unpretentious resort with 16 octagonal bungalows and oceanfront villas nudging up to the beach. More elegant one and two-bedroom suites feature kitchenette, king-size beds, and a Murphy bed in the lounge that opens onto a wide veranda. The beachside bar is a popular place for locals and tourists to mix and features hammocks beneath thatch umbrellas. Water sports are offered, and the resort also has a tour desk, gift store, masseuse, and manicurist. Guests have day privileges at Swept Away's sports complex (US$10 daily). Rates are US$80 to US$110 (rooms), US$140 to US$180 (suites).

*Crystal Waters Villas* (☎ 957-4284, fax 957-4889, PO Box 18) offers very attractive one, two, and three-bedroom air-conditioned villas, each with lounge, kitchen, and patio.

Amenities include a swimming pool, kiddie pool, and Jacuzzi. A housekeeper and cook are included in the rates of US$90 (one-bedroom), US$130 to US$180 (two-bedroom), US$250 (three-bedroom). The office is across the road.

***CocoLaPalm*** (☎ 957-4227, fax 957-3460; ☎ 612-493-5261, 800-896-0987 in the USA, coclap@toj.com, www.cocolapalm.com) is a new beachfront resort – Swiss run – with 43 rooms in octagonal two-story units. Some have king beds; all have cable TV, telephone, safe, refrigerator, and coffee-maker. There's a beachside restaurant, a bar and grill, and a huge pool with Jacuzzi. It offers four types of rooms plus oceanview and poolside Junior Suites. Rates are US$120 to US$150 in summer and US$150 to US$190 in winter. Guests receive privileges at Swept Away.

Another good option is ***Charela Inn*** (☎ 957-4277, fax 957-4414, PO Box 33, chareca@toj.com, www.negril.com/cimain .htm), where the 49 air-conditioned rooms (19 deluxe; four family units) feature beautiful contemporary decor with lots of hardwoods, plus ceiling fans, hair-dryers, telephones, and balconies or patios. It resembles a Spanish hacienda and surrounds a courtyard with garden and a large circular pool. Rates in summer are US$105 to US$135 double for a minimum three-night stay; and include water sports, Sunfish and sailboard instruction, and a sunset cruise. Winter rates are US$158 to US$210 double. Children under 10 stay free.

If you're seeking meditation, check out ***Nirvana*** (☎ 957-4314, 716-789-5955 in the USA), with three one-bedroom and five two and three-bedroom cottages set in Zenlike tropical gardens. The all-hardwood cabins cost US$150 double to US$210 for the oceanfront honeymoon suite in winter (30% less in summer). Each has a dining room and kitchen, and screened wrap-around windows. ***Whistling Bird*** (☎ 957-4403, 303-442-0722 in the USA) is similar, with 24 rooms in 12 deluxe little cottages for US$91 summer, US$103 winter. It's low-key and a great place to relax beneath shady bamboo. There's a restaurant and beach bar.

Of a similar standard is the ***Negril Inn*** (☎ 957-4209, fax 957-4365, PO Box 59), a 1960s Miami-style property that's divorced from the beach by an ugly wall. Its 46 rooms are nicely decorated, however, and facilities include an outdoor gym, massage, a pool, two Jacuzzis, floodlit tennis courts and a basketball court, a TV lounge and billiards room, and a disco. Rooms are US$140 single, US$220 double, all-inclusive. A better option is ***Negril Gardens*** (☎ 957-4408, fax 957-4374, ☎ 800-752-6824 in the USA, PO Box 58), with 65 nicely appointed air-conditioned rooms and two suites in two-story villas with balconies. Garden-view rooms across the road overlook a pool. Summer rates begin at US$120.

***Merrill's Beach Resort*** (☎ 957-4751, fax 957-3121, PO Box 75), a short distance away, is an attractive place with 28 air-conditioned rooms in a two-story unit amid lush landscaped grounds. All have verandas. It offers water sports and a beach bar, and is popular with European tour groups. Winter rates range from US$77 to US$99. It offers an all-inclusive meal package for US$30 daily.

**Hotels – West End** One of the more charming options is ***Llanrissant*** (☎ 957-4259, 305-668-9877, 800-331-6951 in the USA, ctravis9@idt.net, www.beachcliff.com), a centenary two-story, four-bedroom home and the oldest domicile in Negril. The house – simply yet exquisitely furnished, with ceiling fans and breezes easing in through louvered windows – comes fully staffed and includes satellite TV, stereo, plus fax and Internet access. Hammocks hang from shade trees. Snorkeling gear is included. Winter rates range from US$320 to US$500.

***Dreamscape Villa*** (☎ 957-4495, 312-883-1020 in the USA, PO Box 51) has five voluminous and very beautifully furnished deluxe apartments, plus a studio and one suite, all with satellite TV and refrigerator. It has a pool, an outdoor Jacuzzi under a gazebo, and a private lawn with its own pleasant cove and sundeck. Rates are US$80 to US$120, including continental breakfast in your room.

I adore the ***Caves*** (☎ 957-0270, 800-688-7678 in the USA, ☎ 0800-614-790 in the UK, outpost800@aol.com), a boutique resort in the Island Outpost chain, undoubtedly the finest small hotel in Negril, and one beloved of the Hollywood elite. It is set into the cave-riddled cliffs and offers eight hand-crafted, one and two-bedroom wood-and-thatch cottages – each as distinct as a thumbprint – amid lush gardens, with coral walkways leading down to the sea. Rooms feature exquisite hand-carved furniture, batik fabrics, one-of-a-kind art, CD player with CDs, plus ceiling fans and mosquito nets over the king or queen-size beds, and – for many – outside showers (if that doesn't sound appealing, wait until you see them). The cottages are built atop a stone terrace, from which paths wind down to a free-form Jacuzzi studding the rockface, and thence to hanging balconies and a cave with molded benches where you can recline and meditate to the reverberations of pounding waves. There's also a saltwater pool and sauna, plus an Aveda spa offering full treatments in an octagonal gazebo. Yoga is also offered. Rates range from US$400 double to US$725 for the exquisite Macka Tree Suite; rates include all meals and self-service bar.

Another unique and tranquil option is **Jackie's on the Reef** (☎ 957-4997, 718-469-2785 in the USA), 7 miles south of the Negril roundabout, at the southern end of Ocean Drive. Jackie, a transplanted New Yorker, describes it as a 'holistic guest house spa.' It operates as a New Age haven focusing on spiritual renewal. A natural stone cottage is divided into four rooms, each with two handmade wooden beds and an outdoor shower and bathroom enclosed within your own private backyard. Massages are given on a veranda, and meditation, tai chi, and spa treatments are offered by the shore. There's a small cooling pool inset in the reeftop. The facility is far more rustic than the rates might suggest. Rates are US$125 per person in the summer, US$150 winter, including breakfast, dinner, and exercise class. Day packages (lunch and massage) are offered to nonguests.

## PLACES TO EAT

There are almost as many places to eat as to lay your head. Though jerk and patty stalls are being squeezed off the beach, a plethora of rustic eateries along Norman Manley Blvd and West End Rd offer budget snacks and meals. Many food stands have no access to running water and *may* pose health problems. Several restaurants, especially on the cliff top, close after sunset. Others may close during the day in the off-season. Don't neglect the hotel restaurants.

Local delicacies (besides mushroom omelettes) include crab pickled in red peppers. For fast food, try **Shakey's Pizza** or **King Burger** in Sunshine Village in Negril Village.

### Jamaican

Take your pick from several dozen roadside stalls and eateries selling jerk and native dishes for a few dollars.

**Long Bay** Try **Ossie's Shack**, a simple jerk and juice center opposite Paradise View Hotel, on Norman Manley Blvd. I also recommend the **Negril Yoga Centre** for Jamaican health-food dinners such as Rasta pasta, chicken Jamaican style, and curried vegetables in coconut milk (US$5 to US$7).

The **Beachcomber International Restaurant**, 100 yards south of De Buss, has the usual jerk fare, plus peppered steaks (US$5) and lobster (US$8). At night, its drab appearance is enlivened by candlelight.

**Tan-Yah's** (☎ 957-4031), at the Sea Splash Resort on Norman Manley Blvd, has been recommended for its nouvelle Jamaican dishes.

**Negril Village** **Miss Brown's**, on Sheffield Rd a mile east of the roundabout, serves 'mushroom daiquiris,' mushroom omelettes (US$12 to US$20), and mushroom tea (US$6). Be warned – *they're hallucinogenic*. One cup is said to produce a 'mild buzz.' Two cups are quite a trip. Three cups…whoa there! **Tedd's One-Stop**, nearby, also sells mushroom tea.

Sheffield Rd contains several authentic Jamaican restaurants favored by locals. My favorite is **Sweet Spice Restaurant** (☎ 957-4621), with a menu that includes curried goat (US$5), conch steak (US$7), fish (US$5), and pepper steak (US$4). **Country Man** (☎ 940-5219) is a popular 24-hour eatery that serves jerk and BBQ.

**NEGRIL & WEST COAST**

**West End** You can't go wrong at *Chicken Lavish* (☎ 957-4410), on West End Rd, and *Roy & Felix Serious Chicken* (☎ 957-0139), opposite Drumville Cove. Both are bargain eateries and have great atmosphere. The latter serves curried chicken (US$6), pepper shrimp (US$10), and brown-stewed fish (US$9). Be sure to try the 'call and blow' (white chicken meat wrapped in bacon, stuffed with cheese and onions, fried as a ball; US$7). The *Castaway Restaurant*, next to the Rockhouse, features tasty 'angel and horseback' (ripe banana wrapped in bacon and fried; US$2.50), as well as lobster (US$12), conch steak (US$6.50), kingfish steak (US$6), and bargain breakfasts.

The *Hotel Samsara* (☎ 957-4395) has an 'Island Grill Night' on Thursday for US$15, and an all-you-can-eat Jamaican buffet at 6 pm on Sunday, with fire-eaters, limbo, and salsa dancing.

Near the east end of Ocean Drive, the *Hard Reggae Café* (☎ 957-4991) has a large breakfast menu (from US$2), plus lunches from US$5, and daily specials.

The thatched *Rockhouse Restaurant & Bar* (☎ 957-4373), at the Rockhouse resort, offers nouvelle Jamaican treats such as vegetable tempura with lime, ginger, and soy sauce (US$5), specialty pastas (US$11), and kingfish niçoise salad (US$11). Meals are served alfresco or under canopy on a pavilion overhanging the waters. Lamplit at night, it provides a romantic spot, and there's sometimes live music. It's open 7 am to 11 pm daily, and serves large and hearty breakfasts, including muesli (US$5) and pancakes (US$5).

Plenty of places serve patties and pastries. The *Sunset Mushroom Tea Pub*, on Ocean Drive at the southern end of West End, sells mushroom tea.

## I-tal & Vegetarian Food

**Long Bay** For Rastafarian health food, you have several options. Most notable are *Vegetarian I-tal Health Food*, on Norman Manley Blvd, outside Gloria's Sunset, and *Desi Dread's*, on the beach not far from the Negril Crafts Market. Both sell vegetarian dishes for less than US$5.

**West End** *Hungry Lion* (☎ 957-4486) specializes in I-tal dishes and juices. It has a mural of Marcus Garvey and various musical idols to amuse you while you enjoy dishes such as lasagna with callaloo (US$8), vegetarian shepherd's pie (US$10), and sautéed shrimp in garlic herb (US$18). Nearby, *Just Natural*, in a thatch hut in nicely kept gardens on West End Rd, also serves veggie dishes and seafoods, including tuna melt, veggie burger, and burritos.

Farther south, beyond the lighthouse, is *Culture Yard* (☎ 957-0195), a pleasant spot serving I-tal foods such as hemp burgers made from marijuana plant seeds (US$2), jelly coconut, and red pea stew. It's run by a friendly Rasta named Marjori, who offers games and hammocks. And *Jackie's on the Reef* serves health foods and herbal teas (US$6 breakfast, US$8 lunch, US$18 dinner).

## Seafood

**Long Bay** A steadfast beach favorite is *Cosmo's* (☎ 957-4330), with three thatched bars and dining areas near the Long Bay Beach Park. It specializes in conch soup, curried conch, and curried shrimp. Prices range from about US$5 to US$12. Cosmo charges US$2 to use his beach facilities and changing rooms. It's open 9 am to 10 pm.

*Fun Holiday Beach* (☎ 957-3585) has a two-for-one lobster special on weekends, plus a Thursday night buffet and soca beach party.

**West End** Seafood options atop the cliffs include *Drumville Cove* (☎ 957-4369), where you can savor snapper Drumville (baked filet with creamy sauce; US$7), *escoveitched* fish with sautéed onion (US$7.50), and lobster (US$12). *Summerset Village* (☎ 957-4409) offers an all-you-can-eat lobster buffet on Thursday. The *Lighthouse Inn* (☎ 957-4052) serves an excellent red snapper stuffed with callaloo, and steamed or brown-stewed kingfish, tuna, or barracuda (US$8 to US$20).

## Italian

**Long Bay** The Italian-owned *Red Snapper Deli*, just north of Alfred's Ocean Palace, an atmospheric bamboo-and-thatch bar and restaurant fronting the beach, serves a huge

## Legal Lobster?

By law, no lobster can be landed, captured, purchased, or sold between April 1 and June 30. At this time you'll see 'Lobster Closed Season' flyers posted all over Negril. Many restaurants, however, continue to serve lobster (which they claim to have stockpiled before closed season). In 1996, the NCRPS declared a moratorium on serving lobster in the Negril Environmental Protection Area. Obviously, some restaurants are serving illegally caught lobster. Use your conscience: stick to fish or shrimp!

menu of seafood and pastas. It offers free shuttles to and from your hotel. Also on Long Bay is the *Ristorante da Gina Italiano* in the Mariposa Hideaway hotel. And despite its name, the *Conch Hill Natural Food Place*, mid-way along Long Bay, serves a menu heavy with Italian dishes.

Another good bet is the highly ranked *Gambino's Italian Restaurant* (☎ 957-4170), in the Beachcomber Club, serving a wide range of pastas, lasagna, carbonara, and other Italian classics.

Seeking pizza? Try *Chances* (☎ 957-3977), mid-way along Long Bay, or *Mr Slice Pizza*, next to Alfred's Ocean Palace.

**West End** Try *Bella Donna* (☎ 957-0628), where Donna – who proudly claims to be the 'best cook in Negril' – produces Italian-Jamaican fare at her rustic eatery. Live bands perform. Entrees begin at US$10.

Expect to pay US$15 for dinner at the Italian restaurant at *Hotel Samsara* (☎ 957-4395). *Summerset Village* has an Italian 'extravaganza' on Saturday nights.

*Mr Slice Pizza* (☎ 957-9808, 957-3520) charges US$3 per slice; a 14-inch pizza costs US$15 (add US$2 for delivery).

*Archway Café* (☎ 957-4399), farther along on West End Rd, also specializes in pizza but has fish and chips and burgers, too. It offers free delivery.

## Other Cuisines

**Long Bay** My favorite place on the beach is the *Kuyaba on the Beach*, at the Sea Gem hotel. This thatched, multi-tiered stone-and-timber structure has heaps of ambience, enhanced by hammock-seats at the bar. The dining is upscale but unpretentious. The lunch menu features burgers (US$7) and gourmet sandwiches, plus superb pepper shrimps (US$10). For dinner, check out a wide range of pasta dishes (US$11 to US$20), a superb lobster bisque, or the Cuban crab and pumpkin cakes with papaya mustard (US$20). The bruschetta is to die for. A mento bands plays, but Friday is Cuba night with live music.

You might also try *Tamboo Inn* (☎ 957-4282), a bamboo-and-thatch, two-story restaurant lit by brass lanterns at night. Its varied menu includes a breakfast of 'pigs in a blanket' (US$7), pancakes and sausage (US$6), or a fruit platter with ice cream (US$5). Grilled cheese sandwiches, deep-fried lobster niblets, and nine types of pizza are each US$5 to US$22.

**West End** Negril is synonymous with *Rick's Café* (☎ 957-0380), to which scores of visitors skitter, lemminglike, to watch the sunset. This erstwhile rustic bar has gone upscale since it struck pay dirt in the 1970s, and today it's one of the most sophisticated eateries in town, lit by Tiffany lamps and graced by 1920s-era Hollywood posters. Prices have gone upmarket, too (but not with cash – here you purchase beads to spend, for US$1.25 each). Burgers cost US$6. The eclectic, wide-ranging menu also includes pompano Jack filet, conch steak, charbroiled fish platter, linguine Bolognese, plus exotic desserts (US$3). Entrees begin at about US$10 and run to US$21 for curried shrimp. It's open 2 to 10 pm, and has a two-for-one happy hour from 8 pm onwards.

As an alternative, I recommend the restaurant at the *Xtabi* lodge, which offers a marvelous setting on the cliff face and has a varied and reasonably priced menu mixing seafood, Jamaican, and continental dishes. The chef at *Doc's Delight* (☎ 957-4850), in the Negril B&B, cooks gourmet international dinners (baked chicken in honey-peanut

Sunset silhouettes at Rick's Café, Negril

sauce, lobster Thermidor, Châteaubriand, and so on). It's a good option, too, for breakfasts of Belgian waffles and homemade muffins.

A more homely option is the **LTU Pub**, 100 yards south of Rick's Café. This small cliff-side, open-air bar has an eclectic menu with a wide range of specialty burgers (from US$6) and spaghetti dishes, fish and chips, and chicken Bombay, all for about US$8.

The popular **Pickled Parrot** is an American-style bar and grill serving fare ranging from burritos and tacos to burgers, pizza, and seafood. (It recently opened a beachfront grill with similar fare.)

**Peking House** (☎ 957-0229), on West End Rd, is the only Chinese restaurant that I know of in Negril, though **Errol's Sunset Café** (☎ 957-3312), on Norman Manley Blvd, also serves Chinese dishes.

### Cafés

**Cecile's Café** (☎ 957-3586), on Norman Manley Blvd, is a charming spot done up in lively Caribbean colors, with hip music. It serves salads, pastas, and sandwiches from US$5, plus cheesecake and other desserts and cappuccinos (US$3). The **Blue Mountain Coffee Shop**, opposite Merrill's Beach Resort, serves dynamite cappuccinos, espressos, and ice coffees.

In the West End, try **Cheap Charlie's Kaffe**, an espresso bar with pastries and Cuban cigars.

### Groceries

There's a **supermarket** in Sunshine Village, plus small **grocery stalls** dotted along Norman Manley Blvd and West End Rd. The best-stocked store along West End Rd is **Twin Stars** (☎ 957-0172).

### ENTERTAINMENT

Negril is Jamaica's most party-conscious resort town. At any time of the year, Negril is the place to 'ride de riddims.' In fact, it's the only place in Jamaica with live concerts every night in peak season, and there's

HOLGER LEUE

NEGRIL & WEST COAST

almost sure to be some big talent in town. Negril also has a handful of discos, plus the requisite earthy go-go club, but no cinema and nothing in the way of high culture. There are dozens of bars to choose from, from funky shacks catering mostly to locals to thoroughly touristy spots such as Rick's and the sophisticated bars of the all-inclusive resorts.

## Stageshows

Negril's live reggae concerts are legendary. A handful of venues (notably De Buss, Alfred's Ocean Palace, and Risky Business) offer weekly jams, and have a rotation system so they all get a piece of the action. Big-name acts usually perform at MXIII, Hotel Samsara, or Central Park, all on West End, and acts are advertised with billboards. Cover is normally about US$10.

Several previously steadfast venues had closed in 1998 (including Kaiser's, previously the biggest venue), and the scene has become notably more 'touristy' than in prior years as the police have begun to enforce noise abatement laws forcing stageshows to close down by midnight. The scene is fluid.

**Long Bay** *Risky Business* (☎ 957-3008, riskybiz@toj.com) hosts music on Monday, Thursday, and Saturday. *De Buss* has reggae shows on Tuesday and Thursday. *Alfred's Ocean Palace* (☎ 957-4735) plays host on Tuesday and Friday night, when it's *the* place to be. It also has concerts on Sunday. *Roots Bamboo* (☎ 957-4479) hosts live reggae concerts on Wednesday and Sunday. *Fun Holiday Beach* has live reggae on Saturday (with limbo and fire-dancers) and Monday (Ladies Nite, with free drinks all night for women), plus a Soca Beach Party with two-for-one rums at 8 pm Thursday.

The *Long Bay Beach Park* comes alive on Sunday when an 'Oldies Beach Party' is held from 10 am to early evening.

**West End** The *Negril Yacht Club* (☎/fax 957-9224, www.cwjamaica.com/~negrilyacht/) hosts free live reggae, Thursday through Sunday, and the *Sunset Bar*, at Mariner's Inn (☎ 957-0392), also hosts live reggae at

sunset. The *Lighthouse Inn* hosts a 'mento yard' at 7 pm on Wednesday.

You'll also find regular sound-system jams where DJs play shatteringly loud music – usually dancehall with some Eurodisco – on speakers the size of railroad boxcars. The most popular jams are in the Negril Hills (see the Negril Hills section, later in this chapter). Try the *One Love Restaurant*, at the rear of Coral Seas Plaza in Negril Village.

You'll find information about upcoming events posted on streetside poles.

## Bars

Negril has dozens of bars, running the gamut from dark and down-to-earth rum shops serving dreadlocked locals (the most authentic are on Sheffield Rd) to chic upscale options with satellite TV, neon, and other contrivances. The competition is fierce; many offer happy hour incentives to lure you for sunset, notably along the West End, where the bars are lively in early evening before petering out as the beach bars take over.

**Long Bay** My favorites on the beach include the Sea Gem hotel's *Kuyaba* for atmosphere with hammock-seats beside the bar; and the funky *Boat Bar*, a tiny place formed around an old fishing boat turned into a bar, with a floor of bottle tops.

Several 'sports bars' have opened in recent years. *Margueritaville* (☎ 957-4467), a sibling to the smash-hit club in Montego Bay, is a lively spot that boasts a basketball court, assorted music and other entertainment, and offers a free shuttle. The resort *Legends* has a popular sports bar, with walls festooned with sports paraphernalia and Hollywood posters. If only the music weren't so loud! *Risky Business* and *Winners* (☎ 957-9473) are other sports bars.

**West End** You can savor the almost carnal sunsets from any bar along the shoreline, but *Rick's Café*, atop the cliffs on West End Rd, is the prime gathering place. The happy hour at Rick's begins *after* sundown, when the crowd begins to drift away. Several bars have happy hours at about 5 or 6 pm, timed to steer you away from Rick's. A little down the road, the *LTU Pub* offers a less touristy alternative, as does the tasteful bar at the *Rockhouse* resort.

The *Pickled Parrot* is also fun. It has moved from the beach to the West End, where you can plunge down a waterslide into the briny blue. It has a happy hour from 3 to 5 pm and serves snacks.

To commune with locals, try *Mi Yard* on West End Rd. It's open 24 hours and draws a late-night crowd into the wee hours, when you can swig shots of white rum and slap down dominoes with locals.

*Garcia's Rockin' Reggae*, on West End Rd, has a pool hall with music.

Watch for the opening of the *Smoke House*, a serious cigar smoker's emporium, touted to open at the Rockhouse (see Places to Stay), with coffees and liquors.

## Discos

The most happening disco in town is *Compulseion Disco* (☎ 957-4169), above Negril Plaza. The US$5 entrance fee buys two drinks (on Wednesday, a US$15 cover includes all local drinks). It's open until 5 am Wednesday to Saturday and has happy hour from 10 pm to 1 am. It gets hot inside, and the dancing can get decidedly raunchy. Local women – many of them prostitutes – are unabashed.

*Limits*, at Negril Inn, is modestly upscale. The disco at Hotel Samsara had closed in 1998.

Nonguests can also obtain passes for entry to the discos in the following upscale all-inclusive resorts: Sandals Negril, Hedonism II, Couples, Beaches, and Grand Lido. The passes aren't cheap (expect to pay US$25 to US$65), but once inside the gates you can booze and party to your heart's content without having to shell out another cent.

## Go-Go Clubs

*Close Encounters* (☎ 957-0423), upstairs in King's Plaza, offers the usual fare of erotic stage acts until 4 am. You can't miss it – between gigs the dancers hang out on the roadside balcony, naked but for high heels or sometimes a g-string. Entrance costs US$3

(beers cost US$2.50). Many of the dancers are also prostitutes, with the attendant health risks to bear in mind.

## Beach Parties

*Blue Whale Divers* (☎ 957-4438) hosts a beach party every Tuesday, with kayak races, three-legged races, egg-and-spoon races, and wet T-shirt contests. *Risky Business* (see above) sometimes hosts a beach bonfire with DJ music. And the *Blue Lagoon Country Club* (☎ 957-9777) has a beach party on Saturday nights.

You can purchase a night pass to Hedonism II (US$65), where the beach parties are salacious – and hilarious – and you can partake of all activities and booze without additional cost.

## Comedy, Karaoke & Other

Tired of reggae? Then head to *Kuyaba* at the Sea Gem hotel on Friday night, where live Cuban musicians perform at 7:30 pm. Marvelous! It hosts mento on other nights. *Club Palm* (☎ 957-3039), at Traveller's Beach Resort, has jazz on Wednesday (US$7 including one drink), stand-up comedy on Thursday, with a 'ladies night' and special show (women get free entry plus half-price drinks), a talent contest on Friday, and 'wrestlemania' and Reggae Comedy Jam on Sunday.

For karaoke, try the *Mariner's Inn* on Tuesday and Thursday.

## Children's Entertainment

*Anancy Fun Park* (☎ 957-4100 ext 381), opposite Poinciana Beach Hotel, is a children's entertainment complex that features a learning center, a folk and heritage museum, donkey cart rides, fishing and boating lakes, nature trail, carousel, miniature steam train ride, go-carts, miniature golf course, and video arcade. It's open 1 to 8 pm Tuesday to Sunday (entry costs US$2 to US$5). Guests at the hotel can buy a US$50 per week 'Anancy Package.'

## SHOPPING
## Arts & Crafts

Itinerant locals hawk carvings, woven caps, hammocks, jewelry, macramé bikinis, and

T-shirts on the beach and along West End Rd, where there are some splendid carvings and wicker items. You can't walk by without a sales pitch. Don't be hustled into a purchase you don't want. Partly for this reason, the Negril Chamber of Commerce has been moving vendors off the beach and streets and concentrating them in crafts centers. On West End Rd, be sure to check out the Yin & Yang arts and crafts store, with a huge range of jewelry; it's opposite the Rockhouse.

There are three main crafts centers: Rutland Point Craft Centre, opposite Couples Negril; the Negril Crafts Market just north of Negril Plaza; and the A Fi Wi Plaza in Negril Village. Competition is fierce. Haggling is part of the fun. Look at it that way and you'll get farther without losing your cool.

Negril Plaza, Coral Seas Plaza, and Sunshine Village also have good souvenir shops. I recommend the Kuyaba arts and crafts boutique at the Sea Gem (☎ 957-4318).

### Other Items

Most upscale hotels have well-stocked gift stores and boutiques. Tajmahal's (☎ 957-4910) has duty-free stores at the Grand Lido Hotel and Beachcomber Club selling jewelry, watches, and the like. There's even a United Colors of Benetton at the Beachcomber. And Sunshine Village has several duty-free stores.

Victor's Records on West End Rd can outfit you with reggae tapes.

Looking for a sarong? Check out Sarongs to Go, on West End Rd.

Photo Colour Lab (☎ 957-4594), next to the JTB office in Coral Seas Plaza, offers developing (US$15 processing per color roll), video production, and custom B&W work. It also provides passport and visa photos (US$6) and sells film. It's open 8 am to 5 pm Monday to Friday, 8 am to 4 pm Saturday. On West End Rd, Photo Print (☎ 957-0435) has film and photo supplies.

A new shopping center – Times Square – was being built at press time opposite De Buss on Norman Manley Blvd.

### GETTING THERE & AWAY
### Air

Negril Aerodrome is at Bloody Bay, about 7 miles north of Negril Village.

Negril wood carvings meet their maker.

CHRISTOPHER P BAKER

NEGRIL & WEST COAST

Air Jamaica Express (☎ 957-5251) has two flights daily between Montego Bay and Negril (US$37 one-way) and one daily from Kingston's Tinson Pen (US$52 one-way). Special students' and seniors' fares are offered.

Air Negril (☎ 957-5325, fax 957-5291) has regular, nonscheduled service between MoBay and Negril (US$60 one-way) using new 14-seat Cessnas.

Timair (☎ 957-5374) serves Negril.

### Bus

Minibus service between Negril and Montego Bay is frequent. The two-hour journey costs about US$3. You may need to change buses in Lucea (check the final destination written on the side of the vehicle). Be prepared for a hair-raising ride – the drivers are singularly reckless. Minibuses also leave for Negril from Donald Sangster International Airport in Montego Bay (the price is negotiable, but expect to pay about US$10).

In Negril, buses for Montego Bay, Savanna-la-Mar (US$1), and Kingston (about four hours) depart from Sheffield Rd, just east of the roundabout. You can also wave down the Montego Bay bus on Norman Manley Blvd.

Tour buses cost US$20 to US$25 each way. Caribic Vacations (☎ 957-3309, 953-9878), Tropical Tours (☎ 957-4110), and Tourwise (☎ 957-4223) offer transfers between Montego Bay airport and Negril.

### Taxi

A licensed taxi between Montego Bay and Negril will cost about US$70. In MoBay, call the Jamaica Union of Travelers Association (JUTA; ☎ 979-0778). You should be able to negotiate a rate for about US$50 to US$70 with an unlicensed driver. Negril is 52 miles east of Montego Bay, approximately a 90-minute drive.

## GETTING AROUND

Walking short distances is OK, and it's especially pleasant to stroll the beach. However, Negril stretches along more than 10 miles of shoreline, and it can be a withering walk. At some stage you'll most likely need transport. Upscale resorts at the north end of Long Bay have shuttles into town, and several hotels on the West End run shuttles to the beach. I've walked the length of Norman Manley Blvd and West End Rd several times, but it's a hot and sweaty trek.

### To/From the Airport

There's no scheduled bus service between the airstrip and hotels. A taxi will cost a whopping US$7 to US$10 for a journey between the airport and Negril Village or any point in between. Even a half-mile journey to Rutland Point will cost US$7.

### Minibus

Minibuses cruise Norman Manley Blvd and, to a lesser degree, West End Rd. You can flag them down anywhere; rides usually cost less than US$2. The majority of vehicles are heading to Montego Bay, and your request to go just a few miles may be viewed with disdain.

### Car & Motorcycle

Cars and Jeeps are more expensive than elsewhere in Jamaica. Consider renting one in Montego Bay. In Negril, expect to pay at least US$45 per day (plus insurance) off-season for a small car and US$65 per day for a convertible Suzuki from Jus Jeep (☎ 957-0094, fax 957-0429), Coconut Car Rental (☎ 957-4291), or Vernon's Car Rentals (☎ 957-4764), next to Whistling Bird on Long Bay and also at Advanced Travel Service (☎ 957-4057), upstairs in Negril Plaza. At least a dozen other car rental booths line Norman Manley Blvd and West End Rd. Most require a hefty deposit.

There are plenty of places renting motorcycles. Scooters average US$25 to US$35 a day; motorbikes US$40 to US$55. A few companies to consider are Tykes Bike Rental (☎ 957-0388) and Dependable Bike Rental (☎ 957-4764). Salmon's Bike Rentals (☎ 957-4671), outside Westlea Cabins, charges US$30 a day for scooters. Kool Bike Rentals (☎ 1-771-6858 cellular), at the Negril Yacht Club, charges US$25 for a scooter and US$60 for a Honda CB600. Ask for Steve or 'Bigfoot.' Wright's Bicycle Rental (☎ 957-4908) charges US$35 per day for a scooter, US$40 for a dirt bike, and US$60 for a Honda Shadow.

Irie Bike (☎ 957-5555) rents scooters and offers a full-day scooter excursion to May-field Falls (US$70 single, US$110 double). Happy Bike (☎ 957-3181), on Norman Manley Blvd, has 90cc scooters for US$33 per day and 175cc ones for US$39. It also offers guided tours.

Helmets are not mandatory and hardly anyone wears one, but you should! The roads are potholed and often have patches of sand and gravel. Remember, too, that you may not feel the effects of the sun while riding with a breeze that cools you down. Use sunscreen.

### Taxi

A nonstop parade of taxis runs through Negril. Licensed taxis display a red license plate and are mostly white Toyota Corolla station wagons (estate cars). Fares are regulated by the government (about US$2 per 2 miles), but few drivers use their meters. Call JUTA (☎ 957-9147). You can order taxis from Will's Taxi Service (☎ 957-5249), Easy-Going Cabs (☎ 957-3227), or Dependable Taxi Service (☎ 957-4764). There are taxi stands at the Negril Crafts Market and in front of Coral Seas Plaza. If you take an unlicensed cab, you should bargain the fare *before* getting in: US$5 should be a maximum fare.

A much cheaper bet is a 'robot' or shared taxi – usually an aged and battered vehicle – that picks up passengers en route. They run the length of Norman Manley Blvd and West End Rd and can be flagged down anywhere along the route. The fare from the round-about to the airport or lighthouse should never be more than US$2.

Henry Woodcock (☎ 957-0182, 1-819-9314 cellular) runs a 28-passenger shuttle bus for tours and airport transfers.

### Bicycle

You can rent mountain bikes from US$7 a day. Most motorcycle rental agencies listed above have bicycles, as does Indian Skonk Bike Rental (☎ 957-0870). If you rent a bike overnight, make sure that it is securely locked in a well-lit area. Consider taking a large chain and padlock with you. Check to ensure that insurance will cover any loss.

# Negril to Tryall

Northeast from Negril, the A1 leads to Montego Bay, hugging the coast of Hanover parish most of the way (an expressway was under construction at press time). It's a pleasing drive as the road wriggles past small fishing villages and winds in and out of tiny coves. The only town of note is Lucea. Most travelers buzz on by without a glance at the intriguing historic buildings, but you can happily spend a couple of hours here.

If you're driving, be careful on the section of road near the Great Morass immediately north of Negril: motorists are tempted to speed. Minibus drivers display reckless abandon.

## GREEN ISLAND HARBOUR

Immediately north of Negril, the A1 swings around a wide expanse of swampland – the Great Morass – good for spotting crocodiles if you have the spirit to explore the mangroves. After 10 miles you pass the shores of a deep cove – Green Island Harbour – where pirogues line the thin, gray-sand shore. There's a forlorn Presbyterian church.

**Hurricane Park** (☎ 819-9923) is a tree-shaded spot with a bar serving seafood to day visitors. A similar, more appealing, recreational site is **Half Moon Beach**, 800 yards farther west and named for its sands like crushed diamonds that help create the illusion that you're on the moon's surface. You may strip to your birthday suit. Snorkeling gear can be rented. And simple meals are served at a thatched restaurant. Dirt-bike races are occasionally held on the erstwhile airstrip behind the beach (it is now closed to prevent drug-trafficking). It's open 8 am to 10 pm daily (the US$2.50 entrance is good toward a meal or drink purchase).

## Rhodes Mineral Springs & Beach

This recreational site, 2 miles west of Green Island Harbour, has several thatched bars and a restaurant backing a small but attractive beach where hot mineral springs bubble up. Follow the beach west and you may see crocodiles at the mouth of the river.

Horseback riding is offered. Choose from three trips (US$30 to US$40). The Scuba World Dive Shop (☎ 957-6290, 1-995-9345 cellular, scubaworld@cwjamaica.com) offers diving.

A beach party is hosted on Sunday night.

## Places to Stay

You can camp at *Half Moon Beach* for US$10 per tent, and there are two very basic wooden cabins with bare-bones furnishings for the same price. The restaurant caters sandwiches, burgers, and simple Jamaican snacks.

*JJ's Guest House* (☎ 956-9159, 718-968-7469 in the USA), just east of Green Island Harbour, is a modest yet comfortable place atop a breezy hill with distant views of the ocean. There are eight rooms, each with two single beds, ceiling fans, and private bath with hot water. You dine on a rooftop patio. There's a bar and a plunge pool. It's 400 yards up a dirt road from the highway. Winter rates are US$35 to US$45.

*Rhodes Mineral Springs & Beach* (☎ 957-6334, fax 957-8333, PO Box 16) has two handsome air-conditioned cottages on the beach. One sleeps two for US$80; the second is family-size and costs US$100 year-round. Both have private bath with hot water, plus kitchen. Lower rates are offered for stays of five days.

At Orange Bay, Jasmine McGregor rents *Falcon Crest* (☎ 957-6072), an old house for up to six people, with a minimum one-month stay required. There's a kitchen and lounge plus three bedrooms with private bath, hot water, and ceiling fans. The price is negotiable.

## Places to Eat

You can eat cheaply at the roadside *jerk stalls* at Green Island Harbour, where you'll also find *Mandela Green* (☎ 956-2607), a popular bar and dance spot.

## BLENHEIM

This tiny hamlet, 4 miles inland of Green Island, is too small to appear on most maps, but it's important as the birthplace of national hero Alexander Bustamante, father of Jamaican independence and the island's first prime minister. The rustic three-room wooden shack where Bustamante was born has been reconstructed on the original site as a national monument. The **Sir Alexander Bustamante Museum** (c/o National Heritage Trust; ☎ 922-1287, fax 951-1703), which stands all alone on a hilltop amid bamboo, is impressive for such an out-of-the-way spot and includes photographs and other memorabilia telling of the hero's life. There are no refreshments, but public toilets are available and there's a picnic area to the rear. It receives very few visitors. It's open 9 am to 5 pm daily. There's no charge.

A memorial ceremony is held in Blenheim in Busta's honor each August 6.

## Getting There & Away

**Bus** You can catch a bus or minibus in Lucea. Most of the buses that travel to Grange Hill (note the beautiful stone church on a knoll on the south side of town) and Savanna-la-Mar pass through Kingsvale, where you can walk to Blenheim, but it's a stiff, hilly journey of three miles or so.

**Car** Blenheim can be approached from Lucea via Dias, where Hanover St leads past the Baptist Church and continues west to Blenheim (it's not signed, however). You'll need to ask directions.

The easiest route is from Davis Cove, 2 miles north of Green Island Harbour. Blenheim is signed from here, though you'll still need to ask directions as you progress. Take the road that leads inland immediately west of the bridge over Davis Cove River. The road passes through cane fields before climbing through heraldic stands of bamboo. You'll come to a hilltop T-junction after 2 miles; take the left road downhill and continue to a steep dirt road off to the right that begins immediately before the second of two tiny bridges. The road loops uphill 400 yards to the Bustamante museum.

## LANCE'S BAY

Lance's Bay, about 4 miles west of Lucea, offers a couple of small yet tempting beaches. Most notable is Gull Bay Beach, a pocket-

## National Hero Busta

Alexander Bustamante, one of Jamaica's revered national heroes, was born on February 24, 1884, on the Blenheim Estate, where his father was an impoverished overseer. The boy – christened William Alexander Clarke – left Jamaica with limited education in 1903 and worked in several countries before returning to his homeland in 1932 (with the surname Bustamante).

He was already in his 50s when he entered public life by speaking out against the appalling social and political conditions of colonial Jamaica. This charismatic figure organized the local labor force and formed the Bustamante Industrial Trade Union, for which he was imprisoned by the British colonial government following islandwide riots in 1938.

In 1944, he formed the Jamaica Labour Party (JLP) to contest the island's first general election held under universal adult suffrage. The JLP won a resounding victory. 'Busta' thus became Jamaica's first prime minister, a post he held until 1954, the year he was knighted by Queen Elizabeth II. Busta enjoyed unusually cordial relations with the Queen: at a state reception for Commonwealth prime ministers at Buckingham Palace, he once greeted the monarch with the words 'Hello honey!' and a warmly received embrace.

Following independence, Jamaica became part of the West Indies Federation, and Bustamante was the Jamaican representative of the Democratic Labour Party. In 1962 he steered the nation to secession from the federation. Bustamante then led the JLP to victory in the Jamaican general election later that year, thereby becoming the first prime minister in an independent Jamaica. He retired from active politics in 1967 but remained influential. He was named a national hero prior to his death in 1977.

size cove lined by shimmering white sand. At Cousin's Cove, just west of Lance's Bay, a farmer named Ron has a cave – **Ron's Rat Bat Cave** – on his property, about 800 yards inland. He charges US$10 for an hour-long guided tour. The forbidding chambers are replete with stalagmites and stalactites, pendulous fruit bats, a mineral pool good for a dip, and even ancient, if barely discernible, petroglyphs said to have been daubed by Arawak Indians.

A North American, Linda Stewart, (☎ 956-6234) offers horseback riding (US$60 half-day, including lunch; US$40 for children). Her twee wooden cottage is 100 yards beyond Ron's cave. She sometimes rents the cottage to riders. The rooms cost US$25 double, including breakfast, and are basic but have electricity, private bath (cold water), and balcony with an ocean view. Linda hopes to have a telephone soon.

*Hideaway Cottages* offers small, well-kept air-conditioned cabins at Lance's Bay. The pink-and-green cottages are set back from the road in well-tended gardens and have a porch with chairs.

NEGRIL & WEST COAST

The only eatery of note is the rustic *Carolina Sunset Inn*, on the oceanfront just before Lance's Bay.

## LUCEA

'Lucy' (population 6000), as the town is commonly known, is built around a harbor ringed by hills on three sides. (Animal Hill is named for the families – the Wolfs, the Lyons, the Mairs, and the Hoggs – who once lived there.) Twenty-five miles east of Negril Village and about the same distance west of Montego Bay, Lucea is small enough for visitors to walk everywhere.

Back in early colonial days, Lucea was more active than Montego Bay. Only the 'molasses pier' remains of the once-busy shipping wharves (molasses is still loaded onto cargo ships from huge tanks next to the pier). The town still abounds in old limestone and timber structures in 'Caribbean vernacular' style, with gingerbread wood trim, clapboard frontages, and wide verandas. The oldest dates to the mid-1700s. Lucea has appeared as a set in several movies, including *Cool Runnings* and *Wide Sargasso Sea*. The Hanover Historical Society ('the Barracks'; ☎ 956-2584), PO Box 35, formed in 1989, is active in the town's preservation.

'Lucy' is a somnolent place, except on Saturday when the market is in full force and stalls spill out onto the streets. You can walk around with relatively little hassle.

Local residents have set up a small-scale 'visitor in the home' program similar to the JTB's Meet the People. Contact JTB offices for information.

### History

Lucea is one of Jamaica's earliest settlements. The first written record of Lucea dates back to 1515, when King Ferdinand of Spain commended his governor in Jamaica for moving settlers to the site after the capital of Nueva Sevilla was abandoned. The town grew on the shores of Lucea Harbour, which extends inland for one mile. In 1774 historian Edward Long estimated that 300 ships at a time could be sheltered here. Lucea had by then been named a free port by the English. The infamous pirate Henry Morgan even used Lucea Harbour to shelter his ships, and later owned 4000 acres locally.

By the mid-18th century Lucea was the center of an important sugar-growing region, and the town prospered as a sugar port and market center. Jews from Europe settled and established themselves as merchants, shopkeepers, clothiers, shoemakers, and goldsmiths.

Following emancipation, free peasants prospered in Hanover parish and supplied produce to much of the rest of Jamaica. The 19th century saw many fine edifices built by skilled artisans (many of them former slaves) including Lucea market and courthouse. Main St still retains a few old merchant residences, with timber columns supporting the upper stories.

Lucea lends its name to a locally grown yam, which in the 19th century was exported in large quantities to expatriate Jamaicans working on the plantations and railway construction in Cuba and Central America. 'Lucea yams' are still an important crop, along with pimento and ginger.

### Information

**Money** Scotiabank (☎ 956-2553) faces the roundabout in the center of town. National Commercial Bank (☎ 956-2204) has a branch on Main St. The Jamaican National Building Society (☎ 956-2344) has an official exchange bureau.

**Medical Services** Dr Chapman's New Era Medical Centre is in Island Plaza on Main St (open 8 am to 6 pm weekdays, until noon Saturday). The Family Care Pharmacy is also here, or try Dr David Stair or Dr Taylor Watson (☎ 956-2930). Lucea hospital has an emergency department (☎ 956-2233, 956-3836); it's on the headland behind Hanover Parish Church.

**Emergency** There are police stations on Main St (☎ 956-2333) and on Watson Taylor Drive (☎ 956-2222).

### Things to See

Lucea can be explored on foot in one hour. Begin your walking tour at **Sir Alexander**

**Bustamante Square**, centered on a small fountain fronting the handsome courthouse that was formally opened by Queen Elizabeth II on her state visit in 1966. Note the vintage fire engine (1932) beside the courthouse.

The **courthouse** has limestone balustrades and a clapboard upper story topped by a clock tower supported by Corinthian columns. The clock was sent to Lucea in 1817 by mistake – it was actually intended for the Caribbean island of St Lucia. The residents (who had ordered a more modest clock from the same company) decided to keep the more elaborate godsend and passed the hat around to pay for it. It has supposedly worked without a hitch ever since, under the maintenance of the Williams family who were given the responsibility for its running over 100 years ago. If you think the cap on the tower resembles the helmet worn by the Prussian Imperial Guards, you're correct. It was donated by a German landowner who designed it.

On the east side of the square is bustling **Cleveland Stanhope market**. A walk north

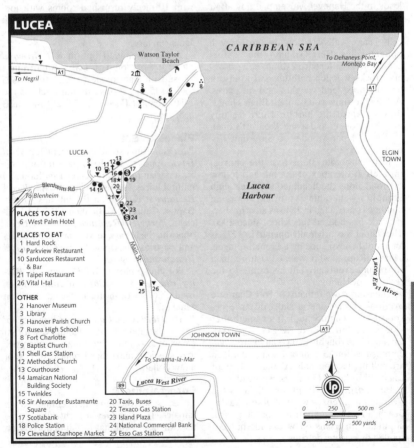

**LUCEA**

CARIBBEAN SEA

Watson Taylor Beach

To Dehaneys Point, Montego Bay

To Negril

LUCEA

Blenheim Rd
To Blenheim

ELGIN TOWN

Lucea Harbour

Lucea East River

**PLACES TO STAY**
6  West Palm Hotel

**PLACES TO EAT**
1  Hard Rock
4  Parkview Restaurant
10  Sarducces Restaurant & Bar
21  Taipei Restaurant
26  Vital I-tal

**OTHER**
2  Hanover Museum
3  Library
5  Hanover Parish Church
7  Rusea High School
8  Fort Charlotte
9  Baptist Church
11  Shell Gas Station
12  Methodist Church
13  Courthouse
14  Jamaican National Building Society
15  Twinkles
16  Sir Alexander Bustamante Square
17  Scotiabank
18  Police Station
19  Cleveland Stanhope Market
20  Taxis, Buses
22  Texaco Gas Station
23  Island Plaza
24  National Commercial Bank
25  Esso Gas Station

Main St.

JOHNSON TOWN

To Savanna-la-Mar

Lucea West River

0      250      500 m
0      250      500 yards

NEGRIL & WEST COAST

up the main frontage road curls past some of Lucea's finest historical houses, many in a near state of decrepitude, and deposits you atop the headland with a fine view east over Lucea Harbour. At the hillcrest is **Hanover Parish Church** (☎ 956-2253), established in 1725. It's architecturally uninspired but has several interesting monuments – including one of planter Simon Clarke by the noted British sculptor John Flaxman – and a Jewish quarter within the walled cemetery recalling the days when Lucea had a lively Jewish community.

A sideroad that begins 200 yards west leads to the **Hanover Museum**, a tiny affair housed in an old police barracks that include the burned-out remains of prisoners' cells, where walls are now overgrown with bougainvillea. Bert Graham, the genteel curator, looks after such exhibits as a prisoners' stocks, wooden bathtub, and a miscellany of pots, lead weights, and measures. Ask him to show you Captain Bligh's hand-drawn map of the harbor. There's a tiny gift shop, toilets, and a snack bar. It's open 10 am to 4 pm Monday to Saturday. Entrance is US$2.

Retracing your steps past the church, turn left at the apex of the hill and follow the road along the headland to **Rusea High School**, a venerable red-brick Georgian building constructed in 1843 as an army barracks. It has housed the school since 1900. The school was originally opened in 1777 as an act of benevolence by a French refugee, Martin Rusea, who washed ashore in a storm and eventually left his estate to the residents of Hanover.

The overgrown remains of **Fort Charlotte** overlook the channel a short distance beyond Rusea High School. It's named after Queen Charlotte, wife of King George III of England. The roughly octagonal fortress had embrasures for 23 cannons, some of which are still in place on rails. A small colony of frigate birds hover like kites overhead.

Beyond the school playing field to the west is the breeze-swept **Watson Taylor Beach**, a gray-sand affair of modest appeal, popular with locals on weekends but despoiled by eclectic detritus.

## Places to Stay

The musty smelling **West Palm Hotel** (☎ 956-2321) is an old wooden building, just behind Hanover Parish Church, with 23 simple rooms from US$30 (US$35 with air-con). Some have narrow single beds; others have queen-size beds. All have basic furnishings and private bath with hot water. The hotel is popular with businesspeople, and locals gather at the bar out back. It has a modest restaurant.

The modern **Global Villa Guest House** (☎ 956-2916, fax 956-3109), 5 miles west of town on A1, is a clean, modern property with 10 nicely furnished rooms with louvered windows and tile floors from US$40. It has a TV lounge, bar, and restaurant serving Jamaican fare.

A recommended option is **Driftwood** (☎ 956-2370), on Third St, a small guest house with eight modest rooms for US$25 to US$35 in a house dating back to the 1780s. **Crystal View** (☎ 957-9225) is a B&B near town.

## Places to Eat

No restaurants stand out except for **Vital I-tal**, opposite the Esso gas station. This Rastafarian restaurant serves I-tal food and natural juices. Locals gravitate to **Sarducces Restaurant & Bar**, on the hill next to the Baptist Church on Blenheim Rd, and the clean **Parkview Restaurant** (☎ 956-3168), opposite the library, serving Jamaican dishes and pastries. Seeking Chinese? Try **Taipei Restaurant**, on Main St.

For cheap patties, try **Hammonds Pastry Place**, next to **Chicken Joint** serving fried chicken. Both are in Island Plaza on Main St.

The **Hard Rock Café** west of Lucea is *not* part of the internationally famous restaurant chain, but is a funky little shack serving rice and peas, jerk, and other Jamaican dishes for a few dollars.

## Entertainment

Lucea is not the most happening spot in Jamaica. Try **Twinkles**, a nightclub next to the Jamaican National Building Society on Main St.

*Long Acre Restaurant & Nightclub*, reached via a long tree-lined driveway 2 miles west of Lucea, stages reggae shows in an atmospheric oceanfront setting. There's a bar but – despite its name – no food. It's signed off the road.

## Shopping

Check out the works of Lloyd Hoffstead, a well-known local painter and sculptor who has a gallery on Hanover St (☎ 956-2241), 100 yards east of the Texaco gas station. His work is of varying quality, but there are some good sculptures and paintings (open 9 am to 5 pm Monday to Friday). There's also a small workshop for disabled people at the entrance to the fort where you can buy crafts.

## Getting There & Away

Buses and 'coasters' arrive and depart Lucea from the open ground opposite the market. Lucea is a mid-way terminus for buses traveling between Montego Bay and Negril, and you may need to change vehicles here. Touts will attempt to shepherd you onto their bus, but no bus leaves before it is completely full, so your best bet is to choose the fullest bus. A bus between Lucea and MoBay or Negril costs about US$1.20. A minibus costs about US$3. From Lucea, minibuses also operate to Frome (US$1), Savanna-la-Mar (US$2), and Kingston (US$8).

The B9 leads south from the courthouse to Frome and Savanna-la-Mar.

## MOSKITO COVE

This long, slender inlet, 4 miles east of Lucea, is a popular place to anchor yachts. It's rimmed with mangroves and a few rustic jerk stalls and beer shacks. **Bigga's Royal Dwarf Factory**, roadside, is where a friendly Jamaican named Bigga does naive carvings and masks to order.

Beyond Moskito Cove, the road crosses a beautiful, wide-open grassy plain that slopes gently toward the ocean. Drive with caution! Cows often wander aimlessly along the road. Look, too, for the stack (rock pillar) offshore that some say resembles Queen Victoria in profile.

## MAYFIELD FALLS & MINERAL SPRINGS

A series of languid ridges – the Dolphin Head Mountains – rise inland of Moskito Cove. The wild hills' appeal is their abundant birdlife and many cascades. The grandest of these are at Mayfield (☎ 815-2681), a working tropical farm and tour attraction with 5 acres of land near Pennycooke, about 10 miles south of Moskito Cove, in an area called Glenbrook on the border of Westmoreland and Hanover parishes.

You'll cross a bamboo-and-log bridge to then follow the sun-dappled rivercourse, clambering over riverstones to reach the three falls and 21 pools where you can take a refreshing dip and even swim through a cave or enjoy a natural 'Jacuzzi' in any of several delightful swimming holes shaded by glades of bamboo. Take your swimming gear and sneakers or flip-flops. You can learn about ackee, breadfruits, and other Jamaican fruits, vegetables, and flowers, and even join in traditional African music and dance during show time (2:30 pm Tuesday and Friday). Geese and other waterfowl abound. There are hammocks beneath shade trees, plus volleyball. Entrance costs US$12, or US$20 with lunch.

## Getting There & Away

From the A1, take the road inland from Moskito Cove via Cascade. The route is signed but there are several turnoffs; you should ask your way to be sure. You can also reach Mayfield Falls from Tryall or Hopewell via Pondside (see the Montego Bay & Northwest Coast chapter); or by turning north at Savanna-la-Mar and taking the Banbury or Amity Cross routes (15 miles) along a road that is deplorably potholed.

Caribic Vacations (☎ 957-3309 in Negril) offers full-day excursions from Negril and Montego Bay for US$45 and US$50 respectively, including transport and lunch.

You can arrange a 'Mayfield Nature Pure Tour' in advance at Shop 4, Negril Plaza (☎ 957-3268, fax 957-3253).

## KENILWORTH

Just west of the Maggotty River east of Moskito Cove you'll see a turnoff to the left for the Human Employment & Resource Training Trust (HEART Trust), about a mile along a dirt road at Kenilworth (formerly called Maggotty). The HEART Trust was established in 1982 as a residential academy to provide vocational and personal development training to young Jamaicans. It operates under the Ministry of Education & Culture. It occupies 206 acres of an old sugar plantation acclaimed as the best example of old industrial architecture in Jamaica. The 17th-century ruins are on the left at the base of the hill; the HEART academy rises up the slope. Tourists are welcome. Don't be put off by the daunting wire-mesh gate. The guard will let you in if you ask (no charge).

Most prominent among the estate ruins are the sugar boiling house and distillery and the long rectangular sugar mill, a two-story limestone building with a semicircular flight of stairs leading up to an arched doorway. The walls have oval Palladian windows. A graveyard, 400 yards up the hill beyond the ruins, includes the tomb of Thomas Blagrove, an early owner. According to the inscription, 'his humane treatment of his servants, in a region not abounding in such examples, induced their cheerful obedience.'

As yet unfulfilled plans call for the ruins to be restored: the venerable mill, for example, has been touted to become a performing arts theater. And plans to develop a tour and to build a small guest house and restaurant and conference center have yet to evolve. For further information, contact Samuel Boyd (☎ 953-5315), Kenilworth HEART Trust/NTA Academy Sandy Bay PO, Hanover.

# Negril to Savanna-la-Mar

Tourism has been slow to develop along the southern shore of Westmoreland, a parish dependent on the sugar industry, with dismal Savanna-la-Mar the only town of any import. There are few beaches.

Roads fan out from Savanna-la-Mar through the Westmoreland Plains. This flat, mountain-rimmed area, planted almost entirely in sugarcane, was the scene of much violence during the labor agitation of the 1930s that helped shape Jamaica's contemporary politics. The plain is drained by the Cabarita River, which feeds swamplands at its lower reaches. The fishing is good, and a few crocodiles may still live in more secluded swampy areas, alongside an endemic fish – the 'God-a-me' – that can live out of water in moist, shady spots. The river is navigable by small boat for 12 miles. This region, too, is undeveloped for tourism except for a singular gem called Roaring River.

The eastern portion of Westmoreland is hilly and modestly populated, with mountains hemming up to the coast. Several slender beaches with active fishing communities provide a slice of Jamaican life. This section of coast, centered on Bluefields, southeast of Ferris Cross, is generally considered part of the 'South Coast,' and is gaining new stature as a center for nascent tourism (see the Southwest Coast chapter).

## NEGRIL HILLS
This range of low-lying hills rises east of Negril's West End. The raised limestone upland is wild and smothered in brush. The only habitations are on the eastern flanks, in cozy hamlets sprinkled along the single road that provides access from Negril: Whitehall Rd leads south from Sheffield Rd (the junction is opposite Sweet Spice Restaurant) and runs to the hamlet of Orange Hill and swings east through the hills via the village of Retirement and eventually links to the A2 for Savanna-la-Mar.

A drive or cycle ride into the Negril Hills reveals a bucolic Jamaica miles removed from the hedonistic beach scene. Goats forage the margins and cattle munch contentedly in tiny roadside pastures in the lee of rugged formations. The only site of note is **Whitehall Great House**, in ruins following a fire in 1985. The surrounding plantation grounds provide a stage for horseback rides (note the massive silk-cotton tree considered one of the largest in Jamaica). Don't be fooled into paying US$5 for a tour by the locals who hang out and attempt to attach themselves as self-ascribed 'guides.'

Jerk chicken special, Negril

Xtabi Lodge, Negril

Got whatcha want, mon!

Negril's Long Bay beach

The courthouse in Savanna-la-Mar

Grazing down by Roaring River, east of Negril

East of Retirement, a badly eroded side-road loops down to **Homers Cove** and **Little Bay**, where handsome little beaches (sadly denuded by sand mining) provide for relatively peaceful bathing. There are a few food stalls. Little Bay is imbued with the kind of laid-back feel that pervaded Negril before the onset of commercialization. It's a great place to commune with Rastas and other Jamaicans who live in ramshackle homes and exist from fishing, by their entrepreneurial wits, and a carefree axiom. The area is popular for reggae and dancehall sound systems that lure the local crowd from miles around, but foreigners are few and far between.

Bob Marley used to hang out here in the 1970s. A sign points the way to **Bob Marley's Spring**, where he bathed.

### Places to Stay

You can rent guest houses with locals, but most of the housing hereabouts may be a bit grim for all but the most ascetic tastes. Try *Tony's Ocean Rest* (☎ 909-9976), which has been recommended.

The only beachside spot of worth is *Coconut Cottages by the Sea* (☎/fax 997-5013; ☎ 608-836-5460, fax 836-9391 in the USA), an upscale place run by North Americans and featuring stone-and-wood cottages with cathedral ceilings and patios. Some share outdoor showers offering ocean views. There's a restaurant, and tours are offered.

I heartily recommend *Wendy Lindo's B&B* (☎ 1-999-5793 cellular), south of West End in the Negril Hills (see Guest Houses in the Negril section, earlier in this chapter).

Nearby, *Ibis Too* is a cottage for rent atop the hill at the junction of Beaver Ave and William Hogg Blvd. It has a pool plus three rooms in the villa.

### Places to Eat

*Jamaican Jurassic Park*, at Retirement, is a funky bar in a little well-tended garden with lots of plants and huge metal plants and pterodactyls sitting atop the rocks. It serves basic Jamaican fare.

### Entertainment

*Jamaican Jurassic Park* hosts regular sound systems and stageshows for a local crowd, as does *Jah Elvis Cultural Centre*, on the south side of Mt Airy.

## LITTLE LONDON

This depressing village, 11 miles east of Negril (and 7 miles west of Savanna-la-Mar), once had a significant number of East Indians whose ancestors were brought as indentured laborers following emancipation. Today their descendants are little in evidence.

Most villagers still work in the sugar fields, or tend rice grown in the marshlands east of town. Others eke a living from the sea: a rough road leads south from Little London to Hope Wharf, a poor fishing hamlet.

I'm not aware of anywhere to stay in Little London, and I can't imagine why you would want to stay. *Winnie's Kingfish Kitchen*, a half mile west of Little London, is the only eatery of note. It serves seafood, patties, and natural juices.

Any of the buses traveling between Negril and Savanna-la-Mar will drop you in Little London. You can catch a bus or minibus to Montego Bay for about US$1.50 and US$4 respectively.

---

### Little Bay Mangrove Project

The shoreline between Salmon Point and Hope Wharf is rapidly disappearing due to sand mining and the bulldozing of mangroves for development. Locals say a lot of beach has vanished. The mangroves once trapped sediment that flows from the New Savannah River, and today the mud is flowing out to sea, where it is adversely affecting the reefs and fisheries.

Locals have formed the Little Bay Citizens Association, and alongside NEPT/NCRPS, the group has begun to replant mangroves and other shoreline trees to stabilize the beach, reduce erosion, and trap sediment.

---

NEGRIL & WEST COAST

## FISH WORLD & AQUA TECH

This fish farm (☎ 955-4929) is the place to cast your lure for tarpon, though here the feisty fish are placid. The tarpon and snook live chock-a-block in large ponds, although you can also fish the river or the ocean by boat. Call ahead if you want your fish fried fresh after you catch it (you can also 'fish' for crayfish called *janga*). Fish World is popular with locals who scoop up their fish the easy way – with nets. It's like hunting elk in the suburbs.

The 600-acre property is beside the Cabarita River about 4 miles east of Little London and 3 miles west of Savanna-la-Mar. It's a swampy place, part of the morass that once took up much of the Westmoreland Plains before being drained for King Sugar in the 18th century. The plains still flood occasionally, when the Cabarita River overflows its banks. The birding is fabulous. And crocodiles might be seen on guided nature tours. There are paddle boats and ocean kayaks. It's open 10 am to 6 pm.

Fish World offers *campsites* for US$10, with outside toilets, showers, and access to a kitchen.

## SAVANNA-LA-MAR

With a population of 16,000, Savanna-la-Mar ('the plain by the sea'), the capital city of Westmoreland, is the largest town in western Jamaica. 'Sav,' as it is locally known, offers few attractions, though shops lend a sense of prosperity to the unappetizing town.

Sav was founded around 1730 and grew modestly as a sugar shipping port during the colonial era. It has an unremarkable history, except where Mother Nature is concerned. Hurricanes swept the town in 1748, 1780, 1912, 1948, and 1988. Great George St has acted like a great gutter for wind-driven swells, and in 1912 the schooner *Latonia* was left high-and-dry a mile from shore.

## Orientation

Sav is virtually a one-street town. Its axis is mile-long Great George St, which runs perpendicular to the A2 ending at the old seafront fort. The market is east of the fort on the foreshore of Wisco Pier. Most other roads extend off Great George St.

## Information

**Money** Most of the national banks are represented, including Scotiabank (☎ 955-2601), at 19 Great George St, and National Commercial Bank (☎ 955-2623), at 68 Great George St. Nearby in Citizen's Plaza, you'll find the Jamaica Citizens Bank (☎ 955-3300), which also represents Western Union.

**Post & Communications** The post office (☎ 955-2205) is on the west side of Great George St, 200 yards north of the courthouse. UPS (☎ 955-9637), 82A Great George St, is open 7 am to 7 pm daily.

You can make telephone calls and send faxes from the Telecommunications of Jamaica office (☎ 955-2520) at 43 Great George St, opposite the Mutual Security Bank; or from the Cable & Wireless office (☎ 955-9700), in the Savanna-la-Mar Commercial Plaza.

**Travel Agencies** There's a National Travel Service office (☎ 955-2437) at 46 Great George St.

**Libraries** The parish library (☎ 955-2795) is open 9 am to 6 pm Monday to Friday, 9 am to 1 pm Saturday.

**Medical Services** Sav-la-Mar Hospital, northeast of town, has a 24-hour emergency service (☎ 955-2133). You'll find several doctors' clinics near Uptown Mall, including the Western Medical Centre (☎ 955-2188), which is open 8 am to 11 pm daily. The Greysville Pharmacy (☎ 955-9427), on Great George St, is open 9 am to 9 pm daily.

**Emergency** The police station (☎ 955-2758) is adjacent to the courthouse on Great George St. In an emergency, call ☎ 110 for fire brigade or ambulance, or ☎ 119 for the police.

## Great George St

The English colonialists never completed the **Savanna-la-Mar Fort** at the foot of Great George St. Parts of it collapsed into the swamps within a few years of being built. Although much of its stone walls are still mostly intact, the fort is not worth the drive.

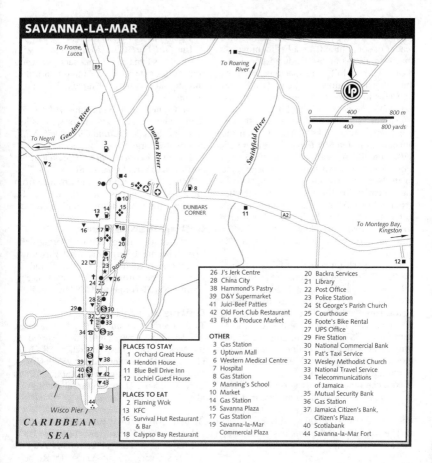

**SAVANNA-LA-MAR**

To Frome, Lucea

B9

To Roaring River

To Negril   Goodens River

Dunbars River

Smithfield River

0   400   800 m
0   400   800 yards

DUNBARS CORNER

A2

To Montego Bay, Kingston

Great George St
Rose St

CARIBBEAN SEA

Wisco Pier

| | |
|---|---|
| 26 J's Jerk Centre | 20 Backra Services |
| 28 China City | 21 Library |
| 38 Hammond's Pastry | 22 Post Office |
| 39 D&Y Supermarket | 23 Police Station |
| 41 Juici-Beef Patties | 24 St George's Parish Church |
| 42 Old Fort Club Restaurant | 25 Courthouse |
| 43 Fish & Produce Market | 26 Foote's Bike Rental |
| | 27 UPS Office |
| **OTHER** | 29 Fire Station |
| 3 Gas Station | 30 National Commercial Bank |
| **PLACES TO STAY** | 31 Pat's Taxi Service |
| 1 Orchard Great House | 5 Uptown Mall |
| 4 Hendon House | 6 Western Medical Centre |
| 11 Blue Bell Drive Inn | 7 Hospital |
| 12 Lochiel Guest House | 8 Gas Station |
| | 9 Manning's School |
| **PLACES TO EAT** | 10 Market |
| 2 Flaming Wok | 14 Gas Station |
| 13 KFC | 15 Savanna Plaza |
| 16 Survival Hut Restaurant | 17 Gas Station |
| & Bar | 19 Savanna-la-Mar |
| 18 Calypso Bay Restaurant | Commercial Plaza |
| | 32 Wesley Methodist Church |
| | 33 National Travel Service |
| | 34 Telecommunications of Jamaica |
| | 35 Mutual Security Bank |
| | 36 Gas Station |
| | 37 Jamaica Citizen's Bank, Citizen's Plaza |
| | 40 Scotiabank |
| | 44 Savanna-la-Mar Fort |

Its innards are drowned by the sea to form a small cove where locals swim.

Many of the old stores that line the entire length of Great George St retain their wide, shady piazzas. The most interesting building is the **courthouse**, built in 1925 at the junction of Great George and Rose Sts, where there's a fountain made of cast iron, inscribed on each side with the words, 'Keep the pavements dry.'

**St George's Parish Church**, opposite, was built in 1905. It's uninspired, but has a stately pipe organ that was dedicated in 1914.

At the north end of town by the roundabout known as Hendon Circle is the very handsome **Manning's School**, built in 1738 after a Westmoreland planter, Thomas Manning, left his land and buildings 'for keeping a free school in the parish of Westmoreland to instruct the youth.'

## Places to Stay

The pickings are slim. *Hendon House* (☎ 955-3943) is a 250-year-old, blue-and-white two-story timber house, 50 yards north of Hendon Circle. The entrance is to the side,

NEGRIL & WEST COAST

not at the locked front door, as appears. The place has a funky charm, reminding one reader of something from a Fellini movie. A spiral wooden staircase leads upstairs to 12 rooms. They're lofty and spacious, with fans and jalousie windows, and cost US$17 and US$23 with shared bath, or US$26 with private bath and decrepit plumbing.

Another old stone-and-timber two-story great house that looks delightful from the outside is the *Lochiel Guest House* (☎ 955-9394), on the A2 east of town. Inside, it's gloomy and rundown, however, though some of its 14 rooms costing US$20 and US$23 are appealing (try the one at the front on the ground floor). All have utility furniture and hot water in private bathrooms. Eight new rooms in a two-story block to the rear offer more modern decor and cost US$28. Meals are not served.

In a similar vein is *Orchard Great House* (☎ 955-2737), beside the road at Strethboghe (also known as Hertford), about 2 miles northeast of Sav on the way to Roaring River. This aged, stone-and-wood home has 22 meagerly furnished rooms for US$24 with fans, US$31.50 with air-con. It also has four octagonal self-contained cottages for monthlong rental. There's a restaurant and bar and a swimming pool.

You can rent two houses (one 'large,' one 'small') amid lush gardens at *Tambrin Hill* (☎ 955-2852, PO Box 210), an old sugar estate once owned by Alex Haley, author of *Roots*.

The *Blue Bell Drive Inn*, east of town on A2, also has cheap, basic rooms.

### Places to Eat

I recommend *J's Jerk Centre*, a tiny outdoor place with little thatch umbrellas. The jerk chicken costs US$3 per quarter (add US$2 for *festival*). The owner also serves steam fish for US$2.50. For patties, pastries, and desserts, check out *Juici-Beef Patties* next to Scotiabank, or, a better bet, *Hammond's Pastry*, where Russell and Dorna Hammond make the best traditional coco-bread around. It's opposite *D&Y Supermarket*.

North of the hospital, *Ann T's Country Kitchen* sells natural juices, fish, and lobster on the shady veranda of an old house.

Across the street is *Yvonne's* (☎ 955-9563), a well-kept bar serving snacks.

The *Old Fort Club Restaurant* (☎ 955-3362) serves Jamaican staples such as curried goat. It has a 'fish fry' at 7 pm on Saturday, and an 'old hits party' Thursday to Sunday evening.

For Chinese, try the *Flaming Wok* (☎ 955-2235), which does take-out as well as sit-down meals, as does *China City* (☎ 955-2435), on Great George St.

There's a *Kentucky Fried Chicken* at the north end of Great George St.

You can buy fresh fish and produce from the market at the base of Great George St, but the sanitary conditions aren't up to par.

### Getting There & Away

Several buses and minibuses operate daily to both Montego Bay and Negril. Buses also depart on a regular basis from the Parade in Kingston; the three-hour journey will cost about US$1.80 (or about US$8 by minibus).

### Getting Around

**Taxi** Several companies offer taxi services. Try Pat's Taxi Service (☎ 918-0431), opposite the Wesley Methodist Church at 88 Great George St. Backra Services (☎ 955-3660) has a 24-hour taxi and rent-a-car service. Island Taxi (☎ 955-9722), at 126 Great George St, also offers 24-hour service.

**Bicycle** Foote's Bike Rental (☎ 955-4029), behind J's Jerk Centre, rents bikes for US$6 per day, and also does bike repairs. Also try Smiley's Cycle (☎ 955-3275), 15 Ricketts Ave, for bike supplies and repair.

### FROME

Frome lies at the heart of Jamaica's foremost sugar estate. It sits in the center of the rich alluvial plain that has made Westmoreland the island's most productive sugar-growing parish. The plains are dominated by a sugar-processing factory built in 1938 by the West Indies Sugar Company and today owned by the Jamaican government. The factory, south of the town of Grange Hill, processes the entire sugar crop of Hanover and Westmoreland parishes.

When the factory opened, it became the setting for a major labor dispute that spread nationwide. During the Depression of the 1930s, many small factories were bought out by the West Indies Sugar Company (then a subsidiary of the English company Tate & Lyle). Unemployed workers from all over Jamaica converged seeking work. Although workers were promised a dollar a day, the men who were hired received only 15 cents a day and women only 10 cents. Workers went on strike for higher pay, passions were running high, and violence erupted. When the crowds rioted and set fire to cane fields, the police responded by firing into the crowd, killing four people. The whole island exploded in violent clashes. The situation was defused when Alexander Bustamante (born locally in Blenheim) mediated the dispute. His efforts gave rise to the island's first mass labor unions and the first organized political party under his leadership (see Government & Politics in the Facts about Jamaica chapter).

A monument at a crossroads north of the factory gates reads: 'To labour leader Alexander Bustamante and the Workers for their courageous fight in 1938. On behalf of the Working People of Jamaica.'

Free tours of the factory can be arranged by reservation (☎ 955-2604, 955-2641). No high heels or sandals are allowed.

Frome also boasts two attractive churches, including **St Barnabas Anglican Church** in Teutonic style.

Buses and minibuses marked 'Grange Hill' operate on a regular basis from Savanna-la-Mar, Lucea, Negril, and Kingston (if coming from Kingston, be sure not to take a bus headed for Grange Hill in St Thomas parish).

## ROARING RIVER & BLUE HOLE

Nature lovers and anyone seeking an offbeat experience should spend an hour or two at Roaring River, a natural beauty spot where mineral waters gush up from the ground in a meadow full of water hyacinths and water lilies. It's a marvelous setting with a towering silk-cotton tree overgrown with epiphytes. An old stone aqueduct takes off some of the water, which runs turquoise-jade. Steps lead steeply up to a cave in a cliff face that is the mouth of a subterranean passage lit by electric lanterns (you can enter the caves only with guides from the cooperative, who have keys to the cave gate). Inside, a path with handrails leads down to the chambers full of stalagmites and stalactites. Take your swimming gear to sit in the mineral spring that percolates up inside the cave, or in the 'bottomless' blue hole outside the cave.

In winter, a mento band plays inside the cave (one guy uses the stalactites as an 'organ'). Harmless fruit bats, which roost in the recesses, flit past.

A guided tour costs US$10 adults (US$15 including lunch), US$5 children. The well-dressed guides are registered in a cooperative: the Roaring River Citizens' Association (☎ 995-2094, 979-7987 in Montego Bay, fax 952-2868) in the landscaped compound – Freedom Village – on the right as you enter the hamlet. There's secure parking, plus a reception lounge, changing rooms, playground, and crafts shops.

*Warning*: Unregistered touts will try to stop you as you approach Roaring River. They'll try to get you to hire one of them as a guide and will tell you that you can't drive up to the Blue Hole without a guide. It's bull! I've received several reports of heavy-handed extortion in which tourists have been threatened by these con artists. Don't hire them, and don't fall for their intimidating bluster.

### Blue Hole Ital Gardens

The narrow lane continues beyond Roaring River for about a mile uphill through the village to Blue Hole Ital Gardens, a beautiful sinkhole, surrounded by a landscaped garden full of ginger torch and heliconia on the private property of a Rasta called Esau. Entry – overpriced – is US$6, but grants a chance for a cool dip with the fish in the turquoise waters. The source of the Roaring River is about 400 yards farther up the road, where the water foams up from beneath a matting of foliage.

### Places to Stay

The superbly situated *Sunset Hills Cottage Rental* is a solid, two-story wooden cabin atop a cockpit (steep-sided hillock) east of Roaring River, with vast views over the cane fields and distant cockpits. It has electricity and a kitchen. The turnoff is a little more than 400 yards before you arrive at Roaring River. A dirt road leads through fields, then steeply uphill – a 4WD is essential – for half a mile. It's run by a North American named Beatrice. There was no one there when I called by. Ask for Zeffy Fogo at Roaring River.

*Blue Hole Ital Gardens* (☎ 999-5791) has two very rustic but utterly charming cottages for rent for US$30 per night at the edge of the tumbling brook (the 'waterhouse' cabin sits *over* the stream). Each has a spacious veranda. One is big enough for a family. Bamboo-enclosed toilets and showers are alfresco. It's the quintessential counterculture lifestyle retreat, with the bounty from the fruit trees for breakfast. You can also camp for US$10 per spot. The owner, Esau, was planning to add outside toilets.

A fella called Benjie also rents simple rooms farther up the road.

### Places to Eat

A restaurant at the Roaring River Citizens' Association compound serves curried chicken and other Jamaican fare.

There are two other good places to eat. Both are rustic, rough-hewn affairs. *Chill Out View* sits atop a hill overlooking the silk-cotton tree and burbling spring. It serves Jamaican fare for a few dollars. Better still is *Lovers Café*, overlooking Blue Hole I-tal Gardens, half a mile north. Papaya and other fruit juices cost US$3. It also serves salads (US$3), a veggie dinner (US$6), grilled fish (US$8), and I-tal dishes, washed down by herb teas. Try the 'Herbal Roots Tonic' love potion, claimed to be a potent aphrodisiac.

### Getting There & Away

Petersfield is a modest little town in the center of the sugarcane fields, 5 miles northeast of Savanna-la-Mar, from where a taxi will cost US$2 (taxis often try to double the fee for tourists). Roaring River is at Shrewsbury Estate, about a mile north of the main crossroads in Petersfield. You can catch a bus in Savanna-la-Mar as far as Petersfield. From there it's a hot walk or rough ride down the potholed road through the cane fields.

Organized tours to Roaring River are offered by companies based in Montego Bay and Negril. Check at the JTB offices for suggestions.

## FERRIS CROSS

Ferris Cross is a major crossroads hamlet on the A2, 5 miles east of Savanna-la-Mar. Here, the A2 turns southeast and follows the coast to Black River and the south coast. Another road – the B8 – leads northeast to Galloway (3 miles), where it begins a steep climb to Whithorn and Montego Bay.

### Paradise Park

This 1000-acre working cattle ranch (☎ 1-999-5771 cellular, fax 955-2997), PO Box 44, Savanna-la-Mar, attracts locals on weekends. It offers 90-minute plantation tours at 11 am and 2 pm, plus horseback rides (US$4) and pony rides (US$1) for the kids. 'Busha' Clarke will take you on rides down to the beach and through palm jungle used as a setting for the movie *Papillon*. Ostensibly it's open 9:30 am to 4 pm Monday to Saturday, but you should call ahead, as the small 18th-century wooden great house was in dilapidated condition in late 1998. Paradise Park is along the banks of the Sweet River, a mile west of Ferris Cross.

# Southwest Coast

The southwest coast – comprising St Elizabeth parish and the narrow coastal strip of east Westmoreland and south Manchester parishes – is one of Jamaica's new tourism frontiers. Along the shore there are few picture-postcard beaches (the shore is much rockier, the water murkier, and the sand darker than on the north coast), with only a fistful of exceptions.

But the area is replete with attractions, such as the Great Morass, Bamboo Avenue, and YS Falls, a beautiful spot to rival Dunn's River Falls near Ocho Rios. And the area is the gateway to the southern half of Cockpit Country. Three of Jamaica's prime wildlife-rich ecosystems are here, and the area is establishing itself as a node for the nation's nascent ecotourism.

The region is heavily touted by the Jamaica Tourist Board (JTB), which incorporates St Elizabeth – centered on the Treasure Beach area – with Manchester and promotes the two as the 'south coast.'

The area is poised for change. In 1998 ground was broken on the region's first major resort – a US$85 million Sandals all-inclusive property – near Whitehouse, where a 400-villa residential complex is also rising. And a championship golf course – the first in the region – is slated.

The spotlight, however, is increasingly shining on Treasure Beach, with its deserted long beaches brightened by colorful fishing boats hauled up to the dunes. The area is also an important center of market gardening. St Elizabeth is Jamaica's breadbasket: melons, peppers, scallions, tobacco, corn, and similar produce grown here supply the rest of Jamaica.

The lifestyle is as yet virtually unsullied by tourism (the area appeals to travelers whose idea of a good time is watching fishermen return to the beaches, where women wait with tubs filled with ice for the fish). It has a unique lazy calm based on a traditional life that keeps locals rooted and hopeful. Its people are mellower than elsewhere in

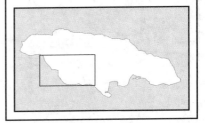

Jamaica: everyone wishes you a safe journey, fewer people ask you for money, and the ones who do are more inclined to offer thanks.

Many local residents see the arrival of the large-scale resorts as a threat (others look forward to the employment opportunities, regardless of the cost to community life) and think the region's future lies in a more sensitive kind of tourism, different from the hustle-and-concrete-resort tourism of the north coast. They don't want another Negril or Montego Bay. They'd prefer to benefit from the prosperity that tourism provides without irrevocably changing their environment and lifestyle. Several community-based movements have evolved to help define the region's future.

St Elizabeth has its own cultural anomalies. Miskito Indians from Central America were

# SOUTHWEST COAST

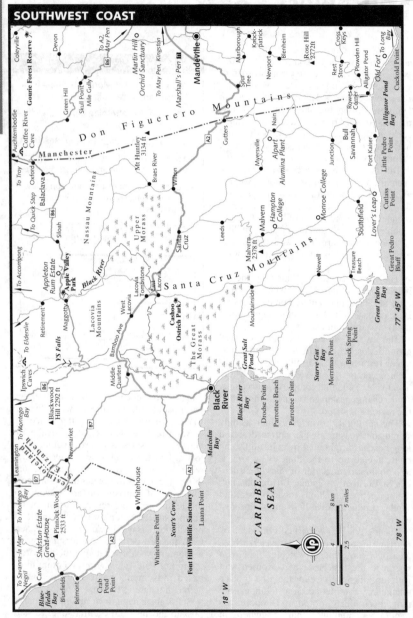

brought to Jamaica to help track Maroons during the 18th century and eventually were given land grants in St Elizabeth. The Miskitos, plus 19th-century Scottish castaways and German settlers, are partly responsible for the high percentage of mixed-race peoples concentrated in regional pockets. This century the area has suffered from high rates of emigration; many of the laborers who migrated to Panama, Costa Rica, Guatemala, and Cuba to work on railway construction and banana plantations came from this area.

The main routes are plied by buses and minibuses traveling between Montego Bay, Negril, and Kingston, but away from the A2 many sites of touristic interest are ill-served by public transport.

### Geography

The southwest coast is an intriguing mix of dry savannas, swampland, and mountains. The western plains, centered on the town of Black River, are known for the Great Morass, a swampy marsh and forest that is a rare habitat for crocodiles and waterfowl. Farther east, the plains – which slope gently upward to the north and east – are lush with cattle pastures, market gardens, and to a lesser degree, sugarcane fields. The area is one of the first cleared by the Spaniards for cattle. (Santa Cruz, in particular, was known for its vast droves of cattle and horses, and the tradition lingers.) It is also still possible to see buildings of 'Spanish Wall' (masonry of white lime, sand, and stone between a wooden frame), a construction method passed down from the 16th century.

The plains are hemmed in to the west by a range of hills called Surinam Quarters, whose scarp faces falls sharply to the coast; to the north by the Nassau Mountains and Cockpit Country; and to the east by the Don Figuerero Mountains of Manchester parish. Dividing the plains north to south are the Santa Cruz Mountains, a steep-faced chain that slopes to the sea and – *whoosh!* – drops 1700 feet at Lover's Leap.

### Climate

The area has two distinct climates associated with the temperate uplands and the relatively dry, yet hot, plains. When you tire of the humidity of the north and east coast, this is the place to come. The southwest coast has a relatively dry, balmy climate, while the highlands are moist and refreshingly springlike. Treasure Beach, lying in the rain-shadow of the Santa Cruz Mountains, is dry and much of the southern plains are covered with thorn-scrub and cactus.

### Organized Tours

Tour operators in Montego Bay, Negril, and Ocho Rios offer tours that combine a swim at YS Falls and a boat ride into the Great Morass or a visit to the Appleton Rum Estate. (See the Organized Tours sections in respective chapters.)

Tours from Kingston are offered by Galaxy Leisure & Tours (☎ 931-0428, fax 925-6975), 75 Red Hills Rd, and JUTA Tours (☎ 978-8703), 75 Old Hope Rd.

A US-based company, Calypso Island Tours (☎ 510-366-5116, 800-852-6242), offers a nine-day Outback Jamaica eco-adventure tour focusing on the southwest coast.

# Whitehouse & Environs

The strip of narrow coast of southeast Westmoreland parish is shadowed by the steep slopes of Surinam Quarters, which rise east of Ferris Cross. Forested hills edge the twisty road. The few lonesome beaches attract contemplative sorts who like to slumber in hammocks away from the rest of the world. But the area is awakening from its Rip Van Winkle slumber. Plans are moving ahead for two major resort developments that have many local residents concerned about the disruption of their bucolic ways. The area is politically favored, as it's the constituency of Prime Minister PJ Patterson.

### BLUEFIELDS

This sleepy fishing village, 12 miles southeast of Savanna-la-Mar, has a long sliver of beach popular with locals and Kingstonians escaping the capital city for weekends at local guest houses. The town has a rich history despite its offbeat appearance. The Spanish built one of its three settlements in Jamaica on this site.

Bluefields Bay provided a safe anchorage and reliable source of freshwater for Spanish explorers and, later, British naval squadrons for over four centuries. Many pirates based themselves here, including Henry Morgan, who in 1670 set out from Bluefields Bay to sack Panama City (Bluefields is supposedly named after Bleevelt, a French pirate).

Surinam Quarters, inland from Bluefields, is named for the colonists who were settled here after the English traded Surinam to the Dutch for New Amsterdam (New York) in 1667. Most of the colonists raised indigo and, later, sugar (planters here gave the first impetus to sugar production on the island). Many Scottish, who came over from Darien in Panama where a settlement they had founded failed, also settled the area, while others fled Scotland after the Battle of Culloden in 1745. You'll see many Scottish place names in the area (Auchindown, Kilmannoch, and Culloden, for example). Campbell – a common Scottish name – is a familiar name hereabouts.

Side roads from the one-road village lead into the green hills to ramshackle old plantation homes. The English naturalist Philip Henry Gosse (1810-88) lived at Bluefields House in 1844 and 1845, where he gathered materials for his two books, *A Naturalist's Sojourn in Jamaica* and *Birds of Jamaica*. The house garden has a breadfruit tree said to be one of the originals brought from the South Seas by Capt William Bligh in 1793.

Six-mile-long Bluefields Bay consists of a series of small coves. Mangrove thickets separate narrow beaches where colorful fishing boats are drawn up on poles and nets hung out to dry like laundry. You can even see fishing boats and pirogues being carved from cotton trees in the traditional manner. Fishing is the way of life for most families. Booby birds, frigate birds, and pelicans roost in the mangroves.

A recently built bypass skirts the shore, where **Bluefields Beach Park** (☎ 955-8257) has been created, with vendors, public telephones, parking, and restrooms, which cost J$20 to use (less than US$0.60).

A small mausoleum filled with memorabilia honors Belmont-born reggae superstar Peter Tosh, who died in 1987. (Also see 'Peter Tosh' in the Reggae'n'Riddims special section.)

Locals sell reggae tapes, and ask for a donation if you view the tomb, painted red, gold, and green and festooned with press clippings. A reggae festival is held each mid-October on Tosh's birthday. The turnoff to the mausoleum is 200 yards west of Belmont Cabins (see Places to Stay, later in this chapter).

You'll see kids standing by the roadside holding lobsters up for sale. Locals are also known for their colorful hammocks, strung up for sale along the road.

### Information

The police station (☎ 955-8156) is opposite the turnoff for Shafston Estate Great House at the east end of town. If your emergency is stress-related, Terry Williams, founder of the Bluefields Trust, offers massage.

### Fishing Trips

Fishermen will take you out. Errol's Deep Sea offers fishing and reef trips. Fees are negotiable, but expect to pay about US$50 or more. Women should not go unless accompanied by a trusted friend. Also see the Whitehouse section, later in this chapter.

### Places to Stay

**Budget** *Shafston Estate Great House* (☎ 997-5076) is a budget traveler's dream. This run-down historic house run by Frank and Rosie Lohmann has a stunning hilltop setting that is well worth the arduous climb. You're rewarded with fabulous views from the veranda down over the coast and forested hills as far east as Negril. You can't see the house until the final approach, when it suddenly appears amid pimento fields framed by a huge silk-cotton tree (one of the biggest in Jamaica). Alas, the setting is now spoilt by an appallingly ugly metal tower that the owner has recently built. It's used for swinging on a chain, but looks unsafe.

Camping costs US$17.50 per person, including meals. Water and toilets are available. Wooden bunk beds in a dormitory cost US$25 per person, including three meals daily. There are also 10 basic rooms in the old house. Those with shared baths cost US$30/50 single/double; rooms with private bath are US$10 extra. Ten simple yet charming rooms are in a newer block with screened windows and clean, tiled communal unisex showers and bathrooms for US$60/90, including meals. The place is popular with European youth, who relax in hammocks on the veranda or laze in a cool dipping pool. There's also a pool table and darts and a small bar serving cocktails for US$3.50. A restaurant was planned. There are cats and dogs – and their excrement – underfoot.

Turn north off the A2 opposite Bluefields police station. After 200 yards, turn left at a Y-fork, then turn right 400 yards farther uphill. From here it's a steep 2-mile climb up a dirt road. For a free pickup if you can't make it, call the house from the public telephone outside the police station.

The oceanfront *Sunset Cottage* (☎ 955-8007), on the A2, has simple one and two-bedroom, air-conditioned units with fans, kitchenettes, and living rooms from US$20 double. And *Belmont Garden Cottage*, about 100 yards east, also has a twee cottage in a garden. Better yet is *Belmont Cabins*, fronted by a pleasant thatched bar and restaurant and offering six handsome wooden cabins with fans, verandas, and private bath for US$25 single or double. It's run by Lundell Gooden, a gracious host.

The *Casa Mariner* (☎ 955-8487) at Cave, 2 miles north of Bluefields, is modest. Ten meagerly furnished rooms with private bath and hot water cost US$28, and three rooms with air-con cost US$43. Facilities include a large bar with pool tables and a breezy upstairs restaurant. Another restaurant on a jetty over the water is good for watching herons feeding amid the mangroves.

The ambitiously named *International Yacht Club & Lounge*, also east of Cave, advertises villas for rent.

**Top End** If you hanker for the tranquil life and have money to burn, contact Braxton and Debbie Moncure (☎ 202-232-4010, fax 703-549-6517, www.bluefieldsvillas.com), 726 N Washington St, Alexandria, VA 22314. They run five deluxe, fully staffed waterfront villas in Bluefields: *San Michele*, *Milestone Cottage*, *Cottonwood*, the *Hermitage*, and *Mullion Cove*. Rooms are decorated with carved and inlaid sideboards, mahogany rockers, antique armoires and dresses, and hand-embroidered Irish linen on canopied mahogany beds. Asian throw rugs adorn the floors. Each villa has a private pool (except Cottonwood), plus bicycles, snorkeling and fishing gear, sailboat, and croquet sets; they share a tennis court. Each has its own resident chef. Birdie, the manager, will take you touring in the minibus for an additional fee. Weekly low-season (May to December) rates range from US$2400 to US$3750 double (depending on the villa) and up to US$9000 for 12 people at Mullion Cove. High-season rates are approximately 30% more.

### Places to Eat

Bluefields is a good place to buy jerk fish, pork, or chicken and enjoy a picnic with your toes in the briny and a Red Stripe in hand. The *jerk stalls* that once lined the beach are now in Bluefields Beach Park, across the road, including Jerry's Meals on Wheels, which was housed in an old bus and is now *Fresh Touch Restaurant*, selling jerk, roast fish, and natural juices.

At the far southeast end of the bay is the rustic *KD's Keg & Fish Joint*.

At Cave, try *Ocean Park Seafood Restaurant*, which doubles as a nightclub.

### Entertainment

There are several local rum shops where you can sup white rum and beer and enjoy a game of dominoes with locals. *Casa Mariners*, *Belmont Sands*, and *KD's Keg* are

## The Bluefields Project

Like many areas in Jamaica, the Bluefields region (population 7000) has seen agricultural, housing, and other development that has resulted in degradation of forests, soils, and other resources. Locals fear the coming of tourism, which poses new threats: farmers are being forced from their lands by rising real estate prices, and fishermen are subsisting on dwindling fish stocks resulting from mangrove destruction and overfishing.

Unlike in most other areas, Bluefields' residents are taking charge with an initiative that promotes sustainable development within the communities of Cave, Mearnsville, Brighton, Belmont, and McAlpine.

The Bluefields Project started in 1988, when the Bluefields Trust was formed by Terry Williams. In 1989 the Bluefields People's Community Association (BPCA) was formed to promote small businesses and establish links between environmental and economic sustainability. A Resource & Training Centre was opened, and local farmers were given courses in permaculture (sustainable agriculture). Local women have been trained in dressmaking and childcare, and a horticultural nursery and environmental education center were set up. In 1998, Radio Bluefields was introduced, broadcasting news and acting as a forum for viewpoints as part of the efforts to prepare local communities for tourism. For information, contact the Bluefields Project (☎ 955-9828), Box 22, Bluefields PO, Westmoreland. A similar group is the Bluefield People's Community Association (☎ 955-8792).

Donations can be made though the following international organizations:

Co-Operation for Development
118 Broad St, Chesham, Bucks HP5 3ED, UK

CUSO Finance Dept
135 Rideau St, Ottawa, Ontario, Canada

Nature Conservancy International Program
1815 N Lynne St, Arlington, VA 22209, USA

all fun, especially on weekends, when reggae music is cranked up.

### Getting There & Away

Buses that operate from Negril and Savanna-la-Mar to Black River all pass through Bluefields.

## WHITEHOUSE

Whitehouse is a large fishing village and a great place to sample provincial coastal life. It stretches for about a mile along the A2, parallel to a series of beaches, where large motorized boats and hand-carved pirogues are drawn up, massive lobster pots lie in great piles, and trucks unload huge blocks of ice. The Whitehouse Fishing Cooperative supplies much of the island with wahoo, tuna, barracuda, bonito, snapper, kingfish, marlin, and lobster taken on the Pedro Banks, about 80 miles to sea.

Follow the dirt road past Alexander's Seaview Shopping Plaza to reach the main beach, where locals gather when the night's catch is brought in. The fish market bustles as higglers bargain with fishers. A crafts and vegetable market is held on Wednesday and Saturday.

Just west of town is South Sea Park, an upscale residential community with villas and homes along the coral shorefront.

The area is expanding and is slated to be the area's first large-scale, all-inclusive resort – Beaches – being built by the Sandals chain to open in 2000 at Auchindown, an unspoilt stretch of coast between Bluefields and Whitehouse. Sandals promises to spend considerable sums to minimize the resort's environmental impact and intends to build boardwalks through the mangroves and lagoons, in which crocodiles and tarpon live. The habitat is fed by the Robin's River, but such is the political power of the Sandals entity that it has ostensibly received permission to redirect the river (hardly an eco-sensitive move). The site will include an 18-hole golf course.

Local developers Ronnie Thwaites and Peter Probst are developing a 400-home upscale residential resort southeast of Whitehouse. Other developers with eyes on the cash-register are even lobbying for a cruise port!

## Information

There's a Jamaica Citizens Bank at the west end of town. The Whitehouse Pharmacy (☎ 963-5409) is next to the bank, and South Sea Pharmacy (☎ 963-5489) is in the village center near Alexander's Seaview Shopping Plaza.

Dr Maung Myint has an office in the plaza in Whitehouse village, open 7:30 am to 12:30 pm and 3:30 to 5:30 pm weekdays, and 8 am to noon Saturday. The police station is about 400 yards farther east.

## Activities

You can hire a fishing boat to go snorkeling for around US$15 per hour. Better yet, hop aboard with local fishermen for a trip to the fishing banks, but be prepared for some arduous work at sea, pulling up lobster and fish pots on lines. This will definitely test your sea legs. The price will depend on your negotiating skills. Herman, a local boatman in Bluefields, provides rods and reels and can take up to four people for about US$20 per hour. It's best to leave at dawn.

Peter Probst at Natania's (see Places to Stay, below) can arrange snorkeling or fishing.

## Places to Stay

The *Pear Tree Pub*, in the center of Whitehouse, has basic rooms for US$5.

Despite its funky name, *Roots Uprising Guest House* (☎ 963-5550, 995-9164, 139 South Sea Park) is a contemporary home owned by a Swiss woman named Jenny Húeskn. She has five spacious rooms that share a large bathroom for US$30 to US$50 per room. Jenny prefers to rent to groups: her house can accommodate up to 10 people and costs US$1500 weekly with a housekeeper. There are mosquito nets over the beds. You can camp on the lawn – or on the roof (Jenny will provide a net) – for US$10.

*White Castle* (☎ 963-5406), about 4 miles northeast of Whitehouse, is a gleaming white modern building with blue awnings on a forested hillside. It has fabulous views from the 10 modest, air-conditioned rooms

for US$30. You can use the kitchen; three rooms have their own kitchens for US$50. A pool is in the works. The turnoff to the hotel is unmarked; it's 50 yards west of the 'Fishpot' roadside stand.

I recommend *Culloden Café* (☎ 963-5344, lyons@cwjamaica.com), at Little Culloden, a mile northwest of Whitehouse. Its charming owners have a cottage with kitchenette and double bed, living room, and porch with hammock for US$50 including continental breakfast. It has a beachfront terrace with shingly pocket-size beach and private shade trees. Best yet, there's the best restaurant for miles at hand (see Places to Eat, below).

*Natania's* (☎/fax 963-5342), next door, is a modestly decorated home-away-from-home run by live-in owners Peter Probst – a New Yorker – and his Jamaican wife, Veronica. A wide outdoor dining veranda looks over well-tended lawns and lush gardens that fall to the rocky shore, where multi-tiered terraces are built above the coral and fitted with artificial beaches for sunning (clothing optional). Water sports are offered, and there's a large pool, sun deck, and beachside bar. The eight rooms have ceiling fans and wide jalousie windows, but – alas – most beds have soft sponge rather than firm mattresses, and the bathrooms are measly. Room rates are US$65 a double in summer. At press time, Peter was planning on selling.

At the far southeast end of South Sea Park is the *South Sea View Guest House* (☎ 963-5172, fax 963-5000). This modern villa has eight air-conditioned rooms, each with private bath, king-size bed, cable TV, and hand-painted tropical murals. There's a swimming pool and steps lead to a rocky cove good for bathing. Upstairs rooms cost US$55 double (it also has a package for US$750 per couple per week including two meals daily).

Other options at South Sea Park include *White House Beach Villa* (which happens to be pink), and *Tan Tan Beach Villa* (☎ 963-5176), fronting a tiny cove with a private beach. The latter has five modestly furnished rooms with fans and cold water only. It's overpriced at US$50 a double including breakfast. Also at South Sea Park, *Hospitality Inns & Villas* (☎ 963-5500) has eight rooms in an attractive modern two-story house of free-form design, with tile floors and an atrium lounge. Decor is ho-hum, but rooms are spacious and have fans (some have small TVs) and cost US$50 high season. One room for US$10 more has a huge tub-shower in a cavernous bathroom. There's a small restaurant and bar.

In late 1998 ground had *finally* been broken on Sandals' *Beaches Whitehouse* (☎ *800-726-3257, 305-284-1300, fax 284-1336 in the USA; ☎ 800-545-8283, 416-223-0028, fax 223-3306 in Canada; ☎ 0800-742742, 020-7581-9895, fax 7823-8758 in the UK),* due to open in 2000. The 310-room resort, which will be for singles, couples, and families, will feature a sports complex, a children's park, and the southwest coast's first 18-hole golf course.

### Places to Eat
First choice – and a rare bargain – should be *Culloden Café* (see Places to Stay, above), run by Ann Lyons – from Minnesota – and her English hubbie, John Belcher, who bartends and 'gets credit for all but the food.' And what food! The simple restaurant boasts a terra-cotta floor and veranda overlooking the lawn and ocean, but you can also dine on a tiny patio down by the shore. Typical of daily specials are couscous and vegetable salad (US$6), carrot honey ginger soup (US$3), and blackened kingfish (US$12). Leave room for the key lime pie (US$3), and wash it all down with superb homemade limeade. It's closed Tuesday.

The *Red Snapper Restaurant*, at the South Sea View Guest House, offers breezy alfresco dining overlooking the ocean. Its Jamaican fare includes curried or grilled lobster (US$16), and chicken'n'chips or steamed fish (US$7). *Natania's* also welcomes nonguests for meals in a more homey environment on the patio for US$5. Lunch includes tuna melt, burgers, and other American fare.

*Mi Deh Yah* (☎ 963-5979) is open 24 hours! It cooks seafood to order, including lobster (US$16), served on a breezy oceanfront terrace in a landscaped park.

There are rustic eateries in the center of Whitehouse. You can buy breads, patties,

and the like at the *Seaview Pastries, Bakery & Snack Counter*, and there's a *grocery* store plus *produce market* (Wednesday and Saturday) near Alexander's Seaview Shopping Plaza.

### Entertainment
Things should waken up soon, but at press time, nightlife was limited to a few local clubs such as *Club Classique*, in the village, and *Belmont Sands* nightclub, at Culloden, whose reggae rap on Saturday might bust your eardrums.

Sophisticates should call in at *Culloden Café* where there's a cozy little TV lounge and bar and the 'largest library in Jamaica' perfect for postprandial pleasure. I recommend a Cuban cigar and 12-year-old Scotch malt.

## SCOTT'S COVE
Twenty miles southeast of Savanna-la-Mar, the A2 sweeps around this deep little inlet where dozens of food and beer stalls line the shore. It's a good place to buy fried snapper and *bammy* – a pancake of fried cassava – with onions and peppers for a dollar or two (the vendors will race up as soon as they see your car halt). The cove is full of brightly painted fishing boats.

Immediately southeast is an area of bull-thatch palms that extends into the Font Hill Wildlife Sanctuary. The most important tree economically, it is used for weaving baskets and other straw-work regarded as among the island's best.

Scott's Cove forms the parish boundary between Westmoreland and St Elizabeth. Beyond lies St Elizabeth, where the landscape takes a dramatic turn.

## FONT HILL WILDLIFE SANCTUARY
This 3150-acre wildlife reserve – one of the least disturbed natural ecosystems in Jamaica – is owned by the Petroleum Corporation of Jamaica. It stretches along 2 miles of shore.

Much of the sanctuary is made up of scrubby acacia and logwood thickets. Closer to the shore is a maze of interconnected lagoons and swamps, with water colors varying from deep blue to jade green and brown. The birding is fabulous. Herons and egrets are common, as are jacanas, whistling ducks, blue-winged teals, and eight endemic bird species that include the pea dove, white-bellied dove, and the ground dove – the smallest dove in the world.

More than 200 American crocodiles still exist at Font Hill – one of the densest populations in Jamaica. Their numbers, however, continue to decline. A tagging and census of crocodiles was initiated in 1989, led by the well-known Jamaican crocodile expert Charles Swaby. As a boy, Swaby used to hunt crocodiles in the Black River, Parrotee Swamps, and Font Hill (he has captured 2000 crocodiles in his career but has never been bitten).

The swamps are accessible by canoe at high tide. Be careful – the water level drops at low tide.

The beach is a magnificent little strip of golden sand shaded by sea grapes and fringed by reef. Offshore you'll find great snorkeling and bathing. Dolphins even come into the cove. A great spot for picnics, the beach is very popular with locals. A trail leads from here via the sanctuary and back to the shore at Luana Point, beyond which, hidden around a headland accessed by the sand flats, is a resplendent beach nestled in a deep bay. The spot is popular with locals for trysting, despite attempts by Anthony Anderson, the former overseer (now deceased), to put a stop to that 'nonsense!'

The sanctuary has a restaurant, gift store, bar, and picnic booths, and a boardwalk, interpretive center, and marina. Font Hill was under new management at press time and was closed until further notice (ostensibly pending completion of additional facilities).

Peter Marra – once an ornithologist here – leads bird trips. Make reservations via Robert Sutton at Marshall's Pen (☎ 904-5454) in Mandeville.

Font Hill is 2 miles east of Whitehouse. Watch for the sign that reads 'Fonthill Private Property – Wildlife Sanctuary.' A dirt track leads to Font Hill Beach.

# Black River & Environs

Black River is the principal town of St Elizabeth parish. It sits on the west bank of the mouth of the aptly named Black River in the nape of Black River Bay, where waters are a scintillating jade-blue. There are plenty of attractions close by, notably Bamboo Avenue, the Great Morass (great for spotting crocodiles and birds), and Cashoo Ostrich Farm.

## BLACK RIVER
Peaceful and picturesque now, with plenty of snoozy charm, the town of Black River (population 4000) is a far cry from the heady days of the 18th and 19th centuries when it prospered from the logging trade. Black River was a center for the export of logwood, from which a Prussian-blue dye was extracted for export; English lords had their ermine robes stained by logwood dye. Logwood still grows hereabouts, though the ships stay away since the port closed in 1968 (a few fishing trawlers still land their catches here).

Early prosperity brought electric power to Black River in 1893, when it was installed in a house called Waterloo, the first such installation in the country. In 1903 the first motorcar was imported to Jamaica by Waterloo's owner. Back then, the town had a horse racetrack and an active gambling life, and a mineral spa at the west end of town was popular with the well-to-do. It was recently restored and reopened as the Abundant Spring Mineral Bath (☎ 965-2255).

Many buildings disappeared in a huge explosion that leveled the town center in 1900, though the town still boasts many fine examples of Caribbean vernacular structures. Some are on their last legs, but a recent restoration project has saved others.

### Information
**Tourist Office** The JTB office (☎ 965-2074, fax 965-2076) is on the upper floor of the Hendriki Building beside the bridge at 2 High St. It has a modest supply of literature.

## BLACK RIVER

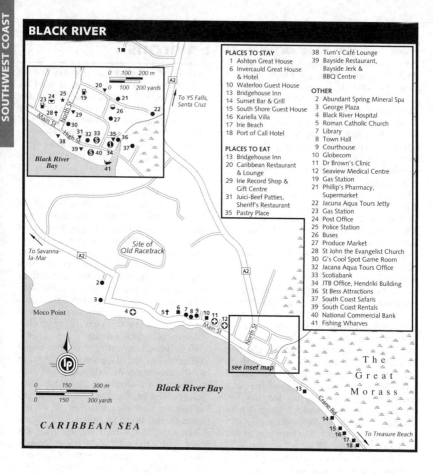

**PLACES TO STAY**
1 Ashton Great House
6 Invercauld Great House & Hotel
10 Waterloo Guest House
13 Bridgehouse Inn
14 Sunset Bar & Grill
15 South Shore Guest House
16 Kariella Villa
17 Irie Beach
18 Port of Call Hotel

**PLACES TO EAT**
13 Bridgehouse Inn
20 Caribbean Restaurant & Lounge
29 Irie Record Shop & Gift Centre
31 Juici-Beef Patties, Sheriff's Restaurant
35 Pastry Place

38 Turn's Café Lounge
39 Bayside Restaurant, Bayside Jerk & BBQ Centre

**OTHER**
2 Abundant Spring Mineral Spa
3 George Plaza
4 Black River Hospital
5 Roman Catholic Church
7 Library
8 Town Hall
9 Courthouse
10 Globecom
11 Dr Brown's Clinic
12 Seaview Medical Centre
19 Gas Station
21 Phillip's Pharmacy, Supermarket
22 Jacuna Aqua Tours Jetty
23 Gas Station
24 Post Office
25 Police Station
26 Buses
27 Produce Market
28 St John the Evangelist Church
30 G's Cool Spot Game Room
32 Jacana Aqua Tours Office
33 Scotiabank
34 JTB Office, Hendriki Building
36 St Bess Attractions
37 South Coast Safaris
39 South Coast Rentals
40 National Commercial Bank
41 Fishing Wharves

**Money** You can cash traveler's checks or arrange cash advances at Scotiabank (☎ 965-2251), at 6 High St, or at National Commercial Bank (☎ 965-2207) across the road. Global Travel (☎ 965-2651, 965-2203), 46 High St, acts as a Western Union agent for cash transfers from abroad.

**Post & Communications** The post office (☎ 965-2250) is next to the police station on North St. You can make international calls at the nearby Telecommunications of Jamaica office (☎ 965-9915), and at Globecom

on High St, at the Waterloo Guest House; the latter offers fax, email, and Internet services.

**Laundry** Try the Squear Laundromat on George Plaza. Ostensibly it's open 24 hours.

**Medical Services** Emergency services are available at the Black River Hospital (☎ 965-2212), a half mile west of town, housed in an old army barracks. Dr John Brown has a clinic (☎ 965-2305) at 48 High St. Seaview Medical Centre, 100 yards farther east, is open 24 hours. Phillip's Pharmacy is on North St, a block north of High St.

**Emergency** The police station (☎ 965-2232) is on North St, 200 yards from the shore. For emergencies, call ☎ 119 for the police or ☎ 110 for an ambulance or fire brigade.

## Things to See & Do

High St is lined with ramshackle, colonnaded, Georgian-style timber houses with gingerbread trim. At the east end is the **Hendriki Building**, dating from 1813.

Historic structures worth checking out include the porticoed **courthouse**, facing the ocean on Main St, and the **town hall** with lofty pillars and fronted by an enormous banyan tree. Nearby is the yellow-brick **Parish Church of St John the Evangelist**, built in 1837 at the main road junction. Note the tombstones outside the southwest entrance. They commemorate local merchant Duncan Hook (1741-79) and his four children by a 'free mulatto,' who lies beside him. Like many white men of his time, Duncan had a special Act of Assembly passed to grant his lover and children the same legal status as white people. Without it they could not have been buried in the churchyard.

One of the most impressive buildings is the **Invercauld Great House & Hotel**. Another is the **Waterloo Guest House**. Both are splendid examples of the classic Jamaican vernacular style, with shady wooden verandas and gingerbread trim (see Places to Stay, below).

The main reason most people visit Black River is to take a boat ride into the Great Morass in search of **crocodiles** and birds (see Boat Tours under Great Morass, later in this chapter). Several timid but menacing-looking beasts hang out, jaws agape, at the end of the piers on both sides of the river. At the east end of town (just east of the Hendriki building) is an old iron bridge, a good spot for watching great swathes of hyacinths floating out to sea and from which you might also see the occasional crocodile waiting for tidbits thrown by tourists from the riverside berths. ('Charley,' one hanger-out croc, likes to be petted!)

The rusty cranelike scale on the west bank was once used for weighing logwoods.

## Horseback Riding

Ashton Stable at Ashton Great House north of town (see Places to Stay, below) offers three two-hour trail rides, including one to the beach; they cost US$14.

## Special Events

The Black River Horticultural Show is held each Easter. Every May Black River hosts the South Coast Fishing Tournament; for information, call the South Coast Fishing Club (☎ 965-2074).

## Places to Stay

In town, **Waterloo Guest House** (☎ 965-2278, fax 965-2072, 44 High St) is an old Georgian edifice, recently renovated but still in rickety condition and offering the fuddy-duddy charm of an older, offbeat property. There are five meagerly furnished rooms with fans in the old house, plus 16 carpeted, more stylish air-conditioned rooms with TV and hot water in a new annex, for US$23 to US$34. All have private bath with showers. It attracts German guests.

Several hotels are on Crane Rd, which runs along the shore east of town for several miles. One of the best is the **Bridgehouse Inn** (☎ 965-2361, 14 Crane Rd). Its 14 rooms have private bath with hot water and air-con. It has a bar and TV lounge, and a restaurant that is popular with tour groups. A single or double costs US$29 in high season.

**South Shore Guest House** (☎ 965-2172, 33 Crane Rd), a 12-bedroom hotel, has a breezy outdoor bar and restaurant. Rooms are spacious, though basic, with utility furniture, fans, and large bathrooms, plus verandas fronting a narrow beach for US$25, or US$30 with TV and hot water. In similar vogue, try the neighboring **Sunset Bar & Grill** (☎ 965-2113), which also has rooms. Farther along is **Irie Beach** (☎ 965-2756), offering six uninspired, carpeted, modest rooms with TVs for US$34 to US$50. It has an elegant little restaurant.

The **Port of Call Hotel** (☎/fax 965-2410, 136 Crane Rd) has 19 rooms, plus a pool and

Jacuzzi, and restaurant and bar. It looks appealing from the outside, but the interior is disappointing, with meager utility furnishings and a restaurant resembling a military mess hall. Most rooms have a TV and telephone. Those upstairs have air-con. Rates are US$29 single/double downstairs, or US$34 upstairs. The hotel charges US$60 one way for Montego Bay or Kingston airport transfers (US$30 for each additional passenger). It rents bicycles.

The venerable **Ashton Great House** (☎/fax 965-2036, PO Box 104, Luana, Black River) has a magnificent setting on a hill beside the A2, about 2 miles north of town. Spacious albeit slightly dowdy rooms have telephones and private bath with hot water. Rooms cost US$50 double. The pool and huge sun deck offer fantastic views over the 185-acre grounds and, beyond, the Black River plains and bay.

More impressive is the centenarian **Invercauld Great House & Hotel** (☎ 965-2750, fax 965-2751, PO Box 12, Black River). The house – a typically Georgian structure with gable roofs, bay windows, valances, and intricate fretwork – was recently restored to haughty grandeur and is furnished with period antiques and replicas. It has 20 rooms that vary in size and mood. More modern units (spread throughout expansive grounds) feature 52 air-conditioned rooms and suites with private baths and balconies. The hotel has an airy dining room, pool, tennis court, and gift shop. Executive suites have king-size beds and private verandas. Rates are US$68 to US$74, and US$80 for junior suites, and US$97 for superior suites. Tours are offered.

You can rent a private bungalow, **Kariella Villa** (☎ 965-2725, 44 Crane Rd). It sits in a lush, landscaped garden and has three bedrooms said to have marvelous views.

Also try Ferne Spencer at South Coast Rentals (☎ 965-2651, fax 965-2697) at 17 High St, above Bayside Restaurant.

### Places To Eat

The best place around is the **Bridgehouse Inn** on Crane Rd. It serves excellent seafood and Jamaican dishes such as curried goat, washed down with health drinks made of beetroot juice and Irish moss (entrées begin at US$8).

In town, the **Caribbean Restaurant & Lounge** is a clean, shady outdoor eatery serving Jamaican specialties for less than US$5. On a budget? Try **Turn's Café Lounge**, at the corner of High and North Sts; it's open 24 hours. A more elegant option popular with locals is the self-proclaimed 'pastry and pub' **Bayside Restaurant**, on High St. The **Bayside Jerk & BBQ Centre** is at the rear, overhanging the sea. For inexpensive spicy patties and pastries, I like the **Pastry Palace**, just north of the Hendriki Building at the east end of High St; try **Juici-Beef Patties**, Jamaica's ubiquitous fast-food patty chain, next to **Sheriff's Restaurant** on High St.

For an ice-cream soda (US$2.50) or milk shake (US$1.50), head to the earthy bar at the front of the **Waterloo Guest House**. It has a modest restaurant with an inexpensive Jamaican menu.

A barbecue with live music is held at the **Jerk Pit** at Ashton Great House each Friday, Saturday, and Sunday evening (US$15). You'll dine alfresco surrounded by pasture, with the great house illumined on the hillock above.

There are plenty of grocery stores, including a **supermarket** on the bottom floor of the Hendriki Building. Try your bargaining skills for fish, meat, or produce at the colorful **produce market**, held near the bus station on Friday and Saturday. You can buy natural I-tal food and juices at **Irie Record Shop & Gift Centre**, on North St.

### Entertainment

A sound system is usually set up on weekends at the **Abundant Spring Mineral Bath**, west of town, and the DJ cranks it up loud enough to waken the dead, drawing the local youth. 'Oldies' are played here on Sunday. In town on North St, **G's Cool Spot Game Room** has video games, table football, and the like. Most of the bars are gloomy, although the **Invercauld Great House** draws the town's middle class, and the faded albeit renovated bar in the **Waterloo Guest House** is steeped in aging ambience.

## Getting There & Away

You can catch buses to Black River from most major towns, as it's on the main route between Kingston and Negril. Buses arrive and depart Black River from behind the market, just west of the river.

South Coast Rentals (☎ 965-2651), at 17 High St, rents cars, and the Port of Call Hotel rents bicycles to all-comers.

## THE GREAT MORASS

This 125-sq-mile wetland – Jamaica's largest extant marshland – extends inland from the mouth of the Black River. It is separated by the narrow Lacovia Gorge into the Lower Morass and Upper Morass. Several rivers feed the Morass. The main source, however, is the Black River, Jamaica's longest river, which rises near Coleyville as Hectors River and flows west as the boundary between Manchester and Trelawny parishes before disappearing underground near Troy. Many tributaries add to its considerable size as it meanders through the flatlands of the Great Morass. It is navigable for about 12 miles upriver.

The Spanish called it the Río Caobana (Mahogany River), because of its black color. Although the waters are stained by tannins from decomposed vegetation in the Great Morass, most of the blackness you see is not the water; it's the dark peat of the riverbed.

The Morass is a complex ecosystem and a vital preserve for more than 100 bird species. With luck you'll see cinnamon-colored jacanas, egrets, whistling-ducks, water hen, seven species of herons, and red-footed coots strutting atop the lily pads. The Morass also forms Jamaica's most significant refuge for crocodiles. About 300 live in the swamps. Don't be surprised to find a 9-foot-long crocodile dog-paddling alongside your boat and begging with a cold-eyed stare for a treat. You can easily see them along the riverbanks in town, where a couple of well-known crocs regularly haul out to sun on the docks (see Boat Tours, below).

Feisty game fish are plentiful, including snook and tarpon. The Morass even has its own endemic fish: a small species called a God-a-me that can live out of water in moist leaf litter and mud. On rare occasions, endangered manatees may even be seen near the river estuary.

The vegetation changes upriver as the watercourse narrows. In places the mangroves are so thick and tall that aerial roots form tunnels. Beyond the confluence of the YS, Middle Quarters, and Black Rivers, red mangroves give way to saltgrass marsh and jungle-thick swamp forest rooted in peat, and the vista broadens into marshy meadows of tall sedges, reeds, and saw grass. Between the mangroves and marsh are a variety of riverine plants such as wild cane, bulrush, wild ginger, quaco, potato slip, floating water hyacinth, and the insect-eating bladderwort. The decaying vegetation gives off methane gas, which bubbles up.

## Taming & Saving the Great Morass

In 1783 loyalist refugees from the North American colonies were settled in the Morass and unsuccessfully attempted to produce rice and indigo. For two centuries, the region was heavily logged. In the 1970s the government-owned Black River Upper Morass Development Company was formed to develop the Morass. The company partly drained the Morass and laid roads in preparation for rice cultivation. The project eventually fell through.

In recent years, several corporations have established commercial shrimp and fish ponds, the latest business ventures in a 200-year history of converting the swamps to commerce. Local fishers also gain access in their dugout canoes, tending funnel-shaped shrimp pots made of bamboo in the traditional manner of their West African forebears.

The Black River & Great Morass Environmental Defense Fund is spearheading an attempt to have the area declared a national park. Conservationists have been pitted against developers. The marsh is polluted by pesticides and other agricultural runoff from the draining. Plans have been proposed for a manatee and yellow-snake breeding program.

For more information, contact the Forestry & Soil Conservation Dept (☎ 924-2612),

Ministry of Agriculture, 173 Constant Spring Rd, Kingston.

## Boat Tours

A number of places in Black River offer Great Morass tours. South Coast Safaris (☎ 965-2513, fax 965-2086), at 1 Crane Rd, offers 90-minute journeys 7 miles into the wetlands. Owner Charles Swaby guides many of the trips himself aboard his *Safari Queen*. His tours leave at 11 am, 12:30 pm, 2 pm, and 4 pm Monday and Saturday, plus 9 am on other days. Trips cost US$15 per person, including drinks; US$29, including buffet lunch and a visit to YS Falls; or US$60

including transfers from Negril, US$65 from Montego Bay, and US$80 from Ocho Rios. The trips leave from the old warehouse on the east bank of the river. The midday tours are best for spotting crocodiles; early and later tours for birding.

St Bess Attractions (☎ 965-2374, 965-2229), behind the Hendriki Building, offers a similar tour – the 'St Elizabeth Safari' – at 9:15 am, 10 am, 10:30 am, 2 pm, and 2:30 pm.

Jacana Aqua Tours (☎/fax 965-2466), 12 High St, also known as Ride de River Tours, charges US$15 for safaris at 90-minute intervals, 9 am to 4:30 pm daily; or US$30 for an 'Irie Safari Tour' combining the Black River

---

## What a Croc!

Saltwater crocodiles, once common around virtually the entire coast of Jamaica, are now relegated to a few areas along the island's south coast, most notably the Great Morass. They were once so numerous that one of the earliest laws in Jamaica proclaimed that an 'alligator' should be on the Coat of Arms.

They're formidable looking beasts. An average adult male can grow to 12 feet; alas, they're usually killed before they have a chance to attain full maturity.

The American crocodile – called an 'alligator' in Jamaica – is very different from the larger and very aggressive Nile crocodile. The former is shy, afraid of people, and eats relatively small amounts (mostly fish) utilizing conical teeth well-adapted for capturing slippery prey. It goes long periods without eating, and can survive on 10lb of food a week.

Early morning is a good time to see crocodiles, when they are sunning on the banks to restore heat lost at night. A legacy of the dinosaur period, the crocodile maintains a body temperature of 77°F by alternating between shade, water, and sun. It hunts at night.

When submerged, its beady eyes watch above the water. When it sinks, special valves seal its orifices.

The animal inhabits mangroves and can be seen in the Black River Great Morass, riverside in the town of Black River, Alligator Hole (Canoe Valley), Font Hill Reserve, and, to a lesser degree, Negril. Like the virtually extinct manatee, crocodiles were once abundant in the Black River. Ruthless hunting has greatly reduced their numbers. The crocodile has a very high death rate in Jamaica, primarily due to deterioration in swamplands, over-fishing (ironically, since crocodiles cull the slowest and weakest fish members, they improve fish productivity), and alteration of estuary configurations, which has altered water flows adversely. They have been protected since 1971.

and YS Falls, or the Cashoo Ostrich Farm and Appleton Rum Estate. Jacana has a resident crocodile called 'Freddie' who hangs out beneath the shade of the tour boat and whom you can lure onto the riverbank and hand-feed! He generally hauls out unsolicited at mid-day to bask on the dock. Tours depart wharfside from a jetty just north of the bus station, where you can also buy tickets.

A similar tour is offered by Black River Tours (☎ 965-2774), run by a charismatic American named Charles Wills.

Caribic Vacations (☎ 952-5013), with offices in Montego Bay and Negril, offers a boat safari tour each Wednesday from Ocho Rios (US$82) and Negril (US$75), and on Thursday from Montego Bay (US$74). Several other tour operators offer similar tours from these resorts.

You can also hire a guide to take you upriver in his canoe or boat for about US$10 to US$20 roundtrip. Ask near the bridge in town. Donovan Bennett at St Bess Attractions will also rent you a boat and oarsman. Ganja is grown in significant quantities in the morass, and stumbling on a major plot is a good reason not to go exploring solo.

Middle Quarters Rafting offers bamboo raft trips plus sea-kayaking on the Black River. (See the Middle Quarters, later in this chapter.)

Take a shade hat and plenty of mosquito repellent.

## PARROTTEE

This extension of the Great Morass south of Black River is dominated by marshlands and two large freshwater lakes – Great Salt Pond and Wallywash Pond – that attract waterfowl (especially grebes, ducks, and waders). Only birders will find them of interest; Great Salt Pond is sadly littered with trash.

You can follow marshlands south from Black River about 5 miles along the coast to a rustic fishing village called **Parrottee Beach**. The dirt road dead-ends half a mile south of Parrottee. Beyond lie a series of lonesome beaches totally undiscovered by travelers. They're difficult to get to but worth the effort if you're seeking total seclusion.

You can camp amid the sand dunes, although I don't recommend this if you're alone.

If you plan on following this coastal route southeast for Treasure Beach, note that the going is tricky. Follow the paved road that winds inland through the marshes from Parrottee. You'll reach a crossroads. Head straight across up the hill if you're heading for Treasure Beach (this is a dramatic drive as the road winds and dips along cliff tops studded with yucca and agave). Alternately, take the road to the right through parched savanna; just before you reach the closed gates to a private cattle ranch, take a left and follow the muddy track to a T-junction. The low hills in front of you are coastal dunes smothered in vegetation. If you turn left and follow the track past lonesome dark-sand beaches, you'll eventually merge with the Treasure Beach road.

***Touch Class Beach Club*** is, despite its name, a rustic but atmospheric bar at Parrottee. It's a cool place to hang out at night, playing dominoes with locals and listening to reggae.

## MIDDLE QUARTERS

This small village on the A2, 8 miles north of Black River, is renowned for its women higglers who stand at the roadside selling delicious 'pepper shrimps' – pronounced 'swimp' locally – cooked at roadside grills. They're well named: you'll need a bottle of beer ready to put out the fire! Also make sure that they're fresh that day. Local fishermen still set out from Middle Quarters to catch mullet and freshwater shrimp (actually, they're crayfish, not shrimp) in traps made in centuries-old African tradition from split bamboo. US$0.30 will buy a good-sized shrimp; US$2 will buy a bagful.

Middle Quarters Rafting offers bamboo raft trips (US$15 per person) plus sea-kayaking (US$5 per hour) on the river. It provides safety vests. It's alongside the A2 just south of Middle Quarters.

You can hop aboard any of the buses plying the A2. Minibuses also serve Middle Quarters from Kingston (US$8).

## NEWMARKET

At Middle Quarters, a little trafficked road – the B7 – leads uphill, northwestward, 8 miles to Newmarket. Newmarket formerly lay to the west of the Westmoreland parish boundary, but residents always considered themselves part of St Elizabeth parish. In 1960, after lengthy petitions, the House of Representatives passed a special law granting the town its desired status and slightly altered the parish boundary. In 1979 the small country village was flooded and remained so for an entire year when the underlying rock became saturated and the water table rose above ground level. Forty-one people drowned. Plenty of rickety old buildings still stand, creating a mellow time-worn feel to this out-of-the-way hamlet.

Newmarket bustles on Wednesday morning, when people flock for a produce market that begins before sunrise.

B7 continues north to Struie and Montego Bay.

## YS FALLS

These unspoiled cascades are the most dramatic of Jamaica's falls and rival those of Dunn's River Falls. Eight beautiful cascades fall 120 feet, separated by cool pools perfect for swimming. They're hemmed in by limestone cliffs and surrounded by towering trees lush with epiphytes and orchids. The falls are on private property – the YS Estate, 3½ miles north of the A2 (the turnoff is a mile east of Middle Quarters). The entrance is just north of the junction of the B6 toward Maggotty (this road is horrendously potholed). Look for the YS House and the remains of an old sugar mill near a bridge over the river. Today the estate raises racehorses and a herd of 700 hardy native Jamaica Red cattle.

A tractor-drawn jitney takes visitors from the car park to a parking area beneath a giant guango tree near the cascades. Alternately, you can walk. (It's a mile-long trek through grassland to the falls; in parts you might have to wade in the river. Don't worry about crocodiles, which aren't found this far inland.) You may be able to drive to the falls with permission.

There are eight iron gates to be opened and closed (your vehicle will need high ground clearance).

You'll find picnic grounds and a tree house. After sipping a rum punch you might be inclined to play Tarzan and swing on a rope into the pools. Be careful! The eddies are strong, especially after rains, when the falls are torrential. A stone staircase and pathway follows the cascades upriver. There are no lockers, however, so you'll need to keep an eye on your stuff while you bathe.

YS Falls is one of the few spots in Jamaica without any hustlers, and the owner, Tony Browne, intends to keep it that way. Browne is descended from the Marquis of Sligo, the colorful governor of Jamaica when slavery was abolished in 1834. Back then, old maps of Jamaica spelled the property 'Wyess,' which according to Inez Knibb Sibley's *Dictionary of Place Names in Jamaica*, is thought to be derived from a Gaelic word for 'winding.' Browne, however, believes the name YS comes from the initials of a Captain Scott, who received the grant for services during Oliver Cromwell's invasion in 1655, and his partner Mr Yates. Together they began producing sugar and rum. Their produce was branded Y&S for Yates and Scott.

The property closes for the last two weeks of October, though that may change, as YS Falls is firmly on the tourist map. The property is open 9:30 am to 4:30 pm daily except Monday (last admission is at 3:30 pm). Entrance costs US$9 for drop-in visitors, including a guide. There's a gift store, a grocery selling quality Jamaican items, and *Micky's Grill*, a thatched restaurant serving fish and chicken dishes, plus burgers for J$50 to J$70 (US$1.50 to US$2).

### Organized Tours

St Bess Attractions (☎ 997-6055) operates tours to YS every half hour from 9 am to 3:30 pm from Black River, as does South Coast Safaris (also in Black River). Most tour operators in major resort towns include YS as a regular stop on their roster of sightseeing tours.

## Getting There & Away

Buses travel via YS Falls from the Shakespeare Plaza in Maggotty. You can walk to YS Falls from the junction on the A2, but it's about 3 miles and hot work. Buses will drop you there. From Mandeville, a minibus will cost about US$2.

## IPSWICH CAVES

These limestone caverns, about 5 miles north of YS Falls, are full of stalactites and stalagmites, badly stained by soot from kerosene torches and cigarettes. The cave entrance is at Ipswich, an almost derelict hamlet on the old railway line between Montego Bay and Kingston. In 1978 I took a ride on the Governor's Coach Tour, a tourist-oriented railway journey that for many years trundled from Montego Bay to the Appleton Rum Estate and stopped at Ipswich for a peek inside the caverns. The train no longer operates, but you can still hire a guide to lead you into the stygian chambers for a small fee.

The turnoff is off the B6, about 2 miles north of YS Falls. It leads dramatically up through cockpits and is horrendously potholed. Beyond Ipswich it climbs to Elderslie. You'll be glad for a 4WD.

## BAMBOO AVENUE

This photogenic archway of towering bamboo has been made famous on touristboard posters. The 2½-mile-long tunnel shades the A2 between Middle Quarters and Lacovia. Bamboo Avenue was planted by the owners of Holland Estate, which formerly belonged to John Gladstone, father of the British prime minister (you can see the Holland sugar factory to the south). The bamboo forms an enchanting tunnel. The grove is maintained by staff from the Hope Botanical Garden in Kingston.

In the fall, the 5km Holland Bamboo Run (☎ 929-9200) goes from Bamboo Avenue to Santa Cruz.

You can buy snacks and drinks at *Travelhalt*, midway along the tunnel.

## LACOVIA

This sprawling village, 2 miles east of Bamboo Avenue, straggles along the A2 for almost 2 miles and is divided into West Lacovia, Lacovia Tombstone, and East Lacovia. The town was the site of a former Spanish ford across the Black River, and a skirmish between the Spanish and English was fought here in 1655. (The name is derived from *la caobana*, Spanish for 'mahogany,' which was an important local export product.)

This nondescript hamlet alternated with Black River as the capital of St Elizabeth in the mid-18th century. They had a great rivalry, and official meetings moved between towns. During the late 19th century, an important fiber-making industry was based here using bamboo as the raw material. The industry was run by Jews, who formed the majority of the population since Spanish times. Today, cashew farming is important, and locals stand at the roadside selling nuts.

The only site of interest is at Lacovia Tombstone, named for its two side-by-side tombstones in the center of the junction at the east end of town in front of the Texaco gas station. An unlikely legend says that the two young men who lie buried here killed each other in a tavern duel in 1738. One of them, Thomas Jordan Spencer, was a distant ancestor of Princess Diana, according to the coat of arms – that of the Spencers of Althorp – on the marble-topped tombstone.

### Places to Stay & Eat

*Carlyn Resorts* (☎ 966-6636), in East Lacovia, is a wood-and-stone two-story structure with five rooms. They're small and basic but clean, and have private bath (no hot water) and fans for US$25 high season. There's a restaurant downstairs that serves seafood; it's a good place to dine while watching the Black River flow by.

You can buy burgers and other snacks at *Best One Pastries & Bakery*, a fast-food joint 20 yards west of Carlyn Resorts. The *English Bar & Restaurant* is a clean, pleasant eatery in West Lacovia.

### Getting There & Away

All the buses running along the A2 pass through Lacovia, which is served directly from Kingston by bus (about US$1.50) and minibus (about US$4).

## CASHOO OSTRICH PARK

Ostriches in Jamaica? Yup! The Cashoo Ostrich Park (☎ 961-1960, fax 961-2132), set on 100 acres of farmland about 4 miles south of East Lacovia, is a breeding farm. At press time, it had about three dozen ostriches, a bird native to Africa. Most of the birds here are females; the males are culled before they reach sexual maturity to avoid testosterone flavoring the meat. Your guide will indulge you with trivia: ostriches weigh up to 350 pounds, produce eggs weighing 5lb, can run up to 50mph, and can cover 20 feet in one stride.

The facility includes a large fruit orchard and herb garden, plus a petting zoo with an emu, donkeys, hens, ducks, geese, and swans. There's a kid's playground, soccer field, badminton court, and a bar by the river with hammocks beneath shade trees. You can fish for tilapia (US$3.50 per pound), but watch for the crocodiles, which sometimes crawl into the fishing ponds. A 'mat' (race-track) for ostrich races is being planned. Meanwhile, you can saddle up for horse-back rides.

Boat trips are offered into the Great Morass (US$4.30). A campground is planned.

The park is open 10 am to 4:30 pm Tuesday to Sunday. Entrance costs US$5.

## SANTA CRUZ

Santa Cruz (population 5000) is a bustling market town, a dormitory community for the Alpart alumina plant nearby at Nain to the southeast, and the most important commercial center in southwest Jamaica. During the past few decades it has grown modestly wealthy on revenues from the local bauxite industry. Before that, Santa Cruz was a market center for horses and mules bred locally for the British army. A livestock market is still held on Saturday. Otherwise there's no reason to make a stop.

Santa Cruz is bounded to the north by the swamp of the Upper Morass. The area was extremely unhealthy in centuries past, and many early settlers succumbed to fever. In the 18th century, several plantation owners granted land north of Santa Cruz to Moravian missionaries from central Europe, and

several churches that still stand may be of interest (the area is accessible by road from **Wilton**, 3 miles east of Santa Cruz; the road continues north into the Nassau Mountains).

### Information

Scotiabank (☎ 966-2230), 77 Main St; National Commercial Bank (☎ 966-2204), 7 Coke Drive; and Citizens Bank (☎ 966-2047), 1 Coke Drive, all provide foreign exchange and cash advance services.

Dr Oliver Myers (☎ 966-2106), 23 Coke Drive, is one of several clinics near the police station. There are a couple of pharmacies, including Premier Pharmacy (☎ 966-9032), 26 Coke Drive, and Phillip's Pharmacy (☎ 966-2113), 72 Main St.

The police station (☎ 966-2289) is 200 yards south of the town center on the road to Malvern.

### Places to Stay

*Danbar Guest House* (☎ 966-9382, 966-4478) is a beautiful home in secluded gardens, signed, at the west end of town. It has five rooms cooled by fans for US$34. Some share a bathroom with cold water only. The homey lounge is a surrealistic zoo of gaily painted ceramic animals. Heaps of plastic flowers do little to enhance the ambience, but the mood is welcoming. Meals can be prepared to order.

*Chariots Hotel* (☎ 966-3860), at Leeds, 4 miles south of town at the base of the Santa Cruz Mountains on the road to Malvern, is modern and spacious. It has 20 modest rooms from US$34, some with air-con, and suites with king-size bed for US$100.

### Places to Eat

*Veggie Bite* is a vegetarian restaurant in Phillip's Plaza, on the A2. For Chinese, try the *Flying Dragon*, next to *Juici-Beef Patties*, where you can pick up vegetarian or meat patties for US$0.50. *Paradise Patties*, next to the Shell gas station, also sells patties and burgers.

For a break from jerk chicken and rice and peas, try the *Rotiraja* for Indian cuisine. Three miles east of town, *One-a-Way Drive Inn* serves roast and steamed fish.

You can buy baked goods at *Hind's Restaurant & Bakery* (☎ 966-2234) in Santa Cruz Plaza. It also serves Jamaican fare for breakfast, lunch, and dinner.

## Entertainment

At the east end of town is *Blinking Safari Club*, a bar and disco. Another rustic nightclub popular with locals is *Occasions* at Braes River, 2 miles north of the A2 (the turnoff is at Wilton, 3 miles east of Santa Cruz). And the *Supreme Club*, at the junction of Main St and Coke Drive, also puts on live bands when nude go-go dancers aren't performing ribald acts.

The *Sun Cinema*, opposite the Esso gas station at the west end of town, is one of Jamaica's few regional cinemas.

## Getting There & Away

Santa Cruz is a main stop for buses going between Kingston and Black River. Minibuses serve Santa Cruz from Black River (US$1.50).

If you want to head into the Nassau Mountains, you can catch a bus or minibus from Santa Cruz to Balaclava for about US$0.40 and US$1, respectively.

Buses leave from the south side of the junction of the A2 and Centre Drive at the east end of Santa Cruz. Minibuses leave from opposite Scotiabank at the west end of town.

## Getting Around

Several companies rent cars, mostly to executives from the local alumina factory, but they'll be happy to take your tourist dollars. Two to consider are Praise Tours & Auto Rental (☎ 966-9020), at 109 Main St at the east end of town, and Southern Comfort Car Rental (☎/fax 966-9726), at Shop No 45 in Santa Cruz Plaza on Main St.

## GUTTERS

Gutters, 10 miles east of Santa Cruz, sits astride the border of St Elizabeth and Manchester parishes at the foot of Spur Tree Hill – a long, steep, winding climb up the Don Figuerero Mountains to Mandeville. There's no village here, but the site is a major T-junction with a road that runs south

to the Alpart alumina factory at Nain, and to Alligator Pond and Treasure Beach.

Several restaurants sit at the base of the hill, though it's far better to stop to admire the view midway up at the *Hill View Jerk Centre* and *Charmers Restaurant*.

Gutters is the unlikely location for one of Jamaica's hottest nightspots – *Jim's HQ Lounge*. It's elegant by rural Jamaican standards. Many Jamaicans proclaim it the top nightclub outside Kingston. On weekends it gets packed, particularly with Jamaicans from Mandeville 10 miles east. Entrance costs US$3 and includes one drink. An outdoor terrace relieves the pressure. Jamaica's leading DJs spin the discs. Sunday is oldies night, and there are occasional fashion shows and beauty contests.

Buses plying the A2 between Mandeville and Black River pass through Gutters. You can also get here from Kingston by minibus from the Parade for about US$5.

# Nassau Mountains & Cockpit Country (South)

The plains of St Elizabeth are bordered to the north by this low, narrow range of deeply forested hills that merge into the rugged Cockpit Country. Few roads penetrate the hills, where the sparse population is mostly involved in subsistence farming.

Between the Nassau Mountains and Cockpit Country is the wide Siloah Valley, carpeted with sugarcane and the famous Appleton rum factory at its heart.

The Cockpit Country forms a highland barrier that divides north Jamaica from the south. Moreover, it divides the parishes: the northern portion lies in Trelawny and St James parishes, and is accessed via Montego Bay. It is easily accessed from the south via Troy: the usual approach is to make the full-day's hike across the Cockpit Country from Troy to Windsor, or vice versa. Also see the Cockpit Country (North) section in the Montego Bay & Northwest Coast chapter.

# MAGGOTTY

The regional center of the Nassau area is this village laid out on a bend of the Black River at the western end of the Siloah Valley, where the river turns south and begins its descent to the St Elizabeth plains. This regional market center is now a source for hydroelectricity generated by a series of waterfalls. An alumina plant stands amid the cane fields northeast of town, and was once a major contributor to pollution of the Black River (the rusting hulk – closed in 1973 after only four years operation – was brought back to life in 1997).

The upper river has been used for canoeing and raft trips offering Class III rapids deep in the Black River Gorge, south of town. You can hike through the gorge, which features a series of 28 roaring cascades with intermittent pools good for swimming. It's an hour's relatively easy trek to the bottom, but the return journey is a stiff hike.

## Apple Valley Park

This 418-acre family nature park (☎ 963-9508, fax 963-9561), on the south side of Maggotty, surrounds an 18th-century great house. The park is centered on two small lakes full of fish, geese, and ducks, and offers fishing (the owners charge for each catch; US$3 per pound) and a variety of touristy activities that appeal mostly to Jamaicans. There are paddle-boat rides, and canoe rides are available on the Black River. There's traditional mento-band entertainment and other shows. The bar and restaurant atop the canopied causeway are good places to relax over a Jamaican meal. Much of the park is a forest reserve good for birding. The owners also operate a tractor-pulled jitney from the old railway station in Maggotty: it travels through the spectacularly gloomy Black River Gorge to the cascades.

It's open 10 am to 5 pm daily except Monday and Wednesday. Entrance costs US$7 (US$4.30 children) on weekends, US$5.75 weekdays.

## Cycling

Contact Manfred's Jamaican Mountain Bike Tours (☎ 705-745-8210 in Canada, manfreds@peterboro.net) about its week-long program based at Apple Valley with daily excursions; bike rides average 25 miles, as far afield as Treasure Beach, YS Falls, and Oxford Caves. Some days are 'demanding,' with moderate hill climbing and some off-road. Trips are geared to moderate riders. A support vehicle is provided. Trips are offered in mid-winter only and cost CAN$1100 or US$799 land only, including transfers between Montego Bay and accommodations at the Apple Valley guest house. You can rent a bike for US$25 per day.

## Places to Stay

There are camping sites for US$4.50 per person at **Apple Valley Park**, which also has rustic cabins for US$18 double. Patrick and Lucille Lee, the Chinese-Jamaican couple who run Apple Valley, also have bunks for US$10 per person in their 18th-century, red-roofed great house south of town atop a hill 1½ miles into the 200-acre property, with a wide veranda overlooking the valley. It has five bedrooms and four bathrooms, plus a lounge. Lucille will cook for you, but guests also have kitchen privileges. It's reached from behind the police station.

Nearby, and marginally better, is **Poinciana Guest House**, a delightful old house on the hill behind the post office, 100 yards south of Apple Valley Park. It has six modestly furnished rooms with private bath for US$17. There's hot water (when the heater works), and a homey TV lounge. Six more rooms are in an annex. Meals are prepared. Ask for Miss Williams at the Happy Time Restaurant.

## Places to Eat

The open-air restaurant at **Apple Valley Park** sits on a causeway between two lakes and serves traditional Jamaican dishes. You can catch carp, silver perch, or red snapper yourself (US$2 per pound to cook). The Lees also run the pleasant, air-conditioned **Valley Restaurant** (☎ 963-9508), opposite Apple Valley Park, and open only on weekends or by reservation on weekdays. It offers many Jamaican dishes, including vegetarian options. Set breakfasts are US$3, and dinners are US$6.

Otherwise, the most significant spot is the **Shakespeare Tavern**, in the Shakespeare Plaza at the north end of the village.

More basic options include the **Seven Stars Restaurant** and **Happy Time Restaurant** in the village.

There's a **supermarket** in the village center, opposite the Seven Stars Restaurant. You can buy bread, patties, and pastries at the **Sweet Bakery**, next to the Valley Restaurant.

## Getting There & Away

Maggotty is 7 miles north of Lacovia. The road is well paved. There's a roundabout immediately on the north side of town: the road to the northwest leads to Elderslie and Accompong; the B6 to the east leads through the Siloah Valley to Balaclava and thence to Mandeville – a superbly scenic drive. A badly potholed road leads west from the Seven Stars Restaurant in Maggotty to YS Falls.

Buses stop and depart from opposite Shakespeare Plaza, at the north end of Maggotty.

## ELDERSLIE

This forlorn congregation of meager houses and ramshackle huts is scattered on the southwest edge of Cockpit Country in what was once a thriving banana-producing area. The narrow road from the roundabout at Maggotty (newly paved in 1998) winds uphill interminably through cockpits. Elderslie is 15 miles south of Maroon Town (see Montego Bay & Northwest Coast chapter), to which it is linked by badly deteriorated road that passes over and through some of the most rugged terrain you'll find on the island. The road southwest from the village center will take you to Ipswich and YS Falls.

Many local youth earn a living turning hardwoods into carvings, although very few tourists call by.

**Wondrous Cave**, near Elderslie, has an underground lake. Westin Thomas will guide you there. You can find him at the village social center. He allows **camping** beside the river next to the cave.

## ACCOMPONG

This lonesome village (population 1100) clinging to a hillside on the southwest side of the Cockpit Country is the sole remaining village in western Jamaica inhabited by descendants of the Maroons, though few of its residents are 'real' Maroons. It touts itself for that reason, but is perhaps more interesting as a point for exploring the region of Cockpit Country known as Me No Sen You No Come.

The village, which crouches on the flank of a steep hill, is named after the brother of the great Maroon leader Cudjoe (Accompong is a common name among the Akan-speaking Cormantyne tribes of West Africa). The settlement was founded in 1739 following the treaty between the Maroons and the English. In 1795, when a second war with the British broke out, the Accompong Maroons remained neutral. At the end of hostilities, all other Maroon settlements were razed, but Accompong was allowed to remain.

The village still enjoys aspects of quasi-autonomy, and is headed by a 'Colonel' elected by secret ballot for a period of five years (the current leader, Colonel Meredie Bowe, is a policeman in Montego Bay). He appoints a council, which he oversees. Oft-touted reports that the Maroons enjoy virtual autonomy in legal matters are exaggerated, as shown in 1986 when the police raided Accompong and seized a large quantity of marijuana. Despite pleading immunity under the terms of the 1739 treaty, many council members were sentenced to jail. The inhabitants refuse to pay government taxes, which might explain the dire state of the roads! The village elders defend their autonomy fiercely and for that reason have strongly opposed the creation of a Cockpit Country National Park.

Locals take pride in their heritage and are quick to use it for economic ends. Accompong exists on the largesse of tourists, and you may be hit up for money for the smallest excuse. Local youths may accost you immediately to tout themselves as guides, and you may even be told that there's an entrance fee to the village, which is false. Don't believe any local who tries to play on a long-forgotten custom that visitors can enter the village only by invitation. Attempts to part tourists from their money are not exclusive to Accompong, but its inhabitants seem particularly creative.

Anthropologist Katherine Dunham recalls her stay in Accompong in 1946 in *Journey to Accompong*.

## Post & Communications

A public telephone (☎ 1-997-9101) serves the whole village. It's cellular and has limited service (and supposedly doesn't accept incoming calls). You can buy phone cards across the road at Peyton Place Pub.

## Things to See & Do

Accompong is centered on the tiny 'Parade Ground,' where a Presbyterian church looks over a small monument honoring Cudjoe (the statue next to it is that of Leonard Parkinson, another Maroon freedom fighter). The **Accompong Development Centre** is opposite the monument. Here you can watch local women and children making belts, clothes, and carved gourds. It contains a measly museum containing an *abeng* horn, a musket, and other motley miscellany (open on January 6, Independence Day; but it can be opened on request for a whopping US$15 that includes a village tour).

Guides can be hired to take you to the rather paltry **Peace Caves**, where Cudjoe signed the 1739 peace treaty with the British. The US$15 fee is steeper than the cave entrance, which is almost an hour's walk away in the valley below. There's nothing else to see, and as a tourist site Accompong is much overrated.

## Accompong Maroon Festival

This traditional ceremony is held each January 6 – the anniversary of the treaty signed between Maroon leader Cudjoe and the British, giving freedom to the Maroons. Abeng horns and drums are played; the lively music, feasting, and dancing end with a reggae party. For information, call Kenneth Watson (☎ 952-4546).

## A Renaissance of Pride

The Accompong community faces a difficult task in maintaining its cultural autonomy. The village is recovering from three decades of emigration and the legacy of cultural suppression by European missionaries who tried to convince the community that their African roots, based in spirituality and medicine, were evil. Several prize artifacts (as well as Cudjoe's home) have been destroyed. The Maroon 'Koramanti' (Cormorante) language became extinct. Traditional health and sanitation systems have degenerated, traditional agricultural techniques have withered, and as much as two-thirds of the adult population has left. With the nearest school 8 miles away and no transportation to it, youth are enticed to find an easier life in the cities.

But the traditional spiritual beliefs and medicines are finally experiencing a revival as young people discover a new pride in their roots. A community center was recently completed, and a Maroon Museum and a skills center are planned. Permaculture (sustainable agriculture) training has been initiated. The village has an ongoing Maroon Health Project that focuses on supporting primary health through the use of traditional medicines.

A booklet, *Welcome to the World of Maroon Traditional Medicine*, available in Accompong, is worth the steep price tag of J$200 (about US$5.70).

## Places to Stay & Eat

The cellar of **Peyton Place Pub**, a bar and grocery store on the town square, has been converted into a guest house with three small, simple, but clean rooms for US$10. They're very cool and even have windows. They share a small shower and toilet. The bar serves basic fare for a few dollars and is a colorful place to sup with locals.

Neverly Wilson rents two thatch huts with hot water at the lower end of the village.

And Miss Cawley, on the Elderslie road, also has rooms.

The ***Star One People of the Culture Club*** is another popular bar that also serves basic meals, as does a colorfully painted shack at Harmony Hall (also called Whitehall), a mile south.

## Getting There & Away

From Montego Bay, buses depart from Creek St for Maggotty, where you can catch a bus outside Shakespeare Tavern to Accompong.

Accompong lies off the Maggotty-Elderslie road: turn right in Retirement (there's no sign, so it's best to ask directions), and follow a horribly rocky and pot-holed road uphill. In Accompong, the road loops back to join the Maggotty-Elderslie road farther west.

Montego Bay's Maroon Attraction Tours (☎ 952-4546, fax 952-6203), 32 Church St, is the 'official' tour company offering excursions to Accompong from MoBay for US$50, including breakfast in Maroon Town, plantation tour, and a village walk with the Colonel.

You can travel more informally on trips arranged by the owners of Linkage Guest House (☎ 952-4546), at 39 Church St in Montego Bay, who are Maroon descendants and offer trips for about US$50 per person.

## APPLETON RUM ESTATE

The Appleton sugar estate and rum factory (a mile northeast of Maggotty) enjoy a magnificent setting in the midst of the Siloah Valley. The valley is ringed by the Nassau Mountains to the south and the escarpment of the Cockpits to the north. The yeasty smell of molasses hangs over the cane fields, luring you toward the largest and oldest distillery in Jamaica. The factory has been blending the famous Appleton brand of rums since 1749. It is owned by J Wray & Nephew, Jamaica's largest rum producer.

There's a well-stocked gift store, and a snack bar serves food from 9 am to 5 pm.

## Organized Tours

A guided factory tour is a must. Call-ins are welcome. You'll view a video before setting out on a walking tour of the distillery, where your guide will provide arcane details on fermentation that make you realize how little has changed since founder John Wray perfected his rum technique in the mid-18th century. You'll even taste rum samples in the 'John Wray Tavern.' Factory tours cost US$12, including rum tasting and a small bottle of rum. Lunch with coffee costs US$6.

A scale model of the factory shows the entire operation.

The famous Governor's Coach Tour (a journey by railway from Montego Bay) no longer operates, but it has been replaced by a similar motorcoach excursion, the Appleton Estate Rum Tour. It departs from MoBay daily, and from Ocho Rios (US$65) and Runaway Bay (US$62) on Tuesday and Wednesday. The excursion includes a distillery tour, plus a boat ride into the Great Morass. Contact Caribic Vacations (☎ 953-9878 in Montego Bay, ☎ 957-3309 in Negril, ☎ 974-9106 in Ocho Rios) or Jamaica Estate Tours Ltd (c/o Appleton Rum Estate; ☎ 963-9019, fax 963-2243).

## SILOAH

The village of Siloah is scattered along an old railway track east of the Appleton factory, which employs virtually the entire population of the town. You can drive north from here to get to Quick Step (see below). Take the paved road to the north immediately east of Siloah.

There's a Scotiabank a mile west of town on the B6. The People's Co-Operative Bank offers Western Union service.

***Dragon's Inn*** is a basic restaurant and bakery; the ***Bamboo Cove*** is rustic, but more atmospheric. For fudge, ice cream, and other desserts, visit the ***Ultimate Snack Counter*** across the road.

At least one minibus runs between Kingston (west of the Parade) and Siloah.

## QUICK STEP

This remote mountain hamlet, 8 miles north of Siloah, offers magnificent views over a portion of the Cockpit Country known as the District of Look Behind. It's eerie and extremely forboding: a chaos of honeycombed limestone cliffs hewn into bizarre shapes and cockpits (deep forested bowls up to 500 feet across). Look Behind is so named because English soldiers involved in the guerrilla war against Maroons had to look over their shoulders to avoid being ambushed.

North of Quick Step, the road peters out. Hiking trails lead into the heart of the Cockpits, but you are well advised to hire a guide. One trail takes you to Nogo; another leads to Windsor Cave, a full-day's hike. It's easy to get lost and this is no place for that. *Don't attempt it alone!*

You may be able to rent rooms locally.

## BALACLAVA

Balaclava sits atop a ridge at the east end of the Siloah Valley. If you're climbing uphill from the west, it's worth resting at the ridge crest to take in the view of the valley laid out below, smothered in sugarcane as flat and green as a billiard table. Around Balaclava sugarcane gives way to citrus groves.

The town has a bucolic charm. An attractive Anglican church and the disused railway station are about the only buildings of interest.

### Information

For information, stop anywhere in town and inquire for Mrs Myrtle McFarlane (☎ 963-2201), a self-appointed tourism information officer. Everyone knows Myrtle!

There's a Western Union in town.

In an emergency, call the police station (☎ 963-2233).

### Places to Eat

An inexpensive, basic place to eat is *Freddie's Place Club Restaurant*, at the east end of town. Two more basic budget options are *Le Grand Club & Restaurant*, opposite the old railway station, and *JC's*, next to the police station, just east of the bridge. For groceries and pastries try *Bala-Ramadama*, near the gas station.

### Getting There & Away

Buses and minibuses stop at the gas station in the center of town. A bus departs at about 11 am for Mandeville (US$0.60), and

another for Montego Bay at 3:30 pm (US$1). Balaclava is also served by bus from Santa Cruz, and a minibus runs to and from Kingston for US$5.

Beware the dangerous railway crossing hidden atop the hill on the west side of town en route to and from Siloah.

## AUCHTEMBEDDIE

Two miles northeast of Balaclava, the B6 turns southeast for Mandeville; another road (the B10) leads north and climbs into and through the Cockpits via Auchtembeddie and drops to Troy on the border with Trelawny parish. The B10 is one of the most spectacular drives in the country. You climb up through a series of dramatic gorges, with the road clinging to the sheer face of the Cockpits.

This limestone country is a choice spot for spelunkers, who head for **Coffee River Cave** at Auchtembeddie. The Jamaica Caving Club (☎ 927-2728), c/o Dept of Geology, University of the West Indies, has mapped about 9000 feet of passages, many of which are underwater. They are totally undeveloped for tourism, but local guides will be willing to escort you for a negotiated fee.

## TROY

This nondescript hamlet, 3 miles north of Auchtembeddie, is the southeastern gateway to the Cockpit Country. Troy sits in a valley bottom and is surrounded by sugarcane fields. It is also a center of yam cultivation, which grow on tall runners. **St Silas church** is worth a look.

A dirt road leads 2 miles north from the center of Troy to Tyre, an even smaller hamlet on the edge of the Cockpits (see the Montego Bay & Northwest Coast chapter map). Beyond Tyre, the road turns to an unpaved track then eventually fades into a bush-enshrouded trail as it dramatically cuts into the Cockpits. From here you can hike to Windsor; see the Cockpit Country (North) section in the Montego Bay & Northwest Coast chapter. Allow a full day for the hike (about 15 miles), but don't attempt it alone, as there are several forks and it is easy to get lost. Ask around and any of a dozen locals will be willing to guide you into the Cockpits for a negotiable fee.

Mrs Chillie has a small **guest house** overflowing with plastic flowers and other kitsch. Rooms share a bath with cold water only and cost US$15. Guests can use the kitchen. Look for the two white houses in a courtyard on the right, 200 yards north of Troy Square.

There are a couple of simple eateries, and the **Rich Man Poor Man Pub** for entertainment.

# Treasure Beach & Environs

The coastal strip southeast of Black River is unique in several ways. The area is sheltered from rains for most of the year by the Santa Cruz Mountains, so there is none of the lush greenery of the north coast. Instead, you'll find acacia trees and cactus towering up to 30 feet. In places, the landscape is reminiscent of an East African setting. Because of the extremely dry climate, farmers have had to apply ingenuity to make the most of the land. They've developed a 'dry farming' technique of laying guinea grass on the soil for mulch.

The region is unsullied by tourism. It's possible here to slip into the kind of lazy, no-frills tropical lifestyle almost impossible elsewhere on the island's coast. The area's residents have a countrywide reputation for conviviality unique to the island.

The Santa Cruz Mountains divide southern St Elizabeth in two. They rise from the sea a few miles east of Treasure Beach and run northwest in a great wedge. The mountains were a popular holiday spot during the late 19th century and earlier this century. Today the green slopes are intensively farmed and the area is relatively prosperous. In parts the scenery is reminiscent of England, with roads lined with limestone walls.

The most dramatic route into the Santa Cruz Mountains is up the west-facing slope from the village of Mountainside. The road switchbacks steeply for several miles, offering marvelous views. The more leisurely route is via Southfield, 10 miles east of Treasure Beach. East of Southfield lies Alligator Pond (see the Spanish Town & South Coast chapter), secluded in a deep valley with the Don Figuerero Mountains forming the steep-faced eastern wall.

## TREASURE BEACH

Treasure Beach is a gem for travelers in search of the offbeat. You won't find a more authentically charming and relaxing place in Jamaica.

Treasure Beach is the generic name given to four coves – Billy's Bay, Frenchman's Bay, Calabash Bay, and Great Pedro Bay – that stretch for several miles south of Starve Gut Bay. Their rocky headlands separate lonesome, coral-colored sand beaches. The long palm-backed curve of Treasure Beach is the node. The area remains largely untouristed. The sense of remoteness, easy pace, and graciousness of the locals (mostly farmers and fisherfolk) attract small handfuls of foreign travelers seeking an away-from-it-all, cares-to-the-wind lifestyle. Many have settled – much to local pride. To think that someone would leave behind the USA or Europe to live in their remote little place!

Each morning 'donkey women' ride down from the hills to sell their fruit and vegetables, while fishermen prepare their boats to sail out to the Pedro Keys, a teeming fishing ground from which they return at sunset to land their catch. Each bay has its own cooperative.

Amenities are limited. At night the lanes are dimly lit. Water sports haven't yet caught on, although the waves are good for bodysurfing (beware of a sometimes vicious undertow). Calabash Bay is said to be kindest to swimmers. It's backed by the Great Pedro Ponds, which are good spots for birding. This portion of coast also draws hikers who follow trails used by fishermen. And with luck you may even see marine turtles coming ashore to lay eggs (the endangered creatures are protected by law, but many local fishermen still catch them for their meat and shells).

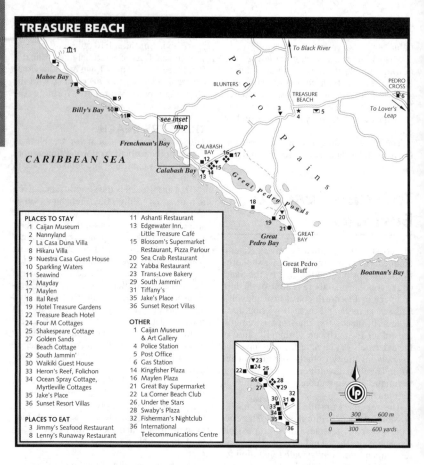

**TREASURE BEACH**

**PLACES TO STAY**
1 Caijan Museum
2 Nannyland
7 La Casa Duna Villa
8 Hikaru Villa
9 Nuestra Casa Guest House
10 Sparkling Waters
11 Seawind
12 Mayday
17 Maylen
18 Ital Rest
19 Hotel Treasure Gardens
22 Treasure Beach Hotel
24 Four M Cottages
25 Shakespeare Cottage
27 Golden Sands
   Beach Cottage
29 South Jammin'
30 Waikiki Guest House
33 Heron's Reef, Folichon
34 Ocean Spray Cottage,
   Myrtleville Cottages
35 Jake's Place
36 Sunset Resort Villas

**PLACES TO EAT**
3 Jimmy's Seafood Restaurant
8 Lenny's Runaway Restaurant

11 Ashanti Restaurant
13 Edgewater Inn,
   Little Treasure Café
15 Blossom's Supermarket
   Restaurant, Pizza Parlour
20 Sea Crab Restaurant
22 Yabba Restaurant
23 Trans-Love Bakery
29 South Jammin'
31 Tiffany's
35 Jake's Place
36 Sunset Resort Villas

**OTHER**
1 Caijan Museum
   & Art Gallery
4 Police Station
5 Post Office
6 Gas Station
14 Kingfisher Plaza
16 Maylen Plaza
21 Great Bay Supermarket
22 La Corner Beach Club
26 Under the Stars
28 Swaby's Plaza
32 Fisherman's Nightclub
36 International
   Telecommunications Centre

The area's reclusiveness is about to change. Word is getting out that this area offers something special. Developers are buying up land, and it can be only a matter of time before the first major resorts appear. A Citizens' Committee has been formed and meets monthly to regulate impending development. Much of the current popularity is thanks to the efforts of mom-and-son team, Sally and Jason Henzell. The Henzell family – Jason's dad, Perry, directed the hit movie *The Harder They Come* – has been coming to Treasure Beach for generations,

and Jason's grandma kept up a constant stream of bad press to national newspapers to keep visitors away! Today, her daughter and grandson play a reverse role at Jake's Place (see Places to Stay, below).

Virtually everyone has white ancestors to a greater or lesser degree. It's said that Scottish sailors were shipwrecked near Treasure Beach in the 19th century, accounting for the preponderance of fair hair, green eyes, and reddish skin. The elders are prudish folks, and nude bathers are likely to be chased off with a stick (the antics of the

Bamboo Avenue, a $2^{1}/2$ mile natural tunnel north of Black River

Westmoreland plains from Haddah

Getting their kicks

Fishers at Whitehouse

Rainy day in Belmont

Parrot fish at rest, Belmont

Fishing boats, Black River

Born to shop, Black River

go-go dancers at the Fisherman's Bar, however, show there are two sides to a coin).

Treasure Beach is particularly popular with easy-going Yanks from Cape Cod. And in 1998, the hit-movie *How Stella Got Her Groove Back* had spawned a significant 'rent-a-Rasta' trade here, with middle-aged foreign women reclaiming their youth in the arms of much younger local men.

## Information

**Tourist Office** There's no information bureau, but the bulletin board at Trans-Love Bakery (☎ 965-0486) is an unofficial source.

**Money** You'll find a Workers Bank in Maylen Plaza. It's not geared to serving travelers, but will change traveler's checks. The nearest major bank is located in Southfield, 10 miles east of Treasure Beach; and a Scotiabank (☎ 965-8257) and National Commercial Bank (☎ 965-8611) at Junction, 5 miles farther east.

**Post & Communications** The International Telecommunications Centre (☎ 965-0062) offers telephone and fax service. It's 100 yards east of Jake's. The tiny Treasure Beach post office is on a hillside just west of Pedro Cross.

**Travel Agencies** Global Travel (☎ 965-0547) is a full-service agency in Maylen Plaza.

**Medical Services** Dr VM Elliott has an office at Maylen Plaza (open 7 am to 10 pm Monday, Tuesday, Friday). Joshua Lee Stein (☎ 965-0583), a trained physiotherapist, offers massages – what he calls 'stress relief therapeutics' – and does the rounds on his tricycle with folding massage table in tow; he charges US$35 per hour. (For an appointment, call or inquire at Trans-Love Bakery). You can choose your massage indoors or outdoors, at your guest home or Joshua's house.

**Emergency** There's a police station on the hillside about 2 miles east of Calabash Bay.

## Caijan Museum & Art Gallery

This totally offbeat museum (☎ 990-6641), in the hills a mile west of Billy Bay, is run by Rastafarian 'architect' Brother John Deer (formerly of Nannyland; see Places to Stay, below) in his house – looking like a Greek troglodyte monastery built into the bare rock wall – and packed with antiques and an eclectic array of miscellany: bottles, a Singer sewing machine, and honorifics to Bob Marley and other heroes. A dauntingly steep path to the museum begins at a derelict Ford Prefect beside the road. You can also camp or stay in a cottage here (see Places to Stay).

## Fishing

Jason Henzell at Jake's Place arranges boat rides (US$30 to US$50) along the coast and into the Great Morass. He can also arrange a fishing trip into the briny blue (about US$25) with locals. You can negotiate for a fishing boat from locals on the beach, but I recommend using someone with experience to negotiate on your behalf. The best way to do it is to put the word out in a bar. The local grapevine will do the rest. Arrange the trip a day or so in advance. There's no rush in Treasure Beach! A night at sea is tiring business, and you will probably be expected to pull fish traps.

## Organized Tours

Rebecca Wiersma of Treasure Tours (☎ 965-0126) offers one-day excursions locally and far afield, from golfing in Mandeville to boating trips on the Great Morass or at Alligator Hole to see manatees.

Recommended for fishing trips is local fisher Allan Daley (☎ 965-0552), Treasure Beach PO, Newcombe Valley District, St Elizabeth. He also does a tour along the coast to Black River, plus a safari trip for US$20. He's said to have 'a lovely manner with tourists.'

Damian's Cycling Tours (☎ 965-0215, or contact Jake's) offers mountain biking locally, plus hiking and snorkeling. Manfred's Jamaican Mountain Bike Tours includes Treasure Beach on cycling trips from Apple Valley Park (see the Maggotty section, earlier in this chapter).

Julie Kolipulos acts as a freelance guide and offers day-long walking tours (US$30). She hangs out at the Trans-Love Bakery.

## Special Events
Jake's Triathlon, begun in 1995, draws competitors from around the world each April. In 1999 more than 100 participants ranging from world-class triathletes to recreational athletes took part in the event, which features a 800m swim, 18km mountain bike ride, and 6km cross-country run. There's no entry fee. Call Jake's (☎ 965-0552) or check it out online at www.islandlife.com.

In mid-October, the Great Jamaican Canoe Race and Hook'n'Line Fishing Tournament is an antidote to the big-wig powerboat sportfishing scene on the north coast. Locals compete with hook and line using their canoes. The three-day event features the 'Great Jamaica Canoe Race,' a bikini contest, and music and dance. This is another Jason Henzell creation; contact Jake's.

## Places to Stay – Budget
**Camping** An intriguing option is *Nannyland*, an offbeat, countercultural kind of place at Mahoe Bay. Camping is on a sliding scale up to US$20, and there are outside bathrooms, water, kitchen, hammocks slung between trees, and trails leading down to a lonesome red-sand beach with coral tidepools. The cactus garden is full of beat-up antique trucks (US$3 general admission). The owner – a Rasta who told me that her name is Celia 'Bitch' – has a reputation locally for not liking white folks, and she sure acted that way when I called by!

*Four M Cottages* (☎ 965-0131) has camping about 400 yards from the beach for US$10. You can also camp under a thatchroof shelter at *Ital Rest* (☎ 965-0248), where there are cooking facilities plus outdoor showers and toilets for US$10 per site; tents and foam mattresses are rented for US$3. And you can camp for US$10 in the grounds at the *Caijan Museum* (☎ 990-6641). It's best to call between 5 and 6 pm.

**Guest Houses & Cottages** *Nannyland* (also see Camping) has two nice, albeit rustic, options: a tree house and a cabin perched at the edge of the cliff. Both cost US$20. And John Deere rents a stylishly funky cottage at the *Caijan Museum* for US$25. There's no electricity, but the location and stunning views make amends.

*Shakespeare Cottage* (☎ 966-2091), 200 yards east of the Treasure Beach Hotel, has the cheapest rooms around, starting at US$5. At Calabash Bay, *Golden Sands Beach Cottage* (☎ 965-0167) is a budget guest house with four basic but well-kept rooms with kitchenettes and private bath (cold water only) for US$20 to US$25.

In the center of Treasure Bay, *Ocean Spray Cottage* and *Myrtleville Cottages* (☎ 965-6438) have one and two-bedroom units for rent immediately north of Jake's. Nearby is the simple *Waikiki Guest House* (☎ 965-0448), with four rooms, each with fans and cold water in a private bath for US$20 per room, but prices are negotiable. It faces a tiny beach. Waikiki also has a one-bedroom cottage and two two-story cottages. The restaurant *South Jammin'* (☎ 965-0136) also has a cottage for rent to the rear, with cold water and fans for US$25.

Another option for longer stays is *Maylen* (☎ 965-0695), where 33 simply furnished rooms with fans rent for US$150 weekly (some share bathrooms).

## Places to Stay – Mid-Range
Effie Campbell has a modern house with six rooms of varying size at *Four M Cottages* (☎ 965-0131, PO Box 4, Mountainside, St Elizabeth), opposite the Treasure Beach Hotel. Windows are screened, and there are mosquito nets over some beds. Rooms can get hot although they have fans (but no air-con). Each has a private bath with hot water (tepid when I stayed there). Guests have kitchen privileges. The gazebo bar is a popular spot for sunset drinks. Effie charges US$25/35 single/double (no credit cards accepted). It's popular with German tourists.

A more atmospheric out-of-the-way place is *Ital Rest* (☎ 965-0248, Great Bay District, Calabash Bay PA, St Elizabeth), run by two Rastas, Jeanne and Frank Genus. It's surrounded by pastures and scrub forest amid grounds full of fruit trees about 400 yards from Great Bay. The couple rent four exquisite, rustic, two-story, all-wood thatched cabins with view, showers, and toilets, and solar electricity for US$50 low season, US$70 high season. Kitchen facilities are shared. The couple also has a beautiful 'treetop' room for US$30 double low season, US$40 high season. There's a small thatched bar and Jeanne serves home-cooked Jamaican fare. The beach is about a five-minute walk.

Nearby is the *Hotel Treasure Gardens*, a modern, jury-rigged affair with an ugly pool.

I highly recommend *Nuestra Casa Guest House* (☎ 965-0152), a B&B at Billy's Bay. This little gem – perhaps the best bargain around – is run by Lillian Brooks, a delightful English lady who exudes typical Yorkshire hospitality, and her son Roger, a burly chap with giant-size humor. A wide veranda has rockers, and a rooftop sun deck is shaded by umbrellas. Her recently renovated three-bedroom house, in a reclusive hillside setting, is tastefully decorated. Two rooms share a bathroom; a third has its own. All have lofty wooden ceilings. It's a tremendous bargain at US$35 double per room. Rates go down the longer you stay and are US$30 per night for a two-week stay, or US$25 for three weeks. Breakfasts (English or Jamaican) are US$5. Lilly prefers couples and cricket fans.

Nearby, between Frenchman's and Billy's bays, is *Seawind* (☎ 965-0582, fax 965-0582, PO Box 40, Treasure Beach), on a headland overlooking a pocket-size beach. This five-bedroom house has private bath with hot water and costs US$65 high season. Meals are cooked to order.

The erstwhile Olde Wharf Hotel is now a youth center.

## Places to Stay – Top End
*Hikaru Villa* (☎ 203-247-0759, 800-526-2432, c/o the Noels, 141 Ridgefield St, Hartford, CT 06112) is a fully staffed, four-bedroom beachfront villa with private tennis court and a sun terrace with 50-foot lap pool overlooking the beach. It abounds with Jamaican *maho* hardwood and rents from US$1025/1325 weekly low/high season for up to four people (more for additional people).

Mrs Patsy Kinkead rents *Sparkling Waters* (☎ 609-771-6193, 800-350-7620; c/o Terry Springer, 675 Appenzell Drive, Hummeltown, PA 17036), with a two-bedroom guest house with TV and VCR, and patio facing the beach for US$850 weekly; and a two-bedroom villa with cathedral lounge, plus TV and VCR for US$1100 weekly. You can also inquire at Trans-Love Bakery (☎ 965-0486).

A pleasant traditional option is the *Treasure Beach Hotel* (☎ 965-2305, 800-742-4276 in North America, fax 965-2544, PO Box 5), a rambling property nestled on a hillside overlooking the beach and once known as a nudist resort. The 36 recently renovated air-conditioned rooms include 16 new, spacious, deluxe oceanfront suites with king-size four-poster beds, cable TVs, tile floors, and patios. A large lounge has a TV for rainy days. There are two swimming pools and a whirlpool, plus volleyball court, and sailing and snorkeling are offered. The dining terrace overlooks the gardens. Standard rooms cost US$80/90 single/double in summer; US$90/100 in winter; deluxe rooms are US$103 in summer, US$130 winter, single or double. The hotel also has an all-inclusive plan and an inclusive 'Treasure Plan' featuring daily nature tours for US$138 per person.

*Jake's Place* (☎/fax 965-0552; 800-688-7678, 305-531-8800 in North America; ☎ 0800-614-790 in the UK; jakes@toj.com, www.intimate-jamaica.com/ij-sc01.htm) gets my vote for the 'chicest shack' between Negril and Kingston, and has been billed by one posh magazine as 'the best hotel in the world under 100 pounds a night.' Eclectic and endearing are understatements for this rustic, rainbow-colored retreat run by Sally and Jason Henzell, who aimed to attract 'talent on the way up.' This is the only hotel in the world that has *never* cut the grass and can get away with it. The place is totally offbeat. Local kids and fishermen looking like ragamuffins (there are no pretensions in Treasure Beach; Jake's is strictly 'no dress code') wander in and out as if they own the place. And cats and Jack Russell terriers scamper about.

There are four double rooms perched over the sea, three cottages, a three-bedroom villa (rooms can be rented separately) like a mini Moroccan *ksar*, and a one-up/one-down house – featuring an exterior spiral staircase, terra-cotta tile floors, tile-and-brick-glass walk-in showers, and exquisite handmade beds. The decor follows Greek and Moslem motifs (Sally, who was art director on her husband Perry's classic reggae movie, *The Harder They Come*, was inspired by Catalan architect Antonio Gaudi), with onion-dome curves, blood-red floors, and walls and rough-hewn doors inset with colored bottles and glass beads. The beds are metal frame contraptions. Rooms have ceiling fans, candles aplenty, and large shuttered windows for cross ventilation. At night bullfrogs sit on your porch grabbing bugs attracted by the porch light. The exquisite pool – also studded with colored bottles and lamplit at night – is shaded by a spreading tree, with a cascade falling to the sea and a tiny beach.

Jason operates fishing trips, boat rides, mountain bike tours, and other activities. Jake's has its own restaurant that is the trendiest place around at night. Local mento bands perform, and moonlight poetry readings are hosted. In case you're wondering, 'Jake' is a parrot! He now resides at Trans-Love Bakery, where he fell in love with their female parrot. Rooms start at US$75 and rise to US$150 for Seahorses.

Jake's Place handles reservations for **Heron's Reef**, a one-bedroom cottage, with a living and dining area plus kitchen, and its own beach renting for US$75 nightly; **Folichon**, next door, a four bedroom, two bathroom home that sleeps up to eight people, with a kitchen and housekeeper for US$150 nightly or US$1000 per week; **Treasure Cot**, a two-bedroom cottage with a lounge boasting near-wrap-around windows (US$115 nightly); and **Abalone**, a four-bedroom villa for US$250 that can be divided.

**Sunset Resort Villas** (☎ 965-0143, 800-786-8452 in North America, fax 965-0555) takes up five acres on Calabash Bay and has two fully-staffed villas: a three-bedroom villa costs US$230 nightly; a nine-room villa can be rented for US$935, or individual rooms for US$85 to US$120. The two spacious and elegant villas share a pool and a basketball court.

Ted Tatham offers the homey, four-bedroom, three-bath, and fully staffed **Blue Marlin** (☎/fax 965-0459, PO Box 5) on an expansive greenswath beside the beach at Great Bay for US$1200 weekly, up to four people, US$120 extra per guest, in high season; it's 20% less in low season.

Other places to consider include **La Casa Duna Villa** (☎ 215-297-5642, fax 297-0255 in the USA), a modern three-bedroom villa with cook and housekeeper at Billy's Bay; **Rainbow Tree** (☎ 703-759-5333 in the USA), a splendid, contemporary five-bedroom villa on six acres; **Mayday** (☎ 965-0125), a handsome modern cottage near Calabash Bay; **Coyaba** (☎ 965-6222); and **Unforgettable Inn**, about 3 miles east of Treasure Beach at Fort Charles, where rooms cost US$850 a week double including all meals. **Villa Caprice** (☎ 965-2265, fax 965-2032, PO Box 7, Black River) is set in lush gardens with a pool. It has four air-conditioned bedrooms. Last but not least is **Lyric** (☎ 416-698-6855 in the USA), a stone-walled villa that sleeps six and has its own pool (from US$700 weekly).

Villas are available from US$150 a week through Treasure Tours (☎ 965-0126), at Calabash Bay, and South Coast Rentals (☎ 965-2651), 17 High St in Black River.

## Places to Eat

*The* place to savor a leisurely breakfast in typical Treasure Beach fashion is **Trans-Love Bakery** (☎ 965-0486), run by Ralph, a friendly transplanted German. It serves omelettes (US$4), muesli (US$3), and fruit salads. The portions are huge! You can also buy fresh-baked sugar buns, cakes, sesame rolls, quiche, and French bread. It does a special Sunday breakfast (hopefully Martin, an elderly local, will have forgiven his tiff with the owners and be back to play slide guitar). It's open 8 am to 2 pm.

*South Jammin'* (☎ 965-0136) is also open for breakfasts and offers shady patio or indoor dining. Its lunch and dinner menu includes steamed fish, pepper steak, curried goat, and lasagna (US$6 to US$13).

At night folks head to the open-sided wooden restaurant at *Jake's Place* featuring low lighting and hip music. You can also dine poolside on the patio out back. The menu varies, but typical Jamaican gourmet dishes include 'lobster Szechuan' (US$14), stuffed crab backs (US$7), and vegetable pasta (US$4). Try the killer rum punch or rum coconut with pineapple juice. Filling lunches include vegetarian treats such as lima-bean soup (US$3). Drinks are served at a spot overhanging the ocean.

*Tiffany's* (☎ 965-0300), an elegant and romantic eatery named after the movie *Breakfast at Tiffany's*, is open noon to 10 pm. The eclectic menu includes burgers (US$4), T-bone steaks (US$9), curried goat (US$6), and salads. You feel totally out of place being served by waiters all dressed up as if the place were in Paris. The equally pleasant *Yabba Restaurant* at Treasure Beach Hotel serves Jamaican and continental dishes in the US$7 to US$20 range on an open veranda overlooking the sea.

More rustic options include *Sea Crab Restaurant* at Great Pedro Bay, serving tasty seafood dishes for less than US$5; and *Blossom's Supermarket Restaurant*, near Maylen Plaza. Nearby *Pizza Parlour* (☎ 965-0170) serves pizza by the slice and whole.

At Calabash Bay you'll find the *Little Treasure Café*, with a pleasant gazebo area where Chef Gordon serves burgers and seafoods; and *Edgewater Inn*, another simple seafood diner in spitting distance. The *Sunset Resort Villas* restaurant is open to the public; it specializes in pizza. Inland, *Jimmy's Seafood Restaurant* (☎ 965-0160) uniquely serves Chinese dishes.

Farther west, I recommend the thatched *Ashanti Restaurant*, serving reasonably priced seafood dishes. Nearby, at Hikaru Villa, is *Lenny's Runaway Restaurant*, doing bargain-priced meals to order.

You can stock up at any of a dozen small *groceries* on the main road, including *Great*

*Bay Supermarket*. Fresh fish is always available on the beach. There's a *pastry shop* in Swaby's Plaza, and a large *supermarket* at Southfield, 10 miles east of Treasure Beach.

## Entertainment

Most of the locals go to bed early, except on weekends. *Fisherman's Nightclub* (up a dirt road behind Tiffany's) is mostly the domain of local youth ogling the go-go dancers performing ribald acts, though there's also a pool hall and bar at the back, and a bamboo bar with TV at the front. Locals also hang out, listening to reggae and swigging stiff shots of overproof rum at Yaboo Restaurant's *La Corner Beach Club* and at *Under the Stars*, where you'll be charged J$50 (less than US$2) for use of the beach.

For dancing, head to *Casablanca Nite Club* in Kingfisher Plaza. *Jake's* also has a dance floor under floodlit trees. The *Galaxy Games Center* at Maylen Plaza has video games.

## Shopping

One of the best craft stores is on the front lawn at Jake's Place (see Places to Stay, above), where Jason Henzell also operates the Caribbean Candle Factory, making wax pineapples, Rasta-shaped candles, and peeled banana candles. Monique's Variety Store sells souvenirs and T-shirts, as does Tropical Treasures in the Maylen Plaza, and Treasures Gift Shop at Kingfisher Plaza.

## Getting There & Away

There is no direct bus service to Treasure Beach from Montego Bay, Negril, or Kingston. If you're coming from MoBay, take a minibus to Savanna-la-Mar (US$2). From there, a minibus to Black River costs US$1.70; then catch a minibus to Treasure Beach (US$1.70): the 'Cherry B' and 'Butty B' run between Black River and Trans-Love Bakery, departing every 90 minutes or so Monday to Saturday. Minibuses operate from Santa Cruz (US$1.50).

Unlicensed taxis hang around Trans-Love and the bus station in Black River (about US$2). They're 'robots' and will pick up passengers along the route.

## Treasure Beach Foundation

Jason Henzell recently founded BRED – the Treasure Beach Foundation – dedicated to fostering heritage pride, sports, health, and education among the community. Work includes restoring decrepit housing, sponsorship of a soccer team (Treasure Beach United) and a basketball team (Treasure Beach Riprise) plus construction of a new wing and introduction of computers at local schools.

If you wish to donate to the nonprofit foundation, contact Treasure Beach Foundation (☎ 965-0635, fax 965-0552), Calabash Bay PA, Treasure Beach, St Elizabeth.

---

Jake's Place arranges transfers from MoBay for US$75 (up to four people).

Countrystyle Community Tours (☎ 962-3725, fax 962-1461, paulov@infocharn.com) offers 'the Community Experience of Treasure Beach' (US$50), including visits to a private home, a goat farm, and Lover's Leap, plus lunch at Jake's Place. Add US$40 for hotel transfers.

### Getting Around

Hitching is a popular option, but there's not much traffic along the single shoreline road. Renting your own wheels is best.

Jake's Place arranges car and motorcycle rental, as does the Waikiki Guest House. Jake's charges from US$65 daily for jeeps, US$40 for small motorcycles, and US$30 for scooters. You can rent bicycles and motorcycles from Native Bike Rental (☎ 965-0140) in Maylen Plaza: bicycles cost US$5 daily with a US$50 deposit; motorcycles begin at US$30 for a 80cc Honda, up to US$70 per day for a 750cc machine, with a US$200 deposit.

Jake's Place arranges transfers by taxi.

### MALVERN

This village straddles the Santa Cruz Mountains at a refreshing 2400 feet, a looping 15 mile drive northeast from Treasure Beach

(and 11 miles south from Santa Cruz via Leeds). Years ago, Malvern was favored as a summer resort for its temperate climate, which rarely exceeds 80°F. The tourist trade died long ago, and today Malvern serves as an agricultural and educational center.

Malvern is dominated by the cream-colored Hampton College (a girls school founded in 1858), which has a beautiful setting looking across the deep vale toward the Don Figuerero Mountains. It's the building with the blue-and-red roof, about a mile south of Malvern Square, the village center. Munro College (a boys school founded in 1856) is 4 miles farther south. Both are private and were established by charitable trusts.

A small number of other interesting historic houses remain, including photogenic Deep Dene, 200 yards west of the junction in the village center. Today it is the Blenheim Moravian Teacher Training College.

The slopes around Malvern are flecked with pine forest. A precious stand of bull thatch, or sisal, also grows in the hills above town. The material is still used locally to make straw hats and baskets.

### Information

The People's Co-Operative Bank represents Western Union. The tiny Workers Bank serves the needs of the local community; don't anticipate being able to change large sums (open 9 am to 2 pm Monday, Wednesday, and Friday, and 9 to 11 am Thursday and Saturday).

The post office is 50 yards west of the junction in the town center. The police station (☎ 966-2355) is immediately east.

There's a Texaco gas station in town.

### Places to Stay & Eat

I'm not aware of a hotel in town. Ask around for a room. Reputedly, guests have been accepted at *Deep Dene* (☎ 966-5148).

One of the few places to eat is *Dolly's Restaurant*, next to the gas station, serving Jamaican staples and ice creams.

You can buy produce and groceries at *Stephenson's Supermarket*, behind the gas station on Malvern Square. *Paraguas Tavern* and the *Malvern Meat Shop*, which sells patties and pastries, are both at the main junction in town. You'll find a *bakery* in the central plaza.

### Getting There & Away
If you're traveling from Kingston, you can take a minibus west of the Parade.

### LOVER'S LEAP
You need a head for heights to stand by the cliff edge at Lover's Leap, a mile southeast of Southfield, where the Santa Cruz Mountains plunge over 1700 feet into the ocean. The headland is tipped by a red-and-white-hooped **lighthouse**. The views stretch for miles; the best are from the upper-story veranda of the restaurant. The blunt mountain face causes warm onshore winds to rise, and John Crow buzzards soar on the thermals at eye level. Far below, waves crash ashore on jagged rocks.

Lover's Leap is named for two young slaves who supposedly committed suicide here. According to legend, the woman was lusted after by her owner, who arranged for her lover to be sold to another estate. When the couple heard of the plot, they fled and were eventually cornered at the cliffs, where they chose to plunge to their deaths. No one seems sure whether the story is true or not.

The site is now a privately owned enterprise with a tiny cactus farm, herb farm, children's play area, souvenir shop, and a modest restaurant. It's open 10 am to 6 pm daily (US$3 entrance).

Far below is **Cutlass Beach**, named for its shape. You can hike with a guide (US$14 per group) from the restaurant: a stiff one-hour down, and an even more stiff two-hour climb back. With luck you may see wild mountain goats, which locals like to hunt.

### Places to Stay & Eat
The only accommodations nearby are at *Lover's Leap Guest House & Eating & Drinking Lounge* (☎ 965-6004), about 400 yards north of the lighthouse. The modest hotel has 10 carpeted rooms for US$30. They're well lit and clean, with fans and private bath, but smell of mothballs. It has an outdoor bar and grill.

The uninspired *Lover's Leap restaurant* serves meager sandwiches, burgers, milk shakes, and cocktails.

## ALLIGATOR POND
Alligator Pond – the most authentically unspoiled coastal spot on the island – is about as far from Montego Bay and packaged tourism as you can get. Although Kingstonians crowd in on weekends, this large fishing village remains totally undiscovered by foreign travelers and offers a genuine, offbeat Jamaican experience. Part of the reason is its lonesome location: Alligator Pond is hidden at the foot of a valley between two steep spurs of the Santa Cruz and Don Figuerero Mountains. Both run right up to the coast, effectively cutting Alligator Pond off from the rest of the country. If you stand at Lover's Leap and survey the region from a distance, the mountains east of Alligator Pond resemble an alligator's head – hence the name.

The village is set behind a deep-blue bay backed by dunes. The main street is smothered in wind-blown sand. Each morning local women gather on the dark-sand beach to haggle over the catch delivered by fishermen. Be sure to bring your camera! It's not for the squeamish, however, as you're likely to see octopus, squid, eels, and fish getting their brains bashed out or being gutted. Pigs roam the beach in search of morsels. Local youths surf wooden planks; modern fiberglass boats and colorful old pirogues carved from tree trunks line the long beach.

The **Sandy Cays** lie about 20 miles offshore. They poke out of the ocean a few feet, and fishermen sometimes retreat there to process their catch. The cays – lined with white-sand beaches – are an excellent location for bathing (clothing is optional here), while the snorkeling and scuba diving are good at **Alligator Reef**, about a 20-minute boat ride from shore. It too has a fine beach.

On the coast 2 miles west of Alligator Pond is **Port Kaiser**, dominated by an alumina plant and shipping facility owned by Kaiser Bauxite Company.

At **Rowes Corner**, 2 miles north of Alligator Pond, the first elementary school for black children in Jamaica was established by Moravian missionaries in 1823. A memorial commemorates the event.

## Fishing

You can hire a fisherman to take you out fishing for a negotiable fee. If you join local fishers on their forays, be prepared to witness a disturbing disregard for the law, such as fishing the coral reefs with line and trapping and taking lobster (protected seasonally) year-round. You should report any fishing that uses dynamite – a devastating practice that still occurs along the southwest coast.

## Scuba Diving

You can scuba dive at the Sandy Cays to see coral mounds such as Drop-Drop and Saletsat, where nurse sharks and giant rays gather to feed on the waste fish processed by fishermen at sea. The only local dive operator had closed its doors in 1998.

## Places to Stay

*Venus Sunset Lounge & Accommodation*, a mile east of Alligator Pond, has four simply furnished rooms (more are to be added) with fans, shared bath, and cold water for US$30. It sits amid lawns and has a thatched bar and basic restaurant overlooking a tiny beach.

Next door is *Breakers*, a simple guest house that has a large indoor restaurant, but I have never been able to rouse anyone here when I've dropped by.

## Places to Eat

The beach is lined with funky stalls catering to fishermen. Take your pick of a dozen or so places selling fish and lobster dishes. By far the best is *Little Ochie Pub* (☎ 990-6178), run by Marcia: it has tremendous atmosphere, with thatched tables and chairs on the beach, including some built into thatch-roof old boats raised on stilts. Locals play dominoes, and middle-class Jamaicans crowd in on weekends. Specialties include curried conch (US$6), roast fish (US$4.50), and lobster (US$8). The *Sea Breeze Restaurant*, behind Little Ochie, tries to compete.

Another atmospheric spot is the *Red Lobster Seafood Pub*, located a mile north

of Alligator Pond, at the junction for Port Kaiser. It's painted bright orange and green.

You can buy lobster for US$6 per pound from local fishermen, but refrain from doing so between April 1 and June 30, when it's illegal to catch, sell, or purchase lobster; but not all the fishermen heed the law. Endangered marine turtles are also caught by locals, despite being protected by law. *Don't buy turtle meat or turtle jewelry!*

## Getting There & Away

Minibuses operate between Alligator Pond and west of the Parade in Kingston. Alligator Pond can be reached via a paved road from Mandeville via Gutters (at the base of Spur Tree Hill on the A2) or via Newport and Rowes corner, where the road switchbacks down dizzyingly. A minibus operates from Mandeville via Gutters (about US$2), and there's a second on weekends. At least one minibus also runs between Bull Savannah and Kingston.

Bull Savannah squats on the eastern brow of the Santa Cruz Mountains with Alligator Pond at the mouth of the valley far below. The road between them is a steep, winding roller coaster. Drive carefully.

## LONG BAY

Long Bay, east of Alligator Pond, is a rare pristine spot. Virtually the entire 15-mile shoreline, which is hemmed in by mountains, is composed of mangroves and reeds that make up the Long Bay Morass – a nirvana for birders. Blue crabs, African perch, and freshwater tropical fish are abundant. There are crocodiles, too. And the swamp is the last refuge in Jamaica for endangered manatees, which can easily be seen at Canoe Valley at the far east end of Long Bay.

With boardwalks and an interpretive center, this could be an ecotourists' mecca. For years the government has talked of creating the Canoe Valley Wildlife Refuge. The area begs for national park status, which would head off the developers. Alas, no progress had been made at press time and the area – which was made accessible by road only in 1996 – is already littered with roadside trash.

The paved road begins in Alligator Pond and extends eastward behind the Morass as far as Alligator Hole (Canoe Valley). I consider this highway one of the preeminent drives in Jamaica. For the first few miles, the road dips and winds past tall cacti and scrubby savanna, and the coastal vistas are fantastic. Watch out for goats grazing the scrub (signs read: 'We love our kiddies'). After about 3 miles the cacti and scrub give way to swampland towered over by thatch palms. The sheer face of the Don Figuerero

## Mermaid or Manatee?

Long Bay Morass is a rare and precious haven for the West Indian manatee. Many thousands of these elephantine marine mammals inhabited the coastal waters of Jamaica and other Caribbean islands in the days before Columbus. When European ships began arriving in Caribbean waters, sailors told tales of mermaid sightings, but manatees may have inspired the rumors. Over the past five centuries they have been hunted voraciously for their meat, blubber, and hides. Today they are protected under the Wildlife Protection Act, but that is no shield against Jamaican fishermen, who still kill them. Less than 100 are thought to remain.

The animal belongs to the order *Sirenia*, the only aquatic mammals that subsist on vegetation. Three species – including the West Indian manatee – and the marine dugong of the Indo-Pacific make up the order. All face extinction.

The manatee is an extremely gentle and loving creature that spends much time nuzzling. They are extremely slow to reproduce; mature females produce a single calf once every two or three years, and the cow-calf bond is extremely close. The animals have deep-set eyes, blunt snouts and whiskered lips, bodies like plump wine sacks, and paddlelike tails. They have no external ears.

The slow-moving beasts normally cruise at 2 or 3mph, feeding on sea grasses in shallow coastal waters and estuaries. Daily, each individual can consume up to 10% of its body weight (they can weigh up to 2000lb). Manatees can grow up to 15 feet long. They also like to drink the freshwater that bubbles up from subaqueous springs, such as at Canoe Valley. You're not likely to see one elsewhere in the wild.

For more information, contact the Natural Resources Conservation Dept (☎ 929-5070), 53½ Molynes Rd, PO Box 305, Kingston 10. In the USA, contact the Save the Manatee Club (☎ 800-432-5646, www.savethemana tee.org), 500 N Maitland Ave, Maitland, FL 32751.

Mountains edges right up to the road on one side, with the swamp right up against it on the other. It has sharp bends. Drive carefully – take a corner wide and you'll end up with the crocodiles!

The area is uninhabited, with the exception of a meager facility at **Gut River**, 6 miles east of Alligator Pond. Gut River is one of half a dozen spring-fed streams that percolate out of the limestone mountains and meander to the sea through a morass of mangroves and reeds. Here the mineral spring emerges from a deep cleft and feeds a miraculously azure pond where the occasional flash reveals mullet and big crabs 20 feet down. Large dragonflies hover over the jewel-like water. The pool grows shallower toward its mouth, where the water is trapped behind a sand spit that hides a lonesome red-sand beach.

The site is poorly run by two fellows from Mandeville: Patrick Reid and Mitch Burey. On weekends Jamaicans crowd in from Kingston and Mandeville for ear-splitting reggae. Lots of jerk chicken and curried goat served at a small, funky restaurant gets washed down by Red Stripe beer. When the crowd leaves, garbage is strewn everywhere, and nobody bothers to clean it up. There aren't any accommodations here.

A group of Rastas have built a house next door.

**God's Well** is a sinkhole in the morass that drops to a cave at about 158 feet. Scuba divers occasionally test the waters (God's Well is for experienced divers only – the first diver to tackle it died). Believe it or not, divers have even been known to swim the 'Suicide Run,' a 2-mile swim to the ocean through the seemingly impenetrable swamps. Yes, the chance of bumping into a crocodile is very real, but locals advise: 'Dem alligators no problem, mon…Dem coward. 'Im see you come close, mon, 'im swim fast, fast can go!'

## Getting There & Away

Unless you're driving, you'll probably have to take a taxi from Alligator Pond. It should cost no more than US$8 roundtrip. A minibus travels to Gut River from Mandeville on weekends.

# Central Highlands

Jamaica's cool, crisp central highlands are a world apart from the steamy coastal lowlands. Jamaica's resort-driven tourism has bypassed the uplands, which were popular last century as a vacation retreat, when the towns of Christiana and Mandeville became social centers for wealthy Jamaicans and Europeans. The trade has since died, but the charms remain. Today the towns are important agricultural centers.

Parts of England or Germany come to mind around Mandeville and Christiana, with rolling hills, bucolic valleys grazed by cattle in fields fringed by hedgerows and stone walls, and intensively farmed mountain slopes that rise northward to almost 3000 feet, forested in pine and oak. At higher elevations clouds sift through the quasi-alpine forests.

To the south and west is a wedge-shaped upland plateau – the Don Figuerero Mountains – running north to south, with a west-facing, ruler-straight escarpment, the base of which forms the political and physical boundary between St Elizabeth and Manchester parishes. The deeply forested northern slopes of the Don Figureros drop into a narrow and beautiful valley that runs northwest to Balaclava (see the Southwest Coast chapter), and reminds me of a setting from England's Yorkshire Dales, providing a fabulous excursion from Mandeville. North, the Mocho Mountains rise to Christiana and crest at Mt Denham (3254 feet) on the border with Trelawny parish before falling away to the Dry Harbour Mountains (see the Montego Bay & Northwest Coast regional map). The tail of the Mocho Mountains filters east into Clarendon parish.

In the south of Manchester parish is Alligator Hole, a good spot to sight the endangered manatee (for more information, see the Spanish Town & South Coast chapter).

In the 18th century, the area became an important center for coffee cultivation. Sugar estates were entirely absent. Although slaves worked the coffee estates, the harsh

## Highlights

- Mandeville, the most pleasant town on the island, perfect for a highland escape
- Birding at Marshall's Pen with Robert Sutton
- Hiking and caving in Gourie Forest Reserve
- Dinner at Bloomfield Great House – a culinary treat
- A scenic drive through Mile Gully

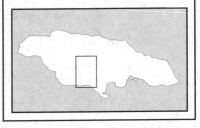

plantation system never took hold. Following emancipation, the newly freed slaves settled as independent farmers and continued to grow coffee. In latter years, citrus farms became important, and cattle now grow fat on the lush pastures. Bauxite is also mined near Mandeville, bringing further prosperity to the region. The relative wealth of the area is evident in the scores of immaculate white houses, farmsteads, and villas spread across the lush hillsides.

## Mandeville

The town of Mandeville (population 13,700) sits in the very center of Manchester parish, on the eastern flank of the Don Figuerero Mountains. Manchester parish, established as a separate parish in 1814, was named for the Duke of Manchester, who was governor of Jamaica from 1808 to 1827.

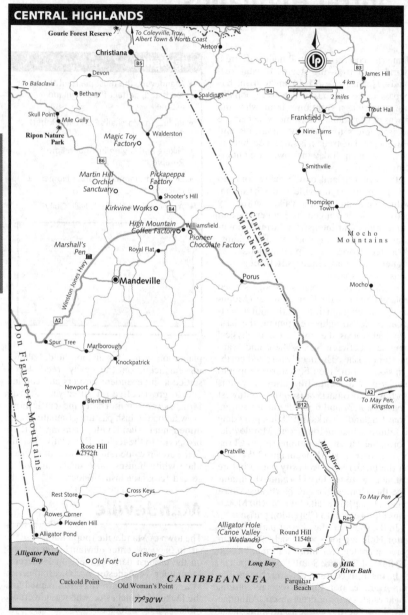

# CENTRAL HIGHLANDS

Gourie Forest Reserve

To Coleyville, Troy,
Albert Town & North Coast

Christiana

Alston

B5

James Hill

B3

Devon

0        2        4 km
0              2 miles

To Balaclava

Spaldings

B4

Bethany

Frankfield

Trout Hall

Skull Point
Mile Gully

Nine Turns

Ripon Nature
Park

Walderston

Magic Toy
Factory

Smithville

B6

Martin Hill
Orchid
Sanctuary

Pickapeppa
Factory

Shooter's Hill

Thompson
Town

Kirkvine Works

B4

Mocho
Mountains

High Mountain
Coffee Factory

Williamsfield

Pioneer
Chocolate Factory

Marshall's
Pen

Royal Flat

Mandeville

Porus

Mocho

Spur Tree

Marlborough

Knockpatrick

Toll Gate

A2

Newport

To May Pen,
Kingston

B12

Blenheim

Rose Hill
2772ft

Pratville

Milk River

To May Pen

Rest Store

Cross Keys

Rowes Corner
Plowden Hill

Alligator Pond

Alligator Hole
(Canoe Valley
Wetlands)

Round Hill
1154ft

Rest

Alligator Pond
Bay

Old Fort

Gut River

Long Bay

Milk
River Bath

Cuckold Point

Old Woman's Point

CARIBBEAN SEA

Farquhar
Beach

77°30'W

Don Figuerero Mountains

Winston Jones Hwy

Clarendon

Manchester

CENTRAL HIGHLANDS

Mandeville – the most prosperous and pleasant town on the island – spreads across a rolling plateau. It has a strong English feel that has attracted a large number of English retirees in recent decades, alongside North Americans who have arrived with the bauxite industry. It is pervaded by a sense of modernity and sophistication outside the tourist realm, and in some ways deserves to be seen as Jamaica's second city.

## HISTORY

Mandeville began life as a haven for colonial planters escaping the heat of the plains. The town was established only in 1816, following a petition from the region's isolated coffee planters. It was named after Lord Mandeville, eldest son of the governor. The parish authorities laid out the town according to a strict order: first the courthouse, then a parsonage, jail and workhouse, and lastly a church (all four buildings still stand).

In the 19th century, the city prospered as a holiday retreat for wealthy Kingstonians and planters, and attracted a considerable population of English retirees from other colonial quarters. Many early ex-pats established the area as a center for dairy farming and citrus and pimento production. Jamaica's unique, seedless citrus fruit, the ortanique, was first produced here in the 1920s and is now grown in large quantities by Alcan, the North American bauxite company, which owns considerable acreage locally.

Alcan opened operations here in 1940. Relatively high wage levels lured educated Jamaicans, turning what was then a sleepy retreat into a city of cultured energy. Alcan has built large residential areas for its employees, many of them North Americans whose presence has had a distinct 'Americanizing' effect, bringing a middle-class savoire faire to the town. Today Mandeville's economic fortunes are tied to those of the bauxite industry.

## ORIENTATION

Mandeville is spread across rolling hills in a maze of wriggly streets with no apparent order. The center is compact enough to walk almost everywhere. At its heart is an historic village green, called Cecil Charlton Park after a former mayor. The 'green' is ringed by Park Crescent, from which roads radiate out like spokes on a wheel: Manchester Rd leads southeast, Ward Ave and Brumalia Rd lead west, and Main St leads north.

Main St is the main artery and runs north to Caledonia Rd: at the T-junction, Caledonia Rd leads east to Williamsfield; west of the junction it turns south and runs back into town parallel to Main St, and continues south as Perth Rd. Main St and Caledonia Rd are linked by North Racecourse and South Racecourse, shaped in a great oval that is the legacy of a horseracing track that stood here in the 19th century. Between North and South Racecourse, Main St is split into northbound and southbound lanes by a narrow median (the northbound lane is Hargreaves Ave).

A major bypass – the Winston Jones Hwy (A2) – skirts the northern edge of town, dropping eastward to Williamsfield (and the junction of the main roads to Christiana and Kingston) and westward to St Elizabeth parish. New Green Rd links the highway with the junction of Caledonia Rd and Main St; Greenvale Rd links the highway with Perth Rd.

## Maps

The 'Discover Jamaica' road map issued by the Jamaica Tourist Board (JTB) includes a separate map of Mandeville. Hotels issue a sketchy hand-drawn map of the town.

## INFORMATION
## Tourist Offices

The JTB does not have an office in Mandeville. The best information source is the Central & South Tourism Committee, based at the Astra Country Inn, with a Visitor Information Service (☎ 962-3725). It has a meager supply of brochures.

The Jamaica Information Service (☎ 962-0827) has an office in Shop F3 at Caledonia Plaza; most of its information is of practical use for local citizens. The Mandeville Hotel publishes a handy pamphlet guide to the town.

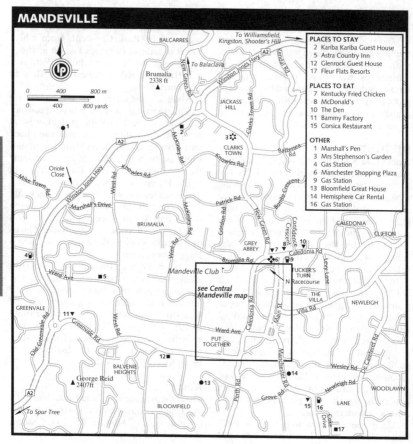

# MANDEVILLE

**PLACES TO STAY**
2  Kariba Kariba Guest House
5  Astra Country Inn
12  Glenrock Guest House
17  Fleur Flats Resorts

**PLACES TO EAT**
7  Kentucky Fried Chicken
8  McDonald's
10  The Den
11  Bammy Factory
15  Corsica Restaurant

**OTHER**
1  Marshall's Pen
3  Mrs Stephenson's Garden
4  Gas Station
6  Manchester Shopping Plaza
9  Gas Station
13  Bloomfield Great House
14  Hemisphere Car Rental
16  Gas Station

## Money

There are plenty of places to change foreign currency or arrange cash advances. Scotiabank (☎ 962-1083) is at the junction of Ward Ave and Caledonia Rd; the CIBC (☎ 962-1480) is at Park Crescent. The National Commercial Bank has three branches: one in the Manchester Shopping Plaza (☎ 962-8600), another that faces Mandeville Plaza (☎ 962-2161), and a third at 9 Manchester Rd (☎ 962-2886). All have 24-hour ATMs. If you need to receive or send money by remittance, contact Western Union (☎ 962-1037) in the Brumalia Town Centre.

## Post & Communications

The post office (☎ 962-2339) is on South Racecourse. If you need to send packages, use UPS (☎ 962-5135), which has an office at Shop 33 in the Manchester Shopping Plaza. Letters to North America cost US$11 (more to Europe). UPS offers guaranteed next-day delivery service; it's open 7 am to 7 pm daily. There are plenty of public telephones sprinkled around town, but for international calls go to the Cable & Wireless office on Hargreaves Ave.

## Travel Agencies
You'll find lots of agencies around town. Try Sterling Travel (☎ 962-2203) in Caledonia Plaza; International Travel Services (☎ 962-2123) at 36 Manchester Rd; or Global Travel Service (☎ 962-1183) in the Manchester Shopping Plaza.

## Bookstores
The best bookshop is Booklands, in the Manchester Shopping Plaza, with a wide range of magazines. Several stationery stores sell books and magazines, including the Book Shop (☎ 962-9204) in Villa Plaza on Main St, and Books & Things (☎ 962-0049) at 1 Buena Vista Circle. Haughton's Pharmacy, on the southwest side of the village green, also has a reasonable selection of international magazines.

## Library
To brush up on local history, drop by the Manchester Parish Library (☎ 962-2972) at 34 Hargreaves Ave.

## Medical Services
Mandeville is well served by nine medical centers and about 40 doctors. The town's two hospitals – Mandeville Hospital (☎ 962-2067) and the privately run Hargreaves Memorial Hospital (☎ 962-2040) – are both on Hargreaves Ave and have emergency centers. For less urgent treatment, try the Gateway Medical Centre, on Caledonia Rd, or the Caledonia Medicare Centre (☎ 962-3939). Villa Plaza also has a doctor's office, X-ray lab, and pharmacy, plus the Maxicare Dental Centre (☎ 962-9279) at 29 Main St. Likewise, Consolidated Health Services (☎ 962-0320), at 14 Caledonia Rd, is a full-service clinic next to the Manchester Shopping Plaza.

Pharmacies include the Caledonia Mall Pharmacy (☎ 962-0038), at Shop G5, 3 Caledonia Rd; Grove Court Pharmacy; and Haughton's Pharmacy (☎ 962-2246), on the 'green' at 18 W Park Crescent, which is open 8 am to 8:30 pm Monday to Saturday, and 9 am to 7 pm on Sunday.

## Emergency
Call the police at ☎ 119. The police station (☎ 962-2250) is on the north side of the village green. For an ambulance or fire truck, call ☎ 110.

## THINGS TO SEE & DO
### Cecil Charlton Park
This tiny English-style green, also known as Mandeville Square, lends a charming village feel to the town center. On the north side of the square is the **Mandeville Courthouse**, a handsome building of cut limestone with a horseshoe staircase and a raised portico supported by Doric columns.

The **Rectory**, the oldest home in town, adjoins the courthouse. Both it and the courthouse were completed in 1820. The original rector gained a considerable income from selling baptismal certificates. In addition, he caused an outcry by also renting out the building as a tavern. It later became a hotel and is now a private home.

On the south side is a produce market that bustles daily. Civic leaders believe that it is too congested and poses a health risk (it was closed by health inspectors in 1998) and hope to relocate it. A **cenotaph** stands on the south side of the square, commemorating Jamaica's dead from the two world wars.

**St Mark's Church**, likewise on the south side of Cecil Charlton Park, was also established in 1820. It's not Westminster Abbey, but the timber clerestory is impressive. During the slave rebellion of Christmas 1831, nonconformist missionaries suspected of inciting the rebellion were jailed in the organ loft. The churchyard includes graves of English soldiers who died during a yellow fever epidemic.

### Bloomfield Great House
This immaculate historic home (☎ 962-7130, fax 961-0549, bloomfield.g.h@cwjamaica.com), at 8 Perth Rd, sitting atop a hill southwest of the town center, is Mandeville's pride and joy. The two-story structure is built in a traditional Caribbean vernacular and fairly gleams after a fine renovation. The house is about 170 years old (the exact date is uncertain) and began life as the center of

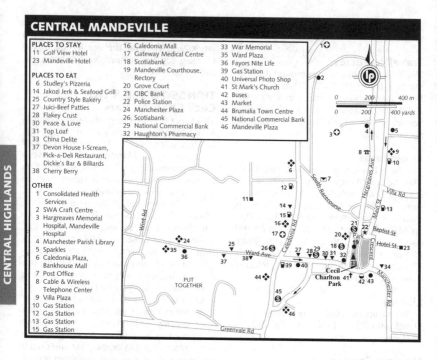

## CENTRAL MANDEVILLE

**PLACES TO STAY**
11 Golf View Hotel
23 Mandeville Hotel

**PLACES TO EAT**
6 Studley's Pizzeria
14 Jakozi Jerk & Seafood Grill
25 Country Style Bakery
27 Juici-Beef Patties
28 Flakey Crust
30 Peace & Love
31 Top Loaf
33 China Delite
37 Devon House I-Scream,
   Pick-a-Deli Restaurant,
   Dickie's Bar & Billiards
38 Cherry Berry

**OTHER**
1 Consolidated Health
   Services
2 SWA Craft Centre
3 Hargreaves Memorial
   Hospital, Mandeville
   Hospital
4 Manchester Parish Library
5 Sparkles
6 Caledonia Plaza,
   Bankhouse Mall
7 Post Office
8 Cable & Wireless
   Telephone Center
9 Villa Plaza
10 Gas Station
12 Gas Station
13 Gas Station
15 Gas Station

16 Caledonia Mall
17 Gateway Medical Centre
18 Scotiabank
19 Mandeville Courthouse,
   Rectory
20 Grove Court
21 CIBC Bank
22 Police Station
24 Manchester Plaza
26 Scotiabank
29 National Commercial Bank
32 Haughton's Pharmacy

33 War Memorial
35 Ward Plaza
36 Fayors Nite Life
39 Gas Station
40 Universal Photo Shop
41 St Mark's Church
42 Buses
43 Market
44 Brumalia Town Centre
45 National Commercial Bank
46 Mandeville Plaza

---

a coffee estate and, later, a citrus plantation. Most recently it housed Bill Laurie's Steak House. New owners – husband-and-wife team, Ralph Pearce and Pamela Grant – have invested considerable money, a sense of taste, and an exemplary attention to detail to restore the home to gracious grandeur (as if with the wave of a magic wand). It's now one of Jamaica's finest art galleries and premier restaurants.

The gleaming mahoe and buttlewood floors, the rails of the balcony extension carved with Caribbean motifs, the infinite attention to decor are the masterly expression of Croatian architect Snjezana Hercigonja. Bloomfield offers one of the finest dining experiences on the island as well (see Places to Eat), with dining rooms that double as galleries displaying an eclectic range of art featuring works by many of Jamaica's leading artists, as well as an international repertoire, including Australian landscapes

by Ralph's mother. Eleanor Strudwick is a local resident artist; her Eleanor's Arts & Crafts is one of five studios and stores that make up the gallery downstairs. Casual visitors are welcome to browse the galleries. The entrance is 200 yards south of Manchester College, on the opposite side of the road at the crossroads.

### Huntington Summit

Somewhere between the sublime and the ridiculous, the extravagant Huntington Summit mansion (☎ 962-2274), 25 Racecourse, in May Day, 2 miles southeast of the town center, is the yang to Bloomfield's yin. The octagonal home is of palatial proportion, with wrap-around plate-glass windows and artificial cascades tumbling into a swimming pool where waters feed into a pond in the lounge. The centerpiece of a farm (replete with a series of cages overfilled with birds and rabbits) and stables called Manchester

Green, the home is fascinating for its eclectic and ostentatious furnishings that reflect the catholic tastes of its owner, Cecil Charlton, a millionaire farmer, politician, and self-promoter who served as Mandeville's mayor for 20 years during the 1970s and 1980s. He made much of his money as owner of the Charles-Off betting shops, but also served as chairman of the corruption-ridden National Water Commission (see Government & Politics in the Facts about Jamaica chapter).

The home is open to the public daily except Wednesday and Saturday, by appointment. There's no charge, but a donation is urged.

## Marshall's Pen

This 18th-century great house (☎ 904-5454) is another impressive historic edifice and nature retreat, and a perfect antidote to Huntington Summit. It stands in the midst of a former coffee plantation turned cattle-breeding property on the northwest side of town. The house is fronted by beautifully landscaped gardens beneath huge fig trees hung with epiphytes and vines. Marshall's Pen is splendid for birding: more than 100 species have been recorded here, including 25 of the 27 species endemic to Jamaica.

The property was formerly owned by the Earl of Balcarres (governor of Jamaica from 1795 to 1801) when it was an estate of 4000 acres. Today the 300-acre property is owned by Robert Sutton, Jamaica's leading ornithologist, and Anne Sutton, an environmental scientist. The couple are gracious hosts. Robert can trace his ancestry to the first child born to English parents in Jamaica in 1655. He is happy to share his encyclopedic knowledge – he has been described as someone who 'could coach Alistair Cooke on urbane civility' – and will reminisce on any subject you raise.

It's a treat to don rubber boots and binoculars and set out with the Suttons and their several dogs swarming happily at your heels. Robert is co-author with Audrey Downer of *Birds of Jamaica: A Photographic Field Guide*. He also escorts a weeklong birding trip that includes the Cockpit Country and Blue Mountains.

The stone-and-timber house, built in 1795, began life as the center of a coffee estate. The forecourt in front of the parking area was once a 'barbecue' used for drying the beans. The Suttons' home has wood-paneled rooms brimming with antiques, leather-bound books, artwork, and other museum-quality pieces. You can tour the mini-museum and marvel at the vast and eclectic collection, which includes oriental memorabilia, shells, and postage stamps, and even ancient Arawak relics. If Robert or Ann aren't at home, then Robert's father, Arthur Sutton, will be delighted to show you around. He was born in 1900 and is as fascinatingly erudite as his famous son.

Entrance costs US$10 and is by appointment only. Visiting at early morning or evening is best. Overnight stays can sometimes be arranged in advance for birders, if convenient for the family (see Places to Stay, later in this chapter). Contrary to prevailing information, horseback rides are *not* available.

The house is northwest of the Winston Jones Hwy, about 3 miles from the town center. Take Oriole Close off the highway (there's a sign for 'Somerset Quarries' at the junction). Turn right onto a paved road after 100 yards; the estate entrance – an unmarked stone gateway – is about 400 yards farther on the right. Follow a dirt road half a mile up to the house, past fields grazed by red poll cattle. Mosquitoes abound; take repellent.

## Roxborough

Right Excellent Norman Manley, who was prime minister from 1955 to 1962, was born in 1894 at Roxborough, 6 miles east of Mandeville. Manley was born of a lower-middle-class white family and spent his early years on a run-down estate managed by his widowed mother, who remarried a black man and was shunned by all but her closest friends. Manley became a champion athlete, won a Rhodes scholarship and entered Oxford to study law, but enlisted (along with his brother Roy, who was later killed in action) in an artillery regiment during WWI, earning the Military Medal for valor. He returned to Oxford to complete his degree and took top honors in law at Gray's Inn. (He married his English-born cousin Edna

Swithenbank, who would go on to become Jamaica's foremost sculptor. (For more on Edna Manley, see 'First Lady of the Jamaica School' in the Facts about Jamaica chapter.)

Fire gutted the house in 1968, but the gardens, with spreading poinciana trees, are maintained by the National Trust of Jamaica. It's not worth the drive, but you might drop by in passing to admire the views across the hills of Manchester and Clarendon from a raised tableau inset with a marble plaque. Much of the estate is currently being mined for bauxite.

## Mrs Stephenson's Garden

Mrs Stephenson's Garden (☎ 962-2909), at 25 New Green Rd, is worth a browse. This well-manicured, well-ordered garden has been planned and planted, and pruned and mulched by a stalwart who is really an artist. Carmen Stephenson can be seen on any day doing earnest battle with a prickly rose bush or coddling her rare white anthuriums with equal solicitude. Her garden is a riot of color, a drunkenness of scents, difficult to dampen in even the wettest of weather. Keen amateur gardeners descend year-round to 'tut-tut' at the lay-out or gasp at the collection that includes orchids and ortaniques. Casual visitors are welcome during daylight hours (US$2).

## HIKING & HORSEBACK RIDING

John Nightingale offers hikes and horseback rides at Perth Great House (☎ 962-2822), 13 Perth Rd, a Georgian great house dating to 1760. And Pamela Goodwyn, a former horse-jumping champion, offers one-hour rides at Godfrey Lands for US$50. For reservations, contact Countrystyle Community Tours (☎ 962-7979, 962-7917), at the Astra Country Inn. You may also be able to arrange rides through the Manchester Club (☎ 962-2403).

## GOLF & TENNIS

For years, *the* social scene in Mandeville has revolved around the Manchester Club (☎ 962-2403), a private club off Brumalia Rd, northwest of the town center. The nine-hole golf course (which has 18 tees) was laid out in the 1860s, making it one of the oldest

country clubs in the Americas. It's a tight layout and quite challenging despite being relatively short (US$13). Caddies are compulsory (US$13). Ex-pat residents and guests of local hotels can use the facilities, including the three night-lit tennis courts and squash courts (both US$4.50 per hour).

## SCUBA DIVING

Excuse me? Yes, there's scuba diving in these mountains. Ralph Pearce of Bloomfield Great House (☎ 962-7130) teaches classes in the heated pool to the rear of the property, with PADI certification dives on the north coast (about US$200). He also offers referral certification dives; trips are in conjunction with the Kingston Scuba Club.

## ORGANIZED TOURS

Kariba Holidays & Leisure Tours (☎ 962-8006, fax 962-5502), at Kariba Kariba Guest House (see Places to Stay, later in this chapter), offers a two-day 'Jamaica Off the Beaten Track' tour featuring visits to Black River, YS Falls, Bamboo Avenue, Mandeville, and the Appleton Rum Estate (US$180). He has other tours and can customize tours.

Countrystyle Community Tours (☎ 962-7979, fax 962-1461, paulov@infocharn.com), at the Astra Country Inn, has a full-day 'Highlights Tour' of Mandeville (US$40 per person) that aims to put tour participants in touch with local Jamaicans. It also offers specialist guides – ordinary people who show guests their way of life – for US$10 per hour. It also offers tours to Treasure Beach, Ocho Rios, and Oracabessa (all cost US$50).

## SPECIAL EVENTS

The Manchester Horticultural Society Show (☎ 962-2328) is held in late May at Mrs Stephenson's Garden.

Golf enthusiasts time their visit to coincide with Jamaica's oldest golf tournament, the Manchester Golf Week, held in late July at the Manchester Club (☎ 962-2403); contact the Jamaica Golf Association (☎ 975-4287). It's followed in August by Tennis Week at the same location. The Jamaica Horse Show is also held at the Manchester Club in July.

## Community Tourism

You won't be long in the Mandeville area before you hear about 'community tourism,' an attempt to foster opportunities for locals wishing to participate more fully in Jamaica's tourism industry. Key to the movement is the desire to promote tourism throughout the central highlands and south coast while avoiding the mistakes of other resort areas.

The dynamo behind the movement is Diana McIntyre-Pike, co-owner and manager of the Astra Country Inn (☎ 962-3725), and director of Countrystyle Ltd, PO Box 60, a company that specializes in providing alternatives to 'sea and sand' vacations. She helped form the Central & South Tourism Committee, funded in part by the national Tourism Action Plan. The group sponsors special-interest tours, community guides, skills training, and assistance with tourism development at the village level. McIntyre-Pike has also set up the Countrystyle Institute for Sustainable Tourism to assist in professional development of the community, which offers a wide range of courses from community guide training to environmental waste management.

Promoters of small-scale community tourism fear that as south-coast tourism blossoms, government bureaucracy will spoil things. 'Whatever development takes place, it must complement our lifestyle, not change our way of life,' says McIntyre-Pike. A common complaint is that the government is not listening to the locals. This is especially true for the southwest coast, where big developers are finding favor with politicians in Kingston.

Organizers such as McIntyre-Pike are hoping to avoid overdevelopment by forging a connection between tourists and the citizenry. Many locals have opened their properties as guest houses. Others are taking visitors on family outings or guided excursions. Plans involve attracting small cruise ships to Port Kaiser or Black River (see the Southwest Coast chapter), from which passengers would be taken to villages and eco-attractions. And as the big resort chains move in, the program aims to foster exchanges for resort guests wishing to overnight with local families. In addition to promoting an interchange of cultures, small businesses are also being developed, such as a village program to manufacture 'South Coast Fashions.'

The Oracabessa Foundation, in St Mary parish, performs a similar function. (See 'Community Development' in the Ocho Rios & North Coast chapter.)

**CENTRAL HIGHLANDS**

## PLACES TO STAY

Mandeville is one of the few places in Jamaica with genuine guest houses, where you're a guest in a family home.

### Guest Houses

***Kariba Kariba Guest House*** (☎ 962-8006, fax 962-5502, PO Box 482), beside the Winton Jones Hwy, is a beautiful new home built of fieldstone run by Derek and Hazel O'Connor, a friendly English couple. It was in the final phase of construction at this writing, with handsome tile and hardwood floors, a large lounge with arches and exquisite detailing, and large rooms with balconies. A swimming pool is to be added. Rates for two rooms with private bath are US$45; two rooms with shared bath cost US$35, including breakfast. Dinner and lunch cost US$5 each.

If you're not fussy about decor, try ***Glenrock Guest House*** (☎ 961-3278, 3 Greenwall Rd), a homey place with seven carpeted bedrooms with fans and louvered windows, plus private bath with hot water. Rooms cost US$29 to US$34. Free breakfasts are included with longer stays.

Another option is ***Hillside Guest House*** (☎ 904-8717), about 3 miles south of town on Manchester Rd. It's open in summer only and has eight rooms with private bath for US$23.

Serious birders may be able to stay at *Marshall's Pen* (☎ *904-5454, PO Box 58*), which has three bedrooms in the main house, plus five self-catering apartments in a converted coffee warehouse. Costs range from US$25 per person per night. Meals can sometimes be arranged. Note that this is not a hotel or guest house; rooms are made available at the owners' discretion, and only to devout birders or nature lovers.

## Hotels

The *Mandeville Hotel* (☎ *962-2460, fax 962-0700, PO Box 78*), at the bottom of Hotel St on the east side of the green, is the island's oldest hotel, dating to the 1890s. Before that it served as a barracks for English troops. A partial renovation has brought the main facility up to par, but rooms to the rear remain dowdy. Self-contained units with kitchenettes are also available nearby. The restaurant is popular with local businessfolk and overlooks a pool. It has a pub. Room rates vary from US$65 to US$125. Apartments cost US$180 to US$210.

There's a homey charm to the *Astra Country Inn* (☎ *962-3725, fax 962-1461, 62 Ward Ave*), on the western outskirts of town. It has 20 well-lit rooms with tile floors (some with king-size beds) plus options for TVs and telephone, including suites with kitchenettes. The decor was jaded at press time, but a renovation was scheduled. Facilities include a pool, an English-style pub, and a pleasant dining room serving tasty Jamaican cuisine from produce grown in the hotel's organic garden (a food plan costs from US$20 daily). Coffee is delivered to your room as a wake-up call. Rates range from US$40 to US$65; it's US$110 for a suite. A breakfast option costs US$10.

*Fleur Flats Resorts* (☎ *962-1053, 10 Coke Drive, PO Box 485;* ☎ *416-445-0209 in Canada;* ☎ *305-252-0873 in the USA;* ☎ *020-7964-0047 in the UK*) offers spacious, fully furnished apartments that sleep four people in comfort for US$57 (one bedroom), US$86 (two bedrooms). Rooms have TVs and phones. The family oriented resort is a 20-minute walk from the town center. The

couple who owns it are extremely gracious and friendly.

The *Golf View Hotel* (☎ *962-4471, fax 962-5640, 7B Caledonia Rd, PO Box 189*) is a rambling, motel-style property surrounding a small pool in an ugly concrete courtyard. Rooms have contemporary decor, tile floors, fans, cable TVs, louvered windows, and tub showers and cost US$55 to US$80. Spacious air-conditioned suites have walk-in showers and four-poster beds for US$60 one-bedroom, US$80 two-bedroom. Beware the dangerous stairs!

## PLACES TO EAT

Among the town's several dozen restaurants, you'll find a variety of international cuisines.

### Jamaican

The *Mandeville Hotel* – which has a poolside barbecue each Wednesday night – and *Astra Country Inn* both have notable restaurants. At the former I recommend the chicken and red snapper in a piquant sauce. The Astra grows much of its produce in a private garden. Its natural health breakfast costs US$5, and Jamaican dishes begin at US$7. Sandwiches and other snacks cost US$2.

You can get a cheap breakfast at *Cherry Berry* (☎ *962-4726*), opposite Scotiabank, or *Tweeties Café* in Brumalia Town Centre, across the road from Tweeties Fried Chicken. Tweeties' menu also features fish and chips, pizza, and sandwiches.

The *Corsica Restaurant* (☎ *962-2786*) is clean and pleasant and serves Jamaican fare for US$6, plus fish and chips for US$9.

The *Jakozi Jerk & Seafood Grill*, on Caledonia Rd, is one of the town's more popular eateries and has outside dining. *Peace & Love*, on Ward Ave, is also pleasant and offers inexpensive Jamaican fare.

*Bloomfield Great House Restaurant & Bar* (☎ *962-7130, 8 Perth Rd*) is one of Jamaica's pre-eminent restaurants, exemplifying the best of Caribbean nouvelle cuisine (also see the Bloomfield Great House entry earlier). There are several dining options, including the romantic veranda offering panoramic vistas over town, and an inside dining room, open to sensations of the tropical elements through wide-open doors. A private dining room seats 12. A TV room keeps children amused. The creative menu, which changes regularly, includes fresh pastas (about US$15) such as callaloo fettuccine; punjab prawns in mango curry with coconut (US$20); and T-Bone steaks (US$30), harking back to the days when this was Bill Laurie's Steak House. The lunch menu offers caesar salad, pizza, fish and chips, and lighter fare (from US$4). Meals are filling and offer great value. Australian wines are well represented. A small bar (lit by Tiffany lamps) has Red Stripe on tap, plus international favorites such as Corona. A Sunday champagne brunch is offered. The place is justifiably popular with expat residents and middle-class Jamaicans. Free pick-up and drop-off are offered.

### Fast Food
If you need a fast-food fix, *Kentucky Fried Chicken* has an outlet on Caledonia Rd, opposite the Manchester Shopping Plaza. Or try *Hungry Jack's* at Villa Plaza on Main St; *McDonald's* at the junction of Caledonia Rd and Main St; *Tweeties Fried Chicken*, also on Main St, in the Brumalia Town Centre; and *Juici-Beef Patties* on Ward Ave.

There's a food court to the rear of the Manchester Shopping Plaza, with *Indies Pizza*, *Gee's Café* (recommended for its Jamaican breakfasts), plus the *Real Things Health Food Store*. *Studly's Pizzeria* (☎ 962-0082) is in Caledonia Plaza. Another food court is downstairs in the basement, known as Bankhouse Mall, including *Bankhouse Bakery*, *KFC*, and *Sunrise Vegetarian Foods*.

### Chinese
The *Den* (☎ 962-3603, 35 Caledonia Rd) specializes in Asian dishes. Thursday and Friday it offers curry dishes, chicken tandoori, and shrimp simmered in coconut cream. It has a happy hour from 5:30 pm. It's closed on Sunday.

Other reasonably priced Chinese options include the *Bamboo Village Restaurant* (☎ 962-4515, 35 Ward Ave), in the Ward Plaza; the *International* (☎ 962-0527, 117 Manchester Rd); and *China Delite* (☎ 962-9560), also on Manchester Rd.

### Bakeries & Groceries
You can buy one half of Jamaica's famous 'fish and bammy' at Clem Bloomfield's *Bammy Factory* (☎ 963-8636, 40 Greenvale Rd). *Top Loaf,* on Ward Ave, and *Flakey Crust (11 Manchester Rd)*, next door, sell fresh-baked breads, pastries, and patties. The *Country Style Bakery* is a clean bread shop on Ward Ave.

*Jakozi Jerk* has an ice cream counter, and *Devon House I-Scream* has an outlet nearby, 200 yards west of Scotiabank, above the *Pick-a-Deli Restaurant. Cherry Berry,* on Ward Ave, serves iced yogurts and ice cream.

There are several *supermarkets* in town, notably along Brumalia Rd, in the Manchester Shopping Plaza, and on Manchester Rd south of Cecil Charlton Park. You can also buy fresh produce at the *market* on the south side of Cecil Charlton Park, but hygiene is an issue (the market was briefly closed by health inspectors in 1998).

## ENTERTAINMENT
The in-vogue spot in late 1998 was *Fayors Nite Life (☎ 962-2660, 33 Ward Ave)*. It has live music out back and a disco inside. Friday is 'Ladies Nite' (entry is free for women; men pay US$3). It also shows movies on a big screen with surround sound at 7 pm Thursday and at 6 pm Sunday (US$3).

But on weekends half of Mandeville seems to pour downhill 10 miles west to the upscale disco *Jim's HQ Lounge* (see Gutters in the Southwest Coast chapter).

More down-to-earth discos include *Sparkles (41 Main St)* in Leader's Plaza, playing a mix of dancehall, reggae, and soca on weekends; and the recently opened *Ward 21 (☎ 961-4560, 38 Mandeville Plaza)*, featuring sound systems. If deafening dancehall is your thing, also check out *Bally's* on Manchester Rd, 400 yards south of Cecil Charlton Park.

*Bloomfield Great House* has live musical entertainment on Friday nights. The *Mandeville Hotel* hosts live jazz at 7 pm each Wednesday, during its poolside barbecue.

For a beer or cocktail in quiet surrounds, try **Merv's Cocktail Bar**, in Caledonia Plaza or the **Manchester Club** (for members and guests), which hosts occasional barbecues and has a happy hour on Friday.

The **Cecil Charlton Centre** is the town's cinema.

Want to play pool? Head to **Dickie's Bar & Billiards** on Ward Ave, above Devon House I-Scream.

If your taste runs to earthy go-go clubs, join the local men at **Sprint** or **Whispers**, both at Royal Flat, about 3 miles east of town along Caledonia Rd, or a short distance farther, the decidedly raunchy **Club Cariba** at Russell Place Gardens. Entry is free; beers cost US$2.50.

## SHOPPING

Mandeville has 12 major shopping plazas. The largest is Manchester Shopping Plaza on Caledonia Rd.

The town is well off the tourist map, so the supply of crafts is meager. A notable exception is the SWA Craft Centre (☎ 962-2138) on North Racecourse behind the Manchester Shopping Plaza. It trains young adults with only basic education to make a living from crochet, embroidery, weaving, and so on. Its most appealing item is the famous 'banana patch' Rastafarian dolls, complete with a Jamaican passport.

Country Cottage Craft Gift Shoppe (☎ 961-6918), at 37 Main St, sells aromatic oils and soaps, plus paintings and ceramics.

Need film? The Universal Photo Shop, on Ward Ave 100 yards west of the town square, is the only place I know of outside Kingston and the resort towns that sells slide (transparency) film. A 36-exposure roll of Kodak Elite costs about US$14.

You can buy anthuriums at the Paul Cross Nursery beside the Catholic Church on Manchester Rd near Newleigh Rd. Alternately, try Carmen Stephenson's garden at 25 New Green Rd, or her flower shop (☎ 962-2909), Shop 14, Manchester Shopping Plaza.

## GETTING THERE & AWAY

Plans to build an airport capable of accepting international flights (possibly using Alpart's airfield southwest of town) have been touted for years, but no progress had been made at press time.

Mandeville has bus service from virtually every major town in Jamaica. Minibuses depart Kingston from Half Way Tree (about US$5) and buses from the Parade (about US$1.50).

Buses and minibuses depart Mandeville from near the market on the main square. For information call Superior Omnibus Service (☎ 962-2421) at Caledonia Plaza.

Bargain Rent-a-Car offers transfers from Kingston for US$35 per person one-way.

## GETTING AROUND

There is no local bus system. You'll find taxis near the market on Cecil Charlton Park. Otherwise call Manchester Taxi Service (☎ 962-2021).

To rent a car contact Hemisphere Car Rental (☎ 962-1921, fax 962-4131), 51 Manchester Rd; Maxdan Car Rental (☎ 962-5341), Shop 8, 18B Ward Ave; or Prams International (☎ 962-1051), 4 Newleigh Rd.

# Around Mandeville

## SPUR TREE

Four miles southwest of Mandeville is Spur Tree, atop the steep west-facing crest of the Don Figuerero Mountains. From Spur Tree the A2 falls precipitously in a dizzying switchback to Gutters and the plains of St Elizabeth (see the regional map in the Southwest Coast chapter). In colonial days, carriages were hitched to strong draught mules or oxen for the ascent and descent, and occupants transferred to ponies.

At the top of the hill you can look out over the Essex Valley (forming the eastern part of St Elizabeth parish) and the Santa Cruz Mountains. If you pull into the car park of Alpart Farm, you can look down into the Alpart bauxite mine, said to be the largest open-pit mine outside Chile. The valley floor is dominated by the company's alumina plant, 5 miles to the southeast at Nain. At night it glitters!

## SOUTHERN DON FIGUERERO MOUNTAINS

Following Manchester Rd south from Mandeville you'll pass Knockpatrick, where the road is crossed by a great cable conveyor belt used to deliver bauxite from Alpart's mines to the processing plant at Nain, 15 miles to the west. A Rastafarian named Sam operates a roadside thatched bar called *Nature Village*. He's a colorful character, worth stopping to talk to.

The scenic drive continues south until you arrive at Newport, a quaint and photogenic village centered on a large triangle where there are two brightly painted pubs – the *Capricorn Pub* and *Grand Duke Bar* – and a police station.

Farther south you pass through a surreal and powerful landscape of towering rocks north of Rest Store, a tiny hamlet nestling atop the southern crest of the Don Figuerero Mountains. Bring your camera for the spectacular view. From Rest Store, the road begins its winding descent to Rowes Corner and Alligator Pond (see the Southwest Coast chapter). If you turn east at Rest Store, you can loop back to Newport via Cross Keys, which has a magnificently preserved Georgian courthouse and police station atop a hill, fronted by topiary bushes.

## WILLIAMSFIELD

This village lies 1000 feet below and northeast of Mandeville at the base of the Winston Jones Hwy (A2), which links with the B4 at a roundabout at the east end of Williamsfield. There are several sites of interest.

### Williamsfield Great House

This old house was built by Capt George Heron, who built three other great houses and maintained a family in each. You can tour the restored great house by appointment, but it's not one of Jamaica's most interesting, and a modern structure has been added atop the old. It's near Royal Flat, a hamlet on the old Mandeville Rd, 400 yards south of the turnoff from the Williamsfield junction on the Winston Jones Hwy (the turnoff from the old road for the house is signed 'Williamsfield Gardens').

### High Mountain Coffee Factory

You can take a free tour of this processing factory (☎ 963-4211), where coffee herbal teas and coffee liqueurs are produced by the Jamaica Standard Products Co under three labels: Blue Mountain, High Mountain, and Baronhall Estate. It's adjacent to the old railway station just west of the roundabout. Tours are by appointment. Dress lightly, as it is very hot inside. The factory is tiny and the tour not overly interesting, but it has a coffee tasting room and store.

### Pioneer Chocolate Factory

Chocoholics will think they're in nirvana on a visit to the Pioneer Chocolate Company's factory (☎ 963-4216), which is also open for 30-minute tours by advance arrangement. Tours were being discouraged when I called by, however. Try asking for John or Robert Cunningham, who must approve all visits. You can watch the seeds from the cocoa bean being processed into chocolate bars, which you can sample. There's a factory outlet on the roadside, next to the Texaco gas station. It's 400 yards east of High Mountain.

### High Mountain 10K Road Race

Jamaica's largest bicycle road race attracts local and overseas amateurs and professionals. The High Mountain 10K Road Race (☎ 963-4211) is held here every January.

## SHOOTER'S HILL

Shooter's Hill, 2 miles northwest of Williamsfield, marks the base of a steep 4-mile-long climb ascending almost 1400 feet to Christiana. A lookout point midway offers splendid views. Near the top of the hill is **Walderston**, where a road to the right leads off to Spaldings. On the west side of the road, high atop a hill, is the Moravian-built **Mizpah church**, roughly resembling an alpine lodge topped by a four-faced German clock.

### Kirkvine Works

Just north of Williamsfield you'll pass the massive tailings lake full of rust-red liquid toxic waste from the Kirkvine Works, at Shooter's Hill. The alumina plant is owned and operated by Alcan Jamaica, the largest of the four multinational mining corporations operating in Jamaica. It's a joint venture between the Jamaican government and the Aluminium Company of Canada Ltd. The company is the largest single contributor to the Jamaican economy and government coffers. The processing factory is also the country's largest alumina plant.

Huge bauxite deposits underlie much of the surrounding land. The rust-red earth is scooped from open-pit mines and ferried by dump truck and aerial ropeway to the factory to be crushed, washed, kiln-dried, powdered, and refined into alumina (well over 500,000 tons of alumina are produced annually). The processed ore is transported to Port Esquivel at Old Harbour Bay on the south coast and shipped to North America and Scandinavia for smelting into aluminum. The company mines only a small portion of its land holdings at one time. Once mined, the land is restored with pasture and forest and returned to grazing. About 8000 acres are given to livestock and citrus, while another 23,000 acres are farmed by almost 5000 tenant farmers.

You can arrange free weekday **factory tours** through the Astra Country Inn or Mandeville Hotel (see the Mandeville section, earlier in this chapter), or through Mr J Neil at the Kirkvine Works office (☎ 961-7503, 962-3141). A day's notice is usually required. There's a strict dress code: long pants are required, and feet must be covered (no sandals). You can tell the place is run by North Americans: it's the most orderly and efficiently run place in Jamaica, with everything geared to safety.

### Pickapeppa Factory

Yet another 30-minute tour is available by appointment at this factory (☎ 962-2928, 962-2809) at the foot of Shooter's Hill, 100 yards west of the junction. The factory produces Jamaica's sinus-searing world-famous sauce (similar to England's Worcestershire sauce). You'll see workers stirring giant pots of simmering scallions and other vegetables. Otherwise there's not much to see, and it's rather pricey at US$9 (children US$3). There's no sign, but you can't miss the smell.

### Magic Toy Factory

This factory (☎ 1-990-6030 cellular) in Walderston, mid-way up Shooter's Hill, is a must visit. It makes handmade toys and puzzles, refrigerator magnets, exquisite wall plaques, and a miscellany of other creative pieces jigsawed from wood, then varnished and hand-painted in Caribbean colors. The enviable setting, in a vine-clad great house surrounded by palette-bright gardens, is alone worth the drive. The business is the brain-child of Will Robson, a gracious Yorkshireman, and his Jamaican-born wife, Margaret. They were planning to add a tea room on the hillside with views.

It's a great place to stock up on Christmas gifts for the kids for US$1 and up. It's open 9 am to 5 pm weekdays, and weekends by appointment.

## MILE GULLY & ENVIRONS

This modestly prosperous village sprawls along a dry valley that runs northwest from Mandeville in the lee of the forested north face of the Don Figuerero Mountains. The B6 leads northwest from Shooter's Hill, winding, dipping, and rising past lime-green pastures dotted with guango and silk-cotton trees and crisscrossed with stone walls and hedgerows. The area is reminiscent of the Yorkshire Dales and offers grandiose views where the road rises along the edge of cockpits.

The limestone valley is pitted with caves, including **Oxford Caves** near Mile Gully. They're said to abound with stalagmites and stalactites, and colonies of bats flit in and out. If you intend to explore, hire a local guide. You can also visit on a tour offered by the Hotel Villa Bella in Christiana (see the Christiana section, later in this chapter).

About a mile west of Mile Gully, at **Skull Point**, is a venerable blue-and-white 19th-century police station and courthouse at the junction for Bethany. A memorial outside salutes three famous slaves: George Lewis (the 'first evangelist'), Damon (a 'freedom fighter, killed in the struggle'), and James Knight ('Christian martyr'). A ceremony is held each August in their honor. Once, while taking photos of the plaque, I was hailed from the police station by a mysterious voice and discovered that it was a fella in jail, wanting to chat through the bars.

The road from Skull Point climbs sharply to Bethany – a worthy drive that delivers you at the **Bethany Moravian Church** – a simple gray stone building dating back to 1835, dramatically perched four-square mid-way up the hill with fantastic views down the valley. The church is rather dour close up, but the simple interior boasts a resplendent organ.

Another beautiful church – **St Simon's Anglican Church** – sits on a hillside amid meadows at Comfort Castle, 4 miles west of Mile Gully, with huge spreading trees festooned with old man's beard.

### Ripon Nature Park
Ripon, about a mile east of Mile Gully, produces citrus, flowers, coffee, and cocoa and is being developed into a bird sanctuary, wild garden, and eco-park by Derek O'Connor, owner of Kariba Holidays & Leisure Tours (☎ 962-8006) in Mandeville. The garden has more than 500 endemic species including orchids and is centered on an estate dating to 1750. The house is partly derelict, but its palm-lined driveway leads to the orchid garden accessible by trails and open for picnics. A tour includes either breakfast, lunch, or dinner, and a whirl around the old house. Horseback riding is to be introduced, and you can opt for a self-guided or guided walk. Entrance costs US$2.50.

### Martin Hill Orchid Sanctuary
Jamaica has scores of orchid species and more than 100 of them can be admired at this orchideum near Mark Post, about 3 miles north of Mandeville, on the road to Mile Gully and Balaclava (take New Green Rd). About 50,000 plants grow on the 1-acre facility, sponsored by Alcan, which owns the land (call Alcan at ☎ 962-2221 and ask for Mr Stevenson). Among the species represented are 25 Jamaican endemics (including the *Epidendrum scalpeligerum*, not seen for 17 years until recently).

The sanctuary was closed at press time following vandalization by plant thieves, who stole a vast quantity of stock. Security

was to be introduced, and an entrance fee may be charged.

### Getting There & Away
Bus No LS30 operates twice daily between Mandeville and Balaclava via Mile Gully. It should cost less than US$1 to any point where you wish to get off.

If you're driving from Mandeville – a magnificent drive – the B6 continues west 5 miles to Green Hill and a T-junction marked 'St Paul's 5 miles' (to the left) and 'Balaclava 6½ miles' (to the right; see the Southwest Coast chapter). One mile north (to the right) of the junction, en route to Balaclava, is a *very dangerous* spot: you'll climb a short hill that tempts you to accelerate. Unfortunately there's a railway crossing atop the crest, and a hairpin bend *immediately* after. Drive slowly!

# Christiana & Environs

Visitors are often surprised by the cool, cloud-swept heights around Christiana. You'd be forgiven for imagining yourself in the Pyrenees or the highlands of Costa Rica. The air is crisp, clouds drift through the vales, and pine trees add to the alpine setting. The region receives very few foreign visitors, but it's worth the drive for an altogether different Caribbean experience.

The area is an important center for Irish potatoes. Cacao, yams, and coffee production are also important, and during picking season you can watch women with baskets moving among the rows, plucking cherry-red coffee berries.

### CHRISTIANA
Lying 10 miles north of Mandeville at an elevation of 3000 feet and a mile south of Jamaica's mountain backbone, the town of Christiana is the heart of a richly farmed agricultural region where gently undulating hills and shallow vales are speckled with white houses with red roofs. Christiana is a fairly sleepy place, but on Thursday when the higglers come to sell their produce, the roads are so thick you can hardly drive

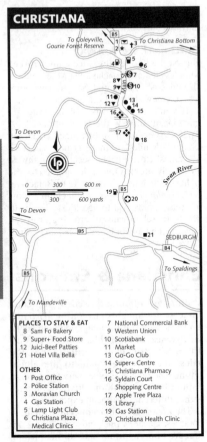

CHRISTIANA

To Coleyville,
Gourie Forest Reserve

To Christiana Bottom

To Devon

To Devon

Swan River

To Mandeville

0        300        600 m
0        300        600 yards

SEDBURGH

To Spaldings

| PLACES TO STAY & EAT | 7 National Commercial Bank |
|---|---|
| 8 Sam Fo Bakery | 9 Western Union |
| 9 Super+ Food Store | 10 Scotiabank |
| 12 Juici-Beef Patties | 11 Market |
| 21 Hotel Villa Bella | 13 Go-Go Club |
|  | 14 Super+ Centre |
| OTHER | 15 Christiana Pharmacy |
| 1 Post Office | 16 Syldain Court |
| 2 Police Station |    Shopping Centre |
| 3 Moravian Church | 17 Apple Tree Plaza |
| 4 Gas Station | 18 Library |
| 5 Lamp Light Club | 19 Gas Station |
| 6 Christiana Plaza, | 20 Christiana Health Clinic |
|    Medical Clinics |  |

looks down over the town from the northern end of sinuous Main St. During the 19th century, Christiana became a hill-town resort popular with European dignitaries and Kingstonians escaping the heat of the plains. The marvelous Hotel Villa Bella recalls that era.

## Information

Three bank branches are located along Main St, including Scotiabank (☎ 964-2223) and National Commercial Bank in the town center (☎ 964-2466). Western Union is represented by the Super+ Food Store (☎ 964-2465), on Main St.

The post office (☎ 964-2279) is on Main St just north of the town center, next to the police station. You can make international calls and send and receive faxes from U-Phone (☎ 964-3407) in the Apple Tree Plaza, 100 yards south of the fire station (open 8 am to 8 pm Monday to Saturday, and 2 to 8 pm Sunday).

Global Travel Service (☎ 964-2714) is a travel agency on Main St.

The small town library is opposite the Jamaica Citizens Bank, south of the town center.

Several doctors' clinics are in Christiana Plaza, off Main St in the town center. These include Dr Glen Norman Day's clinic (☎ 964-2361), open 9 am to 3 pm Monday, Tuesday, Thursday, and Saturday; and Dr Paul Morris' clinic (☎ 964-2299), open 8 am to 5 pm Monday to Saturday. The well-stocked Christiana Pharmacy (☎ 964-2424) is on Main St.

There's another pharmacy across the street in the Syldian Court Shopping Centre, where Dr Khin May has an office, open 8:30 am to 3 pm Monday to Saturday. The government-run Christiana Health Clinic is toward the south end of Main St.

The historic police station (☎ 964-2250) is at the north end of Main St.

## Christiana Bottom

This beautiful riverside spot, in a valley bottom 800 feet below the town, has a waterfall plus picnic spots surrounded by bamboo and lilies. Two sinkholes full of

through town. If you're in Christiana on a Thursday, stay through the evening for Higgler's Night.

The area was settled by German farmers during the 18th and 19th centuries. Many had fought as mercenaries for the English army during the American War of Independence, and they were rewarded with land grants in Jamaica. Their legacy is evident in the fair skin and blue and green eyes of the locals.

Moravian missionaries were also active during that era, and a **Moravian church** crystal-clear water tempt you to take a refreshing dip. There's no entrance fee. You can hike from the center of town, though the going at the lower reaches can be muddy and slippery. Take the road that leads east from Kirby Hardware and the National Commercial Bank; it's 2 miles from here. Take the first left and then the second left. If you still get lost ask a local for the 'blue hole.' Monica Zijdemans at Hotel Villa Bella (☎ 964-2243) can guide you.

## Gourie Forest Reserve

About 2 miles northwest of town, near Coleyville, is this forest reserve of pines, mahogany, and mahoe growing atop and betwixt dramatic cockpits. Orchids grow profusely. The park is laced with hiking trails. Gourie, however, is most noteworthy for having Jamaica's longest cave system. The cave entrance is about half a mile downhill from the cabins.

Two **spelunking** routes have been explored and laid out through the caves. One of the routes is easy; the other is difficult and made more so by the presence of an icy river. Rubber-soled shoes are required and a guide is essential. Entrance is free. There are no facilities.

A good way to visit is with Villa Bella Tours (US$30 for three hours) at the Hotel Villa Bella.

The Forestry Dept of the Ministry of Agriculture (☎ 964-2065) rents two basic wooden cottages. The office is on Main St, but you can reportedly get the keys from the caretaker at the reserve. The US Peace Corps plans to train local guides.

To get to Gourie, turn uphill (southwest) at the radio tower immediately south of the junction that leads west for Coleyville and Troy (see the regional map in the Montego Bay & Northwest chapter). Immediately, take the left at a Y-fork, then right at the next Y-fork and follow the green wire fence.

## Organized Tours

Monica Zijdemans, owner of Villa Bella Tours (☎ 964-2243) leads excursions to places of interest near Christiana for groups of four or more people, including trips to the Oxford Caves (US$30), Martin Hill Orchid Sanctuary (US$10), Lorimar Coffee Estate, the Gourie Caves, and the Moravian churches at Bethany (see Mile Gully & Environs, earlier in this chapter) and Mizpah. Monica also has bird-watching trips with Anne Sutton (see Marshall's Pen in the Mandeville section, earlier in this chapter), who guides trips as far afield as the Blue Mountains, Rocklands, and Rio Grande. The company is located in the Hotel Villa Bella.

JJ's Tours offers guided **mountain bike tours**. JJ, a delightful Canadian, and her husband offer routes of one/two/three days for US$60/70/80, not including accommodations at the Hotel Villa Bella. A support van is provided. Contact the Villa Bella for information.

## Special Events

On Christmas Eve the streets are closed and farming families pour in for a traditional dance celebration – a Jonkanoo – called 'Grand Market Night.' The tradition has died out elsewhere in Jamaica, but here the town puts on a grand Jonkanoo with men on stilts and general festivity in the streets. Even the shops stay open until dawn! (Also see 'Jonkanoo' in the Facts for the Visitor chapter.)

## Places to Stay & Eat

The **Hotel Villa Bella** (☎ 964-2243, fax 962-2765, PO Box 473, www.discoverjamaica.com/gleaner/inns/) is a gracious old country inn perched on a hill at Sedburgh, at the south end of town. Monica Zijdemans is the charming owner of this former grande dame, which retains its original mahogany floors (now somewhat squeaky), 1930s art-deco furniture, and idiosyncratic lighting and plumbing. The 18 homey rooms have deep bathtubs and rent for US$60. Gracious and efficient service recalls the days when Christiana was a center for 'old-style tourism.' Facilities include a reading room and TV lounge, and an elegant dining room and antique furniture. The place is long in the tooth (which is part of its charm) but is gradually being brought back to life following an injection of cash and a new

CENTRAL HIGHLANDS

management team for 1999, with plans for upgrading and expansion. A pool is to be added, and an enclosed patio will provide entertainment.

The hotel also offers one of the best and most reasonably priced dining experiences on the island and is popular with business-folk from Mandeville. The superb menu merges Jamaican cuisine with Japanese and Chinese. Typical dishes include chicken teriyaki (US$7), chicken Szechuan (US$8), and Chinese-style poached fish in ginger and soy sauce (US$8), all using herbs and vegetables from the hotel's garden. I recommend the *sole jamaique* (simmered in coconut milk, lemon grass, and spices) for US$12. Eat on the veranda or the garden terrace, where you can sip homemade ginger beer and admire the flower-filled, 6-acre garden. High tea is at 4:30 pm. And the ackee breakfast is unsurpassed!

*Taste Treats*, on Main St, sells patties and other basic Jamaica snack foods. There's a bakery 50 yards to the east, and *Sam Fo Bakery* is opposite Scotiabank. And *Juici-Beef Patties* on Main St sells patties for a pittance.

You can buy fresh produce at the *market* on Main St.

### Entertainment
Christiana is relatively dull on weekdays. It's a farming community: farmers go to bed early and get up around 4 or 5 am. There are a few reggae bars, most notably the *Lamp Light Club* which hosts occasional live bands. Even this seemingly conservative place has a go-go club – a dark and seedy little place beneath and behind Shaw's Hardware Trading Centre on Main St. *Qualitex*, in the Super+ Centre, has a disco on weekends.

The town comes alive on Thursday nights, when the higglers are in town. And the Hotel Villa Bella hosts an event at 8 pm every last Friday of the month.

### Getting There & Away
This important market town is well served by buses operating on a frequent if somewhat erratic basis from Kingston and Mandeville. You can also take a bus from May Pen and Montego Bay.

### Getting Around
You can walk most places. There's no bus service. If you need wheels, try Lloyd's Auto Rental (☎ 964-3580) in Syldain Court at the southern end of the town center, on Main St: you can pick up and drop off cars at the Hotel Villa Bella, or at the Montego Bay or Kingston airports.

### COLEYVILLE
This small mountain-crest farming village at 2952 feet is 3 miles north of Christiana, astride the border of Manchester and Trelawny parishes. It's cool and windy up here, and Coleyville is often shrouded in swirling mists. Bring a sweater!

On a clear day you have sweeping views of both coasts. Many of the slopes are covered with pine. Irish potatoes grow well in the temperate climate, as do strawberries, for which the village is noted.

North of Coleyville, the B5 begins its descent into Trelawny parish. Another road (beginning at the road junction immediately north of the radio tower) winds northwest-ward, descending through the Hectors River Valley to Troy on the edge of the Cockpit Country (see the Southwest Coast chapter).

### Getting There & Away
You can walk to Coleyville from Christiana (take a sweater or jacket in the event of fog). Buses operate between Coleyville and west of the Parade in Kingston; expect to pay about US$2. There are several minibuses daily to and from Mandeville. Buses to Albert Town from Mandeville or Christiana will also drop you in Coleyville.

### SPALDINGS
Spaldings is a small, often mist-shrouded town at about 3000 feet elevation on the crest of the central highlands 3 miles east of Christiana, to which it plays second fiddle. The hills are planted in market gardens. Ginger and yams are important local crops.

Spaldings is also the site of **Knox College**, a coed religious school founded in 1940 by a progressive educator, Rev Lewis Davidson, who believed that a school should serve to benefit its local community. Hence, the school has its own print works, farm, and even a meat-processing plant.

The B4 continues east, dropping into the Rio Minho Valley (see the Spanish Town & South Coast chapter).

## Information

There's a National Commercial Bank (☎ 964-2268) next to the gas station west of the town square.

The People's Co-Operative Bank, 100 yards east of the square, represents Western Union and is open 9 am to 1 pm weekdays, and until noon on Saturday.

There are public telephones at the post office (☎ 987-9023), 100 yards west of the town center, next to the library.

For emergencies, contact the Percy Junior Hospital (☎ 964-2222) at the west end of town.

Dr Glen Norman Day has a clinic (☎ 964-2361) next to the gas station. It's open 8 am to 3 pm Monday, Tuesday, and Thursday, and until 1 pm Saturday. There's a medical laboratory next door.

Dr J Hayman also has a clinic above the Mid-Island Pharmacy (☎ 964-2209) in the town center. It's open 8 am to 3 pm weekdays, and 10:30 am to 1 pm Saturday.

The police station (☎ 987-9058, 964-2260) is at the east end of town.

## Places to Stay & Eat

Mr Clinton Blackwood has a small *guest house* (☎ 964-2719, 8 Main St).

The best bet is *Glencoe B&B* (☎ 964-2286), a delightful piece of old England at Nash Farm, a mile southwest of Spaldings on the road from Walderston and Christiana. The two-story stone farmhouse is run by Lucy Nash, whose family founded the farm in 1891. The four quaint little upstairs bedrooms boast mahogany floors, antiques, and private bathrooms with hot water. An enclosed wide upstairs veranda forms a wrap-around lounge with a TV and a small library. Rates are US$26 per person, including a farmhouse breakfast.

Several clean, modest restaurants serve Jamaican fare, including *Variations Restaurant*, *Goatee Restaurant*, and the *Little Link Pastry Shop* for pastries and burgers.

## Entertainment

The *Electric Disco*, upstairs on the south side of the square, is the ritziest disco for miles. The local guys gather to sup at the *Up Top Sports Bar & Grill*, on the third floor of the building next to the gas station.

## Getting There & Away

Spaldings is easily reached by bus from Mandeville, where vehicles depart from beside the market on Cecil Charlton Park. At least one minibus operates daily from west of the Parade in Kingston for about US$5.

Buses from Ocho Rios and Runaway Bay to Mandeville pass through Spaldings.

# Spanish Town & South Coast

This is the least known and least visited part of the island, despite its historic importance as the locus of the island's first capital – St Jago de la Vega – established by the Spanish and today called Spanish Town. Spanish Town remains one of Jamaica's largest cities and its major center of industry outside Kingston, to which, by virtue of proximity, it is a sister city. Although desperately in need of restoration, Spanish Town is replete with colonial structures.

Clarendon parish and, to a lesser degree, the neighboring parish of St Catherine, were in colonial days the wealthiest parishes on the island. The southern part of Clarendon was a separate parish known as Vere – a center for the manufacture of indigo dye, made from the root of the indigo plant. The banks of the Rio Minho had many indigo works during Spanish days, when the Spanish panned for gold in the river they called Rio de la Mina (River of the Mine).

The upland region opened up only in the 1920s and 1930s when a railroad was extended into the Minho Valley, giving farmers access to market. Banana plantations were established, and sugar estates expanded into the valley and hills of Upper Clarendon. Sugar remains the mainstay of the area.

The two parishes are spanned by the A2, running east-west between Spanish Town and Mandeville, with the important town of May Pen betwixt, in the heart of the region. (North of Spanish Town, the A1 runs through Bog Gorge then climbs up to Linstead and the central divide before dropping to Ocho Rios and the north coast.) Forays north from the A2 lead up through valleys cut by rivers tumbling from the central highlands. The plains south of May Pen are smothered in sugarcane fields and cattle pastures. Mangroves line the south coast, which holds little appeal for tourists in search of beaches. Nature lovers and hikers can find solitude, however, on the vast hook of Portland Ridge: a totally undeveloped hilly area covered with dense shrub and used as a bird

## Highlights

- Historic Spanish Town, rundown but replete with historic edifices

- Serenity, for an eye-to-eye look at Jamaican wildlife you may never see in the wild

- Pristine Alligator Hole (Canoe Valley Wetland), a last refuge for endangered manatees

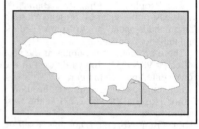

hunting ground. The Milk River, which forms the boundary between Clarendon and Manchester parishes, was once used to irrigate the sugar estates of the Clarendon Plains in the days when crocodiles splashed about in the muddy banks. It is said that there are still 'alligators,' but if so, they're very rare. And Jamaica's 'wildlife zoo' – Serenity Park – is near Old Harbour.

## Spanish Town

The fascination of Spanish Town lies in its troubled, colorful past. The island's third-largest urban center (population 87,000) and the capital of St Catherine parish, it boasts a wealth of historic buildings, most in a sad state of repair. Vandalism, demolition, fires, hurricanes, and time have taken their toll on a city that was the capital of Jamaica between 1534 and 1872.

There are modern buildings, but walking its streets you may sense a malaise, and the

# SPANISH TOWN & SOUTH COAST

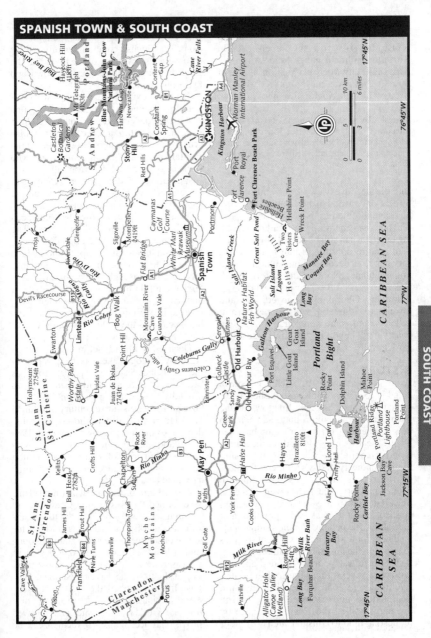

produce markets that dominate the town center are a squalid place, with rotting refuse to give you the creeps. As in Kingston, political gangs hold sway over parts of the town. Michael Crichton, author of *Jurassic Park*, was partly correct when he wrote in his autobiographical book, *Travels*:

Spanish Town was startling in its sprawl and squalor. A shantytown west of Kingston, it was poor, colorful, and charged with menace. There were no tourists here: indeed, there were no whites at all.

But the negative view is not entirely fair. Streets once trodden by Spanish señoritas and sandal-footed friars hold strong appeal. The fine craftsmanship that went into building the town can still be seen if you stop and take time to note the ornate fretwork and carvings that decorate both mansions and humble homes. None of the historic buildings date back to the Spanish era, however, but many Georgian public edifices and townhouses still stand, with 'piazzas' or front galleries, and what were once well-fruited courtyards beyond the high red-brick garden walls.

## HISTORY

After the settlement at Sevilla la Nueva failed in 1534, the Spanish established a new capital at Villa de la Vega – 'the town on the plain' – atop foundations that had been lain down earlier by Christopher Columbus' son, Diego. The town grew modestly as the administrative capital, helped along by a silk-spinning industry (today's Mulberry Gardens district recalls the era when the Spanish planted mulberry trees). However, Villa de la Vega (later renamed St Jago de la Vega) languished, and at its peak had a population of only about 500 people. The Inquisition operated here for a while and even went so far as to imprison the governor and abbot.

The town was poorly defended and was ransacked several times by English pirates. Eventually, in 1655, an English invasion fleet landed and captured the city. The Spaniards stalled the English advance by requesting time to consider their surrender

terms, and used the time to pack up before wisely fleeing north with all their possessions. The English commander ordered his troops to destroy much of the town that the English would rename Spanish Town and make *their* capital.

For the next 217 years, the town prospered as Jamaica's administrative capital. The menacing Victorian prison and gallows were here. So, too, a slave market, Jewish synagogues, and theaters. Taverns served the planters, their families, and entourages, who flocked to Spanish Town from all over the island during the 'dead season' (October to December) on the sugar estates, when the legislature was also in session.

Eventually Spanish Town was outpaced by Kingston, the mercantile capital. The latter's merchants resented Spanish Town's status as administrative capital and in 1755 managed to strong-arm the governor into forcing a bill through the legislature transferring the title to Kingston. The people of Spanish Town, however, petitioned King George II of England, who proclaimed the bill illegal, and the archives were duly trundled back to Spanish Town.

Decline had already set in. When novelist Anthony Trollope called on the governor in the 1850s, he described Spanish Town as 'stricken with eternal death.' Kingston was officially named the capital in 1872, and Spanish Town sank into a century of sloth. In 1988 Hurricane Gilbert did considerable damage to the historic town center. In 1989 an elaborate development plan was unveiled, but lack of vision and common purpose, and an inadequate infrastructure, have held it back.

A small group of Spanish Town residents have formed the Restoration Committee to encourage a sense of pride in the town's historic landmarks. The group is pushing for zoning of commercial activity and promoting guided historic tours. The hope is that as tourists return, old-time guest houses will reopen. In 1987, the Jamaica National Heritage Trust petitioned the United Nations' World Heritage Committee to list Spanish Town as a World Heritage Site. It has received 'provisional acceptance.' If recognized, the

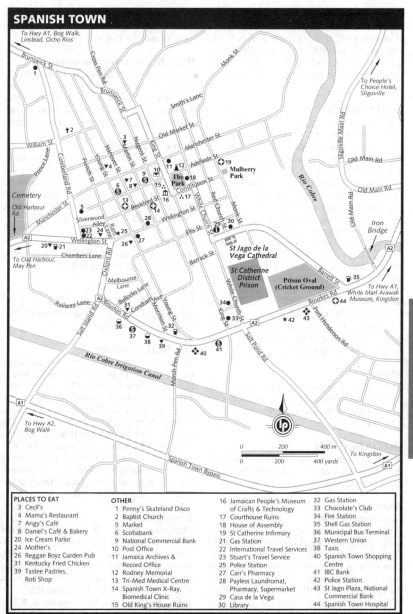

# SPANISH TOWN

To Hwy A1, Bog Walk, Linstead, Ocho Rios

Brunswick St

Cross Pen Rd

Smith's Lane

To People's Choice Hotel, Sligoville

William St

Monk St

Prince Lane

Cumberland Rd

French St

Young St

Harbour St

Nugent St

King St

Martha St

Old Market St

Manchester St

Adelaide St

Mulberry Park

The Park

Constitution St

Red Church St

White Church St

Monk St

Sligoville Main Rd

Old Main Rd

Old Main Rd

Rio Cobre

Iron Bridge

Cemetery

Old Harbour Rd

Manchester St

Silverwood Alley

Rand

Beckford St

Wellington St

Ellis St

St Jago de la Vega Cathedral

St Catherine District Prison

Prison Oval (Cricket Ground)

To Old Harbour, May Pen

Chambers Lane

Melbourne Lane

Bullocks Lane

Barrack St

Barrett St

To Hwy A1, White Marl Arawak Museum, Kingston

Railway Lane

Bourkes Rd

Condrants Ave

Young St

Morrison St

Salt Island Rd

White Church St

King St

Bourkes Rd

Fort Henderson Rd

Salt Pond Rd

Rio Cobre Irrigation Canal

March Pen Rd

To Hwy A2, Bog Walk

To Kingston

To Old Harbour, May Pen

Spanish Town Bypass

0   200   400 m
0   200   400 yards

**SOUTH COAST**

## PLACES TO EAT
3   Cecil's
4   Mama's Restaurant
7   Angy's Café
8   Daniel's Café & Bakery
20  Ice Cream Parlor
24  Mother's
26  Reggae Boyz Garden Pub
31  Kentucky Fried Chicken
39  Tastee Pastries,
    Roti Shop

## OTHER
1   Penny's Skateland Disco
2   Baptist Church
5   Market
6   Scotiabank
9   National Commercial Bank
10  Post Office
11  Jamaica Archives &
    Record Office
12  Rodney Memorial
13  Tri-Med Medical Centre
14  Spanish Town X-Ray,
    Biomedical Clinic
15  Old King's House Ruins

16  Jamaican People's Museum
    of Crafts & Technology
17  Courthouse Ruins
18  House of Assembly
19  St Catherine Infirmary
21  Gas Station
22  International Travel Services
23  Stuart's Travel Service
25  Police Station
27  Carr's Pharmacy
28  Payless Laundromat,
    Pharmacy, Supermarket
29  Casa de la Vega
30  Library

32  Gas Station
33  Chocolate's Club
34  Fire Station
35  Shell Gas Station
36  Municipal Bus Terminal
37  Western Union
38  Taxis
40  Spanish Town Shopping
    Centre
41  IBC Bank
42  Police Station
43  St Jago Plaza, National
    Commercial Bank
44  Spanish Town Hospital

Jamaican government will receive much-needed funding to restore the city. However, as of late 1998, nothing much had evolved, although the past decade has seen the establishment of light industrial factories on the outskirts of town, lending a certain commercial vitality.

## ORIENTATION

The town sits on the west bank of the Rio Cobre. At its center is the Georgian square, the Park (formerly called the Parade), on the site of the original Spanish plaza between King and White Church Sts and Adelaide and Constitution Sts. The Spanish laid out the town on a quadrangular grid around the plaza (although it is easy to become confused and lose your sense of direction in the tight one-way system).

The historic town center is very congested and many of the streets in the city center are blocked by street stalls. At its southern end and accessed via White Church St, the St Jago de la Vega Cathedral is fronted by its own green square. Barrett St leads southeast from here to Bourkes Rd, a major commercial street, to a bypass connecting Spanish Town with May Pen to the west (A2) and Kingston to the east (A1).

## Maps

The 'Discover Jamaica' road map published by the Jamaica Tourist Board (JTB) includes a separate, detailed map of downtown Spanish Town.

## INFORMATION

There is no tourist office. Your best source of information is Casa de la Vega (☎ 984-9684), at 27 Barrett St.

## Money

Scotiabank (☎ 984-3024) has a branch at 27 Adelaide St; Citizens Bank (☎ 984-2939) is at the Spanish Town Shopping Centre at 17 Bourkes Rd, as is the CIBC; and National Commercial Bank (☎ 984-0672) is at the St Jago Plaza on Bourkes Rd, and also at 14 Nugent St (☎ 984-3017). All the banks have ATMs and can cash traveler's checks for either US or Jamaican dollars. If you need to

have money remitted from your home country, there's a Western Union office in front of the bus station on Bourkes Rd.

## Post & Communications

The post office (☎ 984-2082) is at the corner of King and Adelaide Sts. You can make international calls and send faxes from the Telecommunications of Jamaica office (☎ 984-7010) in the Spanish Town Shopping Centre.

## Travel Agencies

There are several agencies to choose from, including International Travel Services (☎ 984-2762), 1 Cumberland Rd; Stuart's Travel Service (☎ 984-3285), 5 Cumberland Rd; and Apollo Travel Service (☎ 984-5040), in the Spanish Town Shopping Centre.

## Library

The public library (☎ 984-2356) is at 1 Red Church St, opposite the cathedral.

## Laundry

If your socks are about to walk by themselves, head to Payless Laundromat (☎ 984-7779), at 13 Wellington St.

## Medical Services

There are plenty of pharmacies, including Carr's Pharmacy (☎ 984-6469) at 58 Young St, and the Spanish Town Pharmacy (☎ 984-1314) in the Spanish Town Shopping Centre at 17 Bourkes Rd. The Tri-Med Medical Centre (☎ 984-2179) is at 35 Young St. The Spanish Town Hospital on Bourkes Rd has a 24-hour emergency department (☎ 984-3031), as does St Catherine Infirmary (☎ 984-3600), at 13 Monk St. The Spanish Town X-Ray and Biomedical Clinic is at the corner of Beckford and Martin Sts.

## Emergency

The police station (☎ 984-2305) is at the corner of Oxford Rd and Wellington St. Another police station is on Bourkes Rd, just west of the junction with Port Henderson Rd. The fire brigade (☎ 984-2251) is on King St a block north of Bourkes Rd.

In emergencies, call the police at ☎ 119. For an ambulance or fire truck, call ☎ 110.

## Dangers & Annoyances

The stereotype of the surly Jamaican has some truth in Spanish Town, one of Jamaica's most hard-edged cities. The bark, however, is worse than the bite. I've walked the streets downtown without mishap. Still, you should be cautious, especially of petty theft. Avoid exploring away from the main downtown streets. And avoid driving near the market (at the western end of Adelaide St), where whole streets are blocked by stalls and piles of rotting, stinking garbage – a stomach-turning sight – and the *higglers* are unsympathetic to vehicles and foreigners.

## WALKING TOUR

Spanish Town's maze of one-way streets – many blocked by the sprawling market – dictate a walking tour. Fortunately, most sights of appeal are encompassed within a compact span. You should begin at the town square, at the junction of King St and Constitution St.

### The Park

Spanish Town's finest old buildings enfold the Park, the town square established by the Spanish as the center of Jamaica's capital city in 1534. Dominating the square is the splendid **Rodney Memorial**, on the north side of the plaza. The elaborate monument was built in honor of Admiral George Rodney, who crowned his four-year service as Commander in Chief of the West Indian Naval Station in 1782, when he saved Jamaica from a combined French and Spanish invasion fleet at the Battle of the Saints. In gratitude, the House of Assembly voted £1000 to erect a monument. They commissioned John Bacon, the leading English sculptor of the time. Bacon's marble statue depicting Rodney dressed as a Roman emperor ended up costing £30,918, and it weighs over 200 tons. One of Rodney's hands is missing; it dropped off when the statue was moved to Kingston during the feud over the capital. Irate Spanish Town residents stormed Kingston to bring Rodney 'home.' He stands within a cupola temple, with sculpted panel reliefs to each side showing the battle scenes. The monument is fronted by two brass cannons from the French flagship.

The building behind the memorial is the **Jamaica Archives & Record Office**. It preserves documentation that records centuries of parochial administration, plus such intriguing gems as secret files kept on National Hero Marcus Garvey. The Clinton Black Reading Room is open to the public 9 am to 4:30 pm Monday to Thursday, 1 am to 3:30 pm Friday.

On the eastern side of the plaza is the red-brick **House of Assembly**, erected in 1762 but subsequently altered and today housing the offices of the St Catherine Parish Council. It has a beautiful wooden upper story with a pillared balcony. The Assembly and Supreme Court sat here in colonial days, when it was the setting for violent squabbles among parliamentarians. During one debate in 1710, the Speaker adjourned a rowdy meeting. However, members who wished to carry the vote locked the doors and held swords to the throat of the Speaker, Peter Beckford, while the Assembly carried their motion. The Speaker's father heard the commotion and summoned the guards, who rushed to the younger Beckford's aid. Unfortunately, in the general excitement, Beckford senior fell down the stairs and was killed.

Moving to the south side of the square, you pass the fenced-off **Courthouse Ruins**. The courthouse was destroyed in 1986 by fire. The Georgian building dates from 1819, when it was used as a chapel and armory, with the town hall upstairs. The Spanish Church of the White Cross had stood here prior to the English invasion.

Finally, on the west side of the plaza is the impressive porticoed Georgian red-brick facade of the ruins of the **Old King's House**, a once-grandiose building erected in 1762 as the official residence of Jamaica's governors. The proclamation emancipating slaves was made from the front steps on August 1, 1838. The building was destroyed by fire in 1925, leaving only the recently restored facade and the stables to the rear.

Today the stables house the **Jamaican People's Museum of Crafts & Technology**

(☎ 984-2452), operated by the Institute of Jamaica. A reconstructed smith's shop and an eclectic array of artifacts from carpenter's tools to Indian corn grinders provide an entry point to early Jamaican culture. A splendid model shows how Old King's House once looked. The museum receives few visitors. There's a small bar and restaurant. Entrance costs US$1 (US$0.50 children). It's open 9:30 am to 4:30 pm Tuesday to Saturday.

From the southeast corner of the square, follow Constitution St east two blocks to **Mulberry Park**. A monastery and Jewish cemetery once stood at this site, where today the St Catherine Infirmary for impoverished people now stands. The park is named for the mulberry trees that were grown here to produce silk. There's not much to see, alas. Banana trees overshadow the remains of the headstones that are scattered around.

### St Jago de la Vega Cathedral

From the square, take White Church St south for three blocks to St Jago de la Vega Cathedral. This Anglican cathedral is the parish church of St Catherine and the oldest cathedral in the former British colonies. It's also one of the prettiest churches in Jamaica, boasting wooden fluted pillars, an impressive beamed ceiling, a magnificent stained-

ROBERT FRIED

Tile in St Jago de la Vega Cathedral

glass window behind the altar, and a large organ dating to 1849 (donations are being sought to restore it). The church stands on the site of one of the first Spanish cathedrals in the New World: the Franciscan Chapel of the Red Cross, built in 1525. English soldiers destroyed the Catholic church and used the original materials to build their own cathedral. The current structure dates from 1714. Note the handsome octagonal steeple with faux-Corinthian columns, and the negroid gargoyles – considered unique in the world – above the south window.

Its baptism and marriage registers date from 1668. Many leading personalities are buried within its precincts. The oldest tomb dates to 1662 and is inset in the black-and-white transept aisle laid by the Spanish.

Exiting the church, walk southeast along Barrett St.

### St Catherine District Prison

Walking southeast along Barrett St from the church, you'll pass behind the St Catherine District Prison. There's hardly anything endearing about it. Hangings have been carried out here since 1714, when the prison was known as the Middlesex and Surrey County Gaol. Today, many prisoners are on death row in narrow cells that date back almost three centuries. Conditions in the prison – Jamaica's largest – were condemned in 1994 by the United Nations Human Rights Committee, and a British Member of Parliament described a recent visit as 'like something out of a nightmare.' It is the site of frequent fatal riots.

Some of the cells face onto the street so that you could, if you wished, hold a conversation with prisoners peering out through the bars.

### Iron Bridge

At the bottom of Barrett St, turn left onto Bourkes Rd and follow it east. There's a stately grandeur to the narrow Iron Bridge spanning the Rio Cobre on the southeast outskirts of town. The span was made of cast iron prefabricated at Colebrookdale, England, and was erected in 1801 on a cutstone foundation that dates to 1675. The only surviving bridge of its kind in the Americas, it is still used by pedestrians.

## BAPTIST CHURCH

This dour church at the corner of William and French Sts was built in 1827 by abolitionist James Phillippo. It was faithfully restored after being badly damaged by a hurricane in 1951.

## WHITE MARL ARAWAK MUSEUM

Contemporary Jamaican culture owes much to the Arawak influence, as displayed at this rather modest museum atop a large pre-Columbian settlement. Archaeological research has been ongoing here since the 1940s. The displays describe Amerindian life and decimation at the hands of the Spanish. Hunting and agricultural implements, jewelry, and carvings are featured. It's administered by the Institute of Jamaica. A reconstructed Arawak village is up the hill behind the museum.

It was closed in late 1998 for renovation. (Previous opening hours were 10 am to 4 pm weekdays.)

The museum is 200 yards north of the A1 – known as the Nelson Mandela Freeway – about 2 miles east of Spanish Town on A1. When traveling east, you'll have to cross the freeway; beware of oncoming traffic!

## GOLF

The Caymanas Golf Course (☎ 926-8144, 922-3386) is an 18-hole course (6844 yards) that was home to the Jamaican Open until 1987. It's set amid low hills 3 miles east of Spanish Town. There's a pool, and a clubhouse with clubs for rent. Caddies can be hired. The club is signed off the A1, but it's easy to miss.

## ORGANIZED TOURS

Historic walking tours are offered by Spanish Town Heritage Tours, housed in the charming old building Casa de la Vega (☎ 984-9684), at 27 Barret St catercorner to the cathedral; it's represented in Kingston by Destinations (☎ 929-6368), at 9 Cecelio Ave.

A full-day tour by Kingston's Limousine Taxi Touring Co (☎ 968-3775) includes Spanish Town.

## PLACES TO STAY

The only hotel I'm aware of is the motel-style *People's Choice Hotel* (☎ 984-2474), 1½ miles northeast of town on Sligoville Rd. It has a restaurant and bar, plus the Spanish Treasure Nightclub. The 60 basic rooms are clean, with fans for US$27; some have air-con for US$45, and TV for US$60. It's noisy when the disco is going. Rooms are also rented by 'short-time' guests seeking a place of coital convenience. It has a pool and Jacuzzi, plus a restaurant. Theft is a problem, according to staff!

## PLACES TO EAT

Spanish Town has little in the way of fine dining, although there are plenty of modest restaurants. Try *Mama's Restaurant*, on Young St, serving hot meals and natural juices and open 7 am to 6 pm daily. It's clean and inviting, as is *Angy's Café*, nearby. *Cameron's* (☎ 984-5031), at Shop 71 in the bus station, is a vegetarian restaurant and health food store.

Snacks are served at the *Wine Bar* at the Jamaica People's Museum, and at the *Reggae Boyz Garden Pub* on Young St, serving snacks and simple Jamaican fare for a few dollars in a pleasant garden patio.

*Devon House I-Scream* has an outlet in St Jago Plaza, where there's a food court that includes the *Shopper's Fair Supermarket*. You can buy produce in the town market, but hygiene is questionable.

*Cecil's*, on Martin St near the corner of Old Market St, is one of the better-looking places. For fast food, try *Mother's* on Ram Lane, *Tastee Pastries*, east of the bus station on Bourkes Rd, or *Kentucky Fried Chicken*, across the street from the bus station. The *Roti Shop*, next to Tastee Pastries, also sells patties, plus rotis and other basic Indian fare. *Daniel's Café & Bakery*, at the corner of Adelaide and Martin Sts, serves fresh-baked pastries and breads. You'll find an *ice cream parlor* next to the gas station on Wellington St.

## ENTERTAINMENT

The best place is the glitzy *Spanish Treasure Nightclub* (☎ 984-2474) at People's

Choice Hotel, on Sligoville Rd (US$3 entrance). It has air-con and opens onto a swimming pool that can be used at night. The mirrored stage is also a venue for exotic dancers. Each night is a theme night: Monday night is 'Swim Nite,' Tuesday is 'Ladies Nite,' and soca and oldies are played on Thursday.

The air-conditioned **Sips Lounge**, at the intersection of Oxford Rd and Wellington St, is another modestly attractive dance spot. Other options include the **Max Club**, just off the A1 in Green Dale east of the Rio Cobre, and **Penny's Skateland Disco**, at the north end of Cumberland Rd.

The **Astor Cinema** is on Brunswick St.

Spanish Town has its share of earthy go-go clubs, including **Disco Packie Tree**, the **Chocolate's Club** on King St, and, on the A1 west of town, **Lust Go-Go** and the more sophisticated **Palace Nightclub** (☎ 981-6922).

### GETTING THERE & AWAY
### Bus

Buses marked 'Spanish Town' depart frequently from both the Parade and Half Way Tree in Kingston. The journey takes 30 minutes and costs about US$0.50.

You can also catch buses for Spanish Town from Black River, Mandeville, Montego Bay, and Ocho Rios. In Spanish Town, buses leave from the well-organized Municipal Bus Terminal on Bourkes Rd.

### Car

Spanish Town is linked to Kingston via the A1 (Nelson Mandela Hwy), a dual carriageway that bypasses Spanish Town to the south and continues to May Pen. The exit is signed: after crossing the Rio Minho, turn right at the Shell gas station onto Barrett St to enter the historic town center. Jamaicans treat the A1 east of Spanish Town as a racetrack. Drive with caution!

Arriving in town from the west on the A2 from Mandeville and May Pen, you'll see the exit sign at the José Martí roundabout, from where Old Harbour Rd will take you downtown. The A1 meets the A2 at the roundabout and turns north to Bog Walk and Ocho Rios on the north coast.

### Taxi

A taxi ride between Kingston and Spanish Town will cost about US$15. There's a taxi stand on Bourkes Rd, east of the bus station.

### GETTING AROUND

Walking downtown is practical, if seemingly intimidating. Guard your valuables!

Driving in Spanish Town is a frustrating nightmare, a maze of narrow, congested lanes and one-way streets.

A couple of places rent bicycles, including Spanish Town Auto & Bicycle Maintenance (☎ 984-6683), 84 Young St, and Winners Cycle Auto Stores (☎ 984-8702), 12 Greendale Blvd, Shop 12.

# North of Spanish Town

From Spanish Town, the A1 leads north over the mountains to Ocho Rios and the north coast. Attractions en route are minimal.

### BOG WALK GORGE

About 7 miles north of Spanish Town the A1 cuts through a great limestone canyon – Bog Walk Gorge – carved by the slow-moving jade-colored Rio Cobre. The road parallels the river for several miles. You drop into the gorge and cross the river via the Flat Bridge, an 18th-century stone bridge.

The gorge is several hundred feet deep and littered with massive boulders. Every rainy season, landslides block the road, disrupting traffic and adding to the damming effect of the narrow gorge. Flat Bridge is frequently under water after heavy rains; the high-water mark of August 16, 1933, is shown on the rock face, when the river rose 25 feet above the bridge!

Drive carefully across Flat Bridge, which has no sides. Several vehicles have been lost over the side.

### Bog Walk

One of Jamaica's oldest towns, Bog Walk was an important rest stop during early colonial days. The town lies at the confluence of the Thomas, Pedro, and D'Oro rivers, which combine to form the Rio Cobre, 5 miles north of Bog Walk Gorge. The one-street town stretches along the old highway for more than a mile. The modern A1 bypasses the town parallel to the old road. Bog Walk has a Nestlé milk condensery, sugar factory, and citrus-packing plant west of town.

### Information
If you need the police, call ☎ 985-2233, or ☎ 119 (emergency). There's a post office (☎ 985-2217), plus a pharmacy in Bog Walk Plaza (☎ 985-2658), and a gas station and Western Union.

### Places to Stay & Eat
I'm not aware of any guest houses in town, but half a mile south of Flat Bridge in the gorge is *Riverside Drive-Inn* (☎ 983-5714), a thatched-roof bar whose hostess, the saucy Queen-I, rents very basic rooms by the night for US$18. She also rents rooms by the hour. At night, go-go dancers perform on a stage down by the river.

In town, *Big Tree Restaurant* (☎ 985-1827), opposite the police station, is the only decent-looking place to eat. Roadside vendors sell bags of oranges along the A1 bypass.

### Getting There & Away
Bog Walk is served by buses and minibuses from Spanish Town and by buses traveling between Ocho Rios and Kingston. In Kingston at least two minibuses operate from the Parade.

## SLIGOVILLE
This small village sits on the upper slopes of Montpelier Mountain (2419 feet), 5 miles east of Bog Walk, at a junction with roads for Kingston (via Red Hills) and Spanish Town.

During the colonial era the area was a popular summer retreat for the white society, and the governor had a home here. When emancipation was proclaimed in 1834, Sligoville was established as the first of dozens of 'free villages' created islandwide. The village was named for the second Marquis of Sligo, governor of Jamaica from 1834 to 1836.

At least one minibus operates between Kingston and Ocho Rios via Sligoville. It should cost no more than US$1.50 from Kingston and about US$5 from Ocho Rios. You can also catch a bus or 'coaster' in Spanish Town.

## LINSTEAD
An important market town in the mid-19th century, Linstead has retained its role as a regional market center and is celebrated in the popular song 'Linstead Market,' which tells of a woman with fruit still unsold in her basket at evening time and her children hungry at home. Everyone who passed by felt her produce for ripeness, then went away without buying even a quattie-worth:

Carry em ackee go a Linstead market,
Not a quattie worth sell.
Lord, what a night, not a bite
What a Saturday night,
Everybody come feel-up, feel-up
Not a quattie worth sell...

On Saturday, higglers still descend on the town from far and wide, and the streets are packed with women selling their yams, corn, tomatoes, and other produce.

The compact and bustling little town is centered on an old clock tower. Also in the center is an Anglican church that has been destroyed by hurricanes several times; the current structure dates from 1911. Otherwise, the town – which has a confusing system of one-way streets – has no touristic appeal.

A highway (the A1) bypasses Linstead, which sits astride the old road to the west.

### Information
There's a Scotiabank (☎ 985-2277), at 42 King St next to the gas station, and a National Commercial Bank (☎ 985-2295), at 29 King St. The post office (☎ 985-2218) is on Main St.

Stuart's Travel Service has an office (☎ 985-2781) at 60 King St.

For medical emergencies, call Linstead Hospital (☎ 985-2241) on Rodney Hall Rd. Pharmacies in town include Gayle's (☎ 985-9858), at 93A King St, and Dixon's (☎ 985-2202), at 43 King St.

The telephone number for the police station is ☎ 985-2285.

### Places to Stay & Eat

If all you need is a dirt cheap place to rest your head, try the **Restwell Guest House & Pub** (☎ 985-7425), down a cul-de-sac half a mile north of town on the old road that parallels the bypass. Six rooms have private bath with cold water only, and cost US$5. They're basic but clean.

For nocturnal pleasure, locals head to the **Razzmatazz Sports Bar & Grill** (4 Begonia Rd), south of the town center. It's the liveliest place for miles.

### Getting There & Away

At least six buses plus minibuses operate between Linstead and both Half Way Tree and the Parade in Kingston. Any of the vehicles traveling between Ocho Rios and Kingston or Spanish Town will also take you. For a nearby challenging drive, take the tortuous Devil's Racecourse (B13) northeast of Linstead.

### DEVIL'S RACECOURSE

East of Linstead, the B13 leads through a broad valley planted with sugarcane and bananas before beginning a tortuous climb north to the mountain-crest village of Guy's Hill, straddling the border of St Catherine and St Ann parishes. The road is precipitous, with dangerous hairpin bends that account for its name. Drive with caution! There's no reason to take this tour unless you like challenging drives.

### EWARTON

Ewarton, on the A1, 7 miles north of Linstead, owes its relative prosperity to the Ewarton Works. Many of the locals are employed here and there is a significant middle class, but even they haven't been able to lend the town a sophistication worth the halt. You may be able to get a factory tour by calling ahead (☎ 985-2301).

North of Ewarton, the road begins its steep ascent over Mt Diablo and the border with St Ann parish.

### Places to Stay & Eat

I'm not aware of any nearby accommodations.

The best place to eat is the **International Whitehouse Seafood Restaurant** (☎ 985-0319, 40 Main St), on the southern fringe of town. Main dishes cost about US$4. **Lifeline** (☎ 985-0142), next door, sells nutritional items, tonics, and vegetarian foods.

### Entertainment

For earthy entertainment, check out **Living Colours**, 3 miles south of Ewarton, with reggae music and go-go dancing. Note the fascinating mural on the outside wall.

### Getting There & Away

A bus journey from Ocho Rios or Kingston will cost about US$1.20 (US$4 by minibus). You can catch a bus or minibus for Ewarton from west of the Parade in Kingston.

# West of Spanish Town

West of Spanish Town, the two-lane A2 runs ruler-straight for Old Harbour and May Pen. The highway is dangerously fast and notorious for its fatal accidents. Use caution!

### GUTTERS

This roadside hamlet, on the A2 about 5 miles west of Spanish Town, is important as the junction for several key nature sites. There's a Texaco gas station at the junction.

### Serenity

This is Jamaica's 'wildlife safari park' (☎ 983-8607), a 35-acre commercial facility boasting a menagerie from around the globe: spider monkeys, dozens of snake species that include a 10-foot-long albino Burmese python, wallabies, pheasants, and ostriches. It features birds from throughout the Americas, including macaws and a large selection of smaller parrots. Local birds include the beautiful Jamaican barn owl. The owner plans to add elephants and camels to give rides.

There's a kids' petting zoo, and pony rides are offered.

Entrance costs US$6 (US$3 children) and includes fishing (including bait and rods) in vast breeding ponds stocked with tilapia. Paddle-boats are available. Meals are served at a Jerk Centre and Macaw Restaurant.

Alas, Jamaicans are behind the times in terms of ecological sensitivity – as reflected by the attitudes of some of the staff, who are afraid or contemptuous of wildlife – and while the owner (Kenny Benjamin, owner of the Guardsman security company; some of the dogs are kept here) may mean well, many of the creatures are in tiny cages that are inadequate by many peoples' standards. If you visit, I urge you to leave a note asking the owners to invest in larger cages for the animals. And the deafening piped-in music detracts from the, er, serenity?

It's about 400 yards north of the gas station.

## Fishing

A road opposite the Texaco gas station runs south from Gutters for about 10 miles through canefields to Bushy Park in the flatlands at the base of the Hellshire Hills, where Nature's Habitat Fish World (☎ 969-2285) and Little's Hobby Hut (☎ 995-8500) have a series of man-made lagoons stocked with tilapia. Both sites are popular with Jamaican families who come down to fish with scoop nets for their supper (US$6 per lb). You can take the fish home, or have it prepared and served roasted or steamed at open kitchens on site.

## OLD HARBOUR

This otherwise nondescript town is famous for its iron clock tower in the town square. The Victorian tower is marvelously preserved, as is the clock, which amazingly was installed shortly after the English invasion in 1655 and, even more amazingly, still keeps good time. The belfry and other renovations date from the 19th century. Other points of interest are the Church of St Dorothy, one of the oldest on the island. The Bodles Agricultural Station (☎ 983-2842) is famous for

research in breeding hardy cattle strains. It offers tours by appointment.

There's a small roadside crafts market on the A2 west of town, immediately east of Sandy Bay.

## Information

Scotiabank (☎ 983-2205) has a branch on the square; next door is a National Commercial Bank (☎ 983-2279). You can have money remitted via Western Union at People's Co-Operative Bank, 400 yards east of the square.

The post office (☎ 983-2383) and the police station (☎ 983-2255) are on the south side of the town square.

There's a doctor's office on Darlington Drive. It's open 9 am to 5 pm Monday to Friday, until 2 pm on Saturday.

## Colbeck Castle

The origins of this now-ruined great house are shrouded in mystery. It is thought to have been built by Colonel John Colbeck, who landed with Oliver Cromwell's invasion army in 1655 and rose to become a landowner in St Catherine. Its square towers at each corner had slave quarters beneath. The fortified relic stands amid scrubby grounds grazed by goats, 1½ miles northwest of Old Harbour and reached by following the road north from the clock tower. At the three-way split, take the middle route, which leads to the ruins that loom on your left. Carry on, cross the bridge, and take the first left. The dirt road leads half a mile to the ruins, though the going can be rough in poor weather.

## Places to Eat

Many eateries serve inexpensive Jamaican fare. Try *Midnite City Restaurant*, the *Paddock*, or *Tee Gee's*. You can satisfy your sweet tooth at *Homey Crust Bakery* or the *Topic Ice Cream Parlor*. *Juici-Beef Patties* serves fast-food burgers, sandwiches, and spicy patties.

## Entertainment

The *Border Line Lagoon Niteclub*, on the A2 east of Old Harbour, is a reggae club that also has go-go dancing, as does **Whispers**, 2 miles west of town. Farther west, beyond Sandy Bay, **Sunrise GQ Club, Restaurant & Cocktail Lounge** (☎ 986-8482) has a ladies night on Thursday (free entry to women), dancehall on Friday, and oldies on Sunday (US$3 entrance).

### Getting There & Away
Buses traveling to Kingston or Spanish Town from Mandeville pass through Old Harbour. If you're coming from Kingston, look for Kenneth Dennis' minibus (No ST641); he charges about US$2.

### OLD HARBOUR BAY
This large fishing village, 2 miles south of Old Harbour, is the site of the south coast's largest fish market. The access road from the A2 is opposite Bodles Agricultural Station. Fishermen land their catch midmorning, and it makes a photogenic sight with the nets laid out and the colorful pirogues drawn up on the otherwise ugly shore. The village is a squalid place of tin and wood shacks and is prone to flooding in rainy season.

Christopher Columbus was here in 1494 and named the bay Puerto de la Vaca (Cow Bay) for its large population of manatees (sea cows). The animals have since been decimated. The Spanish established a shipbuilding facility at Port Esquival, a mile west of Old Harbour Bay. The name recalls Juan Esquival, Jamaica's first Spanish governor (1509-19). Today it's the site of a bauxite shipping terminal.

### Places to Eat
You can sample fried fish and boiled lobster prepared on the beach at any of several dozen rustic rum shops and steamed fish joints. Try **Ebony Rose Café** or **Cacique**. Another good bet is **Ocean Breeze Restaurant** at the rear of the fish market. The most salubrious place is **Auntie's Hot Spot**, half a mile inland from the shore. **Seamech Restaurant**, 200 yards before the shore, is also recommended. You can buy ice cream nearby at **Taste Right**.

The **Pretty Woman Nightclub** is the hot spot; it's the typical rum shop serving up the requisite exotic go-go.

### Getting There & Away
You can catch a bus from Old Harbour. A bus also runs daily from the Parade in Kingston.

## GOAT ISLANDS
Offshore of Old Harbour Bay are two large islands, Little Goat and Great Goat, sheltering Galleon Harbour to the east. The last endemic Jamaican iguana was seen here in the 1940s, and the animal was considered extinct until 1990 when a small population was discovered in the Hellshire Hills (see the Kingston & Environs chapter). There are a few beaches along the mangrove-lined shores.

During WWII, the US Navy built a base on the larger island. The barracks are used nowadays by a few fishermen.

## COLEBURNS GULLY
This off-the-beaten-track valley extends northwest from Spanish Town into the central highlands. The road via Guanaboa Vale leads north 5 miles to **Mountain River Cave**, a National Trust site of archaeological import. Guides Percival Pierson or Linton Wright will lead you down one steep mile and across the river, where the cave entrance is barred by a grill gate to which they have the key. Inside, you'll discover Arawak petroglyphs painted in black on the walls and ceiling. Many date back up to 1300 years. There are birds and beasts such as frogs and turtles, as well as human figures and abstract designs, most of them quite meager and indecipherable to amateur eyes. This is not Lascaux!

The caves are about 2 miles above Guanaboa, where the path is marked by a sign. The steep track is sweaty going, but there's a good spot for swimming in a small river with waterfall.

At the top of the valley is the village of **Lluidas Vale**, set in a beautiful green trough (also called Lluidas Vale) filled with cane fields of the old Worthy Park Estate. A roadside monument commemorates Juan Lubolo, a former slave turned guerrilla leader in the 17th century. His band of escaped slaves lived autonomously during the Spanish occupation here. Lubolo switched sides after the English invasion in 1655 in exchange for citizenship. His people thus formed the first free black settlement in the New World. After Lubolo died, English settlers seized the lands. The Juan de Bolas Mountains, which reach 2743 feet, are named after him.

Lluidas Vale is served by buses from Falmouth and Ocho Rios, and from Half Way Tree and the Parade in Kingston, and Spanish Town.

# May Pen & Environs

## MAY PEN

The large capital city (population 41,000) of Clarendon parish, 36 miles west of Kingston, has a strategic location midway between Spanish Town and Mandeville, and on the banks of the Rio Minho. However, it is bypassed by the A2 (Sir Alexander Bustamante Hwy), which runs about one mile south of town. It is a major market town and light industrial center at the heart of a prosperous agricultural district. The town center teems at any time of day and all week, but especially on Friday and Saturday when the market is held south of the main square. Be prepared for terrible congestion, honking horns, and pushy drivers who add to the general mayhem.

There's little of interest to see or do. The only historic building of interest is the ramshackle remains of an old fort that can be seen south of the main square, where the pandemonium reaches a pinnacle, and a closed railway station built in the 1880s. The commercial center stretches from here to the north along the A2 for more than a mile.

## Information

There's no tourist office, but the Jamaica Information Service (☎ 986-2193) has an office on Storks St. There's a small public library on the A2 about 200 yards east of the market square.

**Money** National Commercial Bank (☎ 986-2343) and Scotiabank (☎ 986-2212) both have branches on Main St close to the main square, and CIBC (☎ 986-2578), at 55 Main St, is farther north. There are several money-exchange bureaus on Main St.

**Post & Communications** The post office (☎ 986-2302) is 100 yards northeast of the square. You can make international calls and send faxes from the Cable & Wireless office (☎ 986-2342), on Fernleigh Ave at the west end of town, or from the Telephone & Fax Service (☎ 902-4898, fax 986-7795) on Main St, which is open 8 am to 8 pm Monday to Saturday.

**Travel Agencies** Try Stuart's Travel Service (☎ 986-4542) in May Pen Plaza, or Apollo Travel Services (☎ 986-4946) on Main St.

**Medical Services** May Pen residents must be a sickly bunch, as there are dozens of pharmacies, including Tait's Clarendon Pharmacy (☎ 986-2324), at 34 Main St, open 8 am to 8 pm, and Sunshine Pharmacy (☎ 986-9085), at 7 Fernleigh Ave. May Pen Medical Centre (☎ 986-2717), at 10 Manchester Ave, can assist with routine diagnosis and prescriptions.

If you need emergency attention, call the new May Pen Hospital (☎ 986-2528), 2 miles west of the town center.

**Emergency** For police call ☎ 119. The local police station (☎ 986-2208) is 100 yards west of the main square.

## Halse Hall

This attractive great house (☎ 986-2561), 3 miles south of May Pen, is situated on a hillock surrounded by pastures. During the Spanish colonial period, the property was known as Hato de Buena Vista (Ranch of the Beautiful View). After the English invasion in 1655, the land was granted to Major Thomas Halse, who built the house on an old Spanish foundation. For a time it was occupied by Sir Hans Sloane, the famous doctor and botanist whose collection of Jamaican flora and fauna formed the nucleus of what later became the British Museum of Natural History in London. Thomas Halse and several of his descendants slumber peacefully beneath tombstones on the back lawn.

Today Halse Hall is owned by Alcoa Minerals, which processes the bauxite-rich earth of Clarendon at its Jamalco aluminum

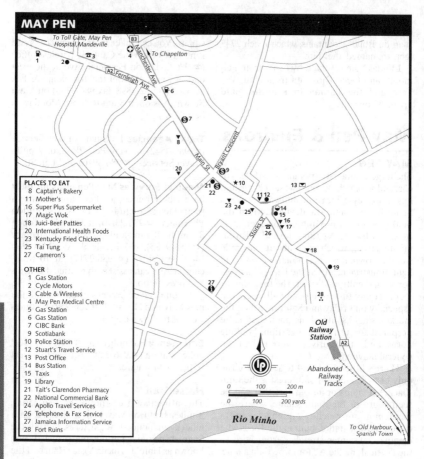

**MAY PEN**

*To Toll Gate, May Pen Hospital, Mandeville*

*To Chapelton*

Manchester Ave

Fernleigh Ave

Main St

Bryant Crescent

Starks St

*Old Railway Station*

*Abandoned Railway Tracks*

*Rio Minho*

*To Old Harbour, Spanish Town*

0    100    200 m
0    100    200 yards

**PLACES TO EAT**
8  Captain's Bakery
11  Mother's
16  Super Plus Supermarket
17  Magic Wok
18  Juici-Beef Patties
20  International Health Foods
23  Kentucky Fried Chicken
25  Tai Tung
27  Cameron's

**OTHER**
1  Gas Station
2  Cycle Motors
3  Cable & Wireless
4  May Pen Medical Centre
5  Gas Station
6  Gas Station
7  CIBC Bank
9  Scotiabank
10  Police Station
12  Stuart's Travel Service
13  Post Office
14  Bus Station
15  Taxis
19  Library
21  Tait's Clarendon Pharmacy
22  National Commercial Bank
24  Apollo Travel Services
26  Telephone & Fax Service
27  Jamaica Information Service
28  Fort Ruins

**SOUTH COAST**

processing plant near Hayes to the south. The company uses Halse Hall for conferences and social functions, including community events. Tours can be arranged by appointment (ask for Mrs Chambers). A sign on the A2 points to Halse Hall.

### Special Events

An annual Denbigh Agricultural Show is held on the Denbigh Showground, 2 miles west of town, during Independence weekend each August. Jamaica's leading farm and cattle exposition displays the best of the

island's agricultural products. For information, contact the Jamaica Agricultural Society (☎ 922-0610, fax 967-4040), 67 Church St, Kingston.

### Places to Stay

The only hotel of any worth is **Versalles** (☎ 986-2775, fax 986-2709, 42 Longbridge Ave), a mile southwest of town. This expansive, modern hotel has lush lawns nibbled by Shetland ponies. It has 48 modestly furnished rooms with telephones and private bath for US$36 single or double 'basic,'

US$59 to US$74 'standard,' and US$89 to US$112 suites. Some rooms have air-con. There's a lap pool, restaurant, and disco.

For a more homey family environment, check out *Fairfield Guest House* (☎ 986-4344, *Lot 63, Fairfield Drive)*; *Pirates Hotel* (☎ 986-2873), at Hartwell Gardens; or *Lions Villa Guest House* (☎ 986-7353, 17 Chapelton Rd).

## Places to Eat

There are dozens of dining options, but don't expect anything cosmopolitan. For Jamaican fare try the *Hot Pot* (☎ 986-2586, 18A Manchester Ave), north on B3, a diminutive spot popular as a hang-out for local guys.

The nicest places are *Bloom's Restaurant*, next to the hospital 2 miles west of town, and, 2 miles farther west, *Big Acre Restaurant & Lounge*. Both serve sandwiches, burgers, and Jamaican staples for a few dollars.

Chinese restaurants include *Tai Tung* on the southwest side of the main square and the *Magic Wok* (☎ 986-2161), 100 yards southeast of the square. A stone's throw away is *Juici-Beef Patties*, serving hot vegetarian and meat patties for US$0.05. *Mother's* also offers patties and baked goods; it's 100 yards west of the square. *Kentucky Fried Chicken* has a franchise next to Stuart's Travel, 100 yards west of the main square. If you're craving pizza, try *Mr Bee's Pizza* (☎ 986-2127), on Fernleigh Ave.

*Cameron's* is a vegetarian restaurant and health food store. You can buy all manner of nutritional products at *International Health Foods* (☎ 986-4640).

For groceries, try *Super Plus* supermarket on Main St, near the plaza. For baked goods, try *Captain's Bakery* at the north end of Main St.

Most restaurants are closed on Sunday.

## Entertainment

The nicest place around is the *Versalles Disco* in the Hotel Versalles, open Thursday to Sunday (US$3 entrance). Thursday is 'oldies' night. The *Temptations Nightclub* (☎ 962-9186, 41 Manchester Ave) is a good place to practice your reggae moves. It has dancehall on Thursday nights; entrance is US$3.

## Getting There & Around

**Bus** The totally disorganized bus station is immediately south of the main square. You can catch buses here to Christiana, Spanish Town, Kingston, Ocho Rios, Mandeville, Negril, Milk River, and Lionel Town. At least two buses operate to May Pen from the Parade in Kingston; it's a one-hour journey and costs about US$1. Minibuses also ply the route via Spanish Town for about US$3.

**Motorcycle** Cycle Motors (☎ 986-4764) on Fernleigh Ave rents motorcycles.

**Taxi** Taxis congregate in a disruptive jumble on the south side of the bus station. You can call a cab with the May Pen Taxi Operators Association (☎ 986-2681) or Path Transport & Services (☎ 986-9882), at 12½ Manchester Ave.

## WEST OF MAY PEN

The A2 continues westward from May Pen across the vast flatlands of the Clarendon Plains to Toll Gate (a toll gate formerly stood at the site of the present village), marking the beginning of a 2000-foot, 9-mile ascent of Melrose Hill that will deposit you near Mandeville, in the central highlands (see the Central Highlands regional map). Midway, at Porus, where the climb begins in earnest, you pass into Manchester parish. The mountainside catches the rains and is densely foliated. Papaya and other fruit hang at stalls along the roadside.

The B12 runs south from Toll Gate to Milk River and the south coast.

Several reasonable restaurants line the A2 near Toll Gate. I recommend *Joan's Place & Fish Stop*, *Sweet 'n' Juicy Rest Stop*, the attractive riverside *Little Paradise Restaurant* at Clarendon Park, or *Coconut Grove*, next to a pig farm (hopefully the wind is with you).

## LIONEL TOWN

Lionel Town is a busy market town, 13 miles south of May Pen. It's totally off the beaten path in the midst of sugarcane fields of the West Indies Sugar Company (a subsidiary of Tate & Lyle Ltd). You'll know you've arrived because of strong odors from the **Moneymusk Sugar Factory**, a mile west of town.

Near Moneymusk, just east of the hamlet of Alley, is the hamlet of **Amity Hall**, boasting a notable Anglican church – St Peter's – with bleached gravestones shaded by giant silk-cotton trees. The 18th-century church has an impressive organ, plus engraved tableaux on the west wall. The rector lives next to the church and has the key. Nearby is an old windmill of imported brick, which now houses the town library and looks like a great mushroom with its wide-flanged roof.

The site was the setting of a 1694 battle between British forces and French invaders who had landed at Yallahs and swept westward, destroying sugar plantations until halted at Amity Hall.

Lionel Town has a gas station and several basic restaurants, including the lively *7/11 Seafood Restaurant & Lounge*, which doubles as a disco.

At least one minibus links Lionel Town with May Pen, and a bus runs daily from Kingston (US$0.50).

## PORTLAND RIDGE

The southernmost extension of Jamaica is a rugged, upland, scrub-covered ridge rimmed by mangrove swamps and offshore coral reefs. There have been proposals to make the peninsula into the Portland Ridge National Park. It's totally away from the tourist path and difficult to access. Adventurous sorts will find it good for lonesome hiking and camping (use caution and do *not* camp alone), and the area has many caves considered excellent for spelunking. Arawaks adorned the walls of many with their petroglyphs. One of the best is Jackson Bay Cave, with about 12,000 feet of passageways, underground lakes, and stygian chambers festooned with formations (you can get there via the Jackson Bay turnoff).

A very rough single-track road continues past the turnoff and leads to Portland Lighthouse. En route you pass through marshland and mangroves, teeming with birds such as oystercatchers. A 4WD is recommended. After 8 miles you reach the boundary of the PWD Hunting & Sporting Club. A sign reads 'No Trespassing!'

*Portland Cottages* are nearby.

## CARLISLE BAY

Carlisle Bay, 7 miles south of Lionel Town, has been touted in some guidebooks for its stretches of coral-colored sand, such as at Jackson Beach. The few mangrove-backed beaches lack for beauty, however, and are the province of fishermen and for residents of May Pen and other inland towns seeking any old patch of sand on weekends. The main village is **Rocky Point**, a melancholy, down-at-the-heels place – deplorably littered! – with lots of burned-out shacks. It's a good place, however, to view the commercial fishing fleet coming and going. You can even hire a boat or ask to be taken on for a night of fishing with the locals. Women should not go unaccompanied by a trusted friend.

The bay is reached by a winding and decrepit road through scrubland grazed by cattle and goats.

### Places to Eat

Expect icy stares from the sullen locals, who seem to resent the presence of 'whiteys' and other foreigners. Try *Black Thunder HQ* and *Beachwave Beachfront Tavern* near the shore, or, your best bet, *Splendor Height Restaurant & Lounge* as you approach town. The latter serves seafood in an enclosed patio.

Rocky Point is known for a local delicacy: turtle eggs in red wine. Endangered marine turtles (and their eggs) are protected by law. Don't support the illegal harvest!

### MILK RIVER BATH

Fourteen miles southwest of May Pen, this well-known spa is fed from a saline mineral hot spring that bubbles up at the foot of Round Hill, 2 miles from the ocean. The waters are a near-constant 92°F. An immersion is said to cure ailments ranging from gout and lumbago to rheumatism and nervous conditions.

A spa first opened in 1794. The current spa – which is attached to the Milk River

Mineral Bath Hotel – is owned by the government and supervised by the Ministry of Tourism (☎ 920-4929). There's a clinical feel and smell to the place. The six time-worn public mineral baths and three private baths are cracked and chipped, though clean.

These waters are the most radioactive waters in the world (50 times more so than Vichy in France and three times those of Karlsbad in Austria). Hence, bathers are limited to only 15 minutes, though you are allowed three baths a day. Imbibing the waters is also recommended by the spa staff as a stirring tonic. They don't mean for you to swig from the pool; they'll give you a tumbler.

The spa is popular with Jamaicans, who tend to hang out in their dressing gowns. It gets crowded on weekends with Kingstonians seeking treatments. It's open 7 am to 9 pm daily. Admission is US$1.25 per bath (children half-price). Massages are offered for US$23 per hour.

Much of the surrounding scrubland is threatened by charcoal-burners, whose work is arduous and pays little more than bare subsistence. You'll see basic kilns and possibly the dust-covered workers themselves begging rides along the road.

About 200 yards north of the spa is the **Milk River Spa Mineral Pool**, an open-air swimming pool open to the public 10 am to 6 pm on weekends and holidays.

### Places to Stay & Eat
The rambling **Milk River Mineral Bath Hotel** (☎ 924-9544, 1-995-4099 cellular, fax 986-4962, Milk River PO, Clarendon) is a homey, white-porched hotel with shady verandas, louvered windows, etched wooden motifs above the doors, well-worn pine floors, and 20 modestly furnished, pleasant rooms for US$42 double with shared bath, US$50 for private bath. Guests are not charged for using the mineral spa. Meals are served in a cozy dining room, where the menu includes Jamaican favorites such as mutton stew and stewed fish. Breakfasts include a health-food special for US$5.

### Getting There & Away
Milk River Bath is accessed off the A2 along a well-paved road via Cook's Gate

and Rest. It can also be reached via the B12 from Toll Gate (on the A2, 9 miles west of May Pen). A bus operates from May Pen three times daily.

## FARQUHAR BEACH
Beyond Milk River Bath, a dirt road lined with tall cacti leads 1½ miles to a funky fishing village at the river mouth. The gray-sand beach backed by mangroves is not very appealing. The village life is fascinating, however, and you can while away hours watching the fishermen tending their nets and pirogues. You can hire a boat and guide to take you fishing or to the mouth of the Alligator Hole River in search of crocodiles and elusive, endangered manatees.

### Places to Stay & Eat
**Diana's Seafood Bar** is a sky-blue shack serving steam fish (US$4.50) and basic Jamaican fare. It's also the local grocery and bar, with a thatched, open-sided hut where local Rastas play dominoes. Diana, a pleasant young lady, also has **Diana's Guest House**, with one room with a double bed and an outside bathroom and toilet, but no electricity (it's lit by a kerosene lamp). Rates are negotiable.

There are a handful of rustic rum shops run by Rastas.

## ALLIGATOR HOLE
A government-owned wildlife reserve of extreme importance, Alligator Hole (also known as Canoe Valley Wetland) is well known for its manatees. They live amid dense, three-foot-tall reeds in the jade-blue pools fed by waters that emerge at the base of limestone cliffs forming the northern edge of the Canoe Valley. Herons, grebes, jacanas, gallinules, and other waterfowl are abundant. Both marine and freshwater fish also survive in the waters, which are lent a mild salinity by the seepage of sea water through the limestone bedrock. The Canoe Valley Wetland was set up as a feeding station for a family of manatees that inhabits the diamond-clear water in which fish-eating crocodiles (called 'alligators' locally) also hover.

After reading the well-done displays (weathered and fading in late 1998), you can take an hourlong trip to the sea by canoe with a guide. The price is based on 'satisfaction' says Paul, one of the site wardens. There's no entrance fee.

Alligator Hole is reached via the B12. The turnoff is a mile north of Milk River, and leads 3 miles via steep Round Hill. A lonesome, narrow paved road also parallels Long Bay, linking the site with Alligator Pond and St Elizabeth, 15 miles west (see the Southwest Coast chapter).

# Rio Minho Valley

The Rio Minho rises in the mountains near Spaldings (west of Frankfield; see the map in the Central Highlands chapter) and flows down to Carlisle Bay. Before reaching the ocean the river drains into the sandy soils of the Clarendon Plains, and the riverbed is usually dry at May Pen. During heavy rains the river becomes a raging torrent. The situation has been aggravated in recent decades by severe deforestation and poor farming practices in the Rio Minho Valley. The area has been totally bypassed by tourism and displays considerable poverty but makes for a fabulous drive on a clear day, when the views from on high at the upper end of the valley north of May Pen are grandiose. Eventually you emerge in the cool heights of the central highlands – the ultimate reward. (See the Central Highlands chapter.)

## CHAPELTON

This picturesque if scruffy little town is very rural-English in feel. It's laid out around St Paul's Parish Church and an old clock tower that has a war memorial at its base. One of the earliest slave revolts on the island occurred in 1690 at Suttons Plantation, southeast of Chapelton. Chapelton is 12 miles north of May Pen.

### Information

There's a gas station in town, plus a National Commercial Bank (☎ 987-2225) at 40 Main St, a post office (☎ 987-2222), and a police station (☎ 987-2244).

Dr Arlene Henry-Dowle has a clinic (☎ 987-2215) west of the church; it's open 7:30 am to 7 pm weekdays (except Wednesday). The regional hospital has emergency services. It's signed, on the right, 200 yards south of the village square. Chapelton Pharmacy (☎ 987-2126) is just before the hospital gate.

### Places to Eat

*Dixon's Restaurant & Bar* and *Sunshine Bar* are both very basic. *Bella Taste Patties*, facing the square, sells patties for J$20 (about US$0.60) and has fruit juices and coconut desserts.

### Getting There & Away

From the Parade in Kingston you can catch a bus that travels via May Pen. Several buses also pass through Chapelton en route to Frankfield from Kingston.

## TROUT HALL

Trout Hall, in the upper Rio Minho Valley 6 miles north of Chapelton on B3, is the regional center of a major citrus plantation owned by the Citrus Company of Jamaica Ltd. You can visit by prior arrangement (☎ 986-2201, 923-4282), 40 Manchester Ave, May Pen, in Kingston.

North of Trout Hall, the B3 climbs 1300 feet in less than 3 miles to James Hill at the crest of the nation's backbone. (See the map in the Central Highlands chapter.)

## FRANKFIELD

West of Trout Hall, the B4 follows the Rio Minho through citrus groves and fields planted with yams to Frankfield, centered on a tiny traffic circle at a three-way junction. The disheveled town has a 'lost in the hinterland' feel. You'll be the first foreign visitor in a while, and eyes will follow you warily as you move through town.

West of town the badly potholed B4 begins a precipitous climb to Spaldings. The road is prone to mudslides. (See the Spaldings section in the Central Highlands chapter.)

There's a gas station, bank, and pharmacy in town.

If you choose to stay overnight, try **Bonnick's Hideout**, a guest house on the road south of town to Smithville. I've not visited, so can't vouch for it.

Numerous buses and minibuses travel between Kingston and the Rio Minho Valley. You can catch these in May Pen, where you can also hop aboard buses No LS311 or LS468 (the journey costs about US$0.40, or US$2 by minibus).

# Kingston & Environs

## Kingston

Dramatically situated between ocean and mountains, Kingston need not be the daunting beginning to a Jamaican vacation so many foreigners assume, despite first impressions – the obvious squalor of shanties as your aircraft comes in low to land at Norman Manley International Airport. While it's true that Jamaica's lively, engaging, teeming, unrepentantly in-your-face capital (population 800,000) is plagued by intractable problems that, just three decades ago, didn't exist in the city, Kingston's negative image belies its many appeals.

The city's history is intriguing. High culture is as developed as anywhere in the Caribbean outside Cuba, boasting attractions that definitely merit a visit, including the National Gallery – a first-rate art museum. And the nightlife is the most cosmopolitan and colorful on the island, with everything from jazz and lively theater to reggae concerts performed with originality and aplomb. The city's yearly calendar is replete with festivals and sporting and other events. There are top-notch hotels, and good restaurants for all tastes. And a wealth of nearby venues for recreation and exploration beckon travelers to explore farther afield.

'Kingston' usually refers to the city-parish of Kingston and the surrounding parish of St Andrew, which are jointly administered and also known as the 'Corporate Area.' Together they cover 191 sq miles, although the metropolitan area measures only 45 sq miles. St Andrew parish extends all the way to the summit ridge of the Blue Mountains. The city is usually divided into two areas: Uptown and Downtown. This chapter adds a third: the surrounding meniscus of hills, including the Hellshire Hills and Jack's Hill, and the outlying regions of metropolitan Kingston, including Port Royal and outlying areas of St Andrew.

The view from the mountains – be sure to drive into the hills – reveals leafy foothill suburbs and, below, the highrise hotels, banks, and office buildings of New Kingston, where the majority of visitors stay, smothered on some days by a thick cloud of vehicle-induced smog. Here, relatively wealthy 'uptowners' lead middle-class lifestyles modeled on those of North America and Western Europe.

Kingston has a huge middle-class and vast acres of well-maintained streets lined with modern houses. It is also a city divided, with

### Highlights

- Bob Marley Museum, a fascinating glimpse into the life of Jamaica's most revered contemporary hero
- The Parade, a pulsing marketplace at the heart of Kingston
- Peaceful Lime Cay, a sun-drenched haven from the hustle and bustle
- Historic Port Royal, a disheveled trove of colonial structures with the promise of a glittering restoration
- Hellshire Beaches, a funky fishing village alive on weekends with the Kingston picnic-and-party crowd
- Horse racing at Caymanas Park
- Black Sovereign Ethiopian Embassy, the Bobo Ashanti Rastafarian commune above Bull Bay

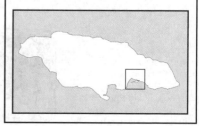

## Life on the Edge

On the edge of Kingston huddle extensive shanty towns. Like Dickensian England, endemic rural poverty continues to encourage an enormous pool of starry-eyed youths to seek a better life in Kingston. For most, the illusion ends in dwellings made of packing cases, fish barrels, tin, and cardboard. To deter squatters, the government has refused to supply public amenities, giving rise to illegal and unsanitary pit latrines.

Shanty towns are occasionally bulldozed by the government. Squatters, however, quickly reclaim land that is cleared, and the lack of basic amenities has not deterred migration from the countryside. Tuberculosis, associated with overcrowded rooms, and typhoid (resulting from inadequate sewage facilities and contaminated drinking water) prevail.

Peripheral location, social stigma, and endemic illiteracy have added to shanty town residents' difficulty finding work. A great percentage of Kingston's *lumpenproletariat* live by pimping, prostitution, and violent crime. Others adapt by 'scuffling' or scraping a living through begging, making handicrafts, and selling the scraps gleaned from garbage dumps such as the 'dungle' on the foreshore in West Kingston. As late as the 1960s, people had actually lived on the dungle. 'Droves of squatters awaited the arrival of the garbage carts, and, as they disgorged their contents, competed for them with the John Crows,' recalls Professor Colin G Clarke.

Monsignor Richard Albert (☎ 905-1575) lives like Mother Theresa among the poor of Kingston. His '1000 A Month Club' is a foundation that sponsors inner-city projects (supporters join the club for J$1000 – less than US$30 – a month).

hovels and highrises side by side. Downtown is dominated by day by city business – the country's financial institutions are here – although most of the historic buildings of note are also here, and well worth a browse. By night, city life is dominated by the urban underclass. It's a sad sight to see the bankers fleeing at 5 pm, when the homeless bed down in bank doorways.

Clamorous Kingston is definitely a Third World city, one with sophistication. Goats run free everywhere, browsing the garbage-filled gutters totally oblivious to your approach by car until the moment you're about to pass them, when the kamikaze herd is sure to dash across your path.

The drift from countryside to city occurring in much of the developing world has been felt here no less forcefully in the past few decades. Kingston's population has more than doubled in the past 30 years, making it, by far, the largest English-speaking city south of Miami. The growth has over-whelmed the city's ability to provide housing and services. The vast shanty towns that push at the city's margins are for the most part hidden from tourist view. Still, in even the more exclusive areas, makeshift homes of corrugated cardboard litter the spare plots of ground.

At times its culture can be darned right intimidating. Seething tensions simmer below the surface and often boil over, making for international headlines that have tended to keep visitors at bay. In some areas, a white face is an invitation to violence.

But this chaotic and vibrant city is the heartbeat of Jamaica and its center of commerce and culture, hustling and bustling with energy.

## HISTORY

On May 10, 1655, an English fleet bearing 7000 men sailed into Kingston Harbour and, after desultory resistance from the Spanish defenders at Passage Fort, captured Jamaica for Cromwell. For several decades the site of the future city was used for rearing pigs. When an earthquake leveled Port Royal in 1692, survivors struggled across the bay and pitched camp with the swine. The refugees promptly succumbed to an epidemic that claimed more than 3000 lives. (The city, which arose on the site of a swamp, continued to suffer many epidemics in ensuing years.)

Within two months of the disaster, the Council met aboard HMS *Richard and Sarah* and decided to build a city 'equal to Port Royal in everything.' A town plan was drawn up on a grid pattern, centered on an open square.

Though devastated repeatedly by earthquakes and hurricanes, the port city prospered throughout the 18th century, becoming one of the most important trading centers in the Western Hemisphere and an important transshipment point for slaves destined for the Spanish colonies. Though Britain later abolished the slave trade, Kingston continued to flourish as an entrepôt for the Spanish empire.

By 1800, the population had reached 11,000. As the city expanded, the wealthier merchants moved to the cooler heights of Liguanea, where they built more expansive homes. Many built lookout towers atop their homes to check on the movement of ships in and out of the harbor (Vale Royal, the current prime minister's official residence, is a good example). The merchants became peeved that the official capital was sleepy Spanish Town, which Kingston had eclipsed. In 1755, Governor Admiral Charles Knowles bowed to political pressure and transferred his government's offices to Kingston. His successor revoked the act, however, and it wasn't until 1872 that the capital was officially transferred.

The 1907 earthquake leveled much of the city. Many important buildings were destroyed, and most of the fine houses ringing the Parade burned down.

In the 1960s, the Urban Development Corporation reclaimed the waterfront, and several historic landmarks, including Victoria Market, were razed to make way for a complex of gleaming new structures: the

## KINGSTON & ENVIRONS

**PLACES TO STAY**
1 Stony Hill Hotel
3 Elmundo's Guest House
4 Cozy Heights
5 Mountain Valley Hotel
6 Crowne Plaza
9 Jonraine Country Inn
10 Springburn House
11 Abahati Hotel
13 Maya Lodge
14 Hollywood Villa
17 Ivor
19 Artland Guest House
20 Olympia Crown Hotel
33 Inez Bogue Hotel
36 La Roose
48 Hellshire Beach Club

**PLACES TO EAT**
1 Stony Hill Hotel
6 Crowne Plaza
9 Forbidden Heights
11 Pearl's Café
17 Ivor
18 Blue Mountain Inn
19 Artland Guest House
31 Rodney Arms
36 La Roose
45 Jamaica Gates Sea Café & Bar

**OTHER**
2 Texaco Gas Station
7 Manor Hill Plaza
8 Mr Carby's Aviary
12 Foxy's Pub
15 Produce Market
16 Constant Spring Golf Club
20 Memories Disco
21 Jamaica College
22 University Hospital
23 Bus Station, Papine Market
24 Gas Station
25 Jamworld Entertainment Centre
26 Tuff Gong Recording Studios
27 Mico Teachers College
28 Up Park Camp
29 Gun Court
30 Cactus Disco

32 Plaza Concord
34 My Friend's Place
35 Jewels
37 Fort Augusta (Prison)
38 Bellevue Hospital
39 Rockfort Mineral Baths
40 Rockfort
41 Fort Nugent
42 Apostles Battery
43 World Meditation Centre
44 Royal Jamaica Yacht Club
45 Jamaica Maritime Institute
46 Harbour View Shopping Centre, Harbour View Drive-In Cinema
47 Rodney's Lookout
49 Two Sisters Cave

Ferry

A1

To Spanish Town

Waterford Rd

Caymanas Park Racetrack

Passage Fort Drive

Passage Fort

Portmore

To Fort Clarence, Hellshire Beaches

Naggo Head Drive

Port Henderson

Dawkins Drive

Dawkins Lagoon

Augusta Dr

Portmore Pkwy

Forum

Salt Island Creek

Green Bay

Fort Clarence

Great Salt Pond

Fort Clarence Beach Park

Fisherman's Beach

Fishing Village

Bush Reef

Hellshire Beaches

Hellshire Hills

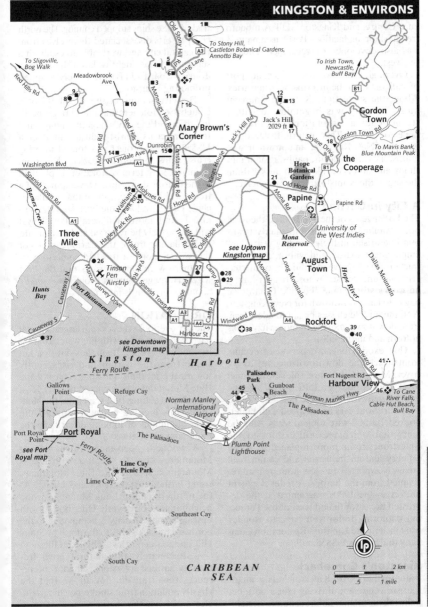

# KINGSTON & ENVIRONS

To Sligoville,
Bog Walk

Red Hills Rd

Meadowbrook
Ave

To Stony Hill,
Castleton Botanical Gardens,
Annotto Bay

Old Stony Hill Rd

Long Lane

To Irish Town,
Newcastle,
Buff Bay

B1

Gordon
Town

Mannings Hill Rd

Mary Brown's
Corner

Jack's Hill Rd

Jack's Hill
2029 ft

Skyline Drive

Gordon Town Rd

To Mavis Bank,
Blue Mountain Peak

the
Cooperage

Red Hills Rd

Molynes Rd

Dunrobin Ave

W Lyndale Ave

Washington Blvd

A1

Constant Spring Rd

E Kings House Rd

Hope Rd

Old Hope Rd

Hope
Botanical
Gardens

B1

Papine

Papine Rd

Spanish Town Rd

Barnes Creek

A1

Three
Mile

Waltham Park Rd

Hagley Park Rd

Molynes Rd

Half Way Tree Rd

Old Hope Rd

see Uptown
Kingston map

Mona Rd

Mona
Reservoir

University of
the West Indies

August
Town

Hope River

Dallas Mountain

Hunts
Bay

Causeway N

Marcus Garvey Drive

Port Bustamente

Tinson
Pen
Airstrip

Spanish Town Rd

Slipe Rd

Camp Rd

Carib Rd

Mountain View Ave

Long Mountain

Causeway S

see Downtown
Kingston map

A3

A1

Harbour St

Windward Rd

A4

Rockfort

Windward Rd

Kingston        Harbour

Ferry Route

Harbour View

Fort Nugent Rd

To Cane
River Falls,
Cable Hut Beach,
Bull Bay

Gallows
Point

Refuge Cay

Palisades
Park

Gunboat Beach

Norman Manley Hwy

The Palisadoes

Port Royal
Point

Port Royal

see Port
Royal map

Ferry Route

Norman Manley
International
Airport

Main Rd

The Palisadoes

Plumb Point
Lighthouse

Lime Cay
Picnic Park

Lime Cay

Southeast Cay

South Cay

CARIBBEAN
SEA

0    1    2 km

0    .5    1 mile

KINGSTON & ENVIRONS

Bank of Jamaica, the Scotia Centre, the now-defunct Oceana Hotel, the Jamaica Conference Centre, and Kingston Mall. A modern freight shipping facility – Port Bustamante – was also developed on reclaimed lands to the west.

Overnight, Kingston became a major port of call on Caribbean cruising itineraries. About the same time, Kingston's nascent music industry was beginning to gather steam, lending international stature and fame to the city. This, in turn, fostered the growth of New Kingston, an uptown area of multistory office blocks, banks, restaurants, shops, and hotels developed in the 1960s on the site of the Knutsford Park racecourse.

## A City in Decline

The boom years of the 1960s lured the rural poor, swelling the slums and shanty towns that had arisen in the preceding years. Unemployment soared, and with it, crime. The fractious 1970s spawned politically connected criminal enterprises whose trigger-happy networks still plague the city. Commerce began to leave downtown for New Kingston. And the middle classes began to edge away from downtown, moving to more ritzy areas uptown and in the hills.

That exodus began a period of decline from which the downtown has yet to recover. Many of the once splendid colonial town houses decayed into 'yards,' or zinc hovel tenements that have become littered with burnt-out cars and scarred with bullet-pocked, barbed-wire-topped walls. And the piers that welcomed cruise ships to the waterfront are no more, replaced by an oil refinery and an industrial and commercial area – Newport West – on swampy land reclaimed from the harbor. A redevelopment project in the 1980s was aimed at the depressed areas south and west of the Parade, but exploring today you have to wonder what exactly the Kingston Restoration Company did with its US$30 million.

## Kingston's Comeback

Prior to the 1970s, Kingston was a major tourism venue and thriving cruise port, but political turbulence and economic destabi-lization during the late 1970s and 1980s sent the city into a tailspin, destroying the tourist trade. Cruise ships stopped coming. The north coast resorts disassociated themselves from the capital city and were able to establish a separate market identity. Even the Jamaica Tourist Board (JTB) effectively stopped promoting Kingston.

The city seems on the threshold of a comeback. Hoteliers and the JTB are pushing to dispel the city's negative image and to resurrect its tourist industry. In 1995, a US$50 million project was touted to bring cruise ships and tourists back to Kingston. A major, long-term restoration is planned in the historic downtown. Development of a free port has been proposed that would include Port Royal and the Fort Augusta Peninsula. And, most significantly, Port Royal will supposedly be restored and turned into the Williamsburg of the Caribbean. As of this writing none of this had come to pass, but there were definite signs that the Port Royal Heritage Tourism Project was *finally* about to turn words into deed.

## ORIENTATION

The city overlooks the seventh largest natural harbor in the world, with the waterfront on its southern border. It spreads out in a fan shape from the harbor and rises gently toward the foothills and spur ridges of the Blue Mountains, which encusp the city. It's a magnificent setting, best seen from the Hellshire Hills looking northeast toward the Blue Mountains or looking down from the mountains themselves.

A wooded, steep-faced ridge – Long Mountain – rises to the east, with Dallas Mountain, a spur of the Blue Mountains, rising farther east, parallel and higher. At the northern end of Long Mountain is the neighborhood of Beverly Hills, dotted with upscale homes. The city is hemmed in to the northeast by Jack's Hill, to the north by Stony Hill, and to the northwest by Red Hills.

Unfortunately, this natural bowl frequently suffers inversions, climatic occurrences that trap the hot air, so that the ghastly pollution from smoke-belching vehicles and from the factories east of town settles over the harbor and city, creating Los Angeles-like smog.

## Downtown

The historic area just north of the waterfront forms the city center. Ocean Blvd, Port Royal St, and Harbour St parallel the waterfront. King St, the main thoroughfare, leads north from the waterfront to the Parade, surrounding a bustling square at the heart of the historic district.

Most buildings of historic interest lie within a four-block quadrant northeast of the Parade. From here, E Queen St runs east to the Norman Manley International Airport and Port Royal. W Queen St runs west for four blocks, then tilts and becomes Spanish Town Rd, which cuts northwest (toward Spanish Town) through Tivoli Gardens and the industrial estates of southwest Kingston, an altogether depressing drive lined with slums and shanty towns.

## Uptown

Marescaux Rd and Slipe Rd lead north from downtown to 'uptown.' The two roads meet at Cross Roads, a major junction marked with a clock tower that is the unofficial boundary with New Kingston, immediately to the north. Knutsford Blvd, the main north-to-south artery, bisects New Kingston. Half Way Tree Rd leads northwest, turning into Constant Spring Rd, which leads to Manor Park and Stony Hill.

Northeast of New Kingston lies the middle-class residential area of Liguanea,

## Restoring Port Royal

In the early 1960s, the Port Royal Company of Merchants planned a development project with Walt Disney Productions to convert Port Royal into a theme park. Nothing evolved then, but suddenly things look promising.

In April 1995 ex-Premier Edward Seaga unveiled an ambitious scheme that would make Port Royal a free port, with hotels, restaurants, attractions, and entertainment. Independently, that same month Pragma Development Ltd was formed to restore Port Royal to its former glory and turn Port Royal into a theme destination for cruise ship visitors, with the addition of major cruise ship facilities.

The Port Royal Heritage Tourism Project, spearheaded by Robert 'Bobby' Stephens (former Director of Tourism for Jamaica), had completed its conceptualization phase as of late 1998 and, ostensibly (this *is* Jamaica) was set to begin restoration and construction of an 80-acre theme park at this writing, beginning with the creation of Chocolata Hole Bay, a 17th-century docking area with a new cruise ship pier, entertainment center and arcade, Jamaica music museum, and Fine Arts Centre. In addition to restoring the dilapidated buildings, workshops will be created to make pewter mugs and other period crafts. A special tour boat will be introduced, with underwater portholes for viewing the sunken city. And sound and light shows will bring the past alive, as will reenactments with townsfolk in period costumes. Plans also involve making Port Royal into a scuba diving mecca.

Leading cruise ship interests seem enthused by the idea, and predictions are that half a million cruise visitors will arrive each year.

The project includes the construction of new health and other facilities for the existing community, members of which have been elected to serve as directors.

For further information, contact Port Royal Development Company (☎ 960-3598, fax 960-3599, info@portroyal-jamaica.com, www.portroyal-jamaica.com), 12 Worthington Terrace, Kingston 5.

## KINGSTON NEIGHBORHOODS

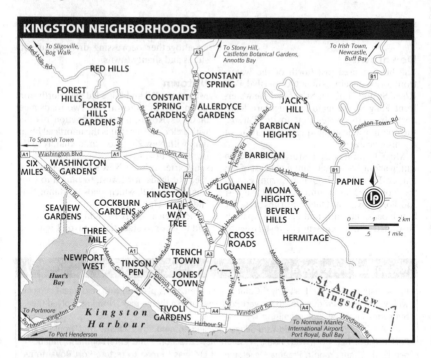

up Hope Rd from Half Way Tree. Hope Rd ascends gradually past Mona Heights to Papine, the gateway to the Blue Mountains and the University of West Indies campus at Mona.

### Maps

You can obtain copies of the JTB's 'Discover Jamaica' map from the JTB headquarters (see the Tourist Offices section below). It features a good 1:34,000 scale street map of Kingston.

The Survey Dept at 23½ Charles St has more detailed city maps designed for planners (see the Maps section under Planning in the Facts for the Visitor chapter).

### INFORMATION
### Tourist Offices

The JTB (☎ 929-9200, fax 929-9375) has its headquarters in the ICWI Building, 2 St Lucia Ave. It has a limited collection of tour-

ist literature, plus a small research library on the ground floor. Another JTB office is located in the arrival hall at Norman Manley International Airport (☎ 924-8024).

The Jamaica Information Service (☎ 926-3740) at 58A Half Way Tree Rd offers statistical and general information on the island.

Ilean and Malcolm McInnes offer tourist advice at their Bench & Bar Restaurant (☎ 967-4443, fax 967-0766), downtown at the corner of Port Royal and Duke Sts.

### Foreign Embassies & Consulates

More than 40 countries have embassies and consulates in Kingston. Some are listed in the Facts for the Visitor chapter. Others you'll find in the telephone directories.

### Money

**Banks** Uptown, you'll find more than a dozen banks along Knutsford Blvd in New Kingston, and dozens more elsewhere. Most have foreign-exchange counters as well as 24-hour ATMs. Very few ATMs are linked to international networks, so it may be difficult to get cash using cash cards issued by foreign banks. There's no problem, however, in receiving cash advances against credit cards during bank hours. Banking hours are 9 am to 2 pm Monday to Thursday and 9 am to noon and 3 pm to 5 pm on Friday.

Scotiabank (☎ 922-1000) has its main foreign-exchange center immediately east of the Jamaica Conference Centre at Duke and Port Royal Sts. National Commercial Bank (☎ 922-3940) has its centralized foreign exchange department at 77 King St. Citibank (☎ 926-3270, fax 929-3745) has a branch at 63 Knutsford Blvd. For Citibank's international department, call ☎ 960-2340.

The following leading banks have branches throughout Kingston:

CIBC Jamaica
  (☎ 929-9310) 23 Knutsford Blvd
  (☎ 922-3751) 58 Duke St
  (☎ 926-7408) 78 Half Way Tree Rd
  (☎ 922-6126) 1 King St
  (☎ 924-2521) Manor Park Plaza
  (☎ 923-4821) 6 Newport Blvd

Jamaica Citizens Bank
  (☎ 922-5850) 4 King St
  (☎ 926-5492) 15A Old Hope Rd
  (☎ 926-2098) 12 Constant Spring Rd
  (☎ 920-0652) 16A Half Way Tree Rd
  (☎ 927-9431) Sovereign Centre
  (☎ 960-2341) 17 Dominica Drive
  (☎ 924-8666) Manley International Airport

National Commercial Bank
  (☎ 929-9050) 32 Trafalgar Rd
  (☎ 926-6709) 94 Half Way Tree Rd
  (☎ 926-1970) 21 Constant Spring Rd
  (☎ 968-4560) 90 Slipe Rd
  (☎ 922-8885) Duke St
  (☎ 922-6710) Duke & Barry Sts
  (☎ 926-6077) 14½ Half Way Tree Rd
  (☎ 923-5391) 211 Hagley Park Rd
  (☎ 929-1922) 94 Half Way Tree Rd
  (☎ 922-3980) 124 Harbour St
  (☎ 922-3690) 121 King St
  (☎ 968-0990) 1 Knutsford Blvd
  (☎ 929-8950) 30 Knutsford Blvd
  (☎ 925-9039) Manor Park Plaza
  (☎ 927-7780) 133 Old Hope Rd
  (☎ 923-9004) 54 Second St
  (☎ 926-6623) 2 Oxford Rd

  (☎ 925-3313) 105 Red Hills Rd
  (☎ 927-0463) UWI Mona Campus
  (☎ 928-4230) 89 Windward Rd

Scotiabank (Bank of Nova Scotia)
  (☎ 922-1810) 30 Duke St
  (☎ 925-7560) 105 Red Hills Rd
  (☎ 922-1420) 35 King St
  (☎ 922-8890) 60 E Queen St
  (☎ 926-8034) 1 Knutsford Blvd
  (☎ 926-4325) 6 Oxford Rd
  (☎ 926-1530) 86 Slice Rd
  (☎ 927-4371) 125 Old Hope Rd
  (☎ 960-8097) 10 Constant Spring Rd
  (☎ 929-4192) 4 Ellesmere Rd
  (☎ 926-1540) 88 Half Way Tree Rd
  (☎ 923-5681) 128 Hagley Park Rd
  (☎ 923-7045) 236 Spanish Town Rd

**Traveler's Checks** Grace Kennedy Travel (☎ 929-6290) at 19 Knutsford Blvd, Kingston 5, acts as the local Thomas Cook representative. It cashes Thomas Cook traveler's checks free of charge. Stuart's Travel Service (☎ 929-2345) at 9 Cecelio Ave represents American Express.

**Wire Remittances** Western Union has an office at 20 Tobago Ave in New Kingston (☎ 926-2454, 888-991-2056), and downtown in Woolworth's on King St (☎ 922-2284).

## Post & Communications

The main post office (☎ 922-2120) at 13 King St is open 8 am to 5 pm Monday to Thursday, 9 am to 4 pm on Friday, and 8 am to 1 pm on Saturday. It gets crowded. A better option is the New Kingston Post Office (☎ 926-6803) at 115 Hope Rd. Other branches are located throughout the city (see the Blue Pages in the telephone directory). For information on parcel post, call ☎ 922-9430.

Federal Express (☎ 960-9192) is at 40 Half Way Tree Rd, at the junction of Norwood Rd. DHL has offices at 60 Knutsford Blvd (☎ 929-2554) and 54 Duke St (☎ 922-7333). AirPak Express (923-0371) is at Tinson Pen Airport. UPS (☎ 968-8288) at 30 Dominica Drive offers the cheapest express service; it's open 7 am to 7 pm daily. It also has an office at Norman Manley International Airport (☎ 924-8457). UPS offers a money-back guarantee of next-day delivery to the

USA and Canada. It will cost you about US$11 to send a letter to the USA; you can even send a package up to 5lb for US$17.50.

You can make international calls and send faxes from most hotels, but many add a hefty service charge. There are plenty of public call boxes, including at the Cable & Wireless headquarters, uptown, at the junction of Oxford St and Half Way Tree Rd; and upstairs in the New Kingston Shopping Mall.

A cheaper alternative is to make calls from the Jamintel Centre, operated by Telecommunications of Jamaica (TOJ; ☎ 922-6031, 888-967-9700) at 15 North St, at the corner of Duke St. It has a message service at 9 East Parade (☎ 922-9613, 888-924-9700), and you can also send cablegrams from here. It's open 9 am to 5 pm. (See the yellow pages for additional TOJ offices.)

You'll also find similar services in the Jamaica Conference Centre (☎ 922-9160, fax 922-7816) at 14-20 Duke St.

You can rent cellular phones at TOJ's Cellular Centres at 136 Ripon Rd (☎ 929-2355, 960-4244), 9 Carlton Crescent, 116 Constant Spring Rd, and Shop 13 at the corner of Princess St and Ocean Blvd; or from Cable & Wireless Caribbean Cellular (☎ 968-4000).

For directory assistance, call ☎ 114; for operator assistance, call ☎ 112; for an international operator, call ☎ 888-922-2170 or 888-991-2170.

### Email & Internet Access
Most upscale hotels catering to business travelers provide email access. The Crowne Plaza and the Courtleigh Hotel & Suites both have in-room dial-up access.

Innovative Superstore (☎ 978-3512), in the Sovereign Centre on Hope Rd, offers email and Internet access for US$3 per 30 minutes. Telecommunications of Jamaica (☎ 888-991-2222) provides toll-free Internet assistance.

There are dozens of computer retailers; see the yellow pages.

### Internet Resources
Scores of websites are dedicated to offering information on Kingston. You can find all kinds of sites and links at fantasyisle.com/kingstn.htm. A good general source is www.realjamaica.com/kingston.htm.

### Travel Agencies
There are dozens of travel agencies. Two reputable companies are Grace Kennedy Travel (☎ 929-6290, fax 968-8418) at 19 Knutsford Blvd and Stuart's Travel at 9 Cecelio Ave (☎ 929-2345) and Shop 7 at 38 Constant Spring Rd (☎ 929-4222).

International Travel Services (ITS) is also recommended. It has offices throughout Kingston, including 2 Belmont Rd (☎ 926-6540), 13 Constant Spring Rd (☎ 926-6303, 888-991-2406), and downtown at 9 King St (☎ 922-6114).

### Bookstores & Libraries
Kingston lacks a *really* well-stocked bookstore. Most bookshops are primarily office supply and stationery stores. The following are relatively well-stocked:

Bookland
   (☎ 926-4035) 53 Knutsford Blvd
Book Traders
   (☎ 928-9081) 7 Norman Rd
Kingston Bookshop
   (☎ 922-4056) 70B King St
Sangsters Sovereign Centre
   (☎ 926-0710)
The Book Shop
   (☎ 926-1800) 15 Constant Spring Rd
The Book Place
   (☎ 941-1615) Manor Park Plaza
Times Stores
   (☎ 922-4690) 8 King St
   (☎ 926-7410) Tropical Plaza
   (☎ 927-9726) Liguanea Plaza

Most hotel gift shops stock a limited selection of novels, travel guidebooks, and cultural and historic guides to Jamaica. All the Write Things (☎ 968-2307), in the grounds of Devon House, has a comprehensive selection of books on Jamaica and the Caribbean.

You can buy leading international magazines and newspapers at the above stores, as well as at most pharmacies.

The Jamaica Library Service (☎ 926-3315) is headquartered in the St Andrew Parish Library on tree-lined Tom Redcam Ave. It's open 9 am to 6 pm Monday to Friday and 9 am to 5 pm Saturday.

The National Library of Jamaica (☎ 922-5533) at 12 East St in the Institute of Jamaica, incorporates the Caribbean's largest repository of audiovisual aids, books, maps, charts, paintings, and documents on West Indian history. The library is open 9 am to 6 pm Monday to Friday and 9 am to 5 pm Saturday. No bags or briefcases are allowed.

The Jamaican National Heritage Trust (☎ 922-1287) in Headquarters House at 79 Duke St maintains archives on the island's architectural history.

The Scientific Research Council (☎ 927-1771) has a public library in Hope Gardens, at the top of Hope Rd. You may also be allowed to use the three libraries of the University of the West Indies; call the loan and reference desk (☎ 927-2123).

## Universities

'You-wee,' as Jamaicans call the University of the West Indies (UWI; ☎ 927-1660) campus, lies southeast of Mona Heights, in northeast Kingston. Visitors are free to enter the campus, which has several sites of historical interest.

UWI has campuses in Barbados, Jamaica, and Trinidad. The Kingston campus offers degrees in agriculture, arts and general studies, education, engineering, law, medicine, natural sciences, and social sciences, and also includes a teaching hospital with 500 beds.

The No 66 bus departs the Parade and passes the UWI campus en route to Hermitage (US$0.30). Buses Nos 77, 78, and 79 also leave the Parade for August Town, passing the campus en route.

## Cultural Centers

The British Council (☎ 929-6915), 69 Knutsford Blvd, Kingston 10, promotes everything British and hosts soirées and cultural events. Likewise, Alliance Francaise de la Jamaique (☎ 925-8876), 3 March Drive, Kingston 8, has an outlet in Kingston to promote French culture.

Contact the Jamaica Cultural Development Commission (☎ 926-5726) for a list of other cultural centers.

## Laundry

You'll be hard-pressed to find self-service laundries. Among the few are Speedy's Laundromat (☎ 924-5846) at 108 Red Hills Rd, Constant Spring Fabricare (☎ 905-2065) at 104 Constant Spring Rd, and Quick Wash Coin Laundry (☎ 920-2713) at 1 Union Square.

There are plenty of laundry services, including Dryclean USA at 17 Constant Spring Rd (☎ 920-6772) and 12 Northside Drive (☎ 977-4339); and Supercleaners, which has branches in the Sovereign Centre (☎ 978-5116), Lane Plaza in Liguanea (☎ 978-0705), E Queen St (☎ 922-7688), and Manor Park Plaza (☎ 969-6646), and the Liguanea Fabricare Centre (☎ 927-7525) on Old Hope Rd. Most laundries offer same-day service as well as drycleaning.

## Toilets

You'll find restrooms in the Kingston Mall (US$0.35), and at Nelson Mandela Park at Half Way Tree. They're unsavory places, best avoided.

## Luggage Storage

There are no rental lockers at the Norman Manley International Airport or anywhere else for that matter. Theft is too great a problem. Most hotels permit guests to store luggage with the concierge for up to a week or so at no extra charge.

## Medical Services

Kingston has more than half of Jamaica's doctors, four public hospitals, and a plethora of medical clinics.

Medical Associates Hospital (☎ 926-1400), 18 Tangerine Place, Kingston 10, is a private facility that offers emergency ambulance service and medical assistance.

St John's Ambulance (☎ 926-7656) offers free ambulance services in Kingston; AmbuCare (☎ 978-2327) and Deluxe Ambulance Service (☎ 923-7415) both offer 24-hour emergency service.

Wings Jamaica (☎/fax 923-6573, 923-5416), based at Tinson Pen Airport, offers air ambulance.

Private hospitals include:

Andrews Memorial Hospital
  (☎ 926-7401)
Medical Associates Hospital
  (☎ 926-1400) 18 Tangerine Place
Nuttall Memorial Hospital
  (☎ 926-2139) 5 Caledonia Rd
St Joseph Hospital
  (☎ 928-4955) 22 Deanery Rd

Eureka Medical Centre (☎ 929-1820) at 1 Eureka Rd also has an emergency ward.

The following public hospitals all have emergency departments:

Bustamante Hospital for Children
  (☎ 926-5721)
Bellevue Hospital
  (☎ 928-1380) 6¹/₂ Windward Rd, Kingston 2
Kingston Public Hospital
  (☎ 922-0210) North St
University Hospital of the West Indies
  (☎ 927-1620) UWI campus, Mona

If you put your back out carrying all the reggae tapes you've purchased, you can find relief at the Physiotherapy Centre (☎ 929-6766) at 12 Tangerine Place.

Biomedical has a clinical diagnostic laboratory (☎ 926-4191) at 8A Caledonia Ave, Kingston 5.

**Pharmacies** Kingston has no shortage of pharmacies. Uptown try Moodies Pharmacy (☎ 926-4174) in the New Kingston Shopping Centre at 30 Dominica Drive. Downtown try Kent Pharmacy (☎ 922-3323) at 8 Carvalho Drive. Farther afield are Constant Spring Pharmacy & Medical Centre (☎ 924-2786) at 1418 Constant Spring Rd and the well-stocked Manor Park Pharmacy (☎ 924-1424) at 186 Constant Spring Rd.

**Medical Services for Women** Gynae Associates (☎ 929-5038) at 23 Tangerine Place, Kingston 10, specializes in women's medicine. Dr Valerie Dean (☎ 929-8201), an obstetrician and gynecologist, has a clinic at 22 Old Hope Rd. You can have mammograms taken at the Jamaica Cancer Society (☎ 927-4265) at 16 Lady Musgrave Rd, Kingston 5. The Women's Centre of Jamaica (☎ 929-7608) at 42 Trafalgar Rd may be able to provide information on medical services for women.

The Woman's Crisis Centre (☎ 929-2997) has 24-hour counseling for women.

**Medical Services for Children** If you have kids needing medical attention, call the Bustamante Hospital for Children (☎ 926-5721) on Arthur Wint Drive, Kingston 5. There's also a Childcare Medical Centre (☎ 988-5086) at 6 Portmore Drive in Portmore, west of Kingston.

## Emergency

In case of an emergency call the police at ☎ 119. Call the fire department or ambulance service at ☎ 110.

The police maintain a hotline (☎ 927-7778), and a tourism liaison (☎ 922-9321) at 79 Duke St.

Downtown police stations are located at East and Sutton Sts, and on E Queen St. Uptown stations are located off Maxfield Ave, just south of Hagley Park Rd; and on Old Hope Rd. A complete listing of police departments and branches is given in the 'Emergency Numbers' page at the front of the Jamaican telephone directory.

## Dangers & Annoyances

Be cautious when driving or crossing the street. Otherwise, despite its reputation, Kingston is no more threatening to tourists than is Montego Bay, Negril, Ocho Rios, New York, or Chicago, as long as you avoid the 'yards' or ghettoes.

New Kingston and upscale residential areas such as Liguanea and Mona are generally safe for walking, as are most main roads and downtown, where tourists (white and black alike) may find comfort in being in the company of Kingston's middle-class business elite by day. Avoid wandering west of the Parade when exploring downtown. Stick to the main streets – if in doubt ask your hotel concierge or manager to point out trouble areas.

Foreigners, especially white tourists, stand out from the crowd. Fortunately, visitors to Kingston are not hassled to anywhere near the degree they are in the north coast resorts. I've walked many miles on Kingston's streets and only infrequently have I ever been hustled. Still, many Kingstonians, especially the down-and-outs, are by nature suspicious or scheming a rip-off. Don't loiter!

If you feel uncomfortable, it might help to consider whether the threat is mostly what you *perceive* it might be. My comfort level increased markedly as I became more familiar with the city and as I came to realize that my initial lack of comfort was due to my *anticipation* of trouble. Nonetheless, constant alertness is called for, especially during periods of discontent.

Many Kingstonians respond aggressively to having their photographs taken. This is usually from fear of police informers and the like.

Although crime in Jamaica is limited to small pockets outside of the tourist path, the big picture isn't pretty. The island averages three murders per day, and 75% of these occur in Kingston – the murder capital of the Caribbean, second among metropolitan areas in the Americas only to Washington, DC. More than half of the murders resulted from domestic disputes, and the rest were mostly drug-related or politically inspired murders in the ghettoes.

Be wary of visiting during sporadic periods of tension, when localized violence can spontaneously erupt.

## DOWNTOWN WALKING TOUR

Kingston's downtown is concentrated enough to permit a walking tour taking in most of the major sites. A good place to begin is at Kingston Harbour.

### The Waterfront

For several blocks, the waterfront is paralleled by Ocean Blvd, a breeze-swept 400-yard-long harborfront boulevard meagerly landscaped with a thin grass strip and shady palms. Virtually nothing remains of the orig-inal colonial waterfront that served as a center of social activity centered on a weekend market – known as Christmas Grand Market – held at the foot of King St. It fronted Victoria Pier, where for over three centuries royalty, dignitaries, and other rich and famous folk first set foot in Jamaica.

Start at the **Bank of Jamaica**, the national mint and treasury at the east end of Ocean Blvd, on Nethersole Place, fronted by a tall concrete statue of Noel 'Crab' Nethersole (minister of finance from 1955 to 1969), who earned his nickname for his strange walk. Inside you'll find a small **Museum of Coins and Notes** (☎ 922-0750) displaying Jamaican currency through the centuries. It's open 9 am to 4 pm Monday to Friday. Entry is free.

Go west half a block along Nethersole Place to get to the **Jamaica Conference Centre** (☎ 922-9160, fax 922-7816), 14-20 Duke St, built in 1982 as the venue for meetings of the United Nations' International Seabed Authority. Its impressive architecture and facilities were built to United Nations' standards and are worth popping inside for a guided tour, not least to admire the intriguing wicker basket and bamboo ceilings and walls like upended Murphy beds (closer inspection reveals that they're woven mats). The names of those who worked on the construction of the center are engraved on a mosaic of metal tiles on the facade outside the main entrance. It reads 'One one coco full basket,' which roughly translates as 'everyone's contribution makes something complete.' Two cafeterias offer views over the harbor. The lobby contains a Scotiabank money exchange, Air Jamaica ticket office, and public telephones.

Thence turn onto Ocean Blvd and head west past the emotionally charged *Negro Aroused* statue at the foot of King St (actually, this is a replica; the original is in the National Gallery). This eloquent bronze statue depicting a crouched black man breaking free from bondage is the work of Jamaica's foremost sculptor, the late Edna Manley, wife of ex-prime minister Norman Manley and mother of ex-prime minister Michael Manley. One block west, looming

# DOWNTOWN KINGSTON

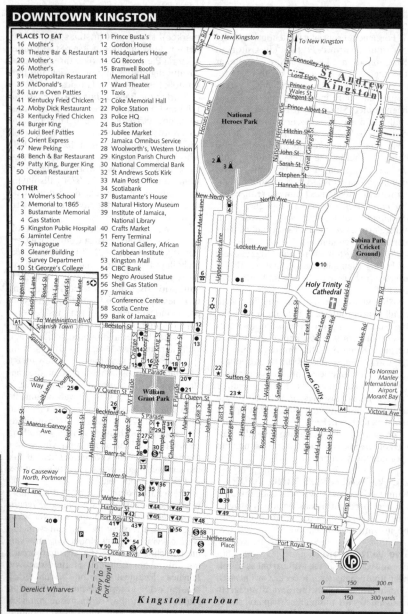

**PLACES TO EAT**
16 Mother's
18 Theatre Bar & Restaurant
20 Mother's
26 Mother's
31 Metropolitan Restaurant
35 McDonald's
36 Luv n Oven Patties
41 Kentucky Fried Chicken
42 Moby Dick Restaurant
43 Kentucky Fried Chicken
44 Burger King
45 Juici Beef Patties
46 Orient Express
47 New Peking
48 Bench & Bar Restaurant
49 Patty King, Burger King
50 Ocean Restaurant

**OTHER**
1 Wolmer's School
2 Memorial to 1865
3 Bustamante Memorial
4 Gas Station
5 Kingston Public Hospital
6 Jamintel Centre
7 Synagogue
8 Gleaner Building
9 Survey Department
10 St George's College

11 Prince Busta's
12 Gordon House
13 Headquarters House
14 GG Records
15 Bramwell Booth
   Memorial Hall
17 Ward Theater
19 Taxis
21 Coke Memorial Hall
22 Police Station
23 Police HQ
24 Bus Station
25 Jubilee Market
27 Jamaica Omnibus Service
28 Woolworth's, Western Union
29 Kingston Parish Church
30 National Commercial Bank
32 St Andrews Scots Kirk
33 Main Post Office
34 Scotiabank
37 Bustamante's House
38 Natural History Museum
39 Institute of Jamaica,
   National Library
40 Crafts Market
51 Ferry Terminal
52 National Gallery, African
   Caribbean Institute
53 Kingston Mall
54 CIBC Bank
55 Negro Aroused Statue
56 Shell Gas Station
57 Jamaica
   Conference Centre
58 Scotia Centre
59 Bank of Jamaica

National Heroes Park

Sabina Park
(Cricket Ground)

Holy Trinity Cathedral

William Grant Park

Kingston Harbour

Derelict Wharves

0    150    300 m
0    150    300 yards

over the harborfront, is the erstwhile Ocean Hotel, which opened two decades ago to cater to business travelers. Alas, it flopped dismally, as the target clientele preferred Uptown (the hotel remains closed). Its pink facade hints at the embarrassment.

Turn right (north) on Orange St to get to the National Gallery (see below).

Head back to Ocean Blvd, and continue to its western end, where the rickety old wharves are a gathering point for fishing boats pelicans use for lounging. The **Crafts Market** is here, too, in an old iron building constructed in 1872. Although gloomy within (beware of pickpockets), it's a great place to buy wicker and straw goods or carvings and other souvenirs. It's open daily except Sunday.

**National Gallery** The highlight of a waterfront walk – indeed, of any visit to Kingston – is the National Gallery (☎ 922-1561), opened in 1984 in the Roy West Building at 12 Ocean Blvd. It's open 11 am to 4:30 pm Monday to Friday. Works encompassing international notables from the English Bloomsbury set to contemporary Cuban painters are represented, but above all, the gallery, part of the Institute of Jamaica, displays Jamaican works from the 1920s to the present, and boasts particularly good collections by John Dunkley and Edna Manley, represented downstairs in the AD Scott Collection. Note, too, the bronze statue of Bob Marley by Christopher Gonzalez in the foyer; it is a draft of a statue that was intended for Celebrity Park but was considered uncomplimentary by Marley fans. You be the judge.

The 10 rooms in the permanent gallery are arranged by decade. The Jamaican School, housed on the first floor, is best represented by the works of Dunkley and Manley. One whole room is dedicated to the contemporary intuitive works of Mallica 'Kapo' Reynolds, a charismatic sect leader whose marvelous mahogany figurines and other works are overtly religious. A collection of particularly interesting works by Osmond Watson melds Christian and Rastafarian imagery. Be sure to see *Nine Night* by David Pottinger, depicting trance-like mourners at a ritualistic grievance ceremony; and Karl Parboosingh's *Ras Smoke I* (1972), an evocative oil on canvas of a Rastafarian smoking his chalice. The abstract works of Carl Abrahams are well represented, melding into the more surrealistic art of Colin Garland and the ethereal works of the gallery's former curator David Boxer. All the big names in the Jamaican artistic pantheon are represented: from Gloria Escoffrey and Barrington Watson to Rastafarian Everald Brown. (Also see Arts in the Facts about Jamaica chapter.)

Entrance is 'by contribution' (US$0.75 minimum). Guides are free, but tips are welcome. Nicky Morris is recommended.

An Annual National Exhibition is held December through the spring as a showcase for the best of recent Jamaican art. Temporary exhibits rotate throughout the year.

The meagerly furnished **African Caribbean Institute** (☎ 922-4793), in the building to the north of the gallery on Orange St, houses a motley museum dedicated to Afro-Caribbean culture and including displays on the National Hero Marcus Garvey. It's open 9 am to 3:30 pm weekdays.

## The Parade & Around

In colonial days, **King St** was the main thoroughfare leading from Victoria Pier to the Parade. It still is, and retains many beautiful old buildings with wide sidewalks shaded by columned verandas. Note the decorative carvings and long Corinthian columns at the Mutual Security Bank building at the corner of King and Harbour Sts, and the ornate wrought-iron railings on the upper floors of the buildings farther up the street. The public buildings between Water and Barry Sts that house the Treasury and Law Courts, Main Post Office, and Accountant General Department (in the old Bank of Jamaica) were built of concrete after the 1907 earthquake.

Half a mile up King St you reach the **Parade**, the streets surrounding William Grant Park at the bustling heart of the downtown mayhem. The gleaming white edifice facing the park's southeast corner is **Kingston Parish Church**, today serving a much reduced congregation of true Kingstonians – those 'born under the clock' (within earshot of its bell). Like many structures hereabouts, the original church was destroyed in the 1907 earthquake and was replaced (in concrete) by the existing building. Note the tomb dating to 1699, the year the original church was built. Admiral Benbow, the commander of the Royal Navy in the West Indies at the turn of the 18th century, lies beneath a tombstone near the High Altar. There's also a memorial to Benbow sculpted by John Bacon, one of many notable marble plaques commemorating soldiers of the West Indian regiments who died of fever or other hardships during colonial wars. Beautiful elegiac prose is inset in the south wall in honor of Edward Baker, midshipman, who died in battle at sea off Santo Domingo in 1796. The organ, in fine working fettle, dates to 1722.

The South Parade, packed with street vendors' stalls, is known as 'Ben Dung Plaza' because passersby have to bend down to buy from street hawkers whose goods are displayed on the ground. The place is clamorous and disgustingly littered, and stores blast reggae music loud enough to drive away even the most determined visitor (locals seem inured).

Both the North and South Parade are major bus thoroughfares, which adds to the pandemonium. A new bus terminal three blocks west, slated to open in 1999, should ease traffic congestion.

Betwixt North and South Parade is **William Grant Park**, which originally hosted a fortress erected in 1694 with guns pointing down King St toward the harbor. The fort was torn down and a garden, Victoria Park, laid out in 1870, with a life-size statue of the queen on a pedestal at its center. She has since been replaced by a bust of Sir Alexander Bustamante; Her Majesty's statue is now a few steps away on the east side of the park. The statue, which faced down King St in its former location, is said to have been turned around 180 degrees during the 1907 earthquake and sure enough, she looks 'not amused' amid the clamorous hurly-burly. All important announcements were traditionally proclaimed from its base during colonial days. The park was renamed in 1977 to

honor black nationalist and labor leader Sir William Grant (1894-1977), who preached his Garveyite message of African redemption here.

You can sit on the red-brick benches to admire the bougainvilleas and note the social life. At the center of the park is a four-tiered whimsical fountain shaped like a wedding cake. It's often dry, and is occasionally illuminated by spotlights at night, and there is a tiny playground for children. Statues include those of ex-Premier Norman Manley and Edward Jordon (1800-69), a Jamaican patriot who rose to become Speaker of the House of Assembly, but who, as an abolitionist, faced trial for sedition and treason.

Head west along W Queen St. Stretching three blocks from the Parade is the **Jubilee Market** (also known as Solar Market), a cacophanous hive of produce vendors' stalls that has been on this site since the 18th century and was in the process of being rebuilt at press time (see the Shopping section, later). For white visitors, the place can be a bit daunting, bordering as it does on Trench Town, within which some archly 'anti-white' feelings are harbored. (See 'the Yards.')

The wide North Parade is more placid than the South Parade. Barracks once stood on North Parade, which served as a parade ground for British soldiers. Public hangings took place here in colonial days, when the area was the center of social life.

At the northwest corner of the park is a little castlelike structure with a pink, turreted facade: **Bramwell Booth Memorial Hall**, the headquarters of the Salvation Army, built in 1933.

The impressive sky-blue facade with white trim at the park's northeast corner, on the north side of the North Parade, belongs to the **Ward Theater** (☎ 922-0453), home to the Little Theater Company. The site formerly housed the Kingston Theater, built in 1774. The Ward, which dates from 1907, is the fourth theater on the site. It's named for Colonel Charles Ward, custos of Kingston, who donated the theater to the city in 1912. Ward was a partner in the famous liquor firm of J Wray & Nephew, Ltd, which had its start at the Shakespeare Tavern. At the

The sky-blue Ward Theater

tavern, next door to the Kingston Theater, John Paul Jones made his debut as a professional actor in 1768 while in-between ships and before going on to become a famous US naval hero. The doors are usually open and visitors are welcome to nose around.

**Coke Memorial Hall** faces the eastern side of William Grant Park. This crenelated building has an austere red-brick facade in the dour tradition of Methodism. The structure, named after Dr Thomas Coke, founder of the Methodist Missions in the West Indies, dates to 1840, but was remodeled in 1907 after sustaining severe damage in the earthquake. Coke was one of many Methodist missionaries dedicated to the fight to abolish slavery and, like his cohorts, faced the ire of the colonial authorities. Today it gets little use, but the caretaker is usually around with the key to let you inside for a peek.

### Duke St & Around

From the park's southeast corner, Laws St heads east one block to Mark Lane, leading one block south to **St Andrew Scots Kirk**. This church is the most intriguing historical gem in Kingston. The octagonal Georgian brick structure serves the United Church of Jamaica and Grand Cayman. It was built from 1813 to 1819 by a group of prominent Scottish merchants and immediately christened the 'handsomest building in Kingston.' It is surrounded by a gallery supported by Corinthian pillars. Note the blue St Andrew Cross in the stained glass window. You'll be amply rewarded if you visit during a service,

when its acclaimed choir, the St Andrew Singers, performs.

Duke St, paralleling Mark St one block farther east, has several buildings of historic importance. Law firms still have their offices here, as they did in colonial days, when the street established itself as the node of Jamaica's political life. Duke St stretches for almost 2 miles north to south, with buildings of note widely dispersed.

**Bustamante's House** is at its southern end, near the corner of Water Lane, at 1A Duke St. This is the site of National Hero Sir Alexander Bustamante's office, where he wrote his campaign letters to the *Daily Gleaner* and conducted a money-lending business.

**Headquarters House** This trim little townhouse-turned-museum is at 79 Duke St, one block north and one east of North Parade. The house of brick and timber was originally known as Hibbert House, named after Thomas Hibbert, reportedly one of four members of the Assembly who in 1755 engaged in a bet to build the finest house and thereby win the attention of a much sought-after beauty. It seems he lost the bet (but no one is sure if his cronies fared better). In 1872, when the capital was moved from Spanish Town to Kingston, the house became the seat of the Jamaican legislature and remained so until 1960, when Gordon House was built across the street.

Since 1983, Headquarters House has housed the Jamaican National Heritage Trust (☎ 922-1287), which has its offices in the former bedrooms and in an extension recently added. Visitors are welcome to roam the rest of the building, including the former debating chamber on the ground floor, holding portraits of Jamaica's National Heroes, original furniture, and an impressive public gallery of mahogany. Upstairs is a look-out tower of the type commonly built by wealthy merchants to spy incoming vessels in yesteryear. The basement is an Aladdin's Cave brim-full with art and offbeat relics. Entrance is free.

**Gordon House** Jamaica's parliament meets at Gordon House, immediately north of

Headquarters House (☎ 922-0200), at the corner of Duke and Beeston Sts. The rather plain brick-and-concrete building was constructed in 1960 and named after National Hero the Right Excellent George William Gordon (1820-65), a 'free colored' son of a Scottish plantation owner. Gordon became wealthy and, as a member of the Assembly, championed the rights of the poor and oppressed, for which he paid with his life (see 'Morant Bay Rebellion' in the Blue Mountains & Southeast Coast chapter).

You can visit Gordon House by prior arrangement to watch how the Jamaica parliament conducts business (generally a somewhat soporific affair, occasionally enlivened when firebrands such as Edward Seaga take the floor). Entrance to the public galleries is free. The legislature has a single chamber, where the House of Representatives and the Senate meet at different times: the former at 2 pm on Tuesday (and sometimes, in pressing business, on Wednesday at the same hour), and the latter at 11 am on Friday. When not in session, the marshal sometimes lets visitors in at his discretion. If parliament is in session, you won't be allowed to drive along Duke St between Heywood and North Sts.

**Jewish Synagogue** Jamaica's only synagogue, the United Congregation of the Israelites, sits on the corner of Duke and

## The Yards

The ghetto areas of West Kingston are true urban jungles. Acre upon acre of these festering 'yards' or tenements spread out west from the Parade, where much of the city's population growth in recent decades has been concentrated in areas such as Trench Town and Jones Town, and in sterile housing projects such as Majesty Pen and Tivoli Gardens. The latter were conceived as 'model communities' by ex-Premier Edward Seaga while he was minister of finance in the 1960s.

The region that is known as the 'West' was once a calm residential zone. Alas, during the strife of the 1970s, the middle classes debunked and moved to the safety of the suburbs. The poor masses filled the void and conditions rapidly deteriorated, drawing hoodlums, criminal-politicians, and other predatory elements, called 'yardies,' who recruited gang members from the mass of unemployed youths and carved out their turf in the low-income ghettoes. The situation was exacerbated by politicians such as Seaga, who shamelessly curried votes by patronizing the 'dons' who lorded over the violent gangs or 'posses.' They even provided arms to the gangs and inspired them to intimidate constituents who supported political opponents. Certain areas were said to 'eat only when their party is in power.' The ghettoes became divided politically in a sectarian battle for hearts and minds.

It's easy to tell which party rules behind the stockades. Up-front, no-nonsense wall murals act as territorial markers that tell the tale of a city at war with itself. Some of the worst ghettoes are in East Kingston, where affiliations have traditionally been with the JLP. While I was in Kingston in October 1994, a shooting spree left seven people dead; when I was there in March 1995, 12 people died in a blood-letting. Both incidents were blamed on the Shower posse (named because they 'showered' their victims with bullets) from Tivoli Gardens, a long-time JLP stronghold and the heart of Seaga's constituency. And during my visit in October 1998, four people died in riots sparked by the arrest of a Trench Town 'don.'

The ghettoes are no-go zones for out-of-towners (even people from neighboring areas dare not enter the 'opposition's' turf). If you want to visit, you *must* seek permission from a guide respected in the area and go with him – to do otherwise is dangerous business.

Charles Sts. The attractive whitewashed building was built in 1912 (its predecessor was toppled by the 1907 earthquake).

Today its congregation is tiny, the majority of Jews having left Jamaica during the heady years of the Manley era. But the place is worth a visit, not least for its fine mahogany staircase and gallery. Sand muffles your footsteps as you roam – a momento laid to remember the days of the Inquisition, when Jews fleeing persecution in Spain were forced to practice their faith in Jamaica in secret. It is usually locked, though the caretaker is often around on weekdays to open up on request for a small donation.

### East St & Around

East St runs parallel to Duke St and is two blocks east, sloping south (one-way for traffic) from National Heroes Park to Ocean Blvd.

**Institute of Jamaica** Toward the southern end of East St, the Institute of Jamaica (☎ 922-0620), 12 East St, is the nation's small-scale equivalent of the British Museum or the Smithsonian. It was established in 1879 for 'the encouragement of literature, science, and art.' The institute hosts permanent and visiting exhibitions, and features a lecture hall, plus the **National Library** with reading rooms and libraries full of Jamaican newspapers and texts dating back more than two centuries. The institute is open 9 am to 5 pm Monday to Thursday, and until 4 pm on Friday.

Also here is a **Natural History Museum**, accessed by a separate entrance around the corner on Tower St. The dowdy collection offers an array of stuffed birds and an herbarium displaying tropical cash crops, rounded out by an eclectic miscellany – musical instruments and Taino artifacts, for example – playing a historical note. It's open 9:30 am to 4:30 pm Monday to Thursday, and until 3:30 pm on Friday. Groups are admitted by appointment only (US$2 per person).

Other divisions are scattered throughout the city, including the **African Caribbean Institute** and the National Gallery (see National Gallery, earlier in this chapter), both at 12 Ocean Blvd.

**Other Downtown Sites** The huge building near the junction of North and East Sts is the **Gleaner Building**, home to Jamaica's leading newspaper. Seven blocks east, the imposing **Holy Trinity Cathedral** is the center of Roman Catholicism on the island. Admiring its dome and four minarets, visitors can immediately see the Spanish Moorish influence and understand why the Cathedral has been described as a 'reinforced concrete version of St Sophia,' the famous church in Istanbul. Its pipe organ is said to be unmatched in the Caribbean. A Jesuit boy's school, **St George's College**, stands next door.

## Marescaux Rd & Around

Marescaux Rd, north of National Heroes Park, is lined with lignum vitae, the national flower. The tree flowers in early summer, a mauve bloom that turns to bright yellow, attracting a species of white butterfly.

**National Heroes Park** The 74-acre oval-shaped site at the north end of East St was formerly the Kingston Race Course (the first horse race was run in 1816, the last in 1953). During the 19th century, a rivalry between 'east' and 'west' Kingston often erupted into 'wholesale organized fisticuffs' here. Today it is a forlorn, barren wasteland grazed by goats. The only bright notes are the flame trees that burst into bloom each spring.

At the park's southern end, **National Heroes Circle** contains a group of statues and memorials, most in dreary realism style. The tomb of Sir Alex Bustamante is a flat marble slab beneath an arch resembling the handle of a wicker basket. More interesting is the Memorial to 1865, commemorating the Morant Bay Rebellion with a rock on a pedestal flanked by bronze busts of Abraham Lincoln and a black slave with a sword.

Ex-Premier Norman Manley is also buried here. So, too, is Marcus Garvey, whose body was flown from England in 1964 and reinterred with state honors.

Note the bust of General Antonio Maceo, the Cuban nationalist hero who was given refuge in Jamaica following the failure of

## Jamaica's National Heroes

Jamaica has its equivalent of George Washington and Joan of Arc – individuals who, by force of character, spirit, and example, have been deemed worthy of special status as National Heroes, earning the honorific title, 'the Right Excellent.'

Jamaica has seven National Heroes:

**Paul Bogle** (unknown-1865) was an independent smallhold farmer and a black Baptist preacher. As a champion of the underclass, he led the march on Morant Bay in 1865 that spun out of control and became the 'Morant Bay Rebellion.' A bounty was placed on Bogle's head. He was captured by the Maroons and executed by the British. (See 'Morant Bay Rebellion' in the Blue Mountains & Southeast Coast chapter.)

**Alexander Bustamante** (1884-1977), a firebrand trade unionist and founder of the Jamaica Labour Party, championed independence and became the independent nation's first prime minister, 1962-1967. (See 'National Hero Busta' in the Negril & West Coast chapter.)

**Marcus Garvey** (1887-1940) is considered the father of 'black power' and was named Jamaica's first National Hero in 1980. He was born in St Ann's Bay, and in his youth became involved in movements to improve the lot of black people. He traveled abroad widely before founding the Universal Negro Improvement Association and devoting his lifetime to the cause of black nationalism. (See 'One God, One Aim, One Destiny' in the Ocho Rios & North Coast chapter.)

**George William Gordon** (1820-65), a mixed-race lawyer, assemblyman, and post-emancipation nationalist, was the son of a Scottish plantation owner and one of his slave mistresses. The 'free colored' was self-educated and rose to become a successful landowner and businessman and a powerful advocate of nationalism. He was elected to the Assembly, where he

the Cuban War of Independence (the bust is a gift from the Cuban government). The Simón Bolivar Monument, dedicated to the liberator of South America, stands in bronze outside the park, in front of the Ministry of Education. Bolivar survived an assassination attempt while in Jamaica, where he lived in exile for seven months.

**Wolmer's School** A venerable educational establishment, Wolmer's School was founded in 1729 at the bequest of a Swiss-German goldsmith. It has produced many notable figures.

**Mico Teachers College** The intriguing wooden colonial structures north of Wolmer's School house one of the oldest teacher-training colleges in the world: Mico Teachers College. The college was originally established by the Lady Mico Charity as a primary school in 1834 to educate ex-slaves following emancipation. The impressive main building dates from 1909.

Mico is the sole survivor of several Mico colleges founded throughout the West Indies. All were created with the income accrued from a £1000 bequest that, in 1670, Lady Mico's nephew chose to forgo rather than marry one of his six nieces. The dowry was thus invested, with a portion designated as ransom to free Christian slaves from the Barbary pirates. When piracy declined, the money, which had grown into a considerable sum, was used to create the Mico colleges.

Many distinguished Jamaicans were also trained here.

**Up Park Camp** 'The Camp,' midway down Camp Rd (which runs parallel to Marescaux

## Jamaica's National Heroes

was despised for championing the rights of the poor. As a Baptist minister, he ordained Paul Bogle as deacon. When Bogle led a march on Morant Bay courthouse that erupted into the Morant Bay Rebellion, political opponents seized the opportunity to brand Gordon responsible. He was arrested and taken to Morant Bay, where he was summarily tried and executed the same day. (See 'Morant Bay Rebellion' in the Blue Mountains & Southeast Coast chapter.)

**Norman Manley** (1893-1969) was a lawyer who founded the People's National Party, fought for political autonomy for Jamaica, and became the self-governing island's first prime minister prior to independence. (See Roxborough in the Mandeville section of the Central Highlands chapter.)

**Nanny** (dates unknown) was a legendary leader of the Windward Maroons in the 18th century. She was born and raised in the mountains (like most Maroons, she was of Ashanti origin) and was never enslaved. Nanny rose to become spiritual leader of the Maroons; folklore attributes her with magical powers. Little else is known about her. (See the Nanny Town section in the Port Antonio & Northeast Coast chapter.)

**Sam 'Daddy' Sharpe** (1801-32), a town slave named for his owner, was a deacon at the Burchell Baptist Church in Montego Bay. He was hanged by British authorities for his role in leading the 1831 slave rebellion that engulfed the western parishes. (See 'Preaching Resistance' in the Montego Bay & Northwest Coast chapter.)

Within a few years, several candidates are expected to be named National Heroes by the Jamaican Parliament. Among them are ex-prime minister Michael Manley, reggae superstar Bob Marley, and Olympic gold-medal winner Merlene Ottey, who would thus become the first living National Hero.

---

Rd) is the 200-acre headquarters of the Jamaica Defense Force (and formerly of the British army in Jamaica). The southern entrance is called Duppy Gate for the legend of a colonial officer whose ghost appears at night to inspect the guards.

Anyone interested in Jamaica's military history might pop inside the small **Jamaica Defense Force Museum** (☎ 926-8121), also called the Military Museum, in front of Up Park Camp. It displays uniforms, weapons, and medals of the West Indies Regiment and the Jamaica Infantry Militia that existed between 1602 and 1906. It's open by appointment.

**Gun Court** Immediately south of Up Park Camp is the Gun Court, whose tall barbed wire fences and guard towers have a conspicuous purpose: to keep dangerous criminals in. The Manley government established the high-profile prison in 1972 to house prisoners convicted of gun crimes. Prison conditions are extremely harsh and have been condemned by several human rights organizations, but it remains popular with the Jamaican public.

## UPTOWN
### Half Way Tree
This important neighborhood, road junction, and major bus terminal (and a bottleneck for traffic) was an important colonial-era crossroads village – St Andrew – on the road from Spanish Town to Liguanea and the Blue Mountains. Half Way Tree is named for a venerable silk cotton (kapok) tree that stood here until the 1870s and whose shaded base became the site of both a tavern and market. Today the spot is marked by a clock

tower erected in 1813 as a memorial to King Edward VII, whose bust sits on the south side of the tower.

Avoid lingering in and around Nelson Mandela Park, a small landscaped park on the northeast side of Half Way Tree. There is a taxi stand near the park's southeastern corner.

**St Andrew Parish Church** This brick church (☎ 926-6692), at the corner of Hagley Park Rd and Eastwood Park Rd, is popularly known as 'Half Way Tree Church.' It's thought that a church has been here since 1666. The original apparently toppled in the 1692 earthquake, and the foundations of the existing church were lain that year. The exterior is austere and unremarkable, but the stained-glass windows and organ are worth a peek inside. Services are held at 6:30 and 7:30 am Sunday, at 9 am Tuesday and Friday at 9 am, and at 6:30 am Wednesday.

## Hope Rd

Most of the sites of interest in Uptown are located along this road, which runs from Half Way Tree to Papine, at the foothills of the Blue Mountains.

**Devon House** The only site of any great appeal in New Kingston is Devon House, nestled in landscaped grounds on the west side of Hope Rd at its junction with Waterloo Rd. The beautiful ochre and white house was built in 1881 by George Stiebel, a Jamai-

can wheelwright who hit pay dirt in the gold mines of Venezuela. The millionaire rose to become the first black custos of St Andrew. His house decayed, but was restored after the government bought it in 1967 to house the National Gallery of Jamaica, which has since moved to its present location downtown.

Antique lovers will find it worthwhile to poke around inside. Note the trompe l'oeil of palms in the entrance foyer. Stiebel even incorporated a game room with whist and cribbage tables, a sewing room, and a gambling room discreetly tucked away in the attic.

The house is a favored spot for wedding photographs, and the tree-shaded lawns attract couples on weekends. Tourists flock to the courtyard behind Devon House, which is ringed by quality souvenir and craft shops, plus the I-Scream ice cream store, and Brick Oven Bakery, which has reactivated the old oven in the original kitchen. The former stables and carriage house today are home to two of Jamaica's more famous restaurants. (See Places to Eat, later in this chapter.)

Devon House (☎ 929-7029), 26 Hope Rd, is open 9:30 am to 5 pm Tuesday to Saturday. It costs US$6 to enter, including a guided tour.

**Jamaica House** Half a mile farther up Hope Rd on the left is a one-story structure faced by a columned portico and fronted by expansive lawns. Gladioli fringe the driveway and add a splash of color. Initially built in 1960 as the residence of the prime minister, the building today houses the prime minister's office. You are restricted to peering through the fence.

**King's House** Hidden amid trees behind Jamaica House is the official residence of the governor-general. Reopened to the public in 1995 after a lengthy restoration, it lies along a driveway that begins at the junction of E King's House Rd and Hope Rd.

King's House (☎ 927-6424) was initially the home of the Lord Bishop of Jamaica. The government purchased the grandiose home in 1872 to house the English governor. The original, however, was badly damaged in the 1907 earthquake. Today's visitors

Devon House

explore the remake, built in 1909 to a new design in reinforced concrete. The dining room contains two particularly impressive full-length portraits of King George III and Queen Charlotte by Sir Joshua Reynolds. The house sits in a 200-acre setting of park land, which includes a giant banyan tree that legend suggests is haunted by duppies.

You may never get to dine with royalty, but the governess hosts free afternoon teas as part of the Meet the People program. Contact the JTB (☎ 929-9200) for information and reservations. King's House is open 9 am to 5 pm, Monday to Friday, by appointment.

**Bob Marley Museum** The most visited site in Kingston is the reggae superstar's former home (☎ 927-9152, fax 978-2991) at 56 Hope Rd. An Ethiopian flag flutters above the gate of the red-brick manse that Marley turned into his Tuff Gong Recording Studios (the studios are now in southwest Kingston; see the Farther Afield section). One wonders if Marley would turn in his grave to see his beloved home now such a temple of commercialism.

Dominating the forecourt is a gaily colored statue of the musical legend; in his arms is a guitar, while a soccer ball and portrait of Haile Selassie rest at his feet. Some of the guides are deathly solemn, but the hourlong tour provides fascinating insights into Bob Marley's life, events from which are depicted on a six-panel mural *The Journey of Bob Marley Superstar*, painted on the inside of the compound wall.

His gold and platinum records (*Exodus*, 1977; *Uprising*, 1980; and *Legend*, 1984) are there on the walls, alongside Rastafarian religious cloaks, Marley's favorite denim stage shirt, and the Order of Merit presented by the Jamaican government. One room upstairs is decorated with media clippings about the superstar. Another contains a replica of Marley's original record shop (Wail'n Soul'm). And his simple bedroom has been retained as it was, with his star-shaped guitar by his bedside. During your visit, he'll be talking to you through hidden speakers.

HOLGER LEUE

Outside, the guide will point out the bullet holes that ripped through the rear wall of the house during an assassination attempt in 1976. Nearby is the tree beneath which Marley would smoke ganja and practice his guitar. The former recording studio out back has metamorphosed into an exhibition hall and theater, where the tour closes with a fascinating film of his final days.

The bamboo Queen of Sheba Restaurant in the forecourt can appease your hunger with dishes such as I-tal stew (US$5), brown stew chicken and fish (from US$5.75), and fruit juices.

The museum is open 9:30 am to 4:30 pm daily. Tours depart hourly except 1:30 pm (entrance costs US$10, children US$5, students US$8). The last tour is at 4 pm. No cameras or tape recorders are permitted.

### Vale Royal

The prime minister's official residence is at the apex of Lady Musgrave and Montrose Rds. The beautiful house was constructed in 1694, when it was known as Prospect Pen and owned by Sir Simon Taylor, said to have been the richest man in Jamaica. The government bought it in 1928.

The lookout tower on the roof was a common feature of the day, when merchants used spyglasses to keep watch on the movement of ships in Kingston Harbour.

# UPTOWN KINGSTON

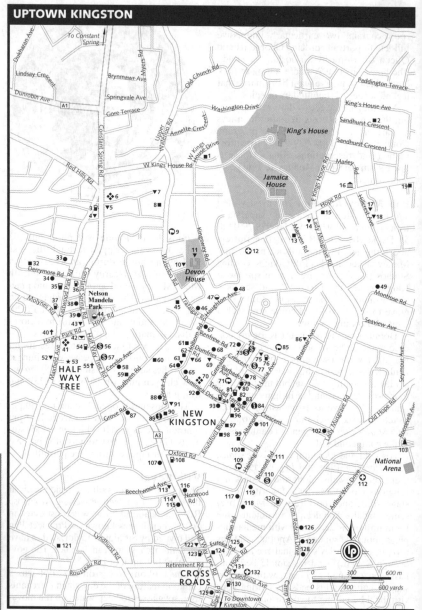

# UPTOWN KINGSTON

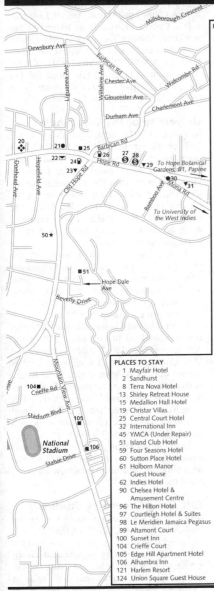

**PLACES TO EAT**
4 Taco Bell
5 McDonald's
7 Moonstruck Café,
   Galley's Pizzeria
8 El Dorado Room
10 The Grog Shoppe,
   Devonshire Restaurant,
   Mahogany Tree Bar
11 Devon House I-Scream,
   Brick Oven Bakery
14 Boston Jerk,
   Friends on the Deck
16 Queen of Sheba Restaurant
17 Raphael's
18 Café Bella
23 Baskin Robbins
29 McDonald's
31 Chilito's
32 International Inn
43 Tastee Pastries
52 Bombay Restaurant
62 Plantation Terrace
63 Akbar
66 Indies Pub & Grill
69 Garden City Restaurant
75 McDonald's
80 Burger King, Pizza Hut,
   Bullseye Steakhouse &
   Salad Bar
81 JamRock Sports Bar & Grill
86 Red Bones Blues Café
91 Chelsea Jerk Centre & Lounge
98 Pavilion, Port Royal,
   The Brasserie
102 Café Spartan
111 Carlos' Café
113 King's I-Tal Vegetarian
   Restaurant
114 New World Chinese
   Restaurant
122 Burger King
123 KFC
131 Doreen's Restaurant

**PLACES TO STAY**
1 Mayfair Hotel
2 Sandhurst
8 Terra Nova Hotel
13 Shirley Retreat House
15 Medallion Hall Hotel
19 Christar Villas
25 Central Court Hotel
32 International Inn
45 YMCA (Under Repair)
51 Island Club Hotel
59 Four Seasons Hotel
60 Sutton Place Hotel
61 Holborn Manor
   Guest House
62 Indies Hotel
90 Chelsea Hotel &
   Amusement Centre
96 The Hilton Hotel
97 Courtleigh Hotel & Suites
98 Le Meridien Jamaica Pegasus
99 Altamont Court
100 Sunset Inn
104 Crieffe Court
105 Edge Hill Apartment Hotel
106 Alhambra Inn
121 Harlem Resort
124 Union Square Guest House

**OTHER**
3 Gas Station
6 King's Plaza
9 German Embassy
11 Treasure House of
   Flowers & Art
12 Andrews Memorial Hospital
16 Bob Marley Museum
20 Sovereign Centre
21 Caribbean Art Gallery
22 Post Office
24 Gas Station
26 Gas Station
27 Scotiabank
28 National Commercial Bank
30 Ligueana Fabricare Centre
33 KMTR
34 Irie FM
35 Countryside Club
36 Gas Station
37 Gas Station
38 Odeon Cinema
39 Skateland Disco
40 St Andrews Parish Church
41 Half-Way Tree Plaza
42 Post Office
44 Taxis
46 Women's Crisis Centre
47 Limo Taxi Tours
48 Zanzibar
49 Vale Royal (Prime
   Minister's Residence)
50 Police Station
53 Police Station
54 Gas Station
55 Holy Cross RC Church
56 CIBC Bank
57 Scotiabank
58 Stuart's Travel Service
64 Sangster's Liqueurs Co.
65 New Kingston
   Drive-In Theater
67 JAMPRO
68 Chances
70 Lychee Garden,
   New Kingston
   Shopping Mall
71 Canadian Embassy, DHL
72 Island Car Rentals
73 Scotiabank
74 Citibank
76 Gas Station
77 CIBC Bank
78 Grace Kennedy Travel
79 Air Jamaica, Bookland
81 Asylum Disco
82 FedEx
83 Epiphany
84 JTB Office
85 British Embassy
87 Bolivar Art Gallery
88 Chelsea Galleries
89 Jamaica Information Service
92 BWIA International Airways
93 Ras Art & Craft
94 Gas Station
95 Wassi Art Pottery
96 Jonkanoo Lounge
97 Mingles
98 Gallery Pegasus
101 New Kingston Theater
102 Spartan Health Club
103 Celebrity Park,
   Bob Marley Statue
107 Cable & Wireless
108 Gas Station
109 US Embassy,
   Mutual Life Building
110 Scotiabank
112 Bustamante Hospital
   for Children
115 Gemini Club
116 FedEx
117 Cellular Centre
118 Palaise Royale
119 Avis
120 Gas Station
123 Gas Station
125 Carib Cinema
126 Jamaica Cultural Centre
127 Little Theater
128 Parish Library
129 Carib Cinema
130 Gas Station
132 Nuttall Memorial Hospital

**KINGSTON & ENVIRONS**

## National Stadium & Celebrity Park

There's a so-called Celebrity Park on the north side of the National Stadium (☎ 929-4970) on Arthur Wint Drive, although the only statue at present is the famous one of Bob Marley holding his guitar.

The stadium – venue for most of Jamaica's sporting events of importance – was built in 1962 to coincide with independence celebrations, and that year it hosted the Commonwealth Games. Adjoining it is the indoor National Arena, hosting smaller events.

## FARTHER AFIELD
## Hope Botanical Gardens

Anyone familiar with Kew Gardens in London may be disappointed in those at the uppermost end of Old Hope Rd. The 200-acre gardens, which contain the Caribbean's largest collection of botanical plants, still haven't recovered from the blow they suffered when Hurricane Gilbert roared through in 1988. Still, it's worth a browse.

The gardens date back to 1881, when the government established an experimental garden for indigo and sugar on the site of the former Hope Estate, which had been established by Richard Hope, an officer in Cromwell's army that invaded Jamaica in 1655. Part of the Hope Aqueduct, built in 1758 to supply the estate, is still in use. The original garden remains as an experimental crop station. This century has seen the addition of various elements of a botanical garden. The Ministry of Agriculture, which administers the gardens, maintains a research station and nursery, although the gardens have been in steady decline for some decades.

Among the attractions of the gardens are cycads, or 'sago palms,' from the antediluvian era. There's a cactus garden, sunken garden, forest garden, orchid house, greenhouses, a small aquarium, ornamental ponds, and a maze. The aviary is an excellent site for bird watching.

A basic children's amusement park called Coconut Park adjoins the gardens to the northeast and has rides; a small zoo has a motley display that includes monkeys, lions, and tropical birds.

The gardens are open 6 am to 6 pm daily February to April and September to December, and until 7 pm May to August. Entrance is free. Coconut Park is open 10 am to 6 pm weekends (US$1). The zoo is open 10 am to 5 pm daily and costs US$0.60. For zoo information call ☎ 927-1085. No cars are allowed in the main entrance off Old Hope Rd, but there's parking 400 yards farther east; turn left and follow the sign to Coconut Park.

## University of the West Indies

Kingston's UWI campus is worth a visit. It's built on the grounds of the former Mona sugar estate. The old **aqueduct** that bisects the campus once brought water from the Hope River to turn the old sugar works, which still stand at the northern end of the campus' circular street, Ring Rd. In the late 18th century the aqueduct also supplied water to the city. Goats, horses, and cattle graze the campus lawns.

Another legacy from plantation days is the chapel of limestone that stands foursquare near the campus entrance. Formerly a sugar warehouse at Gales Valley Estate in Trelawny near Montego Bay, it was dismantled stone by stone and reassembled in Mona.

Two of Jamaica's most famous **artworks** can be found on the outside walls of the Assembly Hall and the Caribbean Institute of Mass Communications. The elaborate murals are the work of Belgian artist Claude Rahir. Also of note is the metal bird by famous Jamaican sculptor Ronald Moody on the inner Ring Rd, opposite the Institute of Social and Economic Research. It represents *savacou*, a mythical Carib Indian bird of war.

The **Norman Manley Law School** contains a room dedicated to the ex-premier, replete with some of his office furniture and personal memorabilia.

## Tuff Gong Recording Studios

Bob Marley's son Ziggy Marley runs the studios (☎ 923-9383, 923-5814, fax 923-4657, tuffgong@cwjamaica.com) at 220 Marcus Garvey Drive in southwest Kingston. Drop-in visitors are welcome. Free tours are hosted, and you may bump into your favorite artist recording his or her future hit (entry to the

Inside Tuff Gong Studios

actual recording studio is at the discretion of the artist renting the studio at the time). A gift store (in the building to the rear) sells T-shirts, tapes, crafts, and a miscellany of Marley mementos, with discs spun by a colorful DJ, Selvyn.

## ACTIVITIES
### Golf
Golfers have two options. Constant Spring Golf Club (☎ 924-1610) is an 18-hole championship course at the foot of the mountains. The 6196-yard, par 70 course is short and noted for tight fairways and contoured greens. It boasts a swimming pool, bar, and tennis, squash, and badminton courts. Visitors can use the club facilities for US$20 daily. Six miles west of Kingston, Caymanas Golf Course (☎ 926-8144, 922-3386) is a 6844-yard, par 70, 18-hole course that features elevated tees and uphill shots to small, bunkered greens. There's a club house with clubs for rent, and a pool (see Spanish Town in the Spanish Town & South Coast chapter). It's in the hills north of Spanish Town Rd.

### Other Activities
Runners' and walkers' favorite spots include the Palisadoes and the Mona Reservoir, normally around sunrise and sunset. A pass for entry to the Mona Dam costs US$35 for one year from the National Water Commission, 4a Marescaux Rd, and grants access to a track and reservoir with waterfowl (the steep price pays for security, but one-time visitors may gain entry for a nominal day fee). You can also jog for free at the Police Officers Club on Hope Rd. If you're into social running, the Hash House Harriers meet at the Royal Jamaica Yacht Club at 5 pm each Friday (see the Palisadoes, later in this chapter).

Entry at the public Olympic-size pool at the National Stadium (☎ 929-4970), c/o Institute of Sports, costs US$1.

There are numerous gyms. The best by far is Spartan Health Club (☎ 927-7575), 9 Lady Musgrave Rd, superbly outfitted with modern equipment, a steam room, and aerobics room. Non-members are charged US$14 for use.

You can rent bicycles at any of the following shops:

Cycle Shop
  (☎ 926-6822) 79 Half Way Tree Rd
God Bless Cycle
  (☎ 937-4476) 176 Spanish Town Rd, Shop 11
LK Bicycle Centre
  (☎ 978-2814) 74 Lady Musgrave Rd
Mars Cycle Centre
  (☎ 977-5404) 122 Waltham Park Rd

## ORGANIZED TOURS

JUTA, Ltd (☎ 926-1537), 85 Knutsford Blvd, Kingston 5, has a 'Kingston Highlight Tour' and also offers customized guided tours. Galaxy Tours – at 81 Knutsford Blvd (☎ 968-8122) and 75 Red Hills Rd (☎ 931-0428, fax 925-6975) – runs a series of specialty city tours, ranging from cultural outings and shopping trips to 'Reggae the Night Away.' Pro Tours (☎ 978-6113), 7 Lady Musgrave Rd, has a Kingston art tour and 'Uptown' tour each Wednesday, Thursday, and Saturday.

Heritage Tours (☎ 938-2578) offers half-day tours of the city and environs for US$25 per person (based on four people), with guides well-versed in Kingston's history and culture. They'll pick up and drop at your hotel for free.

Island Car Rentals (☎ 926-8861, 929-5875, fax 929-6787) has a series of chauffeured tours, including a 'Bob Marley Tour' (US$43 per person), an historic and cultural tour of Kingston (US$43 to US$51 per person) or Port Royal (US$50), a 'Jamaica Heritage Tour' (US$51), and a 'Blue Mountain Tour' (US$64).

The Touring Society of Jamaica (☎ 975-7158, fax 975-3620, www.touringjamaica.com), c/o Island Outpost, PO Box 118, Ocho Rios, St Ann, offers some intriguing trips and excursions, mainly for Jamaican residents, but tourists, of course, are welcome. Want to visit the Cifuentes y Cia cigar factory where the Macanudo, Jamaica's finest cigar, is made? Or are you more interested in the nitty-gritty dancehall scene? No problem.

Other area tours are provided by the following companies:

Gemini Tours
  (☎ 968-2473 Kingston,
   ☎ 952-8202 Montego Bay)
  2 Eastwood Ave, Kingston 10
Infinity Tours
  (☎ 960-9290, fax 960-9301,
   infinity@infochan.com)
  12-14 Oxford Terrace, Kingston 5
Intimate Jamaica
  (☎ 960-3598, fax 960-3599,
   intimjam@infochan.com)
  12 Worthington Terrace, Kingston 5
Pleasure Vacation Tours
  (☎ 924-4140, fax 924-1756)
  1531 1/2 Constant Spring Rd, Kingston 8

## SPECIAL EVENTS

Kingston has a full calendar of annual festivals and events (also see the Blue Mountains & Southeast Coast chapter, for nearby events).

The highlight of the calendar is Carnival, a weeklong cultural and musical festival held over Easter each April and featuring soca on the waterfront, parades and floats, costumed bands, and the spectacular Road Parade. Each year it differs in theme and venue, but in 1998 was centered on the Cinema Two complex. Charter tour operators offer packages from the USA. Contact JTB offices worldwide.

See below for other major happenings.

### January

National Exhibition
  Goes all month (see December listings)
Jamaica School of Dance Concert Season
  (☎ 926-6129, 922-5988) at the Little Theater
  features creative, Caribbean-themed dancing
LTM Pantomime
  Runs through April (see December listings)

### February

Bob Marley Birthday Bash
  (☎ 927-9152) in early February brings reggae
  fans to the Bob Marley Museum
United Way Jazz Concert
  (☎ 929-4302) benefits the organization and
  features regional and international jazz artists.
  It is held mid-month at the Wyndham Hotel.
  Contact the Mutual Life Gallery
UWI Carnival
  (☎ 927-1660) lasts a week and is staged by university students from throughout the Caribbean

Shell/Sandals Limited Overs Cricket Competition brings together the national teams of Jamaica, Barbados, and Trinidad and Tobago at Sabina Park

Carib Cement International Marathon
(☎ 928-6231) attracts top national and international athletes who run the streets of Kingston and along the Palisadoes to Port Royal. Entry is US$3

## March

JAMI (Jamaica Music Industry) Awards
(☎ 960-1320) feature guest performers from reggae to classical. Contact Pulse Investments, Ltd

Jamaica Orchid Society Spring Show
a three-day flower show, is held in UWI's Assembly Hall

Miss Universe Jamaica Beauty Pageant
determines who represents the island in the Miss Universe contest

## April

Devon House Craft Fair
(☎ 929-7029) lays out arts and crafts displays, plus Jamaican foods, at Devon House in mid-April

Cable & Wireless Test Cricket
is an international cricket match at Sabina Park featuring the West Indies team

## May

Jamaica Horticultural Society Show
in the National Arena. Contact JTB offices

All-Jamaica Tennis Championships
(☎ 929-5878) is a series hosted late May through mid-July at the Eric Bell Tennis Complex

## July

National Dance Theater Company's Season of Dance
(☎ 926-6129) is a summerlong season of performances

Mello-Go-Round
(☎ 926-5726) is a presentation of various performing arts held at either the National Arena or Randy Williams Entertainment Centre

## August

Independence Day Festival & Street Parade
(☎ 926-5726) features the National Festival Song Competition (held at the National Arena), the Gospel Song Festival (at the Randy Williams Entertainment Centre), and a traditional Jonkanoo street parade, live music, and modern dances

## September

Miss Jamaica World Beauty Pageant
(☎ 927-7575) is a gala crowning pageant and a social highlight in the Kingstonian calendar. The winner represents Jamaica in the Miss World contest. It's sponsored by the Spartan Health Club

## October

Oktoberfest
(☎ 927-6408) celebrates German heritage with oom-pah-pah music, dancing, and, of course, a beer drinking contest. Contact the Jamaica German Society

Foska Fun Run
in late October is a 12K road race from Manor Park Plaza to the Police Officers Club on Hope Rd, including a 2K 'Kiddies & Family Fun Run'

Shell/Sandals Cricket Competition
(☎ 967-0322) held at Sabina Park (as well as in Montego Bay) features regional teams. Contact the Jamaica Cricket Association

Caribbean Heritagefest
(☎ 926-5726) is a two-day event in mid-October at the Jamworld Entertainment Complex, Portmore, outside Kingston. It features food and crafts fairs, folk theater, traditional dance and drumming, and musical performances

## December

Devon House Christmas Fair
(☎ 929-7029) promotes a colorful display of arts, crafts, and culinary delights at the Devon House

LTM Pantomime
(☎ 926-6129) is a witty satire with a gala opening on Boxing Day (December 26) at the Ward Theater, and runs through January. (It continues through April at the Little Theater)

National Exhibition
(☎ 922-1561) is where Jamaica's finest artists showcase their work December to February at the National Gallery

## PLACES TO STAY

Kingston has about 2000 hotel rooms, most in small, locally owned properties. The classier hotels – all located in New Kingston – cater mostly to business travelers. You'll find many guest houses in the classified advertising sections of local newspapers. Standards vary widely. Several fine hotels are located in the hills overlooking Kingston and offer the advantage of cooler temperatures and grand vistas (see the North of Kingston section, later in this chapter).

Budget properties are mostly dingy. The majority of budget hotels are uptown on the south side of New Kingston; some are on the fringe of trouble-filled districts.

Kingston hotel rates are usually the same year-round. All rates quoted are for nonresidents (most hotels offer lower rates for Jamaican citizens).

## Places to Stay – Budget

The much-troubled **YMCA** at the junction of Hope and Trafalgar Rds was to be rebuilt and may have reopened by the time you read this. It has burned down twice in recent years and has lain idle for a long time, but at press time was being rebuilt by the Jamaica Social Investment Fund (for updates, call ☎ 926-3414 or 888-991-2356).

*Harlem Resort* (☎ 926-7872, 2 Walker Ave, Kingston 5) lies on the northern edge of Trench Town. Some of the 25 rooms have private bath and TV and cost US$16. All have fans. Cold water only. There's a tiny restaurant.

*Hollywood Villa* (☎ 969-1518, 7 W Lyndale Close, Kingston 20) has five basic rooms, each with fan and TV; US$17 includes breakfast and cold water. The owners will do your laundry. In the same price range is *Steve's Guest House* (☎ 922-1691, 1 Connolley Ave). The 17 carpeted rooms have private bath (some with hot water), fans, and TV. Rooms with TV and waterbed cost US$20.

Another option is the *Chelsea Hotel & Amusement Centre* (☎ 926-5803, fax 929-4746, 5 Chelsea Ave), next to Chelsea Jerk Centre. Older rooms are dark and basic (US$20, or US$25 with TV); modern rooms for US$45 in a new block are slightly better, but still overpriced. All feature air-con and hot water. A fifth night is free. The owners claim not to offer 'short time,' but it has a reputation as a 'love' motel. There are exceptions: a sign reads, 'No room will be rented to two men!'

A very pleasant hostess, Dorothy Hansen, runs *Artland Guest House* (☎ 923-4647, 111 Waltham Park Rd) on the corner of Molynes Rd, Kingston 11. She offers 28 modestly furnished rooms in two buildings; the more expensive rooms have air-con and TV and cost US$20 to US$28.50, and all rooms have private bath (cold water only). There's a lounge plus small bar and restaurant. One mile east is the *International Inn* (☎ 929-4437, 14 Derrymore Rd, Kingston 10), with nine basic cubicle-type rooms for US$21 to US$26 all offering air-con and private bath with cold water. It has a popular restaurant and bar.

The *Central Court Hotel* (☎ 929-1026, 47 Old Hope Rd, Kingston 5), near the junction of Old Hope and Hope Rds, has 32 air-conditioned rooms and one and two-bedroom suites with fans, TV, and telephone, plus hot water. It has a seafood restaurant. Room rates begin at US$22 (US$2 more for TVs).

At the southern end of Half Way Tree Rd is *Union Square Guest House* (☎ 929-9264, 40 Union Square, Cross Roads, Kingston 5). It has 15 rooms with color TVs and hot water. Rates range from US$21 with fans to US$30 with air-con.

Pickings are virtually nonexistent downtown. I've seen inside a few guest houses on the edge of downtown, but all were hovels.

## Places to Stay – Mid-Range

**New Kingston** New Kingston has some reasonable options. *Holborn Manor Guest House* (☎ 926-0296, 3 Holborn Rd) has 12 rooms with fans and phones but modest, dowdy furnishings and cold water only. Rooms with TV cost US$32/35 single/double (including breakfast). You'll pay US$5 less without TV, but there's a TV lounge where you can sink into crimson, crushed-velvet sofas.

Next door is the *Indies Hotel* (☎ 926-2952, fax 926-2879, 5 Holborn Rd, Kingston 10). It, too, has utility furniture, plus carpets and bright floral spreads in its 15 spacious rooms (most with air-con; all with TV and telephone) – and there's hot water here. Year-round rates are US$35 to US$55 single, US$57 to US$61 double. A bar and restaurant is in the courtyard. Take an upstairs room for sunlight.

A popular option with locals is the *Mayfair Hotel* (☎ 926-1610, fax 926-7741, W

*Kings House Drive, Kingston 10)*, behind Devon House. The columned portico entrance hints at grandeur within, but the 32 air-conditioned rooms – which cost US$40 to US$50 single, US$50 to US$60 double, US$66 to US$110 suites – are fairly basic, clean, and well lit, with utility furniture, TVs and telephones, and a pink motif. Its best feature is the views toward the Blue Mountains. A buffet is hosted poolside on Wednesday and Saturday nights.

One of my favorite options in this price bracket is the **Sandhurst** (☎ 927-8244, 70 *Sandhurst Crescent, Kingston 6)*, in a quiet residential neighborhood in Liguanea. It verges on the eccentric: note the atmospheric lounge with dark hardwood walls and South American tapestries. Nat King Cole was playing on the PA when I was there. The 43 spotlessly kept pale-blue rooms with their black-and-white-tile floors, utility furniture, and plastic flowers conjure up images of Miami during the 1960s. The rooms are somewhat gloomy and stuffy. Some have TV and telephone and private veranda. Rooms cost US$44 to US$46 single, US$48 to US$54 double, or US$65 double with air-con. A dining terrace has views toward the Blue Mountains and over a pool.

The **Shirley Retreat House** (☎ 927-9208, 7 *Maeven Rd, Kingston 10)* is operated by the United Church of Jamaica and has four simply furnished, well-lit rooms with hardwood floors, pleasant fabrics, fans, and private bath with hot water. There's a TV in the lounge (two rooms have small TVs, and one has air-con). Rates are US$45/55 single/double including continental breakfast. Meals are cooked on request.

Nearby is the pleasant **Medallion Hall Hotel** (☎ 927-5721, fax 978-2060, 53 *Hope Rd, Kingston 8)*, down the road from the Bob Marley Museum. It has 14 rooms with adequate furnishing and private bath for US$50/60. There's a modest restaurant and English pub.

The **Sunset Inn** (☎ 929-7283, fax 968-5185, *1A Altamont Crescent, Kingston 5)* offers an advantageous location in the heart of New Kingston. Alas, the 11 rooms are dowdy with little light, though large bathrooms make

amends. Studios (small, with no kitchenette) cost US$53; one-bedroom units with kitchenette are US$57 to US$62. All have TVs, telephones, and fans. Take an upper-story room to catch the breeze.

Another reasonable option is **Sutton Place Hotel** (☎ 926-1207, fax 926-8443, 11 *Ruthven Rd, Kingston 10)*. The contemporary design features unusual classical touches (pediments, octagonal columns, and Mediterranean window grills), but the hotel is soulless. The 160 modest-size, air-conditioned rooms (US$68 single or double, year-round) have cheerful tropical fabrics, TVs, and telephones. A small pool and an unexciting restaurant and bar are in the grounds. It also has two-bedroom apartments with kitchens for US$88.

Boasting contemporary furnishings, **Altamont Court** (☎ 929-4497, fax 929-2118, 1 *Altamont Crescent, Kingston 5)* is an attractive alternative with lush foliage and 55 modern, clean, air-conditioned one-bedroom studios for US$90 and suites for US$120, each with telephone and satellite TV. Facilities include an attractive restaurant and a small pool with bar.

**Farther Afield** *Cozy Heights* (☎ 969-5341, *19A Stilwell Rd, Kingston 8)* offers six rooms for US$30 with fans and private bath with hot water. There's a dining room, small pool, and a TV in the lounge.

The **Abahati Hotel** (☎/fax 924-2082, 7 *Grosvenor Terrace, Kingston 8)* is in a reclusive setting in a quiet, upscale neighborhood in Constant Spring, at the base of Stony Hill. It offers a cool location at 600 feet elevation. The owners were half-heartedly refurbishing the 1950s-style Miami hotel. The 12 rooms – which cost US$30 to US$50 – are carpeted and clean, with lots of light but tired furniture. Some have air-con. Spacious gardens and a pool offer a chance to relax. The hotel's highlight is a pleasing restaurant – Pearl's Café.

Fitness devotees should check into the **Olympia Crown Hotel** (☎ 923-5269, fax 901-6688, 53 *Molynes Rd, Kingston 10)*, 100 yards east of the Four Roads junction in northwest Kingston. This modern, motel-style property has 90 rooms for US$34 to US$43 with fan, US$52 with air-con and cable TV. There's a large-screen TV in the lobby, plus a fully equipped fitness center with steam room and massage, tennis courts, and even a jogging track and the Memories Disco.

*Crieffe Court* (☎ 927-8033, fax 978-8382, 10 Crieffe Rd, crieffe@cwjamaica.com) is a well-kept hotel run by a super friendly and helpful man named Ron. There's nothing inspirational in the basic decor, but the 20-room hotel is spotless and the twin-bedroom rooms, costing US$40, are spacious. Unfortunately, they're also dark (the heavy window screens keep out the light). Ron also has studios with kitchens from US$52. All rooms have fans, TVs, and hot water; upstairs rooms have a balcony. All have double beds. Potted plants abound, and the small restaurant has a tree growing through the floor.

In the foothills on the northwest edge of town is *Springburn House* (☎ 969-6850, 1 Springburn Ave, Kingston 19), in a 1950s-style house behind Meadowbrook High School, with 15 rooms, two with shared bath. There's hot water and all rooms have air-con, TV, and telephone, but the decor is dated. Rates are US$50/60 single/double.

*Elmundo's Guest House* (☎ 931-0795, 66 Mannings Hill Rd, Kingston 8) is similarly priced.

An option for those wishing their own catering facilities is the *Edge Hill Apartment Hotel* (☎ 978-1720, fax 978-0536, 198 Mountain View Ave, Kingston 6). You'll pay US$68 for studio apartments, with kitchenette, that sleep up to three people. The rooms are uninspired and overpriced, and are modestly furnished with utility furniture. But they're clean and feature carpets, two double beds, TV, telephone, and ceiling fan. Edge Hill has a seafood restaurant and rooftop lounge.

## Places to Stay – Top End

**New Kingston** Self-catering apartments are a popular option for Jamaicans. Pick of the litter is *Christar Villas* (☎ 978-3933, fax 978-8068, 99a Hope Rd, Kingston 6). It's handily situated in Liguanea, just below the Sovereign Centre and just above the Bob Marley Museum. You can choose from modern studio apartments for US$88 and one and two-bedroom suites for US$70 to US$140. Rates include tax and free airport transfer. Upper-story suites tend to get hot (suites have air-con in one bedroom and ceiling fans in the others), but are spacious, pleasantly furnished with deep-cushioned chairs, and have a full kitchen and comfy beds. You can always cool off in the pool, and there's a self-service laundry, restaurant, and a gym. Rooms have satellite TVs but no phones.

The least glitzy hotel is a venerable English-style, German-run hotel, the *Four Seasons* (☎ 926-8805, 800-526-2422, fax 929-5964, 18 Ruthven Rd, Kingston 10, www.hotelfourseasonsja.com). (It is not part of the international Four Seasons chain.) The original Edwardian home exudes an aged European ambience with its mahogany wall panels and doors, gilt chandeliers, and French curtains. The hotel is comprised of four separate buildings with 76 air-conditioned rooms, all with private bath. Rooms in the original house, though modest, are spacious, lofty, airy, and light, with old prints on the walls. Some have half-canopy beds and mahogany furniture. Some have small bathrooms with showers only; others are larger. Rooms in the garden units are unappealing, with knocked-about utility furniture and a dowdy atmosphere, though a renovation was planned for 1999. A new 40-room block centered on a swimming pool and bar to the rear offers a more amenable, resort-style ambience, plus direct-dial phones, in-room safe, and air-con (upstairs rooms have raised wooden roofs). Telephones and TVs are standard. Rates year-round (single or double) range from US$76 to US$115 (business discounts are offered for longer stays).

Two upscale highrise hotels dominate the New Kingston skyline. The first is the *Hilton Hotel* (☎ 926-5430, 800-445-8667 in North America, 0845-7581-595 in the UK, fax 929-7439, 77 Knutsford Blvd, Kingston 5), formerly the Wyndham, in the midst of the financial and diplomatic center. The Hilton is strongly oriented toward the business traveler, and boasts contemporary architecture and furnishings and a full complement of facilities. It has 300 rooms, including 14 suites. The spacious rooms are elegantly furnished and have a small work desk, direct-dial telephones, and cable TV. Other features include a fitness center, boutique, two tennis courts, 16,000 sq feet of meeting space, and the Jonkanoo Lounge for night owls.

Nearby is the **Courtleigh Hotel & Suites** (☎ 929-9000, fax 926-7744, 85 Knutsford Blvd, courtleigh@cwjamaica.com), another splendid contemporary option that is a rebirth of the venerable, now defunct Courtleigh Hotel on Trafalgar Rd. This attractive property has deluxe rooms and one-bedroom suites featuring four-poster beds and tasteful mahogany furnishings, plus cable TV, direct-dial telephones, hair-dryers, work desk, and in-room data-ports for Internet access. The building and 40 rooms are handicap accessible. Suites have kitchenettes. In addition, there's a state-of-the-art business center, a respected restaurant, and the renowned Mingles Pub, plus pool bar, small gym, and a coin-operated laundry. Rates are US$115 deluxe, US$190 one-bedroom suite, and include continental breakfast. Two-bedroom suites are available.

The intimate, all-suite **Terra Nova Hotel** (☎ 926-2211, 926-9334, 800-526-2422 in North America, fax 929-4933, 17 Waterloo Rd, Kingston 10, www.cariboutpost.com/terra_nova) has among the most beautiful and sophisticated rooms in town. Though the colonial mansion was built in 1924 (as a wedding gift), the 35 spacious, newly refurbished junior suites – US$165 single or double (US$25 additional person), including taxes and service charge, plus breakfast – in three two-story wings have a contemporary feel, with evocative Edwardian decor in deep maroons and dark greens. King-size beds and cable TV are standard. And thumbs up for the marbled bathrooms. Try to get an upper-story room. The lounge is an Old World contrast, with 1930s English floral prints and lots of green silks. The El Dorado dining room is one of the most elegant eateries in town, plus there's a patio restaurant and La Fresca poolside bar and grill. The hotel is a 15-minute walk from the business district.

The luxurious, 17-story **Le Meridien Jamaica Pegasus** (☎ 926-3690, fax 929-5855, 81 Knutsford Blvd, www.meridienjamaica.com; ☎ 800-543-4300 in North America; ☎ 0800-317006 in the UK; ☎ 2-262-4940 in Australia) has 350 air-conditioned rooms, including 13 suites and three luxury suites. It even has 'female business traveler rooms' and nonsmoking floors. It also offers a panoply of facilities and a selection of restaurants, including the very elegant Pavilion for international dishes. It has a slight edge over the Hilton with its full-service business center and the Knutsford Club – a more exclusive enclave of rooms and suites catering to businessfolk. Rates are US$180 single, US$190 double (US$15 extra in the Knutsford Club), and US$275 to US$570 for suites.

**Farther Afield** The **Alhambra Inn** (☎ 978-9072, fax 978-9074, 1 Tucker Ave, alhambra@cwjamaica.com) is an attractive, two-story property with 20 air-conditioned rooms in Spanish style with red-tile, terra-cotta floors, heavy woodwork, and wrought-iron. It's designed to lure convention business and offers gracious furnishings, cable TV, telephones, and spacious bathrooms. Upstairs rooms have lofty ceilings and king-size beds. Rates are US$75 single, US$85 double including taxes. Facilities include a restaurant, two bars, and a pool in the courtyard.

The **Island Club Hotel** (☎ 978-3915, 800-554-735 in the USA, fax 978-3914, 1 Hopedale Ave, Kingston 6), perched at the base of Beverly Hills, was looking severely unkempt at this writing and is probably on its last legs. Its higgledy-piggledy, pink-painted units are offset one atop the other like disarranged building blocks tumbling down the exposed limestone cliff. The red-brick pathways are steep, and there are lots of steps. The air-conditioned rooms are very airy, with lots of windows, lace curtains, and hardwoods. Features include telephones and TVs, and fax machines and computers are available upon request. A tiny fitness center was locked, and the small pool looked more fitting for reptilian reproduction when I last called by. Rooms cost US$76 (US$20 additional person, including tax).

The ultra-modern and gracious *Crowne Plaza* (☎ 925-7676, 800-618-6534, fax 925-5757, 211A Constant Spring Rd), formerly the Forte Belle Suites, is one of the more luxurious of Kingston's hotels, located in the hills of the Manor Park suburb. The 57 one-bedroom and 20 two-bedroom suites (all with minibar, cable TV, mini-safe, iron and ironing board, kitchens, and balconies) feature panoramic views and autumnal colors. The top floor has a more contemporary vogue. 'Super suites' are huge and boast four-poster beds. It's clearly aimed at business travelers; 'smart' work desks, for example, feature Internet linkage in all rooms. It's decorated in an elegant, modern take on the Edwardian style, and there's a full business center and limousine transfer service. Other highlights include a gym, pool, jogging trail, and tennis court, plus a piano bar, and award-winning restaurant. Rates begin at US$99.

## PLACES TO EAT

Kingston has more fine restaurants than you can shake a stick at, plus a multitude of fast food joints and roadside snack stalls.

### Jamaican

**Downtown** The *Ocean Restaurant (8 Ocean Blvd)*, facing the harbor at the base of Ocean Towers, serves inexpensive Jamaican fare, including goat, fish, and chicken dishes. For steamed fish, festival, and other Jamaican fare try *Genise's Restaurant* on Mark Lane.

You'll find many others as you wander about downtown.

**Uptown** The *Chelsea Jerk Centre & Lounge* (☎ 926-6322, 7 Chelsea Ave), 100 yards east of Half Way Tree Rd, is *the* place for jerk. Mouth-searing jerk pork and chicken dishes cost about US$3. Also consider *Doreen's Restaurant* at the junction of Old Hope Rd and Caledonia Ave; *Cleo's* on Kingsway Ave, off Hope Rd; and *Boston Jerk* at the corner of Hope and Lady Musgrave Rds. You'll also find plenty of jerk stands scattered along Red Hills Rd. You can smell the spice from afar.

The *Grog Shoppe* (☎ 968-2098), on the grounds of Devon House, serves ackee crepes, baked crab backs, roast suckling pig with rice and peas, as well as more recherché nouvelle Jamaican dishes for upwards of US$6. You can dine alfresco beneath a kapok tree on the patio or in the old stable. There's live jazz on Tuesday. The *Devonshire Restaurant* (☎ 929-7046) at Devon House, serves continental dishes with Jamaican accents. It has a dress code and is closed on weekends. Reservations are advised. The *Mayfair Hotel* has a traditional Sunday brunch.

The *Indies Pub & Grill* (☎ 920-5913), opposite the Indies Hotel on Holborn Rd, and *Pollyanna's* (☎ 927-9575), on Stanton Terrace, are both popular. The latter also has Chinese specialties. Indies has pizzas (US$7), burgers (US$2), fish-and-chips, and Jamaican dishes. You can dine outside or in the air-conditioned lounge, which resembles a traditional English pub.

The *Hot Pot* (☎ 929-3906, 2 Altamont Crescent) is a Kingstonian favorite, offering true Jamaican food, such as ox-tail soup.

Chef Patrick Anderson at *Pearl's Café* (☎ 924-2082, 7 Grosvenor Terrace, Kingston 8), in the Abahati Hotel, has won awards for his nouvelle Jamaican cuisine, such as shrimp with curry (US$12).

Favored for *really* top-notch cuisine is *Red Bones Blues Café* (☎ 978-6091, 21 Braemar Ave), where imaginative cuisines such as drunken codfish in avocado halves, and chicken stuffed with cream cheese and herbs, are served in two dining rooms showcasing handworked walls and trompe l'oeil ceilings: one is 'light and lunchtime airy,' the other 'night-time romantic.' Local food artist Norman Shirley has teamed up with Jamaica's foremost architect, Evon Williams, and the artist Zoda, to produce this gem. It's beloved of Kingston's social elite.

**Farther Afield** Several restaurants are good enough to lure Kingstonians a bit out of their way, notably *Strawberry Hill* and *Blue Mountain Taverna* (see the Blue Mountains & Southeast Coast chapter); plus *Ivor* (see the North of Kingston section, later in this chapter).

## Fast Food

McDonald's and the like have made a big imprint on Kingston in recent years. The major shopping centers have fast-food outlets. Some, such as Sovereign Centre, have food courts – whole floors that are dedicated to fast-food outlets.

**Downtown** *Burger King* is at the corner of Harbour and Duke Sts, and *Kentucky Fried Chicken* is at the corner of Port Royal and King Sts.

*Patty King*, at the corner of Harbour and Duke Sts, charges less than US$1 for patties and has a daily special. You can also buy filling and savory patties for less than US$1 at *Luv n Oven Patties* (22 King St). *Taste Patties* is on Orange St, one block south of the Parade. And *Mother's* has several outlets and also sells meat patties and burgers.

**Uptown** *McDonald's* has several outlets, including on Constant Spring Rd just south of King's Plaza, which contains a *Taco Bell*.

Lots of places sell patties for less than US$1. Try *Brick Oven Bakery* (☎ 968-2153), behind Devon House.

For finger-licking ribs, head to *Rib Kage* (☎ 905-1858, 149 Constant Spring Rd). It's by far the best spot for down-to-earth barbecued dining.

The widest menu is offered at *JamRock Express*, next to the JamRock Sports Bar & Grill on Knutsford Blvd. This food-to-go outlet rounds out its salads and pastrami, corned beef sandwiches, and the like with croissants, bagels, and a great range of desserts.

## I-tal & Health Food

Uptown, try *King's I-tal Vegetarian Restaurant* (☎ 929-1921, 16 Slipe Rd), south of the junction of Oxford St and Half Way Tree Rd. It's a favorite of reggae stars, attested by signed photographs on the walls. It serves ackee stew, and even tofu, as well as veggie patties and natural juices. It's upstairs, a block north of the New World Chinese Restaurant.

Another good, inexpensive place is *Emperial Kish-Inn* (2 Hillview Ave), off East-wood Park Rd, with homemade desserts and spicy savories such as soy mince.

*Café Spartan* (☎ 927-7575, 9 Lady Musgrave Rd), in the Spartan Health Club, offers pumpkin soup, stew peas, chicken and pineapple salad, and tuna salads for US$1.50 to US$6. *Lyn's Vegetarian Restaurant* (7 Tangerine Place) has similar fare at similar prices.

Also try *Minnie's Ethiopian Herbal Health Food* (☎ 927-9207, 170 Old Hope Rd). Minnie is Mignon Phillips, Bob Marley's former personal cook. She creates mouth-watering stews, dumplings, fried fish and festival, and vegetarian I-tal.

*Natural Vitamins* is a health food store in the Sovereign Centre.

## Continental

**Downtown** The best is the *Bench & Bar Restaurant* (☎ 967-4443) at the corner of Port Royal and Duke Sts, across from the Scotia Centre. It's favored by office workers for breakfast and lunch; the fare includes sandwiches, ratatouille, chicken creole, lasagna, steaks, kebabs, prawn cocktail, seafood, and daily specials (US$5.75). It's open 7 am to 5 pm weekdays (closed on weekends). The place is run by Malcolm and Ilean McInnes, two gracious hosts (and gourmands to boot) who also run the acclaimed Blue Mountain Taverna, in Mavis Bank (see the Blue Mountains & Southeast Coast chapter).

**Uptown** The regal *El Dorado Room* (☎ 221-9334), in the Terra Nova Hotel, sets a standard for upscale dining. The European menu has hints of the Caribbean, as well as steadfast Jamaican favorites such as pepperpot soup and grilled snapper. Bring a sweater against the frigid air-conditioning. The hotel also has a less expensive outdoor restaurant, favored by the Kingstonian business elite. It serves continental fare at high prices, though the chicken with guava sauce (US$15) is recommended. There's a daily salad bar. It also hosts the annual Heritage Week Food Festival in mid-October with cuisines representing a different element of Jamaica's cultural potpourri highlighted each day.

## Chinese

**Downtown** Try the *New Peking Restaurant* on Church St, *Orient Express* (*135 Harbour St*); or the slightly more upscale *Metropolitan Restaurant* on Church St, one block north of Barry St.

**Uptown** An inexpensive option is the popular *Lychee Garden* (☎ *929-8619, 30 Dominica Drive)*, upstairs in the New Kingston Shopping Mall. Even cheaper options include *New World Chinese Restaurant* (☎ *926-5836)* on Half Way Tree Rd, *Hong Kong* (☎ *920-9799)* at 7th Avenue Plaza, and *1-2-3 Fast Food* at the junction of Hope and Lady Musgrave Rds.

Despite stiff prices, the *Jade Garden* (☎ *978-3476, 106 Hope Rd)* in the Sovereign Centre is popular and gets full on weekends. A highlight is the huge aquarium. Don't expect to eat for much less than US$25 a head.

## Indian

The Indian legacy is alive and well in Kingston. The best restaurant is *Akbar* (☎ *926-3480, 11 Holborn Rd)*. The splendid decor is primarily warm ochers and pea-green, and fabrics, paintings, and other touches evocative of Mughal style are enhanced by music. The reasonably priced menu is huge and includes tandooris and vegetarian dishes, with appetizers for US$1 to US$11 and entrees from US$8 to US$21. The food is excellent. There's an outside terrace. It's open noon to 4 pm and 6 to 11 pm daily, and offers a buffet lunch special for US$14.

## Other Cuisines

One of the best spots is the *Moonstruck Café* (☎ *968-4811, 21 Central Ave)*, formerly the Café Central, hidden in a cul-de-sac behind the Terra Nova Hotel at the top end of Central Ave. It serves Italian fare such as bruschetta (US$5.50) and pastas (from US$13), plus seafood such as spicy blackened snapper (US$17), and fried calamari (US$5.70). Seafood specials are served Friday night. For pizza you can't beat *Galley's Pizzeria*, above the Moonstruck Café. Gourmet veggie pizzas cost US$10 (6 inches) and

US$17 (12 inches). There are even smoked salmon and pesto pizzas.

In similar vogue is *Carlos' Café* (☎ *926-4186, 22 Belmont Rd)*, a trendy bar that serves stuffed crab backs (US$7.50), pastas, surf-n-turf, and – on Mondays – real Alaskan king crab.

For seafood head to *Fish Place* (*136 Constant Spring Rd)*, known for its spicy conch soup, superb steamed fish, and scallop and lobster dishes, most in the US$15 range. *Heather's Garden Restaurant* (☎ *960-7739, 9 Haining Rd)* is also known for its tasty, moderately priced seafood.

*Bullseye Steakhouse & Salad Bar*, above Kenny Rogers Bar on Knutsford Blvd, has a salad bar from US$6, plus burgers, steaks, and fish-and-chips (US$10).

Seeking Mexican? Head to *Chilito's*, a modishly trendy spot on Hope Rd, 100m above the junction with Mona Rd.

Two sisters run the splendid *Café Bella* (☎ *978-5002, 19 Hillcrest Ave)*, an acclaimed bistro serving Mediterranean fare. Try the bruschetta for a starter. For Italian meals, the cognoscenti head to *Raphael's* (☎ *978-1279, 7 Hillcrest Ave)*, where moderately priced pasta, veal, and seafood dishes are served alfresco under a spreading lignum vitae tree.

## Cafés & Ice Cream

A visit to *Devon House I-Scream* (☎ *929-7086)*, the popular ice-cream shop behind Devon House, will set you back US$2 for a two-scoop cup. Also try *Newbury Shakes n Cones* at Mary Brown's Corner offering exactly that, made of Jamaican fruits.

## Groceries

There's no shortage of supermarkets. Try any of the major shopping malls. For produce, head to Papine market at the top end of Hope Rd, or the market on Constant Spring Rd.

## ENTERTAINMENT

Everywhere else on the island the nightlife is touristy; in Kingston it's not. You won't find limbo or fire-eaters here. Instead, you can savor top-notch discos, ballet, classical music, theater, and down-to-earth reggae concerts performed for locals, not tourists. Brian 'Ribbie' Chung and Chris 'Gypsy' Cargill set the hip scene. They're the fellas behind Cactus – the Portmore club where upper St Andrew scions get the groove on with dancehall divas – and Asylum – today's in-vogue disco – and JamRock Sports Bar & Grill – absolutely *the* place to see and be seen.

Kingston's middle classes have suddenly discovered salsa and the Latin beat. At this writing everyone was taking dance classes, and clubs were vying to add Cuban dancers to their repertoire of evening fare.

The private party scene is intense. Strawberry Hill, where parties are held regularly, is a center of the upper-crust scene. Socialite Michael Fox also hosts popular 'Moonlick' parties at Wildflower Lodge during fullmoon weekends. (See the Blue Mountains & Southeast Coast chapter for more details on both.)

Any Ticket (☎ 937-1279), 3 Lancelin Ave, Kingston 10, is a ticket office for entertainment and sporting events that take place in Kingston.

## Bars

At press time, *the* in-vogue place of choice was undoubtedly the *Jam Rock Sports Bar & Grill* *(69 Knutsford Blvd)*. This classy, sophisticated spot draws an upscale crowd. It has TVs all around and plays world beat music. Gotta get those buffalo wings? Then check it out on Tuesday night. It offers beers and Appleton rums for US$1 during 'happy hour,' 4:30 to 6:30 pm Monday to Saturday.

Another sports bar is *Half-Time*, also on Knutsford Blvd. And *Friends on the Deck*, at the corner of Lady Musgrave and Hope Rds, is a trendy bar with finger food.

The *Moonstruck Café* (☎ 968-4811, 21 Central Ave), a compact, classy, outdoor nightspot, is popular with the middle-class crowd and expat residents. The patio bar is a venue for karaoke. There's a pool table and, upstairs, a top-notch pizzeria. (Also see Places to Eat, above.)

Another in-vogue spot is *Carlos' Café* (☎ 926-4186 22 Belmont Rd), an open-air bar with lively tropical decor enhanced by a warm neon glow, and pool table, video poker,

table football, and – on Thursday nights – Cuban dancers who are helping make Latin music the 'lick' (the latest fashion). It serves food (see Places to Eat, above), and has a 'crab night' on Monday. It hosts karaoke on Friday. Entry is free; beers cost US$3.

The bar at the *Hilton Hotel* has karaoke on Friday. And karaoke is also the forte at the *Crowne Plaza* on Wednesday, *Chaser's Restaurant & Lounge* (29 Barbican Rd) on Monday, and *Twyn Citi* (☎ 929-8361, 2 Congrave Park) in Portmore on Thursday. On other nights, Chaser's is a popular spot for middle-class Jamaicans, and the music is deafening. *Crossings New World Café* (☎ 978-3547, 94 Old Hope Rd) is more mellow.

Many of the clubs listed below under Discos also have bars popular on weekdays. For example, *Peppers* (☎ 952-2219, 31 Upper Waterloo Rd) serves snack foods in its outdoor bar and is popular with the professional crowd.

*Priscilla's* (109 Constant Spring Rd) is also favored by professionals who are drawn for the city-views, mellow ambience, and R&B music on weekends. *Raphael's* (☎ 978-1279, 7 Hillcrest Ave) is another trendy place on weekend nights, with a quiet outdoor ambience; likewise, the *Mahogany Tree Bar*, next to the Grog Shoppe at Devon House. While in the vicinity, be sure to stop in at the *Magnum Specialist* (109 Constant Spring Rd), a natural juice bar off Half Way Tree, known for attracting a potpourri from ragamuffins to well-known reggae stars.

## Discos & Nightclubs

Choose from seedy to sophisticated. Dress accordingly, as Kingstonians have a dead-on fashion sense.

Friday is *the* night of the week for Kingstonians, and the only night when things get going much before midnight, beginning with 'after-work jams' at upscale clubs. Most dance spots have a 'Ladies Nite' (usually Thursday, with free entry or drinks for women), which are generally advertised in the *Gleaner* and other newspaper entertainment sections.

Want an earthy, *really* Jamaican experience? Then head to a dancehall club. The dancehall scene is fluid and as of this writing no single venue seemed to have replaced House of Leo (which has closed) as *the* place to be seen. Dress code for the ladies is, apparently, as little and as tight as possible, and the more gaudy the better (tighter than tight 'batty rider' shorts – hot pants – are de rigeur). The police are attempting to force dancehalls to close by midnight because they're a noise nuisance.

The *Countryside Club* (☎ 929-9403, 7 *Derrymore Rd)*, just off Half Way Tree Rd, is contrived but pleasant, offering wooden dining terrace and lawns, a restaurant and bar, plus dancing to live music, especially Latin sounds on Thursday nights, when Cuban cabaret is featured. On Saturday, the Latin scene shifts to the *Jonkanoo Lounge*, in the Hilton Hotel, which along with *Mingles*, in the Courtleigh Hotel on Knutsford Blvd, attracts an older, more sophisticated crowd. Mingles has a Latin beat on Saturday, with salsa, merengue, and lambada.

At press time, the newly opened *Asylum* (☎ 929-4386), above Jam Rock Café, at the base of Knutsford Blvd, was another happening scene, packing in crowds on Tuesday, Thursday, and Friday nights. *Mirage* (☎ 978-8557, 106 Hope Rd)*, in the Sovereign Centre, once Kingston's most elite disco, had lost its magic in 1998, when it briefly closed (cover charge is US$5). It has a dancehall night on Tuesday.

Other modish and popular discos include *Peppers* (☎ 952-2219, 31 Upper Waterloo Rd)*, an outdoor venue that plays vintage oldies on Wednesday (and has big-name stageshows monthly) and *Epiphany* (☎ 929-1130, 1 St Lucia Ave) in New Kingston.

There's also a modestly attractive disco – *Memories* – in the Olympia Crown Hotel, hosting fashion parties on Saturday, and jazz and oldies on Sunday.

*Cactus* (☎ 998-5375), upstairs at the Portmore Plaza in Portmore (see the Port Henderson section, later in this chapter), has long been a favorite of Kingston's professional set. It was given a new, livelier decor in 1997 and features dancehall (Wednesday) and reggae, and an oldies party on Sunday (US$5 entrance). Thursday is Ladies Nite,

with free drinks for women. Nearby is *Extremes* (☎ 939-2950), in Portmore Mall, a disco popular with the local crowd; it has dancehall on Sunday.

The Friday 'oldies nite' at the *Rodney Arms* near Portmore was defunct at press time, but rumored to be soon resurrected.

For oldies, try *Priscilla's* on Constant Spring Rd, or the *Turntable* (☎ 924-0164, 18 Red Hills Rd)*, Thursday through Sunday. It hosts classic 'oldies' on Thursday, with the gamut from James Brown to the Stones.

*Zanzibar* (☎ 926-7883, 7 Haughton Ave) is a relatively new nightclub hosting occasional parties, including toga parties that, I'm told, can get rather wild.

I can't vouch for *Father's Rhythm & Blues HQ* on Manning Hills Rd, but if R&B is your thing, maybe this is an option.

## Stageshows & Sound-Systems

Kingston has frequent live stageshows, which are announced in newspapers and on streetside billboards. Top-name artists often perform at the National Arena, as do international R&B stars such as Whitney Houston and Roberta Flack.

Look, too, for impromptu sound-system street parties ('jump-ups'), where the speakers are banked mile-high, food vendors are on hand, and all are welcome. Promoters usually charge a small gate fee to pay for security. There's usually at least one on a weekend, often at a private home. Look for posters advertising Stone Love, the biggest name in sound-system productions.

An outside street party for the 'masses' takes place on Tuesday nights at *Front Line* on Red Hills Rd. Inner-city groups play outdoors for free, and vendors set up their stalls. Great fun!

Ask around, too, for unadvertised all-night jams, which are mostly private affairs at which you'll probably be made welcome. A good source is the Tuff Gong Studios (☎ 923-9383, 923-5814). Talk to Bragga, one of the security guards (he knows the local scene well).

## Theater

Kingston boasts vibrant performing arts year-round. At the forefront is the highly acclaimed *Little Theater* (☎ 926-6129, 4 Tom Redcam Drive). Founded in the 1960s by the Little Theater Movement, the theater incorporates the Jamaica School of Drama, the island's first. You can watch rehearsals and even take a backstage tour by appointment. The theater puts on plays, folk concerts, and modern dance throughout the year. The main season is July through August, and a 'mini-season' is held each December. The 'Likkle' Theater is famous for its lively slapstick Christmas pantomime (see the National Pantomime section under Arts in the Facts About Jamaica chapter). You may not understand much of what's said, but you're guaranteed to have fun.

No less acclaimed is the National Dance Theater Company, which hosts a rich repertory that combines Caribbean, African, and Western dance styles. It has a fiercely loyal following and sells out quickly. The *Ward Theater* (☎ 926-6129), on the north side of the Parade, is home to both the Little Theater's annual pantomime and the National Dance Theater Company. The Jamaica Folk Singers and other companies also perform here. Entrance is US$3 (gallery), US$6 (parquette), or US$7 (dress circle).

The *Barn Theater* (☎ 926-6469, 5 Oxford Rd) also hosts plays.

Look for performances by the University Singers, who are justly acclaimed for their repertoire of Caribbean folk and popular music, choral, madrigals, jazz, African songs, and pantomime; and by the Cari-Folk Singers, a group of longtime friends dedicated to preserving the Jamaican folk genre and whose 400-song repertoire blends ska, rock-steady, folk, and contemporary styles. Both groups appear notably during the autumn season of concerts.

## Go-Go Clubs

At least two go-go clubs in Uptown attract a foreign clientele as well as locals: *Gemini Club* (☎ 920-0013) on Half Way Tree Rd; and the slightly more upscale *Palaise Royale* (☎ 929-1113, 14 Ripon Rd), which features a pool table and video games. The clubs are hassle-free. Both offer free entry on weekdays but cost US$3 on weekends (the fee

includes one drink). Expect to be solicited by the dancers for 'off-duty' pleasure. (See the caveats in the section on Prostitution in the Facts for the Visitor chapter.)

*Chances* (☎ 968-3682, 5 Dumfries Rd) also has go-go dancing on Sunday (US$14, including hors d'oeuvres), but big-name sound-systems also set up. More earthy options include the *Get-Away Club* (60 Lyndhurst Rd) and the *Highland Club* (82 Manning Hills Rd), which has exotic dancing from 1 pm on.

## Jazz

Live jazz is hosted in the basement of the *Mutual Life Centre* (☎ 926-9024, 2 Oxford Rd) every last Wednesday evening of the month; in the mini-bar of *Le Meridien Jamaica Pegasus* on Friday night; and in the *Talk of the Town* on the 17th floor of the Pegasus on the last Wednesday of each month.

The *Grog Shoppe* (☎ 929-7027), on the grounds of Devon House at Hope and Waterloo Rds, hosts jazz at 7 pm Tuesday, and live blues at 7 pm Wednesday. *Crossings New World Café* (☎ 978-3547, 94 Old Hope Rd) also has jazz on Tuesday.

A 'Friday Evening Jam' at *Boon Hall Oasis* (☎ 942-3064) in Stony Hill features jazz and contemporary sounds from 6 pm to midnight. Otherwise it's open 9 am to 5 pm Monday to Saturday. (See the North of Kingston section, later in this chapter, for details on getting to Boon Hall Oasis.)

## Cinemas

Three cinemas showing first-run Hollywood movies are located uptown: the relatively dour *Odeon Cinema* in Half Way Tree; the comfy, new, five-screen *Carib Cinema* in Cross Roads, replacing the old grand dame (which burned down); and *Palace Cineplex 1 & 2* (106 Hope Rd) in the Sovereign Centre. Entrance is usually about US$5. Jamaicans stand when the national anthem is played before the movie. Often there's an intermission.

There is a drive-in cinema at Harbour View, east of town (entrance is US$6); the New Kingston Drive-In Theater is on Dominica Drive.

## Harbor Cruise

Buddy Francis returned the venerable *Caribbean Queen* to service in 1998, when he began operating party cruises around Kingston Harbor. It's offered on a charter basis only, not on a scheduled basis.

## SPECTATOR SPORTS
### Cricket

It's not just cricket! It's West Indian cricket. And the place to see it is Sabina Park (☎ 967-0322), downtown not far from the Holy Trinity Cathedral. National teams from English-speaking Caribbean islands play at the Red Stripe Cup each January, the Shell/Sandals Overs competition in February, and the Cable and Wireless Test series in April.

### Track & Field

The National Stadium on Arthur Wint Drive hosts major sporting events such as cycling and track and field. It seats 30,000 spectators. Kingston plays host to the annual Carib Cement International Marathon (☎ 928-6231) held each February. It's US$3 to enter.

### Horse Racing

Races have been held in Kingston since 1816, first at Kingston Race Course (the site of today's National Heroes Park). It was moved to Knutsford Park in 1953, but has since been replaced by the highrises of New Kingston; it then moved in 1959 to Caymanas Park (☎ 939-0848) at Portmore on the southwest fringe of Kingston, where 'de excitement caan dun!' Racing takes place each Wednesday and Saturday, as well as on public holidays.

The International Karting Road Race is held in late November on the streets of Kingston. Contact Abe Zaidie (☎ 926-9342).

Motor-racing fans should check with Motor Racing Jamaica (☎ 960-9100, www.kasnet.com/racingjamaica), or the Jamaica Motoring Club (www.jamaicamotoringclub.com), which hosts local rallies.

Equestrian fans (and the social elite) head to the Annual International Show Jumping Extravaganza and Horse Trials held each November at Caymanas Polo Grounds at Caymanas Park.

## SHOPPING

Kingston has plenty of troves, beginning with the roadside stalls on the Parade and around Half Way Tree. Everything you could want for the home is displayed, along with locally made leather goods at bargain prices.

Several modern shopping malls are concentrated on Constant Spring and Hope Rds. Two of the largest are Sovereign Centre at 106 Hope Rd and New Kingston Shopping Mall on Dominica Drive.

### Crafts Stalls & Art Galleries

The waterfront Crafts Market at Pechon and Port Royal Sts hosts dozens of stalls selling wickerwork, carvings, batiks, straw hats, and other crafts. It's hassle-free, and prices here are lower than elsewhere on the island. Watch your wallets! Ras Art & Craft (☎ 929-3920), at 17A Dominica Ave at the junction with Knutsford Blvd, is also a good place to scout Rastafarian T-shirts, woolen 'tams,' and leather goods.

Bolivar Art Gallery (☎ 926-8799, fax 968-1874), 1D Grove Rd, has works by Jamaica's leading artists, but also offers fine books, antiques, and maps. Babylon Jamaica (☎ 926-0416), 10A W King's House Rd, specializes in Rastafarian art. The Art Gallery (☎ 960-8939) at 10 Garelli Ave also has a branch in the Wyndham Hotel. It offers a large range of original paintings by top artists, as well as antique silver collectibles, jewelry, hand-blown Venetian-glass, furniture, and T-shirts exclusive to the gallery.

Also selling the best of Jamaican creative talent is Artisan (☎ 978-3514) at 106 Hope Rd in the Sovereign Centre, and Patoo (☎ 924-1552) at 184 Constant Spring Rd in the Manor Hill Plaza. The latter is a casbah of local treasures (Tortuga puddings laced with rum, Busha Brown sauces, potpourri baskets, reproduction furniture, ceramic tableware and decorative ornaments, and rugs and mats by Faith Centre Weavers). It also has an in-house coffee bar plus a reading nook and art gallery.

Chelsea Galleries (☎ 929-0045) in the Island Life Centre on Chelsea Ave displays works by Jamaica's leading artists. Painter Barrington Watson owns the Contemporary

Art Centre (☎ 927-9958) at 1 Liguanea Ave, which is a hub of artistic activity. Gallery Pegasus (☎ 926-3690), a small gallery in the basement of Le Meridien Jamaica Pegasus on Knutsford Blvd, has revolving exhibitions of works by Jamaica's leading artists. At the Grosvenor Gallery (☎ 926-3691) at 1 Grosvenor Terrace, you'll find some of the best art in Jamaica displayed in five exhibition rooms. Solo exhibits fill the front rooms, with a permanent exhibit at the rear, in addition to an antique showroom. The Mutual Life Gallery (☎ 929-4302), in the Mutual Life Centre at 2 Oxford Rd, also maintains exhibits by leading contemporary Jamaican artists.

For pottery, check out Clonnel Potters Gallery on a quiet corner of Village Plaza on Constant Spring Rd. It sells exquisite thrown and slip-cast pieces in stoneware and porcelain, as does Treasure House of Flowers & Art (☎ 978-6344) on Hope Rd.

### Clothing

Mijan Caribbean Clothing (☎ 977-5133) at 20 Barbican Rd, and Wright Style Clothing (☎ 968-8520) at Devon House, sell quality Jamaican designs. Also try Ciao Bella, at 19 Hillcrest Ave, selling in-vogue designs and with the benefit of the Café Bella at hand. Patoo (☎ 924-1552), in the Manor Park Shopping Centre, is a good bet for batik sarongs.

### Flea Markets

A flea market is held on Sunday on Dominica Drive, near the New Kingston Theater. Local markets include Papine Market on weekends at the top end of Old Hope Rd, or the crowded Jubilee Market (also called the Coronation Market), immediately west of the Parade. At Jubilee Market, every kind of fruit and vegetable, crafts, cheap clothing, and bric-a-brac are laid out for sale. Be prepared to avoid heaps of rotten fruit, honking cars, and rickety wooden handcarts on tiny wheels being pushed through the throng. You'll be the only out-of-towner and the experience can be daunting, particularly for white people, who are not always welcome. *Don't* go wandering any farther west without a guide who's respected locally. Leave valuables and all but a minimum of money in your hotel safe. And be alert. This is a *real* Jamaica experience!

### Furniture

Several Kingston companies make top-of-the-line furniture and sell it abroad. Some exporters can fulfill local orders, too. Medallion Galleries (☎ 923-9017), 1 Nanse Pen Rd, Kingston 11, produces Queen Anne and Chippendale furnishings; Creative Wicker Ltd (☎ 929-3019), Shop 1, 6 St Lucia Ave, makes wicker products.

The Jamaica Furniture Guild (☎ 929-1292), 13 Dominica Drive, Kingston 5, represents leading exporters and can help you buy furniture here and ship it home.

### Music Stores

If you're shopping for reggae cassettes or CDs, check out High Times (☎ 922-5538) at Shop 42 in the Kingston Mall, next to the National Gallery. The staff can sleuth the most obscure soundtracks and even make up compilation tapes.

Downtown, there are several music stores on Orange St north of the Parade, a magnet for anyone seeking the latest (or not so recent) vibes. One of the best is GG Records, on the corner of the Parade. Prince Busta's (one block north) and Rockers International, at 135 Orange St, are both good for oldies. Another good spot is Music City, on E Queen St.

You can also buy from a superb reggae selection at Tuff Gong Studios (☎ 923-9383) on Marcus Garvey Drive.

### Rums & Liquors

Sangster's (☎ 926-8888), purveyors of Old Jamaica rum-based liqueurs, has a factory outlet at 17 Holborn Rd. It's open 8:30 am to 5 pm weekdays.

If you'd like a cigar to go with your drink, stop by Jamaica Tobacco Retail Store (☎ 925-1547), 31 Upper Waterloo Rd, Kingston 10.

### GETTING THERE & AWAY
### Air

Norman Manley International Airport handles international flights. Domestic flights depart and land at Tinson Pen Airport. (See the Getting There & Away chapter for information on Norman Manley International Airport. For more on Tinson Pen Airport, see the Getting Around chapter.)

Air Jamaica (☎ 929-5689, 922-4661), 51 Knutsford Blvd, is open 8:30 am to 4:30 pm weekdays. (See Airlines in the Getting There & Away chapter for international airlines that have offices in Kingston and at Norman Manley International Airport.)

Air Jamaica Express (☎ 923-8680, 305-670-3222, fax 305-670-2992 in the USA) has 12 flights daily from Tinson Pen to MoBay (US$49 each way), plus two flights daily to Port Antonio (US$37 each way), and one to Negril (US$52 each way). Students and seniors are offered a US$25 one-way fare between Kingston and MoBay.

Airspeed Express (☎ 937-7072, fax 923-0264) offers air tours, transfers, and charters, as does Tropical Airlines (☎ 920-3770, 937-0978 at Tinson Pen), Jamaica AirLink (☎ 923-0486, fax 923-0264) and Aero Express (☎ 927-4921). All offer nonscheduled service to MoBay, Negril, and Port Antonio.

## Bus

Buses and 'coasters' run between Kingston and every point of the island. Most arrive at and depart from the chaotic and crowded terminal at Beckford and Pechon Sts, five blocks west of the Parade, or from Half Way Tree. The downtown station is in an intimidating area that is not safe for wandering.

Buses to Ocho Rios (four daily) and Port Antonio (four daily) cost about US$1.50; those to Montego Bay (four daily) cost about US$3. Buses for Spanish Town (hourly, 6 am to 6 pm, plus additional evening service; US$0.70), Mandeville (six daily; US$1), and Black River (four daily; US$1.50) depart from Half Way Tree.

The companies that operate the franchises do not publish timetables (see the Getting Around section below). Service is terribly crowded. Hopefully things will improve in coming years as the Transport Licensing Authority extends its reforms of the bus system. At press time, work was about to begin on a new bus terminal west of the Parade which should bring order to the chaos. (See

the Getting Around chapter for information about Jamaica's bus system.)

**Minibuses** You can catch a minibus to almost every town and village on the island from the Parade. They operate from the same terminals as buses, and all caveats regarding travel by bus apply (also see Getting Around). Minibuses to Montego Bay (120 miles) cost around US$8 to US$12. Minibuses to Ocho Rios cost around US$5 to US$8. There are frequent services to both destinations.

**Private Transfers** Most tour companies and car-rental companies offer private transfers. Island Car Rentals (☎ 926-8861, 926-5991, fax 929-6987), for example, charges US$120 to MoBay, US$70 to Ocho Rios or Mandeville, and US$80 to Port Antonio.

## GETTING AROUND
## To/From the Airport
### Norman Manley International Airport
Kingston's international airport is midway along the Palisadoes, about 17 miles southeast of downtown Kingston. A couple of robberies in mid-1994 led the US Embassy in Kingston to issue an advisory urging visitors to be cautious while traveling to or from Kingston airport by car, especially at night, but the drive is usually without incident. Police patrols have been increased. Check for the latest information (see Dangers & Annoyances in the Facts for the Visitor chapter).

**Bus** The bus stop is opposite the police station beside the customs exit from the arrivals lounge. Bus No 98 operates on a regular basis (usually about every 30 minutes) between Norman Manley airport and the west side of the Parade (US$0.75). The X97 minibus also operates between the airport and West Parade (US$1.50). It's a 25-minute journey.

**Car** Island Car Rentals has an office at the airport (☎ 924-8075, fax 924-8389). The company is extremely reliable, with modern, well-maintained vehicles and efficient service.

**Taxi** There are plenty of taxis outside the baggage-claim area. JUTA (☎ 927-4534, 926-1537), 85 Knutsford Blvd, Kingston 5, is the only authorized taxi company. A taxi to New Kingston will cost US$15 to US$21, depending on destination.

**Private Transfer** Limo Taxi Tours (☎ 968-3775, fax 944-3147) at 3A Haughton Ave, Kingston 10, offers limousine service from Norman Manley airport, plus regular airport transfers. Pleasure Tours (☎ 924-1471, fax 924-1756), 153¹/2 Constant Spring Rd, Kingston 8; and JUTA Ltd (see above), also offer transfers (US$15 per person one-way). JUTA also has representatives at the airport who can assist you. Island Car Rentals charges US$30 single or double, or US$55 three to seven passengers for chauffeured transfers.

**Tinson Pen Airport** Just off Marcus Garvey Drive, Tinson Pen is a basic facility. If you're lucky, a taxi may be waiting outside. Otherwise you'll have to call one; it should cost about US$8 to New Kingston.

A bus into downtown runs past Tinson Pen. Other buses operate between Portmore and the Parade and pass along Marcus Garvey Drive (the fare to the Parade is about US$0.30). A taxi will cost about US$7.

## Bus

The British established a good bus system. After independence, the system sank into notorious decline. Fortunately, things were about to change radically at press time as part of a three-year plan to eradicate the mega-problems that have plagued Kingston's bus system for years. (See 'Kingston Bus Blues.)

**The Situation at Press Time** Here's how things looked in early 1999, when masochists (and the poor) were still relegated to enduring travel aboard crowded tropical ovens commanded by cesspool-mouthed *'ductas* and *'ductresses.*

The city and environs are divided into five zones, including Spanish Town, Portmore, and the Blue Mountains. You may be able to

obtain a free bus map from Jamaica Omnibus Service at 80 King St, but don't count on it. Alternately, try the two companies that monopolize services: KMTR (☎ 968-2441, 968-7777) at 11 Hillview Ave and the National Transport Co-op Society (☎ 968-1010) at 26 Lyndhurst Rd. Buses stop only at official stops. They start running around 5 am and stop at 10 pm. The chaotic bus system has two major terminuses: downtown at the junctions of Beckford and Pechon Sts (just west of the Parade), and uptown at Half Way Tree, where bus stops are scattered along the roadsides. New street signs went up in 1995, making it a lot easier to determine which buses go where. You may still need to ask locally, however. If arriving at the chaotic downtown terminal, it's a good idea to take a taxi for travel to other points in Kingston.

Fares in 1998 were determined by a six-stage system according to distance: from J$10 to J$25 (less than US$1, regardless).

**Now the Good News** In October 1998, Jamaica took delivery of 150 new Mercedes-Benz buses to be used in Kingston by the Jamaica Urban Transport Co Ltd (JUTC), formed in July 1998 to replace the existing franchise system. JUTC is owned by the government and private sector interests and was due to take over operations of all public passenger buses in Kingston.

In January 1999, the city will begin doing away with the cash system and will introduce a 'smartcard,' to operate on the same basis as a telephone card and be available at the same outlets. You can purchase your card for whatever value you want and the cost of each bus journey will be automatically deducted by machines aboard the buses. You can call for information at ☎ 929-1287.

A new bus terminal is planned downtown for south of the Jubilee Market, west of the Parade. Eight additional new terminals will be created, including at Papine, Constant Spring, and Half-Way Tree.

## Car Rental

Many car-rental companies have offices downtown and at Norman Manley International

## Kingston Bus Blues

Many things are dysfunctional in Jamaica, and chief among them is the Kingston bus system, which devolved into a Kafkaesque nightmare in 1983 when the government shut down the state-owned Jamaica Omnibus Service and turned the system over to hundreds of private bus owners. Timetables became a thing of the past. Overcrowding exceeded 200% capacity at peak hours, when traveling by bus was nightmarish. Bus crews raced one another to reach bus stops first, with bullying touts to usher people on board at each stop. And tickets were rarely issued, leading to wholesale graft. The system has been called a 'lucrative cash cow,' with no accountability. The day's receipts would simply be handed over in cash to the hundreds of individual bus owners after the crews had taken their cut.

In 1994, Kingston residents barricaded the streets to protest the chaotic and problem-plagued system. The government introduced a new system in March 1995 with a pledge to end decades of overcrowding, lack of timetables, callous treatment by bus crews, and a lack of tight accounting. The Transport Licensing Authority divided Kingston into five franchise areas, with two companies and a cooperative given the franchises. The companies were supposed to adhere to timetables and issue tickets, but things seemed only to deteriorate. Angry Kingstonians again barricaded the streets. In September 1995, the chastised government announced that it was reversing a 12-year-old policy and re-entering the bus service business. But still, nothing changed. Finally, in 1998, the Authority began a total overhaul of the system (see the Getting Around chapter) that finally promises to breathe fresh air into Kingston's corrupt and festering bus system.

Airport. The majority offer free airport shuttles. Jamaica's largest and most reputable car-rental company, Island Car Rentals, has its main office (☎ 926-5991, 888-991-4255, 800-892-4581 in North America, fax 929-6987, www.islandcarrentals.com) conveniently located at 17 Antigua Ave, at the top of Knutsford Blvd in New Kingston. There's also an outlet at the Hilton Hotel at 77 Knutsford Blvd.

See Rental Companies under Car Rentals in the Getting Around chapter for other companies with offices in Kingston and at the Norman Manley International Airport.

**Driving in Kingston** Kingstonians are fast and aggressive drivers, lane discipline is tenuous, and two-way streets become one-way without warning. It is easy to miss a turn or end up going the wrong way (Kingstonians simply throw the car in reverse). Watch for cars backing down one-way streets or coming at you head-on. Even the most innocuous mistake can result in a torrent of foul-mouthed abuse. That said, driving around Kingston isn't really so bad.

Parking downtown can be a problem. Your best bet is the public parking garage between Barry and Tower Sts, and Church and Temple Sts.

Few Kingstonians rely on street names, so it is invaluable to have a Kingston map on hand.

### Taxi

Taxis are numerous except when it rains, when demand skyrockets. Use licensed cabs only: they are usually white Toyota Corolla station-wagons (estate cars) or older model European cars painted black-and-yellow. All have red PPV license plates. The rate cards quoting government-established rates are often out of date. Ask the fare and determine if the meter is working before you get in (usually it isn't). If not, don't get in until you've settled on a rate for the journey (determine whether the quoted fare is in Jamaican or US dollars).

You can call a cab from Blue Ribbon (☎ 928-7739), Checker (☎ 992-1777), Metro Cab (☎ 929-6918), and Yellow Cab (☎ 922-

6444). Other companies are listed in the yellow pages.

JUTA Tours (☎ 926-1537, 927-4534) runs a slightly more expensive taxi/limousine service for tourists.

Fares from New Kingston to downtown are about US$3.50 to US$6.

# West of Kingston

## PORTMORE

Portmore (population 90,000) is a sprawling, nondescript middle-income residential suburb that stretches for miles across the plains west of Kingston. Although located in St Catherine parish, it is a commuter town for the capital, to which it is linked by the Portmore-Kingston Causeway, a spit reaching into Kingston Harbour.

The city is expanding westward under the aegis of the Urban Development Corporation, which in 1965 conceived a plan to develop Portmore as a 'twin city' to Kingston. The project, which calls for the development of 27,000 acres, is nightmarish in its conception, with identical pre-fab cement houses arrayed in endless rows of criss-crossing streets. Shopping malls, entertainment centers, and fast-food joints add color to an otherwise drab environment.

On the north side of Portmore is the **Caymanas Park Racetrack** (☎ 988-7258) where horses race twice weekly (US$0.35 to US$1.10 entrance). East of Caymanas Park, at a site now occupied by the Jamworld entertainment complex (also known as Portmore Festival Village), are the ruins of **Passage Fort**. Jamworld is where, briefly, Reggae Sunsplash was held (see the Facts for the Visitor chapter).

Portmore Parkway links Portmore with the Causeway and Kingston. It is paralleled to the east by Augusta Drive, running along the harbor shoreline. The breeze-blown shore – **Port Henderson Beach** – is popular with Kingstonians, but there's barely a beach to speak of and the thin strip of sand is disgustingly littered. Behind the spit is Hunt's Bay, full of discarded rubber tires amid the mangroves.

The Causeway is lined with jerk shacks. Concord Plaza is a small complex midway along Augusta Drive, with a pharmacy, bank, and grocery.

## Fort Augusta

This fort, at the northern end of Augusta Drive, dates back to 1740, when an existing swamp was partly filled to create Mosquito Point. The fortress – named for the mother of King George III – guarded the western end of the harbor. What you can see today is not the original fort, which was destroyed when lightning struck the magazine holding 3000 barrels of gunpowder, killing 300 people and shattering windows up to 15 miles away. The huge crater was filled in and the fort rebuilt. It's fairly well preserved. The original limestone turrets are in place, but portions of the outer walls have collapsed into the bay. The fort is now a prison.

## Port Henderson

At the head of the spit on the western side of the entrance to Kingston Harbour (at the southeast corner of Portmore), Port Henderson contains some fine examples of 18th and 19th-century architecture and is well worth the visit for the views across the harbor, especially at sunset, when Kingston glistens like hammered gold.

In Spanish colonial days, travelers destined for Villa de la Vega (then the capital) alighted here. This was the landing site, too, of the English invasion fleet that in 1655 ended Spanish rule over Jamaica. Around 1770, the mouth of the river silted up and a village – Port Henderson – was founded farther south at the western end of the spit. It grew into a major port and the embarkation point for Spanish Town. Later, after a mineral spring was discovered, it became a fashionable spa resort.

Today the site is a funky fishing hamlet called **Forum** with pirogues and nets drawn up on the beach. About 200 yards uphill from the Rodney Arms (see below) is the well-preserved ruins of a semicircular gun emplacement replete with cannon, and an old fort and battery – the **Apostles Battery** – in various stages of restoration.

Turn left (south) at the roundabout at the west end of Augusta Drive to get here.

**Rodney Arms** This restaurant and pub is housed in a beautifully restored Georgian limestone building that was once the Old Water Police Station, where pirates and miscreant marines were detained. It is named after Admiral George Rodney, who commanded the naval station at Port Henderson.

**Fort Clarence** Continue along the pot-holed road for a half-mile uphill, and you'll reach Fort Clarence, which is today the headquarters of the Jamaica Defense Force (JDF). Signs read 'Restricted Area: No Unauthorized Person Allowed Beyond this Point.' A barbed wire fence underscores the point. At least the views over the bay are worthwhile from this lonesome spot. A dirt track – 4WD essential – curls up and around the fort and pushes through the undergrowth, but dead-ends a half-mile farther.

**Rodney's Lookout** Between Forum and Fort Clarence is Rodney's Lookout, reached via a trailhead just before the JDF camp. The trail leads uphill to the ruins of Admiral George Rodney's former house. Grasspiece Lookout is nearby.

## Places to Stay

**Camping** You can pitch a tent at the *World Meditation Centre*, directly below the Apostles Battery. The Rasta owner of the site charges US$5 to camp (he lives in the old stone hut above the Apostles Battery). Bring your own food and water. The breezy campsites sit on little terraces on the rocky shore over the water, with cactus all around. It's a fantastic setting, with views across the harbor.

**Hotels** Augusta Drive is lined with hotels, though why you would want to stay here beats me. Many are 'short time' motels (usually hidden behind high walls) that rent rooms on a hourly basis.

*Inez Bogue Hotel* (☎ 998-6804), opposite the Concord Plaza, is a modest, modern hotel with 50 rooms for US$22 and a swimming pool and restaurant.

*La Roose* (☎ 998-4654) offers nine clean yet modestly furnished rooms with fans for US$27. An air-conditioned suite costs US$54. All have private bath with hot water; some have TVs and telephones. Its fairly elegant restaurant specializes in seafood.

In a similar vein is the *Arizona Inn* (☎ 998-4666, Lot 8, Block M, Port Henderson), featuring 11 simply furnished rooms with lofty ceilings, fans, spacious bathrooms, and TVs – encased in iron cages! It's a very breezy location. There's an outside dining terrace, with a small dance floor and a disco on weekends. The hotel also has an intimate little indoor restaurant with a large wooden bar and lounge with cozy chairs. Rates vary from US$31 to US$49 for a family room, and US$57 for a suite with spa.

Appropriately named, the gleaming-white *Jewels* (☎ 988-6785), 400 yards west of La Roose, has 25 air-conditioned rooms aired by the breezes that channel down the corridors for US$46 to US$71. Rooms are nicely if simply decorated with bright tropical fabrics, and upstairs rooms have lofty wooden ceilings. Bathrooms have hot water but are small.

*Arizona*, *Lands End*, *Cupid*, *Occasions*, and *Portmore Inn* are 'short time' hotels.

## Places to Eat

You can hang out with locals at seafood restaurants on Augusta Drive, including *My Friend's Place*, a popular, narrow little bar with outdoor patio dining. Seafood dishes cost less than US$2.

Don't leave without treating yourself to a meal at the *Rodney Arms* (☎ 988-1063), popular with Kingstonians on weekends. It's a marvelous place to enjoy the views across the harbor or to watch the local fishermen laying out their nets to dry while you sample crab back, seafood platter, shrimp, fish, and other seafood dishes from Mrs Olive Stuart's kitchen. Prices range from US$13 for steamed fish to US$23 for curried garlic lobster. It's open 4 to 11:30 pm, and 1 to 10 pm Sunday. The snapper is a specially big, spicy, and fine fish dish. Oysters are offered on weekends at the Rodney Arms' *Rathid Oyster Bar*, which also serves garlic shrimp, garlic crab, and a special flambé rum drink (US$3). The oyster bar is one of several shady dining terraces on wooden decks on the hillside, which has shade trees, and oddities such as a cannon, fountain, and small water cascade. Waiters in bow ties add a note of elegance.

You can buy fresh fish at Forum.

## Entertainment

The *Cactus Disco* in Portmore is one of Kingston's better nightclubs and is extremely popular on weekends (see Discos & Nightclubs in the Kingston section, earlier). The *Zanadu Night Club*, in Concord Plaza on Augusta Drive, is one of several go-go clubs.

## Getting There & Away

Port Henderson is reached via the Causeway, which begins in Kingston at the southern end of Hagley Park Rd (at its junction with Marcus Garvey Drive), leaps across the westernmost point of Kingston Harbour, and traverses a narrow spit. Note that no eastbound traffic *into* Kingston is allowed along the Causeway between 4:30 and 7 pm; no westbound traffic is allowed between 6:30 and 9 am.

Buses to Portmore operate from Half Way Tree and Three Miles (at the junction of Hagley Park Rd and Spanish Town Rd) as well as from the Parade (US$0.50). Alternately, take a minibus from the Parade to Port Henderson or Portmore.

The NTCS (☎ 968-1010), ostensibly, operates an air-conditioned executive bus service, with 'ground hostesses.' No standing is allowed. There's even a daily paper and a glass of orange juice. It costs US$1.20.

## HELLSHIRE HILLS

One look at the Hellshire Hills and it is easy to appreciate their great natural tourism potential that lies entirely untapped. The area is a 100-sq-mile, totally uninhabited upland region due south of Portmore. The hills are like an inverted circular shield, enveloped on three sides by the Caribbean and covered in knife-sharp limestone and inhospitably thick scrub and tall cactus. The only humans to be found here are occasional wild-pig hunters, charcoal burners, and scientists studying the endangered Jamaican iguana,

for whom the Hellshires are a last refuge (see 'the Jamaican Iguana').

The area receives less than 30 inches of rainfall a year. The unusually porous limestone (a variety called honeycomb) soaks up all the rain it receives. What little surface soil exists is suitable only for cactus and thorny scrub, known as 'dry limestone forest.'

The Hellshires are an important habitat for migrant birds, and a last refuge for diverse species of rare plants and animals: the endangered yellow snake, the Mabuya maboua skink, and the coney, Jamaica's only native land mammal (bats excepted). Hunting (and more recently, the encroachment of human habitations) has decimated the population of the coney, or Jamaican *hutia*, a large, guinea pig-like rodent that is now restricted to a few parts of eastern Jamaica. The coney is protected and rarely seen.

Although once favored as a haven by runaway slaves, the Hellshires have never been populated. The scrub forest is protected under the Forestry Act of 1937, but the law is not enforced. Charcoal burning, slash and burn agriculture, squatting, and other destructive forest uses occur without control. And the area is threatened by encroaching urbanization. The eastern half of the hills has been earmarked for housing and resort development by the Urban Development Council (UDC). The All Hellshire Environmental Group successfully launched an effort to have the government declare a Hellshire Hills Protected Area that incorporates the wetland fringe. Nonetheless, urbanization appears to be gaining speed.

## Hiking

The Hellshires are perfect for hiking – if you can rough it. There are no facilities. If you plan on exploring, hire a guide familiar with the area, take plenty of water, and stay on the trails; the limestone terrain is pitted with scrub covered sinkholes and it is all too easy to break a leg, or worse. Don't underestimate this environment!

## Organized Tours

A good way to see the area is on the one-day 'Iguana Project' trip, offered by the Jamaican

## The Jamaican Iguana

The endemic Jamaican iguana *Cyclura collei* is Jamaica's largest land animal, sometimes growing up to 2m long. Once common throughout the southern scrublands and tropical dry forests, during the past two centuries it has suffered from the effects of forest degradation and the predation of mongooses, feral pigs, cats, and dogs. In the 1940s, the iguana was thought to be extinct.

In 1990, however, an iguana was discovered by a hunter in the Hellshire Hills. The 'lost' species had managed to survive for half a century, undetected, within sight of the nation's capital.

A Jamaican Iguana Research & Conservation Group was immediately formed, headed by Dr Peter Vogel, a zoologist at the University of the West Indies in Kingston. Vogel and his team discovered a small remnant population in the central and western section of the hills. Possibly only a few dozen adults have survived. Because the survival rate of young iguanas is very low, many eggs were removed from nests, incubated at Hope Zoo, and the baby iguanas raised for eventual release to the wild.

Unfortunately, hunters are pushing into the remotest regions, threatening to finish off the remaining iguana population. The forest continues to be degraded by charcoal burners, and large-scale mining operations and urban expansion on the Hellshire boundaries are slated.

For further information, contact the Jamaican Iguana Research & Conservation Group (☎ 927-1202, fax 927-1640), Dept of Zoology, University of the West Indies, Kingston 7.

---

Iguana Research & Conservation Group (☎ 927-1202), c/o Dr Peter Vogel, Dept of Zoology, University of the West Indies, Kingston 7. The cost, US$60 to US$120 per person, includes transfers from Kingston, lunch, and an 8-mile guided hike.

### HELLSHIRE BEACHES

This series of narrow, white-sand beaches is on the fringe of the eastern Hellshire Hills. A line of batteries once stretched along this shoreline, though virtually nothing remains. The beaches are reached via a road that leads south from Portmore via Braeton Newtown (a southwesterly extension of Portmore) to Hellshire Point, 8 miles south of Braeton.

The road meets the coast at **Great Salt Pond**, a circular bay overgrown on its perimeter with briny mangrove swamps where snook, mullet, stingrays, and reportedly even crocodiles ('alligators') can be seen. Fort Clarence overlooks the northeasternmost point of the bay.

Lying at the southeasternmost point of Great Salt Pond is **Fort Clarence Beach Park** (☎ 968-4409), popular with Kingstonians on weekends. It frequently hosts beauty contests and live reggae concerts. It's open 10 am to 5 pm Wednesday to Friday, and 8 am to 6 pm weekends, and costs US$3/US$1.50 adults/children. The park is closed on Monday and Tuesday, except on public holidays. It has showers and toilets plus secure parking. A restaurant and bar are open weekends only.

A road to the left of the second, more southerly roundabout leads east to the main beach, called **Fisherman's Beach**. The beach is appealing enough and the water warm, but the main interest is the social scene, based around a compact and funky village with dozens of gaily painted huts and stalls selling beer, jerk, and fried fish and *festival* (fried biscuit or dumpling). The place gets crowded and noisy on weekends. If you visit before noon you can watch the fishing pirogues come in with their catch. On any day of the week, though, it's a fascinating visit, a slice of the 'real' Jamaica up close – the ramshackle hamlet is a fishermen's and Rasta haunt.

Halle J Watersports (☎ 998-9422, 770-1355) offers trips to Lime Cay (see Lime Cay

Spanish Town schoolkids

Marshall's Pen, Mandeville

Mandeville Courthouse

LEE ABEL

Hanging at the Kingston Harbour docks

LEE ABEL

Kingston lights up at sunset

& Environs, later in this chapter) and Port Royal, and offers Jet Skis, water-skiing, snorkeling, and inflatable sea bikes. You can also rent horses.

A reef protects the northern end of the shore, where the swimming is safe. (See the Outdoor Activities chapter for suggested dives and snorkeling sites.)

From Fisherman's Beach, the road winds south along a dramatic, virtually uninhabited shore – an incredible piece of Jamaican real estate – with rocky coves and occasional sandy beaches with turquoise and jade-colored shallows. To the west, the cactus-covered land slopes to the Hellshire Hills.

After 2 miles you'll reach **Two Sisters Cave** and **Arawak Museum**. Both have been closed 'for development' for several years. Blind river bass live in the brackish water that fills the pools at the base of the cave. Ancient petroglyphs can also be seen in the second cave. A sign nearby warns that bathing is prohibited due to 'bacterial contamination.'

### Places to Stay & Eat

The only hotel is the **Hellshire Beach Club** (☎ 989-8306), a modern, handsome, two-story complex that opened in 1998 with 60 air-conditioned rooms, all with private bath and shower, for US$34. It has a pool, bar, and restaurant. It's about 200m from the beach and is popular with beach-goers making out.

Dozens of shacks sell jerked, fried fish and other Jamaica fare for pennies.

### Getting There & Away

Buses operate to Hellshire Beaches from Half Way Tree (No 1) and the Parade (No 10) about every 30 minutes on weekends, less frequently mid-week (US$0.40 for the 30-minute journey). You can also catch minibuses from the Parade.

# East of Kingston

Kingston is hemmed in to the east by Long Mountain, which extends right up to the shore, forming a narrow bottleneck for the A4, the only road east out of town. Beyond Long Mountain lies a narrow coastal plain.

About 4 miles east of downtown, at Harbour View, a road to the right at the traffic circle (roundabout) leads along the Palisadoes, a thin scrub-covered sand spit with a few beaches, the Norman Manley International Airport, a nascent wildlife refuge, and, at its tip, Port Royal, the setting for Jamaica's most colorful history.

## ROCKFORT MINERAL BATHS

These private mineral baths are immediately west of the cement factory 3 miles east of downtown Kingston. Rockfort (☎ 938-5055, fax 928-6096) has one large public pool, and 11 private pools of varying sizes, all with whirlpools and wheelchair access. Reopened in 1994 after a facelift, it provides pleasant bathing in amiable surroundings and attracts Kingstonian families on weekends. The slightly saline and moderately radioactive water rises from a cold spring. One hour is the maximum allowed. The flow is continuous, with water entering the pool from above and exiting below. There's a cafeteria and juice bar, plus changing rooms and lockers. The public pool is open 6:30 am to 6 pm Monday to Friday, 8 am to 6 pm weekends (US$2 entrance, US$1.20 children). Private pools are open 8 am to 6 pm daily (US$14 two people, US$20 four people, US$33 eight people, US$40 12 people).

Adjacent to the baths is an English fort – Rockfort – with cannons.

Bus No 99B operates from the Parade and Half Way Tree and travels along Windward Rd as far as Harbour View (US$0.30). The No 99A returns via Half Way Tree. You can also take the No 98, which departs from the Parade and passes Rockfort en route to Port Royal.

## FORT NUGENT

The English considered the point where Long Mountain comes down to the coast – a place called Harbour View – a perfect location for defense. Thus, on the hill sits the ruins of a Martello Tower built in 1806 as part of Fort Nugent, which guarded the eastern approach to Kingston.

Turn inland onto Fort Nugent Rd at the Harbour View roundabout.

## THE PALISADOES

The Palisadoes is a narrow, 10-mile-long spit that forms a natural breakwater protecting Kingston Harbour. It extends due west from Windward Rd. At the western end, reached via Norman Manley Hwy, lies the historic city of Port Royal, set on a former cay that the Spanish called Cayo de Carena, where they careened their ships.

The spit is underlain by a submerged coral ridge topped by sand, silt, and gravel that was deposited over thousands of years by westerly currents. It earned its name for the defensive palisade that was built across the spit to defend Port Royal from a land-based attack. It consisted of a 'stout wall with a six-gun redoubt.'

The Palisadoes is sparsely vegetated, fringed on its harbor side by mangroves that shelter a small number of crocodiles and nesting colonies of pelicans and frigate birds. Environmentalists are campaigning to have the mangroves protected as a wildlife reserve.

### Dangers & Annoyances

In 1994, the US State Department issued a travel advisory for Norman Manley Hwy. Apparently there have been a series of robberies, but I have driven it with no problem numerous times. The Palisadoes is a popular site for health-conscious Kingstonians jogging or walking.

### Gunboat Beach

This beach, on the inner shore of the spit, due east of the airport, is popular with working-class Kingstonians, but the sea is too dirty for swimming. Gunboat Beach is accessed by a spur road that leads from Norman Manley Hwy to the Royal Jamaica Yacht Club. There are jerk stalls and loud music on weekends.

### Norman Manley International Airport

The airport lies inside the elbow at the spit's widest point. It dates from WWII, when a wide expanse of marshy flats on the harbor side of the Palisadoes' elbow were filled and built up. (See the Getting There & Away section under Kingston, earlier in this chapter.)

### Plumb Point Lighthouse

The 70-foot-tall, stone-and-cast-iron lighthouse lies midway along the Palisadoes at its elbow. It was built in 1853 and still functions (it ceased to do so only once, during the 1907 earthquake). Where today cactus and scrub grow, there once thrived a coconut palm plantation. A stone monument records the planting of the first of 20,000 trees during the 19th century.

Despite the lighthouse's presence, in 1997 a freighter ran aground nearby on the windward side of the spit. This is a fascinating sight, though the freighter is rapidly rusting away.

### Royal Jamaica Yacht Club

This elegant club (☎ 924-8685) and marina is open to bona-fide members of international yacht clubs only. Berthing costs US$1.30 to US$3.70 per foot, depending on location. It has a fine swimming pool and sundeck, nice restaurant, and a patio bar. You can also rent sailboats, yachts, and cruisers at Royal Jamaica Yacht Club.

### Places to Eat

Other than in Port Royal and the Yacht Club, the only facility along the Palisadoes is the *Jamaica Gates Sea Café & Bar* at the head of the peninsula.

## PORT ROYAL

Port Royal is a dilapidated, ramshackle place of tropical lassitude, replete with important historical buildings sadly collapsing to dust for want of restoration. It's a fascinating spot, worth much more than a cursory visit. Today's funky fishing hamlet was once the pirate capital of the Caribbean and was (supposedly) briefly the wealthiest city in the New World. Later, it was the hub of British naval power in the West Indies, but the remains give little hint of the town's former glory. Its inhabitants today mostly make a living from fishing. Their livelihood took a blow in 1998 when a crippled Cuban tanker loaded with sugar dumped its load along the coast, killing off fish stocks; at press time, the vessel was listed in the harbormouth.

Many locals show their birthright as descendants of pirates and slaves – many are of

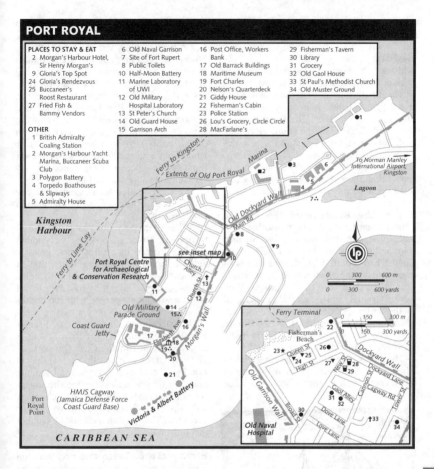

## PORT ROYAL

**PLACES TO STAY & EAT**
2  Morgan's Harbour Hotel,
   Sir Henry Morgan's
9  Gloria's Top Spot
24  Gloria's Rendezvous
25  Buccaneer's
    Roost Restaurant
27  Fried Fish &
    Bammy Vendors

**OTHER**
1  British Admiralty
   Coaling Station
2  Morgan's Harbour Yacht
   Marina, Buccaneer Scuba
   Club
3  Polygon Battery
4  Torpedo Boathouses
   & Slipways
5  Admiralty House

6  Old Naval Garrison
7  Site of Fort Rupert
8  Public Toilets
9  Half-Moon Battery
10  Marine Laboratory
   of UWI
11  Old Military
    Hospital Laboratory
12  St Peter's Church
13  Old Guard House
14  Garrison Arch

16  Post Office, Workers
   Bank
17  Old Barrack Buildings
18  Maritime Museum
19  Fort Charles
20  Nelson's Quarterdeck
21  Giddy House
22  Fisherman's Cabin
23  Police Station
26  Lou's Grocery, Circle Circle
28  MacFarlane's

29  Fisherman's Tavern
30  Library
31  Grocery
32  Old Gaol House
33  St Paul's Methodist Church
34  Old Muster Ground

ruddy complexion, with distinctly Caucasian features. They can appear reticent – even sullen and surly – and are slow to warm to strangers. But join them at Gloria's Rendezvous on a Saturday night and you'll experience their warm side.

Local developers have long touted the city as a prime possible marine archaeological attraction. The potential is undoubtedly enormous. Nowhere else does a sunken city lie next to shore in a mere 30 feet of water, with a fort and other colonial remnants on dry land to boot. While much lip service has

been devoted to restoring Port Royal, virtually nothing had been done to date. Fortunately, at this writing it looked as if the ambitious, much-hyped Port Royal Heritage Tourism Project was about to become reality, turning the offbeat, dilapidated town into the Caribbean's premier cruise-ship port of call. By the time you read this, wholesale change may have restored parts – or even all – of Port Royal into a recreation of the star it once was. (See 'Restoring Port Royal,' earlier in this chapter.) Hopefully they'll give the town a new sewer system!

Most tourist sites open 9 am to 4 pm Monday to Friday and 10 pm to 5 pm weekends.

## History

Although the Spanish used to careen their ships on the isolated cay on which Port Royal was later built, they never settled nor fortified it as the English did within one year of arriving in Jamaica in 1655. The English called the island 'Cagway' or 'the Point.' Here they built Fort Cromwell (renamed Fort Charles after the Restoration in 1662). Within two years General William Brayne was able to report that 'there is the faire beginning of a town upon the poynt of this harbor.'

**Era of the Buccaneers** This was the period when England was sponsoring freelance pirates in their raids against Spanish ships and possessions. Almost as soon as the English had captured Jamaica, buccaneers – organized as the Brethren of the Coast – established their base at Port Royal. They were alternately welcomed and discouraged by the authorities according to the dictates of England's foreign policy. (See the Rise of the Buccaneers section under History in the Facts about Jamaica chapter.)

The lawless buccaneers were big spenders who disposed of their loot 'in all manner of debauchery with strumpet and wine.' The

Buccaneer galleon

wealth flowing into Port Royal attracted merchants, rum-traders, vintners, prostitutes, and others seeking a share of the profits. Townsfolk even invested in the expeditions in exchange for a share of the booty, and great celebrations took place when the raiders returned. (By tradition, the governor, who then lived at Port Royal, was the first person allowed to step aboard when the ships dropped anchor; he claimed one-tenth of the booty.) No number of taverns or whorehouses seemed enough to slake their thirst (40 new licenses were issued for taverns and rum shops in 1661 alone).

The clergy called it 'the wickedest city on earth' and proclaimed that damnation would follow.

Although the governor's court was moved to Spanish Town in 1664, the vice-ridden town continued its stratospheric growth, aided by an insatiable new trade: that of Guineans whose ships arrived with holds of 'black ivory' (slaves). By 1682 Port Royal was a town of 8000 people, with 800 houses 'as dear-rented as if they stood in well-traded streets in London,' for as Francis Hanson recorded, 'in Port-Royal there is more plenty of running Cash (proportionally to the number of its inhabitants) than in London.' There were fortresses all around, plus two prisons and, reflecting the town's cosmopolitan nature, two Anglican churches, a Presbyterian church, a Jewish synagogue, a Roman Catholic chapel, and a Quaker meeting house.

**Earthquake & Destruction** At noon on Tuesday, June 7, 1692, a great earthquake convulsed the island, and the doomsayers were vindicated: Port Royal was destroyed. The wharves and streets nearest the water's edge keeled over like stricken ships. Fort Carlisle, Fort James, Fort Rupert, and Fort Walker sank beneath the waves. Nine-tenths of the town disappeared underwater, where it remains. (Fort Rupert, though, gradually rose back up to settle on land, where its remains can be seen today.) The massive quake was followed by a huge tidal wave that washed one ship, the *Swan*, into the center of the town, where it rested on the rooftops,

Don't even think of attacking Port Royal – Fort Charles stands ready.

providing shelter for those fortunate enough to scramble aboard. More than 2000 people died, many having fallen into great fissures before being 'squeezed to pulp' when a second tremor closed the gaping holes like pincer jaws. Many of the survivors were claimed by the pestilence that followed, caused by the hundreds of unburied corpses.

**Resurrection** Port Royal's heyday of infamy was over. Even before the earthquake, official English policy had changed, and sea-rovers who would not give up piracy were hounded and hanged at Gallows Point, a promontory at the harbor mouth of Port Royal (the last hanging was in 1831). The English government had not written off Port Royal, however. The defensive works were repaired in time to repel a French invasion mounted against Jamaica in 1694. Piracy was briefly revived to help finance the rebuilding. Gradually Port Royal regained its stature as a merchant town and as center of the turtling industry. The town refused to die, despite a great fire in January 1704.

The greatest impetus to Port Royal's resurrection was the near-constant state of war in which England found itself with Spain, France, and Holland throughout the 18th century. The wars marked the beginning of a 250-year term as headquarters of the British Royal Navy in the West Indies. As the British Navy built up its strength in the Caribbean, the ships came to rely increasingly on Port Royal for repairs and supplies, and as a muster point for battle fleets.

Six forts and a militia of 2500 armed men protected the naval station, which was supported by a prosperous merchant town of 2000 buildings. The advent of peace in 1815 spelled the end of Port Royal's naval glory, and a fire that year consumed much of the town. Struck by one calamity after another, the old port sank into decline. In 1838, Jamaica ceased to be a separate naval command. With the development of steam warships in the early 20th century, Port Royal's demise was sealed. The naval dockyard closed in 1905, and although the defenses were maintained through both world wars, they have since been left to decay. A rehousing scheme was initiated in 1951, following a devastating hurricane.

## Orientation

Approaching the town, Norman Manley Hwy runs beside a long brick wall enclosing the old British Admiralty Coaling Station, naval garrison quarters, and naval dockyard. You enter town through a breach in the old town wall to the main square, or Muster Ground, overlooked by the Half-Moon Battery on the left. A parapetted town wall of cut limestone blocks (popularly known as Morgan's Wall) leads along Tower St to Nelson Square, the old parade ground once known as Chocolata Hole. In 1988, Hurricane Gilbert did much damage to the old barrack buildings, but Fort Charles still stands, as does the redbrick Garrison Arch, which is all that remains of a former wall. At the tip of the spit is HMJS Cagway, headquarters of the Jamaica Defense Force Coast Guard. Other historical attractions lie scattered around the perimeter.

**Maps** The Institute of Jamaica Publications (☎ 929-4785), 2a Suthermere Rd, Kingston 10, produces an excellent map called 'Port Royal: A Walking Tour.' It includes brief information on the sites to see. The map is included with the book *Port Royal* by Clinton V Black (Institute of Jamaica Publications, 1988), which you can buy in the gift store of Morgan's Harbour (see Places to Stay, later in the Port Royal section).

## Information

There are public telephones at Morgan's Harbour and outside the police station (☎ 967-8068) on Queen St. The post office and Workers Bank are housed in the old barracks near the fort (open 8 am to 4 pm Monday to Friday). There's a well-stocked library (☎ 967-8391), open 9 am to 5 pm Monday, Tuesday, and Thursday to Saturday.

## The Sunken City

Two-thirds of 17th-century Port Royal lies hidden from view, 30 feet deep in the harbor offshore of the naval hospital. A beacon about 100 yards offshore marks the site of

one of the sunken forts: Fort James. Legend says that the buoy marks the site where St Paul's Church (not to be confused with today's methodist church) sank in 1692 (fishermen claim that in rough seas they can hear the tolling of church bells beneath the sea).

Underwater 'excavations' have been ongoing since 1959, when the National Geographic Society sponsored an expedition. Many expeditions have since explored the 'Sunken City,' which you can explore by glass-bottom boat or on scuba-diving trips (permit only) from Morgan's Harbour resort. (See Scuba Diving, later in the Port Royal section.)

## Old Naval Hospital

The dilapidated hospital sits at the northwest side of town. It was built in 1742 atop a part of the old city that had sunk in the earthquake, but fire destroyed the original. The existing 380-foot-long structure is remarkable for its prefabricated cast-iron framework especially designed to withstand both earthquake and hurricane; it was shipped as ballast from Bradford, England. The structure dates back to 1819 and remained in use until 1905.

The **Port Royal Centre for Archaeological & Conservation Research** (☎ 967-8072) has been headquartered here since 1968, but on two recent visits it seemed as inactive as the city it attempts to preserve. Alas, the Archaeological and Historical Museum, once housed here, is no longer, and none of the staff seems to know what has happened to the motley collection of relics – pewter tableware, medicine bottles, a copper still, and even Ming porcelain – dragged up from the Sunken City. (One of the more fascinating trinkets was a pocket watch whose hands had rusted away long ago, but were etched on the face by coral at 11:43 am, the moment of the 1692 earthquake.) Old horse-drawn carts in the forecourt are held together by humidity and bailing wire.

The hospital is set to become the principal attraction of the restored Port Royal, housing an archaeological museum, pirate museum, shops, restaurants, and other attractions.

The Marine Laboratory of the University of the West Indies is immediately south of the hospital. It is not open to the public.

## Fort Charles

Jamaica's latitude and longitude are measured from the flagstaff of Fort Charles (☎ 967-8438), a weathered redoubt originally laid in 1655. It alone withstood the 1692 earthquake (the other five forts in Port Royal all sank into the sea). Being 'not shook down but much shattered,' it was rebuilt of red brick in 1699 and added to several times over the years. It was originally washed by the sea on three sides, but silt gradually built up and it is now firmly landlocked.

At its peak, 104 guns protected the fort – making it one of the most heavily defended in the Caribbean. Many cannons still point out from their embrasures.

A Horatio Nelson Museum and light-and-sound show are touted as part of the proposed Port Royal Heritage Tourism Project.

Entrance is US$4. There's a snack bar in the old artillery store. It's open 9 am to 5 pm Monday to Thursday, 9 am to 4 pm Friday (closed Good Friday).

**Maritime Museum** This marvelous museum stands in the courtyard and contains a miscellany of nautica from the heyday of the British Navy, plus a fabulous model of the 'Jamaica Producer' cargo ship presented by the Jamaica Banana Producers in 1936. Nelson lived in the small 'cockpit' while stationed here, and his quarters are replicated. A plaque on the wall of the King's Battery, to the right of the main entrance, commemorates his time here. Local legend suggests that the three cement crosses placed in the outside wall beneath the artillery lookout point mark where Nelson's three wives are buried.

**Giddy House** A small hut sits alone amid scrub-covered, wind-blown sand 100 yards to the southwest of Fort Charles. The red-brick structure was built in 1888 to house the artillery store. The 1907 earthquake, however, briefly turned the spit to quicksand and one end of the building sank, leaving the store at a lop-sided angle. It is known as the Giddy House because it produces a sense of disorientation to people who enter. It is filled with sand and litter.

### Lord Horatio Nelson

Many of England's greatest naval heroes served at Port Royal. Most notable was Admiral Horatio Nelson (1758-1805), British Naval Commander during the Revolutionary and Napoleonic Wars.

Nelson arrived in Port Royal in 1777. While awaiting the return of the frigate *Hinchinbrooke*, which he was to command, he was briefly given command of Fort Charles, despite being only 20 years old. At that time Jamaica was on a war footing and expected a French invasion. Nelson spent much of his time pacing the platform still known as 'Nelson's Quarterdeck.'

The following year, Nelson participated in an expedition to Nicaragua, where he succumbed to fever. He returned to Port Royal, where he was attended by a famous black faith healer, Cubah Cornwallis, mistress of William Cornwallis (whose name she had taken), the brother of the general who surrendered Yorktown to the Yankees in 1781.

At Nelson's Quarterdeck a tribute tablet to Britain's greatest naval hero reads: 'In this place dwelt Horatio Nelson. You who tread his footprints remember his glory.'

**Victoria & Albert Battery** Next to the Giddy House is a massive gun emplacement and equally mammoth cannon – part of the easternmost casement of the Victoria & Albert Battery that lined the shore, linked by tunnels. The cannon keeled over in the 1907 earthquake.

## Old Gaol House

The only fully restored historical structure in town is the sturdy Old Gaol House, made of cut stone on Gaol Alley. It predates the 1692 earthquake, when it served as a women's jail. Today it houses a small crafts store.

## St Peter's Church

Despite its nondescript exterior, St Peter's Church is worth a stop. Built in 1725 of red brick, it today boasts a faux-brick front of cement. Note the floor paved with original black-and-white tiles, and the beautifully decorated wooden organ loft built in 1743 and shipped to England in 1996 for restoration. The place is replete with memorial plaques, such as 'Mr R Smirke, naval cadet, who fell from aloft at Belize' in 1856. Note, too, the monument by the sculptor Roubiliac that commemorates Lieutenant Stapleton of HMS *Sphinx*, who was killed when a cannon he was firing exploded. Most noteworthy is the plaque to Capt Augustus James Champion de Crespigny, describing an 1810 incident:

[T]aking to a small boat pulled into the very muzzles of the enemy's guns and evidently saving five men that were near drowning by the *Achilles* barge being such, his conduct was so noble that he gained…the envy of the French commanding officer, who at last ordered his men to cease firing on him.

The communion plate kept in the vestry is said to have been donated by Henry Morgan, though experts date it to later times.

Most intriguing of the curiosities is a churchyard tomb of Lewis Galdye, a Frenchman who, according to his tombstone

was swallowed up in the Great Earth-quake in the Year 1692 & By the Providence of God was by another Shock thrown into the Sea & Miraculously saved by swimming until a Boat took him up.

Eventually he grew to become a prosperous *asiento* (slave trader), assemblyman, and the church warden.

### Naval Dockyard

The old naval dockyard lies to the east of Morgan's Harbour (see Places to Stay, below). Its perimeter walls still stand, as does the Polygon Battery and torpedo slipways, though most of the buildings within are gone. The old coaling station lies immediately to the east. Most of the famous ships of the British Navy from the 18th century to the age of steam berthed here. Today it occasionally hosts live reggae concerts, and will hopefully soon be restored and landscaped, with the creation of a Fine Arts Centre, as part of the Port Royal Heritage Tourism Project.

### Naval Cemetery

Half a mile east of the dockyard, also enclosed by a brick wall, is the intriguing naval cemetery, where sailors lie buried beneath shady palms. Alas, the cemetery's most ancient quarter, which contained the grave of the famous buccaneer Sir Henry Morgan, sank beneath the sea in 1692.

### Yachting & Sport Fishing

Port Royal has a full-service marina (VHF channel 68; radio call 'Morgan's Harbour') at Morgan's Harbour Yacht Marina. Fresh water, gasoline, diesel, laundry, showers, chandler facilities, and customs clearance are offered. The marina rents boats and yachts, and offers deep-sea fishing (US$400 half-day, US$650 full-day, US$300 for four hours of drop-line fishing).

### Scuba Diving

Morgan's Harbour Yacht Club has a full-service scuba diving facility, the Buccaneer Scuba Club (☎ 967-8030, fax 967-8073), offering three to seven-night dive packages (US$261 to US$669 single, US$186 to US$494 per person double) plus PADI courses from basic to open-water certification, as well as a 'Discover Scuba' day-program (US$65). A single dive costs US$30, and US$40 at night. Dive equipment can be rented, as can snorkeling equipment. It has a 'Reef & Wreck Snorkel Dive' for US$15 per hour.

The harbor and adjacent waters have abundant coral reefs, such as the **Edge** and **South East Cay Wall**, where you can swim with nurse sharks, turtles, and dolphins; and explore wrecks such as the *Texas*, a warship covered in black coral. The highlight, however, is the Sunken City, scheduled to open to commercial dive operations. At press time, diving the sunken city was by permit only, accompanied by a Coast Guard diver. To verify the status, call the Jamaica National Heritage Trust (☎ 922-1287).

### Exploring Kingston Harbour & Mangroves

Morgan's Harbour has trips by rubber Zodiac to the mangrove swamps in Kingston Harbour (US$12). A few crocodiles still

Sir Henry Morgan

inhabit the inner sanctums, and the mangroves are also a nesting site for frigate birds and pelicans. When I toured the area, we edged a little too close to the frigate bird rookery and spooked a young bird. It failed to get the wind in its sails and dropped in a panic into the water where it flapped about and kicked madly. Finally it lifted off right in front of us so that I had to duck to avoid being struck by its hooked beak!

Dolphins are once again making regular appearances in the harbor.

Morgan's Harbour Yacht Marina also has sunset and night harbor cruises (US$250 for up to 30 people). You can rent canoes for US$7.

### Organized Tours

Limousine Taxi Tour Co (☎ 968-3775, fax 944-3147), 3A Haughton Ave, Kingston 10, and Pro-Tours (☎ 978-6139), 7 Lady Musgrave Rd, Kingston 5, offer guided half-day tours from Kingston (US$31).

### Places to Stay

Built in 1950 but renovated in 1997, the *Morgan's Harbour Hotel* (☎ 967-8030, fax 967-8073; ☎ 800-852-1149 in the USA; ☎ 020-7930-8600, fax 7930-9232 in the UK) is an atmospheric, upscale hotel within the grounds of the old naval dockyard. It has 63 spacious, elegant, air-conditioned rooms (from US$130/150 single/double), all with terra-cotta tile floors and French doors opening onto balconies. Cable TV is standard, as are firm king-size beds with headboards of gleaming dark hardwood. Rooms are decorated with original prints by Jamaican artists. Among the facilities are a swimming pool, gift store, Sir Henry Morgan's restaurant, and a handsome outside bar with an old anchor chain for its foot rail. It's very romantic at night when lit by ships' lanterns. The hotel offers special dive packages, plus a two-night package for US$125/150 single/double, including breakfast, tax, and service charge.

### Places to Eat

*Gloria's Top Spot (5 Queen St)* is famous islandwide for its reasonably priced seafood. Don't confuse it with *Gloria's Rendezvous* at the west end of High St, next door to *Buccaneer's Roost Restaurant* (☎ 967-8053), another down-to-earth eatery serving seafood for under US$4. For cheap patties, try *Circle Circle*, which also has ice cream and baked goods.

*Sir Henry Morgan's*, in Morgan Harbour Hotel, is popular with the Kingstonian middle-class, especially for Sunday brunch. You can opt to dine on a shaded terrace with views toward the Blue Mountains. The dinner menu is heavy on seafood and includes grilled lobster, jerk pork, and Jamaican specialties, plus salads and sandwiches. Try the sherry trifle, Black Forest gateau, or sweet potato pie for dessert (US$4.50). Prices range from US$6 to US$35.

Vendors sell fried fish and bammy on the main square, where a motley collection of ramshackle stalls lean one against the other. Washed down with beer, your lunch should cost less than US$3. You can purchase supplies at *Lou's Grocery*.

### Entertainment

Port Royal is a great place to gain a taste of down-to-earth Jamaican life. *The* place to be on a weekend is the welcoming *Gloria's Rendezvous*, one of my favorite spots on the island on a Saturday night, when local men of all ages – from youths in the latest hip-hop fashion to geezers in yesterday's duds – filter in and warm up at the bar to await the arrival of the women – from young women in spandex 'batty riders' to grannies in more conservative garb. By midnight, everyone is dancing to ska, twist, and disco music. Rum flows freely. And eventually the wining turns truly salacious…with young couples simulating copulation to the whistles and cheers of the crowd.

***Buccaneer's Roost*** has a video game room, CD juke box, pool table, and darts.

There are several funky bars on the square, notably ***MacFarlane's*** (otherwise known as the Angler's Club) and ***Fisherman's Tavern***. MacFarlane's has tremendous 'color' on Friday nights when a mountain of speakers is built 20-feet-high in the square and ska music reverberates across the harbor. Locals wash in and out of the funky watering hole, overindulge in white rum, and pick fights while bartenders boogie at the bar. 'There are a few scalawags, but mostly it's harmless stuff,' I was told. ***Morgan's Harbour Hotel*** sometimes has live bands and dancing.

Go-cart racing is advertised at an offbeat racetrack on the north side of the airport, but there has never been any sign of activity when I've called by.

### Getting There & Away

**Bus** A bus runs from the Parade in downtown Kingston several times daily (US$0.60).

**Taxi** A licensed taxi ride from New Kingston to Port Royal will cost you about US$35 one-way. A 'robot' (unlicensed cab) costs US$20. Norman Manley International Airport is only a five-minute taxi ride away but costs US$15. Morgan's Harbour Hotel offers free airport transfers to guests.

**Ferry** A ferry sails from the waterfront at the foot of Princess St, on Ocean Blvd in Kingston. It's a 30-minute journey and costs US$0.10 one-way (US$0.20 on weekends and public holidays). The ferry departs Kingston at 6, 7, and 10 am, noon, and 3, 5, and 7 pm, and departs Port Royal for Kingston 30 minutes later.

## LIME CAY & ENVIRONS

Lime Cay is one of half a dozen or so uninhabited sand-rimmed coral cays sprinkled like jewels amid the turquoise and aquamarine waters about 2 miles offshore from Port Royal. The cay is tiny and can be circumnavigated in five minutes. It's the perfect spot for sunbathing and snorkeling. Kingstonians flock there on weekends for picnics hosted by Port Royal locals. A 'picnic park' has even been established.

Ivanhoe 'Rhygin' Martin – the cop-killer folk hero immortalized in the movie *The Harder They Come* starring reggae singer Jimmy Cliff – was killed here in 1948.

**Maiden Cay** is a smaller, shadeless option nearby, popular with nudists.

En route to Lime Cay, you'll pass what little remains of **Rackham's Cay** (it's rapidly disappearing beneath the waves), named for the infamous Jack Rackham, one of scores of pirates hanged here in metal-casing after execution. Nearby is **Gun Cay**, named for the cannons that can still be seen, legacies of a British fortification.

### Getting There & Away

To get to Lime Cay, you can rent motorized boats (called 'canoes') from fishermen in Port Royal for US$14 roundtrip; or a canoe at Morgan's Harbour marina (US$8 to US$12 per person, minimum four people). The latter has yacht charters to Lime Cay (US$10 per person, minimum 10 people) and can arrange packaged lunches and barbecues (US$10 to US$14).

Morgan's Harbour marina has a two-hour tour of the cays (US$10), plus a one-hour tour of both Lime Cay and the harbor mangroves (US$10). Trips depart hourly from 10 am to 5 pm on weekends, and upon request on weekdays.

## CANE RIVER FALLS

These falls are a popular bathing spot for locals, following the example of Bob Marley, who immortalized the place in song: 'Up to Cane River to wash my dread. Upon a rock, I rest my head.' As a foreigner, your presence will generate considerable, though usually harmless, interest.

The turnoff is just beyond Seven Mile, about 2 miles east of Harbour View roundabout. (See the regional map in the Blue Mountains & Southeast Coast chapter.)

## CABLE HUT BEACH

A short distance farther east along the coast road you'll arrive at this uninspiring beach, popular with Kingstonians. You can eat at any of several jerk stalls and beachside 'recreation centers' highlighted by **Paradise Cove**. There's a nicer, more private beach a short distance east – **Brooks Bend Beach** – with showers and changing room.

Hostelries are limited to the *Caribbean Villa Hotel* (☎ *928-6541, Lot 7, St Thomas Rd, Kingston 17)*, 400 yards east of Harbour View roundabout. It claims a 'harbor view,' though the view is far from salubrious. It serves local and Chinese dishes in the restaurant. The 10 modest 'bungalow' rooms cost US$12 to US$20. (See the regional map in the Blue Mountains & Southeast Coast chapter.)

## BULL BAY

Bull Bay is a small town 9 miles east of downtown Kingston. (Bull Bay is adjacent to the smaller cove of Cow Bay, named for the manatees – 'sea cows' – that were once prevalent.) East of town, beyond a spur of the Blue Mountains called the Queensbury Ridge, a rugged dirt road on the far side of the bridge over the Chalky River will take you into the hills, ending at a Rastafarian commune of the Bobo Ashantis (see below).

Beyond Bull Bay, the main road climbs the scrub-covered hill before making a hairpin descent to Grants Pen and St Thomas parish (see the Blue Mountains & Southeast Coast chapter). Near the summit, on the left, you'll pass a **monument to Three Finger Jack**, one of Jamaica's most legendary folk heroes. The marker was erected by the National Heritage Trust to recall the deeds of Jack Mansong, who, in 1780 and 1781

fought, often singlehandedly, a war of terror against the English soldiers and planters who held the slave territory. Strong, brave, skilled with machete and musket, his bold exploits were equalled only by his chivalry.

Apparently, 7-foot-tall Mansong won his moniker after losing two fingers of one hand in a fight. The slave began his exploits after being sentenced to death for inciting rebellion. He escaped and took to the hills, so beginning life as an outlaw and highway robber. He made the Queensbury Ridge his home and preyed on travelers along the roads near Bull Bay. He is regarded as Jamaica's 'Robin Hood,' as it is said that he never robbed the poor. He was eventually captured in 1781 by three Maroons, who stuck his head on a pole and marched to Spanish Town to collect a £300 reward. Mansong's fame was such that a pantomime based on his life ran for nine years in London's West End.

## Black Sovereign Ethiopian Embassy

This rather makeshift camp painted in the Rasta colors of red, gold, and green is the home of the Bobo Ashantis and sits on the rugged mountainside above Bull Bay. About 100 Rastafarians live here and make a living from farming or their skills on the street (members donate 10% of their earnings to the commune). The government considers them squatters.

The commune – 'Dis not Jamaica, mon. Dis is Jah-mekya (God made her)' – originated in 1958, when it was founded by the Right Honorable Prince Emmanuel Charles Edward, revered by his gaily robed followers as a black Christ. It is referred to as a 'school of redemption' that is all about 'uniting all nations in peace and harmony.' Male elders are referred to as 'my lord.' Women are addressed as 'honorable empress.' Everyone greets their fellows in passing with the term, 'Blessed!'

Guests are welcome as long as they respect 'manners and principles.' You are led to a room festooned with portraits of Haile Selassie. Here you're greeted by the head priest, who will give you a spiel rich in clever metaphor that offers a fascinating insight into Rastafarian philosophy, including Rasta interpretations of history and politics. You're requested to empty your pockets and turn to give praise to Haile Selassie, an act that you may be asked to repeat each time someone enters and bows to pray to this unlikely god. Of course, you'll be hit up to pay a donation for your visit, and may be persuaded to fork out a hefty US$20 for a slender copy of *Black Supremacy*, the Rastafarian 'bible.'

You are welcome to stay overnight for as long as you wish, but you must contribute 'something' and 'come to salvation' through performing duties on 'campus.' Cameras are welcome.

You can contact the group at Ethiopia Africa Black International Congress, 10 Miles, Bull Bay PO, St Andrew.

It's a little more than half a mile uphill from the bridge on the A4, 20 yards east of the Red Lion Pub. You can hike. If you drive you'll need 4WD. (See the regional map in the Blue Mountains & Southeast Coast chapter.)

### Getting There & Away
The No 97 bus from Half Way Tree and the Parade goes to Bull Bay (US$0.30). Other buses and minibuses operate from the Parade. (See the regional map in the Blue Mountains & Southeast Coast chapter.)

# North of Kingston

A crescent of steep rimmed mountains arc around Kingston: Red Hills to the northwest, Stony Hill to the north, and Jack's Hill to the northeast. The views over the city are magnificent and the climate amenable, explaining why Kingston's monied class have built their fine houses here.

There are no sites of interest, although a chap called Mr Carby has an exotic birds aviary at 16 Kirkland Crescent.

## JACK'S HILL
Jack's Hill is a steep-faced ridge that marks the first step into the mountains north of Kingston. Skyline Drive runs along its crest, providing superb views over the city. The Jack's Hill Community Center is the headquarters for **Project Plant** – the Mammee River Agricultural and Environmental Development Project – a community reforesta-

tion and environmental education program funded by the United Nations Development Program. The project takes its name from the Mammee River, which flows through the area, and is intended to benefit local farmers. The goal is to achieve sustainable management of the watershed and sensitive utilization of the hills north of Kingston for agroforestry and ecotourism.

## STONY HILL
The old coaching route over the Grand Ridge, now the A3, leads up Stony Hill and crosses the westernmost ridges of the Blue Mountains.

The A3 descends through the **Wag Water Valley** to the flatlands of the north coast. Bamboo lines the valley sides. It's a very windy road with many hairpin turns and potholes. Many Jamaican drivers do not slow down merely for hairpin bends or because the road narrows, but you should!

About 12 miles north of Half Way Tree, a turnoff to the right at Coakley leads to the **Temple Hall Coffee Estate** (☎ 942-2340), where coffee was introduced to Jamaica by governor Sir Nicholas Lawes in 1728.

## CASTLETON BOTANICAL GARDENS
Seventeen miles north of Half Way Tree, the road bisects Castleton Gardens, which are spread over 30 acres on the banks of the Wag Water River, astride the boundary of St Andrew and St Mary parishes. Many exotic species introduced to Jamaica were first planted here.

The gardens date back to 1860, when 400 specimens from Kew Gardens in London were transplanted on the former sugar plantation owned by Lord Castleton. The gardens, which rise up the hillside on the west side of the road, eventually became the most richly stocked garden in the Caribbean. More than 1000 species of natives and exotics are displayed. The upper level includes two towering Norfolk pines. Nearby are labeled specimens of Strychnos, from which strychnine poison is extracted.

Entry is free. Castleton is open 7 am to 5 pm daily (until 6 pm some months). On the eastern (lower) side of the road is a picnic area with cafeteria and toilets. The guides are unpaid (they're not allowed to charge), but tips are welcome. Ask for Roy Bennett, who has been the senior guide for almost 40 years. He's very helpful and you'll be delighted to hear him expound on the garden while you explore.

## PLACES TO STAY
### Budget
Reportedly, you can *camp* on the riverbank at Castleton for a token fee of US$2. There's water. A lively little jerk center called *Desert Rose* is about 100 yards north of the gardens.

You can also camp at *Grass Piece Farm* in the hamlet of Leinster, reached by a road to the left (west) from the bridge 1½ miles north of Castleton. The owners, Annie and Roger Robinson, also rent a *cabin*.

At Jack's Hill, *Maya Lodge* (☎ 702-0314, 702-0112, PO Box 216, Kingston 7) is hidden in a trough below Skyline Drive and was once an institution among budget travelers seeking 'alternative accommodations' when it was owned by Peter Bentley, who ran Sense Adventures from here. Its offshoot, Destinations, is still based here and offers hikes in the Blue Mountains; Bentley now lives in Australia. You can reach Destinations through Maya Lodge or at its Kingston office (☎ 929-6368), 9 Cecelio Ave. Maya Lodge's new owners are slowly upgrading and have raised prices considerably, though it still has the feel of a youth hostel. Fifteen campsites – US$10 per person – are cut into the steep hillside amid tall grass and bamboo; you need to bring your own tents and equipment. Wooden cabins sleep up to four people but have neither electricity nor hot water for US$23 single, US$35 double, US$57 four people. If you don't mind the comings and goings, you can rent a two-person open loft above the office. There are also double rooms for US$57 with shared bath; one room has a private bath. Hot water was to be added at press time. Sometimes there is only meager fare available at the café, but you can bring your own food. Campers can cook outside for US$3 per use (there's an outdoor eating area under thatch with rough-hewn tables and benches). A cooked breakfast costs US$3, and dinner US$7. Maya Lodge is close to two streams good for quiet contemplation, as the radio in the lodge always seems to be on, and there's a constant stream of people in and out. It is no longer a bargain.

Valerie Phipps maintains Maya as a resource for hikers heading into the Blue Mountains. There's a reference library, and you can hire guides here for between US$50 and US$100 daily. Blue Mountain hikes are also offered. You can even rent canoeing equipment. You can also camp for US$10 per tent nearby at *Rasta Perch*, a primitive hillside hut that is home to Leonard 'Baps' Cole and is reached by a steep half-mile trail off Jack's Hill Rd. 'Baps' is an elderly Rasta who is partial to blowing on an *abeng* (conch shell horn) and playing his bamboo flute. You'll need to bring all your own equipment.

### Mid-Range
The rambling, slate-roofed *Stony Hill Hotel* (☎ 942-2357, PO Box 111, Kingston 8), in the hills 5 miles north of Half Way Tree, boasts fabulous views over Kingston and is one of the more unusual hotels around. A working Model-T Ford stands in the forecourt, which is embellished with mosaics of historical motifs. This old-world charmer has 35 rooms, all with private bath with hot water, large windows with views, and an intriguing blend of homey 1960s decor and modern art, for US$71. Potted plants and bougainvillea arbors abound. The modestly elegant restaurant is open to nonguests and is popular with tour groups. There's a pool, plus a bar that's a 1950s time warp. The turnoff is on a dangerous hairpin bend by the Texaco gas station.

The *Mountain Valley Hotel* (☎ 924-2313), on Old Stony Hill Rd, Kingston 8, is an old-style, rather jaded guest house with 14 rooms for US$34. It has a pool in a concrete sundeck. It's 400 yards north of the junction with Long Lane.

Nearby *Talk's Hotel* has been recommended. Reportedly it's a ramshackle, five-story makeshift place clinging to the hillside at Stony Hill and offering fabulous views.

**Sunset Ridge Guest House** (☎ 977-1568, 20A Skyline Drive, Kingston 7), at Jack's Hill, has 12 rooms at US$60.

## Top End

One of the best bargains in the suburbs is the **Jonraine Country Inn** (☎/fax 944-3513, 7 W Kirkland Heights, Forest Hills), a millionaire's home leased to Lorraine Fong. The exquisite contemporary Spanish-style villa sits 1000 feet above Kingston at Kirkland Heights, on Red Hill. It stairsteps up the hillside, offering breathtaking views over the city. The main house has seven spacious rooms, all tastefully decorated, with sponge-washed walls, atrium lounge, and a twee bar upstairs. Lorraine loves to host, and you'll be looked after with true hospitality. It's a bargain at US$70 double, including a full breakfast. If you want to feel like a millionaire, check in!

Make reservations early for a stay at **Ivor** (☎ 702-0510, fax 702-0380, Skyline Drive, Jack's Hill, Kingston 6, ivor@colis.com), which squats at 2000 feet atop Jack's Hill and offers fabulous vistas over Kingston. The charming house was built in the late 1870s, and has lost none of its traditional style. The three rooms are individually and beautifully furnished. You can relax on rockers on the veranda, which is lit at night by old brass lanterns. The owner, Hellen Aitken, is very charming and helpful. This gem costs US$100/115 single/double, including continental breakfast.

## PLACES TO EAT

**Forbidden Heights** (☎ 944-3513), the restaurant of the Jonraine Country Inn (see above), allows you to dine while savoring incredible views over town. The cuisine is superb: chicken in oyster sauce, chicken wings, fish, and shrimp. Entrees begin at about US$10. It has an all-you-can-eat crab night on Wednesday (US$16). It's open 6 to 11 pm daily except Sunday.

Another good bet is **Ivor** (see Places to Stay, above), popular with middle-class Kingstonians. Meals are by reservation only; book well ahead. A four-course dinner costs US$24 per person, and a three-course lunch

is US$16. It also serves snack lunches and afternoon teas. The menu changes daily, but typically includes pumpkin soup, jerk shrimp, roast pork, lemon and thyme chicken rolls, snapper with mustard and capers, and such desserts as sherry trifle and cappuccino creme caramel.

**Boon Hall Oasis** (☎ 942-3064), tucked into a nook at Stony Hill (turn on Seaview Rd, opposite the Petcom gas station, then take the third left on Airy Castle Rd), is popular for its traditional Jamaican buffet. It serves meals at 3 pm and 6 pm to 9 pm, and afternoon tea is 3 pm to 6 pm. A calypso band plays during Sunday buffet brunch (11 am to 3 pm). Also offering views from the hills is **Stony Hill Hotel** (☎ 942-2357), popular with tour groups for its buffet (US$18.50).

## ENTERTAINMENT

At Jack's Hill, you can't beat a rum shop called **Ringo's Club**, nearby on Peter's Rock Rd, playing scratchy old records to accompany conversation with slightly soused locals.

## GETTING THERE & AWAY
### Bus

A No 12 bus from Barbican will take you to Papine where you can get a minibus to Jack's Hill. You can also get to Jack's Hill via minibus (US$0.50) from opposite the Texaco station at Barbican between 5:30 and 10 am, and 3 to 10:30 pm. The No 74 and No 76 buses run to Barbican via Slipe Rd from the Parade, at Duke St and E Queen St, and bus No 54 departs from the West Parade.

### Car

Constant Spring Rd leads from Half Way Tree to the Manor Park roundabout and becomes the A3, or Stony Hill Rd.

For Jack's Hill, take either Skyline Drive from its junction with Gordon Town Rd, half a mile north of Papine (it's about 4 miles from here to Jack's Hill); or, from Hope Rd, take E King's House Rd to Barbican and from there, Jack's Hill Rd. It's 3 miles uphill. Foxy's Pub sits at the hilltop crossroads in Jack's Hill. From Foxy's Pub, a rugged road – Peter's Rock Rd – leads 100 yards downhill to the Maya Lodge.

# Blue Mountains & Southeast Coast

If you tire of reggae and beach-bumming and want to cool off in fern-festooned forests, head to the Blue Mountains at the eastern end of Jamaica.

The steep-faced Blue Mountains rise northeast of Kingston and soar in green pleats to a knife-edged backbone (the Grand Ridge) that extends west-northwest and east-southeast for 30 miles. The mountains average 12 miles wide. The chain is flanked to the east by the lower John Crow Mountains; to the west are the less distinct Port Royal Mountains.

The parish of St Thomas, east of Kingston, lies in the shadow of the Blue Mountains and, as a source of touristic interest, in the shadow of the rest of Jamaica. Very few foreign visitors pass through this corner of the country, one of the island's least scenically attractive areas, with few appealing beaches and few places of historic interest.

## Highlights

- A meal, spa treatment, or night of romance at Strawberry Hill
- The trail to Blue Mountain Peak, for the greatest high in Jamaica
- Lonesome Cinchona Botanical Gardens
- Old Tavern Estate, for the best coffee in the world
- Morant Point Lighthouse – getting there is half the fun, and you'll have the beach to yourself

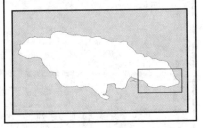

## Blue Mountains

The Blue Mountains dominate the eastern parishes of St Andrew, St Thomas, Portland, and St Mary, rising swiftly from the coast to a series of rounded peaks culminating in Blue Mountain Peak (7402 feet), the highest point in Jamaica. Others include Mt Horeb, Stoddard's Peak, Half a Bottle, and Catherine's Peak. The latter, which dominates Kingston and is topped by a tall radio antenna, was named for the first person to climb it, Catherine Long, who reached the top in 1760.

Many of the humble and gracious mountain folk are caught in a culture of poverty. Some villages still lack electricity. Most of the children lack shoes. And a large portion of the grown men (at least those fortunate enough to own a piece of land) get up at the crack of dawn to tend steep-pitched plots. The farmers grow coffee and vegetables (they supply Kingston), as did their forebears following the 1838 abolition of slavery, which allowed former slaves to establish small farmsteads in these mountains. On weekends the higglers pile into trucks and vans for the journey down the mountain to ply their produce in the markets. Ask a local farmer what he grows and he'll tell you yams, carrots, scallions, coffee, and thyme. 'And what about ganja?' you may mischievously ask, for it, too, is an important cash crop hereabouts.

The ranges east of Blue Mountain Peak (and the upper northern slopes) are virtually uninhabited. Wild indeed!

Dirt roads link hamlet with hamlet, luring you off the tourist path to appreciate life in the mountains. Many roads are rutted, rain-washed tracks full of holes and huge rocks. Often they deteriorate into muddy stairways that your car negotiates with wheezing difficulty. Fancy clutch skills are called for, and 4WD is essential.

Fill up on gas in Kingston as there are no gas stations in the Blue Mountains; the nearest is at Papine.

# BLUE MOUNTAINS & SOUTHEAST COAST

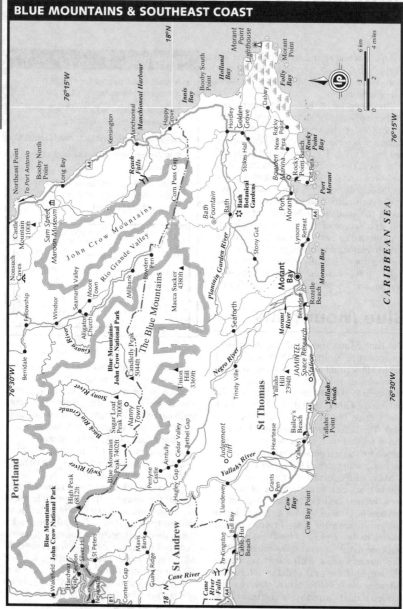

Few locals own a vehicle. The wiry old men and women toting baskets of vegetables and bundles of firewood on their heads will be grateful if you stop and give them a ride.

## ORIENTATION

The few roads and hamlets are concentrated on the southwestern slopes, closest to Kingston. The B1 snakes up and over the mountains, providing easy access to most places and sites of interest. Simply follow Hope Rd uphill to Papine, a market square and bus station, where Gordon Town Rd leads into the mountains. At the Cooperage, the B1 forks left steeply uphill for Strawberry Hill and Newcastle. Gordon Town Rd continues straight from the Cooperage and winds east a mile up the Hope River Valley to Gordon Town, then steeply to Mavis Bank and Hagley Gap, the gateway to Blue Mountain Peak.

## GEOLOGY

The mountains take their name from the haze that tints their heights. They're composed of sedimentary, igneous, and metamorphic rocks dating back 140 million years. These are the oldest rocks on the island, born of volcanic convulsions beneath the sea during the Cretaceous period – a result of the jostling of the Caribbean and North American tectonic plates that still occurs. The mountains have been on the rise for at least the past 25 million years, though their major uplift took place within the last five million years.

The range is still imperceptibly rising along major fault lines at a rate of almost 1 foot per 1000 years. When the faults shift, great landslides tumble into the plunging valleys, leaving raw gashes of red earth and rock. Since rainfall is high, streams and waterfalls are numerous and the mountains are deeply incised by plunging rivers.

## CLIMATE

The Blue Mountains are much wetter than the rest of Jamaica. Moisture-laden trade winds blowing from the northeast spill much of their accumulation on the mountains, which forms a rain shadow over Kingston and the southern parishes. The summer months (June through September) provide the best weather for exploring. December to April is also a good time, though slightly cooler. Temperature drops 3°F to 4°F for every 1000-foot rise in elevation (it can freeze in the early morning above 5500 feet). Intervening months experience heavy rains. Torrential rains of 12 or more inches in 24 hours are not unknown, and usually result in serious flooding.

## FLORA

The Blue Mountains are a botanist's dream, with more than 500 flowering plant species (about 240 of which are endemic to the island), including 65 species of orchid, the majority of which have flowers so small as to be barely noticeable. An endemic of note is the 'Jamaica rose' *(merianias)*, whose pendulous, roselike blossoms glow like tiny lanterns when struck by sunlight. A great many species are exotics introduced by English settlers during the last century as ornamentals: azaleas, bright-pink begonias, eucalyptus from Australia, bamboo from the Far East, ginger lilies imported from Asia, and cheesebury and rhododendrons from the Himalayas.

Native tree species include boarwood, whose name derives from the folk belief that wounded hogs tear the bark with their tusks and rub their wounds with the sap. Another is *Chusquea abietifolia*, which remarkably, flowers synchronistically, and only once every 33 years. The event was first reported in 1885, when it flowered both in Jamaica and at Kew Gardens in England. It last flowered in 1984 and is due again in 2017.

Vegetation changes with altitude. The upper slopes are swathed in ferns (more than 50 species), bromeliads, and antediluvian tree ferns – *Cyanthea* – that grow to 35 feet tall and live more than 150 years. Toward the summits, cloud forest enshrouds the hiker.

## FAUNA

The mountains are home to eight species of frogs and the Jamaican coney, a fish species whose demise within this century can be blamed on the voraciousness of the

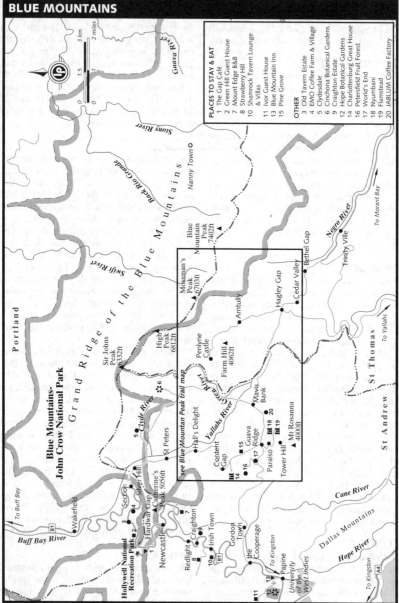

# BLUE MOUNTAINS

**PLACES TO STAY & EAT**
1 The Gap Café
2 Green Hill Guest House
7 Mount Edge B&B
8 Strawberry Hill
10 Shamrock Tavern Lounge & Villas
11 Ivor Guest House
13 Blue Mountain Inn
15 Pine Grove

**OTHER**
3 Old Tavern Estate
4 EMO Coffee Farm & Village
5 Clydesdale
6 Cinchona Botanical Gardens
9 Craighton Estate
12 Hope Botanical Gardens
14 Charlottenburg Great House
16 Petersfield Fruit Forest
17 World's End
18 Nyumbani
19 Flamstead
20 JABLUM Coffee Factory

Blue Mountains-
John Crow National Park

Grand Ridge of the Blue Mountains

Portland

St Thomas

St Andrew

Hollywell National Recreation Park

Blue Mountain Peak 7402ft
Mossman's Peak 6703ft
High Peak 6812ft
Sir Johns Peak 6332ft
Catherine's Peak 5056ft
Farm Hill 4062ft
Mt Rosanna 4000ft

see Blue Mountain Peak trail map

non-native mongoose. Birdlife is more pro-lific. Among the commonly seen species are the 'doctorbird,' Jamaican blackbird, Jamaican tody, rufous-throated solitaire, white eyed thrush, rufous-tailed flycatcher, the ring-tailed pigeon, and the crested quail dove, or 'mountain witch.' Butterflies are also numerous, including the transparent 'glass wing' butterfly. The large swallowtail is found not in the Blue Mountains, but in the John Crow Mountains to the east.

## DEFORESTATION

Vegetation on the north side of the mountains differs markedly from that on the south. The north side is lusher – the forest begins at about 2000 feet – but the south side has been cleared to between 3000 and 4500 feet, mostly for vegetable farming, coffee, and fruit trees. Blue Mountain ecology is fragile and soil erosion is a major problem.

Deforestation in the Blue Mountains has a long history. During the 18th and 19th centuries much of the hills were cleared to supply the coffee houses of Europe. Since the demise of the coffee industry, eucalyptus and pine have taken hold, while in some places the slopes have been conquered by savanna-type grasses, introduced from Africa early this century. Be careful hiking: tangled grass stems hide gullies, causing serious injury to unwary livestock and hikers.

Every year the pressure increases to cultivate higher slopes. Squatters, charcoal burners, and timber pirates have continued to fell trees. And both the Coffee Industry Board and Forestry Industry Development Co were recently allocated former forest reserve for clearance (the Forestry Dept has had a history of political corruption and has been accused of turning a blind eye to ongoing violations). Fortunately, in 1997 the Natural Resources Conservation Authority (NRCA), the body entrusted with managing Jamaica's national parks and protected areas, scored a noteworthy victory when it halted the Coffee Expansion Project on the upper flanks of the Rio Grande Valley. The past few years have seen a genuine committed effort to make good on a growing eco-sensitive ethic, and the park is very much a reality.

Even Mother Nature has been a vandal. The forests suffered miserably during Hurricane Gilbert in 1988, when extensive forest cover was lost.

A good introduction to Blue Mountain ecology is the *Blue Mountain Guide* (edited by Margaret Hodges), published by the Natural History Society of Jamaica.

## BLUE MOUNTAINS-JOHN CROW NATIONAL PARK

On February 28, 1993, the first steps were taken to control logging; the Blue Mountains-John Crow National Park was created to protect 193,260 acres. It is managed by the Natural Resources Conservation Authority (NRCA) under the Protected Areas Resource Conservation Project (PARC), a regulatory body set up in 1991 as a joint venture between the USAID (Agency for International Development) and the Jamaican government.

The park includes the forest reserves of the Blue and John Crow Mountain Ranges and spans the parishes of St Andrew, St Thomas, Portland, and St Mary. Forty percent of the higher plant species are endemic to the area, and the forests harbor many endangered species, including the Jamaican hutia, giant swallow-tail butterflies, and yellow-billed parrots.

Community participation is seen as critical to policing the park. Local advisory committees have been established to involve the communities, so that they derive benefit from protecting the forests. Ecotourism is being promoted, and locals are being trained as guides. As yet the park has gone virtually unnoticed by nature lovers, despite its many attractions.

See Ecology & Environment in the Facts about Jamaica chapter for details.

### Information

There are ranger stations at Hollywell and Portland Gap, and at Millbank in the Rio Grande Valley (see the Port Antonio & Northeast Coast chapter), plus an administrative office (☎ 977-8044) at Guava Ridge, near Mavis Bank, St Andrew. It's open 10 am to 4 pm weekdays.

Entry to the park is free at this writing, but plans called for the introduction of fees by the year 2000, when visitors will have to purchase a permit (about US$5) from the ranger stations or the Jamaica Conservation & Development Trust (☎ 960-2848), 95 Dumbarton Ave, Kingston 10.

For more information, contact the national park office at Guava Ridge, the Jamaica Conservation & Development Trust, or the NRCA (☎ 923-5125) at 53 Molynes Rd, Kingston 10.

## Hiking

'To really appreciate the Blue Mountains you must go there, accept the challenge, and walk the trail to the summit,' says writer Ivan Goodbody. The Blue Mountains are a hiker's paradise. Dozens of trails lace the hills, many carved by British soldiers over a century ago. Others were used in the heyday of coffee by mule trains and were kept open by foresters and farmers who used them (until recent decades) to transport their produce to market in Kingston. Many have since become overgrown, but others remain the mainstay of communications for locals, the vast majority of whom do not own cars. No roads penetrate the northeastern slopes, and here it is still possible to savor the isolation that for two centuries made the area a Maroon redoubt.

Trails (called 'tracks' locally) are rarely marked. When asking directions of locals, remember that 'a few chains' can mean several miles, while 'jus' a likkle way' may in fact be a few hours of hiking. Hiring a guide is highly recommended. Within the Blue Mountains-John Crow National Park, hiking trails have been categorized as guided, nonguided, and wilderness. Work continues on a 'Grand Ridge of the Blue Mountains Trail,' similar to the US Appalachian Trail, with huts for sleeping along the way. The trail will run from Morces Gap in the west (access is from Jack's Hill in Kingston) via Blue Mountain Peak, to Corn Puss Gap in the John Crow Mountains.

You'll rarely be far from a village or homestead where hospitable country folk are certain to assist you.

Jack's Hill (see the Kingston & Environs chapter) provides a good base for hikes. Trails lead uphill to Peter's Rock and the peak of Mt Horeb (4850 feet). Another trail ascends from Peter's Rock to Hollywell National Recreation Park. An old trading route, the **Vinegar Hill Trail**, begins here and ascends via Catherine's Peak (5056 feet) before dropping down to Chepstowe, near Buff Bay, on the north coast.

**Organized Hikes** Members of the Veterans Hiking Group take weekend hikes throughout the Blue and John Crow Mountains. Non-members are welcome. There's no fee, but you should contribute to transportation costs. Contact Ian Wallace, c/o the Forestry Dept (☎ 924-2667).

Maya Lodge (☎ 702-0314, 702-0112), PO Box 216, Kingston 7, at Jack's Hill on the Skyline Drive northwest of the B1, remains the prime resource center and is the base for the Jamaica Alternative Tourism, Camping & Hiking Association (JATCHA) and for the Destinations tour company. It will help customize an itinerary for hiking and other special interest travel. Destinations (formerly Sense Adventures), offers guided hikes, including day hikes from US$17 per person (departing at 8:30 am); and an overnight 'Blue Mountain Peak Trek' that includes 4WD transfers to Penlyne Castle, dinner, accommodations, and breakfast for US$170 per person (minimum two people). Some trips start at Maya Lodge; others begin at Hollywell or Penlyne Castle. (See the Outdoor Activities and Kingston & Environs chapters for further details.)

Nature N U Tours (☎ 977-5607), 3 University Drive, Elleston Flats, Kingston 7, also specializes in guided tours of the Blue Mountains. Weekend trips cost US$28.50 to US$43 per person, and use the cabins at Portland Gap. It also offers hiking around Clydesdale and Cinchona.

Blue Mountain Adventure Tours, at Section, also offers guided hikes. Costs range from US$25 to US$50 per day, depending on the group size. You can ask for a specialist guide with knowledge of birds and botany. The company has no telephone, but you can call park headquarters (☎ 977-8044) at Guava Ridge to make arrangements.

Sun Ventures (☎ 960-6685, fax 929-7512), 30 Balmoral Ave, Kingston 10, offers hikes, including one to Blue Mountain Peak with an option for a night hike with camping at the peak. Other hikes follow trails on the northern slopes and a rugged three-day hike along the Grand Ridge. Hikes begin at US$50 per person for day trips (US$35 per person in groups of three or more people), and US$75 for overnight trips (US$55 for three or more people), including transportation.

The Touring Society of Jamaica (☎ 975-7158, fax 975-3620, lyndalee@islandoutpost .com, www.touringjamaica.com), c/o Island Outpost, PO Box 118, Ocho Rios, offers a more esoteric range of upscale trips, including hiking around Cinchona, for groups of six people or more from US$250 per day.

**Freelance Guides** Guides can be hired from Maya Lodge for about US$25 for half-day, US$35 full-day.

You can also hire guides nearby at Foxy's Pub, in Jack's Hill. Look for Michael 'Sweet Pea' Barrett, who has been guiding since he was a teenager; or the Mitchell brothers (Tony and Chris), both of whom are experienced and courteous guides. Outdoor adventure expert, Stephen Cohen, also recommends Norman 'Willie' Graham, who leads tours on his organic farm, and the elderly Leonard 'Baps' Cole.

Freelance guides hire themselves out at Penlyne Castle, Hagley Gap, and Mavis Bank (see relevant sections, later in this chapter).

On overnight trips, you're expected to buy the guide's food and pay for his accommodations.

For locale-specific information, see the Hiking sections and the Blue Mountain Peak section in this chapter.

**Maps** If you hike alone, buy the Survey Dept 1:50,000 or, better yet, the excellent 1:12,500 Ordnance Survey topographic map series, available from the Survey Dept (☎ 922-6630), 23½ Charles St, PO Box 493, Kingston. Four different sheets – numbers 13, 14, 18, and 19 – cover the area around

Blue Mountain Peak; you may need to buy all four (US$5 each), depending on the route you intend to follow. The maps are available in England from Ordnance Survey, Romsey Rd, Southampton SO9 4DH.

**Guidebooks** An absolute prerequisite to hiking alone is *A Hiker's Guide to the Blue Mountains*, by Bill Wilcox, who describes a wide range of hikes. It was published in 1985, but not much has changed.

**Water** Although increased use of pesticides has led to an increase in river pollution, upper-course streams are usually clean enough to drink from (many harbor freshwater crayfish, called *janga* – not to be mistaken for *ganja* – that can grow up to a foot long). Experienced hikers know to drink from the fresh rainwater in the reservoirs of the cupped leaves of bromeliads. Take a cloth with you to strain out dead bugs and decaying vegetation.

## CYCLING

The Blue Mountains are good for exploring by bicycle. You'll need a sturdy mountain bike. Take plenty of water, as well as a puncture repair kit. The going can be steep and arduous, but you'll generally be warmly welcomed by locals. If you want a fairly tame organized bicycle tour, call Blue Mountain Tours (☎ 974-7075, fax 974-0635), 152 Main St, Ocho Rios, which offers a downhill bicycling tour that begins at 5060 feet and descends to the north coast. The company also offers customized trips along mountain trails, including a two-day trip with a visit to the Old Tavern Estate (US$150).

Neil Chin operates Wilderness Tours, 1 Annex Cres, Barbican, Kingston, offering mountain bike tours with a gourmet three-course meal at Strawberry Hill, southwest of Newcastle (US$150).

You can also take guided mountain bike tours with Go Active Vacations (☎ 944-8431, 991-4292) at Mt Edge; owner Michael Fox offers a one-day trip to Wildflower Lodge (US$120), a two-day trip to Wildflower and Bath (US$160), and a local half-day trip (US$60).

## ORGANIZED TOURS

The Touring Society of Jamaica (see Organized Hikes, above, for contact information) offers a series of Blue Mountains tours and excursions, including a 5-day tour called 'Jamaica's Historic Gardens' that features Castleton and Cinchona and costs US$2300. Short walks around Irish Town are US$10 per hour, or stroll along the Gordon Town and Fairy Glade Trails for US$35 to US$50. It also organizes a half-day birdwatching tour (US$25), and the Blue Mountains are included on its eight-day 'Birding Jamaica' tour (US$3345 for two people).

The Touring Society of Jamaica also has a series of special events for Jamaica residents, including dinner lectures and slide presentations at Strawberry Hill, and a series of garden tours, including weekends at Strawberry Hill, visits to Cinchona Botanical Garden, and a Strawberry Hill Garden Tour & Sunday Brunch (US$43).

Pro Tours Ltd (☎ 978-6113), 8 Lady Musgrave Rd, Kingston 5, offers a Blue Mountain tour from Kingston, Montego Bay, and Ocho Rios. Island Car Rentals offers a series of personally chauffeured tours, including historic and cultural tours of the Blue Mountains (US$64).

## SPECIAL EVENTS

Strawberry Hill (☎ 944-8400, fax 944-8408, strawberry@toj.com, www.islandoutpost.com/StrawberryHill) hosts a calendar of special events, including the Dewars Classic Backgammon Tournament in July; a series of 'Torch Night' concerts, billed as a 'sizzling showcase of Jamaica's best music makers,' in fall; a Halloween Party; the Jamaican Art & Fine Craft Fair in November; and the Christmas Craft Fair.

## THE COOPERAGE

Two miles above Papine via Gordon Town Rd is the Cooperage, a hamlet named for its community of Irish coopers who made the wooden barrels in which coffee beans were shipped in the 19th century. The historic Blue Mountain Inn, a former coaching inn housed in a former coffee plantation house, overlooks the Mammee River. It was once ritzy enough to serve Lyndon Johnson and members of the British royal family and today is an acclaimed restaurant.

The Mammee River Rd leads left from the T-junction above the inn and follows the river valley uphill. The road was cut in 1896 to link the military camp at Newcastle. It hugs the mountainside and its entire length is one switchback after another. The views are breathtaking, but drivers should leave the gawking to passengers. The road is narrow, overgrown with foliage, and the corners are blind, so honk your horn frequently. Take particular care on weekends when the road gets busy. Two and a half miles uphill, a road to the left follows the Mammee River to Maryland and Peter's Rock, overlooking Jack's Hill.

The road straight ahead at the Cooperage leads to Gordon Town, Mavis Bank, and Blue Mountain Peak.

Buses to Redlight, Hardwar Gap, and Gordon Town all pass the Cooperage.

### Places to Eat

The *Blue Mountain Inn* (☎ 927-1700, 927-2606) so exudes olde English charm that you might imagine yourself in the Yorkshire Dales, surrounded by stone walls, suffused in the warm glow of a log fire, and the welcome of soft-cushioned sofas and chairs. This rambling restaurant, full of period pieces, has a carved mahogany bar and a dining room over the river where the likes of feta salad, spicy cajun shrimp, duck a l'orange, and rack of lamb are served at dinner (7 pm to 10 pm). Lunch is provided for groups.

### IRISH TOWN

Mammee River Rd climbs to Irish Town, a small hamlet where the coopers lived during the last century. Potatoes are still an important crop, reflecting the Irish influence. Farther uphill is Redlight, a hamlet apparently named for the fact that it served as a brothel for soldiers from the Newcastle barracks.

In an emergency, call the Irish Town police station (☎ 944-8242).

### Bamboo Lodge

This private home, just before Irish Town, served as a recuperation station for fever-stricken sailors during the last century. Lord Nelson came here as a 20-year-old to recover from dysentery and was attended by a noted herbalist, Couba Cornwallis, mistress of the Earl of Cornwallis, the governor at the time.

## Craighton Estate

Craighton Estate (☎ 944-8224), 6½ miles above the Cooperage, is a coffee plantation built in 1805. Today it is owned by Ushima, the largest coffee company in Japan. Coffee is still grown. Tours are available on Tuesday and Thursday by appointment. Visits cost US$20. It's open 9 am to 5 pm only.

## Places to Stay & Eat

**Strawberry Hill** (see Special Events for contact information) is a superlative retreat suspended 3100 feet up, just north of Irish Town. The property is owned by Chris Blackwell, the impresario who launched Bob Marley to fame through his label, Island Records. (Marley convalesced here after being shot in 1976.) The 12 Caribbean-style cottages range from studio suites to a four-bedroom, two-story house – Highgate – built into the hillside by local villagers who were trained as craftsworkers during the property's five-year evolution. Each cottage is a statement in elegance, from hand-molded hardwood sofas, to stereos with CD players, chic bedside lamps, Jamaican spice colognes, and Sperod's Olive Oil soaps in the terracotta tubs.

Just imagine settling in a hammock on your veranda, listening to reggae riffs carried uphill on the breeze, while far below, Kingston twinkles like myriad fireflies. Your dark mahogany four-poster bed, a mile off the floor, will be lined with crisp linen sheets and an electric blanket perfect for chilly nights. Relax under the plump down comforter and marvel at the phosphorescent flickering of fireflies flitting about the room.

There's even a full-service Aveda spa with sauna (spa retreat packages are available), and a pool was added in late 1998 to the garden where Hawaiian landscape architect Stephen Haust planted several growing zones into 6 acres, providing each cottage with a unique landscape.

Rates for the one to three-bedroom units (some with kitchen) range from US$280 to US$590 per night, including breakfast. From mid-April to mid-December, rates go down to US$175 to US$575. For information and reservations, contact Island Outpost (see Accommodations in the Facts for the Visitor chapter for all contact information). Transfers are included, and a helicopter is available at additional cost. The staff reflect Blackwell's principle that with professional training and guidance the local labor pool provides the highest standards.

Strawberry Hill hosts special events (see Special Events, earlier in this chapter).

Many Kingstonians make the longish drive to Strawberry Hill for some of the finest nouvelle Jamaican cuisine on the island. Among the savory dishes are curried pumpkin soup (US$4), soy bean roti stuffed with curried vegetables (US$13), and jerk lamb loin with roasted garlic (US$20). Reservations are advisable. Locally born master chef, James Palmer, offers residential cooking courses (US$2500).

The modest **Shamrock Tavern Lounge & Villas**, at Irish Town, has rooms, plus a lively bar with video games, but the receptionist wouldn't let me in or give me any additional information on the hotel.

## Getting There & Away

You can take a bus or minibus from Papine (US$0.30), passing Irish Town en route to Redlight and Newcastle.

## NEWCASTLE

Newcastle hangs invitingly on the mountainside high above Irish Town. The road climbs tortuously to 4000 feet where, 13 miles from Kingston, you suddenly emerge on a wide parade ground square guarded by a small cannon. The military encampment clambers up the slope above the square. Newcastle was founded in 1841 by Field Marshall Sir William Gomm, Commanding Officer of the British Forces in Jamaica. Back then, soldiers stationed on the Liguanea plains were dying of yellow fever. Gomm fought a battle against the British bureaucracy to establish a training site and convalescent center in the more salubrious hills. 'We have carried the hill!' he wrote. With the granting of independence in 1962, the camp was turned over to the Jamaica Defense Force.

The square offers a fantastic view of Kingston. With good fortune you may even arrive to watch recruits being drilled. Note the insignia on the whitewashed stone wall, commemorating those regiments stationed at Newcastle (it dates back to 1884, when it was started by the North Staffordshire Regiment). A turnoff on the square leads up through the camp and continues to Catherine's Peak.

Reportedly you can nip into the Sergeant's mess for a quick tipple. Since this is a military camp, visitors are allowed only around the canteen, shop, roadways, and parade ground.

### Hiking

A path marked **Woodcutter's Gap** begins from the road above the parade ground and leads through a thicket of wild ginger lilies before linking with the Fairy Glade Trail (see Hiking in the Hollywell National Recreation Park section). Green Hills Trail, Fern Walk Trail, and Woodcutter's Trail also begin north of Newcastle.

A camp store – the Tuck Shop – is around the corner, west of the parade ground. It sells groceries, pastries, and sodas, and is a good place to get your provisions for hiking.

### Places to Stay & Eat

Several cottages – *the Roost*, *Stepping Stone*, and *Blue Mist* – are available for rent near Newcastle. For more information contact the Touring Society (see Organized Hikes, earlier in this chapter). You can also rent some of the military cottages by contacting Newcastle Hill Station (☎ 944-8230).

*Tree Tops* (☎ 974-5831, fax 974-5830), just below Newcastle, is another handsome house set amid gardens, with two bedrooms and views over Kingston.

A good option nearby is *Mount Edge B&B* (☎ 944-8151, 1-816-8597 cellular, ☎ 888-991-4292). The all-wood house has two rooms for US$35 double, including

breakfast, for the 'rock room,' and US$45 for the 'room with a view,' plus a spacious lounge with kitchen and wide glass windows to all sides. The owner, Michael Fox, offers three bike tours from Mt Edge (see Cycling, earlier in this chapter). The place is an official bird-watching station.

The colorful roadside *Mount Edge Fruit Bar & Café* has a full bar.

Fox also hosts occasional 'Moonlick' parties during full-moon Fridays.

## HARDWAR GAP

Two miles above Newcastle you reach Hardwar Gap, at the crest of the Grand Ridge. The Gap Café sits on the hillside just below the summit and Hollywell National Recreation Park. The Gap is a fabulous place to rest and take in the vistas over a soda or cappuccino (see Places to Eat, below). The original house was set up as a way station for buggy traffic in the 19th century. With the advent of motorcars, a 10 shilling charge was levied for overnight stays (guests had to provide their own food and bed linen). Accommodations are no longer offered.

The café also has the Dis 'n Dat Gift Store selling a full stock of Jamaican food and gift items. Walkways lead down through the beautiful gardens.

## HOLLYWELL NATIONAL RECREATION PARK

The mist-shrouded uppermost slopes are densely forested with rare primary montane forest. Hollywell National Recreation Park, 200 yards above the Gap Café, protects 300 acres of this remnant woodland, lush with dozens of fern species, epiphytes, impatiens, violets, nasturtiums, and wild strawberries and raspberries (many exotic species were introduced as fodder plants for army horses in 1841) growing in the lee of soapwood and dogwood. Pine trees dominate. In 1988, Hurricane Gilbert did extensive damage. Many trees have been replaced, and the tropical climate has assisted in rapid revegetation. If you're a birder, bring binoculars. Doctorbirds, todies, and solitaires are among the many easily spotted species.

The Doctorbird

The park – which is actually part of Blue Mountains-John Crow National Park – is administered by the Jamaica Conservation & Development Trust (☎ 960-2848, fax 960-2850, jcdt@greenjamaica.com, jamcondt@uwimona.edu.jm), Dumbarton Avenue, Kingston 10, PO Box 1225, Kingston 8.

A ranger station is on the right a short distance beyond the entrance. (The toll gate is not always occupied.) The park has view points and picnic spots.

## Hiking

Hollywell is tremendous for hiking. Trails lead off in all directions through the ferny dells, cloud forest, and elfin woodland. With a bit of luck or better-than-average skill at map reading you can even find the Cascade, Jamaica's second-highest waterfall, plunging sheer off the north slope off Hartley Hill (4363 feet).

The **Fairy Glade Trail** is occasionally closed for rehabilitation; it has been abused by people taking wild plants. This four-hour trail is a rough scramble through the tropical montane and elfin forest to the summit of Mt Horeb (4037 feet). A new trail – **Oatley Mountain Trail** – was due to open at this writing, with educational signs leading through the forest to a river that's good for bathing. You'll pay for access and must be accompanied by a guide.

Another trail – negotiable by 4WD – leads down to Peter's Rock and Jack's Hill.

## Places to Stay

**Camping** is allowed for US$3 per person. There are water faucets and toilets.

You can rent rustic **cabins** with twin beds and basic kitchen for US$5 per cabin for up to four people; bring your own bedding and food. Advance reservations are essential via the Blue Mountains-John Crow National Park office (☎ 977-8044; ask for Roger Williams). Holiday and weekend stays should be booked several weeks in advance. It's open 8:30 am to 5 pm weekdays.

## Places to Eat

The atmospheric **Gap Café** (☎ 997-3032, 923-7055, fax 923-5617) sits on the hillside at 4200 feet, beside the entrance to Hollywell, 2 miles above Newcastle. You can choose elegant dining either indoors or alfresco beneath a canopy on a two-tier wooden terrace with wrought-iron furniture. A 'Jamaican special' breakfast costs US$12. High tea is also served (US$2). And the eclectic lunch menu includes curried Caribbean shrimp, shepherd's pie, sandwiches, and delicious pastries by Colin ('pastry chef extraordinaire'). A cup of Blue Mountain coffee costs a steep US$3.50! But you're drinking in the view and atmosphere too. Dinner is by reservation only. It has a well-stocked gift store. The café is open 10 am to 5 pm weekdays, until 6 pm on weekends (closed Good Friday). Bring mosquito repellent.

## Getting There & Away

Buses operate twice daily between Papine and Buff Bay, on the north coast, via Newcastle, Hardwar Gap, and Section. It costs about US$0.30.

**BLUE MOUNTAINS**

## SECTION

Heading north from Hollywell, the road drops steeply toward the hamlet of Section and then more gently curls its way down to Buff Bay, 18 miles north. As soon as you crest the ridge, the vegetation on the north-facing slope is noticeably lusher. You'll pass several cottages with colorful gardens. The most dramatic is Green Hill Guest House (see Places to Stay, below), surrounded by azaleas, fuchsias, hydrangeas, rhododendrons, magnolias, and nasturtiums.

A turnoff to the right at Section leads a mile to **Silver Hill**. The road is lush with ferns that brush against your car. Silver Hill is a ridgetop crossroads where the main road – horrendously eroded – loops south and drops to Content Gap, eventually linking up with the road from Gordon Town to Mavis Bank. A dirt road to the left drops to Silver Hill Coffee Factory (visitors are welcome). After touring the factory, check out the small-time operation of James Dennis, one of scores of small landholders hereabouts who make their income from coffee and form the Portland Blue Mountain Coffee Co-Operative Society.

Mr Dennis spends his time hiking up and down the mountains and tending his precious coffee beans (he will 'grind' some for you by filling a hollow log and beating the beans with a stout hardwood shillelagh – average price is about US$15 per pound).

Many of the farmers hire out as guides. The Blue Mountain Adventure Tours hiking group is based in Section.

The **Fishdone Waterfall**, midway between Section and Buff Bay, on the north coast, makes a pleasant spot to stop for a swim (turn left just above the white bridge).

## Old Tavern Estate

About 400 yards downhill from Green Hill Guest House is a small, anonymous cottage that you would surely pass by if you didn't know that its occupants, Alex and Dorothy Twyman, produce the best of the best of Blue Mountain coffee (their coffee was named 'Best in the Caribbean' in 1998). The old wooden house is perched on the cliffside at 3900 feet, overlooking coffee

groves, with marvelous views toward Buff Bay. If you plan on visiting a coffee farm, make it the Old Tavern Estate. The Twymans welcome visitors by prior arrangement only to their Old Tavern Estate (☎/fax 924-2785), PO Box 131, Kingston 8. No visitors are accepted on Fridays.

Although the Twymans' coffee is acclaimed as the best on the island, until recently they weren't allowed to sell an ounce due to Kafkaesque government regulations. Mr Twyman wanted to sell his beans under his own estate label instead of seeing them blended with lesser beans from other Blue Mountain farms. The coffee board consistently denied Mr Twyman a license to process and roast his own coffee and sell it as 'Blue Mountain' coffee because it was processed on site, not at an official JABLUM processing plant. Laws defining 'Blue Mountain coffee' currently are based on where coffee is *processed*, not where it's grown. Mr Twyman stopped selling his beans to the coffee board in 1982 and began storing his unroasted beans at a warehouse. (Handily, he discovered that coffee that's aged before it is roasted is highly prized. Apparently, aging enhances the bean's flavor by mellowing it. So the Twyman family was sitting on a mountain of the finest and most expensive coffee beans in the world.)

Finally, in 1997, after a tempestuous battle with vested political powers, the Twymans were begrudgingly granted his exclusive license to grow, process, roast, and sell a 'single estate coffee' under his estate label – the *only* estate on the island so permitted. (It was a bittersweet victory: that same day, their son, Mark Twyman, was murdered under suspicious circumstances.) Father and son had been planning to build a hospitality center, but the plans are on hold.

See 'Hallowed Grounds' in the Facts about Jamaica chapter for more details on the politics of Blue Mountain coffee.

The farm currently has 90,000 bushes raised semi-organically and at a low density to protect against disease in the wet climate (other farms have high-density bushes and use lots of fungicides and pesticides). And where other estates pick their berries before or shortly after cool rainy weather sets in, Mr

Twyman lets his mature on the bush through winter (as long as eight months), so that they develop a more robust, mellow flavor. The estate produces no more than 30,000lb per year. Mr Twyman's estate-roasted coffee is a bargain at US$25 per pound. It's sold in special bags with one-way valves that permit carbon dioxide (given off by beans) to escape, without permitting oxygen (which causes oxidation) in. You can have orders of 5lb or more shipped by FedEx (from US$175 to the USA, US$200 to elsewhere). The Twymans are also considering introducing 'roast-your-own' coffee for visitors, who can sample their coffee and their homemade mead, honey, and coffee liqueur.

A trail leads down through lush ferns and moist forest to a stream with freshwater crab and shrimp. The remains of the original tavern can also be seen amid the coffee bushes.

Understand that you're visiting a working farm. If he has time, Mr Twyman or his elder son, David, may give you a guided walk through the farm.

You can order Twyman coffee in North America from the Great Estates Coffee Company (☎ 800-334-0928, www.coffeereview .com), which also publishes *Coffee Review* magazine.

The Touring Society of Jamaica offers a tour to the Old Tavern (US$75), as does Pro Tours Ltd (☎ 978-6139). See Organized Hikes and Organized Tours, earlier in this chapter.

### Places to Stay & Eat

You can camp at *EMO Coffee Farm & Village* (☎ 977-1749), clinging to the hillside 1 mile above Section.

The basic *Green Hill Guest House & Cottages* (☎ 997-4087, fax 952-6591, PO Box 467, Montego Bay), owned by the Institute of Jamaica, are part of a delightful-looking home in a magnificent setting amid bright-flowering plants, a mile north of Section. The inside is more ascetic. The six bedrooms, which cost US$20 per person, have hardwood floors and are bare but for the beds, one of which is a magnificent antique four-poster. The rooms share one bathroom with a deep tub. There's a small lounge and meals

are cooked in a large kitchen by a cook (don't forget to tip). You can enjoy marvelous views from a wide veranda when the clouds fade. With investment, this could be a classy gem. For now, it is a place only hardy budget travelers could love.

James Dennis lives in a three-story cinderblock *house* – testament to the popularity of his fine coffee – where he sometimes puts up guests for about US$20. You can also *camp*. Jerk chicken and simple Jamaican fare are served at a small *restaurant* across the way.

## GORDON TOWN

Gordon Town, at 1200 feet, is a neat village centered on a wide square with a police station (☎ 927-2805), post office, and even a tiny courthouse. It began life as a staging post for Newcastle in the days before the Mammee River Rd was cut from the Cooperage. The old parochial road still exists, though it is really a track: the Gordon Town Trail.

Local lore says the town was named for the Scottish regiment, the Gordon Highlanders, who were once billeted here. Others say its name is derived from that of Dr John Gordon, who purchased the botanical gardens – Spring Gardens – that had been established here about 1770, but have since disappeared. (For more information, see *Botanic Gardens of Jamaica* by Alan Eyre.)

'Brother' Joseph Wolfe, an aging Rastafarian, was hoping to build a riverside tourist spot a 30-minute hike from Gordon Town, where you can bathe in pools. He sells coffee (US$5 a pound) and fresh vegetables. He's a delight to talk to…and quite photogenic.

To reach Cinchona, Mavis Bank, and the trail to Blue Mountain Peak, turn right at the square and cross the narrow bridge.

### Hiking

The Gordon Town Trail begins in Gordon Town and follows the Hope River Valley via Mt Industry and Redlight. Another trail leads from Gordon Town to Sugar Loaf (7000 feet), Content Gap, Top Mountain, and Cinchona. The 13-mile track is very popular with youth groups and gets quite busy on public holidays and weekends.

A third track leads via Flamstead and Bellevue, Mt Rosanna, Governor's Bench, and Orchard to Mavis Bank (10 miles).

## Places to Stay & Eat

The *Tip Toe Inn*, a rum shop just below the square, reportedly has rooms. The most atmospheric place to eat is *King's Jacket Bar & Lounge*, half a mile above Gordon Town.

## Getting There & Away

Buses and 'coasters' operate between the Parade in Kingston and Gordon Town via Old Hope Rd and Papine (US$0.30). Other buses operate from Half Way Tree in Kingston.

## WORLD'S END

This pretty roadside cottage clings to the mountainside at 2500 feet, 3 miles from Gordon Town. Despite its Hansel-and-Gretel appearance and outside walls painted with murals, World's End (☎ 926-8888, fax 929-8465, sangseroldja@toj.com), in Gordon Town, is a factory that produces world-famous rums and liqueurs. The company has suffered economic difficulties of late and went into receivership in 1998, but was still open for visitors at press time.

It was created by Dr Ian Sangster, who was born in Scotland and came to Jamaica to teach in 1967. The chemist founded Sangster's Old Jamaica Spirits in 1974. From humble beginnings using a 10-gallon blending pot, an analytical balance, and a Scottish genius for distilling, Sangster parlayed two barrels of aged rum into a thriving business. Sangster concocted his beverages from natural extracts of fruits and spices, cane sugar, and mellow aged rum. You can learn how on tours by appointment. Inside, you can watch how the three ingredients are 'married,' a process apparently helped by the diurnal temperature range (from 50°F at night to 92°F by day).

Sangster's cream liqueurs were touted as aphrodisiacs in the movie *Higglers*. You can also purchase Golden de Luxe Rum (winner of the Gold Medal for rum in the 1987 International Wine and Spirits Competition), Coconut Rum, and White Rum (111 proof) which, claims Sangster, 'adds a little power to the smoothness in cocktails.' Each liqueur has its own reproduction ceramic bottle, such as the Port Royal Decanter, a hand-crafted flagon, and its own exquisite label showing an historic scene.

You can sample the goods on a hillside patio beneath shade trees with views down the valley.

## GUAVA RIDGE

Guava Ridge (2 miles above World's End) is the site of a hilltop junction for Pine Grove, Content Gap, and Cinchona (to the left), with Mavis Bank and Blue Mountain Peak straight ahead. En route you'll pass a turnoff for **Petersfield Fruit Forest**.

A road to the right (see the Blue Mountain Peak Trail map, later in this chapter), signed for 'Bellevue House' 50 yards east of Guava Ridge, leads through patches of forget-me-nots and forests of pine and eucalyptus to several summer homes, including **Nyumbani**, the retreat of the Manley family, and **Flamstead**, former great house – now in ruins – of Governor Edward Eyre (see 'Morant Bay Rebellion,' later in this chapter) and a lookout from which Horatio Nelson and other British naval officers once surveyed the Port Royal base, sending their messages with mirrors. The area has been laid out with roads for commercial development. The view over the Palisadoes and Kingston Harbour is fabulous.

Flamstead is 4 miles from Guava Ridge; the road is tortuous and badly eroded. You can visit Flamstead coffee plantation (☎ 960-0204) by prior appointment. Carlyle Dunkley, former Minister of Tourism, also has a coffee farm (☎ 977-1917) here and accepts tourists.

A dirt sideroad from the Flamstead road leads up to Paraiso, where there's a ranger station for the Blue Mountain National Park.

## CONTENT GAP

About 3 miles north of Guava Ridge is the hamlet of Content Gap, a center of coffee production by small-scale farmers. A trail leads downhill from here to Gordon Town.

Another heads uphill from the water tank at Content Gap to **Charlottenburg** (☎ 978-3530, 927-0752), a well-preserved great house with antique furnishings and still extant buildings that served as slave quarters. The mile-long walk takes about 20 minutes. It's open 9 am to 5 pm Tuesday, Thursday, and Friday, by reservation only.

### Places to Stay & Eat
*Pine Grove* (☎ 977-8001, fax 922-5895, Content Gap PA, St Andrew) is a popular Kingstonian family retreat on a bluff with a 360-degree view. Its 16 small and simply furnished rooms are charming, with two double beds, full kitchens, small verandas, and TVs. Private baths have hot water. The tranquil setting is made more so by the pretty, English-style gardens reached via red-brick pathways and terraces. Bamboo and eucalyptus abound. The all-wood restaurant with wicker furniture is popular with Kingstonians for dinner and Sunday brunch. Meals are by reservation only, even for guests. Pine Grove maintains its own coffee farm. Rooms are US$60 to US$75 double; studios with kitchenettes cost US$80 to US$85.

You may be able to stay at *Charlottenburg Great House* (☎ 978-3530, 927-0752, 927-2585, 1 Dublin Castle Close, Gordon Town) by prior arrangement.

### CLYDESDALE
Clydesdale is a derelict old coffee plantation and a popular spot for budget accommodations. The estate was taken over in 1937 by the newly formed Forestry Dept, which established a nursery. The much-battered water wheel and coffee mill machinery are partially intact. It has picnic spots and a small waterfall where you can skinny-dip. The **Morces Gap Trail** begins here.

The turnoff from the horrendously potholed 'main' road to Section is 2 miles beyond Content Gap, just above the hamlet of St Peters. To reach Clydesdale, cross the Chestervale Bridge over the Brook's River. Immediately you'll reach a Y-fork beside Anthony Wolfe's store. Take the left, steeply uphill for Clydesdale and Cinchona. It's a terribly rocky drive, suited for a 4WD only,

along a track much damaged by landslides. After a mile, you'll reach Clydesdale.

### Places to Stay
*Clydesdale* has a hostel-type dormitory and modestly furnished cabin. For reservations, contact the Forestry Dept (☎ 924-2667), 173 Constant Spring Rd. You must pick up your cabin reservations in advance in Kingston. Bring your own food. You can also camp at Clydesdale, which has water, toilets, and basic kitchen facilities for US$5; and there's riverside *camping* at Anthony Wolfe's, at Chestervale Bridge (see above). He'll sell you spice cakes, eggs, fruits, and other produce from his store, which was being rebuilt at this writing.

You can camp for US$1.50 per tent at *Eco-Holiday Village* (☎ 929-1226, 929-6163 in Kingston), which also has 560 bunk beds in dormitories (US$6 per person) amid breeze-swept pastures surrounded by pine forest. Campers can bring food (but can't use the kitchen) and a cook will prepare meals, which are also prepared on request for those using bunks (US$2.50 for three meals). Self-contained flats and cabins with kitchens cost US$17 single, US$28.50 double; with private bath and hot water they cost US$40 double. It has a laundry service and its own sick bay. The facility was built as a camp for juvenile delinquents and has the feel of a military compound. It is still used by police, youth, and church groups, who are catered to with volleyball, netball, and soccer fields, plus a bar and 'tuck shop' (snack bar). A games center with video games and an auditorium were planned. Guided hikes are offered. The turnoff is about 500 yards above the turnoff for Clydesdale after you cross the Chestervale Bridge.

### CINCHONA BOTANICAL GARDENS
Cinchona, at about 5000 feet, is one of the most spectacularly situated botanical gardens in the world, with fabulous views north to the peaks and down the valleys of the Clyde, Green, and Yallahs Rivers. It was founded in 1868 when Assam tea and cinchona (an Andean plant) were planted – the latter for quinine, which is extracted from

the bark, to fight malaria. The plantation proved unprofitable, however, and was abandoned. The grounds were later turned into a garden to supply Kingston with flowers.

In 1903 the Jamaican government leased Cinchona to the New York Botanical Garden and, later, the Smithsonian Institute, as a propagation station and laboratory for tropical plants. Cinchona has been kept up rather than maintained. Today it takes up a mere 30 acres, much of the land where cinchona and Assam tea were once cultivated having passed into coffee. It gets virtually no visitors, but is well worth the journey. Cinchona is a veritable Who's Who of botanical species: rubber trees, eucalyptus, oleander, juniper, cork oak, pecan, peach, and red-barked Blue Mountain yacca, Canary Island pines, massive rhododendrons, and azaleas that explode riotously in spring. Summer brings blue agapanthus and other lilies out in bloom.

The old governor's house (built of mahogany and pine) sits atop the gardens, fronted by lawns and looking a bit dilapi-dated (Hurricanes Allen in 1980 and Gilbert in 1988 gave it a thorough beating), although it is still chock-full of weathered antiques. The government has set about restoring Cinchona, but it is slow going. The **Panorama Walk** begins to the east of the gardens, leading through a glade of towering bamboo and opening to staggering views. Half a dozen other tracks snake off into the nether reaches of the mountains, including the 10-mile Vinegar Trail that leads to Buff Bay. No one should attempt to go any farther without a guide; you might be able to hire one of the gardeners.

### Places to Stay

You can *camp* here for US$5, but you must reserve in person at the Forestry Dept (☎ 924-2667), 173 Constant Spring Rd, Kingston. Guest cottages are planned.

### Getting There & Away

Finding Cinchona may prove difficult without a guide. A 4WD is essential. Con-tinue uphill from Clydesdale for 2 miles until you reach a three-way junction. A house and coffee nursery called Top Moun-tain sit on a knoll overlooking the junction (there's another farmhouse directly ahead; the Ministry of Agriculture maintains an experimental vegetable farm and temperate fruit orchards here). Take the steep uphill track that leads north past Top Mountain. Keep left at the Y-junction and continue aiming uphill. It's a vertiginous drive; don't underestimate the road. The ruts are deep enough to hang up your chassis and leave your wheels spinning thin air. You may have to walk the final mile.

The Touring Society of Jamaica offers excursions to Cinchona (see Organized Tours, earlier in this chapter).

## MAVIS BANK

Mavis Bank, a one-hour drive from Kingston, is a tidy little village in the midst of coffee country (see the Blue Mountain Peak Trail map, later in this chapter). It's a perfect base and gateway to the real Blue Mountains. Everyone around here is notice-ably more friendly than in Kingston. They're country folk, inclined to say 'hello' instead of giving you a sullen stare. Locals joke that the police from Kingston are posted here when they're in need of some R&R.

The People's Cooperative Bank (☎ 977-8010), in the village center, represents Western Union and is open 9 am to 3 pm weekdays. The police station (☎ 977-8004) and post office are just below Blue Mountain Taverna. There's a public telephone here.

A shy young man named Carlton Hall produces some wonderful carvings in lignum vitae. He has a workshop up the hill, catercorner to the Blue Mountain Taverna, which sells his works.

### Mavis Bank Central Coffee Factory

The JABLUM coffee factory here is one of four coffee-processing plants through which all legally defined Blue Mountain coffee must pass. It's owned by Keble Munn, former Minister of Agriculture and a descendant of National Hero George William Gordon. Munn's grandfather, Victor Munn, set up a pulpery here in the 1920s to process coffee brought in from outlying districts. There's a small 'museum' with historical artifacts and photos of Keble Munn through the ages (there he is in 1923, at three years old, raking coffee in knee-breeches). The factory – brick buildings centered around a huge patio covered with drying coffee beans – is in a hollow below the road as you approach the village. Ask chief 'cupper,' Norman Grant, to kindly demonstrate 'cupping' (tasting), the technique to identify quality coffee; he sucks a spoonful of liquid coffee in to cause a fine spray that hits the taste buds at the back of the mouth.

The factory was in receivership in 1988 (much to the despair – or delight – of knowledgeable coffee growers). The coffee is marketed ready-roasted and vacuum-sealed under the JABLUM and Mavis Bank labels, though much is sold to the Coffee Industry Board. You can tour the factory (☎ 977-8005, fax 977-8014, c.munn@gte.net) by appointment before 3:30 pm daily; it's open 8 am to 4 pm. A tour is US$8.50.

The factory is accused of polluting the Yallahs River, causing diarrhea and skin diseases among residents who rely upon it for their water supply.

Also see 'Hallowed Grounds' in the Facts about Jamaica chapter.

### Hiking

You can hire guides from a small rum shop called Hikers Guide Rest Point. It even offers mules for hikes to Blue Mountain Peak. The trail begins at Churchyard Rd and leads steeply uphill for 5 miles to Penlyne Castle; see Organized Hikes under Blue Mountain Peak, later in this chapter.

In the village center, Climb Every Mountain (☎ 977-8541; ask for Miss Campbell) offers a tour guiding service. It rents tents and camping equipment, and does 'walkabouts' as well as trips to Blue Mountain Peak.

Forres Park Guest House & Farm offers guided tours of Blue Mountain Peak (US$43 by day, US$57 by night). Malcolm McInnes, of Blue Mountain Taverna, also offers tours in his 4WD, plus hikes, including to the top of Blue Mountain Peak.

### Places to Stay & Eat

You can rent rooms from locals, as well as with owners Jill and Paul Byles at *Paraiso* (☎ 977-8007, 924-9505), a farmstead between Guava Ridge and Mavis Bank.

The *Forres Park Guest House & Farm* (☎ 977-8141, 927-5957 in Kingston, fax 978-6942), between the coffee factory and village, is a working coffee farm with an enviable hillside setting, with lush gardens and tiers of coffee bushes flowing downhill like folds of green silk. It offers six rooms in the main lodge and three basic wooden cottages with red concrete floors and pine furniture for US$20 single, US$25 to US$30 double. Meals are cooked by request.

A surprising spic-and-span gem is the *Blue Mountain Taverna* (☎ 977-8223, fax 977-8440, taverna@in-site.com, www.in-site .com/taverna/), a three-story house on the 'square' in Mavis Bank. This 'home away from home' is run by Ilean (a Jamaican raised in England) and Malcolm McInnes (a transplanted Scot), and has four carpeted, simply furnished rooms, each with en-suite bath, heater, a quilt, and plenty of blankets, and walls that meet at odd angles. The couple are the most gracious hosts imaginable, and engaging raconteurs to boot, especially over a glass of whisky, conversing into the wee hours in a cozy lounge with piano, stereo, large-screen TV, and VCR. (Malcolm might even play his dulcimer for you.) Rates are US$40 single, US$65 double, US$75 triple. The McInnes, who are a blessing to the community for their exemplary contributions, offer transfers for out-of-towners from their Bench & Bar Restaurant, in downtown Kingston.

The Taverna is a member of the Ring of Confidence (see the Accommodations section in the Facts for the Visitor chapter).

You owe it to yourself to make the trip from Kingston simply to eat at Blue Mountain Taverna. Ilean was for years a successful restaurateur in London, and Malcolm is a gourmand and wine-lover. The are four tiny dining areas, including the roadside café, an Upstairs Balcony serving local and international dishes, and a small garden area with views toward the Peak – perfect for breakfast (from US$5) and a 'wicked' Calypso Coffee laced with rum to get the day going. Home-made fruit punch and ginger beer are served, and there's a large cellar of international wines. Lunches and dinners (you can eat any time up to 10 pm) cost from US$8. Be sure to try the Blue Mountain Coffee Rum Cake, which the McInnes hope to export commercially. A 'Gourmet Night' special costs US$120 double including accommodations, breakfast, and gourmet dinner in a formal dining room. Delightful!

### Getting There & Away
A bus runs from Papine in early morning, and again in early afternoon via Gordon Town and Guava Ridge to Mavis Bank (US$0.75). A taxi from Kingston to Mavis Bank costs about US$13 (or US$1.50 per person sharing a 'robot' or a minibus). If you're driving, turn left for Mavis Bank at the unmarked T-junction, 1½ miles east of Guava Ridge (the road ahead leads to Tower Hill).

### HAGLEY GAP
This ramshackle village sits abreast a hill east of Mavis Bank (the road is 'bad to 'ell'), and is the gateway to the Blue Mountain Peak (see the Blue Mountain Peak Trail map). It's a center for cultivation of pimento, which often lies scattered on the ground to dry. The road forks in the village, where a horrendously denuded dirt road for Penlyne and thence Blue Mountain Peak begins a precipitous ascent (4WD only), as if scaling a cliff.

Beyond Hagley Gap, the 'main' road continues downhill to the Negro River and, beyond, the remote hamlets of Woburn Lawn and Cedar Valley, where Pippa Fray offers rooms for rent (☎ 925-5651, 925-4955). You'll eventually end up on the coast road near Eleven Mile and Bull Bay.

A post office is located 200 yards beyond the village center, on the left.

### Places to Eat
You'll find several funky little eateries, high-lighted by *Taylor Square Pastries*, the Rasta-hued *Jah Errol I-tal Corner* and *Toppy's Bar*, all funky rum shops serving inexpensive I-tal food.

### Getting There & Away
You can catch a bus from the Parade that runs to Hagley Gap via Bull Bay and Cedar Valley (US$0.40).

If driving, continue straight from Mavis Bank and you'll pass through Mahogany Vale and, half a mile beyond, across the Yallahs River. The road then climbs steeply, gradually deteriorating all the way to Hagley Gap. Several landslides have made the pace arduous; 4WD is recommended.

### PENLYNE CASTLE
Penlyne Castle is the base for 7-mile hikes to Blue Mountain Peak (see the Blue Mountain Peak Trail map). Most hikers stay overnight at one of the two lodges here before tackling the hike in the wee hours, as they have since at least 1925 when a Miss Steadman opened Wildflower Lodge to hikers. The dirt road ascends less than a mile beyond Whitfield as far as Abbey Green (a historic coffee estate now going to seed), after which you must abandon your vehicle and hike. Another one-hour hike leads to a waterfall at Sally River.

Everyone gets around on donkeys.

Bring warm clothing. One minute you're in sun-kissed mountains. The next, clouds swirl in and the temperature plunges.

### Places to Stay & Eat
**Camping** Camping is allowed for US$5 at *Whitfield Hall* (see below) if the hostel is full. The campground is on a wide lawn beneath eucalyptus. There are picnic tables, benches, and a BBQ pit, as well as water, toilets, and a basic kitchen.

**Hostels** *Wildflower Lodge (☎ 929-5394/5, 10 Ellesmere Rd, Kingston 10)* is a substantial hardwood structure with an atmospheric dining room with a huge hardwood table and benches. There are hammocks in the dining room and on the veranda, which faces south-east down the mountain. It has 36 bunks in basic rooms with communal bathrooms with solar-heated water for US$14, plus three

Coffee plots in the Blue Mountains

Tasty sips at Mavis Bank

Coffee factory, Mavis Bank

Local transport for coffee farmers – and their beans

A little extra light at the Morant Point Lighthouse

Newcastle and the Blue Mountains from Strawberry Hill

more-appealing private rooms with private bath downstairs for US$40, and a two-bedroom cottage at the bottom of the garden for US$57, which sleeps up to six. Breakfasts cost US$7; lunch and dinner cost US$8.50. You also have use of a large but basic kitchen. The lodge offers horseback rides and guides for the climb, and has a well-stocked gift shop selling film. Adult camps are held on weekends year-round, and children's summer camps in July and August.

About 400 yards uphill, nestled amid pine trees, is *Whitfield Hall* (☎ 927-0986, c/o John Algrove, 8 Almon Crescent, Kingston 6), a more basic option with bunks for up to 40 people. It gives off true hostel ambience. The dark, gloomy lounge has a huge fireplace (there's a US$5 firewood charge), a smoke-stained ceiling, and aged hardwood floor. An old grandfather clock stands like a silent sentinel. The lounge also contains a piano and an asthmatic antique pump organ. Brass gas lamps provide illumination. Guests share two basic bathrooms with toilets and deep tubs (cold water only), plus a small kitchen (bring your own food; you can buy canned peaches here for US$1.75). You can cook for yourself, but locals will cook on request. Bunks cost US$14 per person (US$9 children; US$7 Peace Corps and students). You can hire mules (US$34) and guides (US$3 per person; US$14 to the peak).

A friendly Rasta, Jah B – pronounced 'jarbee' – has a basic but cozy wooden *guest house* (☎ 977-8161, c/o Joyce in Mavis Bank), on the left 400 yards below Wildflower Lodge. It has three rooms with four bunks apiece, plus a shared shower and flush toilet, for US$12 per person. Jah B cooks I-tal meals (about US$7) amid a cloud of ganja smoke and a nonstop volley of friendly banter. He offers transfers from Kingston in his beat-up Land Rover and will guide you up Blue Mountain Peak for US$43.

### Getting There & Away

Penlyne Castle is reached via a dirt road that ascends precipitously from opposite Toppy's Bar in Hagley Gap. Only 4WD vehicles can make the journey, which is dauntingly rugged. You'll reach a T-junction after 3 miles, with Penlyne Castle to the left and the hostels to the right. Jeeps can be rented in Hagley Gap to take you up the tortuous, gutted road (reportedly US$20 for up to six people).

Most hotels in the Blue Mountains offer 4WD transfers to Penlyne Castle. Whitfield Hall and Wildflower Lodge offer transfers by Land Rover from Mavis Bank (US$20 up to six people; US$3 per person for seven or more) or Kingston (US$41; or US$5 per person).

**Warning** The Wildflower and Whitfield transfers are untrustworthy in late evening, when drivers often don't show up (or refuse to continue), stranding people in Mavis Bank. Be sure to arrange a transfer for no later than mid-afternoon.

### BLUE MOUNTAIN PEAK

It's a 3000-foot ascent from Penlyne Castle to the summit of Blue Mountain Peak (7402 feet) – a three or four-hour hike. It's not a serious challenge, but you need to be reasonably fit, especially to tackle the arduous switchback to a ridge called Lazy Man's Peak.

The well-maintained trail is threatened by erosion, and also by trash from those with no respect for the wilderness. Be a responsible hiker! Don't litter or take off-trail short-cuts, which leads to soil erosion. Wooden signs advise you to 'Stay on the Path.' Rock slides, mud pools, and drop-offs are among the potential hazards if you stray. One of the saddest sights is the dilapidated hut defaced by graffiti near the summit.

Most hikers choose to set off from Penlyne Castle in the wee hours to reach the peak for sunrise. Don't hike without a guide at night. Numerous spur trails lead off the main trails and it is easy to get lost. These mountains are not kind to those who lose their way. Your guide will rouse you at about 2 am. Fortified with a breakfast of coffee and cereal, you set out single file in the pitch black along the 7½-mile trail (you'll need a flashlight and a spare set of batteries – just in case). Midway, at Portland Gap, there's a ranger station and hut on a ridge, surrounded by ginger lilies and hydrangeas.

## BLUE MOUNTAIN PEAK TRAIL

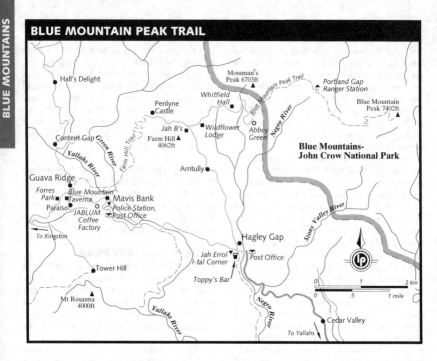

As you hike, reggae music can be heard far, far below, competing with the chirps of crickets and the *sshhhhh sshhhhh* of katydids singing to attract mates. Myriad blinkies and peeny-wallies will be doing the same, signaling, with their phosphorescent semaphore. With luck, you might pass a 'blinking tree' where the beetles collect and glow en masse, sometimes synchronistically like a lighthouse. Eerie! Even better is if you choose to hike on a moonlit night.

You should arrive at the peak around 5:30 am, while it is still dark. The lights of Kingston glimmer to the southeast, and those of Port Antonio to the north. Dawn is sublime. First, a sliver of pink light arcs the eastern sky. The star-filled sky soon grades through every shade of purple and blue. Your stage is gradually revealed: a flat-topped hump, marked by a scaffolding pyramid and trig point (in the cloud it is easy to mistake the *real* summit for a smaller

hump to the left of the hut near the summit). A short trail leads to the edge of the peak. To the southeast is the distinctive hump of Sugar Loaf.

From the peak (which casts a distinct shadow over the land below), Cuba can be seen hovering on the horizon, 90 miles away. After a brief celebratory drink and snacks, you'll set off back down the mountain, arriving at Whitfield or Wildflower in time for brunch.

You don't have to set off at an ungodly hour. By setting out a few hours later, say 5 am, you may still make the top before the mists roll in, and you will have the benefit of enjoying the changing vegetation and unraveling scenery with greater anticipation for what lies ahead (and above). You pass through several distinct ecosystems, including an area of bamboo and primordial giant tree ferns farther down. Farther up is cloud forest, dripping with filaments of hanging lichens and festooned with epiphytes and moss. Near the top is stunted dwarf or elfin forest, with trees such as hirsute soapwood and rodwood no more than 8 feet high – an adaptation to the extreme cold.

### What to Bring

Although hiking boots or tough walking shoes are best, sneakers *(buggas* or *puss boots)* will suffice, though your feet will probably get wet. At the top it can be icy with the wind blowing, and temperatures can approach freezing before sunrise, so wear plenty of layers. Rain gear is also essential, as weather can change rapidly. Clouds usually begin to form in early morning, followed by a cold breeze.

### Guides

Guides can be hired locally at Hagley Gap, Penlyne Castle, or from Maya Lodge at Jack's Hill; rates are around US$20 per half-day or US$30 for a full day.

### Altitude Sickness

A few people experience dizziness or drowsiness at elevations as low as 7000 feet. Don't overnight at the top if you feel sick.

### Organized Hikes

Maya Lodge (☎ 702-0314, 702-0112), PO Box 216, Kingston 7, organizes an overnight 'Blue Mountain Peak Trek' that includes 4WD transfers to Penlyne Castle, dinner, accommodations, and breakfast for US$170 per person (minimum two people).

### Places to Stay

Most hikers overnight at Wildflower Lodge or Whitfield Hall (see the Penlyne Castle section, earlier), but there are closer options. A funky *cabin* (little more than a lean-to) 40 feet below the summit can be rented for US$2.50 from the Forestry Service (☎ 924-2667), 173 Constant Spring Rd, Kingston. A barrel at the summit collects rainwater (it normally has a fair share of dead bugs and detritus – use a clean cloth as a strainer). The Forestry Service also maintains a more substantial, dimly lit *cabin* halfway up the trail at Portland Gap

(almost 2½ miles above Abbey Green). It stocks a few biscuits and drinks. You can *camp* outside, where there's a cooking area and water from a pipe. Again, this is by reservation only. The terribly run-down hut has a fireplace, but holes in the roof can douse the fire (a waterproof cover for your sleeping bag is a good idea if you decide to overnight here).

# Southeast Coast

Jamaica's southeast corner is the island's ugly duckling and one shunned by most tourists. It's drier than its northern neighbor, Portland parish, and gets progressively drier farther west where the narrow coastal plain is covered with scrub. The south-facing coast is also much gentler than that of Portland to the northeast, with mostly unappetizing gray-sand beaches. Only a limited tourist infrastructure exists, although numerous guest houses cater to Kingstonians escaping here for the weekend. Life revolves mostly around small fishing villages where the work is still performed by canoe and net. The exception is Morant Bay, the only town of note, which rose to moderate importance in the late 18th century as an export port for sugar.

The remote area is one of Jamaica's poorest, as reflected by the pitiful living conditions of the plantation workers on the flatlands east of Port Morant. Conditions have always been harsh, and the area figured prominently in rebellions during the colonial era.

## YALLAHS & ENVIRONS

East of Bull Bay and the parish boundary between St Andrew and St Thomas, the A4 from Kingston makes a hairpin descent to Grants Pen, then winds through scrub-covered country, rising and falling until it reaches the coast at the village of Yallahs, 10 miles east of Bull Bay. Cattle and goats wander the streets of town.

At press time the finishing touches were being put on a bridge over the wide gully of the Yallahs River, 2 miles west of town. It's about time! During heavy rains the ford was often impossible (the bridge, however, seems more like a dam – it has a couple of tubes for water to pass under – and it, too, will probably flood) and vehicles had to take a circuitous route up the river valley to Easington and cross an iron bridge to return to the coast. The Yallahs River begins 4500 feet up in the Blue Mountains, but the lower river is usually dry. The many boulders along the lower riverbed attest to the power and threat of flash floods.

Immediately east of Yallahs is a gray shoreline called **Bailey's Beach**. It's of limited appeal, but you can watch fishermen working their nets and pots offshore.

## Yallahs River Valley

A road leads north from Yallahs through this rugged valley. The valley has been the scene of horrendous flooding in past years, aided by deforestation on the mountain slopes. The Yallahs Valley Land Authority works to foster conservation.

About 3 miles north of town, you cross the river near Heartease, where it is said to be possible to witness Revivalist spirit-cult meetings occasionally held on the eastern riverbank near the old bridge.

At the village of Llandewey, 7 miles northwest of Yallahs, you gain a fine view of **Judgement Cliff**, a sheer cliff that looms up 1000 feet, the result of a 1692 earthquake that destroyed Port Royal and caused the mountainside to collapse. According to local folklore, the great landslide buried a venal slave owner (hence the name).

You can continue along the winding, deteriorating road as it begins to claw its way through the lower ridges of the Blue Mountains. At the hamlet of Bethel Gap, a dirt road leads east sharply uphill to Hagley Gap and Mavis Bank; you'll need a 4WD. Just north of Bethel Gap, at the village of Cedar Valley, the 'main road' loops east and follows the Negro River valley back to the coast at Morant Bay.

## Places to Stay

Wally Bailey, the friendly owner of *Bailey's Beach Resort* (☎ 982-5056, PO Box 16, Yallahs, St Thomas), lends his name to the beach on which he has 14 basic and simply furnished cottages cooled by fans and sea breezes for US$15 to US$22. Private baths have cold water only. The bar hosts a disco on weekends. The sea was farther out in 1972 when Wally built his hotel; now the waves eat at the foundations.

*Arntully Guest House* is an old great house at the foot of the Blue Mountains, in a valley about 2 miles north of Cedar Valley. The rooms are said to be 'comfortable' and rates moderate. You'll need 4WD to get there and should bring your own food.

### Getting There & Away

A bus and several minibuses operate from the Parade in Kingston.

## YALLAHS TO MORANT BAY

Two large lakes east of Yallahs, the **Yallahs Ponds**, are enclosed by a narrow, bow-shaped sandspit that is 4 miles long and up to a mile wide. The ponds are exceedingly briny due to evaporation (the large pond is 14 times saltier than the ocean). Antediluvian life-forms flourish, including algal bacteria that often turn the ponds a deep pink, accompanied by a powerful smell of hydrogen sulfide ('bad egg gas'). On breezy days a salty froth is often whipped up and blows across the road.

You can still see the remains of an old stone **signal tower** built on the sandspit in the 1770s by the English to communicate with Port Royal. It is listed as a national monument.

On the hillside just beyond Yallahs Ponds is the **JAMINTEL space research station**, in operation since 1971. The giant dish links Jamaica to the international satellite network. You may be able to arrange a tour by appointment; call ☎ 982-2309.

The shoreline farther east – known as **Greenwall** – has cliffs with turquoise waters below. A series of long, dark-gray beaches extend eastward. Fishermen use them, and you'll see colorful pirogues drawn up. A few miles east you pass **Rozelle Beach**, the main breeding ground for the indigenous (and endangered) blue swallowtail butterfly.

## Places to Stay

Joe Corniffe has basic rooms and camping at his *Gold Mine Camp & Club* (☎ 926-2548), on the left at Lyssons near Botany Bay, 6 miles east of Yallahs.

## MORANT BAY

It's easy to drive straight past this town without realizing it. Morant Bay (population 8000), the only town of importance along the south coast, squats on a hill behind the coast road. Most of the town's early colonial-era buildings were burned in the Morant Bay Rebellion of 1865. Still, there are a few points of interest around the town square.

The Morant River, west of town, is crossed by Jamaica's longest bridge.

## Information

**Money** You'll find a branch of the National Commercial Bank (☎ 982-2225) at 39 Queen St opposite the Texaco gas station. Scotiabank (☎ 982-2310) also has a branch on Queen St, catercorner to the Jamaica National Building Society, which has a foreign exchange bureau. Western Union is represented by Marville's Gift Centre, in Morant Bay Plaza.

**Post & Communications** The post office (☎ 982-2109) is on Queen St. You can make international calls and send and receive faxes at the Telecommunications of Jamaica office (☎ 982-2200) at 2 Church St or at Cable & Wireless (☎ 982-1967) in Morant Bay Plaza.

**Medical Services** Princess Margaret Hospital (☎ 982-2304), 54 Lyssons Rd, 800 yards east of town, can provide emergency treatment. Clinics include the Morant Bay Medical & Dental Clinic (☎ 982-2517) in Morant Bay Plaza on the A4, and George's Medical Clinic, 200 yards east of Queen St (follow it around); and also at 4 Queen St (☎ 982-2334) and 14 Queen St (☎ 982-1107). There's another clinic run by Dr Lampart (☎ 982-2343) on Lyssons Rd, and Dr Maurice Stanhope has a clinic (☎ 982-2519) at 6 East St. Lloyd's Pharmacy (☎ 982-2400) is opposite the library on Queen St.

**Emergency** The police station (☎ 982-2233) is at 7 South St, next to the old courthouse.

## Things to See

The town's National Hero, Paul Bogle (see 'Morant Bay Rebellion') is memorialized by the **Paul Bogle statue**, which stands in a little square in front of the courthouse. The work, by noted sculptor Edna Manley, powerfully depicts the national hero standing grimly, elbows out, hands clasped over the hilt of a machete. (Another plaque commemorating Bogle can be found at his chapel, nearby at Stony Gut.) The attractive **courthouse** was rebuilt in limestone and red brick after being destroyed in the 1865 rebellion. It's topped by an octagonal wooden belfry.

Catercorner to the courthouse is a handsome, ochre-colored **Anglican church** dating to 1881.

Nearby is a plaque commemorating those who died in the 1865 struggle and whose bodies were left to rot on the refuse dump. In 1965, excavations turned up 79 skeletons in a mass grave between the courthouse and the remains of a small, 18th-century **fort**, which retains three small cannons on their carriages. The bodies were re-interred below the fort, where a memorial in a tiny park records that 'they did not die in vain.'

## Special Events

October 11 is **Paul Bogle Day**, when a party is held in the town square and a 6-mile road race sets out from his home village of Stony Gut.

## Places to Stay & Eat

*Morant Villas* (☎ 982-2422, fax 982-1937, 1 Wharf Rd) sits amid lawns and tall palms atop a bluff on the coast road just east of town. It has 22 simple yet clean rooms with fans and private bath with hot water for US$30. There are also 10 studios with kitchens for US$48, plus suites for US$71. A restaurant and bar serves seafood for US$6 to US$12. The hotel offers tours by minibus.

On the A4, about 400 yards east of Morant Villas, is *Chef's Seaview Restaurant* (☎ 982-2449), which looks over turquoise waters and has three basic rooms with fans. A simple restaurant has an outside patio.

*Caravan Jerk Pork*, on Hope Rd, offers cheap mouth-searing jerk dishes. To cool off

## The Morant Bay Rebellion

Following emancipation in 1838, the local black population faced widescale unemployment and extreme hardship, conditions exacerbated by heavy taxation and the harshness of local magistrates. In the 1860s, Paul Bogle, a black Baptist deacon in the hamlet of Stony Gut, organized passive resistance against the oppression and injustice of the local authorities and planters in St Thomas. He was supported by George William Gordon, a wealthy mulatto planter who had risen to become an assemblyman.

On October 11, 1865, Bogle and 400 supporters marched to the Morant Bay courthouse to protest the severe punishment meted out to a destitute who had been arrested on a petty charge. An armed militia shot into the crowd and a riot ensued in which 28 people were killed, and the courthouse and much of the town center were burned to the ground. The countryside erupted in riots. Bogle fled with a £2000 bounty on his head, but was soon captured by Maroons (who had agreed to act as bounty hunters in their peace treaty with the British; see the History section in the Facts about Jamaica chapter) and hanged the same day from the center arch of the burned-out courthouse. Meanwhile, Gordon was arrested in Kingston, ferried to Morant Bay, condemned by a kangaroo court, and also hanged.

Governor Edward Eyre ordered reprisals. The militia swept through St Thomas, razing more than 1000 houses and summarily executing more than 430 people. The British government was outraged by Eyre's reaction (a tribunal found that the punishments were 'excessive...reckless...and...at Bath positively barbarous'), and forced the Jamaica House of Assembly to relinquish its power to Parliament. Thus the island became a Crown colony, leading to reforms of the harsh judicial system.

Paul Bogle

---

afterwards, try a **Devon House I-Scream** at the east end of Queen St.

### Entertainment

Try the **Sapphire Star Club** at the east end of Queen St. **Chef's Seaview Restaurant** has a dance floor and stage with go-go dancing on weekends.

### Getting There & Away

Three buses daily operate between Morant Bay and the Parade in Kingston, with additional minibus service. Buses arrive and depart from beside the Shell gas station on the A4 at the west end of town.

## SEAFORTH

This prosperous agricultural town is the southern gateway to the Blue Mountains. It's reached via a well-paved road that leads north from the large roundabout immediately west of Morant Bay and follows the wide, level valley of the Morant River inland through banana plantations.

From Seaforth, a paved road leads west and ascends the Negro River valley to

Trinity Ville, then deteriorates as it climbs more steeply to Cedar Valley and Hagley Gap, where the hiking trail to Blue Mountain Peak begins. Another road heads east across the foothills to Bath.

## RETREAT

Retreat is a small beachside residential community about 3 miles east of Morant Bay. It sits between two of the few pleasant beaches along Jamaica's southern coast. The aptly named **Golden Shore Beach** is hidden from view from the road. Watch for the hand-painted sign.

The beach extends east 2 miles to **Prospect Beach**, a 'public bathing beach' maintained by the UDC. The area is a popular relaxation spot for locals and Kingstonians, many of whom maintain holiday homes at Retreat.

### Places to Stay & Eat

On the main road a mile east of Retreat is **Brown's Guest House** (☎ 982-6205), beside the A4. The bungalow is run as a B&B and has five large rooms painted in gaudy tropical colors. Each has private bath with hot water. Rooms cost US$23. It's a homey place with simple 1960s utility furniture. You walk through a coconut grove to reach the beach. Alternately, try **Saunder's Beach Cottage** (☎ 982-2215), 400 yards farther east and reached by a dirt road that leads down to the shore. The modest house has simple rooms for about US$10. Nearby, at Prospect Beach, **Bluemah Palace** (☎ 982-6250) offers basic rooms, a restaurant, and a Friday night 'jam.'

Also appealing is **Goldfinger's Guest House** (☎ 982-2644, Lot 21, Retreat, St Thomas), which has modest rooms with private bath for US$100 double.

At Golden Shore Beach, **Golden Beach Resort** (☎ 982-9657) has 15 rooms in a condo-style unit set amid landscaped grounds. They're clean and boast refreshing, contemporary furnishings. Downstairs rooms have fans and patios with grills and cost US$33, or US$37 with TV and telephone. Upstairs rooms have air-con for US$43. There's a small restaurant for alfresco dining.

For something more elegant, try **Whispering Bamboo Cove** (☎ 982-2912, 105 Crystal Drive, Retreat). It's a gleaming-white, contemporary, villa-style hotel with a columned portico entrance and wrought-iron lamps on the walls. The 10 rooms are airy, spacious, and tastefully furnished with tropical fabrics and antique reproductions. Light pours in through French doors. Rooms cost US$57 to US$80 and have cable TV and telephone, plus king-size beds and wide patios or balconies. Solar-powered heating guarantees hot water. The gracious restaurant opens onto lawns. A separate, self-contained, two-bedroom cottage with kitchenette costs US$86.

The UDC has a down-at-the-heels **bar** and **restaurant** at Prospect Beach. A funky jerk shack called **Paradise Cove** has more color. The most atmospheric place is a funky bay-front eatery called the **Shipwreck Seafood Bar & Restaurant**, 5 miles east of Retreat. Traditional Jamaican dishes cost less than US$3, and you can look over a bay where fishing pirogues are beached.

### Getting There & Away

Lee Chong Young operates a minibus (No STBW586) to Retreat from the Parade in Kingston.

## PORT MORANT

This small one-street village lies at the head of a deep bay. It offers nothing of interest except a marina equipped with necessities.

There's a National Commercial Bank opposite the gas station, and a nearby police station (☎ 982-2018).

### Bowden Marina

About 11½ miles east of Port Morant, a road to the right leads to a threadbare marina (☎ 982-8223) rimmed by mangroves in the middle of Bowden Bay. Oysters are farmed here. Berthing costs US$0.50 per foot. There are showers and restrooms, plus gasoline, diesel (US$1.50 per gallon), and water. There's not much to make you want to anchor here, except perhaps necessity.

Unbelievably, it hosts an annual Invitational Fishing Tournament (☎ 977-1078, fax 977-2061) in mid-March.

## Places to Stay & Eat

There are cheap roadside *cabins* (☎ 982-8244) west of the village, and *Coconut Place*, a pleasant eatery and entertainment center nearby.

The best place to eat is *Young's Bar & Restaurant*, on the A4 opposite the turnoff for Bath. You'll pay about US$2 for curried goat, ackee and codfish, and other staples. Half a mile east of town, *Ace's Beach Club & Restaurant* has an unappealing setting, but its seafood dishes cost less than US$2. It hosts dancehall.

## Getting There & Away

You can take a bus or minibus from the Parade in Kingston. At least one bus (No MB127) continues east as far as Golden Grove.

## BATH

This down-at-the-heels village, 6 miles north of Port Morant, lies on the bank of the Garden River, amidst sugarcane and banana plantations. The town owes its existence to the discovery of hot mineral springs in the hills behind the present town in the late 17th century. A spa was developed, and socialites flocked in and built town houses here. Today, it's a run-down, melancholic place whose relative poverty attests to the pitiful wages paid to plantation workers. Perhaps for this reason, locals are somewhat surly and slow to warm to foreign visitors.

The one-street town has a post office, police station (☎ 982-2115), and a Shell gas station.

## Bath Botanical Gardens

At the east end of town is an old limestone church shaded by royal palms that flank the entrance to the second-oldest botanical gardens in the Western Hemisphere, established by the government in 1779. Many of the exotics introduced to Jamaica were first planted here: bougainvillea, cinnamon, mango, jackfruit, jacaranda. Most famous is the breadfruit, brought at such cost from the South Pacific by Capt William Bligh aboard the HMS *Providence*. The garden has seen better days (Hurricane Gilbert

pummeled it badly in 1988, and it is frequently inundated when the river floods its banks). The garden will be of interest only to serious horticulturists.

## Bath Fountain

Local legend says that in the 1690s a runaway slave discovered hot mineral springs that cured the injuries he had received while escaping. He was so impressed by the miracle that he returned to tell his master. In 1699 the government bought the spring and an adjoining 1130 acres, created the Bath of St Thomas the Apostle, then formed a corporation to found the town of Bath and administer mineral baths for the sick and infirm. Thirty slaves built the road and the hospital that offered free treatment to the desperately ill. The waters are high in sulfur, magnesium, lime, and other minerals and have therapeutic value for treating skin ailments and rheumatic problems. Back then it was generally believed that the waters would cure everything from venereal disease to nervous spasms.

By the mid-18th century the springs had been usurped by gentry seeking cures for the 'dry bellyache' caused by overindulgence, for as Lady Nugent recorded in her famous diaries: 'they ate like cormorants and drank like porpoises.' It wasn't long before the unusual effects of the water had created a new demand: the historian Edward Long recorded that drinking the water:

[D]iffuses a thrilling glow over the whole body; and the continued use enlivens the spirits, and sometimes produces the same joyous effects as inebriation. On this account, some notorious topers have quitted their claret for a while and come hither, merely for the sake of a little variety in their practice of debauch, and to enjoy the singular felicity of getting drunk on water.

Two springs issue from beneath the bath house. The water can be scorching (it varies from 115°F to 128°F). You soak in a deep, ceramic-tiled pool (US$4 for 20 minutes). The homey spa also offers full-body massages for US$35, plus facial, scalp, and other massages (US$25). It's open 8 am to 9:30 pm Tuesday to Sunday. On weekends it's best to arrive early, before the crowds from Kingston arrive. To get there, turn up the road opposite the church and follow the winding road 2 miles uphill.

Guides may try to sell you swallowtail butterflies. These exquisite butterflies are endangered. *Don't buy!*

## Hiking

A trail leads from Bath Fountain up over Cuna Cuna Gap to the Rio Grande Valley, Moore Town, and the north coast. You might want to try to hire a guide in Bath. Experienced hikers, however, can obtain Sheet 19 (showing St Thomas parish) and Sheet 14 (which shows Portland parish) of the Ordnance Survey 1:12,500 map series from the Survey Dept at 23½ Charles St, Kingston. They cost US$5 each.

## Places to Stay & Eat

Your only option is the *Bath Fountain Hotel & Spa* (☎ 982-8410), a recently renovated, pink colonial hotel that dates to 1747 and contains the spa baths on the ground floor. The modestly furnished bedrooms are clinically white (appropriately, the hotel is called 'the hospital' locally). You can choose between rooms with shared bath for US$30, or private bath for US$50 (or US$60 'deluxe'). It has a small restaurant.

There are a few rustic riverside *restaurants* on the road below the spa, and a few little *rum shops* in town.

## Getting There & Away

There is one bus daily between the Parade in Kingston and Bath, where it stops outside the church. At least two minibuses also serve Bath from the Parade. It's about a two-hour journey (US$0.50 by bus, US$2 by minibus). A bus also operates between Morant Bay and Bath (about US$0.20).

Bath is 6 miles north of Port Morant. The drive is incredibly scenic. Beyond Bath, the road continues east for 6 miles to the crossroads at Hordley and is abysmally potholed.

## GOLDEN GROVE

Golden Grove, 6 miles east of Port Morant, is a desperately poor hamlet of corrugated-

tin and wood huts on stilts, dominated by the plantations of Tropicana Sugar Estates, east of the road, and the banana plantations of Fyffes to the west. Few dwellings have running water. The town does, though, have a gas station.

The area around Golden Grove was first settled in 1656 by 1600 white planters from the island of Nevis (including the governor of Nevis, Major Luke Stokes) induced by a command from Oliver Cromwell. Within four months, more than half the settlers had died of fever, including Stokes and his wife. Many of the locals are descended from Africans from Sierra Leone who settled on the sugar estates in the decades following emancipation.

To the west of Golden Grove, a sideroad leads from the A4 and loops eastward through the cane fields, eventually depositing you at the tiny hamlet of Old Pera, where a ruined windmill sits on a hilltop overlooking the rocky coves. Another dirt road (2 miles east of Port Morant) leads to New Pera, gateway to **Rocky Point Beach,** where fishing pirogues are drawn up. Locals pour in on any weekend to splash in the shallows and jive to ear-shattering reggae and rap.

## Stokes Hall

The Stokes family is commemorated by Stokes Hall (a mile south of Golden Grove), which was built by the major's three sons who survived the fever and prospered. The thick-stone-walled house is one of few buildings of note in St Thomas parish, with its fortified towers at each corner. The ruins are protected by the Jamaica National Trust. From on high you have a restricted view over the sugar fields and Duckenfield sugar factory to the southwest. You'll have to hunt to find Stokes Hall, however, as it is hidden behind thick foliage atop a hill; there are no signs, but follow a dirt road toward the ocean for about a mile.

## Places to Stay & Eat

You can feast on fish with rice and peas for US$3 or less at a basic *restaurant* at Rocky Point Beach. A Rasta, 'One Love Woody,' offers cheap *rooms* in the tiny fishing hamlet.

## Getting There & Away

You can reach Golden Grove from Kingston by bus No 127, which departs from the Parade, and from Port Antonio by bus No LS289.

The roads that lead to New Pera and Old Pera branch several times in the cane fields. Ask directions from locals.

## MORANT POINT

To the east of Port Morant is a large, marshy peninsula – Morant Point – that juts out into the Atlantic Ocean in the shape of the head of a barking dog. The peninsula is smothered in swamp and sugarcane, and is crossed by a maze of dirt tracks.

## Morant Point Lighthouse

This 100-foot-tall, red-and-white-striped edifice marks Morant Point, the easternmost tip of Jamaica, and the southern end of **Holland Bay**, a lonesome and spectacularly pretty white-sand beach.

The 18-foot-wide cast-iron tube was erected in 1841 by freed African slaves from Sierra Leone. It's the oldest lighthouse on the island and is listed as an historic monument.

Ask the lighthouse-keeper to show you the way to the top. The powerful view and the windy silence make for a profound experience as you look out over rippling fields, as green as ripe limes, toward the cloud-haunted Blue Mountains. I was the first tourist in over three weeks, according to the lighthouse-keeper. It's well worth the arduous drive along a warren of muddy tracks that wander through the cane fields.

Entry is free.

## Getting There & Away

Although you can get there by foot or car from Dalvey, the lighthouse is more easily reached by car from the gas station on the A4 in Golden Grove. It's a labyrinthine course, however, and there are lots of lefts and rights to choose from. You'll need a guide to lead you; ask at the gas station. 4WD is recommended.

Minibuses and bus No MB112 (US$0.60) go as far as Dalvey from Kingston and Morant Bay. Alternately, take bus No LS289 from Port Antonio to Golden Grove (US$0.50).

## HORDLEY

One mile north of Golden Grove is a cross-roads named Hordley. The road going west leads to Bath. The A4 continues east and returns to the shore at Holland Bay, the southernmost point of the windward coast. Soon you are climbing sharply uphill along the flanks of the John Crow Mountains (the view down across the coastal plains is marvelous). At Hector's River, 6 miles from Hordley, you pass into Portland parish.

It's 31 miles from Hordley to Port Antonio along a wide, well-paved road with little traffic.

# Language

## UNDERSTANDING PATOIS

When Jamaicans speak patois, the discussion may be incomprehensible to visitors. It might sound like a chaotic babble without rules. But there are rules. They're just different from those of traditional English grammar.

Some words are unexpectedly present, for example, where others are unexpectedly missing. New words are invented and slip into general parlance as quickly as others fall from grace. And vowel sounds go sliding off into diphthongs. Like Yorkshire folk, Jamaicans often drop their 'h's' (thus, 'ouse' instead of 'house') and add them in unexpected places (for example, 'hemphasize'). Jamaicans usually drop the 'h' from 'th' as well: hence, 't'ree' for 'three,' and 't'anks' for 'thanks.' 'The' is usually pronounced as 'de' and 'them' as 'dem.' They also sometimes drop the 'w,' as in 'ooman' (woman).

Jamaicans also often use transliteration, as in 'flim' for 'film,' and 'cerfiticket' for 'certificate.' They rearrange syllables and give them their own inflections. In patois, the word 'up' is used to intensify meaning: thus, cars 'mash up.' Patois words are usually spelled out phonetically.

In order to express the mood of the moment, 'Jamaica talk' infuses words with intonation, repetition, gesture, imagery, and drama. It is not a static, written language, but an oral, vitalic thing that infuses life into inanimate objects. Thus, one does not forget to mail a letter; instead, 'dat letter jus' fly out of mi mind.' And a waiter does not simply drop a tray full of crockery; 'dat wurtless t'ing jump right out of mi hands.' Among a people that superstitiously believes in *duppies* (ghosts), such reasoning permits individuals to disclaim responsibility for their actions.

Such animate imagery, a carryover of West African proverbs, infuses Jamaica talk with life and becomes a catalyst in the crystallization of sayings based on the wisdom of experience, often using living creatures as teachers. In the context of a society torn from its roots and oppressed, the islanders have evolved countless sayings that express simple warnings about behavior and interpersonal relationships. Thus, 'Every day you goad donkey, 'im will kick you one day.' Or, 'When you go to donkey's house, doan't talk about ears.' And 'If you play with puppy, 'im lick your mouth.'

Jamaican patois is liberally laced with sexual innuendo and slang, often of an extremely sexist nature, as personified by the 'slackness' of the modern DJ culture. Cuss words abound, especially the word 'rass,' an impolite term that originally meant 'backside' or 'arse' but whose meaning now varies according to circumstance. It's a word visitors to Jamaica should know, as it's one of the most commonly used (and misunderstood) words. Generally it is a term of abuse, as in 'Im a no good rass!' (mild), or when used with Jamaicans' most offensive (yet common) derogatory term, 'Im a rass blood clot' (a menstrual pad). It can also be used as an endearment ('Hey, rass, gi mi smallers') or in a similar vein to describe a superlative ('Dat gal pretty to rass, mon!').

Patois is not gender specific. Everyone and everything is simply 'im' or 'dem.' Possessive pronouns such as 'my' and 'mine' are often replaced with 'a fi,' which can also be an intensifier, as in 'A fi mi bike' ('It's *my* bike'). And plurals are often either ignored (as in 'five finger') or signified by the word 'dem,' as in 'De byah dem go to school' ('The boys have gone to school'). Note how the present tense is used to convey a past action.

And since you'll not be able to walk far without being asked for money, it helps to know enough patois to comprehend what you're hearing. Expect to hear 'Gi mi a smallers no bass' ('Give me some money now boss'); 'bass' means boss and is often used to address persons in authority or those able to dispense favors.

There are several Jamaican pocket-guides to understanding patois, including *Memba de Culcha: Chief Words, Phrases, Proverbs & Riddles in Jamaican Dialect*, by Cecily Reece-Daly (National Books, Detroit).

## Colonial Carryovers

Many words in the Jamaican lexicon are carryovers from early English colonial days – true Shakespearean English. The language is imbued with terms otherwise considered archaic. One of the most obvious is 'chain,' the old English measurement (22 yards), which is still used liberally, though rarely accurately. Similarly, you may be served a drink in a 'goblet.'

A few terms derive from slave days. Thus visitors can expect to be called 'massa' (master) or 'mistress.' The term 'pickaninny' is still used for children, despite its racist connotations in western culture; for example, the bus conductor might say 'pickney stan' up an gi big people seat.'

## African Heritage

Scores of words have been passed down from Africa, mostly from the Ashanti, Cormorante, and Congolese languages. Thus, a Jamaican may refer to a fool as a 'bo-bo.' A commonly used word is 'nyam,' which means 'to eat.'

## Sayings & Proverbs

Jamaicans use plenty of metaphors and proverbs. They will tell you 'Cockroach no business in a fowlyard' ('Mind your own business'). If a Jamaican tells you, 'De higher monkey climb, de more 'im expose,' he or she is telling you that your boasting is transparent and that you're acting pretentiously, exposing more than you should.

Some phrases you'll hear may not mean what they suggest. 'Soon come,' for example, is a common refrain, but don't hold your breath! The phrase *really* means the subject will arrive eventually – almost the opposite of what you would expect. Likewise, 'jus' up de road' or 'jus' a likkle distance' can mean miles or the other side of town.

The most common greeting is 'Everyt'ing cool, mon?' or 'Everyt'ing irie?'

## 'Jamaica Talk'

A good preparatory source is the movie *Dancehall Queen,* with dialog in thick, at times impenetrable, Jamaican dialect. Here's a sampling of words you'll be sure to hear while strolling through the streets.

**ago** – to be intent on doing something, as in 'me ago duntown'

**agony** – sexual act, or style of dancing that suggests it

**almshouse** – anything negative

**arms house** – violent posture, common during sound-system clashes

**atops** – Red Stripe beer

**Babylon** – the establishment, white society

**bakra** – slave owner, white man

**baldhead** – non-Rasta; person of unsound viewpoint

**bandulu** – hustler, criminal, or the act of being swindled

**bangarang** – commotion, sometimes associated with rival, deafening sound-system noise

**bankra** – basket

**bashment** – a large dance or party; anything fabulous

**batty** – bottom or rear end, as in 'Yu batty too big, mon!' (as heard from a woman who doesn't give a damn for a propositioner's looks)

**batty boy** – gay man

**batty riders** – tight lycra hot-pants for showing off one's batty, favored by dance-hall queens

**bawl** – call out, especially in anguish

**beenie** – small

**big up** – to inflate or promote oneself, as in 'Big up yo chest, mon!'

**blood** – a respectful greeting, as in 'Wh'appen blood?' Also a swear word, most often used with 'claat' (see Understanding Patois, above)

**bly** – a chance or opportunity; sometimes a feeble excuse

**bomba** – commonly used abusive term, usually allied with 'clawt,' as in 'Get de bomba-clawt car out mi way!'

**Bobo dread** – a Rastafarian follower of Prince Emanuel Edwards

**boonoonoonoos** – fabulous, greatest; street or beach party

**boops** – a man who keeps a woman in idle splendor (Men, watch out if a woman tells you, 'Mi wan' you fi mi boops.')

**brawta** – additional

**breadkind** – any starchy vegetable used as a side dish in lieu of bread

**bredda** – friend, usually male

**bredren** – male friends

**brownings** – brown-skinned women; also a 'well-heeled' woman showing off her status

**buck** – to meet someone

**bumper** – rear end or backside

**burn** – to smoke ganja

**busha** – overseer of a slave plantation

**byah** – boy

**carry go bring come** – to spread gossip

**chalice** – a Rastafarian's holy ganja pipe (also known as a 'clutchie')

**charged** – stoned or drunk

**check** – to appreciate, especially a point of view or a person's physical attraction; also to pay a visit

**chillum** – a pipe for smoking ganja

**cho** – an expression to signify that the speaker is becoming annoyed

**chronic** – particularly potent ganja

**clawt, claat** – one of the strongest and most frequently heard Jamaican expletives (see Understanding Patois, above)

**coolie** – an East Indian

**cool runnings** – no problem

**cool yu foot** – slow down, relax

**copasetic** – cool, 'irie'

**cork** – full

**cotch** – relax, rest; also means to brace or support something, as well as a place to sleep

**cris** – from 'crisp,' meaning attractive or top-rate; 'Im a cris, cris t'ing!' ('He's handsome!')

**cris-biscuit** – anything 'cris' or excellent

**crub** – dance salaciously, as in 'wining'

**culture** – used to signify that something is Rastafarian

**cuss-cuss** – an argument

**cutchie** – ganja pipes

**dally** – the opposite of to linger; to go

**dawta** – a respectful term for a young woman

**de** – the

**degeh** – measly or pathetically small, usually used in a derogatory sense

**deh-deh** – to be someplace, as in 'Mi deh-deh!' ('I'm here!')

**deportees** – used cars, imported from Japan

**dibby-dibby** – pathetic, especially a competitor's weak sound system

**do** – please, as in 'Do, me a beg yu'

**don** – male authority figure

**downpresser** – a Rastafarian term for an oppressor

**dread** – a Rastafarian; also a terrible situation

**dunzer** – money; also known as 'smallers'

**duppy** – ghost

**facety** – cheeky, impertinent, as in 'Yu facety to rass, gal!' ('You're rude, girl!')

**fiyah** – a Rastafarian greeting

**flex** – how one behaves; to party wildly

**ganga-lee** – a gangster

**ganja** – marijuana; also known as 'de 'oly 'erb,' 'wisdom weed,' 'colly weed,' 'kaya,' 'sensie,' and 'tampie'

**ginnal** – a swindler or con artist

**gorgon** – a person to be feared

**gow** – empty boast

**gravilishas** – greedy

**grind** – see 'flex'

**guidance** – a Rastafarian parting term, meaning 'May God be with you'

**guinep** – a small green fruit, often sold by the bunch at the roadside

**gwan** – go away

**gyal** – woman

**heartical or 'eartical** – an esteemed person, someone with integrity; authentic

**herb or 'erb** – marijuana (see 'ganja')

**higger or 'iggler** – a market vendor, usually female; also a person who bargains

**him or 'im** – he, she, her, his, it

**hottie-bottie or 'ottie-bottie** – an attractive woman

**Idren** – brethren, used by Rastafarians to mean friends

**irie** – alright, groovy; used to indicate that all is well; also a greeting ('Everyt'ing irie?')

**iron bird** – airplane

**I-tal** – natural foods, health food, purity

**iyah** – a greeting

**Jah** – God; an Old Testament name, popular with Rastafarians
**Jamdung** – Jamaica (also known as Jah-Mek-Ya, as in 'God's work')
**janga** – shrimp, crayfish
**Joe Gring** – a man with whom a woman has an affair while her husband or boyfriend is away
**jook** – pierce or stab

**kingman** – husband
**kiss mi...** – not an invitation, but a common profane exclamation, as in 'Kiss mi rass!'
**kiss me neck** – to express surprise

**labba labba** – talk
**labrish** – gossip
**leggo beast** – rowdy person
**let off** – to give
**level vibes** – no problem
**lick** – to smoke; also to be in-vogue; also to strike a blow
**lick shot** – a gun fired at a dancehall to express appreciation
**lion** – upright, usually describes a righteous Rastafarian
**lovers rock** – romantic reggae

**maarga** – thin (from meager), as in 'Da boy deh maaga' ('That man there is skinny')
**mantel** – good-looking man, usually one who's promiscuous
**market mammie** – a higgler
**massah** – mister; derived from 'master' of slavery days and now used for any male, particularly one in authority
**mash up** – to have an accident
**massive** – a noun used to describe a crowd
**matey** – girlfriend who is one of several sexual partners
**men** – used in the singular for a gay man
**mule** – childless woman
**myal** – white magic, used to do good, that incorporates use of herbal medicines and control of 'duppies'

**naa** – won't, as in 'Mi naa go dung deh' ('I won't go down there')
**natty** – dreadlocks; also 'natty dread'; also used for a Rastafarian

**nuff** – plentiful; also used as a greeting with 'respect,' as in 'Nuff respect!'

**obeah** – illegal black magic that incorporates use of herbal medicines and witchcraft
**one love** – parting expression meaning unity

**peeny-wally** – insect that flashes phosphorescent
**pickney** – child or children, shortened version of pickaninny
**pollution** – people living in spiritual darkness
**posse** – a group of young adults who form a clique
**prentice** – young man
**punny printers** – extremely tight 'batty riders'

**queen** – respectful term for a woman, usually a Rastafarian woman

**ragamuffin** – a no-good person
**ramp** – to annoy someone or interfere, as in 'De gyal ramp wid me!'
**rass** – a backside; also one of the most violent cuss words (also see Understanding Patois, above)
**reach** – arrive, as in 'De bus not reach yet, mon!'
**reality** – the ghetto reality or a hard life
**reason** – to debate or discuss
**red-eye** – envious or greedy person
**renk** – foul-smelling; extreme rudeness
**respect** – commonly used greeting and farewell
**rhaatid** – like 'rass,' but a gentler and more commonly used expletive; its meaning depends on intonation and facial expression, but usually expresses surprise
**riddim** – Jamaica's reggae has it
**risto** – a member of the elite (derives from aristocrat)
**roots** – coming from the people or communal experience
**roughneck** – a scoundrel or ragamuffin
**rude boy** – a ghetto criminal or vandal
**runnings** – whatever is happening; also means crafty business schemes
**rush** – to be the focus of things

**samfi-man** – a con man

satta – invitation to sit, usually to meditate
sipple – slippery
skank – to con; also an early 1970s dance move
sketel – a beautiful and promiscuous woman, one with many boyfriends
skin-out – abandon whatever one is doing to have sex, usually at a stageshow
skylark – to dawdle or idle
slack – sexually explicit lyrics
smaddy – somebody
soke – fool around, as in 'No soke wi' mi' ('Don't mess with me')
stageshow – live music event
stoosh – airs of superiority, condescending behavior
structure – one's body, as in 'A fi mi structure!' ('It's my body!')
sufferer or suffrah – poor but righteous person

swimp – shrimp

talawah – small but powerful, as in 'De byah likkle but 'im talawah'
tea – any hot drink
ting – thing or woman, as in 'A mi ting, she' ('That's my girlfriend'); also used for genitals (male or female)
trace – to cuss someone
trash – to dress up, to be well turned-out

wine – sensuous dance movement
wolf – a Rastafarian imposter
work – sex

yard – a Jamaican's home
yardie – a gangster-type from the ghettoes, used by Jamaicans to mean anyone from Jamaica
yush – greeting used by rude boys

# Glossary

Also see the 'Jamaica talk' list in the Language chapter.

**abeng** – goat horn
**ackee** – tropical fruit popular as a breakfast dish
**all-inclusive resort** – a resort-hotel where all activities, meals, beverages, entertainment, etc, are included in the room rate
**Antilles** – the Caribbean Islands
**Arawak** – indigenous pre-Columbian inhabitants of Jamaica

**balm** – folk medicine
**bammy** – pancake-shaped cassava bread
**bongo** – small drum; someone with strong African roots
**busha** – plantation overseer

**calabash** – gourd whose hardened shell serves as a vessel for holding liquid
**callaloo** – spinach-like vegetable
**cassava** – root crop used as a breadkind
**Carib** – a warlike indigenous pre-Columbian people
**cay** – a coral isle
**charcoal-burners** – people who eke a meager living burning mangrove to make charcoal
**cimaroon** – Spanish term for escaped slave
**cockpits** – limestone hillocks separated by canyons
**custos** – colonial-era representative of the Crown at parish level

**dancehall** – type of reggae, popularized through the 1980s, in which DJs perform over pre-recorded music; place where dancehall is performed (usually an open space)
**dancehall queen** – a female habitué of dancehall clubs
**dreadlocks** – uncut, uncombed hair, as worn by Rastafarians
**dub** – a remixed version of a recording with the vocal removed
**duppy** – ghost

**endemic** – native, or regularly found here (usually refers to species of flora and fauna)

**festival** – fried biscuit or dumpling
**free colored** – offspring of white slave owner and black slave; accorded some special rights

**ganja** – marijuana
**General Consumption Tax (GCT)** – charge of between 6.25% and 15% on most hotel bills and some restaurant or store purchases
**go-go** – exotic dancing that is a staple of Jamaican nightlife

**JABLUM** – Jamaica Blue Mountain coffee processors
**Jah** – Rastafarian term for God
**Jamdung** – Rastafarian term for Jamaica
**Jamintel** – Jamaica International Telephone
**JAPEX** – Jamaica Product Exchange
**JATCHA** – Jamaica Alternative Tourism, Camping & Hiking Association
**jerk** – meat or fish smoked and seasoned with tongue-lashing sauce
**JLP** – Jamaica Labour Party
**JTB** – Jamaica Tourist Board
**JUTA** – Jamaica Union of Travelers Association

**Maroons** – community of escaped slaves who were antagonistic to British during colonial period; also their contemporary descendants
**mento** – first indigenous Jamaican music
**MoBay** – slang for Montego Bay

**NEPA** – Negril Environmental Protection Agency
**NRCA** – Natural Resources Conservation Authority
**NWC** – National Water Commission
**Nyahbinghi** – Rastafarian council site

**obeah** – witchcraft; practice of witchcraft
**Ochi** – slang for Ocho Rios

**PADI** – Professional Association of Dive Instructors

**parish** – one of 14 political districts

**patty** – thin crusty pastry filled with meat or vegetable, usually spiced

**pirogue** – canoe hollowed from large tree trunk; long wooden fishing boat

**plantocracy** – the community of plantation owners as a social and political entity

**PNP** – People's National Party

**pollution** – Rastafarian term for people living in spiritual darkness

**ragga** – type of digital reggae epitomizing dancehall music since 1985

**Rasta, Rastafarian** – adherent of religious philosophy, Rastafarianism, whose main tenets hold that blacks are one of the 12 Lost Tribes of Israel, that Emperor Haile Selassie is divine, and that Selassie will lead Rastafarians to Zion

**rum shop** – local bar, usually utilized by working classes

**Sandals** – a foremost chain of all-inclusive resort hotels

**soca** – combination of soul and calypso music

**sound system** – a mobile disco using giant speakers, such as a dancehall

**spliff** – a joint (marijuana rolled in paper)

**steel band** – music group composed of drummers using oil drums

**SuperClubs** – a foremost chain of all-inclusive resort hotels

**toast** – when a DJ talks or sings over a record in a dancehall

**TOJ** – Telecommunications of Jamaica

**USDEA** – US Drug Enforcement Agency

**wine** – salacious dancing

**Xaymaca** – Arawak term for Jamaica

**yabbas** – earthenware pots

**Zion** – the Promised Land (Ethiopia) in the Rastafarian religion

# Acknowledgments

## THANKS

Many thanks to the travelers who used the last edition and wrote to us with helpful hints, useful advice, and interesting anecdotes:

Cindy Aber, Simon Aggus, Hanny Aichman, Kevin & Judy Amborn, Joan Attridge, Keith & Ann Barnard, Jackie Beckford, Arturo Bodenstedt, Merv & Christina Bolenback, Seve A Burch, Jessica J Burke, Charles Byles, Christine Campbell, Claire Chick, Pauline Connelly, Stephan Cornips, David Crawford-Emery, Paul Deacon, Simon deQuesnay, Bruce English, Christine English, Julie Ferguson, M Freeman, Jens-Uwe Geis, Mike Gerrard, Katharina Gode, Rosemary Grave, Viktor Håkansson, Ronny Haklay, Richard Hastings, Russell Heppner, John Hickman, Martin Iacampo, Jr, Karen Irvine, Justin Jaworski, George Kechagioglou, Dan Kovicic, Lars Kraemer, Dominique Lavie, Pam Loveland, Paul Marshman, April McBeth, Malcolm McInnes, Jaana Nurmela, Bob Olajos, Adrian Parker, Theresa Paulka, Sean Peterson, Caroline Pfriender, Diane Phillips, Sven Plein, Rob Polomsky, Tom & Anne-Marie Purnell, Jan Ritzmann, James Robinson, Johan RootzTn, Valentina Salapura & Michael K Gschwind, Wins Sébastien, Irma Sokolnicki, Lydia Strzebnick, Donna Tai, Sheryl Thomas, Craig R Travis, Judith Watson, Tori Wilson, Rebecca Woods, Barbara Zampelli.

# Lonely Planet Journeys

**J**OURNEYS is a unique collection of travel writing – published by the company that understands travel better than anyone else. It is a series for anyone who has ever experienced – or dreamed of – the magical moment when they encountered a strange culture or saw a place for the first time. They are tales to read while you're planning a trip, while you're on the road or while you're in an armchair in front of a fire.

These outstanding titles explore our planet through the eyes of a diverse group of international writers. JOURNEYS books catch the spirit of a place, illuminate a culture, recount a crazy adventure or introduce a fascinating way of life. They always entertain, and always enrich the experience of travel.

### FULL CIRCLE
#### A South American Journey
*Luis Sepúlveda (translated by Chris Andrews)*

'A journey without a fixed itinerary' with Chilean writer Luis Sepúlveda. Extravagant characters and extraordinary situations are memorably evoked: gauchos organising a tournament of lies, a scheming heiress on the lookout for a husband, a pilot with a corpse on board his plane ... *Full Circle* brings us the distinctive voice of one of South America's most compelling writers.

**WINNER 1996 Astrolabe – Etonnants Voyageurs award for the best work of travel literature published in France.**

### GREEN DREAMS
#### Travels in Central America
*Stephen Benz*

On the Amazon, in Costa Rica, Honduras and on the Mayan trail from Guatemala to Mexico, Stephen Benz describes his encounters with water, mud, insects and other wildlife – and not least with the ecotourists themselves. With witty insights into modern travel, *Green Dreams* discusses the paradox of cultural and 'green' tourism.

### DRIVE THRU AMERICA
*Sean Condon*

If you've ever wanted to drive across the USA but couldn't find the time (or afford the gas), *Drive Thru America* is perfect for you. In his search for American myths and realities – along with comfort, cable TV and good, reasonably priced coffee – Sean Condon paints a hilarious road-portrait of the USA.

'*entertaining and laugh-out-loud funny*'– *Alex Wilber, Travel editor, Amazon.com*

### SEAN & DAVID'S LONG DRIVE
*Sean Condon*

Sean and David are young townies who have rarely strayed beyond city limits. One day, for no good reason, they set out to discover their homeland, and what follows is a wildly entertaining adventure that covers half of Australia.

'*a hilariously detailed log of two burned out friends*' – *Rolling Stone*

# Index

Bold indicates maps.

629

### T

## Boxed Text

# MAP LEGEND

## BOUNDARIES

- ·—·—·—· International
- ·····—·····— Parish

## HYDROGRAPHY

Water

Coastline

Beach

River, Waterfall

◎ Swamp, Spring

## ROUTES & TRANSPORT

- Freeway
- Toll Freeway
- Primary Road
- Secondary Road
- Tertiary Road
- Unpaved Road
- Pedestrian Mall
- Trail
- Walking Tour
- Ferry Route
- Railway, Train Station
- Ⓜ Mass Transit Line & Station

## ROUTE SHIELDS

A1 Highway

## AREA FEATURES

- Park
- Ecological Reserve
- Cemetery
- Building
- Plaza
- Golf Course

## MAP SYMBOLS

| | | |
|---|---|---|
| ✪ **NATIONAL CAPITAL** | ✈ Airfield | ▲ Monument |
| ◉ **Parish Capital** | ✈ Airport | ⊾ Mosque |
| ● **LARGE CITY** | ∴ Archaeological Site, Ruins | ▲ Mountain |
| ● **Medium City** | ⑤ Bank | 🏛 Museum |
| ● Small City | 🍺 Bar | Observatory |
| ● Town, Village | ◗ Baseball Diamond | One-Way Street |
| ○ Point of Interest | 🏃 Beach | 🌳 Park |
| | ⊖ Bus Depot, Bus Stop, Ferry | 🅿 Parking |
| | 🕍 Cathedral | )( Pass |
| | ⌒ Cave | ⚲ Picnic Area |
| ■ Place to Stay | † Church | ★ Police Station |
| ▲ Campground | ⬟ Dive Site | 🚽 Pool |
| ⏏ RV Park | Ɵ Embassy | ✉ Post Office |
| ⌂ Hut, Chalet | ✕ Footbridge | Shipwreck |
| | 🐟 Fish Hatchery | ❖ Shopping Mall |
| ▼ to Eat | ⁂ Garden | ✿ Synagogue |
| 🍷 ace to Drink) | 🏯 Gas Station | 🏰 Stately Home |
| ☕ | ◎ Hospital, Clinic | ☎ Telephone |
| | ❶ Information | 🏃 Trailhead |
| | 🗼 Lighthouse | Winery |
| | ☀ Lookout | 🐘 Zoo |

*Note: Not all symbols displayed above appear in this book.*

---

## NET OFFICES

3122, Victoria
819 6459
:om.au

ifornia 94607
275 8555

### UK

10A Spring Place, London NW5 3BH
☎ 020 7428 4800 fax 020 7428 4828
email go@lonelyplanet.co.uk

### France

1 rue du Dahomey, 75011 Paris
☎ 01 55 25 33 00 fax 01 55 25 33 01
email bip@lonelyplanet.fr
3615 lonelyplanet *(1,29 F TTC/min)*

eb: www.lonelyplanet.com *or* AOL keyword: lp
anet Images: lpi@lonelyplanet.com.au